Building Enterprise Solutions with Visual Studio™ 6

SAMS

Don Benage and Azam A. Mirza

with
Greg Sullivan, Larry Millett, Michael D. Sallee,
J. "Eddie" Gulley, Marc Cantril, Cameron K. Beattie,
Jody C. Socha, Ronald W. Terry, David Burgett,
Wen Lin, Anthony J. Taylor, Joe Lengyel,
Daniel P. Egleston, Chris H. Striker,
Gregg D. August, Tim White, Jay Lindhorst,
Matthew Baute, Eric M. Brown, John Pickett,
Chris Zeigler, Don Lykins, Mark A. Wolff,
Patrick E. Tobey, Brad Rhodes, Yanni Xiao,
Linda Callender Pannock, and Beth Farson

Building Enterprise Solutions with Visual Studio™ 6

SAMS

Building Enterprise Solutions with Visual Studio™ 6

Copyright © 1999 by Sams Publishing

International Standard Book Number: 0-672-31489-4

Library of Congress Catalog Card Number: 98-87556

Printed in the United States of America

First Printing: December, 1998

01   00   99   98   4   3   2   1

Trademarks

Warning and Disclaimer

EXECUTIVE EDITOR
Bradley L. Jones

ACQUISITIONS EDITOR
Kelly Marshall

DEVELOPMENT EDITOR
Matt Purcell

MANAGING EDITOR
Jodi Jensen

PROJECT EDITOR
Dana Rhodes Lesh

COPY EDITORS
Rhonda Tinch-Mize
Maryann Steinhart
Sydney Jones
Linda Morris

INDEXER
John Sleeva

PROOFREADER
Cindy Fields

TECHNICAL EDITORS
Diane Macdonnell
Sakhr Youness

SOFTWARE DEVELOPMENT SPECIALIST
Dan Scherf

TEAM COORDINATOR
Carol Ackerman

INTERIOR DESIGNER
Ruth Lewis

COVER DESIGNER
Anne Jones

Contents at a Glance

V | Team Development with Visual Studio

VI | Appendix

Table of Contents

21 Dynamic HTML 601

22 Creating Applets and Applications with Visual J++ 643

23 Using Microsoft Transaction Server to Build Transactional Web Pages 671

Foreword

Yesterday's MIS requirements—automating everyday business tasks and tracking basic corporate information—have become routine. Today, organizations require information technology to provide a competitive advantage as well. Business applications must be able to expand the company's products and services into new areas, such as the Web. New applications must be as scalable and reliable as existing systems, but they must also be more flexible, support robust architectures, and be easier and faster to build. At the same time, organizations need the ability to support teams of developers, possibly spread across the globe.

Use this book to build solutions and to make the right choices from the start. This book teaches you how to use Visual Studio 6 for the full life cycle of multitier application design, development, and deployment. Topics include user interface development, middle-tier component development and assembly, database design and programming, performance analysis, and team-based development support. The authors of this book are "black belt" developers themselves and share their knowledge about Visual Studio 6 so that you can get a jump start building powerful, scalable systems. This book is the perfect guide to architecting a successful solution with Visual Studio 6.

Lizzie Parker
Visual Studio 6 Technical Product Manager
Microsoft Corporation

About the Authors

G. A. Sullivan is a noted leader in providing high-quality software development services through the application of leading-edge information technology. The company specializes in developing core business applications for its clients. As a Microsoft Solution Provider Partner, G. A. Sullivan is a recognized leader in the development of distributed multitier and client/server applications for both traditional and Web-based environments. G. A. Sullivan is also one of the fastest growing technology companies in the United States. The company was ranked among the top 500 fastest growing private companies in America according to *Inc.* magazine's *Inc.* 500 list in 1997 and again in 1998.

G. A. Sullivan provides a full range of service offerings, including project management, high-level IT consulting, and staff augmentation. Consultants provide expertise in any area within the software development life cycle, including project management, technical team leadership, system/business analysis, software engineering, database administration, and technical/user documentation.

G. A. Sullivan believes that technical leadership is a key component to continued success and thus participates in the industry through a variety of speaking and publishing engagements. In addition to writing technical publications, the company publishes a technical white paper series, writes articles for trade publications, and presents technical seminars, executive briefings, and informative roundtable discussions on leading-edge technology topics at locations across the country.

For information, contact G. A. Sullivan at the following address:

G. A. Sullivan
55 West Port Plaza, Suite 100
St. Louis, Missouri 63146
Email: corporate@gasullivan.com
Web site: www.gasullivan.com
Phone: (314)213-5600
Fax: (314)213-5700

Dedication

This book is dedicated to the employees, friends, and extended family of G. A. Sullivan.

Acknowledgments

A project of this size involves the hard work and dedication of many people. We would like to thank all the software developers, authors, editors, and their families for the hard work and support they contributed. To the many people at Microsoft who made this book possible and helped us along the way, our sincere thanks. To all the people at Macmillan whose professionalism and effort helped us produce a quality product, thank you. And to the many other people—friends and customers of G. A. Sullivan who pitched in with assistance—we extend our sincere gratitude. Thank you for all your help.

In addition, we would like to thank the following people for their special efforts and assistance: Lizzie Parker, Dave Mendlen, Tracey Trewin, Tim Brodhacker, Lloyd Arrow, Simon Poile, Martyn Lovell, Chris Kaler, Stew MacLeod, Margo Hathaway, Sandy Geduldig, Cindy Salmonson, Jody Detzel, and Deana Woldanski.

Tell Us What You Think!

As the reader of this book, *you* are our most important critic and commentator. We value your opinion and want to know what we're doing right, what we could do better, what areas you'd like to see us publish in, and any other words of wisdom you're willing to pass our way.

As the executive editor for the Advanced Programming team at Macmillan Computer Publishing, I welcome your comments. You can fax, email, or write me directly to let me know what you did or didn't like about this book—as well as what we can do to make our books stronger.

Please note that I cannot help you with technical problems related to the topic of this book, and that due to the high volume of mail I receive, I might not be able to reply to every message.

When you write, please be sure to include this book's title and author as well as your name and phone or fax number. I will carefully review your comments and share them with the author and editors who worked on the book.

Fax: 317-817-7070

Email: `adv_prog@mcp.com`

Mail: Bradley L. Jones
          Executive Editor
          Advanced Programming team
          Macmillan Computer Publishing
          201 West 103rd Street
          Indianapolis, IN 46290 USA

Introduction

Building Enterprise Solutions with Visual Studio 6, a book written by professionals for professionals, is about Microsoft Visual Studio 6. Authored by a team of senior software developers and information system consultants, this book is designed to guide you through the complex design, implementation, and development issues associated with Microsoft Visual Studio. The authoring team is composed of software developers from G. A. Sullivan, a premier software development consulting company and Microsoft Solution Provider based in St. Louis, Missouri.

One of the most alluring features of this book is its up-to-date information. The authors worked hard to produce a time-critical, technically complete "how-to" book that offers in-depth coverage of the most important elements of the Microsoft Visual Studio suite of products, including the latest releases of Microsoft's development tools such as Visual Basic 6, Visual C++ 6, Visual J++ 6, and Visual InterDev 6. This book provides thorough coverage of how to use these products to create applications for modern client/server, multitier, and Internet-enabled enterprise environments. It also includes sufficient notes, tips, and cautions to ensure that you avoid common pitfalls and learn new techniques with a minimum of wasted time.

Who Should Use This Book?

This book is aimed at *software developers* of client/server and Internet/intranet (I-net) enabled applications who are responsible for creating and deploying applications by using the Microsoft development tool suite, and *information system managers* faced with planning issues. You'll learn how to design and develop applications and components by using Microsoft Visual Studio and its individual products. This book provides excellent advice for developers who must implement applications in a Microsoft BackOffice environment with Windows NT Server, Internet Information Server (IIS), Microsoft Transaction Server (MTS), SQL Server, and the Microsoft Message Queue (MSMQ). It also provides good advice for technical managers on how to use Microsoft products to build state-of-the-art systems that will improve their business footing and leverage their automated information systems to maximize return on investment.

With the variety of material presented in *Building Enterprise Solutions with Visual Studio 6* and with its high quality of content, up-to-date material, level of detail, and easy-to-follow "how-to" format, this is the all-encompassing book you will quickly come to depend on to supply answers to your Microsoft Visual Studio questions. Although the products that make up the Microsoft Visual Studio suite are described separately within the book, special attention is paid to integration issues and techniques. Portions of the book are also devoted to providing background material to enhance your understanding of critical concepts and of how to be really effective with Microsoft Visual Studio in the enterprise.

How This Book Is Organized

This book is organized in a logical sequence, starting with a discussion of Microsoft Visual Studio basics, an overview of the product, and background material on creating database applications—a key area of concern for most developers. The chapters in Part II, "Creating COM Components," focus on the important new techniques for creating component-based applications with Microsoft's object technologies such as the Component Object Model (COM), the Distributed Component Object Model (DCOM), and Web-based technologies such as ActiveX and Java. Separate chapters are devoted to Visual Basic and Visual C++, each an important language included in Visual Studio. Part II also includes a chapter on creating COM components for MTS.

The chapters in Part III, "Developing Internet, Intranet, and Extranet Applications," are devoted entirely to the most active area of recent growth—that of applications designed to run in I-net environments. Detailed coverage is provided on both the client and server sides of these applications. This includes information on creating Web browser–based applications and using Microsoft's addition to Internet Information Server known as Active Server Pages (ASP). The use of Visual InterDev and Visual J++—major elements of Microsoft's strategy for I-net applications—is covered in detail, including the use of design-time controls with Visual InterDev and the creation of browser-based applets with Visual J++. Part III also includes coverage of Dynamic HTML, server-side scripting, and the techniques for integrating existing applications into an I-net infrastructure. The use of MTS to create transactional Web sites is included, as well as a chapter on the new packaging and deployment features in Visual Studio 6.

The chapters in Part IV, "Developing Scalable Distributed Applications," focus on the more traditional client/server development techniques, with a special emphasis on creating distributed applications by using a multitier (or n-tier) architecture and multiple databases. Using Visual Basic with both RDO and ADO is covered. Also, five chapters are devoted exclusively to using Microsoft Transaction Server to create scalable, transaction-based applications for hardcore, line-of-business use. In addition, coverage is provided on using the Microsoft Message Queue with Visual Basic.

The final chapters of the book, in Part V, "Team Development with Visual Studio," deal with the tools that help teams of programmers work together. These tools include Visual SourceSafe, the Visual Modeler, the Microsoft Repository, and the new Visual Studio Analyzer. Using each tool is described, in addition to background information on the rationale for using these powerful additions to the Visual Studio suite.

Part I: Application Development with Visual Studio
The chapters in Part I provide an introduction to the Visual Studio suite of products:

- Chapter 1, "An Inside Look at Visual Studio," introduces you to this suite of products. It describes what's in the box and why Visual Studio is an important addition to a developer's tool set. It also provides guidance on who can best use a tool suite such as Visual Studio and details some of the primary advantages it offers.

- Chapter 2, "Using Visual Studio to Create Applications," explores the basic use of the Integrated Development Environment (IDE) known as Developer Studio, which is used by Visual C++, and the new IDE called the Microsoft Development Environment used by Visual J++ and Visual InterDev. It also introduces the IDE for Visual Basic and basic techniques for creating applications.

- Chapter 3, "Debugging Enterprise Applications with Visual Studio," introduces you to various debugging techniques that are useful in the different IDEs provided with Visual Studio 6. You will also learn about debugging SQL Server stored procedures and Web-based script.

- Chapter 4, "Creating Database-Aware Applications with Visual Studio," provides important information on designing databases and database applications. It describes the database design tools in Visual Studio that support these activities. It also introduces some concepts that are developed in more detail later in the book, such as multitier architectures, distributed databases, and partitioning client/server applications.

- Chapter 5, "An Inside Look at Microsoft Transaction Server," introduces you to one of the most important and exciting elements of the Visual Studio suite. MTS is the engine for Microsoft's component software strategy and plays a key role in implementing COM-based multitier application architectures. This chapter provides an overview of this important technology.

- Chapter 6, "An Inside Look at Active Server Pages and the Internet Information Server," describes Microsoft's Web server and the features it provides. It also outlines techniques that you can use to build Web-based applications, providing a foundation for the chapters in Part III on building applications with Web technologies. The built-in Active Server objects are discussed in detail, and their purpose and usage are described.

- Chapter 7, "An Inside Look at the Microsoft Message Queue," introduces a relatively new member of the server tool suite offered by Microsoft. MSMQ provides a powerful message delivery mechanism built on a sophisticated, enterprise-ready architecture. It is designed for organizations that span a single building or have offices around the globe. This chapter describes MSMQ's most important features and capabilities.

- Chapter 8, "An Inside Look at Microsoft SQL Server," provides an introduction to the features of Microsoft's high-end database product that are important to software developers. In addition to the basics, Chapter 8 provides important information on data warehousing, an important element of many modern software development project.

Part II: Creating COM Components

The chapters in Part II explore Microsoft's object technologies and describe how to create applications with ActiveX controls and COM-based components:

- Chapter 9, "Using Microsoft's Object Technologies," discusses the object-oriented and object-based technologies that form the underlying infrastructure for creating modern applications. Many of the names and abbreviations related to this area are defined and put into their historical perspective, clearing up the confusion that exists due to the changing meanings of some of these terms. A solid overview of the Component Object Model and the Distributed Component Object Model is provided. A brief discussion of the competitive CORBA technology and its relationship to COM/DCOM is also provided.

- Chapter 10, "Creating Reusable Components," explores the strategies and techniques you can employ to build software components that are reusable. This is an area of great concern and interest for many developers, and something of a holy grail for the industry as a whole. This chapter describes concrete steps you can take today to start leveraging reusable components instead of starting from scratch with each new project.

- Chapter 11, "Using COM Components and ActiveX Controls," describes how to use controls and components built with COM and ActiveX-based tools in traditional client/server environments and those based on Web servers and browser-based clients. It also discusses the integration of ActiveX and Java.

- Chapter 12, "Creating ActiveX Controls with Visual Basic," covers the techniques used to build ActiveX controls. You are guided step by step as you create your first control. Then more advanced controls are described, including constituent controls, aggregate controls, and user-drawn controls.

- Chapter 13, "Creating ActiveX Controls with Visual C++," follows a similar course as the previous chapter except it describes the use of Visual C++ rather than Visual Basic. You are again guided through creating your first control, and then progressively more advanced controls and features are described.

- Chapter 14, "Creating COM Components for MTS," prepares you for additional MTS chapters occurring later in the book. All the basics of creating components for MTS, without discussing implementation in a particular language, are introduced in this chapter. Coverage includes state management, the use of object contexts, and the MTS programming model.

Part III: Developing Internet, Intranet, and Extranet Applications

The chapters in Part III provide detailed coverage on building applications for the Internet or private intranets and extranets:

- Chapter 15, "Clients, Servers, and Components: Web-Based Applications," provides a broad, conceptual look at the entire architecture of the typical I-net environment. A comparison is made with traditional client/server environments, and issues related to partitioning your application into client- and server-based components are discussed.

- Chapter 16, "Creating Web Browser–Based Applications with Visual Basic," provides an in-depth discussion of a powerful new capability added to Visual Basic that allows applications to be hosted in an ActiveX-compatible Web browser. This chapter discusses design considerations and how to create ActiveX documents. It also introduces the use of the Web browser as an application framework and describes both client- and server-side issues when you're developing Web-based applications.

- Chapter 17, "Server-Side Programming," explores key issues surrounding the use of code on the Web server. In particular, it describes the pros and cons of locating code on the server, the techniques that are available to the programmer writing server-side scripts, and some of the pitfalls that you should avoid.

- Chapter 18, "Developing Active Content with Visual InterDev," provides an in-depth introduction to Visual InterDev, the primary Web development tool in Visual Studio. It describes the IDE and the various wizards provided to help you get your Web development off to a good start. It also describes how to use both client- and server-side ActiveX components in your Web-based development.

- Chapter 19, "Advanced Visual InterDev Concepts," describes advanced techniques you can use to build powerful Web-based applications. It explores the use of client-side components. Team-based development with Visual InterDev is also described.

- Chapter 20, "Visual InterDev Design-Time Controls," describes a powerful feature of Visual InterDev known as *design-time controls*. This chapter describes some of the built-in design-time controls that allow you to manage database access more easily and format results from a Web server, and it describes the ability to include standard elements on multiple pages automatically.

- Chapter 21, "Dynamic HTML," describes an important new development in the evolution of the Hypertext Markup Language (HTML). Dynamic HTML is based on an object model proposed by Microsoft to the World Wide Web Consortium (W3C) and adds both an exposed object model and comprehensive event model for developers to use when building advanced Web-based applications.

- Chapter 22, "Creating Applets and Applications with Visual J++," examines the capabilities of Microsoft's implementation of Java, Visual J++. This chapter describes how to create applets and applications and the difference between the two.

- Chapter 23, "Using Microsoft Transaction Server to Build Transactional Web Pages," describes the integration of two mid-tier tools—Web servers and MTS. Using these tools together creates synergistic capabilities that can add power and flexibility to your application-building toolset. This chapter introduces these capabilities.

- Chapter 24, "Packaging and Deploying Web-Based Applications," examines the new features added to Visual Studio 6 that aid the developer in creating applications that are easier to deliver to the desktop and install. Microsoft has added many new capabilities in this area in the latest release of Visual Studio—with a focus on dramatically reducing the cost of deployment. Learn how to use these new features with your applications.

Part IV: Developing Scalable Distributed Applications

The chapters in Part IV describe the tools and techniques you can use to build applications that use multitiered architectures and distributed databases:

- Chapter 25, "Clients, Servers, and Components: Design Strategies for Distributed Applications," provides an overview of distributed applications—what it means to describe an application as *distributed*, the different types of distributed applications, and the tools that exist for creating them. The implications of I-net technologies for this type of application also are discussed. A number of important topics are covered, including the services paradigm and two-tier versus three-tier client/server applications.

- Chapter 26, "Building Client Front Ends with Visual Basic," explores classic two-tier client/server application development. Visual Basic is used to create a front-end application that connects to a back-end server running Microsoft's SQL Server database using ActiveX Data Objects (ADO). It also describes how to access ODBC-compliant databases and the Data Form Wizard.

- Chapter 27, "Creating COM Components for MTS with Visual Basic," describes the techniques for building MTS components using Visual Basic in an easy-to-follow how-to format. This is the first of three related chapters that describe the language-specific requirements for creating mid-tier components for an MTS environment.

- Chapter 28, "Creating COM Components for MTS with Visual J++," follows the same outline as the previous chapter, but uses a different language. In this chapter, Visual J++ is used for creating mid-tier components.

- Chapter 29, "Creating COM Components for MTS with Visual C++," completes the group of language-specific chapters on building MTS components. Visual C++ is used in this chapter, but the development parallels the previous two chapters to make comparison and contrast as easy as possible for multilanguage developers.

- Chapter 30, "Creating Data Access Components for MTS with Visual Basic and ADO," continues the MTS coverage with a discussion of how to encapsulate all data access in the mid-tier. The process of creating components with Visual Basic that use ADO to access back-end data sources such as SQL Server is described.

- Chapter 31, "Using Microsoft Transaction Server to Enable Distributed Applications," details how to use the MTS Explorer administrative tool supplied with MTS to package components and implement them on mid-tier computers on your network. It also describes how to monitor the status of currently executing multitier applications.

- Chapter 32, "Using MSMQ with Visual Basic," provides an introduction to programming for the Microsoft Message Queue. Complementing the introduction to MSMQ provided in Part I, this chapter provides specific examples of how to add items to a queue, read queues, and use them as elements of your application architecture.

Part V: Team Development with Visual Studio

The chapters in Part V provide information on the additional tools in Visual Studio that allow groups of programmers to work together effectively:

- Chapter 33, "Using the Visual Component Manager and the Microsoft Repository," describes the use of the Visual Component Manager—a front end for the Microsoft Repository—which stores several types of information important to developers (including models and source code) in a single store. The underlying design and features of the Microsoft Repository are also described.

- Chapter 34, "Using the Visual Studio Analyzer," reviews the capabilities of an important tool that is new to Visual Studio 6—the Visual Studio Analyzer. This powerful new analysis tool captures and displays an "under the covers" view of the events and actions of multitier applications as they are executing.

- Chapter 35, "Using Visual SourceSafe," provides detailed guidance on how to use the SourceSafe source code management tool for source control and version tracking. This tool's capabilities are described for both traditional and Web-based environments. This chapter also covers how to perform different tasks by using the graphical interface provided.

- Chapter 36, "System Modeling and the Microsoft Visual Modeler," provides an overview of the recently released Unified Modeling Language (UML) and the use of modeling as an aid to the development of good software. The features and capabilities of the Microsoft Visual Modeler are described. This chapter also covers code generation and reverse engineering.

Conventions Used in This Book

Special design features enhance the text material:

- Notes
- Tips
- Cautions
- Troubleshooting boxes

N O T E Notes explain interesting or important points that can help you understand the described concepts and techniques.

 T I P Tips are little pieces of information that help you in real-world situations. Tips often offer shortcuts or alternative approaches to make a task easier or faster.

CAUTION

Cautions alert you to an action that can lead to an unexpected or unpredictable result, including loss of data. The text provides an explanation of how you can avoid such a result. Pay careful attention to Cautions.

 TROUBLESHOOTING

Troubleshooting boxes provide commonly asked questions about problems or challenges typically encountered by users. These troubleshooting tips are presented in the form of a commonly asked question and its answer.

Rather than have you wade through all the details relating to a particular function of an application in a single chapter or part before you progress to the next topic, this book provides special cross-references to help you find the information you need. These cross-references follow the material they pertain to, as in the following sample reference.

▶ **See** "Another Section or Another Chapter," **p. xx**

This book also uses various typesetting styles to distinguish between explanatory and instructional text and text you enter. Onscreen messages, program code, commands, and text that you are to type appear in a special monospaced font. Placeholders, or words that you replace with actual code, are indicated with monospace italic.

When a line of code is too long to fit on one line of this book, it is broken at a convenient place and continued to the next line. A code continuation character (➡) precedes the continuation of a line of code. (You should type a line of code that has this character as one long line without breaking it.)

Key combinations that you use to perform Windows operations are indicated by joining the keys with a plus sign: Alt+F4, for example, indicates that you press and hold the Alt key while pressing the F4 function key.

Application Development with Visual Studio

CHAPTER 1

An Inside Look at Visual Studio

by Greg Sullivan

In this chapter

Enterprise Application Architecture

Enterprise applications are large and important, and they are built for business organizations. Large applications have many users, a great deal of data, and a high volume of transactions on that data. These applications require large teams of developers to successfully build and implement them. Finally, enterprise applications are built to serve an important business purpose and, necessarily, to be able to bend and grow in a world of changing business requirements.

This book is about enterprise application development. Specifically, it's about using the latest integrated software development tool suite from Microsoft to build Web applications and multitier applications and to integrate client/server and Web technologies. This bundle of development tools is known as *Visual Studio* and is ideally suited for creating and deploying these software solutions.

Whether your users are inside your organization, external to your organization, or both, the key to creating an enterprise application today is to build it from the ground up so that it is scalable. An enterprise application that is built to be scalable must be built from a solid architecture. It must also be properly designed in order to protect the investment in creating the application. With a solid architecture and sound design, you will provide your organization with the most flexibility as business conditions change throughout the life of the application.

How are scalable applications built? The answer lies in the architecture of the application model. It isn't possible to build scalable applications without planning an effective and flexible application model. First analyze and then architect, design, and build. Always use object-oriented design and construction techniques. Building scalable applications isn't magic, but it isn't nearly as difficult as many think, provided proper attention is given to the architecture model.

 TIP Settling on an application model prior to beginning any enterprise application development process is a necessary step. Not only does it lay down the ground rules for all to follow, but it also helps by taking a huge problem and breaking it into smaller, more manageable pieces.

The reasons applications are built vary from application to application. Regardless of the initial motivation for the investment, most certainly the "business rules" will change over the life of the application. An application built with a well-thought-out architecture, that is truly scalable, can best accommodate changing external conditions.

Not only is a scalable application flexible enough to accommodate change, but it also can accommodate scheduled or random increased capacity requirements. For example, say you own a company that manufactures parkas and sells them worldwide directly to the end customer. You sell 1,000 parkas a day via Internet sales and telesales throughout the year, with the exception of September through December. During these months you average 25,000 parkas a day.

N O T E Scalable applications can accommodate changing business requirements, whether temporary or permanent. ▪

With a scalable order entry and inventory system, you can accommodate the additional temporary demands placed on your applications by simply adding more hardware for those months. Of course, you will need more Internet server capacity to ensure adequate response time to your Internet customers. You will also need more server capacity for data and back-end processes to accommodate the additional telesales staff you will have working the phones. Yes, it is possible to consider temporary hardware as a reasonable alternative, especially if you outsource application operation to an Internet service provider (ISP)—a trend in enterprise application implementation.

Scalable applications must be distributed. The software components that become objects must be able to work on any computer, anywhere on the network. Data must be distributable across multiple physical database servers. Finally, processes must be distributed across the layers, or tiers, of the application.

Microsoft recently introduced the Windows Distributed Internet Application (DNA) Architecture. It provides a logical model for how enterprise applications should be built. Windows DNA is simple in concept. Within its logical model, Windows DNA clearly defines how many of Microsoft's development tools and server products should work together in building and implementing enterprise applications. Windows DNA also describes how the products of other industry vendors, such as the Oracle database management system, fit into this application architecture. Figure 1.1 depicts Windows DNA.

At the heart of Windows DNA is the business process layer, which represents the middle tier in a three-tier architecture. It is in this tier that the business rules must be placed in order to build the most flexible and scalable application.

 T I P Even though Windows DNA describes a three-tier architecture, it might be necessary to build enterprise applications in four tiers in some situations. In cases where the number of users and the number of transactions are large, it is useful to add a layer to balance the load for the application servers. This service abstraction tier is often left out—to the demise of many projects.

As such, business rules are isolated from details of data management and access, as well as complex user interface issues. This provides for the flexible growth of an application in a changing business environment in that developers have only one place to visit to accommodate new business requirements. Windows DNA is covered in detail in Chapter 9, "Using Microsoft's Object Technologies."

Part
I
Ch
1

FIGURE 1.1
Windows DNA provides
an abstraction to the
three logical tiers
needed to build
scalable enterprise
applications.

DNA Architecture

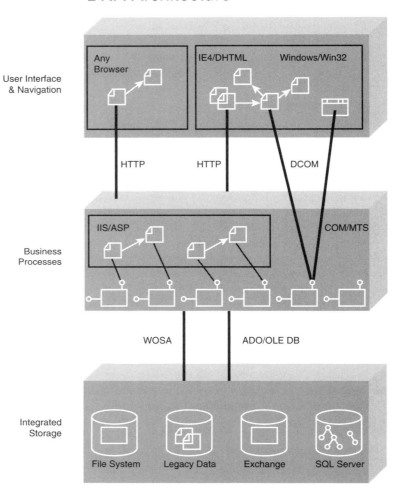

NOTE   The significance of Windows DNA cannot be underestimated when it comes to enterprise
application development. Windows DNA must be the model for the architecture of each
and every enterprise application developed with Visual Studio.

What Is Visual Studio?

Visual Studio is a product bundle including most of Microsoft's most powerful software development tools for building enterprise applications and their associated software components. Similar to the way it has bundled desktop products in Microsoft Office (for end users) and server products in Microsoft BackOffice (for network administrators), Microsoft has put together a suite of products in a package targeted at software developers.

ON THE WEB

Microsoft maintains a page on its corporate Web site dedicated to Visual Studio, at `http://www.microsoft.com/vstudio/`. I encourage you to stay current with Visual Studio developments and updates with frequent visits to this site.

However, unlike Microsoft Office and Microsoft BackOffice, Visual Studio is a truly synchronized product suite. All the development languages within Visual Studio now possess the same version number. At a closer look, there is much more to this than a simple marketing twist. Within Microsoft, the teams for each developer product work under the Visual Studio product umbrella, sharing common goals and incentives, as opposed to simply repackaging the individual products into a product suite after the last one is released. In fact, all development tools in Visual Studio from the 6 release forward will release together. This is the best indication of Microsoft's commitment to integrating the full breadth of development tools into an integrated tool suite.

The initial release of Visual Studio occurred in March 1997 and was labeled Visual Studio 97. As with any initial release of a new software product, Visual Studio 97 had some identifiable shortcomings. A significant missing feature was a common front end shared by all tools because the development tools didn't yet share the Integrated Development Environment (IDE). Although the current release doesn't yet fulfill this goal entirely, it is another big step in the right direction.

The current release is Visual Studio 6. This is the version number also shared by most of the development tools contained in the product package. Even though the product releases will be simultaneous, the product announcements and marketing will continue to take place on an individual product basis, as well as for the entire Visual Studio package. This is because Microsoft continues to sell individual tools in Visual Studio separately. More than likely, the individual product announcements will be spread out across different time periods prior to the simultaneous release of each individual product and the entire Visual Studio product package.

The primary development tools that comprise the Visual Studio package are as follows:

- Visual C++
- Visual Basic
- Visual InterDev
- Visual J++
- Visual FoxPro

You can buy each Visual Studio product separately; however, if you're in a team environment developing an application that requires more than one of these languages, Visual Studio offers several advantages:

- It's well suited to the mixed-language programming often required for distributed application development.
- It's specifically designed to accommodate team-oriented software development and contains many features supporting a team and its individual software engineers. The chapters in Part V, "Team Development with Visual Studio," explore this aspect of the product.
- Microsoft has priced the license fees for Visual Studio so that licensing the suite amounts to less than purchasing all the components individually. Depending on the licensing model used, the savings can be significant.

Visual Studio is available in two package options: Professional Edition and Enterprise Edition. Both editions are intended for use by serious application developers who are developing in a desktop or distributed application development environment. The Enterprise Edition adds products and tools that enable you to deal more effectively with database access and enterprise scalability issues.

N O T E Because this book is about using Visual Studio for enterprise application development, its focus is on the Visual Studio Enterprise Edition.

Goal for Visual Studio

To understand better the role of Visual Studio in software development today, you need to examine some goals for the product. Clearly, the concept of integrating design, development, and development tracking tools into one package can ease some of the burdens associated with software development, if the integration is implemented appropriately. Following is a review of some of the most important objectives set forth by Microsoft for Visual Studio:

- Object-oriented software engineering—Developing component-based software is the cornerstone of modern-day software development. Microsoft bases Windows development on its Component Object Model (COM); consequently, the need for a tool suite that integrates component development and application building is tremendous. Visual Studio provides the capability to craft software components and glue them together into solutions in a cohesive and consistent development environment.

- Internet development—Using Internet technologies for commercial application development, whether exposed to the entire Internet or secured on an intranet, solves two of the biggest problems plaguing software development in recent years. One of the most perplexing problems in client/server application development in a Windows environment is software distribution. Another significant problem is computer communications. Internet technologies minimize the impact of both problems. Consequently, the demand for a comprehensive tool suite for Web-based application development is an important objective for Visual Studio.

- Multitier application development—Client/server application development remains in high demand and works well with the incorporation of Internet technologies. Adding new tiers to applications enables you to isolate business rules and application services.

It's critical for Visual Studio to support current multitier application development initiatives and additional techniques in the future.

▶ **See** Chapter 25, "Clients, Servers, and Components: Design Strategies for Distributed Applications," **p. 727**

▓ Embrace and extend—Industry vendors other than Microsoft have developed popular leading-edge technologies for software developers. Microsoft has announced publicly its intention to *embrace* certain of these technologies and *extend* them in the Windows environment. The best example of this is Microsoft's acceptance of Java technology introduced by Sun Microsystems. Visual J++ is Microsoft's implementation of Java for use in building Web-based applications. As promised by Microsoft, Visual J++ embraces Java technology and extends it to operate effectively in Windows environments. (Its integration support for ActiveX and Java components is evidence of this.)

▓ Mixed-language software development—Using multiple programming languages for developing applications is desirable in many cases. Combining the most popular languages and development tools into Visual Studio accommodates mixed-language software development.

▓ Team software development—Software developers work in teams made up of component builders, solution developers, object modelers, application architects, documentation specialists, end users, and others. An important goal of Visual Studio is to provide a tool suite that enables each development team member to interact with development-related information in a manner consistent with that particular role. A perfect example of this is the versatility the Visual Component Manager (VCM) offers in encouraging software reuse.

This is a short list of some of the most important aspects of Visual Studio. With the introduction of Visual Studio, Microsoft has shown that it understands the needs of software developers and software development teams to have tools that work better together and take advantage of the most powerful technologies. Future versions of Visual Studio and its associated products are expected to continue to enhance developer productivity.

What's in a Name?

Before I provide a brief description of each product included with Visual Studio, bringing some clarity to the product names might be helpful. Microsoft now makes a practice of making product code names available to the public. Some products in Visual Studio have had code names similar to actual product names (of other products), causing some confusion over which product is which.

Visual Studio—the entire product package and the focus of this book—was code-named *Boston*. One product included with Visual Studio is Visual InterDev, originally code-named *Internet Studio*. Because this code name was widely used in industry press, some people confused *Internet* Studio with *Visual* Studio. As if the word *studio* wasn't overused enough, the name of the Visual Studio IDE is *Developer Studio*, so we now have Visual Studio (the entire product package) and Developer Studio (the IDE shared by some of the Visual Studio products) as officially released products. Internet Studio, simply a code name for Visual InterDev, is no longer valid.

Visual Studio Professional Edition

The most basic version of Visual Studio is the Professional Edition. This product package contains all the primary component-building and application-development tools available from Microsoft. It also contains an Integrated Development Environment for some of the products. The Professional Edition of Visual Studio includes the following tools:

- Visual C++ Professional Edition—Visual C++ is the most powerful development tool included with Visual Studio. Not surprisingly, it's also the most difficult to become proficient in. Its most common use is in developing ActiveX software components, but it's also used to develop entire applications. Visual C++, which includes the Microsoft Foundation Class (MFC) library and the Active Template Library (ATL), is covered in detail in Chapter 13, "Creating ActiveX Controls with Visual C++," and Chapter 29, "Creating COM Components for MTS with Visual C++."

- Visual Basic Professional Edition—Of all the development tools included in Visual Studio, Visual Basic provides the best combination of power and flexibility. It enables you to create ActiveX software components and assemble them into applications for deployment in client/server environments or on the Internet. Because Visual Basic is one of the most widely used tools in Visual Studio, it's covered throughout this book in great detail. In particular, detailed coverage is provided in Chapter 12, "Creating ActiveX Controls with Visual Basic"; Chapter 26, " Building Client Front Ends with Visual Basic"; and Chapter 27, " Creating COM Components for MTS with Visual Basic."

- Visual InterDev—Most new enterprise applications today are developed as client/server applications on Internet technologies, often referred to as *Web-based software development*. Visual InterDev is the development tool included with Visual Studio that specifically targets developers who create Web-based applications. In contrast to Microsoft FrontPage, a Web page development tool intended for desktop users, Visual InterDev is specifically targeted at application developers. The chapters in Part III, "Developing Internet, Intranet, and Extranet Applications," explore Web-based application development and how to use Visual InterDev in this type of development activity.

- Visual J++—Sun Microsystems has popularized the use of the Java programming language as an effective means for developing Web-based applications. Although Microsoft and Sun compete in many ways, Microsoft has licensed the technology from Sun and incorporated it into Visual J++. This tool helps you develop Java applets and applications in a Microsoft visual programming environment consistent with other development-tool user interfaces. Visual J++ can also be extended to integrate Java with ActiveX. You can find out more about using Visual J++ in Chapter 22, "Creating Applets and Applications with Visual J++."

- Visual FoxPro—At its heart, Visual FoxPro is a relational database system. Based on the dBASE programming language, it has evolved from the FoxBase data management tool acquired by Microsoft several years ago. In its current form, Visual FoxPro has grown into a full object-oriented application development system that enables you to build client/server and Internet-based applications on top of the relational database system incorporated into the tool. Visual FoxPro is included as a product in Visual Studio;

however, it isn't covered in this book. For additional information on the use of Visual FoxPro for database application development, see Que's *Special Edition Using Visual FoxPro*.

In addition to these development tools, Visual Studio Professional Edition includes a special edition of the Microsoft Developer Network (MSDN) Reference Library on a CD. This edition of the reference library is geared specifically to Visual Studio software developers, with an index and cross-reference of documentation associated with all the Visual Studio products. It comes with Visual Studio and includes interesting articles, samples of source code, text from reference books, and consolidated product documentation. A complete subscription to the MSDN library is available to Visual Studio licensees for a special price. The MSDN library is an important tool for any software engineer developing software in a Windows environment with Microsoft tools; a complete subscription is highly recommended.

ON THE WEB

When you subscribe to MSDN, you can stay current by visiting MSDN on the Web. The site can be found at http://www.microsoft.com/msdn/.

Visual Studio Enterprise Edition

Visual Studio Enterprise Edition includes the development tools contained in the Professional Edition; however, the Enterprise Editions of Visual C++ and Visual Basic are substituted for their Professional Editions. The Enterprise Editions contain enhancements designed to provide an improved environment for multitier, client/server application development, Internet application development, and data management.

The Enterprise Edition of Visual Studio also includes other products and tools intended to extend the functionality of Visual Studio Professional Edition or to enhance support for software development in teams. Briefly, some of the more prominent products and tools are as follows:

- SQL Server Developer Edition—This full version includes all the features of SQL Server, including relational database management, data replication, database administration tools, and an extensive stored procedure development environment. Although a full version of SQL Server is provided with the Enterprise Edition of Visual Studio, its use is limited to software development activities such as building and testing applications. This enables you to use test databases without disrupting users of live data in production databases.

- Microsoft Transaction Server (MTS)—A full version of Microsoft Transaction Server is included, but with a license limiting its use to building and testing applications. When applications that use MTS are implemented in a production environment, a full license for the product is required. MTS is built on Microsoft's Distributed Component Object Model (DCOM) and includes the Microsoft Distributed Transaction Coordinator (DTC). MTS is at the heart of enterprise application development. As such, complete coverage is given to it in Part IV, "Developing Scalable Distributed Applications."

- Visual SourceSafe—Effective software development in a team environment requires a source control system. Microsoft offers Visual SourceSafe for this purpose. It enables the control and management of the source files associated with any type of development project, including Visual Studio projects. It can also be used to manage source files for Web site development and end-user documentation. Visual SourceSafe is covered in Chapter 35, "Using Visual SourceSafe."

- Visual Component Manager—This new product from Microsoft enables you to organize software components for Visual Basic and other development tools within and external to Visual Studio. It enables your development teams to create a database of software components and object models, along with the associated documentation. This tool accommodates a more efficient form of software reuse and represents an important step in the right direction with respect to efficient object-oriented software engineering. Objects are stored in the Microsoft Repository and are available to developers through VCM. The Microsoft Repository is based on a design specification jointly prepared by Microsoft and Texas Instruments Software. Both VCM and the Microsoft Repository are covered in detail in Chapter 33, "Using the Visual Component Manager and the Microsoft Repository."

- Visual Modeler—The Visual Modeler is an object-modeling tool from Microsoft. The Visual Modeler is a component-based application design tool appropriate for designing desktop or distributed applications. This product is provided by Microsoft through its affiliation with Rational Software Corporation, a leading vendor of object-oriented design tools for many years. The Visual Modeler is covered in detail in Chapter 36, "System Modeling and the Microsoft Visual Modeler."

- Visual Studio Analyzer—This is arguably the most significant addition to this release of Visual Studio. The Visual Studio Analyzer plugs a previously large hole in enterprise application development. This new tool enables enterprise application developers to monitor applications as they run. Although traditional debuggers have provided this capability on single machines in the past, the Visual Studio Analyzer takes debugging to the next level by tracking execution for a distributed application. In this manner, execution can be traced from component to component, across the entire computing environment. The Visual Studio Analyzer is introduced and explained in detail in Chapter 34, "Using the Visual Studio Analyzer."

- ActiveX Data Objects (ADO)—ADO provides access to most of the popular relational database systems. It also provides access to a broader range of databases, including nonrelational databases. Furthermore, ADO is one of the most efficient and effective data access methods available for Web-based database development. Full coverage of ADO is provided in Chapter 30, "Creating Data Access Components for MTS with Visual Basic and ADO."

- SQL Server debugging tools—The Transact SQL debugger enables you to debug SQL stored procedures interactively from within Visual C++ and Visual Basic.

Microsoft likely will continue to extend the power of this product package by adding new tools to the Enterprise Edition that are targeted at complementing the primary development tools included in the Professional Edition. The license fee for the Enterprise Edition is typically 50 percent to 100 percent more than the Professional Edition, depending on the type of pricing used.

Licensing

Visual Studio is licensed per developer—that is, you must pay a license fee to Microsoft for each developer *seat* on your team. Although you might also license each Visual Studio product individually, there's a pricing advantage to acquiring the Visual Studio license as opposed to the individual licenses. The size of the advantage depends on current pricing of the entire package and the individual components, as well as the selection and number of tools required for your development effort.

Microsoft now offers licenses to Visual Studio in three forms. First, there are license fees for the Professional and Enterprise Editions at full price. Second, Microsoft offers a discount to full price if you're upgrading from certain previous versions of the primary development tools included in Visual Studio. Finally, to encourage more people to switch to Visual Studio, Microsoft offers a discount to those with certain competitive development products. The competitive and version upgrade discounts are typically available through rebate coupons provided by Microsoft.

ON THE WEB

Stay current with Microsoft pricing for Visual Studio, including competitive and version upgrade discounts, by checking its Web site at http://www.microsoft.com/vstudio/.

System Requirements

Visual Studio requires a powerful computer with a substantial amount of hard disk space and memory. In fact, if all products are installed at their maximum size, the total hard disk space requirement can exceed 1.7GB. The minimum processor required to execute Visual Studio is a Pentium operating at 90MHz or higher.

Visual Studio is available to operate on Windows 95 or Windows NT Workstation 4 or later. Components and applications developed with Visual Studio might need to support execution on Windows 95 or Windows NT. If so, it's recommended to maintain a development computer with both operating systems for testing purposes. This increases the hard disk requirement, but the cost of storage is trivial compared with the cost of inconvenience to developers in testing software.

The minimum acceptable RAM for Windows 95 or Windows NT Workstation is 24MB. Microsoft recommends 32MB RAM; however, it's prudent to use at least 64MB RAM. Additional RAM is important when testing database applications with SQL Server access on the same computer, in which case RAM in excess of 64MB is highly recommended.

CAUTION

Processor, RAM, and hard disk requirements for Visual Studio 6 are greater than for the previous version, Visual Studio 97. Before upgrading to Visual Studio 6, be certain to review your computer configuration to ensure that it is adequately equipped.

In addition to these requirements, a CD-ROM is necessary. It's possible to use a VGA monitor; however, a Super VGA monitor of at least 17 inches in size is highly recommended. A mouse or compatible pointing device is required.

Hard disk requirements vary, based on which edition of Visual Studio is installed. It's possible to split installation across multiple drives (with the restriction that only the shared components can be separate). It's also possible to execute Visual Studio from the installation CD-ROM with a minimal portion of it installed on your hard drive. Figure 1.2 shows all of Visual Studio installed on a single drive.

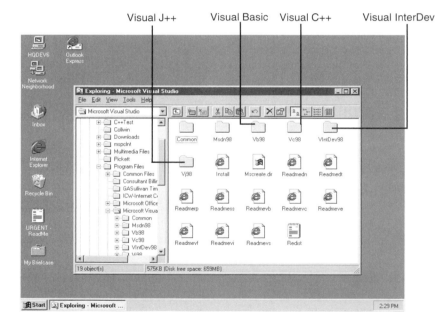

FIGURE 1.2
By default, all Visual Studio products install in the same program group.

Table 1.1 depicts the typical and maximum storage required for each product in Visual Studio Professional Edition. Installing the individual products is optional.

Table 1.1   Storage Requirements for Visual Studio Professional Edition

Tool	Typical Disk Storage	Maximum Disk Storage
Visual C++	266MB	370MB
Visual Basic	54MB	94MB
Visual InterDev	81MB	98MB
Visual J++	86MB	104MB
Visual FoxPro	85MB	90MB
MSDN	57MB	493MB
Totals	629MB	1.25GB

In addition to more products, Visual Studio Enterprise Edition includes larger versions of Visual C++ and Visual Basic, as shown in Table 1.2.

Table 1.2   Storage Requirements for Visual Studio Enterprise Edition

Tool	Minimum Disk Storage	Maximum Disk Storage
Visual C++	302MB	403MB
Visual Basic	116MB	135MB
Visual InterDev	81MB	98MB
Visual J++	86MB	104MB
Visual FoxPro	85MB	90MB
SQL Server	80MB	95MB
SNA Server	50MB	100MB
MSDN	57MB	493MB
Totals	857MB	1.52GB

Internet Explorer 4 is required for both the Professional Edition and the Enterprise Edition of Visual Studio. This adds a maximum of 59MB in hard disk requirement (43MB in a typical installation). Windows NT Option Pack is also required when installed on Windows NT Workstation. This consumes 20MB in a typical installation and a maximum of 200MB in a full installation.

Whether or not you are in a team development environment, it is prudent to use Visual SourceSafe (not shown in the Tables 1.1 and 1.2) for source code control. If so, Visual

SourceSafe should be installed on a network server to which all the team's developers have access. 128MB of hard disk space is required for the basic server installation. 141MB is the maximum necessary.

The server-side installation of Visual SourceSafe is the only part that is required. However, it is recommended that each developer install the client portion of Visual SourceSafe on his or her workstation. A basic client installation requires 59MB, with a maximum of 72MB for a full install.

The Role of Visual Studio in Software Development

Software applications created with Visual Studio are developed by assembling individual software components. The software engineers who "glue" software components together to form the entire solution are sometimes referred to as *solution developers*. Software engineers playing the role of component builders develop the software components used to build applications. These software components are purchased from industry vendors or developed by component builders on your application development team.

ON THE WEB

Microsoft offers a formal certification for software engineers. It has recently been completely revamped to better match the actual work performed by developers in a desktop or distributed application development environment.

The details of the Microsoft Certified Professional (MCP) program can be found on Microsoft's Web site at http://www.microsoft.com/mcp/.

Some software development tools are designed to develop components, whereas others are created for assembling components into solutions. Given the significance of this approach to software development, it's no surprise that Visual Studio contains a combination of tools suited to one or the other purpose—or, in some cases, to both purposes. Moreover, in the world of multitier application development, software components are needed in client-side application development and in server development. Again, Visual Studio includes tools for both. Table 1.3 shows Visual Studio's development tools, with an indication as to whether they can create or assemble components. You can use component producers to create software components, and component consumers can assemble software components into applications.

Table 1.3   Visual Studio Server Components and Client Components

Tool	Server Components		Client Components	
	Producer	Consumer	Producer	Consumer
Visual C++	✓	✓	✓	✓
Visual Basic	✓	✓	✓	✓
Visual InterDev	✓		✓	
Visual J++	✓	✓	✓	✓
Visual FoxPro	✓		✓	
SQL Server	✓			

As Table 1.3 shows, Visual C++ and Visual Basic can produce and consume software components. Visual InterDev and Visual FoxPro are available only to assemble software components into solutions. Visual J++ is designed to create software components in support of Java applet or application development. Finally, SQL Server delivers the capability to use database server-side software components through extended stored procedures.

What's in Visual Studio for You

Visual Studio represents a breakthrough in many ways to the world of software development. Although other development tool suites have existed before its introduction, this product varies in that it's backed by Microsoft's muscle. Microsoft is committed to improving the integration of Visual Studio products and continuing to enhance the capabilities and efficiency of software development teams. Already, Visual Studio means many things to many people.

Software development teams faced with selecting tools often debate the relative merits of a given tool, based on its power and flexibility versus its productivity. Typically, the most powerful and flexible software development tools are the most difficult to learn and the most inefficient because they're lower level in nature, require more in-depth knowledge of the underlying technology, and are more difficult to debug when problems arise.

On the other hand, the tools that tend to yield the shortest development times are usually less powerful or less flexible. Although throwing together a simple database application quickly is possible with a database tool such as Microsoft Access, it can't begin to match the performance or features of a full-blown implementation of the same database in SQL Server. This example is simply one of the tradeoffs facing developers, administrators, and managers when selecting development tools (and production servers).

As a Development Manager

The most appealing feature of Visual Studio from the perspective of a development manager is the opportunity for a more organized development environment. The tools in Visual Studio and their integration simplify the task of administering a complex development environment. This provides an opportunity to lower software development costs through more efficient coding practices and also by giving software engineers the tools to write code with fewer errors. Specifically, the Visual Studio development environment offers the following benefits from the perspective of a development manager or development team leader:

- Flexibility—Because Visual Studio includes development tools geared toward component builders and solution developers, it offers tremendous flexibility. Some tools, such as Visual Basic and Visual InterDev, are quick to learn and thus are within the reach of the vast majority of the software development community. Others, such as Visual C++ and Visual J++, require a more in-depth knowledge of Windows and Internet programming concepts. Nevertheless, they're important tools for developing large-scale client/server and Web-based applications.

- Simplicity—The introduction of development tool suites has changed development *tool* selection decisions to development *environment* decisions. This greatly simplifies the process of selecting the right tools for the job. To further simplify the process, Microsoft supports most of the important industry and de facto standards in software development (for example, Microsoft's support of Java from Sun Microsystems).

- Consistency—A common thread across most Visual Studio development tools is the visual programming environment. This provides a high level of consistency as developers move from tool to tool over the course of their careers.

- Support—Visual Studio includes a CD-ROM containing a version of the MSDN Library. Owners of Visual Studio also can register for the online version. The combination of a local CD-ROM and the online service for MSDN is valuable for troubleshooting technical problems that arise during software development.

- Integration—One of the biggest reasons for moving your development environment to a complete tool suite is integration. The most obvious form of integration is in the user interface, which Visual Studio offers in the Developer Studio IDE. Another important form of integration is the interaction of the tools with one another; for example, most of the files created with the design tools in Visual Studio can be used by the development tools as well, greatly reducing the overhead associated with communication between design and development team members.

- Team composition—Software development teams in the Visual Studio development environment can consist of individuals with various levels of experience and talent. This goes beyond the roles of component builder and solution developer. For example, nonprogrammers can work on the team in Web page development with a straightforward tool such as Microsoft FrontPage, and their work can be integrated into Visual InterDev.

- Control—Controlling access to all files associated with a software development project is important for development managers and team leaders. This goes beyond controlling source code files to include documentation and design files. Visual SourceSafe provides a safe way to control and monitor access to files in a team development situation.

As an Application Architect

The biggest difference between the Professional and Enterprise Editions of Visual Studio is that the Enterprise Edition contains several tools pertaining to application design, including the

Visual Modeler and Visual Component Manager. The best news is that application architects and object modelers now have tools for design purposes that integrate tightly with the development tools.

You can generate source code for Visual C++, Visual Basic, and Visual J++ from object models created in the Visual Modeler. You can even extract source code from a source module and create an object model to import into the Visual Modeler. This two-way interface is valuable for application architects and object modelers.

The other great news for the Visual Modeler is that it supports the emerging standard for object modeling: the Unified Modeling Language (UML). UML has been developed by several key object-oriented industry leaders employed by Rational Software Corporation, one of the leading object-modeling tool vendors, and has been licensed by Microsoft. At least 25 other leading vendors in the software industry support UML. This means that object models created in other tools that support UML can be imported into Visual Studio, and object models created by the Visual Modeler can be exported to non-Visual Studio tools that support UML.

ON THE WEB

Rational Software Corporation maintains up-to-date information about UML at its Web site at `http://www.rational.com/uml/index.shtml`.

As a Component Builder

Developing software components to support COM has always been difficult and time-consuming. With the advent of ActiveX technology, the job became simpler in some respects and more complex in others. It remains possible to develop ActiveX components with Visual C++, but it's also now possible to develop these components with Visual Basic.

The advantage of developing ActiveX components in Visual Basic is that the developer is shielded from many of the complexities associated with COM. This simplifies the process of developing software components, makes the process of developing software components accessible to a broader group of developers, and—most important—reduces the cost of software development (by saving time) without a sacrifice to project quality.

> **CAUTION**
>
> The fact that ActiveX components can now be developed with Visual Basic is no reason to avoid learning the fundamentals of COM and ActiveX technology.

You can use the development tools in Visual Studio to develop several different types of software components. In particular, component builders can create Java applets, ActiveX controls, and Active Server Components with Visual Studio. The purpose of the various components and the details about building them are topics to which an entire section of this book is dedicated. See the chapters in Part II, "Creating COM Components," for complete coverage of these components and important issues related to their construction and use.

Another advantage Visual Studio provides to component builders is the Microsoft Repository, a tool that catalogs and stores software components. The Microsoft Repository, in conjunction with its front-end Visual Component Manager, can also store object models and documentation associated with the models and components. Because the Microsoft Repository supports UML, it's possible for other non-Visual Studio tools to interoperate with Visual Studio through the Microsoft Repository. If you accept UML as the standard by which your software components are designed and developed and by which your object models are created, the Microsoft Repository will prove to be a valuable tool regardless of which UML-based development tool suite you're using.

As a Solution Developer

Mixed-language development is a foregone conclusion in software development today, so software engineers will have some advantage if the user interface for the different languages is the same. Microsoft has recognized this need and delivered a common user interface called the *Developer Studio IDE*.

Although all the visual programming tools included in Visual Studio share similar user interfaces, it's advantageous for the IDE to provide access to each development tool. It's anticipated—although not absolutely guaranteed—that future versions of Visual Studio will share one, and only one, IDE.

Visual Studio is available to host only on a 32-bit Windows platform—Windows 95 or Windows NT Workstation 4 or later. Moreover, Visual Studio is designed to target the development of 32-bit Windows applications. Of course, these applications are available only for execution on Windows 95 and Windows NT operating platforms.

From Here...

In this chapter, you learned what Visual Studio is, who Visual Studio is for, and what it means to the various people involved in software development. You also saw what tools make up Visual Studio and how Microsoft licenses the entire product package. Finally, you explored the role Visual Studio plays in enterprise application development.

For more information on some of the topics addressed in this chapter and the steps to take next in your exploration of Visual Studio, see the following chapters:

- To get started with your Visual Studio installation, see Chapter 2, "Using Visual Studio to Create Applications."

- To learn about Microsoft's approach to object-oriented technology and how it affects software development, see Chapter 9, "Using Microsoft's Object Technologies."

- To learn more about enterprise application development and the role of Visual Studio, see Chapter 15, "Clients, Servers, and Components: Web-Based Applications."

- To learn the full power of using Visual Studio to develop applications in a distributed computing environment, see Chapter 25, "Clients, Servers, and Components: Design Strategies for Distributed Applications."

CHAPTER 2

Using Visual Studio to Create Applications

by Don Benage

In this chapter

In Search of the Perfect IDE

For years, Microsoft has had a goal to deliver a single Integrated Development Environment (IDE) for all its programming tools. Developers learned how to use this environment and then write code in the language of their choice. They could even use multiple languages much more easily than if each language had its own unique IDE. With Visual Studio 97, the previous release, Microsoft had moved closer to their goal and offered the capability to use all language products within just two IDEs. Research continued on a new ultimate IDE for all languages with the hope that the final goal could be attained in this release, Visual Studio 6.

As so often happens in the real world, two steps forward can necessitate one step back. As work continued on the new IDE, it became obvious that the job of integrating all languages into a single environment would take longer than anticipated. With milestones and ship dates looming, Microsoft had some tough decisions to make. It was eventually decided that the current release, Visual Studio 6, would require the use of three separate IDEs. Visual Basic (VB) would retain its own IDE, Visual C++ would continue to use Developer Studio (the closest thing to a shared environment in the Visual Studio 97 release), and an entirely new IDE would be introduced and shared by Visual InterDev and Visual J++.

This approach was made with those developers who spend all day using Visual Studio in mind. Rather than trying to force the issue and deliver a single environment that was a compromise for one or more of the languages, each language continues to operate in an environment that is both powerful and flexible. Every effort was made to standardize the look and feel, and the operational characteristics, of those elements that could reasonably be standardized. Menus, toolbars, and function keys are still not entirely uniform, but progress has been made. Although there are three IDEs to contend with, they do share many common elements.

The biggest cost to those who use multiple languages on a daily basis, or engage in cross-language debugging scenarios, is the requirement for additional memory to handle the increased size of a multi-IDE working set and the added time and inconvenience of launching these separate environments. This is a better option than providing a substandard environment for one (or more) of the languages and forcing developers working in that language to spend all day struggling to overcome its weaknesses.

The three different IDEs are summarized in Table 2.1.

Table 2.1   IDEs Used in Visual Studio 6

Name	Executable	Language(s)
MS Development Environment	DEVENV.EXE	Visual J++, Visual InterDev
Visual Basic IDE	VB6.EXE	Visual Basic
MS Developer Studio	MSDEV.EXE	Visual C++

This chapter covers some of the rudimentary tasks you need to know to use Visual Studio. If you're an experienced developer who has already worked with a Microsoft language product, you might want to review the initial section on setting up Visual Studio, skip the remainder of the chapter, and proceed directly to the more advanced material in the rest of this book. If you're new to Microsoft's tool suite, this chapter helps you to get started.

Setting Up Visual Studio

Part

I

Ch

2

Installing Visual Studio presents some special challenges because of the size of this large suite of tools. Most people probably won't need to install the entire suite. It would be a rare developer who has skills in using all the languages and tools that are part of Visual Studio. If you're sharing a system with several people who work at different times, however, or want to be able to experiment with the entire tool set, you might still want to install the entire product.

To install the entire Enterprise Edition, you need more than 2GB of disk space. If you don't install all the online help files but instead run them from CD-ROM, you can save a substantial amount of space. However, the shared components alone require up to 300MB. You also should remove earlier standalone versions of any languages in the suite (for example, Visual Basic 4). Finally, you should allow plenty of time for the operation. Installation times vary widely depending on the speed of your computer's CD-ROM drive, hard disk(s), and internal clock; however, installation of everything can easily take more than two hours.

If you have been using the Visual Studio 97 release, especially if you have been using all the tools in the suite, you should strongly consider installing the new release on a clean build of Windows (whatever flavor you might use). Although you might be able to successfully upgrade to the new release without reinstalling, a tool suite of this size and complexity is a considerable investment in time and resources. If problems develop, it's a real benefit to know that you started with a clean version of the operating system, applied the latest service patch, and then installed the Visual Studio suite. Your chances of resolving a difficult or intermittent problem are much higher under these circumstances than if you upgrade over a release that has already been in operation for months.

Of course, you should also make a backup of all your data, source code, project files, design documents, and any other data on your machine before proceeding with the installation/ upgrade. Although developers sometimes play a bit fast and loose with suggestions made for mere mortals, this would be a good time to be safe.

Finally, as this book went to press, no service patches for the Visual Studio 6 product had been released. Undoubtedly, service patches for Visual Studio 6 will be offered in the future and should usually be downloaded and applied. In general, Microsoft patches are always cumulative so that you'll require only the most recent one; you don't need to apply a series of patches in order (see the later section "Applying a Service Patch" for more information).

All these potential hurdles notwithstanding, after you assemble the CD-ROMs and any appropriate service patches, uninstall any old versions, and check your hard disk to verify that you have enough space, you're ready to proceed. Although the process can be time-consuming, it's not difficult if you follow the basic guidelines offered in the following sections.

N O T E If you're installing multiple language and server products, you'll be asked to restart your machine after some of the individual products are installed. It's recommended that you take the time to restart your machine any time you're prompted to do so, even if you intend to install additional products. This isn't always required. If the setup program doesn't prompt you to restart, you might safely proceed with the next product without rebooting.

Installing Visual Studio

The setup program for Visual Studio 6 Enterprise Edition (the only version described in this chapter) is a tremendous improvement over Visual Studio 97. The process is much more integrated with this release. When you launch the setup program, as described shortly, you'll first need to install the latest release of Internet Explorer (IE), version 4.01. IE is used as a vehicle to deliver help, online documentation (for the Windows NT Option Pack), and besides, it's not an option. The setup program won't continue until you install IE.

You should install the Microsoft Developer Network (MSDN) Library last because this component checks to see which other components you've installed and adds support information for only those tools and languages it finds. To ensure that you have the support files for all the languages and tools you're using, install the MSDN Library after everything else is properly set up.

The language tools are generally all on Disc 1, the server-based tools on Disc 2, and some additional support files on Disc 3. However, to run the integrated setup program, you always start with Disc 1.

To install Visual Studio, follow these steps:

1. Insert Disc 1 from the CD-ROM set into your CD-ROM drive.

   Depending on your computer's configuration, the setup program might launch automatically via the AutoPlay feature of Windows NT 4 or Windows 95/98. Otherwise, you can manually launch the setup program by double-clicking the Setup.exe file in the root directory of the CD-ROM drive.

2. The Installation Wizard for Visual Studio 6 Enterprise Edition dialog box appears. It describes the operation of the Wizard using Next and Back buttons and gives you a chance to choose the View Readme button to review the Readme file for Visual Studio 6. Choose the Next button.

3. The End User License Agreement (EULA) is displayed. Review it and click the I accept the agreement radio button. Choose Next to continue.

4. You're prompted to enter Your Name, Your company's name, and the product's ID number. You usually can find the CD Key on a yellow sticker attached to the back of one of the CD-ROM envelopes. Enter the requested information and choose Next to continue.

5. At this point you'll probably be prompted to install Internet Explorer 4.01. In some cases you might be prompted to install a new version of IE 4.01 even though you're already running a version you believe is 4.01. The Visual Studio setup program insists on IE 4.01, build 4.72.3110.8 or greater. Don't fight it. Click the Install IE 4.01 check box, and choose Next to continue.

6. The Internet Explorer 4.01 service pack 1 Active Setup dialog appears. Follow the instructions and set up IE 4.01. Restart your computer. Close the annoying IE Welcome dialog (you can't uncheck the Show this next time you log in check box until the second time you've been annoyed). The Visual Studio 6 Installation Wizard continues by confirming that you have successfully installed IE. Choose Next to continue.

7. The Enterprise Setup Options menu appears (see Figure 2.1). You can select Custom, Products, or Server Applications. Choosing products allows you to install preconfigured products (for example, Visual Basic with appropriate tools and server options). Selecting Server Applications skips the workstation tools and languages and proceeds directly to server setup options. Click Custom and then choose Next.

Part

I

Ch

2

FIGURE 2.1
The Installation Wizard for Visual Studio 6 guides you through the installation process for all languages, server applications, and add-on utilities.

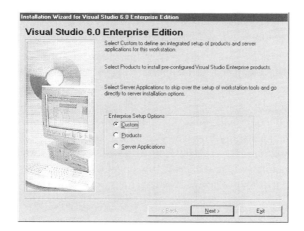

8. You are now offered an opportunity to select a folder as the location of the common files shared by Visual Studio 6 applications. The minimum space required for the folder is 50 MB. The amount of free space on the currently selected drive is displayed. Either accept the default, or Browse for a folder of your choice. Choose Next to continue.

9. The Welcome dialog for Visual Studio 6 Enterprise Setup is displayed. You are reminded to close any running applications and encouraged to read and follow the End User License Agreement. Choose Continue.

10. The Product ID number for your copy of Visual Studio 6 is displayed, and you are encouraged to write it down for use when you fill out your registration card or when calling for product support. You can also retrieve this number later by choosing Help, About from the menu in any of the products you are installing. Choose OK to continue.

11. The Visual Studio 6 Enterprise—Custom dialog is displayed (see Figure 2.2).

FIGURE 2.2

The Custom dialog can be used to select exactly which products and options you want to install.

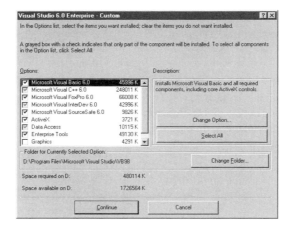

12. The Custom dialog is preset to a full list of products with a suggested set of optional features appropriate for most users. The space required for each product, as well as the total space required and available, is displayed in the dialog. You can explore and change the optional features that will be installed by selecting a product in the Options window and choosing the Change Option button.

13. After you have made your selections and double-checked the space requirements to be sure you have enough disk space, choose OK to begin the installation process.

14. Depending on the individual products to be installed by Enterprise Setup, various dialogs are presented that provide you with information and ask you to make some choices. For example, when installing Visual C++ you are asked if you want to register environment variables necessary to run build tools from a command prompt. A SourceSafe dialog describes optional database formats that affect whether or not your new database is compatible with older SourceSafe clients.

15. After gathering any additional information required, Enterprise Setup displays a progress bar in addition to an informational panel that describes some of the new features of Visual Studio 6 (see Figure 2.3). You might be prompted to insert a different CD during the installation process.

16. Remember that if you're prompted to restart your machine, you should take the time to do so (see Figure 2.4). The Installation Wizard restarts and allows you to continue after rebooting. If you aren't prompted to reboot, you can continue with the next step immediately.

FIGURE 2.3

The new features of Visual Studio 6 are displayed in addition to a progress bar.

FIGURE 2.4

At various points, you will be asked to reboot your machine so that Windows can complete the installation process.

17. After installing all the language products and tools you selected, the Installation Wizard prompts you to install MSDN. Insert the MSDN Disc 1 in your CD drive and choose Next to continue.

18. The Welcome dialog for the MSDN Library—Visual Studio 6 is displayed. You are again urged to read and follow all End User License Agreements and to shut down any running programs. Choose Continue.

19. A dialog again displays your product ID number. Click OK to continue. The License Agreement for MSDN is displayed in a window. Click I Agree to continue.

20. The MSDN Library—Visual Studio 6 Setup dialog is displayed. You can choose Typical, Custom, or Full. You can also choose Change Folder to select the location where the MSDN files will be installed. Choose Custom.

21. The Custom dialog is displayed (see Figure 2.5). You now have the opportunity to select those components that you want to install directly to your hard disk. This allows you to use these files without requiring the CD and also improves performance. You must select the first entry to install the Text Index in order to use MSDN without the CD.

FIGURE 2.5

In addition to the explicitly listed options, there is a selection called All Other Files that encompasses older content and requires over 300MB.

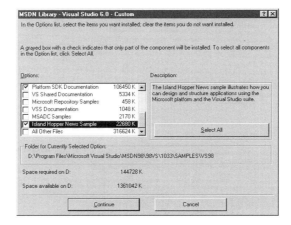

22. Once again you will see a progress bar in front of an informational panel, this time describing the MSDN Library. When setup of MSDN has completed, a dialog announces success. Choose OK to continue.

23. The Installation Wizard for Visual Studio 6 resumes and offers the option to install Other Client Tools (for example, InstallShield). If you want to install any of these tools, select the product name in the Client Tools list box, and choose Install. Otherwise, choose Next to continue.

24. The Server Setup dialog appears. You have the option to install Visual SourceSafe Server or to launch the BackOffice Installation Wizard to guide you through the setup of other Server products. If you intend to use SourceSafe and want to install a SourceSafe database on this machine, select that option in the Server Components list box and choose Install. Otherwise, skip to step 27.

25. You will be prompted to change CDs. Insert Visual Studio 6 Disc 2 and choose OK to continue. After a Welcome dialog with the customary warning about License Agreements is shown, you will see the Visual SourceSafe Server Setup dialog (see Figure 2.6).

FIGURE 2.6

This setup program is used to install a shared Visual SourceSafe database and the administrative tools and to create a shareable NetSetup program to allow client installation from this machine.

26. Choose the Server button to continue. Again, you will see a progress bar and an informational panel describing the new features of the product. After the installation is complete, you will be prompted to restart your machine. After rebooting, the Installation Wizard continues.

27. Select Launch BackOffice Installation Wizard from the Server Components list box and choose Install. The BackOffice Server Setup dialog appears (see Figure 2.7).

Part

I

Ch

2

FIGURE 2.7
The BackOffice Server Setup provides an integrated setup of limited license versions of Microsoft's server products for use as a development test bed.

28. You can select the various option buttons on this dialog to see additional descriptive information about the option displayed in the right half of the window. In addition, you can choose More Information to see additional information about a selection. Select the appropriate option, and choose Next. Custom will be described here.

29. A Disk Space Requirements dialog is displayed, with requirements based on a standard set of options before you are given a chance to revise those selections. This gives you an opportunity to quickly identify any potential major problems with disk space shortages on a particular drive so that you can change locations or product selection to resolve those issues. After reviewing the disk space dialog, choose Next to continue.

30. The BackOffice Programs and Their Components dialog is displayed (see Figure 2.8).

FIGURE 2.8
This dialog is used to customize the installation of server products in the BackOffice family.

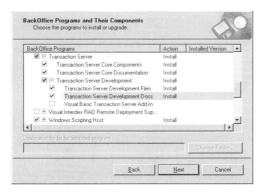

31. Top level items are displayed in a list box. To see what options are included, click any of the plus signs to the left of a product name to expand the hierarchy and view its subcomponents. If necessary, you can choose Change Folder to change the location of a particular product. Choose Next to continue.

32. The Administrator and Service Accounts for BackOffice Programs dialog is displayed (see Figure 2.9). Use this dialog to associate appropriate service accounts with server applications such as Microsoft Transaction Server (MTS) and SQL Server.

FIGURE 2.9

You can define any necessary administrative and service accounts for your BackOffice server applications in this dialog.

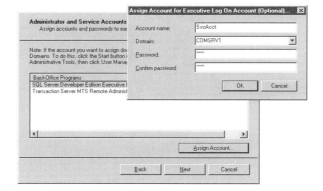

N O T E   Service accounts provide a security context in which Windows NT-based services run. They are similar to standard user accounts, but have the special user right Log On as a Service. If you haven't already defined service accounts, you can do so at this time using the User Manager for Domains application (which you can find by selecting Start, Programs, Administrative Tools, User Manager for Domains from the menu).

33. Select a product and choose the Assign Account button. Make appropriate entries in the Account name, Domain, Password, and Confirm Password text boxes. Choose OK.

34. After assigning accounts for all appropriate BackOffice products, choose Next to continue.

35. Some BackOffice products (for example, SQL Server) display additional dialogs to gather more configuration information (see Figure 2.10).

36. After all information has been gathered, a confirmation dialog shows the products, options, and locations that you have selected. Choose Back if you need to make any changes. Otherwise, choose Next.

37. The BackOffice Component Installation dialog is presented to show the progress of the installation. In addition to a progress bar, it lists the products to be installed and indicates with an arrow the current product being installed. Those products that have already been installed are indicated by a check mark.

FIGURE 2.10

All additional BackOffice configuration dialogs are presented before the actual setup process begins.

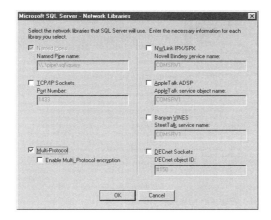

38. A final dialog indicates that the process is complete. Choose Finish to exit the BackOffice Installation Wizard. You will be prompted to reboot your machine. After rebooting, the Installation Wizard for Visual Studio 6 starts one last time and prompts you to Register Over the Web Now! Check the Register Now check box if you want and choose Finish. You're done!

After you install all the languages, tools, server applications, and SDKs you plan to use, you're ready to apply any service patches that have been released. This important part of the installation process can save you hours of aggravation later. Although running your new tool suite might be tempting, it's a good idea to check the Microsoft Web site if you haven't already done so, download any appropriate patches, and apply them at this time.

Applying a Service Patch

Microsoft provides service patches, which include a cumulative set of all bug fixes, for all products used for corporate information systems, including their operating systems. As this book went to press there weren't any service patches for Visual Studio 6 yet, but you can check to be sure by visiting the following Web site.

ON THE WEB

Service patches are available at no charge (except connect time) on Microsoft's Web site at `http://msdn.microsoft.com/vstudio/sp/default.asp`. The Web page provides complete instructions for installing the latest patch. In general, installation requires nothing more than simply running a setup program, verifying that the default actions to be taken are acceptable, waiting for some files to be copied, and then rebooting your machine after the patch is applied.

In addition to the service patches there is a wealth of troubleshooting information in Microsoft's *Knowledge Base*, an online database of problems and their fixes (see the later section "Finding Help").

Using Developer Studio

Developer Studio is a powerful IDE that supports application development with Visual C++. In the previous release of Visual Studio, you could also use it to view much of the online information available to support your development efforts. In this release, online information is viewed through HTML Help, a new application designed to provide the same searching and organizational characteristics as those previously offered within Developer Studio, which is now used only for developing applications in Visual C++.

Many new features have been added to make Visual C++ 6 and the Developer Studio IDE easier to use and more productive. Table 2.2 shows some of the new features in this release.

Table 2.2   Developer Studio's New Features

Feature	Benefit
Edit and Continue debugging (ENC)	Fix a bug and continue without having to stop, recompile, and rebuild
IntelliSense	Provides information about methods of a class or interface in a drop-down box as you type
Speed enhancements	Improved compile and build times
ATL Object Wizard	Allows you to insert an ActiveX Template Library object into a Microsoft Foundation Class project

To give you a quick feel for using this environment, walk through the following example. You'll use the AppWizard to create a basic Win32 application complete with its own project and workspace and to run it. For debugging techniques, see Chapter 3, "Debugging Enterprise Applications with Visual Studio."

To use Developer Studio for these tasks, follow these steps:

1. Choose File, New from the menu. In the New dialog box, click the Projects tab (see Figure 2.11).

2. Select Win32 Application from the list. In the Project Name text box, enter a name for your new project (for example, HelloWorld).

3. In the Location text box, enter a path for the folder where you want to store your project and workspace files. You can also click the ellipsis (…) button to browse for an appropriate location. Click OK.

4. Select Create New Workspace to create a workspace that you can use to save the configuration of all the various windows you might create.

5. At the prompt to confirm the creation of a new folder, click OK. Another dialog box confirms that your project and workspace are created. Click OK.

6. A Win32 Application—Step 1 of 1 dialog appears. You can use this dialog to create an empty project, a simple Win32 application, or a typical Hello World application. Select the third option and choose the Finish button.

FIGURE 2.11
The New dialog box allows you to create new workspaces, projects, applications, and other types of files and documents.

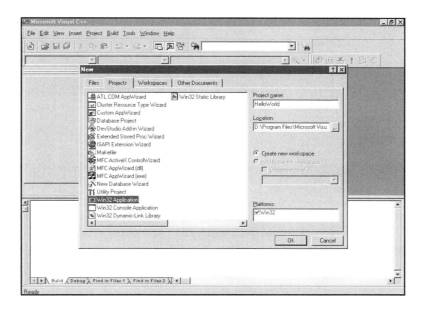

7. After the AppWizard runs, your display should look something like Figure 2.12 except that you haven't yet built an executable application or opened any of the files to inspect them. Select the FileView tab in the window at the upper left if it is not already visible. Double-click on the HelloWorld.cpp file to open it for viewing or editing.

FIGURE 2.12
The HelloWorld application has just been built with the results appearing in the Build tab of the output window at the bottom of the screen.

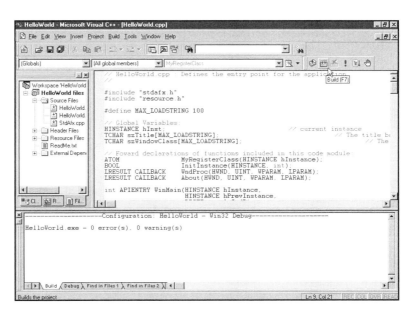

8. To build the application, click the Build button (the second button from the left on the Build minibar—see Figure 2.13). If the Build minibar isn't visible now, right-click anywhere on the toolbar area and select it from the pop-up menu.

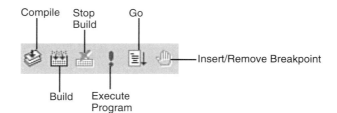

FIGURE 2.13
The Build minibar has toolbar buttons that control the build and debug processes.

9. The results of your build process appear on the Build page of the output window at the bottom of the screen. (If the output window isn't visible, choose View, Output from the menu.)

10. Assuming that you had no (serious) errors (as should be the case if you've followed the example exactly), you can now run the application and experiment with some simple debugging techniques. Click the Execute Program toolbar button to run your new application. The results should look something like Figure 2.14.

FIGURE 2.14
A typical Hello World application in action.

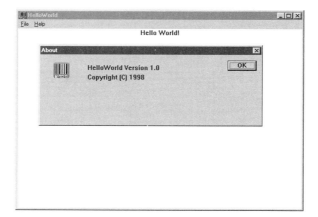

You've created a project and learned how to compile and link your application into an executable program or module. This rudimentary process is the basis for any build process you might run. But Developer Studio is used for more than just building applications. It's also a powerful debugging tool that helps you find any errors in your code and correct them. You'll find detailed descriptions of various debugging tasks in the next chapter.

▶ For more information about debugging, **see** Chapter 3, "Debugging Enterprise Applications with Visual Studio," **p. 55**

Using Visual Basic's Development Environment

This section introduces you to the main features of the Visual Basic 6 environment and helps you become comfortable with its features. Over the course of its history, Visual Basic's IDE has been the first to offer innovative features such as IntelliSense. With IntelliSense, as you enter a command the IDE automatically offers help with the syntax, describes both required and optional parameters, and streamlines the job of entering the remaining code. Because its focus is to provide an environment and language that simplifies programming tasks while still providing powerful capabilities, it has often been the first language to receive new features targeting ease of use.

Visual Basic 6 continues this tradition and has been enhanced. Table 2.3 shows some of the new features that have been added to VB and its IDE.

Part
I
Ch
2

Table 2.3   Visual Basic's New Features

Feature	Benefit
Data Environment Designer	A data modeling tool that allows you to design hierarchical data objects
Data Object Wizard	Generates code for data access classes and controls
WebClass Designer	Creates cross-platform, cross-browser Web applications within VB
Package and Deployment Wizard	Aids in the creation of Setup programs or Web-based installation files

You can get more information on these tools in other chapters of this book. For example, the integrated visual database tools are discussed in Chapter 4, "Creating Database-Aware Applications with Visual Studio." In this section, you'll get a quick look at the Visual Basic environment by using the VB Application Wizard to create a fully functional application shell to which you can add customized logic to create many different types of applications.

To use the Visual Basic IDE, follow these steps:

1. Launch Visual Basic by choosing Programs, Microsoft Visual Studio 6, Visual Basic 6 from the Start menu.

2. The Visual Basic IDE appears (see Figure 2.15).

    Depending on your preferences, you might also be presented with the New Project dialog box. If you don't want this dialog box automatically displayed in the future, select the Don't Show This Dialog in the Future check box. The various types of projects that you can create with Visual Basic appear in the dialog box.

FIGURE 2.15
The Visual Basic IDE is visible behind the New Project dialog box, which you can open at any time by choosing File, New Project from the menu.

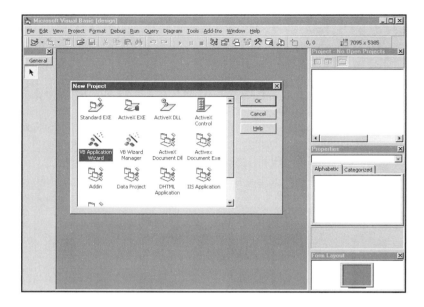

3. For the purposes of this example, click the New tab in the New Project dialog box. You can browse the different types of projects supported by VB to find the one that you are interested in creating.

4. Select the VB Application Wizard icon and choose OK. An Introduction dialog is displayed. If you use this wizard regularly and have saved settings that you want to reuse, you can select a profile to load using the drop-down list box, or by choosing the ellipsis button and browsing for the file containing a profile that was previously saved. Because this is likely the first time you have to run this wizard, you won't have a profile available yet. Choose Next to continue.

5. The Interface Type dialog is displayed (see Figure 2.16).

FIGURE 2.16
Use the Interface Type dialog to select your application's appearance.

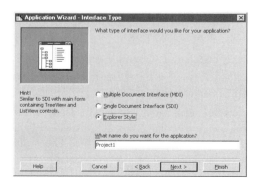

6. For this example, select an Explorer Style interface. Then enter a name for the application. Choose Next to continue.

7. The next dialog allows you to configure the menus for your application. A standard set of menus, including File, Edit, View, and Help, are displayed by default in a two-pane format. You can add, change, or delete menus (in the left pane) and menu items for the selected menu (in the right pane) using this dialog. When you are happy with the menu layout, choose Next to continue.

8. A similar two-pane display, the Customize Toolbar dialog, is presented (see Figure 2.17). Select among the available buttons in the left pane, and then click the right-arrow button to move your selection into the right window, causing it to become active and appear on the toolbar mockup near the top of the dialog. You can include separators anywhere you like to keep related buttons grouped together and improve legibility. Choose Next to continue.

Part

I

Ch

2

FIGURE 2.17

This dialog provides complete control over which toolbar buttons will be displayed in your application and the layout of the toolbar.

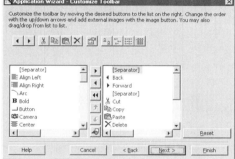

9. For applications that will eventually be distributed in multiple languages, it's desirable to use a resource file to store the strings used in the application. For this example, select No on the Resources dialog and choose Next to continue.

10. The Internet Connectivity dialog is displayed (see Figure 2.18). If you would like your application to support Internet connectivity, select Yes in this dialog and then indicate which URL you want the browser to initially display. Select No for this example and choose Next to continue.

FIGURE 2.18

Internet connectivity can easily be added to any VB application with the Application Wizard.

11. The next dialog allows you to select a variety of standard forms and form templates that you might want to include in your application. The different types of forms are listed in the following:

   - Splash screen at application startup
   - Login dialog
   - Options dialog for custom settings
   - About box
   - Generic dialog
   - ODBC Login
   - Tip of the Day
   - Web Browser

12. Click the check boxes on any of the forms or templates you'd like to include in your project. Once your project is created, you can customize any of the forms you have selected to suit your specific needs. Choose Next to continue.

13. The Data Access Forms dialog is presented. You can easily create forms that are based on tables or queries from your databases. You can select existing forms, or choose the Create New Form button to create a form from scratch. This example doesn't make use of a data form, so choose Next to continue.

14. You have finished. If you want, you can save a profile for use the next time you use the wizard. You can also view a report summarizing the activity of the wizard. Choose Finish to complete the wizard.

15. An Application Created dialog is displayed to confirm the successful conclusion of the wizard process. Choose OK to close the dialog, and your new application complete with forms is displayed, ready for your modifications (see Figure 2.19).

16. Find the Run button on the toolbar (a right arrow near the middle) and click it to compile and run your application.

Although this overview of the Visual Basic IDE is but the tip of the iceberg, it should provide you with a basic feel for its use. Use the sample application you've just created to try things and experiment on your own. At any time while using the IDE, press the F1 key for help. In addition to the online help, the last section in this chapter presents other sources of help you might find useful.

FIGURE 2.19

A sample application created by the VB Application Wizard with a slightly modified splash screen form visible in the fore-ground.

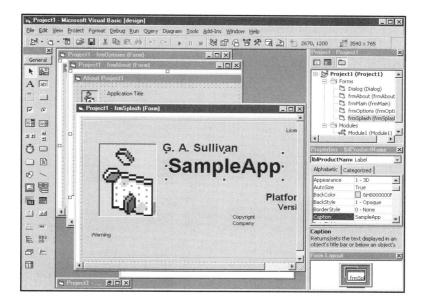

Using the Microsoft Development Environment for Visual InterDev and Visual J++

The newest IDE in the Visual Studio suite is shared by both Visual J++ and Visual InterDev. These two products have both been dramatically updated in the Visual Studio 6 release as you might expect for what is essentially their second major release. The IDE they share is known as the Microsoft Development Environment, and it is well suited to the development of Web-based projects and the other types of projects these languages support.

In order to take full advantage of this environment, you need to have an Internet Information Server (IIS) Web server to use as a development platform as you create your Web-based applications. This could be a remote server on another machine or a personal Web server on your own machine. The Web server must be running the current version of FrontPage Server Extensions for all the features of this IDE to operate properly.

In the following example, a remote server named HQSRV3 is used to contain and deliver the Web content and application(s) that you will create. It was created by installing the Windows NT Option pack on a Windows NT Server machine. The Option Pack includes IIS, MTS, Microsoft Message Queue (MSMQ), and other server-based components. You can use the instructions in the first section of the chapter to launch the BackOffice Installation Wizard if you want to create a new Web server.

Some of the main features of the new IDE are listed in the Table 2.4.

Table 2.4   Features of the Microsoft Development Environment

Feature	Benefit
Toolbox	Visual Basic–like group of user interface elements and controls that can be placed on a page.
Tabbed views	Select Design, Source, or QuickView to see form based design, underlying code, or preview what the final display in a browser will look like.
Extensive Drag & Drop	In addition to ActiveX controls, you can drag/drop HTML fragments, newly designed design-time controls (DTCs), and HTML-intrinsic controls.
Properties window	VB-like properties window for setting and changing the properties of most anything visible in the IDE.
IntelliSense	Displays methods and properties of any object it knows of (including Active Server Pages [ASP] objects, ActiveX Data Objects [ADO], and objects built in VB and Visual C++).

To create a new Visual InterDev Web project, follow these steps:

1. Launch Visual InterDev by choosing Programs, Microsoft Visual Studio 6, Visual InterDev 6 from the Start menu. The Microsoft Development Environment is displayed, with a New Project dialog (see Figure 2.20).

FIGURE 2.20

You can create a wide variety of projects using the Microsoft Development Environment.

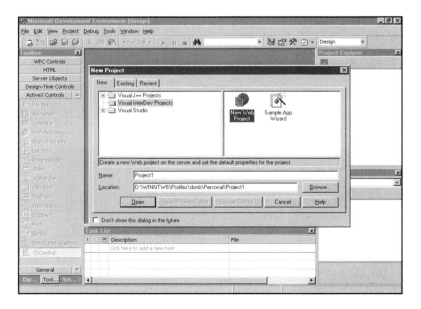

2. The first dialog in the Web Project Wizard is displayed. With this dialog you can select the Web server you want to use, and the mode you want to work in—master or local. Master mode automatically updates the Web application on the server, while local mode gives you explicit control of when updates occur. Make your selections, and choose Next to continue.

3. You should briefly see a dialog advising you that the Web server is being contacted. If there are no difficulties contacting the server, Step 2 of 4 will be displayed (see Figure 2.21).

FIGURE 2.21

Use this dialog to select an existing Web application on the server or create a new one.

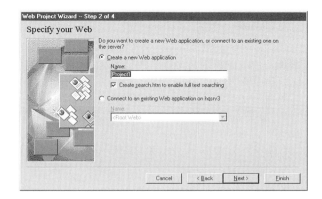

N O T E   An application, as used here, is nothing more than a collection of related Web pages stored in a folder that is generally defined as a virtual directory on the Web server.

4. After you have created a new application or connected to an existing one, choose Next to continue. The next dialog (Step 3 of 4) is displayed. It is used to determine the layout of your Web pages (see Figure 2.22).

FIGURE 2.22

A variety of predefined Web page layouts are available to choose from.

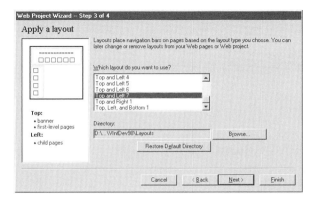

5. Select a layout for the Web pages in this application. You can select a layout in the list box labeled <u>W</u>hich Layout Do You Want to Use? A preview of the layout appears in the pane at the left of the dialog. Choose <u>N</u>ext to continue.

6. The Step 4 of 4 dialog is displayed (see Figure 2.23). Select a theme from the list of available themes. The Blueprint theme is shown in the example. Choose <u>F</u>inish to complete the wizard.

FIGURE 2.23

In addition to the standard themes, a collection of additional themes can be optionally installed during the setup of Visual InterDev.

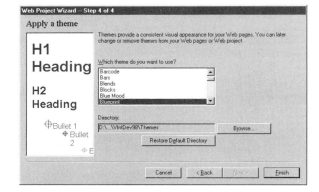

7. A series of dialogs will inform you of progress (creating project file, copying script library, and so on). When the process is complete, you have a new, Web-based project sitting on your test server.

8. To modify any of the elements on the Web Server, you must first get a working *copy*. Alternatively, if you simply want to see what's there, you can get a read-only copy without locking any of the files to which another developer might desire access.

9. Right-click on the Search.HTML page and select Get <u>W</u>orking Copy from the pop-up menu. The page is displayed in the tabbed editor window, and a small lock icon appears to the left of the document's icon indicating that you now have this locked for updating.

10. Right-click on the same icon again and choose View in <u>B</u>rowser from the menu. You should see something like the display in Figure 2.24.

11. You can make changes to the local copy of any of the pages in this application, add new pages, and then Release Working Copy to transfer the updated pages back to the Web server.

FIGURE 2.24

You can preview a page in the browser of your choice or select the QuickView tab to see a similar view without launching a separate browser.

Finding Help

Each language product in Visual Studio has multiple options for getting help—some particular to the individual language and some shared across all Visual Studio products. In this section, you learn how to use various sources for additional information.

With the rapid rate of change that's now common among software development products, the tool many developers prefer to use first is Microsoft's Web site. Microsoft has made a large and ongoing investment in providing a wealth of background information, bug fixes, downloadable update files, and the latest news through http://www.microsoft.com.

Visual Studio's primary Web page is at http://msdn.microsoft.com/vstudio. Go here for the latest news, pricing and upgrade information, frequently asked questions (FAQ), white papers, data sheets, evaluation guides, and ordering information.

You can download service patches from http://msdn.microsoft.com/vstudio/sp/default.asp. Here you'll find not only the latest service patch itself, but also instructions for applying it, a list of the problems it fixes, FAQs, and links to related Knowledge Base articles describing specific problem scenarios. You can download the appropriate patch directly or order a CD-ROM containing the patch because it might be quite large.

As mentioned earlier, the Microsoft Knowledge Base is a large database of known problems and their fixes. Although you can't always find your specific problem in the Knowledge Base, it's usually worth checking to ensure that the difficulty you're experiencing hasn't already been diagnosed and fixed. To search the Knowledge Base, go to Microsoft's home page and choose the Search button at the top of the page. This displays a query page that allows you to enter key words and select the specific areas within the Microsoft Web site you want to search. The Knowledge Base is listed as one of the available areas to search.

In addition to the various online options, a wealth of information is on the Visual Studio CD-ROMs. Although this information is obviously not as up-to-date as the Web site, it's available anytime and is a great source of background information and tutorial-type information that isn't subject to change frequently. During installation, you can choose to install this information directly to your hard disk, or leave it on the CD-ROMs. If you have lots of hard disk space, it's clearly faster and easier to access this information directly from the hard disk. However, because of the vast amount of supporting information included in Visual Studio (more than 1GB), most people are willing to trade the moderate inconvenience of having to occasionally swap CD-ROMs for the savings in disk space.

You can view the MSDN Library CD-ROM directly in the new HTML Help application. This application is installed automatically when you run the Setup program for the MSDN library. It includes a built-in query capability to search for information on any topic.

ON THE WEB

Another great resource is the MSDN Web site. This has become a focal point for new information on technologies and tools for software developers. In addition to product information, white papers on important technologies, and links to other important resources for developers, this site also features regular columns highlighting a particular product or tool. You can find this site at `http://msdn.microsoft.com/developer/`.

You've learned about the primary Web-based and CD-ROM–based resources available to Visual Studio users in search of additional information. These resources, combined with the information found in the rest of this book, should help make you an effective developer of applications with the latest techniques, designed to run in the sophisticated environments found in most organizations today.

From Here...

For more information on some of the topics addressed in this chapter and where to go next in your exploration of Visual Studio 6, see the following chapters:

- For further insight about debugging applications, see Chapter 3, "Debugging Enterprise Applications with Visual Studio."

- To learn how to use Visual Studio to develop database applications, see Chapter 4, "Creating Database-Aware Applications with Visual Studio."

- To learn about Microsoft's approach to object-oriented technology and how it affects software development, see Chapter 9, "Using Microsoft's Object Technologies."

- To learn how to use Visual Studio to develop applications for the Internet or your own intranet, see Chapter 15, "Clients, Servers, and Components: Web-Based Applications."

- To learn how to tap into the full power of using Visual Studio to develop applications in a distributed computing environment, see Chapter 25, "Clients, Servers, and Components: Design Strategies for Distributed Applications."

CHAPTER 3

Debugging Enterprise Applications with Visual Studio

by Michael D. Sallee

In this chapter

Debugging Fundamentals in Visual Studio

Since the creation of the first compiler, the development community has been demanding better and better techniques for eliminating programming errors. Over time, compiler developers have addressed this challenge by continually improving and integrating their products. In today's world a single compiler is not enough. Developers commonly use multiple programming languages on multiple platforms. This situation can make debugging errors a difficult and tedious task.

Visual Studio provides state-of-the-art development environments for each of its programming tools. It provides one of the most tightly integrated environments on the market today. To understand how Visual Studio assists the developer in removing errors from an application under development, I'll examine where errors can be introduced during development.

- Typing errors frequently occur when developing an application. Visual Studio provides wizards that enable much of the application to be autogenerated for you. However, at some point typing is still required. All the Visual Studio development environments provide editors that display reserved words and comments in different colors. They also use IntelliSense, which is a technology that automates routine tasks and simplifies complex ones. It's used in Visual Studio to assist with code completion. For example, the Auto List Members feature automatically displays a drop-down list of available options appropriate to a given situation. For example, if `Mike` is an instance of a class with a property (`employeeID`) and two methods (`submitTimecard` and `getPaycheck`), when `Mike` followed by a period is typed, a list is displayed containing the options (`employeeID`, `submitTimecard`, and `getPaycheck`). Additionally, if one of the methods is selected, the Auto Quick Info feature displays the parameter list.

- Compilation errors result from incorrectly constructed code. If you incorrectly type a keyword or variable, omit some necessary punctuation, or simply use a variable wrong, a compilation error is generated. Visual Studio explains the error and requires the error to be fixed before the executable is generated. This type of error generates only when compiling takes place.

- Traditional programming languages, such as Visual C++, Visual Basic, and Visual J++, are compiled on demand within their respective development environments. Web-based programming languages using Hypertext Markup Language (HTML), script, or Active Server Pages (ASP) are called *interpretive languages* and work a little differently. They are all runtime compiled; that is, they are compiled and executed each time the uniform resource locator (URL) is navigated to.

- Runtime errors are errors that cannot be detected until the code is executed at runtime. An example of a runtime error is when a calculation results in a division by zero. If you are executing in debug mode when a runtime error occurs, Visual Studio halts execution at that line of code, allowing the situation that caused the error to be examined.

- Logic error is another way of saying the application, or code fragment, doesn't perform as expected. This can be the result of bad design, poor code structure, or typing error. Often logic errors can only be detected by testing the application and analyzing its results.

This chapter covers some of the tasks you need to understand to debug applications in Visual Studio. The first section covers the basics of debugging in Visual Studio. The remaining sections are divided into development problem areas, which are subdivided by the applicable Visual Studio development tools. A developer having a particular problem can simply turn to that problem area or development tool and begin. Because of the similarities in the environments, it's not necessary to study the debugging tasks for development tools you don't use.

This section covers the rudimentary fundamentals of debugging in Visual Studio. A developer experienced with any one of the development tools (Visual Basic, Visual C++, Visual J++, or Visual InterDev), should probably skip this section and focus on his particular problem area described later in this chapter.

This section addresses the problem of debugging in Visual Studio as the same for all its development tools. However, because of the differences among the development environments, the information presented might vary slightly for a particular development tool.

The debugging tools provided by Visual Studio are designed to help you with troubleshooting logic and runtime errors. These tools are also ideal for observing the behavior of code that has no errors.

Debugging is the process of correcting or modifying your code so that your project can build cleanly and run as expected. When it comes to debugging, there is no fixed sequence of steps. This chapter gives you the general steps required to find most logic or runtime errors in your application.

The better you understand conditions surrounding an error, the faster you can find a suitable solution. Each development environment in Visual Studio allows you to see what your application is doing when it runs. It also provides access to the current state of your application, including the values of variables, expressions, properties, and the names of active procedure calls.

A sample Debug toolbar is shown in Figure 3.1. There are slight variations in the Debug toolbar between the different development environments, but the basic functionality is the same. The Debug toolbar contains the most common commands and tools available to support your debugging session. The ToolTip feature displays the function of a particular toolbar button when the mouse is positioned over the icon. The following list briefly describes each debug tool's purpose (as it appears on the Debug toolbar, from left to right).

FIGURE 3.1
The Debug toolbar.

- Run/Continue/Go—Causes the application to begin running. If the application is in break mode, selection causes the application to resume running.
- Break—Causes the application to stop execution (or break), as if a breakpoint had been encountered.
- End—Terminates the running application.

- Toggle Breakpoint—Marks or unmarks a line of code in the application as a breakpoint.
- Step Into—Runs the next executable line of code in the application and steps into procedures.
- Step Over—Runs the next executable line of code in the application without stepping into procedures.
- Step Out—Runs the remainder of the current procedure and breaks at the next line in the calling procedure.
- Locals Window—Displays the current value of local variables while the application is in break mode.
- Immediate Window—Allows you to run code or query values while the application is in break mode.
- Watch Window—Displays the values of selected expressions.
- Quick Watch—Lists the current value of an expression while the application is in break mode.
- Call Stack—Shows the list procedures that have been called but not yet completed while in Break mode.

Visual Studio provides many ways to set breakpoints. Most of the development environments support clicking to the left of the line at which you want to break on. When a breakpoint is set, Visual Studio inserts a red circle at the beginning of the line. The Visual Basic development environment also highlights the entire line. Placing the cursor on the line you want to break at and clicking the Toggle Breakpoint icon on the Debug toolbar also sets a breakpoint.

The Debug toolbar is initially displayed floating, or not attached to the environment window. It can be moved, docked, or closed to suit your debugging needs. If the Debug toolbar is accidentally closed, it can be redisplayed by right-clicking on the white space in the development's toolbar area and selecting Debug.

While running, a break can be forced by clicking on the Break icon on the Debug toolbar. This forces a break at the currently executing line of code. This feature is useful when an operation in your application seems to be taking an inordinate amount of time to complete. This might perhaps be a result of coding an endless loop. Selecting the Break icon allows the situation to be examined.

Regardless of how a breakpoint is reached, when at one, the capabilities of the debugger are available. Sometimes you can determine the cause of a problem by running portions of code. More often, however, you will also have to analyze what's happening to the data. You might isolate a problem in a variable or property with an incorrect value, and then have to determine how and why that variable or property was assigned an incorrect value.

With the debugging windows, you can monitor the values of expressions and variables while stepping through the statements in your application line by line. There are four main debugging windows supported by Visual Studio: Immediate window, Watches window, Locals window, and Call Stack window. To display these windows, either click the corresponding command on the View menu, or click the corresponding button on the Debug toolbar.

The Immediate window, shown in Figure 3.2, shows information that results from debugging statements in your code or that you request by typing commands directly into the window. The Immediate window is very useful for testing alternative lines of code when the current one has been found to fail. It can use all the variables available in active memory, as well as calls to available functions. The window also enables active variables to be set. For example, to display the result of the variable i divided by 5 in Visual J++, type i/5 in the Immediate window. In Visual Basic the equation must be preceded with either a ? or the word print. The Immediate window isn't supported in Visual C++.

FIGURE 3.2

The Immediate window.

The Watches window, shown in Figure 3.3, shows the current watch expressions, which are expressions whose values you decide to monitor as the code runs. A break expression is a watch expression that causes break modes to be entered when a certain condition you define becomes true. In the Watches window, the Context column indicates the procedure, module, or modules in which each watch expression is evaluated. The Watches window can display a value for a watch expression only if the current statement is in the specified context (within current scope). Otherwise, the Value column shows a message indicating that the statement isn't in context. For convenience, the Watches window fully supports drag-and-drop functionality. To add a watch variable, simply drag the variable from the Code window and drop it on the Watches window. Right-clicking on the variable and selecting Add Watch from the pop-up menu also adds a watch variable.

FIGURE 3.3

A sample Watches window.

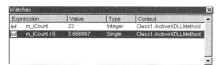

The new Quick Watch feature makes it easy to examine the current value stored in a variable while the debugger is in break mode. Position the mouse pointer over the variable and hold it steady for a moment. A small window (similar to a tool tip) opens to display the current value of that variable.

The Locals window, shown in Figure 3.4, displays the value of all variables within the scope of the currently executing procedure. As execution proceeds from procedure to procedure, the content of the Locals window changes to display only the variables applicable to the currently executing procedure.

Part

I

Ch

3

FIGURE 3.4

The Locals window.

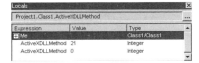

A variable that represents an object appears in the Locals window with a plus sign (+) displayed to the left of its name. Clicking the plus sign expands the variable, displaying the properties of the object and their current values. If one or more of the properties is an object, they are also displayed with a plus sign to their left. They too can be expanded until there are no more object properties.

The Call Stack window, shown in Figure 3.5, displays the stack of all procedure calls that haven't yet completed. As procedures call additional procedures, the call stack increases in size. Likewise, the call stack decreases in size when a procedure is exited.

FIGURE 3.5

The Call Stack window.

Extending the functionality of these windows, Visual Studio provides an additional tool for variable examination. It's automatically invoked when the mouse pointer is placed over any variable. After a short delay, the value of that variable is displayed. This capability is limited, however, because it cannot display very long strings or object properties like the Debugging windows can.

If you can identify the statement that caused an error, a single breakpoint might be all that's required to locate a problem. More often, however, you know only the general area of the code that caused the error. Breaking at the start of that area and stepping through the code line by line can often help isolate the problem. All the Visual Studio development environments support three types of stepping. They are Step Into, Step Over, and Step Out.

Step Into runs code one statement at a time. When you use Step Into to step through code, any call to a function or procedure that has debug information available for it will be stepped into. For example, if the next executable line of code is a call to the procedure ProcessReport, when Step Into is selected, the procedure is called and execution stops on the first executable line of the procedure. If no debug information is available for the procedure, the entire procedure runs and execution stops at the line following the call.

Step Over is similar to the Step Into, except for calls to procedures or functions. Step Over won't look for any debugging information for a given call. It executes the call as a unit and halts execution on the subsequent line. Suppose, for example, that your code calls the procedure ProcessReport twice in a row and the current line is the first call. When Step Over is selected, the procedure runs and execution stops at the second call to the procedure.

Step Out is similar to Step Into and Step Over, except it advances past the remainder of the code in the current procedure. Execution is halted after the last line of the procedure has been executed, but before the procedure is exited. For example, if you were executing a procedure named ProcessReport, when Step Out is selected all remaining lines of the procedure are executed and break mode is resumed in the calling procedure following the call to the procedure.

Exiting Debug mode can be accomplished in a couple ways. It is automatically exited when the application successfully terminates. Selecting the end button on the Debug toolbar can also exit debug mode.

Debugging ActiveX DLLs in Visual Studio

This section describes procedures for debugging ActiveX DLLs in Visual Studio.

ActiveX DLLs are what is known as in-process components. This means that they are loaded or mapped directly to the client's address space. The client process is able to invoke the DLL's functionality directly as if it were built as part of the same project. It's quite common in a three-tier development effort for an ActiveX DLL (server) to be developed by a separate developer or team of developers than the user application (client).

When developing an ActiveX DLL, it's important to eliminate code defects prior to releasing the DLL for use by the client application. By definition an ActiveX component is software used by other programs, so it cannot test itself. A *tester application* must be created that fully exercises the functionality of the component. An ActiveX DLL can, however, be debugged using a single instance of the development environment.

ActiveX DLLs in Visual Basic

This section provides specific instructions for debugging ActiveX DLLs in the Visual Basic development environment.

Visual Basic has a very robust environment for debugging ActiveX DLLs. The ActiveX DLL project and the tester application project can be combined into a single Group project. The projects exist as individual projects, but the grouping enables multiple projects to be open within the same environment at the same time.

When a Group project (or group of projects) is opened, the list of projects can be seen in the Project window. The Project window displays the startup project name in bold. For debugging purposes it must be set to the tester application.

When working with a Group project in Visual Basic, you can build each project individually or select Build Project Group from the File menu to build all the projects at once. In real-world applications several dependent DLLs might be loaded into the project group, requiring the projects to be built in dependency order. The build order associated with the build group option is set when the projects are added. To successfully use the build group option, either add the projects in dependency order or manually edit the group project file. The manual edit solution isn't recommended because it's possible to corrupt the project file.

The following steps provide enough information for an average developer to determine how to enter Break mode in a Visual Basic ActiveX DLL. It isn't intended to be a step-by-step procedure:

1. Create your ActiveX DLL using Visual Basic.

▷ For more details on how this is accomplished, **see** Chapter 12, "Creating ActiveX Controls with Visual Basic," **p. 337**

2. Compile the project into an ActiveX DLL by selecting Make <project name> from the File menu and confirming the filename. Visual Basic automatically registers the component in the system Registry.

3. Create a Group project by adding the tester application project. This can be an existing project or a new one. The tester application is added by selecting File, Add Project from the menu and selecting either a new Standard EXE project or an existing project.

N O T E In a Project Group the startup project is displayed in bold text in the Project window.

4. Notice that the project window, shown in Figure 3.6, now contains two projects and the title reads Project Group—Group1. Right-click on the ActiveX DLL project. Select the Project Properties option to display the ActiveX DLLs properties window.

FIGURE 3.6

A sample project group window.

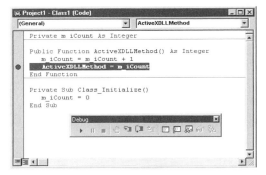

5. Click on the Component tab and ensure that Project Compatibility is enabled, as shown in Figure 3.7. Close the Properties window.

6. Set the tester application project as the driver application. Right-click on the tester application project in the Project window and select the Set as Start Up option.

7. With the test client project highlighted, select References from the Project menu.

FIGURE 3.7
The Project Properties dialog showing a DLL with Project Compatibility.

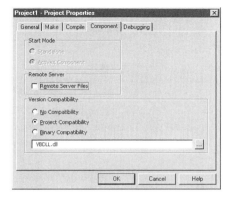

8. Find and select a reference to the ActiveX DLL project in the reference list. When a DLL project exists in a Group project, there will be two references to it in the list: one for the DLL and one for the project. Visual Basic treats references differently, so when debugging in a Group project, ensure that all DLL projects contained in the group are referenced by the project reference and not the DLL reference. Project references are those whose reference location ends in .vbp rather than .dll. If your project won't break at breakpoints set in the ActiveX DLL project, it's likely that the calling project references the .dll reference instead of the .vbp reference.

9. Add code to the tester application as required to exercise the functionality of the ActiveX DLL. Although not required in Visual Basic, it's generally a good idea to compile the tester application and remove any errors before running.

10. Set breakpoints in either the ActiveX DLL or in the tester application code and run. Debug as outlined in the section "Debugging Fundamentals in Visual Studio."

ActiveX DLLs in Visual C++

This section provides specific instructions for debugging ActiveX DLLs in the Visual C++ development environment.

In Visual C++ the client application is defined as the startup application for the ActiveX DLL. This enables the ActiveX DLL to be debugged from a single development environment.

It's important to remember that C++ has multiple-build types. You must build a debug version of the ActiveX DLL to successfully perform the following procedures. The debugging information is generated only for debug builds. If you don't want to debug the test client, it isn't necessary to build a debug version of the calling application.

The following steps provide enough information for an average developer to determine how to enter Break mode in a Visual C++ ActiveX DLL. It isn't intended to be a step-by-step procedure.

1. Create your ActiveX DLL using Visual C++.

▷ For more detail on how this is accomplished, **see** Chapter 13, "Creating ActiveX Controls with Visual C++," **p. 385**

2. Compile the project into an ActiveX DLL by selecting Build, Rebuild All from the menu or by clicking on the Rebuild All Icon on the Debug toolbar.

3. Register the DLL by using the regsvr32.exe utility located in /WinNT/System32 directory. It is important to remember that Visual C++ doesn't automatically do this for you.

TIP To quickly register ActiveX DLLs, use Windows NT Explorer to navigate to the DLL. Bring up the Open With dialog by double-clicking the DLL. Select Regsvr32 and click the OK button. From this point on, you merely have to double-click the ActiveX DLL from Windows NT Explorer to register the DLL.

4. Create a Client application to exercise the desired functionality of the DLL.

N O T E It's important to note that it isn't required that the tester client application be written in Visual C++. It can be written in any Visual Studio development language capable of creating an executable. ▪

5. Set the test client as the startup application by selecting Project, Settings from the menu, which displays the Project Settings window shown in Figure 3.8. Click the Debug tab and select the general category. Then enter the location of the client application in the Executable for Debug Session text area.

FIGURE 3.8
The Project Settings window.

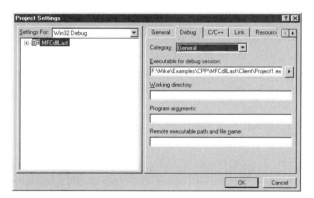

6. Set breakpoints in the DLL where desired and run the application. Debug as outlined in the section "Debugging Fundamentals in Visual Studio."

ActiveX DLLs in Visual J++

This section provides specific instructions for debugging ActiveX DLLs in the Visual J++ development environment.

Debugging ActiveX DLLs written in Java uses some technology found in Visual Basic and some found in Visual C++. Similar to Visual Basic, the ActiveX DLL project and the tester application project can be combined into a single Group project. The projects exist as individual projects, but the grouping enables multiple projects to be open within the same environment at the same time.

When a Group project (or group of projects) is opened, the list of projects can be seen in the Project window. The Project window shows the startup project in bold. When testing ActiveX DLLs you need to set it to the tester application. It's also important that the tester application reference the appropriate ActiveX component, which in this case is the ActiveX DLL project. The way in which Visual J++ references the component is similar to that found in Visual C++. A reference class is built, and calls are made to the class. The process is outlined later in this section.

When working with a Group project in Visual J++, you can build each project individually or select Build Project Group from the File menu to build all the projects at once. In real-world applications several dependent DLLs might be loaded into the project group, requiring the projects to be built in dependency order. The build order associated with the build group option is set when the projects are added. To successfully use the build group option, either add the projects in dependency order or manually edit the group project file. The manual edit solution isn't recommended because it's possible to corrupt the project file.

When working with an ActiveX DLL written in Java, it's important to remember that the client uses the DLL the same as any other ActiveX DLL. Just because it is written in Java, it isn't given any additional portability features or made any more Web accessible. This isn't an attempt to downgrade the capabilities of Java; it's a reality of making Java an ActiveX DLL.

The following steps provide enough information for an average developer to determine how to enter Break mode in a Visual J++ ActiveX DLL. It isn't intended to be a step-by-step procedure.

1. When creating your ActiveX DLL using Visual J++, ensure that the project type of COM DLL is used. This is accomplished by selecting File, New Project from the menu to display the New Project dialog box. Click on the New tab and select Visual J++ Projects, Components, and COM DLL from the Open Project dialog box (see Figure 3.9). Enter a project name and select the Open button.

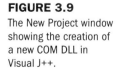

FIGURE 3.9
The New Project window showing the creation of a new COM DLL in Visual J++.

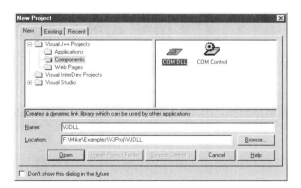

Part

I

Ch

3

2. When the wizard completes, a COM project is available with a single Java class. Modify the Project Properties and make this class a COM class. To do this, select Project, Project Properties from the menu to display the Project Properties dialog box. Choose the COM Classes tab and make sure that the check box is checked for wizard generated class.

3. Add code to implement desired functionality in the class.

4. Compile the project into an ActiveX DLL by selecting Build from the Build menu. Visual J++ automatically registers the component in the system Registry.

5. Create a Group project by adding the tester application project. This can be an existing project or a new one. The tester application is added by selecting File, Add Project from the menu and selecting the desired test project. For the purposes on this demonstration, from the New tab, choose Visual J++ Projects, Applications, Windows Application. (Make sure the Add to the Current Solution option button is selected.) Enter a project name and select the Open button. Visual J++ builds a Java Form.

6. Add a button to the form, where the functionality of the ActiveX DLL is called. This is done by selecting the WFC Controls tab on the Toolbox and dragging the Button control onto the form.

7. Create a COM wrapper for the ActiveX DLL. To do this, highlight the tester project and select Add COM Wrapper from the Project menu. When the COM Wrappers dialog is displayed, find and select your ActiveX DLL project from the Installed COM Components list and press the OK button.

8. Notice that the tester project now contains two items, the form and the COM wrapper class.

9. Set the tester application project as the driver application. This is done by right-clicking the tester application project in the Project window and selecting the Set as Start Up Project option.

10. Add code to the tester application as required to exercise the functionality of the ActiveX DLL. Compile tester project by selecting Build Project from the Build menu.

11. From here, set breakpoints in either the ActiveX DLL or in the tester application code and run. Debug as outlined in the section "Debugging Fundamentals in Visual Studio."

Debugging ActiveX EXEs in Visual Studio

This section describes procedures for debugging ActiveX EXEs in Visual Studio.

From a client application's point of view, ActiveX DLLs and ActiveX EXEs are invoked in exactly the same way, making the usage of one over the other transparent at design time. Unfortunately, debugging the component requires you to know which one you are using because you must debug them differently.

ActiveX EXEs are what is known as out-of-process components. This means that they run in their own separate address spaces. COM must package requests from the client, transmit data to the server via Remote Procedure Calls (RPCs), receive the data on the server side, and then invoke the server appropriately. COM accomplishes this by adding proxy code to the client and stub code to the server at compile time.

The following sections demonstrate debugging ActiveX EXEs in Visual Studio.

ActiveX EXEs in Visual Basic

This section provides instructions specific to debugging ActiveX EXEs in the Visual Basic development environment.

The following steps provide enough information for an average developer to determine how to enter Break mode in a Visual Basic ActiveX EXE. It isn't intended to be a step-by-step procedure:

1. Create your ActiveX EXE using Visual Basic.

2. Compile the project into an ActiveX EXE by selecting File, Make <project name> from the menu and confirming the filename.

3. Set breakpoints in the ActiveX EXE as desired.

4. Run the ActiveX EXE. The Debugging tab of the Project Properties window is displayed in Figure 3.10. The dialog has three options:

FIGURE 3.10

The Debugging tab of the Project Properties window.

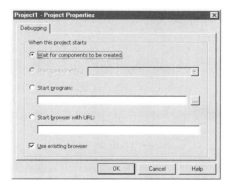

- Wait for Components to Be Created (default)
- Start Program
- Start Browser with URL

5. Ensure that Wait for Components to Be Created is selected and click on the OK button.

Part

I

Ch

3

N O T E Both Start Program and Start Browser with URL will accomplish your goal of debugging the ActiveX EXE in Visual Basic, but in general it's best to select Wait for Components to Be Created. This enables full control over both the client and the server application, which is why it's used in this example. In your particular application, one of the others might be a better selection.

6. In a second instance of Visual Basic, create a tester application project by selecting new Standard EXE project.

7. Select References from the Project menu. The References window for the project is displayed containing a list of all available COM components (ActiveX EXEs and ActiveX DLLs) identified in the Registry.

8. Find and select the ActiveX EXE project in the list and click the OK button.

9. Edit the project to add calls to the ActiveX EXE as desired to fully exercise its functionality.

10. Run the application. When a breakpoint is hit on the server side, the Visual Basic containing the ActiveX EXE is brought to the foreground and the client waits until execution resumes. Debug as outlined in the "Debugging Fundamentals in Visual Studio" section.

ActiveX EXEs in Visual C++

This section provides instructions specific to debugging ActiveX EXEs in the Visual Basic development environment.

It's important to remember that C++ has multiple build types. You must build a debug version of the ActiveX EXE to successfully perform the procedure. The debugging information is generated only for debug builds.

The following steps provide enough information for an average developer to determine how to enter Break mode in a Visual C++ ActiveX EXE. It isn't intended to be a step-by-step procedure:

1. Create your ActiveX EXE using Visual C++.

2. Compile the project into an ActiveX EXE by selecting Build, Rebuild All menu item or by clicking on the Rebuild All icon on the debug tool bar.

3. Set breakpoints in the ActiveX EXE as desired.

4. Run the ActiveX EXE by selecting Start Debugging and Go from the Build menu or by clicking on the Go icon on the Debug toolbar.

5. Open a second instance of the Visual C++ development environment and create a test client project.

6. In the test client project, add calls to the ActiveX EXE to exercise its functionality.

7. From here, run the application. When a breakpoint is hit on the server side, the Visual C++ environment containing the ActiveX EXE is brought to the foreground and the client waits until execution resumes. Debug as outlined in the "Debugging Fundamentals in Visual Studio" section.

Occasionally it might be required to debug an application that is already running. Visual C++ fully supports attaching to running processes. This functionality is sometimes necessary when debugging ActiveX EXEs and is critical for debugging Windows NT services.

> **CAUTION**
>
> Never attach to a process unless you know what the process is. When a process is attached to debugging, it's taken over by the Visual C++ development environment. When the project is exited, the environment is closed, and the attached process is terminated. Some processes, usually system processes, cause Windows to halt if they are stopped.

It's best to only attach to your own Visual C++ applications, which have been compiled with debugging information. Remember, when you finish debugging the application, it will be terminated. So make sure this won't cause you or other users problems before proceeding.

The following steps provide enough information for an average developer to determine how to enter Break mode in a Visual C++ ActiveX EXE. It isn't intended to be a step-by-step procedure:

1. From the Build menu, click Start Debug and Attach to Process. The Attach to Process dialog appears (see Figure 3.11).

FIGURE 3.11
The Attach to Process dialog.

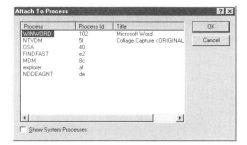

2. Select the process you want to debug and Click OK. Look for statements in the status bar at the bottom of the screen stating that symbols for the application and its DLLs have been loaded.

3. Select the Break icon from the Debug toolbar. This forces the application into break mode. An assembler listing might be displayed, but not to worry. This will be resolved soon enough.

4. Open a source file associated with the application. An alternative approach is to open the Call Stack window and double-click one of the processes.

5. Set breakpoints in the source as required. Begin the process running again by selecting Start Debugging and Go from the Build menu or by clicking on the Go icon on the Debug toolbar.

6. When at a breakpoint, debug as outlined in the "Debugging Fundamentals in Visual Studio" section. When you stop debugging the application, the application will be terminated.

Part I
Ch 3

Debugging Web-Based Script in Visual Studio

This section describes procedures for debugging Web-based Script in Visual Studio. The discussion applies to server-side scripts for Microsoft Internet Information Server (IIS).

Web-based development presents a series of challenges, which add difficulty to application debugging. This difficulty is often more complex than typical client/server debugging. Client/server development can encompass multiple machines, but doesn't have the multiple machines running different operating systems compiling and executing the same program.

You must remember that on the Web when a URL is entered in a browser, the URL is translated to a file of some type. Limiting my discussion to HTML and script, the file is runtime compiled by both IIS and then by the browser. IIS actually passes the results of its compilation to the requesting browser. For files containing only HTML, or HTML and client-side script, IIS just transmits the file without change to the client or browser.

When the file contains server-side script, the server processes the commands sequentially. The Web server will begin transmitting the file until it encounters server-side script. It then processes the encountered script. When the script completes, it resumes transmitting the file to the client.

It's interesting to note that there might be many independent blocks of server-side script in a single file. The client processes the file as it is received. The blocks of server-side script might generate more lines, which are sent to the client as part of the file. The server-generated lines can be either client-side script or HTML.

The result of all this is that it can be difficult to determine within which machine the problem resides: the client or the server. Visual InterDev seamlessly integrates both server-side and client-side debugging into a single environment, making it much easier to debug Web applications.

To enable server-side debugging in Visual InterDev, the Visual InterDev Server must be installed on your IIS server. The Visual InterDev Server is what makes it possible to halt server-side execution and step or continue based on developer input.

Visual InterDev Server is available as part of Visual Studio. To install, start Visual Studio setup from your installation media and select Server Applications and Tools (Add On Only) and Visual InterDev Server Components. Then just follow the prompts for the complete installation. After you have installed the proper tools, some options need to be set in Visual InterDev itself. The following steps outline the general procedure required to enable Visual InterDev to support script debugging:

1. Open the project that requires debugging.

▷ For more information on opening or creating Visual InterDev projects, **see** Chapter 18, "Developing Active Content with Visual InterDev," **p. 527**

2. Highlight the project by single-clicking the project in the Project window.

3. Enable client-side debugging by setting the Enable Client Debugging option to True in the Properties window.

4. Enable server-side debugging by setting the Enable Server Debugging option to True in the Properties window.

N O T E Both server-side and client-side debugging add overhead, resulting in a performance hit when selected. It's recommended that, when possible, you enable only one of the options at a time. ▦

5. Add breakpoints and run the project. Debug as outlined in the "Debugging Fundamentals in Visual Studio" section.

Debugging Database Applications in Visual Studio

This section describes procedures for debugging database applications in Visual Studio.

Visual Studio has integrated database support into each of its development tools. Developers using Visual Studio Enterprise Edition can view, implement, edit, and debug SQL Server stored procedures (T-SQL) and Oracle subprograms (PL/SQL). The integrated SQL editor includes a color-coded editing environment.

This integration requires some additional setup. The server must be SQL Server version 6.5 and Service Pack 3 or later. For Windows NT 4, the SQL Debugger interface and Remote Automation component can be set by running Sdi_nt4.exe. The components are located in \Program files\Common Files\Microsoft Shared\SQL Debugging.

There is no setup required for the client, other than a complete installation of the Enterprise edition of the development environment. For environment-specific steps for debugging stored procedures refer to the following sections.

Part
I
Ch
3

SQL/Stored Procedures in Visual Basic

The T-SQL Debugger is fully integrated into Visual Basic, as it is with the other development environments. With Visual Basic, however, it is an Add-In that must be enabled. To enable the T-SQL Debugger, follow these steps:

1. Start the Add-In Manager by selecting Add-In Manager from the Add-Ins menu. The Add-In Manager dialog is displayed.
2. From the Available Add-Ins, find the VB T-SQL Debugger option and double-click it. The Load Behavior changes to Loaded. If you desire integrated Visual Basic and SQL debugging, described later in this section, click the Load On Startup option.
3. Click the OK button to close the dialog. Notice the T-SQL Debugger menu option is now available from the Add-Ins menu. It also a T-SQL Debugging Options menu option from the Tools menu.
4. Start the T-SQL Debugger by selecting it from the Add-Ins menu. The Visual Basic Batch T-SQL Debugger window is displayed, as shown in Figure 3.12.

FIGURE 3.12

The Visual Basic Batch T-SQL Debugger window.

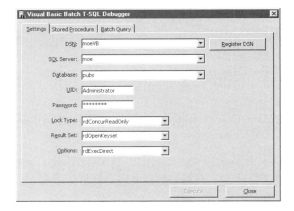

5. Enter a Data Source Name (DSN) and then enter the password. This assumes that you already have a DSN registered on your machine. If you don't, fill in the information on the menu and press the Register DSN button.

6. Click the Stored Procedure tab to view the stored procedure information pane, as shown in Figure 3.13. The names of all the existing stored procedures are available in the drop-down menu. This window also shows how the query will be executed: the parameters, the data type of each parameter, and the value to be assigned to each parameter when the query is executed.

FIGURE 3.13

Stored procedure options are shown on the Visual Basic Batch T-SQL Debugger window.

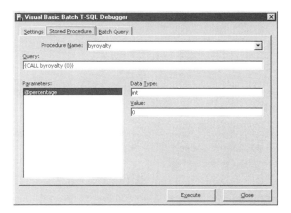

7. Select the stored procedure to debug and enter values for any input parameters. Do this by clicking the parameter from the parameter list and changing the entry in the Value text box.

8. Click the Execute button. This starts the Automation Manager and brings up the T-SQL Debugger.

9. The T-SQL Debugger sets breakpoints much like Visual C++. You click the line where the breakpoint is desired, and either click the Insert/Remove Breakpoint icon on the Debug toolbar or right-click and select Insert/Remove Breakpoint.

10. To begin debugging, click the Go icon on the Debug toolbar or right-click and select Go.

To perform runtime debugging of stored procedures (Visual Basic code and SQL), select T-SQL Debugging Options from the Visual Basic's Tools menu (see Figure 3.14). This allows you to turn on or off the decision to automatically step into stored procedures. With this option turned on, the T-SQL debugger is automatically activated whenever you step into a method that executes a stored procedure. When the stored procedure is exited, the environment returns to debugging Visual Basic Code.

FIGURE 3.14
The T-SQL Debugging Options window.

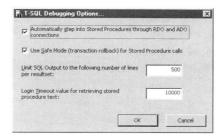

Part

I

Ch

3

Other options on the Tools menu are as follows:

- Use Safe Mode—When selected, this causes any design-time queries to be automatically rolled back when the transaction is complete.

- Output Window Rows—Limits the number of rows that appear in the T-SQL Debugger output window when debugging design-time queries.

- Login Timeout—Sets the amount of time that the debugger waits to connect to the database before timing out.

As an alternative method for running the T-SQL Debugger, while stepping through Visual Basic code that accesses the database using either ActiveX Data Objects (ADO) or Remote Data Object (RDO), right-click on a stored procedure in the Data View window. Then choose the debug command from the UserConnection designer.

SQL/Stored Procedures in Visual C++

SQL debugging is fully integrated into Visual C++ Enterprise Edition. This section outlines the steps required to perform SQL debugging using the Visual C++ development environment. The following procedure assumes that you must have set up an ODBC data source for your SQL Server. If you haven't already done this, it must be done before continuing.

1. Create a database project by selecting New from the File menu. Under the Project tab select Database Project as the project type. Enter a name for the project. Ensure that Create New Workspace is selected and click the OK button. The Select Data Source dialog is displayed.

2. Choose SQL Server as your data source. If you didn't include the login and password in setup information for the data source, you might get the SQL Server Login dialog box. If this happens, enter a valid Login ID and Password and click the OK button.

3. In the Workspace window select the Data View tab. Then double-click the database. The database shows up in the list as XXX(YYY), where XXX is the database name that the data source pointed to and YYY is the name of your SQL Server.

N O T E   Steps 4 and 5 create a new stored procedure. If you want to debug an existing stored procedure, expand the Stored Procedure folder associated with the database. Then double-click the stored procedure in the list. The procedure is displayed in the SQL editor. Proceed with step 6.

4. With the database chosen, select New Database Item from the Insert menu. The Insert Database Item dialog is displayed.

5. Select Stored Procedure from the Database Item list box and then click the OK button. The prototype for the new stored procedure appears in the SQL editor.

6. Edit the Stored Procedure as desired. Save the Stored Procedure by selecting Save from the File menu. When a new stored procedure is saved, it's stored in the Stored Procedures folder associated with the database.

7. Right-click in the stored procedure editor window. When the menu is displayed, select the Debug option. The Automation manager starts. When the instruction pointer (yellow arrow) appears, you're debugging your stored procedure. Use the Debug Toolbar to finish stepping through and debugging the stored procedure.

8. The results of running the stored procedure show up in the Output window under the Results tab.

SQL/Stored Procedures in Visual InterDev/Visual J++

This procedure outlines the steps for debugging stored procedures in both Visual InterDev and Visual J++. Because both use the same development environment, the steps are the same for each.

SQL Debugging is only available in the Enterprise Edition of Visual InterDev/Visual J++. The following procedure assumes that you have already set up an ODBC data source for your SQL:

1. Create a database project by selecting New Project from the File menu. In the New Project dialog, select the New tab and choose a Visual Studio, Database Projects, New Database Project. Enter a project name for the new project and click the Open button. The Select Data Source dialog appears.

2. Choose SQL Server as the data source and click the OK button. The new project is created and the Data View tab is displayed showing the database selected. The database shows up in the list as XXX(YYY), where XXX is the database name the data source points to and YYY is the name of your SQL Server.

3. In the Data View window, expand the tree for the database.

N O T E Steps 4 and 5 create a new stored procedure. If you want to debug an existing stored procedure, expand the Stored Procedure folder associated with the database. Then double-click the stored procedure in the list. The procedure is displayed in the SQL editor. Proceed with step 6. ▓

4. With the database highlighted, select Add Database Item and Stored Procedure from the Project menu. The prototype for the new stored procedure is displayed in the SQL Editor.

5. Change the name of the stored procedure and select the Save icon from the standard toolbar. The development environment takes care of the steps required to save it as a stored procedure. Notice that the name of the new stored procedure now appears in the Stored Procedure folder associated with the database.

6. Edit the Stored Procedure as desired and save.

7. On the stored procedure edit window, click to the right of each line where you want the program to break. A red dot appears, which indicates that a breakpoint is set.

8. To start the debugging session, right-click in the stored procedure editor window. When the menu is displayed, select the Debug option. The Automation manager starts. When the instruction pointer (yellow arrow) appears, begin debugging your stored procedure.

9. When execution of the stored procedure has finished, the results of running the stored procedure show up in the Output window under the Database Output drop-down menu option.

From Here...

In this chapter, you looked at the problem of debugging applications developed with different languages, using different toolsets, and targeting different platforms. Among the components you debugged were ActiveX DLLs, ActiveX EXEs, and SQL Server Stored Procedures. You started with the basics of application debugging, and finished with a look at how each problem can be solved using the appropriate Visual Studio development environment.

For more information about building, debugging, and deploying enterprise applications with Visual Studio, see the following chapters:

- See Chapter 4, "Creating Database-Aware Applications with Visual Studio," for an overview of building data-driven applications.

- See Chapter 34, "Using the Visual Studio Analyzer," for a look at Microsoft's newest tool for analyzing distributed applications.

- Chapter 11, "Using COM Components and ActiveX Controls," provides a good overview of programming with Microsoft's object technologies.

- To learn more about enterprise application development and the role of Visual Studio, see Chapter 25, "Clients, Servers, and Components: Design Strategies for Distributed Applications."

Part
I

Ch
3

Creating Database-Aware Applications with Visual Studio

by J. Eddie Gulley

In this chapter

Looking at Database Design Issues

Modern development of client/server (CS) applications requires the orchestration of many different components. Often, these components have to be designed, developed, and tested separately from within many nonintegrated tools. This lack of integration increases the learning curve, increases costs, and decreases productivity for developers.

Picking up where Visual Studio 97 left off, Visual Studio 6 brings together a complete toolkit for CS application developers. Included with the Visual Studio 6 Enterprise Edition, the visual database tools provide database design and management support to developers through the Integrated Development Environment (IDE) for Visual InterDev, Visual J++, Visual Basic and Visual C++ Enterprise editions. These tools tightly integrate the project workspaces and open database connectivity (ODBC) compliant relational databases for full life cycle development of complex CS applications.

Before you dive into the design tools, you need to consider some of the issues involved in the design of a solid database on which your CS application will operate. These issues are as important to address as those involving language selection, overall system architectures, and other tasks required in the development of accurate, stable applications.

Some of the more important issues to consider in good database design are

- The logical and physical design of the database
- The location of server-side logic in SQL Server stored procedures versus middle-tier components

By neglecting these issues, you deprive your client/server project every chance at success. Worse, you could doom it to failure.

The Necessity for Database Design

The importance of good logical and physical design in relational databases is easy to underestimate. The necessity for appropriately capturing requirements early in the life cycle is important in all components of a CS application, but is perhaps more necessary in the context of the back-end database. The database in a CS architecture is normally much less resilient when changes are made later in the development cycle than other components. This is true because the database in the CS model is usually the foundation for the entire system.

Front-end applications have three functions: They allow data to be input by users, they pass data to middle-tier business logic components for calculation or persistent storage in the database, and they present results back to users. These requirements for user-services components create an inherent dependency on the middle-tier components and—even more important—on the data-services components in the CS model. Thus, even minor changes to the database structure can flow throughout the CS model, causing even more changes to the dependent components. Changes to front-end graphical user interface (GUI) components usually don't require changes in other layers.

One accepted way of lessening the risk of changes to the database is to make a habit of documenting the structure of your database.

Documenting your structure not only provides you with a graphical picture of your database but also allows you to think through your design. A graphical method of doing this is entity-relationship (ER) diagramming, which provides a picture of the tables and their relationships with other tables in the database (see Figures 4.1 and 4.2). Such a picture of the database allows developers and users to see database design decisions in an understandable and standardized format. Developers can easily walk through the diagram with end users to ensure that requirements are met. By being able to visualize the database design, you can easily see how data is stored and perhaps see problems inherent in a particular database design. It's beyond the scope of this book to teach you the intricacies of data modeling and design, but you're highly encouraged to seek out other sources of instruction on this important development concept.

FIGURE 4.1

The Logical Data Model represents a process or processes in the context of the users or actors of that process.

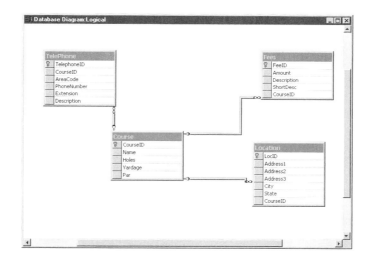

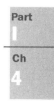

Part

I

Ch

4

FIGURE 4.2

The Physical Data Model represents how a logical model is stored physically in a relational database.

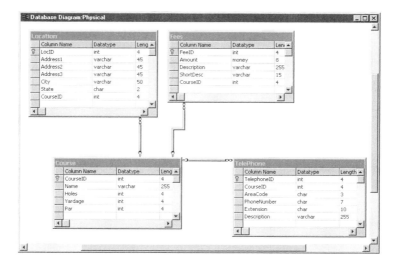

A good ER diagramming tool serves to define the database at various levels of abstraction. A logical model of the database provides a method for communicating with and soliciting feedback from end users during the analysis phases of development (refer to Figure 4.1). This logical view also provides end users and other database users with only the information they need for their purposes, and hides details important only to database designers and developers. The physical model in Figure 4.2 provides a detailed view of the design of the database and provides for the actual representation of the schema applied to the database. The physical database schema consists of tables, columns, and relationships from the logical model, as well as individual column data types, defaults, table and column constraints, indexes, and table constructs for resolving many-to-many relationships. With Visual Studio 6, designers can not only provide graphical representation of the database, but can also use that model as a means of creating the physical data structures within the relational database management system (RDBMS) through script generation and execution against an ODBC-compliant database, such as Microsoft SQL Server.

ON THE WEB

You can get more information about data modeling or ER diagramming from Web pages of computer-aided software engineering (CASE) tool vendors. For background on the concepts of and standards for ER diagramming, visit the National Institute of Standards and Technology's (NIST) Web site at `http://www.itl.nist.gov/div897/pubs/index.htm`. Here, you can view or download Federal Information Processing Standard (FIPS) Publication 184 "Integration Definition for Information Modeling (IDEF1X)." IDEF1X, the NIST standard for data modeling, is implemented in most major database CASE tools.

Visual Studio Database Design Tools

The visual database tools encompass a full range of features to give you control over the physical database schema required for your Visual Studio 6 project. Four components make up the visual database tools:

- Database Designer
- Source Editor (for stored procedures and triggers)
- Query Designer
- Data View

The Database Designer provides a graphical depiction of your database structure. The Database Designer provides a great tool that takes the drudgery out of modeling and creating database structures, without requiring you to learn constructs of complex Data Definition Language (DDL). The Database Designer also allows you to experiment with the design of your database without affecting the physical database until you're ready to do so. This capability to experiment lends itself well to the iterative development cycles popular today. The Database Designer also lets you make changes to a database while automatically migrating data to the changed structure, as long as that data doesn't violate any rules of the changed structure.

The Source Editor for SQL Server provides a modern development environment for stored procedures and triggers. In traditional stored procedure development, you couldn't set breakpoints and step through code. You would try to compile the completed procedure and receive vague error messages—no line numbers, no ability to view the value of a variable. Visual Studio's Source Editor provides intelligent compilation and debugging support, plus the capability to step into stored procedures and SQL statements embedded in your application. You can set breakpoints and watch variables, just as you can with almost all programming language IDEs. It sure beats using trial and error and print statements to narrow down where the errors are occurring in the source code.

The Query Designer enables you, either graphically or in SQL, to create and execute queries against ODBC-compliant databases. Anyone familiar with the query-by-example (QBE) feature in Microsoft Access will welcome the ability to apply the same concept to more powerful CS databases.

The Data View component provides a graphical browser to a connected database. Data View resembles and acts as an explorer for your database. You can view your database diagrams, tables, triggers, stored procedures, and views from within your development environment. Prior to Data View, you often had to run a separate application, such as the MS SQL Server Enterprise Manager, to obtain an organized look at the objects in your database. Although this isn't necessarily a problem, having this capability built into your normal environment lets you view your entire system from within the same integrated development component.

The next section and the section "Developing Stored Procedures with Visual Studio 6" provide more detail on how to use the Visual Database Tools. These two components focus more on the design issues previously introduced and are newer additions to Microsoft's programming tools.

Part

I

Ch

4

Using Data Modeling with Visual Studio 6

The purpose of this section isn't to teach you how to perform data modeling but to show you how to use the Database Designer to depict your database design graphically and create the database objects required to physically implement your design. Before you begin, you must create the necessary devices for storing your database and create a blank database to access through the Data Designer.

Exploring Your Database with the Data View

The Data View component provides an Explorer-type interface to enable you to browse your database. With the Data View you can browse the database objects themselves, such as the diagrams, tables, views, stored procedures and triggers you have previously created. Objects are visually organized in the Data View by the project connection it relates to. If you have multiple connections to multiple databases, individual databases are contained in their own connection folder along with the objects contained in that database connection.

N O T E   A little time spent learning the security model of SQL Server will greatly aid you in troubleshooting during development and integrated testing of large CS applications. SQL Server security knowledge can also boost your productivity when chasing down vague error messages that, at their root, are merely a matter of database object permissions.   ▥

The SQL Server security model is broken down into three modes: Integrated, Standard, and Mixed. With Integrated Security, SQL Server uses Windows NT's authentication services for login validation for all connections. Only trusted connections are enabled when using Integrated Security. Standard Security uses SQL Server's own login process. Mixed Security enables SQL Server to service login requests based on whether the requesting connection is trusted. Under Mixed Security, SQL Server uses Integrated for trusted connections and Standard for nontrusted connections.

To view the Data View window from inside the Visual Basic IDE, choose Data View Window from the View menu. The first time you open the Data View from a project you need to add a data link to your project. You can create a data link within the Data View by following these steps:

1. Open the Data View by choosing the Data View Window from the View menu.

2. Right-click on the Data Links folder and choose Add a Data Link from the context-sensitive pop-up menu. This displays the Data Link Properties dialog, as shown in Figure 4.3, with the Provider tab active.

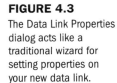

FIGURE 4.3

The Data Link Properties dialog acts like a traditional wizard for setting properties on your new data link.

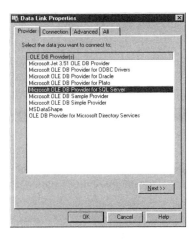

3. Select the type of data you want to connect to by selecting the appropriate OLE DB Provider from the list as shown in Figure 4.3. After you have selected your provider, choose the Next command button.

N O T E   If your OLE DB provider isn't reflected in the list, make sure that it has been properly installed on your machine. You might need to refer to the specific provider's user documentation to troubleshoot installation and registration of these types of components.   ▥

4. To complete the Connection tab of the Data Link Properties dialog, provide the server name for your database and the appropriate user ID and password information, and select the database on the provided server with which you want to connect. Figure 4.4 shows a completed Connection tab with appropriate information.

FIGURE 4.4

The Connection tab on the Data Link Properties dialog allows you to enter the server, database, and login information for your connection.

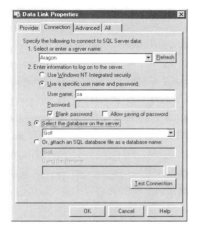

5. After you have completed the Connection tab, you can test your connection by selecting the Test Connection button. To complete the Connection tab, choose the OK button. If the test is unsuccessful, you need to first ensure that your data source is running and available. The most frequently noted problem is a mismatch in client and server network libraries or that the data source is not running. Refer to your data source's documentation for specific troubleshooting techniques.

6. You can now name your data link by highlighting the data link name in the Data View and changing the text as desired.

After you have created a data link in the Data View, you can browse the objects in the connection. Objects contained in the connection are organized by type. The objects are stored by type in folders underneath the connection, as shown in Figure 4.5.

FIGURE 4.5

The Data View hierarchically represents the database connection objects within folders for each object type.

Objects within the individual folders are further represented by the tables and columns contained within each folder. Within the Data View you can explore objects to just about any level of granularity. For instance, to browse individual properties of a particular column in a table contained in the Data View, expand the Tables folder in the Data View. Then expand the particular table containing the column you want to view by right-clicking on the column and choosing Properties from the pop-up menu. Figure 4.6 shows a properties dialog for a column.

FIGURE 4.6
With the Data View, you can browse objects down to the individual column level. Here you can see the properties for a column in the Data View.

The Data View also acts as the main entry point for managing other objects in your projects, such as the database diagrams, views and stored procedures you have created. Whichever object type you select to manage with the Data View calls the controlling database tool for that object. For instance, if you select diagrams from the Data View, the Database Designer application loads and enables you to manage or create new diagrams. Selecting a view brings up the graphical query designer to create your view. Selecting a stored procedure brings up the SQL Source Editor to create and alter stored procedures.

More information on managing each object type from the Visual Database Tools is provided in the following sections.

Creating a Diagram with the Database Designer

A developer's edition of SQL Server is included with Visual Studio 6 Enterprise Edition. You can create devices and databases within SQL Server with either the SQL Enterprise Manager or the ISQL interface. After the devices and databases have been created, create a connection or data link in the Data View as outlined in the previous section, "Exploring Your Database with the Data View." Now you're ready to design your database with the Database Designer.

N O T E Specific details on creating and managing devices and databases for SQL Server are found in the *SQL Server's Administrators Companion*. ▪

The Database Designer enables you to create individual tables by right-clicking on the Table folder from within the Data View and choosing New Table from the pop-up menu. You can create multiple tables and relationships between multiple tables by right-clicking on the Database Diagrams folder in the Data View and choosing New Diagram from the pop-up menu.

A blank database diagram is now open onscreen. To begin creating tables in your diagram, follow these steps:

1. From the blank diagram, right-click and select New Table from the pop-up menu.
2. At the prompt for the name of the new table, enter a name and click OK.
3. A blank table appears in which you can begin entering column names and the necessary properties for your table. The Database Designer lets you choose the appropriate data type and precision for each column. By default, the columns are set up to enable NULLs unless you deselect this option in the table designer.

Table 4.1 lists the properties you can set for each column with the Database Designer.

Table 4.1   Column Properties

Property Name	Definition
Column Name	Name you want to use for the column. All column names must be unique within a table and conform to SQL Server rules for database object identifiers.
Datatype	System- or user-defined data type for the column.
Length	Used to specify the maximum number of characters for char types or digits for numeric types.
Precision	The total number of digits that can be stored on either side of a decimal point.
Scale	The total number of digits that can be stored on the right side of a decimal point. The scale value must be equal to or less than the precision for the column.
Allow Nulls	Used to specify whether a column should allow NULL values. If NULLs are allowed (True), you can provide a default.
Default Value	Used to denote a default value for insertions. Defaults can be literal values or Transact SQL function calls such as the getdate() function for returning the current system date and time. If a default isn't provided, columns that don't explicitly provide a value will be assigned NULL.

continues

Table 4.1 Continued

Property Name	Definition
Identity	The identity property allows columns to contain auto-generated values to uniquely identify each table row. Identity columns are handy for sequential numbers as unique identifiers.
Identity Seed	Beginning value for future generations in an identity column. The next insertion into the table begins with this seed value. If not given, this value defaults to 1.
Identity Increment	Amount that an identity value increments from the previous record in the table. For instance, if the identity increment value is set at 10, each subsequent insertion adds 10 to the previous row's column value to generate the current identity value.

CAUTION

Before making a decision on the nullability of a column, make sure that you understand the consequences of multiple-value logic and SQL queries. Careful consideration given to this contentious issue can possibly prevent subtle logic errors from finding their way into your code. NULLs can be said to have multiple possible values, such as the attribute not applying to a particular record, the value not being known for a record, or the value known but not captured yet for a record. Queries that include columns containing NULLs must account for the possible logical meanings of the NULL values; also, care certainly should be taken to properly constrain such queries.

Figure 4.7 shows a completed table named Course. This table and the others represented in Figures 4.1 and 4.2 are used throughout this chapter and Chapter 8, "An Inside Look at Microsoft SQL Server." The T-SQL Data Definition Language scripts for creating the entire sample database are listed in Chapter 8.

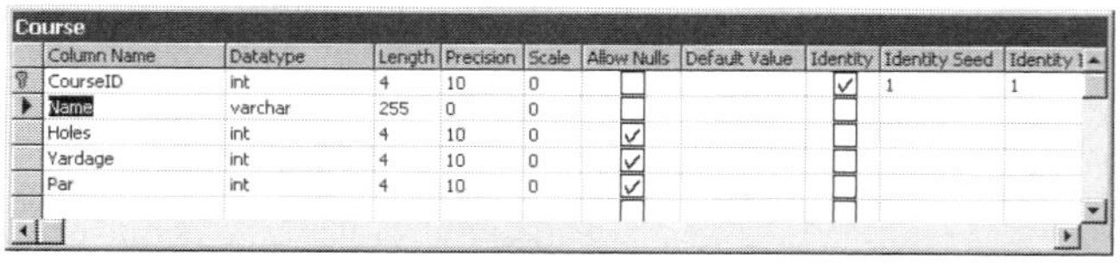

FIGURE 4.7
The Database Designer can represent the logical or physical view of a database. Here is the physical view of the sample Course table.

The only thing left to do for this table is to denote the primary key(s) by following these steps:

1. Select any rows that represent a key field.

2. Select the appropriate column's record selector and then right-click on the column and select the Set Primary Key item from the pop-up menu. The key icon on the key column's record selector column denotes a primary key for this table.

   Choose to either save your diagram or continue adding more tables. To save the table to the database, choose File, Save from the menu. When prompted to enter a name for the diagram, enter an appropriate name or, if previously saved, leave the name and choose OK.

   The Database Designer displays a dialog with a list of tables that have changed or will change on the physical database and prompt you to save the changes to the database. You can choose Yes, No, or Save Text File as shown in Figure 4.8.

FIGURE 4.8
The Database Designer change list: Choose Yes to save the listed changes to the database.

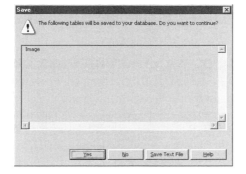

Part

I

Ch

4

3. After you have chosen to save the changes to your database, the designer prompts you to save the changes to a script file. A script file can come in handy when you don't have appropriate permissions to alter the database. If you choose to save the file, it will be saved in your project directory.

In more formal development shops, you might work under more guarded database access. In these cases, you'll want to save your diagram to a text script file, submit it to your database administrator (DBA) for review, and let him run the script against the database for object creation.

Figure 4.9 shows your new Golf database diagram. A new table called Images has been created as a result of the previous steps. Now all you need to do is add a relationship between your Images table, which can be used to store a course's binary image, and your parent Course table.

FIGURE 4.9
The sample database diagram with an images table.

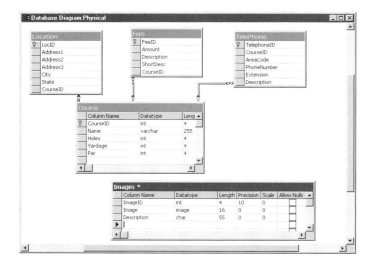

Creating Table Relationships with the Database Designer

After you create more than one table on the diagram, you might need to relate one or more tables. Table relationships are represented by foreign key constraints on dependent table columns. For instance, an image record might be related to a course record through a foreign key relationship on the CourseID column. This requires that any image record entered into the Images table must reference through its CourseID column a valid CourseID record in the Course table.

To create foreign key relationships in a database diagram, drag the parent table's key columns to the child table's foreign key column (see Figure 4.10). After you draw the required relationship, you're prompted with the Create Relationship dialog box shown in Figure 4.11.

FIGURE 4.10
A dashed line between two tables in a database represents foreign key relationships in progress.

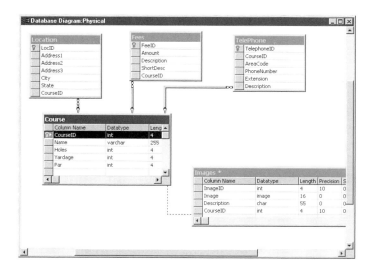

FIGURE 4.11

The Create Relationship
dialog box shows which
columns in the parent
and child tables will
serve as foreign keys
and references.

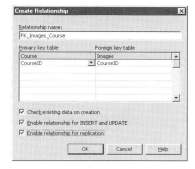

The dialog box in Figure 4.11 defaults to an appropriate name for the foreign key constraint
that will be created, and it enables you to verify that the correct columns in the parent and
child tables are included in the constraint. By default, other options are also enabled, such as
checking existing data, if any, against the new column constraint and checking the relationships for inserts and updates and for replication. Generally, you should accept the defaults
unless your database requirements dictate otherwise.

After the relationship is created, you will see the related tables attached on the diagram
through a three-dimensional bar with a key icon on the parent end and a double-link chain on
the child end (see Figure 4.12). This notationally represents a one-to-many relationship in
entity-relationship diagramming.

FIGURE 4.12

Relationships are
graphically represented
with a key for the
parent (or one side) of
the mix and a chain for
the child (or many side)
of the relationship.

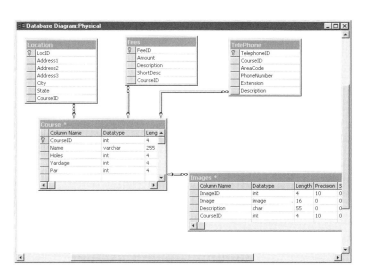

Part
I
Ch
4

Continue adding tables and relationships as necessary to complete the diagram of your database. After you finish, you can save all changes to the database immediately or generate a
script file as noted earlier.

Navigating Database Objects and Diagrams with the Database Designer

You can also experiment further with the diagram. For instance, right-click any object to bring up menu options for different views of objects (see Figure 4.13). You can view each table with full column names and parameters, just view the tables and key field columns, or just view tables with name spaces. You can also choose to view properties of any object on your diagram. By looking at the properties for a table, you can examine and alter indexes and other constraints for that object.

FIGURE 4.13

A table object's contextual right-click menu has many options for navigating and configuring objects as well as accessing an object's properties.

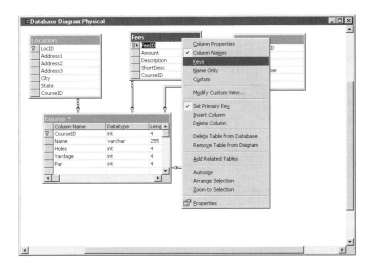

The Database Designer also lets you create smaller views of a large diagram. This is often helpful in large CS projects in which the database contains hundreds of tables and a developer is concerned only with a portion of the database that deals with a particular set of tables. You can create diagram views easily by inserting a new diagram and dragging the required tables from the Data View to the blank diagram.

Another use for the diagramming tool is to experiment with different layouts of tables and relationships without affecting the underlying database until the design is finished. You can accomplish this by creating a diagram, dragging existing tables to it, and altering their structure as desired. Just remember not to save the diagram to your database until you're sure that the design is what you want, or you'll lose any previously created structures.

With some experimentation and practice, you should be able to create complex databases with the Database Designer included with Visual Studio. This can bring more of an engineering approach to development projects and get developers and users interacting during the requirements phase for more successful projects.

Developing Stored Procedures with Visual Studio 6

If you've ever had to develop stored procedures for SQL Server, you're aware of the lack of tools to support this development. Unlike application developers, SQL procedure programmers haven't historically had tools such as advanced editors, debugging facilities, or even good ways to test stored procedures. Often, you had to enter your procedure code into a text editor or directly into the ISQL interface provided with SQL Server. There was no on-the-fly syntax checking, color coding, or consistent indentation for procedure development. Debugging and testing were even worse—you often submitted your completed procedure to the SQL engine and received error messages, which gave you only enough information to figure out the problem if you had a great deal of experience.

Debugging your procedures meant placing print statements at key points throughout to try to identify which areas were properly processed and which weren't. Testing stored procedures required you to set up the affected database objects with data to meet referential integrity requirements and then manually enter procedure calls with correct parameters. After that, you had to run select queries against affected tables to identify whether your procedure affected the underlying data correctly.

Visual Studio 6 brings the SQL developer into the modern age. Fairly complete support is provided in Visual Basic 6 as an included add-in, and is integrated into the Visual InterDev and Visual C++ 6 IDE. You can now use your familiar editor for entering procedure code, with all the frills you're used to in your favorite development environments. Properly indented text, color coding, and syntax checking are all available in the editor.

Another new feature included with Visual Studio 6 is SQL stored-procedure debugging, which uses the same debugging components available with VC++ and Visual InterDev. VB has a separate Transact SQL (T-SQL) debugger provided as an add-in, available automatically when testing your Active Data Objects (ADO) code or separately on demand.

If you're familiar with the Visual C++ IDE and debugging facilities, you'll be up and running fairly quickly with procedure development and debugging. If you're familiar with VB, you'll soon learn about the Transact SQL debugger and see how you can be as productive with your SQL development as you are with the rest of your application code tasks.

Part

I

Ch

4

Installing T-SQL Debugger

Begin by ensuring that T-SQL debugger is installed. If you chose to install all the enterprise tools when you installed Visual Basic, you should have a new option, T-SQL Debugger, on the Add-Ins menu. If not, you'll need to repeat the setup process, choosing a custom install and opting to Select All for the enterprise tools selection.

In addition to installing the T-SQL debugger on your client machine, you need to ensure that your database installation is SQL Server 6.5 and is running at least Service Pack 3. Then you need to run the Sdi_nt4.exe setup program on your SQL Server machine. This setup program is a server-side setup for SQL debugging. It needs to be installed on the machine housing your SQL Server, which can be the same as your development machine. You can find the Sdi_nt4.exe application on the client machine on which you installed Visual Basic in the \Microsoft Visual Studio\Common\Tools\SQL Debugging\SvrSetup directory.

NOTE To verify the server installation, ensure that SDI.DLL is resident in your \MSSQL\BINN directory on a Windows NT installation of SQL Server, or \MSSQL\BIN on a MS-DOS, 16-bit Windows, or Windows 9x-based client. ▨

Using T-SQL Debugger

You can access the T-SQL Debugger via one of several methods: explicitly during procedure design time, implicitly by stepping through the application code that makes calls to your stored procedures, or explicitly from within a database object's contextual right-click menu in the Data View.

NOTE To automatically step into a stored procedure, make sure that you've selected Automatically Step Into Stored Procedures in the T-SQL Debugger options. You can access the T-SQL Debugger options by choosing Tools, T-SQL Debugging Options from the Visual Basic menu. ▨

You can explicitly invoke the debugger during design-time by choosing Add-Ins, T-SQL Debugger from the menu. This brings up the Batch T-SQL Debugger dialog box (see Figure 4.14).

FIGURE 4.14

The T-SQL Debugger settings enable you to establish parameters for your debugging session.

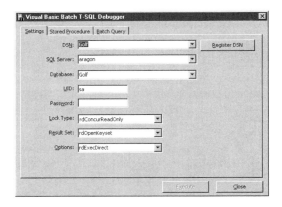

On the first tabbed page, enter information pertaining to the data source name (DSN) with which you want to access the database. Available sections include

- ▨ DSN
- ▨ SQL Server
- ▨ Database
- ▨ UID
- ▨ Password
- ▨ Lock Type
- ▨ Resultset

The Lock Type property in the T-SQL Debugger dialog box refers to the type of concurrency control the debugging session should have over the resultset being affected. The named items in the list box refer to Remote Data Objects (RDO) constants that refer to specific values that can be assigned to the LockType property of RDO resultset objects. Table 4.2 describes the available lock types.

Table 4.2 Available Lock Types

Lock Type	Description
rdConcurReadOnly	Resultset is read-only. No modifications can be made to the data.
rdConcurLock	The resultset locks all associated data pages. *Pessimistic* in that it assumes that no other users will need the same data.
rdConcurRowVer	*Optimistic* lock type in that it assumes that no other user will attempt to change the affected data, so it doesn't lock any of the affected pages. Requires row identifiers to be compared against the records in the resultset. If the identifiers match, the modification takes place; if not, an error is generated.
rdConcurValues	Version of optimistic lock where no data pages are locked. Requires row-by-row comparison of values before changes can be committed.
rdConcurBatch	Optimistic locking where no locks are held but where each change is accumulated in a batch. When the batch is applied, each record is modified according to rules of a lower-level parameter. Status values of each record in a batch are returned.

The resultset parameter on the T-SQL Debugger refers to the type of cursor to use with the RDO resultset object in the debugging session. Table 4.3 describes the available resultset types.

Table 4.3 Available Resultset Types

Resultset	Description
rdOpenKeyset	Dynamic type cursor where you can still see records changed by other users but not those added by others. You also can't access records deleted by another user.

continues

Table 4.3 Continued

Resultset	Description
rdOpenForwardOnly	Static type cursor in which you can see records only as they were when you retrieved the recordset. You can't see records added, modified, or deleted by others since you opened your cursor. You can only scroll forward with this cursor type.
rdOpenStatic	Similar to forward-only cursor, except that you can scroll forward or backward.
rdOpenDynamic	All data additions, modifications, or deletions made to the data in your open cursor are visible. Scrolling in any direction is enabled.

The Options selection for the T-SQL Debugger session refers to how the session should present its SQL statements to the SQL Server: either directly through the SQLExecDirect ODBC API function when rdExecDirect is selected, or by preparing a stored procedure for each statement when rdNone is selected.

After the DSN information is entered, you can change to the Stored Procedures page, which is very helpful in the debugging and testing process. This page enables you to

■ Select stored procedures already in the database

■ Show the actual call string with parameter values

■ Set input parameters

■ Insert parameters into the call string

After you select your stored procedure and enter values for any input parameters, you can click the Execute button.

CAUTION

Stored procedures are designed to manipulate or alter data in your database. It's strongly suggested that you select the Use Safe Mode (transaction rollback) for Stored Procedure Calls option in the T-SQL Debugging options. This way, any changes a stored procedure might make can be rolled back on completion of the debugging/testing session.

Now you should be in the T-SQL Debugger interface itself (see Figure 4.15). The interface is made up of a code window (for viewing the actual procedure code being debugged), a Local Variable watch window, a Global Variable watch window, and a procedure output window. The simple toolbar gives you ready access to all the debugging options available.

FIGURE 4.15
The Code window in the T-SQL Debugger isn't for developing but for viewing code as you step through it in a debugging session.

Code window ⎯

Local Variables watch window

Procedure output window

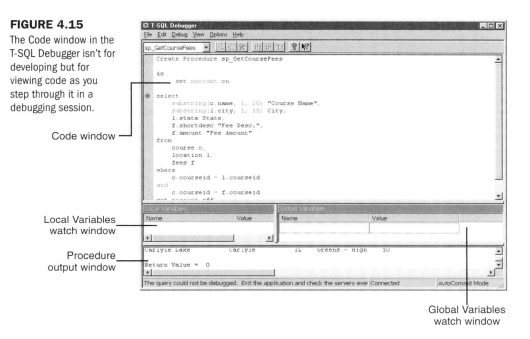

Global Variables watch window

The debugging options available in the T-SQL Debugger are as follows:

- Run
- Set and clear breakpoints
- Step to subexpressions
- Step into subexpressions
- Step over subexpressions
- Run to cursor
- Resultset
- Stop
- Restart

You also can invoke a separate Call Stack window and a temporary table dump window for viewing the related output. Experienced SQL procedure developers will definitely recognize these features as ones long awaited. If you take time to learn the features well, you should benefit from increased productivity.

Creating and Editing SQL Server Stored Procedures

In addition to the debugging facilities provided, Visual Studio 6 enables you to create new stored procedures or edit existing ones from within the Microsoft Developer Studio IDE. Data View provides a graphical hierarchy of all database objects for the database related to the data source you have in your project.

To create a new stored procedure, follow these steps:

1. Right-click the Stored Procedure folder.

2. Select New Stored Procedure from the pop-up menu to bring up a code page with a simple Create Procedure statement already entered (see Figure 4.16). You need to add a name for your procedure on the procedure name placeholder.

FIGURE 4.16
Stored procedures are written by using the SQL source editor.

3. Add any necessary input parameters and begin entering any necessary declare statements for local variables. A simple return statement is added for you, but you'll need to develop any serious error-handlers or output parameters.

   As you enter procedure code, notice that SQL keywords are color-coded in one color and your own identifiers in another. The color coding and other syntactical options are configurable by choosing the Tools, Options menu. These simple but effective visual indicators are great debugging tools for anyone familiar with developing procedures with the old tool sets. It's pretty easy to notice an error in a keyword when it's not the appropriate color. When everything is black text on white, subtle errors are almost impossible to see.

 TIP As you write your procedure code, having a printed copy of your data model close by is often handy so that you can look up identifier name spellings, data types, and table keys and indexes. Or, you can use the Data View explorer from within the same IDE to explore the properties of tables and columns as you write your procedures.

After you enter your procedure code, compile it into the SQL Server database. One of the more common errors is that objects referenced by the procedure aren't already in the database. With the Data View just a mouse click away, you can quickly inspect referenced objects and pick out misspellings or invalid datatypes from your procedure code.

4. To run a stored procedure after you develop it, just right-click the procedure code window. As shown in Figure 4.17, you can also right-click to debug the procedure. Debugging a procedure successfully will submit it to the SQL Server for compilation and error checking.

FIGURE 4.17
The context menu available by right-clicking within the SQL Source editor window enables you to save to database or debug your stored procedure.

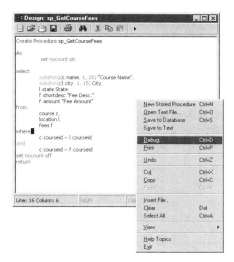

5. After the procedure is compiled, the T-SQL Debugger prompts you to enter any input parameter values and run the procedure. Resultsets, other SQL Server output (such as rowcounts), and any error conditions are displayed in the output window along the bottom of the IDE (refer to Figure 4.15).

After your procedure is successfully compiled and run, notice that it's added to the Data View hierarchy. It's also ready to be debugged, which you can do either during your application debugging, inline with application code, or from the code window by right-clicking the procedure code window and selecting Debug from the pop-up menu.

As you can see, Visual Studio 6 has added some great SQL Server database design and development tools to the CS developer's toolkit. With a little work and experimentation, you should become a more productive database developer with these tools.

SQL Stored Procedures for Server-Side Logic

CS systems that use a RDBMS, such as SQL Server for data storage and retrieval, often must integrate large amounts of Structured Query Language (SQL) statements into middle-tier components. These middle-tier components must enable the insertion, editing, deletion, and retrieval of data stored in the RDBMS. Often, much data-specific logic is required before these services can be fulfilled. For instance, the data might need to be validated from end-user entry before being inserted, or special business rules might need to be applied to the data before it's affected.

When the logic for data manipulation is placed into the middle tier, the full advantages of the RDBMS engine aren't realized. Middle-tier component languages usually aren't designed for manipulating large sets of data, but for processing of individual records one at a time or for performing calculations on a few discrete values.

SQL is a mathematically based language designed for the manipulation and processing of large amounts of related data. By encapsulating the logic for data manipulation in stored procedures, the services necessary for fulfilling the data manipulation are performed in the same CS layer where that data is stored. Common sense tells you that this is a better partitioning of services within layers in the CS model and should provide better performance than SQL statements embedded in external language components. In most cases, the techniques used in external languages require multiple translations of the SQL string before the string is sent to the SQL engine. These multiple translation layers come from passing SQL strings through data-access libraries, such as ODBC. This adds overhead in the processing of the SQL commands.

Some of the more technical reasons why stored procedures are good choices for data-manipulation logic include performance and security. The main performance gain in using stored procedures is the location of the processing. Stored procedures are precompiled and executed within the context of the SQL Server engine. This negates network latency in execution speed because the processes that manipulate data reside in the same memory and processing space as the data structures that store the data. In a networked environment, this can equate to large performance gains.

You can actually use stored procedures as a security tool. User permissions over database objects must be tightly controlled in a CS environment. Stored procedures can let you build up a distinct layer between the physical storage of data and the users of the data. Rather than give users permissions over all tables in which data is stored, you can restrict them to permissions over the execution of stored procedures. Users don't need to have select permissions on a table if they have permissions over a stored procedure that, after some validation logic, does the selection for them and returns a resultset. In this model, rather than build an elaborate management scheme of a hierarchical groups-and-permissions structure on top of tables, you can give users permission to execute a few stored procedures that act as a public interface to the underlying data storage.

N O T E Many other sources cover these concepts for stored procedure development. One good reference is Stephen Wynkoop's *Special Edition Using Microsoft SQL Server 6.5*, Second Edition, published by Que Corporation.

Using the Query Designer

The Query Designer in Visual Studio 6 is a great tool for developers and end-users alike. It works for any ODBC-compliant database and provides more than the typical query-by-example (QBE) type of query-building capabilities.

With the Query Designer you can graphically select the tables, columns, joins and constraints for your query, as well as enter direct ANSI SQL for query development.

Before you can add a query to your project, you need to add a data connection to the project. Do this by right-clicking on your project's name space in the project explorer window. Choose the Add Data Connection option from the pop-up menu. You will be prompted to select a Data Source from the dialog. Choose your data source and select OK. If necessary you will also be prompted to enter your user ID and password to log into the database.

Access the Query Designer from within the Microsoft IDE by right-clicking on your previous data connection name in the Project Explorer. Choose the Add Query or Add Item option from the contextual pop-up menu. In the Add Item dialog you can choose to create database queries, stored procedures, tables, views and triggers with various types of SQL scripts or batches.

From the New tab of the Add Item dialog box, select Database Query and then enter a query name in the Name box, as shown in Figure 4.18. Click Open and the Query Designer appears, ready to start a new query. The Query Designer is made up of four panes: the graphical workspace, the constraints specification grid, the SQL code viewer, and the output results window.

FIGURE 4.18

The Add Item dialog enables you to select several different types of SQL scripts or queries to create.

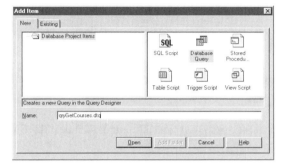

You can drag tables into the graphical workspace from the Data View. Figure 4.19 shows the query designer with two tables from the Data View and columns selected to query.

FIGURE 4.19

The Query Designer is based on four distinct functional panes rather than a wizard approach.

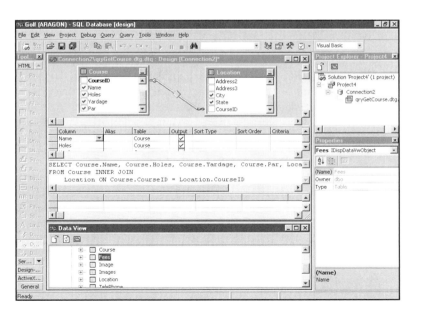

You can see the SQL statement being built in the SQL code viewer as you drag tables from the Data View and select columns in the items on the Graphical workspace. Additional criteria such as constraints, grouping, sorting and custom ordering can be specified in the constraints specification grid.

You can run your new query by selecting <u>R</u>un from the <u>Q</u>uery menu or <u>R</u>un from the pop-up menu you get by right-clicking on the query window itself. After you have built and run your query, you can view the output in the bottom pane of the Query designer.

As you have seen, Visual Studio 6 provides plenty of help to CS developers in an enterprise setting. With the Visual Database Tools and all the Visual Studio offerings you are well on your way to productive development.

Looking at Distributed Computing

Today's systems are often a mix of architectures and technologies. What most of them have in common is that they're of a distributed nature. A *distributed system* is a dynamic collection of computers linked by a network, running software designed to provide an integrated computing environment to users. Distributed systems can range from single-purpose applications that support business processes to full-service computing facilities that service a broad range of users with a broad range of resources.

Given these complex tasks, a distributed system must be designed and developed in levels of abstraction or architectures. One main design paradigm has emerged to deal with the complexity of distributed systems: client/server.

The following sections will help you understand what client/server is and how Visual Studio 6 helps in the development of distributed systems.

Client/Server Computing

CS computing is at the heart of the Information Technology (IT) industry today. As organizations have moved from a centralized computing environment to client/server, the very description of client/server computing continues to evolve. Generally speaking, client/server computing is the splitting of processes into two or more parts, the client and the server:

- The *client* is the requestor of services in the CS mix. The best example of client processing is today's GUI interfaces. Most business systems development projects have as a chief component the development of a GUI to accept user input and interface with server-side processes for persistent data support, process-intensive tasks, or retrieval of server-managed data. This requesting role often enables the tag user services to be attached to the processing that takes place on the client end of the CS mix.

- The *server* is on the receiving end of this mix. The server accepts client requests for processing or data retrieval. This processing usually involves enforcement of business-rule logic, provision of an interface to a persistent data store such as a relational database server, or communications with other resource managers to fulfill the client's request. The server is often labeled as the business services or data services layer in the CS mix.

As shown in Figure 4.20, function calls implement communication between the client and the server. The client component calls a server function. The client passes parameters (param) to the server function arguments (args). The server processes the request and then returns success/failure codes or provides requested data. The client in turn receives the return from the server and acts on any errors, returns success to its client application, or displays data back to users.

FIGURE 4.20

In the client/server mix, two processes cooperate to perform a system service. One (the client) invokes a function, which takes arguments (args) by passing parameters to the server process.

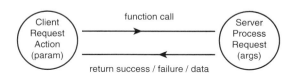

To facilitate communication between the client and server across a network, client components must be able to locate and invoke functions on server components. They must also be able to map parameter values to native datatypes. Different machine architectures require that this interprocess communication be able to marshal or translate data from one architecture to another to provide for correct parameter value representation on the client and server.

In reality, any component in a CS environment can act as a server and a client. Often, a component might act as a client to other servers and as a server to other clients. These client and server components can exist within the context of a single machine, but they usually operate in a multiuser environment (see Figure 4.21).

Figure 4.21 shows a typical distributed system. Users are connected to a local network and share network resources, such as file and print services. Applications share data from an RDBMS. Modern business systems increasingly extend this local distributed model by integrating Web and other Internet access with the local resources, as well as opening up access to external networks for geographically separated business units or for integration with customer or supplier systems. This orchestration of disparate components and resources creates unique design issues and goals, which you must address in the distributed system.

Part
I

Ch
4

FIGURE 4.21

In the simple distributed
system model, clients
(workstations) request
services and resources
from network servers
hosting services such as
file, print, and database
services.

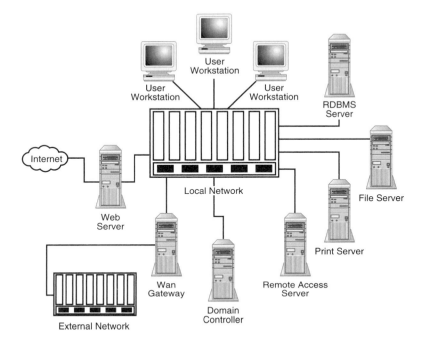

Client/Server Design

Distributed CS components have unique issues and goals, which must be addressed in their design. Some of these goals and issues are

- Support for resource sharing
- Concurrent processing
- Scalable processing
- Openness
- Fault tolerance
- Transparency

Some of the earliest implementations of distributed systems included sharing of print and file services on a local network. Most network operating systems provide for this level of resource sharing by providing such services as standard naming, location directory, and file-handling functions. More recent developments in resource sharing include opening up resources beyond the local boundaries, wide area network (WAN) integration and access to enterprise data, and I-net and remote users.

With the opening up of local networks in distributed computing, concurrent processing and scalability issues increase in importance. *Concurrency* indicates the need for multiple users or user processes to request the same services and the need for server processes to execute in parallel to fulfill all requests in an efficient manner. *Scalability* is concerned with the ability of resource managers to service multiple requests simultaneously on an increasingly more frequent basis as larger numbers of users or clients are added to a distributed system.

Openness as a design goal is the capability of a distributed system to remain extensible across disparate user platforms and components. This requirement often demands resources to operate over multiple protocols and provide standard access facilities. The rapid acceptance of standards for database access—such as a common interface for RDBMS servers in the form of the SQL language—is a good example of openness across distributed systems.

Fault tolerance is the capability of systems to recover from failure. Distributed systems must provide hardware redundancy and software recovery features to provide a fault-tolerant environment. Fault tolerance is also related to the capability of a distributed system to provide the necessary high availability of shared resources. Very few businesses could operate without a high degree of systems availability, a need increased by the interrelated demands of a distributed system.

Transparency in distributed systems is the distributed environment's capability to isolate users from the complexities of the distributed implementation. Users shouldn't need to concern themselves with how data is accessed across local or wide area environments. For maximum productivity and efficiency, the distributed system needs to have the appearance of a single system to the user. Transparency is also an important abstraction technique for developers. Developers shouldn't need to know implementation details of shared resource managers, but should be provided with standard interfaces to integrate their components with others.

Part

I

Ch

4

Distributed CS Technologies in Visual Studio

Visual Studio provides many tools and development technologies to support the requirements of distributed CS systems. In this section, you'll see how the technologies and tools in Visual Studio 6 support the development of systems that in turn support the major design issues and goals.

With Visual Studio, you can design and develop distributed client/server systems by taking advantage of standard integrated tools and technologies. Visual Studio 6 supports the following:

- Concurrency and scalability, which are supported with COM and DCOM and enable you to take advantage of MTS and RDBMS through standard ODBC interfaces.

- Openness, which is provided through the use of ODBC and OLE DB as a standard interface to data providers. COM and DCOM act as an open interprocess communication mechanism to enable client and server processes to communicate in a distributed environment.

- Fault tolerance, which is provided with the integration of technologies within the operating system and SQL Server engine and with transaction capabilities built into MTS. SMP support for multithreaded applications also provides process-level fault tolerance.

- Transparency, which is provided through the use of object-oriented language features of the development languages included in Visual Studio 6. VB and VC++ provide for COM and DCOM support in isolating developers from external implementations.

- Resource sharing, which is directly supported for the development team by the inclusion of Visual SourceSafe as a team development tool for managing the version control and configuration management of source code. SQL Server is also a major player in the resource-sharing requirements. Data-access technologies enable you to build a common database for multiple applications built with different application development tools so that they can access the database and interface with common procedures and business logic services.

Distributed Data Access

Visual Studio 6 reinforces its strength of being an enterprise-class client/server development environment. As such this latest version provides greater support for OLE DB through the use of the ADO 2 library of objects for access to relational data sources and Microsoft's Universal Data Access (UDA) strategy for access to distributed storage components.

Microsoft's UDA provides a variety of techniques for the enterprise to access data across a wide variety of storage types and platforms. Visual Studio 6 also remains backward compatible with earlier versions by offering support for the tried and true Data Access Objects (DAO) and RDO object libraries.

In developing an enterprise architecture, many things must be considered when designing components for the client/server mix. In addition to building applications by strategically applying various client techniques (such as those presented elsewhere in this text) and focusing on transaction-oriented middleware (such as Microsoft Transaction Server and Message Queue Server), one of the most important things to consider is how to access the data. When you build your databases beyond the individual application and begin thinking in terms of the whole organization, you need to think of data access in terms of more than one application requiring database support.

Databases in the enterprise are required to serve data to a range of demanding clients: traditional Visual Basic applications, Internet applications using Active Server Pages built in Visual InterDev, and newer Java components written in J++. Furthermore, there might be VB, Java, or C++ components being hosted in a Transaction Server context as middleware application components.

OLE DB is the next generation data access offering from Microsoft. Finally, with Visual Studio 6, you have support for the latest in data access technologies enabling you to further integrate your legacy and newer relational data with a mixed platform of application services. Included in the Visual Studio edition of the Microsoft Developer Network CD, the Microsoft Data Access Components (MDAC) provide a roadmap to designing your data access strategy. Included in the MDAC are three components:

- Microsoft OLE DB Reference
- ActiveX Data Objects Reference
- Microsoft ODBC Reference

These three resources offer in-depth coverage of the core data access technologies available to Visual Studio developers.

From Here...

In this chapter, you learned about the importance of good database design and how it affects your application development projects. You learned how to use the tools provided in Visual Studio 6 to help design databases, and got an overview of distributed computing and multitier architectures.

For more information on the topics covered in this chapter, see the following chapters:

- For further insight into the use of ActiveX components, see Chapter 10, "Creating Reusable Components."
- To obtain additional information on Web-based applications, see Chapter 15, "Clients, Servers, and Components: Web-Based Applications."
- For further information on developing applications for multitier distributed environments, see Chapter 25, "Clients, Servers, and Components: Design Strategies for Distributed Applications."

Part

I

Ch

4

An Inside Look at Microsoft Transaction Server

by Larry Millett

In this chapter

In May 1997, Microsoft announced that a distributed transaction processing system based on a Microsoft platform (Windows NT Server, SQL Server, and Microsoft Transaction Server) had achieved a billion transactions per day. The day before, IBM had announced a similar result, using Windows NT Server, DB2, and Transarc Encina. Microsoft touted the event as a major milestone in the development of high-volume, highly scalable distributed systems based on relatively inexpensive off-the-shelf hardware and software. IBM pointed out that for larger systems using similar tools, a billion transactions a day was commonplace. In both cases, a transaction processing (TP) monitor was a critical component.

A *TP monitor* is an operating system extension that provides transaction support and efficient management of shared resources. Programs executing in a TP monitor environment can invoke its services to handle some of the most difficult problems in distributed computing. Services provided vary from one implementation to another and can include language extensions, a runtime environment, management consoles, and other useful elements. Microsoft Transaction Server (MTS) extends the traditional TP monitor to a component-based architecture, integrating closely with Microsoft's implementation of the Distributed Component Object Model (DCOM).

Microsoft introduced its TP monitor, MTS, in January 1997. As its name implies, MTS provides support for distributed transactions including two-phase commit (2PC). The distributed transaction services build on the Distributed Transaction Coordinator (DTC) service shipped with Microsoft SQL Server 6.5. However, MTS also provides many other services including security, concurrency, multithreading, shared state, and resource pooling. Both types of services are essential for scalable component-based software development.

For developers of distributed applications, MTS is as important a tool as Visual Studio. MTS extends the Component Object Model (COM) and Distributed Component Object Model (DCOM) to provide an industrial-strength platform for highly scalable enterprise applications. MTS also simplifies many issues for developers, including resource management, distributed transactions, threading, and error handling.

This chapter begins with a review of distributed processing and multitier client/server architecture. This review leads to a discussion of the importance of transactions in a distributed application. After laying this groundwork, the discussion turns to an overview of component integration services provided by MTS. The chapter closes with a look at the details of installing MTS.

ON THE WEB

For the latest information about MTS, visit the official MTS Web page at http://www.microsoft.com/NTServer/Basics/AppServices/TransSvcs/. Microsoft maintains a list of answers to frequently asked questions about MTS at http://support.microsoft.com/Support/transaction/content/faq/. For more information about CORBA, visit http://www.omg.org/

Looking at Goals for Distributed Processing

Not so long ago, a really big application required a really big computer. In Microsoft's vision, large applications will run on a number of inexpensive Windows-based computers. This distributes the processing load and provides a variety of other benefits. Some of these techniques have existed in the past, but have been available only on large, expensive platforms, costing hundreds of thousands, or even millions of dollars. Part of the attraction of these tools is that they are now available on low-cost, commodity-priced computing platforms. This puts the technology within the reach of much smaller organizations.

The focus of this discussion is on enterprise applications such as billing, payroll, and inventory management. It also includes applications specific to particular industries, such as banking, finance, manufacturing, and retailing. In medium-to-large organizations, such applications might manage gigabytes of data, and provide simultaneous access to hundreds of people. An ideal platform for enterprise applications should have the following characteristics:

- Economical to acquire, deploy, and maintain.
- Very reliable (used to run the business!).
- Automated failure recovery with little or no loss of information.
- Capable of handling (very) large amounts of data.
- Capable of supporting hundreds of simultaneous users.
- Strong security features (with auditing).
- High availability of data (no long lock times).
- Enables rapid development and deployment of new applications.
- Supports existing applications.
- Simplifies component reuse.
- Straightforward programming model so that developers can be quickly and economically trained.
- Industry standard protocols and programmatic interfaces.
- Appropriate and affordable for small, medium, and large systems.
- System costs grow gradually as the size of the system grows, with no large increases at certain points in the growth path.
- Capable of continuing to evolve to meet unforeseen challenges.

Taking a collection of small computers, some networking equipment, some software, and a group of trained and talented people and producing a system that can meet these requirements is still a mix of science and art. Microsoft claims that for many distributed applications, MTS can dramatically reduce complexity and development time. In theory, a component can be developed for a single-user standalone computer; MTS provides the necessary infrastructure for integrated multiuser deployment. At first glance, it's a remarkable claim, and on closer examination, the difficulties seem truly overwhelming. Still, MTS substantially fulfills Microsoft's claims.

Part

I

Ch

5

Microsoft has two goals for MTS: provide a robust, scalable infrastructure for component-based applications, and simplify development of such applications. The component architecture of choice is, of course, ActiveX. Because MTS manages security, transaction processing, concurrency, and resource pooling, developers can concentrate on correctly implementing business logic.

Microsoft has designed MTS to play a specific role in a specific application architecture—the component based multitier client/server architecture. Before discussing MTS in more detail, I will review the architecture.

Working with Multitiered Architectures

For several years, Microsoft has heavily promoted a component-based software architecture. A component is simply a unit of software that implements a well-defined group of tasks, or services. An application is a suite of cooperating components. Of course, COM is the preferred model for these components, and ActiveX is the preferred implementation of COM.

MTS is used to deploy mid-tier logic implemented in the form of ActiveX components. These objects receive requests from clients, apply some sort of logic (for example, business rules) to the requests, and then call on appropriate resource managers to resolve the requests. These components can be developed in-house or purchased from third-party software vendors.

After these components are written or acquired, they're combined to form packages sharing resources (for example, memory) and security settings. MTS also manages a shared pool of ODBC data connections to various data providers, which can be traditional database servers or files on a mainframe.

Because MTS can manage links among many clients accessing many resource managers (for example, databases) while applying application logic, the application architecture you can create with these building blocks has some very desirable characteristics:

- Scalable—Applications can be implemented by using one server, or scaled to many multiprocessor servers handling hundreds of users.
- Distributed—Applications that span multiple machines are coded in a manner almost identical to an application designed to run on a single computer.
- Multiuser—MTS automatically provides thread management, assists with shared memory management, and offers other capabilities that make it easier to take existing single-user components and run them safely in a multiuser environment.
- Reliable—MTS uses transaction protocols such as XA and OLE TX (a COM-based protocol) to ensure *atomicity*: discrete units of work are always done completely or not at all. Data accessed through MTS resource managers remains in a consistent state, even with many users accessing diverse resources on multiple machines.

Microsoft promotes a logical three-tier design approach, in which the work of an application is divided into presentation services, business logic, and data services. Presentation services provide interaction with users of the application, typically via a graphical user interface (GUI).

Business logic applies common business policies to users' interaction with data. Data services provide durable storage and retrieval of business information. Note that this is a logical model, and it doesn't imply that a particular application will have three components or that it will run on three machines. The three-tier model is, however, a very effective tool for designing component applications.

The three-tier framework doesn't imply any physical implementation; it's simply an approach for grouping services into components. The traditional two-tier client/server approach divides the services into two categories: data management and everything else. Grouping all three types of services into a single component results in a monolithic application.

Many simple applications and many older PC-based applications are *monolithic*: A single component provides the user interface, data storage, and all processing. This architecture allows developers to carefully tune the interactions of every part of an application. However, it also forces developers to build every part of an application. This approach can lead to weird interactions between implementations of data storage and business logic.

In a traditional, or two-tier client/server application, a database server implements data management functions, and a client application implements other functions, with business logic arbitrarily divided between the client application and the database server. Figure 5.1 shows the typical components of a two-tier client/server application.

FIGURE 5.1

In a two-tier application, business logic is divided arbitrarily between the database server (stored procedures) and the client application.

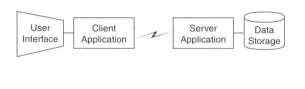

A traditional client/server requires less up-front design and can often be implemented quickly. Because two-tier applications require less communication, response time for individual users might be better than in more complex client/server models. The two-tier model is often a good choice for an application with a small number of users and a limited growth path.

Two-tier applications often don't scale well to large numbers of users because they don't share database resources efficiently. Database contention increases substantially as the number of users increases. Update distribution is notoriously difficult, and changes in the client component must be carefully coordinated with changes in the server component. Because the two-tier model requires a high-bandwidth connection to the database server, it's a poor choice for an Internet-based application.

In the three-tier model, a database server implements data services, mid-tier components implement common business logic, and a presentation component provides a user interface. This model has two primary advantages over the two-tier model: First, database resources can be shared more efficiently, and second, business logic is implemented in a more centralized manner. Increased communications might result in slightly slower response times for individual users when compared with a two-tier implementation. However, response time in a good three-tier implementation will remain quite stable as the number of users increases. Decoupling the presentation layer from business logic also results in much simpler update distribution. A three-tier architecture works well for Internet-based applications because it results in much less processing in the presentation layer.

Although the example in Figure 5.2 describes three tiers, nothing inherent in the design of MTS limits it to this structure. You can break a computing system into more than three logical tiers, and MTS makes implementing various system architectures, including multitier designs, straightforward. The three-tier model is natural in some respects and is starting to be widely used, but need not be the only deployment alternative with MTS.

FIGURE 5.2
This sample MTS environment shows various elements of a three-tier architecture.

N O T E The operating systems and applications installed on PCs have become much larger as they've grown in sophistication. With the advent of the HTTP-based Web browser, application developers started exploring the capability of using this relatively thin tool as the basis for server-based applications. The traditional application architecture with its executable files and dynamic link libraries (DLLs) has been characterized as fat because of the amount of information (programs, configuration files, and data) that must be stored on the client.

Browsers (from Netscape, Microsoft, and others) continue to get fatter as more features are added, however. Also, browser-based applications haven't yet reached the level of performance and sophistication offered by the more traditional Win32 client. It remains to be seen how fat the thin client will need to become to match the functionality offered by Win32 clients. ▨

▶ For a more detailed comparison of two-tier and three-tier architectures, **see** Chapter 25, "Clients, Servers, and Components: Design Strategies for Distributed Applications," **p. 727**

Microsoft very explicitly designed MTS to support mid-tier components for a distributed three-tier application. MTS documents use special terms to identify various components:

- Base client—The application running on a user desktop. The base client corresponds to the user services layer in the three-tier model.

- MTS Component (or application component)—A COM component that executes in the MTS environment. A MTS component must be a DLL, must provide a type library, and must implement a class factory. An MTS component can correspond to the business services layer in the three-tier model and can be invoked by a base client or by another application component.

■ Resource dispenser—A service that manages nonpersistent data, such as the Microsoft ODBC 3 Driver Manager and the MTS Shared Property Manager (SPM). A resource dispenser corresponds to the data-services layer in the three-tier model.

■ Resource manager—A system service that manages durable data, such as Microsoft SQL Server. A resource manager can cooperate with the DTC to implement distributed transactions. A resource manager corresponds to the data-services layer in the three-tier model.

In Figure 5.3, Base Client 1 interacts with a single application component. Base Client 2 invokes one application component, which in turn invokes two others. The secondary components implement a distributed transaction spanning two resource managers. Base Client 3 uses two mid-tier components: one updates a database, and both share data via a resource dispenser.

FIGURE 5.3
Base clients invoke MTS components, which invoke resource dispensers, which invoke resource managers.

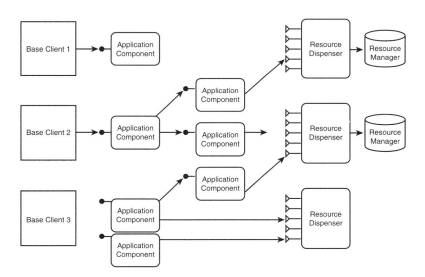

Understanding the Importance of Transactions

Sooner or later, the developer of a distributed application encounters the problem of coordinating simultaneous updates to multiple data stores. The data store might be a file, one table in a database, or a group of tables spanning several databases. The factors making group updates difficult include coping with system failures and ensuring that other applications see a consistent view of the data. The solution to this common problem is the transaction.

A *transaction* is a permanent series of updates to persistent data, which guarantees that all updates occur or none. If the data is consistent before the update, it will be consistent after the series of updates. For example, a program might implement a transfer of funds between two bank accounts. The program must ensure that the proper amount is transferred out of one account and transferred in to the other account. Before the transfer, each account is internally consistent (all transactions sum to the current balance), and all accounts are collectively consistent (account balances for a depositor sum to his total balance with the bank). The transfer must preserve both consistencies. This means either that both parts of the transfer succeed, or that if any part fails, no change is made to either account. The capability to guarantee this sort of consistency is sometimes called *transactional integrity*. In 1983, Andreas Reuter identified four criteria for transactional integrity:

- Atomicity—The transaction succeeds as a single unit or fails as a single unit. If the transaction succeeds, all data sets consistently reflect the result. If the transaction fails, all data sets should consistently reflect the state before the transaction.

- Consistency—The transaction preserves internal consistency (as defined by the application) for each data set. Processing might temporarily generate an inconsistent state, but reestablishes consistency before the end of the transaction.

- Isolation—Other applications accessing data involved in a transaction see the prior state or the end state, but not any intermediate state. When a transaction begins, other applications are blocked from accessing data until the transaction completes.

- Durability—When a transaction completes, the updates to the data sets are permanent and can't be lost because of hardware or software failure. In general, this means that when a transaction completes, all results have been physically written to disk (not just to cache).

Collectively, these criteria for transactional integrity are known as the *ACID test*.

The atomicity and isolation criteria have important implications for application developers. Because the intermediate states of a transaction aren't visible outside the transaction and because each transaction is all or nothing, transactions appear to execute separately and sequentially. This means that an application using transactions can ignore concurrency issues, which can be a substantial simplification.

Transactional Integrity in SQL

Every major database management system (DBMS) includes transaction-management functions. For the DBMS application, each table is a separate data set, and updates to multiple tables frequently require transactional integrity. The Transact SQL language in Microsoft SQL Server includes many transaction-management commands. These three are fundamental, and are found in every dialect of SQL:

- `BEGIN TRANSACTION`
- `ROLLBACK TRANSACTION`
- `COMMIT TRANSACTION`

N O T E   Any persistent data storage mechanism can implement transactions. The best known implementations today are the major database servers such as Microsoft SQL Server, Oracle, Sybase, and Informix. For simplicity, the rest of this chapter discusses transactions as implemented in Microsoft SQL Server.

The BEGIN TRANSACTION command marks the beginning of a sequence of operations that must satisfy the ACID test; COMMIT TRANSACTION marks the end. The ROLLBACK TRANSACTION command indicates that the transaction has failed: All operations back to the BEGIN TRANSACTION command will be undone (rolled back). The COMMIT TRANSACTION command indicates that the transaction has succeeded: All operations will be made permanent (committed).

Sometimes, it's appropriate to nest transactions. Assume two tables for a bank example: an AccountActivity table, listing each deposit, withdrawal, or transfer for each account; and a BankAccount table listing each account (including a current balance). Then the Transact SQL commands to transfer $1,000 from account 11111 to account 22222 might look like Listing 5.1.

Listing 5.1 AELST01.TXT—An Example Involving Two Accounts in Two Bank Branches

```
BEGIN TRANSACTION

    BEGIN TRANSACTION

    INSERT AccountActivity (AccountNumber, ActivityType, ActivityDate,
    ➥Amount)
    VALUES ('11111', 'Transfer', getdate(), -1000.00)

    IF @@error != 0 BEGIN
        ROLLBACK TRANSACTION
        RETURN
    END

    UPDATE BankAccount
    SET CurrentBalance = CurrentBalance - 1000.00
    WHERE AccountNumber = '11111'

    IF @@error != 0 BEGIN
        ROLLBACK TRANSACTION
        RETURN
    END

    COMMIT TRANSACTION

    BEGIN TRANSACTION

    INSERT AccountActivity (AccountNumber, ActivityType, ActivityDate,
    ➥Amount)
    VALUES ('22222', 'Transfer', getdate(), 1000.00)

    IF @@error != 0 BEGIN
        ROLLBACK TRANSACTION
        RETURN
    END

    UPDATE BankAccount
    SET CurrentBalance = CurrentBalance + 1000.00
    WHERE AccountNumber = '22222'
```

Part

I

Ch

5

continues

Listing 5.1   Continued

```
IF @@error != 0 BEGIN
    ROLLBACK TRANSACTION
    RETURN
END

COMMIT TRANSACTION

COMMIT TRANSACTION
```

Although admittedly oversimplified, this scenario does show basic transaction management. The BEGIN TRANSACTION and COMMIT TRANSACTION commands mark the beginning and end of a group of operations (inserts, updates, or nested transactions) that must collectively satisfy the ACID test. If any one operation fails because of an error condition, the entire transaction rolls back to the state at the outermost BEGIN TRANSACTION command. This is implemented by the conditional ROLLBACK TRANSACTION command after each operation.

N O T E   Database servers implement transactions through logs. Every physical write to the data is accompanied by a log entry. Because a series of physical writes is generally required to take a database from one consistent state to another, the log also records consistent checkpoints. If the system should crash in the middle of a sequence of physical writes, the server (on restart) reverses the updates recorded in the log back to the last recorded consistent checkpoint. The BEGIN TRANS-ACTION and COMMIT TRANSACTION instructions force the database server to establish a new consistent checkpoint in the log; the ROLLBACK TRANSACTION instruction forces the server to roll back to a specific checkpoint. After a server determines that it won't need to roll back beyond a given checkpoint, it discards all entries before that checkpoint.

T I P   Most databases support partial rollback of nested transactions. Check your database documentation for details.

If a single program can execute the funds transfer, and if all tables involved reside on a single server, the DBMS can provide all necessary transaction management services. In fact, creating a stored procedure to improve performance and encapsulate the function makes sense. When a transaction spans multiple database servers, or when multiple applications participate in a transaction, however, some middleware is required to coordinate the transactions. MTS fulfills that role.

Two-Phase Commit

Sometimes an application must update two or more distinct data sets, and the updates must satisfy the ACID test. Suppose that a bank customer wants to transfer funds between accounts at two different branches, and each branch maintains separate account databases. In this case, the standard transaction management provided by SQL Server won't suffice.

Suppose that account 11111 resides at Branch A, and account 22222 resides at Branch B. The funds-transfer application can issue the BEGIN TRANSACTION, INSERT AccountActivity, and UPDATE BankAccount commands separately at Branch A and Branch B. The application can send a commit instruction to Branch A, wait for confirmation, and then send a commit to Branch B. On a good day, everything works just fine. But if the network connection to Branch B fails after Branch A is committed and before Branch B gets the commit message, Branch A is updated and committed, while Branch B is in an inconsistent state. The application won't meet the atomicity (all or nothing) criteria of the ACID test.

The solution is a protocol known as *two-phase commit (2PC)*. This protocol adds a commit coordinator process and an extra state: ready to commit. A database in this state can durably commit or roll back a sequence of operations. Before issuing a commit transaction, the commit coordinator issues a prepare-to-commit instruction to each database. When all databases involved achieve the ready-to-commit state, the commit coordinator issues a commit 2PC instruction. Figure 5.4 shows a simplified view of a successful 2PC transaction.

FIGURE 5.4

A two-phase commit for a successful transaction involving two database servers, a commit coordinator, and a client application.

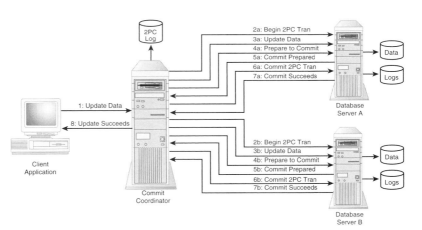

Normally, everything succeeds. However, if one database server experiences a hardware failure or network connection failure before the final commit instruction, data can be restored to the ready-to-commit state, still ready to commit or roll back.

When a single module invokes all components of a distributed transaction, error handling is relatively simple. However, a distributed transaction involving multiple components invoking operations on multiple databases and using multiple 2PC protocols can fail in a bewildering variety of ways:

- Normal application logic causes a database server to abort a local transaction. A database server can also abort a local transaction because it can't achieve a ready-to-commit state.
- A database server fails to respond to a Commit 2PC Tran instruction.
- The commit coordinator fails after issuing a Prepare to Commit or Commit 2PC Tran instruction.

Part

I

Ch

5

■ A database server or network connection can fail at any time during the 2PC transaction.

■ Some combination of faults occurs.

Coping with all the various ways in which a 2PC transaction might fail requires sophisticated design and programming. Because distributed applications must often support transactional integrity, it makes sense to encapsulate 2PC management functions in a server—a TP monitor such as MTS.

N O T E   Theoretically, no protocol can guarantee that every transaction commits or rolls back without intervention. 2PC is probably the best possible protocol, but occasionally an administrator will have to manually force transactions to abort or commit. ■

Although you need a basic understanding of 2PC to take full advantage of MTS, a complete analysis of Microsoft's implementation is beyond the scope of this book. Suffice it to say that the basic 2PC mechanisms described herein reliably provide transactional integrity, with automatic problem resolution, in most failure situations. However, a few conditions still require human intervention. This means that an application that uses the 2PC features in MTS will require knowledgeable administrators.

N O T E   Microsoft DTC, the MTS component that acts as a 2PC commit coordinator, originally shipped as a component of Microsoft SQL Server 6.5. DTC can interact with other TP monitors by using OLE Transactions (the native 2PC protocol for MTS) or X/Open XA (supported by many UNIX databases, including Informix, Oracle, and DB2). For details of Microsoft's implementation of 2PC, see the *Microsoft SQL Server Programmer's Toolkit, Guide to Microsoft Distributed Transaction Coordinator.* ■

Database Access in MTS

Visual Studio includes a number of data access components such as Remote Data Objects (RDO), ActiveX Data Objects (ADO), OLE DB, and Remote Data Service (RDS, formerly known as the Advanced Data Connector). Different tools suit different purposes. Still, as shown in Figure 5.5, all database access methods lead to ODBC.

N O T E   Only about 30% of corporate data resides in relational databases. With its Universal Data Access initiative, Microsoft is trying to provide access to the nonrelational 70%. ADO, OLE DB, and RDS are all designed for universal data access, although, of course, they work quite well with relational databases. ■

▶ For more information about using ADO with MTS, **see** Chapter 30, "Creating Data Access Components for MTS with Visual Basic and ADO," **p. 873**

FIGURE 5.5

All data access methods from MTS lead to ODBC, including RDS, ADO, RDO, and OLE DB.

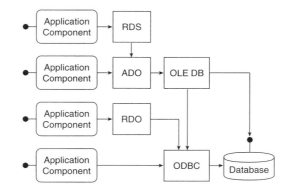

MTS provides two important functions beyond basic database access: distributed transaction support and database connection pooling. The ODBC 3 Driver Manager plays an important role in both functions. ODBC has always used a driver manager; with MTS the driver manager takes on new responsibilities. Figure 5.6 shows how the ODBC driver manager fits between an application and an ODBC driver.

FIGURE 5.6

The ODBC Driver Manager handles communication between an application and ODBC drivers.

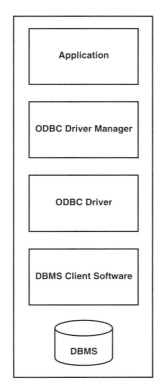

N O T E When using ADO or OLE DB with an ODBC data source, the OLE DB/ODBC bridge
component replaces the ODBC driver manager.

To support distributed transactions from MTS, an ODBC driver must meet three requirements:

- The driver must be fully *thread safe*—It must be able to handle concurrent calls from any thread at any time.
- The driver must not have *thread affinity*—That is, it must enable one thread to establish a connection, another thread to use the connection, and another thread to disconnect.
- The driver must support the `SQL_ATTR_ENLIST_IN_DTC` connection attribute (used to enlist a connection on a transaction).

CAUTION

Thread safety is uncommon and thread affinity is common among popular ODBC drivers. These problems can manifest as a memory-access violation in the MTS Explorer.exe process from within the driver, when the ODBC driver manager begins to close inactive connections.

For database access from an MTS component, choose ADO or RDO. Direct ODBC seems to offer efficiency (by eliminating an intermediate layer), but in most cases developers end up implementing their own class hierarchy. A lot of focused effort went into the development of ADO and RDO; it makes sense to use what's there. OLE DB is another low-level interface for access to any tabular (rows and columns) data source; ADO encapsulates access to OLE DB and is usually a better choice.

Microsoft introduced RDO with Visual Basic 4. RDO is a lightweight encapsulation of the ODBC API, designed specifically for access to a remote DBMS. With Visual Studio 97, Microsoft released RDO 2, a substantial revision. RDO 2 includes several features not available in ADO 1:

- Events on the `Engine`, `Connection`, `Resultset`, and `Column` objects
- Asynchronous queries
- Queries as methods
- Robust batch mode
- Close integration with Visual Basic and related tools such as the Connection Designer and T-SQL Debugger

N O T E Microsoft has indicated that RDO will be maintained but not updated in the future.

ADO encapsulates the OLE DB interface. Although not specifically designed for DBMS access, ADO can access relational databases, ISAM, text, hierarchical, or any tabular data source, as long as an OLE DB Provider exists. ADO is an implemented as an ActiveX component, so any ActiveX-enabled application or language can use it.

Microsoft is clearly encouraging developers to move from RDO to ADO. The company claims that future versions of ADO will provide a superset of RDO 2, a more sophisticated interface, and an easier programming model. ADO also supports Web page data access via RDS.

Role of the DTC in Transaction Processing

SQL Server has included support for the 2PC protocol in the past. Application programmers using the C/C++ programming languages could access 2PC functionality by using the DB-Library interface provided by Microsoft for developing SQL Server applications. Procedures were provided on servers that allowed them to take on the role of commit coordinator.

The inclusion of DTC in MTS adds important new components to help implement distributed transactions and make the management of 2PC a more practical undertaking. Each server has a full DTC service that coordinates transactions with other servers. By using the DTC, a server can take on the role of commit coordinator for certain transactions. Also, the DTC can help resolve problem (or in-doubt) transactions by communicating with other DTC services that run on other servers involved in a transaction.

A client-side interface to DTC is available for Windows NT, Windows 95 and Windows 98. This interface allows developers to create applications using distributed transactions and leverage the facilities provided by the full DTC service running on SQL Servers. The client components of DTC don't include a full DTC service, even on Windows NT clients. Also, the DTC client is available only for 32-bit versions of Windows (Windows 95, Windows 98, and Windows NT).

 A stored procedure running on a SQL Server can possibly launch a distributed transaction on behalf of a 16-bit client. Therefore, older Windows clients can still benefit from DTC functionality.

A set of management utilities has been added to the Microsoft Transaction Server Explorer (MTS Explorer) and the SQL Enterprise Manager (a pair of administrative utilities). The utilities include graphical tools that allow you to dynamically monitor the state of transactions on servers running the DTC service. You can open multiple windows to monitor transactions occurring on multiple servers from a single workstation. An administrator also can manually resolve problem transactions arising from equipment or application failure.

Most developers prefer the use of MTS Explorer, although database-centric developers find the SQL Enterprise Manager to be very useful as well. There's overlapping functionality between these two tools.

Many application developers haven't seen much need for administrative utilities in the past. The MTS Explorer is an exception—it's designed specifically to configure the MTS application environment, as well as make specific settings for your application components. It's used far more often by a lead developer than by a network administrator in typical enterprise network environments, although there are clear benefits if these two groups coordinate with one another.

Part

I

Ch

5

N O T E   Although SQL Enterprise Manager can run on Windows 95 or Windows 98, the DTC utilities are available only when using SQL Enterprise Manager on a Windows NT computer ▦.

Component-Based Transactions

MTS provides a component-based approach to transactions. Because MTS manages transactions, a developer can develop individual operations without regard to transactional integrity. This not only simplifies development, but also results in greater flexibility and better reusability in the middle tier.

Suppose, for example, an application records timesheets for a consultant. A timesheet includes some header information (consultant ID, date range) and some detail information (date, project ID, hours). Adding a new timesheet to the database clearly calls for transactional integrity: You want a complete timesheet saved, or no timesheet saved. Updates to an existing timesheet, however, might involve changes to header information only, or updates to individual detail entries. Trying to develop transactional code to handle every possible scenario can be quite difficult. MTS, however, enables individual operations to be composed dynamically into a transaction at runtime. This allows the developer to write database operations as if they were independent.

When deploying application components, you need to control their participation in transactions. To achieve the highest level of reusability and flexibility, these decisions aren't made when the code is being written, but when the components are deployed. MTS provides four levels of transaction support for a component:

- ▦ If a component is flagged as Requires a Transaction, it will automatically be executed within a transaction at runtime. If it's called by another component that has already begun a transaction, it will participate in that same transaction. If it's executed on its own outside the scope of any other transactions, a new transaction is created to ensure that the work done by this component is completed or rolled back.

- ▦ A component that Requires a New Transaction always spawns its own transactional boundaries. A situation that might call for such behavior is a component that writes audit information to a log. In such a case, you might want the work of this component to be durable, even if the work of a calling component must be rolled back.

- ▦ A component that Supports Transactions can go either way, with respect to transactional behavior. If it's called within a transaction, it participates. If the calling process isn't using a transaction, no transaction is started by this component. This varies from the previous two choices in that it's possible for this component to execute outside transactional boundaries—something that never happens with the first two choices.

- ▦ The final choice, Does Not Support Transactions, is used primarily in cases where the underlying work being done is simply not transactional in nature. Some actions can't be rolled back, and some resources might be required that were never designed to support transactional behavior. These can still be used in a component, but without the benefit of transactional integrity.

Using MTS Component Integration Services

In addition to its support for transactions, MTS provides several features for enhanced scalability, security, and efficient administration:

- Process and thread management
- Just-in-time object activation
- Database connection pooling
- The Shared Property Manager
- Distributed security service (to control object invocation and use)
- Microsoft Transaction Explorer (a graphical tool for system administration and component management)

Process and Thread Management

The MTS Executive provides an execution environment for MTS components. An MTS package consists of one or more ActiveX components that share an execution context (a process). Because all components in a package share a process, execution is more efficient. When components execute inside an MTS process, MTS can provide two important performance benefits: just-in-time object activation and resource pooling.

An MTS application component can execute in one of three basic scenarios: in-process, out-of-process, and remote.

NOTE Some Microsoft documents seem to imply that with MTS, all components run in-process with the base client. This isn't true. An MTS component might run in-process with the base client, but for most enterprise applications the remote server model makes the best sense. The in-process confusion probably arose because every MTS component must be built as an in-process server (a DLL) and because all components in an MTS package execute in a common process. ▓

To run MTS components in-process, the base client must run on a system with MTS running and all components installed locally. The application component runs inside the base client's process. This method provides optimum performance but no process isolation: On any internal error in a component, MTS immediately shuts down the base client and all its active components.

> **CAUTION**
>
> Although running MTS components in-process with the base client provides optimum performance, this approach might compromise security. When a base client successfully invokes a component, MTS doesn't revalidate security for calls between components within the same server process. When MTS components run in-process with the base client, the base client gains access to all components within that server process.

Part

I

Ch

5

A local Transaction Server component executes on the same computer as the client application, but in a separate process managed by the Transaction Server. The client communicates with the component through the COM proxy/stub mechanism. Each message from a base client to an MTS component must cross a process boundary, which incurs some overhead, but this model enables MTS to provide full security and fault isolation. Scalability, however, is limited to the number of base clients and MTS components that can run on the same, single server.

Finally, an MTS component might run on a separate computer from the base client, using DCOM. The client communicates with the component through the DCOM proxy/stub mechanism. Communication between the base client and MTS components takes place at network speeds—milliseconds rather than microseconds. This model provides the best scalability for large numbers of base clients.

ON THE WEB

For a base client running on Windows 95, in-process and local execution aren't an option (MTS isn't available for Windows 95). MTS does support Windows 95 base clients for remote execution, but Windows 95 might need an upgrade for DCOM support. For the latest information on DCOM for Windows 95, see `http://www.microsoft.com/oledev/`.

Windows 98 includes integrated support for DCOM.

You might have to configure DCOM security settings (impersonation and authentication levels) on both client and server computers. The default values for these settings—`Identify` for impersonation, `Connect` for authentication—work properly for MTS but might not be appropriate for your application. Impersonation must be set to `Identify` or higher.

Microsoft recommends using MTS Explorer rather than the DCOM configuration utility (`dcomcnfg`) to change security settings at the package level. Using MTS Explorer ensures consistent security settings for all components in a package.

Just-in-Time Object Activation

In a typical high-volume transaction-processing environment, a large number of base clients invoke a large number of transactions. In MTS, each transaction requires a new instance of a component. Unfortunately, object instantiation takes a long time. It's as though you had to assemble your car before driving to work each day, disassemble it (and put the pieces away) on arrival, reassemble the car to drive home, and take it apart again on your safe return. It's much simpler just to park, lock the car, and take the keys.

Unfortunately, when a large number of people drive to work and park their personal automobiles, parking becomes scarce and traffic becomes dense. Similarly, if every base client maintains its own instance of a component, server resources are strained and performance suffers.

Microsoft's solution to this problem is just-in-time activation. In the ActiveX programming model, a client doesn't explicitly destroy a server component; it just releases the server. Normally, after a server is released by all clients, it destroys itself. However, MTS can deactivate and then reactivate the application component on demand. In fact, MTS can even deactivate an object while a client maintains a reference (provided that the object isn't involved in an active transaction) and doesn't need to maintain any private state information.

To let MTS know when an object isn't involved in a transaction, and has no private state to maintain, you must use the IObjectContext.SetComplete and IObjectContext.SetAbort functions. When a component calls one of these functions, it indicates that it has completed its work and doesn't need to maintain any private state for its client.

To perform some action on object activation or deactivation, implement the IObjectControl interface (IObjectControl for Visual C++ and Visual J++; ObjectControl for Visual Basic). This interface includes three functions:

- Activate()—Enables an object to perform context-specific initialization at each activation (fetching Registry settings, for example). MTS calls this method before any other methods are called on the object.

- Deactivate()—Enables an object to perform any necessary cleanup before it's recycled or destroyed. MTS calls this method at object deactivation.

- CanBePooled()—Returns True if the component supports pooling; otherwise, it returns False. MTS calls CanBePooled() immediately after the Deactivate method.

The Visual Basic code example in Listing 5.2 implements ObjectControl.

Listing 5.2   AELST02.TXT—Implementing `ObjectControl`

```
Option Explicit

Implements ObjectControl

Private Sub ObjectControl_Activate()
 'Initialize member variable for object context
 Set m_oContext = GetObjectContext()
 'A good place to fetch registry entries
End Sub

Private Sub ObjectControl_Deactivate()
 'Explicitly release reference to object context
 Set m_oContext = Nothing
 ' Deallocate any objects created since activation
End Sub

Private Function CanBePooled() As Boolean
 CanBePooled = True
End Function
```

Part

I

Ch

5

N O T E   According to Microsoft, object pooling and recycling isn't implemented for custom components in MTS. MTS invokes the CanBePooled function but ignores the result. Implementing the function now, however, enables a component to take advantage of resource pooling and recycling when MTS implements this feature.

When a base client initially creates an MTS component (by calling `CreateObject` or `CoCreateInstance`), MTS checks for an inactive instance of that object. If an inactive instance is available, MTS returns a reference to that object; if no inactive objects are available, MTS initializes the object in a deactivated state. When the client invokes a method on a deactivated object, MTS first invokes `ObjectControl.Activate`.

N O T E In Visual C++, calls to `QueryInterface`, `AddRef`, or `Release` won't activate an object. ▪

MTS deactivates an object when the object calls `SetComplete` or `SetAbort` and returns to the caller, or when the last reference from an external client is dropped.

For the component developer, it's important to understand that just-in-time activation might actually result in destruction of an object while a client still holds a reference to that object. This is why it's important to use stateless components whenever possible.

 T I P The `IObjectContext.SetComplete` and `IObjectContext.SetAbort` methods notify MTS that a component has completed a transactional operation (with success or failure) and has no state to maintain. MTS will deallocate an object after it calls one of these methods.
To notify MTS that a component has completed a transactional operation (with success or failure), but must maintain state, use the `IObjectContext.EnableCommit` and `IObjectContext.DisableCommit` methods.

Database Connection Pooling

MTS uses the ODBC driver manager as a resource dispenser to provide database connection pooling. When a component running in the MTS environment closes a database connection, MTS captures the connection and holds it open. When another component requests a database connection for the same data source with the same login credentials, MTS returns the pooled connection. This is transparent to components: They call the standard open and close methods on all database objects. However, it makes a big difference in performance and scalability.

Typically, opening a database connection is a slow and expensive operation. For this reason, a program will often acquire a connection at startup and hold it open until shutdown. This improves performance for the program, but impairs scalability. Connection pooling eliminates the high overhead associated with opening a connection, and enables a component to open a connection only when needed and to release it immediately upon completion of each operation.

Successful pooling of database connections in MTS requires attention to two details: connection state and security. Server-side connection state can cause side effects that are difficult to reproduce and eliminate. Connection pooling requires a tradeoff between database security and application scalability.

Many database servers maintain a substantial amount of state for each connection. For example, an application might create a connection local temporary table (CREATE TABLE #MyTemporaryTable ...). If an MTS component creates a temporary table and doesn't drop it before releasing the connection, a subsequent component using the connection and trying to create or use the same temporary table might fail. Another pitfall is changing the current database (USE ThatDatabase); MTS can't detect this context change, and will reuse the connection as though the original database were still current. Many servers also maintain connection local system variables (such as @@rowcount).

Shared database connections require a tradeoff between security and scalability. The user account is an inherent attribute of a connection and can't be changed. Using multiple accounts for ODBC connections will effectively prevent reuse. One approach might be to have users enter a valid account and log in from the base client, but use a common account within MTS. This approach provides user authentication but doesn't enforce access polices. This limitation can be overcome by defining user roles for an MTS component.

The Shared Property Manager

The Shared Property Manager is one of two resource dispensers included with MTS. SPM enables safe multithreaded access to application-defined process-wide variables. Possible applications include a Web page hit counter or shared state for a multiuser application.

Traditional global variables aren't safe for use in a multithreaded or multiuser application because concurrent access might lead to inconsistent results. As an example, Figure 5.7 shows Thread 1 and Thread 2 updating a global variable x, where Thread 1 sets x = x + 1, Thread 2 sets x = x * 2. Depending on the sequence of reads and writes, the result can be 2, 3, or 4. The case in which the result is 2 is clearly incorrect: Thread 2 reads x while Thread 1 updates x—a dirty read.

SPM provides a locking mechanism that enables safe concurrent access to shared state.

N O T E SPM doesn't provide transactions for shared properties because properties are nondurable data.

All objects sharing a property must run in the same server. One way to accomplish this is to limit use of a shared property group to objects created by the same component, or to objects created by components implemented within the same DLL. Remember that an MTS package generally equates to an MTS process. If two DLLs use the same shared property group and an administrator installs the DLLs in separate packages, the two packages couldn't share properties.

SPM objects should be created only from within an MTS component, never from the base client.

Part

Ch

5

FIGURE 5.7

A simple, global variable (x) can lead to inconsistent results in a multithreaded application.

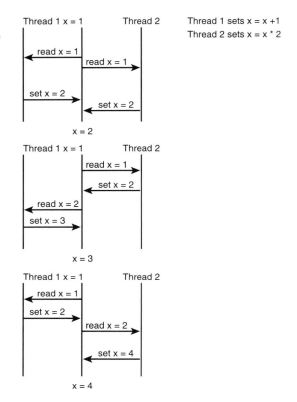

NOTE The Receipt component of the MTS sample bank application included in MTS illustrates a simple application of shared properties. ▪

SPM provides a solution to the problem of shared variables in a multithreaded environment. This is one more way in which MTS allows you to focus on business logic by simplifying multiuser programming issues.

Distributed Security Service

MTS uses declarative role-based security to control application security. The security model is resource-based—each package has its own list of roles (basically groups) and users. Roles for a package are defined, renamed, and deleted using MTS Explorer, but the role names must be hard-coded into components. An MTS component can limit access to resources or functions based on roles and can determine at runtime whether a client has access to that role.

> **CAUTION**
>
> For MTS objects running in-process with the base client, security is effectively disabled.

A *role* is a symbolic name for a group of users. You define and associate roles to MTS components, whereas the MTS administrator defines roles for a package and assigns users to the roles. It's important that the MTS administrator uses the same role names (spelled correctly!) as used in code.

N O T E Roles and security information for a package can't be modified or defined while an instance of that package is running in MTS. ▨

Security in MTS uses only three methods from the `IObjectContext` interface (`ObjectContext` object):

▨ `GetObjectContext` returns a reference to an MTS object's object context. The object context includes the identity of the caller.

▨ `IsSecurityEnabled` returns `False` if the MTS object is loaded in-process with the base client.

▨ `IsCallerInRole` returns `True` if the identity of the direct caller of the object is associated to a specific role. If security isn't enabled (the MTS object is loaded in-process with the base client), `IsCallerInRole` returns `True`. If security is enabled and the identity of direct caller of the object isn't associated to a specific role, `IsCallerInRole` returns `False`.

TIP When an MTS component runs in-process with the base client, `IsCallerInRole` always returns `True`. The `IsSecurityEnabled` method determines whether security checking is enabled. This method returns `False` when running in-process. Always call `IsSecurityEnabled` before using `IsCallerInRole`.

Microsoft Transaction Explorer

MTS Explorer is the tool used to package components and then to deploy the packages. This administrative console is a graphical utility that lets you manipulate and control the components that build a multitier MTS architecture. In addition to these component-based activities, you also can use MTS Explorer to start and stop the DTC, change the service account settings, or perform other administrative tasks. Each time an MTS component's interface changes during development, for example, the component has to be removed from any MTS packages and reinstalled.

The MTS Explorer included with MTS 2 is one of the first tools to use the new Microsoft Management Console (MMC). Specific tools are created as *snap-ins*, which are actually just ActiveX controls written according to specific guidelines. Figure 5.8 shows the MTS Explorer.

FIGURE 5.8

The MTS Explorer with the ConsBill2 package expanded in the left pane and contents in the right pane.

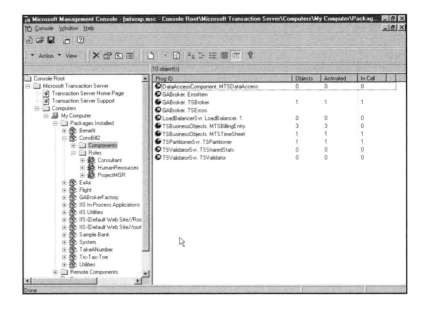

 ON THE WEB

You can download a paper describing the MMC and its extensibility from Microsoft's Web site at http://msdn.microsoft.com/developer/sdk/techinfo/.

Transaction Server Explorer uses a two-pane display. The left pane is presented in hierarchical fashion, showing the computers being managed. If you select an object in the left pane, its contents appear in the right pane.

 TIP

Right-clicking an object generally opens a context-sensitive menu with choices pertinent to the object selected.

Another important operation you perform with MTS Explorer is to configure role-based security. The need for this type of security is easy to understand when you reflect on an environment where many clients are sharing mid-tier business logic. If you want to control access to these components or the behavior of the components depending on the calling process, role-based security becomes an obvious choice.

▶ **See** Chapter 31, "Using Microsoft Transaction Server to Enable Distributed Applications, " **p. 899**

Using Existing Components with MTS

A COM DLL that doesn't implement any specific MTS functions can still gain substantial benefits from running in the MTS environment:

- The capability to run as an in-process server, a local server, or a remote server
- Database connection pooling through the ODBC 3 resource dispenser
- Improved fault isolation for out-of-process servers
- Simplified deployment through MTS Explorer

Installing an existing component to run under MTS is as easy as creating a new package, adding the component to that package, and then setting the `Transaction Support` property for the component to `Does Not Support Transactions`.

MTS support for legacy components can even be leveraged for non-ActiveX code. It's often quite simple to develop an ActiveX wrapper for a legacy application; that ActiveX component can then be added to MTS. The simple MTS programming requirements for transaction support make it possible to create a wrapper that supports transactions. For more information, see the section "Understanding the Importance of Transactions," earlier in this chapter.

Packages of Components

After you purchase off-the-shelf components, write your own, or both, you can create collections of components called *packages*. The programming techniques required for creating these components are described in Chapter 14, "Creating COM Components for MTS."

You can manage a package of components as a unit. The components in the package can share security settings and can access other shared resources through the use of the MTS SPM. They also can share a pool of ODBC connections to database resources. Allocating memory and processing on a one-to-one basis with clients becomes inefficient when handling large numbers of clients. A shared pool is more efficient and scales better as the number of clients grows.

When access to distributed database resources is required, the services of Microsoft's DTC (described earlier in the section "Understanding the Importance of Transactions") are used to efficiently provide a message-based architecture that can maintain the atomic nature of transactions across machine boundaries. Communications with database resource dispensers are handled by using various protocols:

- OLE TX
- Transaction Internet Protocol (TIP)
- XA
- SNA LU 6.2 (through Microsoft COM Transaction Integrator for CICS and IMS)

The MTS development environment provides a very flexible programming environment. As already noted, the focus of most developers is on creating components designed for single-user environments without regard for distributed applications issues. They can work in various languages, including those listed in Table 5.1.

Part

I

Ch

5

Table 5.1   Languages Supported for MTS Development

Language	Manufacturer
Delphi	Inprise
C++Builder	Inprise
Visual Basic	Microsoft
Visual C++	Microsoft
Visual J++	Microsoft
PowerBuilder	Sybase/Powersoft

After components are created, they're packaged to facilitate setting security and deploying on a particular machine. Packages can be managed effectively by using the Transaction Server Explorer. You can even split a package for deployment across server boundaries by partitioning the package for multiple-machine installation.

Installing MTS

MTS 2 is a built-in feature of Windows NT Server 4 Standard and Windows NT Server 4 Enterprise Edition. In addition, existing licensees of these operating system platforms can obtain MTS through the Windows NT 4 Option Pack. MTS 2 is also included in the BackOffice server components on Disk 2 of the Visual Studio install set.

ON THE WEB

The Windows NT 4.0 Option Pack is available for free download at http://www.microsoft.com/ windows/downloads/contents/products/nt4optpk/.

The NT 4 Option Pack installs Microsoft Internet Information Server (IIS) 4, with MTS as a supporting utility. However, it's not always appropriate to install IIS on an application server. This section reviews the install procedure from the Visual Studio disks.

Where to Install MTS

Install MTS on computers acting as application servers and on computers running IIS 4 with Active Server Pages. Developers building mid-tier components will also benefit by installing MTS. Finally, because IIS 4 integrates so closely with MTS, you should install MTS on any Internet server running IIS 4.

Machines that invoke MTS-based components running on Windows NT Server require a Microsoft Windows NT Server Client Access License (CAL). Machines that already have an existing CAL for access to services such as print services and file sharing don't need to acquire an additional CAL in order to use MTS Clients.

System Requirements

MTS 2 runs on NT 4 (Server or Workstation) with Service Pack 3. It will also run on Windows 95 (with DCOM support installed) or Windows 98; However, these platforms don't work well as secure, highly scalable application servers.

MTS requires a minimum of 32 megabytes physical memory, 30 megabytes free disk space, a CD-ROM drive, mouse and display.

Installing from the Visual Studio Disks

Follow these steps to install MTS from the Visual Studio Disks. The procedure ends with a system restart, so you should close all other applications before beginning. If you have not installed any other Visual Studio components on the machine, you will have to install the latest Internet Explorer 4.01 with all the latest patches before proceeding.

1. Insert Visual Studio Disk 1 into your CD-ROM drive. If setup doesn't begin automatically, run Setup.Exe from this disk.

2. Click Next until you get to the Server Setups screen. Select the option to Launch the BackOffice Installation Wizard and click Install (see Figure 5.9).

FIGURE 5.9
The Visual Studio Server Setups screen allows you to install the Visual Source Safe Server or launch the BackOffice Installation Wizard.

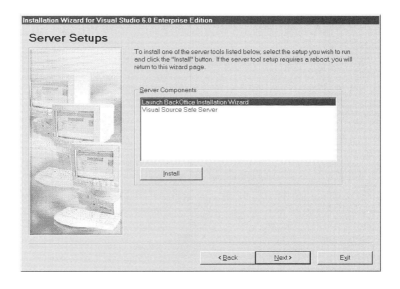

3. Switch to Visual Studio Disk 2 when prompted.

4. Select the BackOffice components to install. To install MTS, you must select the Windows NT 4 Option Pack.

5. At the Windows NT 4 Option Pack Setup dialog, click custom.

6. Select components to install. When selecting MTS, click the Show Subcomponents button

7. At the Transaction Server dialog, select all options, including Transaction Server Development (see Figure 5.10). Click OK. Click Next.

FIGURE 5.10

By default, the MTS development components aren't installed.

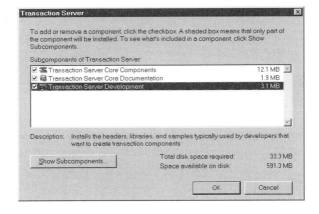

8. Specify the installation folder. Click Next.
9. If you want to enable remote administration for this instance of MTS, select Remote and enter a login and password for an administrator account (see Figure 5.11). Click Next.

FIGURE 5.11

An administrator account is required to enable remote administration of MTS.

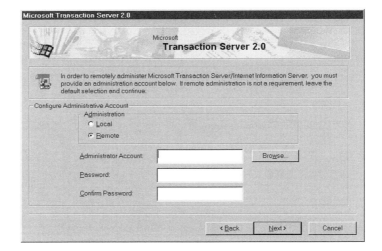

10. The system will copy files onto your hard disk. When copying is complete, click Finish.
11. Reboot.

Connecting Clients to MTS

Client systems connect to MTS via DCOM. For Windows NT Server 4 and Windows NT Work-station 4, Service Pack 3 or later is recommended. For Windows NT 3.51 Server or Worksta-tion, Service Pack 5 is required. For Windows 95, DCOM for Windows 95 is required. Win-dows 98 includes integrated DCOM support.

▶ For more information about registering MTS components on client machines, **see** "Exporting Packages," **p. 913**

From Here...

MTS 2 integrates closely with IIS and Microsoft Message Queue (MSMQ). Microsoft consid-ers MTS a core component of the NT Server operating system, and of its Distributed Internet Application (DNA) strategy. In fact, MTS 2 is probably the last version of the product; in the future, it will be inseparable from the operating system.

Microsoft plans to continue evolving MTS into the future, where it will become a key compo-nent of multi-machine architectures. Microsoft has publicly announced plans to add data-depen-dent message routing (useful in partitioning large applications) and durable queues, which would maintain the queue of messages even in the event of catastrophic failure. These and other features will likely be delivered by, or derived from, the MSMQ Server. It will be interest-ing to see how these technologies are combined to extend and improve the powerful features already included in the current release of MTS.

In this chapter, you learned how a TP monitor improves scalability for distributed component applications. You also learned the ACID criteria for transactions and the two-phase commit protocol. You were introduced to MTS, a powerful tool for implementing multiuser, distributed applications.

See the following chapters for related information:

- For a review of COM and DCOM technologies, see Chapter 9, "Using Microsoft's Object Technologies."

- For information on the overall architecture of I-net environments, see Chapter 15, "Clients, Servers, and Components: Web-Based Applications."

- For information on the overall architecture of traditional client/server environments, see Chapter 25, "Clients, Servers, and Components: Design Strategies for Distributed Applications."

- For information on creating applications specifically designed for Microsoft Transaction Server, see Chapter 14, "Creating COM Components for MTS."

- For information on deploying applications using Microsoft Transaction Server, see Chapter 31, "Using Microsoft Transaction Server to Enable Distributed Applications."

Part

I

Ch

5

An Inside Look at Active Server Pages and the Internet Information Server

by Azam A. Mirza

In this chapter

What's New in Active Server Pages and Internet Information Server 4

The basic software component that brings together the power of I-nets is the World Wide Web (WWW) server software. Web server software gives clients access to corporate information and data by facilitating information publishing, application execution, and data retrieval.

Most Web server software packages—such as Microsoft Internet Information Server (IIS), various Netscape server products, and O'Reilly WebSite—provide a comprehensive set of setup, management, and administration facilities. In most cases, a basic and functional Web server can be installed, set up, and made operational within an hour. Also, all server packages include sophisticated system administration utilities, such as the Server Manager utility included with IIS.

Until recently, most Web servers stored static information for access by clients. With the introduction of technologies such as Java applets, ActiveX controls, and database-access tools, Web servers have become more than just facilitators for publishing static information. Web servers now can provide powerful capabilities, such as user authentication, connectivity to database servers, dynamic page creation based on user actions or database queries, and data encryption. The list isn't exhaustive, but is intended to provide a measure of advances that have been made in the last year or so in terms of the capabilities of Web server software.

Microsoft's IIS deserves special mention because of its tight and robust integration with Windows NT Server and the security subsystem in particular. This tight integration enables IIS to use the built-in Windows NT Server security model for user authentication and password validation. User access to the Web can be controlled by authenticating users against the Windows NT domain user lists. File and directory access from the Web can be controlled by setting permissions for user groups through the Windows NT security mechanisms. Traffic analysis and performance monitoring can be performed by using the Windows NT Performance Monitor utility, and logging can be performed by using the Windows NT event log.

Microsoft has also provided additional functionality to the core Web server product through add-on products and tools. This chapter discusses these tools and technologies in further detail.

IIS 4 was released as part of the Windows NT 4 Option Pack, which provides a new set of services that enable the development of the next generation of Internet-enabled applications for the Win32 platform and also provides a peek into distributed world of the upcoming Windows NT 5.

ON THE WEB

For more information about the Windows NT 4 Option Pack, or to download a free version from the Microsoft Web site, visit `http://backoffice.microsoft.com/downtrial/optionpack.asp`.

The Windows NT 4 Option Pack includes the following services for Windows NT Server:

- Internet Information Server 4
- Microsoft Transaction Server (MTS) 2
- Microsoft Message Queue Server (MSMQ) 1
- Internet Connection Services (ICS) for Microsoft Remote Access Service (RAS)

MTS and MSMQ are discussed in detail in other chapters. This chapter concentrates on IIS 4 and the upgraded Active Server Page (ASP) included with it.

▶ **See** Chapter 5, "An Inside Look at Microsoft Transaction Server," **p. 107**

▶ **See** Chapter 7, "An Inside Look at the Microsoft Message Queue," **p. 167**

New Features in Internet Information Server 4

IIS 4, in conjunction with Windows NT and other Microsoft Internet technologies, makes it easy to publish, share, and access information and also to build and deploy scalable, reliable, and industrial-strength Web-based applications.

To support the building of these distributed business applications, Windows NT 4 Option Pack provides easier setup and administration of the Web server through an integrated setup for all components, and introduces new administration tools for IIS that make it easier to manage your content and configure complex Web sites. New features in IIS 4 include

- Microsoft Management Console (MMC)—The new MMC provides Windows-based administration for IIS, MTS, and Index Server. It's the tool for server administration and management that will be used in Windows NT 5. The MMC uses snap-ins (a concept similar to the add-ins in Visual Basic) for providing administration facilities for various server products. MMC uses a user interface similar to the Windows Explorer tree structure for exposing various administration properties and methods available. Figure 6.1 shows the MMC with the IIS administration tree node expanded.

- Web-based administration—In addition, IIS 4 can also be managed from any Web browser supporting JavaScript and frames. The included Hypertext Markup Language (HTML)-based Internet Service Manager enables secure remote administration using any Web browser. Figure 6.2 shows the HTML-based Internet Service Manager.

- Hypertext Transport Protocol (HTTP) 1.1 support—HTTP 1.1 standard support for improved Internet performance and functionality through transfer chunk encoding, persistent connections (or Keep Alives),pipelining, and HTTP PUT and DELETE.

- Host headers—IIS 4 supports host headers that enable multiple Web sites to share a single Internet Protocol (IP) address. This allows Web administrators to have multiple virtual Web sites running from the same server and to redirect users to the appropriate site based on the Uniform Resource Locator (URL) they enter in the browser.

Part

I

Ch

6

FIGURE 6.1
MMC provides a centralized location for managing all your IIS Web servers.

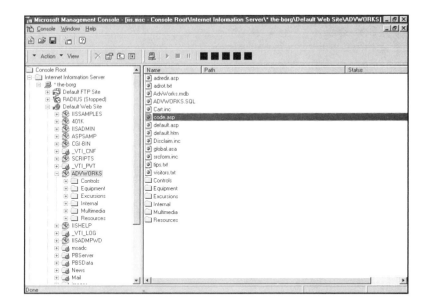

FIGURE 6.2
The Internet Service Manager provides secure Web administration using any Web browser.

■ Multiple hosts, multiple site operators—Administrators can be assigned to various Web sites individually, without having to be Windows NT Server administrators. Different administrative users can be assigned to different sites on the same server, with administrative access to their respective sites only. Operators can set properties that affect only their respective site, and not the operation of the entire Web server.

- Content control—Complete administrative control over all server settings. Properties such as logging, security, and default documents can be set for an entire Web server, individual sites, or for individual files and directories.

- Configuration backup—Save configuration settings for all Web and FTP sites, and restore a configuration to return IIS to a previous state. Replicate IIS configuration to maintain servers with exactly the same settings.

- Custom errors—Provides support for sending customized error messages to users when they encounter server errors (such as file not found or password required). ASP pages can be used to provide dynamic help or suggestions.

- Database components—Improved performance and reliability of database access with updated versions of the ActiveX Data Objects (ADO) and an open database connectivity (ODBC) driver for Oracle databases. Microsoft's ODBC driver for Oracle databases adds additional performance and control features including access to PL/SQL packages and XA/DTC support for MTS. Remote Data Services enables client-side data caching in Web applications to reduce server traffic and overhead.

- Per-site bandwidth throttling—Limit the maximum bandwidth available to a site. Limits can be placed on a per-server or per-site basis.

- Per-site performance monitoring—Measure performance characteristics of both the entire server and the individual sites, including new counters to monitor ASP components.

- Digital certificates—Microsoft Certificate Server issues and manages Internet standard X.509 digital certificates. IIS 4 can authenticate users using digital certificates, and map them back to the Windows NT directory by user or groups. Contents of certificate fields are available to ASP applications for personalization.

- Simple Mail Transfer Protocol (SMTP) and Network News Transfer Protocol (NNTP) Support—IIS 4 includes built-in support for SMTP and NNTP. Any client using SMTP- and NNTP-compliant protocols can access these services on the Web server.

- Indexing and searching—New and improved features make it easier to integrate with Microsoft Index Server to expedite searches. Index Server search pages can be created with ASP to take advantage of dynamic query building. Content filters for Microsoft Office 97 and PDF documents are supplied.

- Online documentation—HTML-based help system, optimized for easy access and quick navigation with full search and indexing capabilities.

IIS 4 provides a powerful and compelling upgrade for sites running earlier versions of the Web server software. It provides tremendous improvements in the areas of server management, reliability, availability, scalability, and Web-based application development.

New Features in Active Server Pages

Microsoft ASP is a *server-side scripting* environment that you can use to create and run dynamic, interactive Web server applications. With ASP, you can combine HTML pages, script commands, and ActiveX components to create interactive Web pages or powerful Web-based applications. ASP applications are easy to develop and modify.

IIS 4, included with the Windows NT 4 Option Pack, includes an upgraded ASP engine that makes it easier to build powerful Web-based applications. These features include

- Microsoft Script Debugger—The biggest enhancement in ASP from earlier versions is the inclusion of a script debugger that can be used to debug server-side scripts running in the IIS environment. The Script Debugger supports line-by-line execution support, checkpoint setting, watch variables, and trace procedures to locate problems and interactively test ASP applications written in any supported scripting language. The Script Debugger can also be used with client-side scripts.

- Transactional scripts—ASP pages and the objects used on the page can be run as a transaction. Transaction support allows you to commit or abort all work done on a page-by-page basis. ASP transactions are limited to each ASP page. You must commit or abort transactions on an ASP page before moving on. Transactions protect your applications from failures that might cause loss of data.

- Out-of-process ASP applications—ASP applications can now be run out-of-process in their own memory space separate from the Web server. This protects other ASP applications, and the Web server, from crashing in case an application fails. It also makes it possible to stop an application and unload its components from memory without stopping the Web server.

- File upload capability—You can now use the Posting Acceptor component to allow users to upload files to the Web server. You can write ASP scripts that send email to the appropriate person with information passed from the Posting Acceptor, such as the location and name of each uploaded file.

- ASP application root directory—The root directory of an ASP application can now be a physical directory within your Web site. Previously, the root directory had to be a virtual directory. You can use the MMC or the Internet Service Manager to indicate the root of an ASP application. You must put .asp files in an application tree for the Web server to detect changes to the files and automatically reload them.

Building Web Applications Using the Active Platform

As part of its strategy to deliver components that enable Microsoft BackOffice as the backbone of Internet technologies, Microsoft has added a high-level component to IIS that delivers cross-platform support, open standards, and a tightly integrated set of tools for delivering dynamic Web content to users.

The Active Platform is an open architecture based on industry standards for creating Web sites and Web-enabled applications for I-nets. Active Platform provides a means for Web developers to create Web content that can be used across hardware platforms and operating systems.

ON THE WEB

Microsoft's Web site, http://www.microsoft.com/, contains extensive information about Active Platform and other Internet technologies. It's a good idea to visit the site periodically for the latest information about Microsoft tools and products.

The Active Platform leverages such technologies as HTML, scripting mechanisms (such as VBScript and JScript), Microsoft Component Object Model (COM), Java support, and the underlying operating system services to deliver dynamic, interactive, and customizable content to client desktops on the Internet and intranets.

By providing a high-level platform that sits on top of IIS and the operating system, Microsoft has created a platform that frees you, the Web developer, from worrying about underlying details and operating system idiosyncrasies. You can build Web sites that conform to the Active Platform specs and not worry about the hardware platform and operating system that the site will run on.

Active Platform not only brings uniformity to the server side for Web-enabled applications, but it also encompasses the client side with the same open architecture to deliver a cohesive means of displaying content residing on Active Platform servers.

There are three main parts to the Active Platform that make it possible to create, deploy, and use powerful Web-enabled applications for the Internet and intranets. These include the following:

- ActiveX technologies
- Active Desktop
- Active Server Pages

Figure 6.3 shows the relationship among the various Active Platform components. The following sections describe these technologies in more detail.

FIGURE 6.3
Active Platform technologies form the basis of the Microsoft Internet initiative.

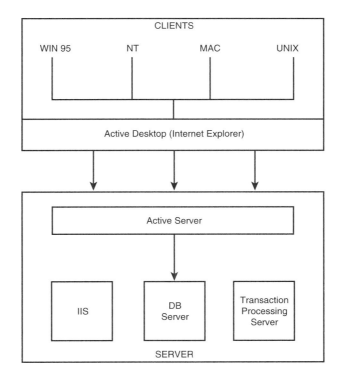

ActiveX Technologies

ActiveX technologies refer to the tools and standards that work together to bring dynamic, interactive content to your Web site. ActiveX technologies are software standards, components, and tools that work on various operating systems and heterogeneous networks to enable the Active Platform. The following are some of the technologies included in the ActiveX standard:

- Dynamic HTML (DHTML)—This extension to HTML technology enables Web developers to create dynamic, on-the-fly Web pages. DHTML pages are created in response to the completion of an ActiveX application and display the results to the user. For example, an ActiveX database access object might query a relational database, obtain the resultset, create a DHTML page to display the resultset, and then send the DHTML page to the client browser for display to the user.

▶ For more information about developing content using Dynamic HTML, **see** Chapter 21, "Dynamic HTML," **p. 601**

ON THE WEB

For more information about Dynamic HTML, refer to the Microsoft Web site at `http://www.microsoft.com/workshop/author/default.asp`.

- Language-independent scripting support—Full support is provided for scripting mechanisms, such as VBScript and JScript. ActiveX supports open scripting standards that provide scripting support in various languages and on all supported platforms. Scripting can be executed on both the client browser and the Web server components through the use of an ActiveX scripting engine.

N O T E IIS supports compilation-free execution of server-side scripts.

- System services—ActiveX provides access to operating system services through its component architecture model. Active Platform can access operating system services on supported platforms such as Windows, Macintosh, and the various flavors of UNIX, which will be supported through third-party vendors in the near future.

- Development tools—Support for ActiveX is incorporated into all Microsoft development tools for creating ActiveX components. These include Microsoft Visual InterDev, Microsoft Visual C++, and Microsoft Visual Basic. ActiveX components can be written in any language that supports the creation of such components.

- Java support—ActiveX technologies provide full support and interoperability for the Java technology and Java applets. The Microsoft Java Virtual Machine (JVM) and the Visual J++ development tool provide support for accessing ActiveX objects from Java applets. This provides support for building Java applets that can interface with operating system services through an ActiveX object. For example, the Java specification does not allow for applets to gain access to file system services. However, by building an ActiveX object that works as a bridge between the operating system and the Java applet, developers can gain access to these resources from the Java world.

N O T E   ASP, discussed later in the "Active Server Pages" section, includes JVM for running Java
applets and applications.

- ActiveX Data Objects—ActiveX provides a new mechanism for accessing databases by using ODBC. ADO is similar to Data Access Objects (DAO) and Remote Data Objects (RDO), used by Visual C++ and Visual Basic, and provides developers with a means to access the data stored in corporate relational databases. Developers can create Hypertext Markup Language (HTML) pages with scripts that take advantage of ADO constructs to access databases or create ActiveX controls that are data aware.

N O T E   Microsoft Visual Basic and Visual C++ are two of the Visual Studio products that can be
used to create data-aware ADO controls.

These ActiveX technologies and tools encompass the entire Active Platform on both the client side and the server side. Some are implemented as standalone tools for enhancing the Active Platform environment, while others implement specific functions on the client side and the server side.

The Active Desktop

The Active Desktop is the client component of the Active Platform environment. The Active Desktop enables the creation of applications that run on the client systems under a multitude of operating systems and hardware platforms.

The Active Desktop provides developers with a means of writing applications to a common interface to ensure their capability to run on multiple operating systems and hardware platforms. The Active Desktop includes support for language-independent scripting, DHTML, system services, and ActiveX component technology. The Active Desktop provides the following advantages over proprietary solutions:

- A single delivery mechanism for providing user interface objects
- Support for language-independent, client-side scripting capabilities
- Support for the DHTML technology
- Support for client-side ActiveX components and controls created with such tools as Microsoft Visual Basic 5
- Support for Java applets through the JVM, the Java runtime compiler, and the Java JIT (Just-in-Time) compiler

Active Desktop is fully integrated with the Microsoft Windows 95/98 and Windows NT operating systems. It provides full support and access to the extensive set of APIs available for the Windows operating system environment. The main delivery mechanism for the Active Desktop is Microsoft Internet Explorer Web browser.

N O T E   Microsoft Internet Explorer 4 provides a look at the first steps of integration between the
Windows GUI shell and the Internet Explorer browser through the use of the Active
Desktop.

Figure 6.4 presents an example of a Web site using ActiveX components and being accessed through the Microsoft Internet Explorer Active Desktop.

FIGURE 6.4

The Microsoft Network Web site provides an ActiveX-enabled Web experience.

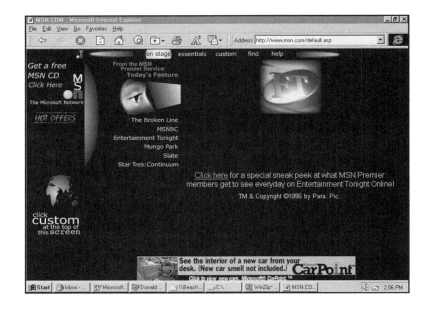

ActiveX controls used as part of the Active Desktop environment provide a powerful way of adding functionality to your Web site.

Active Server Pages

Internet Information Server 3 and 4 include components for enabling your Web site for Active Platform. The component that provides server-side ActiveX functionality is called ASP. ASP is nothing more than an HTML page with embedded server-side scripts written in VBScript or JScript. The script is executed on the Web server. It then generates a pure HTML page as the result of the script execution, and that page is sent to the browser. Figure 6.5 illustrates how ASP works on the Web server.

Because an ASP page is nothing more than an HTML page with a .asp extension, all HTML tags are allowed in the ASP file. ASP files also provide the capability to dynamically generate HTML tags on the server before the page is sent to the client browser.

N O T E   *Active Server Pages* denotes the product that has previously been referred to as the ActiveX Server and code-named Denali.

FIGURE 6.5

The Web server parses the ASP file, and only the generated HTML is sent to the client browser.

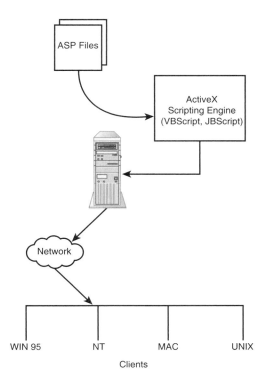

ASP is a high-level component that takes advantage of the scalable, high-performance capabilities of Windows NT Server to provide developers with a rich environment for creating server-side Web applications. ASP includes full support for Windows NT Server system services, database access, transaction processing, and message queuing. In particular, ASP provides support for the following key functionality:

- Active Server objects—ASP provides support for hosting component objects commonly referred to as the ActiveX components. Development tools such as Visual C++, Visual Basic, Visual J++, and PowerBuilder provide support for building reusable components for use by ASP. Active Server Objects are different from ActiveX controls in one respect: They don't have any user interface elements because they only run on the server machine.

- Active Server scripting—ASP provides support for executing scripts on the server. ASP can parse scripts that are written in VBScript, JScript, Perl, or any other supported scripting language.

- State management—ASP adds support for state management to the WWW. HTTP is a stateless protocol that provides no capabilities for tracking and managing application, user, and Web-server states.

- Database connectivity—ASP provides support for connecting your Web site to a relational database system through the use of ADO and server-side scripting.

Part

I

Ch

6

Active Server Scripting

Server-side scripting can be used to create dynamic Web content. Developers can use scripting languages such as VBScript or JScript to write applications that can respond to user-supplied information, user queries, or conditional logic. Server-side scripting enables developers to customize the content of a Web page to different scenarios and display a different version of a Web page every time a client browser accesses it.

Server-side scripting also enables you to customize your Web pages based on the capabilities of the client browser being used by the user. For example, certain browsers might not support ActiveX controls. In such scenarios, you can develop a page that displays without using the controls.

Until recently, most Web content was static in nature, with a small amount of interactivity and dynamism provided by common gateway interface (CGI) scripts. CGI scripts are complex and inflexible by nature. By using ASP and VBScript or JScript, you can produce dynamic Web content more easily and quickly.

N O T E   In addition to VBScript or JScript, which are supplied with ASP, third-party scripting engines can also be developed and plugged into ASP to provide support for other scripting languages. ▧

As evidenced by the installation process for ASP, IIS provides the hosting environment for the Active Server Scripting Engine. An ASP scripting engine is nothing more than an Internet Server Application Programming Interface (ISAPI) application that is loaded by IIS at startup.

N O T E   ASP is not a scripting language, but merely an environment for parsing script commands based on the scripting engine being used. ▧

When IIS encounters a request for an ASP file, it compiles and executes the file's scripts, on-the-fly. The output produced is an HTML page that is sent to the client browser. This compile-free environment is one of the greatest advantages of ASP.

You can switch easily among installed scripting engines by using the following script:

```
<SCRIPT LANGUAGE=VBScript RUNAT=Server>
```

or

```
<SCRIPT LANGUAGE=JScript RUNAT=Server>
```

The default scripting language for ASP is VBScript, but you can switch freely among various scripting languages.

Obviously, scripts are programming languages. As such, you must use a specific syntax and follow certain requirements when producing applications with them. The following sections discuss some of the constructs and syntax requirements enforced by the ASP scripting engine.

Delimiters

Delimiters differentiate HTML tags from plain text and mark the beginning and end of a script unit. HTML uses the < and > signs to mark HTML text. ASP uses <% and %> as a variation on the HTML delimiters to designate sections of ASP scripts. For example,

```
<% name = "John Smith"%>
```

assigns the value John Smith to the variable name. ASP uses the delimiters <%= and %> to enclose output expressions. For example,

```
<%= name %>
```

sends the value John Smith to the browser in the preceding example.

Statements

A *statement* is a complete scripting unit that expresses an action, declaration, or assignment. The For...Next loop construct or the If...Then...Else conditional construct is an example of a statement. Statements can also contain HTML code. For example, in Listing 6.1, HTML code is freely mixed with VBScript.

Listing 6.1   Mixing of Different Scripting Languages and HTML Code Is Freely Supported by ASP

```
<%
Loop
If tRangeType = "Table" Then Response.Write "</TABLE>"
If tPageSize > 0 Then
  If Not fHideRule Then Response.Write "<HR>"
  If Not fHideNavBar Then
    %>
    <TABLE WIDTH=100% >
    <TR>
      <TD WIDTH=100% >
        <P ALIGN=<%= tBarAlignment %> >
        <FORM <% "ACTION=""" & Request.ServerVariables("PATH_INFO") &
        ➥stQueryString & """" %> METHOD="POST">
          <INPUT TYPE="Submit" NAME="<%= tHeaderName &
          ➥"_PagingMove" %>" VALUE="  &lt;&lt;  ">
          <INPUT TYPE="Submit" NAME="<%= tHeaderName &
          ➥"_PagingMove" %>" VALUE="  &lt;  ">
          <INPUT TYPE="Submit" NAME="<%= tHeaderName &
          ➥"_PagingMove" %>" VALUE="  &gt;  ">
          <% If fSupportsBookmarks Then %>
            <INPUT TYPE="Submit" NAME="<%= tHeaderName &
            ➥"_PagingMove" %>" VALUE="  &gt;&gt;  ">
          <% End If %>
          <% If Not fHideRequery Then %>
            <INPUT TYPE="Submit" NAME="<% =
            ➥tHeaderName & "_PagingMove" %>" VALUE=" Requery ">
          <% End If %>
```

continues

Listing 6.1 Continued

```
          </FORM>
          </P>
        </TD>
        <TD VALIGN=MIDDLE ALIGN=RIGHT>
          <FONT SIZE=2>
          <%
          If Not fHideNumber Then
            If tPageSize > 1 Then
              Response.Write "<NOBR>Page: " & Session
              ➡(tHeaderName & "_AbsolutePage") & "</NOBR>"
            Else
              Response.Write "<NOBR>Record: " & Session
              ➡(tHeaderName & "_AbsolutePage") & "</NOBR>"
            End If
          End If
          %>
          </FONT>
        </TD>
      </TR>
      </TABLE>
  <%
  End If
End If
%>
```

Script Tags

ASP supports VBScript as the default scripting language. The expressions, commands, and procedures used within script delimiters must be valid for VBScript; however, other scripts can be freely used within ASP through the use of the `<SCRIPT>` and `</SCRIPT>` tags. By using the RUNAT and LANGUAGE attributes within the script tags, you can change the scripting language and use any other script commands freely. Listing 6.2 illustrates the point.

Listing 6.2 Easily Switch to JScript By Using the Script Tags Within the Same ASP Page

```
<SCRIPT RUNAT=SERVER LANGUAGE=JSCRIPT>
 function MyFunction ()
 {
   Response.Write("MyFunction Called")
 }
</SCRIPT>
```

Procedures

A *procedure* is a collection of script commands that are organized and executed together. Primary scripting language procedures can be defined freely within an ASP file. You can even mix and match different scripting language procedures by using the `<SCRIPT>` and `</SCRIPT>` tags.

Visual InterDev and IIS use VBScript as the primary scripting language. This is defined by the ASP DLL supplied by Microsoft. However, you can change your primary scripting language by using the syntax

```
<SCRIPT LANGUAGE=JScript RUNAT=Server>
```

at the beginning of your ASP page.

Procedures can be defined within the scripting delimiters <% and %>, as long as they are written in the primary scripting language. Procedures can be contained within the same file they are called from, or they can be placed in a separate ASP file and included within the calling file by using the server-side <!--#INCLUDE FILE=...> construct.

To call procedures, include the name of the procedure in a command. For VBScript, you can also use the Call keyword when calling a procedure. If the procedure you are calling requires arguments, however, the argument list must be enclosed in parentheses. If you omit the Call keyword, you must also omit the parentheses around the argument list. If you use Call syntax to call any built-in or user-defined function, the function's return value is discarded. If you are calling JScript procedures from VBScript, you must use parentheses after the procedure name; if the procedure has no arguments, use empty parentheses.

Listing 6.3 illustrates creating and calling procedures by using two different scripting languages (VBScript and JScript).

Listing 6.3 Procedures Can Be Invoked by Using a Variety of Methods Based on the Scripting Language Being Used

```
<HTML>
<BODY>
<TABLE>
<% Call Echo %>
</TABLE>
<% Call PrintDate %>
</BODY>
</HTML>

<SCRIPT LANGUAGE=VBScript RUNAT=Server>
Sub Echo
    Response.Write _
    "<TR><TD>Name</TD><TD>Value</TD></TR>"
    Set Params = Request.QueryString
    For Each p in Params
      Response.Write "<TR><TD>" & p & "</TD><TD>" & _
      Params(p) & "</TD></TR>"
    Next
End Sub
</SCRIPT>

<SCRIPT LANGUAGE=JScript RUNAT=Server>
function PrintDate()
{
```

Part

I

Ch

6

continues

Listing 6.3 Continued

```
var x
x = new Date()
Response.Write(x.toString())
}
</SCRIPT>
```

ActiveX Server Objects

ASPs provide support for five server objects. These objects are unusual because they are built into ASP and don't need to be created before being used in Active Server scripts.

The Active Server objects include

- The Application object
- The Session object
- The Request object
- The Response object
- The Server object

The following sections provide detailed information on using these objects as part of your ASP-based Web sites.

The Application Object

The Application object is used to store and share Web-based, application-specific information between users. Developers can define variables as part of the Application object, which are available to all instances of a particular Web application and to all users accessing that application.

N O T E In ASP parlance, an *application* is defined as a collection of .asp pages stored within the same virtual Web directory and all its subdirectories. A *virtual Web directory* is an alias for a physical location of a Web site directory. For example, the virtual directory alias \MyWeb might be used to define a physical path such as \\MyServer\InetPub\wwwroot\MyWeb\Production.

The Application object supports the following methods:

- Lock—Prevents other users from accessing and modifying the Application object properties and variables while a particular user is accessing it.
- Unlock—Releases a locked Application object for use by other users. If the Unlock method isn't explicitly invoked on a locked object, the object is automatically unlocked when the object times out or the script execution ends.

The Application object can be used to create variables and store values that are available to all instances of the application. For example, Listing 6.4 provides a counter that is incremented every time a user accesses the particular ASP page that includes the given script.

Listing 6.4   Using `Application` Object Variables to Store Information

```
<%
Application.Lock
Application("Counter") = Application("Counter") + 1
Application.Unlock
%>
```

The preceding example provides a sample mechanism for keeping track of the number of times a certain Web page has been accessed. The Lock and Unlock methods ensure that two users don't access the same variable simultaneously.

N O T E   If an attempt is made to modify a locked object, the request is queued until the object becomes available or the Web page times out. Either a Web page timeout can be set as part of the page definition, or a global timeout can be used that is set on the Web server itself and applies to all Web pages by default. For example, a page might have a timeout value of 300 seconds. If a user accessing the page does nothing for more than 5 minutes after the initial page load, the page is reloaded from the server rather than the local cache when the user tries to refresh it. ▒

All variables declared within the context of the Application object are discarded when the application ends. The data stored within the Application object variable must be saved to persistent storage if it is to be used later. The VBScript procedure code sample in Listing 6.5 provides an example of storing and tracking the number of page hits to a text file on the server.

Listing 6.5   Application Object Variables Must Be Saved to Disk If They Are to Be Used Between Different Application Sessions

```
<SCRIPT LANGUAGE=VBScript RUNAT=Server>
Sub SavePageHits()
   SET f = Server.CreateObject("MS.TextStream")
   f.CreateTextFile
   Server.MapPath("/") + "\count.txt", 2, TRUE, FALSE
   f.WriteLine(Application("Counter"))
   f.CloseTextFile
End Sub
</SCRIPT>
```

The Application object also provides support for two events. These events are special, however, and are contained within the global.asa server file.

▶ **See** "Understanding the Global.asa File," **p. 554**

The two events are

▒ OnStart

▒ OnEnd

Part

I

Ch

6

The OnStart and OnEnd events are declared within the global.asa file and are executed when the application starts and ends. These events are used to initialize variables at application startup and to clean up when an application ends. Listing 6.6 provides usage examples for the two events.

Listing 6.6 The `Application_OnStart` Event Used to Initialize Database Connectivity Options

```
<SCRIPT LANGUAGE=VBScript RUNAT=Server>
Sub Application_OnStart
   Application("DataConn_ConnectionString") = _&
      "DBQ=C:\IntraGAS\ei3.mdb;DefaultDir=C:\IntraGAS; "     & _
      "Driver={Microsoft Access Driver (*.mdb)}; "           & _
      "DriverId=25;FIL=MS Access; ImplicitCommitSync=Yes; "  & _
      "MaxBufferSize=512; MaxScanRows=8;PageTimeout=5; "      & _
      "SafeTransactions=0;Threads=3;UID=admin;UserCommitSync=Yes;"
   Application("DataConn_ConnectionTimeout") = 15
   Application("DataConn_CommandTimeout") = 30
   Application("DataConn_RuntimeUserName") = "admin"
   Application("DataConn_RuntimePassword") = ""
End Sub
</SCRIPT>
```

The Session Object

Unlike the Application object, which holds information across multiple instances of the same application and across multiple users, the Session object stores state information about a single user. It provides scope for saving user variables. Except for its narrower scope, the Session object is very similar to the Application object in functionality and usage.

N O T E   Session variables are similar to traditional application global variables. They are available to an application throughout; however, each instance of the application gets its own set of Session object variables. ▨

The Session object supports the following method and properties:

▨ Abandon—The Abandon method is used to destroy all Session object variables and release their memory. If the method is not called explicitly, the variables are destroyed when the Session object times out. Calling the Abandon method within the context of a Web page doesn't destroy the Session object until the page has been processed fully and all scripts on the page have been executed. The code sample in Listing 6.7 illustrates the use of the Abandon method.

Listing 6.7 The Abandon Method Is Queued Until All Script on a Page Has Been Executed

```
<%
Session.Abandon
Session("Counter") = Session("Counter") + 1
Response.Write(Session("Counter"))
%>
```

- SessionID—The SessionID property is a LONG data type that returns the unique identity assigned to the current user session. The server automatically generates the SessionID when a new session is started.

CAUTION

SessionIDs shouldn't be used as unique keys. When a Web server is restarted, the SessionID counter is re-initialized also.

- Timeout—The Timeout property specifies the period in minutes before a Session object is destroyed. If the user doesn't refresh or request a page within the timeout period, the session ends.

In addition to the preceding properties and methods, the Session object supports the OnStart and OnEnd events. These events are identical in functionality to the Application object events, except their scope is limited to the current user session.

The Request Object

The Request object is used to query information from the client browser. The information is passed from the client to the server through an HTTP request. The server, to retrieve the information from the HTTP message, uses the Request object.

Five types of variables can be passed to a server application from the client by using the Request object. Each of these variables has its own collection within the Request object. The Request object contains the following collections:

- QueryString
- Form
- Cookies
- ServerVariables
- ClientCertificate

The syntax for accessing the variables stored within the Request object collections is very simple, as illustrated in the following:

```
Request[.Collection](Variable)
```

Part

I

Ch

6

The collection name is optional and can be omitted. If the collection is not specified, all the collections within the `Request` object are searched. The search occurs in the order the collections are listed earlier. The following sections discuss the `Request` object collections in more detail.

The `QueryString` Collection The `QueryString` collection provides a parsing mechanism for the `QUERY_STRING` HTTP tag. It provides access to the HTTP string contained after the question mark (?), as in the following example. The HTTP string `http://www.gasullivan.com/user.asp?id=azamm&name=azam` can be retrieved by using the `Request` object `QueryString` collection:

```
ID = Request.QueryString("id")
Name = Request.QueryString("name")
```

If more than one value is assigned to the same variable, the variable is stored as an array. Using an optional index parameter, you can access the multiple values.

```
Request.[QueryString]("variable")[.index]
```

To determine the number of values stored within a variable array, use the optional count property:

```
Request.[QueryString]("variable")[.Count]
```

The index parameter can have any value between 1 and the number of values stored in the array.

To access multiple values stored within the same collection variable, use a numeric index after specifying the variable—for example,

```
Name1 = Request.QueryString("name").(1)
Name2 = Request.QueryString("name").(2)
```

Finally, if you need to access unparsed `QueryString` data, you can gain access to it by using the `Request.QueryString` without any parameter values.

The Form Collection The `Form` collection is used to retrieve values posted to an HTTP request by an HTML form, using the `POST` method. A form is a part of the HTML standard and supported by all browsers. Web sites employ forms to collect information from users by implementing text boxes, check boxes, option buttons, and list boxes. Usually there is a Submit button on a form (see Figure 6.6). The submit button is used to trigger the `POST` method, which passes the entered information back to the server in an HTTP `Request` object.

 TIP The user registration page used by most Web sites is an example of an HTML page that uses a `Form` collection along with the `POST` method to collect user data.

The `Form` collection has the following syntax:

```
Request.Form(parameter)[(index)¦.Count]
```

The `Request` object allows access to the data from a form within the ASP. The `parameter` value specifies the name of the form element from which the values are to be retrieved.

The `index` parameter is an optional value that allows access to multiple values within a parameter. It can have values between 1 and `Request.Form("<parameter>").Count`.

FIGURE 6.6

The Login to Sample Web page is used to obtain the login ID and password using the `Submit` and `Post` methods.

The Web page —

The source window showing the code used to generate the login page —

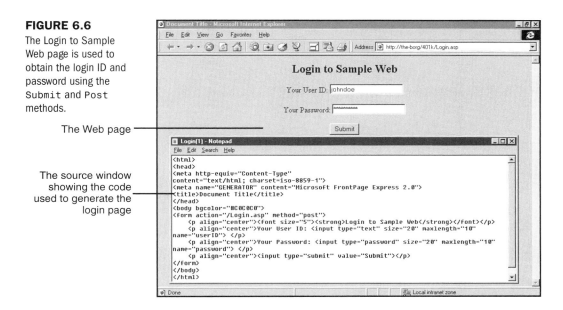

For example, consider the form in Listing 6.8, which is used to collect userID and password information from users logging onto a Web site.

Listing 6.8   The `Form` Collection Is Used to Retrieve Data Entered Through an HTML Form

```
<%@ LANGUAGE="VBSCRIPT" %>
<html>

<head>
<meta http-equiv="Content-Type"
content="text/html; charset=iso-8859-1">
<meta name="GENERATOR" content="Microsoft FrontPage Express 2.0">
<title>Document Title</title>
</head>

<body bgcolor="#C0C0C0">

<form action="/Login.asp" method="post">
    <p align="center"><font size="5"><strong>Login to Sample Web</strong>
    ➥</font></p>
    <p align="center">Your User ID: <input type="text" size="20"
    ➥maxlength="10" name="userID"> </p>
    <p align="center">Your Password: <input type="password" size="20"
    ➥maxlength="10" name="password"> </p>
    <p align="center"><input type="submit" value="Submit"></p>
</form>
</body>
</html>
```

Part

I

Ch

6

The preceding form generates a request of the following type:

```
userID=azamm&password=pass
```

By using the Form collection, you can access the login information and validate the user. The validation routine can look something like this:

```
UserID = Request.Form("userID")
Password = Request.Form("password")
```

The values are retrieved from the Form collection and assigned to local variables for validation.

The Cookies Collection The Cookies collection is used to retrieve the cookies sent through the HTTP request. A *cookie* is analogous to an INI file or registry entries in the sense that it is used to store preferences, user information, and other pertinent user data. Any information can be stored, passed, and accessed through a cookie.

By definition, cookies are stored on the client machine for fast retrieval at a later time. For example, cookies are used to provide personalized Web content to users. User preferences and tastes are stored in cookies on the client machine to customize the content being displayed to the users each time they log on to a Web site.

The Cookies collection of the Request object is used only to read cookies from a client machine. The Response object mentioned later in this section is used to write cookie information to a client machine.

The syntax for requesting cookie information is

```
Request.Cookies(cookie)[(key)¦.attribute]
```

- ▓ *cookie*—Specifies a cookie whose value should be read.
- ▓ *key*—An optional parameter used to retrieve subkey values from a cookie.
- ▓ *attribute*—A read-only parameter that specifies information about the cookie itself. The attribute parameter can have the following values:
  - Expires—Write-only value specifying the date on which the cookie expires.
  - Domain—If specified, this write-only value is used to send cookies only to requests within this domain.
  - Path—The cookie is sent only to requests to this path. If this attribute isn't set, the application path is used. This is a write-only parameter.
  - Secure—This write-only parameter specifies whether the cookie is secure.
  - HasKeys—This read-only parameter specifies whether the cookie contains keys.

To determine whether a cookie is a *cookie dictionary* (whether the cookie has keys), use the following script:

```
<%= Request.Cookies("myCookie").HasKeys %>
```

If myCookie is a cookie dictionary, the preceding value evaluates to True. Otherwise, it evaluates to False.

You can use a loop to cycle through all the cookies in the `Cookie` collection, or all the keys in a cookie as shown in Listing 6.9.

Listing 6.9   Iterating Through Keys on a Cookie That Does Not Have Keys Won't Produce Any Output

```
<%
   For Each cookie in Request.Cookies
      If Not cookie.HasKeys Then
%>
         <%= cookie %> = <%= Request.Cookies(cookie)%>
         <%
      Else
         For Each key in Request.Cookies(cookie)
         %>
            <%= cookie %> (<%= key %>) = <%= Request.Cookies(cookie)(key)%>
         <%Next
      End If
   Next
%>
```

The `ServerVariables` Collection   The `ServerVariables` collection is a set of predefined server variables that are used to read information about the server, the operating environment, and the client browsers. Generally, most of the `ServerVariables` collection items are read-only. The syntax for the `ServerVariables` collection is

`Request.ServerVariables(variable)`

The following are the environment variables accessible through the `ServerVariables` collection:

- `AUTH_TYPE`—The authentication method used by the Web server to validate users when they attempt to access a protected Web page. The three methods allowed include the clear text password validation, encrypted password validation, and the Microsoft Windows NT domain validation.
- `CONTENT_LENGTH`—The length of the content provided by the client.
- `CONTENT_TYPE`—Provides the data type of the content provided by the client. Used by HTTP requests that have information attached to them, such as the HTTP POST method.
- `GATEWAY_INTERFACE`—The revision of the CGI specification used by the server. Format is CGI/revision.
- `HTTP_<HeaderName>`—The value stored in the header `HeaderName`. Any header other than those listed here must be prefixed by `HTTP_` for the `ServerVariables` collection to retrieve their value. The server interprets any underscore (_) characters in `HeaderName` as dashes in the actual header. For example, if you specify `HTTP_MY_HEADER`, the server searches for a header sent as `MY-HEADER`.
- `LOGON_USER`—The Windows NT domain login account name being used by the user.

- PATH_INFO—Extra path information provided by the client. Scripts residing on the server can be accessed using their virtual path and the PATH_INFO variable. If the PATH_INFO information is obtained from a URL, the server decodes it before the PATH_INFO variable is passed to scripts.

- PATH_TRANSLATED—A translated version of PATH_INFO that takes the path and performs any necessary virtual-to-physical path mapping.

- QUERY_STRING—Another method of accessing the query information stored in the string following the question mark (?) in the HTTP request.

- REMOTE_ADDR—The IP address of the remote host making the HTTP request.

- REMOTE_HOST—The IP hostname of the remote host making the HTTP request. If the remote host does not have an IP hostname defined, the server leaves this field empty.

- REQUEST_METHOD—The method used to make the HTTP request. Examples include GET, POST, PUT.

- SCRIPT_MAP—Provides the base portion of the URL.

- SCRIPT_NAME—A virtual path to the script being executed. This is used for self-referencing URLs.

- SERVER_NAME—The server's hostname, Domain Name Server (DNS) alias, or IP address as it would appear in self-referencing URLs.

- SERVER_PORT—The server port number the HTTP request was sent to.

- SERVER_PORT_SECURE—A string that provides information about the port handling the HTTP request. This variable can have a value of 0 or 1. If the port handling the request is a secure port, the value is set to 1; otherwise, 0.

- SERVER_PROTOCOL—The name and revision number of the request information protocol. Format is protocol/revision.

- SERVER_SOFTWARE—The name and revision number of the server software honoring the request and running the gateway. Format is name/revision.

- URL—Provides the base portion of the URL.

Listing 6.10 illustrates how to use the ServerVariables collection.

Listing 6.10 Using a Loop Construct to Cycle Through the ServerVariables Collection

```
<%@ LANGUAGE="VBSCRIPT" %>

<HTML>
<HEAD>
<META NAME="GENERATOR" Content="Microsoft Visual InterDev 1.0">
<META HTTP-EQUIV="Content-Type" content="text/html; charset=iso-8859-1">
<TITLE>Document Title</TITLE>
</HEAD>
<BODY>

<HTML><!-- This example displays the content of several ServerVariables. -->
```

```
<TABLE>
<TR><TD><B>Server Variables</B></TD><TD><B>Value</B></TD></TR>
<% For Each name In Request.ServerVariables %>
   <TR><TD> <%= name %> </TD><TD> <%= Request.ServerVariables(name) %>
   ➥</TD></TR>
</TABLE>
<% Next %>
</HTML>


</BODY>
</HTML>
```

The `ClientCertificate` Collection The `ClientCertificate` collection is used with the Secure Sockets Layer (SSL) protocol to provide certification information to the Web server from the client browser.

 TIP

To determine if you are connecting to a Web browser using SSL, examine the beginning tag of a URL. Instead of an `http://` tag, an SSL Web site URL starts with `https://`. SSL is an industry standard, first introduced by Netscape, that enables Web sites to create, store, and display secure, encrypted information to the users. Content stored on SSL-enabled Web sites is encrypted before being transmitted to the client browser, and vice versa. Your browser must support SSL for enabling a secure connection to the Web server.

When a user connects to a secure server, the server requests certification, and the browser responds by sending the certification fields. If no certificate is sent, the `ClientCertificate` collection returns EMPTY.

The syntax for retrieving client certificate information is

`Request.ClientCertificate(Key[SubField])`

- *Key*—Specifies the name of the certification field to retrieve.
- *SubField*—An optional parameter you can use to retrieve an individual field in either the Subject or Issuer key. This parameter is added to the *Key* parameter as a suffix.

The *Key* field can have the following possible values:

- Subject—A list of values that contains information about the subject of the certificate. SubKeys extract the individual pieces of information from the Subject key.
- Issuer—A list of values that contains information about the issuer of the certificate. SubKeys extract the individual pieces of information from the Subject key.
- ValidFrom—A valid VBScript date that indicates when the certificate becomes active.
- ValidUntil—A valid VBScript date that indicates when the certificate expires.
- SerialNumber—A string that represents the serial number. It's a series of hexadecimal bytes separated by hyphens.
- Certificate—A string containing the entire certificate in binary format.

▓ Flags—A set of flags that provide additional client certificate information. The following flags might be set:

  ▓ ceCertPresent—A client certificate is present.

  ▓ ceUnrecognizedIssuer—The last certification in this chain is from an unknown issuer.

N O T E   To use the preceding flags, you must include the client-certificate include file in your ASP page. If you are using VBScript, include Cervbs.inc. If you are using JScript, include Cerjavas.inc. These files are installed in the \Inetpub\ASPSamp\Samples directory on your Web server. ▓

The SubField parameter can have the following values:

▓ C—Specifies the name of the country of origin.

▓ O—Specifies the company or organization name.

▓ OU—Specifies the name of the organizational unit.

▓ CN—Specifies the common name of the user. This SubField is used with the Subject key.

▓ L—Specifies a locality.

▓ S—Specifies a state or province.

▓ T—Specifies the title of the person or organization.

▓ GN—Specifies a given name.

▓ I—Specifies a set of initials.

Listing 6.11 illustrates a method to access ClientCertificate collection values.

Listing 6.11   Using a Loop Construct to Cycle Through the ClientCertificate Collection

```
<%@ LANGUAGE="VBSCRIPT" %>

<!--METADATA TYPE="DesignerControl" startspan
    <OBJECT ID="Include1" WIDTH=151 HEIGHT=24
     CLASSID="CLSID:F602E725-A281-11CF-A5B7-0080C73AAC7E">
        <PARAM NAME="_Version" VALUE="65536">
        <PARAM NAME="_ExtentX" VALUE="3986">
        <PARAM NAME="_ExtentY" VALUE="635">
        <PARAM NAME="_StockProps" VALUE="0">
        <PARAM NAME="Source" VALUE="/401k/cervbs.inc">
        <PARAM NAME="SourceType" VALUE="1">
    </OBJECT>
-->
<!--#INCLUDE VIRTUAL="/401k/cervbs.inc"-->
<!--METADATA TYPE="DesignerControl" endspan-->
<HTML>
<HEAD>
<META NAME="GENERATOR" Content="Microsoft Visual InterDev 1.0">
```

```
<META HTTP-EQUIV="Content-Type" content="text/html; charset=iso-8859-1">
<TITLE>Document Title</TITLE>
</HEAD>
<BODY>


<%
For Each key in Request.ClientCertificate
  Response.Write( key & ": " & Request.ClientCertificate(key) & "<BR>")
Next
%>


</BODY>
</HTML>
```

The Response Object

The Response object is used to send HTML output to the client browser from an ASP. For example,

```
<% Response.Write("Hello World!")%>
```

results in a display of the text on a Web page on the client browser. The Response object has the following syntax:

```
Response.[collection]¦[property]¦[method]
```

The collection parameter contains only a single collection, the Cookies collection, which was defined earlier in the section "The Request Object."

The Response object supports the following properties:

- Buffer—Indicates whether page output is buffered. When buffered output is specified, the server doesn't send any output to the client until all the scripts on the page have been processed or the Flush or End methods have been called. The call to Response.Buffer should be the first line of the .asp file.

- ContentType—Specifies the HTTP content type for the response. The default content type is text/HTML.

- Expires—Specifies the length of time before a page cached on a browser expires. The time is given in minutes, and a value of 0 means immediate expiration of the cached page.

- ExpiresAbsolute—Specifies the date and time on which a page cached on a browser expires. The default value for date is the day the script is run, and the default value for time is midnight.

- Status—The value of the status line returned by the server. Status values are defined in the HTTP specification. The value consists of a three-digit number and a textual description.

Part
I

Ch
6

In addition, the `Response` object supports the following methods.

- `AddHeader`—Sets the HTML header *name* to *value*.
- `AppendToLog`—Adds a string to the end of the Web server log entry for this request. The string must not contain any commas and must not be more than 80 characters. Multiple calls to this method append the strings to the existing entry.
- `BinaryWrite`—Writes the given information to the current HTTP output without any character-set conversion. This method is most useful for writing binary information required by a custom application.
- `Clear`—Erases any buffered HTML output.
- `End`—Stops processing the ASP file and returns the current result.
- `Flush`—Sends buffered output immediately.
- `Redirect`—Sends a redirect message to the browser, causing it to attempt to connect to an alternative URL.
- `Write`—Writes a variable to the current HTTP output as a string. The variable can be data of any type as defined by the VBScript variant data type.

The Server Object

The `Server` object provides methods and properties that enable interaction with the Web server machine. The methods and properties provided by the `Server` object performs very useful purposes. The `Server` object provides developers access to the OLE automation mechanism through the use of Active Server Components.

The `Server` object supports the `ScriptTimeout` property, which sets the amount of time a script can run before it times out. The property has a default value of 90 seconds.

In addition, the `Server` object supports the following methods:

- `CreateObject`—Creates an instance of a server component and provides the capability to create OLE server objects in the Web application. These objects can be written in any language, such as Visual Basic and Visual C++.

▶ **See** "Using ActiveX Server Components in Visual InterDev," **p. 540**

- `HTMLEncode`—Applies HTML encoding to the specified string.
- `MapPath`—Maps the specified virtual path, either the absolute path on the current server or the path relative to the current page, into a physical path.

N O T E   A virtual path defines an alias to a physical path on the Web server. For example, the absolute physical path c:\myweb\data\images\ might be defined as a virtual path with an alias of \images. Virtual paths can be defined using the Internet Service Manager included with IIS. ▨

- `URLEncode`—Applies URL encoding rules, including escape characters, to the string.

From Here...

In this chapter, you learned about IIS and ASP. You learned about Microsoft's Active Platform strategy and how ActiveX controls, ActiveX server objects and ActiveX scripting mechanisms work together to provide an environment for developing rich and powerful Web-enabled applications. Refer to the following chapters for information related to building Web sites and Web-based applications using ASP and IIS.

- To learn about concepts associated with Web-based application development, see Chapter 15, "Clients, Servers, and Components: Web-Based Applications."
- To learn about getting started with Visual InterDev, see Chapter 18, "Developing Active Content with Visual InterDev."
- To learn about DHTML and its advantages, see Chapter 21, "Dynamic HTML."
- To learn about using design-time controls, see Chapter 20, "Visual InterDev Design-Time Controls."
- To learn about server-side programming using ASP, see Chapter 17, "Server-Side Programming."

Part

I

Ch

6

An Inside Look at the Microsoft Message Queue

by Marc Cantril

In this chapter

As you design applications in the future, you should consider including Message-Oriented Middleware (MOM) in the application architecture. MOM provides proven functionality that you might have written in your current applications. Now you can save that development and testing time for portions of your application that don't exist in the commercial marketplace.

This chapter explains how MOM is to applications as electronic mail (email) is to users. One product is discussed in depth, the Microsoft Message Queue (MSMQ). MSMQ is available in the Microsoft NT Server Option Pack and the latest versions of Microsoft Windows NT 4 Server.

Discovering the Need for Message Queues

What is MOM? Electronic mail provides a very simple analogy of the role that MOM serves in applications. With email, an individual user composes a message that might consist of text and file attachments. The user provides a destination address as the message is sent. The sending user isn't concerned about server operating systems, physical distances, or network protocols between himself and the recipient of his message. The email server software will find a way to deliver the mail message to the destination email server. After the mail has been received on the destination email server, it is stored, waiting to be opened and read by the recipient. The recipient doesn't have to be logged on at the time the message is sent, and the sender only expects the recipient to respond as soon as it is convenient. If a critical message needs to be delivered without delay, the sending user should choose a different communication medium such as the telephone or a pager. Finally, when the recipient does check his incoming mail, the message is read. Keep in mind that reading the attachments requires the recipient to have applications similar to those of the sender. If appropriate, a response is composed and sent. This type of interaction is well understood by developers and users alike. Figure 7.1 illustrates the process.

FIGURE 7.1
Electronic mail helps people communicate in a manner analogous to applications exchanging information with MOM.

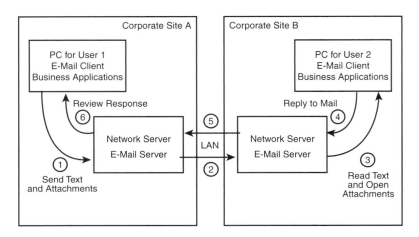

MOM fills a critical space in enterprise software. MOM uses message queues to communicate between components of a single application or multiple applications. In this section, an overview of MOM is followed by a discussion of how MOM can help you optimize resources, support application evolution, and facilitate disconnected application execution.

An Overview of Message-Oriented Middleware

MOM provides a communication infrastructure of queues and message routers. An application writes a message to a queue. The messaging middleware routes the message to the requested queue. Another application (or another component of the same application) reads the message from the target queue and processes the message. The message content is completely managed by the applications reading and writing to the queue.

MSMQ has the capability to record different events occurring during processing. Events such as when the message was inserted in the queue and when the message was removed from the queue can be recorded in event logs. MSMQ also has the capability to reroute communication intelligently if a standard network path is not available for passing messages.

Many people were taught as children to complete one task before starting the next. That philosophy is often effective for reading books, creating wood shop projects, or performing high priority tasks. However, management experts suggest that delegation combined with appropriately timed follow-up can produce higher output and greater satisfaction. The difference between these philosophies is that one promotes serial processing whereas the other encourages parallel processing.

Synchronous programs execute serially. When one program requests services from another program, the first program waits until the second program has responded before continuing. For example, a client application that is designed to pass data from a user to a database might initiate communication with the database as soon as the client begins executing. If the target database doesn't immediately respond to the client application, the client application warns the user that the database isn't available and all activities will stop. The user isn't able to record any data. On the other hand, if the target database does respond but performs its tasks slowly, the user becomes frustrated with the slow application.

That same program might have been written using MOM to execute in an asynchronous fashion. Returning to the prior example, the client application enables the user to enter the data without attempting to connect to the database. When the user attempts to save or commit the data, the program passes the data to a message queue and immediately returns to attend to the user. In the background, another program associated with the database extracts the data from the message in the message queue and inserts it into the database. This background activity occurs when the database is available, without impacting user productivity.

Obviously, certain applications are better candidates for this type of asynchronous communication. An airline reservation system is not be a good choice for asynchronous communication because a business customer in the airport needs to know immediately that a seat has been reserved on the desired plane. A manufacturing order entry application might be a better candidate for asynchronous communication because a customer order must be placed rapidly, but a few minutes delay in posting the order to distribution might be perfectly acceptable.

Figure 7.2 displays the architecture of an MSMQ application. The MSMQ Information Store (MQIS) database is responsible for holding the location of queues and other enterprise settings.

FIGURE 7.2
MSMQ can provide the underpinnings for asynchronous communication from Sales to Distribution.

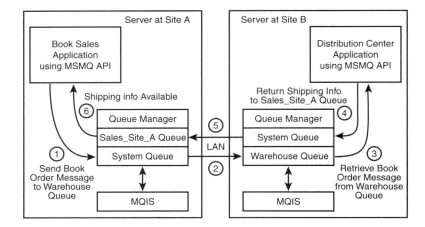

Optimizing Enterprise Resources

MOM can help optimize your enterprise resources. Using MOM in your client applications can boost their performance. The key element is the asynchronous communication. Clients that rely on message queues can quickly read or write to a queue and continue responding to the user, as opposed to forcing the user to wait for network, database, and other infrastructure resources to interactively respond. Asynchronous communication in the client application prioritizes the user's time over system activities. The client application only waits on a response from other enterprise resources when there is nothing else the user can do independently.

Server applications using MOM, on the other hand, check for messages in the queue. If a message exists, the server application processes it and places the results in a return queue for the client application. The server application can be optimized to perform all its important functions with a decreased prioritization on urgent, interactive demands of client applications.

Enterprise developers benefit from MOM because they can dedicate their focus to either the client or the server. They don't have to worry about how the message is delivered from point A to point B. Development staff often fall prey to writing and rewriting applications that move files of data. Yet their project timeframes don't allow sufficient time for testing all the potential points of failure.

Support for Application Evolution

Software development takes place in a very fluid environment where change is continual. Applications that incorporate MOM can increase your ability to keep up with the changes. For example, if your application migrates from a centralized architecture to a distributed architecture, the application might transition from sharing a central message queue to routing messages between distributed queues. These queue reconfigurations can be implemented with minimal impact on the application.

If your application (with MOM) evolves from a homogeneous environment to one with many different operating systems or hardware vendors, you need to purchase message queuing software for those vendor/operating systems. Following installation, queues need to be defined, and the application is ready for use again.

For the corporate development teams, the flexibility to enhance applications while minimizing disruption to the user community is a significant asset. If the users are interested in upgrading a poorly constructed client application (without changing the functionality of a server application), an application with MOM will insulate the changes to the client and away from the server. This technique minimizes the introduction of new defects and lessens the extent of regression testing to the server. In addition, the use of message queues encourages modular development and encourages the creation of test harnesses. Test harnesses can be constructed to place test messages in a queue for routing to the server application and evaluating its response. Likewise, test messages can be placed in a queue simulating a response from a server application to test the reaction of the client application.

MOM can facilitate integration of in-house and newly purchased applications. A newly purchased application rarely completely and cleanly replaces internal corporate applications. An independent software vendor (ISV) application constructed on the MOM paradigm fosters collaboration with enterprise developers, which might need to blend the use of existing applications with new ones. MOM serves as a data-driven programming interface that facilitates integration. The selection process for new applications should include MOM as an important criterion.

Facilitating Disconnected Computing

MOM supports disconnected computing. *Disconnected computing* means that the client application isn't able to access all aspects of its operating environment. For one application, disconnected computing might indicate that the corporate wide area network (WAN) is unavailable. For another application, the client application might be running on a laptop without any network communication. The responsibility of MOM is to deliver messages whenever it is possible. A core assumption of any application using messaging is that the recipient of a message might not be available when the message is sent. Therefore, for applications that are created specifically for users who plan to be disconnected, you should seriously consider MOM. The only constraint is that a local queue manager must be accessible when the client application is disconnected. Without the message queue, the application won't be able to store messages while waiting for a connection.

Part

I

Ch

7

Understanding the MSMQ Architecture

MSMQ is a version 1 product that provides a well-defined and comprehensive architecture for MOM. This section defines the MSMQ interfaces. A brief summary of competing and companion products to MSMQ is also included.

MSMQ Interfaces

Applications communicate with message queues through the MSMQ Application Programming Interface (API). Programs can communicate via C function calls or COM/ActiveX components. The COM/ActiveX API enables the use of tools such as Visual Basic, Visual J++, Visual C++, Delphi, and Microfocus COBOL.

▶ **See** Chapter 32, "Using MSMQ with Visual Basic," for details on using the ActiveX API,
p. 921

Microsoft has also created access to MSMQ from Microsoft Exchange. The MSMQ Exchange Connector facilitates the use of MS Exchange as a client application interface. For example, a supervisor can receive an email informing her of critical events in a workflow. Another example is illustrated in Figure 7.3, in which a job applicant submits his job skills via an MS Exchange form. After the requested information has been recorded, the data is submitted to a corporate Human Resources database for review by hiring managers. The Exchange Connector provides the user with new functionality via the everyday interface that he understands. All the while, the time required to create, test, and install a custom client application is virtually eliminated. In addition to the MSMQ Exchange Connector, the Messaging Application Programming Interface (MAPI) standard is supported, which expands the electronic mail clients that developers can use.

FIGURE 7.3

The Exchange Connector can use MS Exchange forms as a client interface that accepts resumés from job applicants.

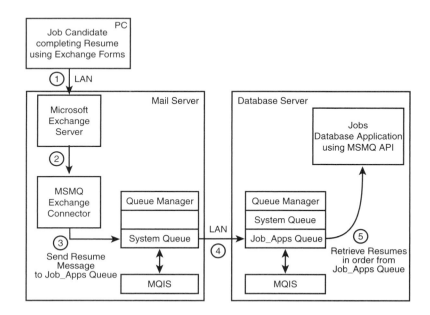

Application developers can also architect and construct I-net applications that use MSMQ functionality. MSMQ is accessible via Microsoft Internet Information Server (IIS) and Active Server Pages (ASP). Figure 7.4 shows the same application functionality previously described. This implementation requires the developer to create a data entry form that executes in a Web browser instead of MS Exchange. The distinction of this design is the ability to painlessly extend the candidate search beyond your corporate network. Now, applicants with Internet access are able to apply for positions also.

FIGURE 7.4

An application for processing resumés can use MSMQ and the Web.

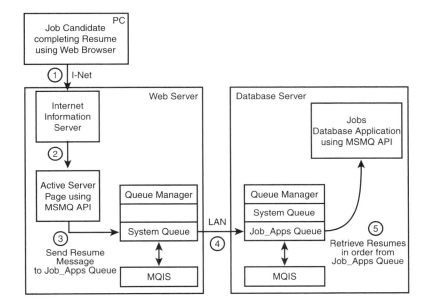

Finally, MSMQ works in conjunction with Microsoft Transaction Server (MTS) and the Distributed Transaction Coordinator (DTC). MSMQ is a resource manager. This combination of products makes your applications scalable and reliable even in environments where network communication is unreliable. When acting as a resource manager, the queue management software confirms that it is ready to send (or receive) a message, but doesn't actually send (or receive) until instructed to commit the transaction.

Competing and Companion Products

The two major competitors on the MOM market are Microsoft and IBM. IBM's MQ series is available on server systems such as the IBM 370 mainframe, Hewlett Packard HP9000, and Digital VAX. Microsoft has focused on PC systems with Windows 95, Windows NT Workstation, and Windows NT Server. However, Microsoft has collaborated with Level 8 Systems to extend the MSMQ API to other operating systems. Level 8 Systems has named its family of products FalconMQ. FalconMQ runs on the UNIX, VMS, AS/400, MVS, OS/2, and Unisys operating systems. Further, the FalconMQ Bridge product enables sending messages between the IBM MQ series message queues and MSMQ message queues.

Part

I

Ch

7

N O T E   Microsoft produces a product called Windows Messaging in addition to MSMQ. Windows
Messaging is a subsystem of MAPI that was named MS Exchange at one time, but the
name was changed when MS Exchange Server was released. Windows MSMQ is a new product with a
different API and architecture. ▩

Examining the Types of Message Queues and Messages

An application designer and developer needs to know how to use the rich functionality of
MSMQ. This section describes the types of queues defined within MSMQ. I discuss the issues
of security and detail the key aspects of sending and receiving messages.

Types of Message Queues

Queues are the heart of MSMQ. Messages are pumped into and out of queues continuously.
MSMQ supports a wide range of queue types. *Application queues* are created at the request of
administrators using MSMQ Explorer (an administrative tool discussed later in this chapter),
or they can be created by applications themselves. *Public* application queues are visible to
MSMQ clients because they are published in a naming service, the Message Queue Information Store (MQIS). MSMQ clients can query MQIS to determine whether a certain public
application queue exists and which computer hosts it. On the other hand, *private* application
queues aren't published in the MQIS. Therefore, an application that wants to send a message
to a private queue must know the specific host of that queue.

The following queues are defined in MSMQ:

- ▩ Application queues—Handle application messages
- ▩ Journal queues for application queues—Receive copies of messages removed from the queue
- ▩ Dead letter queues—Store undelivered nontransactional messages
- ▩ General journal queues—Record messages sent from a source computer
- ▩ Transactional dead letter queues—Host undelivered transactional messages
- ▩ Report queues—Describe routing information on messages
- ▩ Administration queues—Contain acknowledgment messages

Application queues have fewer than 20 properties, and several are worthy of review. The `Quota`
property enables the administrator to control the maximum size for a queue. If the `Journal`
property is set, all messages removed from the queue will be recorded in a journal queue specifically allocated to the application queue. When the `Journal` property is set on a queue, *target
journaling* is enabled. If the `Transaction` property is enabled when an application queue is
created, a transactional application queue will exist. This property must be set if the queue will
be used in conjunction with MTS. A message in a transactional application queue won't send
the message until MTS indicates the transaction should be committed. Transactional queues

cannot receive nontransactional messages, and nontransactional queues cannot receive transactional messages.

N O T E On Windows 95, MSMQ can store up to one gigabyte of messages, whereas on Windows NT 4, MSMQ can store nearly two gigabytes of messages.

Dead letter and transaction dead letter queues are used to store messages that cannot be delivered or have expired. Messages can be recovered from a dead letter queue. A transactional message that is not delivered because it was sent to a nontransactional queue or because of a rollback of the transaction will be placed in the sending computer's transaction dead letter queue, named Xact Dead Letter. A nontransactional message that is not delivered can be placed in the dead letter queue, named Dead Letter, on the source computer, destination computer, or routing computer.

Report queues contain messages describing the route that messages traveled from source to target. Administration queues can store acknowledgments from target application queues verifying that the target queue successfully received the sent message. Administration queues can also contain messages that indicate errors in attempting to deliver messages.

Figure 7.5 shows a few of the properties of a message queue. The ID property contains a globally unique identifier (GUID) for each public queue. The Type ID can be set by applications to identify a class or grouping of queues, which provide a common utility in the application architecture.

FIGURE 7.5

Queue Properties can be viewed with the administrative tool, MSMQ Explorer.

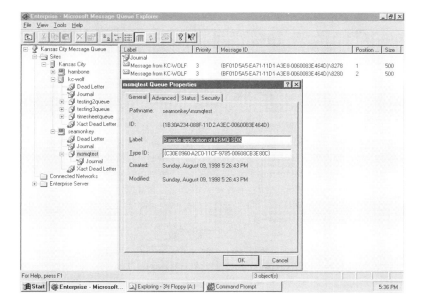

Message Security

You can secure messages in MSMQ in several ways. First, the Windows NT Access Control Lists (ACLs) can be used to protect queues against unauthorized reading, writing, and administrative changes. Second, MSMQ can post events to the NT Security Log. This information can help administrators monitor unauthorized and unsuccessful attempts to interact with queues. Finally, messages can be encrypted and digitally signed while en route to the target queue. When at the target queue, the message is returned to its pre-encrypted value. The Crypto API performs the encryption service.

Message Properties

If queues are the heart of MSMQ, messages are the blood. Messages carry your business data. When messages are routing, business is flowing. Your applications define messages. Messages are formatted by the sender and interpreted by the receiver. Messages can be either ASCII or binary. MSMQ provides a secured pipeline, and you provide the contents.

Messages have over 20 properties that help provide a complete message description. A select few that will prove most valuable are listed in the following:

- The Body property—The content of the message
- The Delivery property—Rules for delivery
- The Transaction property—The transactional delivery flag
- The Priority property—The priority of the message
- The Journal property—Instructions to save a copy
- The Acknowledge property—The type of feedback from the destination
- The Response property—The queue to respond to with feedback
- The Message ID property—The unique identifier for the message

The Body property holds the message of interest that needs to be interpreted by the receiving application. The Delivery property can be either Express or Recoverable. Express messages travel most rapidly because they aren't written to disk during their journey. Recoverable messages are written to disk to avoid data loss in the event of a system crash.

> **N O T E** The maximum size of any one message is four megabytes. Express messages are usually stored in memory; however, they might be written to disk when insufficient resources exist to store the file in memory. When any message is written to disk, it is stored in memory-mapped files with an extension of .mq.

Messages can be marked with a transaction flag, which will guarantee that those messages will be delivered exactly once and in the order sent. Transactional messages must be sent to transactional application queues. Messages that aren't marked with a transaction flag cannot be sent to transaction queues.

MSMQ enables you to set a custom `Priority` property with values from zero to seven. (Zero is the highest priority.) A `Journal` property of the message enables *source journaling*, which indicates that a copy of the message should be placed in the sender's journal queue after it has been sent. The other type of journaling, called *target journaling*, is discussed in an earlier section in this chapter on application queues, "Types of Message Queues." The `Journal` property can also indicate that the message should be placed in a dead letter queue if the message expires before it is sent. The `Acknowledge` and `Response` message properties can be used to provide feedback of the events occurring at a destination queue, such as receiving a message.

All messages are allocated a unique Message ID when they are created. The Message ID is a valuable property to use in your applications. This identifier enables you to link messages sent to other applications with acknowledgments or messages returned from those applications.

▶ **See** Chapter 32, "Using MSMQ with Visual Basic," for examples of creating, sending, and receiving messages in application queues, **p. 921**

Sending and Receiving Messages

The core of the MSMQ API consists of five simple programming interfaces: Locate, Open, Close, Send, and Receive. Messages are always sent asynchronously. However, your application must be able to pass its message to the local queue manager. After that has occurred, the message is stored and ready to be sent at the first opportunity.

Messages are received either synchronously or asynchronously. When applications retrieve messages from an application queue in a synchronous manner, an application can suspend application execution while waiting for a message to arrive. Alternatively, an application might periodically poll an application queue in an effort to process any new messages.

The asynchronous method of retrieving a message is to register a callback with an application queue. When a message arrives, MSMQ communicates that fact to the application, and the application retrieves the message from the application queue.

Installing MSMQ

At this point, you should be convinced that MSMQ will enrich your enterprise applications, and you just can't wait to get started. By now you might be asking, "How do I install this product?" This question is answered in this section, which provides details of licensing, installing, configuring, and testing MSMQ.

MSMQ is included in the current release of Windows NT 4 Server. If you have an older copy of NT 4, you will need to obtain the Option Pack.

ON THE WEB

The Windows NT 4 Option Pack can be installed from the Microsoft Web site `http://www.microsoft.com/windows/downloads/contents/products/nt4optpk/`.

Part

I

Ch

7

The Option Pack is available on CD also. There are two Option Packs, one for Windows NT Workstation and one for Windows NT Server. MSMQ runs on Windows 95 and Windows NT 4 computers using the IP or IPX network protocols. Figure 7.6 displays the opening dialog for the Option Pack installation.

FIGURE 7.6

The Windows NT 4 Option Pack can be installed from the Internet or CD.

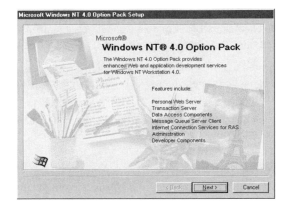

MSMQ must be checked in the main installation dialog in order to invoke installation of MSMQ. Figure 7.7 displays the subcomponents to install during an MSMQ client installation.

FIGURE 7.7

MSMQ isn't installed by default in the Windows NT 4 Option Pack.

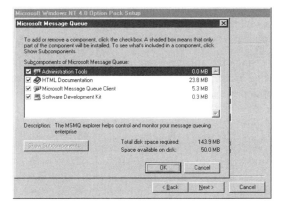

Software Licensing

In corporations, accurately licensing your enterprise software is legally mandatory and morally respectful to software developers. Unfortunately, licensing can become a burden for Information Systems departments, which are more interested in developing software than tracking software licenses. To that effect, Microsoft has made licensing the MSMQ products fairly simple.

MSMQ is included in the license of Windows NT 4 Server (Standard and Enterprise Editions). If your server will be supporting more than 25 clients, cost-based routing, or MS Exchange Connector, you should purchase Windows NT Server Enterprise Edition.

Independent and dependent clients are authorized by the Client Access License (CAL) that is purchased with Windows NT Server. CALs purchased for file sharing and printing services will work for MSMQ client licenses also.

Installation of an MSMQ server requires SQL Server 6.5, either service pack 1 or 3. SQL Server supports storing MSMQ installation details and queue properties in the MQIS. The MSMQ clients don't need SQL Server because they don't have an MQIS. In future releases of MSMQ, the need for SQL Server will also be eliminated for MSMQ servers.

ON THE WEB

For the latest details on MSMQ licensing, browse the NT Server pages at `http://www.microsoft.com/ntserver`.

Documentation

Because MSMQ is a new product, Microsoft is the author of the most available documentation. The installation of MSMQ provides Release Notes, an MSMQ Administrator's Guide, and MSMQ SDK Help. These online documents are well written and logically organized.

ON THE WEB

Some additional resources are on the Internet:

- Microsoft MSMQ Web Site—`http://www.microsoft.com/msmq/`
- Microsoft Developer's Network—`http://www.microsoft.com/msdn/`
- Business Quality Messaging—`http://www.bqm.org/`
- Level 8 Systems Web Site—`http://www.level8.com/falconmq.htm/`
- IBM Web Site—`http://www.software.ibm.com/ts/mqseries/`

MSMQ Topology

Before installing MSMQ, the network administrators, MSMQ administrators, and application designers should design an MSMQ Enterprise. The following are the key components:

- Enterprise—An enterprise defines the totality of the MSMQ environment. An enterprise has a name and a single controller server called the Primary Enterprise Controller (PEC).
- Sites—Sites are subsets of computers defined within an enterprise. Sites often correlate with physical locations of corporate offices. Communication within a site is assumed to be very fast and inexpensive. Sites pass messages to each other through site links; this is *intersite routing*. Passing of messages within a site is *intrasite routing*.

Part
I

Ch
7

■ Connecting networks—*Connecting networks* are defined as computers that can all communicate directly. Typical connecting network definitions are determined by dividing the computers using the IP protocol from those using the IPX protocol within a site.

The next discussion for the project team should center on MSMQ servers, connectors, and clients. MSMQ servers provide the backbone of the MSMQ Enterprise. Servers own message queues and perform message routing. Servers might be assigned special responsibilities in the Enterprise. A *Primary Enterprise Controller* is a single server responsible for holding the configuration of the entire MSMQ installation. This is always the first MSMQ server installed. A *Primary Site Controller* (PSC) is a server allocated responsibilities for knowing about all the computers and queues in a site. *Backup Site Controllers* (BSC) are servers assigned to mirror Primary Site Controllers. Routing servers join connecting networks together. All servers contain the MSMQ Application Programming Interfaces.

Connectors facilitate communication to external products such as Microsoft Exchange, the IBM MQ series message queue, and Remote Access Service (RAS). RAS connectivity might be crucial to fulfill the vision of disconnected application design by enabling the periodic communication with laptops, home computers, or isolated networks.

CAUTION

According to the Microsoft MSMQ installation instructions, the MSMQ RAS connectivity services should not be installed on a Windows NT Server running the NetBEUI protocol of RAS. For maximum reliability of remote access to MSMQ, avoid this configuration.

MSMQ clients are defined as either independent clients or dependent clients. Independent clients have the capability to own queues, along with containing the MSMQ API. Dependent clients rely on an MSMQ server for access to queues, but contain their own MSMQ API. Figure 7.8 shows the book order application from Figure 7.2, with an emphasis on the various MSMQ clients.

FIGURE 7.8
The book order application can be configured with this combination of MSMQ clients and servers.

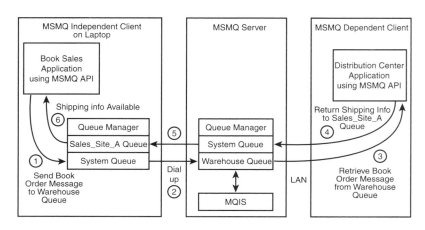

Server Installation

MSMQ servers can be installed on computers running Windows NT 4 Server only. An administrator account is needed for the installation. For proper configuration of the MSMQ security, the administrator should be a domain administrator.

The first MSMQ server installed will be assigned the Primary Enterprise Controller. During this installation, you need to identify the MSMQ Enterprise name (up to 126 characters long), at least one connected network name, and at least one site name (up to 31 characters long).

The installation is initiated by running the setup program for MSMQ. In Enterprise Edition 4, this is found in the MSMQ\Server folder. During the install, indicate that you want to create a server. Next, select PEC. The remaining prompts determine the data device and log device location and size (information for the MQIS implemented in SQL Server), Enterprise name, and connected network name, paired with a protocol (IP or IPX) and site name.

After this first MSMQ server has been installed, refer to the online MSMQ Administrator's Guide for assistance on the details of installing Primary Site Controllers, Backup Site Controllers, and connectors.

Client Installation

The independent and dependent clients can be installed on Windows 95, Windows NT 4 Workstation, or Windows NT 4 Server. Similar to the server installation, proper configuration of MSMQ security requires that the administrator account be a domain administrator. Computers running Windows 95 and Windows NT 4 Workstation install MSMQ from the Windows NT Workstation 4 Option Pack, which offers only client installation.

When installing a dependent client, you need to be prepared to indicate the server on which it depends. That server should be online during the installation. One server can support 15 dependent clients. Figure 7.9 shows the properties of a Primary Enterprise Controller with one dependent client currently online.

> **CAUTION**
>
> The MSMQ dependent client relies on synchronous access to its supporting server. Further, if secured communication is a requirement and encrypted messages are in use, the dependent client might not provide sufficient security. The message will travel on the network, between the dependent client and supporting server, in an unencrypted form. In addition, MSMQ functions on the dependent client cannot be transactional resources.

A client is limited to a maximum of 10 concurrent sessions with other MSMQ clients.

Part

I

Ch

7

FIGURE 7.9

MSMQ Explorer is displaying the computer properties of dependent clients. A computer, named OK, is dependent on the server, KC-Wolf.

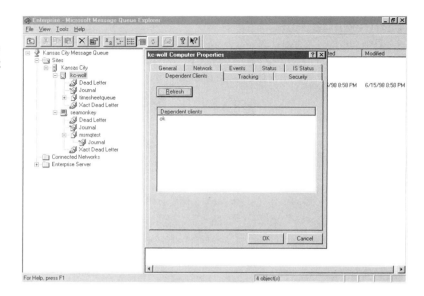

Testing an MSMQ Installation

There are three utilities provided by Microsoft to help you test the installation of MSMQ clients and servers. These same tools can be used for basic troubleshooting if you are experiencing problems in a production system.

Two of the tests are found in the administration tool, MSMQ Explorer. MSMQ Explorer enables you to navigate through the MSMQ Enterprise using a directory metaphor. If you right-click while your pointer is over one of the listed computers, a menu will be displayed that includes an MQPing function. MQPing in MSMQ is similar to the traditional network Ping. You receive confirmation that your computer has the capability to communicate with the selected computer. A small green icon will be displayed if the computer is online; otherwise, a red circle with a strike through it indicates the computer is offline.

Another test function is available in MSMQ Explorer by choosing Tools, Send Test Messages from the menu. Next, click the New Queue button. You need to type in the computer and a new queue to create and test. You can now choose Send, and a test message is sent to that computer and queue. Figure 7.10 illustrates this troubleshooting technique.

FIGURE 7.10

A test function is provided with MSMQ Explorer.

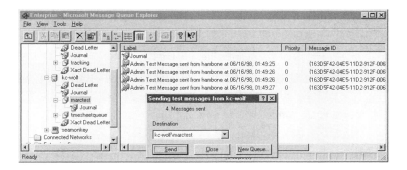

The third utility delivered with MSMQ is called msmqtest.exe. The utility is a C program that can be executed in a DOS command prompt (found in the \Program Files\MSMQ folder). The source code, called msmqtest.c, is also available if you install the Software Development Kit (SDK) for MSMQ. With msmqtest, you can create a queue on the local computer by starting msmqtest in receive mode (msmqtest -r). Now, if you start msmqtest in send mode (msmqtest -s) on any other MSMQ client or server, you will be able to send text messages to computer\queue in receive mode. The name of the queue will always be MSMQTest. The receiver loops infinitely in an attempt to read any message sent to the queue and then prints the value of the Body property to the screen. You can exit the send mode by typing quit. The receiving program can be terminated with Ctrl+C. Figure 7.11 shows several computers sending messages to a receiver.

FIGURE 7.11

MSMQTest is a small sample application useful for trouble-shooting.

```
E:\>cd program files\msmq

E:\Program Files\MSMQ>msmqtest -r

Receiver Mode on Machine: HAMBONE

Waiting for messages...
Message from OK : This is a test message from PC: OK
Message from OK : Are you receiving?
Message from SEAMONKEY : This is a test message from PC: SEAMONKEY
Message from SEAMONKEY : Are you there, Hanbone?
Message from KC-WOLF : This is KC-Wolf. Are the Chiefs ready this year?
Message from KC-WOLF : Over.
^C
E:\Program Files\MSMQ>
```

MQPing is ideal for quickly determining which servers and independent clients are online and available for MSMQ activity. The Send Test Messages method assures you that you have the proper authority to create queues on a remote server or independent client. The msmqtest utility is the only test of the three mentioned that can test proper functionality for a dependent client.

Administering MSMQ

Microsoft has made administration of MSMQ simple. The MSMQ Explorer provides a simple and familiar user interface for users of Windows products. The MSMQ Explorer can be

Part
I

Ch
7

installed on any computer where MSMQ is installed. Therefore, administrators can access their tools whenever and wherever they are needed.

MSMQ Explorer provides the ability to perform some key functions:

- View the MSMQ Enterprise logically, including each MSMQ server or independent client. You can view dependent clients as properties of servers.
- Facilitate configuration of the Enterprise architecture.
- Create and delete queues.
- View the properties of queues, including statistics such as message counts.
- Purge queues of their contents, a process that is valuable for the maintenance of journal queues.
- Alter the security of queues.
- Troubleshoot MSMQ with the `MQPing` and `Send Test Message` functions (described earlier in the chapter in the section "Testing an MSMQ Installation").

N O T E MSMQ Explorer displays up to 20,000 messages for a single queue. If more than 20,000 messages are received, they can be accepted, but they won't be visible in MSMQ Explorer. ▧

Figure 7.12 shows the properties of the Enterprise. MSMQ Explorer is a major reason why MSMQ has been immediately competitive with other MOM products. MSMQ is easier to administer and configure than most.

FIGURE 7.12

MSMQ Explorer displaying the properties of an MSMQ Enterprise.

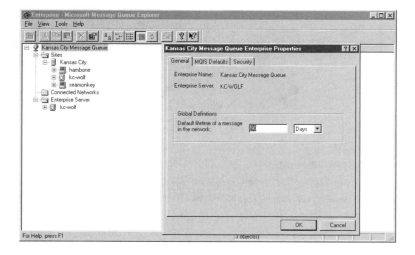

Administrators should keep in mind that they might need more information than can be found in MSMQ Explorer. For example, when troubleshooting an application that uses MSMQ, if the hard disk of the computer reaches capacity, the queues on that computer will no longer be able to accept new messages. Another example is that MSMQ Explorer enables you to examine only connected clients and servers. Disconnected clients and servers are fundamental to the design of MOM applications, and MSMQ administrators have to build tools to cope with that design. Administrators should require the use of troubleshooting tools as fundamental features in enterprise applications, such as specialized application queues that receive messages when clients connect and disconnect. They should insist that application programmers display and log error messages returned from failed MSMQ actions. Administrators should also learn basic network and operating system troubleshooting techniques to be able to examine the health of the systems that host MSMQ servers and clients.

From Here...

MOM should be considered a software infrastructure. Enterprise architects and developers cannot afford to overlook the advantage that this technology can provide to their project teams. If your enterprise uses Microsoft Window 95 and NT heavily, MSMQ will be an excellent product to include in that MOM space. If your environment is mixed, consider the extended product coverage provided by Level 8 Systems.

MSMQ isn't a well-known product, partly because it is relatively new and partly because it is middleware, so you need to stage your design discussions long before the heat of development activities begins. You might have to launch a serious campaign to be sure that your whole team understands the power of the product, endorses the use of MOM, and uses its power in all aspects of application construction. If you are in a position to buy an off-the-shelf application rather than build, put MOM and MSMQ on your shopping list. Applications built with MOM will be more flexible and adaptable in your enterprise.

For examples of how to use MSMQ, see Chapter 32, "Using MSMQ with Visual Basic."

Part

I

Ch

7

An Inside Look at Microsoft SQL Server

*by Don Benage and Eddie
Gulley*

In this chapter

Understanding the Role of the RDBMS

Microsoft SQL Server is the relational database component of the BackOffice family. As a relational database management system (RDBMS), SQL Server is designed to allow organizations to effectively manage information and build powerful database applications for deployment in multiuser networked environments. A developer's edition of SQL Server is included with the Visual Studio development suite. This developer's edition is a full version, which allows SQL Server to be installed and run on Microsoft NT Workstation and is licensed for development purposes only.

The RDBMS is an integral part of most client/server (CS) systems today. An RDBMS is a collection of software components or programs that enables an organization's users and programmers to design, build, and manipulate databases.

Designing the database includes specifying data types, structures, and constraints for the data intended to be stored in the database. These processes are most commonly associated with the physical data modeling tasks in the development life cycle.

Building the database involves the physical storing of data on some storage medium, which is controlled by the RDBMS. Typically this involves the writing of data to the RDBMS server's disk storage subsystem.

Manipulating the database includes querying and updating of data stored in the RDBMS. These tasks are perhaps the most visible to most users of an RDBMS because users and programmers most often identify with the database when they want to get or retrieve data from the database.

SQL Server provides a general-purpose set of applications for end users and programmers to perform database tasks. This allows an organization to take advantage of the RDBMS without having to re-invent the wheel each time a new application is required. Users and programmers can concentrate on the business requirements of their development needs without worrying about writing their own file handlers, query facilities, and other RDBMS features each time.

SQL Server has been developed to support high-volume, online transaction-processing systems (OLTP) as well as to serve as the foundation for newer online analytical processing (OLAP) systems for data warehousing. The management tools and Application Programming Interface (API) libraries provided with SQL Server enable organizations to satisfy even the most challenging development requirements. These tools allow SQL Server to support applications deployed in a traditional CS architecture as well as more modern Internet, intranet, and extranet architectures.

Looking at Microsoft SQL Server

Microsoft SQL Server is based on client/server architecture, which divides processing into two components: a front end, or client component, and a back end, or server component. SQL Server itself constitutes the back-end database server, with which many different front-end client applications communicate, typically over a local area network (LAN). Its built-in data replication, powerful management tools, and open system architecture provide a platform for delivering cost-effective information solutions for organizations of all sizes. SQL Server provides a complete and integrated system of database management software to meet the challenges facing today's organizations when they deploy large-scale distributed information systems.

Microsoft SQL Server is characterized as being a SQL-based, scalable, high-performance RDBMS. SQL Server structures data according to the relational data model, and operations proceed according to the rules of relational algebra, originally put forth by E.F. Codd in 1970. Administrators, users, and application programmers use Transact-SQL (T-SQL) to interact with SQL Server. T-SQL is a Microsoft specific superset of the Structured Query Language (SQL) standard.

N O T E Microsoft SQL Server version 6.5 has been certified by the National Institute of Standards and Technology (NIST) as compliant with the ANSI SQL-92 standard. ■

SQL Server also implements many powerful extensions to the SQL standard. These extensions provide additional functionality within the T-SQL language for such things as more complex SELECT statements as well as extensions for querying data using operators such as CUBE and ROLLUP for data warehousing. T-SQL also contains many common programming language constructs that enable conditional operations and looping and provide the ability to declare and manipulate local and global variables in stored procedures and SQL batches.

SQL Server has been designed to provide for a scalable database server. You can add additional processors to a SQL Server computer (provided the computer you selected supports multiple processors) to achieve performance gains and greater throughput without any significant reconfiguration of SQL Server itself. SQL Server takes advantage of additional processors by utilizing Windows NT's symmetric multiprocessing architectural model.

In the symmetric multiprocessing model, NT schedules individual threads as the basic unit of work. SQL Server is deployed as a single process with a single addressable memory space. SQL Server is able to prepare, execute, and manage user and system tasks as threads inside of its single process. Tasks can then execute simultaneously or in parallel on multiple processors. Some intensive background tasks such as data page scans can even be split across several threads to take advantage of parallel operations.

Microsoft SQL Server has consistently performed well in benchmark testing conducted by the computer industry trade press and various testing laboratories. It is among the top performers available.

As of this writing, the Transaction Processing Council (TPC) has tested Microsoft SQL Server version 6.5, Enterprise Edition, able to process over 16,000 transactions per second.

ON THE WEB

For current benchmarks for SQL Server on a range of machines check out the TPC at http://www.tpc.org/.

Supporting Distributed Transactions

Very often, in CS development, organizations have a need to store data in more than a single data store. In such an environment, SQL Server provides support for transactions that logically and physically must operate on more than one database.

A transaction is a user or system task under SQL Server, such as the updating of a value in a column. A transaction often requires that several SQL commands execute successfully to complete its task. Such transaction support is said to ensure that each transaction maintain its atomicity, consistency, isolation and durability (ACID) properties. For more in-depth coverage of the ACID properties see Chapter 5, "An Inside Look at Microsoft Transaction Server."

SQL Server provides the Distributed Transaction Coordinator (DTC) as a two-phase commit (2PC) protocol implementation to ensure that all transactions in a distributed environment maintain their ACID properties. A full discussion of 2PC is beyond the scope of this book. However, a brief overview will help you to understand the rudiments of this technology and the powerful new components that Microsoft has added to make the use of distributed transactions more practical. This discussion of 2PC is a deliberate simplification designed to help managers and system administrators (SA) understand the role and importance of 2PC in distributed transaction processing.

 For more in-depth coverage of the Distributed Transaction Coordinator, refer to the "Guide to Microsoft Distributed Transaction Coordinator," which is provided with the product.

Sample Transaction Scenario

Assume that you are running an application on a desktop computer that needs to update databases on two SQL Servers as part of a single transaction (see Figure 8.1). Naturally, you want them both updated, or you want the transaction to fail and both servers to be left unchanged. You can try the transaction again later; but most important, the data on each server remains in a consistent state, and the data regarding the proposed transaction also remains consistent. The transaction either happens or it doesn't—all or nothing.

Trying to implement this behavior is harder than it might appear at first. For this technology to be useful, it must continue to work when one or more computers fail at the worst possible moment. Anyone who has used computers for even a short period of time knows that they can and do fail. SQL Servers have the capability to log transactions in a write-ahead log and either commit them or roll them back. Furthermore, this capability is robust enough to handle system failures and power outages. However, this facility alone is not enough to implement distributed transactions.

Suppose that your application has sent update instructions to both databases and is ready to commit the transaction. It could send a commit instruction to the first server (call it A), wait for a confirmation, and then send a commit to B. But what if B, or the communications link between the client and B, fails after A has committed and before B gets the message? The rule has been broken. You didn't achieve an all-or-nothing transaction. You could try sending the commit instruction to both at the same time, but this is really no better.

FIGURE 8.1

A client attempting to work with two SQL Servers as individual entities. The transactional capability of SQL Server alone is not sufficient in this scenario.

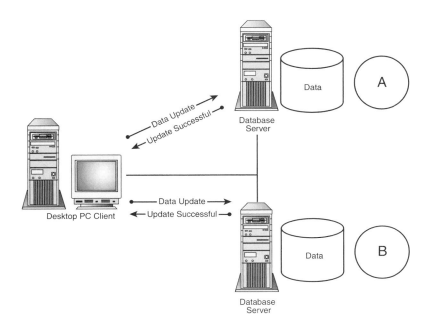

Two additional elements are needed. You must ask your servers to achieve a prepared state in which they can durably commit or roll back. In other words, if the computer fails in the prepared state, it can be restored to the prepared state, still ready to commit or roll back. Additionally, you need a commit coordinator to help this process take place. Of course, the application itself could take on this role, but managing the states of multiple SQL Servers in a durable manner is a lot to expect from a typical application program.

With these additional elements, the following process can occur (see Figure 8.2). When an application is ready to commit its updated information, it notifies the coordinator. The coordinator instructs the SQL Servers to prepare to commit. They each attempt to adopt the prepared state. If one (or both) fails, the coordinator records in a log that the transaction has failed and advises both servers to roll back the transaction. A failed server checks with the coordinator when it is running again and finds out that the transaction should be rolled back. The coordinator also can recover from a failure and remember the status of the pending transaction.

If both servers report that they have successfully prepared, the coordinator records that the transaction should commit and advises both servers to commit the transaction. If a server or communications link fails at this point, all three components (the two SQL Servers and the coordinator) are able to restart and achieve the prepared state again. The coordinator's log reminds them all to commit the transaction. If the commit takes place (as it usually does), the application has successfully completed a distributed transaction.

FIGURE 8.2

A distributed transaction using 2PC protocols. The transaction coordinator is shown as a separate machine for clarity, but could actually be implemented on one of the database servers.

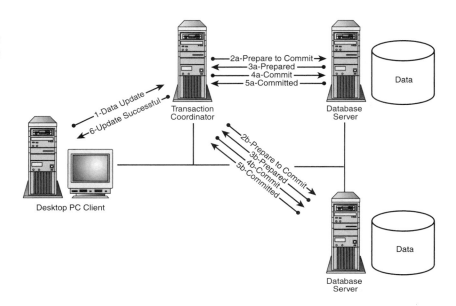

A full analysis of all the possible failures that could occur, at all the worst times, requires a good deal of thought. For this discussion, suffice it to say that the 2PC mechanisms described provide a reliable and automatic problem resolution in most failure situations. A few conditions still require human intervention, however. One such case is an extended outage of a server or communications link that leaves elements in the databases locked. If the locked element is a table of all available rooms at a hotel, the front desk personnel will undoubtedly expect the situation to be resolved quickly.

The Role of the DTC in Transaction Processing

SQL Server has included support for the 2PC protocol in the past. Application Programmers using the C/C++ programming languages could access 2PC functionality by using the DB-Library interface provided by Microsoft for developing SQL Server applications. Procedures were provided on servers that allowed them to take on the role of commit coordinator.

DTC adds important new components to help implement distributed transactions and make the management of 2PC a practical undertaking. Each server has a full DTC service that coordinates transactions with other servers. Using the DTC, a server can take on the role of commit coordinator for certain transactions. In addition, the DTC can help resolve a problem (or indoubt) transaction by communicating with other DTC services running on other servers involved in a transaction.

A client-side interface to DTC is available for Windows NT and Windows 95/98 computers. This interface allows developers to create applications using distributed transactions and leverage the facilities provided by the full DTC service running on SQL Servers. The client components of DTC do not include a full DTC service, even on Windows NT clients. Also, the DTC client is available only for 32-bit versions of Windows (Windows 95/98 and Windows NT).

TIP It is possible for a stored procedure running on an SQL Server to launch a distributed transaction on behalf of a 16-bit client. Therefore, older Windows clients can still benefit from DTC functionality.

In addition, a set of management utilities has been added to SQL Enterprise Manager. The utilities include graphical tools that allow you to dynamically monitor the state of transactions on SQL Servers running the DTC service. You can open multiple windows to monitor transaction occurring on multiple servers from a single workstation. The DTC extensions to SQL Enterprise Manager also allow an administrator to manually resolve problem transactions arising from equipment or application failure.

N O T E Although SQL Enterprise Manager can be run on Windows 95, the DTC utilities are available only when using SQL Enterprise Manager on a Windows NT computer.

For application developers, DTC offers new tools to support distributed transactions. A new statement in T-SQL, BEGIN DISTRIBUTED TRANSACTION, allows the creation of stored procedures that use DTC to coordinate transaction execution on multiple servers. This dramatically simplifies the development of stored procedures involving remote servers. In addition, an API for C/C++ programmers that conforms to the OLE Component Object Model (COM) has been provided for DTC. Using this interface, an application developer can create transaction objects and enlist the services of transaction resource managers and transaction coordinators to process those objects.

At this point, Microsoft SQL Server is the only available resource manager, but a COM Transaction interface definition has been published. Some level of interoperability is offered with several existing transaction middleware products including TUXEDO, and particularly with Microsoft Transaction Server (MTS) 2.

▶ For more information on MTS 2, **see** Chapter 5, "An Inside Look at Microsoft Transaction Server," **p. 107**

Managing DTC with SQL Enterprise Manager

The DTC server components are installed automatically when you set up SQL Server 6.5. You can start the DTC service just like any other service using the Control Panel on the local computer, or using the Services dialog box in the Server Manager utility provided with Windows NT Server. You also can start the service using the SQL Server Manager or SQL Enterprise Manager.

The rest of this section focuses on the DTC capabilities added to SQL Enterprise Manager. This administrative tool has been enhanced with functionality to completely monitor and manage DTC capabilities. To start the DTC service with SQL Enterprise Manager, follow these steps:

1. Start SQL Enterprise Manager.
2. In the Server Manager window, open a server group and select the server you want to manage.

3. If the SQL Server service is not running on the server, click the Services button—the one that looks like a stoplight—on the toolbar. The SQL Server Manager dialog box appears.

4. Click the green Start/Continue portion of the stoplight control. When SQL Server starts, click the Done button.

5. Now click the plus sign to the left of the server name. The services and objects on the server are listed.

6. Right-click the DTC icon. It is typically listed just below the SQL Executive icon and labeled Distributed Transaction Coordinator. Select Start from the pop-up menu. After a brief pause, the icon turns green to indicate the service has started.

The DTC Configuration dialog box allows you to control the behavior of the DTC service. You can configure parameters that affect viewing transactions in the Transactions window, the tracing information sent to the Trace window, and the location and size of the DTC log file. To configure the DTC service, follow this procedure:

1. Start SQL Enterprise Manager.

2. In the Server Manager window, open a server group and select the server you want to manage. If SQL Server and the DTC service are not running, start the services.

3. Right-click the DTC icon. Select Configure from the pop-up menu. The DTC Configuration dialog box appears, as shown in Figure 8.3.

FIGURE 8.3
Use this dialog box to configure the displays that monitor the Distributed Transaction Coordinator service and its behavior.

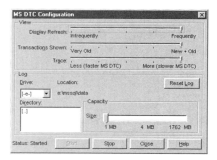

4. Using the Display Refresh slider bar, you can configure DTC to update the display at intervals from 1–20 seconds with a default value of 5 seconds. Updating the display more frequently adds administrative overhead to transaction processing and can cause reduced performance.

5. The older a transaction, the more likely that it will have difficulty completing. The Transactions Shown slider controls how old a transaction must be before being displayed in the Transactions window. You can set values from 1–5 minutes.

6. The Trace slider controls how much trace information is sent to the Trace window. You can specify no tracing, increasing levels of error, warning and informational traces, or all trace information.

7. You can change view settings while the DTC service is running. To change log settings, you must stop the DTC service. You can then change the location and size of the log.

To view the status of active transactions, follow these steps:

1. Start SQL Enterprise Manager.
2. In the Server Manager window, open a server group and select the server you want to manage. If SQL Server and the DTC service are not running, start the services.
3. Right-click the DTC icon. Select Transaction from the pop-up menu. A DTC Transactions window for the selected server appears (see Figure 8.4).

FIGURE 8.4

A DTC Transactions window for the server ARAGON. There is one active transaction.

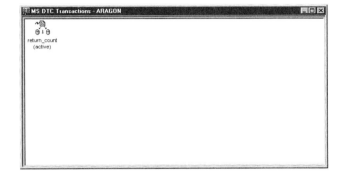

4. You can select another server and open a transactions window for it, as well. It is possible to monitor the transactions on a number of servers simultaneously using tiled or cascaded windows.
5. In the transactions window, you can monitor transaction states and manually resolve in-doubt transactions (see Figure 8.5).

FIGURE 8.5

You can manually resolve in-doubt transactions by right-clicking the transaction in the transactions window and selecting the appropriate action.

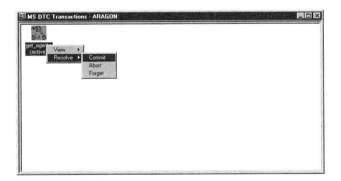

CAUTION

You should not manually force transactions until you thoroughly understand the interaction of all members of a DTC system. Review the "Guide to Microsoft Distributed Transaction Coordinator" carefully before using this utility to resolve transactions.

To view the traces being sent (at the level you configured DTC to provide), follow these steps:

1. Start SQL Enterprise Manager.
2. In the Server Manager window, open a server group and select the server you want to manage. If SQL Server and the DTC Service aren't running, start the services.
3. Right-click the DTC icon. Select Trace from the pop-up menu. A DTC Traces window for the selected server appears.
4. You can select another server and open a traces window for it, as well. It is possible to monitor traces from a number of servers simultaneously using tiled or cascaded windows.

A DTC service maintains statistical information about its performance. To view the statistics that have accumulated for a DTC service, follow these steps:

1. Start SQL Enterprise Manager.
2. In the Server Manager window, open a server group and select the server you want to manage. If SQL Server and the DTC service aren't running, start the services.
3. Right-click the DTC icon. Select Statistics from the pop-up menu. A DTC Statistics window for the selected server appears, as shown in Figure 8.6.

FIGURE 8.6

A DTC Statistics window for the server ARAGON.

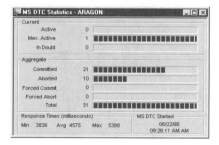

 TIP The statistics for a DTC service are cleared and restarted whenever the DTC service is stopped and restarted.

Exploring Integration with Web Technologies

The Internet today has grown from relatively static informational pages to become an extended platform for hosting robust transactional systems. Microsoft SQL Server has proven to be a solid back end in the new, more distributed CS model known as the Internet. Just as with the older CS model, users of Web interfaces require access to the relational database already pervasive in our organizations.

Intranet applications are being built that extend and often replace traditional LAN-based applications. Extranets are being developed that enable users to transact business online with their business partners and customers. Internet-wide applications are being built which not only extend but also create totally new lines of business and opportunities through true electronic commerce.

Visual Studio 6 provides many tools and technologies to integrate SQL Server with these new applications. The role of SQL Server hasn't changed much in this new model, but its importance has certainly been reinforced as more and more organizations move to the Internet as a way of doing business.

With Visual Studio you are able to use SQL Server as the back end to your Web environment. CS applications can use SQL Server to generate static data on HTML pages or to serve as the transaction processing engine behind an electronic storefront.

SQL Server and Visual Studio are integrated in various ways, but the more important integration features are of two varieties: native SQL Server tools and procedures and SQL Server programmable interfaces or data access libraries, such as OLE DB, provided "in the box with Visual Studio 6. OLE DB makes SQL Server available as a data provider to traditional CS applications as well as Microsoft's Active Platform technologies including Active Server Pages (ASP) and MTS through COM/DCOM interfaces.

Web Integration with the SQL Web Assistant and `sp_maketask`

Web developers often have a need to publish data that doesn't change very often but does so on a predictable basis. The requirement to request data from SQL Server dynamically might not make sense in such cases. Simple price lists, event schedules, employee listings, and other data that doesn't have to be absolutely current can be scheduled to query SQL Server and write an HTML page of resultsets.

Included with SQL Server 6.5 are three new system stored procedures: `sp_makewebtask`, `sp_runwebtask`, and `sp_dropwebtask`. The `sp_makewebtask` stored procedure allows you to define tasks in SQL Server that take a T-SQL query(s) or stored procedure and output the resulting data to a static HTML page. The resulting task is manageable with the SQL Executive task manager.

The `sp_runwebtask` allows you to run a previously created Web task and the `sp_dropwebtask` allows you to drop a previously created Web task from your database and the SQL Executive.

Also included with SQL Server 6.5 is the SQL Web Assistant. The SQL Web Assistant is a utility that essentially wraps the functionality of the sp_makewebtask in an easy-to-use graphical application wizard. This alleviates the necessity for the developer to enter all the possible parameters required and options for the sp_makewebtask stored procedure.

This section is devoted to an overview of how to use the SQL Web Assistant. For the overview, a sample table structure has been created using the following Data Definition Language (DDL) script.

```
CREATE TABLE dbo.Course (
    CourseID int IDENTITY (1,1) NOT NULL ,
    Name varchar (255) NOT NULL ,
    Holes int NULL ,
    Yardage int NULL ,
    Par int NULL ,
    CONSTRAINT PK_Course PRIMARY KEY  NONCLUSTERED
    (
        CourseID
    )
)
GO

CREATE TABLE dbo.Fees (
    FeeID int IDENTITY (1, 1) NOT NULL ,
    Amount money NULL ,
    Description varchar (255) NULL ,
    ShortDesc varchar (15) NULL ,
    CourseID int NULL ,
    CONSTRAINT PK_Fees PRIMARY KEY  NONCLUSTERED
    (
        FeeID
    ),
    CONSTRAINT FK_Fees_Course FOREIGN KEY
    (
        CourseID
    ) REFERENCES dbo.Course (
        CourseID
    )
)
GO

CREATE TABLE dbo.Location (
    LocID int IDENTITY (1, 1) NOT NULL ,
    Address1 varchar (45) NULL ,
    Address2 varchar (45) NULL ,
    Address3 varchar (45) NULL ,
    City varchar (50) NOT NULL ,
    State char (2) NOT NULL ,
    CourseID int NULL ,
    CONSTRAINT PK_Location PRIMARY KEY  NONCLUSTERED
    (
        LocID
    ),
    CONSTRAINT FK_Location_Course FOREIGN KEY
    (
```

```
        CourseID
    ) REFERENCES dbo.Course (
        CourseID
    )
)
GO

CREATE TABLE dbo.TelePhone (
    TelephoneID int IDENTITY (1, 1) NOT NULL ,
    CourseID int NOT NULL ,
    AreaCode char (3) NOT NULL ,
    PhoneNumber char (7) NOT NULL ,
    Extension char (10) NULL ,
    Description varchar (255) NULL ,
    CONSTRAINT PK_TelePhone PRIMARY KEY  NONCLUSTERED
    (
        TelephoneID
    ),
    CONSTRAINT FK_TelePhone_Course FOREIGN KEY
    (
        CourseID
    ) REFERENCES dbo.Course (
        CourseID
    )
)
GO
```

The following script creates a stored procedure to access the sample Golf database. The sp_GetCourseFees stored procedure will be used as the source of the query for the Web task to be created with the SQL Web Assistant:

```
Create Procedure sp_GetCourseFees As
set nocount on

select
    substring(c.name, 1, 20) "Course Name",
    substring(l.city, 1, 15) City,
    l.state State,
    f.shortdesc "Fee Desc.",
    f.amount "Fee Amount"
from
    course c,
    location l,
    fees f
where
    c.courseid = l.courseid
and
    c.courseid = f.courseid

set nocount off
return
GO
```

N O T E The SQL Server Web Assistant is installed by default along with SQL Server 6.5. It is included with Server installations of the SQL Server DBMS as well as with the client-side utilities installation. ▪

To start the SQL Web Assistant from the Start Menu, choose Programs. Then from the Microsoft SQL Server 6.5 program group, choose Microsoft SQL Server Web Assistant. If the SQL Server Web Assistant isn't available from your program group, double-check your SQL Server installation.

After you have successfully started the Web Assistant, you will be presented with the login dialog, as shown in Figure 8.7.

FIGURE 8.7

The SQL Server Web Assistant supports both integrated and SQL Server standard login security.

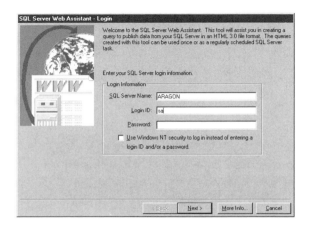

At the login dialog you must enter the name of the SQL Server upon which you want to create the Web task and enter a user ID and password for standard security logins. For integrated NT security logins, check the NT security checkbox and the SQL Server Web Assistant will use your NT user ID and password to log in to the SQL Server. Obviously, any user ID and password account you use with the SQL Server Web Assistant requires that the account have appropriate permissions to access any data required by the query to be used as well as for managing SQL Executive tasks.

N O T E The SQL Server security model is broken down into three modes: Integrated, Standard, and Mixed. With Integrated Security, SQL Server uses Windows NT's authentication services for login validation for all connections. Only trusted connections are allowed when using Integrated Security. Standard Security uses SQL Server's own login process. Mixed Security allows SQL Server to service login requests based on whether the requesting connection is trusted. Under Mixed Security, SQL Server uses Integrated for trusted connections and Standard for nontrusted connections. ▪

After successfully logging in to your SQL Server, you will be presented with the Web Assistant's query selection dialog. This dialog allows you to select whether you want the web task to be based on one of three query types: a T-SQL free form query, a stored procedure, or the output from a graphical database hierarchy selection dialog which acts as an ad-hoc query writer.

If you choose to base your Web task on a database hierarchy, select the tables and columns to include in your select list as well as any additional criteria you might need, such as constraints order by clauses.

An example of the graphical hierarchy dialog is shown in Figure 8.8.

FIGURE 8.8
The Web Assistant provides the option to base your query on a graphical hierarchy.

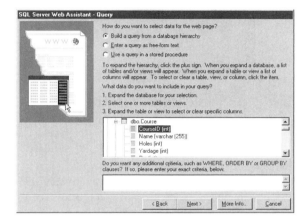

If you choose to base your query on a free-form T-SQL query, you will need to enter a valid T-SQL query in the provided text box as well as choose which database you want to query. Figure 8.9 shows the dialog for a free-form text query.

FIGURE 8.9
Just enter a valid T-SQL statement to base your Web task on a free-form text query.

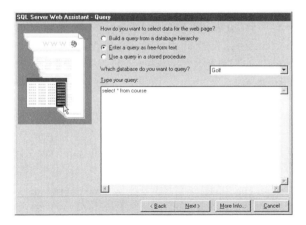

To base your query on an existing stored procedure, select the option to do so. You will then be required to select the database you want to query, as well as an existing stored procedure to use. After you have done so, the stored procedure text will be displayed in a text box. You can specify any input parameter arguments to the stored procedure by using the provided text box. Figure 8.10 shows the dialog for basing your Web task on a stored procedure.

FIGURE 8.10

The dialog shows that you have selected to query the Golf database using the sp_GetCourseFees stored procedure and you will be specifying no arguments.

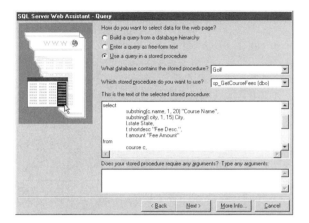

After you have successfully specified how to query data for your Web task, you must specify how to schedule it. The scheduling dialog allows you to decide when your task will run and therefore, when it will refresh the static data on your Web page. The scheduling dialog for the SQL Server Web Assistant has many options for scheduling your task. The following outlines the possible scheduling options and lists the possible criteria to specify on the dialog for each chosen scheduling option:

- Now—The task executes upon clicking the finish button on the final dialog of the SQL Server Web Assistant.

- Later—The task executes at a specified date and time in the future.

- When Data Changes—The task executes upon data changing in a particular table, or column(s) you select using a graphical object hierarchy on the scheduling dialog.

- On Certain Days of the Week—The task executes on days of the week at a specified time you choose on the dialog.

- On a Regular Basis—The task executes a specified number of hours, days, weeks or minutes.

For the sample I have chosen to execute the task On Certain Days of the Week—specifically on Mondays at 4:00, as shown in Figure 8.11.

After your Web task is scheduled, you must specify what file options you require for your Web page. Figure 8.12 shows the dialog where you tell the SQL Server Web Assistant what filename to use, which template if any to use, what your page and query tables will be titled and whether or not to include additional hyperlinked uniform resource locator (URL) addresses and reference text. You can enter a single URL and reference text or choose to enter a list of URLs and text.

FIGURE 8.11

The dialog shows that you have selected to schedule your Web task to run on Monday mornings at 4:00 am. Yes, the scheduler is based on a 24-hour clock.

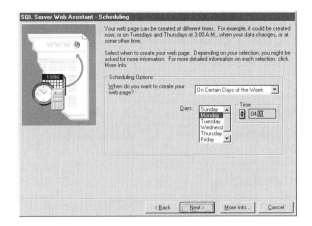

FIGURE 8.12

The File Options page allows you to specify file-based parameters for your Web task.

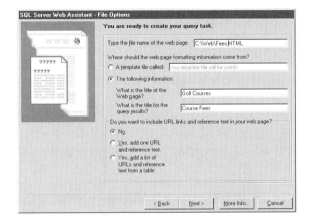

N O T E To learn more about creating template files to merge your task results into, read the SQL Server Web Assistant topic in the "What's New in 6.5" section of the SQL Server Books Online.

After you have your file setup, the SQL Server Web Assistant provides a dialog to specify formatting parameters for your Web task. Figure 8.13 shows the formatting dialog. You can select which HTML header style to use for your results table's title, what font to use for your results, whether to insert an updated date/time stamp on your results page, and whether to include column and view names for your results.

FIGURE 8.13

Limiting the query results to a number of rows option could save your growing database from becoming a bottleneck to your Web site.

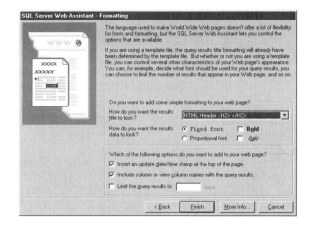

You can also specify a maximum number of rows of data to return from your task. This could prevent a database that has grown from becoming a bottleneck for your Web site. If you find that your database has grown so large that you need to limit the number of data rows to display on static Web pages, you might need to move to a more dynamic data access scheme. Such a scheme would allow a user to enter search parameters to be passed in as constraints for a query to limit the resultsets to only what the user wants to see.

After you have finished with the SQL Server Web Assistant, your task is created, and you can view it and change its execution schedule as needed through the SQL Executive task scheduler. A complete explanation of managing tasks with the SQL Executive is beyond the scope of this chapter, but Figure 8.14 shows the Manage Scheduled Tasks window in the SQL Enterprise Manager.

FIGURE 8.14

The SQL Executive's Manage Scheduled Tasks window can be used to manage your newly created Web task.

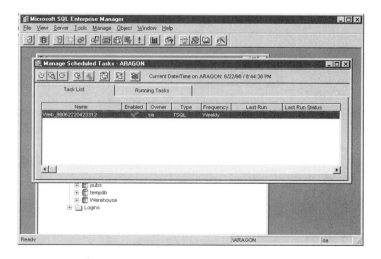

You can also test your task by performing a right mouse click on the task in the Manage Scheduled Tasks window. From the pop-up menu choose <u>R</u>un to execute your task immediately.

A sample run of your task results in the Web page shown in Figure 8.15.

FIGURE 8.15
The sample Web task as a finished, static HTML page.

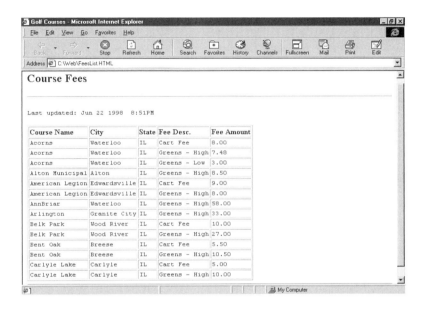

As you have seen, Microsoft SQL Server can play a role in rapidly creating data-driven Web pages for your Internet site. With the flexible scheduling options provided with the SQL Executive, static data pages can be as up-to-date as you choose.

SQL Server Web Integration with External Data Access Libraries

As your Web data access needs grow beyond the relatively static requirements satisfied with the SQL Web Assistant and associated stored procedures, Visual Studio provides you with an almost unlimited variety of ways to request, display and transact business with SQL Server.

Rather than try and provide an extensive survey of the ways to integrate SQL Server with the Web, this section gives you a quick overview of a high-level architecture that allows you to create database-driven Web sites. Some additional references to other chapters will be included for more in-depth information on using Visual Studio to create these architectural components.

Figure 8.16 represents a high-level model of how SQL Server can be integrated with other components included in the Microsoft Active Platform, such as the BackOffice family.

FIGURE 8.16
SQL Server is a vital component in today's Web-enabled world.

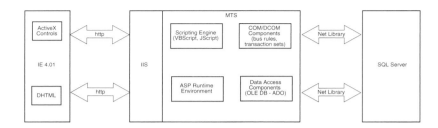

As you can see from Figure 8.16, SQL Server in an Internet architecture using Internet Information Server (IIS) isn't much different from traditional CS systems. The client now, rather than connecting directly to the database server, uses a browser to request ASPs which might invoke server-side scripts. The server-side scripts can access and use data stored in SQL Server through dynamic link libraries (DLLs), which use Active Data Objects (ADO), and data access libraries; this allows connection and query capabilities through all the Visual Studio development tools.

All the Visual Studio development tools—including Visual C++ 6, Visual Basic 6, Visual InterDev 6, and Visual J++ 6—can create COM and DCOM components that provide transactional capabilities with the MTS environment.

▶ For an overview of Microsoft's data access strategy with Visual Studio, **see** Chapter 4, "Creating Database-Aware Applications with Visual Studio," **p. 77**

▶ To find out more about MTS and IIS, **see** Chapter 5, "An Inside Look at Microsoft Transaction Server," **p. 107**, and Chapter 6, "An Inside Look at Active Server Pages and the Internet Information Server," **p. 137**

For an introduction to Web development with all the Visual Studio tools, review Part III, "Developing Internet, Intranet, and Extranet Applications."

After you have a better understanding of how to develop Web applications, you can try more advanced Web architectures with the techniques presented in Part IV, "Developing Scalable Distributed Applications." This section provides insight into building mission-critical applications to handle the often unknown and varying user volumes associated with the Internet.

Using SQL Server and Data Warehousing

Beyond the current demand for SQL Server for traditional OLTP applications and newer electronic-commerce applications on the Internet, data warehousing is another area in which the Microsoft database product provides a great choice. SQL Server provides many query optimization features, and even T-SQL extensions, to support data warehousing.

Depending on the approach you take to data warehousing, SQL Server can offer a complete solution when it comes to the data storage needs of your warehouse. SQL Server can be used in smaller data marts as well as in enterprisewide data warehouses. Before I get into details of data warehouse specific features of SQL Server, I'll take a look at what a warehouse is and the role SQL Server can play in the warehouse.

SQL Server's Role in Warehousing

Without trying to define the industry, this section outlines an implementation using SQL Server. Figure 8.17 shows a reference model of a data warehouse architecture using SQL Server and the Microsoft Repository included with Visual Studio 6.

FIGURE 8.17

SQL Server is a great platform for hosting the latest in data warehousing technologies. Here SQL Server and the Microsoft Repository play key roles in the data warehouse.

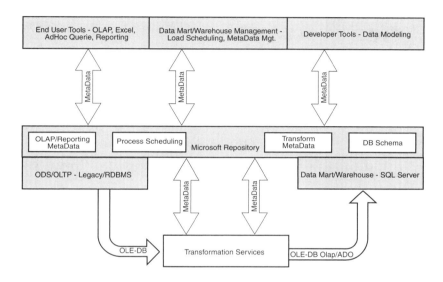

Very quickly, Table 8.1 serves as a glossary for the perhaps unfamiliar terms contained in Figure 8.17. The terms themselves are still somewhat evolving in the warehousing industry and you might very easily find other definitions.

Table 8.1   Component Definitions

Component Name	Definition
MetaData	Data about data. Often used in data warehousing to isolate the star schema from OLAP/query applications, data transformation processes, developer case tools and for storing information about data source files and for management task scheduling.
Operational Data Store (ODS)	An interim data store. Contains operational snapshots of more detail than that typically contained in a data mart/warehouse. Often used as staging area for loading the star schema.
Data Mart	Related collection of data designed to meet the needs of an individual line of business or department. Often contains more detail than the enterprise data warehouse.

continues

Table 8.1 Continued

Component Name	Definition
Data Warehouse	Collection of integrated, subject-oriented databases used for decision support purposes. Often consists of rolled-up aggregates of Data Mart detail or aggregates.
Transformation Services	Processes involved in analyzing, consolidating, cleansing, translating, and validating data before loading a data mart/warehouse.

Microsoft SQL Server, in this model, serves multiple roles. It serves as the physical storage engine for the data mart/warehouse schema, as an existing OLTP or operational data store (ODS), and as the host database for the Microsoft Repository persistent storage.

▶ For more on the Microsoft Repository, **see** Chapter 33, "Using the Visual Component Manager and the Microsoft Repository," **p. 941**

For the purposes of this section I will concentrate on the role most associated with warehousing: the data mart/warehouse data store. SQL Server provides an optimal platform for decision-support–type queries, and as the store for the multidimensional modeling approach used for relational online analytical processing (ROLAP).

Although the SQL Server storage engine and query optimizer are well suited for the performance demands placed on them by high-data volume decision support queries, it is often practical to rethink the way you model your data in a data mart or warehouse. Traditional data-modeling techniques are centered around the normalization of data or the driving out of redundancy to optimize transaction processing.

In *transaction processing* the user often needs to query or manipulate individual data records or transactions to accomplish their work. Small sets of data are involved so the OLTP data model is structured to make small data requests or updates occur in a timely fashion. The partitioning of data across multiple tables with relationships to drive out redundancy is the normal way to model such systems.

In *decision support*, or OLAP queries, there are no manipulations of the data by users. Users place heavier demands on the retrieval of data through queries that might have to scan tables with millions or even billions of rows of data and aggregate certain fields across multiple years of history. Obviously then, databases must be structured for data query speed and allow for the preaggregation of data.

The *multidimensional* (MD), or Star Schema, approach to data modeling is a common technique for modeling your data for OLAP purposes. The Star Schema, conceptually invented by Ralph Kimball, is a great fit for SQL Server in that it allows a RDBMS normally associated with relational modeling to store a physical representation of a multidimensional model of your data.

Figure 8.18 shows a sample star schema data model. Notice that there are two types of tables: a fact table and dimension tables. The fact table is the table named fctFacts, and the dimension tables are those labeled dmn*TableName*.

FIGURE 8.18

The multidimensional data model is optimized for OLAP-type queries.

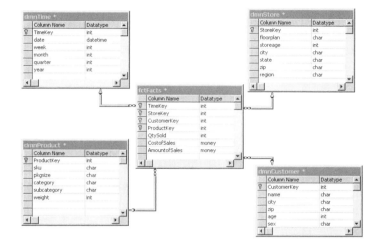

As you can see, the MD model is a bit different from our normal relational model. The design goal behind the star schema is to separate your data into numeric measurements and textual descriptions. The facts like quantity sold or QtySold in the model are the numeric measurements of your business. These facts are the things that you measure to determine your operational performance in your organization. The dimensions in the dimension tables serve to describe the facts. They are separated into tables according to the type of description and which player in your business it is describing, whether that player is your customer, your products, your stores, or your time available to perform your operations.

The time dimension is a special dimension. It's special in that it occurs in almost all MD models. It gives the data mart/warehouse one of their main characteristics: That of being time variant. All measurements in your business happen in relation to events, captured in the time frame in which they happened.

The time dimension is also one of the better dimensions to describe another characteristic of MD data models. The MD model is characterized by allowing users to drill up and down on data. If you look at the dmnTime table in Figure 8.18, you will notice that in addition to the Date field, the time dimension also stores additional descriptive information about the record such as the week, month, quarter, and year the measurement took place. By querying across the dimension you are able to roll up records by aggregates of dimensions.

A quick query as an example will make this a little clearer. The following query is a normal OLAP query for a MD-modeled database:

```
SELECT
    T.Year, P.Category, C.Zip, S.Zip, sum(F.AmountofSales)
    ➥"Sales Amount"
FROM
    dmnTime T, dmnProduct P, dmnCustomer C, dmnStore S, fctFacts
WHERE
    T.TimeKey = F.TimeKey
AND
    P.ProductKey = F.ProductKey
AND
    C.CustomerKey = F.CustomerKey
AND
    S.StoreKey = F.StoreKey
Group By
    T.Year, P.Category, C.Zip, S.Zip
```

With this query in mind, it's easy to envision what drilling up or down means. By changing the query only slightly, such as changing the column in the Time dimension to Quarter, we can drill down to a lower level of detail. This characteristic in MD modeling is important, and you are encouraged to seek out natural hierarchies in your own data to allow this drillable feature.

Another common characteristic used to describe the OLAP query is that of slicing and dicing of data. This concept is a fairly easy one to understand. Take the preceding sample OLAP query and simply remove all references to one of the dimensions such as store. Now you have the same basic query, but without the grouping by store dimension. The store dimension has been sliced out of your resultset.

The MD-modeled database is also practical from a performance standpoint. In typical query optimization you worry about things such as the number and type of joins as well as the index-ing scheme to optimally retrieve and manipulate your data. In the star schema you can basically forget about the performance degradation of performing multiple table joins, and can stick with a consistent indexing scheme.

With the star schema, all your dimensions are keyed by a single field consisting of a 4-byte integer, which is essentially an auto-incremented field. This surrogate key allows you to gener-alize your data identification scheme and isolate it from your production systems, as well as provide you with a nice short integer key to index and join on.

As you will notice in Figure 8.18, the fctFacts table is keyed by its own unique intersection of each of the dimension table's keys. This gives the fctFacts table a composite key with each part being its foreign key back to the individual dimension.

One of the most important considerations to give to the design of your own star schemas is the *grain* of the data or the level of aggregation to store. In larger organizations this is less of a trade-off because they might store detail-level facts in data marts and roll these up to preaggregated facts at the enterprise warehouse level. Just remember that after the grain of the fact table has been determined and loaded, subsequent grain changes filter down to all aspects of the work of extracting, loading, and querying the data.

You have seen that SQL Server, just in its support for the relational concepts, offers a choice in the selection of a data store for your data marts and data warehouses. Now you'll take a look at some built-in features of SQL Server, which extend its usefulness in data warehousing.

T-SQL Extensions: CUBE and ROLLUP

A complete survey of SQL Server and warehouse should cover the two new extensions to the T-SQL language: CUBE and ROLLUP. These two keywords are new with SQL Server 6.5, and act as language extensions for performing OLAP type queries from normal relational database schemas.

CUBE is an aggregate operator, which is meant to serve as an additional option with the GROUP BY clause in a SELECT statement. It serves to further summarize any aggregate function result column in the SELECT statement.

SELECT statements, which group on more than one column, are returned via the CUBE operator with the normal aggregate expected from the GROUP BY clause. Also, every possible combination of summarization among the nonaggregate columns is returned as well.

A brief example will help to illustrate the use of the CUBE operator. The following T-SQL statement selects data from the Golf database found earlier in this chapter. It uses a SELECT statement to pull all golf courses, their location city, and a sum of their fees:

```
SELECT
    substring(C.Name, 1, 12) "Course",
substring(L.City, 1, 12) "City",
sum(F.Amount) "Fees"
FROM
    Course C, Location L, Fees F
WHERE
    C.CourseID = L.CourseID
AND
    C.CourseID = F.CourseID
GROUP BY
    C.Name,    L.City
WITH CUBE
```

The resultset returned from the demo query looks like the following:

```
Course       City         Fees
------------ ------------ ------
Acorns       Waterloo     18.48
Acorns       (null)       18.48
Alton Munici Alton        8.50
Alton Munici (null)       8.50
American Leg Edwardsville 17.00
American Leg (null)       17.00
AnnBriar     Waterloo     58.00
AnnBriar     (null)       58.00
Arlington    Granite City 33.00
Arlington    (null)       33.00
Belk Park    Wood River   37.00
Belk Park    (null)       37.00
Bent Oak     Breese       16.00
Bent Oak     (null)       16.00
Carlyle Lake Carlyle      15.00
Carlyle Lake (null)       15.00
(null)       (null)       202.98
```

```
(null)       Alton        8.50
(null)       Breese      16.00
(null)       Carlyle     15.00
(null)       Edwardsville 17.00
(null)       Granite City 33.00
(null)       Waterloo    76.48
(null)       Wood River  37.00

(24 row(s) affected)
```

As you can see, the CUBE operator returns all possible permutations of the aggregate with the select GROUP BY clause. You not only get totals for each course, as you would with this query without the CUBE operator, but you also receive totals for all course fees in each city as well as a total for all fees for all courses which meet the constraint criteria. The CUBE operator is often called an n-dimensional operator in that the more nonaggregate columns you specify in your query, the more dimensions it creates the summarized aggregates for. This is a feature of most OLAP query products.

The CUBE operator can be very powerful as the source for OLAP-type report generation. The resultset can be parsed as you desire and data presented in any tabular or other layout you desire.

The ROLLUP operator is another aggregate-type function which acts on GROUP BY results in a SELECT statement. It also is an extension to the SQL language provided with T-SQL in SQL Server 6.5.

A quick example demonstrates how ROLLUP operates on your data. After again using the Golf database from earlier in this chapter, the following T-SQL statement will use the ROLLUP operator:

```
SELECT
    substring(C.Name, 1, 12) "Course", substring(L.City, 1, 12)
    ➥"City", sum(F.Amount) "Fees"
FROM
    Course C, Location L, Fees F
WHERE
    C.CourseID = L.CourseID
AND
    C.CourseID = F.CourseID
GROUP BY
    C.Name,    L.City
WITH ROLLUP
```

The resultset returned from the demo ROLLUP query is as follows:

```
Course       City         Fees
-----------  -----------  ------
Acorns       Waterloo     18.48
Acorns       (null)       18.48
Alton Munici Alton         8.50
Alton Munici (null)        8.50
American Leg Edwardsville 17.00
American Leg (null)       17.00
AnnBriar     Waterloo     58.00
```

```
AnnBriar      (null)       58.00
Arlington     Granite City 33.00
Arlington     (null)       33.00
Belk Park     Wood River   37.00
Belk Park     (null)       37.00
Bent Oak      Breese       16.00
Bent Oak      (null)       16.00
Carlyle Lake  Carlyle      15.00
Carlyle Lake  (null)       15.00
(null)        (null)       202.98

(17 row(s) affected)
```

As you can see, the main difference with ROLLUP from CUBE is that the secondary nonaggregate columns, City in this example, are not summarized individually as they were with CUBE. ROLLUP provides for less detail and more summarization. It also is a good source for OLAP-type reports.

From Here...

In this chapter, you learned about roles SQL Server can play across your organization. You learned how SQL Server can be the back end for the more traditional CS architectures, as well as its role in more modern distributed Web environments. Finally, you got to see a brief introduction into SQL Server's role in data warehousing.

For more information on the topics covered in this chapter, see the following chapters:

- To learn more about how SQL Server can participate in distributed transaction, see Chapter 5, "An Inside Look at Microsoft Transaction Server."

- For further information on building Web sites with Internet Information Server and Active Server Pages, see Chapter 6, "An Inside Look at Active Server Pages and the Internet Information Server."

- For further information on developing applications for I-net environments, see Part III, "Developing Internet, Intranet, and Extranet Applications."

- For more information on advanced concepts in distributed, mission critical applications, see Part IV, "Developing Scalable Distributed Applications."

- To obtain additional information about using the Microsoft Repository, see Chapter 33, "Using the Visual Component Manager and the Microsoft Repository."

Creating COM Components

Using Microsoft's Object Technologies

by Cameron K. Beattie

In this chapter

In the early days of personal computing, programmers diligently wrote procedural code to create character-based PC applications, knowing that individual users ran separate copies of the program on their own machines. Programmers rarely needed to be concerned about how a program communicated with other code running on the local machine, let alone worry about how their program interacted with other programs running on a remote machine.

Times change quickly. Today, the computing power available from a typical desktop computer can well exceed the computing power of room-size computers of the early days. It's now commonplace for Internet-enabled computers to browse data from hundreds of thousands of computers interconnected around the globe. Now that computers can readily connect to each other, programmers need the tools and a unified architecture that allows them to write modular programs so that they can communicate in a standard, organized fashion. Object technology provides the power to deliver this functionality, and Visual Studio gives you powerful tools to implement it. This chapter gives you a broad overview of the object technology foundation Microsoft has made available for developing Windows applications with Visual Studio.

Object technologies need an underlying framework that can enable complex and interrelated programs to work together in harmony. The object architecture that Microsoft created—called the *Component Object Model*, or simply COM—is the foundation underlying OLE and ActiveX technologies, and it is Microsoft's solution for providing object-to-object communication. With the enhancements of the Distributed Component Object Model (DCOM), this technology provides communication services across networks to objects physically located on different machines.

Object Technology Basics

No matter which Visual Studio programming language you select for your projects, a basic understanding of COM, OLE, and ActiveX is vital for your success. You can still use Visual Studio programming languages to create procedural code, and sometimes that's necessary and appropriate, but doing so can limit the benefits of using an object-oriented design. This chapter focuses on object-oriented foundations shared by all the Visual Studio development languages, and subsequent chapters provide detailed implementation strategies specific to each language.

Benefits of Object-Oriented Software Development

Users of custom corporate computer applications continue to demand more functionality from their aging systems, and they're becoming less patient about waiting for new functions to be implemented. Because legacy computer systems tend to be monolithic collections of original code, maintenance code, integration code, and lingering "quick-fix" code, these applications have become dramatically more difficult and costly to maintain. Changing key sections of these fragile constructions to add new features is fraught with peril, especially if these applications are part of a mission-critical system. To make matters worse, such applications might be documented only sparsely (if at all), and only rarely are any members of the original programming team still working for the company. If you've ever been faced with the task of extending the life of such an application, you know that there must be a better way to build and maintain enterprisewide computer systems. Fortunately, there is.

Suppose that your company, like many companies, has a legacy application that might give unpredictable results for dates beyond the year 1999. Suppose that, rather than be a single massive collection of procedural code, this application was built from functional modules. Each module has a very specific purpose, and calling that module is the only way for the application to perform that specific task. Thus, in this scenario, one dedicated code module has the task of performing all date calculations, and any other module in the entire application relies on that module for any and all date calculations. To test this program's capability to handle dates beyond the year 2000, you have to test only that date-calculation module to see what happens. If it needs repair, you can change the implementation inside the module, test it, and then plug it back into the program to complete your task. If the date storage and retrieval module also poses a problem, you can use a similar procedure to test, repair, and restore that module. Instead of this scenario, however, most companies are paying staggering costs to update hundreds of thousands of lines of legacy code, in some cases line by line.

With the pace of change in today's business world, companies can no longer afford to create systems that can't be updated easily. This modular approach is available now, and you can implement it using the programming tools in Visual Studio.

These magic little modules are known abstractly as *objects*. You can implement computer-modeled objects in software as discrete components that you can create, modify, or reuse as building blocks for complex, enterprisewide applications. Rebuilding existing functionality from scratch is admittedly quite costly and time-consuming. However, after this foundation is in place, a large portion of desired new functionality can be constructed from previously built components, and you no longer have to start from scratch to create each new application.

Imagine how long it would take for new computers to be developed if computer hardware manufacturers had to start from scratch every time they wanted to build a new computer. Many of the components of a new computer don't require changes since the last model was released, so existing components (such as the power supply, video card, network interface card, or modem) are simply reused. Eventually, when new designs are implemented, the new item can easily replace the previous model with perhaps only a modification of that particular interface.

After the computer is sold to a user, upgrading a component is also simplified by this modular approach. Suppose that you want to upgrade to a faster modem. You can select your new modem from a variety of vendors, and any modem supported by your operating system will work just fine. You don't need to worry whether the modem will work because modems have become a commodity with standard interfaces and communication protocols.

Software developers now actively seek the tremendous advantages of component architecture that hardware developers have enjoyed for years. By using component-based software architectures, you can implement object-oriented designs, yet maintain a large degree of language neutrality. This way, corporations can use existing programming talent in any language supported by the object model implemented on their computer platforms. This language neutrality is accomplished by using programming tools that create components compatible at the binary level. This process allows programmers around the globe to independently develop components or entire applications that will properly communicate together, as long as the interfaces defined between them remain consistent. These components might originally be created for internal applications, but they can then be shared within the company or even marketed to other companies with similar needs.

If you aren't already familiar with object-oriented programming, you will likely need to invest some time to learn how to implement this new technology effectively. The effort you spend now to become proficient with this technology will reward you with increased productivity, job satisfaction, and job security.

After your development team invests the initial time and energy required to become skilled at object-oriented development, the advantages to your company are also worth noting:

- You can reuse many of the objects representing standard business entities and functions, which will reduce the time required to build new programs and the overall cost of maintaining them.
- When maintenance is required, you can easily replace older versions of individual objects with new versions without breaking the application.
- As needs change, you can relocate new objects transparently to new platforms and even to other computers across the network without breaking the applications.
- Large and complex programming projects that seem nearly impossible with other techniques can now be conquered more easily.
- The time and expense required to integrate an existing application with new applications and to perform emergency repairs on applications will gradually decline as more objects are implemented.
- The recovered programmer hours can be redirected toward backlogged projects and new initiatives.

You might be wondering whether your favorite programming language can support object-based application development. A major benefit of COM is that it defines a common binary standard. This means that COM defines an interface as a low-level binary API based on a table of memory pointers, which then enables code modules from different COM-compliant compilers to operate together. Theoretically, you can build a COM-compatible compiler for any programming language that can create memory structures by using pointers, and you can call functions through pointers. Within Visual Studio, Visual C++ and Visual Basic both include COM-compatible compilers.

The result for Visual Studio users is that client objects implemented in Visual Basic can call on the services of server objects written in Visual C++, and vice versa. Each language has certain advantages when creating COM objects, but when used together, they are a powerful combination with which you can tackle nearly any programming challenge you encounter.

A Quick Review of Object-Oriented Programming Terms and Notation

Object-oriented (OO) software development presents a revolutionary improvement in the architecture, tools, and technologies used to build and maintain computer applications. You can choose from a variety of object-oriented methodologies, with most being named for the individuals who proposed them. If you want to investigate them in detail, historically note-worthy object-oriented methodologies include Booch, Coad-Yourdon, Jacobson, Martin-Odell, Rumbaugh, Shalaer-Mellor, and Wirfs-Brock. Despite this array of methodologies, the underlying OO concepts are quite similar. Rational Software Corporation sponsored a significant convergence of OO software development theory by bringing Grady Booch, Ivar Jacobson, and Jim Rumbaugh together to join creative forces. Their collaborative efforts have produced (and continue to refine) the *Unified Modeling Language* (UML), which is rapidly gaining momentum as the industry standard tool set for communicating OO concepts and documenting the artifacts of OO software development. Rational has also produced an OO development methodology called the *Rational Objectory Process*. Others, including Microsoft, are also refining software development methodologies, and there continue to be fresh insights on ways to improve development processes. So even though there are still many ideas about how OO software can be accomplished, at least developers now have a common way to document their OO analysis and design efforts.

ON THE WEB

For more information about Rational's object modeling tools and OO methodologies, visit their Web site at `http://www.rational.com`.

For a comprehensive explanation of the symbols and syntax of the Unified Modeling Language (UML), you can download the current UML specification from: `http://www.rational.com/uml/`.

To preclude any confusion over the meaning of the OO terms used in this book, the following sections give you a brief review of some of the most common terms used in object-oriented software development.

Objects   You can think of a software *object* as an entity that in many ways resembles a physical object. Objects typically have properties that describe their attributes and methods that specify their behavior. *Properties* of objects can be much like properties of physical objects, describing attributes such as color, cost, or size. You can set and lock these properties when designing the program, or you can make them available for users to change during runtime. *Methods* are the named functions or actions that an object is programmed to accomplish when called. Methods are invoked by referencing the object and the method's name. When called, the object behaves as defined by the method to obtain, manipulate, or destroy program data without any requirement to reveal how these tasks are accomplished.

Objects are *portable*, which is to say that they can be relocated and used without modification in any operating environment in which they're supported. Objects are *reusable* because you can use the same object to perform the same task in different programs. Better yet, you can use objects other people have created if you want to quickly add a standard service or function to one of your own programming projects.

For the purpose of object-oriented software development, an individual object is a particular instance created from a particular class of objects. A *class* is a set of objects that you define to have the same attributes and behavior. Classes can be very specific or very general, depending on your needs. For example, you can define a class that encompasses all writing implements, or you can define a class that represents only wooden yellow pencils with No. 2 lead. The *class structure* defines a generic blueprint or model of a new object of that class. Every object belongs to a class and is completely defined by its class structure. To actually bring an object to life in the computer, a specific *instance* of the object must be *instantiated*, which means that a new member of the class is created in memory.

When you define a class in code, you must define all the object's methods, data structures, and interfaces. By default, the methods and data are reserved for the object's exclusive use and are declared as private. If you want to make methods and data available for direct manipulation by other objects, you can declare them as public when you define them in the class structure. Typically, you will define any methods and data you want exposed for clients or used by the user interface as *public* and define the internal elements that implement those services as *private*.

N O T E   C++ programmers have been programming with object classes for years, but the class structure is a relatively new addition to Visual Basic. Support for object classes began with Visual Basic 4 and was further expanded in Visual Basic 5 and 6. As more wizards, integration options, and powerful C++ features (such as classes) have been added to Visual Basic, the stigma against using early versions of VB for anything but simple projects has vanished. Visual Basic is now quite suitable for creating robust and reliable enterprisewide applications.

Object-oriented purists remind us that for an object to qualify as a "true" object, it must support the characteristics of encapsulation, polymorphism, and inheritance. These distinctions are discussed in detail later in the section "OO Advanced Topics."

An object that provides services to another object is acting as a *server*. The object using those services is referred to as the *client*. An object can be a client and a server at the same time—that is, it can request the services of one object while providing services to yet another object. For clarity, it's usually best to focus on a single relationship between two objects at a time, and denote one as the client and the other as the server.

Object Relationships   When trying to design objects, it's handy to have a common method for representing these programming objects graphically. You can use the text syntax `object.method` to denote invoking a particular method of the server object. There are many variations, but Figure 9.1 uses what some refer to as the lollipop type of diagram, which is a typical way to represent an object and its interfaces graphically, and is consistent with UML 1.1. However, UML defines additional enhancements to the basic rectangle to help represent objects in other contexts. Graphically representing memory pointers is outside the scope of UML, but arrows are traditionally used to represent them. A tutorial on UML is beyond the scope of this chapter, and knowledge of UML isn't really necessary for grasping the basic concepts.

FIGURE 9.1

A COM object contains all the methods, properties, and data required by that object.

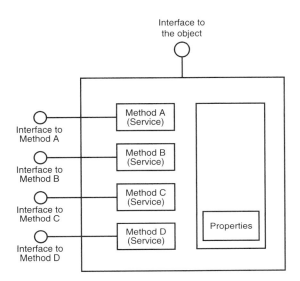

In Figure 9.1, the object is shown as a rectangle. The interface nodes are shown as circles connected to the object or methods by a straight line. Connections to the interfaces are implemented by using memory pointers, which can be drawn as arrows extending from the client object to the interface node of the server object.

When the client and server are operating in the same process space in the computer, the server is referred to as being *in process*, or as an *in-process server*. In-process servers provide the fastest possible service to the client. They are typically objects in the same program, or objects loaded into the same process space ahead of time from an external source such as a dynamic link library (DLL) file. Figure 9.2 shows the relationship between a client and an in-process server.

It's also possible for the server object to operate on the same computer as the client object but in a separate process space. In this situation, the server is called a *cross-process* or *out-of-process server*. Because there are two ways to have an out-of-process server, however, it's more specific to refer to this as a *local server*. For example, your spreadsheet becomes a local server to your word processor when you copy a table of numbers from the spreadsheet and paste it into your word processor. Figure 9.3 shows this relationship.

FIGURE 9.2

This client object has connected to a server object on the same computer and in the same process space, so the server object is acting as a local, in-process server.

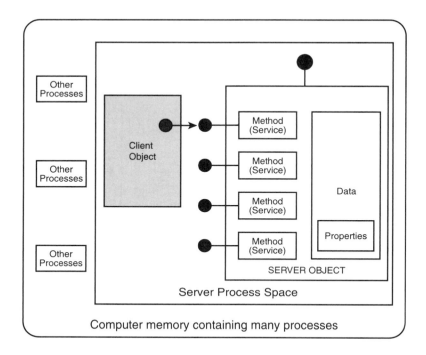

Computer memory containing many processes

FIGURE 9.3

This client object has obtained the services of a server object on the same computer, but outside its process space. In this relationship, this server is a local, out-of-process server.

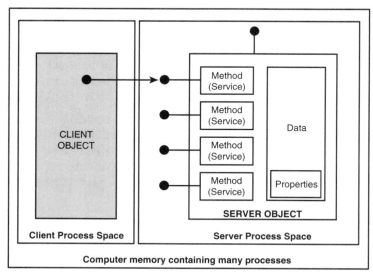

The other way an out-of-process server occurs is when the client and server are on different computers. This once rare situation is rapidly gaining in popularity as objects are distributed across computer networks. The out-of-process object providing the service in this case is called a *remote server*. Performance is typically slower than with in-process or local servers, but the gains in functionality and scalability can be revolutionary, as is highlighted later when discussing distributed computing. Figure 9.4 shows the remote server relationship.

FIGURE 9.4

This client object has obtained the services of a server object on another computer on the network. In this relationship, this server is a remote, out-of-process server.

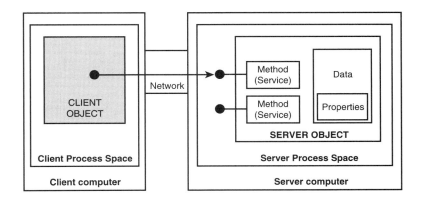

Part
II

Ch
9

You can conveniently group objects that perform very specific tasks in various ways. These object-grouping techniques are an effective way to reuse objects and minimize maintenance.

Perhaps the most straightforward way is to create a new object that can act as a container in which you place the reused objects. This method is referred to as *object containment* because the outer object completely contains the inner objects. The interfaces of the inner objects are visible only to the outer object and can't be accessed directly by external objects. Figure 9.5 depicts this relationship.

FIGURE 9.5

This outer object completely contains or wraps the interfaces and services of the inner objects.

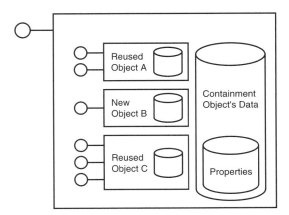

A related grouping method is created by starting with a containment relationship but enabling the outer object to pass along or *delegate* the connecting pointer from the client object directly to the inner object needed to implement the desired function. Referred to as *object delegation*, this relationship is illustrated in Figure 9.6.

FIGURE 9.6

With object delegation, the client object obtains a pointer to the external interface of the server, receives the address of the desired inner object, and then connects directly to the inner object.

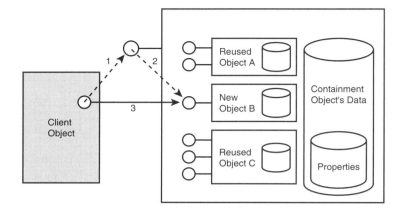

Finally, objects can be collected together, or *aggregated*, by an outer object that enables the inner objects to expose their interfaces directly to client objects. This is perhaps the most complicated case to implement because the clients of the inner objects don't directly see the relationships between the inner and outer objects. This relationship, referred to as *object aggregation*, is shown in Figure 9.7.

FIGURE 9.7

With object aggregation, the client object can directly access the exposed interfaces of each inner object in the server's collection.

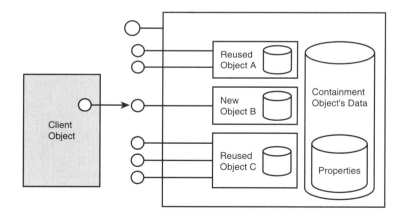

Object-Oriented Versus Procedural Programming

Procedural programming is an approach in which you determine the steps needed to solve a problem and implement them by creating the algorithms in code that act on the data and store the resulting output separately from the algorithms. *Object-oriented programming* is an approach in which you can group a code module's related data and implementation code together into a unified structure, and it acts together in response to requests from other objects. SmallTalk and C-based software development languages have provided this OO capability for years but are extremely cumbersome for all but dedicated experts. Today, with Visual Studio 6, you can use Visual C++, Visual Basic, and Visual J++, separately or in combination, to create robust, enterprisewide object-oriented applications.

OO Software Development Advanced Topics

In object-oriented software development, a discrete combination of code and data must represent each programming object. OO software development also requires a way for client objects to dynamically create new instances of objects based on a given class and to create and destroy server objects as needed while the application is operating. Because some languages accomplish OO objectives more completely than others, many people distinguish between object-oriented languages and object-based languages. *Object-based* languages implement as many of the modular features of object-oriented programming as possible within design constraints that enable simplicity or backward compatibility for that language. For example, although object-based languages such as earlier versions of Visual Basic enabled you to create object-like structures in code, creating another similar object required that you create it at design time, perhaps cutting and pasting code from the first object.

To qualify as a true object, the programming structure must support the characteristics of encapsulation, polymorphism, and inheritance. Entire books have been devoted to this topic, but for the purposes of this chapter, a brief explanation and some simple examples are sufficient to illustrate the basic concepts.

Encapsulation

Encapsulation occurs when the desired services and data associated with an object are made available to the client through a predefined interface without revealing how those services are implemented. The client uses the server object's interfaces to request desired services, and the object performs on command without further assistance. Suppose that you're developing a domestic simulator application. You might want to create a spouse object class in which you define methods for common household tasks, such as methods called WashDishes and MowTheLawn. If a client object (perhaps even another spouse object) determines that it's time to invoke WashDishes, it can make that request via the interface you've appropriately named IWashDishes. The desired result might be that any instantiated Dishes object with a Clean property value now set to False will be cleaned and set to True.

How this method is accomplished is irrelevant to the client. The WashDishes method can be performed with the time-honored Wash in Sink procedure or with any version of the popular Automatic Dishwasher procedure, but the end result will be the same. Similarly, the interface IMowTheLawn will be used to invoke the MowTheLawn method. In this case, the server object might be programmed to trim all Grass objects with a length property of greater than 3 inches down to an even 3 inches. This MowTheLawn method can use the slow but reliable Rotary Mower procedure, the faster Power Mower procedure, or the coveted Riding Mower procedure, but the end result will be the same. In each case, the simulated grass will be an acceptable length, and the requesting client will have no need or desire to know how it got that way.

Objects can even encapsulate their own data from all other objects. By default, an object's data is considered private, and clients must call one of the object's methods to manipulate data or report data values. It's sometimes practical or necessary to expose the data for direct manipulation by client objects, which is accomplished by adding the `public` declaration when you define the object's class structure.

COM fully supports encapsulation, as COM permits a client object to access a server object only through its well-defined interfaces.

Polymorphism

Polymorphism is the capability for different kinds of objects to respond appropriately and differently to the same stimulus. In OO software development, you can see polymorphism as the capability for client objects to access the services of different server objects in the same syntactic manner, even when dealing with different object types.

An illustration will help clarify this concept. Returning to the domestic simulator example, suppose that to make the program more realistic, in addition to the `Spouse` class of objects, you also define object classes representing `Child` and `Dog`. Suppose that you have your program instantiate a spouse object called `Katarina`, a child object called `BabyAlex`, and a dog object called `Rover`. Still trying to make it realistic, you can individually define methods for each object to appropriately simulate the behaviors of walking, eating, sleeping, and speaking. You can then have your program make a call to `Rover.Speak` and compare that result with a call to `Rover.Eat` to see whether Rover's bark is worse than his bite. However, asking the spouse object to speak by making a call to `Katarina.Speak` will give you a dramatically different result than the one produced when you call the dog object to speak. Asking the child object to speak by using `BabyAlex.Speak` might give little or no result until the domestic simulator has run for a sufficient amount of time. Although all these requests are made in exactly the same way—by using the syntax `ObjectName.Speak`—the request produces different results, depending on the object type. This is polymorphism in action.

COM supports polymorphism by enabling different classes of objects to support interfaces with the same name, while enabling these objects to implement the interfaces differently.

Inheritance

Inheritance is the capability to define increasingly more specific objects, starting with the existing characteristic definitions of general objects. Thus, when a more specific class of objects is desired, you can begin the definition by first inheriting all the characteristics of another defined class and then adding to them. Again, an example is useful to help explain this concept.

In the domestic simulator program mentioned previously, suppose you define a class of objects called `Animal` to represent the common attributes of all animals in your simulation. Also suppose that you program the `Animal` class to support characteristics such as breathing and eating. From the `Animal` class, you can create subclasses for `Wild_Animal` and `Pet_Animal`. These two objects will automatically know how to eat, but now you can define that `Pet_Animal` objects will eat only from their food bowls, whereas `Wild_Animal` objects will eat food wherever they find it, including your simulated garden and simulated trash containers. By adding specific characteristics in addition to the common characteristics of the `Pet_Animal` class, you can create classes for `PetDog`, `PetCat`, and any other kind of pet you want to share the house with in your simulation. With all this additional behavior defined in higher-level classes, the polymorphic pet `Rover` can now be instantiated from the `PetDog` class, having completely inherited all the common characteristics defined for a `Pet_Animal` and for `Animal` objects in general.

COM supports *interface inheritance*, the capability for one interface definition to inherit characteristics from another interface. COM, however, doesn't support *implementation inheritance*, the capability for one object to inherit the actual implementation code from another object. Implementation inheritance can be used within each individual COM object because the code is compiled in the same language. Because COM is standardized at the binary level and not the language level, passing the actual implementation code between objects created in different languages will produce unpredictable and potentially disastrous results. This subtle but important difference has sparked an ongoing debate about whether COM truly supports inheritance, and consequently, is truly object-oriented. For comparison, the Common Object Request Broker Architecture (CORBA) specification doesn't require implementation inheritance either, but some CORBA implementations have supported it for certain special cases. In practice, being able to integrate objects created from different development languages is extremely useful and greatly outweighs this one concession to theoretical OO purity.

In the long run, the debate over whether a language is truly object-oriented becomes merely an academic exercise. What matters to you, the programmer, is which characteristics you need for a particular programming project and what language or combination of languages provides the easiest, fastest, and most efficient way to implement them. With Visual C++, Visual Basic, and Visual J++, Visual Studio provides a complete set of object-oriented tools that can accommodate the most simple to the most complex object programming projects.

Progressive Development of Microsoft Object Technologies

In recent years, incredibly rapid progress has been made in advancing the techniques and technologies used for object-oriented programming and modular program communication. These new and improved technologies, with all their new names and integration requirements, have also introduced some confusion to the programming community. A brief look at the incremental steps that brought us to our current state of the art will help clear away some of that lingering confusion.

Microsoft Windows

In the 1980s, if you wanted to do object-oriented programming you could use SmallTalk or C, but programming in those languages was extremely tedious. With the release of the Windows operating system, Microsoft popularized a graphical user interface (GUI) for the personal computer that used a visual object metaphor but didn't fully qualify as object-oriented. The early versions were slow and unstable, but they succeeded in greatly simplifying program-to-program communication via the Windows Clipboard. Users could run more than one program at a time, each in a separate window, and move text or graphics between them by using the clipboard. The interface also enabled you to easily move files and directories simply by dragging and dropping them to new locations.

Although we now take it for granted, being able to copy and paste by using the Clipboard was (and still is) a remarkably handy way to copy data from one document to another. Compound documents were created easily in this manner; unfortunately, it was often difficult to modify the result after the transfer of specially formatted data such as images. To improve the usability of PC applications, Microsoft needed to provide a way for the pasted elements to be edited using the interfaces from their native application environments. To solve this problem, Microsoft created the Dynamic Data Exchange (DDE) protocol, which exchanged data by sending commands between running applications. This was an improvement but was very slow, very difficult to implement, and less robust than if this capability could be provided as a direct service of the operating system.

OLE 1

In 1991, Microsoft improved the object-enabling concept by introducing a technology called object linking and embedding (OLE 1). OLE was a slight improvement to DDE but was still slow and prone to problems because of an underlying architecture that was still a messaging system between applications. On the positive side, OLE-enabled software gave users a more convenient way to store and maintain portions of documents (or entire documents) in a container document. The documents could be from different programs, as long as all the programs were OLE 1 enabled. It was now possible, by double-clicking the embedded portion, to open the document and edit it in its native program's controls without leaving the program used for the container document. For example, you could use OLE 1 to place an Excel spreadsheet within the text of a Word document and edit it within Word. OLE 1 also enabled you to link files so that updates to the original file would be propagated to the linked copies in other documents. OLE 1 became well known, well used, and fairly well understood.

Although this embedding capability was extremely useful, OLE 1 still didn't qualify as a truly object-oriented technology because the data was only referenced from a source file and not encapsulated. If you happened to rename the source data file or move it to a new location on disk, you would also unknowingly render all related OLE links unusable. Perhaps the biggest accomplishment of OLE 1 was that it popularized the idea that documents can act as containers for functional components of other programs.

This modular component strategy also proved quite useful in the development of applications. Microsoft introduced its first version of Visual Basic not so much to pursue the goals of object technology as to simplify application development for the Windows operating system. Visual Basic succeeded in introducing a vast number of programmers to the GUI paradigm, but early Visual Basic programs tended to be more experimental than useful in production environments. These early versions of Visual Basic were acceptable for creating small, specialized programs for single users or small user groups on local area networks (LANs), but didn't provide the performance or scalability required for building large, mission-critical applications.

VBX Components

Visual Basic does have one critical capability most other programming languages lack. Programmers can buy an ever-increasing variety of specialty plug-in components off the shelf from third-party developers. These components, also known as *widgets*, saves tremendous amounts of programmer time and development dollars because programmers can buy (rather than build) many necessary functional pieces for corporate programming projects. It can even be argued that it was the diversity and quality of the secondary add-on component market—not the quality of the base product—that steadily increased the user base and pushed the continuous improvement of Visual Basic.

Because add-on components extended the capability of Visual Basic, they were assigned the .vbx (Visual Basic extension) filename extension and were commonly referred to as VBXs. Although not true objects, VBX components worked extremely well in providing off-the-shelf modular functionality. Although the performance of a VBX component was often disappointingly slow, these modular widgets represented solid progress on the road to better object technologies. As a testament to the versatility and popularity of these widgets, you can still find in use today various niche applications relying heavily on specialized VBX components.

> **CAUTION**
>
> You shouldn't try to use VBX controls with Visual Studio. VBX controls are 16-bit and aren't compatible with the COM-enabled, 32-bit architecture of Visual Studio languages. However, you can still use VBX controls for applications development for Windows 3.1 by using Visual Basic 3 (which is 16-bit) and the 16-bit version of Visual Basic 4.

COM and OLE 2

In 1993, Microsoft created the Component Object Model and laid the technical foundation that has dramatically improved object communication in the Windows environment. COM provided the technical specifications for creating compatible objects and the communication "plumbing" in the Windows operating system required to make it work. The first use of this new programming model came when Microsoft completely rebuilt the OLE functionality by using the new COM architecture. Rather than use a messaging protocol built on top of the operating system (such as DDE or OLE 1), COM provided interprocess communication (IPC) directly as a service of the operating system. Although it was a very different product and approach, Microsoft kept the OLE name, dubbing it OLE 2. OLE 2 eventually provided all the existing features of OLE 1, plus a few more.

With the COM communication architecture, OLE 2.0 could now connect objects outside the process boundaries of an application and could instantly support new versions of objects without changing the source code of the applications that used them. This approach connected binary components actively running in various process spaces. To differentiate this new technology, Microsoft stopped proclaiming that "OLE stands for Object Linking and Embedding" and declared that OLE was no longer an abbreviation; the word *OLE* was the entire name for the technology. OLE is still spelled with all capital letters but is commonly pronounced "olay" instead of "O-L-E."

N O T E With the framework in place to create reusable designs independent of the implementations, COM and OLE 2 architecture can accommodate any new features and technologies
without changing the architecture itself. Many subsequent developments have been built under the OLE
banner, but because of the extensible nature of the OLE 2 architecture, theoretically no technical
reason exists for Microsoft to develop a technology that can properly be named OLE 3. For that reason,
any subsequent mention of OLE in this book without a version number will refer to the OLE 2 set of
technologies.

OCX Components

While the OLE developments were occurring, competition in the visual programming tool
arena was heating up. Borland released the Delphi programming environment, which provided
some serious competition for Visual Basic in the category of simple but powerful GUI development tools. Despite this game of technical leapfrog with the competition, Microsoft continued
to gain market share through an improving product line, brand loyalty from its growing dominance in the desktop suite market, and a highly effective marketing team. Visual Basic advanced from version 3 to version 4, and the 16-bit VBX components were succeeded by OLE-
based 32-bit components called *OLE controls*. Naturally, OLE Controls needed a new name to
distinguish them from their 16-bit VBX predecessors. Microsoft assigned OLE Controls with
the .ocx file extension, and these components became known as OCXs.

OCX components provided modular, 32-bit functionality to all the popular visual programming
languages, including Microsoft Visual C++ and Microsoft Visual Basic. Although OCX components are used in the Visual Basic toolbox just like VBX components had been, OCXs are actually full-fledged COM objects. The process of converting developers from VBX components to
OCX components started gaining significant momentum about the same time that Microsoft
decided to expand the use of the OLE terminology.

The Expanding World of OLE

OLE controls made up one member of a whole family of COM-based technologies renamed
under the OLE banner. Here are the highlights:

- OLE Clipboard—The OLE technology that provides the cut, copy, and paste editor
  functions in the Windows Clipboard.

- OLE visual editing—The OLE technology that enables you to edit, while remaining in
  your current compound document, an object originally created in a different application
  by using the interface and services of that different application. This concept was first
  know as in-place editing and later called in-place activation, before Microsoft renamed it
  Visual Editing and obtained a trademark for the term.

- OLE drag-and-drop—The OLE technology that enables you to select an object from one
  application in the Windows environment and use the mouse to drag it over another
  object and then drop it onto that object. Depending on the behavior defined for the target
  object, the dropped object can be copied, moved, linked, or discarded by using this
  technique.

▒ OLE automation—The Microsoft technology that enables one component to control or automate another application or control. Thus, instead of a component receiving input through the user interface, the component is operated programmatically by another code module. One typical example is allowing your component to access predefined mathematical functions available from an OLE-enabled spreadsheet program such as Microsoft Excel, rather than program them yourself. Like the rest of the OLE components, OLE automation uses the COM architecture to communicate. Of course, the helper program must be installed and available on the user's PC for the OLE automation in your program to function properly.

▒ OLE remote automation—An interim solution for extending OLE automation capability so that it can control objects across machine boundaries. DCOM has encompassed OLE remote automation.

▒ Network OLE and distributed OLE—The names given to the OLE technology that enabled OLE-compatible software components to communicate directly over a network. You can use distributed OLE to perform time-consuming or processor-intensive functions on a network server to relieve the burden on a user's PC. Extensive searches against large databases or complex calculation problems are good candidates for this technology. The idea remains today, but these names and technologies have been encompassed by DCOM.

The confusion over the OLE names was beginning to diminish, just about the same time Microsoft realized that the Internet was a much bigger phenomenon than it had anticipated. Microsoft decided to realign its naming conventions again and return OLE to its roots. The OLE banner was officially removed from all but the original set of technologies related to the linking and embedding of objects into OLE container documents. These three technologies are now grouped into a category called *OLE documents* and are individually named *linking*, *embedding*, and *in-place activation*.

Microsoft Embraces the Internet: OCX Becomes ActiveX

In 1995, the Internet revolution spurred Microsoft's technical (and marketing) ingenuity into high gear. Microsoft originally underestimated the importance of the Internet revolution, but within about a 90-day period in late 1995, Bill Gates completely realigned the Microsoft corporate strategy to include Internet support in almost everything the company was producing.

To boldly signal its entry into the booming I-net revolution, Microsoft created a new high-tech *Active* brand name for present and future I-net related technologies. The company decided to market the remaining OLE technologies as *ActiveX*, which is easier to pronounce than OLE but much harder to define. Because ActiveX is essentially a brand name, expect the collection of technologies in this category to mutate over time.

The naming confusion continued in March 1996 when Microsoft used the new Active brand to rename OLE control components as *ActiveX controls*. This enabled them to operate as COM-compliant components and dedicated their use to the Internet. Sure, you can still use these controls as widgets in the design-time toolbox of your development language, but now all the promotion and commotion revolves around using ActiveX controls to make spectacular Web pages and Web-enabled applications.

Microsoft's Web-centric focus also spurred the company's aggressive push to develop or enhance its other I-net–related technologies. These products and technologies include Active Server Pages, VBScript, Visual J++, and Visual InterDev, which are all included or supported in Visual Studio. COM continues to provide the underlying architecture designed to integrate all this new technology seamlessly.

Active Platform

Microsoft further marked its I-net intentions by declaring that its new I-net architecture for the PC will be named the *Active Platform*. The following technologies are included under the Active Platform umbrella:

- The *Active Desktop* enables the PC desktop to act as an integrated COM container that can hold COM objects such as ActiveX components, provide all the functionality now associated with Web browsers, and connect to I-net broadcast channels. The goal is to completely integrate local PC resources with I-net–based resources into a single, unified user interface. This capability is made available in Internet Explorer 4 and will be included in future releases of the Windows operating systems.

- *Active Server* provides a consistent server-side component programming environment. *Active Server Pages* are used to enable the Web server to present feature-rich Web pages as standard HTML to the client browser.

▶ **See** Chapter 6, "An Inside Look at Active Server Pages and the Internet Information Server," for more information on Active Server Pages, **p. 137**

- *ActiveX technologies* are COM-based technologies that enable components written in different languages on different operating systems to communicate consistently and robustly. All the ActiveX technologies are built to use COM. However, not all COM-based technologies fit under the ActiveX umbrella. For example, MS Office software and Windows operating systems are COM-enabled but aren't considered part of ActiveX.

The marketing experts at Microsoft liked the *Active* part of *Active Platform*, but when the Java proponents began suggesting that Java and the Java Virtual Machine (JVM) could also be considered a platform, Microsoft opted to clearly differentiate its core technologies with the new name *Windows DNA*. The conflict over Java is explored in greater detail later in this chapter in the section "The Scoop on Java-Based Technologies."

More New Names: Windows DNA and COM+

In late September 1997, Microsoft renamed the Active Platform technologies the *Windows Distributed Internet Applications Architecture*, or simply Windows DNA. According to Microsoft, Windows DNA is not a product; it is the marketing term describing the collection of existing and emerging Microsoft technologies that enable you to integrate client/server and I-net programming.

The foundation of Windows DNA technologies is still COM, but COM itself is slated to get some new enhancements and the new name *COM+*. The COM+ enhancements are not available yet, but the anticipated features are discussed later in the section "Objects Over the Horizon: COM+."

Today, the confusion continues among developers over the various names for Microsoft-produced technologies. Nevertheless, it is more important to understand the underlying concepts than it is to keep up with the latest naming conventions. If you're curious what the names were when this chapter was written, Figure 9.8 shows the relationship of some of these OLE/ActiveX technologies to the COM foundation.

FIGURE 9.8
The ActiveX and OLE technologies all have a common foundation in COM.

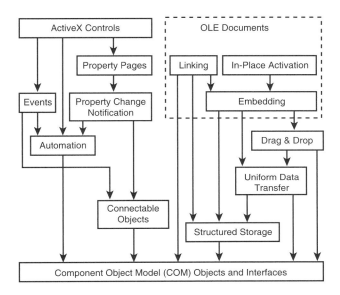

Remote Objects: ORBs and DCOM

For objects to interact between computers and across networks, they must have a common way of communicating. This is accomplished by using an *Object Request Broker (ORB)*, which you can think of as a very intelligent switchboard providing directory and connection services between client and server objects. Various ORBs and ORB-like technologies are now available, and considerable debate has raged over which one is, or should be, the universal standard.

One early entry in this technology category was the Distributed Computing Environment (DCE) from a technology consortium called the Open Group. DCE encompasses an evolving suite of technologies available for various platforms. A wide array of system vendors distributed this DCE technology, including Bull S.A., Cray Research, Data General, Digital, Fujitsu, Hewlett-Packard, Hitachi, IBM, NEC, Siemens Nixdorf, Sony Silicon Graphics, Stratus, and Tandem Computers. Various DCE technologies have been used as a foundation for other technologies released by IBM, DEC, and, yes, even Microsoft.

Another development was CORBA, from the Object Management Group (OMG). The CORBA specification, developed in the early 1990s, has now gained the support of more than 20 major technology vendors, including Apple, Sun, and IBM. OMG has achieved a very impressive membership of more than 700 companies, including Adobe, Apple, Computer Associates,

Digital Equipment, Hewlett-Packard, Netscape, Novell, Oracle, Silicon Graphics, Symantec, Texas Instruments, Unisys, and Xerox. Despite this apparently overwhelming show of support, OMG won't be able to ensure CORBA's status as the single industry standard without the cooperation of the most globally influential company in software today, Microsoft. Unfortunately for OMG, CORBA compliance doesn't fit into Microsoft's plans.

ON THE WEB

For more history about CORBA and the Object Management Group, visit OMG's Web site at `http://www.omg.org/`.

Back at Redmond, Microsoft diligently created its own full-fledged object request broker specifically for the Windows set of operating systems. After years of development rumors, this technology was officially released in 1996 as the Distributed Component Object Model. DCOM extended the COM architecture to provide object communication services at the binary level between computers that use a COM-compatible operating system and are connected via a network.

N O T E   For general discussions about the technology, the term *COM* is commonly used to denote the COM and DCOM technologies.

Objects over the Horizon: COM+

COM and DCOM deliver tremendous functionality, but Microsoft is working to make COM even better. In October 1997, Microsoft announced it was developing enhancements to COM and DCOM to be collectively called *COM+*. These enhancements promise to provide faster performance and improved capabilities and will significantly reduce the complexity of creating COM objects. However, you will still be able to code all the technical details by hand if you want to, but with COM+, the system can do most of the routine work for you.

The target specifications for COM+ have mutated significantly during the development process. For example, the relationship between the Microsoft Transaction Server (MTS) and COM has become so intertwined that in future versions of Windows, MTS features will be wholly encompassed in the COM+ architecture. Some COM+ features initially proposed have been postponed, such as support for a more complete form of object inheritance and improved garbage collection. Here are the highlights of features currently scheduled to be included in the first series of COM+ enhancements:

- Event services—Events can be published by each object for broadcast throughout the system. Other objects can then subscribe to receive the event notifications that they are interested in, thus allowing multiple receivers to use the same event message but for different purposes.

- Load balancing—Requests for object services can be dynamically distributed across connected servers, balancing the load on each server.

- Security—COM+ will provide a role-based security model.

▓ Queuing services—COM+ will provide asynchronous queuing for service requests on objects.

▓ MTS services—COM+ will absorb transaction processing, security administration, and other infrastructure services now provided by MTS.

What would Microsoft innovation be without new names? In the COM+ world, Microsoft's COM ORB is expected to be called the COM Runtime, and the name DCOM will simply refer to the DCE Remote Procedure Call protocol that connects distributed COM objects. COM+ will progressively integrate very tightly with MTS to provide a full-featured and robust computing environment to host any Windows-based, object-oriented system you can imagine and develop. This COM+ and MTS combination has also been dubbed the Component Services Architecture (CSA).

However, because COM+ features might not be available until the next generation of Windows is released, you will still benefit greatly by knowing the basic techniques for implementing COM objects using Visual Studio tools. According to Microsoft, all properly constructed COM objects built now will work equally well or better under the enhancements of COM+.

▶ **See** Chapter 27, "Creating COM Components for MTS with Visual Basic," **p. 809**

▶ **See** Chapter 28, "Creating COM Components for MTS with Visual J++," **p. 835**

▶ **See** Chapter 29, "Creating COM Components for MTS with Visual C++," **p. 855**

▶ **See** Chapter 31, "Using Microsoft Transaction Server to Enable Distributed Applications," **p. 899**

With the announcement of COM+, Microsoft has made its intention clear that now and in the future, the road to Windows-based, object-oriented software is paved with COM.

ON THE WEB

To keep up with the latest news on COM and COM+, visit Microsoft's COM home page at `http://www.microsoft.com/COM/`.

Additional information on Windows DNA and answers to frequently asked questions about DNA are available at `http://www.microsoft.com/dna/`.

Object Technologies Today

COM is Microsoft's way to connect objects, but it isn't the only way. The industry is now grappling with the choice of designing programs to communicate using a designated open standard (such as CORBA) and the technologies based on them (such as Enterprise Java Beans) or to communicate by using COM, the object communication technology that has become the de facto standard for Windows-based computing.

COM/DCOM Compatibility with Other Object Technologies

CORBA-based technologies are the most significant competing object models you'll encounter when supporting enterprisewide integration of your programs created with Visual Studio. For

Part

II

Ch

9

example, IBM provides a CORBA-compliant object architecture for mainframe systems in its System Object Model (SOM) and also in its Distributed System Object Model (DSOM).

ON THE WEB

If your company has IBM-supported mainframe or workstation equipment, you probably want to become more familiar with SOM/DSOM. For more information, visit IBM's home page at `http://www.ibm.com/` and perform a site search for SOM or DSOM.

Other popular CORBA-based ORB offerings are available from Inprise (formerly Visigenic, but they have since merged with Borland to create Inprise) and IONA. Both companies have also created technologies that help you integrate COM and CORBA objects, and both are discussed further in the following section.

COM Versus CORBA: Standard, Stand-Off, Integration, or Assimilation?

CORBA-based solutions are still the main competitors to COM. CORBA has been available much longer and was created from the start to be a nonproprietary, or open, standard, backed by OMG and its alliance of technology firms. COM was created as a proprietary Microsoft development. During October 1996, in an effort to diffuse concerns about it being proprietary, Microsoft announced the creation of The Active Group to guide the evolution of ActiveX and the underlying COM technology. The Active Group was formed under the auspices of The Open Group, another organization dedicated to supporting standards in the software industry.

ON THE WEB

For more information about The Open Group, visit its Web site at `http://www.opengroup.org/`.

For an interesting observation about "Who Owns ActiveX," see David Chappell's cover story from the September 1997 edition of *Byte* magazine. This article also can be found on the Web at `http://www.byte.com/art/9709/sec5/art7.htm`.

Although this appeared to be a positive step toward opening the architecture to the rest of the industry, the track record suggests that Microsoft will retain the deciding vote on any significant changes proposed for COM.

The industry track record also indicates, however, that Microsoft is an extremely tough contender in any market it enters. Microsoft can be counted on to be particularly aggressive in promoting and implementing its object technology because this area is absolutely critical to the advancement of personal computing. In cooperation with Microsoft, Software AG has ported COM and ActiveX support to the Sun Solaris and UNIX family of operating systems with a product called DCOM for the Enterprise (DCOM FTE). Microsoft is working diligently to ensure that every major operating system will soon have COM support. Hence, using Visual Studio to create COM-compliant objects for Windows and UNIX platforms is a safe bet now, and COM objects will have even more utility in the future as COM support spreads to other platforms.

ON THE WEB

For more information on COM and ActiveX support for UNIX-based operating systems, visit Software AG Americas (SAGA) at `http://www.sagus.com/`.

There's still a great debate over which object model you should use: COM or CORBA. It would be nice if these two models were compatible, but because that's unlikely to happen in the foreseeable future, you have to make a choice. Despite all the hype, your choice should be based on what you consider better for your own purposes.

If you're creating applications for the PC desktop, the Object Request Broker de facto standard for Windows-based development is COM, and COM is built into the operating system. Similarly, COM is the clear choice for homogeneous Windows-based programs used across Windows NT-based computer networks.

If, however, your programs need to operate in a network environment that contains a mix of operating systems, including various flavors of UNIX, you might need to integrate your programs by using CORBA-compliant ORB software. In that case, it's wise to standardize on products from a single CORBA-compliant vendor because integration between CORBA-based products has sometimes proven to be very difficult. In the case of Web-based development, Java and Enterprise Java Bean technology is making a strong showing, but it's still not as well suited for enterprisewide integration as the COM and ActiveX combination. Other ORBs might find niche markets where they can survive, but for enterprises where most users have PCs on their desks, the initial standoff between COM and CORBA will likely give way to integration and perhaps finally to assimilation by COM.

ON THE WEB

The Object Management Group maintains a concise set of links to CORBA-related Web sites at `http://www.omg.org/news/corbkmk.htm`.

Perhaps you're wondering whether programs created using Visual Studio (which uses COM) are compatible with CORBA. Such integration isn't yet available out of the box, but third-party tools are now available to help you with this integration.

One popular CORBA-compliant object broker is Orbix from IONA Technologies. Orbix also provides a bridging technology that enables application integration between COM-based Windows platforms and CORBA-based UNIX platforms. Inprise, the freshly renamed company resulting from the merger of Borland and Visigenic, also offers CORBA-compliant VisiBroker object broker and bridging products.

ON THE WEB

More information on Orbix and other IONA products is available at `http://www.iona.com`.

You can find out more about the Inprise VisiBroker product line and the Borland/Visigenic merger at `http://www.inprise.com/visibroker/`.

Part
II

Ch
9

These and other products that help bridge the compatibility gap between COM and CORBA are very useful and will be necessary until the two competing standards either can communicate directly or are merged into a unified standard. Bridging technology provides valuable integration capability; unfortunately, however, as you increase the number of communication layers, the complexity of your programs and the risk for functionality and performance problems also increases. Because COM is quickly being ported to nearly every major computing platform, it might not be long before native COM support is available in all common platforms and Visual Studio programmers will have less need for a COM-to-CORBA interface layer.

Assimilation has also begun under the market pressure of the COM/OLE technologies. In late 1993, a coalition of technology companies—including Apple, IBM, Novell, Oracle, SunSoft, Taligent, and Xerox—backed a compound document architecture standard called *OpenDoc* from Component Integration Laboratories (CILabs). This technology provided some promising competition for Microsoft's COM/OLE technology and prompted a great deal of interest and discussion from the industry, but generated only a meager amount of market share. Being open and standard was just not enough for the OpenDoc alliance to overcome the growing market success of COM-based technologies. OpenDoc's battle to survive amid the growing dominance of OLE technologies was short-lived. The battle concluded in May 1997, when CILabs essentially surrendered by announcing it was discontinuing support of the OpenDoc architecture.

ON THE WEB

CILabs has since been dissolved by its board of directors. At the date of this writing, the company's farewell greetings were posted at `http://www.cilabs.com`.

The battle between CORBA and COM to become the generally accepted ORB standard is nowhere near over. Netscape Communications Corporation is including a CORBA-compliant object request broker and support for the Internet Inter-ORB Protocol (IIOP)—the CORBA-compliant Internet protocol from OMG—in its Enterprise 3 server and Communicator 4 browser. This means Netscape's browsers can use IIOP to connect with remote objects across the I-net.

The incompatibility gap between Microsoft's Internet Explorer and Netscape Navigator/ Communicator is widening, but Microsoft is trying to make this a moot point by using Active Desktop as a preemptive strike to essentially eliminate the need for—and ultimately even the existence of all competing browsers. Unless the U.S. Department of Justice requires otherwise, Microsoft's Windows DNA strategy will integrate all the functions of traditional browser technology directly into the desktop of all future Windows operating systems. Hence, if the PC-using public embraces this new version of Windows, the PC browser battle will essentially be over and Microsoft's COM-based technologies will be the de facto standard.

ON THE WEB

Microsoft maintains Web pages dedicated to OLE and COM topics at `http://www.microsoft.com/oledev/` and `http://www.microsoft.com/COM/`.

The Scoop on Java-Based Technologies

Still another battleground for Microsoft's object technologies is in the I-net arena. This battle has become more intense as a result of the explosive increase in I-net usage and the increasing desire to use I-net for mission-critical, distributed corporate applications.

Sun Microsystems has created a phenomenon of its own with the creation of the Java programming language. Originally created to be a small but powerful means to program applications for small computing devices, it found popularity as a means to create quickly downloadable applets for I-net Web pages. As Java's popularity expanded, so has the scope of what developers are attempting to create by using Java and Java-related technologies.

Part
II

Ch
9

Microsoft's mixed position on this situation is easily misunderstood. Microsoft considers Java to be a great object-oriented programming language and has created the Visual J++ product to provide Java programmers a rich development environment. However, Microsoft considers Java-related technologies to be a very poor choice as an operating system. On all but the smallest computing platforms, the Java Virtual Machine (JVM) that contains and executes the Java applets is essentially an operating system or operating environment built on top of the native operating system. Because Java and Java-related technologies are attempting to be a cross-platform solution, the Java language and the JVM must limit themselves to the lowest common denominator in terms of platform-specific features. Thus, important capabilities available from operating systems (such as Windows) are essentially unavailable to programmers writing pure Java code. The platform-specific implementations of the JVM also introduce the opportunity for incompatibilities, as does the variety of Java development environments. Even if you think you've developed the most pure Java applets or even full-fledged Java applications, you should still test them extensively to make sure that they work correctly on all desired platforms.

With Visual Studio, Visual J++ gives you the option of writing pure Java applets, or you can use the J/Direct interface to allow your applets to access the entire range of Windows-specific APIs. Java purists have panned this platform-specific flexibility for developing Java applets for the PC. Nonetheless, as a programmer supporting Windows-based users, you're faced with a choice: use pure Java to create slower and less functional applets that might or might not work on other platforms, or optimize your code to work in Windows.

Java Beans is another Java-related technology that's not very popular with Microsoft. Sun and IBM developed this technology to give Java applications the same compound document capabilities that ActiveX provides. Java Beans can be visual components that you can add to forms in visual development tools, or they can be nonvisual components that accomplish background tasks. Java Beans are also designed to be cross-platform–compatible, but the current reality is that you still need to test your Java and your Java Beans on each combination of platforms and the JVM that's represented in your user community.

To extend the reach of Java Bean components, Sun has created a specification for creating Enterprise Java Beans (EJB), which is the name for the architecture that enables Java Bean component communication across networked computers. This architecture can also theoretically be used to encapsulate COM components or CORBA components and enable them to work together in the same application. The Enterprise Java Bean specification appears to be a possible alternative to COM-based I-net development, but it is still too early to tell whether actual implementation of the EJB specification will live up to the hype surrounding it. However, because EJB seems to be among the only alternatives to using COM, competing technology companies such as Sun, Netscape, Oracle, and IBM are understandably rallying to support it.

Despite the alliance of industry giants, Java Beans are still the underdogs when compared to the market penetration of Microsoft's COM and the rapidly growing COM+ strategy for I-net development.

Microsoft hopes that as COM gains further acceptance and use throughout the industry, the importance of CORBA, Enterprise Java Beans, and other architectures will diminish along with their market share. Should that happen, Microsoft will have successfully assimilated another major layer of the desktop computing architecture. If not, CORBA and Enterprise Java Beans will remain as alternative distributed object architectures for the desktop and the I-net, and will need to be accounted for when you're integrating and supporting enterprisewide systems.

ON THE WEB

Microsoft's Web site provides current information about its position on these technologies. To find the most recent update, do a keyword search at Microsoft's search page at `http://search.microsoft.com/`. A good starting point to locate more information on CORBA-compliant products is the Object Management Group's Web site at `http://www.omg.org/`.

For more information on Enterprise Java Beans, visit Sun Microsystem's Web site at `http://java.sun.com/products/ejb/` or its Java home pages at `http://java.sun.com/` or `http://www.sun.com/java/`.

COM Outside Windows

Although COM was originally a Windows-only technology, Microsoft and its partners are porting it to every other major computing platform and operating system, including Solaris, MVS, Macintosh, and UNIX. This time the integration rumors are backed by dollars because in addition to its internal efforts, Microsoft has negotiated outside contracts to port COM to some of these other platforms. In association with Microsoft, Software AG has ported ActiveX/DCOM under the name EntireX DCOM to Solaris, Digital UNIX, Linux, and IBM MVS OS/390 operating systems. By the end of 1999, you can also expect to see versions of COM available for HP/UX, IBM AIX, Digital Open VMS, Siemens Nixdorf SINIX, and SCO UNIXWare. Hence, if COM isn't yet supported on your computer system of preference, you probably won't have to wait long until it is.

ON THE WEB

To get the most recent information about COM support for these other operating systems, visit Software AG's Web site at `http://www.sagus.com`. To download the latest trial version of EntireX DCOM for either Solaris, Linux, or Digital UNIX, visit `http://www.sagus.com/prod-i~1/net-comp/dcom/dcomdown.htm`.

Where to Go from Here

To explore specific implementation requirements of COM objects, please continue by reading the following section, "COM Architecture Basics."

However, to go directly to some practical suggestions about how to apply Microsoft's object technologies to real-world development situations, skip ahead to one of the final two sections in this chapter, "Strategies for Using Object Technology with Legacy Applications" and "Strategies for Implementing Object Technologies for New Applications."

Part
II

Ch
9

COM Architecture Basics

This section takes a closer look at the common implementation requirements of Microsoft's object technologies, while still maintaining language neutrality. It provides a quick introduction to COM-related terms and concepts, which are then explained in greater depth in subsequent chapters with language-specific implementation guidance.

Interfaces

The COM infrastructure is built to support communication through object interfaces. In COM, you can think of an *interface* as the communications link between two different objects, and the set of functions available through that link. The interface acts as a fixed contract between objects that defines the expected behavior and the parameters of their interaction. Interface names conventionally begin with a capital I to denote their status as an interface, and the remaining text describes the function or service being exposed. For example, in the Domestic Simulator program mentioned earlier, you might name an interface ISpeak, which will be read aloud as *I-Speak* or *Interface Speak*.

A COM interface is actually implemented as a memory structure called a *VTable*, which contains an array of function pointers. Each element of the VTable array contains the address of a specific function implemented by the object. It's conventional to say that a COM object exposes its interfaces to make its functions available to clients. The object also can contain the data manipulated by the methods, and you can choose to keep this data hidden from the client object. Figure 9.9 shows this structure.

IUnknown One of the most basic rules of the COM specification is that all COM objects must support a specific interface named IUnknown. This interface is the standard starting point for referencing any other interface that the COM object might contain. The COM specification arbitrarily dictates this structure, but it makes sense if you consider that a client object doesn't know what other interfaces are exposed by a server object until the client requests this information by using this predefined interface designed to reveal what interfaces are unknown. A more technical way of stating the relationship is that an object's interfaces must directly or indirectly inherit from IUnknown to be valid under the COM specification. You, the programmer, are responsible for implementing the IUnknown interface for your objects; however, because this operation is so routine, Microsoft programming tools accomplish most of this work in the background or allow you to customize some basic example code. Figure 9.9 also shows how a client must request a pointer from IUnknown to access an object's interfaces.

FIGURE 9.9
You can define a COM interface called `ISample`, which is implemented in memory with pointers to the standard COM methods and to your custom defined methods.

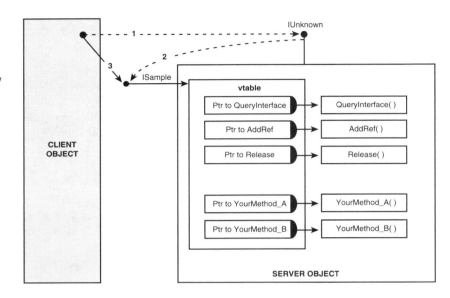

QueryInterface   The object's IUnknown interface must also implement a function named QueryInterface, which reports back to the client whether a requested interface is supported and, if so, provides a means to access it. A successful call to QueryInterface provides the client with a pointer to the requested interface.

Globally Unique Identifiers

Every COM component class and interface must be uniquely identified. This is accomplished by providing a means for you to generate and assign a unique number called the *globally unique identifier (GUID)*. A GUID is a 128-bit integer virtually guaranteed to be unique across space and time until about A.D. 3400 because of the algorithm used to create it. The official pronunciation of GUID is still up for debate, but if your pronunciation rhymes with either fluid or squid, you'll be understood. As illustrated in Figure 9.10, you can use the GUIDGen.exe program provided with Visual Studio to create a new GUID whenever you need to. When creating your new GUID, the program uses an algorithm that includes the current date and time, a clock sequence, an incremented counter, and the IEEE machine identifier if available. The odds against any two people ever creating the same GUID are astronomical. After you create a GUID, you can use it to identify your programming objects and interfaces uniquely. When used to identify an interface, this GUID number is referred to as an *interface identifier (IID)*. When used to identify an object, the GUID number is called a *class identifier (CLSID)*.

FIGURE 9.10

The GUIDGen program included with Visual Studio enables you to create a new GUID in any of four different formats.

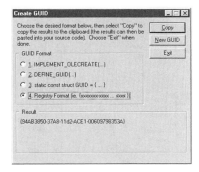

After a particular interface is defined, numbered with a unique IID, and published, it must not be changed; thus, the interface is said to be *immutable*. When you want to update the features of an interface, you must define, number, and publish an additional interface to supplement the older version, retaining any previous versions within the component. If you don't include these previous versions, you'll create version incompatibility problems for your users. You'll see an example of this later in the section "Binary Compatibility and Version Control."

Registering Your Components

After you have a GUID to identify your new object, you must register it with the host system. For machines running Windows, you do this by adding the appropriate information to the Windows Registry, a special system file containing that machine's hardware and software configuration information. When you create and distribute components, you should build your installation program to update the Registry without requiring manual assistance from users. After a component is registered, the operating system will know how and where to access that particular object.

N O T E   According to the current definition, any self-registering OLE component that fully implements IUnknown can be correctly called an ActiveX control. OLE automation servers and most of the widget-type controls from a visual development toolbox are included under the ActiveX controls banner.

Binary Compatibility and Version Control

With the ability for developers around the globe to create objects that must work together, you need to be able to update your objects without causing the failure of existing objects that still depend on your previous version. COM requires that client objects specify the exact server interface they want by using that interface's assigned GUID (as described in the next section, "Creating COM Objects"). Each version must have a different identifier, and QueryInterface returns a pointer to the version the client specifically asks for.

COM enables objects to have multiple interfaces, so any number of versions can be supported simultaneously. When all versions are retained by an object and made available to clients, the old and new clients always work appropriately. When you create a new version of an interface, it's a good practice to change the name or add a version number after the name to avoid any confusion. With proper versioning, you can safely support old and new objects on either side of the client/server relationship. Figure 9.11 shows this concept, using objects from the domestic simulator example.

FIGURE 9.11
Mower objects from different vendors will still get the grass cut as long as COM versioning rules are followed.

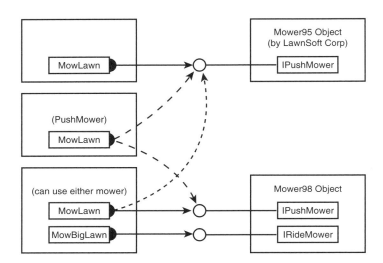

Suppose that you purchased the domestic simulator described earlier. Spouse95 objects created by SimWare are designed to call the PushMower interface (IPushMower) in the Mower95 object when the simulated lawn needs to be cut. Eventually, LawnSoft releases a new version of its mower object, called Mower98, that's the envy of the simulated neighborhood. Some people buy it to upgrade their simulation, but because it's more expensive and not that much better than the mower object everybody started with, most don't buy it. Furthermore, for your simulator to take advantage of this new type of mower, your Spouse object must know that the new mower exists and must know the identifier of the new interface to access it. To allow spouses to be able to use this new variety of mower, SimWare upgrades its Spouse object and releases the Spouse98 version. The Spouse98 object now has two ways to mow the lawn: use the MowLawn object to call the old PushMower interface or use the new MowBigLawn object to call the new RideMower interface.

The whole point of this exercise is that because the versioning was done correctly and each object supports prior interfaces, any combination of spouse and mower objects can successfully mow the lawn. If not, when you drop in a replacement object, you risk breaking the existing object relationships and your application will no longer function correctly. Make it a habit to ensure that your objects fully support your prior interface definitions as well as any new interface definitions in a given object, and your objects will always work together properly.

Creating COM Objects

Clients can create a new instance of an object by making an appropriate call to the object-creation services provided by the COM Library. How this is accomplished depends on the language, but the call always needs to provide the GUID for the class identifier (CLSID) of the desired object.

At the completion of the creation process, the client gets a memory pointer to the new object. It can then use that pointer to ask the object directly for pointers to any other services provided by the object.

COM Library Services

Each platform that supports COM provides a COM Library, which implements a group of functions that supply basic COM services to objects and their clients. The first and foremost service is the means to create a COM object on request. One way to accomplish this is as follows:

1. The client asks the COM Library to create an object of a specific CLSID.
2. The COM Library uses a system utility called the Service Control Manager (SCM) to find the CLSID information in the system Registry, locate the correct server for this class of object, and start it.
3. The COM Library uses the server to create a generic instance of the object and passes an interface pointer to the client.
4. The client asks the object to initialize itself, thus loading any persistent data associated with the object.

Class Factories

If you want to create more than one object at a time, you can repeat the previous creation process, but a more efficient way is to implement and use a class factory. A *class factory* is a service component whose only purpose is to create new components of a particular type, as defined by a single CLSID. The standard interface used for this purpose is appropriately called `IClassFactory`. It's up to the component programmer to provide the class factory for each class, and fortunately, implementing the `IClassFactory` interface is simple and straightforward. If you want to add licensing capabilities to your class factory, you can opt to use Microsoft's newly defined `IClassFactory2` interface, which requires the client object to pass the correct key or license to the class factory before it will create the new instance of the desired class.

Monikers

Another way to accomplish the creation of an object is by using a moniker. A *moniker* is a special type of COM object built to know how and where to instantiate another specific object and to initialize that object with its persistent data. Each moniker can identify exactly one instance of an object. If you want more than one instance of a given class of objects, you need to use a different moniker for each object because each object might have its own unique data.

Suppose that in the human resources application at your firm, employees and their histories are stored as COM objects. If you use monikers, a separate moniker is needed for every single employee in the company. If your employee object, for example, is needed by the system, the system will call up your particular moniker. Your moniker will then create your employee object in memory, load your history information from the persistent data storage, hand the pointer for the employee object back to the requester, and then unload itself from memory.

You can also create a *composite moniker* that activates a group of other monikers. *Absolute monikers* point to OLE documents instead of objects.

Where COM Objects Live

After it's created, a COM object requires a place in memory where it can exist, deliver the services requested by clients, and then unload itself from memory when all the clients report that they're finished with it. To have this existence, a computer object must live within a process or process space with a defined area in the system memory, some instruction code, perhaps some associated data, and some resources for interacting with the system.

A *thread* is the name given to the action of serially executing a specific set of machine code instructions within a particular process space. Computers with processors and operating systems that can execute more than one thread in each process are said to be *multithreaded*. A process capable of multithreading must always have at least one main thread, called the *primary thread*, but can also have many others. In Windows, user-interface threads are associated with each window and have message loops that keep the screen display active and responsive to new user input. Meanwhile, Windows uses worker threads to accomplish other computing tasks in the background. After a thread is initiated, it executes its code until it finishes, is terminated by the system, or is interrupted by a thread with higher priority.

COM supports multithreading by putting objects in the same process space into their own groups, referred to as *apartments*. The purpose and function of apartment threads are comparable to those of the user-interface threads described previously. Similarly, COM uses the term *free threads* to describe what were previously called worker threads. Regardless of the terminology, COM makes multithreaded development easier by handling the communication between these threads and between the various objects.

COM Objects Communicating Together

COM objects must be designed to be well-behaved neighbors. You want to ensure that any COM objects you create correctly implement the rules that enable consistent behavior and reliable communication with other objects. The following sections discuss the most basic rules your COM objects must live by.

Reference Counting

After an object is created, it can take on a life of its own. Because more than one client might be using its services at any one time, each object needs to keep track of its clients so that it doesn't close itself down before all the clients are finished with it. When a client begins using the services of an object, it has the responsibility to call the `AddRef` method to increment the server object's reference counter. Similarly, when the client has finished, it has the responsibility to notify the server object by calling the `Release` method to decrement the reference counter. When all clients have released themselves from the object, the reference counter goes to zero. The object then knows its work is completed and can safely save any persistent data and self-destruct by unloading itself from memory. If a client subsequently needs the object, the object is created again and the reference counting process is repeated.

You must implement the methods for `AddRef` and `Release` as part of the `IUnknown` interface. Because all interfaces inherit from `IUnknown`, the `AddRef` and `Release` methods are then automatically available through any interfaces you define for your object.

COM Objects Across Process and Network Boundaries

COM objects need to be able to communicate with their local neighbors on the same machine, as well as with distant COM objects residing on machines located on the other side of the world. Considerably more complexity is involved with the latter process, but you need to understand both processes to create objects that comply with the COM specification.

Remote COM Servers   Remote COM servers (also known as *cross-process* or *out-of-process servers*) are COM objects providing service from a physically separate computer usually connected via a network. Both computers must be operating with COM-enabled operating systems for this process to work correctly. Remote COM servers typically provide slower performance than their in-process cousins, but they can deliver all the advantages explained earlier for generic OO remote servers, and COM remote servers can provide compatibility between 16-bit and 32-bit clients.

Transparent Connections: Marshaling, Proxies, and Stubs   In COM, a *proxy* is a small binary component activated in the client's process space, which acts as an in-process connector to the server interface, regardless of the server's physical location. A *stub* is a small binary component activated in the server's process space, which acts as an in-process connector to the proxy in the client. With this arrangement, the COM client doesn't need to know where the server object is located because COM creates a proxy or stub as needed, making all servers appear to be in the same process space (see Figure 9.12).

Although a great deal more overhead is necessary to communicate with out-of-process objects than in-process objects, no additional effort is necessary for the COM client. With this architecture, all objects are made available to clients uniformly and transparently.

FIGURE 9.12
COM proxies and stubs provide each remote object with an in-process communication link to other objects across a network.

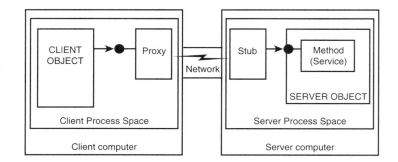

Some extra work needs to happen behind the scenes to make this communication process transparent to the objects. For an in-process server, the client can simply use a pointer to the server, but out-of-process clients have only a pointer to the proxy. COM must support interprocess communication such as Remote Procedure Calls (RPC) to reach the stub, which then communicates through a pointer to reach the server. *Marshaling* is the name given to this process of packaging interface data into an appropriate format for delivery across process or network boundaries. The code module that performs these tasks is called a *marshaler*. For the return trip to the client, the process to unpackage this data is called *unmarshaling*.

Object Automation   If you want to create an object that can be programmed or automated by another object, your object will expose this capability through a specially defined standard interface called `IDispatch`. This interface, also called a *dispatch interface* or *dispinterface*, must implement a standard method called `Invoke` that acts as a channel to receive automation commands from clients. Dispatch interfaces allow you to expose functions and data as methods and properties, which are combined in logical units called *Automation objects*. An application or component that exposes automation objects is called an *OLE Automation server*. An application or component that uses the services of an Automation server is called an *OLE Automation client*. Used by OLE Automation servers, the `IDispatch` interface is generic across programming languages.

COM Object Data

COM objects, much like traditional applications, need to be able to store their data. A COM object can store its data through persistent storage of object data, uniform data transfer, and connectable objects.

A COM object that can store its data by using a fairly permanent medium (such as in a database on a disk drive) is said to have persistent data. Persistent storage is accomplished natively in COM by means of a structure formerly called *OLE structured storage*, now called *Compound Storage*. This structure essentially implements its own independent file system, and the whole thing is stored within a single traditional file on the host machine.

Compared with the traditional file structures, the directories are called *storages,* and the data is stored in file-like structures called *streams.* In much the same way that files contain data specially formatted for the program that created it, streams can hold data in any format designated by the object that creates it. The Root Storage can contain any number of additional storages, also called *substorages,* and any number of streams. Each substorage can also contain any number of additional substorages and streams, with the only limit being the amount of space available on the disk. This entire structure is then physically stored as a single conventional file on the system's disk drive. Figure 9.13 compares the familiar DOS/Windows file structure and the COM Compound Storage system.

FIGURE 9.13

The COM Structured Storage architecture closely resembles the DOS/Windows file system architecture but is stored on a single file on the host system.

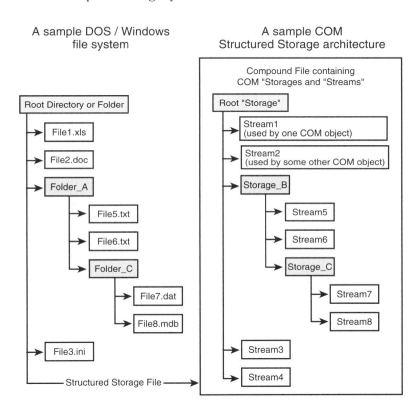

Historically, there have been many ways to exchange data between programs. You can import a data file or copy and paste from the Clipboard, or perhaps a program might read an initialization file. COM has defined a common approach for moving data between objects called *Uniform Data Transfer*. Again, a standard interface, IDataObject, is defined to accomplish this functionality. By calling the IDataObject interface, one COM object (an ActiveX control, for instance) can quickly and easily request data from another object any time new data is needed.

When one object needs data from another object based on data changes, timers, or other spontaneous events, a better technology called *Connectable Objects* can be used to pass the data between objects. The idea behind connectable objects is to set up dedicated incoming and outgoing interfaces used exclusively for interobject communication. Each connection is instantiated with its own Connection Point object within the server object. The client instantiates an internal object called a *sink*, which receives the incoming communication. Standard interfaces defined for this purpose are named `IConnectionPointContainer` and `IConnectionPoint`. The implementation details for implementing these COM interfaces in Visual Basic and Visual C++ are explored in greater detail in subsequent chapters.

Strategies for Using Object Technology with Legacy Applications

For most large organizations, the issue is no longer whether your firm should move to client/server, object-oriented, and distributed computing models, but when and how. Most organizations would like to begin this transition immediately, especially for any new applications, because the benefits of building applications by using object technology are compelling. However, creating new OO systems of significant size and complexity typically requires additional training for the programming staff, a large investment of funds, and months or years to complete. During that time, all the existing applications built with traditional methods still need to be maintained and updated. Furthermore, new and old systems usually have to interoperate during the transition because instant transitions involving multiple systems are rarely possible. This task is indeed daunting, but the sooner your organization determines its strategy for making the transition, the better prepared you can be for implementing it.

When your company is committed to begin the transition, the issue is then how you can economically and sensibly accomplish it. Because aging systems still provide a great deal of functionality, and changing them is getting more expensive every day, many businesses have focused on more urgent problems and secretly hoped for some technical breakthrough to come along and save them before it's too late. Object technologies are no magic bullet, but they can help you solve many of the challenges in creating new systems and updating old ones while maximizing your existing investment in your company's legacy code base.

For most large companies, it isn't wise, practical, or even possible to simply discard the existing mission-critical applications and quickly rebuild them by using object technologies. If this is your situation, you need an incremental strategy that allows you to selectively redevelop, reengineer, and repackage your legacy systems, blending the old processing models with new ones that can all share the same communication framework. COM object technologies can provide that framework.

Each corporate situation presents unique challenges that must be addressed individually, but when you're dealing with these challenges, some common themes emerge. Although there are many variations and combinations, this section explores four basic strategies for applying object technology to the challenge of supporting your legacy computer systems:

- Keep your old systems and interoperate with newly created systems.
- Create new objects around old code to wrap or encapsulate the functions of legacy applications.

- Reengineer legacy applications by using objects to create new multitiered, distributed applications.
- Create object-oriented browser-based interfaces to your legacy data.

Interoperating with Legacy Systems

Many mission-critical legacy systems are stable, reliably do exactly what they're supposed to, and require very little maintenance. Perhaps this claim sounds amazing, but these applications allow your business to continue another day while you and your teammates diligently resolve the most recent crisis or create that rush job application desperately required by your more vocal users.

Part
II
Ch
9

Sometimes there's a compelling reason to change the status quo: The business process changes dramatically, the cost for support becomes unacceptable, or the program can no longer be supported if a serious modification is required or if the language or platform are no longer supported by your company. In such a case, you'll want to start planning the transition and focus on the new system. Because this process will require a great deal of your already scarce programming resources, why not hedge your bets and make use of the legacy system as long as it's practical?

Situations involving this approach include the following:

- *You have a legacy system that's not yet obsolete, but you anticipate it will be within the next 18 months.* Or perhaps you're planning a change to your business processes, which will require a completely different system. Rather than continue to implement short-term fixes on the old system, spend your time and energy to adequately and completely prepare for and implement the new system. The users might accept this approach more readily if you involve them in the requirements, development, and delivery process. Keep the user community updated on your progress in implementing the new system, ask some key users to help test it, and then offer training sessions as soon as practical to ease anxiety about transitioning to the new system.

- *You have a legacy system that manipulates a separate database.* In this case, the old system and the new system can be designed to operate safely while simultaneously using the shared database, and the phase out can happen gradually as functionality is added to the new system. Users can use either system safely during the transition period.

- *You have a mission-critical system that simply can't go down until a replacement system has proven itself.* In this case, a completely separate system must be implemented and tested extensively over time to ensure that it performs to corporate expectations. Both systems must be operated independently until users are fully trained and the new system is trusted. Then a simple and well-publicized transition plan should be implemented to coordinate the movement of all live data and all users to the new system.

- *You have a monolithic system that's extremely costly to modify, and complete replacement would be so cost-prohibitive that it isn't even an option.* This situation is perhaps the most difficult to deal with, as the old system must be maintained in its legacy state for the foreseeable future. Perhaps your best move here would be to encourage your company to take all reasonable steps to retain the legacy programmers. Also, you might want to start a divide-and-conquer plan, in which you explore business reengineering options to begin to move separable business functions onto new systems and away from the great monolithic system.

Object Wrappers for Legacy Code

Another approach is to take existing code modules and embed them inside a new object that acts as a wrapper, completely isolating the legacy code while retaining its functions. This wrapper can encapsulate any or all of the old interfaces—including screen displays, API calls, database interactions, and any other communication elements—exposing them as appropriate COM interfaces. As time, funding, and priorities permit, you can progressively design and implement new objects to replace the wrapped modules from the legacy application.

There are several specific ways to use this wrapper approach. A *database wrapper* accesses and encapsulates just the legacy data, completely bypassing legacy code. A *service wrapper* encapsulates legacy system services, such as printers and communications devices. An *application wrapper* encapsulates the code and data of a legacy system application. Application wrappers can provide the object-oriented equivalent of traditional screen-scraping programs, which emulate the interaction of users on character-based terminals and provide that data through a new graphical user interface. Visual C++ is probably the most common choice for creating these wrappers, but you can also use Visual Basic or Visual J++.

Although wrappers can be a fantastic method for leveraging your legacy programming investments, this approach has a major downside because the old, inflexible legacy code is still hiding inside the object wrapper. The effort to replace the wrapped legacy code with a newly constructed, reverse-engineered object will likely be seen as a very low priority among the users because they have already received the new functionality and now feel comfortable with it. From their point of view, maintaining the new functionality is your problem, not theirs. Replacing a functioning wrapper object might also be a tough sell to management, which probably has a huge list of higher priority new initiatives and maintenance projects that need your immediate attention. With this in mind, it's usually wise to build object wrappers with great care and attention to detail because they might need to last until the underlying function is obsolete to the business, or until a completely new system replaces it.

Reengineering with Objects to Create Multitiered, Distributed Applications

Functions performed by existing monolithic architectures can be reengineered or broken down into a multitiered, object-oriented architecture that's more maintainable, scalable, flexible, and reusable.

The first step is to divide functions into three logical groups representing user services, business services, and data services. This analysis can be more challenging than it sounds:

- The user services group includes all the functions that support interaction with the user, such as forms, menus, controls, and other visual displays. User interfaces on the old system might be simple text-based screens, whereas the new system probably needs a considerably more elaborate graphical user interface.

- The business services group includes the functions that implement the business tasks and rules of the organization. If your company is typical, many of the business rules are undocumented, yet still buried deep within the legacy applications, and must be derived by analyzing procedures and even individual lines of legacy code. When you've discovered them, the business rules contained in the old system must be compared to the rules you want for the new system and adjusted accordingly.

- The data services group includes all the functions related to the storage and manipulation of data. Legacy data storage might be implemented with a flat-file data structure, whereas the new system might need to use a relational database.

Part
II

Ch
9

This logical design might need to be revised as business needs change, but after the initial implementation is accomplished, subsequent iterations of this cycle are much faster and easier. After this logical division of tasks is accomplished, you can design the physical location of the components.

This process can become quite complicated, but fortunately an object modeling tool called Visual Modeler is included in Visual Studio. Visual Modeler provides the basic features needed to construct and document your object classes and relationships, and it can save you a tremendous amount of time.

▶ **See** Chapter 36, "System Modeling and the Microsoft Visual Modeler," **p. 1029**

In most organizations, the legacy system can't be shut down while the new system is under construction. Where possible, use an incremental development process to allow the programming team to deliver a series of small victories instead of an ever-more-anxious period of waiting (and hoping) for the success of one enormous project release.

The first components to build are the ones supporting the lowest level functions of the system. Resist the urge to start with the user interface because you'll quickly become frustrated trying to design interfaces for functions not yet implemented. These low-level functions include such things as data-access components, networking services, and services for hardware and peripherals. Because these functions are potentially needed by any application on the system, migration of these services to reusable components will provide the fastest benefit for other projects that also require these services.

The next components to build are those that support time-consuming computer processes that can be more efficiently accomplished in a separate process space. Performance of the main system can be enhanced greatly by implementing these slower processes as components that can operate in a separate process on the same machine or on a separate, more specialized machine. Functions that fit this category might include fax processing, database report generation, credit-card validation, and computing of numeric solutions by using complex algorithms. When these components are moved onto a separate processor, asynchronous processing can be used by any application on the system modified to take advantage of it.

After these two groups of components are built, tested, and operational, you've formed the foundation that can support a cycle of continuous improvement. Each of the following projects provides the remaining components to one major subsystem of the legacy application. Attempting to complete all the remaining components at one time is a risky endeavor that should be avoided if possible for two reasons:

- The users and management of most organizations like to see steady progress for all the money they're investing in your programming projects. The smaller the scope of the project, the less likely you are to encounter problems that require significant schedule delays.

- Because this technology is still relatively new, it's likely that your programming team will be gaining valuable experience during this process, and schedules are rarely built to accommodate many "experience-building" mistakes. By taking the path of incremental improvement, team members can gain experience as they deliver a steady stream of system enhancement on time and on budget.

Browser-Based Interfaces for Legacy Data

One of the fastest and most exciting approaches capitalizes on the recent explosion in the use of I-net technology. You can create object-oriented interfaces for your legacy data by porting the functionality of your legacy applications to a browser-based implementation. The larger your organization, the more promising the benefits, as long as your company already has the equipment and infrastructure in place to facilitate it. If access to local area networks, wide area networks (WANs), and the Internet from each desktop is commonplace at your organization, this might be your fastest, least expensive, and most flexible option for transitioning away from your legacy systems.

If your company doesn't yet have the infrastructure in place, the benefits of this approach can be so compelling as to become a cost-justifiable reason to start investing in the infrastructure.

This I-net approach relies on the browser on each user's desktop to act as the client container for your interfaces and data. The browser and an I-net connection to the company I-net server computers are the only additions required at the user's computer. With this approach, as soon as you change the content delivered by the central server computer, everyone can use the most recent version.

Visual Studio is particularly well suited to support development of object-oriented browser-based systems. Because DCOM provides your object communication framework, you need to have a DCOM-enabled container for your objects at the user's machine. Your best choice for this container with Windows 95 is Internet Explorer; with Windows 98, the best choice is the Active Desktop. If you're planning to write all your servers by using Visual J++, your user platform options can also include the so-called Network Computer (NC) which is a sparsely equipped network client computer running a standard JVM and little else. Because all your server objects will be accessed across the I-net, that's all that needs to be done at the user's machine.

Visual Studio 6 gives you an even greater degree of flexibility on the server side. Your ultimate goal is to encapsulate all desired services associated with the legacy system into a new set of COM server objects. You can use any of the encapsulation strategies discussed previously, and you can implement it by using COM objects you've created by using any combination of Visual C++, Visual Basic, or Visual J++. Then you can use Visual InterDev to include those objects in a set of Active Server Pages that serves as new the user interface. After your objects and interface pages are developed and tested, you can release them by posting them to a production server platform. Unlike conventional installs (where you interrupt users to install it), with this approach you must notify your users by other means before you can expect them to start using the new system. But like conventional systems, it's a good idea to train the users before unleashing them on mission-critical data systems.

Suppose that your firm's existing inventory database resides on a legacy mainframe computer and is accessed from PCs by using a terminal emulator. You can implement a replacement with new browser-based graphical user interfaces by incrementally creating Active Server Pages to suit the needs of each user group (sales, order fulfillment, finance, and so on). These pages can be delivered from an internal I-net server that was also connected across the network to the legacy mainframe. COM objects created to run on the server provide services by making database calls to the legacy database and delivering the results to the objects operating in the user's browser container. Both the legacy system and your net I-net system can operate simultaneously until all the user groups are provided new interfaces. When the legacy database is migrated to a new system, the calls to the legacy database can be modified and redirected to any standard Structured Query Language (SQL) enterprise database product. If your database product is COM-compatible (such as Microsoft's SQL Server), your task is even easier.

The benefits of this I-net approach can be downright exciting to an Information Systems (IS) department trying to support a large user base. Gone are the hassles of software version control, trying to physically install or upgrade individual copies of your corporate software on hundreds or thousands of geographically separated computers, or trying to use network install utilities to accomplish these tasks. You can at least expect the following benefits from this I-net approach:

- The programming tools enable much greater flexibility and much faster delivery of minor changes than conventional software development cycles.
- As users become more familiar with the browser interface, training can become less of a challenge, compared with teaching a new interface with every program.
- Specialized hardware connections and leased circuits to mainframe computers can be redirected just to corporate I-net servers, or the mainframes can be modified to become I-net servers themselves, thus facilitating the standardization of the communication infrastructure.
- The data shared and services provided within the company can be easily and selectively extended to business partners and existing customers, and advertised online to new customers.

The list of benefits goes on, but even these few things are enough to illustrate the advantages to large organizations with a geographically dispersed user base.

Although this approach has numerous benefits, it does have some significant drawbacks that need to be considered before you commit to it. As with any centralized system, if the network goes down, the entire user community might suddenly lose service. This can be somewhat mitigated by operating mirrored servers at separate locations, so if one server can't be accessed by a given user, that user might be able to establish a connection to an alternative server. Even with mirrored servers, the fragile state of the global I-net communication backbone does pose a significant risk to mission-critical systems. If this risk is unacceptable, you need to stick with more traditional approaches.

Security is also a factor when considering any I-net–based approach. Secure protocols are now available but have yet to gain universal trust. However, many corporate information systems can be operated safely with the minor degree of risk now associated with I-net communication methods. For more information about browser-based interfaces for legacy data, see Part III, "Developing Internet, Intranet, and Extranet Applications."

Strategies for Implementing Object Technologies for New Applications

Each OO methodology has its own lifecycle approach for building applications from scratch, yet there are some common strategies and real-world insights that can greatly improve your project team's chances for success. The first order of business for creating new applications is to gather and document as many project requirements as you can. This step can't be overemphasized. Object-oriented software development enables a great deal of flexibility in designing and adjusting the solution to a given programming problem, but an entire project design might have to be scrapped if critical requirements are omitted during design and then discovered during user testing.

Use every resource at your disposal to ensure that you've captured all the critical requirements of the user's business processes. Rapid prototyping is especially helpful when you're trying to present a new graphical user interface paradigm. By presenting a live demonstration of a sample graphical user interface option for a business process solution, you can often unlock creativity and innovation from users during the design phase before formal development begins. This is a dual-edged sword, however, as user expectations and requirements might also rise significantly. The risk is worth it because this can help you reveal and solve any existing problems with the business processes rooted only in limits imposed by a previous automation system. These risks can be significantly mitigated if you need all new project requirements to first be documented, reviewed for cost and schedule impact, and approved by management before being accepted by your development team. After you document and get approval for your initial set of business requirements, you can then begin the object-oriented analysis and design process.

When designing an application from scratch, the older procedural programming strategy typically used a mixture of two related approaches:

- The top-down approach to programming—Divide large tasks into smaller tasks until each task is simple enough to be implemented directly.
- The bottom-up approach to programming—Write procedures that implement basic tasks, and combine them into progressively more complicated structures until you've created the desired functionality.

A typical approach for OO analysis and design draws on both the top-down and bottom-up approaches, and enhances them. First, examine your problem description from the top, and look for the items, descriptors, and actions involved. The nouns will become candidates for object classes, the adjectives will typically become the properties, and the verbs will become the methods. Then you can start your first iteration of the analysis and design process by establishing the classes and associating each method with the class most responsible for that action. From this starting point, you can concentrate on the bottom-level tasks, adding the properties and further refining the relationships in your architecture. As you proceed through this process and gain additional insight into the problem domain, you will typically reveal new information and dependencies that require you to go back and make revisions to your proposed class structure. As more details are added, your designs can become quite complex.

This analysis and design process, and especially the work required to keep your design documentation up-to-date, can be greatly simplified by using modeling software. As mentioned previously, you can use Microsoft's Visual Modeler for free, or you might want to purchase the more full-featured version called Rational Rose from Rational Software Corporation. Regardless of your choice of modeling tool, learn your modeling software well before attempting to use it to build an object-oriented system from scratch. The development time and money saved by effective use of a modeling tool will make it well worth your effort.

▶ **See** Chapter 36, "System Modeling and the Microsoft Visual Modeler," **p. 1029**

ON THE WEB

For more information about Rational's object modeling tools and OO methodologies, visit its Web site at http://www.rational.com.

The complete UML specification can also be downloaded from Rational's Web site at http://www.rational.com/uml/.

When your preliminary design is acceptable to you and your colleagues, repackage it as a presentation and walk through it with your most supportive user representatives. Even the most elegant object-oriented designs are worthless if they don't satisfy the users' needs. Rapid prototyping is also a valuable tool for testing ideas, to ensure that programmers and users are communicating effectively, and to reveal and facilitate the discussion of any hidden assumptions buried in the individual requirements.

When your most supportive users are happy, test a basic prototype with your least supportive users. Working with these "difficult" users might be uncomfortable, but it will likely yield two very important benefits:

- These more hostile users will tend to make a more determined effort to find the flaws in your project and your logic. Although some portion of this feedback might simply be frivolous griping, many of the comments will reveal places for significantly improving the project. Making peace with hostile users early in the process by negotiating these improvements into the initial design of the project is a much better strategy than avoiding these users and their opinions until you're forced to face them during full-scale user testing and deployment.

- After these initially hostile users become part of the development process, they might join you in feeling some personal ownership in the project, subsequently defending the project to ensure that "their" project becomes a success. Requirements definition, analysis, and preliminary design are critical phases of the development process in which changes can be made more easily and cheaply than subsequent phases, so don't waste the opportunity to capture as many changes as you can while fostering a positive spirit of support among the users.

After you and your users agree on a preliminary object design, resist the urge to immediately begin coding. As a rule, it's cheaper and faster to buy an object than it is to write it yourself, so now start looking for prebuilt objects and frameworks. First look in your own organization. If your organization doesn't have a well-organized object repository, now is the time to start one. Next, look outside your organization for objects that can be obtained from other parts of the same company or from commercial sources. Remember that ActiveX components are COM objects, and you have thousands of commercially distributed ActiveX components to choose from. Only after you truly exhaust your options for reuse should you pass out the coding assignments.

Now that you're ready to begin writing the code, Visual Studio provides you and your team with enormous flexibility. You might need to use any or all of the approaches mentioned previously, depending on the requirements of your project. Language-specific implementation guidance is provided in subsequent chapters for each Visual Studio tool.

After your objects are developed, tested, and put into production, you need to determine who will support them. The project team that originally created the objects for a specific project will likely move on to other tasks, but the objects they put into the corporate inventory will eventually need maintenance. As many other projects reuse your objects, the responsibility for maintenance of a given object can become quite diluted. To avoid abandoning these valuable objects inadvertently, the objects themselves and the repository should be assigned to a project-neutral focal point or team, which at some firms is called the *reuse group*. Perhaps some of the resources saved by reusing objects can be applied to the task of maintaining the object inventory and budgeted independently from the budget lines of the projects that created them.

One final caution: Invest the time needed to prevent the nearly universal problem of poorly documented applications. Properly and fully document your objects, and then include that documentation and the objects in the corporate object repository. You might even need to reuse or maintain some of these objects yourself someday, so take the time to document them appropriately the first time around.

From Here...

Now that you have a general understanding of object-oriented programming and Microsoft's object technologies, it's time to get some language-specific instructions on how to create a few of those versatile COM objects known as ActiveX components:

- To learn how to create ActiveX controls with Visual Basic, see Chapter 12, "Creating ActiveX Controls with Visual Basic."
- To learn how to create ActiveX controls with Visual C++, see Chapter 13, "Creating ActiveX Controls with Visual C++."
- To learn how to create MTS components with Visual Basic, see Chapter 27, "Creating COM Components for MTS with Visual Basic."
- To learn how to create ActiveX components with Java, see Chapter 28, "Creating COM Components for MTS with Visual J++."
- To learn how to create ActiveX controls with Visual C++, see Chapter 29, "Creating COM Components for MTS with Visual C++."

CHAPTER 10

Creating Reusable Components

by Jody C. Socha

In this chapter

Looking at Categories of Reuse

Reuse is alive and well. This statement might seem odd, considering the quantity of pessimistic writing on the subject—namely, that reuse is almost never accomplished in software development shops. But, of course, reuse is accomplished every day. If you don't believe this assertion, look at your own development environment. Chances are, you didn't write the operating system, or systems, that you expect your software to run on. Although there are certainly some exceptions, it is safe to say that the vast majority of people assume that a particular operating system will be in place to provide needed functionality.

Do you need more examples? Consider that almost no one writes his own database connectivity software. Rather, developers almost always use some form of prepackaged software, such as open database connectivity (ODBC) drivers, or Microsoft's Remote Data Objects (RDO) and ActiveX Data Objects (ADO). Consider, also, the large quantity of controls available for use in the development environment. Visual Basic is built around the concept of reusing components—for example, tree views, list views, and image controls—in constructing a user interface. Of course, don't overlook new technologies such as the Microsoft Component Object Model/Distributed Component Object Model (COM/DCOM) or its alternative, the Common Object Request Broker Architecture (CORBA). Building your software around any of these technologies implicitly involves reusing large amounts of code written to make that technology work.

So, why is such a grim view of reuse often taken? Because, there is so much software not being reused. The promise of reuse is incredibly high, but most projects involve only limited reuse of the cut-and-paste variety. Tight deadlines and budgets prohibit development teams from taking a big picture approach to software development. They don't want to accept the responsibility of the extra time or money it takes to consider broader, well-designed solutions that use features such as inheritance and template classes, implemented and documented specifically for reuse. Furthermore, a constantly changing technology-base can cause code written one day to become obsolete the next. Traditionally, the infrastructure hasn't been in place to support reuse in a truly plug-and-play environment.

So, how can an organization achieve the same level of reuse with its own software that it does with third-party software? This chapter attempts to answer that question by presenting a series of steps:

- First, an organization must understand what types of items can be reused. Toward that end, this chapter presents various categories of reusable items, an overview of the technology available for creating those items, and the advantages and disadvantages of reusing them.

- Second, an organization must understand what makes something reusable. This chapter addresses that issue by overviewing various criteria involved in designing a reusable item.

- Third, an organization must invest in technology needed to store, catalog, retrieve, and distribute the reusable components. In this regard, this chapter discusses several tools available from Microsoft and how those tools support reuse.

▓ Last, an organization must develop a strategy for both building reusable components and reusing those components. This chapter discusses organizational issues to address in order to support reuse.

There are many levels of reuse ranging from very concrete software components to more abstract concepts, such as design patterns. This section covers many of these areas by discussing how each area can benefit you and presenting some of the issues associated with them.

Software Components

The term *component* has many different meanings both internal and external to Microsoft Visual Studio. For this chapter, a software component is specifically a single unit of software providing a black box interface for performing a specific function. *Single unit* implies that the code is contained inside of one application. *Black box* means that the component's methods for providing its functionality are not known to the outside world. Finally, the term *specific function* does not mean that the component only performs one task. Rather, the component might provide a set of methods as long as those methods are logically related to each other.

Also, this chapter exclusively discusses using Microsoft's COM model for developing those components. This includes components developed using ActiveX technology because ActiveX is considered an extension of the COM architecture. Although there are a variety of methods for developing components, COM is the method for the future (see Figure 10.1).

FIGURE 10.1
Components simplify the capability to easily extend the functionality of an application.

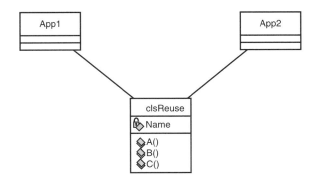

The reasons for using COM are presented in the following:

▓ COM provides a framework for the interfaces between components. Thus, any development language can be used as long it writes to the interface defined by COM.

▓ Because COM only specifies how interfaces should work, it encourages an environment in which developers write to a component's interfaces and not to the component itself.

▓ COM hides the complexities of intercomponent communication. For example, DCOM handles the networking protocols for interactions between different components on different computers. Thus, a developer can focus on the component's main functionality without worrying about networking issues.

■ Using COM enables developers to implement COM-aware applications such as Microsoft Transaction Server (MTS).

Well-written components provide straightforward functionality to the user while hiding the implementation details. On the downside, the user's control over the functionality is severely limited; because it's a black box solution, the user is not allowed to see the component's implementation.

▶ For more information about building COM-based components, **see** Chapter 9, "Using Microsoft's Object Technologies," **p. 217**

One technique that deals with this lack of flexibility is to take advantage of inheritance or aggregation. A second is to not reuse a component per se, but rather reuse the component's interface. These techniques are covered in the next two sections.

Interfaces

Defining and reusing component interfaces are powerful alternatives to actual component reuse. Reusing interfaces merely carries the component reuse to the next level.

Every component under COM creates an interface that defines how other components can interact with that component (see Figure 10.2). It is also possible to create an interface definition independently of an actual component. For example, in Visual C++ (VC++) you will create an Interface Definition Language (IDL) file and compile it to produce the type library in a .tlb file.

FIGURE 10.2
Interfaces provide the capability to plug and play different components, giving various implementations of expected functionality.

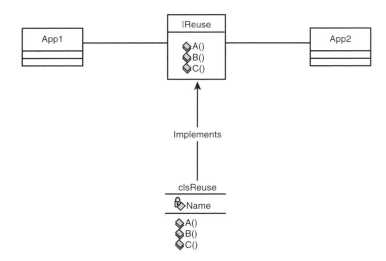

▶ For more information about creating interfaces, **see** Chapter 9, "Using Microsoft's Object Technologies," **p. 217**

N O T E   There is no direct technique to create a .tlb file from Visual Basic (VB). However, you can create a class in VB that is simply a list of properties and methods. After the project is compiled, other applications can then reference it and use it to implement its interfaces. ■

When the .tlb file is created, a VB project can reference that file. Classes in that project can implement the interface by using the `implements` keyword. In VC++, the Active Template Library (ATL) is used in developing interfaces and COM-based classes.

Other applications or components use the component by casting a variable to the interface and creating an object that implements it.

Interface implementation is advantageous because it is easier for the plug and play of components to change how a function performs. This is possible because the Interface Identifier (IID) does not change between components. Only the Class Identifier (CLSID) changes. For example, an application might need to change the destination for outputting logging information from a file to the screen. If a file-logging component is replaced by a screen-logging component, none of the other code needs to change if both components share the same interface. However, reusing interfaces between components can have disadvantages, especially if a reused component actually implements more than one interface. This situation causes the user of the component to implement separate variables that can communicate with each interface. The Visual Basic style code in the following shows an example of this:

```
Dim obj_BaseInterface      as IBaseInterface
Dim obj_DerivedInterface   as clsDerived

Set obj_DerivedInterface = CreateObject("VSExample.clsDerived")
Set obj_BaseInterface = obj_DerivedInterface

Call obj_DerivedInterface.DerivedFunction
Call obj_BaseInterface.BaseFunction
```

CAUTION

Calling the method `DerivedFunction` on the base interface object or `BaseFunction` on the derived interface object generates an error.

As a final note, when reusing interfaces, backward compatibility must be maintained so that code doesn't unexpectedly break.

Inheritance and Aggregation

There are two types of inheritance: implementation inheritance and interface inheritance. With implementation inheritance, a class executes the same method code as another class that it is derived from. Implementation inheritance provides a powerful method for reusing code internal to a project (see Figure 10.3). Currently, implementation inheritance is not available in Visual Basic, nor does the COM model provide it.

FIGURE 10.3

Implementation inheritance provides a way to extend or modify the exact implementation of another class.

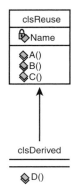

N O T E Microsoft's planned extension of COM, COM+, is supposed to provide a mechanism for providing implementation inheritance. ▨

▶ For more information about inheritance and aggregation, **see** Chapter 14, "Creating COM Components for MTS," **p. 413**

With interface inheritance, on the other hand, a derived class provides exactly the same public method and properties as a base class. It doesn't execute the same code as the base class's implementation of those methods. Likewise, it doesn't need to have the same private methods and properties as the base class.

Interface inheritance is not as powerful as implementation inheritance. However, it is more flexible. Furthermore, it provides the foundation for supporting the technique of aggregation and segmenting application functionality (see Figure 10.4).

Aggregation uses interface inheritance, in which a new class wraps around the base class (see Figure 10.5). Basically, the derived class implements the base class's interface. Then the internal code of the derived class calls into an instance of the base class to provide the base class's functionality. However, the derived class can execute its own code around the calls into the base class, or it might circumvent the base class altogether.

FIGURE 10.4
Interface inheritance provides a way to use the same methods and properties as the base class without having to use the same implementation.

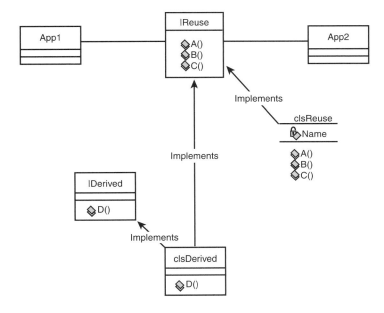

Part III

FIGURE 10.5
Aggregation enables a class to extend the functionality of another class by keeping an internal variable for the base class and calling the identical functions on the base class as necessary.

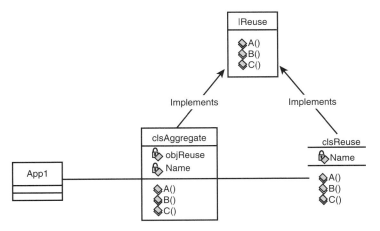

Aggregation provides a method for customizing a component's behavior when the component's internal implementation cannot or should not be changed. On the other hand, it provides extra execution overhead and is dependant on the base class's interface not changing unexpectedly.

Frameworks

*Framework*s are collections of components that work together to provide a more general set of services than components by themselves. Frameworks can be spread across multiple units of code. They might also be incomplete and not provide all the services needed by the user. They form more of a white box approach because the user must become familiar with how the components interact in order to reuse them.

Unlike patterns, which are discussed later, frameworks provide existing code for holding an application together. However, the frameworks might be incomplete and not address every design issue. Examples of frameworks from Microsoft include ATL, Microsoft Foundation Classes (MFC), ADO, and RDO (see Figure 10.6).

FIGURE 10.6
Microsoft's Remote Data Objects provide an example of a framework used to access databases.

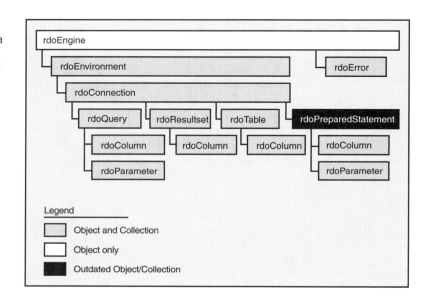

A major advantage of frameworks is that whole sections of code are already written. They also provide more flexibility in their use because not every aspect of how the framework should work is fully defined. A disadvantage of frameworks is that they require the user to understand the framework architecture in order to use it. Furthermore, the user might become trapped into using specific techniques to perform various tasks, such as error handling.

Applications

Similar to frameworks, applications are a set of components working together to provide a set of services. Unlike a framework, an application is complete and can function on its own.

Application reuse is accomplished when the application exposes a set of interfaces enabling access to its internal components. Again, COM is the method of choice for determining the interface. For example, a sales application needs to define methods to determine whether a needed item is in stock. Rather than write the methods, the sales application can call into an interface in an inventory application to check the inventory.

N O T E   Microsoft is actively working with software vendors to develop COM-based interfaces to their applications.

ActiveX (formerly known as OLE) provides a powerful extension to COM for enabling applications to interact with each other. It defines how components can manipulate the behavior of other components. For example, a PowerPoint object is placed in a Word document. When that PowerPoint object is selected, it activates the application's methods. Through the ActiveX interface it takes over the container application providing its own menus and toolbars. Likewise, when the document is printed, Word controls printing the text until the PowerPoint object is reached. ActiveX is then used to call the print method on the object so that PowerPoint controls printing the figure.

▶ For more information about ActiveX, **see** Chapter 12, "Creating ActiveX Controls with Visual Basic," **p. 337**, and Chapter 13, "Creating ActiveX Controls with Visual C++," **p. 385**

An advantage of reusing applications is the capability to compartmentalize functionality into well-defined areas: sales vs. inventory, or Word for text vs. PowerPoint for figures. A disadvantage is the overhead of starting another application into memory to perform even the simplest of functions.

N O T E   COM blurs the line between components, frameworks, and applications. ▨

Thanks to the advent of COM, applications can now be seen as a collection of components assembled to work together. Toward that end, any of the components within the application can be accessed from outside the application, barring any security restrictions. Thus, components built for one application can easily be reused by other applications. However, unless the components were specifically created to be reused, there might be some complications in using them. For example, the components might expect specific error-handling objects to be in place in order to work correctly. The reuser must take the time to create or ensure those same error-handing components (or at least their interfaces) are in place. Alternatively, the user will have to know how the components interact to provide their specified functionality.

N O T E   Microsoft's Visual Basic for Applications (VBA) tool provides an example of the power of this COM-based, component view of applications. Microsoft Office products such as Word have long provided a macro language facility to have Word automatically perform often-repeated tasks. Now, thanks to COM, the macro facility is a variation on the Visual Basic development environment and makes calls to Word's application components to perform these tasks. Furthermore, calls to other applications' components, such as PowerPoint, are now available, which produce an Office-wide development language and not just a Word-specific one. ▨

As an alternative, a few components can be created to provide a simplified interface into the application. These components can then manage the intricacies of how the application works on behalf of the client. Thus, whole suites of functionality can be provided to the outside application with the user requiring knowledge of the application's details.

Part
II

Ch
10

Designs

Reuse does not just include reusing actual code. Designs can also be reused. So if two development efforts must address similar requirements, there is potential for their designs to be reused. Software tools such as Visual Modeler enable this design reuse by allowing projects to import and export sections of models into each other. In fact, using the Microsoft Repository to store models enables reuse of designs across different development tools. This topic is addressed later in this chapter.

The advantage of design reuse is that designs don't lock the developer into any guaranteed implementation or interface. However, reusing a design requires the developer to write the code from scratch.

Patterns

A final area of reuse that has grown out of the object-oriented movement is to not reuse actual code or designs, but rather to reuse ideas for how the code should be written. Patterns identify predictable structures for defining object behavior. Capturing that structure can speed the design and development of it or similar structures in the future.

A pattern provides an outline for the design and can give a developer a powerful head start in laying out that design. However, the developer will still need to flesh out the details of the design, as well as the code.

Designing for Reuse

Large scale reuse can't be accomplished without a plan. There are cases that code is reused in which developers have identified a specific need that some other code satisfies. Often, an organization decides that a piece of software, whether it's well-written or not, should be reused on many other projects regardless of the other project's requirements. The end result is that reusing projects spend more time reusing a component that does not meet their need than building the component on their own.

So, how does one go about building reusable components? Several design and development strategies are needed to make the component truly reusable. The goal is to successfully reuse the component often enough that the savings of reusing it outweigh the costs of developing it. Naturally, this goal can't be accomplished if it costs more to reuse a component than to develop the same functionality from scratch.

N O T E   This chapter doesn't go into exhaustive detail on every reuse design strategy. There are large numbers of books available that discuss these concepts in detail.

Design the Component to Be Reused

The first concept for developing a reusable component is to build the component to be reused. This might sound like common sense, but components are often not built that way. In other words, discussion must occur as to how the component can be reusable to meet a variety of needs and not just one project's specific needs.

If possible, have the component built by an independent project that is responsible for only the component or reusable components. This forces the component to live or die on its own. Also, the independent project is in a better position to coordinate with other projects to determine all the possible uses of the component. It also enables the component's development timeline to meet a variety of deadlines and not just those of one project. If a separate team can't be formed, then, hopefully, those building the component will recognize the needs of other projects that might reuse it.

Keep the Design as Simple as Possible

The most successfully reused components are relatively intuitive, and simple to understand and implement. If long directions on how to use the component or components are required, the component will probably not be reused. This strategy explains why single components and small sets of components are reused on a daily basis, whereas vast frameworks meant to solve many developer problems are often not used.

The same "keep it simple" strategy can be used for more complex setups as long as the complexity is hidden appropriately. A well-chosen set of interfaces can be used to conceal a very complex set of components, thereby simplifying what the user needs to understand.

Build the Components to Meet a Specific Purpose

You don't want to build a component that provides both error handling and logging capability in one. First, this increases the complexity of the component, contradicting the simplicity rule. Second, it forces a user to deal with the logging issues when only error handling is needed. It also prevents the user from writing information other than error messages to a log. Clearly, the functionality should be separated into two components. One component stores the error messages, and the second knows how to write information out to an appropriate log location.

Keep the Design as Generic as Possible

This sounds like a contradiction to the rule of meeting a specific purpose, but it is not. Instead, the objective is to identify all the different ways that a component can support its stated purpose. If there turn out to be too many ways that the purpose can be met, the purpose might be too broad. Look into restating the objective.

For example, a logging object should not limit itself to writing to only a text file. It might be desired to write the log out to a database, to the screen, or to a system event log. Keeping each of these options in mind will help keep the component generic, as well as aid in meeting the next design criteria.

Build the Component to Be As Flexible As Possible

In order to keep the component generic, it must also be flexible. Focus on a component's (or set of components') interfaces and how they can be structured to deal with a variety of issues.

Furthermore, it is entirely possible that the component doesn't exactly meet the needs of the reuser. A well-built component can easily be extended by a user to meet more specific needs.

Consider the logging object again. It was determined that the object needed to be made generic by being able to write to several different destinations. So, how does one build in the flexibility to write to those destinations? There are two options to consider.

In the first method, separate the component into several smaller components forming a logging framework. Thus, there is a generic logging object that knows how to write to a generic log. There are also several supporting objects (file, database, screen, and event log) that know how to write out information passed to them. The logging object can then have the logging destination passed to it through an object reference or some other means. Furthermore, the user can easily extend the functionality of any of these objects by creating a new object that implements the object's interface. The user can then use aggregation to customize the functionality as necessary. This method might be preferable when an application needs to change the logging destination frequently.

In the second method, several different logging objects are implemented, depending on where the information is to be logged. Each of the objects implements the same interface, but the internal implementation of those methods changes depending on the destination. This second method opens the door for the user to write a custom logging object by implementing the standard logging interface. This second method might be preferable when the logging destination doesn't change while the application is running.

Maintaining flexibility does cause potential conflicts with the simplicity rule. Building in flexibility enables the component to do more, which in turn creates more information the user must learn about the component. Maintaining a balance between these two criteria will be a necessary aspect of making a truly reusable component.

Maintain Backward Compatibility

Unless there is specific reason to no longer support an old version of the component's interface, every new release of a component should be backward compatible. Thus, the tremendous amount of work done by an organization is not lost when a new version of a component is released. More to the point, if one application uses a new non-backward-compatible version of a component, and another application does not, then the second application can easily be broken if the first application is installed on the same computer. Consider a component's interface as a written contract, and that the component will always support those methods and properties. Also, consider it your responsibility to share the conversion costs if you decide to break that interface.

As a side result of this issue, care should be taken not to release too many versions of a reusable component. First, this situation creates a configuration control nightmare. Second, maintaining all the interface information on a component adds overhead to the component in terms of both performance and storage.

Analyze Your Applications

Don't just randomly decide which components to reuse. Rather, take the time to research the various applications in use by the enterprise. Search for business functionality that is duplicated from one application to another. Also, research the utility functionality, such as error handling and security, that the applications must perform. Most of the current commercial reuse opportunities come from this area. For example, most applications need access to a database of some kind. From this need stems the popularity of ODBC, RDO, and now ADO.

Watch the Overhead

A downside to building simple, well-defined, flexible components is the potential performance overhead associated with them. To meet these criteria, a component can be internally divided into many separate objects in order to handle the large number of different uses that might be required. As a result, the supporting source code can become rather large in size, larger than expected memory requirements might support, or performance might slow because of the additional function calls needed. Even if a component meets all a developer's required functionality, it won't get reused if it doesn't perform well.

Part
II

Ch
10

Keep Costs in Mind

Initial development costs in terms of time, people, and money are usually higher for reusable component than non-reusable ones. This is because of the additional work the team must take to make the component meet every possible need. The hope is that the savings from reusing the component will exceed the up-front development costs, but, if the component is not built on time or is not built at all because of budget problems, it does no one any good.

Be Prepared to Fail

It's probably not possible to take into account every way that a component will need to perform. So be prepared to start over if necessary. Also, expose the component's interface so that an aggregate component can be built to meet the customer's specific needs.

Alternatively, don't build the component at all. Instead, capture the idea behind a component in a design pattern so that the concept can be easily reused and modified. In fact, design patterns open up opportunities to share design approaches across seemingly unrelated subject areas.

Working with the Toolset

One of the biggest challenges to reuse is determining how to distribute those items appropriately. Typically, one of the drawbacks to being able to distribute reusable items is the lack of a toolset for managing those items and making them available to outside developers. Towards that end, a suite of tools is now available from Microsoft for supporting a team-based development environment. In addition to several other features, these tools provide several levels of support for reusing various aspects of the development environment. An overview of how these tools can support reuse is discussed later in this chapter, and each tool is presented in detail in other sections of this book.

▷ All the tools presented in the following are covered in Chapters 33 through 36 of this book, **p. 941, p. 979, p. 997, p. 1029**

The Microsoft Repository

The most innovative as well as abstract tool is the Microsoft Repository. The repository provides a generic, centralized database for storing information about the development environment.

Featured in the repository are several Tool Information Models (TIMs) that define the type of information captured by a given set of development tools. For example, one TIM can define that the Visual Modeler captures design information about classes, properties, methods, and relationships. When the TIM is configured properly, the Visual Modeler can then export information about the classes and other data for a given model into the repository.

After the information is successfully stored in the repository, it is available for use by other development tools familiar with the appropriate TIM. Thus, one can browse the repository for models that meet specific criteria. When they are found, an outside development tool can then import that model, or portions of the model, for its own use.

The repository itself is simply a database with a set of COM interfaces for accessing that database. Thus, it does not provide the discussed functionality by itself. Rather, external tools work in unison to store and share information into the repository. Thus, the repository provides a foundation for reuse, but not reuse itself. Both the Visual Component Manager and Visual Modeler use the repository as that foundation. Their methods of utilizing the repository are discussed in more detail in the next two sections.

The Microsoft Visual Component Manager

The Microsoft Visual Component Manager was created specifically for the purpose of supporting reuse. Using the Microsoft Repository as its underlying storage structure, the Visual Component Manager provides a powerful tool for storing, browsing, and retrieving objects for use in the development environment. It functions as an add-in for the various development tools provided with Visual Studio and, as such, is able to automatically add and configure selected components into the active development tool's current project.

N O T E The definition of a component when referring to the Visual Component Manager differs from the definition of a component presented earlier in this chapter. In this chapter, the term *component* specifically refers to compiled software. For the Visual Component Manager, a *component* is practically anything, including compiled software, source code, models, and generic documents. ▨

▷ For more information about the Microsoft Repository, and about the Visual Component Manager and the items it stores, **see** Chapter 33, "Using the Visual Component Manager and the Microsoft Repository," **p. 941**

The Visual Component Manager supports reuse by providing a common location for storing information about the various components available for the developer to use. As part of the storage process, referred to as publishing a component, the Visual Component Manager aids in identifying the type of component being stored by grouping the component with other re-lated components, identifying various attributes of the component such as its description, and assigning various keywords to the component.

> **CAUTION**
>
> The Visual Component Manager only stores the location of a component, not the component itself. Thus, if the component is moved without updating the Visual Component Manager, the capability for the Visual Component Manager to interact with that component is lost.

After the item has been added into the Visual Component Manager, its information can be searched to see whether it meets certain criteria. Components in the Visual Component Man-ager can be searched on a variety of attributes including type, keywords, descriptions, author, and others. The capability to group components, along with the assignment of keywords, provides the Visual Component Manager its greatest capability to support finding reuse candidates. For example, components can be grouped by project such as timesheet entry or employee reporting. Or they can be grouped by general type, such as ActiveX Server, or requirements documentation. However, the grouping might not be enough to identify a desired component, so the assignment of quality keywords becomes critical. Thus, you can find a desired component through a search on well-defined keywords, such as timesheet project, client-side component, ActiveX, Visual Basic, employee management, time and billing, or third-party tool. Thus, the Visual Component Manager becomes a powerful catalog for managing your development environment.

 For organizations that intend to use the Visual Component Manager to manage reusable components, especially across projects, one of the first tasks is to develop and publish a thorough list of keywords and their definitions. Although new keywords can be added at any time, a published list will aid in preventing the proliferation of different keywords that mean the same things and aid in avoiding confusion as to the meaning of obscure keywords.

The final aspect of the Visual Component Manager that makes it so powerful is its capability to configure components into the active development tool. For example, if an ActiveX server is found that the developer wants to use, the Visual Component Manager will automatically add the appropriate references to the server into the active tool's project. Thus, the Visual Compo-nent Manager is much more powerful than a simple cataloging tool. It also can retrieve compo-nents on behalf of the developer and automatically configure them for use.

The Visual Component Manager can also be extended to support reuse across the enterprise by utilizing multiple databases for managing components. By default, the Visual Component Manager uses a reserved, Access-style repository database on the local computer. However, the Visual Component Manager user interface can connect to other databases on any computer available on the network. Furthermore, you can use SQL Server to house the component data-bases, which provides a more powerful tool for handling concurrent usage.

To support enterprise reuse, arrange your component databases into a hierarchical structure. For example, set up a component database for each project, for each department, and one for the enterprise as a whole. A developer can then search through his local database, the project database, the department database, and, finally, the enterprise database, for a component that meets his needs. The Visual Component Manager also provides the capability to move or copy component information from one database to another.

CAUTION

For now, when a component is copied to another database, only its information is copied. Thus, the component itself needs to be manually moved to the appropriate destination on the remote database's computer. The component's location will then need to be updated on that remote computer. This is not necessarily the case for a component being copied from a remote computer to the local computer. For some components, the Visual Component Manager provides the capability to install the component automatically.

The Visual Component Manager doesn't help, however, with the larger issues of determining which components to store.

The Visual Component Manager provides a common tool for storing and retrieving reusable components for the individual developer or across the enterprise. Its capability is made possible by the flexibility of the Microsoft Repository's generic storage mechanism.

The Visual Modeler

The Visual Component Manager is not the only tool available for interacting with the repository for supporting reuse. Other tools can store information into the repository as desired with potentially powerful results. An example of this interaction is provided by Microsoft's Visual Modeler tool.

▷ For more information about the Visual Modeler and how it interacts with both the Visual Component Manager and the Microsoft Repository, **see** Chapter 36, "System Modeling and the Microsoft Visual Modeler," **p. 1029**

The Visual Modeler, along with other development tools, stores information in the repository through a specific TIM known as the Open Information Model (OIM). The OIM defines a repository storage schema that is shared by both Microsoft tools and third-party tools. One of the subject areas that the OIM deals with is object-oriented modeling based on the Unified Modeling Language (UML). Information defined by the OIM can be stored in the repository from a Visual Modeler model by selecting Tools, Export to Repository. Likewise, the Visual Modeler can import information about models already stored in the repository by selecting Tools, Import from Repository.

CAUTION

Exporting a model to the repository is different than publishing a model using the Visual Component Manager. Both methods store model information, but only a published model will show up in the Visual Component Manager. Publishing a model is accomplished by selecting Tools, Publish in Visual Modeler.

N O T E The exporting process will prompt you for the repository database to use.

The power in this arrangement is that any tool that is familiar with the OIM is capable of importing and exporting this information. A model built in Visual Modeler can be exported to the repository, and later imported into another design tool, or vice versa. Thus, design work done by a development team is reusable by other development teams, even if they use different design tools.

▶ For more information about Microsoft's Open Information Model, **see** Chapter 33, "Using the Visual Component Manager and the Microsoft Repository," **p. 941**

From here, it is easy to expand on this concept to other types of tools as well. For example, a database modeling tool can share its models with other database tools as long as each tool can read and write information to the same base format. Microsoft is heavily pushing this concept by expanding the subject areas covered by the OIM. The company is also working closely with many other companies in expanding the OIM.

There are, of course, limits to the amount of information that can be shared between tools. For example, exporting a model to the repository from Visual Modeler doesn't include any Visual Basic specific properties assigned to items in the model. Rather, the repository serves as a central point for reusing and sharing common, key information between the tools.

Visual SourceSafe

An alternative to Component Manager for storing and cataloging items is Visual SourceSafe. Similar to the Visual Component Manager, SourceSafe has the capability to insert and retrieve components of any type in and out of the tool. The items can also be collected together into common groups referred to as projects. However, there are several differences between SourceSafe and Component Manager to consider when picking a reuse distribution option:

- SourceSafe uses its own proprietary database structure for storing items and not the Microsoft Repository.

- Furthermore, SourceSafe stores the actual file that is being checked in and not just descriptive information about it.

- On the other hand, because SourceSafe doesn't store descriptive information, there is no advanced search capability as there is in the Visual Component Manager. Thus, a developer needs to know in advance of a specific file to reuse rather than being able to search for one.

- SourceSafe provides a built-in version control mechanism that stores previous versions of files and enables one developer at a time to work on any given file. Component Manager does not. However, the newest release of the Microsoft Repository provides for both version control and check-in/check-out facilities. Thus, it is possible that in the future, the Visual Component Manager will be updated to include this functionality.

- SourceSafe provides built-in security functionality to provide several levels of permissions, on a per project basis. At present, the Visual Component Manager does not provide native security control.

▨ SourceSafe provides the capability to link a file between projects so that the specified file is included in both. Updates to the file in one project are seen from the other project. The Visual Component Manager does not provide this capability directly. Rather, it allows for shortcuts to be specified in one component folder that point to a component in another folder.

▨ The Visual Component Manager will automatically configure a component into a Visual Basic Project or other development tool. With Visual SourceSafe, you must first get the file and then manually add the component and its related files into the project.

For now, the two tools are separate. However, Microsoft is undoubtedly discussing methods for merging the functionality of the two tools. Perhaps, one day, when a component is added to this integrated environment, the component's information is added into a repository-style database whereas the files themselves are stored in a SourceSafe style structure providing the best of both tools' functionality. Until that time, organizations looking to support reuse must choose one or both tools to support component distribution.

▶ For more information about Visual SourceSafe, **see** Chapter 35, "Using Visual SourceSafe," **p. 997**

Microsoft Transaction Server

Utilizing Microsoft's COM architecture provides many advantages in building reusable components that didn't exist before. Many of these advantages are presented in a prior section of this chapter. However, there is one important advantage that was not discussed: COM greatly simplifies the techniques required to distribute the component for use. This advantage is not provided directly by COM, but, rather, is part of MTS.

MTS is a powerful extension to the COM architecture including providing support for transaction control, security, and many other features. The feature of interest in this section is how MTS uses packages to distribute component information and define component interaction.

▶ For an overview on Microsoft Transaction Server, **see** Chapter 5, "An Inside Look at Microsoft Transaction Server," **p. 107**

▶ For information on distribution issues with MTS and the MTS console application, **see** Chapter 31, "Using Microsoft Transaction Server to Enable Distributed Applications," **p. 899**

A package in MTS is a related group of components. All the components in a package run in the same process space. Of interest to this chapter, however, is MTS's package export capabilities. Using the MTS console, an executable file can be created containing the necessary installation information. On the client machine, a user can locate this executable on the network and run it. The executable then performs several key tasks automatically on the client machine:

▨ First, it configures the client machine's registry such that the MTS server is pointed to as the location for running the package's components.

▨ Second, it copies to the client machine those files containing the type library information for the package's components.

▨ Third, it copies over any additional files specified in the special Clients.ini initialization file.

Thus, MTS provides a convenient method for distributing ready-to-run components to client machines. The client machines simply need to run the appropriate package setup executable any time an update is made. This process can possibly be set up to occur automatically. In fact, the clients.ini can enable setup of both the package components.

After the package is successfully installed on the client machine, developers don't need to concern themselves with how to reference the package's components. They can simply create and use those components using standard means. Thus, MTS doesn't break DCOM's advantage of not requiring the developer to know where a component is physically located.

CAUTION

Although a client developer doesn't do anything special to create an MTS component, the same is not necessarily true for MTS components that reference each other. In that case, the MTS components will need to concern themselves with creating the other component in an appropriate context to support transactions.

Part
II
Ch
10

Furthermore, the concept of a package enables software to be partitioned into well-defined functional areas. Thus, if a company identifies a reusable set of components, they can be placed into a package that can be accessed from whatever area needs access to them. There is no need to copy the components over to the new application or prepare separate installation routines. MTS takes care of everything, including setting up process spaces, managing transactions, and handling security. For example, if a company defines a common framework for error handling that it wants used by all applications, these applications need only point at an error-handling package in MTS rather than duplicate the components as necessary.

MTS capabilities can extend across computers. For example, components running under MTS on one computer can reference components running under MTS from another computer. This makes it possible to place a given set of components on only one computer throughout the enterprise. Of course, it might be inefficient—because of the size of the enterprise or the frequency the components will be accessed—to place the components on only one computer. In this case, MTS can be configured to distribute package components from one MTS server to another allowing for component replication.

N O T E COM+ will provide a further extension of COM that will include all the features of MTS plus additional functionality such as load balancing and synchronization. According to Microsoft, COM, DCOM, and MTS are unified under COM+. ▨

The tremendous amount of flexibility provided by MTS does come at some cost, however. First, there is a slight performance cost for separating components into many packages because MTS runs each package in a separate process. Second, there is additional design and development criteria that should be considered when building components for running under MTS.

The bottom line is that COM, MTS, and COM+ finally provide the capability to view applications as a set of interacting components rather than monolithic structures. It allows for the components in the application to be reused between applications. Finally, it supports distribution of components in a timely fashion. This view of the software universe has been a major goal of many software developers over the years. The technology has finally advanced to the point to make that goal a reality.

Component Distribution Tool Summary

As a final note, a short review of the different tools available for supporting reuse is presented in the following. There is some overlap between tool functionality, and with the exception of the Visual Component Manager and the Microsoft Repository, the tools don't interact with each other. As a result, the following list is intended to highlight when and where the tools can be used:

- Visual SourceSafe is intended for managing software and related items still in development. Its version control and check-in/check-out capabilities make it a prime candidate for managing any items that are in a state of flux.

- The Visual Component Manager is better suited to manage finished client-side software components and similar items for direct use in the development environment. It provides the needed cataloging and search capability to find the right component for the job. Also, its provides the capability to automatically install and configure components into the development environment.

- Microsoft Transaction Server is better suited for distributing and running server-side components and related items for use in development or production. MTS will automatically configure client machines for accessing the necessary components.

- The Microsoft Repository provides a generic location for storing a variety of data. The repository is not accessed directly, but is used by other tools such as Component Manager or Visual Modeler to share information.

Understanding the Role of the Technology Center

The final aspect of supporting reuse that must be addressed by an organization is how the organization itself can best be structured to support reuse. In other words, if individual teams are left to themselves to reuse other teams or even their own components, reuse won't happen. Each team's software will always be tailored to suit their needs and won't take into account the extra design effort needed to make the software reusable. Furthermore, a network to distribute the components and design ideas won't be in place to support reuse between organizations. The enterprise needs an internal organization that will take the lead responsibility for promoting reuse throughout the enterprise.

However, reuse should not be the only goal of such an organization. Reuse by itself is too esoteric a concept and won't be successfully accomplished without understanding the goals and objectives of the enterprise. Furthermore, reuse can't be accomplished if proper technologies, concepts, and processes aren't in place that provide an adequate foundation. Reuse is a natural extension of good planning and organization.

Hence, the concept of a technology center is born. A technology center serves as the focal point of promoting reuse throughout the enterprise. It promotes cross-sharing of ideas, provides education, looks for reuse opportunities, and promotes new technology concepts. It serves to do all this and more.

At its heart, the technology center is an independent group that lives or dies by its capability to reduce costs or increase the productivity of other development projects in the organization. Of course, the up-front costs of setting up a technology center will preclude it from making a profit in the short run. However, in the long term, the organization should provide noticeable benefits to the enterprise.

For an organization setting up a technology center, there are several issues that need to be considered. First, the enterprise must set the goals and objectives of the technology center. Second, it must address the resources required to support the center. The next two sections address these issues.

Part
II
Ch
10

Technology Center Goal and Objectives

The technology center should be focused on making the software development process for the enterprise more efficient and productive. To accomplish this task, the enterprise should determine the goals and objectives that the technology center should strive to accomplish. The following subsections cover possible objectives for a technology center. The enterprise must decide for itself what it hopes the center to accomplish. Not all the objectives listed here must be met, and, certainly, items can be added as required. Furthermore, it is conceivable that the list many need to change over time.

As an example of how the list might vary, consider different organizational approaches to establishing a center. The first organization intends the center to be actively involved in the organization's development projects, functioning as a consulting group of sorts. Such a center will focus more on idea sharing between projects and the development process. A second organization might want the center to be actively involved in analyzing and planning overall enterprise development efforts. In this case, analyzing the enterprise structure will lead the list of objectives. In a third case, an organization wants a smaller, less involved center that works to provide infrastructure support. This final group will focus more on providing a library of materials, performing research on new technologies, and providing education to the various groups. For further information, *Object Technology Centers of Excellence* by Timothy D. Korson and Vijay K. Vaishnavi is an excellent source.

Promote Object-Based Technology   All technology centers should adopt promoting object-based technology and concepts as a basic goal. In order to increase the amount of reuse in an organization, an object view of software development needs to be adopted throughout the enterprise. The center can go a long way in promoting these concepts.

N O T E   The term *object based* is used here rather than object-oriented. This was done because not all development tools are truly object-oriented, nor do they all have to be. At present, COM doesn't support implementation inheritance and neither does Visual Basic. Stored procedures in SQL Server aren't object-oriented, and most applications will continue to store data in relational databases well into the future. The idea is to promote the concept of developing applications as a series of interactive objects or components and not monolithic structures of source code.

Promote a Standard Software Development Process   Software is developed using a variety of techniques ranging from ad hoc approaches to well-defined, highly structured processes. A technology center can focus on determining the process to be used throughout an organization. It can help define how that process can differ from one project to the next, based on criteria such as team size. The center can also interact with projects to determine whether they are addressing often-overlooked development tasks such as quality assurance or risk management. It can also research commercially published development processes such as the Microsoft Solutions Framework developed by Microsoft.

Analyze the Enterprise Structure to Look for Integration/Reuse Opportunities   One of the more ambitious goals for a technology center is to get involved with the planning of future development projects. In this situation, the center usually takes on the task of developing an architecture of the enterprise as a whole to find opportunities for integrating different systems or to reuse components between systems. For example, the center might determine that it will be advantageous for the enterprise to develop a common inventory module for use by several different systems rather than each system developing its own module. The technology center won't develop this common inventory module, but can lead the fight to implement the program that will develop it. This objective centers on understanding the business functions and how to align systems to best support those functions.

Promote Idea Sharing Between Projects   As an alternative to analyzing the enterprise, the technology center can just focus on existing projects. Here, the focus is less on business functionality and more on utility functions that applications must perform (such as error handling, reporting, and security). The center can go so far as to develop actual components and frameworks for providing these functions. It can identify components developed by a project that will make good reuse candidates and aid in refining and distributing those components. Alternatively, it can simply document the approaches projects use to solve these and other design issues as a set of patterns that can be reused between projects. In this situation, the technology center becomes a repository for all the ideas being generated within separate projects and serves as a catalyst for sharing these ideas.

Research New Technologies and Concepts   Although all developers and projects are expected to keep up with the latest technology and concepts, the technology center becomes the focus for this type of information. In some cases, the technology center actually obtains, tests, and tries out new tools and ideas in an isolated environment. In addition, the center might obtain commercially available reuse libraries and frameworks and evaluate them on behalf of the organization. This arrangement gives projects a chance to play with new tools without committing to them. In other cases, the center is a clearinghouse of the latest information and is not actively involved in evaluations.

Set Up Technology An extended version of the research step is for the technology center to actually set up the technology to use. There are several variations of this task that can be performed:

■ First, the technology center can mandate standards for use in development projects. These standards can range from coding and user interface standards to designating specific development tools and languages that must be used.

■ Second, the center can set up the infrastructure needed to support various types of reuse. This infrastructure will include arranging tools such as the Visual Component Manager and the Microsoft Repository to provide central points for distributing reuse.

■ Third, if the technology center is involved in planning, it might need to aid in defining the physical locations for where code is located. It might also need to aid in setting up MTS servers and defining what packages will be located on each. This can also involve setting up distribution schemes to integrate data located on disparate databases.

Part

II

Ch

10

Maintain Libraries The name of this objective is deliberately general because there are so many things a technology center can maintain in a library that the list can go on for pages. The bottom line is that there are several areas for which the center can collect and catalog items for use throughout the enterprise—for example,

■ Software components

■ Design patterns

■ Research material

■ Development tools

■ Design tools

■ Magazines and books

Provide Mentoring In this case, the technology center performs as a consultant to assist teams in understanding object technology and other concepts important to the enterprise. In this role, the center can answer questions as necessary or actively participate as members of design and development teams. The center serves to provide expertise on new technologies to meet business requirements defined by the different projects. The theory is that the center will have knowledge of both the latest research and successful techniques used on other projects to guide the new project.

Another aspect of mentoring is to aid management in how to best support object and reuse strategies. The center can provide advice on development tasks, skill sets, and training needed to support new technologies and ideas. It can also familiarize managers with the differences in time and costs associated with different development techniques.

Provide Education Rather than take on the active role of mentoring, the technology center can provide a more passive role of providing education. In this objective, the center arranges for classes on different subjects, prepares its own courses, prepares handouts and documentation on internal standards and processes, and obtains any training material deemed beneficial.

Organizing Technology Center Resources

When an organization has identified its need for a technology center, how does it go about creating that center? This section addresses some of those issues but does not answer them; it is up to each organization to make the determination for itself. In general, the structure will be related to the goals and objectives laid out for the center to accomplish.

Reporting Structure   Reporting structure refers to how the center fits into the rest of the organizational structure for the enterprise. There are two issues to address here. The first issue is the center's authority level. Does it have authority over other projects to affect their timelines and resources, or is it meant to interact with development projects at a peer level? Perhaps it reports to a board made up of representatives from the various projects. Also, does it actively reach out to the various projects, or does it wait for the projects to contact it for information?

The second issue to address is where the center is located. The term *center* can be misleading in that many organizations choose to distribute the center to various locations. This becomes a necessity for larger organizations with many operating locations. Alternatively, the center can be a separate unit unto itself located in a single place.

Staffing   The next issue is determining who should be involved in the center. There are again two issues to address. First, where are the people who will compose the center going to come from? Second, what responsibilities will they perform once on the team?

The first issue depends on the goals and objectives placed on the center as well as the size of the organization the center must support. More aggressive goals and larger organizations will require larger technology centers with more advanced people in them. Clearly, the center shouldn't be composed of brand new people. Rather, the more experienced and qualified employees need to be involved to correctly leverage the center's role in the enterprise.

The second issue also depends on the goals and the size of the organization. In general, there are several positions that might be involved:

- Oversight group—A board or panel composed of individuals from throughout the enterprise who ensure that the goals of the technology center are being met, and refines those goals as necessary.
- Director—As expected, someone will need to take the role of leading the technology center on a daily basis.
- Consultants—For the more active objectives of the center, individuals will be labeled strictly as consultants or mentors. They won't have specific responsibilities. Rather, they will be responsible for aiding the various projects to adopt new concepts and meet their own objectives.
- Other goal-specific positions—The remaining positions will directly support the various goals of the center. An individual or several individuals will be assigned to each area. Such positions can include reuse coordination, process definition, infrastructure support, quality assurance, training coordination, tool acquisition, and research.

Funding   The amount of funding depends on the eventual size of the center and the resources needed for the center to operate. Determining where the money will come from is a trickier issue. There are basically two approaches to funding a center that can be used.

First, the center can have its own set of funds. This helps the center to remain autonomous, so it can meet its stated goals rather than being tied to a specific project for help. However, technology centers can enter a state in which they exist only to support themselves and don't contribute to any projects. This structure is best oriented to a center that is support-oriented with more passive goals.

Second, the center can obtain funds from other projects on a fee for service basis. Thus, when training materials or consulting services are used, a fee is charged for these items to provide the center's funding. Of course, some up-front seed money will be required until the center's first services are acquired. This approach helps to keep the center firmly focused both on the needs of the projects it supports, and on the bottom line. However, it can cause the center to become fractured as it supports many different projects and loses focus on its own goals and objects. Also, the technology center's priorities can easily shift to projects willing to pay large amounts of money and away from smaller projects that might actually need the support more. This structure is best oriented to a center that is consulting oriented with more active goals.

The approaches are not exclusive and can be used together effectively. A mixture of the two can help maintain a balance between the two extremes. This structure is best oriented to a center that is planning oriented with very active goals or to the other two center approaches.

Acceptance   One of the biggest obstacles a technology center will have to overcome is opposition to its need. Some people will just not understand the concept, whereas others will question the benefit of any activity not engaged in specifically building a product. There are, in general, five basic activities that the center or center proponents can perform to gain acceptance for the organization:

- Cost/benefit analysis—Some type of model needs to be developed that demonstrates the potential gains of developing the center. The problem with this type of analysis is that although the costs are easy to quantify, the benefits are often difficult if not impossible to quantify. However, the analysis is still necessary. First, some managers only make decisions based on purely financial reasoning, and, second, the analysis provides a foundation for analyzing the center's progress over time.

- Education—The center can prepare materials and presentations showing the benefits or potential benefits of the organization.

- Funding—The center can be set up to receive at least part of its funding from a fee for service approach. This reduces criticism that the center is not responsive to the needs of various projects.

- Success criteria—Each of the goals and objectives should be mapped to specific criteria to determine whether the center is meeting those objectives.

▨ Test project—Often an initial project of some kind is championed by the center to prove its use to the enterprise. Such a test project can certainly be useful to get the kinks out of the center's roles and responsibilities. However, caution should be taken when using a test project as the sole means of judging the technology center's success. Because of the need to succeed and the fact that the best people in an organization are often put on test projects, they often succeed despite potential risks.

From Here...

Reuse is not an impossible task. With some good organization and strategic planning, an organization can succeed in establishing a solid, purposeful, software reuse initiative. This chapter presents a synthesis of information contained in many other chapters of this book on how reuse can be supported by using Visual Studio. For detailed information on any of the techniques, tools, or topics presented in this chapter, see one of the following chapters:

▨ To learn more about interfaces and about building COM-based components, see Chapter 9, "Using Microsoft's Object Technologies."

▨ For more information about inheritance and aggregation, see Chapter 14, "Creating COM Components for MTS."

▨ For more information about ActiveX technologies, see Chapter 12, "Creating ActiveX Controls with Visual Basic," and Chapter 13, "Creating ActiveX Controls with Visual C++."

▨ For more information about the Microsoft Repository and the Visual Component Manager, see Chapter 33, "Using the Visual Component Manager and the Microsoft Repository."

▨ For more information about Visual Modeler and how it interacts with both the Visual Component Manager and Microsoft Repository, see Chapter 36, "System Modeling and the Microsoft Visual Modeler."

▨ For more information about Visual SourceSafe, see Chapter 35, "Using Visual SourceSafe."

▨ For an overview on Microsoft Transaction Server, see Chapter 5, "An Inside Look at Microsoft Transaction Server."

▨ For information on distribution issues with MTS and the MTS console application, see Chapter 31, "Using Microsoft Transaction Server to Enable Distributed Applications."

CHAPTER 11

Using COM Components and ActiveX Controls

by Azam A. Mirza and Ronald W. Terry

In this chapter

COM Components and ActiveX Controls

This chapter discusses the techniques of using the various types of ActiveX/COM components in an I-net or client/server environment with Visual Basic, Visual J++, and Visual C++. Visual Basic has been a highly successful front-end development tool dealing with capturing and displaying information for users. Although Visual C++ can equally develop the forms and dialog boxes that comprise a user interface, its niche in the client/server development environment has been in the business rules tier. This tier is comprised of objects with little or no user interface and with the primary task of performing the computationally intensive algorithms for data transformations. Visual J++ is the new tool on the block that brings the power of the Java programming language to the Web. Visual J++ is equally suited to building Java Applets for the Web and creating full-scale applications that take advantage of ActiveX components.

Based on the Component Object Model (COM), an ActiveX component exposes its objects for use by another unit of executable code. This implies a client/server relationship in that a client requests objects from the ActiveX server, which in turn performs services for the client. The client itself can be an ActiveX component, which in turn acts as server and exposes objects to another client.

This relationship can be carried out on a single machine where the client and the server reside locally or the client and server can be on separate machines in which the server is called a *remote server*.

A key advantage of ActiveX controls over other comparable technologies is their capability to be used in a wide variety of development tools and programming languages. ActiveX controls aren't used exclusively for Web development. Thousands of business and commercial client/server applications also take advantage of ActiveX controls.

Using ActiveX Controls in Web Sites

ActiveX is a set of technologies that helps you create interactive content for your Web sites. With ActiveX, you can incorporate multimedia, interactive objects, and sophisticated applications that come together to create a truly dynamic experience. ActiveX provides the functionality that brings all this together to create truly energized Web sites.

▶   For more information about ActiveX technologies, **see** Chapter 6, "An Inside Look at Active Server Pages and the Internet Information Server," **p. 137**

A strong point for ActiveX is its integration of existing technologies with the new Web-based technologies such as Java and Hypertext Markup Language (HTML). By leveraging tried-and-true and mature technologies such as object linking and embedding (OLE) and COM/DCOM, ActiveX builds on stable and standards-based technologies for providing functionality in the I-net environment.

▶   For more information about COM/DCOM, **see** Chapter 9, "Using Microsoft's Object Technologies," **p. 217**

ActiveX provides a multitude of benefits for developers embracing World Wide Web technologies, including the following:

- The capability to create rich and interactive content—By leveraging the power of desktop technologies, combined with Web-based technologies, ActiveX provides you with a rich environment and technologies to create great and exciting Web content (see Figure 11.1).

FIGURE 11.1
The Microsoft Network's Web site is an example of using ActiveX components to create a dazzling Web experience.

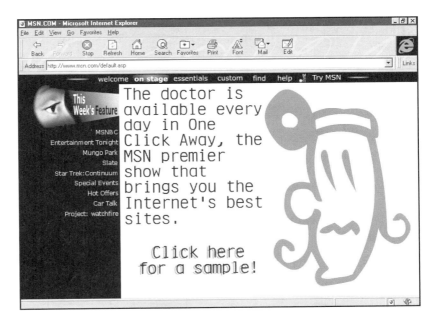

- Thousands of ActiveX controls now available for use in Web applications—New ones are being released every day.
- Open, standards-based and cross-platform support—ActiveX supports widely used Web technologies such as HTTP, Java, TCP/IP, and others.
- Support on multiple platforms—Includes Microsoft Windows, Macintosh, and UNIX.
- Support for the two most widely used browsers—Internet Explorer and Netscape Navigator.

ON THE WEB

To use ActiveX controls with Netscape Navigator, you must use the ActiveX plug-in for Netscape, ScriptActive, from NCompass Labs, Inc., available at NCompass Labs' Web site at http://www.ncompasslabs.com/.

- Creation tools such as Delphi, Visual C++, and Visual Basic—Not only can you create ActiveX controls with these tools, but you can also develop component-based applications by using these tools with ActiveX controls and technologies playing a central role.

Understanding Techniques for Using ActiveX Components in I-net Environments

ActiveX is an open platform for I-net software development. Figure 11.2 shows how ActiveX technologies encompass all aspects of the Web, from clients to servers to development tools to authoring tools to networking technologies.

FIGURE 11.2
Microsoft provides a comprehensive set of products for taking advantage of ActiveX technologies.

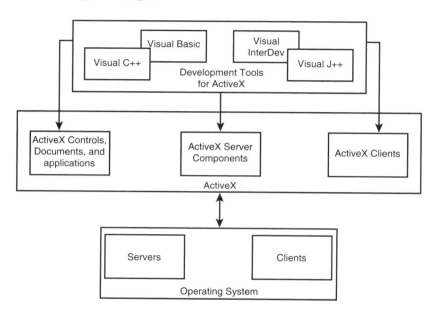

On the server side, Active Server Pages (ASP) and Active Server Components provide support for ActiveX functionality. On the client side, ActiveX controls and the client platforms that support hosting of ActiveX controls provide ActiveX functionality.

▶ For more information about using ASP, **see** Chapter 6, "An Inside Look at Active Server Pages and the Internet Information Server," **p. 137**

Microsoft has released two development products that allow you to take advantage of these ActiveX technologies on the client and the server by making it possible to use ActiveX controls as part of the development environment. These products include Visual InterDev and FrontPage; the next two sections discuss using ActiveX controls in these tools.

▶ For more information about using Visual InterDev to create Web content, **see** Chapter 18, "Developing Active Content with Visual InterDev," **p. 527**

ActiveX Components and Visual InterDev

This section doesn't discuss how to develop Web pages with Visual InterDev. It's more a discussion of the techniques to employ in using ActiveX controls when doing Visual InterDev development.

Visual InterDev is a powerful development environment that provides support for using ActiveX technologies on the server and the client. On the server side, Visual InterDev leverages the power of ASP to provide support for building and using Active Server Components. Figure 11.3 shows how Visual InterDev interacts with ASP and Active Server Components.

FIGURE 11.3

Visual InterDev provides a rich programming environment for using Active Server Components.

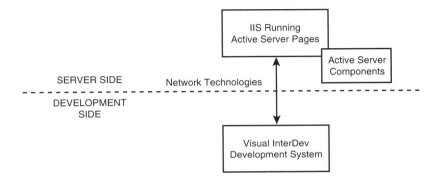

Active Server Components are actually ActiveX controls without any user-interface elements. Active Server Components, also referred to as server-side ActiveX controls, are used to provide two kinds of functionality:

- To gain access to operating systems services
- To encapsulate business rules as part of an application to perform specific tasks such as tax calculations

Tools such as Visual Basic and Visual C++ provide full support for creating Active Server Components. The choice of tool selected for creating Active Server Components depends on your familiarity with the tool and the functionality being developed. As obvious, Visual C++ is a great tool for building components requiring speed and performance. On the other hand, Visual Basic provides a rapid development environment for building components. To get a feel for how Active Server Components work, look at the components provided with ASP, such as the TextStream component.

▷ **See** Chapter 18, "Developing Active Content with Visual InterDev," **p. 527**

On the client side, ActiveX controls provide packaged functionality for building dynamic Web sites. Visual InterDev provides full support for building Web sites that incorporate ActiveX controls for accomplishing various tasks, such as using command buttons, text boxes, and grids. The main distinction between ActiveX controls and Active Server Components is that ActiveX controls employ user interface elements to enhance the look, feel, and functionality of your Web application.

Visual InterDev provides support for using any ActiveX control. It also includes an extensive collection of controls for taking advantage of most Windows graphical elements, such as labels, text boxes, and image controls.

Part

II

Ch

11

The most common method of using client-side ActiveX controls in Visual InterDev is to include them in ASP when you develop Web applications. When a client browser such as Internet Explorer accesses an ASP with an ActiveX control, the control is downloaded to the client machine and then executed as part of the Web page. Figure 11.4 shows the relationship between ActiveX controls, Internet Information Server (IIS) with ASP, and client browsers.

▶ **See** Chapter 19, "Advanced Visual InterDev Concepts," **p. 553**

FIGURE 11.4
Active Server Pages execute on the server and generate an HTML script that's sent to the browser along with any needed ActiveX controls.

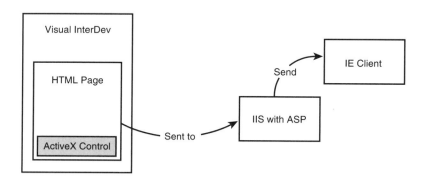

> **CAUTION**
> If you try to access a page that uses client ActiveX controls with Netscape Navigator, the page will load without the ActiveX control and no errors will be generated. Make sure you have the ActiveX plug-in from NCompass Labs installed if you plan to use ActiveX controls with Netscape Navigator.

ActiveX Components and FrontPage (Visual InterDev Edition)

FrontPage is a graphical HTML development tool that helps you build Web pages in a visual environment. Visual InterDev includes a version of FrontPage called FrontPage Visual InterDev Edition. The stripped-down version of FrontPage in Visual InterDev doesn't include support for some advanced functions such as WebBot. One main difference between Visual InterDev and FrontPage is that the latter allows you to insert ActiveX controls into HTML pages in WYSIWYG (what you see is what you get) mode. When FrontPage displays a control in the page, you can use it in a drag-and-drop fashion within the HTML text. Figure 11.5 shows an HTML page in FrontPage with an ActiveX control placed on it.

FIGURE 11.5

The WYSIWYG nature of FrontPage makes it easy to place controls precisely where you want them to appear.

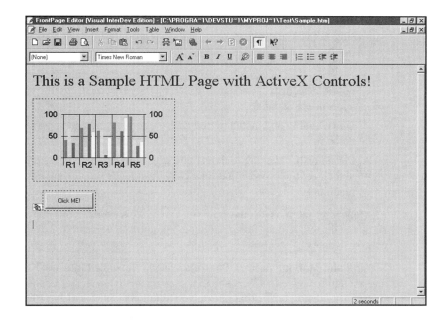

Using ActiveX Components with Internet Explorer

If you've used Internet Explorer to surf the WWW, you've surely come across sites that incorporate ActiveX controls to provide powerful functionality. Internet Explorer is a container application that supports hosting ActiveX controls, Active documents, and so on. Figure 11.6 shows how Internet Explorer interacts with ActiveX control–enabled Web pages.

FIGURE 11.6

As a container application, Internet Explorer handles downloading, displaying, and executing ActiveX controls.

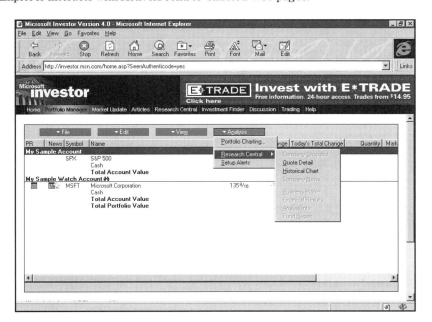

Part

II

Ch

11

As a container application, Internet Explorer takes care of many administrative tasks associated with using ActiveX controls in Web pages. Specifically, Internet Explorer takes care of

- Making sure that the developers have properly signed and marked their ActiveX controls. If an unsigned control is being loaded, Internet Explorer tells the user of a possible security breach and, based on user response and the security settings, takes the appropriate actions.
- Downloading and installing the ActiveX control and all supporting files onto the client machine.
- Periodically checking to determine whether an updated version of the control is available. If so, the browser automatically downloads the newer version and updates the client machine.

The following sections discuss how you can make sure that your controls are appropriately signed and packaged for downloading to client machines and how Internet Explorer handles control updates.

Signing and Marking ActiveX Controls If you've installed Internet Explorer on your machine and tried to navigate to a Web site that uses an unsigned ActiveX control, you're familiar with the security dialog boxes that inform you about possible security problems. The easiest way to get around these dialog boxes is to properly sign and mark your ActiveX controls before deployment.

When installed, Internet Explorer defaults to the High security setting, with the idea that it's safe to have more security than less when going to unknown Web sites. The High setting won't allow you to download any controls that haven't been properly signed and registered by the Web site. You can change the security setting by using the Internet Options dialog box (<u>V</u>iew, Internet <u>O</u>ptions, Security tab).

The signing and marking of controls refer to two distinct operations:

- Developers have registered the controls with an appropriate digital certificate-issuing authority.
- The certificates are incorporated into the controls.

ON THE WEB

VeriSign is the certificate-issuing authority used to obtain digital certificates for ActiveX controls. You can reach VeriSign at `http://www.verisign.com/`.

Signing a control assures that the control's developer is positively identified and that the control hasn't been changed in any way since it was signed. If you make any changes to your control, you must re-sign it. The signature on a control is checked only once when the control is first downloaded. After that, Internet Explorer doesn't recheck the signature on the control.

However, signing the control isn't enough by itself. You must also mark your controls safe for initialization and safe for scripting. What this means is that the control has been marked as safe to be initialized by Internet Explorer and the scripts included with the control are safe for execution. If you mark your control as safe for initializing, you're asserting that no matter what values are used to initialize your control, it won't do anything that would damage a user's system or compromise the user's security. If you mark your control as safe for scripting, you're asserting that your control won't do anything to damage a user's system or compromise security, regardless of how your control's methods and properties are manipulated by the Web page's script. In other words, it has to accept any method calls (with any parameters) or property manipulations in any order without doing anything bad.

During development, you can do some things to make sure that a control is safe for marking. Make sure that the control

- Doesn't manipulate the file system.
- Doesn't modify the Registry except to register and unregister itself.
- Initializes all arrays and indexes correctly.
- Doesn't misuse memory and releases all memory used.
- Validates all input and ensures that the initialization values are within valid limits.

Downloading and Updating ActiveX Controls When Internet Explorer encounters a Web page with an ActiveX control (or multiple controls), it first checks users' local system registries to find out whether that component is available on their machines. If it is, Internet Explorer displays the Web page and activates the control. If the control isn't already installed on the users' computers, Internet Explorer automatically finds and installs the component over the Web, based on a location specified by the developer who created the page.

The Web page developer provides this information by setting the control's CODEBASE property, which specifies a uniform resource locator (URL) location or set of locations where the control can be found and downloaded on the Internet. Internet Explorer then uses this information to locate the control and download the component automatically.

Before a component is downloaded, Internet Explorer displays a message notifying users of the download. Users can choose to cancel the download or to proceed. If the control is digitally signed, a digital certificate provides the name of the software vendor supplying the control and verifies that the control hasn't been tampered with. Figure 11.7 shows a digital certificate displayed for an ActiveX control before it's downloaded.

Part

II

Ch

11

FIGURE 11.7
The digital certificate identifies the control's publisher and the digital certification authority that signed it.

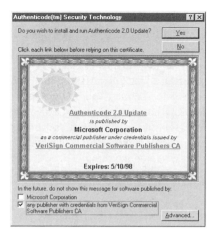

The information is carried by the control itself, so the digital certificate is displayed automatically before downloading, with no development work required by the person who uses that control on a Web page.

N O T E   By default, controls are downloaded into an ActiveX control cache located in the \windows\occache directory. ■

The Component Download Service in Internet Explorer supports versioning, so new versions of the control can be detected and automatically downloaded as required.

ActiveX controls include a mechanism to prevent the unlicensed use of controls in Web pages. The licensing mechanism works by enabling controls to be distributed with a developer license or a runtime license. Under a developer license, developers can use the control for development purposes in tools such as Visual Basic, Visual C++, and Visual InterDev. Under a runtime license, users can only view the control within an existing application or Web page, but can't insert the control into a tool for further development purposes.

 Most controls include a binary file with the .lic extension that includes information about the license. Development tools use this file to determine whether a control can be used in the development environment.

Understanding Techniques for Using Components in Client/Server Applications

ActiveX components come in a wide variety of functionality that seems to be limited only by component developers' imaginations. From user interfaces that capture and display data in an elegant manner to complex behind-the-scenes business calculations, an ActiveX component can become a versatile building block in developing client/server applications.

As with any building block—whether it's a brick for a building or an object for a software application—it's not as important for you to learn the innermost workings or how the building block was produced to be an effective user. Rather, learning the behavior and limitations of the building block, along with being proficient with the techniques and tools used to adhere multiple blocks together, is what's of utmost importance in producing an effective composite structure.

The following sections focus on the different types of ActiveX components typical in a client/server application, their key characteristics, and in which tier they're most effective. The techniques of installing and registering components are also covered. How the component is registered in the Windows Registry determines where the component is located and the security factors involved for client access. You also see how to access remote components (executed on a separate machine) by using the Remote Automation and Distributed COM (DCOM) transports.

Component Types in a Client/Server Environment

You can categorize components used in a client/server environment into three types: ActiveX controls, ActiveX documents, and ActiveX code components. Figure 11.8 shows a typical three-tiered client/server application depicting where each type normally would be incorporated. The front-end or user-interface tier would be composed of forms and dialog boxes consisting of ActiveX controls. These controls would capture or display data for the user and pass/retrieve it to the business tier. The components on the business tier massage the data, perform calculations, and provide results back to the components in the user-interface tier. Also, the business components can pass the data to the data tier. Components in the data tier contain the necessary logic to set and retrieve data from the database.

Part
II
Ch
11

FIGURE 11.8
ActiveX component types in a client/server environment.

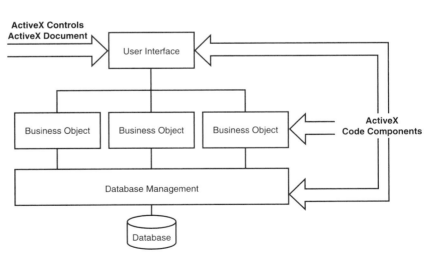

These components can all reside on the client machine, creating what's known as a *fat client*, or be distributed among many machines. For instance, the user-interface tier would reside on the client machine, the business-tier objects would reside on a dedicated machine chosen for performance, and the data-tier objects would reside on the same machine as the database engine.

Deciding how the components will be distributed involves studies based on the environment in which they'll be used. Consider these key issues when distributing components:

- Maintenance—If component maintenance is an overwhelming factor, position the business and data components on a separate machine that all clients can access. By doing so, making updates to business and data components is localized to only one machine. When the components are updated, all the clients who access them are using the updated ones. If the components were installed on client machines, the tedious task of updating every client machine would have to be undertaken.

- Network traffic—As components get distributed across machines, the network traffic inherently increases. If your distributed application's performance is starting to suffer because of high network traffic, you might want to move some of the most frequently called components to the client machines.

- Client access—If the client machine has no access to the network, all components need to be installed on the client.

- Machine performance—Identify the computational-intensive components and locate them on a machine that has the most horsepower.

- User interface—Components consisting of some sort of user interface need to be located on the client machine.

The following sections explain the three different categories of ActiveX components and their uses in more detail, and also include a how-to guide in installing and registering components for use by clients locally or remotely.

ActiveX Controls   *ActiveX controls* are components that provide some form of interface between users and the application, such as a text box or a command button. ActiveX controls are assembled on forms or dialog boxes and are part of the user-interface tier. They expose properties that can be set at design time to adjust the look and feel of the control. Properties can also be accessed at runtime, as well as the controls' methods and events, which enable controls to respond to different needs of the application as it's executing.

ActiveX controls are the most common components. Although they're easily created with any of the Visual Studio development tools (as you've seen in earlier chapters), they're more commonly provided by third-party developers. ActiveX controls are in-process servers that are compiled into files with the extensions of .ocx (most common) or .dll. These files are copied to the client machine hard drive and expose functions that enable the control to register itself through the use of special utilities.

ActiveX Documents   *ActiveX documents* are special components hosted in document containers such as a Web browser, Microsoft Office Binder, Visual Basic Integrated Development Environment (IDE), or a container that you created. Through an additional set of interfaces supported by the ActiveX document, containers can provide a view port into the document's data.

Unlike ActiveX controls, documents are displayed full frame in their host and can take control of their host to some extent (see Figure 11.9). When a document is viewed, the document menus are merged with those of the containers to give users the impression that they're working with an application rather than a container.

FIGURE 11.9
ActiveX documents can reside in many different containers. As shown here, a Word document can reside in Internet Explorer or Office Binder.

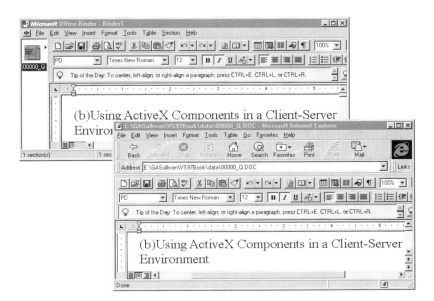

With the popularity of Web-based applications, it's no wonder that the focus of implementing ActiveX documents was placed on Web browsers. Although a container can be easily created by using the SHDOCVW.DLL file installed by Internet Explorer 4, working with documents is addressed in Chapter 15, "Clients, Servers, and Components: Web-Based Applications," where ActiveX components in the Internet environment are addressed.

ActiveX Code Components *ActiveX code components*, formerly referred to as *OLE Automation servers*, have little or no user interface. Code components are used primarily to implement business rules behind the scenes and can reside in all tiers of a client/server application.

Client applications use objects created from the classes exposed by the components and manipulate them through the properties, methods, and events provided. Through the properties, methods, and events exposed to the client—collectively called the *class interface*—components are "glued" together to produce an application.

ActiveX code components can be packaged as in-process or out-of-process servers, with the former residing in files with the .dll extension and the latter in .exe files. Like ActiveX controls, code components expose self-registration functions and are accompanied by a type library (.tlb) file. Visual Basic and Visual C++ development tools use this type library file to obtain information on the component's interface at design time.

How Components Are Installed and Registered

ActiveX components are normally installed by a setup program provided with the application that uses the component and are placed in the System32 directory. If a component isn't associated with any setup program, simply copy the file containing the component to the hard drive. Locating files containing ActiveX components in one location (such as the System32 directory) is a good idea.

According to ActiveX standards, ActiveX components must be self-registering, which, for an in-process control or code component, means implementing and exporting the DllRegisterServer and DllUnregisterServer functions. If the components were installed with an application such as Visual Basic or Visual C++, they most likely were placed in the \Windows\System or System32 directory by their respective setup program and registered with the system Registry behind the scenes.

If the in-process component was developed locally or copied to the local machine without a setup program, the component needs to be registered manually. This is accomplished with the Regsvr32.exe command-line utility located in the \Windows\System or \System32 directory. Regsvr32 takes advantage of several command-line arguments.

The usage for the regsvr32 command-line utility is as follows:

```
regsvr32 [/u][/s][/n][/i[:cmdline]] dllname
```

- /u—Unregister server.
- /s—Silent, display no message boxes.
- /c—Console output.
- /i—Call DllInstall, passing it an optional [cmdline], when used with a /u call, the DLL uninstalls.
- /n—Don't call DllRegisterServer. This option must be used with /i.

To register an ActiveX in-process component, simply choose Run from the Start menu and enter the following:

```
Regsvr32.exe <DLL or OCX File Name>
```

Similarly, to unregister the component, enter the following:

```
Regsvr32.exe <DLL or OCX File Name> /u
```

 T I P If you're registering in-process ActiveX components often, associate DLL and OCX files with the Regsvr32 utility. By doing so, you can just double-click a DLL or OCX file in Explorer to automatically launch the Regsvr32 utility with the file as the command-line argument.

To associate a DLL or OCX with the Regsvr32 utility, locate the file in Explorer. Right-click the file, and then choose Open With. In the dialog box that appears, click Other and select Regsvr32 to open the component file with the Regsvr32 utility and subsequently register the component. If the Always Use This Program to Open This File check box is selected, all files with the same extension are associated with the utility.

For out-of-process servers, the components are automatically registered by executing the server.

Components and Remote Automation

ActiveX clients and out-of-process ActiveX servers communicate through a proxy/stub mechanism automatically supplied by COM. DCOM extends this mechanism across a network, enabling the out-of-process code component to be instantiated and executed on a remote machine, thus distributing the computational load across multiple machines.

DCOM ships with Windows NT 4 and a service pack is available to provide DCOM for Windows 95. For machines not running Windows NT 4 or Windows 95/98 with the DCOM upgrade, Remote Automation is available to provide the same functionality as DCOM. Remote Automation was introduced before DCOM and shipped with Visual Basic 4. Although DCOM is slowly taking over the role Remote Automation held, Remote Automation is still supported by Visual Basic's Enterprise Edition for backward compatibility and for situations where the client process resides on a 16-bit machine.

The following steps are necessary to implement a remote server. Use of DCOM is assumed and, where different, Remote Automation is indicated.

Part

II

Ch

11

1. Install and register the server on the remote machine (the remote server must be an out-of-process ActiveX code component) by simply copying the executable to the server machine and executing it.

2. Configure the access and launch privileges for the component that uses the Racmgr32.exe or dcomcnfg.exe (DCOM only) utility. (Both utilities are discussed later in this section.)

3. Register the server on the client machine by copying the executable to the client machine and executing it. At this point, however, the component is configured as a local server.

4. On the client machine, configure the remote component to run remotely by using the Racmgr32.exe or dcomcnfg.exe (DCOM only) utility.

5. Install and register Autprx16.dll or Autprx32.dll on the client and server machines (Remote Automation). These files are located in the \Windows\System or \System32 directory of the development machine and were installed with Visual Basic.

6. Install and run the Automation Manager (Autmgr32.exe) on the server machine (Remote Automation). This file was also installed in the \Windows\System or \System32 directory with Visual Basic.

7. Run the client application.

Figure 11.10 shows the RemAuto Connection Manager (Racmgr32) utility, which is found in the Microsoft Visual Studio 6 Enterprise Tools program group. The Remote Automation Connection Manager window consists of a list of the classes in your Windows Registry as potential ActiveX components. Two tabbed pages appear on the right: one to configure client access, and the other to configure server connection. The Client Access page is for configuring the remote server's access privileges, which is performed on the server machine.

FIGURE 11.10

The Racmgr32 utility is used on the server machine to configure client access to remote components.

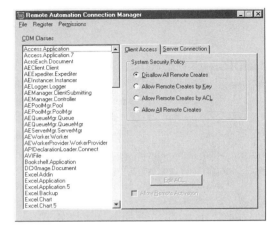

Remote automation provides four levels of access security:

■ Disallow All Remote Creates—Disables the selected class from remote accesses by clients.

■ Allow Remote Creates by Key—Enables the Allow Remote Activation check box at the bottom of the page. This security level enables objects to be created from the selected class by remote clients, as long as the Allow Remote Activation check box is selected.

■ Allow Remote Creates by ACL—Enables remote access from clients specified in an Access Control List (ACL), a list of users or user groups with various levels of access privileges assigned to them. By selecting Allow Remote Creates by ACL, only those users in the ACL will have access to the component and are further limited by their assigned access privilege. To edit the ACL, click the Edit ACL button.

■ Allow All Remote Creates—Enables any object to be created from the selected class.

When invoking the Remote Automation Connection Manager on the client machine, click the Server Connection tab. The Server Connection page has two option buttons and three drop-down boxes that you can use to configure the network connection (see Figure 11.11). When you're selecting a class for the first time, the connection icon toward the top of the page indicates Local. To change this to Remote, right-click the class or the icon and select Remote. However, the type of remote transport and network connection still needs to be configured.

In the Remote Transport section, choose Distributed COM or Remote Automation. If you choose DCOM, notice that only the Network Address drop-down box is enabled (DCOM uses its own network protocol and security). All three drop-down boxes become enabled with the Remote Automation selection. Figure 11.12 shows a sample entry for the selected remote server by using Remote Automation.

FIGURE 11.11

The Server Connection page of the Racmgr32 utility is used on the client machine to configure the connection to out-of-process ActiveX components.

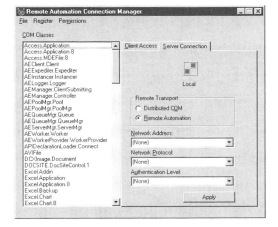

FIGURE 11.12

The MyRemoteServer.Server connection. This component will be accessed on the network machine named *REMCOMP* with the TCP/IP protocol.

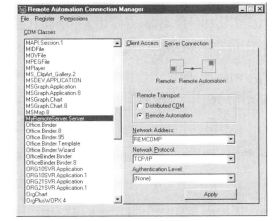

Because the Racmgr32.exe utility is extremely easy to use, you can quickly configure component servers. You can select the local connection and run the client application, and the local component is used. Then select Remote along with Remote Automation, and the component is accessed from the specified network machine by using Remote Automation. Finally, keep the selection at Remote and select DCOM, and the component is accessed on the remote machine by using the DCOM protocol. It's as easy as that.

Another utility is provided for DCOM-enabled machines (Windows NT 4, Windows 98 and Windows 95 with DCOM upgrade) that facilitates configuring DCOM access. You can find this utility, dcomcnfg.exe, in the Windows\System32 directory. Executing this application displays the dialog box shown in Figure 11.13.

Part
II
Ch
11

FIGURE 11.13

The dcomcnfg.exe utility is used to configure the properties and security of components running under DCOM.

This dialog box consists of three tabbed pages:

- Applications—Lists the applications registered as ActiveX servers. Use this page to configure a component by selecting the server and clicking the Properties button.
- Default Properties—Allows you to enable or disable DCOM on the local machine and set default communication properties.
- Default Security—Allows you to identify which clients have access to running components, to launch servers on the local machine, and to change Registry settings for components.

Use dcomcnfg.exe to configure a component to run on a remote machine with the DCOM transport.

N O T E Make sure that the component is installed and registered on the remote machine and registered on the local machine. ▪

Follow these steps:

1. From the Applications page, select the component you want to run remotely and click Properties.
2. Click the Location tab.
3. Select the Run Application on the Following Computer check box and provide the machine name of the remote server.
4. Choose OK twice to save the configuration and to exit the utility.

Likewise, to configure a remote server, follow these steps with the dcomcnfg.exe utility:

1. From the Applications page, select the server component you want to configure and click Properties.

2. Make sure that the Run Application on This Computer check box is selected on the Location page.

3. Use the Security page if you want the component to have a different security configuration from the default (as defined on the Default Security page of the Distributed COM Configuration Properties dialog box).

4. Use the Identity page to set the account that the component will run under.

5. Choose OK twice to save the configuration and to exit the utility.

Now that you've seen the different types of components and how they're installed and registered, it's time to cover how they're used as part of Web pages or applications. For client/server applications, the most popular tools for performing this task are Visual Basic and Visual C++, both part of the Visual Studio suite. Visual J++ can also take advantage of ActiveX components. The rest of this chapter is devoted to using ActiveX components with these development tools.

To learn the techniques of using ActiveX controls and code components, you'll develop a simple dialog box-based application first with Visual Basic and then with Visual C++. This application prompts for a URL and, on the user's request, navigates to the Web site and displays the associated Web page. The following controls and components (installed on your machine when the Visual Studio development tools were installed) will be used:

- Microsoft Rich Text Box (RICHTX32.OCX)
- Sheridan 3D Command Button (THREED32.OCX)
- Internet Explorer (SHDOCVW.DLL)

The two controls, Microsoft Rich Text Box and Sheridan 3D Command Button, are discussed first in the "ActiveX Controls" section. Then, the Internet Explorer Automation object will be incorporated to provide the Web-navigation capability that is covered in the "ActiveX Code Components" section.

Using Components with Visual Basic

After you use an ActiveX component within Visual Basic, you'll come to appreciate the ease with which you can rapidly build component-based applications with this highly successful development tool. What's more, after you work with a particular component and become familiar with the basic steps of incorporating one into a Visual Basic project, using other components will become second nature to you.

ActiveX controls are used by selecting the control from the toolbox and placing it on a form. You can set the control's design-time properties to adjust the look and feel. Properties and methods can also be accessed programmatically. Event-handler functions are incorporated into the form's code to provide logic that needs to be executed in response to a particular event from a control.

Using ActiveX code components requires declaring a variable that's an object of the component. When a call is made to instance the object, properties and methods can then be accessed.

These procedures are discussed in detail in the following sections. Now create a project for the sample application. With Visual Basic running, choose File, New Project from the menu, and select Standard exe.

ActiveX Controls

Using an ActiveX control involves these general steps, explained in more detail in the following sections:

1. Load the control into the current project.
2. Access the control's properties and methods.
3. Handle events fired by the control.

Loading the Control To use an ActiveX control in a project, you need to add the control to the toolbox. Choose Project, Components from the menu to open the Components dialog box. In the list of controls registered with the Windows Registry, select a control and click OK. An icon representing the control appears in the toolbox.

If the control you're interested in doesn't appear in the list box but the .ocx file is installed on your machine (the control might not be registered), click the Browse button on the Components dialog box. In the Add ActiveX Control dialog box, locate the .ocx file and select it to load the control into the project. With the control added to the toolbox, you can use it just like any other control provided with Visual Basic.

Follow these steps to load the Microsoft Rich Textbox and Sheridan 3D Command Button controls into your sample application:

1. Choose Project, Components from the menu to open the Components dialog box.
2. Select the Microsoft Rich Textbox Control item.
3. Select the Sheridan 3D Controls item.
4. Click OK. Six new icons appear in the toolbox. Five of the icons represent the Sheridan 3D controls (of which the Command Button is a member); the sixth one represents the Microsoft Rich Textbox (see Figure 11.14).

You can now assemble the controls on your form.

Place a Microsoft Rich Textbox and a Sheridan 3D Command Button on the form of your sample application. Also place a common label control next to the text box. Your project should look like Figure 11.15.

FIGURE 11.14

The toolbox reflects the components loaded into the projects.

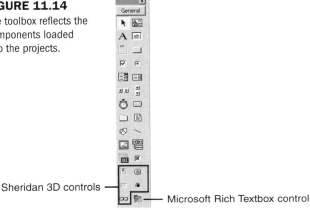

Sheridan 3D controls ——

Microsoft Rich Textbox control

FIGURE 11.15

The Microsoft Rich Textbox and Sheridan 3D ActiveX controls positioned on the main form.

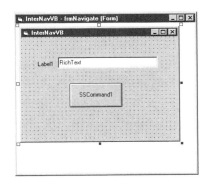

Accessing Properties and Methods   With the control loaded, the properties and methods exposed by the component are most easily viewed with the Object Browser (see Figure 11.16). The list on the left contains the classes or components that are part of the type library selected in the top drop-down box. Selecting the component causes its properties, methods, and events to appear in the right list. The pane at the bottom of the dialog box displays information about the item selected in either list—a convenient way to familiarize yourself with a component before using it in code.

FIGURE 11.16

Use the Object Browser to review an ActiveX component's properties and methods.

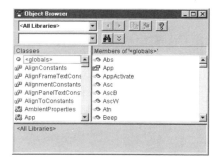

Another way to display control properties that are available at design time is through the Properties window, which normally appears between the Project and Form Layout windows at the right of the IDE. You can use the Properties window to set component properties at design time. Selecting the property displays information about it in the bottom pane of the window. With the property selected, the value can be entered in the column directly to the right of it.

For the example, you'll want to set the Caption properties for the Label and Command Button controls. Also, you'll need to set the Text property of the TextBox control to a blank string:

1. Select the Label control on the form. In the Properties window, locate the Caption property and change the value from Label1 to URL:.

2. In a similar fashion, change the CommandButton's Caption property to Navigate.

3. Select the Rich Textbox control and remove the Rich Text string from the Text property in the Properties window. Your project should now resemble Figure 11.17.

FIGURE 11.17

The final appearance of the sample application with the appropriate properties set.

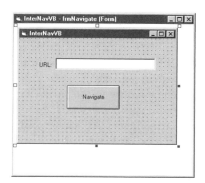

Properties and methods of an ActiveX control can be accessed programmatically. An object of a control is identified by the (Name) property in the Properties window. For example, to obtain the text value of the Rich Textbox identified by the name RichTextBox1, the following code segment would be added:

```
Dim sText As String
sText = RichTextBox1.Text
```

Setting the text value is accomplished with this statement:

```
RichTextBox1.Text = "Hello World"
```

Methods are accessed in the same manner. For example, if you wanted to invoke the `LoadFile` function of the Rich Textbox, the following code would be inserted:

```
Dim sFile As String = "MyFile.rtf"
RichTextBox1.LoadFile(sFile)
```

This code would load a .rtf file into a RichTextBox control.

Run the sample application. Notice that the only operation that can be performed is entering text into the text box. What you really want to happen is the application navigating to the entered URL at the user's command. You'll use the click event fired by the Sheridan 3D Command Button to tell the program to access the text in the text box and navigate to the URL. This leads to a discussion of handling events from ActiveX controls with Visual Basic.

Handling Events   ActiveX controls will fire events predefined by the control's developer, notifying the client process of important events. ActiveX controls provided by vendors usually offer information to be displayed with Visual Basic help, documenting what events they fire.

You can view exposed events from a control loaded into the project in various ways:

Part
II

Ch
11

- Use the Object Browser—Along with the control's properties and methods, the events raised are displayed with a brief description. Figure 11.18 shows a good example, where the Object Browser is showing the Command Button control. As shown in the dialog box, an event called `Click` is raised by the Command Button control, and a description of how this event gets fired is provided in the bottom pane of the dialog box.

FIGURE 11.18
Viewing the Sheridan 3D Command Button's `Click` event.

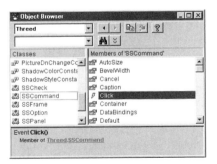

- View the form's code in the Code window—From the left drop-down list, you can select a control or code component to associate code with. The right drop-down list provides the events raised by the component. Selecting an event provides an event prototype in the code section of the form (as seen for the Command Button's `Click` event in Figure 11.19). It's within this subroutine you provide the necessary logic to be executed when this event is fired.

FIGURE 11.19

The Command Button event handler prototype inserted into the form's code.

Returning to the example application, enter the bold line of code in the Command Button `Click` event:

```
Private Sub SSCommand1_Click()

        MsgBox RichTextBox1.Text

End Sub
```

Run the application, type some text into the text box, and click the Navigate button. Did the text in the text box appear in the message box?

You'll now want to add Web-navigation capability to your application using the Internet Explorer component. Using ActiveX code components is the next topic of discussion.

ActiveX Code Components

Using ActiveX code components involves the following steps, which are covered in more detail in the following sections:

1. Load the component into the current project.
2. Instantiate an object of the component class.
3. Access properties and methods of the component.
4. Handle events raised by the component.

Loading the Code Component Code components aren't child windows like controls. Subsequently, they're not dropped onto forms from the toolbox. However, you can load code components into the project, similar to a control. This pulls the type library information into the project, thus allowing you to view the component's properties and methods.

To add a code component, choose Project, References from the menu. The list box in the References dialog box contains ActiveX components registered with the Windows Registry. Selecting a component enables its properties and methods to be accessed at design time.

If the component doesn't appear in the list box, click the Browse button to open the Add Reference dialog box. Locate the file containing the type library information and select it to register the type library with the Registry and provide access to the properties and methods exposed by the component.

Follow these steps to load the Internet Explorer code component into your example project:

1. Choose Project, References from the menu.
2. Select the Microsoft Internet Controls item to load the type library from the shdocvw.dll file.
3. Click OK.

Accessing Properties and Methods With the code components type library loaded, the properties and methods exposed by the component are most easily viewed through the Object Browser, same as for ActiveX controls. To view the Internet Explorer code component properties and methods, do the following:

1. Choose View, Object Browser from the menu.
2. From the top drop-down list, select the SHDocVw library.
3. In the left list box, select the InternetExplorer item. The properties, methods, and events appear in the right list box.
4. Note the class name in the bottom pane. You'll need this, along with the `Application` property, when making a call to create a running object.

ActiveX components are created and manipulated programmatically. These are the basic steps in using a code component within Visual Basic code:

1. Declare a variable of type `Object`.
2. Create and return a reference to the ActiveX object.
3. Access properties and methods with the `(.)` member selector.
4. Release the reference to the object by setting the object variable to `Nothing`.

To incorporate the Internet Explorer component into your example, follow these steps:

1. With the form's code displayed in the Code window, add the following to the declarations section:

   ```
   Dim m_oInternetExplorer As Object
   ```

2. In the form's load event handler, insert the following:

   ```
   Private Sub Form_Load()

       Set m_oInternetExplorer = CreateObject("InternetExplorer.Application")

   End Sub
   ```

3. In the Command Button's `Click` event, add this code:

   ```
   Private Sub SSCommand1_Click()

       m_oInternetExplorer.Navigate (RichTextBox1.Text)
       m_oInternetExplorer.Visible = True

   End Sub
   ```

4. In the form's Unload event, insert the necessary code to release the reference to the object:

```
Private Sub Form_Unload(Cancel As Integer)

    Set m_oInternetExplorer = Nothing

End Sub
```

5. Make an executable file by choosing File, Make <project name>.exe.

6. Make sure that Internet service is up and running. Run the application, type in a valid URL, and click Navigate. You should see the Internet Explorer launch with the appropriate Web page displayed.

Handling Events   Some ActiveX code components raise events similar to ActiveX controls. Visual Basic allows you to provide event handling for ActiveX components with the WithEvents keyword used in the dimension statement. This tells Visual Basic up front that you want to handle events exposed by the component.

To see how to use the WithEvents keyword, handle the Quit event from Internet Explorer and place the reference releasing code there, as follows:

1. Change the declaration statement to read as follows:

```
Dim WithEvents m_oInternetExplorer As InternetExplorer
```

This tells Visual Basic that you want to handle the events raised by the InternetExplorer class.

2. Notice the m_oInternetExplorer item in the left drop-down list. Select it to list all the events raised by the InternetExplorer component in the right drop-down list.

3. Select the Quit event from the right drop-down list.

4. In the Quit event-handler function, add the following message box and relocate the object release code:

```
Private Sub m_oInternetExplorer_Quit(Cancel As Boolean)

    m_oInternetExplorer.Visible = False

    MsgBox "Exiting Internet Explorer"

    Set m_oInternetExplorer = Nothing

End Sub
```

5. Relocate the object creation code to the Command Button's Click event:

```
Private Sub SSCommand1_Click()

    Set m_oInternetExplorer = CreateObject("InternetExplorer.Application")

    m_oInternetExplorer.Navigate (RichTextBox1.Text)
    m_oInternetExplorer.Visible = True

End Sub
```

6. Make an executable and run the application as before.

Using Components with Visual C++

As mentioned earlier, when you become comfortable with using one component, using others of the same type becomes second nature. Using ActiveX components with Visual C++ is no exception. After you use an ActiveX control with the resource editor or use a code component programmatically, you'll use the same techniques repeatedly with each and every ActiveX component you use.

Using ActiveX controls in Visual C++ is similar to using them in Visual Basic when you become familiar with Visual C++'s resource editor. With the control loaded into the project, an icon representing the control appears on the editor toolbar for dropping onto dialog boxes and forms in a similar manner. Visual C++ exposes design-time tools that enable viewing and setting control properties, as well as a test container that enables a control to be tested and its behavior monitored before you incorporate it into applications.

ActiveX code components, on the other hand, are incorporated a little differently in Visual C++ in that they aren't loaded into the project for early binding, as was the case in Visual Basic. To use an ActiveX code component, a container class must be created to encapsulate the interface provided by the component. Before Visual C++ 5, this was accomplished by the ClassWizard, which created source code included into your project that implemented the container class. With Visual C++ 5 and higher, special support for COM has been added to the compiler. By using the new `#import` directive to import a type library, the preprocessor generates the C++ header file describing the interface and a second file containing the implementation, thus eliminating the need to maintain container source code as before.

Part

II

Ch

11

Creating a Microsoft Foundation Class Application with ActiveX Support

Now is a good time to open the project in which you'll be working with the components. You'll be developing the same sample application as you did with Visual Basic in the earlier discussion. Follow these steps to create a dialog box-based Microsoft Foundation Class (MFC) application:

1. Choose File, New from the menu to open the New dialog box.

2. From the Projects page, select MFC AppWizard (exe). Provide the project name and location in the text boxes on the right. Click OK.

3. Select the Dialog Based option and default on the Language drop down. Click Next.

4. In the MFC AppWizard–Step 2 of 4 dialog box, select Automation Support and ensure that ActiveX Controls Support is also selected. By selecting Automation support, your application can use Automation objects exposed by other programs or expose its own Automation objects to other ActiveX clients. With the ActiveX Controls support selected, your application is created with the necessary logic to be an ActiveX controls container. Click Next.

5. Accept the default options on MFC AppWizard–Step 3 of 4 dialog box. Enabling the AppWizard to generate source file comments is helpful if you're new to developing in Visual C++. These comments indicate where in the source code you'll need to provide

some form of functionality. By choosing to link to the MFC library dynamically (the second set of options on the dialog box), your program makes calls to the MFC library at runtime. This selection minimizes the size of your executable. Click <u>N</u>ext.

6. The last AppWizard dialog box appears as shown in Figure 11.20. You should have three classes in the list box. Selecting a class in the list displays information in the text boxes regarding the base class and the associated implementation files that will be generated. Click <u>F</u>inish to have the AppWizard create the project and insert the implementation files. You're then presented with a dialog box summarizing the project. Click OK.

FIGURE 11.20
The last dialog box of the MFC AppWizard summarizes the classes that will be added to your project.

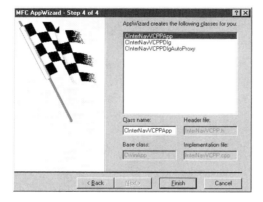

7. Now you can compile your application, even though it has no functionality. Choose <u>B</u>uild, Build <project name>.exe from the menu. After the project finishes compiling, choose <u>B</u>uild, E<u>x</u>ecute <project name>.exe from the menu. Because no functionality has been added yet, clicking either command button halts the execution and returns the Developer Studio to design mode. Click one of the buttons.

8. Your sample application won't need the two command buttons or the TODO caption supplied by the AppWizard. Invoke the resource editor by double-clicking the dialog box resource file in Resource View. You should see the contents of Figure 11.21 onscreen.

FIGURE 11.21
Editing the dialog box resource with the resource editor.

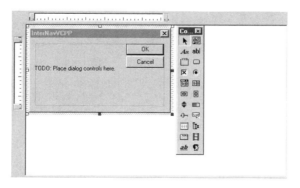

9. Remove the two command buttons and the caption by selecting them and pressing Delete.

You're now ready to proceed with adding the ActiveX controls that will be used in the application. Save your project.

ActiveX Controls

Using an ActiveX Control within Visual C++ involves the following steps, which are discussed in detail in the following sections:

1. Load the control into the project by creating a class to wrap the control's interface.

2. Identify the control's properties and methods, and set the design-time properties.

3. Establish a member variable representing an object of the control's wrapper class.

Loading the Control To load a control into a project, use the Component Gallery (choose Project, Add to Project, Components and Controls from the menu). The Component Gallery stores shortcuts as well as Registry information about registered controls.

If you've installed and registered an ActiveX control and it doesn't appear in the Component Gallery, you must create the shortcut yourself. In Explorer, use the right mouse button to drag the .ocx file containing the control to the Registered ActiveX Controls folder. Choose Create Shortcut(s) Here from the pop-up menu.

To load the two ActiveX controls into your application, follow these steps:

1. Choose Project, Add to Project, Components and Controls from the menu to bring up the Component Gallery dialog box. Double-click the Registered ActiveX Controls folder to display its contents.

2. Locate and select the Microsoft Rich Text control.

3. Click Insert, and then click OK in the message box that asks you to verify your selection.

4. The Confirm Classes dialog box appears, listing all the classes (with their implementation files) associated with the ActiveX control that will be inserted into your project. Click OK.

5. Repeat steps 1 through 4 for the Sheridan 3D Command Button control.

6. If you now view the resource editor as shown in Figure 11.22, notice the addition of two icons on the resource editor's toolbar.

Part
II

Ch
11

FIGURE 11.22

The project's resource editor's toolbar after loading the Microsoft Rich Textbox and Sheridan 3D Command Button controls.

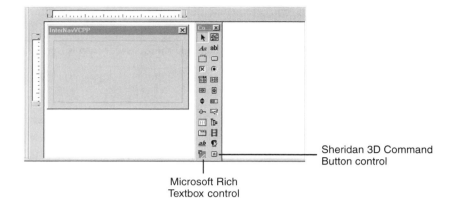

Sheridan 3D Command
Button control

Microsoft Rich
Textbox control

7. Select the Microsoft Rich Text Control from the toolbar and place it on the dialog box.

8. Select the Sheridan 3D Command Button control and place it on the dialog box. Your dialog box should look like Figure 11.23.

FIGURE 11.23

The dialog box resource after placing the Microsoft Rich Textbox and Sheridan 3D Command Button controls on it.

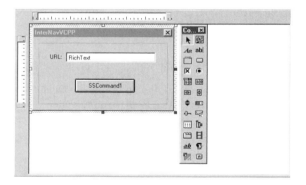

N O T E The label control to the left of the text box is placed on the dialog box in the same way. You can change the label's caption by right-clicking the label and then choosing Properties. On the General page, enter the new caption in the appropriate text box. ▓

 To reposition controls in the dialog box, drag them with the mouse or, with the control selected, use the arrow keys. Likewise, you can resize the control with the arrow keys while holding down the Shift key.

With the ActiveX controls loaded into the project and placed in the dialog box resource, you now can use the properties, methods, and events exposed by each.

Accessing Properties and Methods The ActiveX control's developer designated certain properties to be accessed at design time. You can view these properties and set their values from the control's property page displayed by the resource editor. To access the property page of the Sheridan 3D Command Button control in your application, do the following:

1. With the resource editor in view, right-click the Command Button control. Choose Properties; a dialog box such as the one in Figure 11.24 appears.

FIGURE 11.24

The property sheet for the Sheridan 3D Command Button.

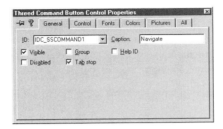

2. The properties are grouped into categories on each page. Display each page to get a feel for what properties the control's developer exposed at design time. Notice that you also can access all properties from the different categories on the All page.

3. On the General page, change the Caption property to Navigate. Play around with the other properties to see how creative you can get with this control's appearance.

The properties for the Microsoft Rich Text control are accessed in the same way. It's a good idea to go ahead and view what properties are exposed by this control for future reference, but you won't need to change any values for this application. You will, however, need to access the Text property of the Microsoft Rich Text Control at runtime.

Part
II
Ch
11

If you remember back to when the controls were inserted using the Component Gallery, several classes were generated and placed into your project. These *wrapper classes* wrap the interfaces to the controls and have member functions for all properties and methods. You can view these member functions through the Class View or by editing the class implementation file. To view the member functions for the Microsoft Rich Text Control wrapper class, follow these steps:

1. With the Class View page displayed in the left pane of the Developer Studio, expand the view of the CRichText class. You'll see a complete list of all member functions that can be used to communicate with the control. You can see a subset of these member functions that begin with the prefixes Get and Set, which are accessory and modifier functions, respectively, that allow you to retrieve and set the controls property values at runtime.

2. Locate the GetText() member function from the expanded list in the Class View. Right-click the function and choose Go To Definition. The implementation file (RichText.cpp) containing the definition (or implementation) of this particular accessory function opens. You should now be viewing the following code in the right pane of the Developer Studio:

```
CString CRichText::GetText()
{
    CString result;
    InvokeHelper(DISPID_TEXT, DISPATCH_PROPERTYGET, VT_BSTR,
    ➥(void*)&result, NULL);
    return result;
}
```

You'll call this function later in the example application to obtain the Text property from the text box.

To make use of the properties and methods exposed by an ActiveX control at runtime, the dialog box class needs a data member that's an object of the control's wrapper class. The ClassWizard provides the support for adding data members of type <control wrapper class> to the dialog box class. You'll want to add a data member of type CRichText to your dialog box to have access to the text property by following these steps:

1. With the dialog box resource in view, right-click the Microsoft Rich Text control and choose Class<u>W</u>izard.

2. On the Member Variables page is a list of control IDs and their respective data member names, if any (see Figure 11.25). Select the IDC_RICHTEXTCTRL1 ID and click the <u>A</u>dd Variable button.

FIGURE 11.25

Adding member variables with the MFC ClassWizard.

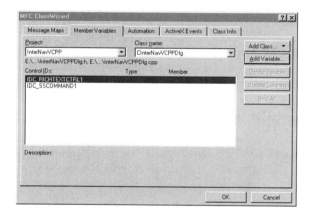

3. Complete the member variable name in the Add Member Variable dialog box. You use this name in your code to reference the object of the control's wrapper class. Click OK to display the data member assigned to the IDC_RICHTEXTCTRL1 ID. Click OK again, and the ClassWizard adds the boldface lines of code to the dialog box class's interface file (see Listing 11.1).

Listing 11.1   Adding a Member Variable

```
// InterNavVCPPDlg.h : header file
//
//{{AFX_INCLUDES()
#include "richtext.h"
//}}AFX_INCLUDES

#if !defined(AFX_INTERNAVVCPPDLG_H__FF98D69A_FFDE_11D0_83C1_
➥000000000000__INCLUDED_)
#define AFX_INTERNAVVCPPDLG_H__FF98D69A_FFDE_11D0_83C1_
➥000000000000__INCLUDED_
```

```
#if _MSC_VER >= 1000
#pragma once
#endif // _MSC_VER >= 1000

class CInterNavVCPPDlgAutoProxy;

///////////////////////////////////////////////////////////////////////////////
// CInterNavVCPPDlg dialog

class CInterNavVCPPDlg : public CDialog
{
    DECLARE_DYNAMIC(CInterNavVCPPDlg);
    friend class CInterNavVCPPDlgAutoProxy;

// Construction
public:
    CInterNavVCPPDlg(CWnd* pParent = NULL);     // standard constructor
    virtual ~CInterNavVCPPDlg();

// Dialog Data
    //{{AFX_DATA(CInterNavVCPPDlg)
    enum { IDD = IDD_INTERNAVVCPP_DIALOG };
    CRichText m_oRichText;
    //}}AFX_DATA

    // ClassWizard generated virtual function overrides
    //{{AFX_VIRTUAL(CInterNavVCPPDlg)
    protected:
    virtual void DoDataExchange(CDataExchange* pDX);     // DDX/DDV support
    //}}AFX_VIRTUAL

    .
    .
    .

#endif // !defined(AFX_INTERNAVVCPPDLG_H__FF98D69A_FFDE_11D0_83C1_
➥000000000000__INCLUDED_)
```

The ClassWizard also adds the following boldface line of code to the implementation file:

```
void CInterNavVCPPDlg::DoDataExchange(CDataExchange* pDX)
{
    CDialog::DoDataExchange(pDX);
    //{{AFX_DATA_MAP(CInterNavVCPPDlg)
    DDX_Control(pDX, IDC_RICHTEXTCTRL1, m_oRichText);
    //}}AFX_DATA_MAP
}
```

4. Invoke the GetText() member function (or any another function, for that matter) of the Microsoft Rich Text control and obtain the value of the text property:

```
CString strText;

strText = m_oRichText.GetText();
```

Handling Events The ClassWizard maps an ActiveX control's events to dialog box class handler functions. The wizard displays all the events that the control can fire. By selecting the events you want your dialog box class to handle, the ClassWizard places the class into an event sink map that connects the event to its handler function.

If you went ahead and compiled and executed the sample application, you'll see the dialog box appear and be able to enter a URL into the text control. But that's about all the functionality the application has at this point. What you really want the program to do is navigate to the URL when you click the Navigate button. Clicking the Command Control button fires an event. The dialog box class handles the event by providing a member function that is invoked when the event is fired. It's within this member function that you'll want to incorporate the necessary logic to retrieve the text from the text control and navigate to the URL.

Because the navigation logic will be handled by the Internet Explorer component (which is covered later in the "ActiveX Code Components" section), an intermediate step will be followed. When the event is handled, logic is put into place to receive the text from the text control and to display it in a message box.

To handle the click event, follow these steps:

N O T E This procedure is the same for mapping all events for all ActiveX Controls.

1. With the dialog box resource in view, right-click the button control and choose Events to display a dialog box containing all the event types the control can fire (see Figure 11.26).

FIGURE 11.26
The events fired by the Sheridan 3D Command Button.

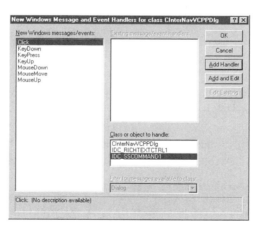

2. Select the Click event from the left list, and then click the Add and Edit button. You're prompted for the name of the member function that will be mapped to the event. Click OK to accept the default name.

3. You're launched into the implementation file where the handler function prototype has been created by the ClassWizard. Enter the following code inside the function:

```
void CInterNavVCPPDlg::OnClickSscommand1()
{
    CString sDisplay;

    sDisplay = "The URL You Entered: " + m_oRichText.GetText();

    AfxMessageBox(sDisplay);

}
```

4. Compile and run the program. Type any text into the text box and click Navigate. The message box should display what was typed.

You also can view and directly maintain the message/event map through the ClassWizard dialog box. Follow these steps:

1. Choose View, ClassWizard from the menu. On the Message Maps page, you should see what's shown in Figure 11.27. The two side-by-side list boxes in the middle of the dialog box contain the objects and events for the class displayed in the upper-right drop-down list.

FIGURE 11.27
The MFC ClassWizard's Message Maps page is used to add and maintain event handlers.

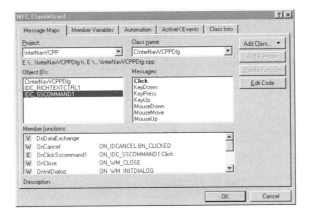

2. Select the command button's ID (IDC_SSCOMMAND1) in the Object IDs list. The events for this control appear in the list on the right.

3. Select the event you want to add a handler function for and click the Add Function button. Accept or change the handler function name and proceed to add logic into the function's implementation.

ActiveX Code Components

Using an ActiveX code component in a Visual C++ project is similar to using ActiveX controls in that a class that wraps the components interface is inserted into a project. It's this wrapper class with which the rest of your application accesses the properties and methods the component developer exposed. What's different is that the ActiveX code component isn't inserted into the project through the Component Gallery, and the component isn't visually edited with the resource editor.

Various techniques are available for loading and using ActiveX code components within Visual C++. To learn these techniques, you'll add the Internet Explorer Automation object to the sample application that you created earlier in the "ActiveX Controls" section to provide the Web navigation functionality this application needs.

Now is a good time to become familiar with the interface to the Internet Explorer component. To obtain information about the component (or any registered component), use the OLE/COM Object Viewer utility provided with Visual C++. This utility displays Registry as well as type library information about the selected component. To view the Internet Explorer component, do the following:

1. Choose Tools, OLE/COM Object Viewer from the menu.

2. From the left list, expand the Automation Objects folder and locate the Internet Explorer entry. Select the entry to see the Registry information (see Figure 11.28).

FIGURE 11.28
The Internet Explorer automation object's Registry entry as viewed by the OLE/COM Object Viewer.

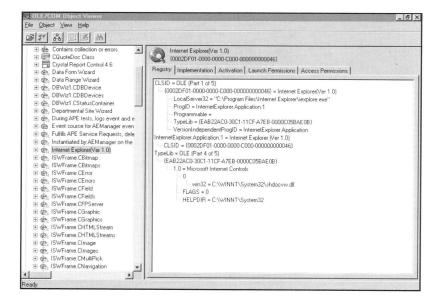

3. The most pertinent information to obtain from this is the ProgID entry. You'll use this value (InternetExplorer.Application.1) in your code to create a running object. Also, the location of the type library is found in the TypeLib/{CLSID}/1.0/0/win32 entry, which for this case is C:\WINNT\System32\shdocvw.dll.

4. In the OLE/COM Object Viewer window, choose File, View TypeLib from the menu and locate the type library file (C:\WINNT\System32\shdocvw.dll).

5. Expand the `interface IWebBrowserApp` entry in the left pane to see all the member functions implemented in the interface in the right pane (see Figure 11.29). It's these member functions that you'll create support for in the wrapper class inserted in your project.

FIGURE 11.29

The `IWebBrowserApp` interface implementation.

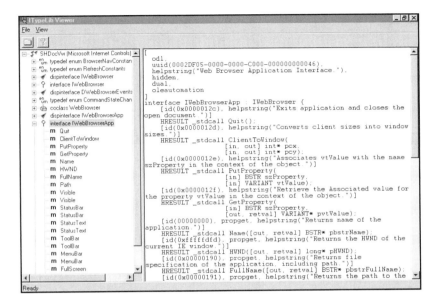

There are two ways to create and insert a wrapper class for an ActiveX code component in Visual C++:

- Use the ClassWizard, which creates and inserts source code into the project for a class based on the ActiveX code components type library.

- Use the `#import` directive. The `#import` directive is used to import the type library of the component into the implementation file of the class that uses the object. The compiler reads the type library and builds the wrapper class for you. This way, there's no source code to maintain in the project.

The ClassWizard Provided with an ActiveX code component's type library, the ClassWizard generates a class that encapsulates each interface listed in the library. The member functions of these classes are tailored to access each property and method included in the library. To create and insert a class for the Internet Explorer component, follow these steps:

1. Choose View, ClassWizard from the menu. Click the Add Class button and select the From a Type Library option.

2. Locate and open the type library file (in this case, C:\WINNT\System32\shdocvw.dll). You should be presented with the Confirm Classes dialog box, which lists the classes that the ClassWizard will generate.

Part

II

Ch

11

3. Select only the `IWebBrowserApp` class and click OK.

4. Click OK again to exit the ClassWizard. Notice an `IWebBrowserApp` class in the Class View, along with the shdocvw.h and shdocvw.cpp files in the File View that contain the implementation.

The `#import` Directive A new feature, first introduced with Visual C++ 5, was the compiler support for COM. By using the `#import` directive with a type library file, the preprocessor generates two header files: one describing the interface to the wrapper class and the other containing the implementation. What's nice is that no source code is added to your project, which subsequently means less code to maintain. The syntax for using the `#import` directive is

```
#import <filename> [attributes]
using namespace <library name>;
```

`<filename>` is the name of the file containing the type library information. This file can be either of the following format or any other file format that the `LoadTypeLib` API can understand:

- A type library file (.tlb or .olb)
- An executable file (.exe)
- A dynamic link library file (.dll) containing a type library resource
- A compound document holding a type library

N O T E Refer to Visual C++'s online documentation for a description of all the available attributes. ■

To prevent name collisions between the imported component and your existing code, the compiler defines a namespace identified by the type library name. A *namespace* is a declarative region that attaches an additional identifier to any names declared inside it. To identify a member of a namespace, the scope resolution operator is used:

```
<namespace>::<member>
```

To avoid typing the scope resolution throughout your code, the using namespace line directly after the `#import` line is incorporated and includes the library name.

To incorporate the Internet Explorer component into your application by using the `#import` directive, follow these steps:

1. Insert the following lines of code into the dialog box class's header file:
    ```
    #import "C:\WINNT\System32\shdocvw.dll" rename("tagREADYSTATE",
    "tagIEREADYSTATE")
    using namespace SHDocVw;
    ```

N O T E You need to rename `tagREADYSTATE` to `tagIEREADYSTATE` to prevent a name collision inside the compiler-generated implementation files. ■

2. In the class declaration section, declare the following data member:

```
IWebBrowserAppPtr m_oIWebBrowserAppPtr;
```

This creates an object of the smart pointer class that encapsulates the interface (to be discussed later in the "Accessing Properties and Methods" section).

Classes Created by the ClassWizard If you use the ClassWizard to incorporate the code component into your project, you'll be creating an object of the class that was derived from the `COleDispatchDriver` class. Member functions inherited from this class provide the means of instantiating the COM object and retrieving and releasing its dispatch :interface. The following are the basic steps of using a class derived from `COleDispatchDriver`:

N O T E Assume that `IChildClass`, a class created by the ClassWizard, exists for these steps. ▪

1. Declare a data member of type `IChildClass`.

2. Call the `COleDispatchDriver::CreateDispatch` function to load the server program and retrieve the `IDispatch` pointer. This increments the object reference count by 1.

3. When you're finished with the component, release `IDispatch` and decrement the reference count by calling the `COleDispatchDriver::ReleaseDispatch()` function.

In the sample application, the ClassWizard created and inserted `IWebBrowserApp` into your project. Use the Internet Explorer component in your application as follows:

1. In the header file for the dialog box class (`InterNavVCPPDlg.h`, in this case), insert the three boldface lines of code shown in Listing 11.2.

Listing 11.2 Adding the Internet Explorer Component as an `IWebBrowserApp` Object

```
// InterNavVCPPDlg.h : header file
//
//{{AFX_INCLUDES()
#include "richtext.h"
//}}AFX_INCLUDES

#include "shdocvw.h"    //Contains the declaration of the IWebBrowserApp class

#if !defined(AFX_INTERNAVVCPPDLG_H__FF98D69A_FFDE_11D0_83C1_
➥000000000000__INCLUDED_)
#define AFX_INTERNAVVCPPDLG_H__FF98D69A_FFDE_11D0_83C1_
➥000000000000__INCLUDED_

    .
    .
    .

// Implementation
protected:
    CInterNavVCPPDlgAutoProxy* m_pAutoProxy;
```

Part

II

Ch

11

continues

Listing 11.2   Continued

```
HICON m_hIcon;

VARIANT vDummy;                    //Argument for IWebBrowserApp::Navigate()
IWebBrowserApp m_oInternetExplorer;  //Declaration IWebBrowserApp object

BOOL CanExit();

.
.
.

#endif // !defined(AFX_INTERNAVVCPPDLG_H__FF98D69A_FFDE_11D0_83C1_
➥000000000000__INCLUDED_)
```

2. In the implementation file for the dialog box class, insert the following boldface lines into the dialog box class's constructor:

```
CInterNavVCPPDlg::CInterNavVCPPDlg(CWnd* pParent /*=NULL*/)
: CDialog(CInterNavVCPPDlg::IDD, pParent)
{
    //{{AFX_DATA_INIT(CInterNavVCPPDlg)
        // NOTE: the ClassWizard will add member initialization here
    //}}AFX_DATA_INIT
    // Note that LoadIcon does not require a subsequent DestroyIcon in Win32
    m_hIcon = AfxGetApp()->LoadIcon(IDR_MAINFRAME);
    m_pAutoProxy = NULL;

    //Initial the dummy argument that will be passed to the
    //IWebBrowserApp::Navigate function
    vDummy.vt = VT_EMPTY;

    //Create an instance of the InternetExplorer.Application object
    //and retrieve its dispatch interface
    m_oInternetExplorer.CreateDispatch("InternetExplorer.Application.1");

}
```

3. Insert the following boldface line of code into the dialog box class's destructor:

```
CInterNavVCPPDlg::~CInterNavVCPPDlg()
{
    // If there is an automation proxy for this dialog, set
    //   its back pointer to this dialog to NULL, so it knows
    //   the dialog has been deleted.
    if (m_pAutoProxy != NULL)
        m_pAutoProxy->m_pDialog = NULL;

    //Release the dispatch interface and decrement the object's
    //reference count
    m_oInternetExplorer.ReleaseDispatch();

}
```

4. Change the code inside the command button's click event handler function to call the `IWebBrowserApp::Navigate` and `IWebBrowserApp::SetVisible` member functions:

```
void CInterNavVCPPDlg::OnClickSscommand1()
{

    m_oInternetExplorer.Navigate(m_oRichText.GetText(),
                                 &vDummy,
                       &vDummy,
                       &vDummy,
                       &vDummy);

    m_oInternetExplorer.SetVisible(TRUE);

}
```

5. Compile and run the application, making sure that you have Internet service provided to you. Type a valid URL in the text box and click the Navigate button. Internet Explorer should be launched and the respective Web page brought into view.

Classes Created by the `#import` Directive If you've used the `#import` directive to create your dispatch interface wrapper class, you'll be using the `_com_ptr_t` template class to access the component's members. `_com_ptr_t`, known as a *smart pointer*, encapsulates a raw interface pointer and handles the creating, reference adding, and releasing of the component object automatically. The `_com_ptr_t` class is hidden in the `_COM_SMARTPTR_TYPEDEF` macro located in the .tlh file created by the `#import` directive. For example, in the shdocvw.tlh file, the following macro is found for the `IWebBrowserApp` interface:

```
COM_SMARTPTR_TYPEDEF(IWebBrowserApp, __uuidof(IWebBrowserApp));
```

This gets expanded by the compiler to the following:

```
typedef _com_ptr_t<_com_IIID<IWebBrowserApp, __uuidof(IWebBrowserApp)>
    IWebBrowserAppPtr;
```

You'll use this class, `IWebBrowserAppPtr`, in your code to use the Internet Explorer component.

Returning to the sample application, follow these steps to incorporate the Internet Explorer component:

1. In the header file for the dialog box class (`InterNavVCPPDlg.h`, in this case), insert the four boldface lines of code shown in Listing 11.3.

Listing 11.3 Adding the Internet Explorer Component as an `IWebBrowserAppPtr` Object

```
// InterNavVCPPDlg.h : header file
//
//{{AFX_INCLUDES()
#include "richtext.h"
//}}AFX_INCLUDES

#import "C:\WINNT\System32\shdocvw.dll" rename
```

Part

II

Ch

11

continues

Listing 11.3   Continued

```
➥("tagREADYSTATE", "tagIEREADYSTATE")
using namespace SHDocVw;

#if !defined(AFX_INTERNAVVCPPDLG_H__FF98D69A_FFDE_11D0_83C1_
➥000000000000__INCLUDED_)
#define AFX_INTERNAVVCPPDLG_H__FF98D69A_FFDE_11D0_83C1_
➥000000000000__INCLUDED_

.
.
.

// Implementation
protected:
    CInterNavVCPPDlgAutoProxy* m_pAutoProxy;
    HICON m_hIcon;

    VARIANT vDummy;                      //Argument for IWebBrowserApp::Navigate()
    IWebBrowserAppPtr m_oInternetExplorer; //Declaration IWebBrowserApp object

    BOOL CanExit();

.
.
.
n
//{{AFX_INSERT_LOCATION}}
// Microsoft Developer Studio will insert additional declarations
// immediately before the previous line.

#endif // !defined(AFX_INTERNAVVCPPDLG_H__FF98D69A_FFDE_11D0_83C1_
       // 000000000000__INCLUDED_)
```

2. In the implementation file for the dialog box class, insert the following boldface lines into the dialog box classes constructor:

```
CInterNavVCPPDlg::CInterNavVCPPDlg(CWnd* pParent /*=NULL*/)
    : CDialog(CInterNavVCPPDlg::IDD, pParent)
{
    //{{AFX_DATA_INIT(CInterNavVCPPDlg)
        // NOTE: the ClassWizard will add member initialization here
    //}}AFX_DATA_INIT
    // Note that LoadIcon does not require a subsequent DestroyIcon in Win32
    m_hIcon = AfxGetApp()->LoadIcon(IDR_MAINFRAME);
    m_pAutoProxy = NULL;
```

```
//Initial the dummy argument that will be passed to the
//IWebBrowserApp::Navigate function
vDummy.vt = VT_EMPTY;

//Create an instance of the InternetExplorer.Application object
//and retrieve its dispatch interface
m_oInternetExplorer.CreateInstance("InternetExplorer.Application.1");
}
```

N O T E When an object of the _com_ptr_t class leaves scope, the Release method of the interface pointer is called automatically. There's no need to explicitly release the reference as was the case for the class derived from COleDispatchDriver.

3. Change the code inside the command button's click event handler function to call the IWebBrowserApp::Navigate and IWebBrowserApp::SetVisible member functions:

```
void CInterNavVCPPDlg::OnClickSscommand1()
{

    m_oInternetExplorer ->Navigate((LPCSTR)m_oRichText.GetText(),,
                               &vDummy,
                               &vDummy,
                                  &vDummy,
                                  &vDummy);

    m_oInternetExplorer ->PutVisible(TRUE);
}
```

4. Compile and run the application.

Using ActiveX Controls with Visual J++

Visual J++ is the Java development tool that allows you to take full advantage of ActiveX technology as part of Java projects. Visual J++ provides full support for the Java Virtual Machine (JVM) on the Win 32 platform. JVM supports the integration between Java and COM, which is the underlying technology for ActiveX. To take advantage of the integration between Java and COM, you must use Visual J++.

The integration of ActiveX and Java allows you to take advantage of the full breadth of options available for developing Web applications. As a Visual J++ developer, you can take advantage of ActiveX controls as part of your Java development efforts to gain access to resources such as the system services. Figure 11.30 shows the integration between Java and ActiveX.

Part
II
Ch
11

FIGURE 11.30

Microsoft's extension of Java to include support for ActiveX results in a rich environment for developers and users.

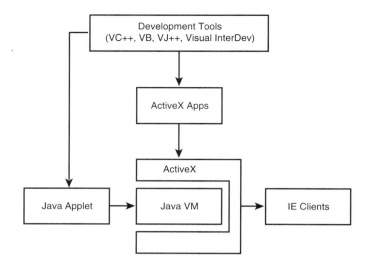

N O T E If you're a Java developer, you can leverage the thousands of available ActiveX controls in your applications by using ActiveX and Java integration in Visual J++. However, this makes your application Win32 specific, and you lose the cross-platform benefits of Java applications. ▪

Because the Visual J++ compiler supports the integration between Java and ActiveX, you can refer to ActiveX controls directly from your Java source code. Visual J++ now supports ActiveX controls as part of its development environment through the use of drag-and-drop toolbars. The use of ActiveX controls in Visual J++ is very similar to the way they are used in Visual Basic.

N O T E The integration of ActiveX and Java in the new Visual J++ 6 is much better, thanks to native support for ActiveX controls. Developers no longer have to worry about importing ActiveX controls into their Java projects and dealing with the type library and GUID issues. ▪

Using an ActiveX Control within Visual J++ involves the following steps, which are discussed in detail in the following sections:

1. Load the control into the project by dragging it from the ActiveX control toolbar.
2. Identify the control's properties and methods, and set the design-time properties.
3. Write event handler code for the events that will be handled by the ActiveX control.

Loading the Control

To load a control into a form, use the toolbar tab from the toolbox window on the left of the Visual J++ IDE. The following steps show you how to use the control in your Java application:

1. Choose the ActiveX Controls menu from the toolbox.
2. Open the form you want to use the ActiveX control on.

3. Drag and drop the control you want to use onto the form.

4. Visual J++ creates the control on the form and adds the appropriate classes to the project for the ActiveX control. Figure 11.31 shows a Calendar control on a blank form. Project Explorer shows the files added to the Java project to support the control.

Project Explorer with the
Calendar control files added

FIGURE 11.31

The Visual J++ IDE now
provides a GUI
environment for hosting
and programming with
ActiveX controls.

Toolbox window

Form with the Calendar
ActiveX control

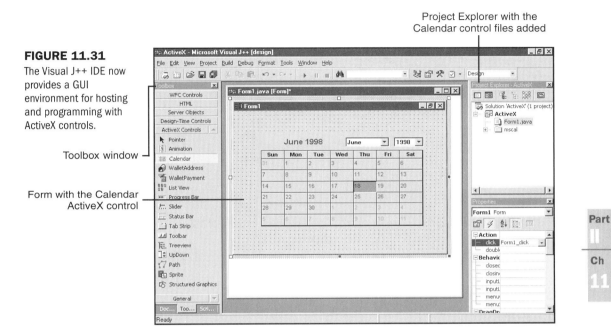

T I P   To reposition controls in the form, drag them with the mouse, or, with the control selected, use the arrow keys. Likewise, you can resize the control with the arrow keys while holding down the Shift key.

With the ActiveX control loaded into the project and placed in the form, you now can use the properties, methods, and events exposed by it.

Accessing Properties and Methods

The ActiveX control's developer designated certain properties to be accessed at design time. You can view these properties and set their values from the control's property page displayed by the property window. To access the property page of the calendar control in your application, do the following:

1. Select the control in the form and its properties are displayed in the property window. You can also display the control properties by right-clicking the control and selecting Properties from the menu. Figure 11.32 shows the Calendar control property window.

Part
II

Ch
11

Properties button
Events button
Alphabetic listing
Categorized listing
Properties
Form1 Form
Appearan
backColc Control
font MS Sans Serif, 11char
foreColo Windowtext
text Form1
Behavior
allowDro false
Misc
acceptBi (none)
autoScal true
autoScrc false
autoScrc 0, 0
borderSt Sizable
cancelBu (none)
context((none)
controlBi true
cursor Default
enabled true
helpButt false
icon (none)

FIGURE 11.32
The property window for the Calendar control.

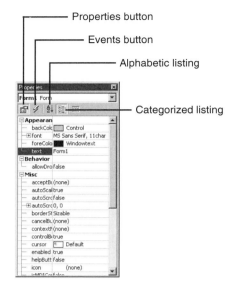

2. The properties are grouped into properties and events. Use the buttons on the property window toolbar to switch between them.
3. To set the value of any property, select the property and enter the new value.

Handling Events

The property window can display all the events that a control can fire. By double-clicking an event that you want to write an event handler for, you can open the code window for the control, and Visual J++ adds the declaration for the event. At this point you are ready to write the code associated with the event. Figure 11.33 shows the code window with the event for the `Click` event highlighted.

Form1.java [Code]*
*/
public void dispose()
{
super.dispose();
components.dispose();
}
private void Form1_click(Object source, Event e)
{
//Place event handler code here...
}
private void calendar1_keyDown(Object source, KeyEvent e)
{
}
/**
* NOTE: The following code is required by the Visual J++
* designer. It can be modified using the form editor.

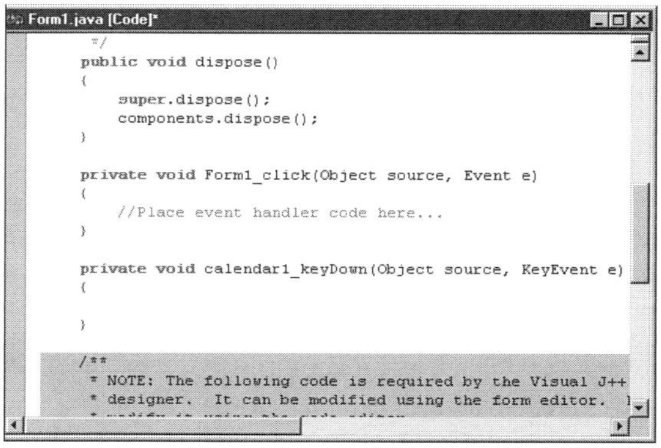

FIGURE 11.33
The code window provides fast access to the event handlers for the ActiveX control.

The new Visual J++ environment brings Java development to the same level of ease of use and familiarity that Visual Basic and Visual C++ provide. Developers familiar with Visual Basic or Visual C++ environments should be able to easily migrate to the Visual J++ environment.

From Here...

This chapter discusses the use of ActiveX controls in various aspects of I-net and client/server environments. You learned about the various issues involved with using ActiveX controls with Internet Explorer, and the security issues involved with ActiveX control usage. ActiveX controls are an integral part of Web-based development with tools such as Visual InterDev or FrontPage. Also, you've learned the techniques to install and register ActiveX components to be accessed on a local or remote machine. You've also seen the steps necessary in incorporating ActiveX components into Visual Basic, Visual J++, and Visual C++ applications.

For more information, see these chapters:

- To learn about the Visual Studio development environment, see Chapter 2, "Using Visual Studio to Create Applications."
- To learn about Active Server Pages and their capabilities, see Chapter 6, "An Inside Look at Active Server Pages and the Internet Information Server."
- To understand the details behind technologies such as COM/DCOM, ActiveX, and Java, see Chapter 9, "Using Microsoft's Object Technologies."
- To learn about creating components with Visual Basic, see Chapter 12, "Creating ActiveX Controls with Visual Basic."
- To learn about creating components with Visual C++, see Chapter 13, "Creating ActiveX Controls with Visual C++."
- To learn about concepts associated with Web-based application development, see Chapter 15, "Clients, Servers, and Components: Web-Based Applications."
- To learn about creating components with Visual J++, see Chapter 22, "Creating Applets and Applications with Visual J++."
- To learn about getting started with Visual InterDev, see Chapter 18, "Developing Active Content with Visual InterDev."
- To learn about advanced concepts associated with Visual InterDev development, see Chapter 19, "Advanced Visual InterDev Concepts."
- For information on where to locate functionality in a client/server environment, see Chapter 25, "Clients, Servers, and Components: Design Strategies for Distributed Applications."

Part

II

Ch

11

CHAPTER 12

Creating ActiveX Controls with Visual Basic

by David Burgett

In this chapter

Introducing ActiveX Controls

In Visual Basic (VB) 6, Microsoft enhances the ability to create ActiveX controls with new features and improved performance. ActiveX controls were introduced in version 5, opening the component development market to the over three million VB developers worldwide. With this new development potential, the market is expected to exceed $650 million in sales in 1998.

▶ For more information about what ActiveX components are and how you can use them, **see** Chapter 11, "Using COM Components and ActiveX Controls," **p. 289**

The ability to create ActiveX controls brings a new level of responsibility to the Visual Basic developer. In programming earlier versions, you never had to be concerned with the implications of using constituent controls (detailed later in this chapter) or ensuring that a design displayed correctly in multiple environments. Likewise, you never had the benefits of writing a commonly used control only once, the ability to add controls to the standard toolbox, or the ability to share your Visual Basic code with not only your C++ programs, but also your Word and Excel documents and your Web pages. With the advent of the Active Desktop in Internet Explorer 4 and Windows 98, you can even write controls that will be permanently available right on your desktop (see Figure 12.1). The icons on the desktop will appear in a layer floating above the ActiveX controls.

FIGURE 12.1
With the Active Desktop, your desktop becomes a container for any ActiveX control.

The new concerns are well worth the added development time. By encapsulating the business rules within the controls, you separate the optimization and enhancement of your program into small, easily managed sections. Suppose that you use a sorted list box control written by another developer. The original developer then improves the sort routine, reducing by 10 seconds the time necessary to sort a long list of items. With no changes to your application, you gain the same 10-second improvement simply by downloading and registering the new control.

▶ For more information about all Microsoft's component technologies, **see** Chapter 9, "Using Microsoft's Object Technologies," **p. 217**

▶ For more information about creating reusable controls, **see** Chapter 10, "Creating Reusable Components," **p. 263**

The four basic types of ActiveX controls, as differentiated by their interface and use of preexisting controls, are listed in the following:

- The simplest ActiveX controls have no visual interface at all; they simply expose some necessary functionality.
- Of the types of ActiveX controls with a visual interface, *subclassed* controls are the easiest to create as they simply add new functionality to or change the default properties of preexisting controls.
- Adding a degree of complexity, you can choose to create a new ActiveX control that combines multiple constituent controls into a single package, commonly called an *aggregate control*.
- To expand the visual possibilities, you can choose to not use any existing controls and create the entire interface yourself.

Invisible ActiveX controls that provide a service to an application are very easy to create and can greatly reduce debug time. Consider the example of an ActiveX representation of a cash register. Although this control could support a graphical interface, most of the functionality of a cash register, such as counting money and computing discounts, is invisible. The CashRegister object can be instantiated by an application, which would then set properties like CurrentDrawerAmount and DiscountPercentage and call methods such as CalculateSalePrice and InsertCash.

N O T E   ActiveX libraries are compiled into EXE or DLL files, whereas ActiveX controls are provided in the form of OCX files.

The CashRegister control will be created as a class within an ActiveX library, which will be compiled into either an EXE or a DLL. ActiveX DLLs are *in-process*, that is, loaded into the same memory process as the calling application. This provides very fast interaction between the application and the library. ActiveX EXEs are *out-of-process*, that is, loaded in a separate memory space. This provides the capability to share data between multiple calling applications, at the expense of access speed. To determine whether to compile your library into an EXE or a DLL, consider how often data will pass between the two, and whether you need one set of data to be shared between multiple calling applications.

Examine the following code, which creates the basis for a remote ActiveX Counter component:

```
Private Counter as Long
Public Function GetCount as long
    GetCount=Counter
    Counter=Counter+1
End Function
```

This simple code creates and updates a counter each time the count is accessed, like those commonly used to track Web page hits. This code can be compiled into an ActiveX DLL to ensure that each client application instantiates its own copy of the counter. Multiple instances of the DLL are instantiated and each applies to a single client application. If the code were

Part

II

Ch

12

compiled into an EXE, each client application could use a single counter, updating the total usage count for all applications independently of each other. Any application, document, or Web page wanting to use the counter would simply need to instantiate a `Counter` object using the `CreateObject` function.

> **N O T E** For the sake of simplicity, I have left the persistence of the Counter data across sessions as an exercise for the reader.

> **N O T E** Visual Basic 6 introduced the capability to create objects on remote machines by passing a server name to the `CreateObject` function. You can now store your ActiveX libraries on a central server used by multiple clients.

Building a Graphical ActiveX Control: The Logo Control

The easiest graphical control to create is the simple subclassed control. Subclassed controls often serve only as a measure of convenience in reducing your workload, but don't underestimate the power a simple enhancement can have.

The most basic subclassed control is one that simply has new default properties set for it. For example, the default value of a check box in Visual Basic is `0 - Unchecked`. You can easily create a control with all the functionality and appearance of a normal check box, but set default value to `1 - Checked`. This might sound like a great expense for little benefit, but it can actually be a great time saver if you use check boxes regularly. After you're acquainted with creating ActiveX controls, you can create this example easily in just a few minutes. Suppose that you could cut your development time by just five seconds per check box. This very simple example would pay for itself in time and energy within a relatively small number of forms.

In this section, you'll build an ActiveX control that's more functional than the check box example. You'll subclass the existing image control to create a logo control that provides a consistent look and feel throughout applications, Web pages, and documents. You can use the control to display your company logo for splash screens, letterheads, or Web pages (see Figure 12.2). After you complete the control, your corporate logo is available in your toolbox right next to your other tools.

FIGURE 12.2

The Logo control makes creating splash screens, letterheads, and Web pages drag-and-drop simple.

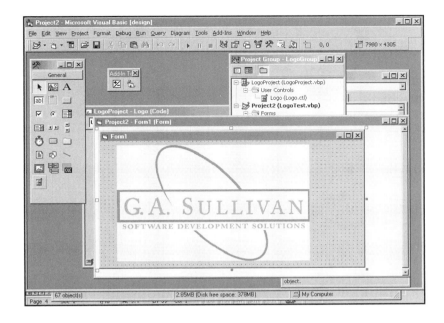

Creating the Corporate Logo Control

To create your corporate logo, open a new ActiveX control project by following these steps:

1. Open Visual Basic or choose File, New, if Visual Basic is already running.
2. Select ActiveX Control from the New Project dialog box (see Figure 12.3).

FIGURE 12.3

Choose ActiveX Control from Visual Basic 6's list of project types and create the necessary form for your first control.

The first difference you'll notice between your ActiveX control project and other Visual Basic projects is the form you'll use to design your control. This form, called a UserControl, differs from a standard application form in that it has no visible border, title bar, or control boxes (see Figure 12.4). The reasons for this will become clear as you develop the control.

FIGURE 12.4

The UserControl form is very similar to a standard VB form, but lacks a title bar and border. These minor differences are very important in differentiating an ActiveX control from a standard EXE form.

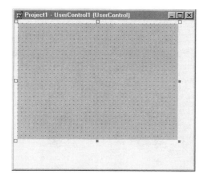

N O T E The latest version of Visual Basic also enables a new type of lightweight UserControl that is windowless and transparent. These UserControls use far fewer resources than standard UserControls and are ideal for creating simple, fast controls. Consult the VB documentation for more information.

Next, notice the new format of the Project Explorer (see Figure 12.5), which creates a hierarchical tree of the various projects and files open in the current project group. This is improved over previous versions of VB that enabled only one project to be open at a time.

FIGURE 12.5

The hierarchical format of the Project Explorer more clearly represents the relationships between the elements and helps you locate a particular element quickly.

The tree hierarchy of the Project Explorer will help you keep track of which controls, forms, and classes belong to a given project, which can be a challenge while trying to debug a control. Multiple projects are now supported, allowing you to maintain ActiveX controls and their test forms in separate projects, but within a single project group. Each project is listed with the filename (if specified) in parentheses.

You should provide easily understood names for the UserControl and project. When you compile your control into an OCX, you will specify a name for it, but when a developer uses the control within the IDE, they will see the name you specify in the control's properties appended with a number to make the name unique. Thus, if you don't change the control's name from the default UserControl1, when a developer places an instance of that control on a form, it will be given the default name UserControl11.

To set the control properties, follow these steps:

1. Right-click the UserControl and choose Properties.
2. Change the Name property to Logo.
3. Choose Project, Project1 Properties.
4. Change Project Name to LogoProject (see Figure 12.6).

FIGURE 12.6
The Project Properties dialog box for Project1 is set in place.

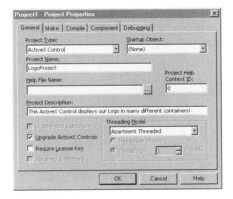

 T I P You can't use the same value for the UserControl name and the project name. Choose a project name that describes the entire set of controls within the project.

The General tab of the Project Properties dialog box allows you to set the name, description, and help file for the control. On the other tabs, you can determine how the control will actually be created, including settings for version information and compatibility, optimization, conditional compilation arguments, and debugging information.

Adding Constituent Controls to the ActiveX Control

To subclass the image control, first add it to your new UserControl. Double-click the image control in the toolbox to create a small image control in the center of your UserControl for displaying the logo of your choice. For the Logo control to act in the desired manner, you must set the properties of the image control as follows:

1. Right-click the Image control and choose Properties.
2. Set the Name property to imgLogo.
3. Set Stretch to True.
4. Set Picture to the image of your choice.
5. Set Left and Top to 0.

N O T E Understanding the constituent controls you use to create a new control is imperative. The choice of an image control rather than a PictureBox control clearly determines the destiny of your new control. The image control lacks many of the methods and properties of the PictureBox control, including a Windows handle to allow manipulation of the control through the Windows API. In return for this lack of functionality, the Image control uses significantly fewer system resources, enabling it to repaint more quickly. Consult the Visual Basic help files for more information on specific controls.

N O T E It doesn't matter where the image resides when you set the Picture property of the Image control. Visual Basic stores the data within the control itself, allowing you to distribute the control as a single file.

The Stretch property determines the state of the image within the control. If it's set to False, the image is displayed with its defined size, despite the size of the control. As a result, only part of the image might be displayed, or the entire image might be visible with a blank area around it. When set to True, the image size is altered to conform to the control. For the corporate logo control, it is important to be able to resize the logo, based on the container. If the control is used in a letterhead, for example, the preferred size will probably be smaller than when it is used as an application's splash screen.

You must remember the distinction between the UserControl and its constituent controls. The UserControl is the interface your end user will see and use. The constituent controls used to create the UserControl (the Image control in this example) are visible only to the creator of the control while the control is in design mode. Properties of the constituent controls are not automatically available to the control as a whole. In order to publish the constituent controls' properties, they need to be exposed as properties of the UserControl.

This is a new concept to most Visual Basic programmers and can cause quite a bit of confusion. With time, the distinction between the UserControl and its constituent controls will become clear. Think of the UserControl as a vending machine in which you can see the selection of candy bars that it holds. Because you can't reach in and directly take a candy bar, the developer of the machine has provided you with the necessary facilities to tell the machine what you want. It is then up to the machine to translate your request into the release of a candy bar.

With this in mind, you now understand that simply setting the Stretch property of the Image control doesn't complete the resizing requirements of the Logo control. Developers using this control will be able to resize only the UserControl, not the Image control contained within the UserControl; therefore, you need to attach the Resize event of the UserControl to the Image within code as follows:

1. Right-click the UserControl (anywhere outside the boundary of the Image control) and choose View Code.

2. Enter the following code in the UserControl_Resize event:

```
imgLogo.height=UserControl.scaleheight
imgLogo.width=UserControl.scalewidth
```

This code forces the image control to be resized every time the UserControl is, in both the design-time and runtime VB environments. The difference between these two environments and the methods for writing conditional code based on the environment is discussed later in the chapter.

Your first control is now ready to use. Before loading your Web site or opening your company letterhead, you should first test the control from the Visual Basic design environment.

N O T E Visual Basic now gives you the option to choose where you want to run your control for debugging purposes. Using the Debugging tab on the Project, Properties menu, you can set VB to create a default HTML page and run your control directly in Internet Explorer. ▪

Testing the Logo Control

The control you're developing can exist only within a container, such as an executable form, a Web browser, or a Microsoft Word document. To test your control, therefore, you must create a container for it by adding a new Standard Executable project to your project group. This is another new concept for Visual Basic users, but greatly simplifies the creation of controls and their independent testing environments.

To add a test container to your project group, choose File, Add Project, and then select Standard EXE from the New tab of the Add Project dialog box. Note that your Project Explorer now has two projects in the project group, with the appropriate files under their respective branches of the tree (see Figure 12.7). When you save your work, you will be prompted to save your new project and its files, as well as the new project group.

FIGURE 12.7

The project group, new to Visual Basic, holds multiple projects, allowing you to create and test ActiveX controls within a single development environment.

Save the new project and files with names that will help you remember this project is only to be used for testing. To test the new control, simply add it to the form as you would any other control.

N O T E The Logo control should be the right-most control in the bottom row of the toolbox. You can rest the mouse pointer over it for a moment to confirm this. ▪

Part
II

Ch
12

N O T E   If the UserControl design window is still open, the Logo control is grayed out and inaccessible. In order to add an ActiveX control to a form, the control itself must be executed. Because Visual Basic cannot execute a control whose design screen is still open, you must close the designer before adding or editing the control on a form. ■

Add a Logo control to the new form by double-clicking it in the toolbox. You'll notice immediately that the image control expands to fill the entire size of the ActiveX control. As instructed, the UserControl's `Resize` event also resized the Image control. When you added the control to the form, the event was fired, and the Resize code was executed (see Figure 12.8).

FIGURE 12.8

The Logo control is placed in a form container.

You can resize the Logo control to ensure that the image is the desired size. The logo control can now be used in a wide variety of containers like any other. You can manipulate the properties and code the events as usual.

For the control to be distributed, you must create an OCX file by highlighting the logo project and choosing File, Make LogoProject.ocx.

You're now ready to use and distribute your logo control to create splash screens, documents, and Web pages. The OCX file containing the control is the only file you must distribute. Insert the Logo control into a Microsoft Word document to create a professional-looking letterhead (see Figure 12.9). Because the control retains its automatic sizing capability, you can use it in multiple documents by resizing it as necessary.

FIGURE 12.9

The Logo control inserted in a Microsoft Word Document.

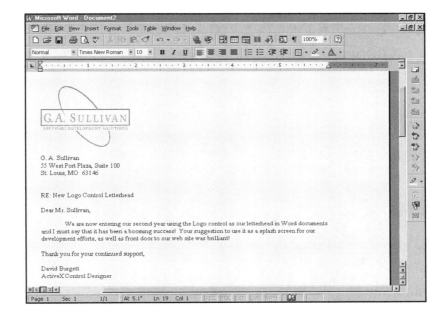

To use an ActiveX control in a Word document, follow these steps:

1. Open a new word document and position your cursor at the insertion point for the Logo control.

2. Again, on the Control Toolbox, click More Controls.

3. Scrolling down the list, locate and click LogoProject.Logo

4. You can position the cursor anywhere inside the ActiveX control to move it or use the sizing handles to resize it.

See the Word help documentation for more information.

Part
II

Ch
12

> **CAUTION**
>
> The .OCX file is the only new file you have created that must be distributed. However, in order to use the control, the standard Visual Basic support file, MSVBVM60.DLL, must be installed, as well as any other support files you used to create your control.

N O T E The .oca files accompanying your .ocx files are cache files created and maintained by the operating system. They're updated whenever necessary, so their date and file size might change frequently.

Creating an Aggregate Control: The Framed Text Box

The second type of graphical ActiveX control you can build with Visual Basic is an *aggregate control* consisting of multiple existing controls grouped together for a particular task. The constituent controls used to build an aggregate control can be those included with Visual Basic, third-party controls, or your own ActiveX controls. When the aggregate is complete, the constituent controls work and appear as a single control to users.

You can create aggregate controls for specific applications, such as a UserInformation control with text boxes to hold a user's name, address, telephone number, and other personal information (see Figure 12.10). Creating such a control allows you to create the control once and use it in multiple applications or Web pages. The business rules applied to entering information are all part of the control, so they will always be consistent and never add to the complexity of the application that uses the control. For instance, rules to validate that phone numbers are entered in the correct format are written as part of UserInformation's code. Use of a single control wherever user information is required also provides consistency between your applications and familiarity for users.

FIGURE 12.10
This form accepts personal user information and instantly filters it through specified business rules.

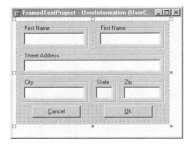

The UserInformation control example is very easy to implement and offers many benefits. Next, you'll create a slightly more challenging aggregate control that incorporates several different types of controls, implements unique properties and methods, and has a custom property page.

N O T E A new event was introduced in VB 6, the `Validate` event. The `Validate` event is fired just before the `LostFocus` event, allowing you to force the focus to be retained on the control until all validations are satisfied. For example, the UserInformation control can use this event to ensure that all required fields have been entered before the user moves to a different control.

Building a More Complex Aggregate Control

To understand the creation of aggregate controls, you'll create a commonly used combination of a text box surrounded by a frame. You've probably used or created an application that uses this technique. A frame control is placed on a form, and a text box control is placed within the frame. The frame's caption is then set to show users the purpose of the text box. This can lead to very user-friendly forms that are easily understood by even the most inexperienced users.

Creating visual consistency between the forms in your applications or across different applications is easy when using this type of framed text control on every data-entry page. The problem with this technique is the added difficulty involved in creating and maintaining two controls for each data-entry field. Each time you need to resize any entry field, you have to resize the frame control and the text box itself. Also, the text box—not the frame—holds the data you're interested in. The text box control is a child control of the frame, not the form, creating additional work if you use any routines that cycle through all the controls on a form.

You can greatly simplify this ritual of creating and maintaining the combination frame and text box control by creating a single FramedText ActiveX control (see Figure 12.11). Begin by following these steps:

FIGURE 12.11

Several examples of the FramedTextBox are placed on a form with simple drag-and-drop ease.

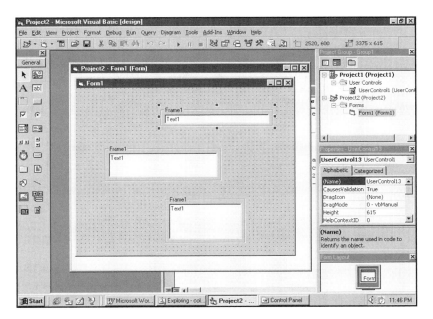

1. Open Visual Basic or choose File, New Project.
2. Choose New ActiveX Control.
3. Name the UserControl `FramedText`.
4. Name the project `FramedTextProject`.

You need to add a frame and TextBox control to the UserControl form:

1. Double-click the Frame control in the VB toolbox. Size isn't important.
2. Click the TextBox control in the Toolbox. Draw the text box within the frame control.

3. Set the following properties for the Frame control:

Name	frmFrame
Left	0
Top	0
Caption	FramedText

4. Set the properties for the TextBox control:

Name	txtText
Left	120
Top	240
MultiLine	True

5. To ensure that the constituent controls always fill the aggregate control, add the following code to the UserControl_Resize event:

```
frmFrame.Width = UserControl.ScaleWidth
frmFrame.Height = UserControl.ScaleHeight
txtText.Width = frmFrame.Width - 2 * txtText.Left
txtText.Height = frmFrame.Height - 1.5 * txtText.Top
```

6. Choose File, Save FramedText.ctl.

7. Close the UserControl design window.

Add a standard EXE as you did for the logo control to test the FramedText control. Add the FramedText control to the form in your EXE. If you notice the time you saved in drawing only a single control, you'll appreciate these time savings more each time you resize the control or set its properties. Resize the control on the form to verify that your code is working as expected.

N O T E   The values given for placement of the text box within the frame and multipliers are just guidelines. Feel free to experiment with these values to create the look you want.

Using the ActiveX Control Interface Wizard to Create Properties for Your Control

Now that you have a FramedText control on the form, notice that the new control lacks many of the properties you need—most importantly, the text and caption properties. You first might think to treat the text box as a property of the control and access the control's Text property accordingly. Remember, however, that constituent controls are private members of the UserControl. As the developer using the control, you have access only to the UserControl and its exposed properties.

You've probably realized that there must be some way to create a new property for the UserControl and to connect that property to the Text property of the text box. Indeed, there is a way—the ActiveX Control Interface Wizard.

Starting the ActiveX Control Interface Wizard   To create the Text property and the others you need, use the ActiveX Control Interface Wizard included with all levels of Visual Basic. To begin, choose Add-Ins, ActiveX Control Interface Wizard.

If the ActiveX Control Interface Wizard doesn't appear on your Add-Ins menu, place it there by following these steps:

1. Choose Add-Ins, Add-In Manager.
2. Double-click on VB 6 ActiveX Ctrl Interface Wizard.
3. Note that the Load Behavior for the wizard changes to Loaded.
4. Click OK.

There is now an entry for ActiveX Control Interface Wizard on the menu.

The first dialog box of the wizard details its benefits. As the dialog box explains, this wizard helps you create your ActiveX control by providing choices about which properties, methods, and events are available to the developer and by writing the basic code necessary to support them. You can disable the introductory dialog box by checking the appropriate box.

If you don't see this dialog box, click the Back button to display it.

The introduction includes two important notes concerning interface design and property pages. The note about property pages simply reminds you to use the VB Property Page Wizard to create them more easily. The note about interface design informs you that it's necessary to add all constituent controls to the UserControl before running the wizard. This requirement is based on the manner in which the ActiveX Control Interface Wizard creates the code for your control. If you add additional constituent controls to your UserControl after running the wizard, these controls might not behave well or might have incorrect property or method assignments. Choosing the constituent controls should be the first task of every ActiveX control design, so this constraint shouldn't hinder the development of your design.

Click Next to move to the Select Interface Members dialog box of the wizard.

Choosing Among Default Properties, Methods, and Events   You can choose which standard properties, methods, and events to include in your control on the Select Interface Members screen. Visual Basic selects those already present, gives you all the standard options, and allows you to create your own as well (see Figure 12.12). The two lists in the dialog box show the available names and the currently selected names.

Part
II

Ch
12

FIGURE 12.12

In the Select Interface Members dialog box, you determine which available properties, methods, and events you'll expose in your ActiveX control.

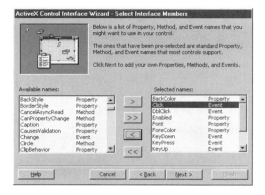

The list on the right shows the properties, events, and one method that are defaults for all visible ActiveX controls. As you examine the list, notice several useful properties VB provides for you, such as BackColor, Enabled, and Font. VB also includes several useful events, such as Click, KeyDown, and MouseMove. The single method provided for you is Refresh, which is useful for all visible controls.

In addition to these useful elements, VB suggests two properties that aren't useful to the FramedText control. The first of these properties is BackStyle, which can be set to opaque or transparent, based on the control in question. To decide whether to include BackStyle in the FramedText control, you must again understand the difference between the ActiveX control and its constituent controls. Your first thought might be to include the property so users can place a FramedText control over other controls (such as a background image), enabling the buried controls to show through the frame. Because BackStyle isn't a standard property of the frame control, however, it's always opaque and will completely cover the UserControl, so users will find the BackStyle property useless and confusing.

 It's possible to create a FramedText control with an applicable BackStyle property, involving little additional difficulty. As an additional exercise, consider redesigning the FramedText control to use four line controls and a label control in place of the frame.

The second property not useful for the FramedText control is BorderStyle. BorderStyle could be applied to the frame control, allowing developers to turn off the frame border and thus the FramedText control. Because you're designing the control to specifically have a frame, however, including the BorderStyle property would be counterproductive.

To remove the BackStyle and BorderStyle properties, select both properties and click the < button.

Adding New Properties and Methods   Now that you've pared the list down to the bare necessities offered by VB, it's time to enhance the functionality and usability of the FramedText control by adding additional properties and methods. As noted before, the properties most prominently lacking from the FramedText control are Text and Caption.

Highlight the following items from the Available Names list and move them to the Selected Names list:

- Properties—`Caption`, `hWnd`, `MousePointer`, `MultiLine`, `PasswordChar`, `SelLength`, `SelStart`, `SelText`, `Text`, `ToolTipText`, `WhatsThisHelpID`
- Methods—`PopupMenu`
- Events—`Change`, `InitProperties`, `ReadProperties`, `Resize`, `WriteProperties`

Click <u>N</u>ext to move to the Create Custom Interface Members dialog box, in which you can define unique properties, methods, and events for which Visual Basic will create the necessary base code (see Figure 12.13). Although you don't need to add any custom interface members for this simple FramedText example, most ActiveX controls require many custom members in order to be useful, as you'll see in the next example.

FIGURE 12.13
In the Create Custom Interface Members dialog box, you can define any custom interface members previously created manually.

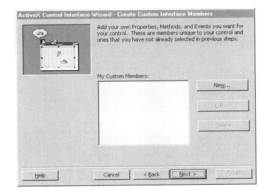

Click <u>N</u>ext to move to the Set Mapping dialog box of the wizard.

Mapping Interface Members The Set Mapping dialog box is the most critical in the wizard because it allows you to map the properties, methods, and events of the constituent controls to the UserControl (see Figure 12.14). Although Visual Basic suggests default mappings, the functionality you want might require a different mapping. If you don't map the interface members to their appropriate controls correctly, your ActiveX control won't function accurately.

FIGURE 12.14
In the Set Mapping dialog box of the wizard, you can map the properties, methods, and events defined on the previous two dialog boxes to their appropriate constituent controls.

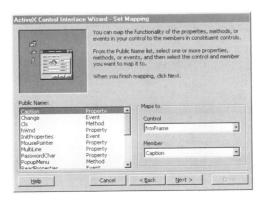

Part
II

Ch
12

Consider the Text property of the FramedText control you're creating. This property should refer to the text box constituent control, not the user control itself. You'll map the Text property of the FramedText control to the Text property of the text box, connecting the two to ensure that a change in one is mirrored in the other. As a result, when the Text property of the FramedText control is changed programmatically or at runtime, VB automatically passes the specified value through to the constituent text control. Because this process is invisible to developers and end users, the Text property appears to be a simple property like any other.

To map the Text property, follow these steps:

1. Choose Text Property from the Public Name list.

2. Choose txtText from the Maps to…Control drop-down list. VB automatically inserts the Text property in the Maps to…Member list box.

3. Map the rest of the properties, methods, and events to the specified UserControl or constituent controls as listed:

UserControl	hWnd, InitProperties, PopupMenu, ReadProperties, Refresh, Resize, WriteProperties
frmFrame	BackColor, Caption, Click, DblClick, MouseDown, MouseMove, MousePointer, MouseUp, ToolTipText, WhatsThisHelpID
txtText	Change, Enabled, Font, ForeColor, KeyDown, KeyPress, KeyUp, MultiLine, PasswordChar, SelLength, SelStart, SelText

CAUTION

You must understand the limitations of the properties you're selecting. The MultiLine property, for example, is read-only. Although you can add a MultiLine property to the UserControl and map it to the text control, the property will remain read-only; trying to change it will cause an error.

4. Click Next to move to the Finished dialog box of the wizard.

Finishing the ActiveX Control Wizard In the Finished dialog box, you can choose to view a summary report. Ensure that the check box is selected and click Finish. The Wizard Summary text suggests tasks yet to be completed, as well as tips for creating fully functional controls (see Figure 12.15).

FIGURE 12.15
The summary report gives you an overview of the work left to be done to make your control effective and stable.

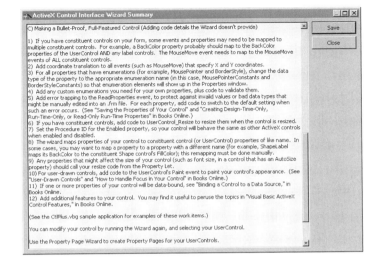

 TIP Pay close attention to Section C of the summary; it offers excellent advice for making your control look and act professionally.

Some of the items listed in the summary are familiar ones, such as adding an EXE to your project to test the control. Other items, such as mapping properties to multiple constituent controls, might be new to you. You might want to map to multiple constituent controls for properties such as `BackColor`, which you previously mapped only to the `frmFrame` control. For example, you might decide to map `BackColor` to the `txtText` control, as well, to ensure the same back color for the frame and text box. You can do this manually as well by adding the following line to the public `Property Let BackColor`:

```
txtText.BackColor() = New_BackColor
```

 TIP You can easily add another property to the FramedText control to allow users to specify separate colors for the frame and the text box. Simply add a new property (as demonstrated later in this chapter), call it `TextBackColor`, and map it to the text control.

Completing the Control with Manually Created Properties and Events

Now it's time to create the properties for your ActiveX control. In the preceding section, you used the ActiveX Control Interface Wizard to map the properties of the UserControl to the constituent controls. The ActiveX Control Interface Wizard also creates the code necessary for the `Text` property, including a call to the `PropertyChanged` procedure, notifying Visual Basic when the property has changed. By examining the code Visual Basic creates for you (see Figure 12.16), you can understand how a property is created.

Part
II

Ch
12

FIGURE 12.16

The FramedTextProject opened to view the property code.

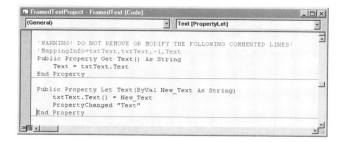

CAUTION

As the comments suggest, the `MappingInfo` line contains internal information for Visual Basic and should not be altered or deleted.

The code created for the `Text` property has two routines: a `Property Get` and a `Property Let`. The word *property* differentiates these routines from standard methods and procedures.

The `Property Get` procedure is straightforward. Whenever the program needs to know the value of the UserControl `Text` property, this function returns the value of the `txtText` control.

The `Property Let` procedure is nearly as simple as you might expect. It accepts a string parameter that holds the new value for the UserControl `Text` property. The procedure updates the `Text` property of the `txtText` control each time the `Text` property of the UserControl is altered.

The third type of `Property` procedure that you need to know about is `Property Set`, which works similarly to `Property Let`, except that it creates a reference to an object rather than a primitive data type. Use `Property Let` as you would use `Let`, with standard variables (such as integer or string), and use `Property Set` as you would use `Set`, with objects (such as forms or controls).

 You can pass extra parameters to your own custom `Property` procedures as long as the parameter list in the `Get` and the `Let/Set` declarations agree. Simply define the parameters you want, and add to the end of the list the parameter holding the value passed into a `Let/Set` procedure.

The function of the extra line in the `Property Let Text` procedure might not be immediately clear. The call to the `PropertyChanged` procedure tells Visual Basic that the property has changed, so VB can update its internal record keeping and store the new value. Remember that the design-time and runtime versions of the controls are actually different instances of the running program. If VB doesn't save the new property value internally, the runtime instance of the control won't reflect property changes made at design time.

VB handles these property value changes through an object called the `PropertyBag`. The ActiveX Control Interface Wizard creates all necessary calls to `PropertyBag` for you in the

ReadProperties and WriteProperties methods of the UserControl. PropertyBag has two methods—ReadProperty and WriteProperty—to move values from the internal storage to the actual control.

The ReadProperty method has a required DataName and an optional DefaultValue parameter. DataName refers to the property being read; DefaultValue is used if no entry is in PropertyBag. Similarly, WriteProperty takes required DataName and Value parameters and an optional DefaultValue parameter. The Value parameter specifies the value to place in PropertyBag in the section defined by the DataName parameter. DefaultValue works a bit differently in WriteProperty, in that WriteProperty writes information to PropertyBag only if the Value specified is different from the DefaultValue.

For example, the ReadProperty method might be called for the FramedText control with a DataName of "Text". This returns the value of the Text property in PropertyBag, or the DefaultValue if the Text property is empty. Similarly, the WriteProperty method, when passed a DateName of "Text", saves the value passed in the Value or DefaultValue in the Text property of PropertyBag.

 T I P   By comparing the Value and DefaultValue and saving only when necessary, VB conserves file space. Thus, you should use DefaultValue whenever possible.

Event notification in your ActiveX control is just as easy as mapping properties. By calling the RaiseEvent method, you can force Visual Basic to respond to any event you choose. For example, in the ActiveX Control Interface Wizard, you specified that the Click event should be mapped to the frmFrame_Click event. Thus, when users click the frame in the runtime environment, the code in the FramedText container's FramedText_Click event is executed.

The problem with this is that the Click event for the FramedText control is fired only when users click the frame portion of the control; it doesn't fire when users click the text box. This disparity emphasizes the individuality of the constituent controls, rather than the desired cohesive whole.

Fortunately, correcting this problem is simple. From the txtText_Click event, call RaiseEvent Click to force VB to fire the appropriate Click event. You could call the frmFrame_Click event instead, but this would add an extra, unnecessary level of procedural calls.

To complete the FramedText control, create RaiseEvent calls in the txtText control for the following events: DblClick, MouseDown, MouseMove, MouseUp.

N O T E   For the Mouse events, be sure to copy the RaiseEvent call from the frmFrame control to ensure that you include the correct parameters.

The FramedText control is now ready to use like any other Visual Basic control. It's manipulated in the design environment and referenced programmatically like all other controls. Test the OCX to ensure that it works correctly. You can now use it in place of the standard text box whenever you want to draw special attention to an entry field.

Part
II

Ch
12

Creating a More Complex Aggregate Control: The TimeSheet Control

To see a much more complex aggregate control, you will create the TimeSheet control, which is similar to a spreadsheet to provide end users with a means of entering billable hours via a company intranet (see Figure 12.17). The TimeSheet control can be used in a standalone application, as seen here, or on a company intranet page. By using a single TimeSheet control in all containers, you can ensure that all data entry conforms to the same set of business rules.

FIGURE 12.17
The TimeSheet control.

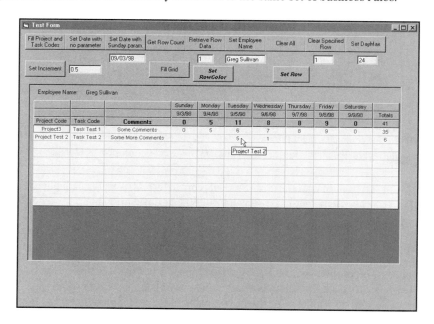

End users will be able to choose a Project Code and Task Code from a list of acceptable options, enter hour amounts for those projects and tasks, and enter any comments about the tasks. The control itself needs to make the acceptable Project and Task codes available, verify and correct all data entered, and provide automatic totaling for all values entered. The control also should accept a project description for every code and display this description in a ToolTip when users pause over any row of time values.

N O T E   The MSFlexGrid control is itself an ActiveX control and is contained within the file MSFLXGRD.OCX. This file must be included with distributions of your TimeSheet control. ▪

This single control can easily be made available to all employees, in house and on site, with business rules built into the control, thus helping ensure that no erroneous time sheets are submitted. This example shows how ActiveX controls can improve efficiency and accuracy while expanding accessibility.

ON THE WEB

This TimeSheet control is an integral part of the G. A. Sullivan Billing Project, created throughout the examples in this book. The source can be downloaded from the G. A. Sullivan Web site: http://www.gasullivan.com/.

▶ For more information about creating the control in J++, **see** Chapter 22, "Creating Applets and Applications with Visual J++," **p. 643**

▶ For more information about creating the control in C++, **see** Chapter 13, "Creating ActiveX Controls with Visual C++," **p. 385**

Building the TimeSheet Control

To begin your control, create a new ActiveX control as before. Edit the project properties to set the Project Name to TimeSheetProject. Set the Name property of the UserControl to TimeSheet.

To display the time sheet information in rows and columns, use the Microsoft FlexGrid control included with VB. The MSFlexGrid isn't a part of the standard toolbox items, so you'll have to tell VB where to find it by adding a reference to MSFlxGrd.OCX (the file extension .ocx shows that the MSFlexGrid is itself an ActiveX control). This example shows the extensibility of ActiveX controls—you're using an ActiveX control as the basis for a new ActiveX control.

Follow these steps to add an MSFlexGrid control to your form:

1. Choose Project, Components from the menu.
2. Select Microsoft FlexGrid Control 5.
3. Click OK.

T I P If Microsoft FlexGrid Control 5 isn't an option on the Components list, you'll have to find the file yourself. Click Browse and locate the MSFlxGrd.OCX file, which should be in the \Windows\System directory.

4. The MSFlexGrid control is now available in your toolbox. Double-click its icon to place the default MSFlexGrid on your UserControl. The example in Figure 12.18 has three fixed rows at the top to serve as headers.

Part
II

Ch
12

FIGURE 12.18

The MSFlexGrid is the main component of the TimeSheet control.

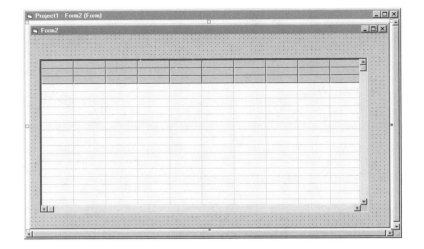

5. By default, the MSFlexGrid has two columns and two rows, with one of each *fixed*. Fixed rows and columns are always displayed in the grid, even when the user scrolls out of right or down out of the initial viewing range. Further, their contents cannot be edited by the user. Your time sheet will have 11 columns—seven for days and one each for project code, task code, comments, and total hours. Base the total row number in the time sheet on how many different projects and tasks any particular employee works on in a given week. As an initial estimate, you can choose 48 as the maximum. You should also set the other necessary setup properties for the MSFlexGrid now, as follows:

Property	Setting
Name	grdTimeSheet
Cols	11
Rows	48
FixedCols	0
FixedRows	3
Left	0
Top	0

Resize the UserControl to the largest convenient size. Resize the MSFlexGrid to fill the UserControl.

6. Like the LogoProject control created earlier in this chapter, you want the TimeSheet control to resize to fill the entire UserControl. Add the following code to the `UserControl_Resize` event:

```
grdTimeSheet.height=UserControl.scaleheight
grdTimeSheet.width=UserControl.scalewidth
```

Using Constituent Controls to Enhance the TimeSheet Control's Functionality

Now that the basic grid is in place for your TimeSheet control, you need to add the constituent controls that will add functionality to the TimeSheet control. One major drawback of the MSFlexGrid is that users can't type directly into the grid. Because the grid is designed to be bound to a database, there's no way to type directly into the control as you would with a text box control.

That said, you might guess that the next control to add to the TimeSheet control is a text box control for data entry. When users type an entry into the TimeSheet, the actual text manipulation will take place in the text control, with the final value being placed into the grid.

When examining the MSFlexGrid, you probably noticed that it supports `KeyDown`, `KeyPress`, and `KeyUp` events, which can be used for text manipulation. So much code is necessary to support all text-manipulation functions inherently handled by a text box that it's worthwhile to tackle the difficulty of incorporating the text box into the control. You'll still have to write code to handle different `KeyPress` events in the grid control; this code determines whether to display the text box or another control. By using the text box, you give your users full editing functions, including cut, copy, and paste.

Follow these steps to create a text box with the appropriate properties:

1. Add a TextBox control to the TimeSheet control. (Size and placement aren't important.)
2. Set the `Name` property of the TextBox control to `txtTime`.
3. Set `BorderStyle` to `0–None`.
4. Set `Visible` to `False`.

Ideally, users of your aggregate ActiveX control should never see its constituent controls as separate controls; the aggregate controls should always appear and work as a single control. For the TimeSheet control, the text box should be invisible to users—they should have a sense that they're editing their text directly in the TimeSheet control itself. For this reason, set the `BorderStyle` of the text box to none (see Figure 12.19).

Part

II

Ch

12

FIGURE 12.19

The text box appears invisible to the user, giving the illusion of a single control.

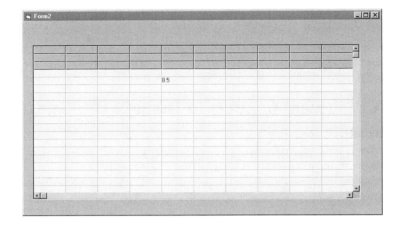

The invisible text box allows you to enter text into the grid seamlessly. By ensuring that the user can't differentiate between the constituent controls, you create a professional-looking, complete control.

To make the txtTime control fully invisible to the user, you need to place it in the appropriate area of the TimeSheet and size it to match the cell being edited. To enable this, place the following code in the KeyPress event of grdTimeSheet:

```
txtTime.Top = GrdTimeSheet.CellTop + GrdTimeSheet.Top
txtTime.Left = GrdTimeSheet.CellLeft + GrdTimeSheet.Left
txtTime.Width = GrdTimeSheet.CellWidth
txtTime.Height = GrdTimeSheet.CellHeight
```

N O T E   The assignment statements for the Top and Left properties work without adding an associated grdTimeSheet property because the top and left of the grid control have been set to 0. This code will be necessary later in the chapter when you move the grid control to allow room for other controls.

Whenever users press a key, txtTime appears inside the cell invisibly and accepts their input. Before this process is useful, however, you need to add four more lines to the KeyPress event of grdTimeSheet:

```
txtTime.Text = Chr(KeyAscii)
txtTime.SelStart = Len(txtTime.Text)
txtTime.Visible = True
txtTime.SetFocus
```

The first line passes the character selected by users to the Text property of txtTime, offering the appearance that users are typing directly into the grid. (The TimeSheet control won't be very user friendly if users have to press a dummy key before they can start entering data.) The second and third lines set the focus to txtTime and place the cursor at the end of the word, so users can continue typing immediately. Again, this helps make the transition between grid and text box seamless, enhancing the illusion that the TimeSheet is a single control.

To test your TimeSheet control, add an EXE to your project, place a TimeSheet control on the default Form1, and run the application. Use the mouse or arrow keys to select a cell, and then begin typing. The text you type will seem to appear directly in the grid itself, lining up within the current cell. Notice that if you type too many characters to fit in the cell, the text automatically scrolls, just as your user will expect. This is another benefit of using the TextBox control.

Now that users can enter data into the TextBox control, you must ensure that the data can be transferred from the text box to the grid after it's entered. Users can signify completion with one of two keys: Enter to accept the data or Escape to cancel any changes and stop data entry.

In the KeyPress event of txtTime, enter the following code:

```
Select Case KeyAscii
    Case Is = 13:
        grdTimeSheet.Text = txtTime.Text
        txtTime.Visible = False
    Case Is = 27:
        txtTime.Visible = False
End Select
```

Try the code again in the executable. You can now enter text into any non-fixed cell on the grid.

Lifetime of a UserControl and the Associated Events

Because users can now enter text into the grid, you need to provide column headers so that they know which data belongs in each cell. These headers should be created within the TimeSheet itself and be visible in the design-time environment. Before you can write the code to accomplish this, you should understand the five important events in the lifetime of an ActiveX control.

An ActiveX control begins its life cycle when the first instance of it is created within a system. This includes creation within a running application, a Web page, or a design-time environment. When an instance of the control is created, the UserControl_Initialize event is fired, giving programmers a chance to set any setup variables necessary.

N O T E The Initialize event is equivalent to the Form_Load event found in standard forms.

Immediately after the Initialize event, the InitProperties or ReadProperties event fires as the control populates its properties. The difference between the two events is chronological. The first time a control is created, the InitProperties event fires, both setting up the properties and filling them. When that instance of the control is re-created, the ReadProperties event fires, simply filling in the appropriate values.

For example, when you place a TimeSheet control on your form, first the Initialize event fires, followed by InitProperties. When you run the application, the control actually ends and restarts. Because this is the second creation of this particular instance of the control, the ReadProperties event fires after the Initialize event.

Part

II

Ch

12

Two events are associated with destroying the control: `WriteProperties` and `Terminate`. `WriteProperties` occurs only when the control needs to save its current data back to the control container. The most common occurrence of this is when a control is deleted from the form in the design-time environment.

The `Terminate` event fires when any instance of the control stops. This includes ending an application, closing a Web page, deleting a control within the design-time environment, or switching between runtime and design time. (The distinction will become more important later in the chapter when you use the `Ambient` property of the UserControl.) The `Terminate` event is used to process any clean-up code before the control is destroyed, such as closing the database for data-bound controls.

Now that you're familiar with the events fired at creation and destruction of your ActiveX control, you can use that knowledge to create column headers for the TimeSheet control. The column headers for the TimeSheet are as follows:

- Project—The code of the project to which the consultant is assigned.
- Task—The code of the specific project task to which this time is billable.
- Comments—Any consultant or client comments.
- Days of the Week—Seven columns for specifying the days of the week, the date, and the total hours worked for that day.
- Total—Total hours billed to the specified Project and Task.

When you first added the MSFlexGrid control to the TimeSheet control, you set the `FixedRows` property to 3. In the grid control, fixed rows appear at the top of the grid, are light gray in color, and never scroll off the page. These rows are to be filled with the column headers.

The lowest of the three fixed rows contain the main headers and the day totals. The top and middle rows hold the day of the week and the date, respectively. Add the code in Listing 12.1 to the `UserControl_Initialize` event. These values represent the static grid headings; the dynamic grid headings are determined at runtime.

Listing 12.1   Values for Static Grid Headings

```
Dim iCounter as integer
With grdTimeSheet
    .TextMatrix(2, 0) = "Project Code"
    .TextMatrix(2, 1) = "Task Code"
    .TextMatrix(2, 2) = "Comments"
    .TextMatrix(0, 3) = "Sunday"
    .TextMatrix(0, 4) = "Monday"
    .TextMatrix(0, 5) = "Tuesday"
    .TextMatrix(0, 6) = "Wednesday"
    .TextMatrix(0, 7) = "Thursday"
    .TextMatrix(0, 8) = "Friday"
    .TextMatrix(0, 9) = "Saturday"
    .TextMatrix(1, 10) = "Totals"
End With
```

Close the UserControl design window and examine the form in the executable. The column headers now appear in the design-time environment and at runtime as well.

Considering Private Versus Public Methods

To fill in the rest of the column headers, you need to write two subroutines that can be called at initialization and any time during the control's life. When writing ActiveX controls, you need to plan carefully which portions of the control should be exposed to future developers and which should be guarded to ensure that they aren't abused. Remember that future developers not only include anyone who uses your control, but also, because controls can be subclassed, anyone who uses any child of your control.

When you define a function or subroutine in an ActiveX control, you must tell the VB compiler whether it's private or public. If you declare it as public, it will be compiled as a normal method of the control and can be called in the form of `Control.MethodName` just like the `Clear` method of the ListBox control. If you declare the subroutine as private, it's available only to other routines within the same module. If you try to call a private subroutine from outside the control, you get a `Method or Data Member Not Found` compiler error.

To display the day totals in the third row, create a private subroutine that you can call anytime a new number of hours is entered into the TimeSheet. Because this is an internal bookkeeping subroutine, making it available to the control's users isn't necessary. Users never have to call a routine explicitly to update the totals as the control handles it implicitly.

Add the code in Listing 12.2 to your TimeSheet control.

Listing 12.2 The `RecalcTotals` Procedure

```
Private Sub RecalcTotals()
   Dim x As Integer
   Dim y As Integer
   For x = 3 To 9
      GrdTimeSheet.TextMatrix(2, x) = "0"
   Next
   For x = 2 To GrdTimeSheet.Rows - 1
      GrdTimeSheet.TextMatrix(x, 10) = ""
   Next
   For x = 3 To GrdTimeSheet.Rows - 1
      For y = 3 To 9
         If Val(GrdTimeSheet.TextMatrix(x, y)) > 0 Then
            GrdTimeSheet.TextMatrix(2, y) = Val
            ➥(GrdTimeSheet.TextMatrix(2, y)) + _
             Val(GrdTimeSheet.TextMatrix(x, y))
            GrdTimeSheet.TextMatrix(x, 10) = Val
            ➥(GrdTimeSheet.TextMatrix(x, 10)) + _
             Val(GrdTimeSheet.TextMatrix(x, y))
         End If
      Next
   Next
   GrdTimeSheet.TextMatrix(2, 10) = Val(GrdTimeSheet.TextMatrix(2, 3)) + _
      Val(GrdTimeSheet.TextMatrix(2, 4)) + _
```

continues

Listing 12.2   Continued

```
        Val(GrdTimeSheet.TextMatrix(2, 5)) + _
        Val(GrdTimeSheet.TextMatrix(2, 6)) + _
        Val(GrdTimeSheet.TextMatrix(2, 7)) + _
        Val(GrdTimeSheet.TextMatrix(2, 8)) + _
        Val(GrdTimeSheet.TextMatrix(2, 9))
End Sub
```

Add a call to `RecalcTotals` to the end of the `UserControl_Initialize` event, and your TimeSheet control will have hour totals across the third fixed row (see Figure 12.20). Next, add another call to the subroutine in the `txtTime_KeyPress` event at the end of the code for `KeyAscii=13`. Test the application; it should now accept and total numeric input in the grid.

FIGURE 12.20

With all column headers in place, the TimeSheet control now resembles a typical time sheet.

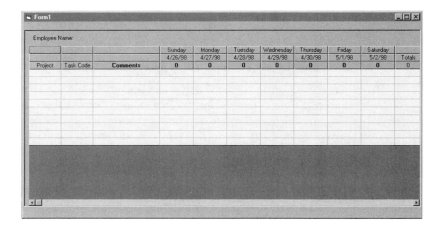

Adding the Rest of the Constituent Controls to the TimeSheet Control

Most of the basic functionality has now been implemented for the time sheet. The columns are labeled and totaled appropriately, and users can enter values into the grid. The only major functions still missing from the TimeSheet control are the capability to choose project and task codes for a row, and the capability to enter comments.

You might have noticed that at this point you can actually enter numeric data in the Comments column by using the `txtTime` control. However, using this control for comment entry limits the comments column by the same business rules applied to the time column, which, when the control is complete, will accept only numeric data. It's possible—and not difficult in code—to determine which column is now accepting the data and apply the business rules accordingly; however, this reduces the readability of the code and complicates debugging. A more readable solution—at the cost of memory overhead—is to add `txtComments` control to accept alphanumeric data for the Comments column.

Set the properties for `txtComments` identical to those of `txtTime`, with the exception of the `MultiLine` property, which should be set to `True` to allow users to enter multiple lines of text in a text box only one line high. The event procedures should be similar as well; you can simply copy most of the code to the new control. For the multiline capability of the text control to be useful, you have to make the control more than one line of text high; therefore, you should adjust the size of the `txtComments` control to be twice the height of the cell being clicked in the `grdTimeSheet_Click` event. Although the text will be squeezed back into a single line when it's placed into the `grdTimeSheet` control, it will be easier to enter long text with the additional visibility.

> **CAUTION**
>
> Make sure that all references to `txtTime` are changed to `txtComments`, and if you add any additional code that references a specific cell of the grid control, be sure to edit the values accordingly. The Visual Basic compiler can't catch these types of errors, and debugging them can be quite difficult.

To complete the TimeSheet control, you need to add two combo boxes to hold the list of acceptable project and task codes. Combining both lists into one control saves coding and a small amount of memory; however, it also diminishes the control's performance speed by forcing it to replenish the list at runtime.

Add two combo box controls to the TimeSheet control and name them `lstProjectCodes` and `lstTaskCodes`. You need to add to the TimeSheet control two public methods, `SetProjectCodes` and `SetTaskCodes`, which will accept an array of strings containing the appropriate data. This array of strings will be used to fill the Project Descriptions combo box, which means end users can choose only from valid projects. The same technique is used for the Task Descriptions combo box. Because the control expects to have a list of project descriptions, the passed array containing the project codes is actually a two-dimensional array that also holds the descriptions (see Figure 12.21).

Part

II

Ch

12

FIGURE 12.21

The Project Code list box ensures that only valid project codes are selected.

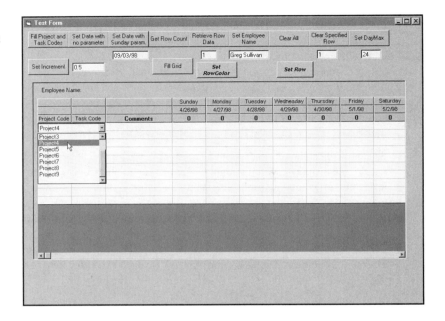

N O T E Visual Basic 6 introduced the capability for procedures to return arrays and for the entire contents of one array to be assigned to another. These combined features allow classes and components to have properties of type array. This could be very useful in an enhanced version of the TimeSheet control.

CAUTION

When creating functions that return arrays, you must use the Exit Function command to return the array. Also, the Visual Basic documentation warns that assigning the local array to the function (that is, FunctionName=LocalArray()) can cause performance issues.

If you've never passed an array to a Visual Basic procedure, don't worry—it's easier than it might seem. Simply declare the parameter as you would for any variable-length array in the procedure declaration, as follows:

```
Public Sub SetProjectCodes(codes() As String)
```

To determine the number of elements passed into the procedure, use the Ubound() function and work with the array parameter as you would any local array.

Carefully Considering Exposed Properties to Make a Control Complete and Useful

The default properties of the combo box control should work fine for the TimeSheet as well. The only property in question is the Sorted property. The TimeSheet control would probably seem more user-friendly if the Project and Task codes were displayed in alphabetical order, so this might be your initial impulse.

Before you do this, however, you should consider your end users' needs. Perhaps the project codes for a given company are customarily in a particular order but not necessarily alphabetical. If users are accustomed to a specific list order, altering that order might actually make the control more difficult to use.

The ideal solution is to allow users to decide whether to sort the combo boxes; however, the Sorted property of combo boxes is read-only at runtime, making such a property fairly difficult to implement in the TimeSheet control.

 TIP

To explore the possibility of including a Sorted property, consider either maintaining two combo boxes for each list or using the Windows API to design the combo box from scratch, programmatically. To use the API, start with CreateWindowEx, any good book on the Win32 API, and a lot of elbow grease, and you should be on your way.

Some properties are easy to create and useful to the control. Because you've already seen how the ActiveX Control Interface Wizard can create the properties for the control, you will now create a property manually to help you understand the internal mechanics involved. You'll create a DayMax property for the TimeSheet control to establish one of the business rules applied to the data entered into the TimeSheet. The DayMax property gives developers a way to control the maximum number of hours that can be entered for any given day. This way, the maximum number of working hours can be set to 8 or some other valid value between 1 and 24, helping to decrease data-entry mistakes.

A property is nothing more than a publicly defined variable, a designated value that the outside world can see. You might decide, therefore, to define a public module-level integer variable for the TimeSheet control and name it DayMax. In this case, any program using the TimeSheet control can set or read TimeSheet.Daymax to any valid integer value. Although this method would work, it offers the control no protection from being set to a negative value or a nonsensical value, such as 10,000. What you need is a way to call a procedure anytime the value changes. Visual Basic properties give you just that, and more.

CAUTION

Be sure to remove any declarations you've made for DayMax before implementing it as a property. If you attempt to define a property and a module variable with the same name, the compiler yields an Ambiguous Name detected error.

Recall the syntax for `Property Get` and `Property Set` (or `Property Let`) declarations:

```
Public Property Get PropertyName() as PropertyType
Public Property Let PropertyName(PropertyValue as PropertyType)
Public Property Set PropertyName(PropertyValue as PropertyType)
```

Define the procedures for the `DayMax` property. Now that you know how to define the property to the world, you need to create an internal integer variable that holds the internal value of the public variable. Define `m_DayMax` as a module-level public integer. The `m_` stands for *member* and is Microsoft's naming convention to help you remember that the variable is an internal member of the control. Create the property by entering the code in Listing 12.3.

Listing 12.3   The Code Behind a Control Property After Sufficient Error Checking Is Included

```
Public Property Get DayMax() As Integer
   DayMax = m_DayMax
End Property
Public Property Let DayMax(ByVal New_DayMax As Integer)
   If New_DayMax >= 1 And New_DayMax <= 24 Then
      m_DayMax = New_DayMax
   End If
End Property
```

Now close the code window and open the executable form. Select the TimeSheet control and examine its properties. The `DayMax` property appears in the Property Browser (like any Visual Basic defined property) and is set to the default value for integers of zero (see Figure 12.22).

FIGURE 12.22

Help descriptions are available even for your custom properties, as shown here for the DayMax property.

T I P To make the DayMax useful, you must set its default value to a valid value, such as 24. This is accomplished in the UserControl_InitProperties event by setting m_DayMax to 24. The component reads this value and displays it in the Visual Basic properties dialog.

Using the ActiveX Control Interface Wizard's Set Attributes Dialog Box

Finish adding the constituent controls to the TimeSheet control by adding a lblEmployeeName label and an associated label captioned Employee: just above the MSFlexGrid control.

Now that all constituent controls have been placed on the TimeSheet control and you have added the DayMax property manually, start the ActiveX Control Interface Wizard to complete the following list of custom interface members:

- EmployeeName property—String, mapped to lblEmployeeName.caption, name of the current employee.
- Increment property—Single; no mapping, Increment amount all numeric data should be rounded to.
- RowCount method—Returns the current number of rows filled with data.
- RowData method—Returns an array filled with the data from the specified row.
- SetDate method—Sets the column headers based on the date passed in or based on the current week.

Use the ActiveX Control Interface Wizard to map the EmployeeName property directly to the associated label. No further work on this property is necessary for now. (The EmployeeName property would be extremely useful in a more advanced version of the TimeSheet control that updates a centralized database or automated payroll.)

The Increment property is a single value used to round data values to the nearest specified increment. For example, if you want to allow your employees to enter time in 15-minute segments, set the Increment property to .25. Now all values entered will be rounded to the nearest quarter hour automatically.

Because the Increment property is nonvisual, don't map it to any of the constituent controls. Having a nonmapped interface member brings up the wizard's Set Attributes dialog box (see Figure 12.23). This dialog box defines settings for any non-mapped properties. You can define the return type and the arguments to simplify method declaration or the data type, default value, and read/write privileges to simplify property declaration.

Part
II

Ch
12

FIGURE 12.23

The Set Attributes dialog box allows you to set read/write access, default values, data types, and help descriptions.

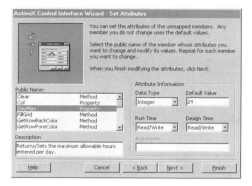

 TIP You can also use the Set Attributes dialog box to define a description for each unmapped property, method, and event. This description will be available to developers via the VB Object Browser and the property window, as seen in the last section of this chapter. If you plan to distribute your control for development use, your users will appreciate a clear, helpful description.

Notice that the ActiveX Control Interface Wizard includes DayMax in the list of properties. This demonstrates the capability to run the wizard multiple times, even after property or method definitions change. As noted before, it's important to have all constituent controls in place before running the wizard, but code changes should not have an adverse effect.

 TIP If you run the wizard multiple times on a single control, you'll probably encounter VB's odd way of dealing with multiple declarations. Rather than replace an old declaration with the newly defined one, VB simply comments out the old code. Although this is excellent for recovering from mistakes made within the wizard, it makes for messy code. Remove these extra comments to make your code more readable.

Set a description and the appropriate values for each custom interface member, and then finish the wizard. Copy the code for the three new methods and test it in the executable. You should be able to change the employee name, view automatic rounding of all hour data entered, and retrieve information about the data in the grid.

Using the AmbientProperties Object

As explained previously, one major difference between ActiveX controls and normal executables is that you create ActiveX controls to run in two distinct states: design time and runtime. The control developers manipulate in the design environment is a running application, the same application that executes in the runtime environment. As the control developer, you must have a way to determine which state the control is being run in so that it can react appropriately. The AmbientProperties object holds this information and much more (see Figure 12.24).

FIGURE 12.24

By using the `Ambient.UserMode` property, you can fill the grid with the control name at design time only. Use discretion with the `UserMode` property; overuse or misguided use can easily confuse your users.

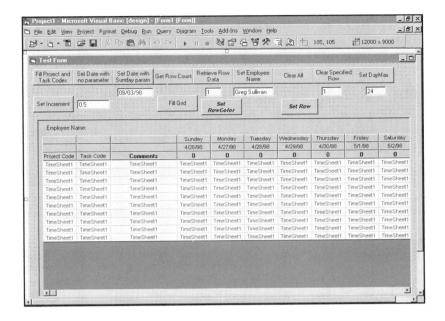

Every container that can support an ActiveX control provides an `AmbientProperties` object (called simply `Ambient`) with which you can determine the properties of that container. VB defines 16 read-only properties within the `Ambient` object, allowing you access to useful container properties such as `BackColor`, `DisplayName`, `Font`, and `UserMode`. The list of ambient properties also includes properties that let you determine if the given control is the default control for the form, the palette being used to paint the control, and even the local language being used by Windows.

`UserMode` is a Boolean value that determines whether the control is being executed for end users or developers. If end users are using the application containing the control, `UserMode` is `True`; otherwise, it's `False`. This property allows you to design controls with different design-time and runtime interfaces, similar to those of the Common Dialog, Timer, and Wizard controls.

To demonstrate use of the `UserMode` property, add code to the TimeSheet control to display the name of the control in each non-fixed cell of the TimeSheet at design time only. Add the code in Listing 12.4 to the `UserControl_Show` event.

Listing 12.4 Adding a Creative Finishing Touch with the `Ambient` Property

```
If Ambient.UserMode = False Then
   Dim x As Integer, y As Integer
   For x = 3 To grdTimeSheet.Rows - 1
      For y = 0 To 10
         grdTimeSheet.TextMatrix(x, y) = Ambient.DisplayName
```

continues

Part

II

Ch

12

Listing 12.4 Continued

```
        Next
    Next
End If
BackColor = Ambient.BackColor
grdTimeSheet.ForeColor = Ambient.ForeColor
```

Now examine the control placed on the executable form, noticing that each cell contains the name `TimeSheet1`, the default name for the TimeSheet control. The final two lines blend the control into its container by setting the control's color scheme to match that of the container. Thus, if you set the `BackColor` of the executable form to another color, close the form, and then redisplay it, the frame around the grid portion of the TimeSheet control reflects the color change as well. This technique works very well if the TimeSheet is used with no border (`BorderStyle = 0`). Run the executable to demonstrate that the `DisplayName` is filled in only at design time.

You probably noticed the problem with this code when you had to close the executable form and reopen it to display the name changes. The code to fill the grid with `Ambient.DisplayName` executes only when the control is drawn on the form. Thus, the `DisplayName` in the grid doesn't update when you change the control's properties. To account for this, the UserControl has an `AmbientChanged` event, which fires whenever one of the ambient properties of the control container is changed.

To use the `AmbientChanged` event, copy the code from the `UserControl.Show` event and paste it into the `UserControl.AmbientChanged` event. Delete the three final lines from the `Show` event to ensure that the colors used to paint the TimeSheet control change only when the related colors of the container change. Leave the code to display the `Ambient.DisplayName` at design time in both events to ensure that the grid is filled when the form is displayed and updated when part of the environment is changed.

 To further optimize your control, use the `PropertyName` parameter passed into the `AmbientChanged` event. You can build a `Select Case` statement to execute only the code necessitated by the property that changed, rather than execute all code each time.

N O T E   The `AmbientProperties` object is container-specific; different containers have different `AmbientProperties` objects and, thus, different ambient properties. For example, `BackColor` is a standard property of the form's `AmbientProperties` object, but not necessarily of a custom container. Your completed control should therefore include code to handle any situation where the control is placed on a nonstandard container that doesn't support the properties you're trying to read.

Now that you have all your properties created and set appropriately, you might be wondering how developers will keep track of them all. Another advanced feature of VB is the capability to group component properties together into logical groups on property pages.

Creating Property Pages

In using Visual Basic, you've probably used a control that contains a custom property page. In fact, you've used one to create the TimeSheet control, the MSFlexGrid. In the ActiveX control designer, right-click grdTimeSheet and choose Properties. Rather than bring up the usual Visual Basic Properties window, the MSFlexGrid displays its own custom Property Pages dialog (see Figure 12.25).

FIGURE 12.25
The MSFlexGrid's custom property page groups the control's properties into five convenient tabs.

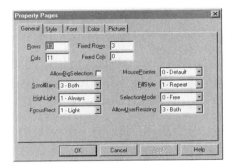

The benefits of using a custom property page are ease of use and better understanding for developers. The custom property page lets you group properties onto tabbed pages, making their purpose more readily understood. The property page for the MSFlexGrid divides its properties into five tabs devoted to General, Style, Font, Color, and Picture properties. On the General page, developers can see at a glance the number of fixed and standard rows and columns without having to scan up and down a typical Properties window. Likewise, with all font-related properties grouped on a single page, developers can see them all quickly and even view a sample based on the current settings.

Creating Property Pages with the Wizard   To add a property page to the TimeSheet control, use the Property Page Wizard to construct the basic page. Choose Add-Ins, Property Page Wizard from the menu.

If the Property Page Wizard doesn't appear on your Add-Ins menu, you can place it there by following these steps:

1. Choose Add-Ins, Add-In Manager from the menu.

2. Double-click the VB 6 Property Page Wizard. Note that the Load Behavior changes to Loaded.

3. Click OK.

The first dialog box of the Property Page Wizard is an introduction, which can be turned off by selecting the check box. The second dialog box of the wizard, Select the Property Pages, shows you a list of the property pages VB suggests you include. Three default property pages are included with VB: StandardFont, StandardColor, and StandardPicture. These same pages are included in the custom property page for the MSFlexGrid.

Part
II

Ch
12

NOTE If you are developing more than one ActiveX control within the current project group, the second dialog you see prompts you to select one control to create a property page for. ▪

Visual Basic has already suggested that you use the StandardFont and StandardColor pages by adding them to the list of selected pages. Select both and click Add to add a new page. Name the page General when prompted and move to the next screen. Choose General at the bottom of the list and click the up-arrow button twice to move it to the top of the list (see Figure 12.26).

FIGURE 12.26

Visual Basic suggests StandardFont and StandardColor property pages and lets you add custom pages with a single click.

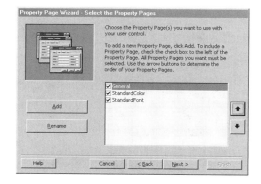

 TIP In addition to the Font, Color, and Picture pages, Visual Basic includes any property pages (.pag files) you have in your project. By adding existing pages to your project, you can reuse property pages for many different controls, with little or no modification.

Ensure that all three pages are selected and advance to the next dialog box, Add Properties. In this dialog box, you can decide which properties belong together on a single page. On the left is the list of Available Properties, and on the right are tabbed list boxes for each selected property page. With the General tab selected, choose >> to move the three available properties into the General list box (see Figure 12.27).

FIGURE 12.27

All similar properties for the control are grouped onto tabs to promote ease of use.

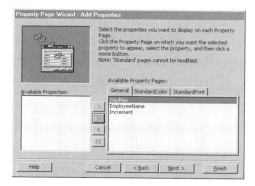

N O T E The `StandardFont` and `StandardColor` pages are maintained directly by Visual Basic; you can't add properties to these pages. ▪

Choose Next to move to the final page of the Property Page Wizard. Choose to view the summary report and select Finish. If you've just created the General property page, VB issues a confirmation that it was created. Respond to the confirmation and examine the summary report closely—it contains a plethora of tips on how to test, bulletproof, and accessorize your property pages.

Close the summary report and open the executable form. Right-click the TimeSheet control and notice a new entry titled Properties. Select this entry to view the custom property pages for the TimeSheet control (see Figure 12.28).

FIGURE 12.28

With just a small amount of work, you can create a fully functional Property Page.

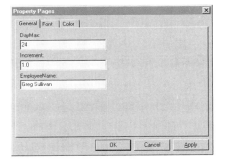

Test the property page to ensure that the changes are applied back to the control. Close the property page and return to the ActiveX control designer. Notice that the General property page now resides in your project window. Double-click the page to view it. Property pages are designed like all ActiveX controls. You can use the property page design window to modify the page any way you like. For example, to personalize the page to your company, you could add a background image of your company logo. You can also specify the location of the controls on the page.

N O T E You'll probably be inclined to resize the General property page to conserve space, but this isn't necessary. When the custom property page is displayed, VB creates a uniform interface by forcing all forms to the size of the largest form. ▪

Creating Property Pages from Scratch At some point, you'll probably find it easier to create your own property pages from scratch than to use the wizard. To do so, choose Project, Add Property Page to create the page. When the page is created, save the form and examine the properties for the ActiveX control. The `PropertyPages` property maintains a list of all included property pages. Check the box next to your new page to include it in the list.

Part

II

Ch

12

To make a designed-from-scratch page functional, you would have to write the code the Property Page Wizard creates for you. Examine the code in the General property page. You'll notice the `PropertyPage` object has two new events in addition to the usual events for forms:

- `ApplyChanges` is called by the Apply and OK buttons and by switching to another property page. Its purpose is to apply all property changes made on the page back to the control. As you would expect, this is accomplished by simply assigning to the control properties the values specified in the text or list boxes on the property page.

- `SelectionChanged` fires when the property page is displayed and when the array of selected controls changes.

The standard Properties window in VB allows you to select multiple controls, displaying only common properties and values for which the value is the same for each selected control. Examination of the basic code created by the Property Page Wizard shows that your new property page doesn't support this. The created code in `SelectionChanged` fills the property page with the values from only the first of the selected controls.

The same limitation exists for the `ApplyChanges` event; although the Visual Basic property window can set a property for multiple selected controls, the default code created by the Property Page Wizard applies the changes to only the first selected control. To alter the code to apply the changes to all controls, create a loop and alter the property value for each control in the `SelectedControls` array. For additional information, see the "Creating Property Pages for ActiveX Controls" and "Property Page Wizard" sections in Books Online help included with Visual Studio.

The TimeSheet control is now complete. This control is a bit different from the previous two controls in that it's not one you are likely to keep in your toolbox permanently. The TimeSheet control has been created to serve a specific purpose on the company intranet page, but don't overlook the other possibilities for this control. It could easily be integrated into a Word document with VBA code to create automated reports and graphs or modified to hold other kinds of spreadsheet-related data, such as expense reports, inventory records, or financial data.

N O T E   As an exercise for the adventurous programmer, try using VB 6's new data source creations feature to make the TimeSheet control expose its data to other controls. This could be extremely useful in building full-featured applications based on the TimeSheet control.

ON THE WEB

All the code for the TimeSheet control is available from the G. A. Sullivan's download area of the Web site: http://www.gasullivan.com/.

Creating User-Drawn Controls

Now that you've written both simple subclassed and aggregate controls, you need to learn about the third type of graphical ActiveX control—*user-drawn*. User-drawn controls are the most complex because you're required to code not only the functionality, but also the interface. Common user-drawn controls include representations of common objects (such as business cards or dice) as well as images created at runtime to demonstrate the drawing process.

To demonstrate the creation of user-drawn controls, you will create a Dice control (see Figure 12.29) that draws a common playing die. This control will be immediately useful in a wide range of games and can be used to easily port your existing games to Web pages.

FIGURE 12.29

Dice is an easy user-drawn control that can be used for games in applications and on the Web.

Follow these steps to create the Dice control:

1. Create a new ActiveX control and name it `Dice`.
2. Set the `FillStyle` property to `0 — Solid`.
3. Name the project `DiceProject`.
4. Run the ActiveX Control Interface Wizard and set the control to have the following properties, methods, and events:
   - Properties—`BackColor`, `BackStyle`, `BorderStyle`, `HasDC`, `hDC`
   - Methods—`Circle`
   - Events—`Click`, `DblClick`, `InitProperties`, `MouseDown`, `MouseMove`, `MouseUp`, `Paint`, `Resize`
   - Custom Properties—`Value`
   - Custom Methods—`Roll`
5. Set all noncustom properties, methods, and events to map directly to the UserControl and set a default value of 1 for the `Value` and `BorderStyle` properties.
6. Add the following code to the `UserControl.Resize` event. This simple code ensures that the newly resized die is always square:
   ```
   UserControl.Width = UserControl.Height
   ```
7. Add the code from Listing 12.5 to the control.

Part
II

Ch
12

Listing 12.5   The DrawPips Routine is the Heart of the Dice Control

```
Private Sub DrawPips()
    Dim PipRadius As Integer

    With UserControl
        PipRadius = .ScaleWidth / 10
        .Cls
        Select Case m_Value
            Case Is = 1:
                Circle (.ScaleWidth / 2, .ScaleHeight / 2),
                ➥PipRadius, .FillColor
            Case Is = 2:
                Circle (.ScaleWidth * 5 / 6, .ScaleHeight / 6),
                ➥PipRadius, .FillColor
                Circle (.ScaleWidth / 6, .ScaleHeight * 5 / 6),
                ➥PipRadius, .FillColor
            Case Is = 3:
                Circle (.ScaleWidth * 5 / 6, .ScaleHeight / 6),
                ➥PipRadius, .FillColor
                Circle (.ScaleWidth / 6, .ScaleHeight * 5 / 6),
                ➥PipRadius, .FillColor
                Circle (.ScaleWidth / 2, .ScaleHeight / 2),
                ➥PipRadius, .FillColor
            Case Is = 4:
                Circle (.ScaleWidth * 5 / 6, .ScaleHeight / 6),
                ➥PipRadius, .FillColor
                Circle (.ScaleWidth / 6, .ScaleHeight * 5 / 6),
                ➥PipRadius, .FillColor
                Circle (.ScaleWidth * 5 / 6, .ScaleHeight * 5 / 6),
                ➥PipRadius, .FillColor
                Circle (.ScaleWidth / 6, .ScaleHeight / 6),
                ➥PipRadius, .FillColor
            Case Is = 5:
                Circle (.ScaleWidth * 5 / 6, .ScaleHeight / 6),
                ➥PipRadius, .FillColor
                Circle (.ScaleWidth / 6, .ScaleHeight * 5 / 6),
                ➥PipRadius, .FillColor
                Circle (.ScaleWidth * 5 / 6, .ScaleHeight * 5 / 6),
                ➥PipRadius, .FillColor
                Circle (.ScaleWidth / 6, .ScaleHeight / 6),
                ➥PipRadius, .FillColor
                Circle (.ScaleWidth / 2, .ScaleHeight / 2),
                ➥PipRadius, .FillColor
            Case Is = 6:
                Circle (.ScaleWidth * 5 / 6, .ScaleHeight / 6),
                ➥PipRadius, .FillColor
                Circle (.ScaleWidth / 6, .ScaleHeight * 5 / 6),
                ➥PipRadius, .FillColor
                Circle (.ScaleWidth * 5 / 6, .ScaleHeight * 5 / 6),
                ➥PipRadius, .FillColor
                Circle (.ScaleWidth / 6, .ScaleHeight / 6),
                ➥PipRadius, .FillColor
                Circle (.ScaleWidth / 6, .ScaleHeight / 2),
                ➥PipRadius, .FillColor
                Circle (.ScaleWidth * 5 / 6, .ScaleHeight / 2),
                ➥PipRadius, .FillColor
```

```
        End Select
    End With
End Sub
```

8. Add a call to the `DrawPips` method in the `UserControl_Paint` event and after the code in the `Property Let` for the `Value` property.

9. Add the following code in the custom `Roll` method:

```
Value = Int(Rnd(1) * 6) + 1
```

Test the control by adding a standard EXE (or viewing it in a Web page) and placing a pair of Dice controls on the form. The controls will be drawing with a single pip in the middle (see Figure 12.30). Add a command button to the form and insert the following code in the `Command1_Click` event:

```
Dice1.roll
Dice2.roll
```

FIGURE 12.30

The Dice control can be used in a control array to make common games.

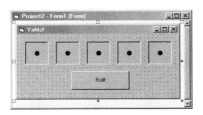

If you examine the properties of the Dice1 control, you will notice that the value for `BorderStyle` is 1, not 1 — `Fixed Single`, as you would expect. The reason for this is that the ActiveX Control Interface Wizard set the property type for `BorderStyle` to Integer instead of the standard enumerated type for `BorderStyles`.

N O T E An *enumerated type* is simply a way to keep two sets of related constants mapped to one another. Suppose that the developer would like to see None and FixedSingle as `BorderStyle` options, but Visual Basic expects to see a numeric value. Creating an enumerated type allows both sides to see what they want and agree on what that means.

In the Declarations section of the control, add the enumeration code from Listing 12.6.

Listing 12.6 Associate the Values the User Wants to See with the Numeric Constants That VB Must Have

```
Enum BorderStyleEnum
    None = 0
    FixedSingle = 1
End Enum
```

Part
II

Ch
12

This code defines the values you'll allow for BorderStyle. To force BorderStyle to allow only these two values, you must change the type definition in the Property Let and Get procedures. They should be the same as shown in Listing 12.7.

Listing 12.7 Adding a Professional Look to Your Control's Properties

```
'WARNING! DO NOT REMOVE OR MODIFY THE FOLLOWING COMMENTED LINES!
'MappingInfo=UserControl,UserControl,-1,BorderStyle
Public Property Get BorderStyle() As BorderStyleEnum
    BorderStyle = UserControl.BorderStyle
End Property

Public Property Let BorderStyle(ByVal New_BorderStyle As BorderStyleEnum)
    UserControl.BorderStyle() = New_BorderStyle
    PropertyChanged "BorderStyle"
End Property
```

If you now examine the BorderStyle property of the control on the executable form, you should see the familiar choices of None and FixedSingle (see Figure 12.31).

FIGURE 12.31

The enumerated types for BorderStyle appear in the Visual Basic Properties window as a drop-down list. Creating control properties that act just like Visual Basic's controls takes only a few lines of code.

 TIP Be sure to define all color properties for your control as OLE_COLOR, not Long, if you want users to be able to choose the color from the palette rather than enter a long integer.

Run the application and you now have the basis for most any dice game. Roll the dice several times to guarantee that the random value generation is working correctly. Your user-drawn control is now finished.

From Here...

By using Visual Basic to create ActiveX controls, you can easily create a single interface for standalone applications, as well as Web browsers and documents. This single-control approach greatly reduces development time and encourages consistency across multiple formats and applications.

The growth of the Internet in the last few years has been phenomenal and shows few signs of slowing. Add to this the increasing popularity of corporate intranets and the integration of Internet Explorer 4 into the Windows operating system, and it becomes clear that the Web browser is quickly taking its place as a necessary piece of software on every computer. With online software purchases on the rise, the capability to issue updates and bug fixes only for the necessary controls (instead of the entire application) becomes important. ActiveX controls give you this capability by automatically downloading and updating themselves when appropriate. Usually, end users need to do no more than confirm the download, making application mainte-nance a breeze across an intranet and simplifying downloads over the Internet.

In addition to these benefits, the capability to add ActiveX controls directly into Microsoft Word and Excel documents changes the entire face of document handling. No longer will documents be static; with ActiveX controls embedded in them, documents can be more responsive, more informative, and more user friendly—all with very little additional development work.

With the advent of ActiveX control creation in version 5 and the many advances made available in version 6, VB solidifies its role as an enterprise development tool.

Refer to the following chapters for more information relevant to ActiveX controls:

- To gain essential background information for understanding and using object-oriented controls, see Chapter 9, "Using Microsoft's Object Technologies."
- To learn how to create the TimeSheet control using Java instead of ActiveX, see Chapter 22, "Creating Applets and Applications with Visual J++."
- To understand the details behind utilizing the ActiveX controls you have created, see Chapter 11, "Using COM Components and ActiveX Controls."
- To learn more about using your COM components with Microsoft Transaction Server, see Chapter 27, "Creating COM Components for MTS with Visual Basic."

Part

II

Ch

12

CHAPTER 13

Creating ActiveX Controls with Visual C++

by Wen Lin

In this chapter

Working with a Simple Control—The SkunkWork Logo

Since the release of Visual Basic 5 Control Creation Edition, many C++ programmers have used it as a tool to create the ActiveX Controls for their applications. This is because of the belief that the development of these controls in Visual C++ was too difficult and required the knowledge of object linking and embedding (OLE). Visual C++ 6 and its Microsoft Foundation Class (MFC) library have greatly simplified and minimized the OLE knowledge required for the creation of an ActiveX control.

MFC is a collection of classes that simplifies the creation of Windows applications. It achieves this by using the object-oriented characteristics of C++ such as polymorphism, inheritance, and encapsulation.

In this chapter, you will use the MFC ActiveX ControlWizard to create visual ActiveX controls that can be incorporated by other Microsoft development tools such as Visual Basic, Visual FoxPro, Visual InterDev, and by Visual C++ itself. The focus of this chapter is on how to use Visual C++/MFC to create ActiveX controls rather than how Visual C++/MFC implements the ActiveX controls. You don't need to have any previous OLE or COM knowledge to write the controls in this chapter, but you must be familiar with MFC.

 T I P Visual C++ includes a tutorial (Circle) for creating ActiveX controls. If you are serious about knowing every facet of ActiveX controls, I recommend the Microsoft Press book *ActiveX Controls Inside Out* by Adam Denning.

The first project described in this chapter is the SkunkWork logo control (SW_Logo). The characteristics for SW_Logo are defined as follows:

- The default bitmap file for the logo is sw_logo.bmp.
- The SkunkWork logo is resizable.
- A notification is sent to the container when the SkunkWork logo is clicked.

Creating an ActiveX Control Using the MFC ActiveX Wizard

To create an ActiveX control of SkunkWork Logo as your first project, follow these steps:

1. Select File, New from the menu.
2. Select MFC ActiveX ControlWizard in the Projects tab of the New dialog box.
3. Select C:\SkunkWork as the project location (or you can select your own directory.)
4. Enter SW_Logo in the Project Name text box (see Figure 13.1).

FIGURE 13.1

Create a new ActiveX control using MFC ActiveX ControlWizard.

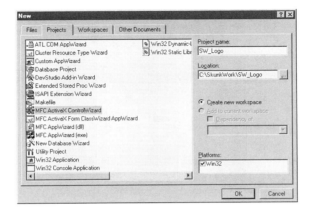

5. Click OK. The MFC ActiveX ControlWizard – Step 1 of 2 dialog box appears (see Figure 13.2).

FIGURE 13.2

You can choose the number of controls and whether to have a runtime license, comments in your source file // TODO, and help files generated in this dialog box.

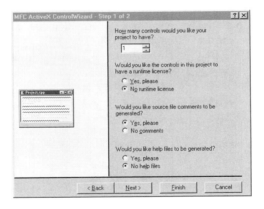

6. You have several options here. You can create more than one control in this ActiveX project. You can require a runtime license to run the control(s). \\TODO comments can be generated in the source code and help files can be generated for the control(s) based upon your choices.

7. For this project you will keep all default settings. Click Next.

8. The MFC ActiveX ControlWizard – Step 2 of 2 dialog box appears (see Figure 13.3).

FIGURE 13.3
You can modify the name of the classes and choose the behavior features of this control. Subclass association and other advanced features can also be chosen.

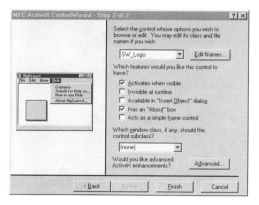

9. By clicking the Edit Names button, you have the chance to modify the names of class, header and implementation files individually. The features chosen for this control are Activates When Visible and Has an "About" Box. No subclass or advanced features are needed in this project.

10. Choose the Finish button. The New Project Information dialog box appears to give you a final review of the control specifications (see Figure 13.4).

FIGURE 13.4
You have the chance to perform a final review of the control specifica-tion.

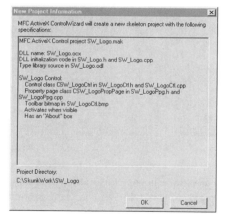

11. Click OK. This project is then created.

In Figure 13.4, the output filename of this project is SW_Logo.ocx. OCX is the extension de-noted for ActiveX controls, which are always linked as a dynamic link library (DLL). The type library file, SW_Logo.odl, is written by Object Description Language (ODL) as a text file. It tells outside containers about the properties, methods, return types, parameter types and the Universally Unique Identifier (UUID) of this ActiveX control object.

The `CSW_LogoCtrl` class inherits from `COLEControl`, which is the backbone of every ActiveX control created by MFC. The `CSW_LogoPropPage` is derived from `CDialog`, so it handles the properties of this control by using the dialog box.

The default attribute of an ActiveX control created by MFC ActiveX ControlWizard is to draw an oval in the center of the outline of the control (see Figure 13.5). In this project, you will remove the code, which draws the oval, and add your own code to create a SkunkWork logo.

FIGURE 13.5

An oval, the default attribute of an ActiveX control, created by the MFC ActiveX ControlWizard.

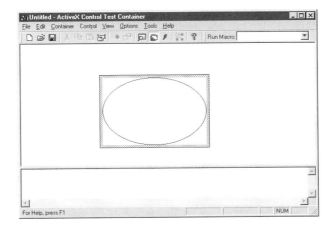

Adding the SkunkWork Logo Bitmap

The next step is to add the SkunkWork logo bitmap file to the control. The first step is to link this file with a resource ID. Later, this ID will be used in your code to refer to the SkunkWork logo bitmap file. To add the SkunkWork logo bitmap resource ID, follow these steps:

ON THE WEB

SW_LOGO.BMP is available at `http://www.gasullivan.com/`. It was created by Image Composer, which is included in the Visual Studio. You can use other bitmap files or use Image Composer to create a new bitmap file as your own logo for this project.

1. Select Resource from Insert menu.
2. Click Import button from Insert Resource dialog box.
3. The Import Resource file dialog box appears.
4. Change Files of types to BMP Files (*.bmp).
5. Select SW_LOGO.BMP and click Import.

After this file is imported, by default it is assigned the resource ID of `IDB_BITMAP1`. You must now change the name of this resource ID. In the Workspace, right-click `IDB_BITMAP1` and then choose Properties from the pop-up menu that appears. The Bitmap Properties dialog box appears. In ID: text box, type `IDB_SKUNK_WORK_LOGO` (see Figure 13.6).

FIGURE 13.6

Import and assign a new resource ID to the SkunkWork logo bitmap file.

Now that the bitmap resource ID, `IDB_SKUNK_WORK_LOGO`, is generated, close the Resource Editor.

Writing the Code for Resizing

Click the ClassView tab in the workspace. Open the `OnDraw` function under `CSW_LogoCtrl` class (see Figure 13.7).

FIGURE 13.7

Open the `CSW_LogoCtrl::OnDraw()` function from the workspace.

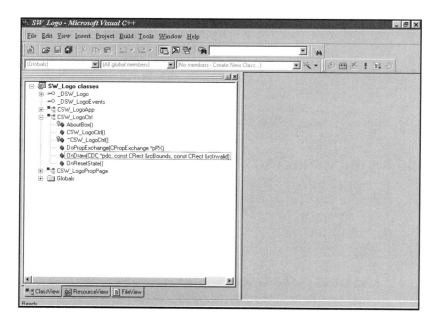

In `CSW_LogoCtrl::OnDraw`, delete the two lines of code underneath the `//TODO` statement. Listing 13.1 shows the `CSW_LogoCtrl::OnDraw` before being modified.

Listing 13.1   AMLST01.TXT—The CSW_LogoCtrl::OnDraw Function Before Modification

```
void CSW_LogoCtrl::OnDraw(CDC* pdc, const CRect& rcBounds, const
➥CRect& rcInvalid)
{
    // TODO: Replace the following code with your own drawing code.
    pdc->FillRect(rcBounds, CBrush::FromHandle((HBRUSH)GetStockObject
➥(WHITE_BRUSH)));
    pdc->Ellipse(rcBounds);
}
```

Enter the code in Listing 13.2 into the CSW_LogoCtrl::OnDraw function.

Listing 13.2   AMLST02.TXT—The CSW_LogoCtrl::OnDraw Function Modified to Support Resizing

```
CDC memDC;
CBitmap picBitmap;
BITMAP bitmap;
CRect rect = rcBounds;

picBitmap.LoadBitmap (IDB_SKUNK_WORK_LOGO);
picBitmap.GetObject(sizeof(BITMAP),&bitmap);

memDC.CreateCompatibleDC(pdc);

CBitmap* pOldBitmap = memDC.SelectObject(&picBitmap);

pdc->StretchBlt( rect.left , rect.top, rect.right, rect.bottom , &memDC,
                 0, 0, bitmap.bmWidth, bitmap.bmHeight, SRCCOPY);

memDC.SelectObject(pOldBitmap);
  ReleaseDC(&memDC);
```

The CBitmap::LoadBitmap function loads the SkunkWork logo bitmap file using the resource ID, IDB_SKUNK_WORK_LOGO. Later the bitmap file is used by the memDC, which is a compatible device context (DC) with the current DC. The CDC::StretchBlt function resizes the logo by stretching the bitmap to fit the current size of the DC.

Firing an Event When the Logo Is Clicked

To add an event to this SkunkWork Logo, follow these steps:

1. Select ClassWizard from View menu (or press Ctrl+W). This opens the MFC ClassWizard.

2. Choose ActiveX Events tab.

3. Select CSW_LogoCtrl from the Class Name: combo box.

4. Click the Add Event button. The Add Event dialog box appears.

5. Select Click from the External Name: combo Box.

6. Choose Stock in Implementation.

7. Click OK. The `Click` event is created (see Figure 13.8).

FIGURE 13.8
Creating a `Click` event for the SkunkWork logo.

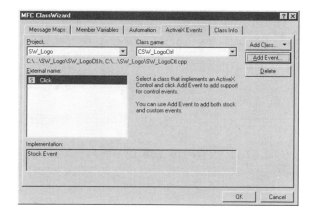

Testing the SkunkWork Logo ActiveX Control

Prior to testing your SkunkWork logo control, you must compile and link this program. Press F7 or click Build button in the Toolbar to compile and link this program.

An ActiveX control must be registered before it can be tested and used. To register an ActiveX control, select Register Control from the Tools menu. After the ActiveX control is registered successfully, the message box in Figure 13.9 appears.

FIGURE 13.9
A message box appears stating that the registering of the ActiveX control was successful.

Now you can test it by following these steps:

1. Select ActiveX Control Test Container from the Tools menu.

2. The Active Control Test Container window appears.

3. Select Insert New Control from the Edit menu.

4. The Insert Control box appears.

5. Select SW_Logo Control from the list (see Figure 13.10).

FIGURE 13.10

Select SW_Logo
Control from the list in
the ActiveX Control Test
Container.

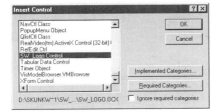

6. Now the SkunkWork Logo ActiveX control is displayed. Click it and the `Click` event is fired (see Figure 13.11).

FIGURE 13.11

The SkunkWork Logo
ActiveX control is
displayed in the ActiveX
Control Test Container.
The `Click` event is
fired by clicking the
logo.

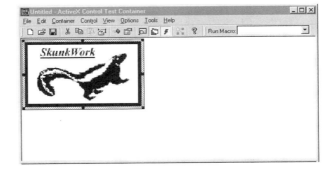

Debugging an ActiveX Control

When it's time to debug an ActiveX control, Visual C++ provides an ActiveX Control Test Container for your use as a debugging aid. To invoke the debug tool, follow these steps:

1. Choose Setting from the Project menu. The Project Settings box appears.

2. Click the Debug tab. Choose ActiveX Control Test Container from Executable for Debug Session (see Figure 13.12).

Part

II

Ch

13

FIGURE 13.12

Choosing the Debug tool in the Project Settings box.

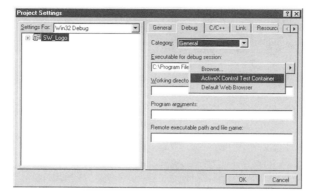

3. Click OK to close the Project Settings box.
4. Press F5 to start the debug session.
5. The ActiveX Control Test Container box appears.
6. Repeat the steps for testing SkunkWork Logo ActiveX Control.

Now you can select a line of code and press F9 to add a break point at any point in the source code at which you want debugging to temporarily pause. This gives you an opportunity to review the current value of variables and investigate the current state of your running application.

▷ For more information about debugging, **see** Chapter 3, "Debugging Enterprise Applications with Visual Studio," **p. 55**

Exploring the Button Control

A button has two states: pushed and released (down and up). To generate the visual effect of a button on a computer monitor, the Button control must have two different paintings corresponding to down and up. You can make it more attractive by using a different color on the background and the caption. Furthermore, you can select a different font and size for the caption. When the button is pushed and released, it fires a click event to notify the container. In this project, you will implement the properties of this control first.

Some properties of the ActiveX controls are implemented so frequently that MFC creates a set of properties, called stock properties, to standardize the implementation. These stock properties have standard names and identifications (Dispid). In this project, you will use BackColor, ForeColor, Font and Caption stock properties (see Table 13.1).

Table 13.1   The Stock Properties of the Button Control

Properties	Description
BackColor	The color for painting the background of the control.
Caption	The text in the control.
Font	The font for the caption in the control.
ForeColor	The color for the caption in the control.

Again, you will use MFC ActiveX ControlWizard to create the Button Control. Open a new project, select MFC ActiveX ControlWizard, type the project name SW_Button, and leave every option as default settings in step 1 and 2. Click Finish button to create the SW_Button project. The next step is to add the Button's stock properties to this project.

Adding Stock Properties to the Button Control

To add Caption, BackColor, Font, and ForeColor properties, follow these steps:

1. Click ClassWizard from the View menu (or press Ctrl+W).
2. Click the Automation tab.
3. In the Class Name list box, choose CSW_ButtonCtrl.
4. Click the Add Property button.
5. The Add Property dialog pops up.
6. From the External name combo box, choose Caption.
7. Under the Implementation, check Stock.
8. Click the OK button to close the Add Property dialog.
9. In the MFC ClassWizard, under External Name, you will see Caption, and under Implementation, you will see Stock Property.v

Repeat steps 4–8. You will add BackColor, Font, and ForeColor stock properties (see Figure 13.13).

FIGURE 13.13

Adding stock properties
to the Button control
using MFC ClassWizard.

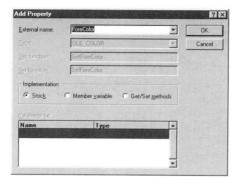

The MFC ClassWizard modifies the dispatch map of the CSW_ButtonCtrl class in
SW_Button.cpp. The dispatch macro adds entries for each stock property (see Listing 13.3).

**Listing 13.3   AMLST03.TXT—The Dispatch Macro Adds These Entries for
Each Stock Property**

```
BEGIN_DISPATCH_MAP(CSW_ButtonCtrl, COleControl)
//{{AFX_DISPATCH_MAP(CSW_ButtonCtrl)
    DISP_STOCKPROP_CAPTION()
    DISP_STOCKPROP_BACKCOLOR()
    DISP_STOCKPROP_FORECOLOR()
    DISP_STOCKPROP_FONT()
//}}AFX_DISPATCH_MAP
 END_DISPATCH_MAP()
```

Click ClassView from the Workspace window. You will see a list of properties, BackColor, Caption, Font, and ForeColor, under the _DSW_Button folder (see Figure 13.14).

FIGURE 13.14

The stock properties
BackColor, Caption,
Font, and ForeColor
added by MFC
ClassWizard in the
workspace.

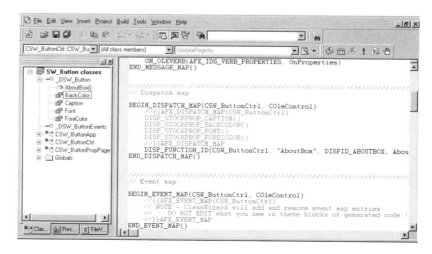

Constructing Property Pages

The properties of the ActiveX controls allow the users to freely manipulate the object of an ActiveX control. A property page serves as an interface for editing and viewing the properties of an ActiveX control. It allows the users of the ActiveX controls to set and view the property value at the design time. MFC provides a macro, BEGIN_PROPPAGEIDS, to construct the property pages for your control's properties. To construct the property pages for stock properties in this project, add the two bold lines in Listing 13.4 into the BEGIN_PROPPAGEIDS macro in SW_ButtonCtl.cpp.

Listing 13.4 AMLST04.TXT—Add These Lines to Construct the Property Pages for Stock Properties

```
BEGIN_PROPPAGEIDS(CSW_ButtonCtrl, 3)
    PROPPAGEID(CW3DButtonPropPage::guid)    // Default (General) page
    PROPPAGEID(CLSID_CColorPropPage)        // ForeColor and BackColor page
    PROPPAGEID(CLSID_CFontPropPage)         // Font page
END_PROPPAGEIDS(CSW_ButtonCtrl)
```

The page count number (3) in the BEGIN_PROPPAGEIDS macro indicates the number of property pages implemented by the control. Here, you have 3 property pages: General, Color (ForeColor and BackColor) and Font pages.

A default property page is created by MFC ActiveX ControlWizard as a part of this project. This page is a dialog associated with a class, CSW_ButtonPropPage, and a dialog ID, IDD_PROPPAGE_SW_BUTTON. In this section, you will add the Caption property to the General property page.

To modify the default property page, follow these steps:

1. Click the ResourceView tab from the workspace. Open the SW_Button resources folder. Under the Dialog folder, double-click IDD_PROPPAGE_SW_BUTTON.
2. The General property page dialog template appears. A TODO statement of the static text control is displayed on the general property dialog box.
3. Right-click the TODO of the static text control and then choose Properties from the pop-up menu that appears. The Text Properties dialog box appears.
4. Type Caption into the Caption: text box and then close the Text Properties box.
5. In the Control toolbar, click the Edit Box control.
6. Place the Edit box control right next to the static text control Caption.
7. Right-click the Edit box control and then select Properties on the shortcut menu. The Edit Properties dialog box appears.
8. Change the ID of the Edit box control to IDC_BUTTON_CAPTION (see Figure 13.15).

FIGURE 13.15
Constructing the
Caption property in
the Dialog template.

Now you need to link the resource ID, IDC_BUTTON_CAPTION, of the Edit box control to a variable so that it can be edited in the program. To make this link, follow these steps:

1. Press Ctrl+W to open the MFC ClassWizard.
2. Click the Member Variables tab.
3. Choose CSW_ButtonPropPage from the Class Name list.
4. Choose IDC_BUTTON_CAPTION and click the Add Variable button. The Add Member Variable dialog appears.
5. Type m_sCaption in the Member Variable name field.
6. Choose Value in the Category list.
7. Choose CString in the Variable Type list.
8. Choose Caption in the Optional Property name list.
9. Click OK.

You will see the new member variable mapping as shown in the following:

```
IDC_BUTTON_CAPTION     CString     m_sCaption
```

Implementing Stock Properties of the Button Control

The next step is to implement ForeColor, BackColor, Font and Caption stock properties. Click ClassView from the Workspace window. Double-click OnDraw(CDC* pdc, const CRect& rcBounds, const CRect& rcInvalid) under the class CSW_ButtonCtrl. Again, you will see the two lines of code generated by the MFC ActiveX ControlWizard. Delete these two lines.

```
pdc->FillRect(rcBounds, CBrush::FromHandle((HBRUSH)GetStockObject(WHITE_BRUSH)));
pdc->Ellipse(rcBounds);
```

To implement the background color of the Button control, add the following code:

```
Crect rect = rcBounds;
pdc->SetBkMode(TRANSPARENT);
CBrush currentBrush(TranslateColor(GetBackColor()) );
pdc->FillRect(rect, &currentBrush);
```

The SetBkMode function with the parameter TRANSPARENT makes the background of current DC not changed before the drawing. The Translate and GetBackColor are member functions of the COleControl. The GetBackColor function returns the color value of BackColor property. The TranslateColor function converts the return color value of the GetBackColor function from the OLE_COLOR data type to the COLORREF data type used by CBrush. The CDC::FillRect function fills the color.

To give this button a pushed look, the frame will be added to the rectangle. Add the following code:

```
pdc->Draw3dRect( rect , 0x00eeeeee, 0x00111111);
```

The CDC::Draw3Drect function will draw a three-dimensional rectangle. The top and left side will be drawn with the color 0x00eeeeee, and the bottom and right will be drawn with the color 0x00111111.

N O T E 0x00eeeeee and 0x00111111 are 32-bit values used for representing a color value. The data type is COLORREF. The format is 0x00BGR, where B is blue, G is green, and R is red.

To get the ForeColor property for the text color of the Caption, add this line:

```
pdc->SetTextColor(TranslateColor(GetForeColor()));
```

The GetForeColor is also the member function of COleControl. It returns the color value of ForeColor property. The TranslateColor function converts the return color value of the GetForeColor function from the OLE_COLOR data type to the COLORREF data type used by the CDC::SetTextColor function that sets the text color in the device context.

To get the Caption property from the property page, add this line:

```
const CString& sCaption = InternalGetText();
```

The InternalGetText is also the member function of the COleControl. It returns the Caption property value.

To get the Font property for the caption, add this line:

```
CFont* oldFont = SelectStockFont(pdc);
```

The SelectStockFont is also the member function of the COleControl. It stores the current font in oldFont and sets the value of the Stock Font property in the device context.

To display the caption on the button, add this line:

```
pdc-> DrawText( sCaption, rect,DT_VCENTER¦DT_CENTER¦DT_SINGLELINE );
```

The DrawText function draws the Caption into the center of the button. The T_VCENTER¦DT_CENTER¦DT_SINGLELINE parameters specify the location of the caption in which it will be drawn in the center of both horizontal and vertical direction with a single line.

The SelectObject function will restore the current system's original font.

```
pdc->SelectObject(oldFont);
```

The completed code of the OnDraw function is listed as the following:

```
void CSW_ButtonCtrl::OnDraw(CDC* pdc, const CRect& rcBounds, const
➥CRect& rcInvalid)
{
    CRect rect = rcBounds;
    pdc->SetBkMode(TRANSPARENT);
    // Paint background color
```

```
        CBrush currentBrush(TranslateColor(GetBackColor()));
        pdc->FillRect(rect, &currentBrush);
        // Draw 3D frame around rectangle
        pdc->Draw3dRect( rect , 0x00eeeeee, 0x00111111);
        // Get ForeColor for Text
        pdc->SetTextColor(TranslateColor(GetForeColor()));
        const CString& sCaption = InternalGetText();
        CFont* oldFont = SelectStockFont(pdc);  // Get Stock font
        pdc-> DrawText( sCaption, rect, DT_VCENTER¦DT_CENTER¦DT_SINGLELINE );
        pdc->SelectObject(oldFont);
}
```

Implementing the Behavior of the Button Control

As mentioned earlier, the behavior of a button is up and down. Now you will implement the Down behavior for painting the button. This allows the user to know that the button is pushed. The button control will be drawn like a button pushed when the mouse button is pressed. The OnLButtonDown and OnLButtonUp message map functions will be used to implement this behavior for down and up by the following steps:

1. Press Ctrl+W to open the MFC ClassWizard.
2. Click the Message Maps tab.
3. Choose CSW_ButtonCtrl from Class name list.
4. Choose CSW_ButtonCtrl in the Object IDs.
5. In the Messages list, scroll down and select WM_LBUTTONUP.
6. Click the Add Function button. You will see the new member function, OnLButtonUp, in the Member functions list.
7. In the Messages list, select WM_LBUTTONDOWN.
8. Click Add Function button. You will see the new member function, OnLButtonDown, in the Member functions list (see Figure 13.16).

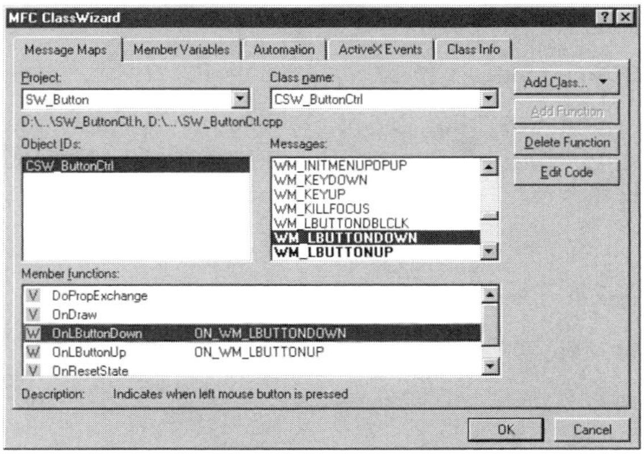

FIGURE 13.16
Adding the OnLButtonDown and OnLButtonUp message map functions in MFC ClassWizard.

9. Click the Edit Code button to edit the OnLButtonDown message map function.

Add the code in Listing 13.5 into the OnLButtonDown function.

Listing 13.5 AMLST05.TXT—The Functionality to Make the Button Appear to Be Pressed Down When the Mouse Button Is Pressed

```
void CSW_ButtonCtrl::OnLButtonDown(UINT nFlags, CPoint point)
{
    CDC* pDc = GetDC(); // Get the current DC

    CRect rect;
    GetWindowRect(&rect);

    pDc->SetBkMode(TRANSPARENT);

    // Paint background color
    CBrush currentBrush (TranslateColor(GetBackColor()) );
    pDc->FillRect(rect, &currentBrush);

    // Draw 3D frame around the rectangle
    pdc->Draw3dRect( rect , 0x0011111111, 0x00111111);


    // Get ForeColor for Text
    pDc->SetTextColor(TranslateColor(GetForeColor()));

    const CString& sCaption = InternalGetText();

    CFont* oldFont = SelectStockFont(pDc);  // Get Stock font

    // Text Output
    pDc-> DrawText( sCaption, rect, DT_VCENTER¦DT_CENTER¦DT_SINGLELINE );

    pDc->SelectObject(oldFont);


    ReleaseDC(pDc);

    COleControl::OnLButtonDown(nFlags, point);
}
```

The code is similar to the OnDraw function. The difference is the CDC::Draw3dRect function that now draws the same color 0x00111111 for left, top, right and bottom sides.

When the mouse button is released, the button control should be restored back to the Up behavior. To implement this behavior, add the code in Listing 13.6 to the OnLButtonUp message map function.

Listing 13.6   AMLST06.TXT—The Button Is Painted to Appear Up When the Mouse Button Is Released

```
void CSW_ButtonCtrl::OnLButtonUp(UINT nFlags, CPoint point)
{
    InvalidateControl();
    COleControl::OnLButtonUp(nFlags, point);
}
```

The `InvalidateControl` function is the member function of the `COleControl`. It will force the control to redraw itself by calling the `OnDraw` function.

Fire a `Click` Event When the Button Is Pushed

When the button is clicked, it will fire a click event to notify its container.

 T I P   MFC provides a set of standard stock events. You can use events, other than the `Click` event here, to modify your ActiveX controls. These stock events are

Event	Description
Click	Fire when a control is clicked.
DblClick	Fire when a control is double-clicked.
KeyDown	Fire when a key is pressed.
KeyUp	Fire when a key is released.
MouseDown	Fire when the control is clicked by the mouse.
MouseMove	Fire when the mouse moves over the control.
MouseUp	Fire when the mouse is released over the control.
Error	Fire when an error occurred to notify its container.
ReadyStateChange	For Asynchronous loading.

To implement a `Click` event to the Button control, follow these steps:

1. Press Ctrl+W to open the MFC ClassWizard.
2. Click the ActiveX Events tab.
3. Select `CSW_ButtonCtrl` from the Class Name list.
4. Click the Add Event button. The Add Event dialog appears.
5. Choose Click in the External Name list.
6. Choose Stock in the Implementation radio control.
7. Click OK.
8. You will see the new `Click` event mapping (see Figure 13.17).

FIGURE 13.17
Adding a stock `Click`
event to the Button
control from the MFC
ClassWizard.

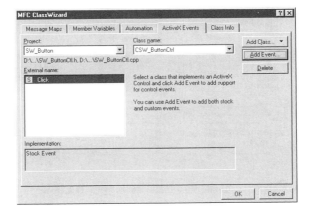

Test the Button Control

To compile and link this program, press F7 or click the Built button in the toolbar. After this process is successful, you register this control by choosing the Register control from the Tools menu. Now you can test the Button control by selecting the ActiveX Control Test Container from the Tools menu. When the ActiveX Control Test Container window appears, select Insert New Control from the Edit menu. In the Insert Control dialog box, select SW_Button Control from the list and click the OK button. The Button control appears. Click SW_Button, and a click event is fired.

To edit the property page of the SW_Button Control, select Properties from Edit menu. The SW_Button Control Properties dialog appears. Now you can type any text for the Caption and change the background color or foreground color in this property page (see Figure 13.18).

FIGURE 13.18
Editing the SW_Button
Control Properties in
ActiveX Control Test
Container.

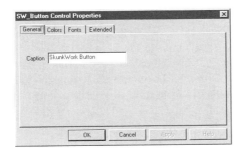

Part

II

Ch

13

Composing an Aggregate Control—The SkunkWork Timesheet Control

It would be less time and effort to create a visual ActiveX control if a dialog template is used as a container to hold multiple controls that can be the MFC standard controls, third-party controls, and your own ActiveX controls. This type of ActiveX control is called an *aggregate ActiveX control* (see Figure 13.19).

FIGURE 13.19
A typical complicated aggregate control includes MFC Edit, List, and Button controls, third-party controls, and your own controls.

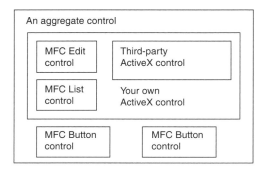

An aggregate control

MFC Edit control

Third-party ActiveX control

MFC List control

Your own ActiveX control

MFC Button control

MFC Button control

Many Visual C++ ActiveX control developers ask, "How can the Resource Editor be used to compose the ActiveX Controls on a dialog template?" Unfortunately, Visual C++ didn't directly provide this functionality, but a solution is provided by the Microsoft Knowledge Base Article Q155973. The previous versions of Visual C++/MFC don't support aggregate controls directly; you must have the OLE and COM knowledge to make it work. The Visual C++ 6 has been improved to minimize the necessary knowledge. The SkunkWork Timesheet control illustrates this solution and shows how an aggregate ActiveX control is implemented in this matter.

N O T E   The Microsoft Knowledge Base Article Q155973 is available at www.microsoft.com/kb or the MSDN Library CD. This article has an example, DlgX, which demonstrates how to create an ActiveX control with a dialog resource. The DlgX requires the subclass of the MFC standard controls inserted at the dialog template resource for message mapping. With the release of Visual C++ 6, it's no longer necessary. ▪

Building the SkunkWork Timesheet Control

In this project, the MFC ActiveX Form ClassWizard project, which is a customized MFC wizard, is provided for you. This project is based on the Microsoft Knowledge Base Article Q155973. The SkunkWork Timesheet control will be created by using the MFC ActiveX Form ClassWizard. To include the MFC ActiveX Form ClassWizard into the set of wizards that can be launched by the Visual C++ Projects wizard, you must first open the MFC ActiveX Form ClassWizard project by completing the following steps:

1. Select Open Workspace from File menu.
2. Locate and open the MFC ActiveX Form Classwizard.dsw.

ON THE WEB

The MFC ActiveX Form ClassWizard is available at http://www.gasullivan.com/.

3. Press F7 or click the Built button from the Toolbar to build this project.
4. After the MFC ActiveX Form ControlWizard is built successfully, the ActiveX Form ClassWizard AppWizard is generated and included in the Visual C++ Projects Wizard.

Now that you have added the ActiveX Form ClassWizard AppWizard, you can use it to create the SkunkWork Timesheet control. To create this control, follow these steps:

1. Select New from the File menu.

2. Select MFC ActiveX Form ClassWizard AppWizard and then type the project name SkunkWork Timesheet (see Figure 13.20).

FIGURE 13.20
Using the customized MFC ActiveX Form ClassWizard AppWizard to create the SkunkWork Timesheet control.

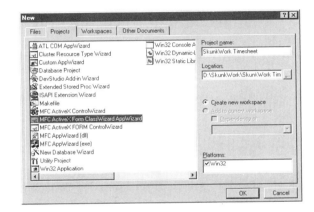

3. Click OK. The project is then created.

4. Click the ResourceView tab from the workspace, open the Dialog folder, and then double-click IDD_FORM. You will see a dialog template. You will use the Microsoft FlexGrid Control, version 6 for this project.

5. Click the Project menu. Choose Components and Controls from Add to Project.

6. The Components and Controls Gallery dialog box appears.

7. Double-click the Registered ActiveX Controls folder.

8. Scroll through and locate the Microsoft FlexGrid Control, version 6. Double-click it.

9. Click OK to insert this component. The Confirm Classes dialog box appears (see Figure 13.21). Click OK.

FIGURE 13.21
Adding the Microsoft FlexGrid control to this project.

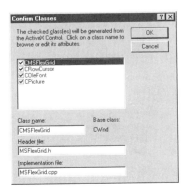

T I P If you are interested in knowing how the MFC ActiveX Form ClassWizard was created, refer to the Microsoft Knowledge Base article Q155973.

You will see the MSFlexGrid icon shown on the control bar. Click this icon and drag it to the dialog template. Extend the size of the dialog template and resize the MSFlexGrid control to match the size of the dialog template. Set the properties of the MSFlexGrid as follows:

Property	Value
FormatString	SkunkWork Timesheet
Cols	11
Rows	48
FixedCols	0
FixedRows	3

Set the Headings of the Timesheet Control

To access the MSFlexGrid control in the program, you need to create a data member of the CXformCtrl to link with the MSFlexGrid control. Press Ctrl+W to open the MFC ClassWizard, click the Member Variables tab, select CXformCtrl from the Class Name list, and click IDC_MSFLEXGRID1 in the Control IDs. Click the Add Variable button. Type m_ctlMSFlexGrid in the Member Variable name field and click OK. The m_ctlMSFlexGrid will be used as a reference to the MSFlexGrid in this program.

Now you want the Timesheet control to resize to fill the entire window. Add the code in Listing 13.7 to XformCtrl::OnDraw.

Listing 13.7   AMLST07.TXT—The Timesheet Control Resizes and Fills the Entire Window

```
void CXFormCtrl::OnDraw(CDC* pdc, const CRect& rcBounds,
➥const CRect& rcInvalid)
{

    if (!m_hWnd)     // It's design-time
    {
        CFormControl::OnDraw(pdc, rcBounds, rcInvalid);
    }
    else    // It's runtime
    {
        m_ctlMSFlexGrid.SetWindowPos(&wndTop,
                                    rcBounds.left,
                                    rcBounds.top,
                                    rcBounds.Width (),
                                    rcBounds.Height(),
                                    NULL);
        f_SetStaticHeadings();
    }
}
```

The f_SetStaticHeading is created as a member function of the CXformCtrl. Add the code in Listing 13.8 to f_SetStaticHeading.

Listing 13.8 AMLST08.TXT—All Headings of the MSFlexGrid Are Set

```
void CXFormCtrl::f_SetStaticHeadings()
{
    // Center all data
    m_ctlMSFlexGrid.SetColAlignment(-1,4);

    // Set headings
    m_ctlMSFlexGrid.SetTextMatrix(2,0,"Project");
    m_ctlMSFlexGrid.SetTextMatrix(2,1,"Task Code");
    m_ctlMSFlexGrid.SetTextMatrix(2,2,"Comments");
    m_ctlMSFlexGrid.SetTextMatrix(0,3,"Sunday");
    m_ctlMSFlexGrid.SetTextMatrix(0,4,"Monday");
    m_ctlMSFlexGrid.SetTextMatrix(0,5,"Tuesday");
    m_ctlMSFlexGrid.SetTextMatrix(0,6,"Wednesday");
    m_ctlMSFlexGrid.SetTextMatrix(0,7,"Thursday");
    m_ctlMSFlexGrid.SetTextMatrix(0,8,"Friday");
    m_ctlMSFlexGrid.SetTextMatrix(0,9,"Saturday");
    m_ctlMSFlexGrid.SetTextMatrix(1,10,"Totals");

    // Display the date heading
    f_DisplayDate();

    // Display hours heading
    f_CalculateHours();
}
```

The f_DisplayDate and f_CalculateHours functions are also created as the member functions of the CXFromCtrl. Add the code in Listing 13.9 to the f_DisplayDate function.

Listing 13.9 AMLST09.TXT—The f_DisplayDate Function Sets the Days of the Week

```
void CXFormCtrl::f_DisplayDate()
{
    // Display whole week of date, starting Sunday.

    CTime tTime = CTime::GetCurrentTime(); // Get current day
    int i;
    CString sDate;

    int nDayOfWeek = tTime.GetDayOfWeek();
    tTime -= CTimeSpan(nDayOfWeek-1, 0, 0, 0);  // Get the Date for Sunday

    for (i = 0; i < 7; i++)
    {
        tTime += CTimeSpan(1,0,0,0);
        sDate = tTime.Format("%x");
```

continues

Listing 13.9   Continued

```
        m_ctlMSFlexGrid.SetTextMatrix(1, i+3, sDate);
    }

}
```

The f_CalculateHours function will calculate the total hours of each day and the total hours of each project. Add the code in Listing 13.10 to the f_CalculateHours function.

Listing 13.10   AMLST10.TXT—The f_CalculateHours Function Calculates the Total Hours of Each Day and the Total Hours of Each Project

```
void CXFormCtrl::f_CalculateHours()
{
    int i, j, k;

    double fDayTotalHours;
    double fWeekTotalHours = 0.0f;
    double fProjTotalHours;

    CString sHour;

    long lTotalRow = m_ctlMSFlexGrid.GetRows(); // total of rows

    //Comput each day total
    for (i = 3; i < 10; i++)  // Column 3 to 9
    {
        fDayTotalHours = 0;
        for (j = 3; j < lTotalRow; j++) // Row
        {
            sHour = m_ctlMSFlexGrid.GetTextMatrix(j, i);
            fDayTotalHours += atof(sHour);
            sHour.Format("%2.1f",fDayTotalHours);
            m_ctlMSFlexGrid.SetTextMatrix(2,i,sHour);


            // Now compute each project hour
            fProjTotalHours = 0;
            for (k = 3; k < 10; k++)  // Column
            {
                sHour = m_ctlMSFlexGrid.GetTextMatrix(j, k);
                fProjTotalHours += atof(sHour);
            }
            sHour.Format("%2.1f",fProjTotalHours);
            m_ctlMSFlexGrid.SetTextMatrix(j,10,sHour);

        }
        fWeekTotalHours += fDayTotalHours;
    }
    sHour.Format("%2.1f",fWeekTotalHours);
    m_ctlMSFlexGrid.SetTextMatrix(2,10,sHour);
}
```

In Figure 13.22, the Timesheet control's heading is all set.

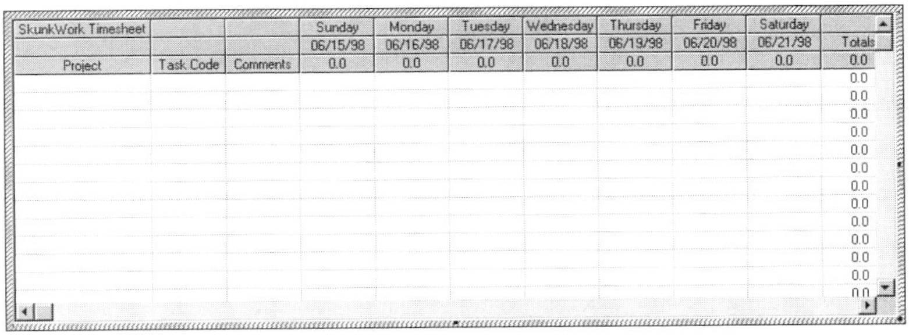

FIGURE 13.22

The heading of the Timesheet control.

Edit a Cell in the Timesheet Control

The MSFlexGrid control doesn't enable you to edit any cell in the grid. The solution is to use an edit control to map the position of the cell you want to edit and then copy the content of the edit control to the cell. To do this, first you must add an edit control with the resource ID, IDC_TEXT_INPUT, to the dialog template (IDD_XFORM). Because this edit control's position is dynamic, you need to create a data member of the CXFormCtrl for this edit control. Use the MFC ClassWizard to create the data member, m_ctlTextInput, associated with IDC_TEXT_INPUT, with CEdit type.

To make the edit control invisible to the user, you need to compute the position of the cell clicked and move the edit control to the location of the cell. Then make the size of the edit control the same as the cell size. The Click event of MSFlexGrid and the ON_KILLFOCUS message of the edit control are implemented to perform this action. Use MFC ClassWizard to generate the member function, OnClickMsflexgrid1, for the Click event and the member function, OnKillfocusTextInput, for the EN_KILLFOCUS message mapping.

Add the code in Listing 13.11 in the OnClickMsFlexgrid1 function.

Listing 13.11 AMLST11.TXT—The Click Event of MSFlexGrid and the ON_KILLFOCUS Message of the Edit Control Are Implemented to Make the Edit Control Invisible to the User

```
void CXFormCtrl::OnClickMsflexgrid1()
{
    // Move IDC_TEXT_INPUT to the cell clicked

    long lRow = m_ctlMSFlexGrid.GetRowSel();
    long lCol = m_ctlMSFlexGrid.GetColSel();

    // if user clicks on column index 10, it's total hour, return it
    if (lCol == 10)
        return;

    // Get a DC
```

Part

II

Ch

13

continues

Listing 13.11   Continued

```
CDC* pDC = GetDC(); // Get a device context
ASSERT (pDC);

// The MSFlexGrid function always return the twips, so we need to
// convert it to pixels 1440 twips = 1 logical inch

// Get dots(pixels) per logical inch, then 1440 twips is divided by it
int nTwipsPerDotX = 1440 / pDC->GetDeviceCaps(LOGPIXELSX) ;
int nTwipsPerDotY = 1440 / pDC->GetDeviceCaps(LOGPIXELSY) ;

ReleaseDC(pDC);

// Converting Twips to Dots (pixels)
long lCellWidth = m_ctlMSFlexGrid.GetCellWidth()/ nTwipsPerDotX;
long lCellHeight = m_ctlMSFlexGrid.GetCellHeight()/ nTwipsPerDotY;

long lCellLeft = m_ctlMSFlexGrid.GetCellLeft() / nTwipsPerDotX;
long lCellTop = m_ctlMSFlexGrid.GetCellTop() / nTwipsPerDotY;

m_ctlTextInput.SetWindowPos(&wndTop,
                            lCellLeft,
                            lCellTop,
                            lCellWidth,
                            lCellHeight,
                            NULL);

m_ctlTextInput.SetFocus();
m_ctlTextInput.ShowWindow(SW_SHOW);

// Clean CEdit Control string and read text back from current
// cell to the edit control
SetDlgItemText(IDC_TEXT_INPUT, "");
CString sData = m_ctlMSFlexGrid.GetText();
m_ctlTextInput.ReplaceSel(sData);
}
```

Add the code in Listing 13.12 in the OnKillfocusTextInput function.

Listing 13.12   AMLST12.TXT—The Click Event of the ON_KILLFOCUS Message Is Shown

```
void CXFormCtrl::OnKillfocusTextInput()
{
    // Copy text from CEdit control to current selected Grid cell


    // Get edit control data
    CString sInputData;
    GetDlgItemText(IDC_TEXT_INPUT, sInputData);

    // User did not input anything or erase content, return
```

```
    if (sInputData.IsEmpty())
    {
        m_ctlMSFlexGrid.SetText("");
        return;
    }

    m_ctlMSFlexGrid.SetText(sInputData);

    // Now check if the user input data in one of column 3 to 9,
    // check if it's a number
    long lCol = m_ctlMSFlexGrid.GetColSel();
    if ((lCol > 2) && (lCol <10))
    {
        double fHour = atof(sInputData);
        if (fHour == 0.0f) // User did not input number
        {
            m_ctlMSFlexGrid.SetText("");
            AfxMessageBox("Please input number here!");
        }

        // Error checking working hour
        if (fHour > 24.0f)
        {
            m_ctlMSFlexGrid.SetText("");
            AfxMessageBox("Are you kidding? No one can work over
            ➥24 hours in one day!");
        }
        // Call calculate hour routine
        f_CalculateHours();
    }

    m_ctlTextInput.ShowWindow(SW_HIDE);
}
```

Test the SkunkWork Timesheet Control

Before you compile this program, you must add a header path to the include files. To add this path, follow these steps:

1. Select Options from the Tools menu. The Options dialog box appears.
2. Click the Directories tab. Choose Include Files from Show Directories for List.
3. Go down to the Directories list. Double-click the blank bar to add a new searching path for the include files.
4. From the Choose Directory dialog box, locate \Program Files\Microsoft Visual Studio\vc98\mfc\src.

Press F7 or click the Build button in the toolbar to compile and link this program. Register the SkunkWork Timesheet control. Then run the ActiveX Control Test Container to test the SkunkWork Timesheet control. In the Insert Control dialog box, you will choose the XForm control from the list instead of the SkunkWork Timesheet control. The reason is that the name of this ActiveX control was XForm when the MFC ActiveX Form ControlWizard was created.

Part
II

Ch
13

N O T E You can modify the registration name by the following steps:

1. Click the ResourceView tab from the workspace.

2. Open and click String Table.

You will see IDS_XFORM, IDS_XFORM_PPG, and IDS_XFORM_PPG_CATION. To change the name of this ActiveX control registration, type SkunkWork TimeSheet in the Caption of IDS_XFORM.

After the SkunkWork Timesheet control is loaded to the test container, resize it, and the SkunkWork Timesheet control will fill the entire window (see Figure 13.23).

FIGURE 13.23

Editing a cell in the SkunkWork Timesheet control.

			Sunday 06/15/98	Monday 06/16/98	Tuesday 06/17/98	Wednesday 06/18/98	Thursday 06/19/98	Friday 06/20/98	Saturday 06/21/98	Totals
Project	Task Code	Comments	12.0	12.0	12.0	12.0	12.0	12.0	12.0	84.0
CCG	IMP									0.0
CNNS	SUPP			8						8.0
SEU98	IMP		12	4	12	12	12	12	12	76.0
										0.0
										0.0
										0.0
										0.0
										0.0
										0.0
										0.0
										0.0

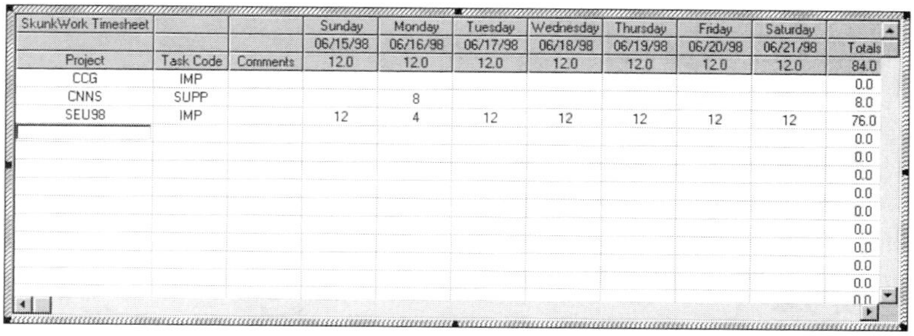

Click the cell. The edit control appears at the location of the cell you just clicked. Right now you can use the mouse to select any cell you want to edit except a few cells that are headings and total hours.

ON THE WEB

The entire code for this chapter is available at http://www.gasullvan.com/.

From Here...

With the release of Visual C++ 6, creating an ActiveX control is not a tough job any more. In this chapter, there is no OLE or COM knowledge needed to create these ActiveX controls. Using the MFC ActiveX ControlWizard, you can create a simple or complicated ActiveX control just by having a good understanding of MFC.

- For an overview of Microsoft's object and component technologies, see Chapter 9, "Using Microsoft's Object Technologies."

- For more information on strategies for creating reusable, see Chapter 10, "Creating Reusable Components."

- For practical guidance on implementing components and controls, see Chapter 11, "Using COM Components and ActiveX Controls."

- To learn about creating components for Microsoft Transaction Server (MTS), see Chapter 14, "Creating COM Components for MTS."

- To learn about building MTS components with Visual C++, see Chapter 29, "Creating COM Components for MTS with Visual C++."

CHAPTER 14

Creating COM Components for MTS

by Larry Millett

In this chapter

Managing Transactions in MTS

In Chapter 5, "An Inside Look at Microsoft Transaction Server," you were introduced to the Microsoft Transaction Server (MTS), the Distributed Transaction Coordinator (DTC), and distributed transaction-processing concepts. This chapter explores the techniques used to create applications for MTS and delves more deeply into the features that support distributed applications.

Creating distributed transactions isn't an easy task. With applications components running on multiple machines connected over a network, many complicated types of error scenarios can occur. Trying to foresee these possibilities and build your application to deal with them appropriately is a monumental job. Microsoft has provided an infrastructure for these applications that greatly simplifies application development in multitier environments.

To get the most out of this chapter, you need a basic understanding of Microsoft's Component Object Model (COM) and Distributed COM (DCOM). You also need to understand the basic concepts underlying distributed transactions and the two-phase commit transaction protocol.

▶ **See** "COM Architecture Basics," **p. 243**

▶ **See** Chapter 31, "Using Microsoft Transaction Server to Enable Distributed Applications," **p. 899**

One of MTS's primary functions is automated support for transactions. Based on transaction requirements declared for each component, MTS automatically begins, commits, and aborts transactions, enlisting database connections and other components as needed. A component's transaction requirements may take one of four values:

- Requires a Transaction—The component's objects must always execute within a transaction. A new object may enlist in its creator's transaction; if the creator isn't executing in a transaction, MTS will create a transaction for the new object.

- Requires a New Transaction—The component's objects must execute within an independent transaction. Even if an object's creator is already in a transaction, MTS will create a new, independent transaction for the new object. This value might be useful for implementing an audit trail component, which records work done on behalf of its creator's transaction regardless of the outcome of the original transaction.

- Supports Transactions—A new object can be enlisted in its creator's transaction, if any. If the creator isn't executing in a transaction, MTS won't create a transaction for the new object.

- Does Not Support Transactions—The component's objects shouldn't be included in a transaction, even when the creator is executing in a transaction. This value should be used only for older components that predate MTS, or inherently nontransactional functionality.

A component's support for transactions is declared in the MTS Explorer when a component is added to a package, or can be set using new transactional properties added in the 6 release of the languages in Visual Studio.

▶ For more information about adding components to packages with the MTS Explorer, **see** Chapter 31, "Using Microsoft Transaction Server to Enable Distributed Applications," **p. 899**

▶ For more information about building MTS components with VB, **see** Chapter 27, "Creating COM Components for MTS with Visual Basic," **p. 809**

▶ For more information about building MTS components with Visual J++, **see** Chapter 28, "Creating COM Components for MTS with Visual J++," **p. 835**

▶ For more information about building MTS components with Visual C++, **see** Chapter 29, "Creating COM Components for MTS with Visual C++," **p. 855**

To provide automatic transaction support, MTS associates an *object context* with each object created in the MTS runtime environment. The object context includes information about the identity of the object's creator and the transaction (if any) in which the object executes. The object context exposes the `IObjectContext` interface. Most newly developed MTS components should support transactions. At a minimum, this means that each of the component's objects will use the `SetComplete` and `SetAbort` methods of the `IObjectContext` interface. The next section discusses the object context in more detail.

Any object that includes a `Begin Tran` statement, or executes SQL that includes a `Begin Tran` statement, should be declared as `Requires a Transaction` or `Requires a New Transaction`. When a component is declared as requiring a transaction or a new transaction, you don't need to include `Begin Tran` statements in the object; MTS automatically provides transaction support.

As an alternative to its automatic management of transactions, MTS allows a base client to directly control transactions with the `ITransactionContextEx` interface. Discussion of the `ITransactionContext` interface, and the corresponding transaction context object, follows discussion of the object context.

Using the Object Context

The object context is central to MTS's implementation of automatic transactions, security, and (eventually) object pooling. Every object executing in MTS has an object context and can obtain a reference to its context with the `GetObjectContext` function. Proper use of the object context is essential for automatic transaction management.

Include a private member variable of type `ObjectContext` in every MTS object. This reference must never be passed outside the object and must be explicitly released when the object is deactivated.

The GetObjectContext returns a reference to an ObjectContext object (interface IObjectContext). This object has a number of methods for transaction control:

- CreateInstance instantiates a new MTS object. Caller and transaction information for the new object's object context is derived from the current object context.

- SetAbort indicates that the object has completed its work and may be deactivated, but the transaction in which it executed should be aborted.

- SetComplete indicates that the object has successfully completed its work and may be deactivated.

- DisableCommit indicates that transactional updates performed by this object can't be committed in their current form.

- EnableCommit indicates that the object has successfully completed its transactional updates but isn't yet ready to be deactivated.

- IsInTransaction returns True if the current object is executing within a transaction; otherwise, it returns False.

- SafeRef returns a reference to the current object (not the object context) that may be passed to other objects.

 T I P A transaction can't be committed while any participating object is executing a method. MTS will behave as though COMMIT is disabled until all method calls return.

The work of a transaction can be divided among several MTS objects. In such cases, your first instinct might be to control the transaction and each subsidiary object from the base client. This approach, however, doesn't effectively exploit the automatic transaction support provided by MTS. A better approach would be to develop one master object that creates instances of the subsidiary objects from its object context. Because the subsidiary objects are created from the master object's context, MTS automatically enlists those objects in the transaction.

A base client creates an MTS object, which uses its object context to create two subsidiary objects, each of which uses its object context to create another subsidiary object. If the first MTS object requires a transaction and the subsidiary objects support transactions, all are automatically enlisted in the same transaction (see Figure 14.1).

FIGURE 14.1
The object context used to enlist subsidiary objects in a transaction.

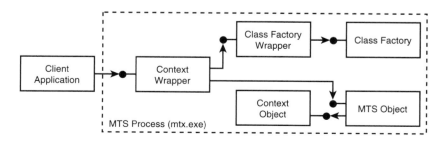

N O T E Don't use `CoCreateInstance` to create a subsidiary MTS object from within another MTS object. You must use `ObjectContext.CreateInstance` so that the new object's context can inherit properties from its client's context and enlist in the client's transaction. ■

Suppose that an application needs to include in a single transaction work performed by two MTS components: `Drive` and `Read`. Suppose also that each component is defined as `Requires a Transaction`, and that we want all work done by the two components to be included in one transaction. A base client implemented in Visual Basic might include the code in Listing 14.1.

Listing 14.1 BALST01.TXT—Using the Object Context

```
Public Sub DriveWhileReading()

Dim objObjectContext As ObjectContext
Dim objDrive As Component1.Drive
Dim objRead As Component2.Read

' Create an instance of Drive, and get a reference to the object context
Set objDrive = CreateObject("Component1.Drive")
Set objObjectContext = objDrive.GetObjectContext

' Use Object Context to create instances of Read within the same transaction
Set objRead = objObjectContext.CreateInstance("Component2.Read")

' do work ñ each component must call ObjectContext.SetComplete or SetAbort
objDrive.Drive("Car")
objRead.Read("Newspaper")

' Clean up
Set objDrive = Nothing
Set ObjRead = Nothing
Set objObjectContext = Nothing

End Sub
```

Using the Transaction Context

The `TransactionContext` object (`ITransactionContextEx` interface) allows a base client to control enlistment of MTS objects in a transaction. Each new instance of `TransactionContext` initiates a new transaction. The base client creates a transaction context and uses that object's methods to control the transaction:

- `CreateInstance` instantiates an MTS component. If the component supports or requires a transaction, the new object is enlisted in the transaction of the `TransactionContextEx` object.
- `Commit` attempts to commit the work of all MTS components enlisted in the current transaction. If any component has called `SetAbort` or `DisableCommit`, or a system error has occurred, the transaction aborts; otherwise, the transaction commits.
- `Abort` aborts the work of all MTS components enlisted in the current transaction.

Using a transaction context to control a transaction from the base client imposes a number of limitations on an application:

- The business logic for composing the transaction is implemented in the base client and isn't reusable.

- To actually enlist subsidiary objects in the transaction, you must create them by using the CreateInstance method of the transaction context object. This subtle requirement is easily overlooked and leads to sporadic failures that are difficult to isolate.

- The transaction context object must run in-process with the base client, which means that MTS must run on the same machine with the base client.

A base client creates a transaction context object and then uses it to create three subsidiary objects, one of which creates its own subsidiary object. The base client controls enlistment of subsidiary objects in the transaction (see Figure 14.2).

FIGURE 14.2
The transaction context used to control subsidiary objects in a transaction from the base client.

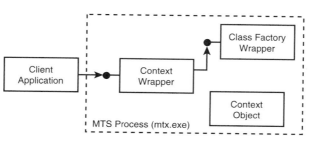

Suppose that an application needs to include in a single transaction work performed by two MTS components: Drive and Read. Each component must be defined as Supports Transactions. A base client implemented in Visual Basic might include the code in Listing 14.2.

Listing 14.2 BALST02.TXT—Using the Transaction Context Object to Control Transaction Properties from the Base Client

```
Public Sub DriveWhileReading()

Dim objTransactionContext As TransactionContext
Dim objDrive As Component1.Drive
Dim objRead As Component2.Read

' Create an instance of TransactionContext
Set objTransactionContext = CreateObject("TxCtx.TransactionContext")

' Use objTransactionContext to create instances of Drive and Read within a
' transaction
Set objDrive = objTransactionContext.CreateInstance("Component1.Drive")
Set objRead = objTransactionContext.CreateInstance("Component2.Read")

' do work ñ each component must call ObjetContext.SetComplete or SetAbort
objDrive.Drive("Car")
objRead.Read("Newspaper")
```

```
' Commit the transaction
objTransactionContext.Commit

' Clean up
Set objDrive = Nothing
Set ObjRead = Nothing
Set objTransactionContext = Nothing

End Sub
```

 TIP To use the `TransactionContext` object in a Visual Basic project, include a reference to the Transaction Context Type Library (txctx.dll). This library includes `TransactionContext` and `TransactionContextEx` objects. The `CreateInstance` method of the `TransactionContext` object takes a string program identifier (`"Appname.Classname"`); the `CreateInstance` method of the `TransactionContextEx` object requires the corresponding GUID strings.

Understanding MTS Component Integration Services

In addition to its support for transactions, MTS provides several features for enhanced scalability, security, and efficient administration:

- Process and thread management
- Just-in-time object activation
- Database connection pooling
- Shared Property Manager
- Distributed security service to control object invocation and use
- A graphical tool for system administration and component management

Process and Thread Management

The MTS Executive provides an execution environment for MTS components. An MTS *package* consists of one or more ActiveX dynamic link libraries (DLLs) that share an execution context (a process). Because all components in a package share a process, execution is more efficient. When components execute inside an MTS process, MTS can provide two important performance benefits: just-in-time object activation and resource pooling.

An MTS application component can execute in one of three basic scenarios: in-process, out-of-process, and remote.

N O T E Some Microsoft documents seem to imply that with MTS, all components run in-process with the base client. This isn't true. An MTS component may run in-process with the base client, but for most enterprise applications the remote server model makes the best sense. The in-process confusion probably arose because every MTS component must be built as an in-process server (a DLL) and because all components in an MTS package execute in a common process.

Part
II

Ch
14

Figure 14.3 illustrates in-process execution. The application component runs inside the base client's process. This method provides optimum performance but no process isolation: on any internal error in a component, MTS immediately shuts down the base client and all its active components.

FIGURE 14.3

An in-process MTS component uses the base client application's execution context.

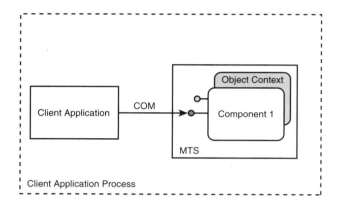

To run MTS components in-process, the base client must run on a Windows NT system with MTS running and all components installed locally.

> **CAUTION**
>
> Although running MTS components in-process with the base client provides optimum performance, this approach may compromise security. When a base client successfully invokes a component, MTS doesn't revalidate security for calls between components within the same server process. When MTS components run in-process with the base client, the base client gains access to all components within that server process.

A local Transaction Server component executes on the same computer as the client application, but in a separate process managed by the MTS Executive (see Figure 14.4). The client communicates with the component through the COM proxy/stub mechanism. Each message from a base client to an MTS component must cross a process boundary, which incurs some overhead, but this model allows MTS to provide full security and fault isolation. Scalability, however, is limited to the number of base clients and MTS components that can run on the same single-client computer.

FIGURE 14.4

MTS components can also run on the same computer as the base client, but in a separate process.

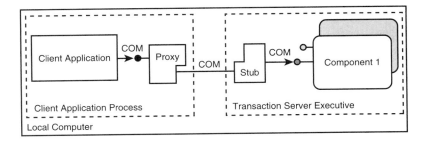

Finally, an MTS component might run on a separate computer from the base client, using DCOM. The client communicates with the component through the DCOM proxy/stub mechanism. Communication between the base client and MTS components takes place at network speeds—milliseconds rather than microseconds. This model, shown in Figure 14.5, provides the best scalability for large numbers of base clients.

FIGURE 14.5

A remote Transaction Server component executes on a separate computer from the client application, in an execution context provided by the MTS Executive.

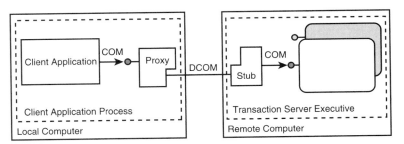

ON THE WEB

For a base client running on Windows 95 or Windows 98, in-process and local execution aren't an option (MTS isn't available for Windows 95/98). MTS does support Windows 95/98 base clients for remote execution, but Windows 95 may need an upgrade for DCOM support. For the latest information on DCOM for Windows 95, see http://www.microsoft.com/oledev.

N O T E You will probably have to configure DCOM security settings (impersonation and authentication levels) on both client and server computers. The default values for these settings— Identify for impersonation, Connect for authentication—work properly for MTS but might not be appropriate for your application. Impersonation must be set to Identify or higher.

You can change default DCOM security settings using the DCOM configuration utility (dcomcnfg), or change settings for an individual package using the MTS Explorer. Microsoft recommends using the MTS Explorer rather than dcomcnfg to change security settings at the package level to ensure consistent settings for all components in a package. ■

Part

II

Ch

14

Object Pooling and Just-in-Time Object Activation

In a typical high-volume transaction-processing environment, a large number of base clients invoke a large number of transactions. In an MTS environment, each transaction requires a new instance of a component. Unfortunately, object instantiation takes a relatively long time. It's as though you had to assemble your car before driving to work each day, disassemble it (and put the pieces away) on arrival, reassemble the car to drive home, and take it apart again on your safe return. It's much simpler just to park, lock the car, and take the keys.

Unfortunately, when hundreds of people drive to work and park their personal automobiles, parking becomes scarce and traffic becomes dense. Similarly, if every base client maintains its own instance of a component, server resources are strained and performance suffers.

Microsoft's solution to this problem is *object pooling* and *just-in-time activation*. In the COM programming model, a client doesn't explicitly destroy a server component; it just releases its reference to the component. Normally, a component released by all clients destroys itself. However, MTS can deactivate and then reactivate the application component on demand. In fact, MTS can even deactivate an object while a client maintains a reference (provided that the object isn't involved in an active transaction and doesn't need to maintain any private state information).

To let MTS know when an object is no longer involved in a transaction, and has no private state to maintain, you must use the `IObjectContext.SetComplete` and `IObjectContext.SetAbort` functions. When a component calls one of these functions, it indicates that it has completed its work and doesn't need to maintain any private state for its client.

To perform some action on object activation or deactivation, implement the `ObjectControl` interface (`IObjectControl` for Visual C++ and Visual J++ and `ObjectControl` for Visual Basic). This interface includes three functions:

- ■ `Activate()` allows an object to perform context-specific initialization at each activation (fetching Registry settings, for example). MTS calls this method before any other methods are called on the object.

- ■ `Deactivate()` allows an object to perform any necessary cleanup before it's recycled or destroyed. MTS calls this method at object deactivation.

- ■ `CanBePooled()` returns `True` if the component supports pooling; otherwise, it returns `False`. MTS calls `CanBePooled()` immediately after the `Deactivate` method.

The Visual Basic 6 (VB6) code example in Listing 14.3 implements `ObjectControl`.

Listing 14.3 BALST03.TXT—Using `ObjectControl`

```
Option Explicit

Implements ObjectControl

Private Sub ObjectControl_Activate()
    'Initialize member variable for object context
```

```
    Set m_oContext = GetObjectContext()
    'A good place to fetch registry entries
End Sub

Private Sub ObjectControl_Deactivate()
    'Explicitly release reference to object context
    Set m_oContext = Nothing
    ' Deallocate any objects created since activation
End Sub

Private Function CanBePooled() As Boolean
    CanBePooled = True
  End Function
```

N O T E According to Microsoft, object pooling and recycling isn't implemented for custom components in MTS 2. MTS invokes the `CanBePooled` function but ignores the result. Implementing the function now, however, allows a component to take advantage of resource pooling and recycling when MTS implements this feature. ▪

T I P The `ObjectControl` interface requires Windows NT 4 Service Pack 2 or greater.

When a base client initially creates an MTS component (by calling `CreateObject` or `CoCreateInstance`), MTS checks for an inactive instance of that object. If an inactive instance is available, MTS returns a reference to that object; if no inactive objects are available, MTS initializes the object in a deactivated state. When the client invokes a method on a deactivated object, MTS first invokes `ObjectControl.Activate`.

N O T E In Visual C++, calls to `QueryInterface`, `AddRef`, or `Release` won't activate an object. ▪

MTS deactivates an object when the object calls `SetComplete` or `SetAbort` and returns to the caller, or when the last reference from an external client is dropped.

Shared Property Manager

The Shared Property Manager (SPM) is one of two resource dispensers included with MTS. SPM allows safe multithreaded access to application-defined process-wide variables. Possible applications include a function to generate sequential (and unique) ID numbers for business forms or the management of any shared state for a multiuser application.

Traditional global variables aren't safe for use in a multithreaded or multiuser application because concurrent access may lead to inconsistent results. In Figure 14.6, Thread 1 and Thread 2 update a global variable x. Thread 1 sets x = x + 1, Thread 2 sets x = x * 2. Depending on the sequence of reads and writes, the result may be 2, 3, or 4. The case in which the result is 2 is clearly incorrect: Thread 2 reads x while Thread 1 updates x—a dirty read. SPM provides a locking mechanism that allows safe concurrent access to shared state.

FIGURE 14.6

Shared between threads, a simple global variable can lead to inconsistent results.

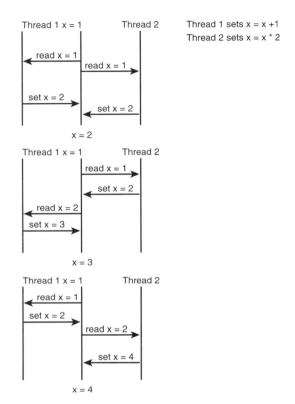

NOTE SPM doesn't provide transactions for shared properties, because properties are nondurable data. ▪

As shown in Figure 14.7, SPM uses a simple hierarchy of three classes:

- SharedPropertyGroupManager (interface ISharedPropertyGroupManager) supports allocation and deallocation of SharedPropertyGroup objects, and indexed, keyed, or enumerated (for each) access to SharedPropertyGroups. A process can have only one instance of SharedPropertyGroupManager.

- SharedPropertyGroup (interface ISharedPropertyGroup) supports allocation and deallocation of individual SharedProperty objects, and indexed, keyed, or enumerated (for each) access to SharedProperty objects.

- SharedProperty (interface ISharedProperty) provides thread-safe access to the value of an individual shared property.

FIGURE 14.7
Each process may have one instance of a SharedPropertyGroup-Manager, which contains a collection of SharedPropertyGroups. Each SharedPropertyGroup contains a collection of SharedProperty objects. Each SharedProperty contains a value (a variant).

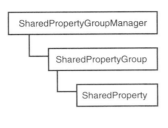

The object-creation methods for SPM include features intended to simplify programming. An attempt to create an instance of SharedPropertyGroupManager when one is already active in the process will succeed, but will return a reference to the existing instance without creating a new one. For example, the following VB code will never fail due to a prior instance of SharedPropertyGroupManager, but will never create a second instance:

```
Dim spmMgr As Object

Set spmMgr = CreateObject("MTxSpm.SharedPropertyGroupManager.1")
```

For SharedPropertyGroup and SharedProperty objects, the create method behaves similarly, but sets a flag (out parameter) to indicate whether a new instance was created or a reference was returned for an existing instance. This flag can be used to conditionally set an initial value (see Listing 14.4).

Listing 14.4   BALST04.TXT—Using the Shared Property Manager

```
Dim spmGroupCounter as Object
Dim spmPropertyCounter as Object
Dim bPriorInstance as Boolean

'Create shared property group spmGroupCounter
Set spmGroupCounter = _
 spmMgr.CreatePropertyGroup("Counter", LockSetGet, Process, bPriorInstance)

' Create the counter SharedProperty.
Set spmPropertyCounter = spmGroupCounter.CreateProperty("Next", bPriorInstance)

' Set the initial value to 0 if this is a new instance
If bPriorInstance = False Then
 spmPropertyCounter.Value = 0
 End If
```

Part

II

Ch

14

Notice that the `SharedPropertyGroupManager` method `CreatePropertyGroup` takes two additional parameters: isolation mode and release mode. Setting isolation mode to `LockSetGet` ensures thread-safe concurrency for all properties in the group. By setting release mode to `Process`, `SharedPropertyGroupManager` will maintain the `SharedPropertyGroup` until the creating server process terminates.

 T I P   All objects sharing a property must run in the same server process with the `SharedPropertyGroupManager`. One way to accomplish this would be to limit use of a shared property group to objects created by the same component, or to objects created by components implemented within the same DLL. Remember that an MTS package generally equates to an MTS process. If two DLLs use the same shared property group and an administrator installs the DLLs in separate packages, the two packages couldn't share properties.

SPM objects should be created only from within an MTS component, never from the base client.

N O T E   The `Receipt` component of the sample bank application included in MTS 2 illustrates a simple application of shared properties.

SPM provides a solution to the problem of shared variables in a multithreaded environment. This is one more way in which MTS allows you to focus on business logic by simplifying multiuser programming issues.

Distributed Security Service

MTS 2 uses role-based security to control application security. The security model is resource-based—each package has its own list of roles (basically groups) and users. Roles for a package are defined, renamed, and deleted by using the MTS Explorer, but the role names must be hard-coded into components. The users associated with a particular role are determined when you deploy the application, and can easily be changed at any time. This task is also done using the MTS Explorer. An MTS component can limit access to resources or functions based on roles and can determine at runtime whether a client has access to that role.

CAUTION

For MTS objects running in-process with the base client, security is effectively disabled.

A *role* is a symbolic name for a group of users. You define and use roles when creating and coding MTS components, whereas the MTS administrator defines roles for a package and assigns users to the roles. It's important that the MTS administrator use the same role names (spelled correctly!) that you did when coding the components.

▶ **See** "Using the MTS Explorer," **p. 901**

N O T E   Roles and security information for a package can't be modified or defined while an instance of that package is running in MTS.

Security in MTS 2 uses two methods from the `IObjectContext` interface (`ObjectContext` object):

- `IsSecurityEnabled` returns `False` if the MTS object is loaded in-process with the base client.

- `IsCallerInRole` returns `True` if the identity of the direct caller of the object is associated to a specific role. If security isn't enabled (the MTS object is loaded in-process with the base client), `IsCallerInRole` returns `True`. If security is enabled and the identity of direct caller of the object isn't associated to a specific role, `IsCallerInRole` returns `False`.

N O T E When an MTS component runs in-process with the base client, `IsCallerInRole` always returns `True`. The `IsSecurityEnabled` method determines whether security checking is enabled. This method returns `False` when running in-process. Always call `IsSecurityEnabled` before using `IsCallerInRole`.

MTS Explorer

The MTS Explorer is a graphical administrative tool for creating and deploying packages, managing security, and monitoring transaction execution. As a developer, however, you'll use the MTS Explorer frequently during development and unit testing. Each time an MTS component's interface changes during development, for example, the component has to be removed from any MTS packages and reinstalled.

 T I P Beginning with the 2 release of MTS, the MTS Explorer was implemented as a "snap-in" for the Microsoft Management Console (MMC).

▶ **See** Chapter 31, "Using Microsoft Transaction Server to Enable Distributed Applications," **p. 899**

Using Existing Components with MTS

A COM DLL that doesn't implement any specific MTS functions can still gain substantial benefits from running in the MTS environment:

- The capability to run as an in-process server, a local server, or a remote server
- Database connection pooling through the ODBC 3 resource dispenser
- Improved fault isolation for out-of-process servers
- Simplified deployment through the MTS Explorer

Installing an existing component to run under MTS is as easy as creating a new package and adding the component to that package. Set the `Transaction Support` property for the component to `Does Not Support Transactions`.

MTS support for legacy components can even be leveraged for non-ActiveX code. It's often quite simple to develop an ActiveX "wrapper" for a legacy application; that ActiveX component can then be added to MTS. The simple MTS programming requirements for transaction support make it possible to create a wrapper that supports transactions. For more information, see the section "Managing Transactions in MTS," earlier in this chapter.

Using MTS with I-net Applications

This discussion focuses on interactions between Microsoft Internet Explorer (IE) and Microsoft Internet Information Server (IIS). Although a wide variety of browsers and servers exist in the market today, the IE/IIS combination provides the richest interaction. However, many of these interactions are proprietary extensions to WWW standards. After you commit to features available only in IE or IIS, there may be some loss of functionality or substantial expense to move to a different platform.

An I-net application may use hypertext transfer protocol (HTTP) to invoke an MTS component in two ways:

- Call an Active Server Page (ASP), which calls the MTS component using DCOM
- Call the MTS component from ActiveX components executing in the Web browser using the Remote Data Service (RDS) (previously known as Advanced Data Connector, or ADC), which in turn uses HTTP

Either approach works well for a thin client. RDS version 1.5 adds updatability for a variety of databases, including SQL Server, Oracle and MS Access. RDS can update tables with at least one unique index, and can update complex result sets, provided the underlying tables have unique keys.

Figure 14.8 shows a typical ASP scenario.

CAUTION

Avoid opening updatable recordsets in RDS where the recordset may contain duplicate rows. An update to a duplicate row could result in data corruption.

N O T E   Microsoft VBScript embedded in a browser-side Web page can't, by itself, access MTS components.

FIGURE 14.8
An I-net application can
use MTS components
via Active Server Pages.

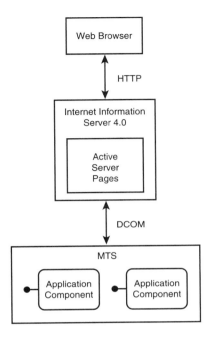

Using Active Server Pages

An Active Server Page can access MTS components via COM or DCOM. Although you can run
the MTS components as an in-process server, any internal error in the MTS component causes
MTS to terminate and may crash IIS. For reliability, it's better to run MTS components out-of-
process.

By default, IIS 3 doesn't allow out-of-process servers. To enable out-of-process components for
IIS, use the Registry Editor (REGEDT32). Go to the following Registry key and set the key
`AllowOutOfProcCmpnts` to 1:

`HKEY_LOCAL_MACHINE\SYSTEM\CurrentControlSet\Services\W3SVC\ASP\Parameters`

Part
II

Ch
14

A new feature added to IIS 4 does allow you to isolate a collection of Web pages as an application and to run them in a separate process. This is accomplished by placing the pages in a folder, defining a virtual directory to point to the folder, and selecting a check box on a property page for the virtual directory (see Figure 14.9).

FIGURE 14.9

This dialog allows you to isolate a Web application in a separate process for improved crash protection.

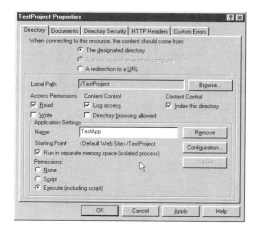

Using Browser-Side ActiveX Components

An ActiveX component executing inside a Web browser can call an MTS component, provided that the component is registered on the Web browser machine. Use the HTML <OBJECT> tag to invoke the MTS component.

N O T E The HTML script needs no special modifications to invoke an MTS component; the component just needs to be registered on the browser machine as an MTS component. Often, the same ActiveX component can be registered as a standalone (without MTS). In that case, the same script will invoke the standalone. ▨

You can also use the <OBJECT> tag to load an MTS component in-process with the browser client (requires MTS installed on the Web browser computer). Figure 14.10 shows an ActiveX component running in a Web browser and invoking a remote MTS component.

FIGURE 14.10
An ActiveX component running in a browser can invoke MTS components just like any other process.

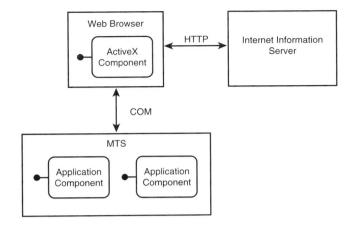

Using Remote Data Services

Microsoft Remote Data Services (RDS) allows an ActiveX component running in a Web browser to retrieve (read-only) data sets from a Microsoft Internet Information Server via ADO. RDS supports a number of protocols:

- HTTP
- HTTP over Secure Sockets Layer (HTTPS)
- DCOM
- In-process server

N O T E RDS was previously known as the Advanced Data Connector (ADC). Microsoft changed the name to Remote Data Services on bringing the technology into its Universal Data Access initiative. ▓

ON THE WEB

For the latest information about the Remote Data Services, visit Microsoft's site at http://www.microsoft.com/data/rds.

Unless your application uses the HTTPS protocol (Secure Sockets Layer), IIS password authorization settings must include Allow Anonymous for RDS to successfully retrieve data with HTTP protocol. Follow these steps to modify this IIS setting (requires stop and restart for the Web service):

1. Run Microsoft Internet Service Manager.

2. Expand the computer icon and right-click the Web site for which you want to change settings. Choose Properties from the pop-up menu.

3. Choose the Directory Security tab, and click the Edit button in the Anonymous Access and Authentication Control frame.

4. Check the Allow Anonymous Access option on the Authentication Methods dialog and click OK (see Figure 14.11). Click OK to close the Web Site Properties dialog box.

FIGURE 14.11
Use the Internet Service Manager to enable Anonymous Access.

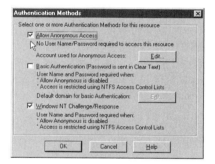

5. Stop the Web service (right-click the Web site and choose Stop from the pop-up menu), and then start the Web service (right-click the Web site and choose Start from the pop-up menu) so that the new settings take effect.

6. Close the Internet Service Manager.

Accessing MTS Components via DCOM and HTTP

Sometimes you may want to access the same MTS component on the same machine via DCOM (over a local area network) and via HTTP (remote Web users). Accessing the component via DCOM simply requires adding it to a package in MTS. To make the same MTS component accessible from IIS, follow these steps:

1. Use Transaction Server Explorer to view properties for the MTS component.

2. Choose the Activation tab.

3. Select In the Creator's Process… and click OK.

From Here...

This chapter gave you a developer's tour of Microsoft Transaction Server. After viewing the programming model for managing transactions, you looked at other services the system provides, including security, database connection pooling, the shared property manager, and just-in-time object activation. After seeing how I-net applications can interact with MTS, you reviewed some programming strategies and pitfalls.

- For a discussion of COM and DCOM, see Chapter 9, "Using Microsoft's Object Technologies."

- For details on using Visual Studio to build software components, see Chapter 27, "Creating COM Components for MTS with Visual Basic"; Chapter 29, "Creating COM Components for MTS with Visual C++"; and Chapter 28, "Creating COM Components for MTS with Visual J++."

- Chapter 31, "Using Microsoft Transaction Server to Enable Distributed Applications," looks at the graphical administrative tool included with MTS, reviewing component deployment, transaction resolution, and security issues.

Part

II

Ch

14

Developing Internet, Intranet, and Extranet Applications

Clients, Servers, and Components: Web-Based Applications

by Anthony J. Taylor

In this chapter

The I-net in the Computing World

The last two years have been an exciting time to be a software engineer. The Internet has had a profound effect on the computing world. Not only have we seen a shift in the way we perceive computers and how they affect our lives, but we also have witnessed a transformation in the way organizations view their core businesses and how computers and the Internet play a role in bringing them into the information age.

The Internet has brought a number of technologies, tools, and languages to the forefront of the computing world. For example, the TCP/IP protocol has become the de facto standard for networking across the globe. The Hypertext Transfer Protocol (HTTP) and Hypertext Markup Language (HTML) protocols have been widely accepted and embraced as the mechanisms for information dissemination across the World Wide Web. The SMTP protocol is fast becoming the standard for global communications through electronic mail. The list goes on and on.

The software development principle has not been insulated from the sweeping changes being experienced by the computing world. The World Wide Web has changed the way we design, build, deploy, and use applications. The Web has made it necessary for programmers to pay attention to the client browser and the Web server as important and necessary ingredients when developing future applications.

This chapter discusses the issues involved with client/server development in I-net environments and the evolution of application development from the mainframe-based monolithic applications, to the various flavors of client/server architectures, to the newly introduced I-net application development paradigm. This chapter explores the pieces that together provide a solution for building I-net applications and how each piece of the puzzle fits into the application development process.

Client or Server?

Deciding what software to put on the client system and what to put on the server is crucial for the success of an I-net project. Performance, security, and upgradeability are three of the key areas that affect software placement. Additionally, if you want to store user preferences, you need to decide where to put the functionality, on the client or the server.

Performance

The response time of the system to the user can be important in having effective software. Putting unnecessary elements on the server will slow the speed of the response by virtue of sending data through network traffic, waiting for the server to validate the data, and then sending a response. Validating data on the client system whenever possible can save much in the response time of the system. This doesn't mean validating passwords, but rather checking to make certain that all required data is present and maybe doing some simple computations. For example, if you are designing a system in which the user can purchase goods, perhaps you will have the client software compute the total and display it to the user without ever going to the server. The user can make an informed decision more quickly and the server doesn't have to continually receive data, do simple processing, and send the data back.

Keeping the database on the server side is a logical way and, most of the time, the only way to design a system. Sending the client a copy of the database would be time-consuming, and it would be difficult to keep the client copy of the database in sync with the server copy.

This scheme for preserving the performance of the system also helps to conserve server resources by reducing the server load. Additionally, it's important to curb the traffic over the network.

Security

By the same token, it's best for some processing to be done on the server. Anything requiring password validation should always be done on the server. Password validation on the client would be impractical and dangerous. The client machine would need access to viable passwords, and an unscrupulous user could gain unauthorized access to the server.

In addition, servers provide a physically secure location for storing sensitive user data and important files. It's much easier to isolate a server in a secure location than to do so for many client machines.

Upgradeability

One other area to consider when designing a system is the upgradeability of the system for the future. Putting certain components on the client machine can cause the need to upgrade every client machine when a software change needs to be made. For example, if you decide that every machine needs to have an ActiveX control to handle certain processing, the control needs to be downloaded or installed on every machine. Later, when you decide that the control is not meeting requirements and needs to be changed, the control again must be installed on every computer. If you had put the processing on the server, you would need to update the software in only one place.

The following are some guidelines summing up where the functionality should be placed, on the client or the server.

For the client:

- Validate user-entered data, such as making certain that required fields are not blank.
- Simple processing and display, such as computing the total cost that a customer has spent.

For the server:

- Access to the database, files, or libraries stored on the server
- Password validation
- Managing client sessions
- Processing of data where the algorithm is confidential

User Preferences

User preferences are settings that enable a Web page to be tailored to a specific desire. For example, if you are browsing a page displaying the current stock market prices, perhaps only the stocks that you are interested in are displayed.

Where to store the information concerning user preferences can be an important and difficult decision. There are two main choices to make; either the user has to log in, or the data has to be kept on the client computer.

ON THE WEB

The Yahoo! Finance Web site (`http://quote.yahoo.com/`) uses a server-side database to store user preferences and portfolio information. It requires users to set up a login ID and password to access the user-preference information.

If the user is required to log in to the system, user preferences can be stored in a server-side database. This is particularly crucial if the information should be restricted to only particular users. For example, in a corporate intranet, the president of the company can have a page tailored to show confidential information, whereas another employee won't have access to the same information.

You can set up client-side preferences in two ways: You can write a client-side component, or, more commonly, you can use magic cookies.

If the security of the data is not an issue, magic cookies can be a solution to custom-tailoring Web pages. The type of user preferences considered here are the layout of the Web page and what nonconfidential data should be displayed. Magic cookies or cookies are information that can be stored on the client machine. The following are some problems with cookies that developers should be aware of:

N O T E Cookie files typically reside on the user's system in the directory
c:\<*Systemroot*>\Cookies: for example, c:\winnt\cookies. A cookie file is a data file, usually with the .dat extension, that stores information in a binary format. ■

- Each browser on a computer has its own cookie file. This means that a user won't get consistent information accessing the same site from the same computer using different browsers.

- Different users on the same machine will get the same information if using the same browser.

- The same user on a different computer won't get the same information.

- A cookie file can hold at maximum 300 cookie entries with arbitrary deletion, which means that entries can be deleted and added without any kind of restrictions once the 300-entry maximum is reached.

- A cookie file can hold at maximum 20 cookie entries for a particular IP address.

■ A user is free to delete or modify cookie files.

■ A user can prevent a cookie from being set or sent.

With all these problems with cookies, why should you use them? The typical user uses a single browser on a single computer and won't edit cookie files. Cookies are extremely useful in maintaining state.

Cookies can be comfortably used to maintain information about where the user has accessed information. For example, when a user accesses `http://www.cookiecentral.com/cookie`, a survey is often displayed. When the user fills out the page, a cookie is set, and then the page is reloaded. Instead of displaying the survey, the new page displays the results. If you had blocked the cookie from being set, the original page would be displayed. No severe damage occurs to the user or the Web site. Similar results occur if the user deleted, modified, or otherwise interfered with the cookie file. Clearly no confidential information should be stored with cookies.

The Evolution of Application Development Processes

Client/server computing has long been viewed as a plausible solution for building line-of-business applications. The main benefits of client/server computing were its distributed nature, its practical use of system resources, and its cheaper deployment cost compared to the older mainframe environments.

A single mainframe machine meant a single point of failure and inefficient use of system resources. Users performing unrelated tasks were forced to share the same system resources. Scalability was an issue because reaching the limits of the mainframe processing power resulted in upgrades to a costlier and bigger machine. Figure 15.1 shows the typical architecture of a mainframe environment.

FIGURE 15.1
The mainframes handled all processing chores, and the clients used terminals to access online resources.

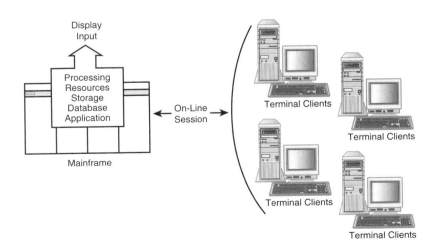

In contrast, client/server computing provides a flexible architecture for building a corporate infrastructure. By breaking up the processing chores between several smaller server machines, it's possible to better use the resources and processing power of the system as a whole. In addition, the clients are more than just dumb terminals; they are capable of handling many processing and user needs, such as running word processing software, without needing the server to accomplish their tasks. Figure 15.2 shows a typical client/server environment model.

FIGURE 15.2

Client/server computing places a larger burden on the user to determine where a particular resource is located.

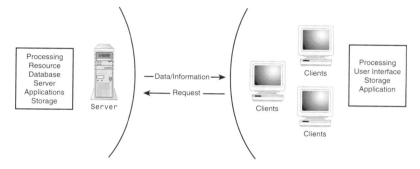

However, client/server computing has its own pitfalls. In many cases, the deployment of multiple-server machines within the enterprise resulted in a management nightmare. Rather than deploying and viewing the servers as a single logical unit, they were deployed and used as single, standalone machines, each working individually. Also, client/server environments demanded more sophistication on the part of the users. Users looking for a particular resource not only had to know where the resource was located but also had to know how to connect to it and use it. The client/server environment, for all its flexibility and power, was also a more difficult environment to learn and use.

For software developers, the jump from mainframes to client/server software development was just as difficult. In the mainframe world, applications were developed, compiled, and executed on the mainframe. The client's purpose was to provide a session into the mainframe system that could be used to execute applications. Figure 15.3 shows the software development life cycle as it exists in the mainframe world.

With the popularity of the client/server environment, software development became more complex and difficult. Processing was now divided between client machines and server machines. Software developers must decide where to put the functionality. Application development has become more than just writing code. Developers have to understand the concepts of application partitioning, user interface design, and networking protocols. Deciding where to put the functionality has become just as important as writing the code to implement it. Decisions must be made to best use the processing power of the clients and the servers.

FIGURE 15.3

The mainframe provides the development and the execution environment for applications accessed through the client.

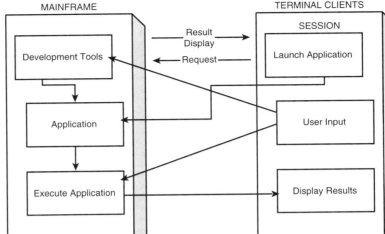

N O T E   For example, an important decision that a developer faces in client/server environments is where to put the database query logic. Should it be implemented using stored procedures or should it be implemented using client-side SQL queries? The correct decision is usually based on the needs and design requirements of the application.

The complexity and difficulty of building client/server applications is offset by the awesome flexibility and power afforded by such an environment. Figure 15.4 illustrates the development life cycle for client/server environments.

Typical client/server development projects include development efforts for building a client user interface and business logic and building and programming a database server. The common term for building database-enabled applications in such a setup is *two-tier client/server*. Figure 15.5 illustrates the two-tier client/server architecture.

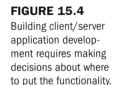

FIGURE 15.4

Building client/server application development requires making decisions about where to put the functionality.

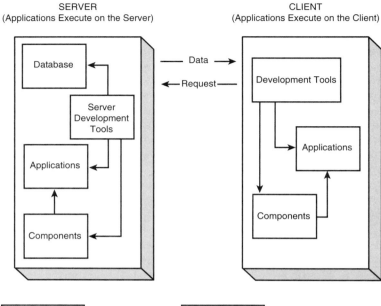

FIGURE 15.5

Two-tier client/server architecture draws the line between the database server and the client component.

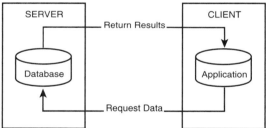

Recent advancement in client/server computing has separated the business logic from the user interface. This is referred to as *three-tier client/server architecture*. The business logic units are modules that are independent of the client and the server and run on their own, providing a communication mechanism between the database and the client. This separates the client from having to handle logic processing and also insulates the client-side developers from having to program database specific logic into their programs. Figure 15.6 illustrates the concept of three-tier client/server computing.

FIGURE 15.6

The business logic unit takes care of connecting to the database server and obtaining data that can then be passed to the client machine for presentation to the user.

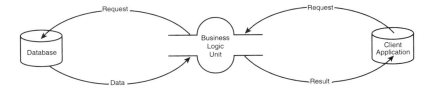

Three-tier client/server architectures afford developers more flexibility in building applications. Client-side developers only need to worry about interfacing with the business logic unit and need not worry about the functionality of the database back end and how to query the database. They are assured of getting the pertinent data in a format they can handle.

The business logic unit handles formulating the appropriate database queries in response to client requests and talking to the database. Modifications can easily be made to each individual part of the system without having to change any of the other pieces in the system. The main benefit of business logic units is their capability to be developed and deployed once and then accessed multiple times from throughout an enterprise using client machines. The OLE Automation mechanism within the Windows operating system environment provides a mechanism for deployment of business logic units.

The logical extension of three-tier architectures is to develop applications that span multiple tiers. The most common example is the use of component-based software development mechanisms to break down an application's business logic units into multiple pieces that can be distributed throughout an enterprise and provide very specific functionality. Figure 15.7 illustrates the concept of distributed, multitier client/server environments.

FIGURE 15.7

Distributed client/ server environments place processing needs where they can best use the available processing power.

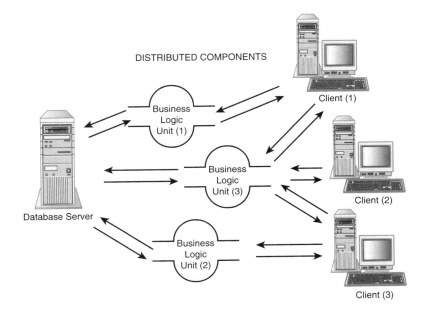

By distributing components throughout machines in an enterprise, multitier architectures better use the processing power available. In addition, upgrades and enhancements to a particular component within an application can be carried out without having to reinstall the whole application on every client machine. Developers can replace the one instance of the component wherever it resides on the network, and all client machines using the component will instantly receive the upgraded functionality.

▷ **See** Chapter 25, "Clients, Servers, and Components: Design Strategies for Distributed Applications," **p. 727**

The I-net architecture model takes the client/server concept to the next level. I-net is just another form of client/server computing that uses the Web browser as the client and a Web server as the back end in its most basic form. However, the I-net architecture provides significant benefits over client/server computing in terms of application development, deployment, and ease of use. The following section discusses the I-net architecture in more detail.

The I-net Architecture

As the world races to connect to the Internet, an unexpected phenomenon is taking place. Corporations trying to determine profitable and beneficial uses for this emerging global network have found a way to enhance the power and usefulness of their own internal networks as well. The intranet, a younger and more contained sibling of the Internet, has emerged. The intranet is a scaled-down version of the Internet, not in functionality or features, but in size and scope. Figure 15.8 presents a sample intranet architecture.

FIGURE 15.8

An intranet can use existing resources within an enterprise to provide an I-net based client/ server environment.

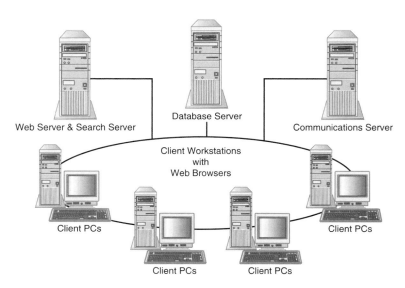

Web Server & Search Server

Database Server

Communications Server

Client Workstations
with
Web Browsers

Client PCs

Client PCs

Client PCs

Client PCs

Intranets are internal, corporatewide networks based on technology used for the Internet. Whereas the Internet provides corporate networks with connectivity to the global network of networks, intranets enable corporations to build internal, self-contained networks that have important advantages over existing network technologies.

> **N O T E** I-net is a collective term that refers to the Internet, intranets, and extranets. *Extranets* are a collection of interconnected intranets.

The I-net process model, and its network connectivity architecture, holds several major advantages over traditional networking architectures. First and foremost, companies are realizing the cost-effectiveness of the I-net architecture. It's relatively inexpensive to set up an internal I-net environment. The technologies at the core of an internal I-net setup are open, standards-based, and widely implemented. The server software for setting up a World Wide Web (WWW) server, often referred to as a *Web server*, is available from a multitude of vendors such as Microsoft and Netscape. The client workstations use inexpensive and easy-to-use Web browser software for connecting to the Web server. The networking infrastructure needed for setting up a basic I-net is already in place in most corporations. In addition, with the integrated Internet Explorer browser in Windows 98, the familiarity and intuitiveness of this model will increase on the user side, as well.

> **N O T E** A rapidly growing intranet might eventually place extensive demands on an existing infrastructure in terms of hardware and networking resources and might necessitate upgrades.

Second, I-nets implement a hybrid architecture that brings together the best features of the client/server process model with those of the host-based process model. The I-net architecture is geared towards ease of deployment, centralized control of information, and simple administration of resources. In the I-net process model, the server is responsible for providing information and requested data to the intended users. In addition, the server holds the key to the graphical user interface presented to the user through the client browser software. Client workstations (typically desktop PCs) use Web browser software to display information sent by the server. The server controls the layout and content of the information. This makes management and administration of information very reliable because it's centralized.

However, the client is not just a dumb terminal. It does perform operations such as information caching and local storage of information downloaded by the user. In other words, the I-net architecture is a process model that takes the best from the client/server world and combines it with the best attributes of the traditional host-based architecture employed by mainframes and minicomputers.

Finally, an important advantage of I-nets is their capability to bring together heterogeneous systems into a common interoperable network. The corporate world has spent millions of dollars and many years trying to connect disparate and incompatible systems into a seamless network. The results haven't been completely satisfactory. Because the I-net architecture was developed from the ground up to connect disparate systems, it lends itself well to the corporate culture in most organizations where different systems such as PCs, Macs, and UNIX-based workstations must coexist.

In terms of software development, the most important and significant benefit of using an I-net environment for building and deploying applications is its capability to create cross-platform applications without the cost of creating and distributing multiple versions of the application. Applications that use the Web browser on the client and use the Web server as an interface between the browser and the application server, or database server, on the back end generate HTML output that can be viewed by users on any platform that supports a Web browser. Figure 15.9 illustrates the concept.

FIGURE 15.9

The Web server provides a single point of entry for all access to back-end application and database servers.

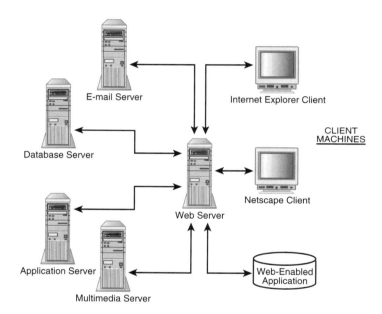

The centralized maintenance and administration of I-net–based applications is another important benefit. The cost of maintenance and enhancements to distributed client/server applications is much greater than the cost of maintenance of I-net applications. Changes made to Web-based applications on the server take effect immediately for all users, eliminating the need for individual changes to each and every client machine. I-net applications that take advantage of client-side components such as Java applets or ActiveX controls can use the automatic download capabilities of the browser to get a newer version of the component when it becomes available.

N O T E   Microsoft Internet Explorer 3 and higher provide an example of a Web browser that automatically checks to see whether a newer version of a client-side component is available for download and upgrades the component on the client machine. The browser does give the user a chance to either accept or reject the upgrade. ▪

The following sections discuss the various components that come together to provide the functionality for building applications in an I-net environment.

The Web Browser as a Client Framework

The use of Web browsers has evolved dramatically in the Web-based environment. Now Web browsers are used not only to access the static data housed on a Web server, but also to change Web content interactively. Before the development of recent technologies, the flow of data was from the server to the client only. Now, however, the application client and application server have a bidirectional flow of control (see Figure 15.10).

FIGURE 15.10
The bidirectional flow of control in the Web-based environment is possible because an operation is defined in a library class but implemented in a subclass in the application.

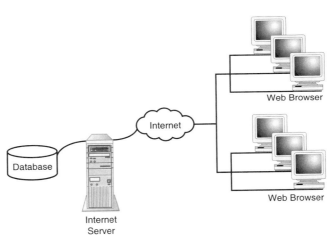

There are many benefits now that the Web browser can be used as a client framework, including

- Reuse of design, saving time and effort
- More functionality because of the bidirectional flow of control
- Less code needed, making updating easier

Many companies have eagerly modified their existing applications to achieve these benefits. Web users no longer are disappointed to find stale information; they can view custom Web content that responds interactively to their responses, whether they click the mouse or press a key.

As Web browsers have evolved for usability as a client framework, other progressions have also occurred. The following sections briefly discuss the changes pertaining to application architecture and the transitions Web developers must make.

The Evolving Application Architecture

As the application development environment evolves, the architecture needed for the new development arena has also progressed.

Web files can not only communicate on a local network, but also can be transferred via a global network to a Web browser, making management of server-side scripts and component files more difficult. Although browser-based applications appear to be the solution to client-centric information, this new environment has its pros and cons, especially with the standards wars taking place.

Of the many proprietary Web browsers, Microsoft's Internet Explorer and Netscape's Navigator are the current leaders. Many Application Programming Interfaces (APIs) also are on the market today—Microsoft Internet Server Application Programming Interface (ISAPI), Netscape NSAPI, WebSite WSAPI, and WebSTAR W*API, just to name a few. With so many vendor products in the marketplace, delivering universally readable HTML pages with features becomes difficult.

N O T E   Despite the push for the convergence of Web-based technology standards, we're beginning
to see exactly the opposite. For example, Dynamic HTML standards have diverged between
Microsoft and Netscape.

How can you resolve the problem, for example, of having a video file on an HTML page with full-motion features many browsers can't view? Do you force one browser to be the standard by which every component is compatible, or do you create alternative images and file types for every Web browser ever used to view a Web page?

Some organizations maintain multiple browsers as the corporate standard. In these cases, often Web pages are created with a descriptive "best viewed with" recommendation for users, indicating the browser type that provides the most functionality with the Web content. Other times, Web applications are created with multiple versions for each browser type that accesses the site. There are occasions when Web developers must create Web pages for text-only browsers, or create content with the least-functional browser in mind for the user community accessing the Web site.

These and other issues must be addressed when determining global standards for HTML, Java, cascading style sheets (features and options to specify style, color, and font for HTML development), and other Web-based technologies.

New Challenges for Developers

As a Web-based application programmer, you face many issues. This paradigm is different. The new browser-based environment uses the connectionless HTTP, which makes maintaining state a challenge.

State is the capability to retain information. To assist with state, cookies offer some help but aren't the end-all solution. A *cookie* is a token file sent to a client browser but not stored on the client computer's hard disk; instead, it resides on the server. Some browsers don't support cookies, so objects that use cookie files must be supported for the browser as well.

Control logic might begin to make sense to you, but you should approach known event-driven functions differently than you do in the traditional client/server development arena. You also use different tools, which are sometimes more primitive in the Web environment than in traditional programming environments.

Controls might be needed to perform services for Web users. When developing Web-based applications, you must answer these questions before using controls within your applications:

- Which control should you use?
- Are custom controls needed? If so, should you purchase or create them?
- Which Web-development technologies are best for the application at hand?
- How do the developed applications use existing technologies?

Suppose that you want to test a Web page before deployment. How will you ensure quality when the audience (possibly the global marketplace) can be using any of a variety of technology architectures? It's impossible to benchmark applications with an almost infinite amount of connectivity combinations possible.

It's clearly evident that today you must stay abreast of the Web-based application environment and the technologies used. Change occurs continually, and smart programmers will be those who maintain a current knowledge of the skills necessary for Web-based application development.

ON THE WEB

For more information on Web site checkers, visit `http://www.websitegarage.com/`. This site has a browser compatibility checker, a load-time check, and a few additional Web checks that might be helpful when developing Web sites and can be downloaded for free.

Static Versus Dynamic HTML: The Old Way Versus the New Way

Hypertext Markup Language is the method used to mark up or tag a document so that it can be distributed on the Web. HTML not modified based on user input is referred to as *static HTML*.

Static HTML files that reside on the Web are only as new as when the files were published. This method is fine for files that seldom change, such as annual tax statements or monthly sales reports; however, when new data is needed, the HTML files need to be published again so that Web users can view the updated material. Listing 15.1 is an example of a simple HTML document.

N O T E To create a simple HTML document, you can use your choice of various text editors. For Listing 15.1, Microsoft Notepad was used. The resulting HTML document will look like Figure 15.11.

Listing 15.1   A Simple HTML Document

```
<HTML>
<HEAD>
<TITLE>Accounting Software Support</TITLE>
</HEAD>
<BODY>
<CENTER>
<H1>Software Support Services</H1>
<HR><H3>At Jones & Jones CPA, we provide quality installation, training,
and customized reporting for the following accounting software packages:</H3>
<BR><TABLE ALIGN=CENTER BORDER=0 WIDTH=70%><TR><TD>
<A HREF="http://www.jones.com/default.htm"><IMG SRC="icon1.gif"
ALT="Jones CPA Software" ALIGN="CENTER" HEIGHT=100 WIDTH=125 HSPACE=20
➡BORDER=0>
<A HREF="http://www.cpasoft.com/index.html"><IMG SRC="icon2.gif"
ALT="CPASoft Solutions" ALIGN="CENTER" HEIGHT=100 WIDTH=125 HSPACE=20
BORDER=0></TD></TR></TABLE>
</CENTER>
</BODY>
</HTML>
```

FIGURE 15.11

The HTML page created from Listing 15.1, viewed in Explorer.

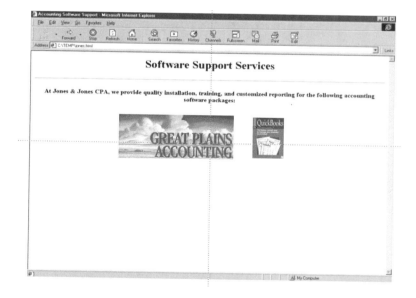

ON THE WEB

For a listing of the available HTML tags, visit the World Wide Web Consortium site at http://www.w3.org/markup/. The Microsoft Site Builder Workshop at http://www.microsoft.com/workshop/c-frame.htm#/workshop/author/ might also be helpful.

As the demand for delivery of dynamic information on the Web has increased, so has the technology used in Web-based application development. Many Web site developers are being approached to publish content on the Web that can be created on demand to meet Web users' expectations. Web users want content fresh, exciting, up-to-date, and tailored to their personal information needs. This new expectation requires a new Web-development method—Dynamic HTML.

Microsoft Dynamic HTML is a feature of Internet Explorer 4 and was developed in collaboration with the World Wide Web Consortium (W3C). Figure 15.12 shows the anatomy of a Web application with Dynamic HTML.

FIGURE 15.12

Dynamic HTML gives users customized views of data from the database.

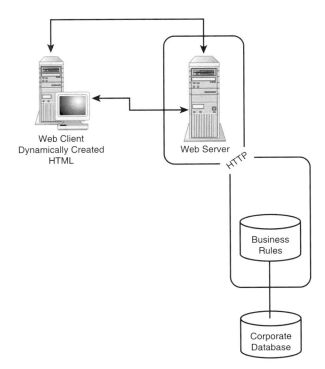

Web Client
Dynamically Created
HTML

Web Server

HTTP

Business
Rules

Corporate
Database

The old way—static HTML—is fine for data that changes as part of a regular business cycle, but today's Web is extremely interactive and changes continually. To update Web content as the data changes, you must use the new way—Dynamic HTML.

You can author truly dynamic Web applications by using Dynamic HTML. You can change any text or graphic element on a Web page without a return trip to the server by using Dynamic HTML—even if the Web page has already been loaded. Web sites will be more inviting because of this flexibility.

Document Object Model (DOM) is the object model provided for HTML by Dynamic HTML. All elements in a Web page are exposed as objects. You can change the look and feel of these objects at any time by modifying their attributes or applying methods. You can also state specifically how you want the positioning and style of page elements by using cascading style sheets (CSS). You can use each x- and y-coordinate and z-order to position each element precisely.

> **CAUTION**
>
> If Dynamic HTML isn't used for a substantial change to Web content, extremely slow performance occurs when an additional round trip to the server is made to display the new text.

Download times with Dynamic HTML are actually shorter than with static HTML. You can even avoid trips to the server by using Dynamic HTML's data-binding feature. Dynamic HTML also gives you more efficiency with the use of animation and graphics. You can decide the allocation for bandwidth consumption between fetches, the consumption of bandwidth packaging, and the elements of design to optimize the users' experiences.

▶ **See** Chapter 21, "Dynamic HTML," to learn more about Dynamic HTML, **p. 601**

The Server: Server-Based Functionality

Although the client has garnered the lion's share of attention in the development community because of its emphasis on the Web browser, the Java language, and the support for applets and controls, the most critical component of any I-net infrastructure is the server hardware platform and operating system. The selection criteria for server platforms include the following:

- High performance
- Scalability (the capability to expand as needs change)
- Powerful operating system administration and management tools
- High throughput hardware systems for both networking and storage media
- Strong security features

Because of the graphical nature of information being handled by I-net–based networks, performance capabilities of the server hardware are an important consideration. In particular, the hard disk subsystem and the network interface must provide good throughput and reliable operation.

The server platform houses a variety of software components to provide various services to I-net users. Some of the major server components of an I-net architecture are

- The World Wide Web server
- The database server
- The communication server

- The search server
- The multimedia services server
- The proxy server

The following sections describe these server components in more detail. Each of these services can be installed on a single machine or can be spread across multiple machines for better performance and manageability.

The World Wide Web Server

The basic software component that brings together the power of I-nets is the Web server software. Web server software gives client machines access to information by facilitating information publishing, application execution, and data retrieval.

Most Web server software packages such as Microsoft's Internet Information Server (IIS), various Netscape server products, and O'Reilly's WebSite provide a comprehensive set of setup, management, and administration facilities. In many cases, a basic and functional Web server can be installed, set up, and made operational within an hour. In addition, all server packages include sophisticated system administration utilities such as the Server Manager utility included with the Microsoft Internet Information Server.

Until recently, most Web servers stored static information for access by clients. With the introduction of technologies such as Java applets, ActiveX controls, and database access tools, Web servers have become more than just repositories for publishing static information. Web servers now provide such powerful capabilities as user authentication, connectivity to database servers, dynamic Web page creation based on user actions, database query resolution, and data encryption. This list is not exhaustive, but is intended to provide an indication of the advances that have been made in the last year or so with the capabilities of Web server software.

Microsoft's IIS deserves special mention because of its integration with the Windows NT Server operating system, and with the security subsystem in particular. Because of this tight integration, IIS offers the following capabilities:

- IIS can use the built-in Windows NT Server security model for user authentication and password validation.
- Authenticating users against the Windows NT domain user account database can control user access to the I-net.
- File and directory access from an intranet can be controlled by setting permissions for user groups through the usual Windows NT permissions mechanisms.
- Traffic analysis and performance monitoring can be performed using the Windows NT Performance Monitor utility.
- Logging can be performed using the Windows NT Event Log.

▶ **See** Chapter 6, "An Inside Look at Active Server Pages and the Internet Information Server," **p. 137**

The Database Server

The database server is a recent addition to the I-net phenomenon. Most Web implementations were using flat files or proprietary systems for storing data and information. However, because most organizations already have large databases installed and operational, it was an obvious choice to use the database as a repository for information being published on the Web.

In addition, corporations provide users access to corporate data through applications written to access the databases. If most data resides in existing relational database systems, and an organization wants to replace its proprietary applications with I-net–based applications, mechanisms are needed to facilitate the flow of information to and from the database servers and the Web server.

Extensions to standards such as open database connectivity (ODBC) and the introduction of standards such as ISAPI have made it possible for Web servers to connect to database servers and access corporate data. The connectivity between Web servers and database servers provides a means for making corporate data available to users. The traditional client/server database applications are being replaced by Web-based database applications. In the years to come, database servers will become an integral part of the I-net infrastructure as more and more database-enabled applications are implemented for use on the I-net platform.

Microsoft provides support for building database-enabled applications using a product such as Microsoft Access or Microsoft SQL Server. Access is a workgroup database designed for small and medium-sized applications with a few megabytes of data at most and a small user base. SQL Server is designed to be the database for the enterprise that can handle large volumes of data and a large number of users. Typical SQL Server database sizes range from a few hundred megabytes to a terabyte with hundreds or thousands of users.

N O T E Visual Studio includes a Developer's Edition of SQL Server 6.5 for use as part of database-enabled development efforts. This edition is only restricted in the number of client connections it supports from the full retail version.

The Communication Server

Communication servers facilitate information exchange between users. They provide functionality for

- Electronic mail (email)—A messaging system for exchanging information between users
- Bulletin boards—A sticky notes system for disseminating information to a group of users
- Discussion groups—A forum for exchanging ideas and engaging in discussions on various topics
- Chat rooms—A place where users can interactively "talk" to each other
- Remote access—Enables users remote connection to the I-net through dial-up networking

Communications servers work in conjunction with Web servers to provide a seamless means for users to interact with the I-net and with each other. Communications servers also provide secure connectivity through email gateways to the outside world. Users can send and receive email messages to people all around the world using their Web browser or other email software packages.

Microsoft Exchange Server is the centerpiece of the communication server strategy Microsoft is pursuing. It's a full-blown workgroup, collaboration, email, and discussion group system that scales very well to large amounts of data and user bases.

The Search Server

Search servers, also called *search engines*, implement powerful search and indexing mechanisms to provide users with a means for finding information. Over time, an I-net site can become a large and complex collection of published information, structured data, and applications. A well-developed I-net site must enable users to do searches on the information in the system based on their own criteria. Most available search servers enable users to search the system using multiple criteria and to define the scope of their search.

Search servers accomplish their task by cataloging and indexing the information being published on the Web site. As new information is added to the Web site, a search engine updates its indices to reflect these changes.

The most critical aspect of search mechanisms is the capability to provide search results in a fast, efficient, and error-free manner. Speed becomes an important issue as the size of a Web site grows. A well-designed search engine can handle large, complex searches and enhance the usefulness of the information.

> **N O T E** Search servers are different from search engines such as Yahoo! and Lycos, which provide a searching mechanism for the entire Internet. Search servers are specifically used to catalog a particular Web site. For example, the search button on the Microsoft Web site uses a search server for user queries.

ON THE WEB

If you'd like to know more about the major search engines, information on specialty search services, or trivia and interesting facts related to major search engines, see `http://searchenginewatch.com/`.

For more information about the Microsoft Search Server, refer to the Microsoft Web site at `http://search.microsoft.com/`.

The Multimedia Services Server

Multimedia servers provide support for high-speed streaming media such as video and audio. Multimedia servers use high-speed links to provide corporate customers access to live or prerecorded multimedia content.

One of the most compelling applications for multimedia servers is to provide support for live audio and video communications. Users can interact with each other through sight and sound rather than using text-based messages.

Another application for multimedia servers is to make it possible for corporations to allow users access to computer-based training classes using audiovisual mechanisms. Users can access video catalogs of seminars and training classes and view them using their browser software or other multimedia clients.

Microsoft NetShow provides support for enabling multimedia capabilities as part of your Web site. Microsoft NetShow enables you to develop and present multimedia presentations and live video feeds as part of your Web site. The NetShow client is needed to view content developed and broadcast with the NetShow Theater Server.

ON THE WEB

For more information about Microsoft NetShow Theater Server, consult `http://www.microsoft.com/theater/`.

To learn about Windows NT Server NetShow Services, visit `http://www.microsoft.com/NTServer/basics/netshowservices/` on the Web.

To compare the two, consult `http://www.microsoft.com/Theater/nsvsnst.htm`.

Proxy Server

Proxy servers enable clients connecting to a corporate network to access the global Internet. Proxy servers provide a high-performance, secure, and reliable means for users to gain access to the Internet from within the corporate intranet.

Proxy servers also control access to Web servers and other I-net resources. They support mechanisms for providing access to the WWW, FTP, Telnet, and other common Internet protocols. In addition, proxy servers also restrict access to an intranet from the Internet world. In effect, a proxy server is a security tool that polices the bidirectional flow of information between I-net networks.

Microsoft Proxy Server provides support for adding firewall and content-caching abilities as part of a Web connection. If you are setting up an Internet connection, the Microsoft Proxy Server provides a secure and cost-effective solution for establishing a secure presence on the Internet.

ON THE WEB

For more information on the Microsoft Proxy Server, visit `http://www.microsoft.com/proxy/` on the Web.

Components of a Dynamic Web-Based Application

Components, or objects, have altered the method of software development and use of systems forever. A business problem can be solved now by reusable software components. Any object can be modified without altering the other objects contained in a framework, or the interaction between them. Initial programming efforts remain intact and can be reused repeatedly in various ways.

Web components vary in their ease of use and application. Each has specific attributes for a particular function, and it's important to match the correct technology with the task needed.

It's not enough to have components themselves. They must exist in a distributed, open environment that permits their execution in a plug-and-play fashion, and one that truly enables the reality of dynamic re-engineering.

Companies are migrating to a component-based environment—not just for the sake of using new technology, but because they see component use and reuse as a solution to their critical business problems. Components are suited for the distributed systems environment because both the data and business logic are housed within objects, enabling them to be located anywhere within a distributed network.

When you're creating interactive Web-based applications, many components are available to assist you. The following sections describe several of the available technologies.

ActiveX

ActiveX is a group of technologies provided by Microsoft that enables you to create active content for the World Wide Web. ActiveX makes interactive Web creation faster and easier. Using ActiveX technology makes the Internet more productive and useful.

ActiveX is a product of the Microsoft object linking and embedding (OLE) technology. Some might wonder whether ActiveX is a new name for OLE because they're both based on the Component Object Model (COM). Although they appear similar, they provide different services to Web developers.

OLE refers only to the technology that enables users to build multiple documents through object linking and embedding. OLE is optimized for desktop application integration and end-user usability, whereas ActiveX is optimized for size and speed to enable controls to respond interactively to events by being embedded in Web-based architecture. All ActiveX and OLE technologies are built on the COM-provided foundation.

▶ **See** Chapter 9, "Using Microsoft's Object Technologies," for more information on ActiveX technologies and COM, **p. 217**

COM is the method that enables two separate software application components to access each other's services. With COM, a software application component applies its functionality as one or more COM objects. Each COM object supports one to many interfaces, which in turn might support one to many methods.

The elements of ActiveX include client and server technologies:

- ActiveX controls—The objects in Web-based applications that make a Web site come alive with user-controllable functions. ActiveX controls are limited only by your imagination. Literally thousands of ActiveX controls are available for functions. ActiveX controls are plug-and-play components that you can use in any application, similar to those included in Internet Explorer 4 (see Table 15.1).

- ActiveX scripting—Enables control from the browser or server of ActiveX controls and Java applets as they function in the integrated environment. VBScript and JScript are two scripting languages discussed later in this chapter. ActiveX scripting enables the creation of standard language runtimes by enabling a host to compile scripts, acquire and call entry points, and maintain the available namespace for you.

- ActiveX document support—Enables Web users to view non-HTML documents (such as Word, Excel, and PowerPoint files) through a Web browser.

- Java Virtual Machine—Enables the integration and execution of Java applets with ActiveX controls by any ActiveX-supported Web browser.

- ActiveX server framework—Provides several Web server-based services, including database access, security, and others.

Table 15.1   ActiveX Controls Used in Internet Explorer

Control	Description
Animated Button	Uses the Microsoft Windows animation common control to display various frame sequences of an AVI, depending on the button state.
Chart	Enables drawing of various chart types with different styles.
Gradient	Shades the area with a range of colors, displaying a transition from one specified color to another.
Label	Displays given text at any specified angle. It can also render the text along user-defined curves.
Marquee	Scrolls, slides, or bounces uniform resource locators (URLs) within a user-defined window.
Menu	Displays a menu button or a pull-down menu. This control acts like a tri-state button when no menu items are specified, or displays a pull-down menu when one or more menu items are specified. It can also display a pop-up menu if the Pop-up method is used.
Pop-up Menu	Displays a pop-up menu whenever the Pop-up method is called, and fires a click event when a menu item is selected.

Control	Description
Pop-up Window	Displays specified HTML documents in a pop-up window. You can use this control to provide ToolTips or previews of links.
Preloader	Downloads the specified URL and puts it in the cache. The control is invisible at runtime and starts downloading when enabled.
Stock Ticker	Continuously displays changing data. The control downloads the URL specified at regular intervals and displays that data. The data can be in text or XRT format.
Timer	Invokes an event periodically. It's invisible at runtime.
View Tracker	Generates `OnShow` and `OnHide` events whenever the control falls within or out of the viewable area.

ON THE WEB

For information about additional ActiveX controls, visit `http://www.microsoft.com/activex/` on the Web.

Java Applets

Microsoft Internet Explorer 3 and higher supports Java applets. Of the many variations of the Integrated Development Environment (IDE) tools for Java development, Visual Studio's Visual J++, Sun Microsystems' Java JDK, and Inprise's JBuilder are a few of the development environments available on the Web.

ON THE WEB

For more information on the Java development environments mentioned in this chapter, see these Web sites:

- Inprise JBuilder: `http://www.inprise.com/jbuilder/`
- Microsoft Visual J++: `http://msdn.microsoft.com/visualJ/`
- Sun's Java JDK: `http://java.sun.com/products/jdk/1.1/index.html`

A platform-specific program called a virtual machine executes an applet. The Microsoft Virtual Machine—available on 32-bit Windows, Macintosh, and Windows 3.1—has been highly acclaimed by the media and developers as the safest, fastest, most functional, and most reliable pure Java on the market.

Java also works with ActiveX, which opens up a vast number of combinations between the two technologies. By extending Java with ActiveX, you can create reusable components. Also thanks to ActiveX technology, you can enhance Java applets with multimedia effects, highly tune performance, and use a wide variety of objects, including ActiveX controls, ActiveX documents, and ActiveX scripting. You can use these applets as building blocks for Web applications.

Java is an object-oriented language that you can integrate with the existing client/server infra-structure. Java is similar to the C++ programming language, except that it doesn't have point-ers, contains a different method for garbage collection, and is extremely strict regarding its object orientation. Sun Microsystems developed Java to be independent of the platform being used.

When using Java Class Libraries, you can create specific use-class libraries or purchase com-mercially developed class libraries.

To call a Java applet, you use a simple HTML tag:

```
<APPLET CODE="Name.Class"
 HEIGHT=500 WIDTH=500>
</APPLET>
```

 TIP Java applets from earlier alpha versions might not execute on newer Java-supporting Web browsers. Check the HTML source code to determine whether the applet will execute. The older Java versions used the <APP> tag; newer versions use the <APPLET> tag.

VBScript

Visual Basic Scripting Edition (VBScript) is a fast, small, lightweight interpreted language used in Web browsers and applications designed to work with ActiveX controls and other embedded objects in HTML documents. Although it's a direct subset of Microsoft Visual Basic, VBScript doesn't include the capability of directly accessing or performing file input/output with the underlying operating system.

N O T E   Now, only Microsoft Internet Explorer 3 and greater fully support VBScript. ▪

ActiveX objects are crucial to productive VBScript coding. When VBScript authors use these controls, Web applications provide a quality appearance to Web users.

VBScript authors can dynamically manage the outcome of an ActiveX control placed directly on the Web page. Code that responds to animate object events can now be created with VBScript.

VBScript procedures are coded either between the <HEAD> and </HEAD> tags or between the <BODY> and </BODY> tags. The code must always be wrapped in <SCRIPT> and </SCRIPT> tags. To ensure that the browser correctly executes the code as VBScript and not another language, make sure that the LANGUAGE indicator is set to equal either VBScript or VBS.

The use of VBScript within an HTML document file is given in the following example, with the actual VBScript code in boldface:

```
<HTML>
<HEAD>
<TITLE></TITLE>
<SCRIPT LANGUAGE = "VBScript">
```

```
<!--
' VBScript code is inserted here
msgbox ("Hello World!")-->
</SCRIPT>
</HEAD>
<BODY>
<SCRIPT LANGUAGE = "VBS">
<!--
' VBScript code can also be inserted here.
msgbox ("Goodbye Cruel World!")

-->
</SCRIPT>
</BODY>
</HTML>
```

 T I P When including your VBScript code within the <BODY> section, always embed the source with HTML comment tags (<!-- and -->) to ensure that the code is hidden from browsers that aren't compatible with VBScript.

ON THE WEB

For more information about VBScript, visit http://msdn.microsoft.com/scripting/ vbscript/ on the Web.

JScript

Microsoft's JScript is a scripting language similar to VBScript in its use. Like VBScript, JScript is used to add interactivity and intelligence to Web-based documents and doesn't produce standalone applets. Now, only Microsoft Internet Explorer fully supports JScript.

JScript resembles the programming language Java but has a few exceptions, as are obvious from the following comparisons:

JScript is	Java is
An interpreted language	Compiled to bytecode before execution on client
Object-based, lacks classes and inheritance	Object-oriented, uses classes with inheritance
Embedded code in HTML	Applet codes separate from HTML
Loose typing with variable data types not declared	Strong typing with variable data declared
Object references checked at runtime	Object references must exist at compile time
Secure, can't write to hard disk	Secure, can't write to hard disk

Because Internet Explorer programmers can code in JScript or VBScript, you must use the LANGUAGE parameter to specify which language is used. In the following example, HTML is extended to enable the dispatching of an event to a JScript user-defined function by the name of callthis():

```
<INPUT TYPE=BUTTON NAME=mybutton VALUE="Click on Me"
onclick="callthis();"LANGUAGE="JavaScript">
```

Another alternative is to extend the <SCRIPT> tag itself, as in the following example:

```
<FORM>
...
<INPUT TYPE=BUTTON NAME=mybutton VALUE="Click on Me">
<SCRIPT FOR="mybutton" EVENT="onClick" LANGUAGE="JavaScript">
alert("Hello");
</SCRIPT>
...
</FORM>
```

With the addition of the FOR and EVENT attributes in the preceding example, Internet Explorer developers can bind a script to a defined object (here, the mybutton button), which is the source associated with an event (in this case, the onclick event). The result of the example will be an alert or pop-up window that displays the word Hello when users click the mybutton button.

ON THE WEB

For additional assistance with JScript, visit http://msdn.microsoft.com/scripting/jscript/ on the Web.

Other Server-Based Components: CGI and ISAPI

Although many server-based components have already been discussed in this chapter, two others are worth mentioning: Common Gateway Interface (CGI) and Internet Server Application Programming Interface (ISAPI). You can create these two server-side extensions in many ways, depending on the programming language and extension used.

Common Gateway Interface   CGI has maintained its long-standing place as a standard in Web interactivity. CGI scripts enable the creation of applications in many different languages. Although Web users can view only the CGI submission, many processes take place to produce the result:

1. Input is passed to the Web server by the Web browser.

2. The input is then passed to a CGI script by the server.

3. After the CGI script processes the input, the input is routed (if necessary) to another application, and then the CGI script sends the output to the Web server.

4. The Web server passes the output back to the browser. This final CGI script output can vary from a newly generated document based on user input to a database's search results.

You can create CGI applications in any executable or interpreted programming language that enables access to operating system environment variables: standard input (`stdin`) and standard output (`stdout`). History shows the Perl language is popular for this purpose; however, many other languages, such as C, AWK, and REXX, have also been used in the creation of CGI applications.

N O T E If an interpreted language is used, the corresponding interpreter must be available when IIS starts the CGI extension application. ■

If server-side extensions are created by using Perl, there's now an alternative to implementing them as CGI applications. ActiveState Tool Corp. (formerly ActiveWare and Hip Communications Inc.) has created an interpreter for Perl (ActivePerl) that's available as an ISAPI application. Legacy and Perl scripts can now be executed without the CGI spawning process, which eliminates much overhead.

ON THE WEB

For more information on Perl and ActivePerl, visit the sites `http://www.ntcenter.rickg.com/ntperl/` and `http://www.activestate.com/`.

Internet Server Application Programming Interface   ISAPI extensions are filters and applications that you can use to create active Web-based applications. An *Internet filter* is a dynamic link library (DLL) that resides on an HTTP server to filter the data traffic that travels to and from the server. You can activate additional processes, such as clicking HTML links or completing an HTML form, by implementing ISAPI extensions into a Web page. These extensions are DLL applications that an HTTP server can load and call. ISAPI applications vary from CGI applications in that they have access to the same resources as the server and are executed in the identical address space as the HTTP server. Figure 15.13 shows the relationship between ActiveX server-side extensions and IIS.

FIGURE 15.13

The overhead with ISAPI extensions is much lower than with CGI applications because ISAPI extensions can be preloaded, can unload DLLs that haven't been called for a period of time, and don't require the creation of additional processes.

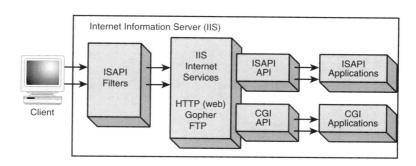

ISAPI filters are templates that you can use to request data dynamically. There might be a level of complexity with ISAPI filters versus ISAPI applications. ISAPI filters require knowledge of the underlying technology executing the template request. With ISAPI applications, however, little or no previous knowledge of the underlying technology is required because the application is used to dynamically create the content.

With ISAPI applications, you're limited by the functionality provided. The tradeoff between ISAPI filters and applications depends on the primary reason for their utilization—ease-of-use versus flexibility. The filter is an in-process control, whereas the application is out-of-process and requires more overhead than a DLL.

From Here...

This chapter looks at I-net architecture and how you can use I-net technologies to build applications that take advantage of the Web browser and Web server concept. I-net development is an extension of the traditional client/server environment that uses standard protocols and communications mechanisms to store, publish, and disseminate information.

- To learn about the database features and tools included with Visual Studio, see Chapter 4, "Creating Database-Aware Applications with Visual Studio."

- To learn about concepts associated with Web-based application development using Visual Basic, see Chapter 16, "Creating Web Browser–Based Applications with Visual Basic."

- To learn about the Visual Studio development environment, see Chapter 2, "Using Visual Studio to Create Applications."

- To learn more about strategies for application development in the enterprise, see Chapter 9, "Using Microsoft's Object Technologies."

- For a discussion of applications for client/server environments, see Chapter 25, "Clients, Servers, and Components: Design Strategies for Distributed Applications."

CHAPTER 16

Creating Web Browser–Based Applications with Visual Basic

by Joe Lengyel

In this chapter

Suppose for a moment that you are a software development professional, building core business applications using Visual Basic. Congratulations, you are one of a million—maybe ten million. Still, you wonder about distinguishing your abilities from the scores of other Visual Basic developers, many of whom are "black belt" programmers. And you'd like to learn more about developing for the Internet, something you are sure will set you apart from the pack. There's good news. You already know how.

To meet the challenges of the active platform while building on the sizable base of experienced programmers, Visual Basic offers ActiveX documents. ActiveX documents enable you to leverage your abilities in Visual Basic for building Internet or intranet (I-net) applications. In this chapter, you will learn to harness the power of this new technology. You will develop and deploy a working ActiveX document application and use it in a browser.

Understanding ActiveX Documents

ActiveX documents, the Web-based building blocks introduced in the fifth version of Visual Basic (VB), are back and better in the sixth version. ActiveX documents enable you to build new Web applications or merge with and enhance the elements of existing I-net sites. Similar to VB forms, ActiveX documents provide a variety of conventional and I-net capabilities, including functionality using the hyperlink object. Although Web development has been possible with VB in the past (ActiveX controls), this ActiveX technology accomplishes the following:

- Leverages the knowledge base of the VB development community to the I-net process model.
- Becomes a Web-development enabler for a larger pool of information systems personnel.
- Facilitates the promotion and reuse of existing enterprise VB components.
- Provides the capability to view and modify existing documents in their resident applications within the browser window.

A real-world example of an intranet scenario will illustrate the benefits of ActiveX documents. Suppose Company ABC has a traditional client/server application that was built in VB. This application is used to manage and administrate all aspects of their business, including order entry, inventory, product lists, and so forth. It has a SQL database that supplies data to the user interface through a remote data object (RDO). When enhancements are made to the application, the VB project is recompiled and rebuilt, and a new copy of the executable is placed on each user's machine.

Now consider that Company ABC plans to expand its operations and open a second office in a different region of the country. It requires use of the same corporate application previously described. This is where ActiveX documents can be very useful. Information systems professionals can migrate the existing VB application to become an ActiveX document application, which can be deployed on a Web or domain server. Users in both company locations can visit the application via their client Web browser. Enhancements to the application will appear without effort because the Web browser determines the runtime requirements of the application and downloads necessary files and components to the user's machine.

This is an example of a Web-enabled application that was built using VB. Many of the screens and program logic are reused from the existing corporate application. The ActiveX document can contain the regular assortment of controls from the VB toolbox, as well as any other licensed ActiveX controls. This example shows that ActiveX documents are a Web development alternative to technologies such as HTML and scripting languages such as JScript and VBScript.

Developing on the ActiveX platform presents a host of new challenges and features for application architects. One difficult task is blending the best components of existing software with new and improved components that were built with the latest tools.

What Is an ActiveX Document?

An ActiveX document can be any particular display of information, such as a word processing document, a data grid, a chart, and much more. You can associate this display of information with browser technologies because this is the tool with which these active viewports of information can be seen. Browsers aren't the only method of viewing ActiveX documents. The use of the term ActiveX, however, typically refers to the ability to view a collection of information in a browser window. For this chapter, an ActiveX document consists of a UserDocument object, code, and one or more controls from the toolbox placed on the UserDocument.

A UserDocument object is the base object of an ActiveX document you develop in VB. Although the ActiveX document concept is not new, building an ActiveX document with UserDocument objects in VB is both new and unique. The UserDocument object is the ActiveX equivalent of a standard VB form. There are differences you will encounter almost immediately, and you need to know these differences.

Development of a standard VB project often begins with a standard form, which becomes the home to various buttons, labels, and code. Development is very similar with an ActiveX document application. You begin with one UserDocument, and similar types of buttons, labels, and code can be added. However, you will encounter differences in the properties and methods of the UserDocument, as well as in other application-specific features, such as navigating between ActiveX documents. Furthermore, the deployment platform is different because client/server development is fundamentally distinctive from I-net development. The distinctions aren't trivial.

You aren't limited to using only UserDocuments in an ActiveX document application. You can add standard forms and modules to your project, as you might to any standard project. An ActiveX document application (an executable or DLL) can consist of numerous UserDocument objects, as well as the regular assortment of forms, controls, and so on. As the full force of development focuses on I-net applications, the standard features of applications that exist today will gradually fade away. This migration ability is a positive attribute, however, because it means the logic and functionality of existing components are reusable.

TIP The first thing to do is familiarize yourself with the properties and methods of a UserDocument. Peruse the property list by selecting View, Properties Menu, or by pressing F4. Review the methods and events by double-clicking anywhere on the surface of the UserDocument.

ActiveX Document Topology

You can think of ActiveX document technology in terms of three layers:

- Documents—The UserDocument objects containing controls and code
- Containers—Browsers, such as Internet Explorer (IE)
- Servers—The VB application housing the ActiveX document(s)

An ActiveX document is made available through a server, which can be a VB executable or DLL. A server is a component that provides the ActiveX document to an ActiveX container such as Internet Explorer. The ActiveX document is served to the browser viewport by the executable or DLL.

The capability to deploy applications for use in browsers enables you to extend your current client/server solutions throughout I-nets. A typical scenario today involves a VB application consisting of a visual front end for presenting data and reporting options to the enterprise users, and an RDO connection to a database for piping data to controls such as text boxes, grids, and list boxes. These applications typically feature reporting functions to provide documentation to customers and executives.

Administrative efforts needed for providing these reports, along with supporting application end users, is not insignificant. Annual maintenance and support are large portions of enterprise budgets. As development technology focuses more on I-nets, the separate distribution and maintenance costs for customers and enterprise users will gradually merge. As customers use vendor Web sites more to retrieve account information, schedules, product lists, and the like, application development will no longer be split between traditional client/server applications and Web applications. Instead, all applications will be browser based or Web applications, and the support and development costs for information systems departments will consolidate into a single focus. A single application will serve customers and enterprise users alike and will be used within a browser. The components in VB contribute to the existing available development tools to make this a bigger reality each day. Organizations that fail to reuse applications and components don't realize the full benefits, and hence don't experience the cost savings.

Selecting a Project Type

VB gives you four options for developing ActiveX projects:

- ActiveX document EXE
- ActiveX document DLL
- ActiveX EXE
- ActiveX DLL

There are major differences between projects that are of the type EXE and those that are DLL. (The differences between document EXEs and component EXEs are explained later in this section.)

▶ **See** Chapter 12, "Creating ActiveX Controls with Visual Basic," **p. 337**

An ActiveX component can be built as an out-of-process component (an .exe file) or an in-process component (a .dll file) with respect to the use of ActiveX objects. Historically, DLLs have served as building blocks in a reusable or shared component capacity. For example, a DLL that facilitates a network logon can be used by each new application that necessitates a network security check. A DLL is an in-process component that runs in the process space of the application that uses it. In-process servers provide accelerated service to the requesting client. An in-process component performs more quickly than its counterpart out-of-process component (an EXE) because no cross-process navigation is required. Therefore, the performance of a DLL exceeds the performance of the same component compiled as an EXE. In-process components do have drawbacks. A natural program breach occurs whenever calls are made from a calling program to an external file. This is the type of breach that might corrupt a program, so special care should be taken to make sure establishment of connections and passing of parameters are done properly. Also, non-COM DLLs must be declared in a VB project file, which means some source code modifications must be made to use the server. By nature, this contradicts the reuse benefits achieved with ActiveX, COM, and DCOM paradigms.

Part

III

Ch

16

> **CAUTION**
>
> With some versions of Internet Explorer, trying to show a modeless form from a DLL fires an error condition. Modeless forms and dialogs enable the focus to be shifted to other forms and dialogs. Modal forms and dialogs must be closed before other actions can be taken. A dangling modeless process creates the error condition within Internet Explorer.

EXEs are out-of-process components that run outside the address space of the client application and within their own process, wherever that might be. For example, most applications you use, such as those in Microsoft Office, are executables. There are two types of out-of-process servers: local and remote. A local server resides on the same computer as the calling application, but in a different process. This describes the arrangement of COM architecture; connecting binary components actively running in various process spaces. A remote server is configured on a different computer. This is DCOM: object communication services at the binary level, between computers that use a COM-compatible operating system, and are connected by some network implementation. One benefit of out-of-process components is the asynchronous performance achieved as a consequence of the separate client and component processing. In other words, EXEs do multitasking.

One very big danger area of ActiveX EXEs is the potential for data disruption. Although this depends on the distribution method, a single server installation of an EXE functions as a single application being used by many users. In this context, no components are installed on the users' machines. In essence, there is only one ActiveX application process taking place, with containers creating separate instances of that process. As a consequence, separate container sessions can simultaneously make transactions, rendering data for one session of the container unexpectedly modified because of changes made through the second container session. Naturally, this problem is an issue within certain contexts. It's not insurmountable—developers deal with these types of issues everyday—but the volume and scope are larger when an I-net is involved.

The performance for an out-of-process component is slower than that of a DLL because of the inability of an executable to make references directly between the client and the component. For example, referrals between a client and a component cannot be made by reference. Instead, a copy of the data must be made in the component, which is a slower process than passing by reference.

One very large benefit of out-of-process servers lies in the capability to distribute them on different computers. Distributed systems mean distributed components serving multitier applications. Distributed components positioned strategically on an architecture yield greatest reuse of human resources and least consumption of technical resources.

ActiveX EXEs are COM objects and can be used in applications that support COM. This means executables created with VB appear, without any special effort on the developer's part, in the list of available object references. When you create a project and designate it as an ActiveX EXE, you are essentially telling VB one of two things:

- This standalone component will be reused in the future as a tool to build new applications.

- This component will be used as a feature of an application, and possibly an ActiveX document application.

ActiveX components are Web-enabled and can be used on ActiveX documents or elsewhere. Knowing the interaction of the two can be a benefit because the same programming approach and tactics can apply to both.

 TIP Just remember that if you want to present an interactive interface for an application that will be deployed in an I-net environment, you should create an ActiveX document EXE; otherwise, create your components with an ActiveX EXE.

Use the following reference to find more information on Microsoft's object technologies and ActiveX components.

▶ **See** Chapter 9, "Using Microsoft's Object Technologies," **p. 217**

Setting Up Project Files

The file set that makes up an ActiveX document application is different than that of a standard application. When you save a form in a standard VB application, there are usually two files created for the one form. The form object is stored in a plain text file, which contains the source code and property values. This file gets an .frm extension. Controls on the form that cannot be stored as plain text are stored in .frx files. If you have ever accidentally deleted or misplaced an .frx file, you know the form has to be virtually re-created.

Similarly, the source code and property values of UserDocument objects and the code behind the document are stored in plain text files. These files receive a .dob (Document Object) file extension. Controls that cannot be stored in DOB files because of their graphical nature are stored in .dox binary files. VB also creates a UserDocument document file when the project is compiled, which receives a .VBD extension and is placed in the same directory as the other project files. The VBD file is the address file for the application to the container. The sample application you will build later in this chapter shows the significance and use of the VBD file.

 T I P After you have compiled your ActiveX document, you can change the extension of the .VBD file; for example, Players.VBD can become Players.NFL. This capability enables the user to make the name of the ActiveX document an intuitive mnemonic of the functionality of the application.

Building an ActiveX Document

The general process of creating an ActiveX document is like creating any other project. The following list gives an overview of the steps to take:

1. Start a new project.
2. Select a project type, either an ActiveX Document EXE or an ActiveX Document DLL. By default, these template projects contain a single UserDocument. Each UserDocument is the core object for an ActiveX document.
3. Add any desired controls to the UserDocument(s).
4. Add other forms, code modules, or more UserDocument objects to the project.
5. Compile and make the project.
6. Deploy the project.
7. View the project in a container.
8. Test and debug the project.

▶ For additional information on creating VB projects, **see** Chapter 26, "Building Client Front Ends with Visual Basic," **p. 761**

In the first exercise, you will make an ActiveX document using an ActiveX Control. The second exercise will focus on building a document from scratch. As you proceed, remember the design issues discussed in the chapter.

 ON THE WEB
This exercise requires the use of Internet Explorer. If you haven't installed IE, do so now. If you don't have a copy, you can obtain one for free at http://www.microsoft.com/ie/.

Design, Development, and Implementation Points

Before you build an ActiveX document, review some design, development, and implementation issues:

▪ An executing ActiveX document is not a standalone application and is meant to be viewed in a browser. When you execute this chapter's sample ActiveX document application in the IDE, you will know the application is running only because the Start button will be disabled. This can make debugging and testing a challenge.

- Containers vary, and it is not always possible to know the capabilities and limitations of the environment in which your ActiveX document will be deployed. You can establish a minimum set of capabilities across containers and environments and work toward that environment. Another alternative is to establish a target container and then program defensively to handle inadequacies with all others. Test your application in a few containers to get an idea of how the ActiveX documents look and operate in the container's viewport. Refer to the section "Integration Issues" later in this chapter for a more detailed discussion on this topic.

- Development for an intranet application can (and probably will) present different development issues, opportunities, and challenges than for an Internet application. Most notably, you will have a more controlled architecture and platform for deployment. If this is the case, you'll be able to maximize functionality without concern for whether the user's browser and workstation support the application.

- Navigating from one ActiveX document to another can vary by container and platform. The performance you achieve in Internet Explorer, for example, might differ from what is achievable in Netscape and other browsers. This is especially important if you have to support a heterogeneous browser environment. Understand the different methods available and the container for which each is designed. Some troubleshooting might be needed in this area.

- Menus developed for individual ActiveX documents can be merged with the menu of the host container. This means the exclusive menu items of the application remain and common menu items default to the container's version.

- Be sure to indicate clearly to users what they are using and where they are located because you don't want users to be unclear about the location or intent of the Web site in their browser. When in doubt, spell this information out plainly. This can be done effectively on the container title bar with labels on each page and with an About box to give the user a mnemonic for remembering the site, as well as some contextual relevance for the site. For example, you will never be unsure you have arrived at the Microsoft home page `http://www.microsoft.com/`.

Creating an Application

In this section you will create two usable ActiveX documents and view them in a container. In the first exercise, you will build an executable with a control built previously in the text. In the second exercise, you will build an executable from scratch. The exercise doesn't guide you through a rigorous application development, but lets you place numerous controls onto a `UserDocument`, write some basic routines, compile and execute the project, and use the application in a container. Nothing you do here will be different from what you have probably already done. Your ability to leverage your investment in the VB learning curve will pay dividends here; in fact, as the scope of your Web development gets serious, this exercise prepares you to handle the greater challenges of I-net development.

Building an ActiveX Document using the TimeSheet Control Before you build an ActiveX document from scratch, consider building a project using a control constructed earlier in the text. In Chapter 12, you created the TimeSheet control, a complex aggregate ActiveX component. With this control constructed, building this project will be simplified. It isn't necessary to use an ActiveX document to deploy an ActiveX control. These controls can be used with HTML editors. But using it in an ActiveX document here demonstrates the versatility of these technologies. To build the ActiveX document using the ActiveX control, perform the following tasks:

Part
III

Ch
16

N O T E You'll need the TimeSheet control to complete the next exercise. If you haven't worked through the exercise to build the TimeSheet control, doing so will be a good experience. If you aren't up for it, you can obtain the control in digital format at `http://www.gasullivan.com/vstudio/vstudio.htm`. All the code bits described in this chapter can be found in digital format at this URL. Save time by performing cut-and-paste operations on the code for the how-to sections throughout this chapter.

1. Open a new project, using ActiveX Document EXE. Remember, this type of project automatically creates the first `UserDocument` object for you, which can be found in the Project Explorer in the `User Documents` folder. The Project Explorer is your window to all the objects within the project, such as modules, classes, forms, and so forth. Because VB enables a developer to have multiple projects open simultaneously, the Project Explorer also organizes your access to all open projects.

2. In the Project Explorer, expand the User Documents folder, select the new `UserDocument` and activate it by either double-clicking it, or by choosing the View Object button located on the toolbar. Activate the Properties list for the `UserDocument` by pressing F4. NOTE: In steps 3 and 4, you assign properties to the objects in the project, then in step 5, you save the objects as files. These are distinct steps that serve exclusive purposes.

3. Provide the new object with the name `TimeSheetDoc` in the `Name` property of the Properties list. The name will now appear in the title bar of the object, followed by `UserDocument` in parentheses. The project has no name at this time.

4. Now supply a name for the project. Choose Project, Project1 Properties from the menu. On the General tab, type `AxTimeSheet` in the space available for the Project Name and click OK. Note that this name now appears in the title bar of the `UserDocument`. Each new `UserDocument` in the project will bear this name as well. The letters `Ax` reflect that this is an ActiveX document project.

5. Save the project by choosing File, Save Project. When you are asked to save the `UserDocument`, use the default name `TimeSheetDoc`. Note that VB provides the default .dob file extension for the `UserDocument`.

6. Next, provide a name for and save the project. Supply the name `AxTimeSheet`. The project should receive a .vbp file extension.

7. To add the TimeSheet ActiveX control to the UserDocument, first you have to add the component to the project Toolbox. Choose Project, Components from the menu. The Components dialog box appears to present a list of controls found in the Windows registry. From the list on the Controls tab, locate the TimeSheet control built in Chapter 12. Check the box next to the control name, and choose OK.

8. Activate the Toolbox and locate the TimeSheet control. Add the control to TimeSheetDoc. Name the control grdTimeSheet. Expand the size of the UserDocument to accommodate the full size of grdTimeSheet.

9. Save the application.

10. Compile the project and correct any errors. Actually, there shouldn't be any errors. You've written no code. This accentuates one strong attribute of using a aggregate ActiveX control. Save the project one final time.

11. Create an EXE by choosing File, Make AxTimeSheet.exe from the menu.

Testing the Application   At this time, the application can be executed. Remember, you won't view and use this application in the Interactive Development Environment (IDE) as a standalone application. You will view and debug the application with the aid of a container. To do this, take the following steps:

N O T E   The CreateToolWindow method, in this context, enables you to create a dockable window in the IDE for the purpose of debugging an ActiveX document. The process of opening a browser window for each test of the application can become tedious. CreateToolWindow partially sidesteps this hassle by facilitating everything in the IDE. Check VB Help for more information on this method. ▪

1. Run the project by choosing Run, Start or by pressing F5. The first time you execute the project, the Debugging options for the project appear. The default options are acceptable. Choose OK to continue.

N O T E   VB 6 provides some choices for debugging ActiveX documents. One option affects the steps you take to view the UserDocument in a browser. The first time you run the application, the debugging options are presented. The default option, Start Component, brings the UserDocument up in the browser automatically. A different option, Wait for Components to Be Created, forces you to start the browser as a separate step and locate the UserDocument after running the VB project. If the goal is to test the application in a browser, the default option is best because it starts a browser up automatically. Debugging options are available in the Project Properties. ▪

2. TimeSheetDoc.VBD loads and appears in the container window.

TROUBLESHOOTING

If you have trouble getting the document to load, check the security settings for Internet Explorer. A security setting of High oftentimes prevents ActiveX controls from loading and registering on the client. Change the setting to Low and attempt to load the document again. Reset your security to High before you browse the Internet again.

3. Use the functionality available in the browser. Select project and task codes. Enter numbers in the cells designated for hours worked. Check for correct tabulation of numbers. Figure 16.1 illustrates the application in the browser window.

FIGURE 16.1
Using TimeSheetDoc featuring the aggregate ActiveX control to log timesheet hours.

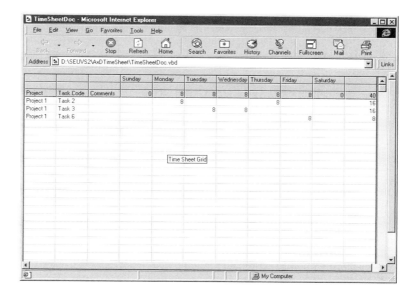

Depending on the sophistication of your applications, the debugging process can be simple or difficult. You will become more accomplished at debugging ActiveX documents with time and experience.

Building an ActiveX Document from Scratch In this section you will create an ActiveX document using the standard assortment of toolbox controls, along with some custom code. You won't be dropping an aggregate control on to a UserDocument. Instead, you'll be building detailed functionality into the user document. You will compile the application and view it in a browser. With this application you depart from business related applications, and develop an application with social implications.

Building the Framework   To build a new ActiveX document, perform the following tasks:

1. Open a new project and choose ActiveX Document EXE.

2. In the Project Explorer, expand the User Documents folder, select the new UserDocument and activate it by either double-clicking it or by choosing the View Object button located on the toolbar. Activate the Properties list for the UserDocument by pressing F4. Remember, you assign properties to the objects in the project and then save the objects as files.

3. Provide the new object with the name FirstUserDoc in the Name property of the Properties list. The name now appears in the title bar of the object, followed by UserDocument in parentheses.

4. Supply a name for the project. Choose Project, Project1 Properties from the menu. On the General tab, type AxGrapeVine in the space available for the Project Name and click OK.

5. Save the project by choosing File, Save Project. When you are asked to save the UserDocument, use the default name FirstUserDoc.dob.

6. Next, provide a name for and save the project. Use the default name, AxGrapeVine.vbp.

7. Activate the toolbox and add a command button to FirstUserDoc. Name the command button cmdSommelier. Type the text Sommelier in the Caption property of the control. Add a second command button, name the button cmdAbout, and type the text About in the Caption property.

8. Add a label control. Type the following text in the Caption property of the label:

   Welcome! You have located The Grape Vine home page. This site provides assistance with selecting an appropriate wine for your next meal or party. Click the Sommelier button at the bottom to review the Options page.

9. It's nice to spice up a home page. Remember, there can be many visitors to a Web site each day. One way is to add an image control. You can set the Picture property to any bitmap (.bmp) or metafile (.wmf) you choose.

   At this time, the ActiveX document looks like the one in Figure 16.2.

FIGURE 16.2
The AxGrapeVine project after addition of controls to the FirstUserDoc UserDocument object.

10. Modify the `Click` event of `cmdSommelier` to resemble the following code segment:

```
Private Sub cmdSommelier_Click()
    OptionsPage.Show vbModal
End Sub
```

11. Modify the `Click` event of `cmdAbout` to resemble the following code segment:

```
Private Sub cmdAbout_Click()
    frmAbout.Show vbModal
End Sub
```

12. Add a form to the project. Choose <u>P</u>roject, Add <u>F</u>orm from the menu. In the Add Form dialog box, choose the Form item and click Open. A new Forms folder containing a blank form now resides in the AxGrapeVine project of the Project Explorer window.

13. Provide the new form with the name `OptionsPage`. The name now appears in the title bar of the object, followed by Form in parentheses.

14. Modify the `Caption` property of `OptionsPage` by typing the following text:

Choose one or more items from the list boxes; click the Suggest button at any time.

15. Add a command button to `OptionsPage`. Name the command button `cmdSuggest`, and type `Suggest` in the `Caption` property of the control. Add a second command button, name the button `cmdHome`, and type `Home` in the `Caption` property.

16. Create a control array containing label controls, one for each of the following:

N O T E   There's an easy way to create a control array. Create the first instance of the desired control by adding it from the toolbox. Perform a copy and paste operation on this control. Upon pasting the new instance of the control, VB gives you the option of creating a control array.

- Appetizers
- Cheeses
- Soups
- Salads
- Pasta
- Red Meat
- Chicken
- Other Meats
- Seafood
- Miscellaneous

17. Add one combo box control for each of the following `Name` properties:

- `cboAppetizers`
- `cboCheeses`
- `cboSoups`
- `cboSalads`

Part

III

Ch

16

- cboPasta
- cboRedMeat
- cboChicken
- cboOtherMeat
- cboSeafood
- cboMiscellaneous

18. Change the `Style` property of each combo box to 2–Dropdown List.

19. Add one text box control for each of the following `Name` properties:

- txtAppetizers
- txtCheeses
- txtSoups
- txtSalads
- txtPasta
- txtRedMeat
- txtChicken
- txtOtherMeat
- txtSeafood
- txtMiscellaneous

20. Make the text property for each textbox blank.

21. Save the application. At this time, the `OptionsPage` form appears as depicted in Figure 16.3.

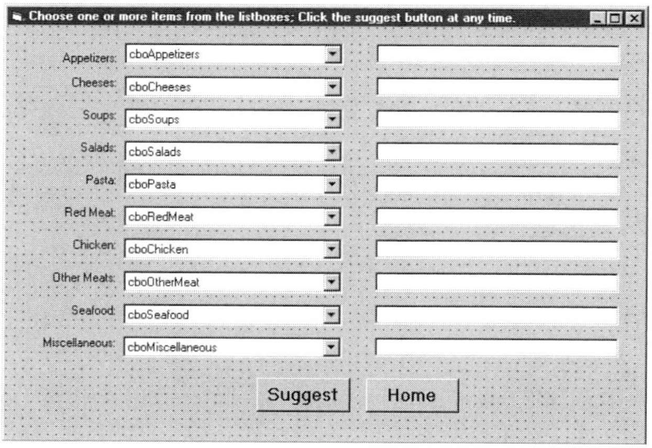

FIGURE 16.3

The `OptionsPage` form after adding all the controls necessary for the `sommelier` function.

Adding Code You will now add the bulk of the logic for the application. Remember, the code can be retrieved from the Web site supporting this text and pasted where you need it.

1. Add the code in Listing 16.1 to the Load event of OptionsPage.

Listing 16.1   List_161.txt—The Load Event of the Form to Center the Form on the Monitor

```
Private Sub Form_Load()
    Me.Left = (Screen.Width - Me.Width) / 2
    Me.Top = (Screen.Height - Me.Height) / 2
    LoadListBoxes
End Sub
```

2. Add the code in Listing 16.2 to the Click event of cmdSuggest.

Listing 16.2   List_162.txt—The Code Behind the cmdSuggestion Control Determines an Appropriate Wine for Each Food Item Selected

```
Private Sub cmdSuggest_Click()
'routine to suggest wines based on selections in combo boxes
MousePointer = vbHourglass
If cboAppetizers.ListIndex <> -1 Then
    Select Case cboAppetizers.ListIndex
        Case 0
            txtAppetizers.Text = "Light-bodied red wines or whites"
        Case 1
            txtAppetizers.Text = "Semi-dry or sweet wines; light, fruity, young
            ➡reds"
        Case 2
            txtAppetizers.Text = "Medium or full-bodied reds"
    End Select
End If
If cboCheeses.ListIndex <> -1 Then
    Select Case cboCheeses.ListIndex
        Case 0
            txtCheeses.Text = "Fruity reds"
        Case 1
            txtCheeses.Text = "Full-bodied reds"
        Case 2
            txtCheeses.Text = "Sweet wines"
        Case 3
            txtCheeses.Text = "Full-bodied reds; fruitier wines"
        Case 4
            txtCheeses.Text = "Creamy whites; champagne; sparkling wines"
    End Select
End If
If cboSoups.ListIndex <> -1 Then
    Select Case cboSoups.ListIndex
        Case 0
            txtSoups.Text = "Medium-bodied reds"
```

continues

Listing 16.2   Continued

```
        Case 1
            txtSoups.Text = "Light white wine"
        Case 2
            txtSoups.Text = "Full-bodied reds"
        Case 3
            txtSoups.Text = "Light-bodied whites"
        Case 4
            txtSoups.Text = "Fruity reds"
    End Select
End If

If cboSalads.ListIndex <> -1 Then
    Select Case cboSalads.ListIndex
        Case 0
            txtSalads.Text = "No wine recommended"
        Case 1
            txtSalads.Text = "High-acidic wines"
        Case 2
            txtSalads.Text = "Dry whites"
        Case 3
            txtSalads.Text = "Fruity reds or whites"
    End Select
End If
If cboPasta.ListIndex <> -1 Then
    Select Case cboPasta.ListIndex
        Case 0
            txtPasta.Text = "Light, fruity reds and blush wines"
        Case 1
            txtPasta.Text = "Full-bodied reds"
        Case 2
            txtPasta.Text = "Light-bodied reds; dry whites"
        Case 3
            txtPasta.Text = "Dry white wine"
    End Select
End If
If cboRedMeat.ListIndex <> -1 Then
    Select Case cboRedMeat.ListIndex
        Case 0
            txtRedMeat.Text = "Medium- or robust-bodied reds"
        Case 1
            txtRedMeat.Text = "Robust full-bodied reds"
        Case 2
            txtRedMeat.Text = "Fruity young reds"
        Case 3
            txtRedMeat.Text = "Full-bodied reds"
    End Select
End If
If cboChicken.ListIndex <> -1 Then
    Select Case cboChicken.ListIndex
        Case 0
            txtChicken.Text = "Medium-bodied reds; white wines"
        Case 1
            txtChicken.Text = "Roses; blush wines"
```

```
            Case 2
                txtChicken.Text = "Crisp, oaky-flavored wines"
            Case 3
                txtChicken.Text = "Full-bodied reds"
        End Select
End If
If cboOtherMeat.ListIndex <> -1 Then
        Select Case cboOtherMeat.ListIndex
            Case 0
                txtOtherMeat.Text = "Medium-bodied reds"
            Case 1
                txtOtherMeat.Text = "Light reds; roses, blush wines"
            Case 2
                txtOtherMeat.Text = "Full-bodied reds"
            Case 3
                txtOtherMeat.Text = "Full-bodied reds; dry whites"
            Case 4
                txtOtherMeat.Text = "Full-bodied, robust reds"
        End Select
End If

If cboSeafood.ListIndex <> -1 Then
        Select Case cboSeafood.ListIndex
            Case 0
                txtSeafood.Text = "Crisp, light whites"
            Case 1
                txtSeafood.Text = "Light reds; crisp, young whites"
            Case 2
                txtSeafood.Text = "Full-bodied whites"
            Case 3
                txtSeafood.Text = "Full-bodied reds"
            Case 4
                txtSeafood.Text = "Full-bodied whites"
            Case 5
                txtSeafood.Text = "Champagne; sparkling wines"
            Case 6
                txtSeafood.Text = "Medium-bodied reds"
            Case 7
                txtSeafood.Text = "Champagne; sparkling wines"
            Case 8
                txtSeafood.Text = "Delicate whites"
        End Select
End If
If cboMiscellaneous.ListIndex <> -1 Then
        Select Case cboMiscellaneous.ListIndex
            Case 0
                txtMiscellaneous.Text = "Dry white wines; champagne"
            Case 1
                txtMiscellaneous.Text = "Beaujolais; fruity reds; blush whites"
            Case 2
                txtMiscellaneous.Text = "Sweet wines; champagne"
        End Select
End If

MousePointer = vbDefault
End Sub
```

Part

III

Ch

16

3. Add the code in Listing 16.3 to the Click event of cmdHome.

Listing 16.3 List_163.txt—The Code Behind the cmdSuggestion Control Unloads the Current Form and Returns the User to the Home Page

```
Private Sub cmdHome_Click()
Unload Me
End Sub
```

4. Create a new procedure and supply it with the name LoadListBoxes. Add the code in Listing 16.4 to the new procedure.

Listing 16.4 List_164.txt—This Procedure Code Loads All List Box Controls with Items from Which the User Can Select

```
Public Sub LoadListBoxes()
'fill the Appetizers cbo
    With cboAppetizers
      .AddItem "Antipasto"
      .AddItem "Pate"
      .AddItem "Toasted ravioli"
    End With
'fill the Cheeses cbo
    With cboCheeses
      .AddItem "Mild"
      .AddItem "Strong/aged"
      .AddItem "Blue cheese, Saga"
      .AddItem "Goat cheese"
      .AddItem "Brie/creamy cheese"
    End With
'fill the Soup cbo
    With cboSoups
      .AddItem "Hearty soup"
      .AddItem "Lighter soup"
      .AddItem "Stew"
      .AddItem "Clam chowder"
      .AddItem "Cheese soup"
    End With
'fill the Salad cbo
    With cboSalads
      .AddItem "Vinegar dressing"
      .AddItem "Herb dressing"
      .AddItem "Creamy dressing"
      .AddItem "Sweet dressing"
    End With
'fill the Pasta cbo
    With cboPasta
      .AddItem "Primavera/vegetable sauces"
      .AddItem "Hearty tomato sauces"
      .AddItem "Shellfish sauces"
      .AddItem "Cream/white sauces"
    End With
```

```
'fill the Red Meat cbo
    With cboRedMeat
        .AddItem "Barbeque"
        .AddItem "Game"
        .AddItem "Grilled or roasted"
        .AddItem "Steak"
    End With
'fill the Chicken cbo
    With cboChicken
        .AddItem "Roasted or grilled"
        .AddItem "Chicken salad"
        .AddItem "Chicken with cream sauce"
        .AddItem "Duck"
    End With
'fill the Other Meat cbo
    With cboOtherMeat
        .AddItem "Veal"
        .AddItem "Ham"
        .AddItem "Pork roast"
        .AddItem "Pork chops"
        .AddItem "Lamb"
    End With
'fill the Seafood cbo
    With cboSeafood
        .AddItem "Grilled"
        .AddItem "Full-flavored fish"
        .AddItem "Swordfish/tuna"
        .AddItem "Fish in cream/butter sauce"
        .AddItem "Lobster"
        .AddItem "Salmon"
        .AddItem "Smoked fish"
        .AddItem "Sole"
    End With
'fill the Miscellaneous cbo
    With cboMiscellaneous
        .AddItem "Fruit"
        .AddItem "Cold cuts"
        .AddItem "Dessert"
    End With
End Sub
```

Part

III

Ch

16

Creating an About the Grape Vine Box As discussed earlier, a good feature of a Web page is to have an About box. Users can refer to this useful tool for understanding the whereabouts and purpose of the Web site, as well as other useful application-pertinent facts. To add an About box to the Grape Vine application, perform the following tasks:

1. Choose Project, Add Form from the menu.

2. In the Add Form dialog box, choose the About Dialog item and choose Open. A new About template form now resides in the Forms folder of the Project Explorer.

3. Change the text property for each label control on the form, using the following example text as a guide:

    - lblTitle—The Grape Vine

- lblVersion—Version 1.0

- lblDescription—The Grape Vine is an online sommelier that suggests wines according to choices made from various food lists. The program can suggest wines for one or more selections. Users should make the final decision on the wine that best complements their tastes.

- lblDisclaimer—Warning: This program protected by copyright laws.

4. Create a new procedure that will center frmAbout when it is loaded. Add the code in Listing 16.5 to the Load event of the form frmAbout.

Listing 16.5   List_165.txt—The Load Event of the Form to Center the Form on the Monitor

```
Private Sub Form_Load()
    Me.Left = (Screen.Width - Me.Width) / 2
    Me.Top = (Screen.Height - Me.Height) / 2
End Sub
```

The form frmAbout appears as depicted in Figure 16.4.

FIGURE 16.4

An About box is a useful mechanism for conveying location and context to visitors of a Web site.

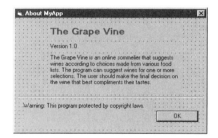

5. Compile the project and correct any syntax errors that occur. Save the project again.

6. Create an EXE by choosing File, Make AxGrapeVine.exe from the menu.

Testing the Grape Vine

At this time, the application can be executed, but remember, this application cannot be viewed in the IDE as a standalone application. You must view and debug the application with the aid of a container. To do this, take the following steps:

1. Run the project by choosing Run, Start or by pressing F5.

2. FirstUserDoc.VBD loads and appears in the container window (see Figure 16.5).

FIGURE 16.5

Viewing the startup page of the AxGrapeVine project in the Internet Explorer.

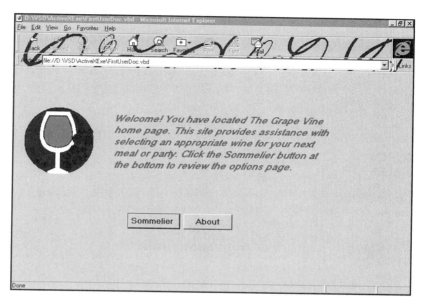

3. Click the buttons to observe the functionality. Click the About button to make the About box appear. Click the Sommelier button to open the OptionsPage form (see Figure 16.6).

FIGURE 16.6

The container viewport while using the Sommelier feature of the Grape Vine ActiveX document.

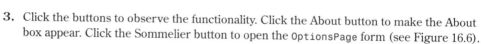

Working with Menus

Now you need to add a menu to the UserDocument. The purpose of the menu in this exercise is to call up the About box in the container viewport. You create this menu for the About box in the VB development environment. If the Grape Vine application is still running, stop it at this time. To create the menu, perform the following tasks:

1. Right-click anywhere on the UserDocument and select Menu Editor.

2. In the Menu Editor, enter &Help for the Caption and mnuHelp for the Name and then click Next. Enter About The Grape Vine for the Caption and mnuAboutGrapeVine for Name. Make mnuAboutGrapeVine a submenu of mnuHelp by selecting the right arrow in the middle of the dialog box. Change the NegotiatePosition entry to Right.

3. When you complete the entries, they appear as in Figure 16.7. Click OK to close the Menu Editor and save the menu entries.

FIGURE 16.7

The Menu Editor depicts the items added to the menu of the ActiveX document.

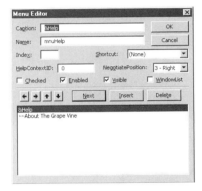

4. Add the following code to the Click event of mnuAboutGrapeVine:

```
frmAbout.Show vbModal
```

5. Save the project and create a new executable.

6. Execute the project by pressing F5. Test the application in IE.

The menu items added in the previous steps now appear on the menu bar of the container. To test the menu items, open the About box. From here, you can augment and enhance the application.

TROUBLESHOOTING

Containers won't exhibit their menus correctly unless the ActiveX document successfully merges the application's Help menu with the container's Help menu. The jump from the .HTM file to the .VBD file interrupts any chance of having this merge occur successfully. The workaround for this is to have the .VBD file load directly. Menu-merging is still an infant capability and a trial-and-error process.

Installation and Configuration Concerns

You have created an ActiveX document and are ready to deploy. This means, in all likelihood, you need to use the Package and Deployment Wizard that comes with VB and Visual Studio. Although you can create a custom setup wizard, the built-in version is robust and really sufficient for most installations.

> **CAUTION**
>
> Exercise caution when modifying any of the features of any setup kit—the fault tolerance for overwriting an important file at a user's desktop might be zero.

Using the Package and Deployment Wizard is much different from setup programs VB offered in the past. Not only is it more integrated into both VB and Visual Studio, but it also offers greater flexibility and options as well, even though it seems simpler to use. This part will be different for you because the scope and consequences can be so diverse. Installing an ActiveX document is much different than installing a standard VB application. No longer do you need heaps of floppies or even a CD-ROM with runtime and dependency files. Certain steps associated with Internet deployment are made easier, but others, including heterogeneous platform issues, make deployment much more challenging. You might be deploying an application for the known world to view, not just the end users down the hall.

The Package and Deployment Wizard manages everything in the context of a package. A package is an assembly of files that constitute the primary and support files necessary to use the application. This term and concept is true of any type of application you build that you use the wizard to deploy. Get used to the term.

Using Internet Package

The package and deployment utility, with your interaction, builds an installation program for deploying the application on clients and servers across LANs, WANS, and I-nets. Although VB still possesses the standard EXE setup program option, there is also a feature for creating an Internet download setup. This enables you to create a setup for ActiveX projects, including projects that contain UserDocuments. The wizard facilitates the installation and use of an application in either of two ways:

- Create a standard installation setup, install the application to a network server, and enable users to contact the application over a network connection.

- Create an Internet download setup, enable users to contact the application via I-net, and install the application for use on the client.

Which method you choose has everything to do with the target location you have in mind during requirements planning and development. In other words, it's about scope. Know your audience. You should use the Internet Package for any I-net–based application.

Understanding Browser-Initiated Setup

By far the biggest paradigm shift you will encounter when deploying active applications is the installation. In the past, software was installed at each client or network share point. Internet setups work much differently. As you build the setup, the wizard collects necessary files and places them in a location you specify. This can be a Web server or a network server. (Eventually the files need to be placed in a location that can be accessed from the I-net.) There they will sit, waiting to be reached by the next browser.

The next time the URL address of the application is specified by some browser out in the ether, the application will be installed at the client computer; that is, the browser drives the installation. As the browser attempts to load the default ActiveX document screen, it performs a comparison of the application requirements and the resources of the local computer. The browser then downloads and registers any differences identified by the comparison. Although the browser handles this workload, it does so objectively, and any missing components prevent the proper installation and subsequent use of the ActiveX application.

See the following reference for a review of I-net architectures.

▶ **See** Chapter 15, "Clients, Servers, and Components: Web-Based Applications," **p. 437**

Stepping Through the Package and Deployment Wizard

In this section, you will step through the process of creating an Internet package, installing the application, and viewing the application in a container. To do this, you will need use of the Package and Deployment Wizard. This utility is available in the Visual Studio 6 program group.

> **N O T E** The Package and Deployment Wizard can also be started from within the VB6 IDE. To enable this, add the Package and Deployment Wizard through the Add-In Manager. When running the wizard directly from VB, the current project receives default focus of the wizard. ▪

The wizard offers you options immediately. The first dialog enables you to select the VB project file and controls how you intend to use the wizard for the session. Figure 16.8 shows the initial dialog. For this exercise, choose the Package option. This is the choice for all yet undistributed applications. The Deploy option enables you to redistribute packages. The Manage Scripts option gives you power to adjust the scripts that package and deploy a previously built package.

FIGURE 16.8

The Package and Deployment Wizard lets you choose the project file and control how the wizard will be used.

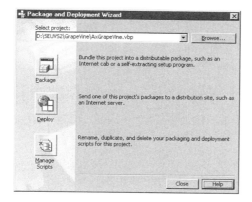

Click the <u>B</u>rowse button and locate the project file `AxGrapeVine.vbp`. After selecting the GrapeVine project, click <u>P</u>ackage to proceed to the Package Type dialog.

N O T E The wizard detects whether the most recent build of the application is older than the saved copies of the individual files in the project. It provides the option to rebuild the executable if it so detects.

Next, select the type of package you want to create. Select the Internet Package option because this application is used in an I-net context through a browser.

The Package Folder dialog box requires you to specify a path where the package will be placed (see Figure 16.9). At this time, select any location your computer has been mapped to. In the future, bear in mind you must choose a location that is accessible via an HTTP transaction by users who might have guest permissions or less.

FIGURE 16.9

The Package Folder window enables users to specify a source location where the wizard can install application files.

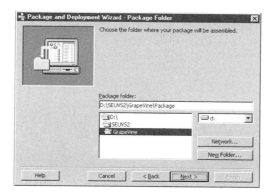

The Include Folder dialog provides feedback on which files are currently associated with the package build (see Figure 16.10). All the files might not be selected even though presented. It's the wizards way of offering suggestions. You also have the choice of adding files to the list that the wizard didn't pick up on its own.

FIGURE 16.10
The Include Folder dialog box enables users to control the files built into the package.

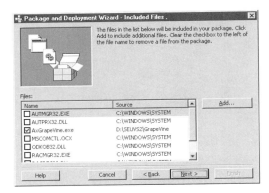

This step usually requires you to make some file additions to the list. Knowing which files to include requires an exhaustive understanding of the support files that must accompany all the components, third-party or otherwise, in your application. Third-party vendors often include a runtime distribution list with their product to assist you. You should always build your package and test it on a clean machine—that is, a machine that doesn't have the runtime components you are distributing—to make sure you won't have problems after the fact. Don't expect the wizard to include all the necessary files by default (it won't), and you will experience iterations of building, testing, and troubleshooting before you meet with success.

The File Source dialog box shown in Figure 16.11 enables you to specify whether parts of your distributed application will be located at a Microsoft Web site (or an alternative web site) and linked to the remaining components. The setup wizard creates a primary cabinet (.cab) file and encloses in it items such as ActiveX controls, EXEs, documents, and DLLs. For ActiveX-based projects, one or more additional .cab files are created to store all additional controls and referenced objects (such as RDO 2).

FIGURE 16.11
The File Source dialog box enables users to specify a source for .cab download.

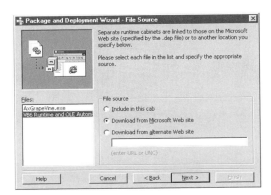

If you are distributing this application across the Internet, it is advisable to choose Download from the Microsoft Web site. If you are distributing this application across your intranet (for example, LAN), choosing either the Include in this cab or an alternative Web site option is more appropriate. For example, an intranet application in an environment with no Internet access can still support ActiveX documents if the necessary .cab files are placed in the setup directory. All the .cab files are available at the Microsoft Web site or on the Visual Basic CD-ROM and can be copied to the network server and used by the application. There are benefits to each method, but generally you want to consider speed, security, and version management. Most important, know the objectives you want to achieve for the application and the enterprise, and choose your installation method accordingly.

Part

III

Ch

16

N O T E Choose Help from the File Source dialog box to get further information regarding your options. ▩

Choose the Include in this CAB option for all files for this exercise. Choose the Next button to continue.

The Safety Settings dialog enables you to personally indicate project components you decide are safe for the user environment (see Figure 16.12). The options include Safe for Initialization and Safe for Scripting. These features are only available for Internet installations. The components are deemed either safe or not. Exercise caution when assigning either of these options unless you're absolutely sure of these assertions. Furthermore, your .cab files must be fully signed before you can make complete use of these features. Click Next to continue.

FIGURE 16.12
The Safety Settings dialog box enables developers to provide an assurance that the components being packaged are safe for download. The browser reads this setting and indicates the status to the user of the browser.

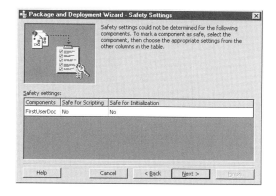

N O T E The term *signed* refers to a digital signature applied to distributed software components to indicate who created the component. It is an assurance by the creator that the component won't damage the user's computer. Signing doesn't completely ensure that an installed component won't damage a user's system, but it does create a path from the user to the creator in case the software harms the system. Developers can be held liable in some instances when installed components create damage. ▩

Figure 16.13 shows the conclusion of the interactive phase of the package construction. Simply provide a useful name for the package and click Finish.

FIGURE 16.13

The Finished dialog box signifies the completion of the wizard steps and enables the user to provide a unique and important package name.

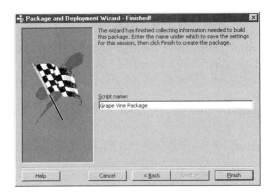

The package will be built in short order.

Included in the package (other than application files) are several files to manage the installation and execution of the application. These files are listed here:

- .htm—Generated Web page that automatically installs and registers .cab files on the users machine and then opens the initial .vbd file in the viewport.
- .inf—Setup-information reference file used during installation of the application.
- .ddf—Project file used by the Setup Wizard to create the .cab file.

Testing the Setup

The .htm file is visited by Internet Explorer to install the application. The other files act in a support capacity during the installation process. To test the setup program, do the following:

1. Start Internet Explorer.
2. Choose File, Open from the menu bar.
3. In the Open dialog box, choose the Browse button.
4. Locate the file AxGrapeVine.HTM. Select this file and choose the Open button. The text box in the Open dialog box fills with the AxGrapeVine.HTM file and path.
5. Choose the OK button.

The HTML page loads and the installation of the application begins. At this time the browser is using the setup files to determine the differences between the local environment and the requirements for the application. It acquires, when possible, the needed files and registers them on the local machine. A warning message might appear, explaining that one or more of the components to be installed is not verifiably safe. This can happen because the safety checks weren't selected during the setup process. Be sure you heed the admonitions of this type of message. If you're not sure of the security implications, you should cancel the setup.

TROUBLESHOOTING

Some browsers won't download components successfully with the browser security level set above medium. You will probably need to take security completely off for some components to work at all. Because this can compromise the security directives of your enterprise, understand how component download affects the development effort. Also, bear in mind that most users choose to cancel download operations from Web sites they have arrived at as visitors or guests. Communicate the download process effectively to all those intended users so that they'll know exactly what to expect and how they are to respond.

The application installation completes in short order, and the FirstUserDoc ActiveX document appears in the browser window.

N O T E Test the setup program on a machine that does not currently contain either a VB IDE or any of the ActiveX components in the project. Test the installation on multiple operating systems and environments to ensure success. ▪

Integration Issues

Serious development always leads to a stage when software integration and implementation become necessary. A basic part of development involves understanding the environment in which the application will be deployed. ActiveX technology developed in VB isn't different from other development tools. There are platforms well suited for VB applications and others that clearly aren't ready to be the target platform. A variety of client/server and I-net development technologies exist because of the diverse platforms on which enterprises and end users function. With that in mind, a discussion about platform capabilities will be beneficial here.

Although there are development tools supported on multiple platforms, Visual Basic is not one of them. Simply put, when you develop in VB, it is done on a PC. A distributed VB application can be used on a variety of platforms, although all-encompassing, cross-platform deployment is not the primary charge of VB; however, an executing ActiveX VB application can be visited by users on a variety of platforms with different browsers. VB does give you the capability to create an Active Server Page (ASP), making the functionality accessible by all browsers, whether running with Windows, Apple Macintosh, or UNIX operating systems. In addition, Visual Basic completely supports open database connectivity (ODBC), making ODBC databases on any platform accessible through common, object-oriented data access mechanisms. For these reasons, it is important to understand and appreciate the concerns that arise in cross-platform environments.

Platforms

Imagine that a Web server can be either an NT or UNIX server; the network operating system (NOS) can be NT, Novell, Banyan Vines, or UNIX; and clients on the network can include Windows NT, Windows 9x, Windows 3.1, Macintosh, UNIX, or OS/2. The collection of technology assembled to achieve enterprise I-net connectivity can be quite diverse, making development a conceptually daunting challenge. Business or organization demands often pair combinations of platforms that seem mutually exclusive. For a developer, supporting the concept can be withering. At the same time, developers demand the programming tools that enable them to assemble open applications to meet these needs. Your biggest concerns as a developer should be the browsers, the installation platform, data access (if any), and security.

The trend in I-net access is to integrate browsing facilities into nearly every facet of enterprise information systems. Content creators and developers are beginning to retire the notion of anything standalone. Instead, they are beginning to think of a whole new online application environment, where the browser offers omnipotent control to the user. This not only provides a more seamless end-user experience, but also enables a new class of exciting I-net development. Many developers have a significant investment in knowledge, tools, and components based on a particular language. Thus, the browser must provide broad support for the creation of ActiveX controls or other software components in popular languages such as VB, Java, and C++. Customers—specifically both application and Web developers—are demanding more from browser architecture. Consider that developers want an open browser architecture that will support all available programming languages and one that is consistent among various user environments, such as Windows and Macintosh. Customers also want tools that support rapid application development with the capability to integrate operating systems and browsers to their proprietary software solutions.

ON THE WEB

Although it isn't necessary, some corporate intranets feature a customized browser. Many intranets are strictly internal and are used with a corporate-established browser. Many organizations desire to create and distribute a Web browser that reflects the specific needs of their organization and end users. In this context, the target for an application is predefined, and development is easier for that reason. A customized corporate browser can be developed with a tool like Internet Explorer Administration Kit. You can find more information about IE's Administration Kit at `http://www.microsoft.com/ie/`.

Browsers

The dominant browsers of the day include the following:

- Internet Explorer
- Netscape Navigator
- Mosaic

N O T E   Check with Microsoft for available Internet Explorer versions per platform. Each new version becomes more sophisticated and offers greater support of ActiveX and HTML technology. Understand the demands that will be placed on your enterprise browser before making any decisions.

Internet Explorer supports a broad range of platforms and is produced in many languages. Microsoft offers IE for the Macintosh, Windows 9x, Windows 3.1, and Windows NT platforms. It is built to take advantage of the strengths of each major platform, thereby providing increased capabilities without burdening users with a new learning curve. Because of UI consistency, end users can take advantage of key operating-system features while easily changing platforms. Invariably, developers find the broadest range of capabilities by targeting IE as a browser.

The merits and demerits of the other browsers won't be discussed, but you can expect the other products to require a special plug-in or added capability before being able to host an ActiveX document.

The only server platform that will readily accept a VB ActiveX document installation is NT Server. Although this seems limiting, consider the market share and inroads NT Server has achieved in recent years. Numerous administrative and security characteristics make NT Server an excellent server platform. Because VB and NT are products of the same vendor, it's a very comfortable marriage.

The PC is the most widely used desktop platform. Although you cannot install a VB application directly to a Macintosh or UNIX workstation, these platforms can use a VB ASP in a browser.

Security

If you are worried about security, that's good. If you aren't sure your environment is secure, that's bad. Most important is to have a security plan and to monitor, revise, and update your security plan and implementation periodically. In this realm, there is database security, network security, and application security. Database security is discussed more in the next section.

Network security can be discussed from the standpoint of Internet users and intranet users. The presence of an Internet server and network firewall by themselves offers good security. Internet users navigate to a Web site using a public URL, and an Internet server translates that address into an internal address, hidden to anyone outside of the enterprise. Effective Internet server administration and management built on a foundation of solid security measures can provide rigorous protection to the network.

ON THE WEB

You can obtain more information about Internet security in a book that discusses the Internet and its numerous topics, including security. You'll find many Internet books at `http://www.mcp.com/mcp_publishers/que/`.

If contemplated and developed correctly, applications can be quite secure. The important point is to establish a series of protective firewalls that accomplish the following:

- Encapsulate in a generic wrapper the processes with which the browser interacts, to hide server and program name details.

Part III

Ch 16

- Encrypt all passwords.
- Develop the application to make bookmarking Web pages inside the verification process impossible.

Data Access

It is very likely your application will interact with a data source. Applications that interact with a database expose a developer to a whole new set of issues:

- Database security
- Data corruption
- Data integrity
- Presentation capabilities
- Interfaces

A serious and legitimate concern for database administrators is to protect enterprise databases from unauthorized access and tampering. Protecting data viewed and used by enterprise users is much less of a concern than exposing corporate data to the world via Web sites. Many Internet users preoccupy themselves by hacking into secure databases and corrupting or illegally using data. People find a way to breach security, even on the most protected networks and databases, so the concern administrators have about protecting the privacy and integrity of enterprise data is very real.

Consider a financial institution that makes account information available to customers through a Web site. Administrators must provide a secure system to prevent unauthorized access to private account data. Implementing the right topology and architecture greatly reduces the threat of security breach. It's important to position the components to hide specific names and paths of servers, executables, databases, and files. This means privileged information should not be readily available by viewing the HTML source code through the View menu of the browser. Because ActiveX documents are based on `UserDocument` objects and not HTML specifically, source code is encapsulated and hidden from end users.

As with any application, data needs to be protected from accidental user corruption. The ability to corrupt data is a function of the privileges the user is given. Obviously, users with read-only permissions have virtually no chance of directly polluting data through the UI, as long as the interface has been developed correctly. Many users, however, are given desktop tools and database access with CRUD (create, read, update, and delete) permissions, in the interest of productivity. It is this type of user, wielding a database access tool, who can cause damage if left unsupervised. Give enterprise users the minimum of permissions. Don't be too quick to give additional authorization to a user who appears more savvy and desires to be more productive. This is exactly the type of user who might take chances and make mistakes at the expense of valuable data.

The biggest fear is unauthorized remote users. There isn't much anyone can do about an unauthorized user with a legitimate password. You can hope this user's access will tip itself off eventually, at which time the password can be changed. Keep close tabs on remote users. Never give remote users more than read privileges unless absolutely necessary. Business processes that require more permissions should be heavily scrutinized. Remember, inadequate database security not only jeopardizes confidentiality of data, but also your ability to maintain database integrity. It is a cost any enterprise can ill afford.

Understand the demands a Web site places on the database, the network, and the company infrastructure. Today's users don't have patience with slow throughput, so determine your expected user volumes, peak demand periods, and appropriate hardware resources accordingly. Optimize the cost-benefit of hardware resources. Often, departments can lease time and Web space from company Web and database servers. The benefits of this arrangement include maintenance of load and cost savings.

Will the application share data between documents and forms? If the answer is yes, particular care must be taken when developing variables and variable scope. Understand these types of implications when targeting for a multicontainer distribution.

Part
III

Ch
16

From Here...

A time and place will come when all applications will have been ported to enterprise intranets and new development will only be active in format. New development will be targeted specifically to I-net solutions and built with ActiveX technology. This chapter discusses how to implement ActiveX documents. You built an ActiveX document application and migrated objects from existing standard applications into your ActiveX application. For more information on some of the topics addressed in this chapter, see the following chapters:

- For information on building applications for a distributed environment, see Chapter 25, "Clients, Servers, and Components: Design Strategies for Distributing Applications."

- For a thorough overview of Web-based application technology, see Chapter 15, "Clients, Servers, and Components: Web-Based Applications."

- To learn more on building front ends with Visual Basic, see Chapter 26, "Building Client Front Ends with Visual Basic."

- For a additional information on the Package and Deployment Wizard, see Chapter 24, "Packaging and Deploying Web-Based Applications."

CHAPTER 17

Server-Side Programming

by Joe Lengyel

In this chapter

Exploring the Strategic Server Use

The need for raw data and information is an accelerant for the pervasiveness of information systems in the workplace and the Internet. At the heart of this pervasiveness is the demand placed on servers. Servers are required to parcel out data efficiently to handle a withering number of requests. Hence, programming for the server takes a great deal of care and preparation. Many issues such as security, speed, and future functionality weigh heavily when deciding which software to use and how to implement the best server for both internal I-net use (an intranet) and external I-net use (the Internet).

When picking the correct way to implement a server, many considerations should be taken into account. What is the purpose? What is most important about what the application does in the present? What does the future hold? Can I get the information to those who need it quickly and efficiently? Is access by unauthorized users controlled? Will the users embrace the application?

This chapter deals with these issues, as well as others, about processing suited for the server. This chapter is an overview of server-side programming and deployment, intended to stimulate important questions and investigation that is rudimentary to the process.

The Internet and intranets are made up of numerous types of building components. Visualize yourself shopping for a new car. You walk the new car lots, looking for a style, color, and price that fits your personality and pocketbook. You narrow the choice down to one car. Now you have to choose between the different options. You want cruise control, rear window defogger, air, power everything, and a CD player. The salesman also points out that the car features a super-charged V6, fuel-injection engine. Sounds good, right? But what do you really know about the engine? You interface with it through the gas pedal. After that, your knowledge wanes. Like most of us, if you have to think about your engine, you don't want it. Well guess what? If you're going to be doing server-side I-net development, you'll need to know more about the engine. Certain topics about I-net development have and will always get more attention. The bells and the whistles of the Web site attract the visitors. The capabilities of the client are the cruise control, air, and power-everything features. This is what matters to most people. But the most critical component of any I-net infrastructure is the server hardware platform and operating system. Like the car engine, this is what makes cruising possible. No small amount of consideration should go into selecting this critical layer. The selection criteria for server platforms include the following:

▪ High performance—Scalable servers and systems are essential in today's computing world. It is not unusual for user loads to increase suddenly and significantly in short periods of time. Any review of Web server audit logs will prove that. Operating systems are described as scalable if they automatically use additional processors. Before purchasing hardware or an operating system, understand the demands that will be placed upon that server. Map those demands against the capabilities to upgrade the hardware. Understand how the operating system will respond to additional processors and memory.

■ Powerful operating system administration and management tools—Depending on the size of the organization, management of various servers can be the responsibility of numerous people or one person (in the case of a small company). The job responsibilities aren't necessarily fewer based on smaller size; administrators of smaller networks have more vertical responsibilities, although those in larger networks have more horizontal responsibilities, or possibly both. In either case, having a rich set of network administration and server management tools is invaluable. Windows NT Server is equipped especially well for this. A powerful GUI administration is useful on all types of software servers.

■ Hardware—High throughput hardware systems for both networking and storage media—Because of the graphical nature of information being handled by I-net–based networks, performance capabilities of the server hardware are an important consideration. In particular, the hard disk subsystem and the network interface must provide good throughput and reliable operation. Furthermore, configuring the software to optimize hardware capabilities is very important. Failure to do so is one leading cause for server underachievement.

■ Strong security features—You must be serious about securing the information processed by your systems. Secure transmission, controlled access, and assigned authorizations are important aspects of a secure computing environment. The operating system should supply you with a high level of confidence that these aspects can be met. But this is only half the battle. The other half must come from within. The organization should construct a well-conceived security model and procedures and measure their effectiveness through frequent auditing.

The hardware platform can host one or more software servers to provide various services to I-net users. Some of the software applications put to use include

■ Web server—An application on the Internet that acts as a host for Hypertext Transfer Protocols (HTTP) and related Web-service activity. It is the basic component that brings together the power of I-nets. Obviously, its greatest purpose is in publishing and disseminating information to wide audiences. This software gives client machines access to information by facilitating information publishing, application execution, and data retrieval.

■ Database server—Relational database servers, such as SQL Server, Oracle, and Informix, are ever more becoming the backbone of information publishing. Although serving database information wasn't necessarily the primary motive behind developing the earliest server-side programming technologies, it has arguably become the most important now. Perhaps the biggest need in the future will be building and administering huge data stores for report and publishing purposes.

■ Component server—A server facilitating the use of DCOM-enabled component applications to operate across the Internet. Microsoft is working with Internet-standards bodies to offer DCOM to the Internet community as an open technology. For networks with predefined transport protocols, this server will also enable COM component applications across intranets. The key point here is strategic and effective partitioning of software

Part
III

Ch
17

components. Because DCOM is an inherently secure protocol, it can be used without being encapsulated in a virtual private network: DCOM applications can simply use the cheap, global TCP/IP network. Most companies don't provide direct Internet access to their desktop computers. All but some dedicated server computers are hidden behind a firewall that typically consists of protocol-level (port-based) and application-level (proxy server) filters.

- Document/index server—These servers support information publishing by providing a means for organizing documents of unstructured data, such as word processing documents. This enables users to quickly search for needed information in documents or other files that are being managed by this type of server. Properties are assigned to each binary file, and the server interprets the properties in response to user requests. Not every organization or company will have a need for a server such as this.

- Firewall/proxy server—These servers enable corporations to provide secure gateways to the Internet. This type of product controls the interchange between a private network and the public Internet network. Configuration possibilities are numerous. For example, the server can be configured to allow only certain people Internet access, what time they do so, and which Internet applications and protocols can be used. Typically, these servers can be configured to support HTTP, FTP, Telnet, Gopher, and other Internet protocols.

- Transaction server—These servers are products that integrate component-based applications with transaction support. They combine the features of transaction processing monitors with the features of Object Request Brokers (ORBs).

Looking at a Technology Review

The technologies available for developing on the server are varied. But they all have the same goals: move processing to a more powerful machine, enable a greater level of security, and centralize the maintenance. Each of these factors is common for all the development technologies discussed in this chapter. Furthermore, most of the technologies discussed in the chapter can and are used in combination with one another. Some are inseparable; others can't be used with another. Developers integrate finished Web components to present a single Web page or site. For example, one Active Server Page (ASP) might be constructed from a series of scripts, some Hypertext Markup Language (HTML), and an ActiveX component.

Answering the question "How are the technologies being used?" is an exercise in understanding the different targets of Web developers and the technological needs inherent in hitting those targets. People responsible for building and maintaining I-net sites don't have complete control over the environment all the time. Oftentimes, a Web developer must adhere to corporate standards when developing a line-of-business site, and can be constrained by the technology (for example, platforms) she has at her disposal. For example, the enterprise might establish Domino as the de facto Web server, although the developer is much more fluent with tools not supported on the Domino platform. Developers find ways around these obstacles. They learn new technologies and adjust. This text is about Visual Studio and the capabilities afforded to the developer who uses the tools in the suite. The focus is about how to use individual products or combinations of products (ActiveX and JScript), together with the products featured in

BackOffice, to build I-net applications featuring best of breed methodologies, programming conventions, and design.

What all this has to do with the server is twofold: The server must support the I-net application and bear some of the load for the application. Each of the server-side methods discussed in the following identifies platform-specific issues. The questions about platform support will be answered. But the chapter is really about how to use the server to perform some of the process load of the I-net application. This is desirable for many reasons, not the least of which are security and performance.

The server is a good location for many of the components, pieces, routines, scripts, or whatever term you want to use. I'll use an example to illustrate a very important reason to place logic on the server. Suppose you want to build a site that provides functionality for querying a database for financial information. It's the kind of site where the user provides a logon to access the confidential areas of the site. In essence, the user logs on, and his logon is validated against a table of valid logons and passwords. It might not be practical to have separate database logons for every site user, especially if the volume is very large. Instead, this validation process might be handled with the use of a generic database logon. The generic logon is used in a script to gain access to the database for validating the user logon. A fundamental database security practice is to provide the minimum amount of permissions necessary to each logon. The generic logon can be given read-only permissions to the minimum views or stored procedures to access underlying tables. Both access and damage are controlled. Considering that, you still won't want to publish a database logon to the general public. Therefore, you'll keep the generic logon and the logic to access the database on a secure server, probably inside of a firewall. Being able to locate important scripts and components on a server really enables you to open up the capabilities of your I-net so much more. Most of today's e-commerce would not be possible without it.

Understanding Server Connections

Making a connection to the server can be one of the biggest decisions behind creating a successful I-net project. Ignoring certain needs could cause serious problems for the future, both during the project and during the life of the application. It is important to recognize that there is not always one solution for every problem. You should weigh each trade-off and design a system that works best for your situation and that minimizes your risk. Each of the following items addresses important considerations for making server connections.

Speed

Speed, in the context of this chapter, can be defined as the rate that a request made from a Web browser is returned. Speed considerations are very important. That is, a slow server response to a browser request is usually intolerable for the user. Users have an idea of how long their type of connection usually takes to return the average Web request. Users know how long they usually have to wait for a response. Regardless, users are never going to wait very long for a response from the server. Anything approaching a minute, even for a 28.8Kbps modem is more than most users are willing to wait. They will typically cancel their connection and choose not to visit the site again, or complain to the appropriate personnel, hoping for improved performance.

That said, speed should not be the number one criterion for developing all sites. Necessary content should never be sacrificed for speed. Instead, necessary content presentation should be adjusted to obtain speed. Don't confuse fluff with necessary content. Don't sacrifice site use for excessive graphics. Each site has a particular brand of user. Thoroughly understand the user's interest in visiting the site. Some sites are novelties and attract users for that reason. However, sites that are used often, for business reasons perhaps, should bear in mind that users consider time extremely valuable. Find the right mix of aesthetics and utility for the site so that it performs quickly on your hardware platform.

Security

Security can really be addressed in two separate contexts: security of the site and security of the content of the site. Securing the site means protecting the software, hardware, and anything else hard and soft from intruders. Hackers are resourceful people with insane amounts of free time on their hands to find cracks in Web site security. Typically, hackers prey on sites not using the full security features of the software. Study, understand, and implement the security at your disposal on your I-net.

Securing the content of the site is a separate matter. For sites publishing nonconfidential information, such as academic schedules, less care is needed. For sites publishing confidential investor information or company customer lists, it is a much more important matter. In these cases, encryption is necessary to make sure that information being distributed via HTTP transactions is safe from interception. Servers supporting encryption techniques, such as Secure Sockets Layer (SSL), should be used.

Scalability

Scalability refers to a Web site's capability to accommodate various numbers of users, with similar performance or response times. Sites that don't scale well perform poorly and leave the users unhappy. Ultimately, the goal is to have a well-frequented site. Part of having a scalable site is assessing potential volumes prior to building the site. Be liberal in the estimates. After that, use a technology that scales well beyond your needs, as opposed to tools that meet the maximum need. The approach should be spend now to save later.

Server Connections

Web servers handle different types of requests from browsers. If the request is for a static HTML document, the Web server software returns the document at the location the user requested. But even static pages, seemingly a cut-and-dried issue, need careful planning. The site can still be scalable. After a close assessment of the capabilities of server hardware, it's important to select a software development tool and approach that will fulfill this need.

If other processing is needed on a request, such as a database query, a different course of action is taken. Some important issues include how to connect to the database server and what software to use to do the processing. Deciding how to connect to a database server can be one of the biggest decisions in creating a successful I-net project. Underestimating traffic volumes and use can make the site practically unusable during peak periods. Ignoring this possibility during development is asking for a complete rewrite of the application. Some key issues to consider are the following:

- Reusing connections—Do as much processing per connection as possible.
- Limit round trips to servers—Along the lines of reusing connections, don't make a connection unless necessary. Batch activities, if possible.
- Limit trips to servers that can be accomplished on the client—Some validations don't need to be performed on a server. A script on the client can handle these. For example, case sensitivity and some date checks can be handled prior to making a trip to the server.
- Invest heavily in hardware that will maximize server throughput—Be sure that you have hardware that will handle the traffic the application creates.
- Carefully develop objects for connecting to database servers—Objects used to handle connections to a database need particular care during development. Using the right database object model, scrolling method, and cursor type can provide the margin of performance that makes the difference.

Developing an I-net application can be daunting. Each has its own set of special considerations. It is important to recognize there is no one solution for every problem. You should weigh heavily all the trade-offs and design a system that works best for the situation which minimizes performance shortcomings. The emphasis of this chapter of course is to aid in the development of I-net applications by providing advice for server-side development.

Working with Server-Side Scripting

In this section, I cover the use of scripting languages to provide server-side functionality for I-net applications. I address VBScript and JScript as tools from various perspectives. I examine their strengths and weaknesses as separate tools; compare the two languages, identifying the best place and time to use them; and discuss the benefits of using scripts to provide dynamic content powered by the server. I will also review the integration of scripts with other server-side components (ActiveX) and HTML to build ASP.

For all of HTML's benefits, you can't do all that you might like to in it. Dynamic content and logic processing are beyond the reach of the markup language. One way to overcome these shortcomings is through the use of a scripting language. Scripting languages are a way to enhance what you can't accomplish using HTML. Scripting enables you to work with variables, logical constructs, and data within HTML code. Scripting is employed extensively today for various purposes both on the client and the server. Examples of client-side use of scripting include checking browser version, validating user input, loading and using ActiveX controls, and generally providing feedback to the user. Here's a review of a client-side scripting scenario.

First, visualize a Web site that accepts user input. These are very common. Let's say that the form is for requesting marketing information from a business. One requirement of the form, however, is that users must supply a complete address to which the promotional materials will be sent. After specifying all necessary information, the user submits her request. But say by accident, the user typed in a 4 digit U.S. postal code. In the United States, there are no 4-digit zip codes. The script validates the user-entered zip code and provides the appropriate feedback, before actually enabling the request to be submitted.

Scripts can be used with controls or applets, too. In the preceding example, you can write an applet that gathers all valid zip codes and actually validates the zip code as well. Scripting languages make this possible. The preceding example describes use of client- or browser-side scripting. In other words, the scripts are embedded in the Web page and executed by the user's Internet browser.

Until recently, most HTTP servers ran on UNIX computers. Extended functionality, such as dynamic content, was accomplished by writing gateway programs using the common gateway interface (CGI) specification. CGI is discussed in more detail later in this chapter. The CGI approach does have its flaws. CGI is not for amateurs. CGI programs are executable programs that interface with the Web server to provide dynamic content and functionality. They can be nasty to create and debug, and certainly are not a trivial endeavor. In addition, CGI programs can be costly to system resources. For each call of the CGI program, the Web server must spin off a separate program. All those processes running concurrently on the server can make a popular Web site very slow. There are other, sometimes better, ways to process user input on the server; today's Web servers support programmable extensions that run in the same process as the server itself and provide extra features that make programming tasks easier. This is where server-side scripting plays a role.

Internet Information Server (IIS) and ASP (the former a Web server, the latter a Web server extension) support scripting languages to add incredible power to a Web site. An ASP is an HTML document that contains embedded server-side scripting. Web servers compatible with ASP can execute these server-side scripts. On the client side, an ASP is a standard HTML document, viewable on any platform using any Web browser. On the server, an ASP uses the power of scripting languages, server processes, and ActiveX components.

There has been a tremendous growth in the use of ASP, because of, in part, the ease of developing powerful I-net applications—Web-enabled client/server applications on the Internet and corporate intranets. ASP dynamically creates HTML based on server-side scripting to connect to databases, track user state and session information, and connect to various COM-based objects. However, the power of server-side functionality is directly proportional to the power of the scripting language executing on the Web server. With this in mind, let's review two scripting languages, VBScript and JScript, and demonstrate how with these scripting languages you can create powerful functionality in an ASP.

Scripting Languages

ON THE WEB

For up-to-date information on scripting, visit http://msdn.microsoft.com.

The European Computer Manufacturers Association (ECMA) is a European-based association for standardizing information and communication systems. The scripting standard known as ECMA-262 is based on a cooperative submission from Microsoft and Netscape. The ECMAScript standard describes a Web scripting language that can enrich and enliven Web pages in a Web browser. ECMAScript is the only standard scripting language on the Web. ECMAScript is based on the ECMA-262 specification, which outlines an object-oriented programming language for performing computations and manipulating objects within a host environment, such as the browser.

Two of the most popular scripting languages today are ECMAScript (a standardized scripting language based on JavaScript), of which JScript is an implementation, and VBScript. JScript 3.1 is Microsoft's implementation of the new ECMA-262 scripting language. Basically, when talking about JScript or JavaScript, I am talking about implementations of the same standard scripting language, ECMA, except that the implementations are marketed by different companies. You can use any scripting language you like for client-side scripts, as long as your audience's browsers support it. In fact, you can use a combination of scripting in your HTML source code. For server-side scripting, especially to build ASPs, you can use JScript, VBScript (or both, as you'll find out), or any other supported scripting language. The following sections cover more information about VBScript and JScript and provide an example of each scripting language used for server-side processing.

ON THE WEB

The complete ECMA-262 specification can be found at http://www.ecma.ch/stand/ecma-262.htm.

ON THE WEB

JavaScript is a scripting language written by Netscape that preceded the ECMA standard.

If you'd like to read up on it, there's an excellent introduction to JavaScript at http://www.cc.ruu.nl/~goyarts/javascript/javascr.htm.

VBScript   VB Scripting Edition, a subset of the VB programming language, is used to develop code scripts for use in Web browsers and other applications that use ActiveX controls, automation servers, and Java applets. VBScript has a lot of similarities to the parent language, but is noticeably thinner and consequently less robust, although excellent for its intended purposes. VBScript is currently available as part of IE and IIS. This means that these products come prepared to enable you to execute VBScripts. The environments you can use to develop scripts variy from simple (Notepad) to complex (Visual InterDev). VBScript brings active scripting to a wide variety of environments.

Part
III

Ch
17

N O T E VBScript is a subset of the Visual Basic for Applications (VBA) language used in Microsoft Office products and the Visual Basic development system. VBA is Microsoft's extensible, strategic application scripting language automation and program objects. VBA provides a complete development environment, including integrated editor and debugging support.

The guiding principles of VBScript are

- Provide the Basic developer with a path to Web development on the client and server
- Bring an easy-to-use-and-understand scripting language to the Web
- Expand the Visual Basic family of languages to platforms not covered by VB or VBA

VBScript enables authors to create scripts using a subset of the Visual Basic language. If you are already a Visual Basic programmer or if you are not a programmer but are looking for a scripting language that is easy to learn, VBScript might be the right language for you. VBScript is implemented as a fast, portable, interpretive language and doesn't include functionality that directly accesses the client machine's operating system or file system. For example, you cannot do file I/O or read the registry on the client machine.

To review, some of the advantages of using VBScript for I-net development are

- Ease of use—VBScript's biggest asset is that it's BASIC, a language designed to be learned quickly. VB brings BASIC users some of the advantages of more complex languages while not losing sight of the fact that the language should be easy to understand.
- User base—VB has been phenomenally successful since its introduction in 1991; there are now over 3 million VB developers. All the VB skills they've learned instantly apply to VBScript. Also, an enormous community exists to provide training, books, and magazines for learning Visual Basic.
- Flexibility—VBScript can be used in a wide variety of applications, and Microsoft is committed to ensuring that wherever script is part of an application, VBScript will be included.

To review, some of the key language features of VBScript are

- Error handling—VBScript has a subset of the error handling provided by VB. This includes the error object and error-condition logic (for example, On Error Resume Next). Error handling is very important when developing server-side code because most of the functionality requires access to external COM objects, which can throw errors.
- Formatting—VBScript has formatting capabilities for dates, numbers, and currency built into the language.
- Class support—VBScript supports three separate classes of objects, making Web development powerful. Specifically, VBScript supports objects provided by the VBScript engine, the browser, and the developer (for example, ActiveX controls and automation servers).
- COM integration—Many COM objects return information in the form of a collection. VBScript has built-in support for iterating through collections.

ON THE WEB

Numerous samples, a tutorial, and other information are all available for testing and viewing at the VBScript Web site at http://msdn.microsoft.com/scripting/.

Prior to VBScript 2, no debugging capabilities existed for the scripting language. Developers basically had to write and test their scripts via the trial-and-error process. With the 2 release, however, Microsoft also released the Script Debugger. This tool, similar to the IDE in VB, enables a developer to observe the performance of a script in a debugging and testing environment. This greatly improves the speed and accuracy of new scripts. Visual InterDev provides a robust environment for developing scripts; it features debugging, IntelliSense, and drag-and-drop capabilities to accelerate script creation.

ON THE WEB

The Microsoft Script Debugger and documentation is available at http://msdn.microsoft.com/ scripting/.

Part
III

Ch
17

JScript   JScript, Microsoft's implementation of an ECMA-compliant scripting language, is an interpreted, object-based scripting language targeted specifically for the Internet. Although it has fewer capabilities than full-fledged object-oriented languages like C++ and Java, JScript is more than sufficiently powerful for its intended purposes; applications for Web browsers or those that use ActiveX controls, Java applets, and Automation servers. It is the first scripting language to fully conform to ECMAScript, the Web's only standard scripting language, and is targeted specifically to the Internet.

Like VBScript, JScript is implemented as a fast, portable interpreter. But JScript is not Java and has nothing to do with Java, nor is it a diluted version of any other language. It is closer in syntax to C or C++. If you are a C or C++ developer, you will probably find JScript to be a very natural extension to what you are already doing.

Like most scripting languages, JScript has its limitations. You cannot write standalone applications in it, for example, and it has little capability for reading or writing files. It's important to note that JScript is not just confined to use in the browser; you can use JScript in most applications in which you can use VBScript. JScript is a loosely typed language. That means you don't have to declare the data types of variables explicitly. In many cases JScript performs conversions automatically when they are needed. For instance, if you try to add a number to an item that consists of text (a string), the number is converted to text. Most programmers would characterize this as undesired functionality because something could happen that wasn't intended, and the programmer might not catch it immediately.

N O T E   JavaScript is not ECMAScript-compliant. JavaScript 1.1 did serve as the basis for ECMA
standards work, but the standards process has resulted in significant language improvements in the areas of Unicode support, IEEE math functions and improved date functions.

To review, some of the advantages of using JScript for I-net development are

■ Broad support—JScript enjoys a broad range of browser support. If your page really must work in any browser, this is the language for you.

N O T E   Most functionality in JScript works across both the IE 4 and Navigator 4 browsers. The key issue here is that Internet Explorer 4 is already fully ECMA-compliant, although Netscape has announced that it intends to support ECMAScript. ■

■ Published resources—If you want to learn JScript, there are tons of books to help you. The publishing of so many texts on the subject stemmed from the excitement that arose when Java was introduced. Since then, Java-anything has received great attention from publishers and developers alike.

■ Similarity to C and Java—If you are a C or Java programmer, the JScript syntax is going to be familiar to you.

To review, some of the key language features of JScript are

■ Dynamic—JScript was designed as a completely dynamic language; that is, you can effectively redefine your program on-the-fly. Although this has a number of potential disadvantages, it does give you the ultimate flexibility in your scripts. This is particularly useful in Dynamic HTML (DHTML) programming because DHTML enables you to dynamically manipulate the object model. If you really want to drive DHTML, you might want to consider using JScript instead of VBScript.

■ Object-oriented—JScript certainly isn't a traditional class-based, object-oriented language, but it does provide an effective alternative based on prototypes. This enables you to reap the benefits of object-orientation without the statically-defined nature of classes.

■ Class support—JScript supports three separate classes of objects, making Web development powerful. Specifically, JScript supports objects provided by the JScript engine, the browser, and the developer (for example, ActiveX controls, automation servers, and Java applets).

■ Regular expressions—A main reason why Perl has such a huge following, regular expressions add the capability to search for expressions in strings. This is exceptionally useful on the server and, increasingly, on the client.

■ Runtime features—Provides the capability to immediately evaluate code at runtime. This enables you to dynamically redefine logic dependent on runtime environment and conditions. This is especially useful when used in conjunction with Remote Scripting, which works with VBScript as well.

When used in IE, JScript is directly comparable to VBScript. Like VBScript, JScript is a pure interpreter that processes source code embedded directly in the HTML. JScript code, like VBScript code, doesn't produce standalone applets, but is used to add intelligence and interactivity to HTML documents. Also like VBScript, JScript supports three separate classes of objects for use within JScript, as mentioned earlier.

ON THE WEB

For information, visit the JScript site at `http://msdn.microsoft.com/scripting/`.

Using Server-Side Scripts

There are numerous reasons for using server-side scripts. They provide so much flexibility and power in such a simple development paradigm. Granted, they might never replace full-fledged programming environments, such as C++ or VB; the differences in capabilities between client/server development tools and scripting languages are still very pronounced. But like many technologies, scripting languages are fast evolving. The capabilities and power of these languages are growing, as is the utility one can get from them.

Scripting is a relatively painless way of adding dynamic content to an ASP, much more so than Internet Server Application Programming Interface (ISAPI) or CGI. As an example, Visual InterDev provides a powerful environment for building scripts and integrating them into HTML pages to construct ASPs. Using tools like InterDev, which facilitate a good deal of drag-and-drop development, scripts can be constructed, tested, and put into production all from the same environment. There's no complicated interfacing with special Web server DLL's, no arcane knowledge of cryptic unpublished functions. Scripting takes advantage of the objects exposed by the browser, Web server, or ActiveX controls. Scripting for ASP is a very readable, understandable way to develop dynamic content.

Scripting empowers more human resources for developing active content than other web development tools, protocols, and specifications. Unlike CGI and ISAPI, scripting appeals and is accessible by the masses, much like VB and Access. People feel courageous and excited about developing scripts. They don't find using the tool formidable and restricted to computer science majors. In a tight market for programmers, with predictions for massive shortages in technical positions, this is especially advantageous.

With the introduction of scriptlet technology, scripting languages can now be used to build reusable collections of functions and procedures. Scriptlet technology enables Web authors to create reusable objects for use within Dynamic HTML. A *scriptlet* is a Web component that you can write using HTML and scripting, which takes full advantage of the capabilities of DHTML. Scriptlets are based on COM, so you can use them to interact with other applications that support COM. On any platform, a scriptlet is just a Web page created with HTML. However, on a Win32 platform, a scriptlet becomes a COM object as well. The scriptlet technology lets you reuse script that you've already written, and add even more functionality to it without altering the original code.

When identifying client and server support for scripting languages, you have to address the topic from two different perspectives. You can write a script in a simple text editor or use a powerful tool like Visual InterDev, but the platform you deliver the script on must support the execution of that script. The browser executes client-side scripts. Not all browsers support VBScript and JScript, and not all client operating systems support all browsers. So there are limitations. IE, which supports VBScript and JScript, is available on Windows, Macintosh, and UNIX (Sparc Station) workstations. Netscape Navigator doesn't support VBScript, but does support JScript. Predetermine the compatibility of your chosen scripting language prior to beginning development.

N O T E   IE4 for the Macintosh doesn't support VBScript as of this writing.

However, this chapter is addressing server-side scripts. Now the question is: To what Web server platforms can VBScripts or JScripts be delivered? On the server, the choice of scripting languages is somewhat predetermined because the scripts will execute on the server, and the environment is controlled. The Web server must support the server-side script, and the operating system must support the Web server. IIS, which ships with Windows NT Server, fully supports VBScript, JScript, and various other scripting languages in ASPs. O'Reilly Software's WebSite Professional supports everything that IIS supports and more. Research the capabilities of the Web server to be used for hosting your site. Understanding any limitations in advance will help you to plan accordingly when developing an I-net application.

ON THE WEB

For a comprehensive comparison of major Web servers, visit O'Reilly's site at `http://website.ora.com/`.

Choosing a scripting language to develop server-side scripts merits important consideration. For many, the choice of programming language takes on an almost religious zeal. If you're a VB programmer, you're certainly not going to want to learn an unfamiliar syntax and a different way of thinking. If you program in C, well, you know about those types. Unfortunately, this rationale exists and can blind a person's decision making to critical and practical facts. Don't let this happen to you. Make decisions on the basis of a well-developed plan that takes into consideration the following types of issues:

- Target hardware platform—On the server, the decision isn't influenced by target platform because you control the server. This assumes that you are using a Microsoft server product. If you are developing for the server, the ability to script external COM objects is probably going to be more important than language features because that's where most of the server functionality will be implemented. For example, the ability to cope with errors raised by COM objects quite probably will outweigh the ability to use extended language features.

- Scripting language features—Understanding the potential of a scripting language requires a review of the language object model, the conditional language features, and the available functions and operators.

- Human resources—Understand the skills and skill levels of your human resources. Do you have experienced programmers on hand, or programming neophytes? Not everything about using scripts is a snap, especially if you intend to employ server-side scripts. Fortunately, scripting is an easy-to-learn technology. So the actual development is not insurmountable. Bountiful samples and documentation on the Web and other media will make learning a scripting language comfortable. But although you make browser-side functionality available in a few lines of code, server-side requires the installation and configuration of numerous software applications. Having people who are adept at those tasks is important.

■ Personal preference—Try to keep personal preferences the least of the priorities. Always use more objective criteria for selecting a technology. Personal preference typically equates to familiarity. All things being equal, now and in the future, you are likely to select what you know. A VB programmer naturally gravitates to VBScript.

A Scripting Example

Here's a review of a server-side script. The following example steps you through creation of an ASP. This example uses a JScript along with some limited HTML. The goal here is to describe environment requirements and execution of a simple example. A serious dynamic site exceeds the scope of this chapter.

To set the stage, consider Figure 17.1. The illustration demonstrates setup for the example you will build and use. You'll be using a Windows NT Server with IIS and ASP installed. By using the following steps, you'll build a single Web page and access it from a browser.

Part
III

Ch
17

FIGURE 17.1
Windows NT Server ships with IIS and ASP, which are used in the scripting example to execute a server-side script.

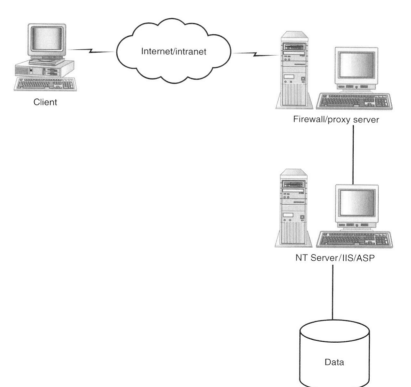

Client

Internet/intranet

Firewall/proxy server

NT Server/IIS/ASP

Data

To build the Web page, perform the following tasks:

1. Open a session of any text editor. Notepad will work just fine.

2. Enter the following HTML into the text document:

```
<html>
<body>
<body bgcolor="#000000" text="#FFFFFF">
```

3. Enter the following VBScript into the text document directly beneath the HTML:

```
<SCRIPT LANGUAGE="JavaScript">
<!--
    // These next lines of code executes when the script tag is parsed.
    var Date = new Date()
    var Hours = Date.getHours()
    if (Hours < 12)
        document.write("Buenos Dias !")
    else
        if (Hours < 17)
            document.write("Buenos Tardes!")
        else
            document.write("Buenos Noches!")
    document.write("<br>Just in case you were wondering, it's " + Date  +
".")
document.write("<br>The background is black. The text is white.")
//-->
</SCRIPT>
```

4. Enter the following HTML into the text, beneath the script:

```
</body>
</html>
```

5. Save the document as My.asp. (Be sure the file hasn't been named My.asp.txt. You can avoid this by choosing Any File as the Save As Type in the Save dialog.)

6. Copy the file to the ASP subdirectory on the server where IIS resides.

7. Open a browser.

8. Choose File, Open to open the ASP file.

9. The browser displays the results My.asp after interpreted and executed by ASP.

Understanding ASP

An approach provided by IIS-compatible Web servers that will appeal to people with HTML and scripting experience is using ASP. ASP is a server-side scripting environment that integrates a set of scriptable objects with HTML, so you can leverage what you already know about creating Web pages. When a browser requests an .asp file from the Web server, ASP parses the requested file from top to bottom, executes any commands, and sends the resulting HTML page to the browser. ASP processes scripting logic server-side, so ASP is a fine cross-browser solution to processing HTML forms on the server. The first release of ASP was with IIS 2.

You can think of ASP as a concept, a product, and an end result. ASP, the product, is an installed component of IIS enabling your Web site for active platform. It ships with IIS, but can be used with Personal Web Server, Peer Web Server, and other IIS-compatible Web servers. ASP, the concept, describes a Web page, perhaps one of many at a site that isn't static. It is active because of the use of scripts, ActiveX components, dynamic HTML, or real-time publishing of database information. ASP, the end result, describes what the users and developers have in a Web site. Users have an interactive site and dynamic content. Developers have an easily maintained site that drives itself by responding to user requests as programmed. In the following section, ASP is addressed. In it you will find a potential-laden tool that will empower you to create interactive Web pages and Web-based applications.

Using ASP

An ASP page is nothing more than an HTML-and-script text file with an ASP file extension. There is nothing to using ASP. ASPs make it easy for HTML authors to activate their Web pages on the server. Customized pages and simple applications can be developed quickly. It's all about using scripts and HTML. ASP works for you, not against you, and doesn't require a lot of direction. After installing ASP, IIS recognizes all HTTP requests for ASP files and processes them server-side.

Part
III

Ch
17

ASP is a high-level component that takes advantage of the scalable, high-performance capabilities of Windows NT Server to provide you with a rich environment for creating server-side Web applications. ASP includes full support for Windows NT Server system services, database access, transaction processing, and messaging queue. In particular, ASP provides support for Active Server Objects, Active Server Scripting, State Management, and Database Connectivity.

ASPs are compatible with any ActiveX scripting language. ASP includes native support for VBScript and JScript, as well as support for third-party languages such as REXX, Perl, and TCL. Multiple scripting languages can even be used interchangeably in the same ASP file. ASP also supports the use of ActiveX components called as objects in an .asp file. ActiveX server components can be created in virtually any language, including Java, VB, C++, COBOL, and more.

▶ For more detailed information on ASP, **see** Chapter 6, "An Inside Look at Active Server Pages and Internet Information Server," **p. 137**

A very important feature of ASPs is the distribution paradigm. Just-in-time compiling automatically recompiles an ASP file upon the next request by a browser. There is no need for manual compilation whenever a change to the page is made. Simply saving the ASP file after your changes are made makes new content available for preview immediately upon the next request.

Getting started with ASP is not complicated. For example, if you acquire Windows NT Server, IIS, ASP, and then whatever you want to use to build the ASP pages (scripts, ActiveX components, HTML, Active Data Objects [ADO], and so on), you have everything you need to do server-side development. IIS is built directly into the Windows NT operating system, and ASP is native to IIS. Thus, it's the best combination to do ASP. Other Web servers, such as WebSite, also support ASP. However, you might find that native features offered and supported by those Web servers work more to your liking than ASP on the same Web server. Deciding to use ASP will probably mean you'll be using it on IIS and Windows NT.

Using the Internet Server API

This section covers the Internet Server Application Programming Interface (ISAPI). Microsoft and Process Server released the ISAPI specification in 1996. From the time of ISAPI's birth, its purpose was to provide the capability to publish dynamic Web content and communications as a competing and improved protocol to the CGI. Microsoft's IIS was released with this interface to enable Web developers to augment the functionality of the Web server to provide dynamic Web content. It can be said that the specification was developed as a means of leveraging the large, talented pool of Windows developers. ISAPI is a standard Internet programming interface to the Win32 platform. For that reason, it became a success. ISAPI was an open specification that enabled vast numbers of developers to create extensions and filters that will run multiple times faster than CGI counterparts.

The predecessor to ISAPI was CGI, created by the lead authors of the earliest Web server. The goal was to enhance Web server functionality with additional useful and necessary capabilities. The idea was that the additional CGI program provided a gateway to information that the server didn't normally process. CGI is discussed in greater detail in the section "Working with CGI."

There are other ways to achieve active content and dynamic Web sites. I have addressed these in the earlier sections that discuss scripting and ASP. ISAPI is a specification that is supported on numerous HTTP servers and isn't tied to a specific platform, although it is inescapably married to IIS. This discussion of ISAPI is to add variety and depth to the topic of creating dynamic Web content using server-side programming. Discussing server-side programming creates natural comparisons of ISAPI to CGI. Those comparisons are emphasized in this chapter.

Specifically, this section refers mainly to ISAPI, with an occasional comparison to Netscape Communication Corporation's Netscape Server Application Program Interface (NSAPI). ISAPI is supported by Microsoft's full line of Web server products including IIS. NSAPI is supported by all Netscape's Web servers (Communications, Commerce, FastTrack and Enterprise) as well as versions 2 and 2.5 of the Netscape Proxy Server. Other HTTP server vendors support one or both of the competing specifications. Table 17.1 lists vendor support for ISAPI extensions and filters.

Table 17.1 Web Server Support of ISAPI

Web Server	Vendor	Extensions	Filters
IIS	Microsoft	Yes	Yes
Peer Web Server	Microsoft	Yes	Yes
Personal Web Server	Microsoft	Yes	Yes
WebSite Pro	O'Reilly	Yes	No
Cyber Presence	Cyber Presence	Yes	No

Web Server	Vendor	Extensions	Filters
Web Commander	Luckman Interactive	Yes	No
Domino	Lotus	No	No
Enterprise Server	Netscape	No	No
Novell Web Server	Novell	No	No
WebStar	StarNine (Quarterdeck)	No	No

Using ISAPI

IIS functions are available to Web developers through ISAPI. There are two good reasons for this implementation:

- The functionality of the Web server software is limited to core competencies.
- The Web server software (hence content) is customizable through the interface.

The creators were right in not building more features into the Web server and instead providing the API. By doing this, they provided the environment for Web developers to create their own scripts that significantly add to the capabilities of a site, while limiting the scope of the server software. This makes improvement of the Web software a more directed affair.

You use ISAPI by creating DLLs in a supported development language. These languages are discussed in more detail later in this chapter. You use the API by declaring and using the helper functions of IIS in your ISAPI DLLs. This is done differently depending on the language chosen to develop the DLL. The library is positioned in a specific directory on the computer hosting the Web server software. When a request is made of the DLL by a browser, the Web server locates the DLL in the directory and loads it into memory. The DLL continues to reside in memory until the Web server is stopped or until the operating system memory manager unloads it.

Why should ISAPI even be considered? This is a good question. A strong case can be made for building a dynamic site of ASP, using a scripting language. One obvious reason is that you can build an ISAPI DLL with powerful programming languages like C++, VB, and Delphi, enjoying the full features these languages provide. Although scripting languages are becoming more sophisticated, they are intended to be light versions of the real thing.

The real answer is that Web site development is preceded with numerous hardware and software considerations. As stated earlier, sometimes there is more freedom and fewer constraints by which to develop a site, and other times there is much less. For example, ISAPI is a Microsoft product, and although other Web server vendors support it, it is only usable on the Windows NT platform. The justification for using one method over another for establishing Web content isn't simply using the latest and greatest tools.

Deciding how to write your system is a function of your requirements and design. More specifically, scalability, portability, time to produce, using current resources, and whether the

Part
III

Ch
17

language has the capability to carry out certain functions all should be paramount in deciding what language or languages to use.

Current resources should be taken into consideration when designing a system. Whether it is with existing software or personnel, the correct design should take these factors into account:

- Personnel—Because there is a great flexibility on how processing can occur on the server, you can base your decisions on what languages to use on the current skill set of the staff. If your current staff includes expert Visual Basic programmers, leverage this ability by using VBScript in your ASP or by writing server-side ActiveX components using Visual Basic. If your staff has been writing JavaScript or JScript in the client-side Web pages, take advantage of this by using JavaScript or server-side Java applets that take advantage of the Java programming language. If the staff has Java experience, maybe they should be using Java on the server.

- Existing software—Using existing software can be key in keeping development costs down and having more rapid development of software. Often, a company has an object that can be used to access data in the database. Typically, the methods to this object are independent of the items in the database so that the same object can be used to access the database via your I-net. This provides several advantages; most importantly, you don't have to rewrite the existing code. Additionally, when you make changes to the database, you will have to change the code in only one place for your entire information system. Separate changes don't need to be made for each system in your organization. Finally, multiple user interfaces can be constructed for various users with the same underlying structure.

N O T E More than just database objects can be reused for I-net purposes. Database objects are ideal for reuse, but other software, such as data processing components, can also be reused. This software can be called from a Web page instead of traditional client software. Other objects share the benefit of using existing code.

- Portability—Portability is an issue that comes up over and over in the corporate computing world. The problem doesn't so much exist on the server side as it does when dealing with client machines. Most corporations have heterogeneous computing environments with multiple desktop environments running on the clients, including Windows, Macintosh, and UNIX-based systems. In the traditional client/server world, creating applications and deploying them on multiple client platforms has always been the biggest obstacle to uniformity of systems within a corporation. The I-net makes it possible, for the first time, to develop applications that can truly be independent of the client machines. By using the client Web browser mechanism and writing applications that take advantage of server-side processing, you can build and deploy applications that can be independent of client-side operating systems.

CAUTION

Keep in mind that client browsers, even though they might support the common mechanisms, are no longer identical in their functionality. Over the years, both Internet Explorer and Navigator have diverged from each other in critical areas such as support for Dynamic HTML and the version of the Java SDK being supported. However, the Web browser still presents the closest thing we have today to a client-independent computing environment.

Proprietary APIs like ISAPI are different from CGI in many ways. These differences lead to some key advantages and disadvantages of using proprietary APIs over CGI.

There are distinct advantages to programming with ISAPI. The biggest advantages are the speed and fewer resources required. Because APIs spawn new threads instead of new processes, there are significantly fewer loads on the server. The time that it takes to generate a new thread instead of a new process is greatly reduced so that a user has a much greater response time when using this system. The memory manager of the operating system can also unload an ISAPI DLL without direction. This means allocated memory can be reclaimed and used for other purposes. Additionally, ISAPI has the capability to further break down HTTP, so more functionality can be achieved with security validation.

One obvious disadvantage of ISAPI is its proprietary nature. ISAPI is only supported on Windows NT, so you are bound to an operating system. Also, if you decide to switch Web servers entirely, new software needs to be written if the new Web server doesn't support ISAPI. Another less obvious but potential problem is the increased complexity of programming. Multithreaded applications by nature are more difficult to design and harder to debug than single-threaded applications. Also, developers have to deal with cleaning up data in memory.

ISAPI Filters

ISAPI filters are different from ISAPI extensions. An extension is a DLL that is an approach for customizing the interactive capabilities of a Web site. An ISAPI extension is a specification which facilitates passing of data that users send to the back-end programs (n-tier objects) provided on the Web or other server. An ISAPI filter, on the other hand, adds to or changes the default behavior of the Web server.

Here is a common example to illustrate the difference. Suppose that you are running a Web service that enables users to view company announcements and other information. Assume that the information is confidential. You want to do two things for every user visiting the site:

1. Authenticate them as a valid user.
2. Customize the content on the basis of who they are.

You can use an ISAPI filter to handle the authentication tasks. Programmatically, you obtain the user's logon and password from a security logon, validate it, and then map it to a generic logon for the group to which he or she belongs. Using a generic group logon is efficient for handling permissions and access, as well as minimizing the account maintenance. You can use an ISAPI extension to handle the content the user views. On the basis of the generic group account, you publish content that is pertinent and accessible to them as users. This example accentuates the differences between the use of the two types of ISAPI DLLs.

ISAPI Versus Other Proprietary APIs

ISAPI and NSAPI are two competing APIs developed by Microsoft and Netscape respectively. Both APIs are designed to accomplish essentially the same task, enabling developers to write applications that can run on the Web server.

Because they are competing APIs, they accomplish this task in different ways, and are obviously incompatible with each other. As is always the case in such scenarios, the individual APIs work best with the development tools and products from the respective vendor. However, there are some issues you must consider when making a decision about which API to use.

ISAPI is a Microsoft standard that works with Microsoft server products and the Visual Studio development tools. However, it is a Windows NT-only solution that cannot be ported to UNIX or other platforms. NSAPI on the other hand works best with Netscape server products and is available on a multitude of platforms including various flavors of UNIX and Windows NT. ISAPI's strong integration with Microsoft tools gives it a distinct advantage on the Windows NT platform, so if you are developing for a Windows-only environment, ISAPI is probably a more flexible and robust choice.

NSAPI can be written in C and C++, whereas ISAPI can be written in C, C++, and Pascal. Being an API, NSAPI can be used with Visual C++. However, most notable from a Visual Studio perspective is the fact that Visual C++ readily supports ISAPI application development through the use of a wizard. The use of the wizard makes it very easy to get started with building an ISAPI application and provides the initial framework necessary to develop more complex applications.

Working with CGI

Not long ago, the first HTTP or Web server was developed. At the time, the Web server had the capability to publish static HTML pages in response to users visiting the uniform resource locator (URL) of the site. The original developers desired a way to create dynamic, customizable content without muddling with the Web server. An additional specification and protocol was developed because, although only certain features were appropriate to include in the server software, other server functionality was inevitably needed. The CGI was born.

CGI is both a method and a specification. There is a particular specification that must be followed to achieve the method of delivering and using a CGI program. CGI is a specification that enables external programs to communicate and respond to queries from Web clients through the Web server. When a client makes a request to a Web server for a CGI program execution, the Web server locates the CGI program in a predefined path. The Web server executes the CGI program and passes the execution parameters it receives from the client to the CGI program. The request and the accompanying parameters are sent as an HTTP request. The CGI program parses the parameter list, executes the program, compiles the results, and sends them back to the client through the Web server.

CGI programs can be written in a variety of languages, including C, C++, Perl, Pascal, and other nonvisual languages. Absent from this list is VB; remember, the original Web server was developed on a UNIX platform, not Windows. In time, the WinCGI specification was created to enable the growing population of VB developers to create Web server extensions.

Using CGI

CGI's niche is really the UNIX platform, which until relatively recently was the predominant Internet platform. As Windows NT has grown in popularity, however, Web servers have made it their target platform. It would be easy to dismiss CGI as an archaic standard not suitable for future Internet development. In many cases, that would be appropriate. But CGI isn't merit free.

As with any connection method, CGI has its advantages and its disadvantages. There are numerous advantages to using CGI:

- CGI can be developed in virtually any language, either as a compiled program or as a script that has environment variable access and can do input and output with `stdin` and `stdout`.

- Almost all Web server software on the market uses CGI, so it is entirely portable from one server to another.

- Because it is the original way to interface programmatically between a Web browser and server, there is a great amount of existing code written in CGI.

- It is relatively easy to program using CGI compared to the proprietary APIs that have been developed. Single process programs are easier to debug than proprietary APIs.

- The nature of CGI applications enables traditional debugging methods. This means that a CGI application can be debugged like any other application. You don't need any special tricks. Such familiarity enables developers to quickly test and debug their software.

- It is virtually impossible to crash the server that a CGI process is running on; a bad CGI program will just crash the process.

CGI is not without drawbacks. The two key disadvantages of CGI are its performance and security problems:

- When a new client makes a call to the server, a new process is spawned. This means that for each new client there is another process on the server. This causes a heavy load on the server. Good CGI development minimizes the costs associated with the constant spawning that a busy site will encounter. Often times, poor server tuning is mistaken for slow CGI. In general, however, CGI doesn't scale well, especially on the Windows platform.

- CGI lets a client run a process on the Web server outside a firewall. This capability poses serious security problems if the proper precautions aren't taken to prevent it. A user could gain access to an unauthorized part of the system.

Part
III

Ch
17

CGI Solutions

You can develop CGI programs in Visual C++ or Visual Basic. To develop CGI programs in Visual Basic you must use the WinCGI programming interface. It is a mechanism that uses INI files to replicate the `stdin` functionality used by the CGI standard to pass parameters to the program. Selection of the language should be made on the basis of factors such as personnel, software reuse, and timing. Table 17.2 lists options for developing and implementing CGI.

ON THE WEB

Two Web sites with links to a wealth of information on CGI are `http://www.progsource.com/cgi.html` and `http://wdvl.internet.com/Software/CGI/`.

ON THE WEB

You can find information about Web server and platform support for CGI at `http://www.cgvb.com/links/lpage.boa/CGI`.

When a request is made to a CGI program, the Web server passes a filename as a command-line argument. The CGI program takes data from this file to determine what information was requested and where the output should be sent, among other data. This file is a temporary file and is generated for each CGI request. The CGI program then makes necessary computations and returns the appropriate data.

Table 17.2   Web Servers, Interface Options, Languages

Platform	Web Server	Interface Option	Languages (Incomplete)
Windows NT	IIS	ISAPI	VB,C, C++, Pascal
Windows NT	UNIX	WebSite Pro	ISAPI, WSAPI,CGI, VB, C, C++, Pascal, WinCGI, Perl
Windows NT	Web Commander	ISAPI, CGI	VB,C, C++, Pascal, Perl
Windows NT	UNIX	Domino	CGI C, C++, Pascal, Perl
Windows NT	UNIX	Enterprise Server	NSAPI, CGI, C, C++, Pascal
UNIX	Novell Web Server	LCGI	Proprietary language
Macintosh	WebStar	CGI,W*API,	C, C++, Pascal, Perl
UNIX	Apache	CGI	C, C++, Perl

Consider Figure 17.2, depicting the implementation of a CGI program.

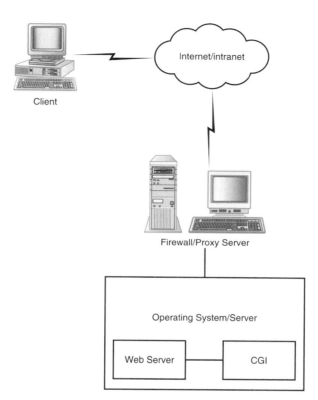

FIGURE 17.2
CGI, the original method for creating dynamic content, runs as a separate process on the server when extending server functionality.

From Here...

This chapter discusses the uses and roles of server-side programming. You have read in-depth information important for making strategic decisions about positioning server-side logic. This chapter also covers various languages and software used for developing server resident programs. For more information on some of the topics addressed here, see the following chapters:

- To obtain help on making partitioning decisions for Web-based applications, see Chapter 15, "Clients, Servers, and Components: Web-Based Applications."

- See Chapter 25, "Clients, Servers, and Components: Design Strategies for Distributed Applications," for an exhaustive look at the aspects of client/server models and considerations in choosing a model.

- For a detailed review of the installation, features, and use of ASP, see Chapter 6, "An Inside Look at Active Server Pages and the Internet Information Server."

Developing Active Content with Visual InterDev

by Azam A. Mirza

In this chapter

Exploring Visual InterDev 6

Microsoft Visual InterDev is a next-generation development tool designed for building dynamic Web applications and enterprisewide Internet and intranet Web sites. Until recently, Web development was predominantly a matter of writing static HTML pages for viewing through a browser; however, the popularity of the Web has created a need for building Web sites and applications that can deliver dynamic and user-specific content.

Visual InterDev leverages the power of two of Microsoft's key Internet technologies to deliver an environment for building dynamic Web sites. It uses the Microsoft Internet Information Server (IIS) as an integral back-end Web server for hosting Web sites. In addition, it uses Active Server Pages (ASP) technology for delivering dynamic Web pages to client browsers.

▶ **See** Chapter 6, "An Inside Look at Active Server Pages and the Internet Information Server," **p. 137**

The Hypertext Markup Language (HTML)- and Hypertext Transfer Protocol (HTTP)-based nature of the Web makes traditional client/server tools less useful for building Web applications. In addition, the HTML interface is not a mature environment and lacks many of the graphical user interface (GUI) features taken for granted when doing client/server development. For example, the standards supported by the various browsers differ widely, with some browsers supporting only Java and others supporting both Java and ActiveX.

ON THE WEB

Netscape Navigator doesn't include native support for displaying ActiveX controls. However, you can access Web sites that use ActiveX controls by downloading the ActiveX plug-in for Netscape, called ScriptActive from NCompass Labs for Windows 95 and Windows NT, from the NCompass Labs Web site at http://www.ncompasslabs.com/.

A critical component of dynamic Web-application development is database connectivity. A truly dynamic Web site is invariably dependent on a back-end database to provide the content. The Web environment presents interesting twists and challenges to maintaining database connections and providing users access to pertinent data.

Microsoft Visual InterDev was designed to address these issues and various others when tackling Web application development. It provides a mating of traditional client/server development methodologies, tools with Web-based technologies, and tools for building robust Web applications.

N O T E To use Visual InterDev, you must be using IIS with ASP and the Microsoft FrontPage Server Extensions. Visual InterDev needs FrontPage Server Extensions to communicate with the Web server. IIS3 is shipped as part of the Windows NT Server Pack 3 and IIS4 is shipped as part of the Windows NT Option Pack. Both IIS versions include ASP code. FrontPage Server Extensions can be found with the Windows NT Option Pack as well. ▨

Migrating from Visual InterDev 1 to Visual InterDev 6

Visual InterDev 6 is the latest incarnation of the popular Web development tool from Microsoft. Visual InterDev 6 includes many enhancements over the previous version. If you have been working with Visual InterDev 1, the move to the new version will be seamless. Version 6 is backward compatible and you can use it to open Web sites and Web projects that were created with the previous version. However, there are a number of changes and enhancements that make it wise to migrate your projects to the new version. This section highlights these changes and how you can take advantage of the new features.

Server Extensions and IIS 4

Visual InterDev 6 includes a new version of FrontPage Server Extensions. These extensions are required to take advantage of the new features and are installed as part of the Visual InterDev install process. In addition, the new server extensions are backward compatible, so you can continue to use your existing Web projects.

The server extensions provide support for a lot of new features, including the following:

- The new scripting object model
- The new data environment
- Design-time controls
- Data commands

All the previously mentioned features are discussed in the following sections, except design-time controls, which are discussed in detail in Chapter 20, "Visual InterDev Design-Time Controls."

Part III
Ch 18

Internet Information Server 4

Visual InterDev 6 includes support for debugging your Web applications. However, to take advantage of the debugging capabilities of Visual InterDev, you must install IIS 4, which is included with Visual InterDev and is also available as part of the Windows NT Option Pack. The debugger provides support for debugging VBScript, JScript and applications written in Java.

Database Connectivity

The database connectivity mechanisms in Visual InterDev 6 have changed considerably from the previous version. In Visual InterDev 1, the database connection was identified by session variables in the Global.asa file. You can view your database connections by opening the Globalasa file.

▶ **See** "Understanding the Global.asa File," **p. 554**

In Visual InterDev 6, the same database connections are now defined by the application variables and are stored in the same Global.asa file. In addition, you can use the Data Environment to add, delete, view and modify your data connections.

▶ **See** "Looking at the Data Environment," **p. 560**

If you are converting a Visual InterDev 1 project to 6 and it includes data connections, those data connections are automatically converted to application variables from session variables. However, the session variables are not deleted from the Global.asa file; they are maintained for backward compatibility with Visual InterDev 1. When you open your project in Visual InterDev 6, it uses the application variables and ignores the session variables, and Visual InterDev 1 does the opposite.

Design-Time Controls Differences

Visual InterDev 6 provides a richer, faster, and more robust environment for creating Web applications, and design-time controls (DTCs) are the main reason. Visual InterDev 6 includes a new version of these DTCs that include major enhancements over their older counterparts. The new DTCs support a full programming model that is exposed to the developer for building robust Web applications. Visual InterDev developers are no longer just restricted to embedded scripts for adding program logic.

▶ **See** Chapter 20, "Visual InterDev Design-Time Controls," **p. 575**

Version 1 DTCs will continue to function in version 6. However, the approach to using DTCs has changed with the new Visual InterDev product. In addition, the controls included with this version of Visual InterDev allow you to develop applications that target any number of Web browsers or you can take advantage of the dynamic HTML programming model included with Internet Explorer 4.

Looking at the Visual InterDev Integrated Development Environment

Microsoft Visual InterDev uses a completely new and richer Integrated Development Environment (IDE) that it shares with Visual J++. The new IDE has several important new features that make it ideal for Web development.

The most important enhancement in the IDE is the inclusion of a graphical editor that allows you to build your Web pages in a WYSIWYG environment. Figure 18.1 shows the new IDE with some of the new features highlighted.

▶ **See** Chapter 2, "Using Visual Studio to Create Applications," **p. 31**

When using the new IDE for building Web applications, the developer is actually working against a live Web site. During development, the parts of the Web site being modified are copied to the local developer workstation. When the developer has finished making modifications, Visual InterDev automatically uploads the latest versions of the modified files to the Web server. However, the new Visual InterDev also includes a local mode that allows the developer to work on his own machine without maintaining a connection to the Web servers.

Toolbox   Editor   Project Explorer   Properties window

FIGURE 18.1
The Visual InterDev IDE
allows developers to
build Web pages using
WYSIWYG tools.

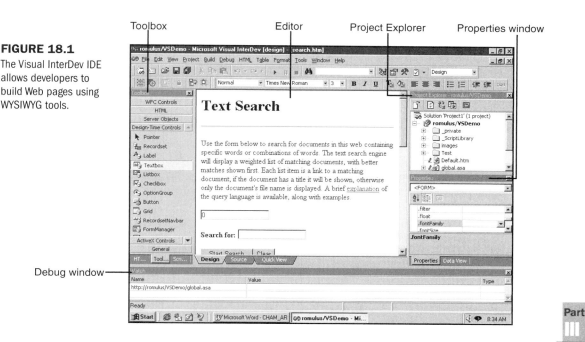

Debug window

N O T E   Typically, developers work against a Web server that acts as the staging server for Visual InterDev development. A *staging server* is analogous to a development machine that is used to develop, debug, and test Web sites before moving the content to a production server. As content is developed, it can be uploaded to the staging Web server and debugged for errors during the development process.

After a Web site has been fully developed and debugged, it can be moved to the production server for use. Visual InterDev provides a simple and powerful mechanism for moving a Web site from the development stage to the production stage.

   Visual InterDev includes a unique and powerful mechanism for graphically displaying the topology of a Web site called the Link View. From the Tools menu, select View Links on the World Wide Web and provide the uniform resource locator (URL) of a Web site to explore its topology.

▶ **See** "Managing Visual InterDev Projects," **p. 570**

The following sections highlight the key features of Visual InterDev that are used to build powerful, dynamic, database-enabled Web applications and sites.

Working with Projects

When working within the Visual InterDev IDE, developers work in the context of a solution. A solution is the hosting place for various Visual InterDev and Visual J++ projects. A developer can have any number of projects open within a solution, depending on the amount of memory available on the machine.

The first step in creating a Web site is to create the project that will host the Web site. A solution within Visual InterDev IDE hosts the project. You can have multiple projects within a solution; however, only one project can be the active project at any given time.

TIP The IDE can host Visual J++ and Visual InterDev projects within the same workspace, thus enabling developers to work on a Java applet in Visual J++ at the same time as they work on a Web site in Visual InterDev. The developers can develop the components and test them on the Web site from within a single IDE. Visual InterDev can then be integrated with Visual SourceSafe to facilitate and organize the development of the solution by the whole team.

To create a project in Visual InterDev, perform the following steps:

1. Select New Project from the File menu. The New dialog box appears, as shown in Figure 18.2.

FIGURE 18.2

The New Project dialog provides a central means to create a host of projects in Visual InterDev and Visual J++.

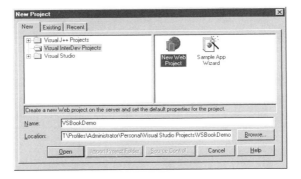

2. Click the Visual InterDev Projects folder and select one of the available project options from the right hand pane. Select the project type you want to create. For creating Web sites, you can choose the Web Project Wizard or the Sample App Wizard.

N O T E The New Web Project enables you to generate a skeleton Web site that you can work from. The Sample App Wizard is geared towards installing one of the sample applications that come with Visual InterDev.

N O T E Because Visual J++ shares the Visual InterDev IDE, the New dialog box also displays possible choices for the Visual J++ environment. Select the appropriate choice from the displayed list.

3. Enter a name for the project you are creating. The Location box automatically updates to display the location where the project will be created. By default, on a Windows NT machine, Visual InterDev stores all workspaces in the directory

<systemroot>\Profiles\<username>\Personal\Visual Studio Projects\ on the local workstation and in the \inetpub\wwwroot\ directory on the server. You can opt to create the project in a new solution or choose to add to current solution.

CAUTION

Make sure that the project name you provide is unique because the system will attempt to create a directory with that name in the default location for creating Visual InterDev projects. Alternatively, you can provide a different location for creating the project.

---

4. Click OK to create the new project. The Visual InterDev IDE updates to display the newly created project.

After you click the OK button on the New dialog box, the Project Wizard starts. The following section discusses the various Visual InterDev project wizards in greater detail.

Project Wizards

By using the project wizards, you get a head start on your Web-development efforts. The wizards are included primarily to provide a starting point and to automate some of the more mundane tasks involved with developing Web applications within Visual InterDev.

 TIP Although it is possible to create a site manually, using one of the wizards as a starting point and then working from the files it creates is a lot faster.

The next two sections discuss the available wizards.

New Web Project Wizard You can use the New Web Project Wizard to create a simple startup Web site. By default, the project created with this wizard will be stored in the publishing root directory of your Web server at \inetpub\wwwroot\<project name> directory.

You can start the New Web Project Wizard by using the steps outlined in the "Working with Projects" section earlier in this chapter and selecting the New Web Project from the project list in the New dialog box. After the Web Project Wizard starts, follow these steps:

1. Provide the name of the Web server this Web project will be connected to, as shown in Figure 18.3. The wizard tries to locate the Web server when you click the Next button.

NOTE The master mode and local mode options, located on the Project Wizard's Web server selection page, allow you to work with a Web server or work independently on your own machine and then manually transfer your files to the Web server.

2. The Specify Your Web dialog box appears, as shown in Figure 18.4. Select the appropriate option for creating a new Web by providing a name for the Web project in the appropriate text box. Click Next to continue.

Part III
Ch 18

FIGURE 18.3
The Specify a Server and Mode dialog box is used to specify a Web server that hosts the project being created by the Web Project Wizard.

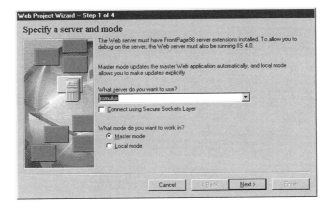

FIGURE 18.4
The Specify Your Web dialog box is used to create a new Web or to connect to an existing Web site for making modifications and changes.

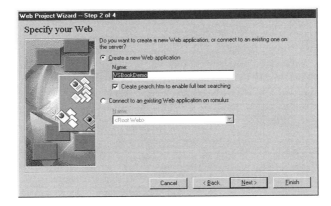

3. The Apply a Layout dialog box appears as shown in Figure 18.5. Layouts provide a means for you to place navigation bars on your Web pages for navigating around your Web site. You can choose a layout from the predefined choices now or add one later. Click Next to continue.

FIGURE 18.5
Layouts provide an easy means of adding standard navigation buttons to your Web pages.

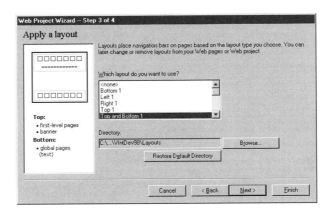

4. The Apply a Theme dialog box appears as shown in Figure 18.6. Themes allow you to provide a consistent look and feel for your Web pages.

FIGURE 18.6

Themes are based on cascading style sheets that can be modified centrally and the changes are applied throughout the Web site.

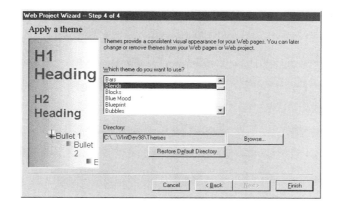

5. Click Finish to create the Web site.

At this point you are ready to start working with your Web site project and add additional files as needed. The search.htm file provides basic functionality for doing full text searches of HTML files within a Web site. First you can customize your home page to suit your needs and then add additional HTML pages that can be accessed from hyperlinks on your home page.

Sample Application Wizard   The Sample Application Wizard provides a convenient mechanism for installing Visual InterDev sample applications provided by Microsoft on the Visual InterDev CD-ROM or on the Microsoft Web site.

To install applications by using the Sample Applications Wizard, follow these steps:

1. Select New Projects from the Visual InterDev File menu. The New dialog box appears.

2. Select the Visual InterDev Projects folder and then the Sample App Wizard. Provide a name for the sample application and click OK to continue.

3. The Sample Application Wizard starts and displays the dialog box shown in Figure 18.7.

FIGURE 18.7

The Sample Application Wizard can also be used to install third-party Web applications.

4. Select a Visual InterDev sample application to install from the list and click Next to continue.

N O T E The Sample Application Wizard installs all components, such as database tables, needed for installing and running the provided sample Web sites. ▪

5. In the Specify a Web Server dialog box, shown in Figure 18.8, supply a name for the Web server where the application will be hosted and a name for the application itself. The default choices are usually appropriate. Click Next to continue.

FIGURE 18.8

The wizard installs the sample application on the selected Web server, where it becomes part of the specified project solution.

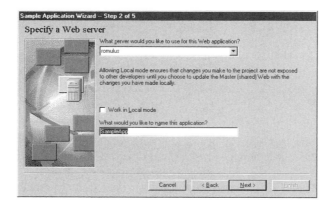

6. If the sample application requires a database, the wizard displays a dialog box for selecting the database, as shown in Figure 18.9. Because the samples being installed can only run using an Access database, the screen displays an Access data source setup option.

FIGURE 18.9

The database list box lists the types of databases that can be used to install the sample application tables.

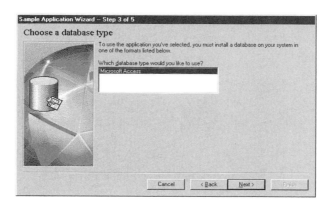

7. Select a shared location where both the Web server and the development clients can access the database, as shown in Figure 18.10. Click Next to continue.

FIGURE 18.10
The shared database directory must reside on a network drive where both the Web server and the development client have access permissions.

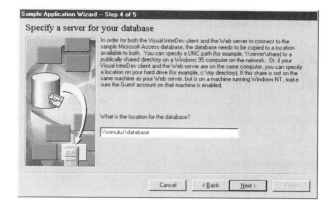

8. Click the Finish button to install the sample application.

To run the sample applications, load the start page in Microsoft Internet Explorer and navigate the application pages.

Adding Content to a Project

After you have created a Visual InterDev project, either manually or by using a wizard, you are ready to add site-specific content to your Web site. The Visual InterDev IDE provides a Windows Explorer-style Project Explorer for navigating through your newly created Web site project. Figure 18.11 shows the Visual InterDev Project Explorer.

FIGURE 18.11
The Project Explorer shows your Web site files and folders in a tree-like structure.

Several methods are available for adding content to a project. The following sections describe each of these methods in detail.

Creating New Files or Folders

Adding new files or folders in Visual InterDev is quite simple. You can create files of various types, including

- Active Server Page—An .asp file that will contain server scripts
- HTML Page—A typical .htm or .html file used by most Web sites
- Style Sheet—For creating cascading style sheets (CSS)
- Text Files—Simple .txt ASCII text files

To create a new file or folder for a project, follow these steps:

1. Select New File from the File menu or right-click the project or folder name and choose New Folder.

N O T E   The New Folder menu option displays a dialog box where you enter the name of the new folder.

 T I P   You can create a new folder as a subfolder of an existing folder by right-clicking that existing folder and selecting New Folder.

2. If you are creating a new file, the New dialog box will be displayed. Select a File type from the available options and provide a name for the file in the text box.
3. Click the Add to Project check box to add the file to the current project or to a different project.
4. Specify a path to the file location if it is different from the default path displayed.
5. Click OK to create a new file and add it to the root level of the project.

 T I P   After a file is created, you can move it to a subfolder within the project by dragging and dropping it on the intended destination folder.

Adding Existing Files or Folders to a Project

To add an existing file to a Visual InterDev project, follow these steps:

1. From the Project Explorer, right-click the project name or folder to which you want to add the file or folder. Figure 18.12 shows the shortcut menu that pops up.
2. Select Add from the menu.
3. You can add a new file at this time or select a file or set of files from the Add Item dialog box, as shown in Figure 18.13. Click OK to continue.

FIGURE 18.12
The right-click shortcut menu provides access to the most commonly used Visual InterDev commands.

FIGURE 18.13
The Add Item dialog box allows you to add files, folders, images or any other item to your project.

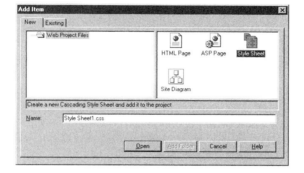

To add an existing folder to a project, follow these steps:

1. From the Project Explorer, right-click the project name or folder to which you want to add the folder.

2. From the shortcut menu, select Add, Add Items.

3. From the ensuing dialog box, select the existing tab and select the folder to add. The contents of the folder are added to the project or folder you selected in step 1.

Using Drag and Drop

The Project Explorer supports full drag-and-drop capabilities. To add files or folders through drag and drop, follow these steps:

1. Click a folder or file in the Windows Explorer and drag it to the Project Explorer in Visual InterDev.

2. Drop the file or folder at the location where you want to add it, and the file or folder is added to the project.

N O T E   The drag-and-drop process copies the files to the Web server and creates a working copy
on the local workstation. ▣

Using Server-Side ActiveX Components

Visual InterDev includes a facility for using ActiveX components in the server environment.
These are ActiveX components that execute on the server and provide a means to integrate
Web applications with traditional client/server applications. Server-side ActiveX components
are used by the Active Server scripting mechanism to provide productivity gains by encapsulating business rules into components.

▶ **See** Chapter 17, "Server-Side Programming," **p. 501**

N O T E   An ActiveX Server component is nothing more than an OLE Automation Server that can be
created by using any tool that supports OLE Automation Server creation. Such tools include
Visual C++, Visual Basic, Visual J++, Delphi, and PowerBuilder. ▣

One of the most important benefits of server-side ActiveX components is their capability to
provide a wrapper mechanism around existing legacy and client/server applications. ActiveX
server components are most easily created with tools such as Visual Basic. The components
can be used in Visual InterDev to integrate into a Web application.

N O T E   An ActiveX server component is distinct from an ActiveX client component in that it doesn't
include any GUI elements. ▣

ActiveX servers provide a reuse mechanism for commonly used code. A variety of applications
and tools are coming out that provide support for ActiveX server components by exposing their
properties and methods as packaged components.

Using ActiveX Server Components in Visual InterDev

Visual InterDev provides scripting support for creating and instantiating ActiveX server components as part of Active Server Page scripts. The sample code in Listing 18.1 uses a server-side
component called `UserInfo` to display information from a database about the user connected to
the Web server.

Listing 18.1   ARLST01.TXT—`UserInfo` Displays Information from a Database

```
Dim UserInformation
Set UserInf = Server.CreateObject("UserInfo.UserInfo")
If Not UserInf.Status Then
     display error code and exit
Else
Set UserInformation = UserInf.GetUserInformation
Response.write UserInformation.FirstName & " "&
➥UserInformation.LastName
End If
```

The preceding sample code performs a variety of tasks through the use of the UserInfo ActiveX server component. The `CreateObject` method instantiated the `UserInfo` object and establishes a connection to the database that is verified by the Status property being set to `True`. After a user connects to the server, the `GetUserInformation` method obtains the user info from the database and displays it by using the `Response` object to write the results to the client.

▶ **See** Chapter 12, "Creating ActiveX Controls with Visual Basic," **p. 337**

▶ **See** "The ClientCertificate Collection," **p. 161**

Distributing Components Using DCOM

The DCOM specification provides mechanisms for distributing objects across the network on different machines. This is a powerful concept that enables you to run your ActiveX components on machines other than the Web server, possibly because the ActiveX server component is nothing more than an OLE Automation Server.

DCOM provides a powerful means of distributing load and processing power across multiple machines within an enterprise; however, the utility (dcomcfg.exe) used to distribute ActiveX server components over different machines can only do this for out-of-process servers.

N O T E The ASP must be enabled to use out-of-process components by setting the following registry key to 1:

HKEY_LOCAL_MACHINE\SYSTEM\CurrentControlSet\Services\W3SVC\ASP\Parameters\AllowOutOfProcCmpnts

You can use regedt32.exe to change the registry setting manually. ▨

A more powerful method of distributing server components is to leverage the power of the Microsoft Transaction Server for distributing in-process and out-of-process server components.

▶ **See** Chapter 31, "Using Microsoft Transaction Server to Enable Distributed Applications," **p. 899**

ActiveX Server Components Included with Visual InterDev

Microsoft supplies prebuilt ActiveX server components with Visual InterDev to accomplish some common and frequently used tasks. These include

- ▨ Advertisement Rotator
- ▨ Browser Capabilities
- ▨ TextStream
- ▨ Content Linking

There are other server objects included with Visual InterDev, such as the ADO objects. These are discussed in other parts of the book. The components that relate only to building Web sites using Visual InterDev are described in further detail in the following sections.

Advertisement Rotator The Advertisement Rotator component automatically cycles through advertisements displayed on a page based on a predetermined sequence. The main purpose of the Advertisement Rotator component is to provide a mechanism for Web sites to display advertisements for revenue generation.

The Advertisement Rotator component uses the Rotator Schedule File to determine the sequence and schedule for displaying various advertisements. The component uses the following files for implementing its functionality:

- Adrot.dll—The Advertisement Rotator Component file, which can be found in the <systemroot>\system32\inetsrv directory.
- Redirection file—An optional ASCII text file used to implement redirection of users to Advertiser sites. It also records the number of users who click an advertisement.
- Rotator Schedule file—An ASCII text file that contains the display schedule for advertisements and how long each advertisement will be displayed. This is a required file that must be present in the specified virtual directory on the server. Refer to the Visual InterDev documentation for the properties and methods supported by the Rotator Schedule file.

The Advertisement Rotator component supports the following properties and methods:

- `Border`—Property that specifies the border size around an advertisement
- `Clickable`—Property that specifies whether an advertisement is a clickable hyperlink
- `TargetFrame`—Property that specifies the target frame that will be used to display the advertisement
- `GetAdvertisement`—Method that determines the next advertisement to display, gets the information from the associated Rotator Schedule File, and formats it as HTML

The code sample in Listing 18.2 shows how the preceding methods can be used to display an advertisement on a Web page.

Listing 18.2   ARLST02.TXT—Displaying an Advertisement on a Web Page

```
<% Set ad = Server.CreateObject("MSWC.AdRotator")
ad.Border(0)
ad.Clickable(FALSE)
ad.TargetFrame(Frame1)
%>
<%
ad.GetAdvertisement("/scripts/adrot.txt")
%>
```

The preceding code sample sets the advertisement properties and then displays the advertisement, using the `GetAdvertisement` method.

Browser Capabilities The Browser Capabilities component provides information on the features supported by a client browser. By knowing the capabilities of a user's browser, developers can tailor their HTML content to more closely match the browser's feature set.

ASP provides a file called browscap.ini, which includes information about the capabilities of various browsers. When a browser requests a page from a Web server, the HTTP header sent by the browser also includes information about itself. The Browser Capabilities component then compares the information in the HTTP header against the browscap.ini file and sends the information to the server.

N O T E The browscap.ini file is located in the <systemroot>\system32\inetsrv\ directory. The browscap.dll component file also resides in the same directory. ▪

The format of the `browscap.ini` file is similar to any other `.INI` files included with Windows. The file includes separate sections for various browsers, which define the properties of the respective browsers. Listing 18.3 shows a few sections of the `browscap.ini` file.

Listing 18.3   ARLST03.TXT—Some Sections of the `browscap.ini` File

```
;;;;;;;;;;;;;;;;;;;;;;;;;
;;; Microsoft Browsers ;;;
;;;;;;;;;;;;;;;;;;;;;;;;;

[Microsoft Internet Explorer/4.40.308 (Windows 95) ]
browser=IE
version=1.0
majorver=#1
minorver=#0
frames=FALSE
tables=FALSE
cookies=FALSE
backgroundsounds=FALSE
vbscript=FALSE
javascript=FALSE
javaapplets=FALSE
platform=Windows95

[IE 1.5]
browser=IE
version=1.5
majorver=#1
minorver=#5
frames=FALSE
tables=TRUE
cookies=TRUE
backgroundsounds=FALSE
vbscript=FALSE
javascript=FALSE
javaapplets=FALSE
beta=False
Win16=False

[Mozilla/1.22 (compatible; MSIE 1.5; Windows NT)]
parent=IE 1.5
platform=WinNT
```

Part
III

Ch
18

continues

Listing 18.3   Continued

```
[Mozilla/1.22 (compatible; MSIE 1.5; Windows 95)]
parent=IE 1.5
platform=Win95

;;ie 2.0
[IE 2.0]
browser=IE
version=2.0
majorver=#2
minorver=#0
frames=FALSE
tables=TRUE
cookies=TRUE
backgroundsounds=TRUE
vbscript=FALSE
javascript=FALSE
javaapplets=FALSE
beta=False
Win16=False
```

The Browser Capabilities component can be used in an ASP file to determine the capabilities of a browser, as shown in Listing 18.4.

Listing 18.4   ARLST04.TXT—Determining Browser Capabilities Using an ASP File

```
<%@ LANGUAGE="VBSCRIPT" %>
<HTML>
<HEAD>
<META NAME="GENERATOR" Content="Microsoft Visual InterDev 1.0">
<META HTTP-EQUIV="Content-Type" content="text/html;
➥charset=iso-8859-1">
<TITLE>Document Title</TITLE>
</HEAD>
<BODY>
<%Set brows = Server.CreateObject("MSWC.BrowserType")%>
Browser <%= brows.browser%>
Version <%=brows.version%>
</BODY>
</HTML>
```

The preceding code sample instantiated a Browser Capabilities object and uses some of its properties to determine the browser name and version information.

N O T E The Browser Capabilities component doesn't have any methods associated with it. ▪

TextStream   The TextStream component, together with the FileSystem object, is used to create, open, read, and write to text files. The FileSystem object is used for the simple purpose of creating and opening text files. It has no properties and includes two methods:

- `CreateTextFile`—Creates a text file with the specified filename
- `OpenTextFile`—Opens a text file with the specified filename

The following code illustrates the use of a `FileSystem` object:

```
Set FSO = Server.CreateObject("Scripting.FileSystemObject")
Set txtfile = FSO.CreateTextFile("c:\test.txt", True)
txtfile.WriteLine("This is a test.")
txtfile.Close
```

In the preceding sample, the `CreateObject` method creates a `FileSystem` object. The `FileSystem` object's `CreateTextFile` method is then used to instantiate a `TextStream` object. The `TextStream` object uses the `WriteLine` and `Close` methods to write to the text file.

The `TextStream` object has the following properties and methods:

- `AtEndOfLine`—Property returns `True` if the file pointer is at the end of a line. This property is read-only.
- `AtEndOfStream`—Property returns `True` if the file pointer is at the end of a TextStream file. This property is read-only.
- `Column`—Property that returns the column number of the current character in a TextStream file. This property is read-only.
- `Line`—Property that returns the current line number in a TextStream file. This property is read-only.
- `Close`—This method closes a TextStream file.
- `Read`—This method reads a specified number of characters from a TextStream file.
- `ReadAll`—This method reads a TextStream file from start to finish and returns it as a string.
- `ReadLine`—This method reads an entire line except for the newline character from a TextStream file.
- `Skip`—This method skips over a specified number of characters when reading a TextStream file.
- `SkipLine`—This method skips an entire line when reading a TextStream file.
- `Write`—This method writes the specified string to the TextStream file.
- `WriteLine`—This method writes a specified string and a newline character to a TextStream file.
- `WriteBlankLines`—This method writes a specified number of newline characters to a TextStream file.

Part

III

Ch

18

Content Linking   The Content Linking component provides a mechanism for creating a table of contents for your Web site. It accomplishes this task by using a Content Linking list file. The Content Linking list file is a simple ASCII text file that includes entries for page URLs and their descriptions.

A sample Content Linking list file is presented in the following:

```
—LINKLIST.TXT—
default.htm   Home Page
about.htm   About the Company
Marketing.htm   Marketing Department Web Page
Acct.htm   Accounting Department Web Page
```

The Content Linking component supports the following methods:

- ■ GetListCount—Counts the total number of items in the Content Linking list file

- ■ GetNextURL—Gets the URL of the next page listed in the Content Linking list file

- ■ GetPreviousDescription—Gets the description line of the previous page listed in the Content Linking list file

- ■ GetListIndex—Returns the index of the current page in the Content Linking list file

- ■ GetNthDescription—Gets the description of the Nth page listed in the Content Linking list file

- ■ GetPreviousURL—Gets the URL of the previous pages listed in the Content Linking list file

- ■ GetNextDescription—Gets the description of the next page listed in the Content Linking list file

- ■ GetNthURL—Gets the URL of the Nth page listed in the Content Linking list file

The example in Listing 18.5 demonstrates the building of a table of contents, based on a Content Linking list file named linklist.txt in the /scripts virtual directory.

Listing 18.5   ARLST05.TXT—Using linklist.txt to Build a Table of Contents

```
<%@ LANGUAGE="VBSCRIPT" %>
<HTML>
<HEAD>
<META NAME="GENERATOR" Content="Microsoft Visual InterDev 1.0">
<META HTTP-EQUIV="Content-Type" content="text/html;
➥charset=iso-8859-1">
<TITLE>Document Title</TITLE>
</HEAD>
<BODY>
<% Set CL = Server.CreateObject ("MSWC.NextLink") %>
<% count = CL.GetListCount ("/scripts/linklist.txt") %>
<% I = 1 %>
<ul>
<% Do While (I <= count) %>
<li><a href=" <%= CL.GetNthURL ("/scripts/linklist.txt", I) %> ">
<%= CL.GetNthDescription ("/scripts/linklist.txt", I) %> </a>
<% I = (I + 1) %>
<% Loop %>
</ul>
</BODY>
</HTML>
```

Working with Client-Side Components

Client-side components are ActiveX controls or Java applets that are integrated into an HTML page and downloaded to a client computer before they can be used by the browser. For the client-side component to run in the browser, both the browser and the operating system must support it.

A powerful feature of dynamic Web sites is their capability to incorporate client-side components. An example of client-side components is the use of Java applets or ActiveX controls to perform various tasks such as animations, scrolling marquees, and advertisements. Figure 18.14 illustrates a Web site that uses ActiveX controls to provide highly powerful Web-based application functionality.

FIGURE 18.14
The Microsoft Investor Web site uses client-side ActiveX controls to provide portfolio-tracking functionality.

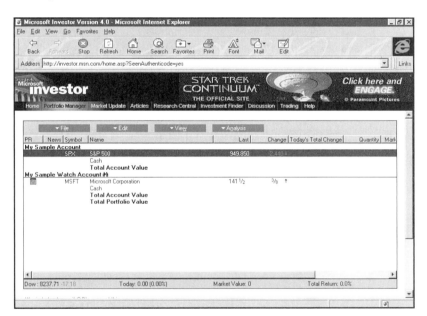

Part
III

Ch
18

Visual InterDev supports two kinds of client-side components:

- ActiveX controls
- Java applets

ON THE WEB

You can download a large number of freeware and shareware ActiveX controls from a variety of Web sites on the Internet. A good place to start is the Microsoft Web site (`http://www.microsoft.com`) or a shareware Web site such as the Cnet's `http://www.shareware.com` or `http://www.download.com/PC/Activex/`.

As previously stated, ActiveX controls are compiled objects that are downloaded to the client machine for execution. For that reason, different versions of compiled ActiveX controls are required for various platforms. Their platform-specific nature enables ActiveX controls to take advantage of operating-system–specific features and capabilities. Most of the ActiveX controls available today are for the 32-bit Windows systems, Windows 95 and Windows NT. These controls can be developed in a variety of languages, such as Visual Basic, Visual C++, and Borland Delphi.

ON THE WEB

To build ActiveX controls for the Macintosh environment, you need to use the Metrowerks Code Warrior SDK, available for the Macintosh environment. For more information, visit http://www.metrowerks.com.

▶ **See** Chapter 12, "Creating ActiveX Controls with Visual Basic," **p. 337**

▶ **See** Chapter 13, "Creating ActiveX Controls with Visual C++," **p. 385**

If you are familiar with Visual Basic Custom Controls (VBXs) or OLE Custom Controls (OCXs), you will have no problem adapting to ActiveX controls. Visual InterDev provides easy mechanisms for incorporating ActiveX controls in your Web applications.

 T I P   Other development environments such as Delphi, PowerBuilder, and Lotus Notes also provide support for using ActiveX controls.

Visual InterDev provides support for using and incorporating client-side components into the Web page. The following sections describe how the Visual InterDev environment can be used to leverage the power of client-side components for building exciting Web sites.

ActiveX Controls in HTML or ASP Pages

ActiveX controls are compiled components that provide specific functionality. Thousands of ActiveX controls for performing a variety of tasks are available for use in application-building tools such as Visual InterDev, Visual Basic, Visual C++, Delphi, PowerBuilder, and many others.

N O T E   Currently, ActiveX controls are supported on the Windows and Macintosh platforms, with support for UNIX slated in the near future. ■

Because ActiveX controls are platform-specific, they aren't portable from environment to environment, and a different compiled version must be supplied for each supported platform. However, the platform dependence allows ActiveX controls to take advantage of platform-specific features and functionality.

Using ActiveX controls in Visual InterDev is very simple and straightforward. To use ActiveX controls on an HTML or ASP page, follow these steps:

1. Open the HTML or ASP page on which the control will be placed.
2. Select the ActiveX Controls tab from the toolbox.
3. Select a control from the list and drag and drop it onto the form in the editor where you want to place it, as shown in Figure 18.15.

FIGURE 18.15
The WYSIWYG editor will display the control in graphical form when it is placed on the Web page.

ActiveX Calendar control

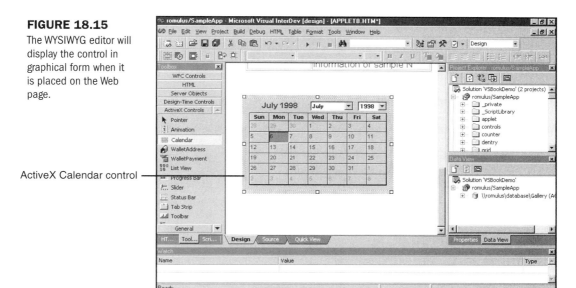

4. Use the properties window to set the properties for the control.

In addition to WYSIWYG development, you can use the source tab on the Visual InterDev editor to view or add ActiveX controls to your Web pages. To do so requires the use of the <OBJECT> tag. The script for the ActiveX control has to be enclosed within the <OBJECT> and </OBJECT> tags and can be scripted in either VBScript or JScript. Figure 18.16 illustrates the script used to insert a sample ActiveX control in an HTML page.

Part
III

Ch
18

FIGURE 18.16

ActiveX controls can be placed anywhere within an HTML page by using the <OBJECT> tag.

ActiveX Calendar control <OBJECT> tag

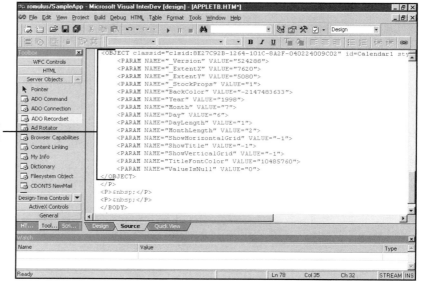

N O T E ActiveX controls are different from Active Server Objects in that they include user interface elements. ■

The syntax of the object tag is as follows:

```
<OBJECT>
ID=identifier
ALIGN=LEFT¦CENTER¦RIGHT
BORDER=n
CLASSID=url
CODEBASE=url
CODETYPE=codetype
DATA=url
DECLARE
HEIGHT=n
HSPACE=n
NAME=url
SHAPES
STANDBY=message
TYPE=type
USEMAP=url
VSPACE=n
WIDTH=n>
```

■ ID—Specifies the name used to identify the ActiveX control, for example, ID="txtName".

■ ALIGN—Specifies the alignment property used to place the control on a page, for example, ALIGN=LEFT.

■ BORDER—Specifies the width of the border if the object is defined to be a hyperlink.

■ CLASSID—Identifies the object implementation through a 128-bit string used by the registry to uniquely identify the object. The syntax depends on the object type: For example, in registered ActiveX controls, the syntax is CLSID:*class-identifier*.

■ CODEBASE—Identifies the code base for the object. The syntax depends on the object.

■ CODETYPE—Specifies the Internet media type for code.

■ DATA—Identifies data for the object. The syntax depends on the object.

■ DECLARE—Declares the object without instantiating it. Use this when creating cross-references to the object later in the document or when using the object as a parameter in another object.

■ HEIGHT—Specifies the height of the object.

■ HSPACE—Specifies the horizontal spacing. This is the space between the object and any text or images to the left or right of the object.

■ NAME—Sets the name of the object when submitted as part of a form.

■ SHAPES—Specifies that the object has shaped hyperlinks. *Shaped hyperlinks* are image areas that are not text-based or do not have a simple rectangular shape.

■ STANDBY—Sets the message to show while the object is being loaded.

■ TYPE—Specifies the Internet media type for data.

■ USEMAP—Specifies the image map to use with the object.

■ VSPACE—Specifies the vertical spacing. This is the space between the object and any text or images above or below the object.

■ WIDTH—Specifies the width of the object.

In addition, you can define and set property settings for ActiveX controls by using the <PARAM> tags within the <OBJECT> and </OBJECT> tags.

The syntax for the <PARAM> tag is as follows:

```
<PARAM NAME=propertyname VALUE=value>
```

■ NAME—Specifies the name of the property to be initialized. For example, most ActiveX controls define a caption property.

■ VALUE—Specifies the value for the property.

You can define as many <PARAM> tags as necessary within the <OBJECT> tags to initialize values for properties. Most properties are optional, however, and don't need to be set in the Web page.

Java Applets

Java applets are programs that can be integrated into HTML pages to provide a variety of functions, including animations, applications, sound, graphics, and audio. Java applets are actual applications written in the Java language, which can be programmed to perform any task imaginable.

▶ **See** Chapter 22, "Creating Applets and Applications with Visual J++," **p. 643**

ON THE WEB

Thousands of Java applets are available as shareware on the Internet. You can use any of these applets as part of your Visual InterDev applications. For more information, visit http://www.javaworld.com.

Java applets are unique in that they are platform independent. Any platform that has a Java virtual machine can run Java applet code with no need to recompile for different platforms.

CAUTION

The platform-independent nature of Java applets makes them unsuitable for utilizing platform-specific functionality. Java applets adhere to the least common denominator philosophy of cross-platform support.

From Here...

In this chapter, you learned about some of the basic features and functionality of Visual InterDev. You learned how to use the Visual InterDev IDE to create projects, how to add content to those projects, and how to use wizards to maximize your efforts. You also learned about using and incorporating server-side and client-side components into your projects.

Refer to the following chapters for information related to building Web sites and Web-based applications using Visual InterDev:

- To learn about Active Server Pages, see Chapter 6, "An Inside Look at Active Server Pages and the Internet Information Server."
- To learn about the advanced features of Visual InterDev, see Chapter 19, "Advanced Visual InterDev Concepts."
- To learn about the Visual Studio development environment, see Chapter 2, "Using Visual Studio to Create Applications."
- To learn about creating ActiveX controls, see Chapter 12, "Creating ActiveX Controls with Visual Basic."
- To learn about creating components with C++, see Chapter 13, "Creating ActiveX Controls with Visual C++."
- To learn about creating components with J++, see Chapter 22, "Creating Applets and Applications Visual J++."
- To learn about the Visual InterDev design-time controls, see Chapter 20, "Visual InterDev Design-Time Controls."

CHAPTER 19

Advanced Visual InterDev Concepts

by Azam A. Mirza

In this chapter

Maximizing Visual InterDev

In Chapter 18, "Developing Active Content with Visual InterDev," you learned about some of the basic features provided by Visual InterDev, and in Chapter 20, "Visual InterDev Design-Time Controls," you will learn about the ActiveX controls that can help you build database-aware Web pages. Now you are ready to learn about some of the exciting advanced features provided by Visual InterDev.

Visual InterDev is designed to be the development tool for building dynamic and powerful Web sites. To accomplish this task, Visual InterDev leverages the power of relational database systems for storing, managing, and producing data to be displayed to users. Most of the world's client/server applications use a database on the back end to provide support for data storage and retrieval, and the dynamic Web world is no different. Visual InterDev includes powerful database connectivity, management, and development tools for building database-aware Web sites.

In this chapter, you will learn about some of these advanced features in greater detail and will also learn how you can leverage the power of Visual InterDev to energize your Web site development effort.

Understanding the Global.asa File

The Global.asa is a special file automatically generated by the Visual InterDev project wizards to hold global functions and variables for the Web application. The Global.asa file is where the Application and Session Object event handlers are stored. Global.asa is also the place where global event handlers for the application are placed. Listing 19.1 lists the bare-bones Global.asa file that is created initially by Visual InterDev if you use the project wizard to create your project.

 T I P The Global.asa file resides in the root directory of your Web application on the Web server.

Listing 19.1   ASLST01.TXT—The Initial Global.asa File

```
<SCRIPT LANGUAGE='VBScript' RUNAT='Server'>

'You can add special event handlers in this file that will get run
'automatically when special Active Server Pages events occur.
'To create these handlers, just create a subroutine with a name
'from the list below that corresponds to the event you want to
'use. For example, to create an event handler for Session_OnStart,
'you would put the following code into this file (without the comments):

'Sub Session_OnStart
'**Put your code here **
'End Sub
```

```
'EventName       Description
'Session_OnStart   Runs the first time a user runs any page in
'your application
'Session_OnEnd     Runs when a user's session times out or quits
'your application
'Application_OnStart  Runs once when the first page of your
'application is run for the first time by any user
'Application_OnEnd   Runs once when the web server shuts down

</SCRIPT>
```

▶ **See** "The Application Object," **p. 152**

▶ **See** "The Session Object," **p. 154**

The Global.asa file is executed whenever a Web application is accessed for the first time and whenever the application ends. The application starts when the first user accesses the application and ends when the last user exits the application. Each individual user access is regarded as an individual session.

N O T E   The Global.asa file isn't displayed to the user. It is a file that is executed on the server without any output being sent to the client browser. ▨

The Global.asa file must be stored in the root directory of the application, and every application can have only one Global.asa file.

In addition, the Global.asa file is used to declare objects that have global scope within the application. Use the <OBJECT> tag to declare objects in the Global.asa file. The syntax for using the <OBJECT> tag in the Global.asa file is

```
<OBJECT RUNAT=Server SCOPE=Scope ID=Identifier
➥{PROGID="progID"¦CLASSID="ClassID"}>
```

- ▨ *Scope*—Identifies the scope of the object. In the context of the Global.asa file, scope is the application or the individual session.

- ▨ *Identifier*—Defines a unique name for the object.

- ▨ *progID*—An identifier associated with the class identifier. The format for *progID* is [Vendor.]Component[.Version].

- ▨ *ClassID*—Specifies a unique OLE object. Either *progID* or *ClassID* must be specified for every object declared.

Listing 19.2 provides an example of an object declaration in the Global.asa file.

Part III

Ch 19

Listing 19.2   ASLST02.TXT—Using Application Object Variables to Store Information

```
<OBJECT RUNAT=Server SCOPE=Application ID=MyConn
PROGID="ADODB.Connection">
</OBJECT>
```

The Global.asa file can also include scripts written in any supported scripting language. To include scripts in the Global.asa file, use the `<SCRIPT>` and `</SCRIPT>` tags. If you include script that isn't enclosed by the script tags, the server generates an error.

One of the major differences in the Global.asa file between the previous version of Visual InterDev and the new version is the way database connections are defined. In the previous version, database connections were defined by `Session` object variables. In the new version, database connections are defined by the `Application` object variables. Listing 19.3 shows the new data connection definition in the Global.asa file.

Listing 19.3   ASLST03.TXT—The `Application` Object is Used to Define a Database Connection and the Data Environment Variable

```
<SCRIPT LANGUAGE=VBScript RUNAT=Server>
Sub Application_OnStart
    '==Visual InterDev Generated - startspan==
    '--Project Data Connection
        Application("VSBookDemo_ConnectionString") =
        ➥"DSN=VSDemo;User Id=sa;PASSWORD=;"
        Application("VSBookDemo_ConnectionTimeout") = 15
        Application("VSBookDemo_CommandTimeout") = 30
        Application("VSBookDemo_CursorLocation") = 3
        Application("VSBookDemo_RuntimeUserName") = "sa"
        Application("VSBookDemo_RuntimePassword") = ""
    '-- Project Data Environment
        Set DE = Server.CreateObject("DERuntime.DERuntime")
        Application("DE") = DE.Load(Server.MapPath("Global.ASA"), "_private/
DataEnvironment/DataEnvironment.asa")
    '==Visual InterDev Generated - endspan==
End Sub
</SCRIPT>
```

▷ For more information about the new features in Visual InterDev 6, **see** Chapter 18, "Developing Active Content with Visual InterDev," **p. 527**

Working with the Scripting Object Model

One of the major enhancements of this version of Visual InterDev is the introduction of a scripting object model, which allows developers to take advantage of object-oriented techniques in building their Web applications.

The Visual InterDev scripting object model defines a set of properties, methods, and events that can be used in conjunction with design-time controls (DTCs) and HTML to build Web pages. You can design your Web pages using HTML and DTCs and then write script for the various page elements to handle interactivity and user responses. It's a very similar concept to writing applications in traditional development tools, such as Visual Basic, using object-oriented techniques.

N O T E The scripting object model is implemented as a set of .asp and .htm files stored in a folder named _ScriptLibrary. The Web project wizard adds this folder to your project. In addition, any time you place a DTC on a page, the scripting object model library is required and is automatically added to your project. Don't change the _ScriptLibrary folder, or its contents, or the scripting object model will cease to function. ▨

The scripting object model adds a great deal of power and flexibility to the Visual InterDev environment. In the past, you had to struggle with HTML and script that was interspersed throughout a page and work with it in a textual context. Now, the combination of the WYSIWYG environment, DTCs, and the scripting object model make it much easier to build Web pages.

The greatest advantage of the scripting object model is the capability to handle generated events by writing script handlers for them. For example, if you have a button on a page, you can handle the button click by writing an `onclick` event handler method. This is a great improvement over the old submit button method, where the user clicked a button, the request was submitted to the Web server, and it sent a response back in the form of another Web page. By using the object model, you can handle the event with a client-side script and eliminate the round-trip overhead.

N O T E Don't confuse the DHTML object model in Internet Explorer with the Visual InterDev object model. In DHTML, a Web page and everything on the page are part of a document object model and can only be accessed by client scripts. However, the Visual InterDev scripting model can be accessed using both client-side and server-side scripts. ▨

▶ **See** Chapter 21, "Dynamic HTML," **p. 601**

Before you can use the scripting object model in your Web page, you must enable it. To do so, complete the following steps:

1. Open the Web page in source view. Right-click on the page, away from any controls or objects. Select Properties from the menu.

2. Figure 19.1 shows the Properties dialog box that appears. On the General tab, click the Enable Scripting Object Model option.

FIGURE 19.1
The Properties dialog box allows you to define scripting platform, language, and ASP settings.

3. Click OK to continue.

4. Visual InterDev adds a metatag to your page that enables the scripting object model for the page, as shown in Figure 19.2.

FIGURE 19.2

The metatag includes the appropriate definition for adding the object model to the page.

Using the scripting object library is quite simple and straightforward. The easiest way to use the object model is to use DTCs to create your Web pages, set their properties, and then write event handlers for the various objects. DTCs are nothing more than a graphical representation of Web elements to ease the development processes. During runtime, the DTCs are converted into textual elements defined by HTML, script, and event handlers.

After you have designed your page using DTCs, writing scripts from them is similar to writing event handlers and functions in a program such as Visual Basic. However, there are a few considerations you need to be aware of that influence how your Web pages will work.

The way you work with the scripting object model depends on the target platform that you will be working with. If you are designing your Web pages for maximum reach and browser independence, you can use the server-side scripting model and ASP pages to take advantage of IIS server objects. However, if you are striving for maximum flexibility and power in your Web applications, you can take advantage of client-side scripting and the DHTML document object model supported by Internet Explorer. The scripting object model extends the DHTML object model.

> **CAUTION**
>
> Where you run your scripts dictates what functions and methods you can and cannot use. For example, if you are writing server-side scripts, do not use functions such as MsgBox. The message box will be displayed on the server and not the user machine.

You can define where a particular script block will run by using the RUNAT attribute of the <SCRIPT> tag, as shown in the following:

```
<SCRIPT RUNAT=Server LANGUAGE="VBScript">
```

If you want the script to run on the client machine, just leave out the RUNAT attribute. Other considerations when switching from client scripts to server scripts include the following:

- In client scripts, you can display messages to the user. However, you cannot use the MsgBox function in server-side scripts. In server-side scripts, you can always use response.write to print a message in a section (such as <DIV></DIV>) that only becomes visible in response to a specific event using client-side scripting to make it visible.

- Client scripts can use the DHTML object model, but server scripts cannot.
- Server scripts must be written in the default scripting language or must include the LANGUAGE attribute in the <SCRIPT> tag.

Using scripting object model methods and properties is very similar to other development environments. You use the familiar dot notation to access properties and methods of objects. For example, if you have dragged a list box design-time control (DTC) onto the page, you can populate it by calling its addItem method, as shown in Listing 19.4.

Listing 19.4 ASLST04.TXT—Using a List Box DTC to Display the List of Department Names in a Web Page

```
<SCRIPT LANGUAGE="VBSCRIPT">
Function LoadListBox()
  ListBox1.additem "Marketing"
  ListBox1.additem "Accounting"
  ListBox1.additem "MIS"
  ListBox1.additem "Purchasing"
End Function
</SCRIPT>
```

Script objects can generate various predefined events. For example, a text box can generate an onchange event when the user enters a value. A button can generate the onclick event when pressed. Listing 19.5 shows an event handler for the onchange event of a text box.

Listing 19.5 ASLST05.TXT—The Input of the txtLogin Field is Saved in a String Variable for Later Use

```
<SCRIPT LANGUAGE="VBScript">
Sub txtLogin_onchange()
  strLogin = txtLogin.value
End Sub
</SCRIPT>
```

TIP Use the Script Outline window to create event handlers. In the Script Outline window, expand the node for the object you are working with, and then double-click the name of the event you want to write a handler for.

N O T E Script object events occur only in response to a user action, not in response to programmatic changes. For example, if you select an item in a list box script object, the onchange event is fired. However, if you change the selection using a script statement, no event is fired.

For a complete reference and samples on the Visual InterDev scripting object model and the properties, methods, and events it exposes, refer to the online documentation for Visual InterDev.

Part
III

Ch
19

Looking at the Data Environment

Visual InterDev 6 introduces a new mechanism for handling database connections and building database-aware Web pages, called the data environment. The *data environment* is actually a repository in your Visual InterDev project that holds the information for connecting to and manipulating databases.

The data environment is exposed as an object in your Web project that can be accessed using script. The data environment object provides a wrapper around the ActiveX Data Objects (ADO), making it easier to work with ADO in your Visual InterDev projects. Within the data environment object, ADO command objects are exposed as methods in script. You can call a command method to execute it and return the recordset referenced by the command or to execute its SQL command or stored procedure.

N O T E   You can only have one data environment in a Visual InterDev project.

The main component of a data environment is the data connection. It defines the connectivity properties for connecting to a database, such as the open database connectivity (ODBC) data source, login ID, and password. To add a data connection to a Web project, complete the following steps:

1. In the project explorer, right-click on the project name or the global.asa file and select Add Data Connection menu option.

2. The Select Data Source dialog box is displayed, as shown in Figure 19.3. Select an existing data source or create a new one and click OK.

FIGURE 19.3

The Select Data Source dialog box displays the ODBC DSNs defined.

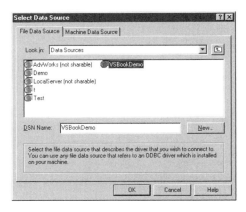

3. A new data connection will be created, and its properties page will be displayed, as shown in Figure 19.4.

FIGURE 19.4

The data connection properties dialog box allows you to customize your newly defined data connection.

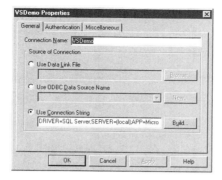

4. Provide an appropriate name for the connection and the source for the connection.
5. The Authentication tab allows you to define design-time and runtime user ID and password information for connecting to the database, as shown in Figure 19.5.

FIGURE 19.5

The Authentication tab allows you to define database login behavior for your connection.

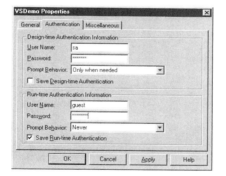

6. The Miscellaneous tab allows you to define timeout values and cursor information, such as client-side or server-side cursors.
7. Click OK and a new data connection will be added to the data environment.

After you have created a data connection, you can add one or more data commands to the data connection. Data commands are similar to the data controls in Visual Basic. They expose a set of data from the database that you can work with. A data command can reference a table, a stored procedure, a view, or a SQL statement. To create a data command object, complete the following steps:

1. Right-click the data connection you added previously and select Add Data Command from the menu. The data command properties dialog box will be displayed, as shown in Figure 19.6.

Part
III

Ch
19

FIGURE 19.6

The data command properties dialog box allows you to customize its properties.

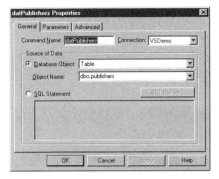

2. On the General tab, provide a name for the data command and select the data connection to use. In addition, specify the source for the data from the drop downs or specify a SQL statement to use.

3. Define any parameters or return values that will be required by your SQL query or stored procedure using the Parameters tab, as shown in Figure 19.7.

FIGURE 19.7

Input parameters required for a stored procedure will be automatically displayed on the Parameters tab.

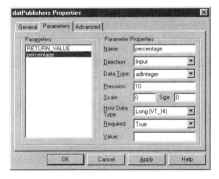

4. The Advanced tab allows you to set values for the recordset type, the number of records to retrieve at a time, and the timeout values, as shown in Figure 19.8.

FIGURE 19.8

The Advanced tab can be used to specify recordset cursor type, lock type, and whether the cursor is server side or client side.

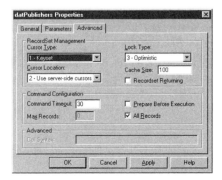

5. Click OK to continue and a new command object will be created in your project.

N O T E You can add as many data commands as you want under a single data connection.

To verify that the data command works as expected, double-click the data command in the project explorer, and Visual InterDev will execute the data command and display the results as shown in Figure 19.9.

FIGURE 19.9

The data results pane is a live view of the data that can be used to add, delete, and modify values in the database.

To use your data command object in a Web page, drag and drop the data command from the project explorer into the page where you want it to appear. A recordset DTC will be automatically added to the page, as shown in Figure 19.10.

FIGURE 19.10

A recordset DTC is required to use a data command in a Web page.

You can now drag and drop fields from the data command in the project explorer on the Web page, and Visual InterDev will create the appropriate text boxes, yes/no fields, and option buttons that are bound to the data in the database. Figure 19.11 shows a page, under construction, based on the data command object created earlier that is tied to the publisher's table in the sample pubs database on a SQL Server database.

To provide navigation capabilities for your records, drag and drop the RecordsetNavbar control from the DTC toolbox onto your page and set its recordset property to the recordset object you created earlier. By default, the RecordsetNavbar control provides Move to First, Next, Previous, and Move to Last buttons. You can use these buttons to move among the records displayed on the page. You can also customize the functionality of these buttons by modifying the script they create.

FIGURE 19.11
The text box DTCs are automatically bound to the fields in the database when the fields are dragged and dropped from the project explorer.

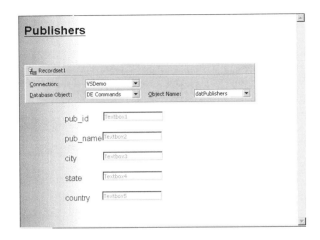

The data environment provides a very powerful and flexible method of creating database-aware Web pages. The capability to create data-aware Web pages with point-and-click functionality is a very strong feature of Visual InterDev 6 and really brings the product to a new level of sophistication and ease of development.

Using the Visual Database Development Tools

Visual InterDev provides strong support for building applications that rely on relational databases to provide interactivity and dynamic content. For that reason, Visual InterDev provides tools and features not only for developing database-enabled Web applications, but also for managing back-end databases.

Visual InterDev database features include the following:

- Support for creating and managing ODBC data sources
- Support for database connectivity by using ODBC in Web applications
- Visual tools for managing data directly by using the Visual InterDev IDE Data View
- Support for design-time ActiveX controls for building data-aware Web applications
- Advanced query designer for building complex database queries

▶ **See** Chapter 20, "Visual InterDev Design-Time Controls," **p. 575**

The tools for core database management and development functionality provided by Visual InterDev are referred to as the Microsoft Visual Database Tools. The Visual Database Tools are not exclusive to Visual InterDev and are shared across other Visual Studio development tools, such as Visual C++ Enterprise Edition and Visual Basic Enterprise Edition. The database tools within Visual Studio, however, are based on ODBC connectivity to the database, and you must have ODBC-compliant drivers available for the database you are trying to use, such as Microsoft SQL Server, Microsoft Access, or Oracle databases. The Visual Development tools include the following:

- Data View—Provides a view into the currently selected database
- Database Designer—A designer for creating, managing, and administering ODBC-compliant databases
- Query/View Designer—Used for building SQL queries to be used in database applications

The following sections discuss these features of the Visual Database Tools in more detail, including database connectivity using ODBC.

Using ODBC Data Sources

An ODBC data source defines how an application connects to a back-end database. Visual InterDev includes support for the ODBC 3.5 database connectivity tools. ODBC services are provided by a driver supplied by the database manufacturer or a third-party vendor. ODBC provides connectivity for both client/server databases, such as SQL Server, and shared file databases, such as Microsoft Access.

> **N O T E**   Visual InterDev includes ODBC drivers for Microsoft Access, FoxPro, SQL Server, and Oracle. Other database drivers are available through third-party developers.

The ODBC driver provides a logical software connection to the database and uses a defined data source to determine the location of the database, how to connect to it, the login information, and the parameters common to all query operations. ODBC 3.5 supports two kinds of database connections:

- Registry DSN—The method of storing database information in the system registry under user and system Data Source Names (DSNs)
- File DSN—The new method of storing data sources as text files, referred to as the file DSN

Both methods provide the same functionality; however, registry-based DSNs are machine specific, whereas file-based DSNs can be shared across multiple machines. The file DSNs provide a very useful method for sharing DSNs across an enterprise by saving the DSN files on a shared network drive.

It is possible to create ODBC DSNs through the Visual InterDev development environment; however, it is important to remember that both the Web server and the Visual InterDev development workstation need an ODBC DSN to connect to the database. The Web server needs the DSN to provide runtime access to the database while users are browsing the Web site. The development workstation needs the DSN for connectivity to the database during development and testing.

T I P   It is a good idea to use file DSNs and store them on a shared directory on the Web server to provide access to these file DSNs from the development workstations.

To set up a shared ODBC file DSN on the Web server, take the following steps:

1. Log on to the Web server and start the ODBC Administrator utility from the Control Panel.

Part

III

Ch

19

2. Choose the File DSN tab and click A<u>d</u>d to start the New Data Source Wizard.

3. From the list of database drivers, choose the driver for which you want to create the DSN and click Next.

4. Provide a name for the data source and then click Next. Make sure that you provide a full UNC path (\\servername\sharename\dsnname) to the DSN file location on a shared drive on the Web server.

N O T E   A UNC (Universal Naming Convention) path refers to a network location using the server name and directory tree, for example, \\MyServer\MyDirectory\MySubDirectory. ▪

5. Click the Finish button to close the New Data Source Wizard.

6. If the DSN you have set up requires additional information, a dialog box is displayed, as shown in Figure 19.12.

FIGURE 19.12

The Create a New Data Source to SQL Server dialog box is displayed to obtain connectivity information for the DSN.

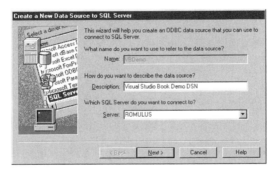

7. Provide the connectivity information on the next few dialogs and click OK to return to the ODBC Administrator utility.

8. Click OK to close the ODBC Administrator utility.

Now that you have added an ODBC DSN, you can use that DSN to add database connections within your Visual InterDev projects. To add a database connection to a project, follow the steps outlined in the earlier section "Looking at the Data Environment."

After you have set up a connection to a database within your project, you can use the various Visual Database Tools to manage the database, build queries, and perform tasks required for doing database application development.

Data View

The Integrated Data View is used to provide a live view into the ODBC data sources being used in a Web application. The Data View is a powerful tool with which you can manage ODBC databases, including support for adding, deleting, and updating of database tables and records. Figure 19.13 illustrates the Data View within the Visual InterDev IDE.

FIGURE 19.13

The Data View uses the familiar Explorer-style IDE to provide access to database objects and properties.

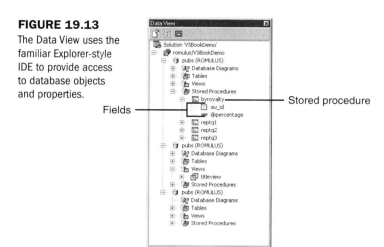

Fields

Stored procedure

The Data View lists the database tables, views, and stored procedures defined within the database. You can view, edit, add, update, or delete anything from this view into the database. The Data View is fairly similar to the SQL Server Enterprise Manager in its capabilities and user interface.

Figure 19.14 illustrates the various views that can be seen in the database and the data stored in the tables. To display the data stored in a table in the right pane, double-click it. Use the data view toolbar to toggle between views.

▶ **See** Chapter 4, "Creating Database-Aware Applications with Visual Studio," **p. 77**

FIGURE 19.14

The Data View displays multiple panes: the Diagram pane, the Grid pane, the SQL pane, and the Results pane.

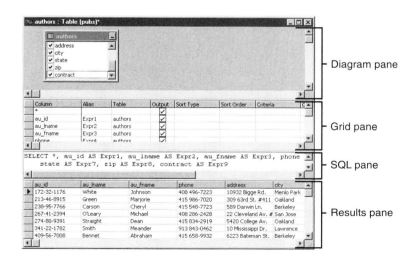

Diagram pane

Grid pane

SQL pane

Results pane

Part
III

Ch
19

T I P   Right-click any object in the Data View Explorer to get to the Properties menu to display the properties of the object.

Database Designer

The Database Designer brings visual ease of use and flexibility to creating and managing remote SQL Server databases. The Database Designer is integrated into the Data View and provides the following two key elements for creating and managing SQL Server databases:

- Table Design mode—Used to define, create, and manage SQL Server table definitions.
- Database diagrams—Used to define foreign keys, constraints, and relationships between tables. In many cases, it easier to use the database designer to manipulate SQL server databases than using the SQL server Enterprise Manager product. An example is renaming a field. This action requires a long process of backing up the data, dropping the table, re-creating it with the new field name, and moving the data back. In the Database Designer, you can easily do this by right-clicking the field and selecting the `rename` command.

▶ **See** Chapter 4, "Creating Database-Aware Applications with Visual Studio," **p. 77**

Query/View Designer

The Query/View Designer is a familiar tool that has its roots in the old Microsoft Query and the query designer built into Microsoft Access. If you have used either of these tools, you will feel right at home with the Advanced Query Designer. Figure 19.15 illustrates the Query/View Designer.

FIGURE 19.15
The Query/View Designer works with any ODBC-compliant database.

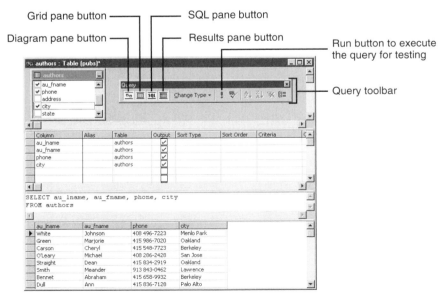

Grid pane button

SQL pane button

Diagram pane button

Results pane button

Run button to execute the query for testing

Query toolbar

To use the Query/View Designer to create queries, take the following steps:

1. Double-click a table in the Data View Explorer to open the table in the right pane.

2. Click the Diagram pane, the Grid pane, and the SQL pane to display the various data views from the Query toolbar.

3. Select any other tables you want to use in the query and drag them to the Diagram pane.

4. Select columns to include in the query by clicking the check box next to the column name. As you select the columns, notice that the Grid and SQL panes update to reflect the changes.

5. Click the Run (!) button in the Query toolbar to run your query and display the data in the Results pane.

6. When you have finished, close the Advanced Query Designer. When you are asked to save the query, provide an appropriate name and location, and save the query. You can now use the query in your application.

Exploring Site Designer

Designing a good Web site takes careful planning and good design. One of the most important considerations in designing a Web site is the structure of the Web site and how different pages within a Web site relate to each other. Defining these navigation links takes time and effort.

Site designer makes it easy to visually create the structure of a Web site using site diagrams. It allows you to quickly prototype the organization of Web pages in a group and view the navigation links between them. Site diagrams are graphical representations of the pages in your Web application that provide information about the navigation structure between pages. Within a site diagram, you can create groups of pages with hierarchical relationships. These groups of pages are called trees. These hierarchical relationships are used to define the navigation links in a site. Figure 19.16 shows a sample site diagram.

Part
III

Ch
19

FIGURE 19.16
The tree-like structure of a site diagram makes it easy to quickly determine the navigation links in a Web site.

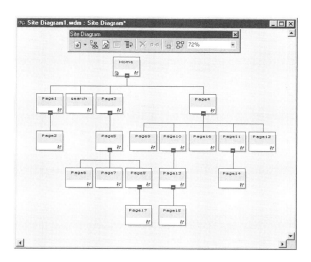

To create a site diagram in your project, complete the following steps:

1. In your Web project, select Add Item from the Project menu.
2. On the new tab, select Site Diagram from the Web Project Files folder.
3. Provide a name for the site diagram and click Open. A new site diagram is created and added to your project.

Site designer automatically adds a home page for the site to the diagram. If no home page exists, site designer creates one and adds it to the project when you save the site diagram.

After you have created a site diagram, you can add pages to it in a number of ways. You can drag and drop files from the project explorer into the site diagram or you can add new pages to your project by adding new pages to the site designer. When you save your site diagram, these pages will be automatically added to the project. You can also add existing pages from other projects or standalone files to your site diagram. All options are available from the Diagram menu that appears on the main menu bar when you open a site diagram.

Managing Visual InterDev Projects

Visual InterDev provides a great deal of functionality for building powerful Web applications. In addition, Visual InterDev includes a set of utilities to provide ancillary functions, such as support for team development, staging and publishing of Web sites, working on multiple projects, and other project management issues. The following sections discuss these functions in further detail.

Team Development

Visual InterDev provides strong support for team development through Visual SourceSafe. Visual SourceSafe is integrated into the Visual InterDev IDE and provides source management for the products included in Visual Studio.

▶ **See** Chapter 35, "Using Visual SourceSafe," **p. 997**

Visual SourceSafe provides source management, version control, and file check-in and check-out capabilities that work seamlessly within Visual InterDev to manage large team-development efforts. Visual SourceSafe works with any type of file, including text, HTML, binary image, and graphics files.

Visual SourceSafe integration for Web projects is server based. The Web server administrator needs to install a copy of Visual SourceSafe on the server. No Visual SourceSafe components need to be installed on Development workstations.

 T I P Because Visual SourceSafe works on the server, the file check-in and check-out operations work over Hypertext Transfer Protocol (HTTP). They can work across firewalls and proxy servers and can span the Internet.

Developers can install client versions of Visual SourceSafe on their workstations to take advantage of other source-management capabilities, such as File Compare and File Merge.

To use Visual SourceSafe with Visual InterDev, take the following steps:

1. Install Visual SourceSafe on the machine running the Web server. Make sure that the Enable Integration option is activated during setup of Visual SourceSafe.

2. Configure the user database on Visual SourceSafe to provide access for two special user types: the Anonymous Internet account for the Web server and the user IDs for Web developers who need access to the source control system.

3. Start Visual InterDev and open the project for which you want to enable source control.

4. Choose Project, Source Control, Add Source Control.

5. Provide the name of the source control database to use with the project, along with the user ID and password.

6. Answer the dialogs that ask for information about project name and so on. The default answers are usually appropriate.

7. Click OK to continue.

Your project will be added to Visual SourceSafe, and you are now ready to check in and check out files from SourceSafe.

Staging and Publishing Web Sites

The Project Explorer within Visual InterDev is a powerful tool that not only provides a view into the contents of a Web site, but also enables you to create, delete, rename, and move files and folders. The support for drag and drop makes it very easy to move files between folders and projects.

Because a single solution can contain multiple projects in the Project Explorer, you can easily move files between distinct remote Web servers. This allows you to host multiple versions of a Web site on different servers and move back and forth between them easily, with simple drag and drop.

For example, you can have two projects open within a single solution that connects to two different servers. One server can be the staging server, where you do most of your development and testing of Web sites. The other server can be the production server, where users connect to browse the Web site. By using drag and drop, you can easily move content from the staging server to the production server and publish your Web site to the user community. Figure 19.17 shows a workspace with two Web projects in one space, where developers can move content back and forth.

FIGURE 19.17
The File View Explorer
enables drag-and-drop
publishing of a Web site.

FIGURE 19.17
The File View Explorer
enables drag-and-drop
publishing of a Web site.

Link View

Visual InterDev also includes a great tool for managing a Web site. Called the Link View, this tool provides a graphical representation of a Web site. Link View can work on any Web site, providing a graphical representation of all the pages within the Web site and the links between them. Figure 19.18 illustrates the Link View produced for the G. A. Sullivan Web site.

FIGURE 19.18
The Link View is a great
tool for troubleshooting
broken links within a
Web site.

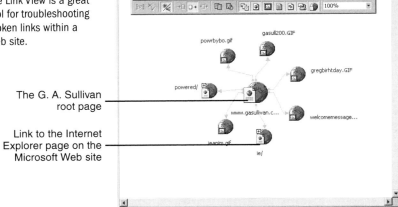

The G. A. Sullivan
root page

Link to the Internet
Explorer page on the
Microsoft Web site

To use Link View, take the following steps:

1. Choose Tools, View Links on WWW.

2. In the View Links on WWW dialog box, provide the URL for the site you are trying to map, as shown in Figure 19.19.

FIGURE 19.19
The URL can be of any
Web site accessible
from the machine on
which Link View is
running.

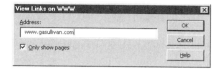

3. The root page is displayed in the middle, surrounded by pages the root page provides a link to.

4. To display the links for any page, right-click on the page and choose View <u>L</u>inks from the shortcut menu.

The arrows shown between the objects in a site are color-coded to indicate the status of the link. The link colors are based on the following scheme:

- Blue—Designates links to currently selected objects
- Gray—Designates links to unselected objects
- Red—Broken links that cannot be resolved for some reason

A view of the links to and from an object can be displayed by clicking the object. This method provides a quick view of all the links to and from a particular Web page. To see the Link View zoomed in and out, choose <u>V</u>iew, <u>Z</u>oom or use the zoom list box on the Link View toolbar.

From Here...

In this chapter, you learned about some of the advanced features and functionality of Visual InterDev. You learned about the scripting object model, the data environment, the Visual Database Tools supplied with Visual InterDev, and project management facilities.

Refer to the following chapters for information related to building Web sites and Web-based applications using Visual InterDev:

- To learn about getting started with Visual InterDev, see Chapter 18, "Developing Active Content with Visual InterDev."
- To learn about Active Server Pages, see Chapter 6, "An Inside Look at Active Server Pages and the Internet Information Server."
- To learn about Dynamic HTML and its advantages, see Chapter 21, "Dynamic HTML."
- To learn about using design-time controls, see Chapter 20, "Visual InterDev Design-Time Controls."
- To learn about server-side programming, see Chapter 17, "Server-Side Programming."
- To learn about the database features and tools included with Visual Studio, see Chapter 4, "Creating Database-Aware Applications with Visual Studio."
- To learn about concepts associated with Web-based application development, see Chapter 15, "Clients, Servers, and Components: Web-Based Applications."

Part
III

Ch
19

- To learn more about using Visual SourceSafe with Visual InterDev, see Chapter 35, "Using Visual SourceSafe."
- To learn about the Visual Studio development environment, see Chapter 2, "Using Visual Studio to Create Applications."

CHAPTER 20

Visual InterDev Design-Time Controls

by Daniel P. Egleston

In this chapter

Exploring Design-Time Controls in Visual InterDev

Visual InterDev 6 takes the initial implementation of design-time controls to a new level by expanding the range of the controls to include standard user-interface elements, recordset controls, form controls, and page controls. These design-time controls also tie in directly to the new scripting object model that was introduced with Visual InterDev 6 and bring the object-oriented programming model to Web development.

Design-time controls exist on two levels. They are presented at design time as visual controls on the HTML or ASP page, giving you the ability to set properties that define the controls' appearance or behavior. At runtime, the design-time controls generate script, which creates a script object, enabling you to write additional script to access the events, methods, and properties of the object.

Following with the recurring Time and Billing sample project, the example, demonstrated in this chapter, is a management tool used to maintain the employee database. The remarkable part of this example is that by using Visual InterDev design-time controls, you can develop an entire database-aware Web application with the capability to add, update, and delete entries, without typing a single line of code, although the events, methods, and properties of the design-time controls are exposed to the developer though the scripting object model.

Establishing a Data Connection

Most of the design-time controls included with Visual InterDev 6 deal with the tedious job of developing database-aware applications for the Web. However, the implementation of any of these design-time controls requires a connection to a database. A data connection provides Microsoft Visual Database Tools access to the database server at design time and design-time controls access at runtime.

ON THE WEB

The files used in the sample application for this chapter can be downloaded from http://www.gasullivan.com/vstudio/.

The data connections used in Visual InterDev 6 projects provide access to data within an open database connectivity (ODBC) database through a data source name (DSN). There are two types of DSNs that can be used in Visual InterDev 6 projects: system DSNs and file DSNs.

System Versus File DSNs

System DSNs store the database connection information in the Windows Registry, and the Visual InterDev project references the DSN name in the script generated by the database connection. By storing the connection information in the Registry, each Web server upon which you choose to run the Web application must have identical Registry entries. This can create problems for enterprise development when you have multiple developer workstations, as well as multiple development and production servers.

File DSNs copy all connection information into the script generated by the data connection, removing any external dependency. This type of connection is often called a DSN-less connection because of its lack of reliance on the DSN after the script has been created. This method of connecting to the database offers easy transfer of the Web application from computer to computer because the connection information is self-contained in the application.

Implementing a Data Connection

Following Visual InterDev's theme of making database-aware application development easy, Visual InterDev 6 provides the functionality to facilitate the creation of a data connection.

Follow these steps to establish a data connection for your Web project:

1. Right-click on the global.asa file within the Project Explorer window.
2. From the drop-down menu, select Add Data Connection (see Figure 20.1).

FIGURE 20.1
Right-clicking on the global.asa file in the Project Explorer window brings up a context-sensitive menu with the option to add a data connection.

3. In the Select Data Source dialog box, create a file data source for the database you want to use. Select New on the File Data Source tab.
4. In the Select dialog box, select the SQL Server driver (or the driver for the data source you want to use) and click Next.
5. Enter the name of the new data source, ConsBill, and click Next.
6. Click Finish to create the data source (see Figure 20.2).

Part
III

Ch
20

FIGURE 20.2

The Select Data Source dialog box with the `ConsBill` file DSN.

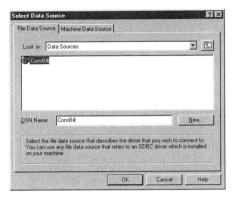

7. In the Create a New Data Source to SQL Server dialog box, enter an optional description of the data source, select the machine name of the SQL Server in the drop-down list, and click Next.

8. Choose the method by which SQL Server will verify the authenticity of the login ID. Windows NT authentication uses a trusted connection between the operating system and SQL Server by supplying your network ID to connect to the database. SQL Server authentication enables you to enter a login ID and password of a user defined within SQL Server. The Client Configuration button launches a SQL Server utility enabling you to configure SQL Server settings for the client machine.

9. Click Next to connect to the SQL Server.

10. Change the default database to the `ConsBill` database (or another database on the SQL Server you want to associate with this data source file) and click Next.

11. Accept the default settings and click Next.

12. Click Finish.

13. In the ODBC Microsoft SQL Server Setup dialog box, a summary of the configuration of the new file data source is shown. In the summary dialog box, the user is provided with a Test Data Source button. This button can be used to verify the successful definition of the DSN settings. The test attempts to connect to the data source, verify the option settings established in the DSN, and disconnect from the data source. If this is accomplished, the test is completed successfully. Click OK to return to the summary dialog box. Click OK.

14. Your new data source should be listed in the Select Data Source dialog box. Select it and click OK.

Upon completing the data connection implementation, the Connection Properties dialog box is displayed with the default connection name, Connection1, and the Connection String property set to use the File DSN you just created.

N O T E The properties can be edited from the Data Connection Properties dialog box, which can
be accessed by right-clicking on the data connection object in the Project Explorer window
and choosing Properties. The properties can also be accessed directly from the Properties window by
selecting the Data Connection object in the Project Explorer window. ▨

The first step in setting the properties of any of the design-time controls is to give an appropriate name to the control, as this name refers to the object using the scripting object model. In
this example, the name given to the `Connection` object is `conConsBill`. The next step is to set
the properties of the control that appear on the tabs within the properties dialog box.

The Authentication tab of the Data Connection Properties dialog box shows an interesting new
feature of the Connection control. The Data Connection control has both design-time and
runtime authentication to the database. In most development environments, developers need
more control over the objects of the database than would be prudent to give to a user at
runtime. These properties enable you to define a design-time user and password, as well as a
runtime user and password. The Prompt Behavior property specifies when the developer or
user will be prompted for logon information:

▨ Always

▨ Only when needed

▨ Only required options when needed

▨ Never

The Save Authentication property for both design-time and runtime authentication specifies
whether the authentication information, User ID and Password, will be saved, so it will persist
at design-time or runtime.

> **CAUTION**
>
> If runtime authentication information isn't defined, the design-time authentication is used to authenticate
> users to the database. This could leave your database objects unprotected from ignorant or malicious users.

Two other properties that are important to the `Data Connection` object are the Connection
Timeout property and the Command Timeout property located on the Miscellaneous tab of the
Connection Properties dialog box. The Connection Timeout property specifies the number of
seconds to wait to open a connection to the database. By default, this property is set to 30 seconds, and, if this time elapses without a successful connection, an ODBC error, `Unable to
connect to data source.`, is returned. Similarly, the Command Timeout property specifies
the number of seconds to wait for a command to return from the database before a timeout
occurs.

Notice that the global.asa file in the Project Explorer window now contains a `DataEnvironment`
entry, which contains the data connection with the default name, `Connection1`. The addition of
a data connection object to a Web application adds a file to the _private directory named
DataEnvironment.asa. This file enables the database tools and design-time controls to access

Part

III

Ch

20

data using a data connection, but has the interesting characteristic of not being viewable by the developer.

The script generated by the data connection stores the connection information in application variables within the `Application_OnStart` event procedure.

N O T E An interesting difference between Visual InterDev 1 and Visual InterDev 6 is the definition of the variables used in defining the database connection. The script generated by the data connection in InterDev 1 stored the connection information in session variables within the `Session_OnStart` event procedure, while the script generated in InterDev 6 stored the information in application variables within the `Application_OnStart` event procedure. Session variables are created each time a new session is started by a user of the Web application. Limiting the number of session variables reduces the overhead required in creating and storing the data connection information in memory for each session. Instead, the connection information is stored in an application variable, which is created at the initiation of the Web application and can be accessed throughout the duration of the application by any user.

When you open the global.asa file, you should see code similar to Listing 20.1.

Listing 20.1   ATSRC01.TXT—Data Connection Code Inserted into the global.asa File Using a File DSN

```
<SCRIPT LANGUAGE=VBScript RUNAT=Server>
Sub Application_OnStart
    '==Visual InterDev Generated - startspan==
    '--Project Data Connection
        Application("ConsBill_ConnectionString") = "DRIVER=SQL Server;
        ➥SERVER=BARBRADY;UID=sa;APP=Microsoft Development Environment;
        ➥WSID=CARTMAN;DATABASE=ConsBill;"
        Application("ConsBill_ConnectionTimeout") = 15
        Application("ConsBill_CommandTimeout") = 30
        Application("ConsBill_CursorLocation") = 3
        Application("ConsBill_RuntimeUserName") = "sa"
        Application("ConsBill_RuntimePassword") = ""
    '-- Project Data Environment
        'Set DE = Server.CreateObject("DERuntime.DERuntime")
        'Application("DE") = DE.Load(Server.MapPath("Global.ASA"), "_private/
DataEnvironment/DataEnvironment.asa")
    '==Visual InterDev Generated - endspan==
End Sub
</SCRIPT>
```

The definition of the database connection in the global.asa file enables the design-time use of the database tools included with Visual InterDev. You can access the objects within the database through the Data View window that can be opened by double-clicking the connection object in the Project Explorer window or by selecting View, Other Windows, Data View from the menu (see Figure 20.3).

FIGURE 20.3

The Data View window showing the table objects of the ConsBill database.

▷ For more information about Visual Database Tools, **see** Chapter 19, "Advanced Visual InterDev Concepts," **p. 553**

Using the Data Command Control

The Data Command control is an object of the data environment that contains references to database objects, such as standard SQL queries, stored procedures, tables, or views. Because the Data Command object is part of the Web application's data environment, the result set of the Data Command is accessible from any page within the application. If the database scheme changes during the development of the Web application, you simply need to edit the command object through the Data Command Properties dialog box, and all references to the command object throughout the Web application are adjusted accordingly. When a Data Command object is added to the data environment of the Web project, a node is added to the tree view of the Project Explorer window as a child node of the Connection object associated with the Data Command. The Data Command node contains information about the database object that is referred to by the data command. A command referencing a database table lists the columns of the table, whereas a stored procedure lists the parameters and returns values of the procedure.

Figure 20.4 shows the Project Explorer window for the Web project example outlined in this chapter. It shows three data commands, referencing a table, a SQL statement, and a stored procedure, of the ConsBill database.

Part

III

Ch

20

FIGURE 20.4

The Project Explorer window showing the entire Web project with the data connection, and the data commands expanded to show their additional information.

▶ For more information about the data environment, **see** Chapter 19, "Advanced Visual InterDev Concepts," **p. 553**

In the first example for this chapter, you add the Data Command control to the data environment using the `ConsBill` connection object, and specifically to give you access to the Employees table of the `ConsBill` database.

To add a Data Command control, follow these steps:

  1. Right-click on the `ConsBill Data Connection` object within the Project Explorer window.

  2. From the drop-down menu, select Add D<u>a</u>ta Command.

  3. In the Data Command Properties dialog box, enter the name of the data command object, `EmployeeList`, into the Command Name textbox (see Figure 20.5). This is the name used to refer to the command object in script.

FIGURE 20.5

The `EmployeeList` Properties dialog box.

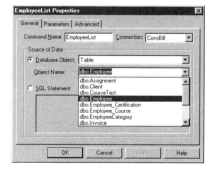

N O T E Notice that within the Data Command Properties dialog box, the Connection Name is automatically set to the ConsBill data connection. ▨

4. Select the radio button next to the Database Object drop-down box.
5. From the Database Object drop-down box, select Table from the list of possible database objects.
6. From the Object Name drop-down, select dbo.Employee from the list of tables in the database associated with the ConsBill data connection.
7. Click OK.

The Project Explorer window now displays the EmployeeList Data Command object with the column name as children of the node, similar to Figure 20.4. There are some additional properties of the Data Command object on the Advanced tab of the properties dialog box that enhances the functionality of the control.

N O T E These properties are inherited by the recordset control, if the recordset control uses the Data Command object as the source of the command. If the Data Command object is reused, define a base set of properties for the Data Command that can be individually customized by changing the properties of the Recordset object. ▨

The Cursor Type property indicates the type of the cursor used with the recordset that inherits the properties of the data command. Table 20.1 lists the possible values of the Cursor Type property and the characteristics of each.

Table 20.1   The Cursor Type Property Values and Their Characteristics

Value	Characteristics
Forward Only	Forward movement through the recordset
Keyset	Forward and backward movement
	Fixed membership
Static	Forward and backward movement
	Fixed membership
	Snapshot of database
Dynamic	Forward and backward movement
	Dynamic membership
	Current state of database

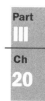

Part
III

Ch
20

N O T E   *Fixed membership* means that the data in the returned recordset is valid for the moment at which the recordset is created; changes to the database won't be reflected in the recordset. *Dynamic membership* means that the recordset reflects changes to the database since the recordset was built. ▨

The Lock Type property specifies the type of locking that the Data Command object uses when building the recordset. The possible values are

   ▨ Read-only—Enables no modifications of the data.
   ▨ Pessimistic—Does as much as possible to ensure successful updates.
   ▨ Optimistic—Doesn't lock records until they are actually updated.
   ▨ Batch Optimistic—Enables for batch updates.

The implementation of the Data Command previously described is the general procedure for creating a data command object. However, slight variations of the preceding steps are required when implementing data command objects for other database objects. The most noticeable variation exists with a standard SQL query. Simply select the radio button adjacent to the SQL Statement text field. At this point, click the SQL Builder button to launch the Visual Database Tools that enable you to generate the SQL statement.

The other variation exists when implementing a database object that has parameters, such as stored procedures. The preceding steps remain the same; however, the Parameters tab of the Data Command Properties dialog box has properties that are only relevant with a database object that has parameters. First, there is a list box with each parameter of the database object. Second, by selecting a parameter from the list, you can view and edit the properties of the parameters. The Direction property defines whether the parameter is an input and/or output parameter, or a return value from the procedure. The Data Type property defines the data type of the parameter and the Value property specifies the default value of the parameter.

Using the Recordset Control

The Visual InterDev design-time controls require the Recordset control to enable the data binding to occur. The Recordset design-time control acts as the host of all other data-bound design-time controls, each of which are bound to a Recordset control to get the data necessary to populate the data-bound controls. As the name implies, the Recordset control defines a set of database records that can be displayed and accessed through the data-bound design-time controls. The Recordset control uses database objects, such as tables, stored procedures, views, and SQL statements to create the set of records to be used by the design-time controls. The Recordset control also has the capability to create a set of records using a previously defined Data Command within the data environment of the Web application. The Recordset control generates code to access database object using ActiveX Data Objects (ADO).

   ▶ For more information about ActiveX Data Objects, **see** Chapter 26, "Building Client Front Ends with Visual Basic," **p. 761**

In this example, you add a recordset control that references the employee table in the ConsBill database—by using the data command created previously—to a Web page. This recordset enables the data-bound design-time controls, those designated by a yellow cylinder in the Design-Time Control tab of the Toolbox window, to be bound to a specific data field of the recordset.

To add a recordset control, follow these steps:

1. Drag the Recordset control from the design-time control tab in the Toolbox onto a Web page open in the editor.

2. Click Yes to enable the Scripting Object Model on the current page.

N O T E   The Scripting Object Model must be implemented for the design-time controls to function properly. By default, when you add the first design-time control to an ASP page, you are prompted to enable the Scripting Object Model to the page. You can also enable the Scripting Object Model for a page by checking the Enable Scripting Object Model checkbox on the General tab of the properties dialog box of the Web page.

3. In the Connection drop-down box, select the ConsBill data connection (see Figure 20.6).

FIGURE 20.6

The Visual InterDev 6 Integrated Development Environment with the Recordset control inserted onto an open Web page.

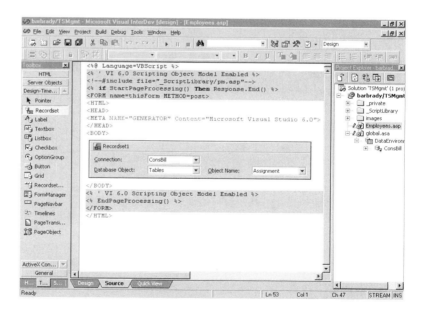

4. In the Database Object drop-down box, select DE Command.

5. In the Object Name drop-down box, select the EmployeeList data command from the list of data commands in the data environment.

Part
III

Ch
20

The same outcome can be achieved by simply dragging the Data Command object from the Project Explorer window directly onto a Web page. This method automatically sets the Connection property to the database associated with the Data Command, specifies the Database Object as a DE Command, and sets the Object Name to be EmployeeList.

The properties of the Recordset control are, not surprisingly, very similar to the properties of the Data Command control. The only difference is the capability to choose a Data Command object from the list of Database Objects. The name of the Data Command object in the Database Object list box is DE Command, and the Object Name list box is then populated with the Data Command objects that are defined within the application's data environment. In fact, when using a Data Command object to define a Recordset, the Recordset properties are inherited from the Data Command object. Nevertheless, it is possible to override the properties inherited by the Recordset control and customize the properties at this point.

Figure 20.6 shows the design-time visual appearance of the Recordset control. The runtime code that is produced by the design-time control can be accessed for each control by right-clicking on the control and selecting Show Run-time Text. The runtime code references the script library to create the recordset object, which performs the database access as defined by the properties of the design-time control.

Listing 20.2 shows the runtime code for the Recordset design-time control, as previously implemented.

Listing 20.2   ATSRC02.TXT—The Runtime Code Created by the Recordset Design-Time Control

```
<!--#INCLUDE FILE="_ScriptLibrary/Recordset.ASP"-->
<SCRIPT LANGUAGE="JavaScript" RUNAT="server">
function _initrsEmployeeList()
{
    thisPage.createDE();
    var rsTmp = DE.Recordsets('EmployeeList');
    rsEmployeeList.setRecordSource(rsTmp);
    rsEmployeeList.open();
    if (thisPage.getState('pb_rsEmployeeList') != null)
        rsEmployeeList.setBookmark(thisPage.getState('pb_rsEmployeeList'));
}
function _rsEmployeeList_ctor()
{
    CreateRecordset('rsEmployeeList', _initrsEmployeeList, null);
}
function _rsEmployeeList_dtor()
{
    rsEmployeeList._preserveState();
    thisPage.setState('pb_rsEmployeeList', rsEmployeeList.getBookmark());
}
</SCRIPT>
```

Figure 20.7 shows the Recordset design-time control when the connection property, database object, and object name do not create a valid recordset. The property that is invalid is represented with a red exclamation mark, and the same indication is given to the Recordset control as a whole.

FIGURE 20.7

The Recordset design-time control with an object name that does not correspond to the database object property. The Assignment object is not a `Data Command` object within the data environment of the Web project.

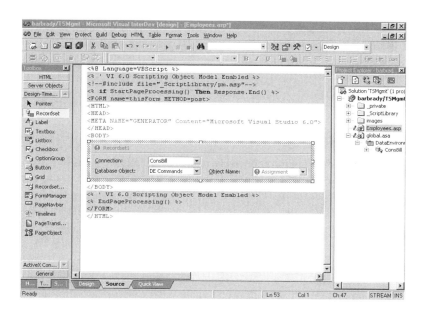

Working with Data-Bound Design-Time Controls

The most difficult part of Web development in the past has been the development of Web applications that enable the user to manipulate data from a data source, whether that be editing, inserting, or deleting data. Typically, multiple pages are developed that look nearly identical, which provide the necessary functionality for the user to perform each of the data manipulation tasks.

Visual InterDev 6 alleviates the need to develop multiple pages for database-aware Web applications with the new data-bound design-time controls. First, each of the intrinsic HTML controls that are used for displaying data were given a design-time existence with the capability to bind the control directly to a data field from a defined recordset within the project's data environment. This enables the developer to simply display the fields for a single record in the recordset. So, there exists an additional design-time control, called the RecordsetNavbar control, that gives the user the ability to scroll through the records of a recordset. The RecordsetNavbar design-time control consists of four buttons that move to the next and previous records, as well as the first and last records in the recordset. The Grid design-time control displays multiple records in a graphical interface with the capability to page through the records of the recordset, but lacking the capability to edit the data.

Part
III

Ch

20

These controls give the developer a lot of control over the creation of data manipulating forms. Yet, without a managing control, multiple Web pages still need to be developed to handle the different types of data manipulations. The FormManager design-time control is the necessary managing control that provides the developer with the notion of modes, which allows for the creating of multipurpose pages.

> **CAUTION**
>
> Don't forget that the data-bound design-time controls are simply intrinsic HTML controls with the same layout limitations as the previous version of Visual InterDev. To create a typical data entry form, you must create tables using the <TABLE> tags to properly format the controls on the form.

Using the Label Control

The label design-time control is a data-bound control best used to display read-only text strings. Placing the label design-time control on a Web page creates a label script object, which displays the text string within HTML <SPAN> tags. The text string can be hard-coded into the caption property of the label control or can be derived by binding the control to a database field by setting the recordset property and the data field property from the associated database. The text string can be formatted by setting the font, size, color, and style properties, which adds HTML <FONT>, <B>, <I> tags accordingly.

The next example walks you through the steps of creating a label for an employee's unique ID, which is stored in an identity column in the database. Each time an employee is added to the database, SQL Server uses a counter to assign a unique integer to the data field, and then increments the counter by a defined Identity Increment. For this reason, the user cannot edit the employee ID. The Label control is the perfect element for displaying the employee ID on the form.

The following steps walk you through the creation of a Label control:

1. Drag the Label design-time control from the design-time control tab in the Toolbox window onto a Web page open in the editor.
2. Enter the name of the Label control, lblEmpID, in the Name text field on the Label Properties dialog box. This name is used to reference the Label object from script.
3. Select the rsEmployeeList recordset from the Recordset drop-down box.
4. Select the EmployeeID data field from the Data Field drop-down box.
5. On the Format tab of the Label Properties dialog box, format the text string by assigning a font face and a size. You can *italicize* or **bold** the text string, as well as change the color of the text.

   The Data Contains HTML property defines whether the text string should be encoded as HTML, causing the text string <B><I>Visual InterDev 6</I></B> to be displayed as ***Visual InterDev 6***.
6. Click OK.

When the previous steps are completed, the Label control is displayed with `databound` as the text signifying that the Label control is bound to a database field. Because the actual text string is the runtime form of the Label control, the visual interface is displayed in all the views within the Visual InterDev editor.

There is an additional property that is important to the implementation of the Label control. The `Scripting Platform` property, which defines the platform, either client or server, where the recordset processes the data, or, if the control is not bound to a data field, enables you to select a platform. The server platform is unavailable in the drop-down box if the control is placed on an HTML page, as no server-side processing occurs.

The `Scripting Platform` is inherited from the recordset to which the control is bound. If the recordset is being processed on the server, there is no choice but to have the scripting platform for the data-bound control at the server. This also means that when the user navigates through the recordset, which changes the data in the control, a round trip must be made to the server to get the next record in the recordset. However, the resources needed to handle the recordset are at the server. The client simply receives a new Web page with the updated data within the control. With a recordset `Scripting Platform` of client, the Web browser uses Dynamic HTML (DHTML) to alter the text displayed in the control from the record.

Using the Textbox Control

The Textbox design-time control is a data-bound control that creates an intrinsic HTML textbox control at runtime, which is used to display editable data. The Textbox control is perfect for building database-aware Web applications with the need to edit the text fields of the database. Placing the textbox design-time control on a Web page creates a textbox script object, which displays a text string in an HTML textbox control within <INPUT> or <TEXTAREA> tags depending on the style property of the textbox design-time control.

This example steps through the creation of a data-bound Textbox design-time control that displays the employee's salary. The Textbox control is best suited for this purpose because the salary field is an updateable field in the `ConsBill` database. As an employee receives a raise, the administrator of the system edits the employee's information using the Textbox control. This example is also interesting because of the use of an expression instead of merely a text string from a database field. The expression enables you to format the salary information using the `FormatCurrency` function.

To implement a data-bound Textbox design-time control, follow these steps:

1. Drag the Textbox design-time control from the Design-Time Controls tab of the Toolbox window onto a Web page open in the editor.
2. Enter the name of the Textbox control, `txtSalary`, in the Name text field on the Textbox Properties dialog box.
3. Select the `rsEmployeeList` recordset from the Recordset drop-down box.
4. Set the Field/Expression property to `FormatCurrency( & [Salary] & , 0)`. Refer to the expression section later in the chapter for more details.

5. Set the Style property to `Textbox`. The possible values of the Style property are

- Text Box—A standard textbox
- Text Area—A multiple line text area for memo fields
- Password—A standard textbox with the characters in the text string substituted with asterisks (*)

6. Set the Display Width and Max Characters to `8`.

7. Click OK.

As this example demonstrates, the Field/Expression property is not limited to a static text string or a single data field. It is possible to build an expression using static text, data fields, and connecting constructs to form a more complex text string.

The Lines property defines the number of lines to be displayed in the text area, if the Style property is set to `Text Area`. The Display Width defines the number of characters that are displayed in the textbox, and the Max Characters property defines the maximum number of characters that are displayed in the textbox.

Using the Listbox Control

The Listbox design-time control is a data bound control that creates an intrinsic HTML list box control at runtime used to display lists of data for the user to make a selection. The Listbox control is best suited for building database-aware Web applications with the need to show a list of items from which the user can make a selection. Placing the list box design-time control on a Web page creates a list box script object, which displays a list box filled with a list of items in an HTML list box control within `<SELECT>` tags. The list box control has the additional capability of being bound to one recordset, while populating the list box from a second recordset.

The following implementation describes how to place a list box control on the Web page and have the data that populates the list box cross-referenced with the data from a second recordset. In particular, the list box is populated with the Employee Type codes from the rsEmpCategory recordset, and the data within the CategoryField from the rsEmployeeList recordset is selected in the list box.

To implement a list box control, follow these steps:

1. Drag the Listbox design-time control from the Design-Time Controls tab of the Toolbox window onto a Web page open in the editor.

2. Enter the name of the Listbox control, `lstEmpType`, in the Name text field on the Listbox Properties dialog box.

3. Set the `Recordset` property to `rsEmployeeList` and the `Field` property to `CategoryCode`.

4. Set the `Row Source` property to `rsEmpCategoryList` and the `Bound Column` and `List Field` properties to `CategoryCode`.

5. Click OK.

Using the OptionGroup Control

The OptionGroup design-time control is a data-bound control that is very similar to the Listbox control. The OptionGroup design-time control creates intrinsic HTML radio button controls that are used to display mutually exclusive options for the user to make a selection. Placing the OptionGroup design-time control on a Web page creates an OptionGroup script object, which displays the choices to the user by using HTML radio button controls within `<INPUT>` tags where the `TYPE` property is set to `Radio`. As with the list box control, the OptionGroup control has the capability of being bound to one recordset, while creating the radio buttons using data from a second recordset.

The OptionGroup control is very similar to the Listbox control. The OptionGroup uses radio buttons instead of a list of items to display the choices to the user, but uses the same cross-referencing technique to select the item of the choices provided. This example leads you through an implementation that is very close to that of the Listbox control. The OptionGroup control displays the Office Location information for the employees.

To implement the OptionGroup Control, follow these steps:

1. Drag the OptionGroup design-time control from the Design-Time Controls tab of the Toolbox window onto a Web page open in the editor.
2. Enter the name of the OptionGroup control, optOffice, in the Name text field on the OptionGroup Properties dialog box.
3. Set the `Recordset` property to `rsEmployeeList` and the `Field` property to `OfficeCode`.
4. Set the `Row Source` property to `rsOfficesList` and the `Bound Column` and `List Field` properties to `OfficeCode`.
5. Click OK.

The OptionGroup control is now data bound, where a radio button is created for each record in the OfficeCode field of the `rsOfficesList` recordset. The selected radio button is chosen by the data in the OfficeCode field of the recordset, `rsOfficesList`.

Using the Checkbox Control

The check box design-time control is a data bound control that creates an intrinsic HTML check box control at runtime used to display Boolean data fields. Placing the check box design-time control on a Web page actually creates a check box script object, which displays a check box control within `<INPUT>` tags where the `TYPE` property is set to `Checkbox`.

Part
III

Ch
20

The Checkbox control is another design-time control that is easy to implement. It is specifically designed to display boolean or bit data types from the database. Because of its checked or unchecked status, it's natural to use the Checkbox control to determine at a glance whether an employee is certified, as is demonstrated in this example. The Certified data field is a bit data field that holds the value 0 or 1 depending on the certification status of the employee.

The following steps walk you through the implementation of a Checkbox control:

1. Drag the Checkbox design-time control from the Design-Time Control tab in the Toolbox window onto a Web page open in the editor.
2. Enter the name of the Checkbox control, `chkCertified`, in the Name text field on the Checkbox Properties dialog box.
3. Enter the caption of the Checkbox control, `Certified`, in the Caption text field.
4. Select the rsEmployeeList recordset from the Recordset drop-down box.
5. Select the Certified data field from the Data Field drop-down box.
6. Click OK.

Using the Button Control

The Button design-time control is a simple control that creates an intrinsic HTML button control at run-time. The only thing that differentiates this button control from a plain HTML button placed on a Web page is the button script object that is created, enabling developers to access the button control through the scripting object model. Placing the Button design-time control on a Web page creates a button script object, which displays a button using an `<INPUT>` tag where the `TYPE` property is either `Button` or `Image` depending on the style property of the design-time control.

The Button control implementation is very simple because for the most part, the Button control simply places an intrinsic HTML button on the Web page. The only additional function of the Button control is the creation of the button script object that enables you to access the button from script, and also enables the functionality of other design-time controls, including the RecordsetNavbar control and the Grid control that uses the `Button` object.

To implement the Button Control, follow these steps:

1. Drag the Button design-time control from the Design-Time Controls tab of the Toolbox window onto a Web page open in the editor.
2. Enter the name of the Button control, btnEdit, in the Name text field on the Button Properties dialog box.
3. Click OK.

The Button control, by itself, has no functionality. However, writing code to handle the events of the button or implementing a managing control, like the FormManager control, enhances the functionality of the Web page.

The previous section gives you an overview of the data-bound design-time controls and how best to implement them on a simple Web page. The complete Web page with all the design-time controls necessary for performing editing of the Employee table in the `ConsBill` database, as shown in Figure 20.8, was created by repeating the general implementations for each design-time control, as previously stated.

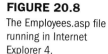

FIGURE 20.8

The Employees.asp file running in Internet Explorer 4.

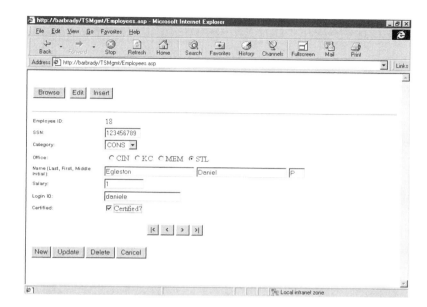

Using the RecordsetNavbar Control

The RecordsetNavbar design-time control is a data-bound control that creates a set of button controls which enable the user to navigate through the records of a recordset. The RecordsetNavbar control provides the functionality for moving to the previous and next records, as well as the first and last records in the recordset. Also, by setting the Update on Move property, the recordset is automatically updated with the data from the controls on the Web page that are bound to the same recordset as the RecordsetNavbar when the user moves to another record in the recordset.

The implementation of the RecordsetNavbar control is very simple. The only properties that must be set are the name of control and the Recordset property that is controlled by the Navbar control. As you might imagine, this is an important control in an application that gives the user the ability to browse records in a recordset.

To implement the RecordsetNavbar Control, follow this procedure:

1. Drag the RecordsetNavbar design-time control from the Design-Time Controls tab of the Toolbox window onto a Web page open in the editor.
2. Enter the name of the RecordsetNavbar control, rsnavEmployees, in the Name text field on the RecordsetNavbar Properties dialog box.
3. Set the Recordset property to rsEmployeeList.
4. Click OK.

Part
III

Ch
20

The RecordsetNavbar control is essential in creating a data entry form with the capability to view the records in the recordset. Navigation through the recordset is facilitated by the code added by the RecordsetNavbar control. The control simply uses the button control and customizes the click events to execute the `MoveFirst`, `MovePrevious`, `MoveNext`, and `MoveLast` functions of the `ADO recordset` object.

The RecordsetNavbar control can be customized by altering the caption used to delineate the buttons and the actions that they represent. Any text string or image can be used as the caption for the buttons.

ON THE WEB

The complete Employee.asp file as seen in Figure 20.8 can be downloaded from `http://www.gasullivan.com/vstudio/`.

Using the Grid Control

The Grid design-time control is a data-bound control that creates a table capable of displaying the records of a recordset. This is the closest design-time control to the Data Range Header and Footer controls of Visual InterDev 1 in the presentation of the data. As with the other data-bound control, and contrary to the Data Range controls in InterDev 1, no extra code is necessary to implement the Grid control. The Grid design-time control creates a grid object, which generates the HTML required to present the data to the user in the table format.

A key concept in the performance of the Grid control is the idea of paging. Paging enables you to limit the number of records that a user views each time. If the user wants to view more records than are displayed on the current page, she can "turn the page" and request the next page from the recordset. Without the use of paging, every record in the recordset would be returned and displayed in the Grid. Depending on the number of records in the recordset, this could cause serious performance degradation. The Grid control does create navigation buttons, similar to those of the RecordsetNavbar control, that enable the user to scroll through the records on the current page and jump to the next page of the recordset.

The Grid control combines the functionality of multiple data-bound controls, including the label control, the textbox control, and the RecordsetNavbar control. The main difference is the formatting that is provided in the Grid control. The properties of the Grid control enable you to specify color schemes, row and column sizes, and the border size of the table, just to name a few of the formatting options. This example steps through the implementation of the Grid control using the same data that was used for the Employee.asp file demonstrated previously.

To implement the Grid control, follow these steps:

1. Drag the Grid design-time control from the Design-Time Controls tab of the Toolbox window onto a Web page open in Design or Code mode in the editor.

2. Set the `Recordset` property to `rsEmployeeList`. This gives you the option of selecting the fields to display in the grid.

3. Select the data fields to be displayed in the grid as shown in Figure 20.9. By default, the display names of the fields are set to the data field names.

FIGURE 20.9
The Grid control displayed with the Internet Explorer 4 browser.

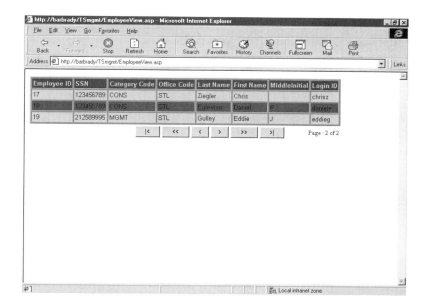

4. Update the display names for each data field.
5. Set the formatting options for the Grid control.
6. Enable the scroll by record option, which enables the user to step through each of the records in the recordset.
7. Set the number of records to be listed on each page. For illustration purposes, the property in this example was set to five to show the paging technique.
8. Click OK.

This control now displays all the information that is available in the Employee.asp file, but in a different format. The Grid control gives you the same flexibility to display the data, without the need to create the table for the data, but without the capability to edit the data.

ON THE WEB

The complete EmployeeView.asp file as seen in Figure 20.9 can be downloaded from http://www.gasullivan.com/vstudio/.

As you can see from Figure 20.9, the Grid control has navigation buttons very similar to the RecordsetNavbar control. The innermost buttons are used to navigate to the next and previous record. The next two buttons from the center are used to move to the next and previous page. Note the page numbering used to show the user how many pages of records are available for viewing. The two outermost buttons are used to navigate to the first and last record in the

Part
III

Ch
20

recordset. Without the property to scroll by recordset, the innermost buttons would not be visible, and navigation could only occur between pages and the first and last records in the recordset.

Using the FormManager Control

The Web page shown in Figure 20.8 is a perfect example of how best to use design-time controls to build data entry pages in a database-aware Web application. However, the problem still exists as to how to manage the multiple data entry modes that are required when performing data entry. The FormManager design-time control acts as the manager for the form and the corresponding controls, manipulating the script objects of the data-bound controls, as well as the associated recordset controls.

The first step in designing a data entry form using the FormManager control is to establish the required modes for the data entry form and the characteristics that distinguish one mode from another. For illustration, the example used in this chapter has three separate modes: Browse, Edit, and Insert.

The Browse mode is characterized by disabling the data-bound controls on the form, causing the data to be displayed read-only. Also, because the form is currently in Browse mode, the Browse button control is disabled, while the other two mode buttons are enabled, disallowing the Browse mode from being selected again.

The Edit mode is characterized by enabling the data-bound controls, so the data is read/write. Because the form is in Edit mode, the Edit button control is disabled, while the other two mode buttons are enabled, and the Update, Delete, and Cancel buttons are made visible to the user.

The Insert mode is very similar to the Edit mode, displaying the data read/write. The Insert button is disabled, and the other mode buttons are enabled, which allows the user to switch modes. The only real difference is the action buttons that are visible. In Insert mode, only the Update and Cancel buttons are visible to the user.

The next item to consider is the transition between modes, and what triggers the transition. Figure 20.10 diagrams the transitions that occur and their triggers. There is a transition from one mode to another on the click of one of the three mode buttons that are not disabled.

FIGURE 20.10
The modes of the data entry form and the triggers that cause a transition between the modes.

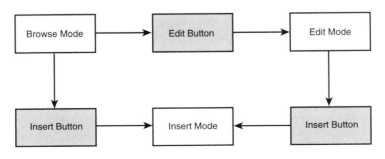

The final item to consider is the action that takes place between modes. An example, shown in Figure 20.11, is if the data form is in Insert mode and the user clicks on the Cancel button, the record update is cancelled, and the user is returned to the Browse mode.

FIGURE 20.11

The actions that occur between mode transitions.

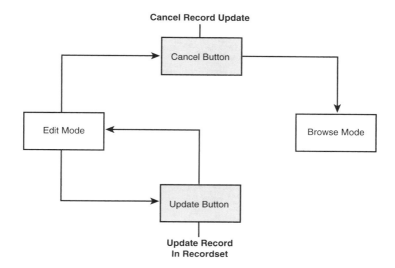

This example completes the Employee.asp file by establishing a managing control that directs the actions and properties of the data-bound controls in the data entry form. By using the design, as specified in the previous section, the FormManager control defines the events that trigger transitions between modes and the actions and property changes that occur between mode transitions.

To implement the FormManager Control, follow these steps:

1. Drag the FormManager Control from the Design-time Controls tab of the toolbox onto a Web page open in the editor.
2. Enter the name, formEmployeeList, in the Name textbox on the Form Mode tab.
3. Enter the names of the modes into the New Mode textbox.
4. For each mode listed in the Form Mode list box, set the appropriate action, as previously specified, to be performed for the selected mode (see Figure 20.12).
5. On the Action tab, specify the mode transitions and the events that triggered the transition to occur.
6. For each transition, specify the actions to be performed between the time of the event and the transition to the next mode (see Figure 20.13).

Part
III

Ch
20

FIGURE 20.12

The Form Mode tab of the FormManager Properties dialog box.

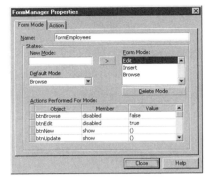

FIGURE 20.13

The Action tab of the FormManager Properties dialog box.

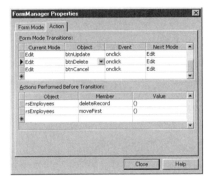

7. Click OK.

As stated in the preface of this chapter, the implementation of the data-bound controls, along with the data connection, data command control, and recordset control, has created a data entry Web page with the capability to look at and edit data from an ODBC data source without typing a single line of code. This is the true power of the Visual InterDev 6 design-time controls, and what sets them apart from the design-time controls of the previous version of InterDev. The time required to develop a complete Web site with database interaction is drastically reduced with the advent of the data-bound design-time controls, which is ultimately the purpose of design-time controls.

Visual InterDev 6 also has added design-time controls that enable the developer to refer to the page as an object, and create transitions between pages of a Web application similar to the animated transitions of Microsoft PowerPoint slide presentations.

Using the PageObject Design-Time Control

The PageObject design-time control enables the page to be treated as an object. With the page treated as an object, developers can write script using the page object. The PageObject design-time control provides access to the methods and properties of the page object and enables you to define custom methods and properties through the properties of the PageObject. The methods and properties of the page object can be referenced in script by `thisPage.property` or by the name provided the object through the `Name` property.

The following steps walk you through the implementation of a PageObject control:

1. Drag the PageObject Control from the Design-time Controls tab of the Toolbox onto a Web page open in the editor.

2. The PageObject is now accessible through script to the developer.

Using the PageTransitions Design-Time Control

The PageTransitions design-time control is used to specify how pages visually move from one to another in the Web browser. Before the advent of page transitions, a Web page suddenly appeared after a link was followed. Taking a page (no pun intended) from Microsoft PowerPoint presentation software, page transitions were introduced to make the transfer from one page to another visually pleasing.

N O T E A page or site transfer cannot occur on a page that uses frames. The page transition won't appear on a page with frames. ■

There are four events that trigger a page transition and are accessible using the PageTransition design-time control (see Table 20.2).

Table 20.2 Four Transitions and When Those Transitions Occur

Transition	Occurs
Page Enter	When the page is loaded or refreshed.
Page Exit	When the page is left and another loaded in its place.
Site Enter	When an external is left and a page from within the Web site is loaded in its place.
Site Exit	When a page within the Web site is left and replaced with an external page.

Part
III

Ch
20

In the case where a Page transition and a Site transition overlap, the Site transition takes precedence over the Page transition, and only one effect is displayed when the page transition occurs.

This ancillary control is simply used to spice up the graphical interface of your Web application. The control gives you the option to choose from nearly twenty different effects for the transitions, giving your Web application some pizzazz, and forcing the users to notice the transition from one site to another, as well as between pages within the Web application. The following steps take you through the implementation of the PageTransitions control.

To implement the PageTransitions control, follow these steps:

1. Drag the PageTransitions control from the Design-time Controls tab of the toolbox onto a Web page open in the editor.

2. Set the Page Enter transition property to the checkerboard effect. Set the Page Exit transition property to the wipe out effect (see Figure 20.14).

FIGURE 20.14
The Page Transition tab of the PageTransitions Properties dialog box.

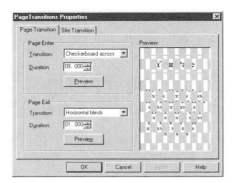

3. Additionally, set the `Site Enter` and `Site Exit` properties to the effects you desire.

4. Click OK.

Besides choosing a transition effect, the only property that can affect the transition effect is the `Duration` property for each of the transitions. The `Duration` property defines the number of seconds the page will last from 0 to 59.99 seconds.

From Here...

This chapter discusses the uses of Design Time Controls. You learned about the new controls included in Visual InterDev 6 and how they are used to create dynamic Web pages. For more information on some of the topics addressed here, see the following chapters:

- For a broad review of Internet technologies for the Active Platform, see Chapter 6, "An Inside Look at Active Server Pages and the Internet Information Server."

- For a detailed review of the features and use of Visual InterDev, see Chapter 18, "Developing Active Content with Visual InterDev."

- To obtain help on making partitioning decisions for Web-based applications, see Chapter 15, "Clients, Servers, and Components: Web-Based Applications."

- See Chapter 25, "Clients, Servers, and Components: Design Strategies for Distributed Applications," for an overview of distributed client/server and multitier architectures.

CHAPTER 21

Dynamic HTML

by Azam A. Mirza and Chris H. Striker

In this chapter

Browsing the Dynamic HTML Features

As the number of World Wide Web (WWW) users has increased, developers of Web-based content have struggled to provide content that approximated the functionality, ease-of-use, and flexibility of traditional software applications. This has been no small task; the Web's nature challenges the fundamental structure of application development. Over the years, various technologies have been introduced that help developers come closer to their goals: new HTML standards, Java applets, ActiveX controls, scripting, and so on. Nevertheless, because a fully exposed object model didn't exist, these technologies necessarily remained only partial solutions at best.

With Dynamic HTML, the landscape has changed. Web-based development is about to take a significant leap forward. Based on the Document Object Model that Microsoft proposed to the World Wide Web Consortium (W3C), Dynamic HTML offers a comprehensive, fully exposed object model to developers. With Dynamic HTML developers can create content that maximizes speed and interactivity—these are no longer necessarily mutually exclusive. Developers can create content that changes in response to user input without having to access the server. Ultimately, many restrictions to Web-based development have been removed.

In this chapter, you will create a single page that demonstrates all the key features of Dynamic HTML: dynamic content, dynamic styles, absolute positioning, multimedia effects, and data binding. To do so, you need to have installed Internet Explorer 4.x for Windows 95/98 or Windows NT 4. For this chapter, I assume that you're familiar with HTML 3.2 and VBScript.

ON THE WEB

Keep in mind that this chapter is a small tip of a relatively large iceberg; to fully take advantage of Dynamic HTML, you need to familiarize yourself with the contents of the Internet Client SDK. For a full treatment of the technologies discussed in this chapter, and especially for complete documentation regarding scripting with Dynamic HTML, refer to the Internet Client SDK from Microsoft at `http://www.microsoft.com/msdn/sdk/inetsdk/asetup/default.htm`.

Dynamic Content

One chief restriction of Web-based development has been that offering content to users is a one-shot deal. Users request a page, the Web server processes the request and offers the page to users, users read the page and send further requests. Change to the page's content was severely limited; with the exception of objects embedded in the HTML code (such as Java applets), the content was necessarily static. New content had to come as another page sent by the server. With Dynamic HTML, this has changed; developers can author pages that dynamically change their content in response to any of the events exposed by the event model, all without going back to the server. Dynamic HTML elements, as well as the information contained in elements, can be removed, added, or modified on-the-fly.

Dynamic Styles

Styles are specified by using Cascading Style Sheets (CSS) or the element attributes. With Dynamic HTML, developers can alter style information at runtime through scripting. Any attribute or property specified in a style can be altered—such as color, size, position, and visibility—all in response to any events exposed by the event model. Internet Explorer 4 supports intelligent recalculation so that the rest of the page responds to any changes; if a change to a particular section of the page forces other elements to move, Internet Explorer handles the moving.

Absolute Positioning

Another main difficulty that Web developers have had to grapple with is the limit on the layout and design of pages. The positioning of elements on a page was restricted to the options offered by traditional HTML. Given this context, Web developers made creative use of tables, frames, and other HTML constructs to present the illusion that their designs broke the boundaries of HTML. In the process, however, these developers spent considerable amounts of time and introduced unnecessary levels of complexity to outsmart HTML.

With absolute positioning, a page's layout is free from old limitations. You can now create attractive designs and user interfaces with the degree of flexibility programmers have come to expect from visual tools such as Visual Basic, Delphi, or Visual C++. The first step toward absolute positioning was taken by Microsoft with its HTML Layout Control—within the confines of the HTML Layout objects, developers were free to position objects anywhere on a 2D plane. Absolute positioning in Dynamic HTML represents the effort to move this capability to HTML itself, using an open standard. It enables positioning on x-y coordinates and z-planes, as well as with scripting animation.

N O T E The HTML layout control (introduced in IE3.x) has been labeled as not secure for scripting in IE4, and Microsoft isn't supporting it any more. Instead, Microsoft is encouraging the use of DHTML objects. ▨

Multimedia Effects

As a sort of extra, Microsoft has offered developers a set of controls with Dynamic HTML that provide multimedia effects to HTML elements and demonstrate some of the eye-catching potential that Dynamic HTML affords. The following is a list of the controls and their descriptions:

▨ The Mixer control lets you control multiple .wav files, as well as which files play in response to particular user actions.

▨ The Path control lets you animate elements on the page by using ticks provided in a fashion similar to a Timer control. The Path control can interpolate positions within ranges of time (specifying position for each tick isn't necessary).

Part
III

Ch
21

- The Sequencer control allows you to time and sequence other controls, scripts, and intrinsic functions. This control can access and manipulate the timed behavior of other ActiveX controls and intrinsic HTML controls, manipulate ActiveX methods and properties, and call scripts.

- The Sprite control allows you to present slide-show animations with graphic images.

- The Structured Graphics control lets you use vector-based images on Web pages, as well as the functionality that vector-based art implies: rotating, scaling, animating, translating, transforming, and so on. Because vector-based images are mathematical descriptions of shapes rather than the bitmap information contained in raster images, overhead is small and speed is improved dramatically.

- The Transitions control lets you use any of several special effects over a range of time to display and hide page elements.

- The Visual Filters control allows you to use any of several filters (such as shadow or spotlight) to enhance the display of visual elements on a page.

Data Binding

Web pages have traditionally been a fairly weak means of accessing databases. Although developers have used common gateway interface (CGI) scripts and other means to provide some of the functionality users have come to expect from true client/server applications, many key elements have been absent. Every distinct view of data required a new request to a server, and there was no means of binding elements on Web pages to a database. Also, users had to wait until a server built and sent an entire page containing data before they could view any of the contents. Finally, generating the HTML to present the data to users was often needlessly time-consuming and sometimes arduous.

Dynamic HTML addresses all the aforementioned limitations through several new data controls. When a page is accessed, Dynamic HTML knows how to regenerate content on-the-fly based on sorting and filtering user input without accessing the server. You can bind HTML elements and form fields to records or fields in records, allowing updates to data sources. You can write pages that begin displaying data as soon as the client receives the first record. Also, by linking HTML elements to a data control using DATASRC, DATAFLD, and DATAFORMATAS attributes, Dynamic HTML allows for automatic generation of table rows from data records. In short, Dynamic HTML provides a new level of database connectivity within the context of the Web.

Now, Microsoft has plans for three data controls to be used with Dynamic HTML: the Tabular Data control (which accesses delimited text files), the Remote Data Service (which allows access to ODBC-compliant databases), and the JDBC control (which allows access to JDBC-compliant databases). Microsoft has indicated, as has been the case with ActiveX controls in general, that it expects other parties to develop data controls.

ON THE WEB

For the latest information about the Remote Data Service, visit Microsoft's site at `http://www.microsoft.com/data/ado/rds`.

Understanding the Dynamic HTML Object Model

What makes all the preceding features possible is the exposed object model. Before Dynamic HTML, only a limited set of elements was available to developers for programmatic control. Only a small number of the attributes of HTML elements were available, as well as a limited number of events. With the introduction of Dynamic HTML, all elements on a Web page are exposed to developers, as well as all attributes and a comprehensive set of events.

N O T E The object model works with whatever scripting language you want to use, be it VBScript, JScript, or any other model-compliant language. Also, pages that use Dynamic HTML still display reasonably well in older browsers that don't support the proposed standard.

Dynamic HTML Object Model Tree

The hierarchy shown in Figure 21.1 in the Dynamic HTML Object Model exposes the highest-level objects in Internet Explorer. The highest-level object is the `window` object, which is the highest-level parent object to all other objects and elements within Internet Explorer. Through these objects, developers have what might be considered metalevel control of the browser relative to the actual content displayed.

FIGURE 21.1

The top levels of the object model exposed by Internet Explorer for use with Dynamic HTML.

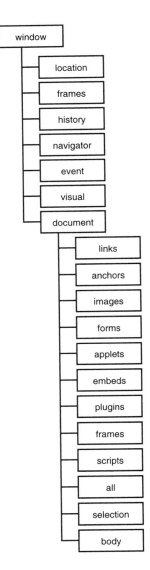

To access the items in the object model, specify the hierarchy from the top down; for example, to get at the links collection of the current document, you might use code such as `window.document.links`.

The `location` property references the address to which the browser points. By manipulating this object, the browser can be set to point to a different address. For instance, the following VBScript code sends the browser to the Microsoft home page:

```
window.location.href = "http://www.microsoft.com"
```

The `history` object represents the list of addresses the browser has recently visited. With scripting, you can send user browsers backward or forward through the list, or take action based on the list's contents.

The `navigator` object, representing the browser, allows you to do a host of useful things. For instance, you can grab the name of the browser, the version of the browser, or the state of the Alt key; you also can check whether users have cookies enabled or Java enabled.

The read-only `event` property returns the event being addressed.

The `visual` object allows you to gather information about the users' viewing capabilities/preferences. With this object, you can determine the color depth at which users are viewing your page, the horizontal resolution, and the vertical resolution.

The `document` object addresses the actual contents of whatever page is loaded in the browser. Under the `document` object are collections for the following items:

```
links           embeds
anchors         plugins
images          frames
forms           scripts
applets
```

Other items of particular note are

- The all collection, which is a collection of all objects on the page. With this collection, you can gain access to every element, no matter what collection it resides in.
- The `selection` object, which references whatever users have selected onscreen at a moment in time.
- The `body` property, which allows access to what might be considered metalevel information within the context of the document. Using this object, you can access and manipulate document-wide properties, methods, and events.

Element Class and Collection

Within a page, every element is available for programmatic manipulation. Dynamic HTML exposes an element model through which all properties, methods, and events are made accessible to scripts. This access is facilitated by the organization of HTML elements. Since the earliest HTML standards, document tags have been arranged in a hierarchical structure. Consider this HTML code:

```
<HTML>
      <HEAD>
             <TITLE>Sample Page</TITLE
      </HEAD>
      <BODY>
             <H1>Section One</H1>
             <H2>Section Two</H2>
             <P><I>Sample Content</I></P>
      </BODY>
</HTML>
```

Here, the hierarchy is clear from the structure of the HTML itself. The <HEAD> and <BODY> tags are directly subordinate to the <HTML> tag. The <TITLE> tag is subordinate to the <HEAD> tag, the <H1> and <H2> tags are subordinate to the <BODY> tag, and so on.

The actual elements are made available to you through collections. Earlier, you read that all elements on a page are exposed through an all collection. To use the all collection with scripting, you might use code similar to this:

```
dim holdItem
holdItem = document.all(1)
```

This code would set the holdItem variable to the second element on the page.

N O T E Keep in mind that an index for a collection always begins with zero and ends with
(*collection*.length) - 1. The length property specifies how many members are in
the specified collection.

Another way to grab elements through script is to grab an element by using the tag itself to access a subset of the all collection:

```
holdElement = document.all.tags("P").item(0)
```

This line grabs the first <P> element on the page.

N O T E The item method is the default for a collection; you can specify it if you want, but the code
works the same way if you omit item.

You can also use the name of the element, as specified in the id attribute for the element. If you wanted to grab the element

```
<P id = "firstelement">Here is some sample code</P>
```

you might use VBScript like this:

```
holdElement = document.all.item("firstelement")
```

The all collection might be considered a good general-purpose tool; however, you can access particular sets of HTML elements through the aforementioned collections (links, anchors, images, forms, applets, embeds, plug-ins, frames, and scripts). Most are self-explanatory. The links collection enables access to the <A> elements that contain href attributes and the <AREA> elements. The anchors collection accesses the <A> elements containing name attributes. The images collection refers to the <IMG> elements; the forms collection accesses all <FORM> elements on a page. The applets, embeds, and plug-ins collections access their respective HTML elements. The frames collection addresses a page's frame structure, and the scripts collection accesses a page's <SCRIPT> elements.

Table 21.1 shows the properties available for every element. (There might be others for specific elements.)

Table 21.1 Element Properties Accessible to Scripts

Property	Access	Description
parentElement as Element	Read-only	Returns the containing element in the structural tree.
tagName as String	Read-only	Returns the tag name represented by the element. The tag name is returned uppercased.
ClassName as String	Read/write	Returns the class specified for the element. Class is uppercased to avoid conflict with the reserved class name.
id as String	Read/write	Returns the ID identifier for the element.
style as Style	Read-only	Returns a style object representing the inline style for the element.
document as	Read-only	Returns the document object containing the element.
left as Long	Read-only	Returns the calculated position of the element in coordinates relative to the window.
top as Long	Read-only	Returns the calculated position of the element in coordinates relative to the window.

Table 21.2 shows the methods available. (Again, there might be others for specific elements.)

Table 21.2 Element Methods Accessible to Scripts

Method	Return Value	Description
scrollIntoView (start as Boolean)	None	Scrolls the element to the first or last line of the display.
contains(element as Element)	Boolean	Returns whether the supplied element is contained within the element's subtree.
getMember (attribName as String)	String	Returns the persisted value for the specified attribute.
setMember (attribName as String, value as Variant)	None	Sets the persisted value for the specified attribute.
removeMember (attribName as String)	None	Causes the attribute to be removed and not persisted into the HTML document.

Event Model

The exposed event model is the last piece of the puzzle. With the event model, you can create pages that respond to user actions. As was the case with the object model, a limited set of events has been available to developers in the past. With Dynamic HTML, the event model is fully fleshed out.

One of the most significant features of the event model is bubbling. As the event model adheres to the hierarchical nature of the object model, events bubble up through the hierarchy until they reach a handler that addresses them. This means you can write generic code that will handle onmouseover events for every element on the page. In the past, you would have had to specify the handler explicitly for every element individually.

Regarding bubbling, remember a couple of key points:

- As events bubble automatically, you need a way to prevent further unintentional event bubbling.

- Some elements have default actions associated with them (to follow the value for the href attribute is the default action of the <A> element). You need a way to override the default action if that's your intention. You can handle both scenarios through the event object, which provides a cancelBubble property and allows you to determine whether you're overriding the default action.

Suppose that you have an image (specified with the <IMG> tag) that you've given the ID parameter Image1. You might want a handler for the onclick event for the document as a whole, but a different handler that executes only when users click the Image1 image. In this case, you need to make certain that after the handler specific to the Image1 element fires, the event doesn't bubble up to the main document onclick handler. You can manage this with code such as the following:

```
<script language = "VBScript" for="document" event="onclick()">
    ElementID = window.event.srcElement.id
    Msgbox("This was processed by the document-wide handler.")
</script>
<script language = "VBScript" for "Image1" event = "onclick()">
    msgbox("This was processed by an element-specific handler.")
    event.cancelBubble = true
</script>
```

In binding events to scripts, you have three options:

- You can specify the script to run within the HTML tag itself:

```
<A onmouseover = "processrollover"language = "VBScript">
```

- You can specify the event information in the script tag (the language independent method):

```
<SCRIPT FOR=... EVENT=... IN=... LANGUAGE=...>
```

- With VBScript only, you can specify the object in the name of the handler:

```
<SCRIPT language = "VBScript">
```

```
Sub object_onmouseover
...
End Sub
</SCRIPT>
```

At this point, to take full advantage of scripting for Dynamic HTML, you need to delve deeper into the event object itself. Tables 21.3 through 21.7 contain detailed information on the `event` object, standard events, and element-specific events.

ON THE WEB

You also can find the information from Tables 21.3 through 21.7 in Microsoft's Internet Client SDK at `http://www.microsoft.com/msdn/sdk/inetsdk/asetup/default.htm`.

Table 21.3   Event Object Properties

Property	Permissions	Description
altKey as Boolean	Read-only	Returns whether the Alt key is pressed at the time of the event.
contains (element as Element)	Read-only	Returns bitmask indicating which mouse buttons are pressed at the time of the event: 0 for none, 1 for left, 2 for right, 3 for both.
cancelBubble	Read/write	Sets or returns whether the event should continue to bubble up through the containership hierarchy. True value on return from a handle cancels further event bubbling for only that event.
ctrlKey as Boolean	Read-only	Returns whether the Ctrl key is pressed at the time of the event.
fromElement as Element	Read-only	Returns the element that the mouse is coming from for the `onmouseover` and `onmouseout` events.
keyCode as Integer	Read/write	Returns a standard numeric ASCII keycode for key events; if set by `onkeypress`, changes the character sent to the object.
returnValue as Variant	Read/write	Sets or returns a return value to the event, a language-neutral way to return values to events, as some languages might not support event notifications as functional routines.
shiftKey as Boolean	Read-only	Returns whether the Shift key was pressed at the time of the event.
srcElement as Element	Read-only	Returns an element object representing the element that first received the notification before it started to bubble.

Part
III

Ch
21

continues

Table 21.3   Continued

Property	Permissions	Description
toElement as Element	Read-only	Returns the element that the mouse is going to for the onmouseover and onmouseout events.
x as Long	Read-only	Returns the horizontal position of the mouse with respect to the origin of the document's physical location at the time of the event.
y as Long	Read-only	Returns the vertical position of the mouse with respect to the origin of the document's physical location at the time of the event.

Table 21.4   Keyboard Events

Event Name (Parameters)	Return Value	Description
onkeydown (keycode as integer, shift as htmlShift)	None	Fired when a key goes down.
onkeypress (keyCode as integer)	Change keyCode to 0 to cancel	Fired when a key is pressed. Changing event.keyCode or integer return value changes the character.
onkeyup (keyCode as integer, shift as htmlShift)	None	Fired when a key goes up. Note that for a shift key, the key is up and so shift state is off accordingly.
onhelp	None	Occurs when help key (F1) is pressed.

Table 21.5   Mouse Events

Event Name (Parameters)	Return Value	Description
onmousedown (button as htmlButton, shift as htmlShift, x as long, y as long)	None	Fired when the left mouse button goes down over the element.

Event Name (Parameters)	Return Value	Description
onmousemove (button as htmlButton, shift as htmlShift, x as long, y as long)	None	Fired when the mouse moves over the element.
onmouseup (button as htmlButton, shift as htmlShift, z as long, y as long)	None	Fired when the left mouse button goes up over the element.
onmouseover	None	Fired when the mouse enters the element.
onmouseout	None	Fired when the mouse exits the element.
onclick	false to cancel default action	Fired when users left-click the element. A click event can also occur when Enter is pressed on a focusable element. The click event follows the onmouseup event when it occurs as a result of a mouse button. For mice with one button, the button is considered the left mouse button.
ondblclick	None	Fired when users double-click the element. The system determines the timing between what constitutes two click events or a click and a double-click.

Part
III

Ch
21

Table 21.6 Focusable Element Events

Property Name (Parameters)	Return Value	Description
onfocus	None	The element is receiving the focus.
onblur	None	The element is losing the focus.

Table 21.7 Element-Specific Events

Event Name (Parameters)	Supported Object(s)	Return Value	Description
onabort	<IMG>	None	Occurs if users abort the download of the image. To abort an image, click a link, click the stop button, and so on.
onbounce (side as String)	<MARQUEE>	None	Occurs when marquee with behavior equal to alternative text hits edge, "bottom", "left", "right", or "top".
onchange	<INPUT TYPE = CHECKBOX>, <INPUT TYPE = FILE>, <INPUT TYPE = RADIO>, <INPUT TYPE = TEXT>, <SELECT>, <TEXTAREA>	None	Occurs when the contents of the object change. This event is fired when the contents are committed, not while the value is changing. For example, for a text box, this event isn't fired while users type, but rather when they commit their changes by pressing Enter or leaving the text box's focus. This code is executed before the code specified by onblur, if the control is also losing the focus.
onerror	<IMG>	None	An error occurs when loading an image element.
onfinish	<MARQUEE>	None	Occurs when motion is complete.
onload	<IMG>, document window	None	Occurs when the element is completely loaded.

Event Name (Parameters)	Supported Object(s)	Return Value	Description
onreadystate change	`<APPLET>`, `<EMBED>`, `<FRAME>`, `<IFRAME>`, `<IMG>`, `<OBJECT>`, `<SCRIPT SRC=...>`, document	None	Occurs whenever the state of the element changes. This is a more detailed version of the `onload` event. Check the `readyState` property for the element. The different states causing this event to be fired occur when the element is loading, when the element is still loading but is now firing events and can be interacted with, and when the element is completely loaded.
onreset	`<FORM>`	None	Occurs when users reset a form. The `onreset` event handler executes code when a reset event occurs.
onscroll (scrollParam as scrollObject)		None	Fired on elements that have an overflow mechanism specified through the overflow CSS attribute. Occurs when the element is scrolled; event doesn't bubble.
onselect	`<INPUT TYPE = PASSWORD>`, `<INPUT TYPE = TEXT>`, `<TEXTAREA>`	None	Occurs when the text selection on a text element changes.
onsubmit	`<FORM>`	None	Occurs when a form is about to be submitted (the `onsubmit` event default action is to submit the form). Event can be overridden by returning false in the event handler. Purpose is to allow client-side validation.
onunload	Window	None	Occurs immediately before the page being unloaded.
onselection change	Document	None	Fires on the document when the user's selection changes.
onzoom (zoomPercent as integer)	Document	Returns integer to override the percent of the zoom	Fires on the window whenever the window is zoomed.

Accessing Document Content

To Dynamic HTML, the content of a page is a single stream of text that begins and ends with the <BODY> tag. The textRange object representing this stream can be manipulated to alter the content on the page. Very few pages, however, offer a stream of text between <BODY> tags with no other elements in between. This is good news for you if you want to manipulate the actual content of a page. The elements between <BODY> tags provide an easy way to break down that stream into easily manipulated component parts.

Keep in mind that the textRange object doesn't automatically exist—you need to create it explicitly by using the createTextRange method. After you create a textRange, methods exist with which you might change the start and end positions, search, or modify all or part of the range. The most basic way to create a text range containing the entirety of a page (everything between the opening and closing <BODY> tags) is a line of VBScript such as

```
Set newRange = document.body.createTextRange()
```

The textRange object itself exposes five properties and a number of methods, as shown in Tables 21.8 through 21.11.

Table 21.8 textRange Object Properties

Property Name	Description
end	Sets or returns the end-character position in relation to the entire stream. If this is set less than the start value, start is also set equal to this value.
start	Sets or returns the start-character position in relation to the entire stream. If start is greater than end, end is also set equal to this value.
htmlSelText	Returns the raw HTML for the selected text.
htmlText	Returns the valid HTML fragment for the text.
text	Sets and returns the text for the range without any of the HTML markup.

Table 21.9 textRange Object Methods

Method	Description
CommonParentElement	Returns the common parent element for the range.
executeCommand (cmdID as long, value as Variant)	Executes a command on the range—for example, changing the text formatting. The following methods provide information when executing command IDs: queryCommandState, queryCommandEnabled, and queryCommandText.

Method	Description
`duplicate`	Returns a copy of the current range.
`isEmbed ([cp as Integer]) as Boolean`	Returns a Boolean that represents whether the specified character is an embedded object. If true, the `parentElement` method can be used to access the embedding object (HTML element).
`parentElement ([cp as Integer]) as Element`	Returns the parent node for the specified character. The character position is scoped to the current range.
`inRange (compareRange as Range) as Boolean`	Returns whether the specified range is within or equal to the current range.
`isEqual (compareRange as Range) as Boolean`	Returns whether the specified range is equal to the current range.
`scrollIntoView (start as Boolean)`	Scrolls the range into view.

Table 21.10 `textRange` **Object Range Movement Methods**

Method Name	Description
`collapse (start as Boolean) as long`	Allows you to create an empty range at the beginning or end of the current range.
`expand (unit as htmlUnit) as long`	Expands the range so that partial units are completely contained.
`move (unit as htmlUnit, [count as Variant]) as long`	Changes the text the range spans over. Doesn't move any text, but instead is used to change what text the range is over.
`moveEnd (unit as htmlUnit, [count as Variant]) as long`	Causes the range to grow or shrink from the end of the range.
`moveStart (unit as htmlUnit, [count as Variant]) as long`	Causes the range to grow or shrink from the beginning of the range.
`setRange (begin as long, end as long)`	Sets the range to the ordinal offsets specified by the method. The offsets are within the scope of the current range.

Part

III

Ch

21

Table 21.11 `textRange` **Object: Inserting Text**

Method Name	Description
`pasteHtml (string)`	Pastes HTML into the current range. The HTML is forced to fit the current context of the document.

Two more methods are particularly useful when working with `textRanges`: `rangeFromText` and `rangeFromElement`.

rangeFromText

The `rangeFromText` method is used in this fashion:

```
document.rangeFromText(text as String, Optional count as Long, Optional flags,
➥range as Object) as TextRange
```

This method is useful for creating text ranges based on a search through the content of a page for a specific known string of text. Table 21.12 lists the parameters.

Table 21.12 `rangeFromText` **Parameters**

Parameter Name	Default If Not Supplied	Description
`count`	Search forward	The string to search for
`Flags`	No flags	`>0` to search forward, `<0` to search backward, `=0` to search only within the supplied range or selection if no range is supplied
`Range`	Start from current insertion point	The range to search in

rangeFromElement

The `rangeFromElement` method creates a text range from the contents of a known element. The method takes only one parameter—the element to be searched for. If you had an element with a specified ID such as

```
<strong id=firstelement>Sample Text</strong>
```

and wanted to create a `textRange` object that contained `Sample Text`, you could use the `rangeFromElement` method like this:

```
Set holdRange = document.body.rangeFromElement(document.firstelement)
```

Using Data Binding in Dynamic HTML

As mentioned earlier in the overview of Dynamic HTML features, data binding is accomplished through the use of new data controls and three new attributes: DATASRC, DATAFLD, and DATAFORMATAS.

The New Attributes

The DATASRC attribute specifies the data control to which HTML elements are being bound by referencing the ID of the data control. It applies to only the TABLE, SPAN, DIV, OBJECT, PARAM, INPUT, SELECT, TEXTAREA, IMG, and MARQUEE elements. If you have a data control with an ID attribute of dcOne on your page, you can bind a table to it with HTML like this:

```
<TABLE DATASRC="#dcOne">
```

N O T E   Remember that in using the DATASRC attribute for tables, you need to put a number sign in front of the ID.

The DATAFLD attribute specifies the field in a record to which an HTML element is being bound. It applies only to the SPAN, DIV, OBJECT, PARAM, INPUT, SELECT, TEXTAREA, IMG, and MARQUEE elements. If you want to specify a cell in a table to which to bind a field in a record from a data source, you can specify it as follows:

```
<TD><SPAN DATAFLD="CompanyName">
```

"CompanyName" is the name of the field.

The DATAFORMATAS attribute specifies what kind of data is being bound. You can specify "html" for data to be considered a string of HTML, "text" for data to be considered text, and "none" if the data is to be taken in raw format. It applies only to the SPAN, DIV, and MARQUEE attributes.

The Data Consumers

Data consumers are the HTML elements that support current record binding (referred to as the elements to which the preceding attributes apply). The following list provides descriptions of the data consumers, with indications as to whether they support editing.

N O T E   Now, only the Remote Data Service (RDS) supports editing; the Tabular Data Control used in the Sample Page later in the chapter doesn't.

- The DIV element doesn't support editing. It displays a block of plain text or HTML text. It re-renders when underlying value in column changes or current record changes.
- The SPAN element doesn't support editing. It displays a block of plain text or HTML text. It re-renders when underlying value in column changes or current record changes.
- The SELECT element supports editing and supplies functionality similar to a list box or a combo box. Binding is supported only for the selected item; multiple selections aren't supported. It works with <OPTION> tags and the index into the <OPTION> group of tags.

Part
III

Ch
21

- The RADIO type INPUT element supports editing and is used to select a single value from a group of options.

- The CHECKBOX type INPUT element supports editing. It is considered individual Boolean selections.

- The TEXT type INPUT element supports editing. It's a text box.

- The HIDDEN type INPUT element doesn't support editing and is accessible for read-only operations.

- The TEXTAREA element supports editing. It's a multicolumn textbox.

- The MARQUEE element doesn't support editing.

- The IMG element doesn't support editing. The bound value should contain only an URL to an image.

- The OBJECT element doesn't support editing. Binding to the default value of an OBJECT is allowed; DATASRC and DATAFLD specify attributes of the <OBJECT> tag. The OBJECT element also can bind to <PARAM> tags of the <OBJECT> tag.

- The APPLET element doesn't support editing. Binding is to the <PARAM> tag corresponding to property name being bound. You can now bind only one <PARAM> tag.

The Data Events

To allow for modifications and updates to data, you need a way to perform client-side validation before the data control sends information to the data source. To cancel an event (for events that can be canceled), you need only to return FALSE by the handler. What follows is a description of the various events:

- onbeforeupdate(can_cancel) fires when the element loses the focus or the page attempts to be unloaded. Fires only if the value in the element has changed since the element received focus. Fires before the onafterupdate() event and the onchange event. One caveat is that onbeforeupdate() fires immediately at the change for the CHECKBOX input type element, the RADIO input type element, the SELECT element, and OBJECTs with an immediate bind flag set.

- onafterupdate() fires following the transfer of data from the element to the data source. Fires only in instances where onbeforeupdate fired. Won't fire if the value is set from script. This event can't be canceled.

- onrowexit() fires just before the data source control changes the current record. Allows for record-level validation before changing records. Boolean value is passed to indicate whether event can be canceled. Also fires when page or the browser is shutting down.

- onrowenter() fires when the current record changes (meaning that new values are available to the control). Allows for preprocessing of the new data. This event can't be canceled.

Exploring Dynamic HTML and Visual Basic

The Dynamic HTML object model is fully accessible from Visual Basic. Visual Basic 6 allows you to develop DHTML applications that are a combination of DHTML code and compiled Visual Basic code. A Visual Basic DHTML application is a browser-based application that executes on the client machine and responds to user requests and actions.

Combining DHTML with Visual Basic allows you to take advantage of the power of the Visual Basic environment with the universal accessibility of HTML. DHTML applications use Visual Basic code to perform some of the same functions that were previously done in scripting or CGI.

A DHTML application in Visual Basic parlance is nothing more than a group of Web pages that require Visual Basic code to handle the events being generated by the user actions. You can design your Web pages using any tool available for creating HTML pages. However, Visual Basic does include a DHTML page designer for building the pages.

The structure of a Visual Basic-based DHTML application is simple. It includes one or more Web pages, a Visual Basic DLL that includes the code for handling the events generated by the Web pages, and a runtime component that hosts the Web pages in a Web browser or Web browser capable control.

Exploring Dynamic HTML and Visual C++

The Visual C++ 6 development environment and compiler provides full support for hosting and building DHTML-enabled Web pages as part of your applications. The support for DHTML is included in the form of a MFC wrapper class called `CHtmlView`. In addition, Visual C++ provides ActiveX Template Library (ATL) support to DHTML for building DHTML-aware controls.

Using the `CHtmlView` Class

The `CHtmlView` class provides support for building MFC applications that are Web aware. `CHtmlView` provides many browser-specific features that allow your application to display DHTML pages. `CHtmlView` provides support for

- Browsing Web sites and local hard drives
- URL and hyperlink navigation
- Forward and Back navigation with history list support
- Support for storing favorites list
- Security

The `CHtmlView` class provides the functionality of the Web browser control in the context of the MFC document view architecture. To base your application on the `CHtmlView` class, the easiest way is to use the MFC AppWizard and specify `CHtmlView` as the view class.

Part
III

Ch
21

ATL and DHTML Controls

Visual C++ provides ATL support for creating DHTML-aware controls. You can create an ATL project that displays a control with Dynamic HTML capability in a Web browser or other container. The ATL DHTML control allows you to specify its user interface through HTML. In addition, the control includes a mechanism for communication between C++ code and HTML.

A DHTML control is similar to any other ATL control, except that the control includes an additional dispatch interface for communicating from the HTML user interface and an HTML resource file. The preferred method of communication between a DHTML control and your C++ code is the `window.external` mechanism provided by DHTML.

A DHTML control is just like any other ATL control, with the following differences:

- A DHTML control implements a dispatch interface for communication between C++ code and HTML. The user interface for the control is specified in HTML, making it necessary to have a cross-language communications interface available.
- It has a resource file for the HTML-based user interface.
- It allows access to the DHTML object model through the member variable `m_spBrowser`, which is a smart pointer of type `IWebBrowser2`. Use this pointer to access any part of the DHTML object model.

The easiest way to create an ATL DHTML control is to use the AppWizard and create an ATL project.

Exploring Dynamic HTML and Visual J++

Visual J++ 6 provides strong support for Java developers to build Web-enabled applications. The Windows Foundation Classes (WFC) for Java include support for DHTML by encapsulating the Dynamic HTML object model. The support for DHTML is included in the com.ms.wfc.html package. To use the package in your Java applications, complete the following steps:

1. Create a new project in Visual J++ by selecting the Web Pages Projects and choosing Code-behind HTML as your project type.
2. This will create a project with three files: two class files (`Class1` and `Module1`) and a sample HTML page (Page1).
3. The `Class1` file extends the `DhDocument` class. `DhDocument` is the class represents the DHTML document. The `Module1` class extends the `DhModule` class that is loaded as an object by the HTML page, and in turn loads the `DhDocument` class.
4. Add the content elements to the `InitForm` method in the `Class1` module. This is where you add the elements that define the look and feel of your page, such as buttons, textboxes and so on.
5. Write event handlers for your elements to provide interactivity with the user. Listing 21.1 shows a sample `Class1` module, Listing 21.2 shows a sample `Module1`, and Listing 21.3 shows the sample HTML page.

Listing 21.1   Building a DHTML-Based Application in Visual J++

```java
// Class1.java Module
import com.ms.wfc.html.*;
import com.ms.wfc.core.*;
import com.ms.wfc.ui.*;

public class Class1 extends DhDocument
{
    DhText sampleText;
    DhButton sampleButton;

    /**
      * The main entry point for the program.
      */
    protected void initForm()
    {
        /**
          * Create elements which you want to access in the document.
          * These can be new elements which your code will add, or
          * preexisting elements which you want to access from a
          * client-side document or server-side template.
          */
        sampleText = new DhText("Hello World! ");
        sampleButton = new DhButton("Click Me!");
        /**
          * Set properties on the elements, or create event handlers.
          */
        sampleButton.addOnClick (new DhEventHandler(this.onClickButton));
        /**
          * Call bindNewElements if the HTML page contains preexisting
          * elements which you would like to access from your code.
          * Pass an array of elements, calling persistID on each element,
          * to specify its ID. For example:
          *     bindNewElements(new DhElement[]
          *{ myElement.persistID("theID") });
          */

        /**
          * Call setNewElements if you want your code to add some new
          * elements to the end of the document.
          */
        setNewElements(new DhElement[] { sampleText });
        setNewElements(new DhElement[] { sampleButton });
    }
        private void onClickButton(Object sender, DhEvent e) {
                sampleText.setText("Hello JAVA world! DHTML Enabled! ");
    }
}

// Module1.java Class
import com.ms.wfc.html.*;

/**
  * This class is hosted on an HTML page as a COM object.
```

continues

Listing 21.1   Continued

```
* When the HTML document has loaded, DhModule will create an instance of
* your document class (which extends DhDocument) and call initForm() on
* the instance.
*/
public class Module1 extends DhModule
{
}

// The Sample HTML Page (Page1.htm)
<HTML>
<HEAD>
<META NAME="GENERATOR" Content="Microsoft Visual Studio 98">
<META HTTP-EQUIV="Content-Type" content="text/html">
<TITLE>Document Title</TITLE>
</HEAD>
<BODY __CODECLASS=Class1>
<OBJECT classid="java:Module1"
        height=0 width=0 ... VIEWASTEXT>
<PARAM NAME=CABBASE VALUE=DHTML.CAB>
</OBJECT>
<!-- Insert HTML here -->
</BODY>
</HTML>
```

Run the preceding example and you should see a simple HTML page display in Internet Explorer that shows a Hello World! caption and a button. Click the button to change the caption on the text label. Notice how the button automatically repositions after the caption is changed to a longer length.

Building a Sample Page

In this section, you will build a page that demonstrates key features of Dynamic HTML. You will walk through the steps of absolute positioning of various elements on the page, which include application of a transition to a graphic element; dynamic changing of a page's content and styles; displaying and hiding of content sections; response to user events on HTML elements; control of HTML with scripting through the object model; and access to a data source using the Tabular Data Control.

While building this page, keep in mind that before Dynamic HTML, you typically would have to build several pages to provide the same degree of functionality and content. What's more, users would have to request these pages one at a time from a Web server, slowing the process considerably.

Step 1: Starting the Project

Before you begin creating your Dynamic HTML page, you must be set up to work within a Web project in Visual InterDev. You must have access to a computer running Personal Web Server (on computers running Windows 95/98), Peer Web Services (on computers running Windows NT Workstation) or IIS 4.x (on machines running Windows NT Server). The computer must have the FrontPage Server Extension installed. As you develop your Web site further, you might find that you need Active Server Pages (ASP) installed as well. You can install the various Web servers from your operating system installation discs and the FrontPage extensions and ASP from the Visual InterDev setup.

You also will need to have Internet Explorer 4 installed. There are several installation options, but everything in the sample page you'll build will work with any of the installations.

If you've already created a Web site with Visual InterDev, you can use it to develop, test, and implement your Dynamic HTML page. If this is the case, start Visual InterDev and open your Web project. Otherwise, follow these steps to create a new Web project on your Web server:

1. Start Visual InterDev.
2. Choose File, New from the menu.
3. Select the Projects tab in the New dialog box.
4. Select the Web Project Wizard to create a new Web project.
5. Enter the name for your new Web project in the Project Name text box.
6. Click OK.
7. Enter the name of your Web server in the Server Name combo box.
8. Select the option to Create a New Web.
9. Select the option to Enable Full Text Searching for pages in the Web.
10. Ensure that the name for your Web has been entered in the Name text box.

After you open a Web project in Visual InterDev, you need to create a new HTML file:

1. Choose File, New from the Visual InterDev menu.
2. Select the Files table in the New dialog box.
3. Select HTML Page.
4. Select Add to Project.
5. Ensure that the path to your Web is entered in the drop-down box.
6. Enter the name for your new HTML file in the File Name box.
7. Click OK.

At this point, you have a new HTML file defined in your Web site.

Part

III

Ch

21

Step 2: Adding the Template

To facilitate building your Dynamic HTML page, replace the comment `Insert HTML here` with the placeholder comments in Listing 21.2.

Listing 21.2 Dynamic HTML Template

```
<!-- HTML for logo -->
<!-- Transition Object -->
<!-- HTML for menu -->
<!-- HTML for sections -->
<!-- HTML for popup window -->
<script language = "VBScript">
'page-level section array variable
'routines to call transition filter upon window load
'routines to process mouseover and mouseout events
'routine to display/hide sub-menu items upon click event
'routine to display content layers upon click event
'routines to handle popup window upon mouseover and mouseout events
'routine to sort table contents via tabular data control
</script>
```

At this point, the HTML for your page should resemble Figure 21.2.

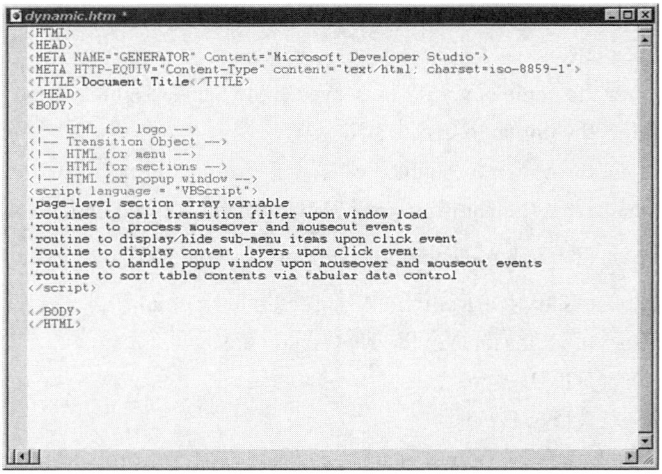

```
<HTML>
<HEAD>
<META NAME="GENERATOR" Content="Microsoft Developer Studio">
<META HTTP-EQUIV="Content-Type" content="text/html; charset=iso-8859-1">
<TITLE>Document Title</TITLE>
</HEAD>
<BODY>

<!-- HTML for logo -->
<!-- Transition Object -->
<!-- HTML for menu -->
<!-- HTML for sections -->
<!-- HTML for popup window -->
<script language = "VBScript">
'page-level section array variable
'routines to call transition filter upon window load
'routines to process mouseover and mouseout events
'routine to display/hide sub-menu items upon click event
'routine to display content layers upon click event
'routines to handle popup window upon mouseover and mouseout events
'routine to sort table contents via tabular data control
</script>

</BODY>
</HTML>
```

FIGURE 21.2
HTML with placeholder comments.

As you build the sample page, you might want to leave the comments in so that you have placeholders marking the various sections of HTML and VBScript.

After adding the template, add the following attributes to the `<BODY>` tag:

- `bgcolor = "white"`
- `topmargin = "20"`
- `leftmargin = "20"`

Step 3: Adding the Graphic

As you build your page, you'll replace the placeholder comments with HTML code and VBScript code. The first task is to place the HTML for the image at the top of the page. Replace the comment HTML for logo with the HTML in Listing 21.3.

Listing 21.3   HTML for the Logo Graphic

```
<img id = "logo" src = "logo.gif" alt="Arcadia Bay"
style="visibility: hidden;" border=0>
```

Replace the logo.gif filename with a file of your own choosing. If the file you want to use doesn't reside in the same physical directory as your HTML page, you'll need to specify the path to your file (for instance, images/mylogo.gif).

At this point, you can view the page as you develop it by opening the file in Internet Explorer or by previewing it in Visual InterDev. To preview the page in Visual InterDev, right-click anywhere in the file editing window and then choose Preview <filename> from the context-sensitive menu.

This opens the InfoViewer Topic window, which acts as Internet Explorer in this case. This window lets you view and use your page from within Visual InterDev just as you would in a separate instance of Internet Explorer.

Notice that nothing appears on the page because the style attribute in the <img> tag for the graphic specifies visibility: hidden. If you aren't already familiar with styles, you might want to review the specification for Cascading Style Sheets and their use with Internet Explorer. To view the graphic, remove the style attribute altogether (remember to replace it if you do so).

Step 4: Adding the Transition to the Graphic

The method you used to include a graphic on your page is fairly standard. It's also boring. Traditionally, Web designers have used techniques such as animated GIFs, Java applets, and Shockwave objects to spice up their pages; Dynamic HTML dramatically expands the available options. With the new multimedia ActiveX controls (included with Internet Explorer and installed automatically during setup), you have a wide range of effects to choose from.

Here, you'll apply a transition filter to the graphic so that it dissolves into view when the page is accessed. Replace the comment Transition Object with the HTML in Listing 21.4.

Listing 21.4   HTML for the Transition Object

```
<OBJECT ID="dissolvein"
CLASSID="CLSID:F0F70103-6A8F-11d0-BD28-00A0C908DB96">
<PARAM NAME="Transition" value="12">
<PARAM NAME="RESTOREBITS" VALUE="0">
</OBJECT>
```

Part
III

Ch
21

You've specified the Visual Transition ActiveX control for inclusion on the page. However, if you view your page now, you'll notice that nothing has changed; your graphic doesn't dissolve into view because nothing on the page links the graphic to the control. To create the link that tells the control to direct the display of the graphic, you need to use scripting.

N O T E The choice of VBScript, JavaScript or another scripting engine is up to you if your target platform includes only the Microsoft browser. Because the object models for Internet Explorer and Dynamic HTML are open, you can choose any engine you like that can address the models. The examples here are presented in VBScript; feel free to translate into another language if you feel more comfortable doing so.

To link the Visual Transition ActiveX control to the graphic, replace the comment routines to call transition filter upon window load with the VBScript in Listing 21.5.

Listing 21.5   VBScript Routines to Handle Transition

```
Sub Window_onLoad()
    logo.style.visibility = "hidden"
    call dissolveLogo()
end sub
sub dissolveLogo
    logo.stopPainting(dissolvein)
    logo.style.visibility = ""
    logo.startPainting(1500)
end Sub
```

If you preview the page now, you should see the graphic dissolve into view. You can control the rate at which the dissolve occurs by changing the parameter for the startPainting method in the dissolveLogo routine.

In Internet Explorer 3.x, a degree of control over the presentation of HTML was available to programmers through scripting. Because the object models weren't fully exposed, this control was necessarily limited. This is no longer the case. Here, VBScript code is accessing the graphic using the ID specified in the <img> tag (logo). Later, you'll see how to use the object model hierarchy to access HTML elements on the page without specifying their ID attributes explicitly. For now, notice that the VBScript routines you just added reference the element with the ID logo, clear the visibility: hidden style setting, and run the graphic through the startPainting method of the Visual Transition ActiveX control. This wouldn't be possible without the object model that Dynamic HTML exposes.

Step 5: Adding the Menu

The next step is to add a menu to your page with items that highlight when the mouse rolls over them. To add the menu structure, replace the comment HTML for menu with the HTML code in Listing 21.6.

Listing 21.6   HTML for the Menu Layer

```
<div id = "menu" style = "position:absolute;left:20;top:75">
<font face = verdana size = 2 color = midnightblue>
<!-- onclick events will go within the a tags below shortly -->
<a id = "one" onmouseover = "processover" onmouseout = "processout"
language = "VBScript">Company History</a><br>
<a id = "two" onmouseover = "processover" onmouseout = "processout"
language = "VBScript">Consultants</a><br>
<!-- insert the html for the submenu here -->
<a id = "three" onmouseover = "processover" onmouseout = "processout"
language = "VBScript">Partners</a><br>
</font>
</div>
```

Notice that the entire structure begins and ends with `<div>` tags, which mark the contained HTML as a separate chunk of elements that can be positioned independently of the rest of the items on the page. As you build this page, notice that the remaining HTML falls within `<div>` tags as well. This way, you can control which chunks of HTML are displayed at any given time.

The opening `<div>` tag contains the information Internet Explorer 4 needs to position the menu on the page. The style attribute specifies absolute positioning with pixel locations for the left and top edges. By changing these settings, you can force the menu to appear anywhere on the page.

If you previewed your page at this point, the menu would appear but simply sit there. This is another point at which developers traditionally had to turn to a Java applet or similar technique to provide feedback to users. Again, by exposing the HTML object model, developers can achieve the same result with much less work. Notice that the `<a>` tags enclosing the menu items contain `id` parameters and references to routines that handle the `onmouseover` and `onmouseout` events. You'll now add these routines. Replace the comment `routines to process mouseover and mouseout events` with the VBScript routines in Listing 21.7.

Listing 21.7   VBScript Routines to Handle Highlights

```
Sub processover
    heldID = window.event.srcElement.id
    set heldObj = document.all(heldID)
    heldObj.style.color = "limegreen"
End Sub
Sub processout
    heldID = window.event.srcElement.id
    set heldObj = document.all(heldID)
    heldObj.style.color = "midnightblue"
End Sub
```

Part
III

Ch

Preview your page again. This time, roll the mouse pointer over the menu items. Notice that they provide feedback by highlighting when the mouse is over them. This is precisely the sort of feedback that was far more difficult to achieve before Dynamic HTML. Make sure that your page looks similar to Figure 21.3.

FIGURE 21.3
Page with logo and
menu in Internet
Explorer, with a menu
item highlighted.

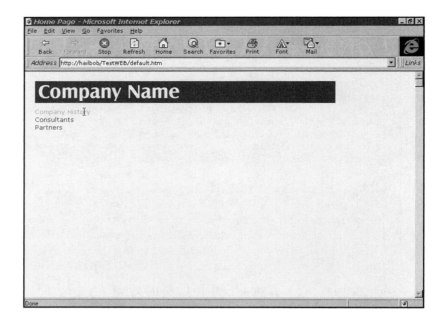

Look at the routines that provide this functionality—`processover` and `processout`. Recall that
the routine that handled the link between the graphic and the Visual Transition ActiveX control
referenced the `<img>` tag explicitly by its `id` attribute; notice that these routines don't, although
they work for each of the three menu items. This is possible because of the event model and
the all collection.

When an event fires, it's sent up through the event model hierarchy until it reaches a handler
or reaches the top level without having found a handler, at which point it disappears. In this
case, the `onmouseover` and `onmouseout` events have handlers specified in the `<a>` tags. Within
the handlers, the first line of code grabs the ID for the element on the page that fired the event.
The construct `window.event.srcElement.id` references the ID for the element that fired the
event that's traveling up the event hierarchy in the current window. The next line sets an object
variable (`holdObj`) to the element with that ID by looking through the all collection for the
document (the all collection can be considered a list of every element on the page). When the
routine sets the object, it sets the color property through the style collection.

Step 6: Adding the Submenu

Designing navigation structures for Web sites has always been tricky—especially for larger
sites. Developers have made innovative use of frames, tables, Java applets, ActiveX controls,
and other objects in their quest for flexible, intuitive navigation. Dynamic HTML makes the
process of developing such structures far easier. In this step, you'll add code for a submenu to
your existing menu.

To begin, add the HTML for the submenu itself to your page. Replace the comment `insert the html for the submenu here` with the HTML in Listing 21.8.

Listing 21.8 HTML for the Submenu

```
<div id = "twochild" style = "display:none">
<font size = 1>
<a id = "four" onmouseover = "processover" onmouseout = "processout"
language = "VBScript">  capabilities</a><br>
<a id = "five" onmouseover = "processover" onmouseout = "processout"
language = "VBScript">  directory</a><br>
<font size = 2>
</div>
```

Notice that this chunk of HTML is contained within a `<div>` tag that has an `id` of `"twochild"`. The `"twochild"` ID is arbitrary—you can name it anything you want. In this case, the name makes it easy to address this element when the element with the ID `"two"` is clicked. The `<a>` tags contain references to the same `onmouseover` and `onmouseout` events that you used before; the items on the submenu will highlight the same as the elements on the main menu. Last, notice that the display style attribute is set to `none`. When you first view the page, the submenu won't show up.

Now add the code that makes the submenu work. First, replace the comment `routine to display/hide sub-menu items upon click event` with the VBScript routine in Listing 21.9.

Listing 21.9 VBScript Routine to Display/Hide the Submenu

```
Sub expandit
     heldID = window.event.srcElement.id & "child"
     set heldObj = document.all(heldID)
     if heldObj.style.display = "none" then
          heldObj.style.display = ""
     else
          heldObj.style.display = "none"
     end if
End Sub
```

Next, add a reference to the `expandit` routine that you just added to the page. You want the routine to be called when users click the second top-level menu item. Change the `<a>` tag with the ID `"two"` so that it reads as in Listing 21.10.

Listing 21.10 Addition of `onclick` Event Reference to HTML `<a>` Tag

```
<a id = "two" onclick = "expandit" onmouseover = "processover"
onmouseout = "processout" language = "VBScript">
```

Part
III

Ch
21

Preview your page. Try clicking the second menu item. You should see the submenu appear and the items highlight when you pass the mouse pointer over them (check your screen against Figure 21.4). Note the method by which the `expandit` routine gets the ID for the submenu—it gathers the ID of the element on which users clicked and appends `child` to the ID. It then looks through the all collection for that new ID. This way, you can handle submenu items for each item on the top-level menu, submenu items for each item on the submenus, and so on, all with the same script. Because the submenu is contained within `<div>` tags nested inside the `<div>` tags for the top-level menu, when the submenu displays, the rest of the menu moves down automatically. (Dynamic HTML handles this for you.)

FIGURE 21.4

The submenu visible on the page, with an item highlighted.

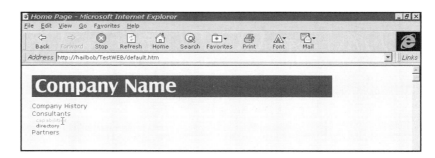

As you build the sample, think of ways to further customize your page. For instance, you might want to make it so that the top-level items stay highlighted when expanded.

Step 7: Adding the Content Layers

Now that your navigation structure is complete, you need to add the content layers that display when you click their respective menu items, as well as the functionality that controls their display. To begin, replace the comment `HTML for sections` with the HTML in Listing 21.11.

Listing 21.11   HTML for Main Content Layers

```
<div id = "partone"
style = "position:absolute;left:180;top:75;visibility:hidden;width:440">
<font face = verdana size = 4 color = midnightblue>
<p align = right>Company History<br>
<font size = 2>
<p align = left>
Placeholder for information about the company<p>
</font>
</div>
<div id = "partthree"
style = "position:absolute;left:180;top:75;visibility:hidden;width:440">
<font face = verdana size = 4 color = midnightblue>
<p align = right>Partners<br>
<font size = 2>
<p align = left>
Placeholder for general information about partnerships.
Sample partner program:<br>
```

```
<ul>
<li>
<!-- surround the following line with <a> tag to trigger popup -->
<font color = indianred>Microsoft<font color = midnightblue>
Solutions Provider Channel
</ul>
</font>
</div>
<div id = "partfour"
style = "position:absolute;left:180;top:75;visibility:hidden;width:440">
<font face = verdana size = 4 color = midnightblue>
<p align = right>Consultants - Capabilities<br>
<font size = 2>
<p align = left>
Sample information about consultant capabilities<p>
</font>
</div>
<div id = "partfive"
style = "position:absolute;left:180;top:75;visibility:hidden;width:440">
<font face = verdana size = 4 color = midnightblue>
<p align = right>Consultants - Directory<br>
<font size = 2>
<p align = left>
<!-- Tabular Data Control -->
<!-- HTML for sort controls -->
<!-- HTML for table bound to data source -->
</font>
</div>
```

Observe that the IDs for the sections you just added correspond to the items in your menu structure. They appear when their respective items are clicked and are hidden when other items are clicked. Also notice that the HTML you just added contains new comments, which will be replaced as you add more functionality to your page. Now add the rest of the code that displays the content layers.

First, you need to change the <a> tags referenced in Listing 21.12 to include the processclick() onclick event.

Listing 21.12 Changing the Menu Item <a> Tags to Add a processclick() Event Reference

```
<a id = "one" onclick = "processclick(1)" onmouseover = "processover"
onmouseout = "processout" language = "VBScript">

<a id = "three" onclick = "processclick(3)" onmouseover = "processover"
onmouseout = "processout" language = "VBScript">

<a id = "four" onclick = "processclick(4)" onmouseover = "processover"
onmouseout = "processout" language = "VBScript">

<a id = "five" onclick = "processclick(5)" onmouseover = "processover"
onmouseout = "processout" language = "VBScript">
```

Part
III

Ch
21

Notice that the calls to the processclick() routine include an index into an array. You need to add VBScript code to your page that provides the values for this array. What's more, this array and its contents need to be accessible to the entire page, as opposed to being accessible to just the routine you're calling (the array needs to have page-level scope). Replace the comment page-level section array variable with the VBScript code in Listing 21.13.

Listing 21.13   VBScript Code for a Page-Level Section Array Variable

```
Dim section(5)
section(1) = "one"
section(2) = "two"
section(3) = "three"
section(4) = "four"
section(5) = "five"
```

Finally, you need to add the actual processclick() routine itself. Replace the comment routine to display content layers upon click event with the VBScript routine in Listing 21.14.

Listing 21.14   VBScript Routine to Handle Menu Item Click Events

```
Sub processclick(num)
    for x = 1 to 5
        if x <> num and x <> 2 then
            set holdObj = document.all("part" & section(x))
            holdObj.style.visibility = "hidden"
        end if
    next
    set holdObj = document.all("part" & section(num))
    holdObj.style.visibility = "visible"
End Sub
```

The processclick() routine loops through the index values into the section array. It grabs the ID for each element that wasn't clicked, appends part to the beginning, and sets the visibility to hidden. If the index number is 2 or the index clicked, the routine skips it (there's no "part two" content section, and you don't want to hide the one users clicked). The routine then grabs the ID for the one users did select, adds part to the beginning of the ID, and sets the visibility to visible for the section referenced by that ID alone. Try viewing the page to confirm that the content sections are displaying appropriately (check your page against Figure 21.5).

FIGURE 21.5

A content layer exposed on the page.

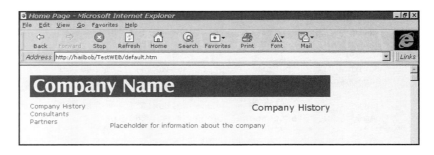

This might be a good place for customization. You might want to make Company History remain highlighted so that you won't need the title in the actual content layer.

Step 8: Adding the Pop-up Window

Another challenge that Web developers have had to face is the display of what can be a great deal of information. Users generally don't like to scroll through unwieldy amounts of information to get to what they want to see. Users also don't like to have to jump from page to page repeatedly to avoid scrolling. Dynamic HTML offers developers an easy way to design pages that get around both problems. In this step, you'll add a pop-up window that appears when users pass the mouse pointer over a particular page section. To get started, replace the comment HTML for popup window with the HTML in Listing 21.15.

Listing 21.15   HTML for the Pop-up Window Layer

```
<div id = "popup"
style = "position:absolute; left:50; top:305; visibility:hidden;width:550">
<center>
<table width = 550 border = 4 rules = none
bordercolor = midnightblue cellspacing = 0
cellpadding = 10 bgcolor = cornsilk>
<tr><td>
<font face = verdana size = 1 color = midnightblue>
<p id = "popuptext">sample text</p>
</font></td></tr>
</table></center>
</div>
```

Again, the code begins and ends with <div> tags. The opening <div> tag contains the same sort of absolute positioning information that you've used with other sections. Remember, you can change all these items programmatically; in this example, however, you'll be leaving the positioning attributes alone.

Next, you need to add the VBScript routine that displays and hides the pop-up window. Replace the comment routines to handle popup window upon mouseover and mouseout events with the VBScript code in Listing 21.16.

Listing 21.16   VBScript Routines to Display/Hide Pop-up Layer

```
Sub processpopup(whichone)
    Set popupElement = document.rangeFromElement(popuptext)
    If whichone = "microsoft" Then
        holdText = "Some info about Microsoft Solution Provider Partners."
    End If
    popupElement.pasteHTML(holdText)
    popup.style.visibility = "visible"
End Sub
Sub wipepopup
    popup.style.visibility = "hidden"
End Sub
```

Finally, locate this HTML that follows the comment `surround the following line with <a>`
`tag to trigger popup:`

```
<font color = indianred>Microsoft 
<font color = midnightblue>Solutions Provider Channel
```

Add the `<a>` tag so that it reads as in Listing 21.17.

Listing 21.17   HTML After Modification to Include Calls to Event Handlers to Handle the Pop-up Window

```
<a onmouseover = "processpopup('microsoft')" onmouseout = "wipepopup"
language = "VBScript"><font color = indianred>Microsoft
<font color = midnightblue> Solutions Provider Channel</a>
```

The `processpopup()` routine first creates a text range from the `<p>` tag within the HTML for
the pop-up window itself. The routine then takes the parameter that's passed when the routine
is called and assigns the correct message to a variable. The routine then uses the `pasteHTML`
method to change the text within the text range to the new text. Keep in mind you can paste
HTML as well as plain text into the element. Finally, the routine displays the pop-up window.
The `wipepopup` routine simply hides the window when the mouse exits the area that called the
`processpopup` routine. Preview your page and check it against Figure 21.6.

FIGURE 21.6

The pop-up window.

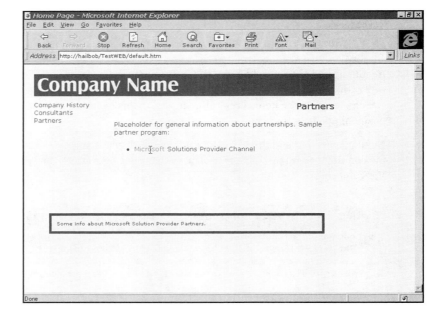

Another idea for customization is to make the pop-up window remain onscreen after the mouse moves off Microsoft, but allow users to drag it any place in the browser and click it to make it disappear.

Step 9: Adding the Data Connection and Bound Data Fields

Web pages become truly useful when they can access data on a server. For quite a while, developers used CGI scripts to access data. More recently, various technologies have been introduced to allow for database connectivity, such as Microsoft's Internet Database Connector and ActiveX Data Objects (ADO). These technologies required round trips to the server to get new data based on the application of filters, sorts, and queries.

With Dynamic HTML, Microsoft has introduced two new controls with which to access data using completely different means. With the Tabular Data control and the Remote Data Service, developers can bring down entire sets of data in one request from the server. Furthermore, page elements can now be bound to the data. By using these controls, developers can create pages that grab data once, present controls that allow users to select and sort subsets of the data, and redraw the page to reflect changes, all without returning to the server. Developers can also allow updates and additions to data sources through the bindings. These capabilities represent a fundamental change in the context of the Web; in the near future, the line between Web sites and applications that had previously been so distinct will fade away altogether.

ON THE WEB

The Remote Data Service and its use is beyond the scope of this chapter. See Microsoft's Web site at `http://www.microsoft.com/data/ado/rds` for information on the RDS.

In this example, you'll use the Tabular Data control; it's far easier to use quickly and is sufficient to demonstrate the principles of binding and refreshing without returning to the server. You'll build a table bound to a data source that displays when users click the directory submenu item. First, you need to ensure that your data source is in place. Make a file called data.txt from the comma-delimited text in Listing 21.18.

Listing 21.18   Data File for the Data Source

```
FirstName,LastName,Address,City,State,Zip,Phone,Fax,EMail
Chris,Stevens,102 NE Bernard Street,St.Louis,Missouri,63102,555-9348,555-9283,
➥cstevens
Lud,Mises,1 Chicago Avenue,St. Louis,Missouri,63182,555-3849,555-2893,lmises
Maxwell,Roach,383 Waltz Street,Cincinnati,Ohio,83728,555-2938,555-8827,mroach
Ray,Snyder,83 First Street,Kansas City,Kansas,77363,555-8837,555-8837,rsnyder
```

Ensure that the data file is in the same directory as your page. Next, you need to place the Tabular Data control object. Replace the comment `Tabular Data Control` with the HTML in Listing 21.19.

Part
III

Ch
21

Listing 21.19   HTML for the Tabular Data Control Object

```
<OBJECT ID=TDC1 CLASSID="clsid:333C7BC4-460F-11D0-BC04-0080C7055A83"
➡WIDTH=0 HEIGHT=0>
<PARAM NAME=DataURL Value="Data.txt">
<PARAM NAME=TextQualifier Value=",">
<PARAM NAME=UseHeader Value=True>
</OBJECT>
```

The `DataURL` parameter specifies your data source, the `TextQualifier` parameter specifies
what character is being used to delimit your data, and the `UseHeader` parameter specifies
whether the first line of your data source contains field names. Next, you need to add the
HTML for the table itself. Replace the comment

```
HTML for table bound to data source
```

with the HTML in Listing 21.20.

Listing 21.20   HTML for a Table with Cells Bound to the Tabular Data Control

```
<center>
<TABLE ID=Table1 DATASRC=#TDC1 border = 0 width = 440>
<TBODY>
<TR><TD width = 440 colspan = 2 bgcolor = midnightblue>
<font face = verdana size = 2 color = white>
<strong><SPAN DATAFLD=FirstName></SPAN>
 <SPAN DATAFLD=LastName></SPAN></strong>
</TD></tr>
<tr><TD width = 220>
<font face = verdana size = 2 color = midnightblue>
<SPAN DATAFLD=Address></SPAN></TD>
<TD width = 220>
<font face = verdana size = 2 color = midnightblue>
Phone: <SPAN DATAFLD=Phone></SPAN>
</TD> </TR>
<tr><TD>
<font face = verdana size = 2 color = midnightblue>
<SPAN DATAFLD=City></SPAN>, 
<SPAN DATAFLD = State></SPAN> 
<SPAN DATAFLD=ZIP></SPAN></TD>
<TD><font face = verdana size = 2 color = midnightblue>
Fax: <SPAN DATAFLD=Fax></SPAN>
</TD></TR>
<tr><TD>
<font face = verdana size = 2 color = midnightblue>
 
</TD><TD>
<font face = verdana size = 2 color = midnightblue>
EMail: <SPAN DATAFLD=EMail></SPAN>
</TD></TR>
</TBODY>
</TABLE>
</center>
```

Preview the page and select the directory submenu item. Check your file against Figure 21.7.

FIGURE 21.7

A table containing bound data. Here, you might make the email field a link that users can click to send email automatically.

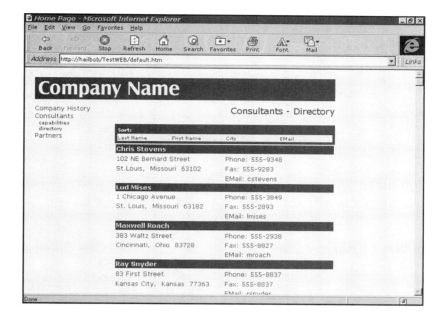

Now look back at the HTML for the table. Notice that the HTML specifies only table cells for a single record from the data source. When a table is bound to a data source with the DATASRC attribute (in the <TABLE> tag), Dynamic HTML knows to repeat the contents of the table enough times to display all the data in the data source. The actual fields in the data source are referenced with the DATAFLD attributes in the <SPAN> tags. The <SPAN> tag tells Internet Explorer that it contains a distinct unit; the DATAFLD attribute within the tag indicates that this field will be acquired from the data source specified by the DATASRC attribute in the <TABLE> tag. Aside from these additions, the rest of the code for the table is standard HTML. Note that the HTML that defines the table is contained within the <DIV> tags for the section with the ID partfive.

Step 10: Adding Sort Capability to the Data Presentation

At this point, the display of data is static; it allows no user interactivity. The last step is to add controls that allow users to sort the data. Typically, this is when you would have to assume a trip back to the server; with Dynamic HTML, this trip is no longer necessary. First, add the table that contains the sort controls. Replace the comment HTML for sort controls with the HTML in Listing 21.21.

Part
III

Ch

21

Listing 21.21   HTML for a Table Containing Sort Controls

```
<table width = 440 border = 4
bordercolor = midnightblue rules = none
cellspacing = 0>
<tr><td valign = top bgcolor = midnightblue
colspan = 4>
<font face = verdana size = 1 color = white>
<strong>Sort:</strong>
</font></td></tr>
<tr><td valign = top bgcolor = cornsilk width = 110>
<font face = verdana size = 1 color = midnightblue>
<span id = "lastname" onclick = "applysort"
onmouseover = "processover"
onmouseout = "processout" language = vbscript>
Last Name</span></td>
<td valign = top bgcolor = cornsilk width = 110>
<font face = verdana size = 1 color = midnightblue>
<span id = "first" onclick = "applysort"
onmouseover = "processover"
onmouseout = "processout" language = vbscript>
First Name</span></td>
<td valign = top bgcolor = cornsilk width = 110>
<font face = verdana size = 1 color = midnightblue>
<span id = "city" onclick = "applysort"
onmouseover = "processover"
onmouseout = "processout" language = vbscript>
City</span></td>
<td valign = top bgcolor = cornsilk width = 110>
<font face = verdana size = 1 color = midnightblue>
<span id = "email" onclick = "applysort"
onmouseover = "processover"
onmouseout = "processout" language = vbscript>
EMail</span></td></font></tr>
</table>
```

Notice that the <SPAN> tags contain references to the same handlers for the onmouseover and onmouseout events, as well as a new applysort handler for the onclick event. Next, add the applysort handler by replacing the comment routine to sort table contents via tabular data control with the VBScript code in Listing 21.22.

Listing 21.22   Handling Data Sorting in the Tabular Data Control

```
Sub applysort
    heldID = window.event.srcElement.id
    set heldObj = document.all(heldID)
    if heldID = "lastname" then
        TDC1.SortAscending=true
        TDC1.SortColumn="LastName"
        TDC1.Reset
    elseif heldID = "first" then
        TDC1.SortAscending = true
        TDC1.SortColumn = "FirstName"
```

```
        TDC1.Reset
    elseif heldID = "city" then
        TDC1.SortAscending = true
        TDC1.SortColumn = "city"
        TDC1.Reset
    elseif heldID = "email" then
        TDC1.SortAscending = true
        TDC1.SortColumn = "EMail"
        TDC1.Reset
    End If
End Sub
```

Preview the page and go to the section that contains the table; check your page against Figure 21.8. Click the fields in the new sort control table at the top of the page. You'll see the data in the table sort in accordance with the field you clicked. This happens without a trip back to the data source.

FIGURE 21.8

The table containing bound data after the city sort is applied. A good idea for this sort of page is to provide filtering as well as sorting capability.

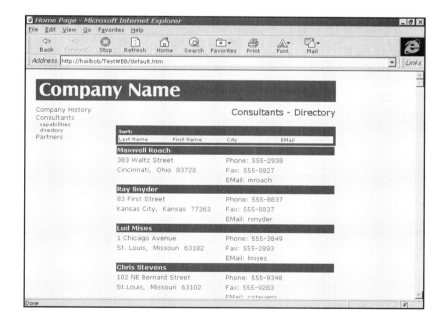

From Here...

As you've probably surmised, Web development has taken a dramatic step forward with the advent of Dynamic HTML. The range of possibilities available to Web developers dwarfs the limited set options that came before; combined with ASP, server-side objects and scripting, and so forth, the day is fast approaching when the line between traditional development and Web development dissolves altogether.

Part
III

Ch
21

- Chapter 6, "An Inside Look at Active Server Pages and the Internet Information Server," discusses the use of ASP on IIS and shows you how to use ASP.

- Chapter 18, "Developing Active Content with Visual InterDev," shows you how to use Visual InterDev to create dynamic Web sites.
- Chapter 19, "Advanced Visual InterDev Concepts," describes some of the more advanced features of Visual InterDev.
- Chapter 20, "Visual InterDev Design-Time Controls," discusses the design-time controls that ship with Visual InterDev (the Data Command, Data Range, and Image controls), and their use in Web pages.
- Chapter 17, "Server-Side Programming," shows you more about writing code for use with ASP.

Creating Applets and Applications with Visual J++

by David Burgett

In this chapter

Introducing Visual J++ 6

Visual J++ 6 is more than just the successor to Microsoft's previous version; it is an evolutionary jump for Java programming. In the few short years since Java's creation, it has undergone many dramatic changes in an attempt to make it more suitable for enterprise development. However, these necessary changes also caused inevitable problems. For example, the new event model introduced in version 1.1 was completely incompatible with the model from the previous version. Although few argued against the benefits of the new event model, many found themselves having to learn the new model and completely rewrite previously finished applets and applications.

The fact that Java could not only survive, but also thrive as a development language while undergoing such radical changes is a testament to its popularity and potential. Visual J++ 6 helps Java recognize some of the potential by taking it up to the next evolutionary rung of the programming ladder and making it suitable for enterprise development. Through the use of Microsoft's leading Integrated Development Environment (IDE), new language features, and an entirely new set of foundation classes that incorporate the entire Win32 Application Programming Interface (API), Visual J++ 6 brings Java development into the real world.

As expected, with all this new power comes a learning curve. Fortunately, however, Microsoft has worked very hard not to alienate those who have preexisting Java code. Even with all the new features in Visual J++ 6, it is still entirely compatible with the current version of the Sun's compiler and can create platform-independent code in addition to Windows-specific code.

It became painfully obvious to both the designers of Java and the developers trying to use it that the first specification for the language would never be acceptable to enterprise developers. Developers had to compromise not only performance in their Java applications, but also native control selection, control over explicit placement of controls, and mature development environments, all in the pursuit of supposed platform independence. Unfortunately, even the promise of platform independence has failed to materialize as each Java Virtual Machine (JVM) acts slightly differently, forcing developers to debug on all target platforms.

Java has come a long way in a very short time. There are now platform-independent foundation class libraries from Sun, Microsoft, and other vendors that enable developers to use all the controls they are accustomed to having in other languages, such as tree controls, tab panels, and splitters. New layout managers and better development environments are enabling more freedom over control placement and advances in JVMs are enabling performance boosts that are closing in on those of compiled applications!

All these advances in Java, the programming language, and in the applications that support Java should help it maintain its booming popularity in the coming years. Whether you are creating applets or applications, Visual J++ 6 makes it quick and easy to write both platform-independent and Windows-specific code.

Creating a Java Applet in Visual J++ 6

To demonstrate the creation of a Java applet in Visual J++ 6, you will create a TimeSheet applet that can be used with the sample application created throughout the book. The TimeSheet applet will be designed after a standard time sheet with numeric entries for each day of the week, an area for comments, and a project and task code describing the work to be done. The project and task codes should be selected from drop down list boxes to ensure that the user cannot enter time under an erroneous project or task codes.

 TIP Forcing the user to select project and task codes from dropdown lists is the first business rule encapsulated in the applet. Incorporating business rules specific to your company is easy and will be demonstrated later in the chapter.

When the TimeSheet applet is finished, you will be able to include it in a Web page viewable in any Java 1.1-compliant browser. Because the intended target for the Java applet is a company intranet page, the TimeSheet applet will be written using standard Java 1.1 code and will use the Abstract Windowing Toolkit (AWT). Keep in mind that the AWT doesn't afford you many of the choices the foundation classes do; however, the major browsers haven't incorporated the foundation classes yet, so use of the AWT is required for multiple browser support.

CAUTION

There is an inclination to include commands unique to the Java 1 specification to make your code more compatible for multiple browsers. Be careful to avoid any elements of the Java specification that have been deprecated, as browser support for these elements is not guaranteed in future versions.

To begin the creation of your TimeSheet applet, open Visual J++. When the New Project dialog appears, choose Applet on HTML from the Visual J++ Projects, Web Pages folder on the New tab. Enter your project name and location, and select Open. Expand the Project Explorer project tree node, and notice that Visual J++ has created not only a default Java applet for you, but also a sample Web page on which to display the applet (see Figure 22.1). Double-click the Page1.htm entry in the Project Explorer to view the Hypertext Markup Language (HTML) designer. Click the Source tab to view the HTML source that Visual J++ has automatically created to display your applet (as shown in Figure 22.2). Select the Design and Quick View tabs to see the HTML graphical designer and the page as it appears in a browser.

FIGURE 22.1

The Project Explorer shows all the files that compose your Visual J++ project.

FIGURE 22.2

By default, Visual J++ creates sample HTML code that displays your Java applet and can be easily enhanced into a fully functional Web page.

 TIP The HTML designer displays an empty square for your applet until you write some code to create an applet interface. Right-click on the square and select Always View As Text to see the actual HTML code.

In the Project Explorer, right-click on Applet1.java and choose Rename to rename Applet1.java to TimeSheet.java. Double-click it to edit the source code. Notice the red, wavy line under the name Applet1 in the class declaration; Visual J++ has already found an error! If you hover the mouse pointer over the word, a ToolTip appears detailing the error (see Figure 22.3). When you rename Applet1, the filename becomes incongruous with the applet name defined within, which causes an error. Change the declaration of the class to read as follows:

```
public class TimeSheet extends Applet
```

 TIP Be sure to update the HTML code to reflect the new class name!

Examine the other code that Visual J++ has created for you in the TimeSheet applet. The first two lines of code import two standard Java classes to provide support for applets and the AWT. By default, Visual J++ creates all applets to conform strictly to the Java specification, enabling them to be displayed in both Internet Explorer and Netscape.

FIGURE 22.3

Visual J++ is constantly checking your source code and can find and help you correct errors even before you discover them.

```
TimeSheet.java [Code]                                    _ □ ×
    import java.awt.*;
    import java.applet.*;

    /**
     * This class reads PARAM tags from its HTML host page and sets
     * the color and label properties of the applet. Program executio
     * begins with the init() method.
     */
    public class Applet1 extends Applet
    {                    ┌─────────────────────────────────┐
        /**              │ Public class 'Applet1' should not be defined in│
                         │ TimeSheet.java'                 │
         * The entry point for the applet.└─────────────────┘
         */
        public void init()
        {
            initForm();

            usePageParams();

            // TODO: Add any constructor code after initForm call.
        }

        private final String labelParam = "label";
        private final String backgroundParam = "background";
        private final String foregroundParam = "foreground";
```

> **T I P** Remember that the import statement doesn't add anything to your code; it simply enables you to call objects and methods without having to specify the entire package hierarchy each time.

Notice next that Visual J++ has created several routines for you as well, most importantly `initForm`. The `initForm` routine sets the background and foreground colors of the applet, defines the default layout and the text for the single default label control, and adds the label to the applet (see Figure 22.4). This procedure can be easily changed to create the necessary controls for the TimeSheet applet.

FIGURE 22.4

The default applet for Visual J++ creates an AWT applet with a single label control placed in the northern region of a `BorderLayout`.

```
TimeSheet.java [Code]                                    _ □ ×
        /**
         * Intializes values for the applet and its components
         */
        void initForm()
        {
            this.setBackground(Color.lightGray);
            this.setForeground(Color.black);
            label1.setText("label1");
            this.setLayout(new BorderLayout());
            this.add("North",label1);
        }
```

The full TimeSheet code used in the sample application incorporates a dynamically built interface, where extra rows only appear on the TimeSheet as they become necessary. The edit controls used to build each line are stored within a vector, and each vector is added to another vector. This enables the applet to keep track of a dynamic number of rows, each comprised of an easily modified number of controls. For the sake of simplicity, the sample TimeSheet control you create will consist of a static set of six rows. To create the components, you must declare them by adding the following code just beneath the `Public Class TimeSheet` declaration near the top of your code:

```
// Component Declaration
public Choice chProject1;
public Choice chTask1;
public TextField tfComments1;
public TextField tfMonday1;
public TextField tfTuesday1;
// Continue declaration for other days
public Label lblTotal1;
public Label lblProject;
public Label lblTaskLabel;
public Label lblComments;
public Label lblMonday;
public Label lblTuesday;
// Continue declaration for other days
public Label lblTotal;
public Label lblMondayRunning;
public Label lblTuesdayRunning;
// Continue declaration for other dayspublic Label lblTotalRunning;
private final int MenuBarHeight=0;
// End of Component Declaration
```

N O T E   The code listed is only a partial listing; you need to duplicate the lines containing Monday
for each day of the week.

When you have declared the variables as stated, copy the declarations for the Choices and the
TextFields and add declarations numbered accordingly for each of the six lines of the
TimeSheet. ▓

Notice that you have also created an integer variable named MenuBarHeight. MenuBarHeight
normally defines the location of all controls on the form, but will be set to 0 and not used in this
example. Using MenuBarHeight makes enhancement of the TimeSheet applet easy by enabling
the developer to add useful items such as date and employee name above the time entry fields.

Now that you have declared variables for each of the visible components, you must add them to
the actual form. Change the default code created in the initForm routine and replace it with
the following:

```
// Create standard labels
setLayout(null);
lblProject = new Label("Project",Label.LEFT);
lblProject.setFont(new Font("Dialog",Font.BOLD,12));
lblProject.setBounds(31,3+MenuBarHeight,62,19);
lblTaskLabel = new Label("Task",Label.LEFT);
lblTaskLabel.setFont(new Font("Dialog",Font.BOLD,12));
lblTaskLabel.setBounds(121,1+MenuBarHeight,51,19);
lblComments = new Label("Comments",Label.LEFT);
lblComments.setFont(new Font("Dialog",Font.BOLD,12));
lblComments.setBounds(262,1+MenuBarHeight,97,19);lblMonday =
➥new Label("M",Label.LEFT);
lblMonday.setFont(new Font("Dialog",Font.BOLD,12));
lblMonday.setBounds(450,1+MenuBarHeight,25,19);
lblTuesday = new Label("T",Label.LEFT);
lblTuesday.setFont(new Font("Dialog",Font.BOLD,12));
```

```
lblTuesday.setBounds(480,1+MenuBarHeight,25,19);
// Continue initialization for other days
lblTotal = new Label("Total",Label.LEFT);
lblTotal.setFont(new Font("Dialog",Font.BOLD,12));
lblTotal.setBounds(664,1+MenuBarHeight,40,19);
// Create labels for running daily totals
lblMondayRunning = new Label("0.0",Label.RIGHT);
lblMondayRunning.setFont(new Font("Dialog",Font.PLAIN,12));
lblMondayRunning.setBounds(441,25+MenuBarHeight,27,19);
lblTuesdayRunning = new Label("0.0",Label.RIGHT);
lblTuesdayRunning.setFont(new Font("Dialog",Font.PLAIN,12));
lblTuesdayRunning.setBounds(471,25+MenuBarHeight,27,19);
// Continue initialization for other dayslblTotalRunning =
➥new Label("0.0",Label.RIGHT);
lblTotalRunning.setFont(new Font("Dialog",Font.PLAIN,12));
lblTotalRunning.setBounds(659,25+MenuBarHeight,40,19);
```

When you add similar code for the other days of the week, you will have completed the code necessary for two rows of column headers at the top of the time sheet. Before you can view your TimeSheet applet, you must compile the Java source code into a CLASS file using Build, Build.

To examine what you have created, open the HTML editor and select the Source tab (see Figure 22.5). Inside the APPLET tag, set the width and height to 800 and 250, respectively. Next, select the Quick View tab to display the HTML page showing where the TimeSheet applet will appear after you've added more code.

FIGURE 22.5

The HTML designer enables you to visually design your HTML pages, as well as directly edit the HTML source.

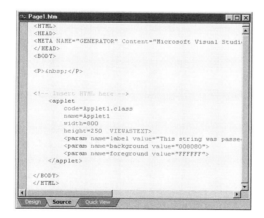

TIP By default, Visual J++ displays an image of the Java applet on the Source tab. To view the HTML representation, right-click on the applet and select Always View As Text.

You have already declared variables for the controls that will accept time entry; you must now instantiate them and add them to the form. In order to facilitate positioning each control properly, you will also define an integer variable, Top. Top will simply be used to calculate the appropriate distance from the top of the applet for each row of controls. Create the time entry fields by adding the code in Listing 22.1 to the initForm routine.

Listing 22.1   Creating the Time Entry Fields to the `initForm` Routine

```
int top=50+MenuBarHeight;
//Create TextFields for time entry
chProject1 = new Choice();
chTask1 = new Choice();
tfComments1 = new TextField("" );
tfMonday1 = new TextField("" );
tfTuesday1 = new TextField("" );
// Continue instantiations for other days
lblTotal1 = new Label("" );
chProject1.setBounds(18,top,77,30);
chTask1.setBounds(95,top,77,30);
tfComments1.setBounds(172,top,270,19);
tfMonday1.setBounds(442,top,30,19);
tfTuesday1.setBounds(472,top,30,19);
//Continue setBounds method for other days
// End of Component Initialization
add(lblProject);
add(lblTaskLabel);
add(lblComments);
add(lblMonday);
add(lblTuesday);
// Continue adding labels for other days
...
add(lblTotal);
add(lblMondayRunning);
add(lblTuesdayRunning);
// Continue adding Running labels for other days
add(lblTotalRunning);
add(chProject1);
add(chTask1);
add(tfComments1);
add(tfMonday1);
add(tfTuesday1);
// Continue adding textfields for other days
  add(lblTotal1);
```

You have now added all necessary code to create the basic TimeSheet applet interface. Rebuild the applet and view the TimeSheet in the HTML designer to ensure that the first row of time entry fields has been properly instantiated and positioned (see Figure 22.6).

The HTML designer will continue to display the old version of the TimeSheet applet until you explicitly refresh it. Select View, Refresh to update the HTML designer to the latest version of your Java applet.

Add code to instantiate and position the other five rows of time entry controls and you have completed the interface design of the TimeSheet applet.

Part

III

Ch

22

FIGURE 22.6
The TimeSheet applet now has all the appropriate labels and a single row of controls to enable time entry.

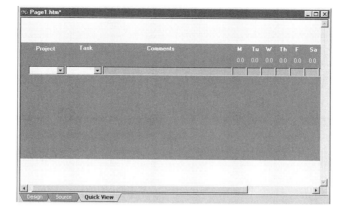

N O T E To properly position the other five rows of time entry controls, you will need to update the Top variable between each row. Insert the following line before calling setBounds() for each successive row:

```
top+=18;
```

 T I P Microsoft Internet Explorer and Netscape Navigator act slightly differently when displaying Java applets. To ensure that your applet displays properly in both browsers, use System.getProperty("java.vendor") to determine which browser is being used. For Internet Explorer, Top will be incremented by 18, whereas Netscape Navigator requires an increment of 22.

Adding Public Methods and Event Handling

The interface for the TimeSheet applet has now been designed and created. However, it is currently only a static display with no user interaction. In order to make the TimeSheet applet useful, you need to add some methods and event handling to it. The methods required will enable the user to add Project Codes and Task Codes to the Choice controls already added to the form. The event handling will need to respond whenever the user enters a time value to update both the row and column totals.

To add a public function to the time sheet control, simply define it as public as shown in the following code:

```
public void addProjectCode(String code)
{
}
public void addTaskCode(String code)
{
}
```

You now have two public methods that can be called from client-side script within the Web page. In order to make the addProjectCode function do something, you must add to it the following lines of code:

```
chProject1.addItem(code);
chProject2.addItem(code);
chProject3.addItem(code);
chProject4.addItem(code);
chProject5.addItem(code);
chProject6.addItem(code);
```

This code will update each Choice control designated to hold Project Codes to display the string value passed into the function. Add similar code to the addTaskCode function to add the parameter value to each Task Code Choice control.

Now that you have defined two public functions, you need a way to test the new functionality of the TimeSheet applet. This can be accomplished using the HTML designer. Select the Source tab to view the HTML code for the applet. Within the <APPLET> tag, define a new parameter Name and assign it the value TimeSheet (see Figure 22.7).

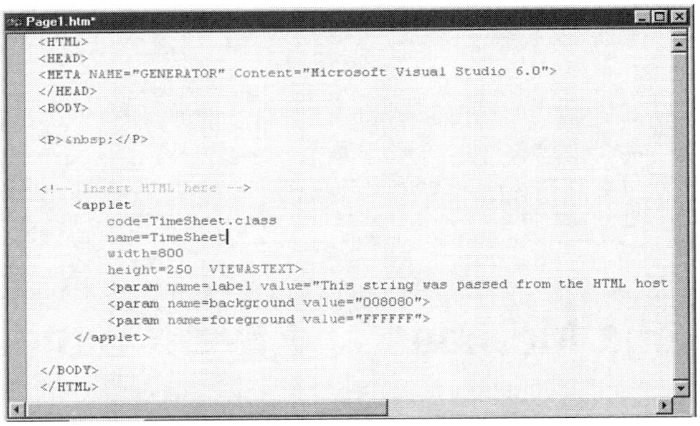

FIGURE 22.7

In addition to the Java code, you can write the HTML code necessary to display the TimeSheet applet on the Web page, right in Visual J++.

```
Page1.htm*
<HTML>
<HEAD>
<META NAME="GENERATOR" Content="Microsoft Visual Studio 6.0">
</HEAD>
<BODY>

<P> </P>

<!-- Insert HTML here -->
    <applet
        code=TimeSheet.class
        name=TimeSheet
        width=800
        height=250  VIEWASTEXT>
        <param name=label value="This string was passed from the HTML host
        <param name=background value="008080">
        <param name=foreground value="FFFFFF">
    </applet>

</BODY>
</HTML>
```

Select the Design tab of the HTML designer. From the HTML tab of the toolbox, drag a Button control onto the HTML designer (see Figure 22.8).

 T I P   The controls on the HTML tab of the toolbox will be grayed out unless either the Design or Source tab of the HTML designer has been selected.

In order to make the HTML button functional, you need to tell it what to do when it is clicked. This is accomplished by adding a client-side JavaScript function to the page and calling that function in the OnClick event of the button.

FIGURE 22.8

The sample Web page Visual J++ creates for you now has a default HTML button that can be used to call functions of the TimeSheet applet.

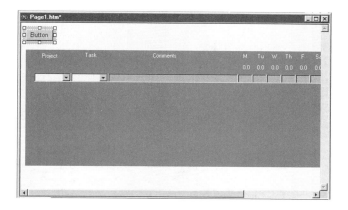

To create the JavaScript function, add the following code between the `</BODY>` and `</HTML>` tags near the bottom of the source code:

```
<script language="JavaScript">
<!--
function addCodes()
{
TimeSheet.addProjectCode("ProjectCode1");
TimeSheet.addProjectCode("ProjectCode2");
TimeSheet.addTaskCode("TaskCode1");
TimeSheet.addTaskCode("TaskCode2");
}
//-->
</script>
```

Now that the client-side JavaScript function is ready to call, all that is left to do is to call it each time the button is clicked. To do this, double-click the button on the Design tab to view the source code for it. Add a new parameter within the `<INPUT>` tag called `OnClick` and assign it the value of `addCodes()` (see Figure 22.9).

FIGURE 22.9

The OnClick parameter of the INPUT tag identifies the action to be taken by the browser each time the user clicks the button.

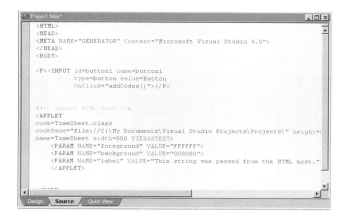

Press F5 to run the application in your Web browser. The TimeSheet applet appears on the page with the button. Press the button to fill sample values into the Project and Task Codes choice controls (see Figure 22.10).

FIGURE 22.10

With just a click of a button, the drop-down lists are now filled with sample Project and Task codes.

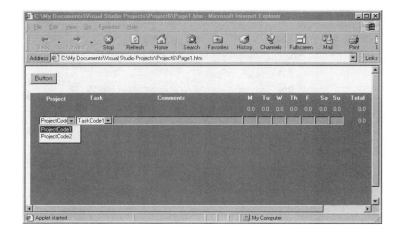

N O T E When run from within Visual J++, both the Java code and the script within the HTML page are being run through a debugger so they will run considerably slower than normal.

Now that you have added two public methods to your TimeSheet applet, it is time to add events that provide more interaction for the end user. You will add code to handle the `keyPress` event.

ON THE WEB

The following section implements a standard Java interface within the code. If you have not used interface implementations in Java previously, refer to the Java tutorial found at `http://java.sun.com/tutorial/`.

The objective is to automatically update the daily totals above each column of time data and the row totals to the left of each Project/Task code combination. In order to do this, you must first tell the Java compiler that you will be implementing all classes of the `KeyListener` interface. Add this code to your class declaration so that it looks like this:

```
public class TimeSheet extends Applet implements KeyListener
```

N O T E If order for the code to compile, you must import `java.awt.event.*`, which contains the definition for the `KeyListener` interface.

You have now informed the Java compiler that you will be implementing all necessary functions to fulfill the `KeyListener` interface requirements. This consists of three public methods: `keyPressed`, `keyReleased`, and `keyTyped`. To fulfill your implementation of the interface, add an empty method for each of these methods, as shown in the following:

Part
III

Ch
22

```
public void keyPressed (KeyEvent e)
{
}
public void keyReleased (KeyEvent e)     {}
public void keyTyped (KeyEvent e)       {}
```

 T I P For more information on the KeyListener interface, see the Java API documentation.

In order for your code to call these events, you must add KeyListeners to all components that handle the events. For simplicity's sake, you will handle only the keyPressed event for the time entry fields (Monday1...Sunday6). In the initForm() routine where you first instantiate the time entry textfields, add an additional line for each appropriate component:

```
tfMonday1.addKeyListener(this);
tfTuesday1.addKeyListener(this);
tfWednesday1.addKeyListener(this);
tfThursday1.addKeyListener(this);
tfFriday1.addKeyListener(this);
tfSaturday1.addKeyListener(this);
tfSunday1.addKeyListener(this);
```

This code causes the applet to call the keyPressed, keyReleased, and keyTyped methods each time any keystroke is registered within one of the textfields. In order to update the time total labels, you will be interested only in the keyTyped event, which is fired after both of the other methods.

 T I P An advanced version of the TimeSheet applet can contain validation code in the keyPressed event to ensure that only numeric entries are entered into the time entry fields.

Finally, you must add code to the keyPressed event to update the total fields based on the new value of each time entry field. To do this, add the following code to the keyPressed method:

```
double dMonday=0.0,dTuesday=0.0;
// Continue declaring variables for the other days of the week
double dRow1=0.0,dRow2=0.0,dRow3=0.0;
double dRow4=0.0,dRow5=0.0,dRow6=0.0;

dMonday+= new Double(tfMonday1.getText().trim()).doubleValue();
dRow1+= new Double(tfMonday1.getText().trim()).doubleValue();
dTotal+= new Double(tfMonday1.getText().trim()).doubleValue();
dTuesday+= new Double(tfTuesday1.getText().trim()).doubleValue();
dRow1+= new Double(tfTuesday1.getText().trim()).doubleValue();
dTotal+= new Double(tfTuesday1.getText().trim()).doubleValue();

// Continue summing the rows for the other days of the week
lblMondayRunning.setText(new Double(dMonday).toString());
lblTuesdayRunning.setText(new Double(dMonday).toString());

// Continue adding to the Running Totals for the other days of the week
lblTotalRunning.setText(new Double(dTotal).toString());
lblTotal1.setText(new Double(dRow1).toString());
```

```
lblTotal2.setText(new Double(dRow1).toString());
lblTotal3.setText(new Double(dRow1).toString());
lblTotal4.setText(new Double(dRow1).toString());
lblTotal5.setText(new Double(dRow1).toString());
lblTotal6.setText(new Double(dRow1).toString());
```

This code simply sums up the time values entered for each column and each row and places that sum in the appropriate total label control (see Figure 22.11).

FIGURE 22.11

With the event-handling code in place, the TimeSheet applet automatically sums each row and column each time any of the time entry fields is changed.

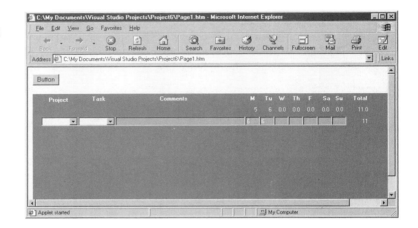

Your TimeSheet applet now has all the basic functionality to enable users to enter time values for given projects and tasks. Now that you have seen how to use Visual J++ to create code using the old methodology, it is time to look at the new functionality that Visual J++ brings to the table.

Working with the Windows Foundation Classes

As mentioned previously, the most visible problem with early versions of Java programming was the limited functionality of the AWT. The problem with the AWT is that its designers were most concerned with platform independence and thus designed the controls within the AWT as peer controls. A *peer control* is one that depends upon its container to create and maintain it. So when a Java program was instructed to create a textbox, the JVM requested one from the operating system it was running on and simply maintained a link to it. The JVM had no real responsibility for the control.

The most prominent problem with this system is that it only enables for inclusion of controls that are available on every target operating system. This excludes many of the common Windows controls such as TreeViews and Splitters because one or more of the target operating systems for Java don't support such controls. Another problem of depending on the operating system for control creation is the slight differences in how each operating system creates the controls. A standard textbox control in a Macintosh environment might be larger than in a Windows environment. This necessitates additional testing to ensure that the interface is acceptable in each operating system's representation.

The solution to these problems is to create a set of peerless controls in a foundation class. This foundation class will be responsible for all aspects of the creation and maintenance of each control. Given this strategy, the JVM accepts the responsibility for creating the control and can ensure that any single control will be created in an identical manner in every environment. It has the added benefit of offering new controls to operating systems with limited selection. Thus, Java programs executing on UNIX platforms can employ Windows-specific controls.

There are two platform-independent foundation classes currently available. Microsoft's Application Foundation Classes (AFC) includes the entire set of standard Windows controls and is compatible with both the 1 and the 1.1 Java specifications. The Java Foundation Classes (JFC), created by Netscape and Sun Microsystems, is compatible only with the 1.1 specification, but it includes a very similar set of controls and will be fully implemented in the 1.2 specification. Both foundation classes offer a rich set of peerless controls. However, neither foundation class is yet standard in any browser, as some of the browsers are still struggling to catch up to the 1.1 AWT specification. When the browsers are advanced to the 1.2 specification, Netscape will definitely support the JFC and Internet Explorer will definitely support the AFC. It is uncertain whether either browser will support the competing foundation class.

Given these two strong foundation classes, why would Microsoft create the new Windows Foundation Classes (WFC)? The WFC is, as the name suggests, specific to Windows. The controls used can only be used in Windows 32-bit operating systems. In addition to offering a rich set of user controls similar to those found in the AFC and JFC, the WFC encapsulates the entire Win32 API, giving Java developers access to all the same Windows functionality that Visual C++ and Visual Basic developers have used for years.

N O T E Keep in mind that using the WFC necessitates that your Java development is targeted only to Windows. Although this dissolves the cross-platform benefits of Java development, Windows developers will likely find the benefits to be well worth the cost.

What the WFC really provides is a layer of communication between Java code and Windows COM controls. All the standard Windows COM controls have been placed inside a package that Java can understand. What this means to the developer is that any ActiveX/COM control can now be used in Windows applications written in Java. The WFC will provide a wrapper around your existing ActiveX control enabling you to drop it onto your Java toolbox in Visual J++. This helps leverage all existing ActiveX development work when making the transition to Java programming.

T I P As you would expect, this extra layer of communication doesn't come without an associated performance hit. You might find it more necessary to port your most often used ActiveX controls to Java for maximum performance.

This layer of communication also works in reverse. Any Java class can be adapted to fit the Windows component model by adding some meta-information. You can then install that class in the toolbox and drop your visual or nonvisual Java class onto a form and manipulate it at design time. You can even export your Java classes as ActiveX controls to be used in Visual Basic, Microsoft Word, or any other ActiveX container.

Also included in the WFC is an encapsulation of the standard HTML elements. These elements have been bound to the Dynamic HTML (DHTML) Object Model and made available in the design-time environment. Each component acts in the same fashion as standard WFC controls and ActiveX controls and is designed through the standard properties dialog.

One of the most important new features in the WFC is the new event-handling model. Recall that the new event-handling model created for the Java 1.1 specification was completely incompatible with the previous version, necessitating large amounts of rewriting for Java developers. Microsoft has worked diligently to devise a new system that will not only be more efficient and easier to implement, but also be completely compatible with the previous models.

Delegates are essentially a way to connect an object to a method. You identify an object and a method, and then you attach them by specifying a calling event. In the Java 1.1 specification, you implement an interface that contains all the necessary methods associated with the event. In the preceding TimeSheet example, you implemented the `KeyListener` interface, which required that you implement the `keyPress`, `keyReleased`, and `keyTyped` methods, despite the fact that you used only one of them.

Using delegates, you do not implement an interface to handle the events. Instead, Visual J++ automatically binds a method reference to the desired control. You need only choose an object, view the available events in the Properties dialog, and enter a name for the event you want to handle. The Microsoft JVM automatically handles the reference and directs execution to the specified code. This brings Java development into very close line with other Microsoft development languages.

Other benefits of using delegates include the capability to call a single method from multiple events. Visual J++ makes it easy to have both an Exit button and an Exit menu automatically call the same method. This not only saves you from having to make a call to one handler from the other, but also saves you the trouble of having to implement `ActionListener` interfaces for both components. You can also set two events of the same control to fire a single method such as the enter and leave events for a text control to ensure that the same validation routine is always called (see Figure 22.12).

FIGURE 22.12

Delegates enable you to call a single method from any number of events in a single or multiple control.

As you have seen, the WFC is more than just another collection of peerless GUI controls. By encapsulating the Win32 API, HTML elements, and offering a delegate-based event-handling model, it clearly paves the way for Java to finally be used as an enterprise-worthy development tool.

Creating Applications with Visual J++

As previously mentioned, the greatest improvement of Visual J++ 6 over the previous version, and in fact all other Java development environments, is the capability to create enterprise applications. Giving developers the ability to create fast Java Windows applications with all the functionality of their Visual Basic and Visual C++ counterparts will help move Java past the hype and into the workplace. Giving those same developers the easiest development environment to work in should help make Java the language of choice for a growing share of applications in the coming years.

In the first three years of its existence, Java has created far more hype than any other language in the history of computer programming. Unfortunately, as such a young language, the applications designed with Java have failed to live up to the hype. There have been some very valiant attempts by large companies to rewrite their flagship applications in Java, most of which have been scrapped before completion. Microsoft recognized this discrepancy and has set out to correct it with Visual J++ 6.

To examine the features of Visual J++ 6 designed to make Java a viable option for Windows development, you will create a simple Windows application that can load, edit, and save files in Rich Text Format (RTF). Best of all, you will do this in a very short amount of time and in less than 10 lines of code.

Begin your SampleProject application by choosing File, New Project. Select Applications under the Visual J++ Projects root on the left pane of the New tab. Notice that Visual J++ enables you to create either a standard Windows application or a console application, or use the Application Wizard to help you create your application. Select Windows Application, specify `SampleProject` as a name, select a location, and click Open.

N O T E   The Application Wizard gives you choices about the type of application to create; whether to include a menu, a toolbar, a status bar, an edit control, and data access; and what type of comments, and it enables you to choose how to package and deploy your new application. You can even save the settings you select to an Application Wizard profile for reuse later.

T I P   If you already have a previous project open, two radio buttons will appear following the location box. Ensure that Close Current Solution is selected before continuing.

In the Project Explorer window, expand the tree under `SampleProject`. Double-click on `Form1.java` to open the WFC form designer. Figure 22.13 shows an example of a form that will be used in the next example. Note the standard Windows button and `richText` controls as well as in the in-place menu editing.

FIGURE 22.13

The WFC Form Designer enables you to quickly create GUI Java forms using that same drag-and-drop paradigm that made Visual Basic popular.

Next, examine the toolbox. Select the WFC Controls tab to view the large array of controls included with Visual J++. Run the mouse over the controls to display the ToolTip over each control featured (see Figure 22.14).

FIGURE 22.14

The WFC includes a wide variety of sophisticated GUI components, including standard Windows dialog boxes as shown here.

Just as is possible in other Microsoft visual design environments, you can customize the toolbox to create just the right set of controls for your project. Right-click anywhere in the toolbox and select Customize Toolbox. The Customize Toolbox dialog splits the available controls into groups of WFC Controls, Applets, Design-Time Controls, and ActiveX Controls. Scroll down the list and notice the Form1 entry on the list indicating Visual J++'s capability to include Java classes (a WFC form, in this case) in the toolbox alongside all other WFC controls. This is a powerful feature that fully supports code reuse in WFC applications. Click Cancel to close the Customize Toolbox dialog.

You are now ready to create your first WFC application! Find the Button control near the top of the toolbox and drag it onto your form as shown in Figure 22.15. Right-click on the button and choose Properties to display the Properties dialog box for this button. At the top of the

Properties dialog, notice the first two buttons on the toolbar just below the combo box. The first button displays a list of the control's properties, and the second refreshes the list to display the control's events. You will use the event list later in the chapter.

FIGURE 22.15
Adding any WFC control to a form is as easy as drag and drop.

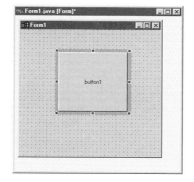

Change the following properties of the button control:

- Name—btnExit
- Text—E&xit

N O T E   The ampersand (&) in the text property indicates that the letter following it will be the access key (or hot key) for the button. In this case, x is the access key, meaning that the button can be selected by the Alt+X key combination.

Move btnExit so that it is near the bottom, right-hand corner of the form. There is one more property that you must set to ensure that the button stays in the same spot, relative to the corner of the form, the new Anchor property. The Anchor property defines which boundaries of the form a control will stay anchored to when the form is resized. In this case, you want the button to maintain its position relative to the bottom and right sides of the form. Set the Anchor property equal to Bottom, Right by selecting and deselecting the cross-hair markers until you specify the proper quadrant (see Figure 22.16).

You now need to write an event handler for the click event of the button to force the application to end when the button is clicked. To do this, double-click on the button to view the event handler for the button's default click event (see Figure 22.17).

FIGURE 22.16

The Anchor property enables you to create a form with controls that retain their relative locations and resize themselves automatically...in just a few mouse clicks!

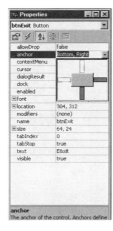

FIGURE 22.17

To create an event handler with Visual J++, all you need to do is double-click the control and begin typing.

Insert the following line of code into the btnExit_Click procedure:

```
application.exit();
```

Select Build, Build to compile the application. In the status bar at the bottom of the design environment, you will see the message Solution update failed. This indicates that errors were found in your application that you need to fix before it can run. To see the Task List that displays all errors found, select View, Other Windows, Task List (see Figure 22.18).

FIGURE 22.18

The Task List shows the description of the error and the file and exact line in which the error occurred.

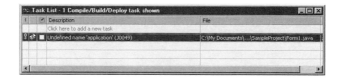

You will see the error Undefined name 'application' (J0049) in the second line of the task list. Double-click the error to move directly to the line within your code that caused the error. Notice the wavy blue line under the word application. This indicates that the error has occurred on this particular word. Rest the mouse over the word to view a ToolTip with additional information from the Task List about the error.

The error has occurred because Java is case sensitive and application should be Application. Erase the line and enter the following instead:

```
Application.
```

Notice that as soon as you press the period key, an IntelliSense dialog box appears, offering you all the methods and properties of the Application object. Select exit from the list and finish the line with a pair of parenthesis and a semicolon as follows:

```
Application.exit();
```

N O T E IntelliSense is smart enough to convert your typing to the proper case, relieving you of having to remember the exact capitalization of every property and method, which can save hours of debugging. ▓

Note that the Task List is automatically updated as you enter code. When you correct the case error and press Enter, the Task List automatically removes the error from the list.

Your btnExit click event handler is now finished. Recall the additional work that was involved in creating event handlers using the AWT. This is the true power of delegates at work, saving you time and effort.

Press F5 to run the application. The IDE jumps into Debug mode, and the application starts (see Figure 22.19).

FIGURE 22.19
A very simple WFC application is completed and running in a matter of just a few minutes.

Examine the running form. Notice that it is indistinguishable from a standard Windows form; it has Minimize, Maximize, and Restore boxes in the upper-right corner and a standard Windows control box in the upper left. Resize the form. Notice how the btnExit control maintains its position relative to the right and bottom sides of the form, as determined by its anchor property. When you consider all the functionality that this simple application framework has in just a couple of minutes of time and one line of code, you can easily see how Visual J++ can knock hours off your development time.

Click the Exit button to end the application and return to the Visual J++ design-time environment. Now that you can start and stop your application, it is time to make it functional. To do so, you need to add a richEdit control to display the contents of Rich Text formatted files. The richEdit control is part of the standard WFC controls collection already available in the toolbox. Drag and drop the richEdit control onto your form and resize it to fill all available space on the form, as shown in Figure 22.20.

FIGURE 22.20

The richEdit control shown here is only one of the many standard controls included in the WFC that are commonly available in other development tools, such as Visual Basic.

Set the following properties of the richEdit1 control:

▓ Name—reDocument

▓ Anchor—Top, Left, Bottom, Right

Run the application again. Resize the form to verify that the reDocument control fills all available space with only a few mouse clicks instead of several lines of code.

By Microsoft standards, all applications should support menu items offering a keyboard alternative to all mouse-usable controls. As you might have guessed, Visual J++ makes creating menus as easy and efficient as possible. To create your menu, drop a MainMenu control anywhere on your form.

 There are actually two menu controls, side by side in the Toolbox. The first is the standard Main menu that resides at the top of your form, and the second is a context menu that can be displayed anywhere on the form. Be sure to check the tool tip to verify that you are adding the correct control to your form.

Notice that as soon as you drop the MainMenu control onto the form, a space for a menu appears near the top of your form and a single menu entry is available, marked Type Here. The menu creation and editing functions in Visual J++ 6 are far and beyond better than all previous schemes included with any development environment. To create a new menu, all you need to do is begin typing. Make sure that the menu item marked Type Here is highlighted and enter &File to create a top-level menu.

As you begin typing in any menu item, you will notice that two more menu items appear, one to the right and one below the one you are currently editing. When you have entered &File for the top level menu, press the down arrow to move to the first second-level menu item below File. Enter the following menu items below File:

▓ &Open

▓ &Save

▓ Save &As

▓ &Close

▓ E&xit

N O T E Visual J++ gives you several ways to complete most tasks. The text property of the menu item holds the value for the caption that appears to the user. You might change this value in the Properties dialog if you prefer. ▓

You now have the basic structure of the menus defined. To set the properties of a menu item, click on the item and press F4 to display the Properties dialog. Set the name properties for each menu item to the prefix mnu and the caption of the item (for example, the first menu item has a caption of File and is called mnuFile).

After the menu items have been named appropriately, click on the File menu to display the entire list, as shown in Figure 22.21.

FIGURE 22.21
Creating menus on a
Visual J++ WFC form is
as easy as clicking and
typing.

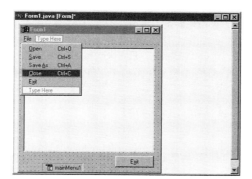

To the right of each caption, you will find a small blank area. Click in this area to display a drop-down list of Speed Keys available for each menu item. Select the following speed keys for each menu:

▓ Open—Ctrl+O

▓ Save—Ctrl+S

▓ Save As—Ctrl+A

▓ Close—Ctrl+C

Again, this is an area where the Microsoft engineers took a long look at how they could improve the interface and speed development. By eliminating the need for additional windows to design the interface, Visual J++ makes menu creation as fast and seamless as manipulating all other controls.

Now that all your menu controls are in place and have appropriate property values set, it is time to write event handlers for the menu items. In order to write code for the mnuOpen control, it is necessary to have a way for the user to be able to select a file from their hard drive or the network. Fortunately, the WFC includes a `fileOpenDialog` that provides a Windows standard way of doing just that. If you have ever had to write Java code to present the user with an aesthetically pleasing File Open dialog, you will most definitely appreciate the ease and speed that the WFC affords you.

Drag a `fileOpenDialog` control onto your form. Set the following properties:

- Name—fodDocument
- Filter—Rich Text Files¦*.rtf

By setting just two properties, you have now completed your standard Windows Open File dialog. All you need to do now is display it upon command.

Double-click on the `mnuOpen` control to display the code for the click event. Enter the following code:

```
fodDocument.showDialog();
if (fodDocument.getFileName()!="")
    reDocument.loadFile(fodDocument.getFileName());
```

This simple code is all you need to enable the user to select a file from any drive he has access to, and display that file in the program. The first line displays the `fileOpenDialog` and waits for the user to either select a file or click Cancel. The second line is used for error checking to ensure that a file has been selected, and the final line loads the contents of the file into the `richEdit` control.

Add a `SaveFileDialog` control to your form and name it `sfdDocument`. It will be used for the Save As menu.

The code for the other menu controls is even simpler. Enter the following code for each of the specified menu items:

- Save:

  ```
  reDocument.saveFile(fodDocument.getFileName());
  ```

- Save As:

  ```
  sfdDocument.showDialog();
  ```

  ```
  reDocument.saveFile(sfdDocument.getFileName());
  ```

- Close:

  ```
  reDocument.clear();
  ```

CAUTION

The Save function is using the last file name selected in the `fileOpenDialog` component to save the file to. If you have displayed and cancelled the `fileOpenDialog` control since opening the file, errors occur when you try to save.

There is one last menu item that you have not set code for, mnuExit. Recall that you have already written code to force the application to quit in the click event handler of btnExit. If you recall the previous discussion of the benefits of delegates, you are probably wondering if you can reuse that code for the mnuExit click event handler. Not only can you do so, but it is surprisingly easy.

To attach the code in the btnExit click handler to the mnuExit click handler, complete the following simple steps:

1. Click the mnuExit menu item.
2. Press F4 to display the Properties dialog.
3. Click the Events button (the lightening symbol) just above the list of properties.
4. Select the click event from the list of events.
5. Click the down arrow on the far right of the Properties dialog and select btnExit_Click() from the resulting list (see Figure 22.22).

FIGURE 22.22
The delegates event model enables you to reuse event handling code for multiple events within one control or every control within your application.

With just a quick list selection from the events list, you have attached the mnuExit item's click handler to the btnExit's click handler code. Run the application again to test the new functionality. Choose File, Open and select an RTF file from the dialog box. It opens in the richEdit control where you can edit it as you please. When you have made changes to the control, choose File, Save to save your changes back to disk. Test the functionality of the other menu items and select File, Exit to test the reuse of the btnExit handler and return to design mode.

Enhancing Your WFC Applications

You now have a fully functioning word-processing application. There is more, however, that you can easily do to make your application more user-friendly, such as adding a toolbar and utilizing the Windows API.

The most important aspect of using a suite of applications like Visual Studio is the capability to mix and match code and objects from different languages. Visual J++ enables you to do just that by giving you the capability to drop ActiveX controls created in either Visual Basic or Visual C++ right onto your form alongside the standard WFC controls. This enables you to leverage your existing code from the other development languages, while using the latest WFC controls, all in a single, integrated environment.

To demonstrate the use of ActiveX controls in your application, add a toolbar control that will duplicate the functionality of the menu items. Select the ActiveX Controls tab in the toolbox to display the list of available ActiveX controls. Drag the Toolbar control onto your form.

> **N O T E**   If the Toolbar control doesn't appear in the list of ActiveX controls, go to the Customize Toolbox dialog and make sure that it is checked. ■

Set the following properties for the Toolbar control:

- ▓ Name—tbSample
- ▓ Anchor—top

At this point, your richEdit control is probably partially covered by the now top-anchored Toolbar control. You will correct this momentarily; first you need to move the btnExit control from the form to the toolbar as follows:

1. Right-click on the btnExit control and select Cut.
2. Right-click on the Toolbar control and select Paste.

Resize the btnExit to fit nicely on the toolbar. Now follow the same procedure as in the preceding steps, except choose Copy instead of Cut and create four more buttons on the toolbar. Change the name and text properties of the buttons to mirror the menu items. When you have finished setting the properties, set the click event handlers for each button to call their respective menu item click handler counterparts. Now you can move and resize the reDocument control to fill all available space below the toolbar.

Your toolbar ActiveX control is now in place and fully functional! You have greatly enhanced the user-friendliness of the control and incorporated code written in another language, all without writing one additional line of code!

The Windows API is full of useful functions that have all been tweaked for maximum performance and fully stress-tested. Having this library available to you can shorten development times and increase stability. To demonstrate this capability, you will call GetTickCount(), a simple Windows API call that returns the number of milliseconds that Windows has been running. This is often used to determine the length of time a given process takes to run.

To access the Windows API, you need to declare the method you will call. Visual J++ comes with a J/Direct Call Builder that helps you select the correct declarations. To view the Call Builder, select View, Other Windows, J/Direct Call Builder (see Figure 22.23).

FIGURE 22.23

The J/Direct Call Builder lets you quickly search through the entire Windows API and automatically pastes the necessary declarations right into your code.

In the Find box, enter GetTickCount. The list scrolls down as you type and highlights the desired method. Click the ellipsis button next to the Target box. In the Select Class dialog, choose Form1 and press OK. Close the Call Builder dialog and move to the bottom of your code. The Call Builder has entered the necessary declaration for you (see Figure 22.24).

FIGURE 22.24

The J/Direct Call Builder automatically enters the API call declaration into your code so that you can keep working without interruption.

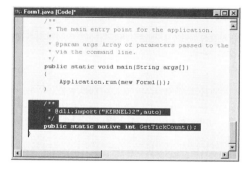

To verify that the API call works, change the code in one of the menu event handlers so that it reads as follows:

```
Long l = new Long(GetTickCount());
    btnExit.setText(l.toString());
```

Run the application and select the menu item whose handler you changed. The caption on the Exit button should now be a very large number, as illustrated in Figure 22.25.

FIGURE 22.25

The button caption now shows the result of a call to the Windows API `GetTickCount` function.

From Here...

This demonstration of using the Windows API focuses on ease of use, not functionality. However, there are thousands of API calls that can quickly and reliably improve the usability of your application by adding functionality such as cut and paste, retrieval of the user's logon name, system information, and almost any other standard Windows functionality.

In addition to the use of ActiveX controls and the Windows API, Visual J++ 6 offers you the capability to save your Java classes as ActiveX controls, build WFC components, mix standard components and Dynamic HTML components, and much more!

- For more information about how to use Visual Studio, see Chapter 2, "Using Visual Studio to Create Applications."
- For more information about using Visual J++ to create COM components, see Chapter 28, "Creating COM Components for MTS with Visual J++."
- For more information about using Java applets as a part of your Web solution, see Chapter 24, "Packaging and Deploying Web-Based Applications."

CHAPTER 23

Using Microsoft Transaction Server to Build Transactional Web Pages

by Joe Lengyel

In this chapter

Looking at Microsoft Transaction Server

One of the big challenges of software development is meeting tomorrow's software needs with software developed yesterday. This means that when software is developed, some kind of vision has to be implemented in a plan that thoroughly considers the future. Object-oriented practices applied to all phases of the software lifecycle greatly assist in achieving an outcome that can meet future needs. Next, you should look for environments that take well-developed software and propel them into a new dimension of performance and implementation ease. This describes Microsoft Transaction Server (MTS).

Not long ago, two-tier client/server applications were the norm of software development. Multitier applications were at the leading edge. Today, multitier applications have replaced the traditional client/server as de facto. There are good reasons for this transition. Two-tier applications don't scale well and they don't port well. In the past, the success of two-tier applications was project oriented. Secondly, Internet popularity has skyrocketed. For Internet applications, logic must be deployed on the middle tier. So developers built business objects and built Web pages. What was needed was middleware that harbored and managed middle-tier business objects, which also promised scalability for object requests from diverse clients, including Internet browsers. The solution, again, is MTS.

This chapter focuses on interactions between Microsoft Internet Explorer (IE), Microsoft Internet Information Server (IIS), and MTS. Although a wide variety of browsers and servers exist in the market today, the IE/IIS combination provides the richest interaction. Now, add Active Server Pages (ASP) and MTS to the mix, and you achieve a superior suite of products that brings shocking power to developing I-net applications.

MTS is designed to simplify the development of the middle tier of multitier applications by providing the infrastructure to execute the business logic. It spares developers from dealing with such issues as connectivity, security, directory, process and thread management, and database connection management. In short, MTS greatly aids developers with the elements required to support robust, production-class, core business applications, regardless of whether they are positioned on the Internet, intranet, or internal local area network (LAN).

Best said, MTS is an enabler built of elements that work together to make implementing and monitoring software objects more practical and powerful. A simple example followed by an explanation of the each element of the MTS framework will be useful here.

Partitioned Applications

Imagine you have built a multitier intranet application. Extensive time was logged for planning, gathering requirements, designing, and implementing a sound, object-oriented masterpiece. The application is tiered in the following manner (see Figure 23.1):

- User Interface
- Interface Logic
- Business Logic
- Data Access Objects
- Database

FIGURE 23.1

A multitier, enterprise application that partitions functionality into useful, flexible layers.

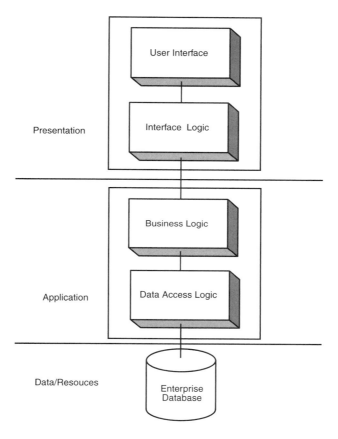

By all indications, the project is a smashing success, and you warm yourself in self-satisfaction. Until the next day, that is. That's when the next project starts—an Internet application providing much of the same functionality of the product you just rolled out, but available to the World Wide Web (WWW) through heterogeneous browsers. By the way, it's due yesterday.

The preceding scenario is not uncommon. There are plenty of solid intranet applications that are being reused to provide Internet functionality. It makes sense, and it is that for which software-reuse pundits are pleading. Good design and development standards put you in a good position to complete the effort with a minimal amount of rework. How would you respond to the situation? Software reuse or cut and paste? If you are thinking cut and paste, you need to take a good look at how your enterprise is building software.

Enterprise solutions should focus on object-oriented approaches to software development. Object-oriented approaches focus on interactions between components (business objects). Figure 23.2 depicts the relationship between components. Each component has a specific job made available to other objects through interfaces. An existing object can facilitate the need for a specific job in a new application merely by supplying interfaces and outcome. Chapter 25, "Clients, Servers, and Components: Design Strategies for Distributed Applications," features an excellent discussion on this subject.

FIGURE 23.2
Object-oriented business objects communicate using interfaces and encapsulate the underlying logic.

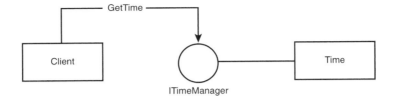

MTS Framework

MTS provides a framework that enables you to implement existing objects to produce the Web site. MTS is composed of the following elements:

- Application components—Application components model the activity of a business. These components implement the business rules and interface with application layers between the user interface and the database. They provide views and transformations of the application state. Application state can be durable or nondurable. Database records represent the durable state of the application. Nondurable data, such as data temporarily stored in variables, is ephemeral.

- Transaction Server Executive—The Microsoft Transaction Server Executive is a DLL that provides runtime services for MTS components. These services include thread and context management. This DLL is loaded into the processes that host application components and runs in the background. Transaction Server also provides a set of resource dispensers that simplify access to shared resources in a server process.

- Server processes—A server process is a system process that hosts application component execution. A server process can host multiple components and can service tens, hundreds, or potentially thousands of clients. You can configure multiple server processes to execute on a single computer. Each server process reflects a separate trust boundary and fault isolation domain.

- Resource managers—A resource manager is a system service that manages durable data. Server applications use resource managers to maintain the durable state of the application, such as the record of inventory on hand, pending orders, and accounts receivable. Resource managers work in cooperation with the Distributed Transaction Coordinator to provide the application with a guarantee of atomicity and isolation.

- Resource dispensers—A resource dispenser is a service that manages nondurable, shared state on behalf of the application components within a process. Resource dispensers are similar to resource managers, but without the guarantee or durability. MTS provides two resource dispensers: the open database connectivity (ODBC) and Shared Property Manager. The ODBC resource dispenser manages database activity through connection pools. The Shared Property Manager provides synchronized access to application-defined, process-wide properties.

- Microsoft Distributed Transaction Coordinator (DTC)—DTC is a system service that coordinates transactions. Work can be committed as an atomic transaction even if it spans multiple-resource managers potentially on separate computers. The inclusion of

DTC in MTS adds important new components to help implement distributed transactions and make the management of two-phase commit a more practical undertaking.

■ Microsoft Transaction Server Explorer (MTX)—You can use the MTX to deploy application components. You can also use it to view and manipulate items in the Transaction Server runtime environment. MTX is a graphical user interface (GUI) for managing and deploying MTS components. Administrators as well as developers can use the MTX to administer, distribute, install, deploy, and test packages. Developers use the MTS Explorer to assemble components into prebuilt packages and to distribute and test components in the MTS environment. In addition, MTX enables you to monitor and manage transactions for your transactional components. This is an especially useful feature for observing the allocation and deallocation of server components.

MTS Packages and Components

All the elements previously described make up the MTS environment. Figure 23.3 depicts the interaction of the elements. They work together in a way that makes developing MTS components the real focus of developers, as it should be. MTS shelters developers from many complex server issues, such as database concurrency, security, context management, and other system-level complexities. This enables developers to focus on the job of software development and implementing business rules. Consequently, developers can write applications as if they run in isolation because components running in the MTS runtime environment can take advantage of transactions. The transaction system, working in cooperation with database servers and other types of resource managers, ensures that concurrent transactions meet the ACID (Atomicity, Consistency, Isolation, Durability) test.

MTS also simplifies building distributed applications by providing location transparency. MTS automatically loads the component into a process. An MTS component can be loaded into a client application process or into a separate, surrogate-server process as a local or remote component, depending on the location.

MTS components are COM components built as DLLs. The term *component* represents the code that implements a COM object. Visual Basic components are implemented through class modules. Visual C++ components are implemented as classes. You can create these components in any language that facilitates creation of ActiveX components. In both cases, these components can be differentiated from other COM components because they execute in the MTS runtime environment.

N O T E MTS imposes specific requirements on components beyond those required by COM. This enables MTS to provide services to the component that would not otherwise be possible. These include increased scalability, robustness, and simplified system management. ■

MTS components are implemented in MTS packages. A package is one or more components that perform related application functions. You can manage a package of components as a unit. The components in a package can share security settings and can access other shared resources. Packages make the job of using components like managing groups of users in NT.

FIGURE 23.3

The elements of MTS work together to create a scalable, transaction processing environment.

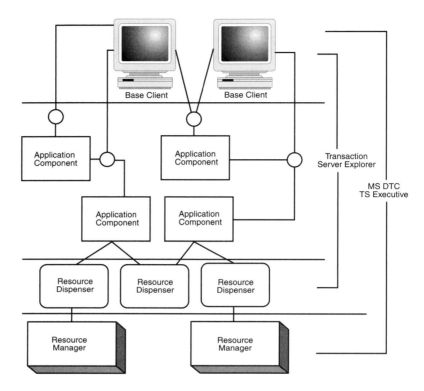

All components in a package run together in the same MTS server process. A package is a trust boundary that defines when security credentials are verified, and defines a deployment unit for a set of components. Packages can be either a library package or server package. A library package runs in the process of the client that creates it. Library packages do not support component tracking, process isolation, or role checking. A server package runs isolated in its own process on the local computer. Server packages support role-based security, resource sharing, process isolation, and process management.

Packages can be managed effectively by using the Transaction Explorer. You can even split a package for deployment across servers by partitioning the package for multiple-machine installation. Figure 23.4 illustrates the relationship between packages and components.

FIGURE 23.4
In MTS, components are implemented through packages.

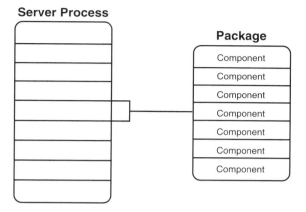

MTS and Software Reuse

MTS provides an infrastructure that is conducive to software reuse. Software reuse is the Holy Grail of software development—much sought after but rarely found. Real software reuse doesn't happen just through the cut and paste of code. And software purists really don't consider software slightly modified as software reused. Software reuse really happens when sof2tware components can be used without any modification. Their use is dictated by the functionality provided through the interfaces exposed. Reuse is about plug and play.

MTS facilitates software reuse, under the correct conditions. Those conditions include fulfilling the concept of developing software for the enterprise, and not simply developing software for a project. Developing software only for a specific project or application typically results in software that cannot be reused. Not only is this expensive, but it's also inflexible. It dissolves into a situation where much time is spent building new applications from scratch, or trying to make new applications out of old applications. The latter method rarely works well. More time is spent trying to decide which code should stay or go, rather than focusing on the vision of enterprise solutions.

MTS promotes software reuse in two ways. First, MTS components are available to any program that calls them, via COM, Hypertext Transfer Protocol (HTTP), or DCOM. Location is not an issue, so strategic placement of components and functionality is fully facilitated and application development is less constrained. Second, the requirements of MTS components demand good programming habits. Good programming habits promote software reuse. For example, embedding procedural code behind a VB form doesn't promote software reuse outside of the cut and paste method. It might be inefficient to reuse the code through form subclassing because a large percent of the form wouldn't be needed. As discussed earlier in the chapter, GUIs should be partitioned from interface logic through object-orientation. The logic in the interface layer can be reused more easily than code embedded behind a GUI. MTS promotes this paradigm. Still, bad MTS components are a possibility. MTS won't prevent you from implementing poorly written code that makes inefficient use of system resources, or that implements incorrect logic. Obviously good planning and building code to correct specifications is crucial. There is no substitute for methodical software development.

MTS and Multitier Applications

One important attribute of an enterprise application is that it is typically mission critical. Large or small, this application must be robust enough to sustain continuous operation, fulfilling business needs. It must be flexible for scalability and deployment, and allow for efficient maintenance, monitoring and administration. Often times, two-tier applications don't fulfill the majority of these requirements. This doesn't mean all two-tier systems fail at meeting all the requirements of enterprise applications. Some meet all the requirements, but don't fulfill software reuse. This is especially true in businesses where programs are built using Rapid Application Development (RAD) tools.

RAD tools are the great enablers of people with moderate to limited backgrounds in software development principles. Consequently, this often means that business applications are inflexible, unscalable two-tier applications that are expensive to maintain and administrate.

To many, building a GUI and writing code to access a database constitutes programming. By a limited definition, this is true. But what more and more companies are finding out is that this approach usually creates a false sense of meeting Information Systems/Information Technology (IS/IT) needs, and that flexibility for the future is compromised. These situations drain IS/IT resources because they don't accommodate modifications to business rules well, and don't facilitate version changes well. Ever try to maintain an application with hard-coded business rules?

MTS promotes multitier development as well. Multitier applications are superior to two-tier applications. Why is this? Two reasons: software reuse and application flexibility and maintainability. First, MTS components can be reused in other applications. Their interfaces are exposed and can be called from other programs. Second, the very fact that you have middle-tier objects packaged in MTS means that you have probably created a more flexible application that is easier to maintain. Changes in business logic don't require a new release of client-side executables.

Understanding Transactional Web Pages

Transactional Web pages raise the bar on the functionality being offered through I-net sites. This isn't referring to Web visitors being able to submit requests for marketing materials or other information. This is referring to businesses being able to deploy distributed applications to support locale and client disperse users with DCOM and HTTP. It's about supporting real-world disconnected architectures the same as hardwire-connected users. It's about the complicated and stressful issues of managing database integrity and use in hyper-distributed environments.

Let's return to the example. What can be the course of action to get an Internet product up and running, with minimal amount of new development, on the basis of an existing multitier application? Reuse is definitely possible with the lower 60% of the tiered architecture. Probably a new user interface suitable for the browser will be needed. There might be an opportunity for reuse with the interface objects, depending on the shape the user interface tier takes on. Otherwise, all the object layers can become packaged components in MTS.

An I-net application can use HTTP to invoke an MTS component in two ways:

1. Call an ASP, which calls the MTS component using COM or DCOM.

2. Call the MTS component from ActiveX components executing in the Web through HTTP.

Either approach works well for a thin client, with the limitation that result sets are read-only. Figure 23.5 illustrates this architecture.

FIGURE 23.5
MTS components can be called from an Active Server Page or an ActiveX component.

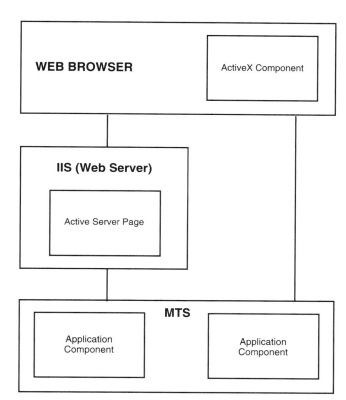

Working with MTS in a Transactional Web Page Solution

In addition to COM and DCOM clients, MTS supports HTML clients through ASP on the server and ActiveX components in the browser. An ASP script can invoke a component running inside of MTS, even components that are also being invoked through DCOM clients. And, an ActiveX component can call an MTS component through the object properties of the ActiveX component. Supporting both HTML clients and COM/DCOM clients from a common component-based middle-tier application that is integrated with legacy systems makes IIS with MTS a powerful application platform for the Web.

With the release of IIS 4, this powerful platform improved. In IIS 4, ASP uses MTS 2 as its application engine. The two technologies ship together in the Windows NT 4 Option Pack, use a common thread pool, and both use Microsoft Management Console (MMC) as a common management console. With IIS 4, ASP scripts run as MTS applications. Developers can configure their Web applications to run out of process, enabling the application to execute in its own MTS package. This provides crash protection for ASP applications.

There is a real need to provide transaction level control in Web pages. Many IS/IT shops have targeted the browser as the strategic client of the future. All applications will be used via a browser. As such, the functionality that we now enjoy in traditional client interfaces must be assimilated into the browser world. Furthermore, the capabilities in the browser must match what we have been accustomed to using in the traditional computing environment. For example, users expect browsers to display and facilitate update of table-like data. Lose the update capabilities and you lose much of the user base.

The real challenge at this level is enabling the users to make the updates, while maintaining the integrity of the data in the background, and offering high scalability. If real-world applications are going to be used in a browser environment, MTS must factor in largely.

N O T E   The exercises in this chapter require a single database table; the data-definition is provided in the following. It's recommended that you create this table in the PUBS database on an Access or SQL Server 6.5 and configure an ODBC resource accordingly. Proceed with an alternative RDBMS system to fit your own research and adjust the following DDL and DML to fit your needs:

```
Create Table MTSTable
(WorkCol    varchar(10)    Default 'Sample')
     Insert into MTSTable Default Values
```

Using Active Server Pages

In this section I discuss how to integrate Active Server Pages with MTS to create and facilitate transactional Web functionality. Specifically, you will step through an exercise that creates an ASP and an MTS component, and calls both from a browser. You will build a Web page that enables you to submit a temperature in Fahrenheit to a database table and retrieve the equivalent temperature in Celsius. The example is simple, but the concepts are important and useful. Figure 23.6 illustrates the environment that was used to develop the exercise.

FIGURE 23.6

The architecture in play when calling an MTS component from an Active Server Page.

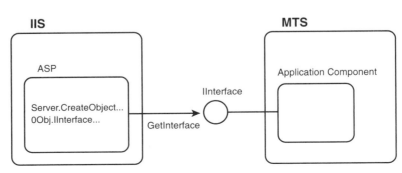

Being able to handle transactions from a Web page is not new. Web developers have been doing that kind of thing for a while, with CGI, ISAPI, and ASP without MTS. Using MTS brings to the setting a whole new paradigm for creating transactional Web functionality. You will build a simple ASP page featuring two ActiveX controls. These controls interact with components within MTS. MTS shepherds transactions to a database. Your environment for performing this exercise can vary. At a minimum you need a browser, a Web server, MTS, and a database. This exercise uses IE, Personal Web Server (PWS), MTS and a database table on SQL Server 6.5. PWS isn't the Web server in which you deploy production-level I-net applications, but this environment is perfect for developing and testing applications and generally getting your feet wet.

CAUTION

An ASP can access MTS components via COM or DCOM. Although you can run the MTS components as an in-process server, an internal error in the MTS component causes MTS to terminate and might crash IIS. For reliability, it's better to call MTS components out of process.

N O T E By default, IIS doesn't enable out-of-process servers. To enable out-of-process components for IIS, use the Registry Editor (REGEDT32 for NT, REGEDIT for Windows 9x). Go to the following key and set the key `AllowsOutOfProcCmpnts` to 1:

`HKEY_LOCAL_MACHINE\SYSTEM\CurrentControlSet\Services\W3SVC\ASP\Parameters`

Building Temperature.ASP   To create the Active Server Page, perform the following tasks:

1. Using any text editor, enter the ASP content in Listing 23.1.

Listing 23.1   LIST231—Building Temperature

```
<%@ LANGUAGE="VBSCRIPT" %>
<HTML>
<HEAD>
<META NAME="GENERATOR" Content="Microsoft Visual InterDev 1.0">
<META HTTP-EQUIV="Content-Type" content="text/html; charset=iso-8859-1">
<TITLE>Temperature Converter</TITLE>
</HEAD>
<BODY>
Converts Fahrenheit to Celsius.
<%
Dim TemperatureObj, Msg, ret
If (Request("PutFahrentheit")) Then
    Set TemperatureObj= Server.CreateObject("Temperature.cTemperature")
        TemperatureObj.PutFahrenheit Request("Fahrenheit")
Else
    Set TemperatureObj= Server.CreateObject("Temperature.cTemperature")
        ret = TemperatureObj.GetCelsius
End If
%>
<BR>
```

continues

Listing 23.1 Continued

```
<FORM METHOD="POST" ACTION="Temperature.asp">
<BR>
Enter Fahrenheit:
<INPUT TYPE="TEXT" NAME="Fahrenheit" SIZE=10 VALUE="32">
<INPUT TYPE="SUBMIT" VALUE="PutFahrenheit">
<BR>
<BR>
Observe Celsius:
<INPUT TYPE="TEXT" NAME="Celsius" SIZE=10>
<INPUT TYPE="SUBMIT" VALUE="GetCelsius">
</FORM>
</BODY>
</HTML>
```

2. Save the file. Provide the name Temperature.ASP.

3. You are finished with this phase of the exercise.

Building the MTS Temperature Component To create the MTS component, perform the following tasks:

1. Start Visual Basic and create an ActiveX DLL project. MTS components must be DLLs because they are in-process servers. By default, a class module will already exist in the project.

2. Set the Name property of the class module to cTemperature. You can activate properties by selecting the class module in the Project Explorer and pressing F4.

3. Choose Project, Project1 properties from the menu. Change the name of the project to Temperature.

4. Next, add a reference to the Microsoft ActiveX Data Object 2.0 Library. Choose Project, References to open the References window. Locate and select the object library reference. Choose OK to continue.

5. Add the code in Listing 23.2 to the class module window.

Listing 23.2 LIST232—MTS Temperature Component

```
Option Explicit
Dim SQL As String
Private Const strConnect = "FILEDSN=MTSSamples"
Public Function PutFahrenheit(vText As Variant) As Variant
        ' obtain the ADO environment and connection
        Dim adoConn As New ADODB.Connection
        adoConn.Open strConnect

    'build and execute the sql
       SQL = "Update MTSTable Set WorkCol = '" & vText & "'"
       adoConn.Execute SQL

        'clean up
```

```
        Set adoConn = Nothing
    End Function

    Public Function GetCelsius() As Variant
        ' obtain the ADO environment and connection
        Dim adoConn As New ADODB.Connection
        adoConn.Open strConnect
        Dim adoRS As ADODB.Recordset
        Dim vTemperature As Variant

        'build and execute the sql
        SQL = "Select WorkCol from MTSTable"
        Set adoRS = adoConn.Execute(SQL)
        vTemperature = adoRS!WorkCol

        'convert F to C
        vTemperature = ((CDbl(vTemperature) - 32) * 5) / 9

        ' clean up
        Set adoRS = Nothing
        GetCelsius = vTemperature
End Function
```

Part

III

Ch

23

6. Save the project to a directory of your choice. Provide the name Temperature.DLL.

7. Compile and make a DLL. Choose File, Make Temperature.DLL from the menu.

8. You are finished with this phase of the exercise.

Building the MTS Temperature Package   To implement the component in an MTS package, perform the following tasks:

1. Start MTS using the MTS Explorer (MTX). The Microsoft Management Console (MMC) facilitates use of MTS. The MMC appears as shown in Figure 23.7.

FIGURE 23.7
Use MMC to manage and observe MTS components.

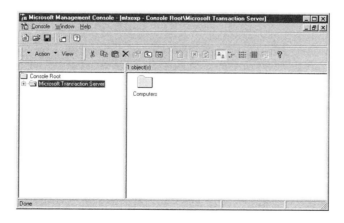

2. Double-click the Computers folder in the right pane of the window. This expands to show the computers currently available for management. Again, for this example, one computer is supporting all software applications.

3. Double-click on My Computer in the right pane of the window. This expands to show the Packages Installed folder, among other elements.

4. Double-click on the Packages Installed folder in the right pane of the window. This reveals the actual packages that have been assembled in MTS. Initially, this displays the samples that have been included with the MTS (if the samples were installed), as well as some system packages. In the future, the package added through this example will appear in this window.

5. At this time, choose New, Package from the Action menu to create a new package containing the VB DLL.

6. The Package Wizard will appear. At this point you can install a prebuilt package or create a custom package. Choose the Create an Empty Package button (see Figure 23.8).

FIGURE 23.8
The Package Wizard steps you through creation of an MTS package.

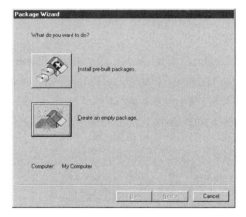

7. Enter a name for the new package. Always use a name that helps describe the functionality of the package. Supply `Temperature` as the package name for this example. Choose Next to continue.

T I P You must have administrator privileges to create packages. If you don't, the package will be created anyway, but won't carry a name. What's more, you won't be able to delete the package you shouldn't have been allowed to create. You must log on with administrator permissions to delete the package.

8. The Set Package Identity window enables you to associate a specific user account with the package. It can be either the current account or another account on a local or remote computer. Interactive User is the default option. For this example, don't change this option. Choose Finish.

9. After choosing finish, the wizard creates the package. It appears in the right pane along with the other packages. At this time the package is empty. You still need to add the VB DLL component to the package. The next section steps you through this process.

10. You are finished with this phase of the exercise.

To add the Temperature.DLL component to the Temperature package, perform the following tasks:

1. Locate and open the Temperature package. The Components and Roles folders are the only contents. Both are empty.

2. Double-click the Components folders in the right pane of the window.

3. Choose New, Component from the Action menu. The Component Wizard appears.

4. At this point you can install a new component or a preexisting component. Earlier in the exercise, you created a VB DLL. This fits the preexisting component description. Choose the Import a Component(s) That Is Already Registered button.

5. A list of COM components appears in the next window. These are in-process servers that have already been registered on the computer where the package resides (see Figure 23.9). Locate and select the Temperature.DLL component.

Part
III

Ch
23

FIGURE 23.9
The Component Wizard locates and presents all in-process servers that can be implemented in a package.

6. The component is added to the package.

> **N O T E**   MTS features a utility to export packages. This utility builds a registration program for you that can be run on client machines that call MTS components via DCOM or HTTP. The export program builds necessary information about the component and the server into the export package. Run the export executable on the client to enable it to locate and call the MTS components in the relative package. If the calling program and the MTS component are on the same computer, the export process is not necessary. Spend some time learning about the Export utility. ▪

Configuring ODBC   An ODBC entry is needed for this exercise. The MTS component uses an ODBC entry to connect to a database, in this case the PUBS database. If you installed the MTS Samples with MTS, an ODBC entry is made. However, it will not have configured to use the correct server or computer. If you intend to use this ODBC entry, you must correct the entry. If you are using your own ODBC entry, make sure it points to the database in which the WorkingTable table resides.

Testing the Temperature Example   Before you test the exercise, be sure to check the following necessities:

-   You need a Web client (IE 4).
-   You need a Web server running (IIS or PWS).
-   You need MTS installed and available through MMC.
-   You need an ODBC data source configured to use the database containing the previous table you created.

To test the sample you've built, perform the following tasks:

1.   Start your Web browser.
2.   Choose File, Open from the menu. The Open File dialog appears.
3.   Locate and select the ASP file you created for this exercise. Choose the OK button to launch the ASP file.

TROUBLESHOOTING

If the file doesn't appear in the browser as expected, check your ASP installation.

4.   Start the Transaction Explorer (through the Management Console).
5.   Position the browser on the screen so that the MTX can be viewed at the same time. This is useful when running the application.
6.   Drill down to the Temperature component. Select the component with a single click in the right pane of the window.
7.   Choose Status View from the View menu. This enables you to observe the activity of the component when it is instantiated in an object context.
8.   Use the buttons presented by the ASP. Note the utilization of the MTS component in the Transaction Explorer window.

The previous exercise, in case you hadn't noticed, is lacking in error handling and transaction control language. It's a simple exercise, and extensive code to accomplish these tasks was omitted for brevity. However, do not underestimate the need for such functionality. It's extremely important and necessary to implement exhaustive error trapping to prevent crashes, and transaction level control to provide a robust computing environment. It's highly recommended that you do so.

Using Browser-Side ActiveX Components

In this section, you will use a browser-side ActiveX component to call an MTS component. You will build a Web page that enables submission of a string value to a database table. The process returns the value in the database table with characters transposed. The example is simple, but the concepts are important and useful. Figure 23.10 illustrates the environment that was used to develop the exercise.

FIGURE 23.10
The architecture in play when calling an MTS component from an ActiveX component within an HTML page.

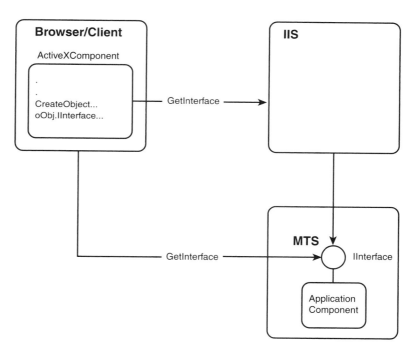

You will build a simple HTML page featuring two ActiveX controls. These controls will interact with components within MTS. MTS will shepherd transactions to a database. Your environment for performing this exercise can vary. At a minimum you need a browser, a Web server, MTS, and a database. This exercise uses IE, PWS, MTS and a database table on SQL Server 6.5. PWS isn't the Web server you would deploy production level I-net applications. But this environment is perfect for developing and testing applications and generally getting your feet wet.

N O T E An ActiveX component executing inside a Web browser can call an MTS component, provided that ActiveX component has been registered on the client, the MTS package registration has been installed on the client, and the MTS component is available in MTS. Use the HTML <OBJECT> tag and script to handle these tasks, as well as to invoke the controls and components. You can also use the <OBJECT> tag to load a MTS component in process with the browser client (requires MTS installed on the Web browser computer). ▨

Building PutGet.HTML First, build the HTML page that calls your MTS components. To do so, perform the following tasks:

1. Open any text editor (such as Notepad) and enter the HTML and Script text in Listing 23.3.

Listing 23.3   LIST233—PutGet HTML

```
<HTML>
<HEAD>
<META NAME="GENERATOR" Content="Microsoft Developer Studio">
<META HTTP-EQUIV="Content-Type" content="text/html; charset=iso-8859-1">
<TITLE>Put and Get HTML</TITLE>
</HEAD>
<BODY>
Put the text in here.
<br>
<OBJECT ID="txtPut" WIDTH=96 HEIGHT=24
        CLASSID="CLSID:8BD21D10-EC42-11CE-9E0D-00AA006002F3">
            <PARAM NAME="VariousPropertyBits" VALUE="746604571">
            <PARAM NAME="Size" VALUE="2540;635">
            <PARAM NAME="FontCharSet" VALUE="0">
            <PARAM NAME="FontPitchAndFamily" VALUE="2">
</OBJECT>
<br>
<br>
<OBJECT ID="cmdPut" WIDTH=96 HEIGHT=32
        CLASSID="CLSID:D7053240-CE69-11CD-A777-00DD01143C57">
            <PARAM NAME="Caption" VALUE="Put">
            <PARAM NAME="Size" VALUE="2540;846">
            <PARAM NAME="FontCharSet" VALUE="0">
            <PARAM NAME="FontPitchAndFamily" VALUE="2">
            <PARAM NAME="ParagraphAlign" VALUE="3">
</OBJECT>
<br>
<br>
<br>
Get the text back here.
<br>
<OBJECT ID="txtGet" WIDTH=96 HEIGHT=24
        CLASSID="CLSID:8BD21D10-EC42-11CE-9E0D-00AA006002F3">
            <PARAM NAME="VariousPropertyBits" VALUE="746604571">
            <PARAM NAME="Size" VALUE="2540;635">
            <PARAM NAME="FontCharSet" VALUE="0">
            <PARAM NAME="FontPitchAndFamily" VALUE="2">
</OBJECT>
<br>
<br>
<OBJECT ID="cmdGet" WIDTH=96 HEIGHT=32
        CLASSID="CLSID:D7053240-CE69-11CD-A777-00DD01143C57">
            <PARAM NAME="Caption" VALUE="Get">
            <PARAM NAME="Size" VALUE="2540;847">
            <PARAM NAME="FontCharSet" VALUE="0">
            <PARAM NAME="FontPitchAndFamily" VALUE="2">
            <PARAM NAME="ParagraphAlign" VALUE="3">
```

```
</OBJECT>
<SCRIPT LANGUAGE="VBScript">
Sub cmdPut_Click
            Dim obj, ProgID
ProgID = "WriteDB.cWriteDB"
Set obj = CreateObject(ProgID)
obj.PutData(TextPut.Value)
Set obj = Nothing
End Sub
Sub cmdGet_Click
            Dim obj, ProgID, Ret
            ProgID = "WriteDB.cWriteDB"
            Set obj = CreateObject(ProgID)
            Ret = obj.GetData
            Set obj = Nothing
End Sub
</SCRIPT>
</BODY>
</HTML>
```

2. Save the file. Provide the name PUTGET.HTML.

3. You are finished with this phase of the exercise.

The preceding page was built using Visual InterDev, a standard product in Visual Studio. You can use any tool that you desire to achieve the same effect as depicted in Figure 23.11.

FIGURE 23.11
The PutGet.HTML page as viewed in a browser.

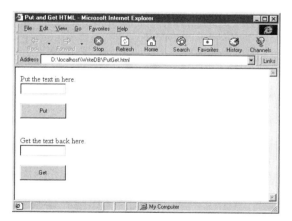

Building the MTS WriteDB Component Second, build the MTS component. This will be a VB DLL. To do this, perform the following tasks:

1. Start Visual Basic and create an ActiveX DLL project. MTS components must be DLLs because they are in-process servers. By default, a class module already exists in the project.

2. Set the Name property of the class module to cWriteDB. You can activate properties by selecting the class module in the Project Explorer and pressing F4.

3. Choose Project, Project1 properties from the menu. Change the name of the project to WriteDB.

4. Next, add a reference to the Microsoft ActiveX Data Object 2 Library. Choose Project, References to open the References window. Locate and select the object library reference. Choose OK to continue.

5. Add the code in Listing 23.4 to the class module window.

Listing 23.4   LIST234—MTS WriteDB Component

```
Option Explicit
Dim SQL As String
Private Const strConnect = "FILEDSN=MTSSamples"
Public Function PutData(vText As Variant) As Variant
    ' obtain the ADO environment and connection
    Dim adoConn As New ADODB.Connection
    adoConn.Open strConnect

    'build and execute the sql
    SQL = "Update MTSTable Set WorkCol = '" & Left(vText, 10) & "'"
    adoConn.Execute SQL

    'clean up
    Set adoConn = Nothing
End Function

Public Function GetData() As Variant
    ' obtain the ADO environment and connection
    Dim adoConn As New ADODB.Connection
    adoConn.Open strConnect
    Dim adoRS As ADODB.Recordset
    Dim sTableValue As Variant

    'build and execute the sql
    SQL = "Select WorkCol from MTSTable"
    Set adoRS = adoConn.Execute(SQL)
    sTableValue = adoRS!WorkCol

    ' clean up
    Set adoRS = Nothing
    GetData = sTableValue
End Function
```

6. Save the project to a directory of your choice. Provide the name WriteDB.DLL.

7. Compile and make a DLL. Choose File, Make WriteDB.DLL from the menu.

8. You are finished with this phase of the exercise.

TROUBLESHOOTING

You might experience difficulties making changes to a VB DLL after it has been added to a package in MTS. MTS references the DLL using a class ID (CLSID). If changes you have made don't appear to be present in the packaged component, delete the component and add it again.

Building the MTS WriteDB Package   Next, implement the VB DLL into an MTS package. To do this, you need MTS installed in the location where the VB DLL is located and registered. MTS is available on the Windows NT 4 Option Pack. If you haven't done this yet, now is the time.

 MTS ships with some good examples that will give you some exposure and experience with the overall MTS environment. It's a good idea to get some practice with MTS using the examples before starting any personal experiments yourself.

To create a package in MTS, perform the following tasks:

1. Start MTS using the MTX. The MMC facilitates use of MTS.

2. Double-click the Computers folder in the right pane of the window. This expands to show the computers currently available for management. Again, for this example, one computer is supporting all software applications.

3. Double-click on My Computer in the right pane of the window. This expands to show the Packages Installed folder, among other elements.

4. Double-click the Packages Installed folder in the right pane of the window. This reveals the actual packages that have been assembled in MTS. Initially, this displays the samples that have been included with the MTS (if the samples were installed), as well as some system packages. In the future, the package added through this example appears in this window.

5. At this time, choose New, Package from the Action menu to create a new package containing the VB DLL.

6. The Package Wizard appears. At this point you can install a prebuilt package or create a custom package. Choose the Create an Empty Package button.

7. Enter a name for the new package. Always use a name that helps describe the functionality of the package. Supply WriteDB as the package name for this example. Choose Next to continue.

 You must have administrator privileges to create packages. If you don't, the package will be created anyway, but won't carry a name. What's more, you won't be able to delete the package you shouldn't have been able to create. You must log on with administrator permissions to delete the package.

8. The Set Package Identity window enables you to associate a specific user account with the package. It can be either the current account or another account on a local or remote computer. Interactive User is the default option. For this example, don't change this option. Choose Finish.

9. After choosing finish, the wizard creates the package. It appears in the right pane along with the other packages. At this time the package is empty. You still need to add the VB DLL component to the package. The next section steps you through this process.

To add the WriteDB.DLL component to the WriteDB package, perform the following tasks:

1. Locate and open the WriteDB package. The Components and Roles folders are the only contents. Both are empty.

2. Double-click the Components folders in the right pane of the window.

3. Choose New, Component from the Action menu. The Component Wizard appears.

4. At this point you can install a new component or a preexisting component. Earlier in the exercise, you created a VB DLL. This fits the preexisting component description. Choose the Import a Component(s) That Is Already Registered button.

5. A list of COM components appears in the next window. These are in-process servers that have already been registered on the computer where the package resides. Locate and select the WriteDB.DLL component.

6. The component is added to the package (see Figure 23.12).

FIGURE 23.12
The WriteDB package containing the WriteDB.DLL.

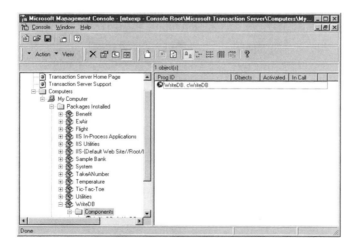

The Transaction Support Property of each component indicates whether the component will execute in the context of a transaction. For this exercise, the default of Does Not Support Transactions was used. Nevertheless, this is a very important property setting. Understand and use this property thoroughly to obtain effective transaction support.

▶ For more information, **see** Chapter 5, "An Inside Look at Microsoft Transaction Server," **p. 107**

Configuring ODBC   An ODBC entry is needed for this exercise. The MTS component uses an ODBC entry to connect to a database, in this case, the PUBS database. If you installed the MTS Samples with MTS, an ODBC entry is made (see Figure 23.13). However, it won't be configured to use the correct server or computer. If you intend to use this ODBC entry, you must correct the entry. If you are using your own ODBC entry, make sure it points to the database in which the WorkingTable table resides.

FIGURE 23.13
The MTS Samples data source entry in the ODBC administration is configured when installing the MTS Sample components.

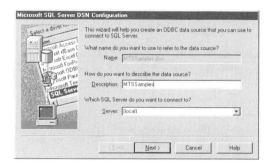

Part
III

Ch
23

Testing the WriteDB Example   Now you will test the application. Before you do this, double-check the environment necessities for this example:

- You need a Web client (IE 4).
- You need a Web server running (IIS or PWS).
- You need MTS installed and available through the Management Console.
- You need an ODBC data source configured to use the database containing the table you created previously.

To test the sample you've built, perform the following tasks:

1. Start your Web browser.
2. Choose File, Open from the menu. The Open File dialog appears.
3. Locate and select the ASP file you created for this exercise. Choose the OK button to launch the ASP file.
4. Start the Transaction Explorer (through the Management Console).
5. Position the browser on the screen so that the MTX can be viewed at the same time. This is useful when running the application.
6. Drill down to the WriteDB component. Select the component with a single click in the right pane of the window.
7. Choose Status View from the View menu. This enables you to observe the activity of the component when it is instantiated in an object context.
8. Use the buttons presented by the ASP. Note the utilization of the MTS component in the Transaction Explorer window.

The preceding exercise, in case you hadn't noticed, is lacking in error handling and transaction control language. It is a simple exercise, and extensive code to accomplish these tasks was omitted for brevity. However, don't underestimate the need for such functionality. It's extremely important and necessary to implement exhaustive error trapping to prevent crashes, and transaction level control to provide a robust computing environment. It's highly recommended that you do so.

From Here...

In this chapter, you learned about using Microsoft Transaction Server with other products to build transactional Web pages. You stepped through an exercise combining an Active Server Page and MTS. Similarly, you called an MTS component from an ActiveX component using a Web browser. Both exercises provide valuable insights into how the technologies come together to provide a powerful toolbox of development opportunities. For more information on some of the topics addressed in this chapter, see the following chapters:

- For more information on distributed computing, see Chapter 25, "Clients, Servers, and Components: Design Strategies for Distributed Applications."

- To learn more about using the Microsoft Transaction Server, see Chapter 31, "Using Microsoft Transaction Server to Enable Distributed Applications."

- A comprehensive study of ASP and IIS can be found in Chapter 6, "An Inside Look at Active Server Pages and the Internet Information Server."

- For a detailed look at developing for I-net applications, see Chapter 19, "Advanced Visual InterDev Concepts."

CHAPTER 24

Packaging and Deploying Web-Based Applications

by Gregg D. August

In this chapter

Exploring Web Pages and Component Downloads

Many corporations are discovering the benefits of creating centralized programming through browser-based intranet applications and using the Internet to reach personnel over the World Wide Web. This chapter describes methods that allow you to add security and licensing to your browser-based applications and effectively place them on an intranet or the World Wide Web.

When using a Web browser, you are actually viewing the output from a text document containing Hypertext Markup Language (HTML) commands. The text document (commonly called a *Web page*) resides at a specific I-net address such as `http://www.gasullivan.com`. The I-net address is technically know as a uniform resource locator (URL), but it is popularly referred to as a *Web site address*. Web servers can be connected to the World Wide Web through the Internet, or can be isolated from the World Wide Web as part of a corporate intranet. Because Web servers are eventually the target of an I-net project, typical development environments consist of at least one development computer and at least one intranet or Internet Web server (see Figure 24.1).

FIGURE 24.1
A typical I-net project development environment.

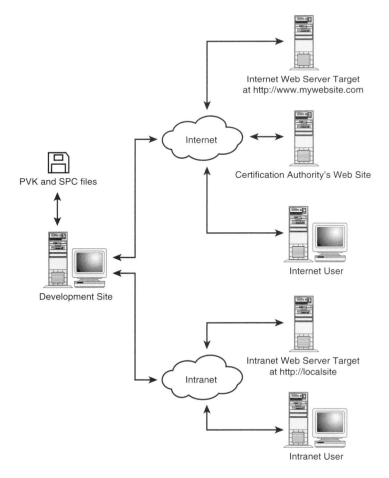

To access a specific Web site, your browser requests the Web site's server to return the HTML code found in the requested Web page. Your Web browser assembles the downloaded HTML code and displays it to you in the familiar Web page format.

Web pages created with standard HTML code are analogous to text documents containing graphic images and hyperlinks. Higher-level HTML such as Dynamic HTML (DHTML) or VBScript can add impressive active content such as buttons, animated text, and simple program procedures to your Web pages. However, you are presented with limitations when using HTML code. One limitation is the inability to distribute proprietary HTML code. A Web page is essentially a text file composed of HTML commands. The file is saved with an .htm or .html extension and is dubbed an HTML file. Your Web browser interprets the commands before it displays anything to you (similar to a .txt file being viewed in Microsoft Notepad). Anyone browsing your Web page can view the downloaded HTML code with a text editor. In addition, HTML applications are somewhat tedious to debug and test.

Despite the fact that DHTML and scripting can enhance the capability of static HTML, it still doesn't compare with the speed or functionality of applications written in, for example, Visual Basic or Visual C++. However, you can add Visual Basic and Visual C++ applications (ActiveX controls and ActiveX documents) to your Web page through the use of Internet download packages.

Part
III

Ch
24

Like Web pages, Internet download packages reside at specific I-net Web sites (usually at the same URL). An Internet download package is a special installation and setup program in the form of a .cab file (also know as cabinet or CAB file). A CAB file is equivalent to a ZIP file and has all the required information to run an ActiveX component on a Web page compressed into it. An Internet download package typically contains an ActiveX control (.ocx) or ActiveX document (.vbd), any essential dependency components (DLLs, EXEs, text, graphic image files, and so on), and an installation-scripting file (.inf).

Microsoft's Internet Explorer (IE) Web browser performs a procedure known as *Internet component download*, which downloads, installs, registers, and runs components from a Web site. IE starts the procedure when it finds a reference to an ActiveX component while assembling downloaded Web pages. During the procedure, IE first reads the component's class ID and version number from the Web page and then scans the Registry to see if it is already installed. If registered, IE compares the registered version number to that referenced in the Web page. If the two versions match, IE runs the component through the path defined in the Registry.

In the event the component is not registered or is registered as an older version, IE reads the HTML code to find the Web browser hosting the component's download package and then starts the Internet Component Download procedure. Before starting the download, IE inspects the package to determine if the enclosed component has the potential to harm your computer and to verify that its author has digitally signed it. Depending on its safety configuration, IE terminates the download immediately, waits for your decision to continue, or ignores all and proceeds with the download. Once downloaded, IE decompresses the CAB file and extracts the control, any necessary dependency files, and the INI file. IE extracts the enclosed files and those from any secondary CAB files and then installs the enclosed files based on information found in the extracted .inf file. The ActiveX component is started only after all files are installed and registered. The Internet Component Download process results in displaying the referenced ActiveX control on the Web page you are viewing.

If the control is licensed, your browser requests a copy of the license key from the Web server. If you have permission to access the key, the Web server returns a copy of it that allows Internet Explorer to create an instance of the control.

Using the Visual Basic Package and Deployment Wizard

Visual Studio 6 includes the Package and Deployment Wizard. It can be used to create a Standard Setup Package, an Internet Package, or build Dependency Files. For the remainder of this chapter, it will be used to guide you through the process of creating a download package from your Visual Basic project and deploying it on an I-net target machine. The wizard can operate as a standalone application, as part of the Visual Basic 6 Integrated Development Environment (IDE), or as an MS-DOS executable (Silent mode) as follows:

- As a standalone application—Select Start, Programs, Microsoft Visual Studio 6.0, Microsoft Visual Studio 6.0 Tools, Package and Deployment Wizard.

- Within the Visual Basic IDE—While in the Visual Basic IDE, select Add-Ins, Add-In Manager, and then pick Package and Deployment Wizard from the available add-ins.

- From an MS-DOS prompt—`PDCmdLn.exe "C:\Myproject.vbp" /p "MyPackageScript" /d "MyDeploymentScript" /i "C:\MyProjectLog.log"`. The /p argument defines the name of a previously saved packaging script, the /d argument defines the name of a previously saved deployment script, and /i argument defines the path used to save output messages that would normally be displayed on the screen.

Creating a Download Package

If you are currently editing the Visual Basic project you intend to package, you need to save it and close Visual Basic. You do not have to compile the project before closing, but doing so will allow you to detect any compilation errors while still in the IDE. The following steps will guide you through creating an Internet download package:

1. Start the wizard as a standalone application. From the wizard's main dialog box, select the Visual Basic project you want to package (see Figure 24.2). You can click Browse if your project is not listed in the drop-down box.

N O T E Figure 24.2 shows the selection of Increment.vbp, which is an ActiveX control created as an example for this demonstration.

FIGURE 24.2

The Visual Basic Package and Deployment Wizard main dialog box gives you the option to bundle your Visual Basic project into an Internet download package, distribute the package, or manage the resulting scripts.

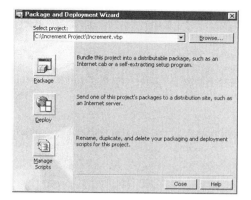

2. Click Package in the Package and Deployment Wizard main dialog box. If the project's source files are newer than the compiled component, the wizard asks if you want to recompile. Click Yes to recompile, No to proceed with the package process, or Cancel to remain in the main dialog box. The wizard then gathers information about your project and proceeds to the next step.

3. The next dialog box allows you to choose a script saved from a previously saved packaging process (see Figure 24.3). A packaging script contains all the steps and information from a previous packaging operation, and allows you to repackage your project repeating most of the steps. You can single-step through and edit a previously saved script. If your project contains previously saved packaging scripts, but you need to create a new one, choose (None). Click Next to continue.

FIGURE 24.3

The Packaging Script dialog box allows you to build a new packaging script or to select and repeat a previous one.

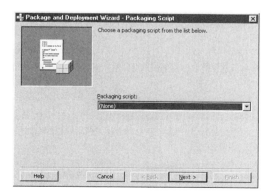

N O T E   The dialog box in Figure 24.3 will not be displayed if there are no previously saved packaging scripts for your project. It has been made to appear at this point as part of this example. ■

4. In the next dialog box, you choose the type of download package you want to create. Because you are creating this package to be used on a Web server, select Internet Package and then click Next.

5. The next dialog box asks you to choose the folder where the package will be assembled. The wizard default is a new folder named Package created in the Visual Basic application folder. You can keep the default location, select a local network folder by clicking Network, or create a new folder by clicking New Folder. Click Next to continue. If the folder already exists, the wizard will give you the choice of selecting a different location. If the folder cannot be found, the wizard prompts you for permission to create it.

6. The wizard analyzes your Visual Basic project, determines the files necessary to run the project, and displays them in the next dialog box (see Figure 24.4). Any file with a marked check box will be included in the download package. You can add additional files by clicking Add, or remove suggested files by clearing the check box.

FIGURE 24.4

The Included Files dialog box shows you the files the wizard deems necessary to include in the download package.

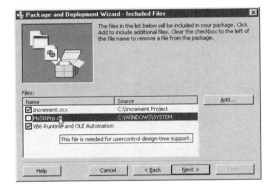

N O T E   The wizard may not find a file if your application does not reference it. For example, if a procedure in your application appends ASCII strings to a local text file that is needed as part of your application, click Add, locate the text file, and include it in the list.

In this example, the wizard has located the file Increment.ocx (which is the project's main executable file), MsStkPrp.dll (which is needed for user control design-time support), and the necessary VB6 runtime files (such as msvbvm60.dll). Notice that the file MsStkPrp.dll is not marked as necessary. Again, you can let the wizard complete the remainder of the process by clicking Finish, or continue stepping through the process yourself by clicking Next.

T I P   Moving your mouse cursor over the name of a file causes a pop-up box explaining why the file is necessary to appear (refer to Figure 24.4).

7. The next dialog box allows you to set locations from which the download package should retrieve its files during installation. Any additional files can be included in your primary CAB file, or can be brought in as secondary CAB files. Highlighting the file will show you the default file source. Pick Include in This Cab to include the file in this (the

primary) CAB file, Download from Microsoft Web Site to retrieve the file through a secondary CAB file supplied directly from Microsoft, or Download from Alternate Web Site to retrieve the file from a Web site of your choice. Retrieving files directly from Microsoft ensures the latest file versions. Retrieving CAB files from alternate Web sites becomes necessary when your application runs locally on an intranet with no access to the Internet, or is located on a different site. For example, if your project runs on an intranet with no access to the World Wide Web, it will not be able to download the VB6 runtime controls CAB from Microsoft. Therefore you need to place a copy of the CAB file on your intranet Web site and enter its URL or UNC (Uniform Naming Code). As before, you can let the wizard complete the remainder of the process by clicking Finish, or continue stepping through the process yourself by clicking Next.

8. The next step requires you to mark components as safe for scripting and initialization (see Figure 24.5). Select the setting for scripting and initialization from the dropdown lists on the right. You can mark your component as safe for initializing when you are absolutely sure that any data used to initialize your component won't cause it to create, change, or delete information or change system settings on a user's computer. You can mark your component as safe for scripting when you are absolutely sure that other components can't access your component's procedures and cause it to create, change, or delete information, or change system settings on a user's computer.

Part
III

Ch
24

FIGURE 24.5
The Safety Settings dialog box allows you to set your components scripting and initialization safety levels.

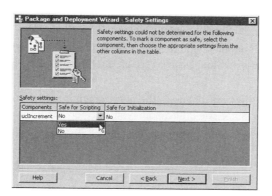

N O T E Internet Explorer 4 analyzes your component's initialization and scripting safety levels before downloading it. You can adjust Internet Explorer 4 safety levels by opening Internet Explorer and selecting View, Internet Options, selecting the Security tab, selecting a security zone, and then picking the zone's security level (see Figure 24.6).

FIGURE 24.6

The Internet Options dialog box located in Internet Explorer 4 allows you to set the security level for different Web content zones.

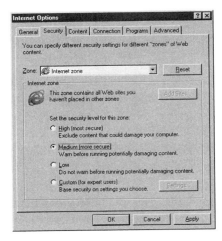

You need to digitally sign your component to properly uphold your claim that your component is truly safe for scripting and initialization. This lets end users be certain that your component will never harm or cause undesirable behavior on their machines—even if someone else uses your component in his own Web page or downloads someone else's Web page that uses your component. Marking a component as safe means that that you are accepting the liability for damages if something goes wrong with your control.

In this example, Safe for Scripting is set to Yes, and Safe for Initialization is set to No. If you are repeating a previously saved script, the Finish button will be available. Click Next to continue.

9. In the final step, the wizard gathers the information from the previous steps and creates the download package. The information you selected can be saved in a packaging script. The wizard selects a default name for the script, but you can change it to better represent your project. In this example the default name is changed to Increment Package. Click Finish to complete the process. The results of the packaging operation can be saved in a report file (see Figure 24.7).

FIGURE 24.7

The wizard displays the results of the packaging operation and allows you to save the information in a Packaging Report.

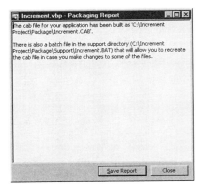

The wizard creates several files during the packaging process:

- Increment.PDM is placed in the same folder as the Visual Basic project files. The PDM file is a text file containing scripting instructions generated during the packaging process. This file becomes associated with the Visual Basic project and will be used to store any additional packaging and deployment scripts built for this project (see Figure 24.8).

FIGURE 24.8

The wizard creates a packaging script (PDM file) and a Packaging Report (TXT file).

- Increment.TXT is the information from the Packaging Report (see Figure 24.8).
- The Package folder contains the deployment files created with the wizard (see Figure 24.9).

FIGURE 24.9

The wizard creates CAB and HTM files and places them in the Package folder.

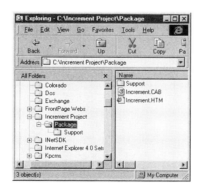

- Increment.CAB is the compressed file that will be deployed as an Internet download package.
- Increment.HTM is an HTML file that runs the new CAB file. You can test your control by launching this file in Internet Explorer. As shown in Listing 24.1, the ID tag is the control's name referred to with HTML scripting, the CLASSID tag is the control's class identifier used by the Registry, and the CODEBASE tag points to the control's CAB file and specifies the control's version number.

Listing 24.1 AXSRC01.TXT—The HTML Code in Increment.HTM

```
<HTML>
<HEAD>
<TITLE>Increment.CAB</TITLE>
</HEAD>
<BODY>
<!--    If any of the controls on this page require licensing, you must
        create a license package file. Run LPK_TOOL.EXE to create the
        required LPK file. LPK_TOOL.EXE can be found on the ActiveX SDK,
        http://www.microsoft.com/intdev/sdk/sdk.htm. If you have the Visual
        Basic 6 CD, it can also be found in the \Tools\LPK_TOOL directory.

        The following is an example of the Object tag:

<OBJECT CLASSID="clsid:5220cb21-c88d-11cf-b347-00aa00a28331">
    <PARAM NAME="LPKPath" VALUE="LPKfilename.LPK">
</OBJECT>
-->

<OBJECT ID="uclIncrement"
CLASSID="CLSID:8E09169E-0716-11D2-A89F-B5F13E6EE6B4"
CODEBASE="Increment.CAB#version=1,0,0,0">
</OBJECT>
</BODY>
</HTML>
```

- The Support folder contains files used to create the CAB file.
- Increment.ocx is the ActiveX runtime control compiled from the Visual Basic project.
- Increment.DDF is the cabinet directive file. It specifies the CAB file structure and which files are to be added (see Listing 24.2).
- Increment.INF is the code download information file. It defines how the control and supporting files will be installed (see Listing 24.3).
- Increment.BAT is an MS-DOS batch file you can use if you need to re-create the CAB file. It runs MAKECAB.EXE using information from the DDF file (see Listing 24.4).

Listing 24.2 AXSRC02.TXT—The Contents of the Cabinet Directive File Increment.DDF

```
.OPTION EXPLICIT
.Set Cabinet=on
.Set Compress=on
.Set MaxDiskSize=CDROM
.Set ReservePerCabinetSize=6144
.Set DiskDirectoryTemplate=".."
.Set CompressionType=MSZIP
.Set CompressionLevel=7
.Set CompressionMemory=21
.Set CabinetNameTemplate="Increment.CAB"
"Increment.INF"
"Increment.ocx"
```

Listing 24.3   AXSCR03.TXT—The Contents of the Code Download Information File Increment.INF

```
;INF file for Increment.ocx
;DestDir can be 10 for Windows directory, 11 for Windows\System(32)
;directory, or left blank for the Occache directory.

[version]
signature="$CHICAGO$"
AdvancedINF=2.0

[DefaultInstall]
CopyFiles=install.files
RegisterOCXs=RegisterFiles
AddReg=AddToRegistry

[RInstallApplicationFiles]
CopyFiles=install.files
RegisterOCXs=RegisterFiles
AddReg=AddToRegistry

[DestinationDirs]
install.files=11

[SourceDisksNames]
1=%DiskName%,Increment.CAB,1

[Add.Code]
Increment.ocx=Increment.ocx
MSVBVM60.DLL=MSVBVM60.DLL
OLEAUT32.DLL=OLEAUT32.DLL
OLEPRO32.DLL=OLEPRO32.DLL
ASYCFILT.DLL=ASYCFILT.DLL
STDOLE2.TLB=STDOLE2.TLB
COMCAT.DLL=COMCAT.DLL

[install.files]
Increment.ocx=Increment.ocx
MSVBVM60.DLL=MSVBVM60.DLL
OLEAUT32.DLL=OLEAUT32.DLL
OLEPRO32.DLL=OLEPRO32.DLL
ASYCFILT.DLL=ASYCFILT.DLL
STDOLE2.TLB=STDOLE2.TLB
COMCAT.DLL=COMCAT.DLL

[SourceDisksFiles]
Increment.ocx=1
MSVBVM60.DLL=1
OLEAUT32.DLL=1
OLEPRO32.DLL=1
ASYCFILT.DLL=1
STDOLE2.TLB=1
COMCAT.DLL=1
```

Part
III

Ch
24

continues

Listing 24.3 Continued

```
[Increment.ocx]
file-win32-x86=thiscab
RegisterServer=yes
clsid={8E09169E-0716-11D2-A89F-B5F13E6EE6B4}
DestDir=
FileVersion=1,0,0,0

[MSVBVM60.DLL]
hook=MSVBVM60.cab_Installer
FileVersion=6,0,81,41

[MSVBVM60.cab_Installer]
file-win32-x86=http://activex.microsoft.com/controls/vb6/VBRun60.cab
run=%EXTRACT_DIR%\VBRun60.exe

[OLEAUT32.DLL]
hook=OLEAUT32.cab_Installer
FileVersion=2,30,4260,1

[OLEAUT32.cab_Installer]
file-win32-x86=http://activex.microsoft.com/controls/vb6/VBRun60.cab
run=%EXTRACT_DIR%\VBRun60.exe

[OLEPRO32.DLL]
hook=OLEPRO32.cab_Installer
FileVersion=5,0,4260,1

[OLEPRO32.cab_Installer]
file-win32-x86=http://activex.microsoft.com/controls/vb6/VBRun60.cab
run=%EXTRACT_DIR%\VBRun60.exe

[ASYCFILT.DLL]
hook=ASYCFILT.cab_Installer
FileVersion=2,30,4260,1

[ASYCFILT.cab_Installer]
file-win32-x86=http://activex.microsoft.com/controls/vb6/VBRun60.cab
run=%EXTRACT_DIR%\VBRun60.exe

[STDOLE2.TLB]
hook=STDOLE2.cab_Installer
FileVersion=2,30,4260,1

[STDOLE2.cab_Installer]
file-win32-x86=http://activex.microsoft.com/controls/vb6/VBRun60.cab
run=%EXTRACT_DIR%\VBRun60.exe

[COMCAT.DLL]
hook=COMCAT.cab_Installer
FileVersion=5,0,1600,1

[COMCAT.cab_Installer]
file-win32-x86=http://activex.microsoft.com/controls/vb6/VBRun60.cab
run=%EXTRACT_DIR%\VBRun60.exe
```

```
[Setup Hooks]
AddToRegHook=AddToRegHook

[AddToRegHook]
InfSection=DefaultInstall2

[DefaultInstall2]
AddReg=AddToRegistry
```

Listing 24.4   AXSRC04.TXT—The File Increment.BAT Used to Re-create the Project's CAB File

```
@echo off
ECHO Use this batch file to make a new cab file. Press CTRL-C to cancel, or
pause
"C:\PROGRAM FILES\MICROSOFT VISUAL STUDIO\VB98\WIZARDS\PDWIZARD\
    MAKECAB.EXE" /f "Increment.DDF"
```

Deploying a Download Package

Once you have created your I-net package you need some means of copying (deploying) it from your development computer to the Web server. If your target Web site is part of an intranet, you can map it as a network drive and simply copy the package from your drive. If your target Web site is located on the Internet you can use any number of available file transfer programs to upload the package. The Package and Deployment Wizard can be used to streamline the upload process.

The following example will demonstrate the deployment of the Increment.vbp project that was packaged in the preceding example. The following steps will guide you through creating and deploying an Internet Download Package to an Internet Web server:

1. Restart the Package and Deployment Wizard if it is not running and select the Visual Basic project you want to deploy. You can click Browse if your project is not listed in the drop-down box (refer to Figure 24.2).

2. Click Deploy in the Package and Deployment Wizard main dialog box. The wizard gathers information about your project and proceeds to the next step.

3. In the next dialog box, you choose which deployment script you want to use. You can single-step through and edit a previously saved script. If your project contains previously saved packaging scripts, but you would rather created a new one, choose (None). Click Next to continue.

4. The next dialog box allows you to choose the package you want to deploy (see Figure 24.10). Select the desired package and then click Next.

FIGURE 24.10

The Package to Deploy dialog box allows you to choose and deploy a previously saved package.

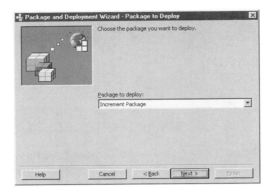

5. In the next dialog box, you are given a choice of deployment methods. Choose Web Publishing for deployment to a Web server. Choose Folder for deployment to a folder on your machine or to one your machine is networked to. In this example, Increment.vbp will be deployed to an Internet Web server, therefore select Web Publishing and then click Next.

N O T E Increment.HTM is a wizard-created Web page containing the HTML code for displaying Increment.OCX control (created for the purpose of demonstrating the Package and Deployment process). The packaging wizard always creates a test Web page containing the ActiveX control you have packaged. This allows you to build a Web page around this control by adding your own HTML code to the page. ■

6. The next dialog box allows you to deploy the files that were previously created in the packaging process and saved in the project's Package folder. Because you chose Web Publishing as the deployment method in step 5, the wizard lists the files ready for deployment. Any file with a marked check box will be deployed (see Figure 24.11). You can keep a file from being deployed by clicking the check box and removing the mark. Click Next to continue.

FIGURE 24.11

The Items to Deploy dialog box allows you to deploy files that were created in the original packaging process.

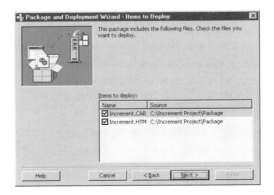

N O T E   If you chose Folder in step 5 as the deployment method, the wizard prompts you to select the target folder and then proceeds directly to step 11. ■

7. In the next dialog box you are given the opportunity to deploy any additional files that were not included in the original package (see Figure 24.12). Web page graphic files, related Web pages, or secondary CAB files are generally chosen at this point. You can choose all items in a folder or select individual files for deployment. No additional files are chosen in this example. Click <u>N</u>ext to continue.

FIGURE 24.12

The Additional Items to Deploy dialog box allows you to deploy files that were not included in the original download package.

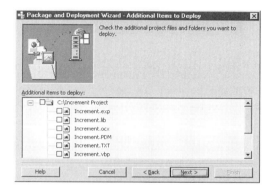

Part
III

Ch
24

N O T E   Any extra files you want to deploy need to be placed within the project folder. ■

8. The next dialog box allows you to choose the target Web site and the Web publishing protocol. HTTP Post and FTP (File Transfer Protocol) are the default selections (see Figure 24.13). Enter the target Web site's URL. You can mark the check box next to Unpack and Install Server-Side Cab to unpack the contents of a deployed cab file on the target server if the publishing protocol supports the operation. In this example, FTP is selected as the publishing protocol, and unpacking server-side CABs is not selected. Enter the target URL and then click <u>N</u>ext.

FIGURE 24.13

The Web Publishing Site dialog allows you to set the target Web site's URL.

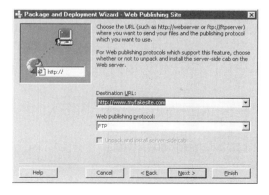

9. If the URL you entered is not saved as a Web publishing site, you are prompted by the next dialog box and asked if you want to save the information as a new Web publishing site (see Figure 24.14). Clicking Yes saves the information in the Registry before continuing. Clicking No continues without saving the information. Click Yes for this example.

FIGURE 24.14

The Package and Deployment Wizard displays this dialog box when you enter a new destination URL.

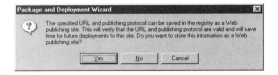

10. The next dialog box asks you to enter a name for the new Web publishing site. Enter the target Web site's URL and then click OK (see Figure 24.15). The wizard then queries the target Web site and determines the validity of the site.

FIGURE 24.15

The Package and Deployment Wizard asks you to name the new publishing site. The new name is stored in the Registry.

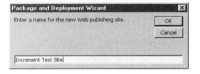

11. If the Web site and publishing protocol are valid, the wizard collects the information needed to deploy the package and asks you to name the new deployment script. Enter a name describing this deployment and then click Finish. The wizard deploys the project to the target machine and then displays the deployment results, which can be saved in a report file (see Figure 24.16).

FIGURE 24.16

The wizard displays the results of the deploy-ment operation and allows you to save the information in a Deployment Report.

N O T E   The Package and Deployment Wizard cannot remove files from the target Web server. Previously deployed files can be removed with an FTP program that handles remote deletion. ▪

Script Management

You can rename, duplicate, or delete previously saved package and deployment scripts from the current project by clicking Manage Scripts in the Package and Deployment main dialog box (refer to Figure 24.2). You can select package scripts by clicking the Packaging Scripts tab (see Figure 24.17), or you can select deployment scripts by clicking the Deployment Scripts tab (see Figure 24.18).

FIGURE 24.17
Manage previously saved packaging scripts with the Packaging Scripts tab in the Package and Deployment's Manage Scripts dialog box.

FIGURE 24.18
Manage previously saved deployment scripts with the Deployment Scripts tab in the Package and Deployment's Manage Scripts dialog box.

CAUTION

Clicking Delete will prompt you to confirm the deletion. Confirming will delete the script immediately, which cannot be undone.

Testing a Download Package

You can test your deployed I-net project on any another machine with access to your project's Web site. There are instances when you may find your ActiveX control downloads and runs properly on your development computer, but fails on a different computer. This usually occurs when a file installed on your development computer and used in the project is overlooked when including files in the download package. A typical example of this is forgetting to include the VB6 Runtime and OLE Automation components during the packaging process. An ActiveX control cannot operate without these runtime components. They are entered on your computer when Visual Basic 6 is installed. When Internet Explorer downloads the package the .inf file will not reference the runtime components, and if they have not been previously installed, your ActiveX control will fail.

N O T E Download problems are typically indicated after Internet Explorer has downloaded your ActiveX Web page; a red *x* appears in the space where your control should be (see Figure 24.19), or nothing appears at all in the window.

ActiveX controls may fail during download if dependent DLLs are not included in the download package, if a licensed control within your control is used without its runtime license, or if an ActiveX control's <OBJECT> tag is defined with an erroneous or missing CODEBASE attribute. ▒

FIGURE 24.19

An ActiveX control download problem that resulted in a red *x* being displayed.

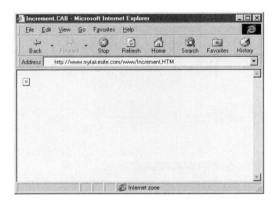

It is best to test your download package on a "clean machine"—a computer that has no trace of the download package or its components. The following procedure will assist you in testing your download package on a clean machine:

1. Install the latest version of Microsoft Internet Explorer.

   You can find it on Microsoft's Web site at http://www.microsoft.com/ie/download. Adjust your Internet Explorer's safety settings to Medium.

2. Uninstall the ActiveX component you intend to download.

   From the task bar click Start, Settings, Control Panel, Add/Remove Programs. Select the name of the ActiveX component. If your ActiveX component is listed as an installed program, select it and click Add/Remove Programs.

   If your ActiveX component was not listed as an installed program you can remove it yourself with a right-click operation. Under Windows 95 or Windows 98, start Windows Explorer, open the Windows\Downloaded Program Files folder, right-click your ActiveX component, and then click Remove. Under Windows NT, start Windows NT Explorer, open the Winnt\Downloaded Program Files folder, right-click your ActiveX component, and then click Remove.

N O T E   Removing an ActiveX component by right-clicking it and then clicking Re<u>m</u>ove is equivalent to unregistering an ActiveX component by using Regsvr32.exe with the /u argument. ▪

When cleaning up your development computer, you may not see the component in the Downloaded Program Files folder. When you compiled your project in Visual Basic, the component was automatically registered and placed in the project folder. You will need to unregister the component by running Regsvr32.exe with the /u switch—for example,

```
C:\Windows\System\Regsvr32.exe /u "C:\Increment Project\Increment.ocx"
```

N O T E   IE 3 used the Occache folder to store downloaded program files. The folder is not removed when you upgrade to IE 4. IE 4 creates the Downloaded Program Files folder instead of using the Occache folder. IE 4 places new ActiveX controls in the Downloaded Program Files folder, but will continue to use any current control remaining in the Occache folder as well. ▪

CAUTION

You may find the following ActiveX controls in the Downloaded Program Files folder. They are used by Internet Explorer and should not be removed:

- ▪ DirectAnimation Java classes
- ▪ Internet Explorer classes for Java
- ▪ Microsoft XML parser for Java
- ▪ Win32 classes

3. Delete temporary files saved by Internet Explorer.

From the Internet Explorer menu, click <u>V</u>iew, Internet <u>O</u>ptions, select the General tab, and then click Delete <u>F</u>iles, OK. This will remove any previously downloaded CAB and HTML files from the Windows\Temporary Internet Files folder in Windows 95 or Windows 98, and the Winnt\Temporary Internet Files folder in Windows NT.

4. Access your Web site with Internet Explorer.

At this point the example control Increment.ocx does not contain an Authenticode Signature. Therefore, Internet Explorer will display the Security Warning dialog box (see Figure 24.20). Click <u>Y</u>es to continue. Because the Increment download package was not set Safe for Initialization (refer to Figure 24.5), you will see a second security warning (see Figure 24.21). Click OK to continue. Internet Explorer then downloads, installs, and starts the ActiveX component (see Figure 24.22). Because this example is running under Windows 95, Internet Explorer saved the downloaded Web page (Increment.HTM) and CAB file (Increment.CAB) in the C:\Windows\Temporary Internet Files folder. It then installed Increment.ocx in the C:\Windows\Downloaded Program Files folder as Increment.uclIncrement. Right-clicking the file and selecting <u>P</u>roperties will inform you about the Web site from which it was downloaded, its dependency files, and its version number.

FIGURE 24.20

Internet Explorer
displays the Security
Warning dialog box
when it encounters an
ActiveX component with
no Authenticode
signature.

FIGURE 24.21

Internet Explorer
displays an additional
dialog box when it
encounters an ActiveX
component that was not
set as Safe for Scripting
or Safe for Initialization.

FIGURE 24.22

The Web page
Increment.HTM with the
ActiveX control
Increment.OCX seen
downloaded, installed,
and running on Internet
Explorer 4.

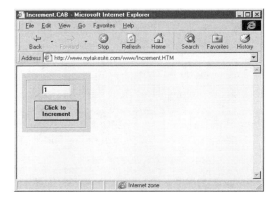

N O T E Increment.uclIncrement is the user control contained within the Increment.ocx
ActiveX control.

Working with Digital Signatures

Deploying your I-net project to a Web site allows other I-net users to download and run your
ActiveX components. Even though you have thoroughly tested your component's code, there is
always a chance that a problem eludes you and ends up causing unintentional harm to a user's
computer. In addition, it is possible for someone else to copy your ActiveX component and

modify it to intentionally cause problems. To reduce users' skepticism about downloading your ActiveX component, you need to assure them that they can find from whom and from where the code comes (Ensuring Authenticity) and that the code has not been tampered with since it was deployed (Ensuring Integrity).

To alleviate these problems, Microsoft developed a procedure known as Authenticode. It is used as a means to encrypt and decrypt Internet download files signed with a Digital Signature. A digital signature is the equivalent of an autographed testimonial of yourself endorsed by an agency that can vouch for your trustworthiness. The endorsing agency is known as a certificate authority (CA), and is responsible for gathering your credentials and supplying you with a Private Key (used for encryption) and a Digital Certificate needed by Authenticode. A digital certificate is composed of a Public Key (used for decryption), your credentials, and the CA's credentials (see Figure 24.23).

FIGURE 24.23

A certification authority supplies you with a private key and with a digital certificate, which is required to add a digital signature to your code.

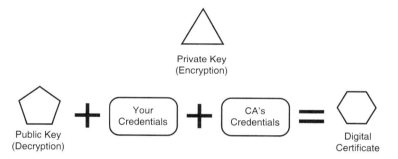

A private/public key pair is an integral part of what is known as *asymmetric algorithms*. Your CA supplies you with a unique pair of keys. The term *key* is used because the algorithms essentially lock and unlock encryption on a file. The private key (also called the *secret* key) is used to generate the public key. The private key is part of a mathematical formula in the encryption algorithm. The encryption algorithm scrambles a file in a manner that only the decryption algorithm can decipher. The public key is part of the formula in the decryption algorithm, and is sent along with the encrypted file. The inventors of these algorithms claim that it would take hundreds of years for someone to backtrack through the encryption formulas without having the public key, and without knowledge of the private key, the public key cannot be decoded. That's why it's important to keep the private key secret.

A sophisticated checksum of the original file can be generated using a hashing algorithm. The resulting checksum is known as a *digest*. (It may also be referred to as a *hash*.) The original file cannot be re-created from the digest, and it is unlikely that two different files will produce the same digest. Because encryption algorithms work more efficiently with smaller files, the digest typically gets encrypted and sent instead of the larger original file.

Signing a CAB File

You can add a digital signature to any .ocx, .exe, .dll, .vbd, or .cab file. You perform the signature procedure outside of the Visual Basic 6 development environment, with tools from

Microsoft's ActiveX SDK. Figure 24.24 depicts the code signing process, which is described in the following steps:

FIGURE 24.24
The sequence of events that takes place when digitally signing a file.

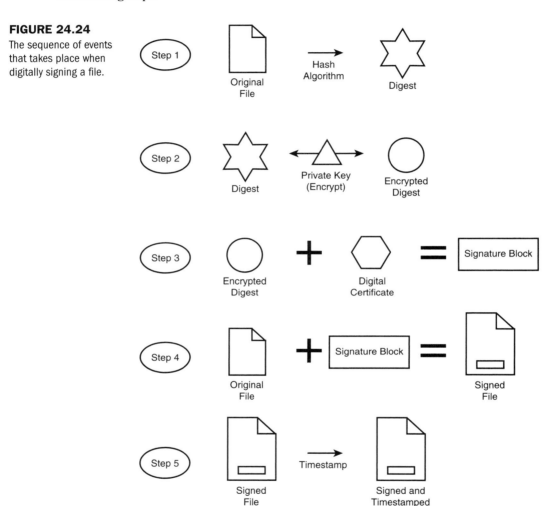

1. Your original file is processed through a hash algorithm creating a digest.
2. The digest is encrypted using your private key.
3. Combining the encrypted digest and your digital certificate creates a data string called a signature block.
4. A digitally signed file is created by adding the signature block to your original file.
5. A digital timestamp is added to your signed file. This puts a time limit on how long the signature is valid.

With the previous explanation in mind, you can use the following procedure to digitally sign your code:

1. Obtain the latest version of Internet Explorer from Microsoft's Web site at `http://www.microsoft.com/ie/download`.

2. Apply to a CA for your credentials. A list of current CAs can be found on Microsoft's Web site at `http://www.microsoft.com/security/ca`. The CA will send you a Private Key (.pvk file) and a Digital Certificate (.spc file). You can apply for individual or commercial credentials. Commercial credentials usually cost more than individual credentials and will require information about your corporation.

   If you are applying as an individual, you can obtain a private key and certificate directly from the CA's Web site at the time of application. The private key and digital certificate are sent to you over the Internet, and placed on a floppy disk. If you are applying as a corporate entity, it will take about a week to receive your private key and certificate.

3. Obtain and install the latest version of Microsoft's Internet Client SDK (INetSDK) from Microsoft's Web site at `http://www.microsoft.com/msdn/sdk/inetsdk`.

4. Modify the .ddf file by adding the entry `.Set ReservePerCabinetSize=6144`. This will allow you to re-create the CAB file with space for the signature block (refer to Listing 24.2). If you create your download package with the Package and Deployment Wizard, this modification is performed automatically.

5. Sign the CAB file used in your download package. You can also sign any file before it is packaged inside the CAB file. Run signcode.exe from an MSDOS prompt to perform the signature procedure. Signcode.exe can be found in the Bin folder of the INetSKD folder. As an example, you would sign and timestamp the file Icrement.CAB as follows:

```
signcode  -spc  a:\mycredentials.spc  -v  a:\myprivatekey.pvk  -n
➥"Increment Control Project"  -i  "http://www.gasullivan.com"  -t
➥"http://timestamp.verisign.com/scripts/timstamp.dll"
➥"C:\Increment Project\Package\Increment.CAB"
```

   In this example, `-spc` specifies your digital certificate, `-v` specifies your private key, `-n` specifies a text string representing the name of the file being signed and will be displayed during the download process, `-i` is the URL that a user can hyperlink to in order to get more information about the content of the signed file, and `-t` is the TimeStamp server's URL, which is provided by the CA.

N O T E This particular timestamp server is located on Verisign's Web site. It creates a certified timestamp on the Increment.CAB file when executed. Timstamp.dll is spelled without an e.

6. Test your signed file by using chktrust.exe, which is located in the same folder as signcode.exe, and is used as follows:

```
chktrust "c:\Increment Project\Package\Increment.CAB"
```

   Chktrust.exe will display `Succeeded` if the file was properly signed.

Testing a Signed CAB File

Test your signed cab file in the same manner as before it was signed. The following procedure will allow you to view the signed CAB file's digital certificate:

1. Clean up your machine by removing the ActiveX component as you did in the previous example.

2. Use the Package and Deployment Wizard to deploy the signed CAB file in place of the unsigned version using the previously saved deployment script.

3. Start Internet Explorer.

4. Because this example was deployed on the World Wide Web, set Internet Explorer's Internet Zone security to Medium (refer to Figure 24.6).

5. In Internet Explorer, enter your Web site's URL and select Yes when the Security Warning dialog box asks if you want to install and run the project (see Figure 24.25). In this example, by clicking the Gregg D August hyperlink, you can view the certificate's properties (see Figure 24.26). The control will download and run as before (refer to Figure 24.22).

FIGURE 24.25

Internet Explorer displays the Security Warning dialog box when detecting a digital signature.

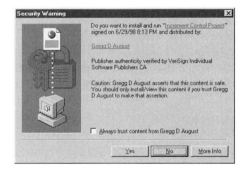

FIGURE 24.26

The Certificate Properties dialog box is displayed when clicking the name hyperlink in the Security Warning dialog box.

Figure 24.27 depicts the digital signature verification process, which is described in the following steps:

FIGURE 24.27

The sequence of events that takes place during the Authenticode procedure in Internet Explorer.

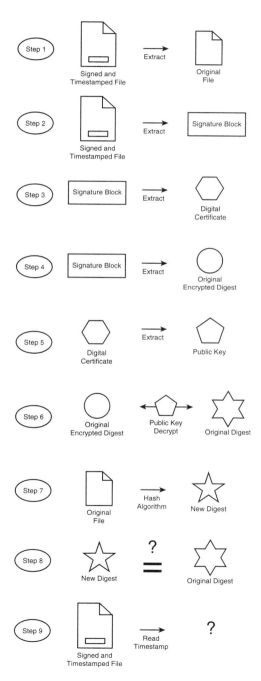

1. The original file is extracted from the downloaded file.

2. The signature block is extracted from the downloaded file.

3. The digital certificate is extracted from the signature block.

4. The original encrypted digest is extracted from the signature block.

5. The public key is extracted from the digital certificate.

6. The original encrypted digest is decrypted using the public key.

7. The extracted original file is processed through the same hash procedure to produce a new digest.

8. If the file has been tampered with since it was deployed, the new digest will differ from the original and the file will be considered invalid. If the file is found invalid, you will be notified and given a choice to cancel the download.

9. If the timestamp has expired, the file is also considered invalid. If the file is found invalid, you will again be notified and given a choice to cancel the download.

Licensing I-net ActiveX Controls

Exposing your ActiveX control on a Web page gives any user the opportunity to exploit it. Copyrights can discourage ethical users from duplicating your user control in their project, but it will not stop someone from adding your downloaded .ocx file to the Components list in Visual Basic and then embedding it as part of his own user control. Fortunately, you can hinder unauthorized replication of your programming efforts by adding license key requirements to your controls.

Licensing an I-net control requires your Web page to reference a License Package File. A license package file resides on the same Web server as the requested Web page, and contains runtime license keys for controls on the page. Unlike design-time license keys, the keys in the License Package File are not installed or registered on a user's computer. With the exception of code used to access the license package file, a Web page written for licensed controls is analogous to unlicensed controls. As Internet Explorer reads the licensed control Web page, it finds a reference to the license package and requests a copy of it from the Web server. The server determines if the Web page controls are licensed to the user, and returns a copy of the license package file if the user's license is valid. If returned, Internet Explorer runs the License Manager (a component included with Internet Explorer) to extract the keys within the license package. Verifying the license keys, Internet Explorer instructs the specific controls to create runtime instances of them. If the controls are not licensed to the user, the Web server will not return the license package file and the specific controls will fail.

Adding an I-net License to an ActiveX Control

Using the following procedure, you can add I-net license support to any ActiveX control created in Visual Basic 6. Carry out the steps in the procedure as follows:

1. Open your ActiveX control project in Visual Basic 6.

2. Add the license key requirement to your control. Using Increment.vbp as an example, click Project, Increment Properties, select the General tab, and then click the Require License Key check box.

3. Recompile the project's .ocx file. Because Require License Key was selected, a Visual Basic control license file (.vbl) is created in the project folder. For example, recompiling Increment.ocx creates the file Increment.vbl.

4. Save your project and close Visual Basic.

5. Start the Package and Deployment Wizard. Create a download package (or reuse a previously saved one) for the licensed control. In this example, the script Increment Package was used to re-create the files Increment.HTM and Increment.CAB in the Package folder within the application's folder.

N O T E Do not include the .vbl file that was created in step 3. This keeps the license key out of the download package, and consequently does not result in it being installed on the user's computer during component download. ▪

6. Resign the new CAB file as shown previously in the chapter.

7. Start Lpk_tool.exe (see Figure 24.28). You use this application to place any necessary license keys in a single license package. Lpk_tool.exe is located in the Bin folder of the INetSDK, which can be downloaded from Microsoft's Web site at `http://www.microsoft.com/msdn/sdk/inetsdk`.

Part
III

Ch
24

FIGURE 24.28

The License Package Authoring Tool (Lpk_tool.exe) allows you to combine individual control license keys into a single license package.

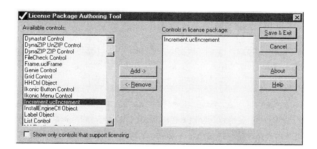

Select the licensed controls used in your Web page from the Available controls list and then click Add. The controls you select will appear in the Controls in license package list. In this example, `Increment.uclIncrement` (the user control in the VB project) is the only control selected because it is the only one contained in Increment.HTM.

Click Save & Exit to create the license package file. Lpk_tool prompts you for a filename and location for the new .lpk file. Save the file in the projects folder so that the Package and Deployment Wizard can access it. In this example the file is saved as Increment.lpk in the Increment project's folder (see Listing 24.5).

N O T E Each Web page uses only one .lpk file. Internet Explorer uses the first License Package
referenced in the page and ignores the rest. However, a single .lpk file can be used on any
number of pages. ▩

**Listing 24.5   AXSRC05.TXT—The License Package Increment.lpk (Note the
Copyright Warning)**

```
LPK License Package
/////////////////////////////////////////////////////////////////////////////
//   WARNING:  The information in this file is protected by copyright law     //
//   and international treaty provisions. Unauthorized reproduction or         //
//   distribution of this file, or any portion of it, may result in severe     //
//   criminal and civil penalties, and will be prosecuted to the maximum       //
//   extent possible under the law.  Further, you may not reverse engineer,    //
//   decompile, or disassemble the file.                                       //
/////////////////////////////////////////////////////////////////////////////
{3d25aba1-caec-11cf-b34a-00aa00a28331}
ADZNAaMT0hGon6zLA/dJSg=
AQAAAA=
b9pnBnAT0hGon6zLA/dJSBQAAAB
nAGcAawBoAGYAaABtAGgAZABlAGYAZgBoAGgAbQBlAG8AZgByAGMA=
```

8. Edit the HTM file to uncomment the license object and point to the new .lpk file (see
   Listing 24.6). An .lpk file must reside on the same server as the Web page using it, so in
   this example VALUE references Increment.lpk in the same relative path as
   Increment.HTM.

N O T E Do not change the clsid number (`clsid:5220cb21-c88d-11cf-b347-
00aa00a28331`), which is the class ID for Internet Explorer's License Manager. ▩

N O T E In this example the Web server does not examine the user's license status and therefore
sends the license keys solely at the request of the License Manager. To take full advantage
of control licensing, you could have your Web server perform a local lookup of users who have authority
to run your controls, check the users' computers for installed runtime licenses, or check the users'
Windows NT authentication before sending keys and allowing controls to operate. ▩

**Listing 24.6   AXSRC06.TXT—The HTML Page Increment.HTM, Modified to
Expose the Reference to the License Package Increment.lpk**

```
<HTML>
<HEAD>
<TITLE>Increment.CAB</TITLE>
</HEAD>
<BODY>
```

```
<OBJECT CLASSID="clsid:5220cb21-c88d-11cf-b347-00aa00a28331">
    <PARAM NAME="LPKPath" VALUE="Increment.LPK">
</OBJECT>


<OBJECT ID="uclIncrement"
CLASSID="CLSID:0667DA6F-1370-11D2-A89F-ACCB03F74948"
CODEBASE="Increment.CAB#version=1,0,0,0">
</OBJECT>
</BODY>
</HTML>
```

9. With the Package and Deployment Wizard's Additional Items to Deploy dialog box, add the .lpk file you created with Lpk_tool, and deploy the .htm, .cab, and .lpk files to your Web server. In this example, the script Increment Deployment was reused with Increment.lpk included in the final deployment.

Part

III

Ch

24

Testing a Licensed ActiveX Control

Once you have deployed your Web page, CAB file and License Package file, you need to make sure your license key downloads properly. The following procedure will provide a means of effectively testing your licensed control:

1. Delete the control license from the Registry. This is absolutely necessary if you plan to download the licensed control on the same computer used to create the control because Visual Basic registers the license key when creating an .lpk file. If for some reason the license key failed to download, the control would still appear to operate correctly because a key is already installed.

   You can use the license ID to locate and remove the license key from the Registry for testing purposes. With a text editor, open your control's .lpk file and locate the license key. Listing 24.7 shows the licensing information from the example file Increment.lpk. To remove this key from the Registry, start regedit.exe and search for the license key in HKEY_CLASSES_ROOT\Licenses. In this example, the license key for the user control Increment.uclIncrement is HKEY_CLASSES_ROOT\Licenses\CBA5CF4D-1121-11D2-A89F-DCDE348A15AF. Delete the key once you have located it.

Listing 24.7   AXSRC07.TXT—The License Information in the File Increment.vbl

```
REGEDIT
HKEY_CLASSES_ROOT\Licenses = Licensing: Copying the keys may be
    a violation of established copyrights.
HKEY_CLASSES_ROOT\Licenses\0667DA6D-1370-11D2-A89F-ACCB03F74948 =
    kcecrcfcfjjchcgjriejcjijpdnikclchcrd
```

2. Clean up your machine by removing the ActiveX component as you did in the previous examples.

3. In Internet Explorer, enter your Web site's URL and download your Web page. If the control license key downloads properly, you will again be prompted by the Security Warning dialog box. Accept the control and continue with the download. If the license does not download properly, your control will not operate, and you will see a red *x* or a blank display (refer to Figure 24.19).

N O T E Failing to deploy the .lpk file, deploying it in the wrong location, or deploying the wrong .lpk file are typical reasons why a licensed control may not display and operate correctly. ▨

From Here...

This chapter has described the mechanics of Internet component download, digital signatures, and control licensing. You've also learned the procedures to digitally sign your CAB files and apply licenses to your ActiveX controls, as well as what to watch out for when testing your download application.

Keep in mind that the procedures in this chapter were demonstrated using a simple ActiveX control project. Larger projects will usually require the inclusion of additional DLLs or EXEs in the download package.

It is also important to know that the procedures in this chapter can be used to package and deploy ActiveX document projects.

▨ For information on control creation in Visual Basic, see Chapter 12, "Creating ActiveX Controls with Visual Basic."

▨ For information on control creation in Visual C++, see Chapter 13, "Creating ActiveX Controls with Visual C++."

▨ For information on creating Web-based projects with ActiveX controls and ActiveX documents, see Chapter 16, "Creating Web Browser–Based Applications with Visual Basic."

▨ Visual SourceSafe also has the ability to deploy a Web-based project. See Chapter 35, "Using Visual SourceSafe," for more information.

Developing Scalable Distributed Applications

Clients, Servers, and Components: Design Strategies for Distributed Applications

by Timothy A. White and Jay Lindhorst

In this chapter

Design Objectives for a Distributed Application

Every year on the Fourth of July, the Boston Pops Orchestra plays a free concert at the Esplanade, culminating in the 1812 Overture. Tchaikovsky's score includes church bells and cannons, rendered by a number of churches in Boston and an artillery detachment at Bunker Hill. Because of their distance from the Esplanade, the cannons must fire and the bells must ring several seconds before the orchestra reaches that point in the score. In fact, because the churches and guns are at varying distances, each is subject to a different delay. Gun crews and bell ringers watch the orchestra on television, and when the performance reaches a predetermined point, each plays their part. Listeners at the Esplanade hear bells ringing all together and cannons firing right on cue with the orchestra.

You can consider the 1812 Overture a distributed application, with the orchestra, the artillery, and each belfry as components. As is typical with most distributed software, success depends upon component interaction. It all works well together because the constraints are simple (the tempo of the performance, the speed of sound, and the relative distances) and roles and interactions are well defined. The bells and cannons do not try to play in time or in close harmony with the orchestra; rather, they aim for subsecond accuracy in their timing. So long as each component performs well and the timing is correct, the bells and cannons produce a delightfully bombastic effect.

Like the 1812 Overture, a distributed application integrates the actions of many components. Distributed application design must focus not only on the details of individual parts, but also on making the distributed components work smoothly together in concert.

This chapter begins with a brief review of design objectives for a distributed system and a review of constraints that sometimes make the objectives difficult to achieve. The balance of the chapter presents design strategies.

A properly designed application fulfills a well-defined business need. In addition, the best distributed applications exhibit several desirable features:

- Performance—High throughput and fast response times.
- Efficiency—Effective, frugal use of available computing resources.
- Scalability—Orderly growth to accommodate increased processing volume and complexity.
- Security—Appropriate access for authorized users.
- Verifiability—A structured quality assurance effort to verify that the application correctly implements specific business requirements.
- Reliability—Infrequent failures and graceful degradation on failure of one or more components.
- Maintainability—Ease of deployment, operation, and enhancement.

Achieving all of these properties for any application requires substantial application of talent, discipline, and experience throughout the development process. Achieving these properties in a distributed application requires careful and sophisticated design, with particular attention to the interactions between components.

The following sections discuss these design objectives in more detail.

Performance

Assuming proper application functionality, application performance is the number one criterion for system quality. System design, architecture, and implementation may be flawless, but if users spend too much time waiting for results, they will be dissatisfied. Applications may perform quite differently in production than in a development environment, due to different network configurations and loads.

It's important to identify specific criteria for application performance (usually in a requirements document). Without objective criteria, performance will be judged subjectively. Important criteria include response time (time to complete one operation), apparent response time (time a user must wait after executing an operation), and throughput (data processed per unit time). Ideally, separate performance criteria should address the best case (no other application active on the network, single user) and the worst case (very heavy network and application loads, many users). Performance criteria should always be stated for the common case (typical application and network loads).

Several studies have shown that people perceive response time under one-fifth of a second as instantaneous. Studies also show that response time over one second can have a negative effect on attitude and productivity. Sometimes, application constraints make subsecond response time simply unattainable; often, asynchronous processing can improve apparent response time.

Overall performance for a distributed application depends as much on component interactions as on individual component performance. Communication delays and resource sharing require special attention.

Efficiency

A distributed application typically uses resources on several computers, as well as network resources. Each individual component must use local resources effectively; the application as a whole must use network resources frugally. Ultimately, inefficiency will manifest as poor performance or poor scalability.

It's important to pursue the right efficiencies. Processor time and memory are cheap and abundant; bandwidth from Europe to North America is typically scarce and expensive. The anticipated growth path for the application will motivate tradeoffs.

Scalability

For a successful application deployed in a successful business, processing demands—number of users, transaction volume, database size—tend to increase. However, this volume typically grows chaotically. A well-designed application grows in an orderly manner to accommodate disorderly growth in demand. The growth plan may include deploying additional instances of some components, adding additional database storage, or redistributing processing tasks.

The best applications also scale down, for cost-effective use by organizations with smaller processing demands (and fewer resources). For example, an order processing system designed for a corporate headquarters might use SQL Server for data management; branch offices might use a scaled-down version with a FoxPro database.

N O T E   It's important to understand the relationship between resource usage and processing volume. Ideally, resource requirements should increase linearly with volume: If volume is n and usage for a particular resource is r, you would like to have $r = kn$, for some constant k. If for some resources $r = kn2$, or worse, scalability is at risk.   ▨

N O T E   For some applications, linear resource usage ($r = kn$) is inherently unattainable. In those cases, load distribution through parallel processing will improve scalability. If the processing load is divided among three instances of the application, resource usage for the three instances $(a^2 + b^2 + c^2)$ will be less than resource usage for a single instance: $(a + b + c)^2$.   ▨

Security

Because a distributed application crosses system boundaries, security becomes more important and more difficult. Generally, each component will execute under a local account context. Remote components, however, need to connect and be provided or denied services, as appropriate.

When a distributed application runs entirely within a Windows NT network, Windows NT's integrated security is the best solution. More comprehensive security solutions can include certificate servers or the distributed security service of Microsoft Transaction Server (MTS).

ON THE WEB

You can find information on programming with the Microsoft Certificate Server at `http://premium.microsoft.com/msdn/library/sdkdoc/appprog_8vjm.htm`.

▶ **See** "Looking at Goals for Distributed Processing," **p. 109**

Verifiability

Testing a distributed system is far more complex than testing a monolithic application. Effective quality assurance requires participation from the earliest stages of the development process. Effective testing requires a parallel test environment that matches, as closely as possible, the production environment.

The most important design features for verifiability are clear separation of services and well-documented component interfaces. Separation of services is discussed later in this chapter in the section "Designing a Distributed Application." Microsoft's Visual Basic help files provide a good example of well-documented interfaces. For example, see the documentation for the TextBox control.

Quality assurance (QA) for distributed applications is more complex than for traditional applications. QA staff should participate in the application design process so that they can develop an effective application test plan.

Reliability

Components in a distributed application must cope not only with local failures, but failures in remote components as well. The number of potential errors mounts in a frighteningly combinatorial way. A well-designed distributed application must degrade gracefully in the event of errors; the best distributed applications automatically recover. A well-designed component manages the effects of a fault locally, rather than propagating the error to other parts of a system.

For efficient administration, a distributed system should pursue a consistent error notification strategy. For example, several components might share a common log file. The Windows NT and Windows 95/98 Event Log is another excellent resource for error notification.

 Microsoft Visual Basic (VB) 6 includes a feature for easy insertion of entries to the Windows NT Application Log or to the file specified by the `LogPath` property in Windows 95/98: the `LogEvent` method of the App object. However, `App.LogEvent` only works in a compiled application; in Debug mode, it will appear to have no effect.

Search VB 6 help for the `LogEvent` method of the App object.

For more information about the Windows NT Event Logs, see Chapter 5, "Checking the Logs," of *Special Edition Using Microsoft BackOffice*, Second Edition, Volume 1 from Que Corporation, ISBN 0-7897-1142-7.

Maintainability

Changes in business result in changes to software, and the pace is accelerating. In a well-designed application, a change to a business requirement results in a change to a single component. To achieve this goal, however, you must encapsulate business logic in middle-tier components.

A complete design must address initial system deployment, ongoing operation, and distribution of updates. As components become more widely distributed, update distribution becomes more difficult to coordinate.

A component-based design is one of the best approaches for long-term maintainability. See the section "The Services Paradigm" later in this chapter.

Design Constraints for a Distributed Application

Constraints are factors in the application environment that limit design choices. It's important to address these constraints in the application design. The 1812 Overture operated under constraints of geographic distribution, subsecond timing, and the speed of sound. Distributed software must operate under a number of common constraints:

Part
IV

Ch
25

- Platform—Hardware, networks, physical plant and operating systems
- Bandwidth—Communications speed and reliability between components
- Resource contention—Cooperative access to shared resources
- Availability—Allowable down time
- Audience—Target users and administrators
- Legacy—Interaction with existing systems
- Political—Organizational and personal relationships

Take a look at each type of constraint in more detail.

Platform

Typically, components of a distributed application must run on a variety of existing hardware under a number of existing operating systems connected by a patchwork of networks. Each component must perform well locally and interact correctly with remote components.

Target platform constraints also include support (or lack thereof) for interprocess communication (IPC), remote procedure calls (RPC), and object request broker (ORB) services. IPC provides local communication between applications running on a single computer; RPC allows an application running on one computer to interact with an application running on another computer. ORB services include object allocation, deallocation, and invocation. For applications running on Windows NT 4 or later (or Windows 95/98 with an update), Microsoft's Component Object Model (COM) and Distributed COM (DCOM) provide all three services. In fact, DCOM provides a good degree of location transparency. In many cases, components can be deployed locally or remotely with no code changes required.

If some components must run on non-Windows platforms, some extra effort will be required. Basically, you will have three choices:

- Implement DCOM on the target platform—To date, COM has been implemented on Windows NT, Windows 95/98, MacOS, some versions of MVS, and several UNIX platforms. However, COM is a well-documented binary standard and could certainly be implemented on other platforms. Although implementing COM and DCOM is a major undertaking, this might be the best approach for some very large projects (on the scale of a nationwide tax processing application for the IRS).

- Use a COM alternative such as Common Object Request Broker Architecture (CORBA)—Microsoft does not currently support CORBA on Windows; however, third-party implementations are available. Leaving aside the technical merits of COM versus CORBA, this approach would result in better platform independence. However, Visual Studio is very tightly integrated with COM, and many powerful features will be lost. For example, VB has built-in support for COM in its `CreateObject()` and `GetObject()` methods; VB has no support for CORBA components.

▶ **See** "COM Versus CORBA: Standard, Stand-Off, Integration, or Assimilation?," **p. 238**

ON THE WEB

Detailed information on CORBA can be found on the Object Management Group's Web site at
`http://www.omg.org/`.

- Use a more primitive mechanism, such as Distributed Computing Environment (DCE) RPC or TCP/IP sockets—As with the CORBA approach, the application becomes more vendor-neutral. However, a non-object-based mechanism (like sockets) provides program-to-program communication, not object-to-object communication. This might seem to be a subtle distinction, but the bottom line is more lines of code.

Microsoft is working to expand the alternatives available for interaction with non-Windows components. This is one of the primary objectives for the Universal Data Access initiative. Technologies nearing release include COM Transaction Integrator (COMTI, LU 6.2 interface to IMS and CICS transaction programs), OLE DB/DDM (access to VSAM and AS400 data sets) and Host Data Replicator (SQL Server replication to DB2). These technologies will be discussed later in this chapter.

ON THE WEB

For the latest information on Microsoft's Universal Data Access technologies, go to `http://www.microsoft.com/data/`.

Bandwidth

A distributed application is, by definition, a communicating application. Good design must take into account the speed and reliability of available communications links. For different cases, available bandwidth may vary from a few bits per minute (voice interactive response) to a few megabits per second (function calls to an in-process Dynamic-Link Library (DLL)).

During application design, it's important to consider patterns of bandwidth availability on the target network. For example, gigabit Ethernet backbone may connect servers, whereas European users connect through a congested 56KB connection. Some client machines might have a permanent network connection; others might connect infrequently by dial-up connections. It's especially important to consider bandwidth constraints when partitioning an application into components (see "Designing a Distributed Application," later in this chapter).

Resource Contention

Sharing resources between processes is one of the fundamental problems in computing. At the most basic level, processes compete for processor time, memory, disk, and network resources. At a higher level, shared resources include rows in database tables, and services provided by other components.

Because database servers provide effective resource-sharing mechanisms, some developers tend to discount this problem in application design. However, resource contention can be an obstacle to scalability, so every effort must be made to minimize resource sharing. Where sharing cannot be eliminated, try to make it nonexclusive.

Availability

An application that must be available 24 hours a day, 7 days a week, without interruptions, requires much more thorough design than a batch job system. Not all applications require long periods of uninterrupted availability; those that do present several special design challenges. First, some method must be found to maintain the system: apply patches and updates, install new devices, defragment disk space, and so on. Second, you must ensure that all resources required by the system (databases, routers, electricity, and so forth) are available on the same uninterruptible basis.

High-availability applications require attention to infrastructure details (backup power supply, redundant network paths), hardware details (redundant storage, hot standby, failover switches) and application features (automatic restart, administrator alert). The most important element in design of a high-availability application, however, is a careful analysis of possible failures and recovery options.

Audience

The audience for an application includes its users, its support staff, and its administrators. Design decisions must take into account the needs of each. For example, users might be working in a high-volume call center where extra seconds waiting for data may cost the enterprise thousands of dollars. This case requires special attention to response time. Also consider users' overall comfort level working with computers; a cashier in a shoe store has different expectations than a developer.

IT support staff require accurate, up-to-date user documentation. Trainers may also need access to requirements and design documents to develop a curriculum.

System administrators need to understand how to install, maintain, and operate the application. For example, they might need to maintain a remote installation by dial-up connections. This case requires attention to performance with limited network bandwidth. Administrators are often neglected when gathering application requirements; remember that the success of an application depends in large part upon successful administration.

An application has at least three audiences: end users, support staff, and system administrators. End users require an appropriate user interface and snappy performance. Support staff require accurate user documentation. System administrators require compliance with security policies, predictable behavior, accurate system documentation, and straightforward installation.

Legacy

Legacy system integration can be a somewhat painful process in developing applications and is a typical constraint of all but a few development efforts. Utilizing the knowledge of experienced staff members can shed light on the legacy system objectives and help to round out the requirement definition for the new system. Dealing with legacy imposed constraints requires tremendous patience and perseverance, but may help to illuminate some requirements of the new system that were not driven out in the original requirements definition process. The constraints of legacy systems and the associated business processes are often derived from needs that are no longer relevant and can provide an opportunity for business process reengineering.

Political

A distributed system often crosses organizational boundaries as well as system boundaries. Different organizations have different priorities, and different expectations for the application. For example, an application developed in Department A may need access to a database owned by Department B. The application may be a crash priority for Department A, but an annoying distraction for Department B. The project manager might win Department B's cooperation by developing a reusable component for looking up supplier information.

Compromises may be required in the use of existing components, design of reusable new components, or use of an enterprise data model. For example, the proposed database schema for a new application might duplicate some information already available in an enterprise database. Database administrators might insist on a modified schema. This may seem a compromise for the application at hand, but can ensure data consistency for the enterprise.

Political give-and-take is a soft skill often disdained by developers. Usually, it's simply a matter of listening carefully to other parties' priorities and finding a way to make your own priorities consistent. By showing respect for other points of view, you can gain respect for your own. After you've earned some trust and respect, you can usually bypass political gamesmanship.

The Services Paradigm

COM is fundamental to Microsoft's strategies for operating systems and tools. COM applications consist of *services* provided by *components*. A service is a group of related functions (an interface) that implements a business requirement; a component is an executable unit of software (EXE or DLL) that implements one or more services. Software design in this model consists of defining services and packaging them into components. Software development consists of building components and integrating them into applications. In some of Microsoft's documentation the terms *services model* and *component-based* are used interchangeably.

The services model provides an approach for turning business requirements into software components. Central to this approach is the idea of a three-tiered framework:

- *Presentation Services* provide interaction with users of the application, typically a graphical user interface (GUI).
- *Business Services* apply common business policies to users' interaction with data.
- *Data Management Services* provide durable storage and retrieval of business information.

The three-tiered framework does not imply any physical implementation; a three-tier application might consist of seven components installed on two computers. Three-tier architecture is a modeling framework, a way of thinking about the services in an application. The traditional two-tier client/server approach typically includes a database component and a desktop component, with business logic divided arbitrarily between the two tiers. Grouping all three types of services into a single component results in a monolithic application.

The services paradigm is particularly well suited to the development of distributed applications and can result in several benefits:

- Encapsulation of complex business logic
- Programming-language independence
- Component reuse
- Reduced project risk

Implementing a service in one component simplifies maintenance when business requirements change. Code changes might often be limited to a single component. As long as the original interface for a service does not change, developers can add new functions or change the implementation of existing functions without breaking other components.

Because COM is a binary standard, it is language-neutral. So long as a component implements its services as advertised, it matters very little whether a component is built with Visual Basic, Visual C++, Visual J++, Delphi, or Symantec C++.

The services approach generally results in components of a good granularity for reuse, particularly in the business services layer. Separating common business policies from application-specific user interactions makes the business services components more generic and better suited to reuse. Effective reuse, however, requires careful component design and developer awareness. (Developers seldom reuse code they don't know about.) Also, a thriving ActiveX control market makes available a wide variety of shrink-wrap components.

Numerous studies have documented that complexity grows exponentially with the size of an application. The services paradigm results in smaller modules with well-defined interfaces. The reduced complexity of each module results in more effective quality assurance. Component reuse also reduces project risk.

Client/Server Implementation Models

Distributed applications generally fall into two categories: cooperating peers, or client/server. In the cooperating peers model, several instances of the same application cooperate to generate a result. In the client/server model, several distinct applications cooperate to generate a result. The client/server approach allows for efficient division of labor and has become the dominant model.

The client/server model might also be subdivided by its connectivity, the way in which the application uses and disseminates information. If the application is connected to the database or network while in use, it is a *connected client*. If there are periods of time when the application will be in use, but not connected to either a database or network, it is a *disconnected client*.

The architectural tiers and connectivity models discussed previously are not mutually exclusive. Every n-tier client/server application falls into the category of either connected or disconnected. The nature of the business, political environment, and degree of risk aversion of the organization drives such architectural decisions.

Within the client/server model, four architectural and connectivity approaches have become popular:

- Traditional (two-tier)
- Three-tier (n-tier)
- Connected
- Disconnected

The Traditional (Two-Tier) Client/Server Model

In a traditional client/server application, a database server implements data management functions, and a client application implements other functions. Business logic often is divided between the client application and database-hosted stored procedures and triggers. For example, a report might use a stored procedure to perform currency conversions on data access and retrieval based on a conversion date computed in the report program. The business logic for determining the conversion date is implemented in the client program; business logic for looking up and applying the exchange rate is implemented in a stored procedure.

A traditional client/server model can be implemented fairly quickly because it requires less up-front design. User response time may also be better than in more complex client/server models. The two-tier model is a good choice for an application with a small number of users and a clearly limited scope.

Two-tier applications usually don't scale well to large numbers of users. Implementation of substantial business logic in stored procedures results in database contention as the number of users increases. Also, the client almost always requires a high-bandwidth connection to the database server; therefore two-tier is not a good choice for remote users. Update distribution can be tricky, as changes in the client component must be carefully coordinated with changes in the server component.

Part
IV

Ch
25

The Three-Tier (N-Tier) Model

In the three-tier model, a database server implements data management functions, a mid-tier application implements common business logic, and a presentation component provides a user interface. When several applications access the same data, it makes sense to encapsulate related business logic in a separate component. For example, a human resources (HR) department will probably have many applications that access personnel data. For all of these applications, business policy might state that all HR staff have access to basic information about employees (name, address, department, supervisor, and so forth), but only supervisors have access to compensation and benefits information, and only managers have access to disciplinary information. A single mid-tier application can retrieve data from the database, apply the access limitations, and pass it along to client applications. As access policies change, only the mid-tier component requires maintenance.

Business data is often subject to integrity rules that cannot be enforced properly by a database server. For example, the database server could enforce the rule that a new order can be created only for an existing customer (a referential integrity constraint). However, the server could not efficiently enforce the rule that a customer with a 90-day past due balance may not place new orders. Although a developer could write an insert trigger or stored procedure to implement the rule, this approach has several shortcomings. First, a trigger would result in longer execution times for inserts, resulting in increased database contention. Second, a trigger or stored procedure enforces the rule *after* the user has filled in all the blanks to create an order. A better approach would be to encapsulate customer information, including available credit, into a mid-tier component for access by the user interface component. Then the application can check customer credit when the user *begins* to create an order.

Components that enforce business rules on data may require a high bandwidth connection to the database server where that data resides. Database response time is typically the largest factor by far in response time for the business object. Where the business rules component in turn serves many other components, those components should be located together on the same server, or on a group of servers with high bandwidth connections. Mid-tier components can also be used to overcome bandwidth limitations by caching data from the database. This approach works well with nonvolatile data.

Sometimes the middle tier includes services that are not strictly business services (graphics processing, transaction management, numerical analysis). Such applications are sometimes called multitier. The same design principles apply, however, so this chapter will not discuss multitier applications separately.

Three-tier applications generally scale much better than two-tier. Implementing business logic in a middle-tier component rather than triggers or stored procedures greatly reduces the number of database queries and thus reduces database contention. When database operations pass through a middle tier, user response time can suffer. However, although mid-tier initialization might slow the first operation, subsequent operations might be much faster. Additionally, not all database operations need to pass through a middle tier. For simple database lookups where the data is unlikely to be used again, direct access from the user interface to the database is appropriate.

Two-Tier Versus Three-Tier: An Example

Consider a sample application: consultant time-sheet submission. First, examine the components for a two-tier implementation. The database server might implement the following services:

- Tables for consultants, clients, assignments, and hours
- Stored procedures to retrieve data for a consultant, a client, current assignments for a consultant, and hours for a specified period
- Referential integrity constraints
- Insert and update triggers to ensure that all hours entered apply to an active consultant, client, and assignment
- Insert and update triggers to ensure that no consultant bills more than 24 hours in one day

■ Insert and update triggers to ensure that no consultant enters hours for a prior month later than the fifteenth of the following month

The desktop component might implement the following services:

■ Database login

■ User interface for hours entry (read-only for prior months)

■ Time-sheet data structures

■ Invoke database stored procedures to look up consultant, assignments, clients, and hours for a specified period

■ Range checking (no more than 24 billable hours/day)

■ Generate and execute SQL statements to update database

■ Error handling for database operations (for example, a trigger rejects an update)

This division of labor capitalizes on the strengths of both the database server and the desktop platform. A single developer using Microsoft SQL Server and Visual Basic can implement the design quickly. Initial deployment should be relatively simple: install database components on the database server, and distribute an install kit to consultants for the desktop component. Subsequent updates, however, will require careful coordination of database changes with distribution of the modified desktop application.

As the business grows, however, one thousand consultants update time sheets within a three-hour period every Monday morning. The implementation of range checking and business policies in triggers results in longer running updates and inserts, and substantial database contention. Contention results in failed database operations (timeouts), resulting in retries, resulting in additional contention, resulting in more failed operations, and ultimately resulting in unhappy consultants. A hardware upgrade might improve the situation, but it's an expensive solution for a problem that occurs only on Monday mornings.

Consider now a three-tier approach. Data services look very much the same, except for the omission of triggers:

■ Tables for consultants, clients, assignments, and hours

■ Stored procedures to retrieve data for a consultant, a client, current assignments for a consultant, and hours for a prior period

■ Referential integrity constraints

The presentation services might include the following:

■ User interface for database login

■ User interface for hours entry

■ Interaction with business services

The presentation layer is quite simple and might be implemented as a Visual Basic application, or as a Web application with scripting and ActiveX or Java components.

The business services layer might include the following services:

- Database login
- Invoke database stored procedures to lookup consultant, assignments, clients, and prior hours
- Time-sheet data structures
- Range checking (no more than 24 billable hours/day)
- Enforce no updates to prior months
- Generate and execute SQL statements to update database
- Error handling for database operations (for example, a trigger rejects an update)

This architecture is substantially more complex than the two-tier implementation. Development will probably take longer simply due to the problems of integrating the separate components. Initial deployment requires installation of database components, distribution of user components, and installation of mid-tier components.

The three-tier model is more complex, but it's also substantially more scalable and flexible. Because triggers do not enforce business logic, inserts and updates are fast and efficient, and the database server can handle heavier loads with less contention.

Now suppose that the consulting company opens branch offices in four cities and that copies of the database are maintained in each city. As consultants enter hours, the entries must update both the local database and the central database at world headquarters. For each implementation, each database would require distributed transaction support. You'll also require integrated account management so that a consultant requires a single login for all databases to which he has access.

The two-tier implementation would require the following changes to the desktop component:

- Add configuration parameters to determine which databases to use
- Implement login to multiple databases
- Generate and execute SQL for distributed inserts and updates
- Implement more complex error handling

The updated desktop component would have to be distributed to all consultants, and distribution would have to be carefully coordinated with database changes. This is a nontrivial problem when dealing with a thousand consultants in five cities. Additionally, database administrators must ensure that the same version of each trigger and stored procedure is installed on each database. As consultants enter hours, triggers fire separately on each database to enforce business logic. In fact, the 24-hours/day constraint is enforced separately in the desktop application and in insert triggers and update triggers on each database.

Now consider changes to the three-tier application. The presentation layer requires no changes. Mid-tier components require the same changes as the desktop application in the two-tier approach:

- Configuration parameters to determine which databases to use
- Implement login to multiple databases
- Generate and execute SQL for distributed inserts and updates
- Implement more complex error handling

The updated mid-tier components must be distributed and installed on application servers at world headquarters and at each branch location, and rollout must be coordinated with database updates. However, coordinated rollout requires cooperation among only a handful of system administrators.

Although a two-tier implementation results in a simpler design and simpler initial deployment, the three-tier model offers superior long-term scalability and flexibility.

The Connected Client Architecture

A *connected client application* is one that maintains a connection to a database and/or a network. This is the most common type of client/server computing. A large part of this book and this chapter is dedicated to technologies that are expanding the connected client architecture and client/server computing in general. Connected client applications are usually built to support some type of online process. They also will typically push some of the functionality or business logic onto the Relational Database Management System (RDBMS) that is being used as a data store.

Connected client applications are typically of the Online Transaction Processing (OLTP) variety. Users work at client workstations entering transaction information into a database, such as a consultant entering time online. These applications offer real-time response to user requests for information and are typically designed around one business process, such as time reporting. In this way, you see the growth of departmentalized computing.

The task of data resolution usually falls to the RDBMS, such as Microsoft's SQL Server. Managing concurrent updates and simultaneous requests for data from multiple users is one fundamental job of the RDBMS. It is also worth noting that the business rules pertinent to these applications are often maintained within the RDBMS in the form of stored procedures, grants and privileges, and user roles.

The Disconnected Client Architecture

A *disconnected client application* is one that is used offline, allowing the user to process data and not be directly connected to a network or corporate data store. This also implies that data must be resolved by some means other than using real-time transactions. It is very common to find the business rules for how the data is managed to be in the form of stored procedures, which allow for batch processing of data received over a given period of time.

Security for transactions must be handled by the local data store, which must be robust enough to handle some form of replication. The replication or dissemination of data, from remote users to corporate data stores, is typically done by periodically connecting to a corporate network by modem and transmitting data. The transmission is usually handled by application logic, making use of automated replication or messaging.

Connected Versus Disconnected: An Example

Once again, consider the consultant time-sheet sample application. This time you must first consider the nature of the application and its user community. The consultant, the user in this example, may be traveling or at a remote location. To implement this solution, you must consider the n-tier connected or disconnected client architectures. The groundwork for the two-tier or three-tier architecture was discussed in the previous section and will remain the same regardless of your connected/disconnected decision.

Some of the connected/disconnected design considerations follow:

- Timeliness of information
- Processing requirements
- Application complexity and maintainability
- Connectivity problems and issues
- Available bandwidth, both concurrency and speed

You will be able to find answers to most of the design issues by doing a thorough analysis of the workflow process in which the application will be used. In the consultant time-sheet example, the timeliness may be daily, weekly, biweekly, or even monthly. The answers will depend on the intended use of the data that the application supplies.

The connected client architecture would make sense if you had identified the following requirements:

- Daily information required
- Minimal processing requirements
- Low complexity with high degree of maintainability required
- Locale will support connectivity requirements
- Available bandwidth capable of supporting concurrent user community at sufficient speed

For cases where real-time budgeting or income projections hang on the hours worked for a given day, daily information may be required. This might entail the consultant dialing in to submit a time sheet daily. For this example, this may seem like overkill, but for many others, this could be vital to the financial well being of the organization. Consider sales representatives who make sales calls daily and generate orders for product: Waiting a week would delay manufacturing, shipment, and payment.

With the time-sheet example, a great deal of processing is probably not necessary to send updated daily time sheets. This will help to alleviate long connected sessions. The shorter the connected session, the less likely you are to encounter connectivity problems. The ability to successfully implement a connected client/server system might depend entirely on the amount of data that is sent back and forth between client and server and the reliability with which it can be delivered.

With the connected client architecture the mid- or second-tier components can be executed remotely, without the user having to have them co-located on his or her machine. This helps to reduce the complexity on the remote machines, for which maintenance can be severe and costly. This also makes delivery of new mid-tier functionality less painful.

One assumption that many people tend to make is that all phone lines are created equal. This is not necessarily the case. Many older hotels have some rather old phone lines that result in cross talk or attenuation on the line. These lines are adequate for voice transmission, but the ones and zeros tend to get misplaced when transmitting data. For the connected client model to work as intended, there must be a level of trust regarding the infrastructure, and the business process must support such decisions. It may be that the user is transmitting from his home or a client site and has some alternatives in regard to communication times and locations.

You may have run into situations where everyone will tend to attempt to connect at the same time, say just before a deadline. If requirements are imposed that time sheets must be submitted by a certain time, the smart bet is that a sizable portion will arrive in the hour immediately preceding the deadline. This means that the communication components at the destination must be able to support this number of concurrent users and offer acceptable performance.

 TIP During the establishment of business rules and the design of the system, factor in the inability of users to communicate for varying periods of time. Determine the impact that this lack of communication has on the business and the system. Then present solutions to both management and the users for dealing with these situations.

The disconnected client architecture would be more applicable if you had identified the following requirements:

- Weekly or biweekly information is sufficient.
- The application is processing intensive.
- High complexity with adequate degree of maintainability is required.
- The locale might not support connectivity requirements.
- The available bandwidth is not capable of supporting concurrent user community at sufficient speed.

You may decide to allow the consultants to record their time into a disconnected application and to transmit the time sheet at a more convenient time. In this example, the consultant would be allowed to enter time into the system at various intervals and then transmit when the opportunity presented itself. This solution would seem to add a degree of flexibility for the consultant, allowing the entry of billable hours while on a flight and then transmitting from the destination as an example.

In the disconnected client model, more processing might be necessary to package up and transmit a week's worth of data, or more. Replication Server, Microsoft Message Queue (MSMQ), and Microsoft Transaction Server (MTS) can aid in this approach. There would also be an increase in processing due to the mid-tier components being housed on a logical mid-tier on the client. For more information regarding Microsoft SQL Server replication, refer to *Special Edition Using Microsoft BackOffice*, Second Edition, Volume 2 from Que Corporation, ISBN 0-7897-1130-3.

▶ **See** "Examining the Types of Message Queues and Messages," **p. 174**

▶ **See** "Working with Multitiered Architectures," **p. 110**

As previously mentioned, the mid-tier components would be housed on the client. The advantages to having them co-located on the client are speed and flexibility. Flexibility and processing speed do, however, come at a cost. The administration and maintenance costs of the mid-tier components will rise, as distribution of new components becomes more difficult.

The ability to transmit data when it is convenient to the user will help belay some of the connectivity problems. Should one site not work on Monday, a different site can be used on Tuesday, or on Wednesday, and so forth. This will allow the user to keep track of his time and process normally regardless of connectivity problems. The flexibility gained by not having to transmit daily is a big factor in using the disconnected client model.

Bandwidth is always a factor, but the flexibility in data transmission can help to alleviate some of the concerns. Time sheets will probably still be tied to a deadline and, as in the connected client model, will arrive en masse at the last possible moments. Adequate communication and a brief introduction of the system and its limitations will help the users adapt to these requirements. This is where a good set of business rules can be your friend.

In the end, connected versus disconnected may very well come down to personal preference. In many cases, you may opt for the solution that best fits your skill set or presents you an opportunity for career growth. At that point it will be up to you to sell your proposal to management, but remember, that also entails delivering the solution, career growth or not.

> **CAUTION**
>
> For bidirectional communication you must pay particular attention to the amount of data that will be transferred to the user on a periodic basis. Large sets of data will increase communication costs and will also increase the costs associated with a user waiting for data to be loaded. One approach is to send only changed information. Another approach is to let the users select what data they need for a given period of time. This allows them to select as little or as much data as they want and suffer the consequences at their own hands.

Designing a Distributed Application

The first step in designing any application is to identify the business objectives for the system, and the constraints under which it must operate: the requirements. One of the most effective approaches to requirements gathering is the *use-case* approach, developed by Ivar Jacobson and others. To oversimplify a bit, a use case is a scenario that describes a business problem to be solved by software. Use cases are very effective tools for identifying the business objectives for a system.

N O T E Unfortunately, Microsoft Visual Modeler 2, which provides an introductory subset of the capabilities of Rational Rose 4, does not support use-case modeling. Visual Modeler is an entry-level product (designed specifically for the first time modeler) and utilizes the standard Unified Modeling Language (UML) as a means to express software design.

At the other end of the modeling-tool spectrum is Rational Rose. Rose 98 is the current version, which provides full roundtrip, multilanguage support for object modeling, using UML 1.1 as the default notation. The extensibility features of Rose also allow integration with other OLE-enabled applications.

Visual Modeler includes tools for class diagrams, component diagrams, and deployment diagrams, but omits the support that Rose provides for use case diagrams, object interaction diagrams (that is, sequence and collaboration diagrams), and statechart diagrams.

Neither tool currently supports activity diagrams, as specified in UML 1.1. ■

ON THE WEB

For the latest information on Microsoft Visual Modeler, visit `http://www.rational.com/msvmuser/`.

For the latest information on Rational Rose (including a free demo version), visit `http://www.rational.com/products/rose/`.

For the latest information on UML, visit `http://www.rational.com/uml/`.

▶ For more information about Microsoft Visual Modeler, **see** Chapter 36, "System Modeling and the Microsoft Visual Modeler," **p. 1029**

After the initial requirements are clear, a design process should include the following steps:

- Model business objects and their interactions.
- Define services and interfaces.
- Identify dependencies among business objects and services.
- Partition the application into components.
- Target components onto platforms.

Typically, this will be an iterative process: decisions in one stage will require changes to an earlier stage.

Model Business Objects and Their Interactions

Top-down structured analysis and design techniques are *algorithm-oriented*; they focus on the steps required to produce a result. These techniques work well for small or medium monolithic applications. Object-oriented (OO) approaches are *interaction-oriented*; they focus on interactions between components. Because OO techniques focus on the most critical aspect of a distributed system design, they are by far the best choice for distributed system design.

To derive an object model from use cases, remember your high school grammar. Nouns from the use cases will show up as entities (classes or objects) in the object model; verbs will show up as interactions between objects. Ideally, the object model should result in several diagrams: *class diagrams* showing classes and their relationships (generalizations, associations, and dependencies), and *sequence diagrams* showing the sequence of interactions between groups of objects for each use case. Figure 25.1 shows a sample class diagram that uses the UML 1.1 notation. Figure 25.2 shows a sample sequence diagram.

FIGURE 25.1
This class diagram shows that Automotive, Truck, and Motorcycle are specializations of Vehicle, a Fleet is an aggregation of Vehicles, and a Vehicle is associated with a Road.

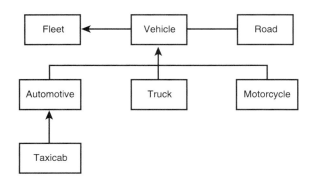

FIGURE 25.2
This UML sequence diagram shows Object 1 sending Message 1 to Object 2, which in turn creates Object 3 and sends it Message 2. After Message 2 returns, Object 2 deletes Object 3, and returns Message 1.

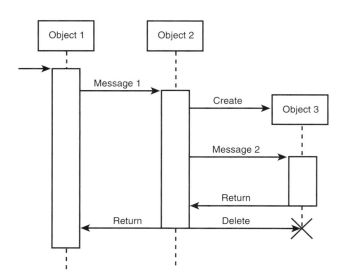

The object interactions identify services for the service-based design approach. The objective for this stage of design is to define in detail the services that the application will implement. A detailed definition of a service is basically a function definition and should include the name of the function, a detailed definition of the formal parameters, and possible return values.

The object model for the application will be a work-in-progress throughout the life of the application. As requirements change or become clarified through subsequent steps, the model will change. At some point in every project, it becomes necessary to "baseline" the object model—identify a specific version as the design for the current release.

Define Services and Interfaces

The object interactions are the services for the service-based design approach. The objective for this stage of design is to define in detail the ways in which the application will invoke services. The invocation details of a service comprise its *interface*. A detailed definition of an interface is basically a function definition. It should include the name of the function, a detailed definition of the formal parameters and possible return values, and any preconditions for invoking the service.

An interface definition should be considered a contract for provision of a service. Early publishing of an interface definition allows developers to treat the service as a black box so that implementation of services can proceed in parallel. After it is published, however, an interface should not change. This is quite difficult to achieve early in a project, but the alternative is chaos. If a service is used by a number of objects, the ripple effect will be widespread. That's why it's important to baseline the object model.

This stage of design is a good time to look for reuse opportunities. Obvious candidates include data management (SQL Server) and transaction management (MTS). You may find that important business logic has already been implemented in a prior project's mid-tier component. Often, a little research will identify a commercial product (ActiveX component or class library) that provides services closely matching project requirements.

Opportunities for software reuse generally fall into three categories:

- Component reuse
- Class library reuse
- Cut-and-paste miracle

Part
IV

Ch
25

Component reuse means binary reuse. An existing component will be incorporated into the new application without access to source code. Good examples include ActiveX controls and the database server. Use of a non-COM DLL is slightly less effective because it requires some source code (header files for C++; function DECLARE statements in VB), and because the interface is subject to change.

Class library reuse is structured source code reuse. An existing well-designed set of source code that addresses a specific problem domain can be incorporated into your project. Examples include the Microsoft Foundation Classes (MFC) and other shrink-wrap class libraries such as Rogue Wave's dbtools.h++. Often, an organization will have an internally developed class library that addresses company-specific problem domains. A well-implemented and well-documented class library can save a lot of design and implementation time.

The cut-and-paste miracle occurs when a department manager remembers an application vaguely similar to the one under development and eliminates several weeks from the implementation schedule because the new project can just reuse most of that code. For small, complex functions that have been correctly implemented once before, the cut-and-paste miracle can save a few hours. Unfortunately, the time saved is usually offset by time spent searching through legacy code for the reusable bits, and time spent melding that code into the new application. The cut-and-paste miracle rarely works as well as expected.

Finally, pause to identify services implemented in the new application that might be useful in subsequent projects. Planning for subsequent reuse does require additional design and implementation time in the schedule.

Identify Relationships Among Business Objects and Services

Software engineers define *coupling* as relationships between software components and *cohesion* as relationships within a component. Generally, cohesion is good, and coupling is bad. A certain degree of coupling, however, is inevitable, and a reasonable goal is for cohesion to be substantially stronger than coupling.

Relationships among business objects and services take a variety of forms. An `Invoice` object, for example, presupposes a `Customer` object; a `ComputeTotal` service for the invoice may depend on a `ComputeTaxes` service. The best tool for identifying relationships is the object model. Relationships between objects appear in the class diagram as aggregation, association, generalization, or dependency relationships. Sequence diagrams show dependencies between services.

An aggregation relation is a *part-of* relation. A taxicab might be part of a fleet; a fleet aggregates vehicles. A generalization relation is a *type-of* relation. A taxicab is a type of automobile, which is a type of vehicle, so a taxicab has a generalization relation to automobile and to vehicle. An association relation is a *uses* relation. A vehicle uses roads, so a vehicle has an association relation to roads. The sample class diagram in Figure 25.1 earlier in the chapter illustrates these relationships.

Generally, generalization and aggregation relations show much stronger coupling between objects than association relations. Objects with a generalization relationship should always be implemented in the same component. Objects with an aggregation relation should be implemented in the same component, unless one or more objects add value as a reusable independent component.

Sequence diagrams show the strength of association relations. The more messages exchanged between a pair of objects, the stronger the relation. The message sequence diagram shows the number of types of messages passed; design should also consider the frequency of each message type. Figure 25.2, earlier in the chapter, shows a sample sequence diagram.

Dependencies also show where requirements changes are likely to have ripple effects. Sometimes, a minor design change can isolate objects or services that are likely to change frequently.

Partition the Application into Components

Partitioning a distributed application is the most challenging part of the design process. Object boundaries, application tiers, dependencies, and deployment issues must all be considered and balanced. A few general guidelines apply:

- *Minimize services implemented in the presentation layer.* A minimalist presentation layer is easily reimplemented on a new platform such as an X terminal or a Web browser.

- *Minimize the number of communications between components.* Each discrete interaction between components introduces round-trip communication delay. Prefer a single, complex procedure call to a series of simpler procedure calls. Stated differently, *maximize the ratio of work-to-connect time.*

- *Minimize coupling between components. Coupling* refers to functional dependencies between components. For example, a mid-tier component might depend on a presentation component to validate a database login. This would require that *every* application that uses the mid-tier component must also use the presentation component for database login.

- *Group services based on the resources they interact with.* This strategy addresses bandwidth constraints. When several objects share a common set of resources, package them in a single component that can be deployed with good access to the needed resources. For example, several mid-tier services might make heavy use of a database; combine those services in a component and deploy it on an application server with a fast connection to the database. Stated differently, *maximize locality of reference.*

- *Use a simulation tool to validate your design.* The Application Performance Explorer (APE) included with Visual Studio 6 can provide useful insights into architectural alternatives. APE will be discussed later in this chapter.

One very effective strategy for partitioning a three-tier application is to classify the services provided by each object as presentation, business, or data. The object and layer boundaries give a good first cut at a partition. Each object will be partitioned into three subcomponents (assuming it provides services in each tier). Then, within each tier, group subcomponents are based on interactions and dependencies within that layer. This same approach works for a two-tier application, or a multitier application.

 T I P   Include closely related objects in one component. This approach will improve performance and maintainability. However, expect the strength of interactions to vary markedly across tiers. Two objects may be strongly related in the data layer but quite distinct in the presentation layer.

Select an Implementation Model for the Application

After creating an object model and incorporating reusable components, select an implementation model. Obviously, reuse decisions will play a substantial role in this decision. The organization's level of experience with client/server computing will also play an important role: groups with less experience tend to develop primarily two-tier applications. Sometimes, an application has very few business services and works better as two-tier.

A traditional client/server application presents relatively few partitioning decisions. The database server provides data management services, and a client application implements business logic and the user interface. In some cases, business logic could be implemented through triggers and stored procedures, or in client code. Generally, stored procedures minimize the number of database calls, improve scalability, and simplify deployment.

For data used by more than one application, or data subject to significant business rules, the three-tier model supports encapsulation of important business logic. Usually, three-tier applications scale more effectively to large numbers of users. Reuse decisions might also motivate a decision for three-tier.

Target Components onto Platforms

In this final design stage, emphasis shifts from abstraction to implementation. Business requirements implemented in the object model must now be reconciled with constraints imposed by the computing environment. Sometimes, partitioning decisions have to be revised.

Often, external factors dictate a particular platform for both the database server and the GUI. For instance, the department database server might run Sybase System 11 on a multiprocessor UNIX system, and target users might run Windows 3.11 on 486-66 machines. Beyond available hardware, platform constraints also include IPC/RPC mechanisms and hosting for other required services such as transaction management.

Presentation Layer Components   For most applications, the presentation layer platform is predefined: whatever sits on the user's desk today. Typically, this includes a range of performance and capabilities. Usually, management exerts substantial pressure to support all existing hardware; however, this can lead to unnecessary compromises in the application. It's always a mistake to hobble a new application to support old hardware. The issue is especially important if DCOM support is at stake. Probably the most important issue is appropriate network bandwidth. A component that makes excessive demands on network resources will perform poorly and might be unstable.

It's generally a good idea to define a minimum platform and a recommended platform. The platform specification should include processor type and speed, memory, available disk space, operating system, and network bandwidth and protocols. As a rule of thumb, when a relatively small number of target users (fewer than 20 percent) have subminimum systems, the hardware upgrade costs will usually be less than the cost to reengineer the application. This is especially true for the transition from 16-bit Windows to 32-bit Windows. If a majority of users have equipment that does not comply with the recommended platform, application performance is at risk.

Limit functionality in the presentation layer to session management (showing windows in the proper order, enabling and disabling controls) and very basic input validation. More complex validation belongs in the middle tier. This generally means that inputs are validated in groups, rather than a field at a time. Identifying these validation groups is an important step in designing both the presentation layer and the middle tier.

Business Services Layer   Components that enforce business rules on data require a high-bandwidth connection to the database server where that data resides. Database response time is typically the largest factor in response time for the business object. Where the business-rules component in turn serves many presentation components, it can make sense to deploy closer to the user.

The business services layer offers deployment flexibility that may not be available for data services or presentation services. Consider whether concurrent processing using the pipeline, parallel, or asynchronous model is appropriate. These three approaches are mutually compatible. Choosing a concurrency strategy can result in modifications to the object model. The concurrent processing models are as follows:

- Pipeline Processing—Application divides a task into stages and processes the different stages concurrently.

- Parallel Processing—Multiple instances of the same application executing against a common task.

- Asynchronous Processing—Application processes run concurrently without synchronization.

When a problem decomposes functionally into a series of sequential tasks, consider a pipeline. Try to design the pipeline for similar processing time at each stage. The design should include a statechart diagram depicting the state of a task as it passes through each stage of the pipeline. This diagram often identifies resource conflicts and processing bottlenecks.

When a problem consists of a number of small uniform tasks, consider a parallel architecture. Parallel processing provides enhanced fault tolerance as well as enhanced throughput. Design should include a statechart diagram for the process.

When a problem includes independent subtasks, consider asynchronous processing. Design should include a statechart diagram for the asynchronous task.

Sometimes, data services can be distributed across multiple databases. When data services require coordinated operations against two or more databases, the application will require distributed transaction support. Microsoft Transaction Server provides good support for distributed transactions, particularly when all databases are hosted on Microsoft SQL Server 6.5 or 7.

Data Services Layer   Most often, an existing database server will provide data management services. If the enterprise has been using the three-tier approach for some time, there should be some opportunity for reuse at both the data services and business services layers.

At the data services layer, it's very important to maximize the amount of work performed per query. For example, inexperienced developers sometimes write an application to query the database individually for each row in a resultset. Visual Studio 6 includes several database access classes (Remote Data Objects [RDO], Active Data Objects [ADO], Data Access Objects [DAO]) for more effective management of resultsets. Most database servers support stored procedures, another way to maximize work per query. There is a tradeoff, however; stored procedures are often difficult to debug and don't fit well into most configuration management tools.

TIP   Use DAO with desktop databases such as Paradox, FoxPro, and especially Access. RDO can provide more efficient access to a database server on the local area network, providing extended access to database errors, and return codes and output parameters for stored procedures. ADO can also provide efficient access to database servers, with fewer advanced features than RDO. All three libraries use Open Database Connectivity (ODBC); Microsoft is nudging developers toward ADO.

ON THE WEB

For a comparison of DAO, RDO, and ADO, see `http://www.microsoft.com/accessdev/articles/av9709.htm`.

For a whitepaper comparison of DAO, RDO, and ADO within Visual Basic, see `http://www.microsoft.com/vbasic/techmat/whitepapers/choosing/default.htm`.

The data services layer is often a hot spot for resource contention. Take care to implement services so as to minimize locking. Avoid cursors; use the minimum workable locking level; avoid long running transactions. In particular, no database transaction should require user input or confirmation. (The users might decide to go to lunch.)

The Application Performance Explorer

The Application Performance Explorer (APE) is a utility provided with Visual Studio 6 to aid in the architectural design of distributed applications. This utility is used to simulate architectural scenarios for distributed client/server applications to help pinpoint performance problems before they are installed into a production environment. The general purpose of APE is to help answer the question of which tasks should be remote and which ones should remain local.

To understand how APE can help in determining a distributed application's architecture, it is necessary to investigate two models of concurrent processing: *synchronous* and *asynchronous* processing.

Synchronous Processing

Synchronous processing is very often thought of in the context of parallel processing. A good example of parallel synchronous processing would be a museum tour. Let's say that at the start of the day, there are 50 people gathered in the museum lobby for the guided tour. The issue in this example is that each room in the museum can only accommodate up to 10 people at once. Therefore, the museum staff divides the museum patrons into 5 groups (group A through group E) of 10 people.

At the start of the tour (the processing), the lucky people in group A enter the first room, while groups B through E must wait. When tour group A continues to the second room, the first room frees up to allow group B to enter. At this point, both groups A and B are "processing" in parallel. This activity continues to the point where eventually all 5 groups are "processing" different rooms in the museum at the same time.

The challenge of the museum curator in this example is obvious. To accommodate the maximum number of visitors, each tour group must spend an equal amount of time in each room. If one specific room in the museum requires a substantially greater viewing time, each tour group that is behind the group currently in this specific room must wait, even though they may have already viewed the entire room they are in.

In the context of client/server processing, when designing a synchronous parallel application (sometimes called a *pipeline application*), it is extremely important for the developer to build components that require nearly an equal amount of processing time. Otherwise, these slower stages of processing become bottlenecks and require additional synchronization to keep the pipeline operating smoothly.

Asynchronous Processing

The background printing feature of Microsoft Word is an excellent example of asynchronous processing. If a document prints at six pages per minute, a 30-page report would require five minutes. By spinning off the printing as a separate task, control returns to the user almost immediately.

The primary design problem for asynchronous processing is error handling. First, the background process has to notify the user process that an error has occurred. Second, and more problematic, by the time an error occurs, the state of the user process has usually changed significantly. In Microsoft Word, for example, a user might have made a substantial number of revisions since printing. It's generally impractical to return to the state at the time of the original request and retry. For a Word user, it's probably acceptable to just print again from the current state of the document.

For client/server applications, database access is an obvious opportunity for asynchronous processing. For example, a background query can retrieve needed data while a user works on a startup dialog. Avoid asynchronous database updates. If the update fails, it might be impossible to return the user to the pre-update context.

Using the Application Performance Explorer

The installation of APE with Visual Studio 6 includes several sample profiles of the remote deployment models described previously. The synchronous and asynchronous processing models are included with both typical performance scenarios and peak performance scenarios to provide a basis for creating custom scenarios to simulate a wide array of distributed application environments. By starting with these included models, Microsoft has made it simple to simulate a potential installation scenario without having to expend significant resources to actually build a distributed application and find performance problems at that time. In reality, no remote deployment installation can be accurately simulated before real construction begins. To help, APE enables the user to actually include existing remote components and an existing database in the simulation environment. Using this feature of APE, it is advantageous to perform "semi-simulation" testing of the deployment environment throughout the construction phase of an application to catch potential performance problems before they occur after production installation.

APE enables the user to create specific simulation scenarios by allowing the easy manipulation of several factors that influence performance in a distributed application. Some of these factors include the number of objects (clients and services) to be created, database options, duration of CPU tasks, and callback options. These simulation scenarios can be saved in the application window to allow quick comparison between several different custom-built architectures.

Part
IV
Ch
25

APE allows the customization of the following factors in remote deployment performance:

- Client options—These options include the number of clients running concurrently in the simulation, test duration, delay between client calls, and whether or not the client passes data to services. For a more real-world simulation, installed remote clients can be specified for the test scenario.

- Service Connection options—These options enable the user to specify a connection type (Remote Automation versus DCOM). These options also enable the user to specify a Remote Application Server that already exists on the network.

- Service options—This set of variables allows the specification of varying database activity, CPU task duration, service binding, and whether to use pre-instantiated objects from a resource pool.

- Database Connection options—These enable the user to specify ODBC, ADO, RDO, or DAO.

- Database options—These options give the choice between the Microsoft Jet Engine, or Microsoft SQL Server. In the case of SQL Server, this allows the APE simulation to use an actual database to run the test against to create a better real-world scenario. Using SQL Server enables the user to test actual performance of the database under varying conditions and also allows the inclusion of Microsoft Transaction Server underneath the Service Options set of variables.

After all the presented options have been specified, the simulation can be easily run by pressing the Start button on the main window. Then all client processes are created, and calls are made to the server processes. All client and server activity is shown in the main window and written to a log file (if the user has specified), as shown in Figure 25.3. If desired, the combination of options selected for this scenario can be saved as a profile so that it can be easily pulled back into the environment for later testing.

FIGURE 25.3

The Application Performance Explorer can validate your design.

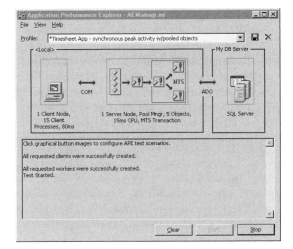

As can be seen by using APE, it is possible to quickly build simulated network configurations and test cases to measure performance under varying conditions. These quick simulated scenarios can help to answer some basic remote deployment questions:

- Where will the processing bottlenecks be?
- How large should a specific component be? Should it be broken into smaller components with less functionality?
- Should CPU-intensive tasks be remoted to faster machines?
- What will happen to performance during peak processing times?

N O T E The Application Performance Explorer source code is in itself an example of a well-designed distributed application. It is included with the Visual Studio 6 installation and can be found in Common\Tools\Ape\Source directory under your Microsoft Visual Studio directory.

ON THE WEB

For more information on the Application Performance Explorer, visit the Microsoft Developer Network Web site at http:// search.microsoft.com/ and search on *Application Performance Explorer*.

Legacy Integration Technologies

Microsoft has amassed an array of tools and technologies that enables you to build distributed applications and to integrate these applications with each other and with legacy systems. Some of these tools are used primarily for moving data to multiple data stores, whereas others are concerned with sharing data and processes between disparate environments. As mentioned earlier in this book, Microsoft tends to use catchy code names. For future reference, for the tools described in this section, the code names are also mentioned. The following Microsoft technologies are discussed in this section:

- The Host Data Replicator (HDR)
- OLE DB provider for AS/400 and VSAM
- COM Transaction Integrator for CICS and IMS (*COMTI*)

The technologies presented here have a common goal. They strive to enable you, as the developer, to focus on business issues and worry less about the back-office issues. The role of the developer is to focus on the business issues and problems at hand, design solutions, and then select the proper tools for the implementation of these solutions. Microsoft has sought to provide you with a rich tool set for nearly all the situations that can arise during the implementation of these solutions. Some of these tools are designed to help you build distributed client/server applications that can be integrated with legacy applications. Others are designed for distributed applications that must make use of multiple databases or handle remote users.

ON THE WEB

The following technologies and tools are presented in cursory fashion. For more details on these and any of the Microsoft products, it is recommended that you visit its Web site, `http://` `www.microsoft.com/`. Be prepared to spend a significant amount of time locating information, but a wealth of technical documentation is provided for each of these tools.

The Host Data Replicator

Many companies that have existing host-based legacy environments use DB2. To answer the call for data transparency with these systems, Microsoft has developed the Host Data Replicator, code-named Cakewalk. The HDR allows replication of database tables between DB2 and SQL Server. It also allows bidirectional replication, in which an entire table is refreshed with a snapshot from the source environment. The HDR uses Microsoft's SNA version 3 for the connectivity to the host environment, while all of the processing resides on the NT server on which the HDR is installed. The HDR supports a variety of replication scenarios, types, and DB2 products.

The HDR supports a myriad of replication scenarios that allow for flexibility and transparency of data between SQL Server and DB2 systems. The HDR supports the following replication features:

- Vertical partitioning—Replication of only selected columns
- Horizontal partitioning—Replication of only selected rows
- Combined partitioning—Replication of only selected columns from selected rows
- Derived columns—Calculated from source data
- SQL—Ability to use SQL expressions to alter data before or after replication
- Data manipulation—Ability to manipulate the data to fit the target's data type or column order

Replication scenarios supported are horizontal, vertical, and combined partitioning. The HDR also supports the use of derived columns, allowing for the calculation of fields during replication. In addition, the HDR provides the ability to use Structured Query Language (SQL) to alter data before or after replication and the ability to manipulate the data type or column order of replicated data.

The HDR provides for three replication time frames:

- On-demand replication
- Scheduled replication
- Recurring scheduled replication

On-demand replication can be implemented through a programmatic interface to provide quasi-transaction-based replication. Scheduled replication is very useful if hour-, day-, or week-old data is sufficient for the business purposes it is intended to serve. Recurring scheduled replication is very similar to scheduled replication, usually set to occur at a specific time or times of the day and over a given period of time.

The HDR supports a variety of DB2 flavors. HDR supports the following versions of DB2:

- DB2 for MVS
- DB2/VM
- DB2/400 for AS/400
- DB2/2 for OS/2
- DB2/6000 for RS6000
- DB2/2 for WinNT

Some organizations might have multiple DB2 environments, but the transparency provided by the HDR can be used with one or more of these DB2 environments and Microsoft SQL Server. This also allows the same set of application code to work using any of the supported DB2 platforms. By writing applications to use the HDR, you can free the dependence of the application on a specific DB2 platform. This allows scalability on the DB2 legacy side of the development environment without changing the code to access it.

For IT shops that have an install base of DB2, it has become much easier to share information with SQL Server databases. This reduces development time for new client/server applications by enabling developers to share data between environments without sacrificing development time in providing middle-ware solutions.

ON THE WEB

For more information on the Host Data Replicator, visit the Microsoft Developer Network Web site at `http://search.microsoft.com/` and search on *Cakewalk* or *Host Data Replicator*.

OLE DB Provider for AS/400 and VSAM

The OLE DB provider for AS/400 and VSAM, code-named Thor, gives you the ability to integrate legacy data with more current relational database systems, such as SQL Server. The OLE DB/DDM driver makes use of two data access methods, Microsoft's OLE DB, and IBM's Distributed Data Management (DDM). OLE DB/DDM opens up the world of legacy data files, VSAM and OS/400 files, to the client/server application developer, you. This enables you to leverage a tremendous resource of many organizations, their legacy data.

OLE DB is a major component of Microsoft's Universal Data Access initiative, which allows for data stored in any form to be accessed through a common set of interfaces. This means that corporate data stored in spreadsheets, relational databases, flat files, or email systems is accessible to the application, greatly simplifying your job as the application developer. This is accomplished by the data stores exposing common interfaces to the data.

OLE DB partitions the database functionality into logical components and allows for these components to communicate by event processing. An OLE DB component can be created to present data in a tabular format while allowing complex application logic to be processed within the component. OLE DB provides a COM-based API for developing robust database applications using any number of data stores and for a variety of platforms. Support for OLE DB falls on the shoulders of the data provider, that is, Microsoft Excel, Microsoft Project, or ODBC SQL-oriented data. OLE DB resides above the data store and below the application, allowing the application developer to interface with the OLE DB APIs without worrying about the underlying data store. It is worth noting that OLE DB is not a replacement for ODBC, but rather enables OLE DB data consumers to utilize ODBC data providers.

IBM's DDM protocol is a standard access method to row-oriented legacy data files, such as VSAM. DDM is available for most host environments. The OLE DB/DDM driver requires no host-side software from Microsoft.

The OLE DB/DDM driver enables you to access VSAM data set members much as you would access files on a Windows NT Server. Because you can not only view the VSAM data set member, but have record-level I/O access, you can utilize this data without first performing costly conversions to SQL Server or other RDBMS formats. The OLE DB/DDM driver also allows access to both fixed and variable record-length records, with full data set navigation. Other features of OLE DB/DDM are file locking, record locking, and record attribute preservation of VSAM files. OLE DB/DDM truly is a single solution for accessing multiple data storage types on multiple disparate platforms.

The following is a list of VSAM file types supported:

- Key-sequenced data set (KSDS)
- Entry-sequenced data set (ESDS)
- Relative record data set (RRDS)
- Partitioned data set (PDS)

▶ **See** "Universal Data Access and OLE DB," **p. 762**

ON THE WEB

For more information regarding the OLE DB/DDM driver, visit the Microsoft Developer Network Web site at http://search.microsoft.com/ and search on *Thor* or *OLE DB provider for AS/400*.

COM Transaction Integrator for CICS and IMS

Microsoft COM Transaction Integrator for CICS and IMS (COMTI), formerly known as Cedar, allows you to create distributed client/server applications using legacy mainframe applications as functional components. COMTI's program-to-program interoperability allows organizations to leverage their existing mainframe applications in a distributed COM-based client/server environment. Using the tools that come with COMTI, you can quickly create Distributed COM (DCOM) components using legacy systems. These components can communicate and interoperate to form very robust applications. COMTI allows for atomic, transaction-based client/server applications to use business logic that is already in place rather than having to rewrite or reengineer legacy business logic. Companies can utilize their existing investment in mainframe programming tools and developers while taking advantage of the more flexible COM- and DCOM-oriented technologies and tool sets to extend legacy systems.

An example of this flexibility is extending a mainframe-based record look-up utility. You could incorporate this functionality into a new Windows-based application, tying it to a pushbutton, and allow the mainframe component to find information, based on a name, and supply this data to your Windows application.

These DCOM components created by COMTI can be used by and run on any DCOM-compliant platform, such as MVS. Developers can use these components in creating client/server distributed applications, which may consist of components running locally, on middle-tier servers, and on the mainframe, passing data between them from a variety of data stores. As in the previous example, a program or utility running on MVS could be created as a DCOM component and utilized by your Windows application.

You can create COMTI components by using the COMTI Interface Builder. The Interface Builder allows you to define the methods and I/O parameters for the host application. This process includes specifying the location and name of the mainframe program, and specifying any default data type mappings. The last step in this process is creating the COMTI type library and registering it with MTS. The COMTI components will reside on the Windows NT Server, not on the legacy host system, and must be registered on any client platforms that they will be called from.

COMTI works by intercepting object method calls and redirecting them to the appropriate mainframe program. COMTI uses the definition, built during the creation of the component, to convert the method call into the appropriate format for the target platform, and sends the method call to the host platform. The connection to the host environment is provided by Microsoft SNA Server 3. Once the mainframe component processes the method call and returns the results, COMTI converts the results from the native host format to a format understandable by the calling object. The results are then sent back to the calling object.

COMTI is a component of MTS, discussed earlier. This allows COMTI to interact and make use of the MTS transaction functionality. COMTI, working with MTS components such as Distributed Transaction Coordinator (DTC) and using the OLE DB/DDM database connectivity, can provide two-phase commit functionality between different database systems running on different platforms. This empowers you, as the developer, to create synergistic applications that make full use of legacy assets while delivering the flexibility and functionality that the organization desires.

COMTI-defined objects can be used with any development tool that supports automation objects. Such tools include Visual Basic and Visual C++ versions 5 and up. You can view these objects using the standard object browser once the object library is added to the application.

ON THE WEB

For more information on COMTI, visit the Microsoft Developer Network Web site at http://search.microsoft.com/ and search on cedar or COMTI.

From Here...

In this chapter, you looked at the problem of designing a client/server application on a traditional network, beginning with Microsoft's strategic services paradigm. Then you looked at some of the factors that influence a design. After reviewing common design objectives and constraints, you learned about concurrent processing approaches, with a comparison of the two-tier and three-tier client/server application models. Finally, you saw all the pieces pulled together into a comprehensive design strategy.

- To learn more about Microsoft's strategies for application development in the enterprise, see Chapter 9, "Using Microsoft's Object Technologies."

- For a more general discussion of distributed applications, see Chapter 17, "Server-Side Programming."

- To learn more about database development in Visual Studio, see Chapter 4, "Creating Database-Aware Applications with Visual Studio."

- For more information on the development of Web-based solutions and applications for I-net environments, see Chapter 15, "Clients, Servers, and Components: Web-Based Applications," and Chapter 11, "Using COM Components and ActiveX Controls."

- For additional information on distributed applications, see Chapter 31, "Using Microsoft Transaction Server to Enable Distributed Applications."

CHAPTER 26

Building Client Front Ends with Visual Basic

by Matthew Baute

In this chapter

Using ADO in Visual Basic: An Overview

One of the first tasks that computers were given was the management of large amounts of data. It's a natural application for a computer system, with its rapid information retrieval and sorting and searching capabilities. It's understandable, then, that a primary area of research and development in the computing community has been the development of powerful yet easy-to-use tools for data management and retrieval.

Playing its part in this ongoing development and refinement of data management tools, Microsoft continues to improve upon its own data access tool suite. Microsoft's strategy is now centered around OLE DB, a technology that features access to both relational and nonrelational data. ActiveX Data Objects (ADO) is the high-level object model made available to Visual Basic programmers and designed to take advantage of the power of OLE DB. This chapter provides an overview of OLE DB and ADO and describes in detail three sample applications. These applications demonstrate how easy building client front ends using Visual Basic and ADO can be.

Universal Data Access and OLE DB

OLE DB is Microsoft's technology to provide *Universal Data Access* (UDA). This technology provides a common data interface to many different data sources. Users frequently need access to data that might exist in spreadsheets, phone lists, email, and so on. Programmatic access to this wide range of data types, formats, architectures, APIs, and so forth has been complex and error-prone. However, the OLE DB API was designed to address how different types of data are accessed and used, and emphasizes commonality in data access and manipulation, such as opening the data source, requesting information, and navigating through the information.

Now that these different applications and data types can be accessed the same way through OLE DB, seemingly impossible things—such as relating joins between a spreadsheet, a database, and an email system—are now possible.

ON THE WEB

You can find more information on Microsoft's Universal Data Access strategy at `http://www.microsoft.com/data/`. Look for more information on OLE DB at `http://www.microsoft.com/data/oledb/`.

Support for accessing relational databases (in particular, for databases compliant with the open database connectivity (ODBC) standard) is included in OLE DB. This is accomplished through the ODBC Provider for OLE DB, a standard component of the OLE DB subsystem.

ActiveX Data Objects

ActiveX Data Objects is the tool set used by Visual Basic programmers to build applications that need to access traditional relational databases or the wide range of data sources made available by OLE DB. ActiveX Data Objects make high-level functionality available to the VB programmer through various objects, methods, and properties that encapsulate low-level OLE DB functions. The intricacies of OLE DB are thus kept hidden from the developer.

With the release of ADO 2, previous data object models such as Remote Data Objects (RDO) and Data Access Objects (DAO) are superceded. ADO is now the data object model recommended by Microsoft for all future development. ADO 2 includes all the functionality of these prior data object models along with new functionality. New features found in ADO 2 include events, asynchronous processing, hierarchical cursors, integration with the T-SQL Debugger, and the new Find method and Sort property.

Conversion from RDO or DAO to ADO is not a trivial task. Although the object models are similar, especially RDO and ADO, they do not map precisely to one another. This requires rewriting code that references the older models when conversion to ADO is undertaken. Although support for RDO and DAO will be continued, these object models will not be enhanced. Conversion of existing applications that use these object models is therefore not required, but might be considered if an application can benefit from the enhanced functionality that ADO provides. Any new development should use ADO as the data object model of choice.

With several new data tools included in Visual Basic 6, ADO is easy to implement in real-world development scenarios. The Data Form Wizard, the Data Project, and the ADO Data Control, all new to VB, provide different ways to quickly get up and running with ADO. Sample applications using each method are demonstrated later in this chapter.

Working with the ADO Object Model

One aspect of Microsoft's Internet strategy was to develop a new data object model that supported the connectionless nature of the Internet. This model needed to support making changes to records exclusively on the client without continuously talking to the server. Changes had to be updated to the server in a single batch.

Microsoft designed ADO in part with this sort of Internet scenario in mind. ADO's UpdateBatch method is the implementation of this asynchronous functionality. UpdateBatch allows the client to pass many changes over the network to the server in a single command. This helps to reduce the number of requests and responses passing between client and server, reducing overall network traffic.

An additional benefit of ADO's design for the Internet is a small memory footprint. Because downloading data over low-speed modems is often quite time-consuming, Web developers need "lightweight" tools that operate well in the bandwidth-hungry Internet environment. ADO fits the bill, featuring high performance as well.

Another important feature of the ADO object model is the capability to create objects independently without having to traverse a rigid object hierarchy. This helps reduce the number of objects needing to be created and improves performance.

Part
IV

Ch
26

ON THE WEB

You can find articles, documentation, news, and other information on ADO at `http://www.microsoft.com/data/ado/`.

The Main ADO Objects

Three ADO objects encapsulate the main functionality needed to perform data manipulation (see Figure 26.1). A brief description of the `Connection`, `Command`, and `Recordset` objects follows. The most frequently used methods for each of the main objects are listed.

FIGURE 26.1
The ADO Object Model has three main objects—the `Connection`, `Command`, and `Recordset` objects.

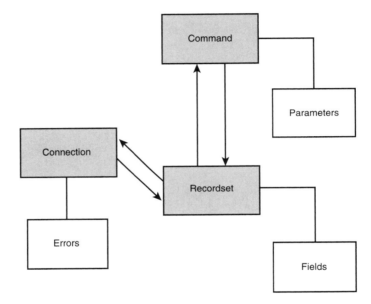

The `Connection` Object   The ADO `Connection` object is used to set database connection parameters and to open a session with a database. The properties of the `Connection` object are designed to enable fine-tuning of the database connection. This object also features transaction processing methods that integrate well with middleware software such as Microsoft Transaction Server (MTS).

▶ For more information about MTS and ADO transaction processing, **see** Chapter 30, "Creating Data Access Components for MTS with Visual Basic and ADO," **p. 873**

Table 26.1 Primary Methods of the Connection Object

Method Name	Description
Open	Establishes a connection with a database
Execute	Runs a query, SQL statement, or stored procedure against a database
BeginTrans	Marks the starting point of a transaction
RollbackTrans	Cancels the current transaction
CommitTrans	Finalizes the current transaction in the database
Cancel	Terminates the execution of a pending asynchronous database command
Close	Closes the current database connection

The Command Object   The ADO Command object is used to execute stored procedures and parameter queries against a database connection. It can be used to add, update, or delete data using Structured Query Language (SQL) statements.

Table 26.2 Primary Methods of the Command Object

Method Name	Description
CreateParameter	Specifies a new parameter for the command to be executed
Execute	Runs a query, SQL statement, or stored procedure against a database
Cancel	Terminates the execution of a pending asynchronous database command

The Recordset Object   The Recordset object is the most important and the most complex object in the ADO object model because it provides a wide variety of functionality for manipulating cursors of data. The number of methods and properties available for use with the Recordset object is quite large, testifying to its flexibility and usefulness.

Table 26.3 Primary Methods of the Recordset Object

Method Name	Description
Open	Establishes a cursor to records in a database
Clone	Creates a duplicate recordset of an existing recordset object
Resync	Refreshes recordset data from the database
MoveFirst	Makes the first record of the recordset the current record

continues

Part
IV

Ch
26

Table 26.3   Continued

Method Name	Description
MovePrevious	Makes the previous record in the recordset the current record
MoveNext	Makes the next record in the recordset the current record
MoveLast	Makes the last record of the recordset the current record
Find	Searches the recordset for a record based on specific criteria
AddNew	Creates a new, blank record in the recordset
Update	Writes any changes made to the current record to the database
Save	Writes the specified recordset to a file
CancelUpdate	Rejects any changes made to the current record since the last update
UpdateBatch	Writes all pending changes in a recordset to the database
CancelBatch	Cancels changes made to any records in a recordset since the last update
Cancel	Terminates the execution of a pending asynchronous database command
Delete	Removes the current record or a group of records from the recordset
Close	Closes the current recordset cursor

 T I P   The new Find method and Sort property of the ADO Recordset object enhance your ability to quickly locate and arrange records within a recordset.

Other ADO Objects

The ADO object model includes several other objects helpful in specific applications that round out the remainder of ADO's functionality. Each of these objects is contained within its own collection. A brief description of each object follows:

- Error (errors collection)—Contains details of errors that occur when working with a Connection object
- Parameter (parameters collection)—Represents an argument associated with a Command object; typically used to represent input/output arguments of stored procedures
- Field (fields collection)—Used to explore information relating to columns of a Recordset object
- Property (properties collection)—Used to access and set built-in or dynamic data-source specific properties

ADO Events

With the introduction of events, ADO's capability to function asynchronously is greatly enhanced. Code can now be written that is triggered when specific events occur with either Connection or Recordset objects.

Most ADO events are combined in pairs. The event that takes place before an operation begins is named Will*Event* (where *Event* is a specified ADO event). The event that takes place when an operation ends is named *Event*Complete. The event name verb and noun are reversed in the naming convention.

Other ADO events stand by themselves, lacking a corresponding pair. The Disconnect event related to the Connection object and the EndOfRecordset event related to the Recordset object are two such events. Unpaired events occur only after data operations have been completed, similar to the EventComplete events of paired events.

The sample code shown in Listing 26.1 (generated largely by the Data Form Wizard described later in this chapter) includes three ADO Recordset events, triggered as the user manipulates data within a Data Grid object on a form.

Listing 26.1   26SRC01.TXT—Paired and Unpaired ADO Events

```
' instantiate ADO events for a recordset
Dim WithEvents adoPrimaryRS As Recordset

Private Sub Form_Load()
  Dim db As Connection
  Set db = New Connection
  db.CursorLocation = adUseClient
  db.Open "PROVIDER=MSDASQL;dsn=SampleApp;uid=;pwd=;"

  Set adoPrimaryRS = New Recordset
  adoPrimaryRS.Open "select ProjectCode,ProjectName,AccountNumber,
➥OfficeCode from Project Order by ProjectCode", db,
➥adOpenStatic, adLockOptimistic

  Set grdDataGrid.DataSource = adoPrimaryRS
End Sub

Private Sub adoPrimaryRS_WillChangeRecord(ByVal adReason As
➥ADODB.EventReasonEnum, ByVal cRecords As Long, adStatus As
➥ADODB.EventStatusEnum, ByVal pRecordset As ADODB.Recordset)
' called before any record manipulation is performed
    Dim bCancel As Boolean

    Select Case adReason
    Case adRsnAddNew
        MsgBox "About to add a new record"
    Case adRsnClose
        MsgBox "About to close the recordset"
    Case adRsnDelete
        MsgBox "You are not authorized to delete records."
```

Part
IV

Ch
26

continues

Listing 26.1   Continued

```
            bCancel = True
        Case adRsnFirstChange
        Case adRsnMove
        Case adRsnRequery
        Case adRsnResynch
        Case adRsnUndoAddNew
        Case adRsnUndoDelete
        Case adRsnUndoUpdate
        Case adRsnUpdate
            MsgBox "About to update the record..."
        End Select

    If bCancel Then adStatus = adStatusCancel
End Sub

Private Sub adoPrimaryRS_RecordChangeComplete(ByVal adReason As
➥ADODB.EventReasonEnum, ByVal cRecords As Long, ByVal pError
➥As ADODB.Error, adStatus As ADODB.EventStatusEnum,
➥ByVal pRecordset As ADODB.Recordset)
' called after any record manipulation is performed
    Select Case adReason
    Case adRsnAddNew
        MsgBox "A new record has been added."
    Case adRsnClose
        MsgBox "The recordset has been closed."
    Case adRsnDelete
    Case adRsnFirstChange
    Case adRsnMove
    Case adRsnRequery
    Case adRsnResynch
    Case adRsnUndoAddNew
    Case adRsnUndoDelete
    Case adRsnUndoUpdate
    Case adRsnUpdate
        MsgBox "The record has been updated."
    End Select
End Sub

Private Sub adoPrimaryRS_EndOfRecordset(fMoreData As Boolean,
➥adStatus As ADODB.EventStatusEnum, ByVal pRecordset
➥As ADODB.Recordset)
    'event called when EOF is encountered for the recordset
    MsgBox "Reached the end of file for the recordset."
End Sub
```

N O T E   Although ADO events are fully supported in Visual Basic 6, they aren't supported in VBScript. ▇

Using Sample Visual Basic/ADO Applications: Project Maintenance

There are several different ways to create client front ends using ADO to access and manipulate data in Visual Basic. This section contains several practical "how-to" applications that demonstrate different methods of creating data management forms using the main features of ADO.

The simplest method of data form creation in Visual Basic is demonstrated with the Data Form Wizard. More complexity and flexibility is introduced through use of the Data Project. Finally, the ADO Data Control sample application demonstrates yet another flexible way to access data in VB.

Setting Up an ODBC DSN

An open database connectivity Data Source Name (DSN) must be created that references the sample Timesheet database application. This can be done either manually, with the ODBC Administrator program, or by using code.

ON THE WEB

The sample Timesheet SQL Server database used in the sample applications can be downloaded at `http://www.gasullivan.com/vstudio/`. Install the database by downloading the SQL script for the Timesheet sample database and then generating the database using the ISQL or ISQL_W tools.

Creating a DSN with the ODBC Administrator   Windows 95/98 and Windows NT ship with an ODBC configuration program called the ODBC Administrator. This program enables you to configure connections to relational databases of many different types. Although a limited number of drivers come preinstalled with Windows, you can load your own ODBC database drivers for less popular database sources and use the ODBC Administrator to configure access to them.

An ODBC DSN contains the basic information needed to connect to a database including the server name and location, the database filename/location, the user ID, and the password. `Connection` settings can also be fine-tuned using this program. Creating a DSN once with the ODBC administrator and then using just the name of the DSN in your programs allow you to hide the complexity of a database connection from users. This also prevents you from having to enter detailed connection information each time you want to connect to the database.

To set up a DSN for the sample application to be used throughout the remainder of this chapter, complete the following steps.

1. From the Control Panel, double-click the ODBC (32-bit) icon. This runs the ODBC Data Source Administrator program, as seen in Figure 26.2.

Part
IV

Ch
26

FIGURE 26.2

The ODBC Administrator provides an intuitive database connection setup environment.

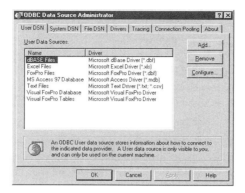

2. Click the System DSN tab to set up a data source that can be accessed by all users on the machine. Creating a user DSN would only allow the current user to access the data source.

3. Click the Add button to configure a new DSN. The Create New Data Source dialog box is displayed (see Figure 26.3), prompting you to choose a database driver from the list of all drivers installed on the machine.

FIGURE 26.3

The database driver is selected using the Create New Data Source dialog box.

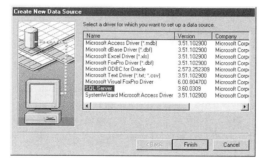

4. Select the SQL Server driver and click the Finish button.

5. The ODBC SQL Server Setup dialog box is displayed (see Figure 26.4). This is where the connection information for the server and database is entered. Click the Options button to display additional dialog box fields.

6. Enter SampleApp in the Data Source Name field. This is the name that will be used to refer to the ODBC connection throughout the sample applications in the following sections. The Description field is optional and can be left blank.

7. Select the SQL Server on your network that you want to use in the Server field.

8. Enter the name of the sample application database in the Database Name field.

9. Click the OK button to save changes.

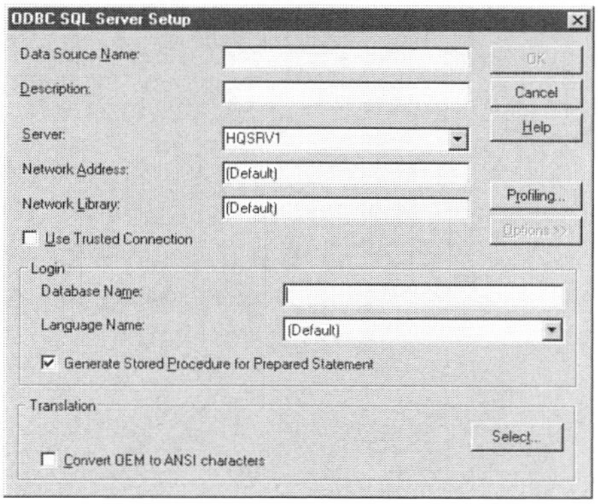

FIGURE 26.4

The ODBC SQL Server Setup dialog box enables the user to enter server and database connection information.

Programmatic Creation of an ODBC DSN   ADO provides the capability to access databases on-the-fly in code. Consider this method when a large number of users are using an application. This prevents each user or an administrator from having to set up a DSN manually using the ODBC Administrator.

This method should also be considered when data sources themselves change. Servers can be renamed, or an application might need to dynamically reference different SQL Servers, depending on the users' departments or other criteria.

A flexible way to implement this scenario is to develop a startup screen from which the user can pick the SQL Server to connect to and enter a valid user ID and password. These choices can be stored in variables and passed to code similar to the following, which connects to the specified server:

```
myADOConnection.Open "Driver={SQL Server};" & _
    "Server=" & SelectedSQLServer & ";" & _
    "UID=" & UserID & ";" & _
    "PWD=" & Password & ";"
```

Although this method can prove quite helpful in certain scenarios, the following sample applications rely on an ODBC DSN being set up manually using the ODBC Administrator. This keeps the demonstration code simple.

Using the Data Form Wizard

The Data Form Wizard is the easiest way to quickly build a client front end to data in Visual Basic using ADO. Perform the following steps to create a simple form providing access to and manipulation of the records in the Project table:

   1. Select Add-Ins, Add-In Manager from the Visual Basic menu (see Figure 26.5).

Part
IV

Ch
26

FIGURE 26.5

The Add-In Manager is used to load the Data Form Wizard.

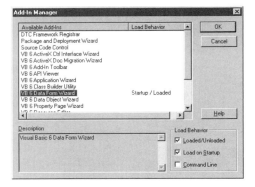

2. Select VB 6 Data Form Wizard in the Available Add-Ins column and check the Loaded/Unloaded and Load on Startup boxes in the Load Behavior section.

3. Click OK to save the settings. The Data Form Wizard will now be available each time you start Visual Basic.

4. Start a new Visual Basic project by selecting File, New Project from the menu.

5. Select the Standard EXE template and click OK.

6. Select Add-Ins, Data Form Wizard to load the wizard.

7. The introductory screen provides the user with the capability to load a data form template from a stored profile. Click the Next button to proceed without selecting a profile.

8. Select Remote(ODBC) on the Database Type screen and click Next.

9. The Connect Information screen enables the user to enter the details needed for the system to access the database properly (see Figure 26.6). Choose SampleApp as the ODBC DSN and click Next.

FIGURE 26.6

The user supplies the Data Form Wizard with an ODBC DSN on the Connect Information screen.

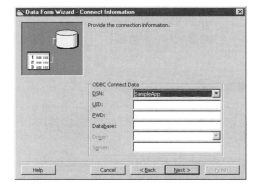

10. Enter the name of the form to be created on the Form screen of the Data Form Wizard as seen in Figure 26.7. Type `frmProjectMaint` in the name field.

Part

IV

Ch

26

FIGURE 26.7

The Form screen is where the new form's name, layout, and type are entered.

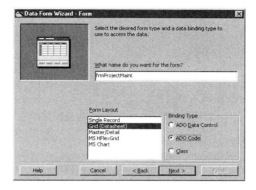

Several options are available on the Form screen that determine the way in which data will be presented on the form.

The choices available in the Form Layout section determine the graphical layout of data on the form:

- Single Record—Data is presented one record at a time on the form (default).
- Grid (Datasheet)—Data is presented in a spreadsheet-like manner using the DataGrid control.
- Master/Detail—Provides the capability to link parent and child records on the same form.
- MS FlexGrid—Displays data in a tabular manner using Microsoft's FlexGrid control.
- MS Chart—Formats data in a chart.

The Binding Type determines the way in which the form is implemented programmatically:

- ADO Data Control—Uses the ADO Data Control for record navigation
- ADO Code—Implements data manipulation solely through ADO code
- Class—Uses a class module to manipulate data

N O T E   The Class Binding Type is unavailable when the MS FlexGrid or MS Chart Form Layout options are selected. Additionally, the ADO Data Control is not available when MS Chart is selected. ▨

11. Select Grid (Datasheet) as the Form Layout option and ADO Code as the Binding Type (refer to Figure 26.7) and then click the Next button to proceed.

N O T E   The Data Form Wizard only supports the ADO object model for data access. Older data access object models such as RDO and DAO are not supported. ▨

The Record Source screen of the Data Form Wizard enables you to choose the table in the database to access, along with specified fields in the table (see Figure 26.8).

FIGURE 26.8

The Record Source screen is where the database table and fields are configured.

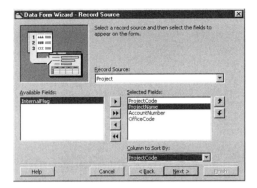

12. Select the Project table as the Record Source and then add all Available Fields to the Selected Fields box, except for the InternalFlag field. This field is calculated internally and should not be accessible to the user.

13. Use the up and down arrows to the right of the Selected Fields box to order the fields as follows: ProjectCode, ProjectName, AccountNumber, and OfficeCode.

14. Select the ProjectCode field in the Column to Sort By field and then click the Next button to proceed.

15. The Control Selection screen enables you to choose which command buttons to place on the data form. Click the Next button to accept the default of all five buttons selected.

16. The last screen of the Data Form Wizard enables you to save the settings you have made to a profile, so you can reuse the form as a template for new forms. Click the Finish button to forego saving a profile.

17. Upon the successful completion of the creation of the data form, a screen is displayed notifying you that the Data Form Wizard is finished (see Figure 26.9). Click OK to close this box.

FIGURE 26.9

The Data Form Created dialog box lets the user know that the new form has been successfully added to the project.

18. Select Project, Project1 Properties from the menu.

19. On the General tab, select frmProjectMaint as the Startup Object and then click OK to save changes. This causes the newly created data form to be the initial form displayed when the application runs.

20. Save and run the application. The fully functional data form is implemented with all the options specified with the wizard, as seen in Figure 26.10. Examine the ADO code that provides the functionality of this form to learn more about ADO methods and properties.

FIGURE 26.10

Looking at the outcome of the Project Maintenance form built with the Data Form Wizard.

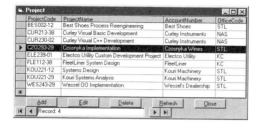

Using the Data Project

Starting with a Data Project in Visual Basic provides you with a complete environment in which tables, queries, fields, and other database objects can be added to forms, used in calculations, and printed with reports. After creating a connection to the database, drag-and-drop functionality can be used to quickly create data fields on a form or report.

The following sample application illustrates the main features of the Data Project. A simple maintenance form is created that enables manipulation of records in the Project table of the sample database. A report that displays and counts all projects is also created using the Data Report tool.

Exploring the Components of a Data Project   The following steps create a new Data Project and enable you to examine the default components and configuration initialized each time a Data Project is created.

1. Start a new project by selecting File, New Project from the menu.
2. The New Project dialog box is displayed as seen in Figure 26.11. Select Data Project and click OK.

FIGURE 26.11

The New Project dialog box enables you to pick a new Data Project.

3. Select View, Project Explorer from the menu, and notice that three objects have been created for you: DataEnvironment1, DataReport1, and frmDataEnv.
   - The DataEnvironment1 object is the Data Environment designer, a tool that enables you to visually connect to database tables, to examine fields, and to perform calculations, which serves as the basis for form and report creation. RDO

programmers will recognize its similarity to the UserConnection Designer, a tool that provides a working environment for RDO data manipulation. Unlike the RDO UserConnection Designer, the Data Environment designer allows multiple connections and supports OLE drag-and-drop functionality.

- The DataReport1 object is the Data Report designer, a banded report generator similar to the Microsoft Access report development tool. Fields are placed in the detail section of the report, while page and report headers display summary information.

- The frmDataEnv object is a blank form created by default. This is the form you will use to develop a simple maintenance screen for editing projects in the sample database.

4. Select View, Toolbox from the menu and notice that an additional tab has been added entitled DataReport.

5. Click the DataReport tab to view the RptLabel, RptTextBox, RptImage, RptLine, RptShape, and RptFunction controls (see Figure 26.12). These controls are used to construct data reports.

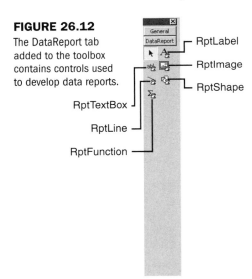

FIGURE 26.12

The DataReport tab added to the toolbox contains controls used to develop data reports.

N O T E The controls on the DataReport tab can only be used on reports and cannot be placed on forms. The controls are disabled when not editing a data report. ▦

6. Select the General tab in the toolbox. The Data Project has added several data controls, including the DataRepeater, ADODC (ADO Data Control), DataGrid, DataList, DataCombo, and MS FlexGrid controls, as seen in Figure 26.13.

FIGURE 26.13

Additional data controls are added to the General tab of the toolbox when a new Data Project is created.

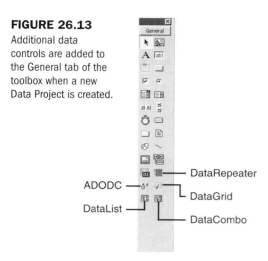

DataRepeater

ADODC

DataGrid

DataList

DataCombo

NOTE The controls added by the Data Project to the General tab of the toolbox, along with all the other controls on the General tab, can only be used on forms and cannot be placed on data reports.

7. Select Project, References from the menu and inspect the references automatically set by the Data Project (see Figure 26.14). Several extra references have been initialized, enabling the developer to begin coding for any of the data objects that have automatically been added by the Data Project.

Part
IV

Ch
26

FIGURE 26.14

Several additional references are automatically set by the Data Project.

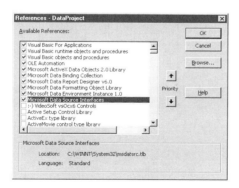

NOTE The Microsoft ActiveX Data Objects 2 Library (Program ID: ADODB) is the main library used when working with ADO and includes the functionality of all the ADO objects. Its default location and filename is C:\Program Files\Common Files\System\ADO\MSADO15.DLL. The Microsoft ActiveX Data Objects Recordset 2 Library (Program ID: ADOR) contains the functionality of only the Recordset object. Because this library contains fewer objects, methods, and properties, it provides better performance. Its default location is the same as ADODB, but it has the filename MSADOR15.DLL.

8. Click OK to close the References dialog box and return to the main window of the Visual Basic Integrated Development Environment (IDE).

Connecting to a Database with the Data Environment Designer

As you can see, the Data Project creates a complete workspace in which to begin developing data forms and reports. The first step in creating a form or report is establishing a connection to the database.

1. Double-click the DataEnvironment1 object in the Project Explorer window. The Data Environment window is displayed, as seen in Figure 26.15.

FIGURE 26.15

The Data Environment window is used to visually configure database connections.

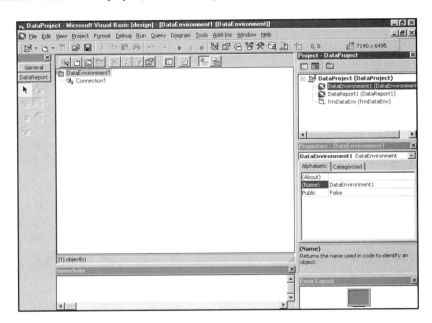

2. A single connection object is created by the Data Project. Right-click the Connection1 object in the top left corner of the main window and select Properties to display the Data Link Properties dialog box.

3. Accept the default OLE DB Provider (Microsoft OLE DB Provider for ODBC Drivers) and select the Connection tab. Select the SampleApp ODBC DSN set up earlier in the Use Data Source Name field, as seen in Figure 26.16.

4. Click the Test Connection button to make sure you are able to talk to the database properly. You will receive a Test connection succeeded message if you don't have any problems connecting.

5. Click OK to return to the main Data Environment window.

6. Right-click the Connection1 object and select Add Command. A single command object is added to the Connection1 object. Right-click the newly added Command1 object and select Properties. The Command1 Properties dialog box is displayed. The Command object enables the user to indicate the specific table, stored procedure, view, or SQL statement to run for the connection.

FIGURE 26.16

The Connection tab of the Data Link Properties dialog box enables you to specify the ODBC DSN.

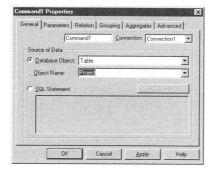

7. Select Table as the Database Object and the Project table as the Object Name as shown in Figure 26.17. Click the OK button to accept the settings.

FIGURE 26.17

Configuring a Command object for the database connection.

8. Expand the Command1 object by clicking on the plus sign to the left of the object. The five fields of the Project table are displayed.

Creating Data Entry Fields on the Maintenance Form Now that a connection to a table in the database has been established, you will use the OLE drag-and-drop functionality of the Data Environment designer to place fields onto the maintenance form.

Step 1: Changing the Control Associated with a Data Field A default control type is assigned to each field based on its data type. This default can be examined and changed by clicking the Options button on the Data Environment toolbar.

1. Click the Options button on the toolbar (see Figure 26.18) to display the Options dialog box. Click the Field Mapping tab to examine the default control that is assigned for each Category/Data Type, as seen in Figure 26.19.

FIGURE 26.18

The Options button.

FIGURE 26.19

The Options dialog box enables the user to change the default control associated with each Data Type.

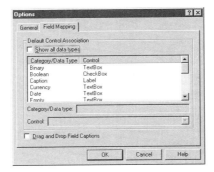

2. Scroll to the bottom of the Category list and notice that the default Control for the Text Category/Data Type is TextBox.

3. Click OK to close the Options dialog box and return to the Data Environment designer.

As you saw in the last step, the TextBox control is assigned to fields with text (adVarChar) Data Types. Because the AccountNumber and OfficeCode fields are foreign keys to other tables in the sample database, change their controls to be Data Combo boxes to give the user the capability to perform lookups to the tables during data entry.

4. Right-click the AccountNumber field and select <u>P</u>roperties.

5. Change the Field Mapping <u>C</u>ontrol to Microsoft DataCombo Control, Version 6 (OLEDB), and click OK to save the settings.

The Details section at the bottom of the Field Properties dialog box contains useful information about the selected field. The DataType of the field is read from the database and is displayed here, along with the field's size, scale, and precision. This quick reference can be helpful when designing forms.

6. Right-click the OfficeCode field and select <u>P</u>roperties.

7. Change the Field Mapping <u>C</u>ontrol to Microsoft DataCombo Control, Version 6 (OLEDB), and click OK to save the settings.

Visual Basic 6 includes several new data controls for working with fields that provide enhanced functionality. Among these are the Data Combo and Data List controls that provide a means to specify the lookup table of lists at design-time.

Step 2: Adding Data Entry Fields to the Form   Fields will now be placed on the maintenance form so that users can modify records.

1. Double-click the frmDataEnv form in the Project Explorer window to activate the form created for you by the Data Project.

2. Change the Caption property of the form to Project Maintenance.

3. Select Window, Tile Horizontally to display both the Data Environment designer and the default form.

4. Drag the Command1 object from the Data Environment window onto the top of the default form. As seen in Figure 26.20, all the fields associated with the Command1 object (the Project table) are placed on the form. Note that DataCombo controls are used for the ctlAccountNumber and ctlOfficeCode fields, as you have specified.

FIGURE 26.20

Dragging the single Command1 object to the Form Designer creates five fields on the form.

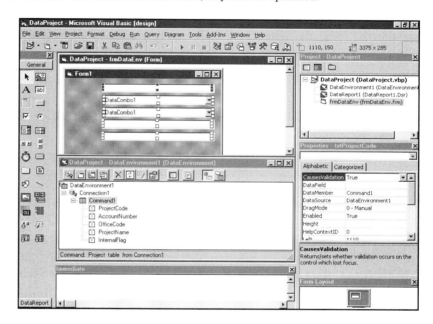

 TIP Dragging the Command object for a Connection object creates data entry fields for all the fields in the table or view specified by the Command object. You can also drag individual fields one by one onto a form.

5. Delete the txtInternalFlag text box (the last control on the form), as this field should not be accessible to the user.

6. Move the ctlAccountNumber and ctlOfficeCode fields below the txtProjectName field and then move these three controls just under the txtProjectCode field.

7. Change the Caption property of the labels that were automatically added to the form to Project Code, Project Name, Account Number, and Office Code. The form should resemble Figure 26.21.

Part
IV

Ch
26

FIGURE 26.21

The maintenance form begins to take shape.

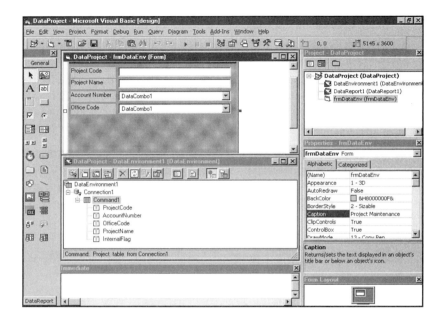

Step 3: Configuring the Lookup Lists for Data Combo Controls The Account Number and Office Code controls must point to the appropriate tables in order for lookup functionality to work properly.

1. Add an additional Command object to the Connection1 object in the Data Environment designer by right-clicking the Connection1 object and selecting Add Command.

2. Name the new Command object Accounts, and select the SQL Statement option.

3. Enter the following SQL statement in the SQL Statement field:

   ```
   Select AccountNumber from Client order by AccountNumber
   ```

4. Click OK to save the settings.

5. Add another Command object to the Connection1 object in the Data Environment designer by right-clicking the Connection1 object and selecting Add Command.

6. Name the new Command object Offices, and select the SQL Statement option.

7. Enter the following SQL statement in the SQL Statement field:

   ```
   Select OfficeCode from Location order by OfficeCode
   ```

8. Click OK to save the settings.

9. To configure the lookup table for the Account Number field, select the ctlAccountNumber DataCombo control in the form window and set the following properties:

   - RowSource = DataEnvironment1
   - RowMember = Accounts
   - ListField = AccountNumber

10. To configure the lookup table for the Office Code field, select the `ctlOfficeCode` DataCombo control in the form window and set the following properties:

- RowSource = DataEnvironment1
- RowMember = Offices
- ListField = OfficeCode

Save and run the project. The default data form is displayed. Try clicking the drop-down arrow of the Account Number and Office Code combo boxes (see Figure 26.22). Lookup lists will be displayed for each field.

FIGURE 26.22

The lookup list for the Office Code data combo box is functional.

Adding Navigation Buttons to the Form   The data form enables the user to edit fields in a record, but there is no way to scroll back and forth between records. Follow these steps to add buttons providing this functionality.

1. Add four command buttons to the data form, aligning them horizontally under the data-entry fields on the form.

2. Change the `Caption` properties of the buttons to `&First`, `&Previous`, `&Next`, and `&Last`.

3. Change the `Name` properties of the buttons to `cmdFirst`, `cmdPrevious`, `cmdNext`, and `cmdLast`.

4. Enter the following code for the `Click` event of the `cmdFirst` button:
```
Private Sub cmdFirst_Click()
    DataEnvironment1.rsCommand1.MoveFirst
End Sub
```

5. Enter the following code for the `Click` event of the `cmdPrevious` button. The `BOF` property is used to trap the error that occurs when the user attempts to move beyond the beginning of file.
```
Private Sub cmdPrevious_Click()
    If Not DataEnvironment1.rsCommand1.BOF Then
        DataEnvironment1.rsCommand1.MovePrevious
    End If
    If DataEnvironment1.rsCommand1.BOF Then
        DataEnvironment1.rsCommand1.MoveFirst
    End If
End Sub
```

Part
IV

Ch
26

6. Enter the following code for the Click event of the cmdNext button. The EOF property is used to trap the error that occurs when the user attempts to move beyond the end of file.

```
Private Sub cmdNext_Click()
    If Not DataEnvironment1.rsCommand1.EOF Then
        DataEnvironment1.rsCommand1.MoveNext
    End If
    If DataEnvironment1.rsCommand1.EOF Then
        DataEnvironment1.rsCommand1.MoveLast
    End If
End Sub
```

7. Enter the following code for the Click event of the cmdLast button:

```
Private Sub cmdLast_Click()
    DataEnvironment1.rsCommand1.MoveLast
End Sub
```

Run the project and change the data in a field of a record in the Project table. Notice that the change is lost when you move to a different record. This is because the default locking type of connection to the database is set to read-only.

8. To change the data locking type, return to the Data Environment window and right-click the Command1 object and select Properties to display the Command1 Properties window.

9. Select the Advanced tab and set the Lock Type to 3 - Optimistic as shown in Figure 26.23. Click OK to save the change. You will now be able to make changes to the data in the Project table using the maintenance form.

FIGURE 26.23
The Advanced tab of the Command1 Properties dialog box enables the user to fine-tune Recordset settings.

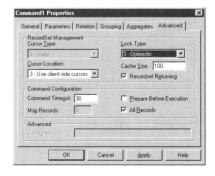

Creating a Project Report Using the Data Report Designer   The Data Report designer enables you to easily create presentation-quality reports using a graphical design environment.

Step 1: Adding Fields to a Data Report   The first and most important step in creating a report is to decide which fields from a table will be placed in the detail section of a report. The purpose of this report is simply to display all the records in the Project table, so the four main fields in the table will be used.

1. Open the DataReport1 and the DataEnvironment1 windows, and select Window, Tile Horizontally, so you can work with both windows at the same time.

2. Set the ReportWidth and Width properties of the DataReport1 object to 8500.

3. Drag the ProjectCode field in the DataEnvironment1 window and to the Detail (Section 1) of the data report (see Figure 26.24).

FIGURE 26.24
Use drag-and-drop functionality to place fields on the data report.

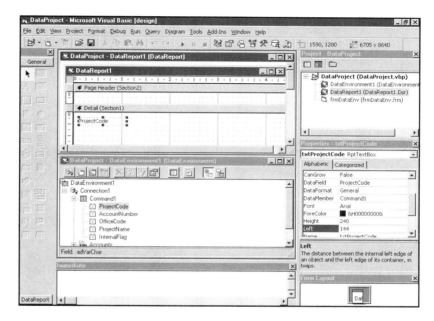

4. Drag the ProjectName field to the Detail (Section 1) of the data report, and drop it to the right of the ProjectCode field.

5. Expand the width of the ProjectName so that the entire contents of the field can be seen.

6. Drag the AccountNumber field to the Detail (Section 1) of the data report and drop it to the right of the ProjectName field.

7. Drag the OfficeCode field to the Detail (Section 1) of the data report and drop it to the right of the AccountNumber field.

8. Resize the OfficeCode field so that it fits completely within the data report window.

9. To make the data fields active, you must assign the data source of the data report. Click the data report and then set the DataSource property to DataEnvironment1.

10. Set the DataMember property to Command1.

Step 2: Configuring the Page Header and Footer   Adding information to be printed at the top and bottom of each page in the report is as simple as placing what you want to print in the proper report band.

1. Drag the Page Footer (Section3) bar so that no blank space is left underneath the four data fields.

Part
IV

Ch
26

2. Using the ReportLabel control from the DataReport tab on the toolbox, place four label controls on the data report in the Page Header (Section2), aligned with the four fields in the Detail section.

3. Change the Caption property of the labels to Project Code, Project Name, Account Number, and Office Code.

4. Use the Report Line control to place a horizontal line underneath the label headings. This line separates the headers from the actual data, making the report easier to read.

5. Right-click in a blank area of the Page Footer and select Insert Control, Current Page Number from the context menu (see Figure 26.25).

FIGURE 26.25

The context menu provides an easy way to add page numbering to a data report.

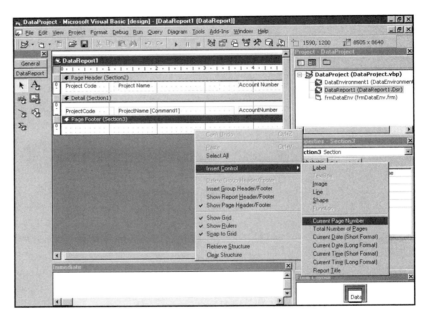

6. Change the Caption property of the page number Report Label control to Page %p.

Step 3: Configuring the Report Header and Footer Adding information printed at the beginning and end of the report is similar to adding a page header and footer.

1. Right-click the data report and select Show Report Header/Footer.

2. Place a Report Label control in the Report Header (Section4).

3. Change the Caption property of the label to Projects Report.

4. Using the Font dialog box, set the font Size to 14.

5. Expand the size of the label so that the entire text of the caption is displayed.

6. Right-click in a blank area of the Report Header (Section4) and select Insert Control, Current Date (Short Format).

7. Right-click to the right of the newly inserted date field in the Report Header and select Insert Control, Current Time (Long Format) (see Figure 26.26).

FIGURE 26.26

A report header is added to the data report.

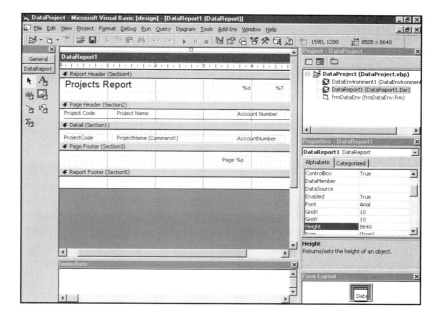

Step 4: Adding a Calculated Field to the Report   To complete the project report, add a calculated field to count the total number of projects at the end of the report.

1. Add a Report Function control to the Report Footer (Section5).
2. Set the DataMember property of the control to Command1.
3. Set the DataField property to ProjectCode.
4. Notice the default FunctionType property of the Report Function control is 0 - RptFuncSum. Because you are trying to count the number of records in the recordset, change this property to 4 - RptFuncRCnt.

The FunctionType property of the Report Function control contains two count functions. The rptFuncRCnt function counts the total number of rows, while the rptFuncVCnt function counts only the total number of non-null rows.

5. Add a Report Label control to the left of the Report Function in the Report Footer.
6. Change the Caption property of the label to Total Number of Projects:.
7. Use the Font dialog box to change the Font Size of the two controls in the Report Footer to 12 point.
8. To complete the report, use the Report Line control to draw a horizontal line just above the two controls in the Report Footer (see Figure 26.27).

Part
IV

Ch

26

FIGURE 26.27

A customized report footer is added to the sample project data report.

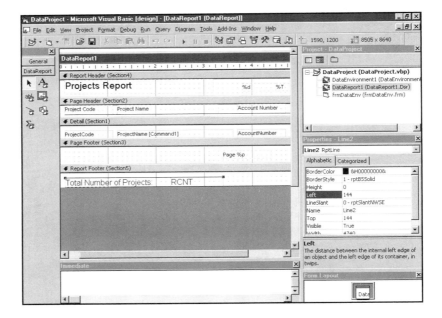

Step 5: Calling the Report from the Maintenance Form   To display the report at runtime, a button must be added to the data form that activates the data report window.

1. Return to the data form and place a command button below the four navigation buttons.

2. Change the Caption property of the button to `Print Project &Report`.

3. Add the following code to the `Click` event of the button:

```
Private Sub Command1_Click()
    DataReport1.Show
End Sub
```

Run the program, and click the Print Project Report button. The report is displayed in Print Preview mode and can be sent to a printer by clicking the printer icon (see Figure 26.28). The `PrintReport` method of the Data Report object can be used instead of the `Show` method if you want to send the report directly to a printer.

FIGURE 26.28
The completed data report is displayed in Print Preview mode.

Using the ADO Data Control

Visual Basic 6 includes a new control called the ADO Data Control, which provides you with the capability to easily connect to a database and work with records. This new control is designed and optimized for use with the ADO object model. It is similar to the intrinsic data control and to the Remote Data Control (RDC), although neither of these controls is able to work with ActiveX Data Objects, and therefore neither is able to access OLE DB data providers.

Unlike using the Data Form Wizard and the Data Project tools, starting from scratch with a blank form and the ADO Data Control provides you with more flexibility when building client front ends to access data in Visual Basic. If you need more functionality than a prebuilt form provides, use this tool to build the form to meet your specific needs.

Both the ADO Data Control and the Data Combo control are used in the following sample application. This program provides the user with the capability of editing, adding, and deleting projects from the sample application database. A sophisticated lookup window is also implemented that allows the user to quickly search for and select a specific record.

Step 1: Creating the Form and Connecting to the Project Table To create the data form with which projects can be added, deleted, or edited, follow these steps:

1. Start a new Standard EXE project.

2. Change the Name property of the form to `frmMain` and the form Caption to Project Maintenance.

3. Set the form's Height to 4100 and its Width to 6000, providing adequate room to add and space controls.

Part
IV

Ch
26

4. Add the Microsoft ADO Data Control 6 (OLEDB) and the Microsoft DataList Controls 6 (OLEDB) to the control toolbox by selecting Project, Components, and checking the appropriate boxes.

5. Click OK. Three new icons appear in the toolbox. Two of the icons represent the DataList Controls; the other represents the ADO Data Control.

6. Set a reference to the Microsoft ActiveX Data Objects 2 Library by selecting Project, References and checking the appropriate box. This enables programmatic access of the ADO objects.

7. Add an ADO Data Control object to the form, and set the following properties:

   - `Name = adodcProjects`
   - `Caption = Projects`
   - `Align = 2 - vbAlignBottom`
   - `Height = 300`

Examine the other properties available at design time for the ADO Data Control. You are given great flexibility over the connections and recordsets you open with this control through such properties as `CacheSize`, `CommandTimeout`, `ConnectionTimeout`, `CursorLocation`, `CursorType`, `LockType`, and `MaxRecords`.

 TIP Properties can be set for controls both at design time using the Properties Window, and at runtime using code. Properties set in code will be more apparent to others viewing your code, but setting properties at design time prevents you from having to write any code at all. You might want to set a property that is unusual or critical to the functioning of a control in code, just for the sake of the documentation it provides.

8. Link the ADO Data Control to the Project table of the sample application by clicking on the ellipsis button in the (Custom) property. This displays the Property Pages dialog box (see Figure 26.29).

FIGURE 26.29.

The Property Pages dialog box allows the user to enter the database and the table, query, or stored procedure to view.

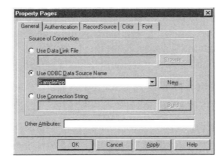

9. On the General tab, select the Use ODBC Data Source Name option and then select the SampleApp ODBC DSN set up earlier.

10. On the RecordSource tab, select 1 - adCmdText in the Command Type field and then enter the following SQL command in the Command Text (SQL) field:

```
Select * from Project order by ProjectCode
```

11. Click OK to save changes.

The adodcProjects ADO Data Control is now connected to the Project table in the database and is ready to begin serving up records, all without a single line of VB code.

Step 2: Adding Data Fields to the Maintenance Form   Now that you have an ADO Data Control successfully connected to the Project table, controls must be added to the form to enable the user to manipulate data.

1. Add two labels and two text boxes to the form. Change the Name property of Label1 to lblProjCode, and the Name of Label2 to lblProjName. Change the Name of Text1 to txtProjCode, and the Name of Text2 to txtProjName.

2. Set the Caption property of the labels to Project Code and Project Name, respectively, and blank the Text property of both text boxes.

3. Bind the text boxes to the ADO Data Control by setting the DataSource property of each control to adodcProjects.

4. Assign the specific field to display in each text box by using the DataField property. The list of fields in the Project table is displayed in a drop-down list when the DataSource has been assigned. Using the DataField property, bind the Project Code text box to the ProjectCode field, and the Project Name text box to the ProjectName field.

5. Add two additional labels and two DataCombo controls to the form. Change the Name of Label1 to lblAcctNum, and the Name of Label2 to lblOffice. Change the Name of DataCombo1 to datcmbAcctNum and the Name of DataCombo2 to datcmbOffice.

6. Set the Caption property of the two labels to Account Number and Office Code, respectively, and blank the Text property of both DataCombo boxes.

7. Set the DataSource property of each DataCombo control to adodcProjects, and set the DataField property of each control to its respective field in the Project table.

8. Change the Style property of both DataCombo controls to 2 - dbcDropdownList. This restricts the user to selection from an entry in the list, preventing new entries.

9. Add two new ADO Data Controls to the form, and name these two controls adodcAccounts and adodcOffices. These two ADO Data Controls are used to read from the lookup tables and populate the list items of the data combo boxes.

10. Select the adodcAccounts control and click the ellipses button in the (Custom) property. Use the SampleApp as the ODBC Data Source Name. On the RecordSource tab, set the Command Type to 1 - adCmdText. Enter the following SQL statement in the Command Text (SQL) field:

```
Select AccountNumber from Client order by AccountNumber
```

This sorts the Account Number lookup window in alphabetical order.

Part
IV

Ch
26

11. Select the `adodcOffices` control and click the ellipses button in the (Custom) property. Use the SampleApp as the ODBC <u>D</u>ata Source Name. On the RecordSource tab, set the Command Type to `1 - adCmdText`. Enter the following SQL statement in the Command Text (SQL) field:

    ```
    Select OfficeCode from Location order by OfficeCode
    ```

12. Because the `adodcAccounts` and `adodcOffices` ADO data controls are only being used for lookup purposes and should not be visible to the user at runtime, set their Visible property to `False`.

13. To link the lookup table of the `datcmbAcctNum` DataCombo control to the ADO Data Control you have just created, set its `RowSource` property to `adodcAccounts`, and its `ListField` property to `AccountNumber`.

14. Similarly, set the RowSource property of the `datcmbOffice` control to `adodcOffices`, and the `ListField` property to `OfficeCode`.

15. Set the Height property of all controls to `300` and align and size them according to Figure 26.30.

FIGURE 26.30

The sample Project Maintenance form begins to take shape, with DataCombo controls and three ADO Data Controls.

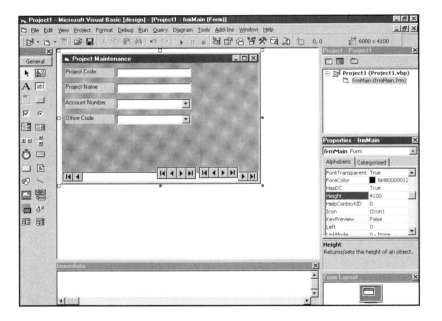

Save and run your form and project. You will be able to scroll through records in the Project table, making changes in any field.

Step 3: Adding an Edit Command Button to the Maintenance Form   Now that data controls have been placed on the Project Maintenance form, enabling users to edit data and scroll through records, place command buttons on the form to provide a finer degree of control over how and when data can be edited. These buttons will also provide the user with a more intuitive interface.

1. Add a command button to the top right of the form. Change the `Name` property of the button to `cmdEdit` and set its `Caption` property to `&Edit`.

2. Add two more command buttons below the data entry fields, just above the main ADO Data Control.

3. Change the Name of `Command1` to `cmdSave` and the Name of `Command2` to `cmdCancel`. Change the Caption property of the `cmdSave` button to `&Save`, and the Caption of `cmdCancel` to `&Cancel`.

4. Adjust the sizing and alignment of the buttons to resemble Figure 26.31.

FIGURE 26.31
Edit, Save, and Cancel buttons are added to the sample Project Maintenance form to provide more intuitive data-entry functionality.

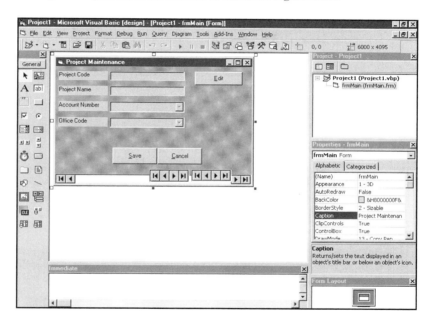

5. Set the Save and Cancel buttons' `Enabled` property to `False`. These buttons will only be available when the user clicks the Edit button and enters edit mode. When the form is first displayed, it won't be in edit mode.

6. Change the Enabled property of all four data entry fields to `False`, and set the `BackColor` property to `&H00C0C0C0&` (light gray). When the form is first opened, the fields won't be editable by the user, and he will be able to see this intuitively because the fields are colored gray.

   A procedure is needed to toggle the entry fields on and off, based on the user's mode. When the user clicks the Edit button, the fields must be enabled and colored white to signify that data entry and modification is permitted. When either the Save or Cancel button is clicked, the fields must be returned to their design-time disabled state.

7. Define a color constant in the general declaration section of the form:

   ```
   Dim vbGray As String
   ```

Part
IV

Ch
26

8. Initialize the form's Load event with the following code to set the color to gray:

```
Private Sub Form_Load()
    vbGray = &HC0C0C0
End Sub
```

9. Add the procedures from Listing 26.2, which toggle the buttons' and fields' Enabled and BackColor properties when edit mode is entered and exited. Notice the Project Code field is not enabled during edit mode. This is to prevent users from changing the Project Code, which is a primary key in the Project table. Doing so would violate referential integrity, as the Project Code is used elsewhere in the database.

Listing 26.2 26SRC02.TXT—Procedures to Toggle the State of the Fields on the Form Based on the Entry Mode

```
'*********************************************************
' Purpose:    Disables all navigation buttons and
'             allows field entry
'*********************************************************
Public Sub DisableButtonsEnableFields()
    cmdEdit.Enabled = False
    adodcProjects.Enabled = False
    cmdSave.Enabled = True: cmdCancel.Enabled = True
    txtProjName.Enabled = True
    txtProjName.BackColor = vbWhite
    datcmbAcctNum.Enabled = True
    datcmbAcctNum.BackColor = vbWhite
    datcmbOffice.Enabled = True
    datcmbOffice.BackColor = vbWhite
    txtProjName.SetFocus
End Sub

'*********************************************************
' Purpose:    Enables all navigation buttons and
'             disallows field entry
'*********************************************************
Public Sub EnableButtonsDisableFields()
    cmdEdit.Enabled = True
    adodcProjects.Enabled = True
    cmdSave.Enabled = False: cmdCancel.Enabled = False
    txtProjCode.Enabled = False
    txtProjCode.BackColor = vbGray
    txtProjName.Enabled = False
    txtProjName.BackColor = vbGray
    datcmbAcctNum.Enabled = False
    datcmbAcctNum.BackColor = vbGray
    datcmbOffice.Enabled = False
    datcmbOffice.BackColor = vbGray
End Sub
```

10. Call the first toggle procedure by entering the following lines of code for the Edit button's Click event:

```
Private Sub cmdEdit_Click()
    If adodcProjects.Recordset.RecordCount <> 0 Then
        DisableButtonsEnableFields
    End If
End Sub
```

11. Enter the following lines of code for the Cancel button's Click event. This code resets the data-entry fields to the original record, before any changes were made. It also uses the CancelUpdate method of the ADO Recordset object, which takes the record out of edit mode:

```
Private Sub cmdCancel_Click()
    txtProjName.Text = adodcProjects.Recordset!ProjectName
    datcmbAcctNum.Text = adodcProjects.Recordset!AccountNumber
    datcmbOffice.Text = adodcProjects.Recordset!OfficeCode
    EnableButtonsDisableFields
    adodcProjects.Recordset.CancelUpdate
End Sub
```

12. Enter the following code for the Save button's Click event. This code writes the changes made by the user to the database for the current record. The Update method of the ADO Recordset object is used to perform the write to the database.

```
Private Sub cmdSave_Click()
    adodcProjects.Recordset!ProjectCode = txtProjCode.Text
    adodcProjects.Recordset!ProjectName = txtProjName.Text
    adodcProjects.Recordset!AccountNumber = datcmbAcctNum.Text
    adodcProjects.Recordset!OfficeCode = datcmbOffice.Text
    adodcProjects.Recordset.Update
    EnableButtonsDisableFields
End Sub
```

Save and run the form. Notice that the data-entry fields cannot be edited without clicking the Edit button. Try entering edit mode by clicking the Edit button. Notice how the ADO Data Control becomes disabled, preventing the user from scrolling through records until editing is completed.

Make a change in a data-entry field and then click the Cancel button. Notice the form returns all fields to the original record, before editing began. Clicking the Save button writes any changes made during edit mode to the database.

Step 4: Implementing an Add Button on the Maintenance Form   The Add button is used to insert a new record into the Project table, and contains functionality similar to the Edit button, with minor changes. In fact, several routines written in the previous step for the Edit button will be revised to keep the overall amount of code at a minimum.

1. Add a command button underneath the Edit button. Change the Name property of the button to cmdAdd, and set its Caption to &Add.

Part
IV

Ch
26

2. Add the following code to the Add button's `Click` event:

```
Private Sub cmdAdd_Click()
    adodcProjects.Recordset.AddNew
    DisableButtonsEnableFields
End Sub
```

When Add is clicked, the code calls the same toggle procedure that the Edit button does. However, when adding a new record, the user must be able to enter the primary key value, the Project Code. Remember that in edit mode this field was not editable because referential integrity had to be enforced.

3. To handle the difference between edit and add modes, define a global Boolean flag in the general declaration section that can be set to denote whether a user is in edit mode or add mode:

```
' Define a flag to denote Edit or Add mode
Dim blnAddFlag As Boolean
```

4. Modify the toggle procedure (as in Listing 26.3) that enables data entry to have an argument passed by either the Edit or Add buttons determining the mode.

Listing 26.3   26SRC03.TXT—Field and Button Toggle Procedure Modified to Handle Edit or Add Mode

```
'*********************************************************
' Purpose:   Disables all navigation buttons and
'            allows field entry
'*********************************************************
Public Sub DisableButtonsEnableFields(Mode As String)
    cmdEdit.Enabled = False: cmdAdd.Enabled = False
    adodcProjects.Enabled = False
    cmdSave.Enabled = True: cmdCancel.Enabled = True
    txtProjName.Enabled = True
    txtProjName.BackColor = vbWhite
    datcmbAcctNum.Enabled = True
    datcmbAcctNum.BackColor = vbWhite
    datcmbOffice.Enabled = True
    datcmbOffice.BackColor = vbWhite
    If Mode = "Add" Then
        txtProjCode.Enabled = True
        txtProjCode.BackColor = vbWhite
        txtProjCode.SetFocus
    Else
        txtProjName.SetFocus
    End If
End Sub
```

---

5. Add the following line of code to the `EnableButtonsDisableFields` toggle procedure to handle the state of the Add button:

```
cmdAdd.Enabled = True
```

6. Modify the Add button's `Click` event procedure to pass the proper argument to the `DisableButtonsEnableFields` procedure and to set the Boolean add mode flag to true:

```
Private Sub cmdAdd_Click()
    adodcProjects.Recordset.AddNew
    DisableButtonsEnableFields ("Add")
    blnAddFlag = True
End Sub
```

7. Modify the Edit button's `Click` event procedure as shown in Listing 26.4 to pass the proper argument to the `DisableButtonsEnableFields` procedure and set the Boolean add mode flag to false, signifying the user is entering edit mode.

Listing 26.4 26SRC04.TXT—The Revised `Click` Event of the Edit Button

```
Private Sub cmdEdit_Click()
    If adodcProjects.Recordset.RecordCount <> 0 Then
        DisableButtonsEnableFields ("Edit")
        blnAddFlag = False
    End If
End Sub
```

8. Edit the `Click` event of the Cancel button as shown in Listing 26.5 to refresh fields only if coming from Edit mode.

Listing 26.5 26SRC05.TXT—The `Click` Event of the Cancel Button is Modified to Handle Both Edit and Add Modes

```
Private Sub cmdCancel_Click()
    If blnAddFlag = False Then
        txtProjName.Text = adodcProjects.Recordset!ProjectName
        datcmbAcctNum.Text = adodcProjects.Recordset!AccountNumber
        datcmbOffice.Text = adodcProjects.Recordset!OfficeCode
    End If
    EnableButtonsDisableFields
    adodcProjects.Recordset.CancelUpdate
End Sub
```

9. Edit the `Click` event of the Save button as shown in Listing 26.6 to handle both Edit and Add modes. Note that a temporary ADO connection is opened to the database to search for an existing Project Code primary key. If the Project Code is already entered, an error message is displayed.

Part
IV

Ch
26

Listing 26.6 26SRC06.TXT—The `Click` Event of the Save Button is Modified to Handle Both Edit and Add Modes

```
Private Sub cmdSave_Click()
    If blnAddFlag = True Then
        ' establish a temporary ADO connection for searching
        Dim adocnnProjects As ADODB.Connection
        Set adocnnProjects = New ADODB.Connection
        adocnnProjects.Open "DSN=SampleApp;UID=;PWD=;"
        ' search for existing entry to ensure primary key is not
        ' duplicated
        Set adorsSearch = adocnnProjects.Execute("Select * from
        ➡Project where ProjectCode = '" _
            & txtProjCode.Text & "'")
        If adorsSearch.EOF = False Then
            MsgBox "Project Code already exists.", vbOKOnly,
            ➡"Project Maintenance"
            txtProjCode.SetFocus
            Exit Sub
        End If
    End If
    ' update the new or changed record in the database
    adodcProjects.Recordset!ProjectCode = txtProjCode.Text
    adodcProjects.Recordset!ProjectName = txtProjName.Text
    adodcProjects.Recordset!AccountNumber = datcmbAcctNum.Text
    adodcProjects.Recordset!OfficeCode = datcmbOffice.Text
    adodcProjects.Recordset.Update
    EnableButtonsDisableFields
End Sub
```

Save and run your form. Try adding a new record to the Project table. Notice the differences between Edit mode and Add mode. In Edit mode you aren't able to change the Project Code field, although in Add mode you are able to enter it. Try adding a record with a Project Code that already exists. You should receive a warning that the record already exists and that you won't be allowed to save.

Step 5: Validating Data Entry on the Form   If you attempt to add a new record on the Project Maintenance form at this point without including a Project Code, the program crashes. This is because it's a required field in the database. In order to trap this type of error and prompt the user to rectify the situation, a validation routine for the form must be written.

1. Add the function from Listing 26.7 to your code in order to ensure that each field on the form has an entry. More elaborate checking could be performed in this routine, dependent on the needs and requirements of each particular field.

Listing 26.7 26SRC07.TXT—Function That Validates Data-Field Entries for the Entire Project Maintenance Form

```
'*********************************************************
' Purpose:   Validate all fields on form to ensure
'            proper entries
'*********************************************************
Public Function ValidateForm()
    If Len(Trim(txtProjCode.Text)) < 1 Then
        MsgBox "Project Code must be entered.", vbExclamation,
        ➥"Project Maintenance"
        txtProjCode.SetFocus
        ValidateForm = False
    ElseIf Len(Trim(txtProjName.Text)) < 1 Then
        MsgBox "Project Name must be entered.", vbExclamation,
        ➥"Project Maintenance"
        txtProjName.SetFocus
        ValidateForm = False
    ElseIf Len(Trim(datcmbAcctNum.Text)) < 1 Then
        MsgBox "Account Number must be entered.", vbExclamation,
        ➥ "Project Maintenance"
        datcmbAcctNum.SetFocus
        ValidateForm = False
    ElseIf Len(Trim(datcmbOffice.Text)) < 1 Then
        MsgBox "Office Code must be entered.", vbExclamation,
        ➥"Project Maintenance"
        datcmbOffice.SetFocus
        ValidateForm = False
    Else
        ValidateForm = True
    End If
End Function
```

Part IV

Ch 26

2. Modify the Click event of the Save button as shown in Listing 26.8 to call the ValidateForm function whenever a user attempts to save an edited or new record.

Listing 26.8 26SRC08.TXT—The Click Event of the Save Button Calls the ValidateForm Procedure

```
Private Sub cmdSave_Click()
    If ValidateForm() = True Then
        If blnAddFlag = True Then
            ' establish a temporary ADO connection for searching
            Dim adocnnProjects As ADODB.Connection
            Set adocnnProjects = New ADODB.Connection
            adocnnProjects.Open "DSN=SampleApp;UID=;PWD=;"
            ' search for existing entry to ensure primary key is
            ' not duplicated
            Set adorsSearch = adocnnProjects.Execute("Select * from
            ➥Project where ProjectCode = '" _
                & txtProjCode.Text & "'")
```

continues

Listing 26.8 Continued

```
            If adorsSearch.EOF = False Then
                MsgBox "Project Code already exists.", vbOKOnly,
                ➥"Project Maintenance"
                txtProjCode.SetFocus
                Exit Sub
            End If
        End If
        ' update the new or changed record in the database
        adodcProjects.Recordset!ProjectCode = txtProjCode.Text
        adodcProjects.Recordset!ProjectName = txtProjName.Text
        adodcProjects.Recordset!AccountNumber = datcmbAcctNum.Text
        adodcProjects.Recordset!OfficeCode = datcmbOffice.Text
        adodcProjects.Recordset.Update
        EnableButtonsDisableFields
    End If
End Sub
```

With the validation routine in place, whenever you try to save a record without entering a Project Code or any other field, you are prompted to enter the required field. Run the project and attempt to save a record with no Project Code. A message box is displayed that warns the user that this is not allowed (see Figure 26.32). This prevents a system error from occurring and gives the user the opportunity to either make the required entry or cancel editing the record.

FIGURE 26.32
The validation routine prevents the user from saving an incomplete record to the database.

Step 6: Implementing a Delete Button on the Maintenance Form Now that you are able to edit existing projects and add new projects to the sample database, you might want to delete existing entries altogether. This is accomplished through the use of a delete button to the form.

1. Add a command button underneath the Add button. Change the Name of the button to cmdDelete and set its Caption to &Delete.

2. Add the code in Listing 26.9 to the Delete button's Click event. Note how the Delete, MoveNext, and MoveLast methods of the ADO Recordset object are used, along with the EOF property.

Listing 26.9 26SRC09.TXT—The Delete Button's `Click` Event Removes the Current Record From the Database

```
Private Sub cmdDelete_Click()
    If adodcProjects.Recordset.RecordCount <> 0 Then
        ' confirm delete
        response = MsgBox("Are you sure you wish to delete this project?", _
            vbYesNo, "Project Maintenance")
        If response = vbYes Then
            adodcProjects.Recordset.Delete
            adodcProjects.Recordset.MoveNext
            On Error Resume Next
            If adodcProjects.Recordset.EOF Then adodcProjects.Recordset.MoveLast
        End If
    End If
End Sub
```

3. Add code to the `DisableButtonsEnableFields` and `EnableButtonsDisableFields` procedures to set the state of the Delete button properly.

Compile and run the program and then try deleting records from the Project table using the Delete button. When you provide a final confirmation for deletion, the record is removed from the database.

Step 7: Implementing Lookup Functionality with the ListView Control   At this point, the Project Maintenance screen is completely functional. The user can add new records, edit existing records, and delete records. Few lines of code are needed to handle ADO data manipulation; the majority of the code deals with the user interface.

The capability to locate a specific record without having to scroll through the entire recordset is a critical feature for a client front end that serves as a database table maintenance screen. The following steps detail how to use the ListView control to build a customized lookup screen the user can employ to quickly locate a specific record within the Project table.

1. Add a new, standard form to the project by selecting Project, Add Form, and then clicking on Form (from the New tab). Set the form Height to 5000 and the form Width to 7000.

2. Change the Name of the form to `frmLookup`, and the Caption to `Project Maintenance Lookup`.

3. Add the Microsoft Windows Common Controls 6 to the control toolbox by selecting Project, Components and checking the appropriate box.

4. Add a label to the top left of the form. Change its Name to `lblProjCode` and its Caption to `Project Code`.

5. Add a text box to the right of the label. Change its Name to `txtProjCode` and blank its Text property.

6. Add a command button to the right of the text box. Change the button's Name to `cmdFind` and its Caption to `&Find`.

7. Add a ListView control to the form under the controls already on the form. Set the following properties for the ListView control:

   - `Name = lstvwLookup`
   - `Height = 3000`
   - `Width = 6700`
   - `Top = 750`
   - `Left = 90`

8. Add two command buttons to the bottom of the form. Change `Command1`'s Name to `cmdOK` and its Caption to `&OK`. Change `Command2`'s Name to `cmdCancel` and its Caption to `&Cancel`.

9. Align all controls on the form similar to Figure 26.33.

FIGURE 26.33
The lookup screen for the Project Maintenance form takes shape.

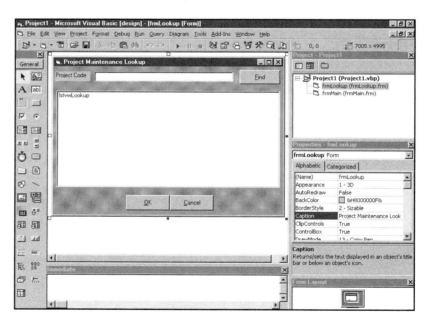

10. Insert the following code in the general declarations section of the lookup form:

```
' Define an ADO Connection to the data source for searching
Dim adocnnProjects As ADODB.Connection
' Define an ADO Recordset object to be used for searching
Dim adorsSearch As ADODB.Recordset
```

11. Add the code in Listing 26.10 to the lookup form's `Load` event. This code defines the columns to be used in the ListView control and opens an ADO connection and recordset to the Project table that will be used to populate the ListView control.

Listing 26.10 26SRC10.TXT—The Lookup Form's Load Event Defines ListView Columns and Connects to the Project Table

```
Private Sub Form_Load()
    ' define the ListView columns
    lstvwLookup.ColumnHeaders. _
        Add , , "Project Code", lstvwLookup.Width / 5
    lstvwLookup.ColumnHeaders. _
        Add , , "Project Name", lstvwLookup.Width / 3
    lstvwLookup.ColumnHeaders. _
        Add , , "Account Number", lstvwLookup.Width / 4
    lstvwLookup.ColumnHeaders. _
        Add , , "Office Code", lstvwLookup.Width / 5

    lstvwLookup.View = lvwReport

    ' open a connection to the database
    Set adocnnProjects = New ADODB.Connection
    adocnnProjects.Open "DSN=SampleApp;UID=;PWD=;"
    Set adorsSearch = adocnnProjects.Execute("Select * from Project order by
ProjectCode")
End Sub
```

12. Add the code in Listing 26.11 to the lookup form's Activate event.

Listing 26.11 26SRC11.TXT—The Activate Event of the Lookup Form Populates the ListView Control with ADO Recordset Data

```
Private Sub Form_Activate()
    lstvwLookup.ListItems.Clear

    ' populate the ListView control with data from the ADO recordset
    Dim myItem As ListItem
    adorsSearch.MoveFirst
    While Not adorsSearch.EOF
        Set myItem = lstvwLookup.ListItems. _
            Add(, , CStr(adorsSearch!ProjectCode))
        myItem.SubItems(1) = adorsSearch!ProjectName
        myItem.SubItems(2) = adorsSearch!AccountNumber
        myItem.SubItems(3) = adorsSearch!OfficeCode
        adorsSearch.MoveNext
    Wend
    txtProjCode.SetFocus
    txtProjCode.Text = ""
End Sub
```

13. Returning to the main Project Maintenance form, add a command button underneath the Delete button. Change the Name of this button to cmdLookup, and the Caption to &Lookup.

Part
IV

Ch
26

14. Add the code in Listing 26.12 to the Click event of the Lookup button. This code displays the lookup form and processes the selection after the user has made a choice. The new Find method of the ADO recordset object is used to quickly locate a record in the recordset with a customizable search string.

Listing 26.12   26SRC12.TXT—The Click Event of the Lookup Button Calls the Lookup Form and Processes the User's Selection

```
'***********************************************************
' Purpose:   Handle the Click event of the Lookup button
'            Show the lookup form and process selection
'***********************************************************
Private Sub cmdLookup_Click()
    If adodcProjects.Recordset.RecordCount <> 0 Then
        ' display the lookup form
        frmLookup.Show vbModal, Me

        On Error GoTo LookupClosed
        If frmLookup.lstvwLookup.SelectedItem <> "Canceled" Then
            adodcProjects.Recordset.MoveFirst
            adodcProjects.Recordset.Find ("ProjectCode = '" &
            ➥frmLookup.lstvwLookup.SelectedItem & "'")
        End If
    End If

ExitLookup:
    Exit Sub

LookupClosed:
    Resume ExitLookup

End Sub
```

15. Add code to the DisableButtonsEnableFields and EnableButtonsDisableFields procedures to handle setting the state of the Lookup button properly.

16. Set the Default property of the Find button on the lookup form to True. This enables the user to press Enter after entering a complete or partial project code to search for.

17. After an entry is selected in the ListView, the OK button should become the default button. Add the code in Listing 26.13 to toggle the form's default button between the Find button and the OK button.

Listing 26.13   26SRC13.TXT—Procedures to Toggle the Default Button Between the Find Button and the OK Button

```
Private Sub lstvwLookup_GotFocus()
    cmdOK.Default = True
End Sub

Private Sub txtProjCode_GotFocus()
    cmdFind.Default = True
End Sub
```

18. To add sorting functionality in the ListView control, add the code shown in Listing 26.14.

Listing 26.14   26SRC14.TXT—The Data in the ListView Control is Sorted Based on the Column Whose Header is Clicked

```
Private Sub lstvwLookup_ColumnClick
➥(ByVal ColumnHeader As ComctlLib.ColumnHeader)
    lstvwLookup.Sorted = True
    ' determine which column header was clicked
    If ColumnHeader = "Project Code" Then
        MySortKey = 0
    ElseIf ColumnHeader = "Project Name" Then
        MySortKey = 1
    ElseIf ColumnHeader = "Account Number" Then
        MySortKey = 2
    ElseIf ColumnHeader = "Office Code" Then
        MySortKey = 3
    End If
    lstvwLookup.SortKey = MySortKey
    ' check the current order and set the order to the opposite of current
    If lstvwLookup.SortOrder = lvwAscending Then
        lstvwLookup.SortOrder = lvwDescending
    Else
        lstvwLookup.SortOrder = lvwAscending
    End If
    lstvwLookup.Refresh
End Sub
```

19. Next add the code in Listing 26.15 to the `Click` event of the Find button. This code searches for a match in the data in the ListView control based on the search string entered in the Project Code text box.

Listing 26.15   26SRC15.TXT—The `Click` Event of the Find Button Searches for a Potential Match in the ListView Control

```
Private Sub cmdFind_Click()
    Dim itmFound As ListItem
    ' search for a record matching the search string
    Set itmFound = lstvwLookup. _
        FindItem(txtProjCode.Text, lvwText, 1, lvwPartial)
    If itmFound Is Nothing Then
        response = MsgBox("Record not found.", vbInformation,
                        ➥"Project Maintenance")
        txtProjCode.SetFocus
        Exit Sub
    Else
        'scroll the window until the record is visible
        itmFound.EnsureVisible
        itmFound.Selected = True
        lstvwLookup.SetFocus
    End If
End Sub
```

Part
IV

Ch
26

20. Finally, add the code in Listing 26.16 to the event procedures listed to handle the remainder of the procedures needed for the proper functioning of the Lookup window.

Listing 26.16   26SRC16.TXT—Routines Needed to Complete the Functionality of the Lookup Window

```
Private Sub cmdOK_Click()
    Me.Hide
End Sub

Private Sub lstvwLookup_DblClick()
    ' same as if OK was clicked
    Me.Hide
End Sub

Private Sub cmdCancel_Click()
    ' let the calling routine know that the cancel button was clicked
    frmLookup.lstvwLookup.SelectedItem = "Canceled"
    Me.Hide
End Sub
```

At this point, test the functionality of the lookup window (see Figure 26.34). Enter the first few letters of a project code to search for, and then press Enter or click the Find button. If a match is found, the ListView window scrolls to the record (if needed) and displays the record.

FIGURE 26.34

The completed Lookup window enables the user to easily search for and select a project.

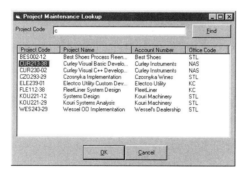

Press Enter or click the OK button to select the highlighted record from the lookup window and return to the Project Maintenance form, making the selected record the current record.

Try clicking the column headings in the lookup window and notice how the ListView control is sorted by the column that is clicked. Click the same column header again, and the data is sorted in reverse order.

From Here...

In this chapter, you learned about OLE DB and ADO and reviewed the main features and objects of the ADO object model. You then learned about several different ways to build data maintenance forms in Visual Basic that access and manipulate data using the methods and properties of the main ADO objects.

- For an introduction to creating mid-tier business logic components in Visual Basic, see Chapter 27, "Creating COM Components for MTS with Visual Basic."

- To learn about developing Visual Basic and ADO solutions in a multitier environment, see Chapter 30, "Creating Data Access Components for MTS with Visual Basic in ADO."

- See Chapter 12, "Creating ActiveX Controls with Visual Basic," for a discussion of how to enhance client front ends with other ActiveX technologies.

- Chapter 25, "Clients, Servers, and Components: Design Strategies for Distributed Applications," explores the intricacies involved with properly designing and developing distributed applications.

Part
IV

Ch
26

Creating COM Components for MTS with Visual Basic

by Eric M. Brown

In this chapter

Looking at and Creating a Simple MTS Component

In this chapter, you will learn the language-specific issues and techniques used to develop COM components for Microsoft Transaction Server (MTS) with Visual Basic. MTS is a powerful extension to the current COM architecture and its use can greatly enhance and strengthen the power of your middle-tier components.

This chapter builds on what you have already learned from Chapter 14, "Creating COM Components for MTS." This chapter deals only with development of components using Visual Basic and presumes you understand the concepts presented in both Chapter 14 and Chapter 5, "An Inside Look at Microsoft Transaction Server."

If you have ever developed a COM dynamic link library (DLL) in Visual Basic, it is likely that this component will run under MTS without any changes. Because DLLs run in the creator's process space, MTS is able to run ActiveX DLLs but not ActiveX EXEs. Microsoft designed MTS in such a way that it is able to run as the stub for most COM DLLs with no changes to the component. This allows components to be developed without regard for whether or not they run under MTS. When developing components that use MTS-specific features, you must not attempt to run them outside of MTS or you will encounter problems.

MTS does provide special features to add additional functionality and capabilities to your components. These features include the ability to do transaction management, to use role-based security, and to share data between components. Before attempting any of the MTS special features or advanced topics, you should create a simple MTS component to become familiar with using Visual Basic and the MTS add-in.

Because most COM components run under MTS, creating a simple component requires only that you install the component under MTS and make no coding changes. MTS does have three events that are fired during the lifetime of any MTS component. These events are as follows:

- `Activate`—Occurs when the component is activated by MTS.
- `Deactivate`—Occurs when the component is deactivated by MTS.
- `CanBePooled`—Returns `True` if the component supports object pooling. Although MTS does not currently support this feature, future versions of MTS will actually implement object pooling.

You can create MTS components that will enable you access to these events by inheriting the MTS Component Interface, `IObjectControl`. To tell your component to inherit this interface, enter the following code just below the Option Explicit line in any ActiveX DLL:

```
Implement ObjectControl
```

N O T E To implement this interface, you will need to have a reference set to the Microsoft Transaction Server Type Library, as shown in Figure 27.1.

FIGURE 27.1

Add the MTS Type Library reference.

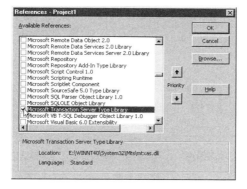

`ObjectControl` is an object that wraps the `IObjectControl` interface in Visual Basic. You are not required to implement `IObjectControl` to develop COM components that work well or run specifically under MTS. Even after implementing this interface in Visual Basic, you can freely move your component in and out of MTS. Implementing this interface allows access to the previously listed events that occur for the component only when running under MTS.

Use the following steps to create your first MTS component:

1. Open Visual Basic or choose File, New Project if Visual Basic is already open.
2. Select ActiveX DLL from the Project New dialog box.
3. Open the Project, References menu and add a reference to the Microsoft Transaction Server Type Library, as shown in Figure 27.1.
4. Click the Open button to create the new project.

Add the code from Listing 27.1 to the code window.

Listing 27.1 CLASS1.CLS—Simple MTS Component

```
VERSION 1.0 CLASS
BEGIN
  MultiUse = -1  'True
  Persistable = 0  'NotPersistable
  DataBindingBehavior = 0  'vbNone
  DataSourceBehavior  = 0  'vbNone
  MTSTransactionMode  = 0  'NotAnMTSObject
END
Attribute VB_Name = "Class1"
Attribute VB_GlobalNameSpace = False
Attribute VB_Creatable = True
Attribute VB_PredeclaredId = False
Attribute VB_Exposed = True
Option Explicit

Implements ObjectControl
Private m_oContext As ObjectContext
```

continues

Listing 27.1   Continued

```
Private Sub ObjectControl_Activate()
    Set m_oContext = GetObjectContext
End Sub

Private Function ObjectControl_CanBePooled() As Boolean
    ObjectControl_CanBePooled = True
End Function

Private Sub ObjectControl_Deactivate()
    Set m_oContext = Nothing
End Sub
```

This component now contains all the code it needs to run under MTS. Actually this component would run under MTS even without inheriting the IObjectContext interface. Compile this component and load it into an MTS package. Although this component will run under MTS, it is useless because it contains no public methods. Add the following line of code to the component to add a public function called Foo to this component:

```
Public Function Foo() as Variant
```

Perform the following steps to see how the MTS add-in works:

1. Check to see that the MTS add-in is enabled. Select the Add-Ins, Add-In Manager menu item. Check the Transaction Server Add-in for VB check box and choose the OK button.

2. Select Add-Ins, MS Transaction Server, AutoRefresh After Recompile of Active Project (see Figure 27.2).

FIGURE 27.2

The Microsoft Transaction Server Add-Ins menu.

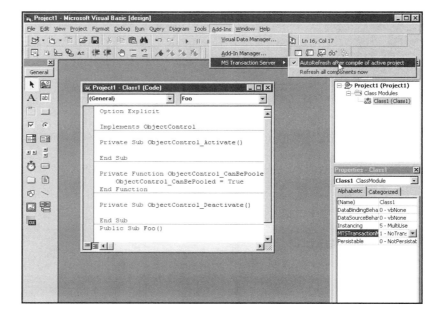

3. Recompile the component and build the DLL. The add-in will automatically update the component in MTS.

Designing middle-tier components is not a trivial task. A well-designed middle-tier component, however, is worth a lot because it can be reused in future projects. Developing middle-tier components can be challenging because they do not have a graphical user interface (GUI). To debug the components you will need to construct a front-end application to call the methods of the middle-tier component.

▶ For more information on designing middle-tier components, see Chapter 25, "Clients, Servers, and Components: Design Strategies for Distributed Applications," **p. 727**

You have seen in this section how to create a simple MTS component. You have also seen how the MTS add-in operates and how it will assist in refreshing the components registered in MTS for you. This section has also shown how little code is actually required to develop a simple component to run in MTS. Because one major advantage of using MTS is the way that it handles transactions, it is worth looking next at developing transaction-aware components.

Developing Transaction-Aware Components

Developing traditional transactional COM components can be a somewhat painful experience, especially if the transaction spans multiple components. Each component needs to know its place within the transaction. The first component in the transaction must start the transaction, and likewise the last component must know to commit the transaction. Another way to handle the problem of transactions spanning multiple components is to build another *controlling* component. This component would be required to know which components appear in the transaction and the order the components should appear so that it could handle beginning the transaction as well as the transaction's eventual commit or abort. The controlling component must be updated if the order of the components in the transaction needs to be changed or if some components need to be added or removed from the transaction.

This architecture becomes even more complex if the main transaction has nested transactions within it. MTS has simplified this issue of developing components that share transactions, have nested transactions, and that need to be moved in and out of transactions after the components have been deployed.

Setting the Transaction Mode at Design Time

To look at the issues involved in creating transaction-aware components, open a new ActiveX DLL project using the same steps as with the previous exercise.

Visual Basic 6 has added to the class properties a new property that enables you to set the different transactional support that a component can have in the property MTSTransactionMode, as shown in Figure 27.3.

Part
IV

Ch

27

FIGURE 27.3

A new class property for `MTSTransactionMode`.

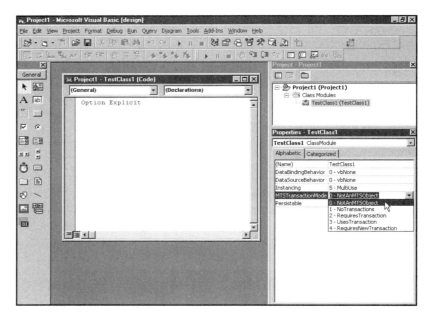

The valid choices for `MTSTransactionMode` for the Visual Basic class are as follows:

- `NotAnMTSObject`—Use this selection if the component does not support MTS.

N O T E   If you select `NotAnMTSObject` as the value for `MTSTransactionMode` and install the component under MTS, the component will be set to Does Not Support Transactions. This setting will not prevent the component from actually installing in MTS. ▧

- `NoTransactions`—Use this selection if the component will run under MTS, but must run outside of any transaction.
- `RequiresTransaction`—Use this selection if the component requires a transaction. If a transaction doesn't currently exist, MTS will create a new one.
- `UsesTransaction`—Use this selection if the component can execute inside of a transaction, but a transaction is not required.
- `RequiresNewTransaction`—Use this selection if this component must execute within its own transaction. MTS will create a new transaction whether or not one already exists. Components that have this selection will commit or abort independently of whether the client's transaction commits or aborts.

Selecting one of these values sets the default value on the Transaction tab of the Properties dialog for the component when it is installed in MTS. This value can be changed at any time (see Figure 27.4).

FIGURE 27.4

Transaction property settings under MTS.

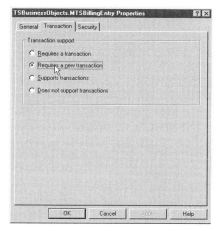

For this component, select UsesTransactions. Change the class name to MTSEmployee. Select Project, References from the menu and add a reference to the Microsoft ActiveX Data Objects 1.5 library.

N O T E The version of ADO that exists on your machine may not be version 1.5. In fact, Microsoft has several different builds of ADO that all report to be ADO 1.5. These builds differ by file date, as well as by what products they were shipped with. At least one build of ADO 1.5 reports that it is ADO version 2 in the reference list. If you have a different version or build of ADO on your machine, just add a reference to the version or build that you have. ▨

Adding MTS Transaction Code

Because the design-time properties and references have been set, you can now begin to add code to this component to support transactions. The code for the MTSEmployee class is shown in Listing 27.2.

Listing 27.2 MTSEMPLOYEE.CLS—The MTSEmployee **Class**

```
VERSION 1.0 CLASS
BEGIN
  MultiUse = -1  'True
  Persistable = 0  'NotPersistable
  DataBindingBehavior = 0  'vbNone
  DataSourceBehavior  = 0  'vbNone
  MTSTransactionMode  = 2  'RequiresTransaction
END
Attribute VB_Name = "MTSEmployee"
Attribute VB_GlobalNameSpace = False
Attribute VB_Creatable = True
Attribute VB_PredeclaredId = False
Attribute VB_Exposed = True
```

continues

Listing 27.2 Continued

```vb
Option Explicit

Implements ObjectControl
Private m_strFirstName As String
Private m_strLastName As String
Private m_strSSN As String
Private m_lngID As Long 'EmployeeID from DB
Private m_oContext As ObjectContext

Public Property Get FirstName() As String
    FirstName = m_strFirstName
End Property
Public Property Let FirstName(strNew As String)
    m_strFirstName = strNew
End Property
Public Property Get LastName() As String
    LastName = m_strLastName
End Property
Public Property Let LastName(strNew As String)
    m_strLastName = strNew
End Property
Public Property Get SSN() As String
    SSN = m_strSSN
End Property
Public Property Let SSN(strNew As String)
    m_strSSN = strNew
End Property
Public Property Get ID() As Long
    ID = m_lngID
End Property

Public Sub Save()
    Dim oDB As New ADODB.Connection
    Dim oRS As New ADODB.Recordset
    Dim strSQL As String
    Dim intAffected As Integer

    On Error GoTo ErrorHandler
    If Not m_oContext.IsInTransaction Then
        Err.Raise vbObjectError + 100, "Save", _
            "This component must run in a transaction"
        Exit Sub
    End If
    oDB.Open "ConsBillDSN", "", ""
    strSQL = "SELECT count(*) from EmployeeID WHERE EmployeeID=" & m_lngID

    oRS.Open strSQL, oDB, adOpenStatic, adLockReadOnly, adCmdText
    If oRS.RecordCount < 1 Then 'no records found so insert record
        strSQL = "INSERT INTO Employee (ID,FirstName,LastName,SSNTaxID) " & _
            " VALUES (" & m_lngID & ",'" & m_strFirstName & "','" & _
            m_strLastName & "','" & m_strSSN & "')"
    Else ' update existing record
        strSQL = "UPDATE Employee set FirstName='" & m_strFirstName & _
            "',LastName='" & m_strLastName & "',SSNTaxID='" & _
```

```vb
                m_strSSN & "'"
        End If

        oDB.Execute strSQL, intAffected, adCmdText
        If Not oRS Is Nothing Then
            oRS.Close
            Set oRS = Nothing
        End If
        If Not oDB Is Nothing Then
            oDB.Close
            Set oDB = Nothing
        End If
        m_oContext.SetComplete
        Exit Sub
ErrorHandler:
        If Not oRS Is Nothing Then
            oRS.Close
            Set oRS = Nothing
        End If
        If Not oDB Is Nothing Then
            oDB.Close
            Set oDB = Nothing
        End If
        m_oContext.SetAbort
        Err.Raise Err.Number, Err.Source, Err.Description
End Sub
Public Function GetProperties(lngID As Long) As Variant
        Dim oDB As New ADODB.Connection
        Dim oRS As New ADODB.Recordset
        Dim strSQL As String

        On Error GoTo ErrorHandler
        oDB.Open "ConsBillDSN", "", ""
        strSQL = "SELECT FirstName,LastName,SSNTaxID from EmployeeID " & _
            "WHERE EmployeeID=" & lngID

        oRS.Open strSQL, oDB, adOpenStatic, adLockReadOnly, adCmdText
        GetProperties = oRS.GetRows ' get the rows as an array
        If Not oRS Is Nothing Then
            oRS.Close
            Set oRS = Nothing
        End If
        If Not oDB Is Nothing Then
            oDB.Close
            Set oDB = Nothing
        End If
        m_oContext.SetComplete

        Exit Function
ErrorHandler:
    m_oContext.SetAbort
    GetProperties = Empty
    Err.Raise Err.Number, Err.Source, Err.Description
End Function
```

Part

IV

Ch

27

continues

Listing 27.2   Continued

```
Private Sub ObjectControl_Activate()
    Set m_oContext = GetObjectContext
    m_oContext.EnableCommit
End Sub

Private Function ObjectControl_CanBePooled() As Boolean
    ObjectControl_CanBePooled = True
End Function

Private Sub ObjectControl_Deactivate()
    Set m_oContext = Nothing
End Sub
```

To understand the code, a walkthrough of the MTSEmployee class is necessary. First, notice that the MTSEmployee implements the IObjectControl interface. In the Activate method of the IObjectControl interface, there is a call to the following method:

```
m_oContext.EnableCommit
```

This method tells MTS that the component has not finished with its work, but that the transactional updates are stable enough that they could be committed at the current point in time. A call to DisableCommit tells MTS that the transactional updates are not stable and could not be committed at this time. This is primarily used by two different types of components: components that require multiple method calls before being able to commit work and stateful components. *Stateful components* use DisableCommit because after a call to DisableCommit, MTS is unable to deactivate the component and reclaim resources. If the client attempts to commit the transaction after the component has called DisableCommit, but before the component has called SetComplete or EnableCommit, the transaction will roll back.

In the GetProperties function a new ADO Connection object and Recordset object are created. One of the design considerations for scalable applications is *state-aware components*. The GetProperties function returns an array of the property values to the calling application, instead of saving the values into the properties and accessing the attributes normally. By having the object return the property values, the actual object is no longer required and it can be deactivated and thereby reduce the amount of resources consumed on the server. In this way, the component can be said to be state-aware or *state-conscious*.

The following line of code tells MTS that the component has completed and can be deactivated.

```
m_oContext.SetComplete
```

If a transactional component calls SetComplete, MTS knows that this component has successfully completed its part of the transaction. In the error handler for this function, the following line of code is called:

```
m_oContext.SetAbort
```

This code tells MTS that there was an error in this component and that it can be deactivated. If a transactional component calls SetAbort, MTS rolls the transaction back. MTS requires all components within a transaction to call `SetComplete` to commit a transaction, but if a single component within the transaction calls `SetAbort`, the transaction is rolled back.

> **CAUTION**
>
> Take care to include only the components in a transaction that are required for the transaction. This will prevent situations where errors in components that don't affect the transaction cause unnecessary rollbacks.

Although you can set the transaction mode that the component will set at runtime, in the MTS Explorer, the mode can be changed to a transaction mode that will cause the component to operate incorrectly. For example, the component you build requires a new transaction, but when it is installed in MTS, the component could be configured incorrectly to Does Not Support Transactions. Because the component needs to run in a transaction, you can verify at runtime that a transaction exists from the following code:

```
m_oContext.IsInTransaction
```

> **N O T E** By calling `IsInTransaction` you will find out only whether the component is currently executing in a transaction, but not whether the component is executing in its own transaction. ▨

Adding transaction support to components under MTS is not a difficult task. MTS actually simplifies the code that is necessary to implement transactions between components, as well as nested transactions among components. MTS also allows components to be moved between transactions after the components have been deployed. MTS enables developers to create transactional components and reduce the amount of code and complexity that would be required to develop traditional components with the same features MTS provides.

Exploring Role-Based Security

Many enterprise applications require security in one form or another. Most applications that use security map a login (either network or application specific) to a set of permissions that allow access to certain functions. Some applications go even further and actually query the network for information on groups and allow security to be assigned to groups instead of only to users. This security information is usually saved in some database table, or possibly hard-coded into the application or component. MTS allows a flexible yet powerful role-based security, which allows business objects to access security via two different schemes: declarative and programmatic security. *Declarative security* means that roles determine which users are allowed access to the interfaces in a component. *Programmatic security* means that the code in the component determines whether the client is allowed to perform the requested operation. These roles are completely dynamic and configurable after components have been deployed.

Accessing role-based security from Visual Basic is a straightforward exercise. You will now create a component called the `TSValidator`. This component is a key piece of the sample Time and Billing application. This component's purpose is to determine whether a person has permissions to see the timesheet he/she is requesting. To create the TSValidator component, open a new ActiveX DLL project using the same steps as in the previous exercise. Then perform the following steps:

1. Open the Project, References menu and add a reference to the SampleApplication TimeBillingExt library. If the Type Library is not in the list of references, use the Browse button to find it.

> **N O T E**   This reference is necessary because this component implements the IValidator
> interface, which is defined in this Type Library. This component implements this interface to
> allow replacement of this component with a similar component of different languages. All versions of
> this component will support this interface, which is how interface inheritance is implemented in
> COM. ▇

2. Set the name of the class to TSValidator.
3. Set the MTSTransactionMode to NoTransactions.
4. Set Instancing to MultiUse.

After you have set the design properties, enter the code from Listing 27.3 into the code window.

Listing 27.3   TSVALIDATOR.CLS—The Source for the TSValidator Object

```
VERSION 1.0 CLASS
BEGIN
  MultiUse = -1  'True
  Persistable = 0  'NotPersistable
  DataBindingBehavior = 0   'vbNone
  DataSourceBehavior   = 0   'vbNone
  MTSTransactionMode   = 1   'NoTransaction
END
Attribute VB_Name = "TSValidator"
Attribute VB_GlobalNameSpace = False
Attribute VB_Creatable = True
Attribute VB_PredeclaredId = False
Attribute VB_Exposed = True
Option Explicit


Implements IValidator
Implements ObjectControl

Private m_objParent As Object
Private m_objObjectContext As ObjectContext
Private m_strMasterConnect As String

Private Sub Class_Initialize()
    m_strMasterConnect = vbNullString
End Sub
```

```
Private Property Let IValidator_Parent(ByVal RHS As Object)
    Set m_objParent = RHS
End Property

Private Property Get IValidator_Parent() As Object
    Set IValidator_Parent = m_objParent
End Property

Private Function IValidator_Validate(ByVal dteDate As Date,
➥ByVal bstrUserID As String) As Boolean
    Dim blnValidUser As Boolean
    Dim oSharedStats As Object

    On Error GoTo IValidator_Validate_Error
    blnValidUser = False

    ' make sure date requested is only 1 week ahead or 6 week behind
    Dim dteFuture As Date, dtePast As Date, dteNow As Date
    dteNow = Date    ' use today's date by default
    dteFuture = DateAdd("ww", 1, dteNow)
    dtePast = DateAdd("ww", -6, dteNow)

    If dteDate >= dtePast And dteDate <= dteFuture Then

        #If MTS Then
            If m_objObjectContext Is Nothing Then
                IValidator_Validate = False
                Exit Function
            End If
            If m_objObjectContext.IsSecurityEnabled Then

                If m_objObjectContext.IsCallerInRole("HumanResources") Then

                    blnValidUser = True

                ElseIf m_objObjectContext.IsCallerInRole("ProjectMGR") Then

                    blnValidUser = DoesUserWorkForCaller(dteDate, bstrUserID)

                ElseIf m_objObjectContext.IsCallerInRole("Consultant") Then

                    If m_objObjectContext.Security.GetOriginalCallerName =
                    ➥bstrUserID Then
                        blnValidUser = True
                    End If
                End If

            End If
        #Else
            blnValidUser = True
        #End If

    End If

    ' Use Shared Property Manager to store statistics. Note that TSSharedStats
    '  is not transactional.  It must, however, be an MTS component.
```

continues

Part

IV

Ch

27

Listing 27.3   Continued

```
    Set oSharedStats = CreateObject("TSValidatorSvr.TSSharedStats")
    If m_strMasterConnect = vbNullString Then
        m_strMasterConnect = GetConnection(bstrUserID)
    End If
    oSharedStats.StoreLastEmployeeID bstrUserID, m_strMasterConnect

    IValidator_Validate = blnValidUser

    #If MTS Then
        m_objObjectContext.SetComplete   ' remove when done
    #End If
    Exit Function
IValidator_Validate_Error:
'    m_objParent.AddError Err.Description, Err.Number, Err.Source

    Err.Raise Err.Number, Err.Source, Err.Description,
    ➥Err.HelpFile, Err.HelpContext

End Function

Private Sub ObjectControl_Activate()
    Set m_objObjectContext = GetObjectContext()
End Sub

Private Function ObjectControl_CanBePooled() As Boolean
    ObjectControl_CanBePooled = True
End Function

Private Sub ObjectControl_Deactivate()
    Set m_objObjectContext = Nothing
    Set m_objParent = Nothing
End Sub

Private Function DoesUserWorkForCaller(ByVal dteDate As Date,
➥ByVal strUserID As String) As Boolean

    Dim adoConnection As New ADODB.Connection
    Dim adoRecordset As ADODB.Recordset
    Dim vConnections As Variant
    Dim strMasterConnect As String
    Dim strSQL As String

    On Error GoTo ErrorHandler

    DoesUserWorkForCaller = False

    If m_strMasterConnect = vbNullString Then
        m_strMasterConnect = GetConnection(strUserID)
    End If

    Call adoConnection.Open(m_strMasterConnect)

    ' get the strUserIDs' projectcode on the date requested
    strSQL = "select E.LoginID from Employee E, Assignment A " & _
```

```
                "where E.EmployeeID = A.EmployeeID and A.Role =
                ➥'ProjectMGR' and " & _
                "A.ProjectCode in (" & _
                "select AA.ProjectCode from Employee EE, Assignment AA " & _
                "where EE.LoginID = '" & strUserID & " ' and " & _
                "and EE.EmployeeID = AA.EmployeeID  and " & _
                "'" & dteDate & "' >= AA.BeginDate and '" &
                ➥dteDate & "' <= AA.EndDate)"

        Set adoRecordset = adoConnection.Execute(strSQL)
        If Not (adoRecordset Is Nothing) Then
            Do While Not adoRecordset.EOF
                If adoRecordset("LoginID") =
                ➥m_objObjectContext.Security.GetOriginalCallerName Then
                    DoesUserWorkForCaller = True
                    Exit Do
                End If
                adoRecordset.MoveNext
            Loop
            adoRecordset.Close
            Set adoRecordset = Nothing
        End If

        adoConnection.Close
        Set adoConnection = Nothing

        Exit Function

ErrorHandler:
        Err.Raise Err.Number, Err.Source, Err.Description, Err.HelpFile,
        ➥Err.HelpContext


End Function

Private Function GetConnection(ByVal strUserID As String) As String
        Dim strMaster As String


        On Error GoTo ErrorHandler

        ' get master database connect string from Registry
        strMaster = GetSetting("Consultant Billing", "MasterDSN", "DSN", "")
        If strMaster = "" Then
          GetConnection = vbNullString
          Exit Function
        Else
          GetConnection = strMaster
        End If

        Exit Function

ErrorHandler:
        Err.Raise Err.Number, Err.Source, Err.Description, Err.HelpFile,
        ➥Err.HelpContext

End Function
```

As you can see, the TSValidator component inherits both the IObjectContext and IValidator interfaces. The function IValidator_Validate contains the code that deals with security. First this function checks to see if the date entered is within a valid range. If the previous check passes, a call is made to determine if security is enabled within the package.

```
m_objObjectContext.IsSecurityEnabled
```

This function returns whether or not security is enabled on the component. Security can only be enabled if the component is configured to run in a server process. If security is not enabled, queries about users in roles always return True. To determine if the caller is in the role "HumanResources", the following statement is executed:

```
m_objObjectContext.IsCallerInRole("HumanResources")
```

The caller (direct caller) is the base client or process that made the call into this component. The function returns True if the caller is in the role as either an individual or group. The business rule implemented here is that if the caller is in the role HumanResources, he or she can do anything. Callers in the role of ProjectMGR can edit a timesheet for anyone on their project. If the caller is in the role Consultant, then a check is made to see if the original caller name is the same as the user whose timesheet is requested by making the following statement:

```
m_objObjectContext.Security.GetOriginalCallerName
```

Using the security object, you can retrieve the names of the caller or creator of this component. The caller or creator names that can be retrieved and a description of each are located in the following list:

- OriginalCallerName—Username associated with the base process that started the call sequence from which the current method was called.
- OriginalCreatorName—Username associated with the base process that started the activity in which the current object is executing.
- DirectCallerName—Username associated with the external process that called the currently executing method.
- DirectCreatorName—Username associated with the external process that called the currently executing method.

See Figure 27.5 for a diagram of these names.

Sometimes a user will not directly have privileges on certain tables in the database. This prevents users from editing data directly in the database, say, by using Microsoft Access. By having an intermediate component running under a different userid, you can have component 2, created from component 1, insert into the database because the direct caller (component 1) does have privileges on the table. This also ensures that no user can directly use the second component without privileges on the database unless they use component 1 to call component 2.

FIGURE 27.5
A diagram of security caller and creator names.

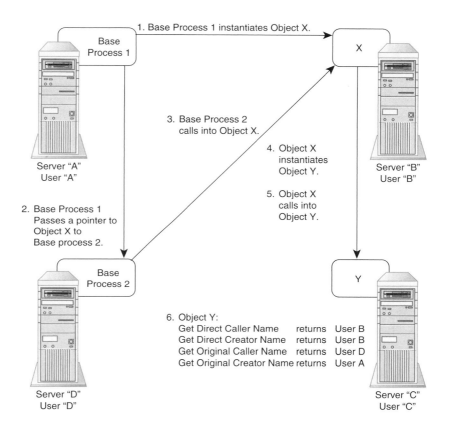

1. Base Process 1 instantiates Object X.

Base Process 1

X

Server "A"
User "A"

3. Base Process 2 calls into Object X.

4. Object X instantiates Object Y.

Server "B"
User "B"

5. Object X calls into Object Y.

2. Base Process 1 Passes a pointer to Object X to Base process 2.

Base Process 2

Y

6. Object Y:
   Get Direct Caller Name   returns   User B
   Get Direct Creator Name   returns   User B
   Get Original Caller Name   returns   User D
   Get Original Creator Name returns   User A

Server "D"
User "D"

Server "C"
User "C"

Creating components to access role-based security in MTS with Visual Basic is straightforward. MTS allows access to simple security (IsCallerInRole, IsSecurityEnabled) as well as advanced security (the Security object). MTS security allows flexible and dynamic security schemes for both programmatic and declarative security. MTS security also allows each business object to easily access the security and to respond appropriately. You can also see that MTS enables you to implement a security scheme in such a way that users have no access to the database except through the business objects that you have developed.

Part
IV

Ch
27

Sharing State Among Components

Sometimes it is important for components to share information regardless of whether or not they exist concurrently. An example of this is a component that generates IDs, counts the number of instances of a component that have been created, or keeps track of the last user to access a particular object. MTS allows sharing of this information through a Resource Dispenser called the Shared Property Manager. The properties that are shared can only be shared between components that execute within the same MTS process (that is, those that are in the same package).

For you to create a component that accesses the Shared Property Manager, perform the following steps:

1. Create a new ActiveX DLL project using the same steps as you did in the first exercise.
2. Open the Project, References menu and add a reference to the Shared Property Manager Type Library.
3. Open the Project, References menu and add a reference to the Microsoft Transaction Server Type Library.
4. Set `ProjectName` to `TSLastUser`.
5. Set the `ClassName` to `LastUser`.
6. Set the `MTSTransactionMode` to `NoTransactions`.

After you set the design-time properties, enter the code from Listing 27.4 into the code window.

Listing 27.4   LASTUSER.CLS—The Source for the `TSLastUser` Component

```
VERSION 1.0 CLASS
BEGIN
  MultiUse = -1  'True
  Persistable = 0  'NotPersistable
  DataBindingBehavior = 0  'vbNone
  DataSourceBehavior  = 0  'vbNone
  MTSTransactionMode  = 1  'NoTransaction
END
Attribute VB_Name = "LastUser"
Attribute VB_GlobalNameSpace = False
Attribute VB_Creatable = True
Attribute VB_PredeclaredId = False
Attribute VB_Exposed = True
Option Explicit

Implements ObjectControl

Dim m_oContext As ObjectContext

Private Sub ObjectControl_Activate()
    Set m_oContext = GetObjectContext
End Sub

Private Function ObjectControl_CanBePooled() As Boolean
    ObjectControl_CanBePooled = True
End Function

Private Sub ObjectControl_Deactivate()
    Set m_oContext = Nothing
End Sub

Public Function GetLastUser() As String
    Dim oManager As SharedPropertyGroupManager
    Dim oGroup As SharedPropertyGroup
```

```
        Dim oProperty As SharedProperty

        On Error GoTo ErrorHandler
        Set oManager = CreateObject("MTxSpm.SharedPropertyGroupManager.1")
        Set oGroup = oManager.CreatePropertyGroup("TSLastUser",
        ➥LockSetGet, Process, blnExists)
        Set oProperty = oGroup.CreateProperty("LastUser", blnExists)

        If blnExists Then    ' the component previously existed
            GetLastUser = oProperty.Value
        End If

        m_oContext.SetComplete

        Set oProperty = Nothing
        Set oGroup = Nothing
        Set oManager = Nothing
        Exit Function
ErrorHandler:
        m_oContext.SetAbort
        GetLastUser = vbNullString
        Set oProperty = Nothing
        Set oGroup = Nothing
        Set oManager = Nothing
        Err.Raise Err.Number, Err.Source, Err.Description
    End Function

    Public Sub SetLastUser(strNewUser As String)
        Dim oManager As SharedPropertyGroupManager
        Dim oGroup As SharedPropertyGroup
        Dim oProperty As SharedProperty

        On Error GoTo ErrorHandler
        Set oManager = CreateObject("MTxSpm.SharedPropertyGroupManager.1")
        Set oGroup = oManager.CreatePropertyGroup("TSLastUser",
        ➥LockSetGet, Process, blnExists)
        Set oProperty = spmGroup.CreateProperty("LastUser", blnExists)

        oProperty.Value = strNewUser

        m_oContext.SetComplete

        Set oProperty = Nothing
        Set oGroup = Nothing
        Set oManager = Nothing
        Exit Sub
 ErrorHandler:
        m_oContext.SetAbort
        Set oProperty = Nothing
        Set oGroup = Nothing
        Set oManager = Nothing
        Err.Raise Err.Number, Err.Source, Err.Description
End Sub
```

Walking through this code, you see that this component supports the IObjectControl interface. The following lines of code outline the objects used in Visual Basic to access the Shared
Property Manager:

```
Dim oManager As SharedPropertyGroupManager
Dim oGroup As SharedPropertyGroup
Dim oProperty As SharedProperty
```

There are three objects used to access shared properties in Visual Basic:

- Shared Property Group Manager
- Shared Property Group
- Shared Property

The Shared Property Group Manager is used to create or access Shared Property Groups. You
can use either CreateObject or the CreateInstance method of the object context to create this
object. The TSLastUser component calls the following method on the
SharedPropertyGroupManager object:

```
Set oGroup = oManager.CreatePropertyGroup("TSLastUser", LockSetGet,
➥Process, blnExists)
```

This method creates the SharedPropertyGroup TSLastUser, if it does not already exist. The
LockSetGet parameter locks the property during a value call. It prevents multiple users from
simultaneously accessing that property. A value of LockMethod for this parameter locks all
properties in the property group exclusively for the current caller as long as the caller's current method is executing. This method is useful if multiple properties in a property group are
dependent on each other. The value Process tells MTS that this property group is not destroyed until the process that created it has terminated. If the value is Standard, the property
group is destroyed when the last client releases its reference to the property group. The value
of blnExists will be True if the property group existed before the call to this component, and
False otherwise.

The following call to the CreateProperty on the SharedPropertyGroup creates the property
LastUser if it does not already exist.

```
Set oProperty = oGroup.CreateProperty("LastUser", blnExists)
```

The value of blnExists is True if the property existed before the call, and False otherwise. You
could just as easily make the call to the method in the following way:

```
Set oProperty = oGroup.CreatePropertyByPosition(1,blnExists)
```

This creates a property in position 1 within the SharedPropertyGroup. This call is equivalent to
the first method mentioned but accesses the property by index rather than property name.
After the shared property is created, the value of the property is set using the following call:

```
oProperty.Value = strUserName
```

The value of the Property object is a variant data type and therefore can be used to store any
data type that can be stored into a variant.

N O T E   You can store both objects and collections into this property if for some reason you need to store a list of objects in a shared property. If you choose to do this, the following statement will generate a type mismatch error:

```
Set oProperty.Value=oCollection
```

The correct statement is

```
oProperty.Value = oCollection
```

When you are assigning the property value to a collection or object, you use `Set` in the assignment as follows:

```
Set oCollection = oProperty.Value
```

The examples that you have seen thus far have all used `CreateProperty` to access properties whether they exist or not. You can access a shared property that exists already by using one of the following methods on the Property Group.

```
Set oProperty = oGroup.Property("LastUser")
Set oProperty = oGroup.PropertyByPosition(1)
```

In this section, you have seen how MTS shares information between components in the same package that may not be concurrently executing. You have seen how to access and create your own resource dispensers, specifically using the Shared Property Manager.

Understanding Error Handling

It is important, in developing components, that you handle all errors and not allow execution to proceed despite the errors. Most Visual Basic developers know that when an unhandled error occurs while an application is running, a runtime error is generated. Handling errors is especially critical when developing MTS components. When MTS detects an unhandled exception, it shuts down execution of the offending thread of execution. This means that if your component has an unhandled exception MTS will shut down the component and prevent any additional problems from occurring.

Another problem that can occur from improper error handling is loss of the error that actually occurred. For example, a client creates an MTS component, which in turn creates another component. If an error occurs in the second component that is not caught by the first component, the error may be lost and a generic error message could be generated. Some error messages may be raised correctly back to the client, but depending on the error that occurs, a message similar to `Method ~ of object ~ failed` could be returned to the client.

The best way handle errors in MTS components is to put an error handler in every function. Before anything else in the function, except maybe declarations, use the following statement:

```
On Error Goto ErrorHandler
```

At the end of each function, put in code that will call `oContext.SetAbort`, if necessary, and code that will reraise any errors that have occurred.

Part
IV

Ch
27

```
Err.Raise Err.Number, Err.Source, Err.Description
```

If you are interested in keeping track of all the errors that have occurred inside several levels of MTS objects, you might consider creating an `MTSErrors` collection object. Whenever an error occurs inside an MTS component, the object can write the error into this collection as well as raise the error. This will create an error stack that the client can walk to see what errors occurred in which components.

Debugging MTS components that do not have good error handling causes the developer many headaches and frustrations. Having a well-thought out and developed error handling architecture will decrease debugging time in complex applications. Having a well-developed error handling mechanism enables you to build complex systems quickly and easily and helps to reduce some of the debugging issues.

Debugging MTS Components

Debugging components can be a time-consuming and frustrating activity, especially if the tools to debug a program are lacking. Debugging device drivers, for example, is typically an aggravating situation because of the debugging tools. Debugging MTS components does have its frustrations, but because of some of the tools provided by Microsoft, debugging components is greatly simplified. There are several strategies to debugging:

- Debugging in the IDE
- Debugging under Visual Studio
- Debugging using WinDbg

Debugging in the IDE

The first thing to remember when developing MTS components is that the code is just Visual Basic code. This means that most of the code can be stepped through in the Visual Basic Debugger. To debug in the Visual Basic IDE, you cannot execute any MTS specific code. This means nothing having to do with the Object Context, Shared Properties, or other specific MTS code can execute. The easiest thing to do is to put in a conditional compile flag—for example,

```
#IF MTS then
```

Define MTS in the Project Properties dialog on the Make tab, as shown in Figure 27.6.

Use this conditional compile flag to bypass any MTS specific code. By doing so, you will be able to debug a majority of the component's functionality using the Visual Basic debugger. This is the easiest debugging technique to use. If you debug this component in Visual Basic first and then load it under MTS and get an error, you will know that the error is related to MTS specific code.

 TIP Don't forget to set the conditional compile flag to the correct value before compiling the component to run under MTS, or your component will not use any MTS specific features.

FIGURE 27.6

Setting the MTS conditional compile option.

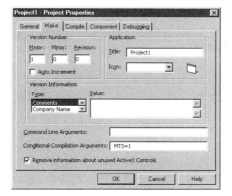

 TIP If you use the conditional compile flag, use `CreateObject` outside of MTS rather than `Context.CreateInstance`.

Debugging Under Visual Studio

You can compile and execute your MTS components under the Visual C++ IDE. The Visual C++ IDE will debug a component only after it has been compiled. You will need to perform the following steps to debug your component in the Visual Studio IDE:

1. Open your Visual Basic component in the Visual Basic IDE.

2. Choose Project, Properties from the menu and select the Compile tab. Select Compile to Native Code, No Optimization, and Create Symbolic Debug Info, as shown in Figure 27.7.

FIGURE 27.7

The settings used for component debugging in Visual C++.

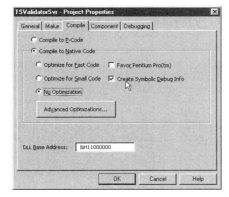

Part

IV

Ch

27

3. Open the MTS Explorer, right-click the package that contains your component and choose Properties. Highlight the Package ID and copy it to the Clipboard.

4. Open the Visual Studio IDE. Open the DLL containing the component to debug. Select Project, Settings from the menu and then choose the Debug tab.

5. Select the MTS executable used to debug your component. This is \winnt\system32\mtx.EXE by default. For Program Arguments, enter /p:{Package GUID} (pasting the value you saved to the Clipboard). You can use the package name instead of the package GUID (see Figure 27.8).

FIGURE 27.8

Setting properties for debugging MTS components in Visual C++.

6. Open the .cls file for the component you want to debug. Set breakpoints in the appropriate places. If you want to display variable information, go to the Tools, Options menu and select the Debug tab. Select the Display Unicode Strings check box.

7. Go to MTS and shut down all server processes.

8. Open the Registry editor and add the following key:

    HKEY_LOCAL_MACHINE\SOFTWARE\Microsoft\Transaction
    Server\Debug\RunWithoutContext

9. In Visual Studio, select Build, Start Debug, Go from the menu.

10. Start your client program and debug your component by stepping through it in the Visual C++ IDE.

 TIP The Visual C++ IDE requires an exact spelling match in order to watch a variable's value.

After you finish debugging your component, make sure you set the optimization options you desire in Visual Basic and remove the symbolic debugging option that you had previously selected. While the RunWithoutContext option allows your component to run outside MTS, your component runs without actually having any of the functionality of MTS enabled. This means that

- SetAbort and SetComplete do nothing.
- Security is disabled.
- There are no transactions.
- CreateInstance is the same as calling CreateObject.

These limitations do hurt your ability to test the full functionality of your component because no MTS functionality is actually enabled. You can test more of the functionality of your component than you could using the Visual Basic debugger, but this technique, while better in some ways, still has some limitations. This technique is very powerful, but there is still one more method that you can use to debug your components.

Debugging with WinDbg

WinDbg enables your component to run under MTS with all of its functionality enabled. The problem with this method is that you cannot step through your program, rather you get status messages as to how the component is running, and you can use those messages to diagnose a problem. Microsoft created a debugger called WinDbg, which is used to debug device drivers, the kernel, and applications. Load your client into the WinDbg application. You can include in the code for your component a call to the following:

```
Call OutputDebugStringA(strError)
```

This call will print out `strError` to the WinDbg window when you launch the client application from inside of WinDbg. If you make this call throughout your component, you will generate a log of messages that you can use to determine what is happening with your component.

Summary

Debugging MTS components requires several tools. Each tool has its pluses and minuses. Debugging in Visual Basic with the conditional compile flag provides the easiest way to change code while debugging but no access to any MTS features. The Visual C++ compiler allows access to the MTS calls but no real MTS Support. The WinDbg option allows access to all of the MTS features, but it is more difficult to determine where errors occur and to therefore fix the errors that have occurred.

The path you should first take when debugging MTS components should be to debug everything you can in Visual Basic. This should get rid of most of the logic problems and simple syntax errors. Then try to run your component and client. Only if you are still having problems should you load your component under Visual C++ to try to determine what is wrong. Only if you are unable to determine the error under Visual C++ should you use the WinDbg option. Using this debugging option will take much more time than the other two options and you should use it only as a last resort.

From Here...

Building scalable applications has become more popular especially since the dramatic increase of Web-based application. Because MTS is a core component used to develop scalable applications, its use will increase in the future. Developing components that run under MTS will also become more prevalent because MTS is an extension of COM/COM+.

Part
IV

Ch
27

By using Microsoft Visual Basic, you can develop components that will run under MTS and take advantage of the special features of MTS. Building reusable transaction components has been simplified with MTS and Visual Basic. Your component can now run its own transactions in certain applications and run inside another component's transaction in other applications by installing the component in two different packages. This enables you to develop flexible and reusable components. You can also develop components with flexible security schemes and components that enable you to share data between components.

For more information on developing MTS and COM components, see the following chapters:

- To learn about Microsoft Transaction Server, see Chapter 5, "An Inside Look at Microsoft Transaction Server."
- For general information on creating COM components for MTS, see Chapter 14, "Creating COM Components for MTS."
- To learn to develop MTS components with J++, see Chapter 28, "Creating COM Components for MTS with Visual J++."
- For information on developing C++ COM components for MTS, see Chapter 29, "Creating COM Components for MTS with Visual C++."
- For information on debugging multitiered application with Visual Studio, see Chapter 3, "Debugging Enterprise Applications with Visual Studio."
- To learn about building data access components for MTS, see Chapter 30, "Creating Data Access Components for MTS with Visual Basic and ADO."

CHAPTER 28

Creating COM Components for MTS with Visual J++

by Eric M. Brown

In this chapter

Looking at and Creating a Simple MTS Component

Java has become one of the hottest development tools primarily because of the ability to use components on multiple platforms and operating systems. Java can be used to create middle-tier components for enterprise development. Although previously Java classes by default were not (and actually still are not) Component Object Model (COM) components, you can add COM support to Java classes very simply and therefore create Microsoft Transaction Server (MTS) components. Understanding how COM works is not essential to developing COM components in Java. In Java, you are as isolated from the inner workings of COM as you are in Visual Basic.

In this chapter, you will learn the specific issues and techniques to develop COM components for MTS with Visual J++. This chapter builds on what you previously read in Chapter 14, "Creating COM Components for MTS." This chapter assumes knowledge of MTS and Java. You will begin by building a simple MTS component and then you will learn how to develop components that take advantage of some more advanced MTS features.

Creating a simple MTS component requires that the component built be a COM component. Classes developed in Java are not by default COM components; therefore, to develop an MTS component, you must first develop a COM component. Under previous versions of Visual J++, building a COM component was labor intensive. It required modifying the IDL that was part of the project to add in the MTS transaction properties, as well as the GUIDs for the class. Microsoft has greatly simplified the development of COM components under Visual J++ 6.

Creating a COM Component

Building a COM class in Visual J++ has some similarities to building a COM component in Visual Basic because most of the complexities of developing COM components are hidden from you. Microsoft has isolated the developer from these details to allow them to focus on developing components that provide some business functionality. To learn to develop a COM component under MTS, you will create the Validator component. Use the following steps to create the Validator component:

1. Open Visual J++ or choose File, New Project if Visual J++ is already open.

2. Select Components in the dialog box and select COM DLL. Name the project Validator, as shown in Figure 28.1.

FIGURE 28.1
Create a new COM component.

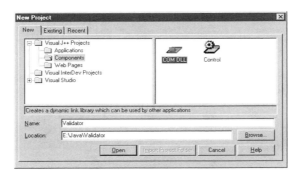

3. Choose Open to create the Validator Project.

The `Validator` component has been created with one public class (`Class1`). Remove `Class1` from the project by right clicking on `Class1` in the Project Explorer window and choosing Remove from Project. Now add a new class by choosing Project, Add Item (Ctrl+D). Select Class and set the name of the class to `JavaValidator`, as shown in Figure 28.2. Choose the Open button.

FIGURE 28.2

Adding a new class to the Validator project.

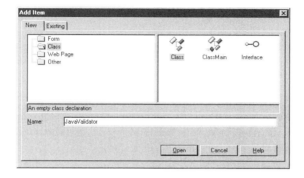

 T I P   You could have just changed the name of the class from `Class1` to `JavaValidator` and saved the file as `JavaValidator.java`.

To set this component to be a COM class, perform the following steps:

1. Right-click the `JavaValidator` class in the Class Outline view and select Class Properties.

2. In the Class Properties dialog box, check the COM Enabled check box, as shown in Figure 28.3.

FIGURE 28.3

Enabling COM support for the `JavaValidator` class.

3. Choose the OK button to apply the changes.

4. Enter the code from Listing 28.1.

5. Select File, Save (Ctrl+S) to save your changes.

Listing 28.1 JAVAVALIDATOR1.JAVA—The JavaValidator Class

```
public class JavaValidator
{
    // this function does nothing
    public String TestFunction()
    {
        return "";
    }
}
```

Compile this component (Ctrl+Shift+B) and you now have a COM component developed within Java. This component installs and runs inside MTS, but it has no interesting behavior, nor does it take advantages of the features that MTS provides.

Implementing IObjectControl

The IObjectControl interface provides a component with access primarily to the object pooling features not currently supported under MTS 2. Inheriting this interface is not required for a COM component to operate properly under MTS. If your component does not implement the IObjectControl interface that does not prevent the component from accessing other MTS specific features (transaction, resource dispensers, or role-based security). Implementing IObjectControl does give a component access to the following three methods that MTS calls on a component running under MTS:

- Activate—Called when MTS activates the component.
- Deactivate—Called when MTS deactivates the component.
- CanBePooled—Called by MTS to determine if the component supports object pooling.

To inherit the IObjectControl interface, in your JavaValidator class, add the following line of code before the declaration of the JavaValidator class:

```
import com.ms.mtx.*;
```

Next, modify the class declaration as shown in the following:

```
public class JavaValidator
    implements IObjectControl
```

N O T E Sometimes after including the import line of code or changing a class to implement the IObjectControl interface, Visual J++ will uncheck the COM enabled check box on the Class Properties box. Before you can compile the component, you need to recheck the COM Enabled check box.

If you attempted to compile the project now, you would generate compiler errors complaining that you have not implemented `Activate`, `Deactivate`, or `CanBePooled`, which are all now required public methods. To add these three methods, enter the code from Listing 28.2 into the editor window.

Listing 28.2 JAVAVALIDATOR2—`Activate`, `Deactivate`, and `CanBePooled`

```
import com.ms.mtx.*;
/***
@com.register ( clsid=CAD73756-12C5-11D2-A647-002078121D67,
typelib=CAD73757-12C5-11D2-A647-002078121D67 )
 */
public class JavaValidator
    implements IObjectControl
{
    private IObjectContext m_ObjectContext;
    // this function does nothing
    public String TestFunction()
    {
        return "";
    }
    public void Activate()
    {
        m_ObjectContext = MTx.GetObjectContext();
    }
    public void Deactivate()
    {
        m_ObjectContext = null;
    }
    public boolean CanBePooled()
    {
        return true;
    }
}
```

In the `Activate` method, you can insert code to save the `ObjectContext` in a private attribute so that you would not have to call `GetObjectContext` each time calling a function of the `ObjectContext` is required. That is all the code that is required to implement `IObjectControl`. Actually saving the `ObjectContext` into a member variable is not even necessary.

CAUTION

Do not attempt to call `GetObjectContext` from inside the Initializer because the component has not been activated yet, and thus there is no `ObjectContext` yet.

As you can see, adding support for `IObjectControl` is a straightforward activity that provides access to the methods that MTS will call on an object. When compiled, this component can be run under MTS or run outside MTS with no code changes. Now that you know how to build a simple MTS component, you need to know how to build transactional components using Visual J++.

Part
IV

Ch
28

Developing Transaction-Aware Components

Building transaction COM components can be a difficult task, especially if the transaction that a component participates in spans multiple components. MTS simplifies development for these components because MTS controls which components belong in which transaction. MTS also enables you to move components between transactions without having to recode your components.

Setting the Transaction Mode at Design Time

To learn to create transactional components, open a new COM DLL project using the following steps:

1. Open Visual J++ or choose File, New Project if Visual J++ is already open.
2. Select COM DLL from the New Project dialog box.
3. Set the Project Name to MTSEmployee.
4. Select the Open button to create the new project.
5. Add a class called Employee and remove Class1 from the project.
6. Enable COM Support for this class.

Visual J++ 6 has added to the Class Properties dialog box a property that enables you to select the different transactional support under MTS that a component can have, as shown in Figure 28.4.

FIGURE 28.4
Setting MTS Support in the class properties dialog box.

N O T E You must enable COM support to enable MTS support.

The valid choices for MTS Support are as follows:

- NotSupported—Use this selection if the component must run outside a transaction.
- Supported—Use this selection if the component can run inside a transaction, but a transaction is not required.

- Required—Use this selection if the component must run inside a transaction. If a transaction does not currently exist, a new transaction is created by MTS.

- RequiresNew—Use this selection if the component must run in its own transaction. MTS will create a new transaction regardless of whether or not a transaction already exists. Components that require a new transaction will commit or abort independently of whether or not the client transaction commits or aborts.

Selecting one of these values at design time will select the default value on the Properties, Transaction tab for the component when installed under MTS. For this component, check the enabled box to enable MTS support and select Required in the drop-down box. This value can be changed at any time in the MTS Explorer, as shown in Figure 28.5.

FIGURE 28.5

Transaction property settings under MTS.

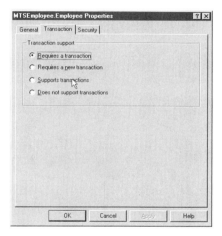

Now that you have set all the design-time properties, you will set the runtime properties to support transactions.

Adding MTS Transaction Code

Your project has all the design-time properties set to enable MTS support, but some code needs to be added to your component to implement the design-time settings. Without adding any runtime code, the component will function under MTS, but will not use its transactional capabilities. The code for the `Employee` class is shown in Listing 28.3.

Listing 28.3 EMPLOYEE.JAVA—The `Employee` class

```
import com.ms.mtx.*;

/**
 * @com.register ( clsid=B9D8DB4C-146B-11D2-A649-002078121D67,
typelib=B9D8DB4D-146B-11D2-A649-002078121D67 )
 * @com.transaction (required)
```

continues

Part
IV

Ch
28

Listing 28.3 Continued

```java
*/
public class Employee
    implements IObjectControl
{
    private String m_strFirstName="";
    private String m_strLastName="";
    private String m_strSSN="";
    private long m_lngID = -1;
    private IObjectContext m_oContext;

    public String GetFirstName()
    {
        return m_strFirstName;
    }
    public void SetFirstName(String strValue)
    {
        m_strFirstName=strValue;
    }
    public String GetLastName()
    {
        return m_strLastName;
    }
    public void SetLastName(String strValue)
    {
        m_strLastName=strValue;
    }
    public String GetSSN()
    {
        return m_strSSN;
    }
    public void SetSSN(String strValue)
    {
        m_strSSN = strValue;
    }
    public long GetID()
    {
        return m_lngID;
    }
    public void SetID(long lngID)
    {
        m_lngID=lngID;
    }
    public void Save()
    {
        if (m_oContext.IsInTransaction())
        {
            // Do Database stuff here
        }
        m_oContext.SetComplete();
    }

    // These methods are for IObjectControl interface

    public void Activate()
```

```
    {
        m_oContext = MTx.GetObjectContext();
        m_oContext.EnableCommit();
    }
    public void Deactivate()
    {
    }
    public boolean CanBePooled()
    {
        return false;
    }

}
```

To understand the transactional code added, a walkthrough of the Employee component is required. In the Activate method of the IObjectControl interface the following method is called:

m_oContext.EnableCommit();

This method tells MTS that the component has not yet finished with its work, but that the transactional updates could be committed at the current point in time. A call to DisableCommit would tell MTS that the transactional updates are not stable and could not be committed at the current point in time. Two different types of components primarily use DisableCommit: first, components that require multiple method calls before committing work, and second, stateful components.

If a client attempts to commit a transaction after the component has called DisableCommit but before calling EnableCommit or SetComplete, the transaction will be rolled back. The call to

m_oContext.SetComplete();

tells MTS that the component has completed its work and can be deactivated. If a transactional component calls SetComplete, MTS knows that the component has completed its part of the transaction. If a transactional component calls

m_oContext.SetAbort();

MTS rolls the transaction that this component is participating in back. If the component does not participate in a transaction, SetAbort and SetComplete perform the same functionality. MTS requires that all components within a transaction call SetComplete before it commits a transaction, but MTS requires only a single component within a transaction to call SetAbort to roll back the transaction. Because of this, take care what components go inside and outside of transactions with other components.

Suppose that you build the Employee component and it requires a transaction under MTS. What is to prevent someone from using the MTS Explorer to reset the Transaction mode to Does Not Support Transactions? You can make a call as the Save method does to

m_oContext.IsInTransaction();

This method tells the component whether the component is running inside or outside of a transaction.

N O T E IsInTransaction will tell the component whether it is operating inside any transaction, but not if the component is executing within its own transaction. ▨

As you have seen, adding transaction support to Java MTS components is simple. MTS simplifies the code that would be required to implement transactions that span multiple components. Microsoft has simplified adding transaction support for MTS at design time in Visual J++ 6 by allowing you to do so at the Properties dialog box instead of having to edit the IDL for the project as was necessary previously. MTS also simplifies the code and complexity that would be necessary to provide the same features that it already provides.

Exploring Role-Based Security

Many applications developed for the enterprise require some type of security. Most applications implement their own security scheme that allows users access to certain functionality. Some applications can query the network to determine privileges for the application. MTS provides a powerful and flexible security scheme known as role-based security.

Role-based security allows business objects to control what functionality a user has access to (programmatic security) as well as what objects a user can access (declarative security). Declarative security is set up using the MTS Explorer. Programmatic security is the code inside the business object that controls what functionality the client can access. Role-based security is based on NT security and enables you to create roles that contain both users and groups.

You will now create the JavaValidator component. This component will demonstrate how to access MTS role-based security. JavaValidator is a key component of the sample Time and Billing application, which is responsible for determining whether a person has permissions to view the timesheet he or she is requesting. To create the JavaValidator component, create a new project by using the following steps:

1. Open Visual J++ 6 or choose File, New Project if Visual J++ is already open.
2. Select COM DLL from the New Project dialog box.
3. Set the project name to TSValidator.
4. Select the Open button to create the project.
5. Create a class called JavaValidator and remove Class1 from the project.

 T I P Right-click the class name in the Project Explorer, and select Rename from the menu to rename the class file from Class1.java to JavaValidator.java. All that you need to do after that is change the declaration of the class inside the file from Class1 to JavaValidator.

6. Enable MTS support on the Class Properties dialog box. Set the Transaction mode to NotSupported.

Under MTS, there are two different levels of security: basic and advanced. Basic security consists of the calls to IsSecurityEnabled and IsCallerInRole. Advanced security enables you to access more complex security features, which will be discussed later. Basic security is available by adding the following line to the top of the class module:

```
import com.ms.mtx.*;
```

To have access to advanced security, you need to add in a COM wrapper for the Microsoft Transaction Server Type Library. To add the COM wrapper, use the following steps:

1. Select Project, Add COM Wrapper from the menu, as shown in Figure 28.6.

FIGURE 28.6
Adding a COM wrapper for the Microsoft Transaction Server Type Library.

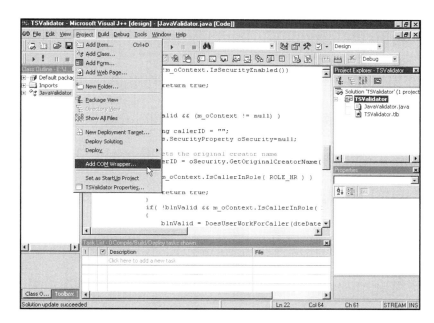

2. Select Microsoft Transaction Server Type Library and click the OK button.

This creates a wrapper class for the Type Library. This wrapper class will create objects that you can directly call from your Java code. It is a very powerful piece of functionality because you can access any COM classes using these wrapper classes and then create instances of COM objects in Java. Because you can wrap the Transaction Server Type Library in a COM wrapper, you do not need the following call:

```
import com.ms.mtx.*;
```

If you would like to use the COM wrapper to create MTS objects, to retrieve the object context, use the following code:

```
mtxas.ObjectContext oContext;
oContext = mtxas.IMTxAS.GetObjectContext();
```

Now that you have access to the advanced security features, add the code into the JavaValidator class from Listing 28.4.

Part
IV

Ch

28

Listing 28.4   JAVAVALIDATOR.JAVA—The JavaValidator **Class**

```java
import com.ms.mtx.*;
import java.util.*;

/**
 * @com.register ( clsid=6FD947E9-148A-11D2-A64A-002078121D67,
typelib=6FD947EA-148A-11D2-A64A-002078121D67 )
 * @com.transaction (required)
 */
public class JavaValidator
    implements IObjectControl
{
    // TODO: Add additional methods and code here
    private IObjectContext m_oContext;
    private static final String ROLE_HR = "HumanResources";
    private static final String ROLE_CONSULTANT = "Consultant";
    private static final String ROLE_PROJECT_MGR = "ProjectMGR";

    // IObjectControl Methods
    public void Activate()
    {
        m_oContext = MTx.GetObjectContext();
    }
    public void Deactivate()
    {
    }
    public boolean CanBePooled()
    {
        return true;
    }

    /**
     * NOTE: To add auto-registration code, refer to the documentation
     * on the following method
     *    public static void onCOMRegister(boolean unRegister) {}
     */

    public boolean Validate(double dteDate, String strUserID)
    {
    boolean blnValid = false;

        // validate that the date is in the valid range
        blnValid = ValidateDate(dteDate);

        // if no context, just return false
        if (m_oContext == null)
        {
            return false;
        }
        else
        {
            // if security is not enabled, just
            // automatically authenticate
            if (!m_oContext.IsSecurityEnabled())
            {
```

```
                        return true;
                }
        }

    if( blnValid && (m_oContext != null) )
    {
        String callerID = "";
        mtxas.SecurityProperty oSecurity=null;

            // Gets the original creator name
            callerID = oSecurity.GetOriginalCreatorName();

        if( m_oContext.IsCallerInRole( ROLE_HR ) )
        {
        return true;
        }
        if( !blnValid && m_oContext.IsCallerInRole( ROLE_PROJECT_MGR ) )
        {
            blnValid = DoesUserWorkForCaller(dteDate,strUserID);
        }
        if( !blnValid &&
                m_oContext.IsCallerInRole( ROLE_CONSULTANT ) )
        {
        if (callerID==strUserID)
                {
                    return true;
                }
                else
                {
                    return false;
                }
        }
    }

    if( m_oContext != null )
    {
        //tell MTS that this object is "complete" for transactional
        //purposes
        m_oContext.SetComplete();
    }

        return blnValid;
}


//private methods

private boolean ValidateDate( double dteDate )
{
    // Insert code here to determine if date is in valid
    // range
    return true;
}

private boolean DoesUserWorkForCaller(double dteDate, String strUserID)
```

Part

IV

Ch

28

continues

Listing 28.4 Continued

```
    {
        // Insert code here to check the database
        return true;
    }
}
```

As you can see, the JavaValidator class inherits the IObjectContext interface. The Validate function contains all the code that deals with security. The function returns True if valid and False if not valid. First, this function checks to see if the date entered is within a valid range. This function ValidateDate is left for the user to implement. If the previous check passes, a call is made to determine whether security is enabled within the package by calling

```
m_oContext.IsSecurityEnabled()
```

Security can be enabled only when the component is running in a server process. If security is not enabled, the Validate function always returns True.

```
m_oContext.IsCallerInRole("HumanResources")
```

This call returns True if the direct caller is in the HumanResources role. This function will return True if the direct caller (caller) is a member of the role either as an individual or as a member of a group. Members of the HumanResources role can edit any time sheet. Callers who are members of the ProjectMGR role can edit a timesheet for anyone on their projects. The implementation of function DoesUserWorkForCaller is left as an exercise for the user. Callers in the Consultant role can edit only their own timesheets. Making the following call checks the last rule:

```
oSecurity.GetOriginalCreatorName();
```

Using the security object provided by the COM wrapper class, you can access the following caller or creator names:

- OriginalCallerName—Username associated with the base process that started the call sequence from which the current method was called.
- OriginalCreatorName—Username associated with the base process that started the activity in which the current object is executing.
- DirectCallerName—Username associated with the external process that called the currently executing method.
- DirectCreatorName—Username associated with the external process that directly created the current object.

It is also possible to access advanced security properties by using the ISecurityProperty interface. This method gives you access to OriginalCallerSID, OriginalCreatorSID, DirectCallerSID, and DirectCreatorSID. This method is not recommended because you are more likely to be interested in the caller or creator name than the Security ID and also because the COM wrapper method is much simpler to implement.

Often, you will want to restrict access to the database. You will not want all users to have direct access to the database. If the users have direct access to the database, they might be able to change data that resides directly in the database through Microsoft Access, bypassing your application and business objects. It is possible that this activity could compromise system integrity.

One way to avoid this is to have the business object be the only object that has rights on the database. The security context that this business object runs under would be able to access the database, so any client that requests the business object's services would be able to access the database, but only through the business object. Allowing only the business object(s) access to the database would require that new applications also use your business objects to access the database.

Accessing role-based security in MTS with Visual J++ is simple. MTS allows access to both simple security methods (`IsCallerInRole`, `IsSecurityEnabled`) using either COM wrapper classes or importing the MTS interface. MTS also allows access to advanced security through COM wrapper classes, which is the most straightforward method, or through the ISecurityProperty interface. MTS provides a powerful and flexible security system that allows groups and users to be assigned to roles, which overlay NT groups and users. MTS provides features that easily allow your components to restrict access to certain function programmatically using role-based security. Finally, MTS also enables you to allow only business objects to have access to the database and to restrict clients from needing that privilege.

Sharing State Among Components

It is necessary or simply easier to sometimes to share state between components regardless of whether they exist concurrently or not. Fortunately, MTS provides such a feature. An example of this would be a component that generates IDs, counts the number of times an object has been created, or keeps track of the last user to access a certain object's resources. MTS allows sharing of this type of information through a Resource Dispenser called the Shared Property Manager. Remember that information can only be shared between components running in the same package (that is, the same MTS process).

To create a component that accesses the Shared Property Manager, perform the following steps:

1. Open Visual J++ or choose <u>File</u>, <u>N</u>ew Project if Visual J++ is already open.
2. Select COM DLL from the New Project dialog box.
3. Select the Open button to create the new project.
4. Set the class properties to enable COM Support.
5. Set the class properties to enable MTS support. Set transaction support to NoSupport.
6. Enter the code from Listing 28.5 into the edit window.

Part
IV

Ch

28

Listing 28.5   CLASS1.JAVA—Java Class That Accesses Shared Properties

```java
/**
 * This class is designed to be packaged with a COM DLL output format.
 * The class has no standard entry points, other than the constructor.
 * Public methods will be exposed as methods on the default COM interface.
 * @com.register ( clsid=C93FA282-14A3-11D2-A64A-002078121D67,
 * typelib=C93FA283-14A3-11D2-A64A-002078121D67 )
 */
import com.ms.mtx.*;
import com.ms.com.*;

/**
 * @com.register ( clsid=C93FA2A3-14A3-11D2-A64A-002078121D67,
 * typelib=C93FA2A4-14A3-11D2-A64A-002078121D67 )
 * @com.transaction (required)
 */
public class Class1
    implements IObjectControl
{
    // TODO: Add additional methods and code here
    private IObjectContext m_oContext;

    public void Activate()
    {
        m_oContext = MTx.GetObjectContext();
    }
    public void Deactivate()
    {
    }
    public boolean CanBePooled()
    {
        return true;
    }
    public Variant GetLastUser()
    {
        ISharedPropertyGroupManager oManager;
        ISharedPropertyGroup oGroup;
        ISharedProperty oProperty;
        boolean blnExists[]= new boolean[1];
        int [] LockMode = new int[1];
        int [] Process = new int[1];
        Variant vntTemp = new Variant("");

        blnExists[0]= false;
        LockMode[0] = ISharedPropertyGroupManager.LOCKMODE_SETGET;
        Process[0] = ISharedPropertyGroupManager.RELEASEMODE_PROCESS;

        oManager = new SharedPropertyGroupManager();
        oGroup = oManager.CreatePropertyGroup("TSLastUser",
                                              LockMode,
                                              Process,
                                              blnExists);
        oProperty = oGroup.CreateProperty("LastUser",blnExists);
```

```
        if (blnExists[1])
        {
            vntTemp = oProperty.getValue();
            m_oContext.SetComplete();
            return vntTemp;
        }
        else
        {
            m_oContext.SetComplete();
            return vntTemp;
        }
    }
    public void SetLastUser(String strNewUser)
    {
        ISharedPropertyGroupManager oManager;
        ISharedPropertyGroup oGroup;
        ISharedProperty oProperty;

        boolean blnExists[]= new boolean[1];
        int [] LockMode = new int[1];
        int [] Process = new int[1];
        Variant vntTemp = new Variant(strNewUser);

        blnExists[0]= false;
        LockMode[0] = ISharedPropertyGroupManager.LOCKMODE_SETGET;
        Process[0] = ISharedPropertyGroupManager.RELEASEMODE_PROCESS;

        oManager = new SharedPropertyGroupManager();
        oGroup = oManager.CreatePropertyGroup("TSLastUser",
                                              LockMode,
                                              Process,
                                              blnExists);
        oProperty = oGroup.CreateProperty("LastUser",blnExists);

        oProperty.putValue(vntTemp);
        m_oContext.SetComplete();
    }
    /**
     * NOTE: To add auto-registration code, refer to the documentation
     * on the following method
     *
     *    public static void onCOMRegister(boolean unRegister) {}
     */
}
```

Here is a walkthrough of the code that you have entered into the editor. You can see that this component implements the IObjectControl interface. The following lines of code outline the three shared property interfaces and can be found in the LastUser method:

```
ISharedPropertyGroupManager oManager;
ISharedPropertyGroup oGroup;
ISharedProperty oProperty;
```

Part
IV

Ch
28

The three shared property interfaces are as follows:

- SharedPropertyGroupManager—ISharedPropertyGroupManager
- SharedPropertyGroup—ISharedPropertyGroup
- SharedProperty—ISharedProperty

The Shared Property Group Manager is used to create and access shared properties groups. The method called on the Shared Property Group Manager object is

```
oGroup = oManager.CreatePropertyGroup("TSLastUSer", LockMode, Process,
➥blnExists);
```

This method creates a property group called TSLastUser. The values of the LockMode parameter can be LockGetSet and LockMethod. LockGetSet locks the property during a value call, whereas LockMethod locks the property exclusively for the current caller as long as the current method is still executing. This is useful if you need to update multiple properties because of dependencies between them.

The valid values of the Process parameter are Process and Standard. Standard tells MTS to destroy the property group whenever the last client releases its reference to the property group. A value of Process tells MTS to destroy the property group whenever the process that created it is destroyed. The last parameter returns True if the property group previously existed and False otherwise.

> **CAUTION**
>
> Attempting to return a reference to a shared property group outside the component that originally referenced the shared property will return an invalid reference.

Following the CreatePropertyGroup method call, the component creates a shared property called LastUser with the following call:

```
oProperty = oGroup.CreateProperty("LastUser", blnExists);
```

The value of blnExists is True if the property existed previously, and False otherwise. If you did not want to create the property by name, but rather by position, you could make the call in the following way:

```
oProperty = oGroup.CreatePropertyByPosition( 1, blnExists);
```

This call would create a property in index position 1 of the shared property group. After you have created the shared property, you access its value with the following method call:

```
oProperty.Value = strUserName;
```

The value of a shared property is a variant; therefore, anything that can be stored in a shared property can be stored in a variant. If you know that a property already exists, you can also retrieve the property by index position or by name by making the following call:

```
oProperty = oGroup.getPropertyByPosition(1);
oProperty = oGroup.getProperty("LastUser");
```

CAUTION

Do not attempt to load an object into a shared property that is running in the same context (that is, one that was created with `CreateInstance`) as the component accessing the shared property, or you will get unexpected results. This is because when the component that created the context goes away, so does the object referenced in the shared property.

N O T E   All the work done previously with the Shared Property Interfaces could also be done by using a COM Wrapper around the Shared Property Manager Type Library. That implementation is not shown, but is similar in nature to the discussion in role-based security where a COM Wrapper was added.

Shared properties provide powerful functionality, which allows sharing of data between two components whether they exist concurrently or not. MTS is flexible enough to allow any object to be stored in a shared property. This section has shown you how to access and create your own resource dispensers by using the Shared Property Manager.

Handling Errors

It is important whenever developing components or applications in general that you handle errors. This is also true when developing MTS components because when MTS detects an unhandled exception, it shuts down execution of the offending thread of execution. This means that if your component has an unhandled exception, MTS will shut down the component and prevent any additional problems from occurring. Not catching errors can also cause, in some cases, the loss of the original error. The error returned is not in any way related to the original root cause of the error.

In the Java language, errors returned from methods are treated as exceptions similar to the way they are handled in Visual Basic. To handle errors under MTS, take care to catch exceptions in every function in which they can occur. This is accomplished by using `try` and `catch` when looking for exceptions. Your COM component written in Java can return errors by throwing an instance of `COMFailException` as shown in the code snippet that follows. This class is provided by the package `com.ms.com`.

```
If (oContext == null) then
    throw new COMFailException("Context is NULL");
```

Keeping track of errors could be important, so you might want to develop your own scheme for handling errors in which you could save the errors in a list. This way you might be able to create a call stack to determine where exactly an error occurred.

Debugging components that do not have good exception handling is a cause of aggravation for the developer. Thinking through the way you handle exceptions will save you time when developing MTS components. Handling exceptions will reduce strange results generated by MTS in mysterious circumstances. Good exception handling will report errors back to the client so you will have a well-behaved and well-developed application.

From Here...

In this chapter, you learned to create MTS components using Visual J++. You learned how simple it can be to develop a simple MTS component implementing the IObjectContext interface. You also learned to access the advanced features that MTS provides including transactions, role-based security, and shared properties. In addition, you learned about the issues and challenges related to developing components in Java, as well as issues and approaches to exception handling in MTS components.

Developing components in Java is becoming increasingly popular. The desire and need to develop MTS components continues to increase due to scalability needs of application primarily caused by the Web. Because MTS is an extension of COM and the predecessor to COM+, MTS development appears to be an integral part of future enterprise development.

For more information on COM and MTS development, see the following chapters:

- To learn more about Microsoft Transaction Server, see Chapter 5, "An Inside Look at Microsoft Transaction Server."
- For general information on creating COM components for MTS, see Chapter 14, "Creating COM Components for MTS."
- For information on how to develop COM components for MTS with C++, see Chapter 29, "Creating COM Components for MTS with Visual C++."
- To learn to develop MTS components with Visual Basic, see Chapter 27, "Creating COM Components for MTS with Visual Basic."
- To learn about building data access components for MTS, see Chapter 30, "Creating Data Access Components for MTS with Visual Basic and ADO."

CHAPTER 29

Creating COM Components for MTS with Visual C++

by John Pickett

In this chapter

Building a Simple MTS Component

Visual C++ is one of the most powerful and complete tools available for building Microsoft Transaction Server (MTS) components. Microsoft's Visual C++ extends the C++ programming environment by providing you with a feature-rich development environment and a vast array of extension libraries.

One of these extension libraries, the Active Template Library (ATL), is the most common tool for developing COM components for MTS. Visual C++ integrates this library into the development environment and uses wizards to greatly simplify the use of ATL classes. ATL, combined with the Microsoft Foundation Classes (MFC), provides the greatest flexibility for building reusable components.

In this chapter, you will become familiar with the issues involved in constructing small, fast, lightweight components for MTS with Visual C++. You will learn how to build the components and explore several techniques to exploit the feature-rich MTS runtime environment, such as enabling object recycling for building highly scalable enterprise applications. Familiarity with COM and the C++ language is assumed throughout the chapter.

The Active Template Library is a template-based library designed to provide developers with the tools to quickly build COM components. Rather than derive from a class to extend the functionality of the class, you create a new class from a template. Often ATL classes inherit from one or more template classes. Inheriting from multiple template classes enables a component to implement more than one COM interface. Components built for MTS are simply extensions to the existing COM support offered by ATL. Components built for MTS are implemented as in-process servers (dynamic link libraries, or DLLs).

To create an MTS-aware project, use the ATL COM AppWizard:

1. Choose File, New from the menu.
2. On the Projects page, select ATL COM AppWizard.
3. In the Project Name text box, enter LoadBalancerSrvr.
4. Set the proper directory in the Location text box. When all the options are set correctly, click OK (see Figure 29.1).

FIGURE 29.1

With the ATL COM AppWizard, you create a new ATL project.

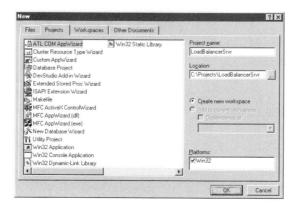

5. The ATL COM AppWizard—Step 1 of 1 dialog box appears (see Figure 29.2). Set the Server Type to Dynamic Link Library (DLL).

FIGURE 29.2
Use these settings for the ATL COM AppWizard—Step 1 of 1 dialog box.

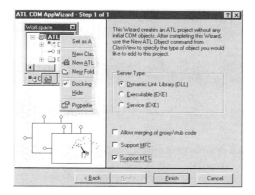

6. Select the Support MTS option.

7. Optionally, select Allow Merging of Proxy/Stub Code when marshaling interfaces is required; otherwise, it is contained in a separate DLL.

8. You may select Support MFC if you want to include the MFC libraries in the project.

9. Click OK when the New Project Information dialog box appears.

N O T E By selecting support for MTS, the ATL COM AppWizard adjusts the Project Build setting to include support for Microsoft Transaction Server. The libraries required for linking to the MTS DLLs are included in the Link properties of the project.

Using ATL to Build an MTS Component

To aid in the creation of COM objects, ATL provides standard implementations for IUnknown, IClassFactory, IClassFactory2, and IDispatch interfaces. ATL implements COM interfaces by inheriting from classes that contain pure virtual functions. To create a simple COM component for MTS, all that is required is to derive a new class from these standard templates.

Follow these steps to create an MTS component:

1. Choose Insert, New ATL Object from the menu to open the ATL Object Wizard (see Figure 29.3).

FIGURE 29.3

Use this dialog box to create a new ATL component.

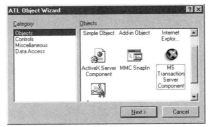

2. Select Objects in the Category list box and MS Transaction Server Component in the Objects list box.
3. Click Next to open the ATL Object Wizard Properties dialog box (see Figure 29.4).

FIGURE 29.4

With this dialog box, you specify the properties for your new ATL object.

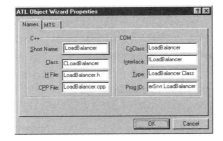

4. Enter LoadBalancer in the Short Name text box, and the wizard will generate the other fields in the dialog box.
5. Leave the default settings for the example and click OK to create the class.

Listing 29.1 shows how the ATL Object Wizard defined CLoadBalancer. CComObjectRootEx provides the default reference counting implementation. The object's class factory as well as the CLSID is provided by CComCoClass. The template class IDispatchImpl exposes the default IDispatch interface for the object.

Listing 29.1   DEFAULTLOADBALANCER.TXT—Default CLoadBalancer Definition

```
class ATL_NO_VTABLE CLoadBalancer :
    public CComObjectRootEx<CComSingleThreadModel>,
    public CComCoClass<CLoadBalancer, &CLSID_LoadBalancer>,
    public IDispatchImpl<ILoadBalancer, &IID_ILoadBalancer,
➥&LIBID_LOADBALANCERSRVRLib>


{
public:
    CLoadBalancer()
    {
    }
```

```
DECLARE_REGISTRY_RESOURCEID(IDR_LOADBALANCER)

DECLARE_PROTECT_FINAL_CONSTRUCT()

DECLARE_NOT_AGGREGATABLE(CLoadBalancer)

BEGIN_COM_MAP(CLoadBalancer)
    COM_INTERFACE_ENTRY(ILoadBalancer)
    COM_INTERFACE_ENTRY(IDispatch)
END_COM_MAP()

// ILoadBalancer
public:
};
```

Now that you have created a simple ATL component, you can begin to extend the component to take full advantage of the features in the MTS runtime environment.

Implementing `IObjectControl`

For components running under MTS, an object can implement the `IObjectControl` interface.

Every object running under MTS is associated with a context. An object's context is similar to the process context that an operating system maintains for a program. A component that implements the `IObjectControl` interface is notified when it is activated and deactivated within a given context. This enables the component to perform context-specific initialization and termination. The `IObjectControl` interface also enables you to specify whether your component can take part in object recycling (see Listing 29.2).

Listing 29.2   IOBJECTCONTROL.TXT—`IObjectControl` Interface

```
interface IObjectControl : public IUnknown
{
public:
virtual HRESULT STDMETHODCALLTYPE Activate( void) = 0;
virtual void STDMETHODCALLTYPE Deactivate( void) = 0;
virtual BOOL STDMETHODCALLTYPE CanBePooled( void) = 0;
};
```

CAUTION

Only the MTS runtime environment can invoke methods on the `IObjectControl` interface. The interface is not available to other clients, including the object itself.

To create an object supporting the `IObjectControl` interface, perform the following steps:

1. Choose Insert, New ATL Object from the menu to open the ATL Object Wizard.

2. Select Objects in the Category list box and MS Transaction Server Component in the Objects list box.

3. Click <u>N</u>ext to open the ATL Object Wizard Properties dialog box.

4. Enter `ImprovedLoadBalancer` in the <u>S</u>hort Name text box, and the wizard will generate the other fields in the dialog box.

5. Select the MTS tab (see Figure 29.5).

FIGURE 29.5

Use the Properties page to select MTS-specific properties for your new component.

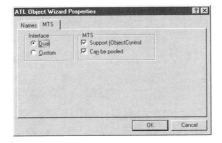

6. Select Support `IObjectControl` to implement the `IObjectControl` interface in the new component and Ca<u>n</u> Be Pooled to indicate that it can participate in an object pool.

7. Click OK to create the component.

The code snippet in Listing 29.3 shows the header generated by the ATL Object Wizard. `CImprovedLoadBalancer` is derived from `IObjectControl`. The three methods exposed by `IObjectControl` (`Activate`, `CanBePooled`, and `Deactivate`) are implemented as public methods in the class. `IObjectControl` is also added to the COM interface map enabling an object's client access to the interface through `QueryInterface`.

Listing 29.3   HEADEREXAMPLE.TXT—`CImprovedLoadBalancer` Class Definition

```
class ATL_NO_VTABLE CImprovedLoadBalancer :
    public CComObjectRootEx<CComSingleThreadModel>,
    public CComCoClass<CImprovedLoadBalancer, &CLSID_ImprovedLoadBalancer>,
    public IObjectControl,
    public IDispatchImpl<IImprovedLoadBalancer, &IID_IImprovedLoadBalancer,
    ➥&LIBID_LOADBALANCERSVRLib>
{
public:
    CImprovedLoadBalancer()
    {
    }

DECLARE_REGISTRY_RESOURCEID(IDR_IMPROVEDLOADBALANCER)

DECLARE_PROTECT_FINAL_CONSTRUCT()

DECLARE_NOT_AGGREGATABLE(CImprovedLoadBalancer)

BEGIN_COM_MAP(CImprovedLoadBalancer)
```

```
        COM_INTERFACE_ENTRY(IImprovedLoadBalancer)
        COM_INTERFACE_ENTRY(IObjectControl)
        COM_INTERFACE_ENTRY(IDispatch)
END_COM_MAP()

// IObjectControl
public:
    STDMETHOD(Activate)();
    STDMETHOD_(BOOL, CanBePooled)();
    STDMETHOD_(void, Deactivate)();

    CComPtr<IObjectContext> m_spObjectContext;

// IImprovedLoadBalancer
public:
};
```

When running under MTS, `CImprovedLoadBalancer` maintains a reference to its ObjectContext through the member variable `m_spObjectContext`. A reference to ObjectContext is obtained in the `Activate` method. It is released in `Deactivate` (see Listing 29.4).

CAUTION

Don't attempt to access an object's context in the constructor. Because the object has yet to be created, there isn't an associated `ObjectContext`.

Listing 29.4   OBJECTCONTROLIMPLEMENATION.TXT—`CImprovedLoadBalancer`

Implementation of `IObjectControl`

```
HRESULT CImprovedLoadBalancer::Activate()
{
    HRESULT hr = GetObjectContext(&m_spObjectContext);
    if (SUCCEEDED(hr))
        return S_OK;
    return hr;
}

BOOL CImprovedLoadBalancer::CanBePooled()
{
    return TRUE;
}

void CImprovedLoadBalancer::Deactivate()
{
    m_spObjectContext.Release();
}
```

N O T E The `Activate` method can initialize a newly created object's state as well as reinitialize the state from a component drawn from the object pool. ▩

Immediately after the object is deactivated, MTS invokes the `CanBePooled` method on the object's `IObjectControl` interface. If the method returns `TRUE`, MTS places the object in the corresponding object pool. The object is released if the method returns `FALSE`. When a client requests an instance of `CImprovedLoadBalancer`, MTS first looks in the object pool for an available instance; otherwise, a new one is created.

By pooling objects in this manner, MTS more efficiently manages the initialization time required for clients to gain access to a component. Object pooling is just one of the techniques MTS uses in providing an environment for building scalable applications.

Supporting Transactions

Performing work within transactions simplifies the task of building scalable components. Transactions isolate one client's work from another's. This prevents clients from interfering with one another during execution. Transactions also help components recover from errors by removing any changes that might have occurred before the error was encountered.

Every MTS component has a transaction attribute that is set in the MTS Explorer. When an object is created, MTS determines whether the object should begin a new transaction, should execute within an existing transaction, requires a transaction, or optionally doesn't use a transaction.

 T I P To change the transaction attribute of a component in MTS explorer, right-click the component and select Properties.

▶ For more information about using transactions in MTS, **see** Chapter 14, "Creating COM Components for MTS," **p. 413**

When a component executes inside a transaction, `ObjectContext` provides several methods in support of the current transaction:

- ▩ `IsInTransaction`
- ▩ `SetComplete`
- ▩ `SetAbort`
- ▩ `DisableCommit`
- ▩ `EnableCommit`

The `IsInTransaction` method tells a component whether it is currently executing in an existing transaction; however, this does not hold true if the component owns the transaction.

`SetComplete` and `SetAbort` are used to declare when a component has completed a unit of work. If the work is successful, call `SetComplete`. Otherwise, call `SetAbort`. When the current executing method returns to the client, MTS will deactivate the component, destroy the object, and recover resources.

For components executing within a transaction, SetComplete indicates that the object updates can be committed. If the component initiated the transaction, MTS attempts to commit the transaction. To cancel any updates, a component calls SetAbort. If any component running within the transaction calls SetAbort, the entire transaction will fail.

To retain state information about an object across multiple method calls, a component calls EnableCommit on its ObjectContext. The component's updates might be committed; however, MTS doesn't deactivate the object. If an object calls DisableCommit, the transaction is aborted when the object that initiated the transaction attempts to commit the changes.

Using Role-Based Security

MTS provides two basic security models—declarative and programmatic. Declarative security is configured with the Microsoft Transaction Server Explorer.

▶ For more information about declarative security, **see** Chapter 14, "Creating COM Components for MTS," **p. 413**

Programmatic security is provided by a component to determine whether the user is authorized to perform the client's request. The IObjectContext interface provides two methods for simple programmatic security:

- IsCallerInRole
- IsSecurityEnabled

The IsSecurityEnabled method determines whether security is enabled. If the MTS component is configured to run in-process with the base client, IsSecurityEnabled returns FALSE. To determine whether the direct caller is in a specific role, a component invokes the IsCallerInRole method on the object's ObjectContext. IsCallerInRole always returns TRUE when the component is running in-process. Listing 29.5 shows an example of programmatic security.

N O T E When a component is included in a library package, the component will run in-process of another hosting package. If IsCallerInRole is called by the component, be sure to define the roles required on the hosting package. ▨

Listing 29.5 SECURITY.TXT—Example of Using Programmatic Security

```
CComPtr<IObjectContext> spObjectContext
GetObjectContext(&spObjectContext)
if( spObjectContext.IsSecurityEnabled() )
    spObjectContext.IsCallerInRole( "Consultants")
```

The MTS security model exposes the ISecurityProperty interface. The ISecurityProperty interface provides access to the security ID of the current caller or creator. Using the security ID, a component can use the Win32 security APIs to provide custom access to its services. A reference to the ISecurityProperty interface is obtained by calling QueryInterface on the object's ObjectContext.

```
spObjectContext->QueryInterface(IID_ISecurityProperty,
➥(void**)pSecurityProperty)
```

N O T E Components written in Visual Basic should use the SecurityProperty object. The object returns the username as a string rather than a security identifier. ■

The ISecurityProperty interface is shown in Listing 29.6.

Listing 29.6   ISECURITYPROPERTY.TXT—The ISecurityProperty Interface

```
Interface ISecurityProperty : public IUnknown
{
public:
virtual HRESULT STDMETHODCALLTYPE GetDirectCreatorSID
➥(PSID __RPC_FAR *pSID) = 0;
virtual HRESULT STDMETHODCALLTYPE GetOriginalCreatorSID
➥(PSID __RPC_FAR *pSID) = 0;
virtual HRESULT STDMETHODCALLTYPE GetDirectCallerSID
➥(PSID __RPC_FAR *pSID) = 0;
virtual HRESULT STDMETHODCALLTYPE GetOriginalCallerSID
➥(PSID __RPC_FAR *pSID) = 0;
virtual HRESULT STDMETHODCALLTYPE ReleaseSID(PSID pSID) = 0;
};
```

Sharing State Among MTS Components

When developing an enterprisewide application, access to and synchronization of global information is an important aspect of system development. MTS provides resource dispensers to manage nondurable information within a distributed environment. The Shared Property Manager (SPM) is a resource dispenser used to share state information among many different components. For example, the SPM can be used to return the next value of a global counter.

N O T E Shared properties are only available to components running in the same MTS package. It is best to share information only in components located in the same DLL. ■

MTS provides three interfaces to create and access shared information:

- ISharedPropertyGroupManager
- ISharedPropertyGroup
- ISharedProperty

ISharedPropertyGroupManager is used to create Shared Property Groups (SPGs) and to gain access to existing groups. To create or access shared properties within a group, the ISharedPropertyGroup interface is provided. The ISharedProperty interface is used to set or retrieve the value of a shared property.

To gain access to a shared property, first create or gain access to an SPG, as shown in Listing 29.7.

Listing 29.7 CREATEGROUPMANAGER.TXT—Creating a Shared Property Group

```
#include <mtxspm.h>

CComPtr<ISharedPropertyGroupManager> spSharedGroupManager;
spSharedGroupManager.CoCreateInstance( CLSID_SharedPropertyGroupManager );
CComBSTR bstrName = "SharedGroup";
VARIANT_BOOL vntExists;

long nLock = LockSetGet;
long nRelease = Standard;
spSharedGroupManager->CreatePropertyGroup(bstrName, &nLock, &nRelease,
➥&vntExists, &spSharedGroup );
if( vntExists == VARIANT_TRUE )
{
    if(nLock != LockSetGet || nRelease != Standard )
    //  isolation and release not as expected
}
```

The CreatePropertyGroup method creates an SPG named SharedGroup if one doesn't exist, or it returns the existing shared group. The value of vntBool returns TRUE if the SPG exists and FALSE if a new SPG is created. The LockModes enumerated type defines two isolation levels for a property group. LockSetGet locks a property during a value call. If LockMethod is passed, all properties of the group are locked by the caller as long as the current method is executing.

 T I P When creating a property group, setting the SPG's isolation level to LockMethod is useful when several properties are dependent on each other.

ReleaseMode is an enumerated type that specifies when the SPG is released. If Standard mode is specified, the SPG is released when the last client releases the group. If Process mode is specified, the SPG is not released until the process in which it was created is terminated.

N O T E You should always determine whether the SPG exists. If it does, check the values returned in nLock and nRelease to determine the LockMode and ReleaseMode for the SPG. ▩

> **CAUTION**
>
> A component should not attempt to pass an SPG reference to another object. If you attempt to pass the reference outside the component that acquired the reference, it is no longer valid.

Listing 29.8 demonstrates how to gain access to a Shared Property (SP) within an SPG. `CreateProperty` creates or returns a new SP by name. An alternative way to create an SP is to call the `CreatePropertyByPosition` method.

After creating an SP with the `CreateProperty` method, you can access the property only through the `Property` method. If the property is created with the `CreatePropertyByPosition` method, the value of the property is accessed through the `PropertyByPosition` method. An SPG can contain properties identified by name and position.

Listing 29.8   SHAREDPROPERTY.TXT—Accessing a Shared Property

```
CComPtr<ISharedPropertyGroupManager> spSharedGroupManager;
spSharedGroupManager.CoCreateInstance( CLSID_SharedPropertyGroupManager );
CComBSTR bstrName = "SharedGroup";
VARIANT_BOOL vntExists;
CComPtr<ISharedPropertyGroup> spSharedGroup;
CComPtr<ISharedProperty> spProperty;

long nLock = LockSetGet;
long nRelease = Standard;
spSharedGroupManager->CreatePropertyGroup(bstrName, &nLock, &nRelease,
➥&vntExists, &spSharedGroup );
if( vntExists == VARIANT_TRUE )
{
    if(nLock != LockSetGet || nRelease != Standard )
    //  isolation and release not as expected
}

bstrName = "Counter";
spSharedGroup->CreateProperty( bstrName, &vntBool, &spProperty );
if(vntExists == VARIANT_FALSE )
{
    // initialize the property if necessary
}
VARIANT vValue;
VariantInit(&vValue);
spProperty->get_Value(&vValue);
```

Handling Errors

It is important for any code to handle errors or exceptions gracefully. This is also true with components running under MTS. When encountering an unhandled exception from a component, MTS assumes the process in which the component is running is unstable. MTS shuts down the process, which can impact any number of other components or base clients. Visual C++ provides powerful, structured exception handling to combat this problem. Exception handling enables components to detect errors and throw the error condition back out to the higher-level code that uses the component. Exceptions provide a path to communicate back to a base client that something unexpected has happened.

When an exception is caught, the ISupportErrorInfo interface enables the component to return error information to a base client. If the ISupportErrorInfo interface is implemented, the component provides an error object to its client.

 TIP

ATL provides the global function AtlReportError to initialize the error object. The error number, source, and description for the error object are the properties set through AtlReportError.

Listings 29.9 and 29.10 show the additions to CImprovedLoadBalancer for support of ISupportErrorInfo.

Listing 29.9   HEADERWITHERROR.TXT—Code to Add to ImprovedLoadBalancer.h

```
class ATL_NO_VTABLE CImprovedLoadBalancer :
    public CComObjectRootEx<CComSingleThreadModel>,
    public CComCoClass<CImprovedLoadBalancer, &CLSID_ImprovedLoadBalancer>,
    public IObjectControl,
public ISupportErrorInfo,
    public IDispatchImpl<IImprovedLoadBalancer, &IID_IImprovedLoadBalancer,
    ➥&LIBID_LOADBALANCERSVRLib>
{
public:
    CImprovedLoadBalancer()
    {
    }

DECLARE_REGISTRY_RESOURCEID(IDR_IMPROVEDLOADBALANCER)

DECLARE_PROTECT_FINAL_CONSTRUCT()

DECLARE_NOT_AGGREGATABLE(CImprovedLoadBalancer)

BEGIN_COM_MAP(CImprovedLoadBalancer)
    COM_INTERFACE_ENTRY(IImprovedLoadBalancer)
    COM_INTERFACE_ENTRY(IObjectControl)
    COM_INTERFACE_ENTRY(IDispatch)
END_COM_MAP()

// ISupportsErrorInfo
    STDMETHOD(InterfaceSupportsErrorInfo)(REFIID riid);

// IObjectControl
public:
    STDMETHOD(Activate)();
    STDMETHOD_(BOOL, CanBePooled)();
```

continues

Listing 29.9   Continued

```
    STDMETHOD_(void, Deactivate)();

    CComPtr<IObjectContext> m_spObjectContext;

// IImprovedLoadBalancer
public:
};
```

Listing 29.10   IMPLEMENTATIONWITHERROR.TXT—The New

CImprovedLoadBalancer

```
HRESULT CImprovedLoadBalancer::Activate()
{
    HRESULT hr = GetObjectContext(&m_spObjectContext);
    if (!SUCCEEDED(hr))
    {
        TCHAR szError [128];
wsprintf (szError, _T("Error!! GetObjectContext returned:  0x%x"), hr);
AtlReportError(CLSID_ImprovedLoadBalancer, szError,
➥IID_IImprovedLoadBalancer, hr);
    }
    return hr;
}

BOOL CImprovedLoadBalancer::CanBePooled()
{
    return TRUE;
}

void CImprovedLoadBalancer::Deactivate()
{
    m_spObjectContext.Release();
}

STDMETHODIMP CImprovedLoadBalancer::InterfaceSupportsErrorInfo(REFIID riid)
{
    static const IID* arr[] =
    {
        & IID_IImprovedLoadBalancer
    };
    for (int i=0; i < sizeof(arr) / sizeof(arr[0]); i++)
    {
        if (InlineIsEqualGUID(*arr[i],riid))
            return S_OK;
    }
    return S_FALSE;
}
```

Debugging MTS Components

Testing and debugging is an important step in developing components for MTS. Although it is not always easy or straightforward, debugging one or more components during system development will be necessary. You will find debugging your components on a single computer much easier than in a distributed environment. A component running successfully on a single computer will run as well when distributed from a remote server. There are several approaches to debugging an MTS component:

- Debugging without MTS support
- Debugging with Visual Studio
- Debugging using WinDbg

 T I P The Application Log in the Event Viewer is a valuable resource in helping to track down errors. MTS provides detailed information about the error as well as the package and object that generated the error.

Debugging Without MTS Support

Executing a component outside MTS is the simplest way to find programming errors; however, services provided by the object context, Shared Property Manager, and IObjectControl interface are not available. To guarantee MTS-specific code is not executed, use a compilation directive to remove all services provided by MTS. An example is shown in Listing 29.11.

Listing 29.11   COMPILEFLAG.TXT—Using a Compilation Directive

```
#ifdef DEBUG_MTS

    spLoadBalancer.CoCreateInstance(CLSID_ImprovedLoadBalancer);

#else
    CComPtr<IObjectContext> spObjectContext;
    spObjectContext.CreateInstance(CLSID_ImprovedLoadBalancer,
    ➥&spLoadBalancer );

#endif //MTS_BUILD
```

CAUTION

If your component implements the IObjectControl interface, the Activate method will not be called. You might need to move initialization code into the constructor when running a component outside MTS support.

To define the compilation directive in the project settings, complete the following:

1. Choose Project, Settings from the menu.

2. Select the C/C++ tab (see Figure 29.6).

FIGURE 29.6

Use this dialog box to customize the ATL project settings.

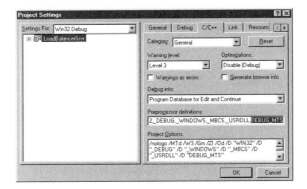

3. In the Preprocessor Definitions text box, add the symbol DEBUG_MTS.

TIP It might be useful to create another project configuration in the workspace. Then you won't have to check the settings; you'll only set the active configuration.

Debugging with Visual Studio

At times it is useful to debug a component running under MTS; however, this task is a bit more tedious. This technique enables you to run the component inside the MTS server process; a debug version of ObjectContext is used in the process.

Follow these steps to debug your MTS component in Visual C++:

1. Shut down the server process using MTS Explorer. Right-click My Computer and select Shutdown Server Process.

2. Open the Registry editor and add the following key:

   HKEY_LOCAL_MACHINE\Software\Microsoft\Transaction
   Server\Debug\RunWithoutContext

3. From Visual C++, choose Project, Settings from the menu.

4. Select the Debug tab (see Figure 29.7).

FIGURE 29.7
With this dialog box, you specify the project debug information.

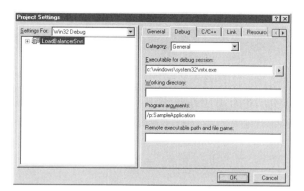

5. In the Executable for Debug Session text box, enter `c:\windows\system32\mtx.exe`.

6. In the Program Arguments text box, enter `/p:[name of package]` to indicate the package containing the component you want to debug.

7. Click OK.

8. Choose Build, Start Debug, Go to begin debugging.

Debugging a component in Visual Studio has the following effect on the `ObjectContext`:

- `CreateInstance` calls the `CoCreateInstance` API; transactions are not available.
- `SetComplete` and `SetAbort` have no effect.
- `EnableCommit` and `DisableCommit` have no effect.
- `IsInTransaction` returns `FALSE`.
- `IsSecurityEnabled` returns `FALSE`.
- `IsCallerInRole` returns `TRUE`.

Because the services provided by the `ObjectContext` are disabled, your ability to completely test a component is limited.

Debugging Using `WinDbg`

In some cases, it might be necessary to debug a component running in the full MTS runtime environment. The downside to this technique is you will not be able to step through each line of program execution. Using the debugger `WinDbg` provided by Microsoft, you can print messages to the `WinDbg` window using this API call:

```
void OutputDebugString(LPCTSTR lpOutputString);
```

By placing calls to `OutputDebugString` in strategic points during program execution, you will gain a feel for the behavior of the object while running under MTS.

Getting started building components is easy using the ATL wizards provided by Visual C++. Implementing the `IObjectControl` interface enables your component to be aware when MTS is activating or deactivating the object. Using Shared Property Groups, role-based security, and transactions will simplify the development effort to create successful MTS components. Shared Property Groups offer access and control to global data. Using transactions enables isolation of work and a greater capability to recover from unexpected errors.

As with any development effort, errors and exceptions must be handled gracefully. This is even more important when running in the MTS environment. An unhandled exception stops the MTS server process, which could impact other components. When you run into problems while your components are running, select the debugging technique that best fits the situation.

From Here...

In this chapter, you learned to create components for MTS with Visual C++. In particular, you explored many of the issues in creating components for MTS.

- For a better understanding of MTS, see Chapter 5, "An Inside Look at Microsoft Transaction Server."
- For more information on MTS components, see Chapter 14, "Creating COM Components for MTS."
- To learn about building MTS components with Visual Basic, see Chapter 27, "Creating COM Components for MTS with Visual Basic."
- To learn about building MTS components with Visual J++, see Chapter 28, "Creating COM Components for MTS with Visual J++."
- To learn about creating data access components for MTS, see Chapter 30, "Creating Data Access Components for MTS with Visual Basic and ADO."
- For information about building distributed applications, see Chapter 31, "Using Microsoft Transaction Server to Enable Distributed Applications."

Creating Data Access Components for MTS with Visual Basic and ADO

by Chris Zeigler

In this chapter

Using ADO in VB: An Overview

Microsoft Transaction Server (MTS) substantially improves scalability and simplifies programming for n-tiered applications. For client applications, a developer can ignore issues of concurrency and scalability, and use mid-tier components as in a single-user application. For mid-tier components, the developer needs only to focus on minimizing state between method calls and to implement a few very simple MTS methods.

The ActiveX Data Object (ADO) library is Microsoft's latest entrant into the field of data access components, and ADO has several features that make it stand out from the crowd. These features, along with special design considerations for MTS support, have placed ADO on the cutting edge of n-tiered client/server development.

First released with VB 4 Enterprise Edition (EE), Remote Data Objects (RDO) made significant advances in ways that applications access data stored in Open Database Connectivity (ODBC) enabled databases. Most importantly, RDO contributes fast access to ODBC without the complexity associated with the ODBC Application Programming Interface (API). ADO builds upon these principals of speed and simplicity and adds interesting new features, including access to other types of nonrelational data. For example, you can use ADO to access data as diverse as mail stores and directory services. ADO was designed with scalability and n-tiered client/server systems in mind, so it is a powerful tool for today's developers designing these types of systems.

Before RDO emerged, Data Access Objects (DAO) introduced the idea of simplifying data access interface for Visual Basic programs. DAO wrapped complex data access code with a simple object layer. RDO, and subsequently ADO, followed this object-oriented data access paradigm. Microsoft's approach to this paradigm in ADO has been positively affected by the need of developers for a scalable architecture. This need has spawned a much flatter object model than those of DAO and RDO. While the benefit of this may not be apparent at first, a flatter object model means fewer objects need to be created to get a specific task done, translating into lower overhead and higher scalability.

The flatter object model ties in well with one of the most important features of ADO, its ability to work in conjunction with MTS. Although ADO eliminates many problems associated with data access for n-tier applications, it is certainly not a panacea. Developers with a large amount of existing data access code that uses RDO should not rewrite that code to use ADO, unless there are apparent gains to be made by doing so. On the other hand, when designing new applications, software developers should seriously consider ADO because of what it can provide.

Working with MTS and Stateless Data Access Components

A primary goal for MTS is to enable an application to expand or scale to meet the needs of a multitude of users. One of the main features that MTS provides to assist in this scalability is just-in-time activation (JITA). JITA makes very efficient use of memory and process resources on the application server, but requires that a new instance of an object be indistinguishable from an existing instance. In other words, only stateless objects can take advantage of JITA.

When an application creates an instance of an object on an application server, that object uses memory and process resources. In many cases, the client application actually makes use of the object for a very small fraction of the time that the object is active. JITA allows the object to be active (using resources) only when the client application actually needs it.

When a client application requests a reference to an object that runs in the MTS environment, MTS returns instead a reference to a context wrapper object. To the client program, this context wrapper object is indistinguishable from the requested object.

This sleight-of-hand gives MTS control over the lifetime of the object. Because MTS maintains the only reference to the object, the Component Object Model (COM) removes the object from memory when MTS releases the reference. Furthermore, MTS can release the reference with no effect on the client. When the object invokes the `SetComplete` or `SetAbort` method, this indicates that the object is stateless: MTS releases its reference and the object is deallocated.

Even though MTS has released its reference and the object no longer exists, the client application still holds a reference to the context wrapper. To the client, this appears to be a valid reference to the MTS object. When the client uses that reference to invoke another method on the object, MTS activates a new reference to the object to carry out the work. This approach works because the object is stateless: The new instance is indistinguishable from the deallocated instance.

N O T E MTS 2 does not implement true object pooling. However, by using JITA and by keeping component DLLs loaded, MTS achieves most of the performance gains of object pooling.

When MTS does implement true object pooling, it will be an enhancement to the JITA process. Before creating a new instance of an object, MTS will first check the object pool to see if an instance of the requested type is available. If so, JITA will invoke the object's `Activate` method (if implemented) and use that instance to do the work requested by the client.

The programming practices described in this chapter work well in the current implementation of MTS, and will fully exploit object pooling when implemented. ▪

When using MTS, objects are not created and destroyed in the same manner as a traditional application. The client expects the component to exist as it was when it was first created. This means that the component cannot contain data left over from a previous activation. Components that behave like this each time they are used are considered stateless objects.

In order to take advantage of JITA, invoke the `SetComplete` or `SetAbort` method of the `ObjectContext` interface. In addition to their transactional semantics, both of these methods signal MTS that the object is now stateless, triggering JITA deactivation.

T I P MTS does not require components to be stateless, although stateless components are more scalable. For components which must maintain state between method calls, the EnableCommit and DisableCommit methods provide transaction management without triggering JITA.

In more concrete terms for the Visual Basic programmer, stateless objects contain no module-level variables that maintain values from the time that one of its methods is called to the next. For example, the data access component in the sample application, MTSDataAccess in the GADataAccess project, does not contain a property that specifies which database connection the data access object is for. If it were to contain this value, and the next client for the object did not want to update the same database, the component would be useless. Any variables that are specific to a certain instance must be reinitialized before they are recycled.

One way to make certain that module-level variables are reinitialized is to implement the Activate and Deactivate event methods in your object. These methods, along with the CanBePooled method, must be implemented when your class is implementing the Object Control interface. They can be used to reset any properties that contain state information. The Activate method is executed when a component is created or when JITA connects the component to a client. The Deactivate method is executed when MTS deallocates the component, either via JITA or because the client has released its reference. The standard VB class events, Initialize and Terminate, cannot be used reliably for this purpose because they are executed only when MTS creates or destroys an object, not when the object is recycled. Imagine that the MTSDataAccess object contained a property, DataSource, whose value it retained between method calls. In order to reset the property for the next base client of the component, you could reinitialize the DataSource property to vbNullString in the ObjectControl_Deactivate event method. Here is a simplified example of this hypothetical data access class:

```
'defined in the Microsoft Transaction Server Type Library
Implements MtxAS.ObjectControl

Private m_strDataSource As String
Private m_objContext as MtxAS.ObjectContext


Public Property Let DataSource(ByVal RHS As String)
    m_strDataSource = RHS
End Property

Public Property Get DataSource() As String
    DataSource = m_strDataSource
End Property

Private Sub ObjectControl_Activate()
    Set m_objContext = GetObjectContext()
End Sub

Private Function ObjectControl_CanBePooled() As Boolean
    ObjectControl_CanBePooled = True
End Function
```

```
Private Sub ObjectControl_Deactivate()
    m_strDataSource = vbNullString
    Set m_objContext = Nothing
End Sub
```

Part
IV

Ch
30

TIP The `Activate` method is a good place to acquire a reference to the context object. The `Deactivate` method is a good place to release all object references.

Another solution to the problem of eliminating state in a component, while still giving it all the data that it needs to perform its duties, is to remove all module-level variables and then create its methods differently. These methods should use arguments to pass all the data that the object needs at the time they are called. In order to keep the method calls simpler, it is important to ensure that only necessary arguments are passed to the method. This will require some thought at design time for the component, so plan ahead.

The following is the `Read` method of the `MTSDataAccess` class that demonstrates how methods can be written to require that all necessary data be passed at the time of the call:

```
Public Function Read(ByVal strConnect As String, ByVal strTableName _
    As String, Optional ByVal strFilterString As String) _
    As ADODB.Recordset

    On Error GoTo ErrorHandler
    Dim rsTemp As ADODB.Recordset
    Set rsTemp = CreateObject("ADODB.Recordset")

    With rsTemp
        'this is essential if using disconnected recordset
        .CursorLocation = adUseClient
        .Open ConstructSQLRead(strTableName, strFilterString), _
            strConnect, adOpenStatic + adOpenForwardOnly, adLockReadOnly

        Set .ActiveConnection = Nothing
    End With
    Set Read = rsTemp

    Set rsTemp = Nothing
    GetObjectContext().SetComplete
    Exit Function

ErrorHandler:
    App.LogEvent Err.Number & " " & Err.Description & TypeName(Me) _
        & ":Read", vbLogEventTypeError
    GetObjectContext().SetAbort
End Function
```

Another way to improve the performance of applications goes hand-in-hand with stateless components: Use the components for as little time as possible, thus allowing other clients to use the same object. The less time that a component is used, the more time other clients can use it, resulting in better scalability. By invoking `SetComplete` and `SetAbort` at the end of each method call, you can let MTS manage the object lifetime using JITA. The client application can acquire and hold a reference to the mid-tier component with no impact on scalability.

Working with MTS and Database Resources

One of the most costly operations in a database application is opening a database connection. Because this operation is so slow, many applications open a database connection at startup and hold the connection open until the program ends. This improves performance for the first application but has a negative impact on scalability. Each open connection requires substantial resources at the database server, and many servers will perform poorly with a large number of connections open. The solution is database connection pooling.

To understand how MTS deals with databases, you must first understand some relevant terms:

- Resource manager—Part of a system that manages persistent data. The best example of this in the sample application is the SQL Server. It manages the data in the system, which is a resource.

- Resource dispenser—A component that handles the nondurable components in a system. The resource dispenser that you are concerned with is the ODBC Driver Manager, which manages the pool of ODBC connections for the system.

Like your own components, the best way to use database resources within an MTS-enabled application is to employ them for as short a time as possible. This means you should get the resource as late as possible, do your work, and then release it as quickly as possible. This method for dealing with database connections is beneficial because it most effectively utilizes a feature called *connection pooling*, where connections are shared among clients. It is important to note that although connection pooling can be done with MTS, the ODBC resource dispenser actually performs the connection pooling.

N O T E   When using ADO with ODBC data sources, the ODBC/OLE DB bridge component replaces the ODBC driver manager. This component acts as an MTS resource dispenser and implements connection pooling.

When using ADO with SQL Server's native OLE DB interface, the OLE DB data provider acts as the resource dispenser and implements connection pooling.

There are several reasons why sharing, or pooling, database connections can be invaluable. Connections, like objects, consume resources when they are created. One of the most noticeable delays in many applications is the amount of time required to obtain a connection. Connection pooling allows several users to use a single connection to a database. For this pooling to work, all users must be using the same database and the same login credentials. This means that each user cannot use his own username and password. This precludes the use of database enforced security and, in cases where it is used, auditing. To simplify things, one database user and password should be established for the application to login. To enforce security in an application, user authentication must be performed in the program itself. MTS and Windows NT provide mechanisms for assisting with security implementation.

Connection pooling does not currently preallocate connections. They are created when they are initially requested, so there will still be a delay when the first ODBC connection is requested. Figure 30.1 shows the Connection Pooling tab of the ODBC Data Source Administrator, which is found in the Windows Control Panel.

FIGURE 30.1

Connection pooling can be configured by using the Windows ODBC Data Source Administrator.

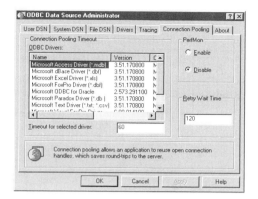

In order for an application to make best use of connection pooling, there needs to be some thought given to the data access components at design time. Traditionally in DAO and RDO, a connection object of some sort was opened to initiate a database connection. The time required to create the connection was usually significant. This time penalty meant that in the past, the connection was usually held open longer. In fact, some applications hold reference to the connection object for the entire time the application is executing. When using ADO, this option is discouraged but could still be used. A better option is to open and close the connection each time it is needed.

To open a result set in RDO or DAO, their respective connection objects usually provide a function that returns the new Recordset object. ADO's approach is to include an ActiveConnection argument on the Open method of the Recordset object. No longer is an open connection needed to create the Recordset object; instead, a connect string can be used as the ActiveConnection argument for the Open method. Conversely, if there is already a Connection object open, it can be passed to the Recordset's Open method. ActiveConnection is also a property of the Recordset object. This can be set to a valid connect string, or a Connection object after the Recordset has been created. When the Recordset is no longer needed, it can be closed using the Close method.

 T I P   When using database connection pooling, always open and close database connections within a single method.

The following code class demonstrates how a connection should be opened and closed within a single method:

```
Private Sub QueryExec(ByVal sConnect As String, ByVal sQuery As String)

    Dim adoConn As ADODB.Connection
    Set adoConn = New ADODB.Connection =

    With adoConn
.Open sConnect  _
```

```
        .Execute sQuery
        .Close
End With
    Set adoConn = Nothing
```

N O T E   In most cases, ADO connect strings are almost identical to RDO connect strings. They vary
slightly depending on the ODBC driver being used.

The ADO connect string includes an optional Provider clause, which defaults to
`Provider=MSDASQL;`—the OLE DB provider for ODBC drivers. Use the provider clause to specify a
non-ODBC data source. To use the Microsoft OLE DB Provider for Microsoft Index Server, for example,
use the clause `Provider=MSIDXS.1;`. █

Another benefit of pooling database connections is limiting the number of licenses that are
needed for a given number of users. For example, if an application holds open a connection for
the time the application is open, a connection is needed for each instance of the application that
is running. This can quickly consume the maximum number of concurrent connections that
are allowed on a database. If connections are pooled, the application can still perform better
while using fewer connections. This means that a database license with a smaller maximum
number of concurrent connections is needed, which in turn translates to a cost benefit. There
is no hard and fast rule for determining how many connections will be needed for a given number of users because this is highly dependent on the amount of data access that an application
performs. The ODBC resource manager does not provide a way to set the maximum number
of connections that will be opened while pooling, so remember to trap for an error if running
out of connections is a possibility.

T I P   MTS does not actually perform the connection pooling. Connection pooling is available to any
application using ODBC (with a thread-safe driver) and the ODBC Driver Manager 3 or above, or to any
application using OLE DB with an OLE DB provider that supports pooling.

Passing Data Between Service Layers

There are many performance problems associated with using several computers to run different service layers in a three-tiered system. Performance problems can arise when passing data
between processes on a single machine, but speed usually will suffer even more when the
components must communicate across a network. One of the big problems is that there are no
convenient ways to pass large amounts of data between layers without incurring performance
penalties because of marshaling. Many three-tiered applications use arrays to pass data between the tiers. These arrays allow a single variant argument, or property, to encapsulate a
large amount of data. For instance, query results can be translated into a two-dimensional array
and returned from a function. Because of the time required to loop through the array, passing
in this manner can slow things down on the back end when bundling the array, as well as on
the front end when unpacking.

With ADO, an easier way to bundle the data is provided by the `GetRows` method implemented in the `Recordset` object. `GetRows` is a function that returns a variant containing a two-dimensional array of all the data in the recordset. There are three optional arguments for the function:

- `Rows`—A long expression that indicates the maximum number of rows to retrieve. This can be especially useful for improving the responsiveness of applications. This is optional; the default is `-1` (all rows).

- `Start`—A string or variant that represents a recordset bookmark indicating where to start retrieving rows in the recordset. This argument, in conjunction with the maximum number of rows, can be used to read blocks of rows at a time. This is optional; the default is the first row in the recordset.

- `Fields`—Useful for limiting the number of columns that should be returned by the `GetRows` call if not all columns are needed. This argument is an array that contains the names of the columns that should be returned. This is optional; the default is all fields.

Part

IV

Ch

30

TIP You should probably steer away from using the Fields argument. It is much more efficient to limit the number of rows in the actual query used to open the recordset. This saves not only the time required to pass unnecessary columns between tiers, but also the time required on the database to retrieve the extra columns.

Although passing arrays works well, it can become awkward, especially when looping through the resulting array and keeping track of the order of the columns in the array. ADO provides another more convenient method of passing data, with a special type of ADO recordset called a *disconnected recordset*. A disconnected recordset is created in the same manner as a regular recordset, but you must use the `adUseClient` option for the `CursorLocation` property of the `Recordset` (set before opening the `Recordset`). After the `Recordset` is created, the `ActiveConnection` property is set to `Nothing` to disconnect the recordset from the database connection. As far as your component goes, the connection is closed now, although in reality, it is put back in the pool. At this point the recordset can be passed to the business services layer to load objects, or even to user services to populate forms.

Most applications should not contain a reference to the ADO library in any project other than the project that contains the data services layer. To allow the other service layers to deal with the recordset, Microsoft has provided a smaller library that just contains the ADO recordset. (It is called the Microsoft ActiveX Data Objects Recordset 2 Library in the Visual Basic references dialog.) Projects in the business services layer or user services layer should have a reference to this library if they need to deal with a disconnected recordset.

`Recordset` objects are helpful for more than just passing data between the layers of an application; in fact, they provide convenient ways of editing that data. When the client cursor is used with disconnected recordsets' data, the recordset can be edited on the client and then sent back to the server to update the data. This is known as a *batch update*.

Understanding ADO in a Three-Tiered Application

In three-tiered development, one of the main concepts is to encapsulate functionality in each respective layer. The data services tier encapsulates reading, writing, inserting, and deleting from the tables in the database. These operations are performed on behalf of the business services layer. In order for the two layers to communicate with each other, there must be some way for them to exchange data. As previously mentioned, ADO provides a recordset object that can be passed in order to transport data from one layer to the other.

One way to update the data in the database is by using disconnected recordsets. Because a disconnected recordset can be updateable, it could be passed all the way to the user interface, updated by the user, and returned to the server to apply changes as a batch. Using updateable recordsets is not an ideal solution in a three-tiered application because it is more difficult to enforce the business rules with the business objects.

An alternate approach is to design the business objects in such a way that their methods accept a recordset as an argument. Using this approach, all business rules can be validated in a single place, a Save method, for example; there is no need to use Property Let routines to verify some business rules, and other routines to verify others. Additionally, all the data is available to the method, yet there is no need for the business object to contain data between method calls. Business objects that are coded this way are merely containers for methods that enforce business rules. This is a very scalable approach, but does not provide immediate feedback to the user when a business rule is violated. Instead the feedback is given when the user applies the changes. When immediate feedback is necessary, business objects with properties are needed.

A business object that contains properties and methods is a more traditional approach. This approach validates business rules both when the properties are set and when methods are performed, and therefore immediately informs the user when a business rule is violated. With this type of business object, it is not beneficial to pass a recordset for rule validation. It is more appropriate to code the business object to call on a separate data access component to retrieve, save, and delete from the database, using primary keys to update or read one row at a time.

For the sake of performance, these data access components should not use updateable recordsets or cursors to perform these functions. Updateable recordsets cause excessive network traffic, as well as consume overhead on either the database server or the computer where the recordset is updated. It is more efficient to design the components to construct Structured Query Language (SQL) statements on-the-fly when asked to perform a certain function. Any function that just reads data should always use a read-only recordset to improve efficiency.

For a practical example, look at the MTSDataAccess component. There are five public methods in this class: Read, Insert, Update, Delete, and GetData.

All these methods except GetData have two arguments in common: a connection string, which enables the component to connect to any database, and a table name, on which to perform the specific operation. The connection string is obtained from the TSPartitioner object, which will be discussed later. When the data access object is asked to read data from a table through the Read function, it constructs a select statement for that table which contains all the columns in the table. Here is the function called from the Read method to create a SQL statement:

```
Private Function ConstructSQLRead(ByVal strTableName As String, _
                                  Optional ByVal strFilterString As String) _
              As String

   Dim strSQL As String

   If (strFilterString = vbNullString) Then
      strSQL = "Select * From " & strTableName & ";"    Else
      strSQL = "Select * From " & strTableName & " Where " &
      ➥strFilterString & ";"
   End If
   ConstructSQLRead = strSQL

End Function
```

For more efficient queries, be sure to design a component that allows the user to limit the number of columns that are requested, instead of requiring that all columns in the table be selected. In this example, all the columns are needed when loading the business objects. As mentioned earlier, the Read method returns a recordset that the business object uses to populate all its properties.

When inserting in the table, the business object passes two arrays to the data access object's Insert method. One array contains a list of the column names in the table; the other, a list of values that should be written into those columns.

The Update method works much the same as the Insert method, but for an Update method it is important for the data access object to know which row in the table will be updated. This means that there are two additional arguments, the column name of the primary key and the value of the primary key of the row that is to be updated.

The Delete method only requires the name of the primary column in the table and the value of the primary key for the row that is to be deleted.

```
Public Sub Delete(ByVal strConnect As String, _
                  ByVal strTableName As String, _
                  ByVal strFilterString As String)

   On Error GoTo ErrorHandler

   Dim cmdDelete As ADODB.Command

   Set cmdDelete = CreateObject("ADODB.Command")

   With cmdDelete
      .ActiveConnection = strConnect
      .CommandText = ConstructSQLDelete(strTableName, strFilterString)
      .Execute
   End With

   Set cmdDelete = Nothing

   Exit Sub
ErrorHandler:
   #If MTS Then
```

```
            GetObjectContext.SetAbort
        #End If

        App.LogEvent Err.Number & " " & Err.Description & _
            TypeName(Me) & ":Delete", vbLogEventTypeError

End Sub
```

The GetData function is unique in two ways: It is used to retrieve data from more than one row, and it may retrieve data from multiple tables. To allow this, GetData accepts an argument that contains a valid SQL statement along with any joins or complex criteria. The GetData function is needed because when an object is loaded there are often related properties that are also loaded. These properties are not saved into the database, but make the data much more useful. For example, the MTSTimeSheet object loads the employee name, which is useful for display purposes, but is not saved with every billing entry. Rather, the employee name is stored in a different table, and the EmployeeID is saved with the time sheet data. Like the Read method, the GetData method returns a recordset for processing by the business object.

```
Public Function GetData(ByVal strConnect As String, _
                        ByVal strSQLStatement As String) _
                As ADODB.Recordset
    On Error GoTo ErrorHandler

    Dim rsTemp As ADODB.Recordset
    Set rsTemp = CreateObject("ADODB.Recordset")

    With rsTemp
        'this is essential when using disconnected recordset
        .CursorLocation = adUseClient
        .Open strSQLStatement, strConnect, adOpenStatic, _
            adLockReadOnly

        '********************************************************
        'NOTE: CANNOT SET THE ActiveConnection PROPERTY TO Nothing UNLESS
        'THE CursorLocation IS SET TO adUseClient
        '********************************************************
        Set .ActiveConnection = Nothing
    End With
    Set GetData = rsTemp

    Set rsTemp = Nothing
    Exit Function
ErrorHandler:
    App.LogEvent Err.Number & " " & Err.Description & _
        TypeName(Me) & ":GetData", vbLogEventTypeError
    App.LogEvent strSQLStatement
End Function
```

 TIP When a business component uses multiple tables to populate its properties, you may want to consider creating a database view to do joins and exclude unnecessary columns. When querying the database to load the components, use the view instead of the base table. This strategy reduces query preparation at runtime and eliminates complex SQL from your Visual Basic code.

An approach that may be more efficient than creating SQL statements at runtime is to use stored procedures in the database to update all tables. This means that for each table there is a stored procedure with a parameter for each column in the table. The stored procedure parameters are filled in by the data access component, and then the stored procedure can be executed using ADO's Command object. This scheme may save some time because the stored procedure does not have to be prepared every time it is executed, unlike the SQL statement, which is prepared at runtime before execution.

As previously mentioned, due to the requirement for partitioning, the data access component needs to be capable of updating tables in multiple data sources. To enable the data access component to be this flexible, it is not designed to store a particular connection or connection string. When the MTSBillingEntry or MTSTimeSheet object is going to perform a database operation such as a Select, it uses the consultant's name and the partitioner object, TSPartitioner, to determine which data source to use. There is a method on the partitioner object with a single argument, the consultant's name. The partitioner object uses the consultant's name to determine in which data source the consultant's information is stored. The partitioner then returns a value containing a connect string for the data source to the MTSBillingEntry or the MTSTimeSheet object. Those objects then pass the connect string to the data access object, which will in turn use it to connect to the appropriate database server. Notice that the data access object connects to the database right before executing the query, and disconnects right after the query is complete. This allows the database connection to be recycled quickly. This code snippet from the LoadForDate method of the MTSTimeSheet business object shows how the TSPartitioner is used to obtain data from a specific data source:

```
Dim oPartitioner As TSPartitioner
Dim oTempBE As MTSBillingEntry
Dim oDataAccess As GADataAccess.MTSDataAccess
Dim dbRS As ADOR.Recordset
Dim strSQL As String
Dim lngEmployeeID As Long


#If MTS Then
    Dim oContext As ObjectContext
    Set oContext = GetObjectContext
    Set oPartitioner = oContext.CreateInstance("GATimeBilling.TSPartitioner")
    Set oDataAccess = oContext.CreateInstance("GADataAccess.MTSDataAccess")
#Else
    Set oPartitioner = New TSPartitioner
    Set oDataAccess = CreateObject("GADataAccess.MTSDataAccess")
#End If
    'get the name of the datasource from the partitioner
    m_strDataSource = oPartitioner.TimeSheetDatabase(m_strUserName)
    Set oPartitioner = Nothing

    'raise an error if the datasource was not obtained
    If m_strDataSource = vbNullString Then
        Err.Raise 4550, TypeName(Me) & ":LoadForDate", _
                  "Invalid or missing datasource"
        LoadForDate = False
        Exit Function
```

Because the data access component does not store the data source connect string (or any other properties for that matter), it fits the definition of a *stateless component*.

Exploring Transactions

One of the most important places that transactions come into play is in the data access tier; after all, it's the work of the data access tier that gets committed or rolled back. The transactions are most important when changing the database and less important with the read methods. Traditionally, in client/server systems, the database management system is responsible for ensuring that transactions are committed and rolled-back successfully at the request of the program. MTS can handle transactions, which allows them to have a much wider scope. In the past it was complicated to design a system with transactions that encompassed multiple data sources or types of data. MTS seamlessly provides this capability. Even if your applications do not span multiple databases, it can be beneficial to use MTS to control transactions because the ease of implementing transactions is unsurpassed in the client/server realm.

> **CAUTION**
>
> Although ADO provides transaction support through ODBC, it should not be used in conjunction with MTS transactions, if only for the sake of simplicity. Furthermore, ODBC and MTS transactions used in conjunction will usually cause unpredictable results.

The central component in MTS transactions is the `ObjectContext`. The `ObjectContext` object contains information to help manage transactions and security, in addition to providing a mechanism for creating new objects on the server side. There is not a method provided for creating the `ObjectContext`, although a reference to it can be obtained. It is implicitly created when an object is activated by MTS. Each MTS component has a context. The context object provides several methods that, when called, will commit or abort a transaction to leave the database in a consistent state.

N O T E   For your Visual Basic components to be able to use MTS transactions and the `ObjectContext`, their projects must contain a reference to the Microsoft Transaction Server Type Library. ▨

For an object to be included in another object's transaction, the child object has to inherit information from the parent's context. In order for the child to get this information, it must be created within the parent's `ObjectContext`. This is done by calling the `CreateInstance` method inside the parent component. For the parent to actually get a handle to its own `ObjectContext`, it uses the `GetObjectContext` method. This method can be called each time the context is needed, or once if the reference is stored in an object variable. The latter is the more efficient way, provided the `ObjectContext` will be used multiple times in a procedure. The following code segment is from the `Save` method of the `MTSBillingEntry` component; it demonstrates how the `GetObjectContext` method can be used to obtain a reference to the `ObjectContext`. Note that in this segment, conditional compilation is used so that the code can be debugged in the Visual Basic environment:

```
#If MTS Then
    Dim oContext As ObjectContext
    Set oContext = GetObjectContext()
    Set oDataAccess = oContext.CreateInstance("GADataAccess.MTSDataAccess")
#Else
    Set oDataAccess = CreateObject("GADataAccess.MTSDataAccess")
#End If
```

To ensure that a child object obtain the correct context from its parent, the child object may not be created from the base client. The base client must create the parent object, and the parent object must create all other objects that are to be included in the same transaction. This is not to say that the base client may not directly reference any of the child objects. An object *may* be passed to the client after it has been created.

In the preceding code snippet, MTSBillingEntry creates a MTSDataAccess object using the CreateInstance method. Remember, this means that the MTSDataAccess object is in the same transaction as the MTSBillingEntry object, so if the transaction is aborted in either component, both components' work is rolled back.

A developer may choose to commit or rollback at any point that seems appropriate. ObjectContext implements two methods that are used to commit or roll back transactions. The first is the SetComplete method. This method is used if the work of the component was successful and the changes to the database should be committed. The second is the SetAbort method which should be used if the processing was not successful and the transaction should be rolled back. Keep in mind that whenever one of these two methods is called, MTS assumes that the object is ready to be reused and the component is immediately deactivated. Your components that have a reference do not have to destroy their references at this point, but beware that if it is used again, you may very well have a reference to a different component of the same class. This is when it is important to limit the amount of state data stored in your objects.

For those components that are designed to hold state, there are two different transaction methods that should be used to ensure that they are not deactivated. These two methods are also implemented in the ObjectContext. The two methods are called DisableCommit and EnableCommit. DisableCommit is used to tell MTS that the transaction should not be committed, but that the object is not ready for recycling and therefore should not be deactivated. The EnableCommit method indicates to MTS that the object is in a state where the transaction can be committed, but that it is not yet at a point where it should be reused.

The MTSBillingEntry component provides a practical example of how to use transactions with data access components. When an update is performed on a database, whether it is an insert, update, or delete, you need to commit the transaction if and only if the entire operation was completed successfully. Because errors are raised to the calling routine when an error occurs, you can be confident that the operation has been completed successfully if the end of the method is reached. Therefore the SetComplete method is called at the end of the Save method. At several points in the Save method there are indications that will show whether an operation can be successfully completed or not. For example, the following code sample is from the MTSBillingEntry component:

Part

IV

Ch

30

```
#If MTS Then
    Dim oContext As ObjectContext
    Set oContext = GetObjectContext()
    Set oDataAccess = oContext.CreateInstance("GADataAccess.MTSDataAccess")
#Else
    Set oDataAccess = CreateObject("GADataAccess.MTSDataAccess")
#End If

    ' Retrieve the assignmentID & rolecode for this project code
    strSQL = "SELECT A.AssignmentID,A.RoleCode, A.EmployeeID " & _
     "FROM Assignment A,Employee E WHERE E.EmployeeID=" & _
     "A.EmployeeID AND LoginID='" & m_strUserName & "' and" & _
     "A.ProjectCode='" & m_strProjectCode & "'"

    Set dbRS = oDataAccess.GetData(m_strDataSource, strSQL)

    If dbRS.RecordCount <> 1 Then
#If MTS Then
        oContext.SetAbort
#End If
        Err.Raise 4501, TypeName(Me), _
          "Assignment ID or Role Code not found for Project Code '" & _
          m_strProjectCode & "' and LoginID='" & m_strUserName & "'"

        dbRS.Close
        Set dbRS = Nothing
        Set oDataAccess = Nothing
        Exit Sub
    Else  ' project code exists only 1 time
        m_lngAssignmentID = dbRS.Fields("AssignmentID").Value
        m_strRoleCode = dbRS.Fields("RoleCode").Value
        lngEmployeeID = dbRS.Fields("EmployeeID").Value
    End If

    dbRS.Close
```

In this example, the data access component is being used to obtain an Assignment ID and a Role code for a given employee on a given project. If a single row that matches all criteria is not retrieved, then an error is raised and the transaction is aborted. If a row is retrieved, variables are set to store the values in several columns from the recordset.

When using this type of error handling, the SetAbort method must be called wherever rules are violated in the method. Another way to handle this is to trap for errors enabling error handling using the On Error GoTo statement. With this kind of error trapping, SetAbort can be called once in the error handler, which eliminates the need for the SetAbort method to be called in many different places in the method. This is the type of error handling that is used in the data access component. Here is the Insert method of that component:

```
Public Sub Insert(ByVal strConnect As String, ByVal strTableName As String, _
    aFieldNames As Variant, aValues As Variant)

    On Error GoTo ErrorHandler

    Dim cmdInsert As ADODB.Command
    Set cmdInsert = CreateObject("ADODB.Command")
```

```
    With cmdInsert
        .ActiveConnection = strConnect
        .CommandText = ConstructSQLInsert(strTableName, aFieldNames, aValues)
        .Execute
    End With

    Set cmdInsert = Nothing

    Exit Sub
ErrorHandler:
    #If MTS Then
        GetObjectContext.SetAbort
    #End If

    App.LogEvent Err.Number & " " & Err.Description & _
      TypeName(Me) & ":Insert", vbLogEventTypeError

End Sub
```

All four of these transaction methods allow components to tell MTS that a transaction should be committed or rolled back. The only missing piece is a way to start transactions. ODBC and most other transactions begin programmatically when they are needed. MTS does not work the same way; rather than programmatically beginning transactions, MTS automatically begins all transactions. This means that the developer designs a component to behave a certain way with transactions, and the transaction is started when the component is activated. There are four transaction modes that MTS defines for components:

- NoTransactions—This is the option that MTS assumes most components will use and therefore is the default for new components when they are imported into their packages. An easy way to tell if a component should be set with this option is whether the component calls either SetComplete or SetAbort. If the component calls these methods, it should not be set up to use this mode.

- UsesTransaction—This option is used if the type of component is not affected, regardless of whether it is in a transaction. If an object of this type is created by an object that is in a transaction, then the new object participates in the transaction. If the object is created by an object that is not in a transaction, then the new object does not participate in the transaction.

- RequiresTransaction—This option should be used if the component needs to be in a transaction. If it is called from an object that is in a transaction already, then there is no problem. If it is called from an object that is not in a transaction, then a new transaction is created for this new object.

- RequiresNewTransaction—This option is used when the new object always needs its own transaction, regardless of whether the calling object is in a transaction. A new transaction is started whenever an object with this mode is activated.

There are two ways to set the transaction mode for the components that you create. When creating objects with Visual Basic, you can set one of these options with the property sheet for the object, as shown in Figure 30.2.

Part
IV

Ch
30

FIGURE 30.2

The Visual Basic Class property sheet allows you to set the MTSTransactionMode.

N O T E If your Visual Basic project is not an ActiveX DLL, it cannot run in the MTS environment, and you will not have the option of setting the MTSTransactionMode on the class property sheet.

The other way that you can set the transaction mode for your components is through the Transaction Server Explorer. The Transactions tab of the property sheet contains the four transaction mode options, as shown in Figure 30.3.

FIGURE 30.3

Use the component property sheet in MTS Explorer to set the transaction mode property.

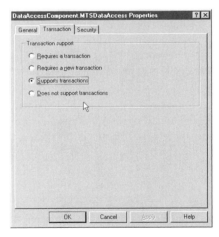

For MTS to handle transactions in a database setting, it enlists the help of the ODBC Driver and the ODBC Driver Manager. Transactions are started by invoking the ODBC Driver Manager each time a database connection is obtained. The driver manager is responsible for examining the component's object context to determine if the component is participating in a transaction. If a new transaction is needed, the driver manager calls a method on the ODBC Driver to begin the transaction. Transactions are committed or rolled back through the same path when the object context's respective function is called.

MTS actually performs automatic transaction processing behind the scenes, without the component explicitly using the `SetComplete` or the `SetAbort` method. The transaction is completed by MTS when the last reference to an object is destroyed. This is important to keep in mind, because if your code never calls `SetComplete`, `SetAbort`, `DisableCommit`, or `EnableCommit`, the transaction is automatically *committed* when the last reference to the object is dropped. For the sake of clarity in your code, you should probably explicitly commit or abort transactions, even though this functionality is provided.

Strategies for Improving Performance and Scalability

Now that I've covered the basic mechanics of using ADO and building MTS components with VB, let's review some techniques for improving performance and scalability:

- Asynchronous query execution allows an application to continue with other processing while waiting for a long-running database operation. The new events in ADO 2 allow your application to be notified when the asynchronous operation is complete.

- Database partitioning distributes the load in the data services tier.

- Multiple recordsets allow an application to retrieve a large amount of complex data with a single database operation.

- Stored procedures allow an application to invoke complex database processing with a single query.

Asynchronous Recordsets and Events

ADO asynchronous recordsets and events are two powerful new additions to ADO 2 that ship with Visual Studio 6. Events, in conjunction with asynchronous operations, allow programmers to speed the execution of their applications and improve the perceived responsiveness of data access components.

Asynchronous recordsets and queries permit applications to begin a time-consuming query, and then continue with other tasks while the query is executing. This allows the user to resume work more quickly. The actual time that it takes to execute the query may not be reduced, but because the user can carry on with other tasks, it makes the application more responsive and certainly more useful. This ability to return control to the user is especially useful when executing large stored procedures or obtaining large amounts of data for reporting purposes. Opening recordsets and running queries are not the only things that can be done with a database asynchronously. Connections also can be opened asynchronously, although connection pooling means that this will only really save time the first time a particular connection is opened.

Events are a vital feature of ADO that allow the application more freedom when using asynchronous database operations. Because other operations can continue while the database is doing its work, the application needs some way of being informed when the database is done, so that the user may be notified, or some other processing started. This is the purpose of events in ADO. When an ADO component, such as a `Recordset`, is declared using the keyword `WithEvents`, Visual Basic allows event procedures to be written that do special processing when they are fired. This is analogous to a command button or any other control's events. When a button is clicked, the `Click` event is fired and the code in the button click event procedure is executed. When declaring an ADO object with events, it must be a class-level variable. To access the event procedures in the Visual Basic development environment, declare the variable `WithEvents`—for example,

```
Private WithEvents m_dbRS As ADODB.Recordset
```

Next, use the object combo box on the top left of the code editor to select the name of the variable that you declared. The procedure combo box on the right side of the editor now contains all the possible events that you can trap for the type of object that you are using, as shown in Figure 30.4.

FIGURE 30.4

The procedure combo box on the right side of the VB editor window contains all the events that can be trapped for a specific object.

To open a recordset asynchronously, use the `adAsyncExecute` option on the `Open` method of the `Recordset` object:

```
Public Sub OpenRecordset(ByVal strConnect, _
    strSQLStatement)

    On Error GoTo ErrorHandler

    Set m_dbRS = New ADODB.Recordset

    m_dbRS.Open strSQLStatement, strConnect, _
    adOpenStatic + adOpenForwardOnly, adLockReadOnly, adAsyncExecute

Exit Sub

ErrorHandler:
    App.LogEvent Err.Description
End Sub
```

To execute stored procedures or other update queries asynchronously, use the connection object. The connection object can be used by creating a new object, attaching the connection to the database, using the `ActiveConnection` property and then running the execute method with the command text and the `adAsyncExecute` option. The event `ExecuteComplete` is raised when the query is complete. Events may also be raised to give messages to the application about the state of the query.

 Events may not always fire when you expect them to. For example, if the query does not take very long to execute, the event procedure may never run.

Database Partitioning

In order to facilitate a large number of users and consequently, an ever-growing amount of data, there must be some way to make the database scalable. An easy way to make the database capable of storing vast amounts of data without causing a bottleneck when large numbers of people need access at the same time is to use multiple servers to hold the data. Instead of replicating all the data on multiple computers, it is more efficient to split some of the data up and store different data on each server.

In the sample application, this partitioning was accomplished by storing data for some consultants on one database and others on another database. The scheme that was used to divide up the consultants was by the first letter of their last name. All the data that is pertinent to the consultants is partitioned in this way. This scheme allows the data to be split up in a logical manner, and the consultant's name can always be viewed to determine on which database server his information resides. The data that is not applicable to the consultant, such as the project or client information, is replicated on all the servers so that there is no need to look at different servers for different types of information. For a given consultant, all the data that is needed for queries can be found on a single server.

Multiple Recordsets

Multiple recordset queries are another time-saving feature of ADO. With multiple recordset queries, several SQL queries can be sent to the database at one time. This is an efficient way of executing queries because it makes the most of the database server's time. There are also fewer trips across the network because the queries are sent in one trip and the recordsets are sent in another. Multiple recordsets could be used in a situation where several business rules are validated with different queries.

Multiple recordset queries are basically the same as a regular query, but contain two SQL statements separated by a semicolon. For example, the following is a valid SQL statement that will return two recordsets:

```
"SELECT * FROM Project; SELECT * FROM Assignment"
```

The results of both queries are sent back in one recordset object even though they may have different columns and totally unrelated data. The recordsets are processed like any other recordset, by looping through it, but when the results of the first recordset have been processed, the next recordset is accessed by using the `NextRecordset` of the `Recordset` object. The `NextRecordset` method returns a reference to the next recordset and is used in the following manner:

```
Set dbRS = dbRS.NextRecordset
```

The recordset that is being set to the `NextRecordset` does not have to be the same one; in other words, the following statement is also valid:

```
Set dbRS2 = dbRS.NextRecordset
```

There is no inverse method in ADO that supports going backward through recordsets.

N O T E   Although SQL Server supports multiple recordset queries, not all databases do.

Using Stored Procedures

Many three-tiered applications make extensive use of stored procedures because they can take much of the processing burden off the business services server. Stored procedures are especially useful when performing extensive database operations that require little intervention. For example, a stored procedure could be very useful when performing a *cascading delete*. A cascading delete is one in which a parent object is being deleted and the operation subsequently removes all the associated child objects. In this instance, it is much more efficient to use a stored procedure to remove all the rows than using several delete statements to delete from each table. Another benefit of stored procedures is the speed at which they execute. There is no need for the database management system (DBMS) to prepare the stored procedure each time it is run. Keep in mind that while stored procedures can also be used to retrieve recordsets from the database, stored procedures are generally less flexible than generating SQL `Select` statements at runtime.

To execute a stored procedure, the ADO `Command` object is used. Executing a stored procedure is much the same as running a query that returns no results. The `CommandText` property of the `Command` object is set to the name of the stored procedure in the database. The `CommandType` property can then be used to tell the command object that the command being executed is a stored procedure. This is useful for optimizing the execution of the command. The `Parameters` collection and the `Parameter` object are then used to define any parameters of the stored procedure. Finally, the stored procedure is executed.

The following code could be used to execute a stored procedure that creates a new task in the consultant billing database. This imaginary stored procedure has two parameters, one for the new task code and the other for the new task description:

```
Private Sub CreateNewTask(ByVal intTaskCode As Integer,
➥ByVal strTaskDesc As String)

    Dim conDBConsBill As ADODB.Connection
    Dim cmdNewTask As ADODB.Command
    Dim prmNewTaskCode As ADODB.Parameter
    Dim prmNewTaskDesc As ADODB.Parameter

    'open the connection to the database
    Set conDBConsBill = New Connection
    conDBConsBill.Open "dsn=consbill"
```

```
'create the new command and set its properties
Set cmdNewTask = New Command
With cmdNewTask
    .ActiveConnection = conDBConsBill
    .CommandText = "CreateNewTask"
    .CommandType = adCmdStoredProc
    .CommandTimeout = 15
    .Prepared = True
End With

'create the first parameter and set its properties
Set prmNewTaskCode = New ADODB.Parameter
With prmNewTaskCode
    .Name = "tskcode"
    .Type = adNumeric
    .Direction = adParamInput
    .Value = intTaskCode
End With

'create the second parameter and set its properties
Set prmNewTaskDesc = New ADODB.Parameter
With prmNewTaskDesc
    .Name = "tskdesc"
    .Type = adVarChar
    .Size = 18
    .Direction = adParamInput
    .Value = strTaskDesc
End With

'append the parameters and execute the stored procedure
cmdNewTask.Parameters.Append prmNewTaskCode
cmdNewTask.Parameters.Append prmNewTaskDesc
cmdNewTask.Execute


conDBConsBill.Close
Set conDBConsBill = Nothing
Set cmdNewTask = Nothing
Set prmNewTaskCode = Nothing
Set prmNewTaskDesc = Nothing

End Sub
```

The parameters collection and the parameter object are vital when using stored procedures, because all but the most trivial procedures have parameters of some sort. To use parameters in the stored procedure, a new parameter object is created. The properties of the parameter object are set, including the name, data type, and the direction (input or output). The parameter is then appended to the already created command object using the `Parameters Append` method.

Understanding Error Handling and Debugging

Many errors that occur in the data access layer can impact the users of the system, but those errors generally do not produce messages that are useful for the user. For example, if a database error occurs, it may stop the functioning of the system, but many times there is nothing that the user can do to correct the problem. Consider a problem with execution of a SQL statement; the user does not need to know that a column does not exist. It is probably a better strategy to inform the user that an error occurred but not to go into detail about what happened. The user can then contact the system administrator to correct the problem, providing that the system administrator has a way to know what happened to cause the error. Visual Basic provides a very convenient method for logging errors of any type. Those errors can be logged to the event log in Windows NT or to a file in Windows 95/98. By using the event log, your error message can be very detailed yet not confuse the user with error codes or table names. The other advantage is that it is not necessary for the user to write down a long error message to tell the system administrator what error occurred. The system administrator merely looks at the NT event log on the appropriate machine to determine what happened.

The procedure for using the event log in Visual Basic is actually quite simple, and utilizes the App object that is available to every VB program. The App object has a method called LogEvent, which accepts two arguments: the LogBuffer (required), which is the actual text that is written to the log, and the event type (optional), which is a long value that indicates the type of the event. There are constants defined for three different event types: vbLogEventTypeError, vbLogEventTypeWarning, and vbLogEventTypeInformation.

TIP Visual Basic programs cannot write to the event log while they are running in the Visual Basic environment. The program must be compiled. If you need to use the event log while debugging in the environment, write an ActiveX DLL with a single class that writes to the event log.

The application log can also be a valuable debugging tool while developing MTS applications. Because components cannot be run under MTS while using the VB environment to debug them, there is no way to tell what parts of an application are doing what. If the application log is used to write an event every time something significant happens, it is possible to tell which parts of an application are performing as expected and which parts are not.

From Here...

This chapter explained how the ActiveX Data Objects and MTS technologies can be used in Visual Basic to create scalable data access components. Visual Basic can be used to create robust and functional data access components for three-tiered applications. Both MTS and ADO provide functionality that increases VB's capabilities and makes development even more rapid than with VB alone. In other chapters you can learn more about other tools in Visual Studio that assist in development of data access components as well as more specifics about how some of the concepts introduced in this chapter, such as MTS, work.

- For more information about MTS see Chapter 5, "An Inside Look at Microsoft Transaction Server."
- To learn more about databases, specifically SQL Server, be sure to read Chapter 8, "An Inside Look at Microsoft SQL Server."

- For more specific information about ADO, read Chapter 26, "Building Client Front Ends with Visual Basic."

- To read about creating MTS objects with VB, see Chapter 27, "Creating COM Components for MTS with Visual Basic."

Part

IV

Ch

30

Using Microsoft Transaction Server to Enable Distributed Applications

by Don Lykins

In this chapter

Managing and Deploying MTS Components

Since the mid-80s, PC software developers have been competing with mainframe programmers for credibility. Arguably the highest performing computers in the world were mainframes and, if an application required more than 300 or so concurrent users, the mainframe choice was automatic. Mainframes offered transaction processing at break-neck speeds, where client/server solutions mainly offered graphical interfaces. A common adage was to leave power processing to the mainframe. However, the late 1990s ushered in a new era of technology called multitier or n-tier computing.

Microsoft Transaction Server (MTS) has enabled a whole new method of designing client/server applications. This method exploits the concept of *components*—discrete units of application code that deliver specific functionality. By deconstructing an application into components, a number of advantages can be achieved. Component-based application architectures enhance flexibility, scalability, and code reuse. In short, applications can now be developed which are scalable, fault-tolerant, and fully extensible. Multitier, component-based architectures have the power to attack jobs reserved for mainframes in the past, and to do so with inherently more adaptable paradigms and tool sets.

Creating components for distributed applications is done with programming languages such as Visual Basic, Visual J++ or Visual C++. In fact, any language capable of creating Component Object Model (COM) components can be used to create components for MTS (although some make it easier than others). However, managing and deploying these components in an n-tier architecture can be complex. Microsoft has made this task easier by creating an administrative console that can be used to configure and deploy multitier applications. Known as the MTS Explorer, it is one of the first applications designed for the newly launched Microsoft Management Console (MMC), a standard framework Microsoft has created to provide a common interface for all administrative applications.

Understanding Multitier Computing

Deploying a component-based system involves many levels of complexity. In the basic form, three tiers of components are created: a client application, middle-tier objects, and a data services tier. The client application, known as the *base client* in the MTS world, can be developed using a variety of COM-based application development tools. To be classified as a base client, it must run outside the MTS environment, usually on a desktop workstation as a standalone application process. However with the increasing popularity of Microsoft's Web-based technology, the use of Active Server Pages (ASP) has slightly changed the definition of base-client applications. Although an ASP-based application is still considered a base client, much of its processing can be done on a mid-tier server running within the same process as other MTS objects, thus creating a hybrid MTS environment

Mid-tier objects are usually COM-based DLLs which run within the MTS runtime environment. They reside in the MTS environment as components, stored in packages, which are created and managed through the MTS Explorer. The middle tier is generally the location of business logic components, which encapsulate the business rules that are followed as a particular organization conducts its daily operations.

The data services layer can be composed of a wide variety of data sources, including traditional databases, but also encompass other forms of structured and non-structured data. Database objects are often just stored procedures residing on the database server.

If an n-tier distributed MTS environment is your objective, careful planning of component design and deployment is required. Development should first be done in a one-tier, single computer environment before deploying to multiservers. This will greatly increase the ability to debug the system at the component level. A component that works well in a one-tier single computer environment will often work just as well in a multitier structure. It is highly recommended that a test environment be established where multiple clients are used to stress test the MTS component.

▶ For more information about creating components for MTS, **see** Chapter 14, "Creating COM Components for MTS," **p. 413**

▶ For a more detailed view of creating MTS components with Visual Basic, **see** Chapter 27, "Creating COM Components for MTS with Visual Basic," **p. 809**

Part
IV

Ch
31

What Is the Microsoft Management Console?

MMC provides a programmable framework for the administration of applications and system resources. Independent Software Vendors (ISVs) can create components, dubbed snap-ins, for managing virtually any type of application or system. A snap-in is an ActiveX control developed to a specific Microsoft Application Programming Interface (API) which runs in the container provided by MMC. Snap-in files are designated with an .msc extension. One such snap-in, known as the MTS Explorer, is used to administer MTS. Every MTS component, whether networked or local, ranging from packages and roles to statistics, is administered through this snap-in developed specifically for MTS by Microsoft.

Using the MTS Explorer

MTS is managed through MMC via the MTS Explorer. If you have installed the Windows NT Option Pack, the most common method of installing MTS 2, the MTS Explorer can be launched by selecting Start, Programs, Windows NT Option Pack, Transaction Server, MTS Explorer. Another alternative, if MMC is already loaded on your workstation, is to locate the file mtxexp.msc through Windows Explorer and execute it directly. The basic MTS Explorer interface will then appear (see Figure 31.1), identifying administrative icons in the left pane, with My Computer icon in right pane.

FIGURE 31.1

The Transaction Server Explorer used within MMC.

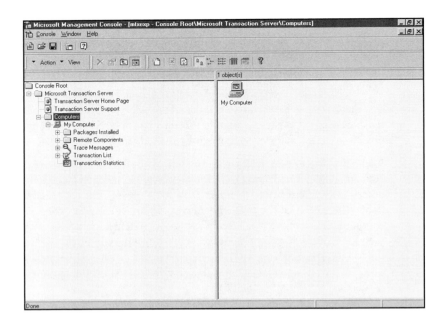

Later in this chapter the administrative capabilities of the MTS Explorer will be discussed.

ON THE WEB

Microsoft maintains a page on its Web site dedicated to system management technology such as MMC. Documents covering this system management strategy can be found at http:// www.microsoft.com/management/. Frequent visits to this site will keep you current on MMC and other related topics.

For the remainder of this chapter, the MTS Explorer will be used to install a sample application designed specifically for this book. This application is a Time Sheet collection application that might be used as a key part of a Consultant Billing system. The application is described in more detail in Appendix A, "The Sample Application Suite." In this chapter, you will learn how to use the MTS Explorer to install mid-tier components on the MTS server, and take the necessary steps to register these components with client computers so they can be called from front-end applications.

The components required to deploy the sample application are listed in Table 31.1. In addition to the DLLs and type libraries that make up the mid-tier components for the application, there is an ActiveX control that manages time sheet information in a grid format (the OCX file), and a front end called TimeEntry.exe, developed in Visual Basic 6.

Table 31.1   Components of the Time Sheet Sample Application

DLLs	Type Libraries	OCXs	EXEs
GABroker	TimeBilling	GASullivanTimeSheet	TimeEntry2
GABrokerFactory	TimeBillingExt		
GADataAccess			
GATimeBilling			
LoadBalancerSvr			
TimeSheet			
TSPartitionerSvr			
TSValidatorSvr			

Part
IV

Ch
31

Creating a Package

A package is nothing more than a group of ActiveX components (DLLs) written to Microsoft's COM specification. In addition to the characteristics of standard COM components, there are a few guidelines specific to MTS that you should adhere to when creating these DLLs. The MTS *executive* is a key element of the MTS runtime environment, intercepting calls to the components in a package and providing services in addition to those built into the components themselves. Packages run in a single process, wrapped by the MTS executive. That is, all DLLs within a package run inside the same process as the parent process mtx.exe. Each package creates an instance of the process mtx.exe. Packages can be distributed on multiple Windows NT Servers, thus providing for increased scalability.

You could develop your applications such that each component (DLL) is included in a different package, which executes on a separate machine, thus creating a completely distributed environment. This extreme case, however, would rarely be appropriate and could decrease overall system performance. Network traffic would increase, as components must constantly communicate between servers. An optimized MTS distributed system will deploy an appropriate number of mid-tier servers to meet the requirements of a particular system, consequently reducing the overhead required to support multiple components on multiple servers.

▶ For a discussion of multimachine architecture when deploying MTS components, **see** Chapter 25, "Clients, Servers, and Components: Design Strategies for Distributed Applications," **p. 727**

N O T E   There are two types of packages: library and server. A library package runs in-process from the client who created it, and a server package runs as its own process. The setup wizard defaults to a server-type package.

Here are the steps required to create a package for the sample Time Sheet application:

1. Launch the MTS Explorer. The remaining instructions assume you will run the Explorer on the mid-tier server on which you are installing components. You can also run the Explorer on a remote computer and register one or more mid-tier servers for administration.

2. After MMC has been launched, you will see the interface for the MTS Explorer, which consists of two panes. The left pane displays a hierarchical view of the computers you have registered and their packages and components. The right pane displays the contents of a selected icon or folder.

3. To begin the process of creating a package, click the plus sign (+) to the left of the Packages Installed icon in the hierarchy of My Computer. This expands the hierarchical display of its contents in the left pane. You will see several packages already installed (see Figure 31.2). Icons of the installed packages appear in the right pane.

FIGURE 31.2

The Transaction Server Explorer displaying currently installed packages.

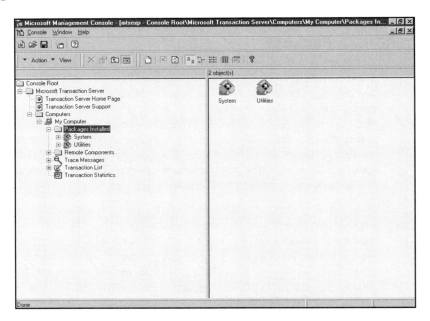

4. To create a new package, click the Packages Installed folder in the left pane. When this is highlighted, choose New, Package from the Action menu. The Package Wizard starts.

5. Click the button labeled Create an empty package.

6. In the next dialog box, enter the name of the new package. In this case enter ConsBill2 and then click Next (see Figure 31.3).

FIGURE 31.3

Use descriptive names when creating a package. This will aid in troubleshooting as your MTS components increase in number.

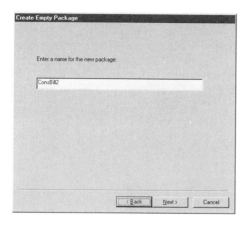

7. Select the package identity by entering a username to administer this package, or you can use the default setting as the current user. The package will run under the account specified (see Figure 31.4).

FIGURE 31.4

In the Set Package Identity window, you can administer the account context under which the package will be run.

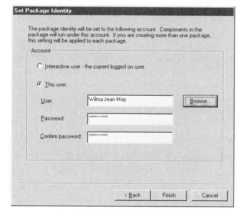

Interactive User means the current user. Whatever active user is currently logged into the machine, if selected, can manage the package. The package will only run if someone is logged into the machine. The package will then use the actively logged-in user as its identity.

This User means that you can specify a user. The package will run with the identity of the user ID specified, even without having a user logged in to the machine.

8. Click the Finish button to complete the package creation.

9. Repeat steps 4 through 7 and create another package named GABroker Factory.

10. Your MTS Explorer window should now contain at least two packages, ConsBill2 and GABroker Factory (see Figure 31.5).

FIGURE 31.5

After packages are installed, they appear in the right pane when the Packages Installed icon is selected.

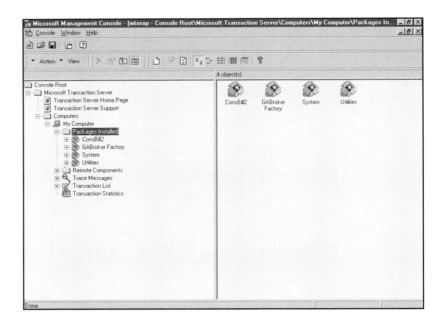

 You can modify package properties such as security, user identity, and description by first highlighting the package and then selecting Properties from the Action menu, or by right-clicking the package and selecting Properties.

Installing Components

Components refer to COM components such as ActiveX controls in the form of DLLs, which execute within the MTS environment as described earlier. A *type library* may also be included to describe all interfaces within a component. This provides important information for the Distributed COM (DCOM) infrastructure used by MTS to pass parameters. Any parameters or arguments required by mid-tier components are passed from the calling client application to the mid-tier server in a process known as *marshaling*. Marshaling is the concept of moving arguments between two processes running in different address spaces. It is the procedure of sending method parameters across process boundaries.

N O T E   A type library is a file that contains descriptions of exposed objects, properties, methods and collections. Object library (.olb) files contain type libraries. Type libraries that are shipped as standalone files use the extension .tlb.

The following are the steps required to install COM components for the Time Sheet application:

1. Install the type libraries first. Click the plus sign (+) to the left of the ConsBill2 package icon. Two folder icons appear, Components and Roles (see Figure 31.6). Click the Components icon and then choose <u>N</u>ew, Component from the Action menu. The Component Wizard starts.

FIGURE 31.6

A package has characteristics defined by components and roles.

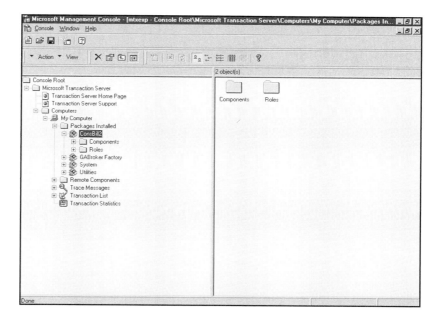

2. Click the button labeled <u>I</u>nstall New Component(s).

   In the Install Components dialog box, click the <u>A</u>dd Files button. Locate the type libraries TimeBilling.tlb and TimeBillingExt.tlb. Add them to the components list. Notice that the <u>F</u>inish button is grayed. This is because you haven't added any COM components yet, just libraries containing descriptions of the objects. Verify that the type libraries are installed correctly (see Figure 31.7).

FIGURE 31.7

A list of installed type libraries appears in the dialog box.

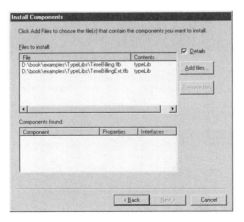

3. Click the <u>A</u>dd Files button, locate the following DLLs, and add them to the package:

- GADataAccess.dll
- GABroker.dll
- LoadBalancerSvr.dll
- GATimeBilling.dll
- TSPartitionerSvr.dll
- TSValidator.Svr.dll

4. Verify that the DLLs are all listed as shown in Figure 31.8. The exact order of the components is not important. The list box Components Found should contain all components, and the Interfaces column should indicate found.

FIGURE 31.8

The components found in the selected files.

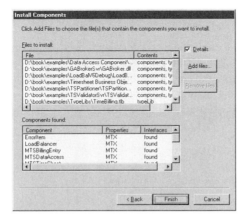

5. Click <u>F</u>inish, and the installation of COM objects for the ConsBill2 package is complete.

6. Click on the plus sign (+) to the left of the GABroker Factory package icon.

7. Click the Components icon and then choose <u>N</u>ew, Component from the Action menu. The Component Wizard starts.

8. Click the button labeled <u>I</u>nstall New Component(s).

9. Click the <u>A</u>dd Files button and add the same two type libraries as in step 2 and the GABroker Factory DLL. Verify the installed component (see Figure 31.9).

FIGURE 31.9
The Components Found list box displays the objects of the GABrokerFactory.dll.

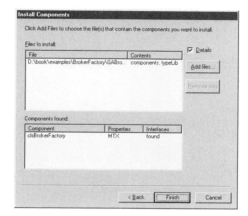

10. Click <u>F</u>inish, and the installation of COM objects for the GABroker Factory package is complete.

11. Click the plus sign (+) to the left of each component of both the ConsBill2 and GABroker Factory package icons. Verify that the components are installed correctly (see Figure 31.10).

FIGURE 31.10
With the Components folder selected, all installed components (DLLs) appear in the right pane.

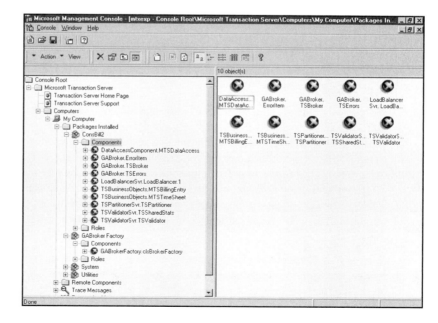

T I P Every time you change a component (DLL), you must remove it from the package and reinstall the component.

Viewing Package Properties

Each package has multiple properties identifying components, such as roles, interfaces, and methods. View the ConsBill2 package and its contents by clicking the plus sign (+) to the left of each component (see Figure 31.11).

FIGURE 31.11

Methods are objects within a component and can be displayed by selecting the Methods folder in the left pane.

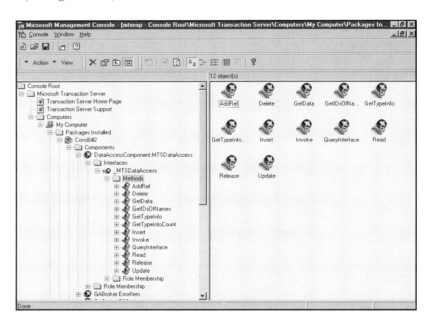

Defining Roles

When designing an application, security should always be considered early in the design cycle. MTS offers an extremely flexible security model defined by the use of roles. Roles enable the security for an MTS package by allowing you to define which users are permitted to invoke specific interfaces within a component. You define roles representing specific types of users that may run the application. As components for the system are being written, the functionality provided by the components may be limited to users who are in a particular role. For example, some of the capabilities of the sample Time Sheet application are only available if the user is a member of the role HR, indicating that he or she is a member of the Human Resources department.

Microsoft recommends defining a parallel set of groups within the Windows NT domain containing the user accounts that will be used to run the application. In other words, if you have defined a role called HR, create a corresponding group called HR Users in your Windows NT domain with User Manager for Domains. You can now enable a particular user to access HR functionality by simply adding him or her to the HR Users group. Spending time defining user access and role security will prove invaluable down the road in any development project.

N O T E   The important point to understand about roles is that when you are *creating* your components you don't know or care who will eventually be assigned to particular roles. During the design of the system, as you capture user requirements, you identify the different types of users that will run the system and you establish corresponding roles. Later, when you *deploy* the application, you can assign appropriate people to the different roles. As people within the organization change jobs and responsibilities, their role membership can be easily changed to match. ▪

After user groups and roles are created and clear links are established between the two, administrative tasks, such as associating every role with a group, become much easier; the tasks are now handled by a Windows NT administrator who simply adds users to the groups. Application components can check role membership before performing an operation by calling the IsCallerInRole method.

Part

IV

Ch

31

CAUTION

An MTS application using role security should check role membership to determine if the caller may continue with a privileged operation. Proper fail-safe mechanisms should be in place to ensure that security violations terminate processing. Such violations/failures can occur when an MTS component is improperly loaded or the component is executed outside the MTS context.

TIP   Within MTS components, all users access the database through the package user ID based on the Package Identity (described earlier in this chapter). Thus database access will not be through the user IDs of those users running the base client application, but through the ID established for the package. If database auditing is required for an application, the business components should contain separate auditing logic.

In the following example, you will define your user ID to have a role of HumanResources and can therefore modify certain data elements in the application that are specific to an employee in the Human Resources department:

1. Click on the Roles folder for the package ConsBill2.

2. To create a new role, click the ConsBill2 Roles folder in the left pane, and then choose New, Role from the Action menu.

3. In the next dialog box, enter the name of the new role, in this case HumanResources (see Figure 31.12). Be sure to spell the name of the role *exactly* as it is shown here. The role definitions for a package must exactly match those roles used when coding system components.

FIGURE 31.12

Roles establish security for an MTS package and establish levels of access.

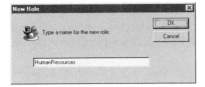

4. Click <u>O</u>K to add this role, and you will see the role added in the right pane.

5. Repeat steps 1 through 4—except this time, add the role ProjectMGR.

6. Repeat steps 1 through 4 again, adding the role Consultant.

7. Verify that all roles are installed correctly for package ConsBill2 (see Figure 31.13).

FIGURE 31.13

Selecting the Roles folder displays the installed roles in the right pane.

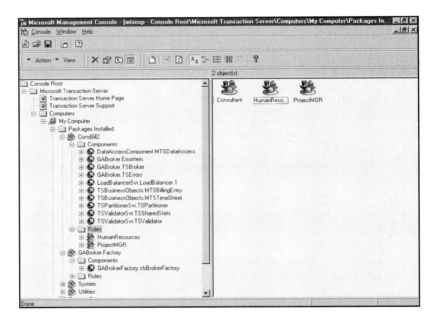

Adding Users to Roles

After you have defined the roles needed by the system and added them to the packages you have created on your mid-tier computer, you are ready to add specific users and groups to those roles. Just as network file sharing and printer access permissions are easier to manage if the users are placed in groups, so too with role permissions. You can assign individual users to a role with the MTS Explorer, and in some special cases this may be warranted, but in general it is best to assign one or more groups to a particular role.

If you have followed the suggestions given earlier in the chapter, you have already defined a set of Windows NT groups that match up with the roles defined for the sample application. This simplifies role management because now role membership can be managed by the same people who normally control network access permissions, using the same administrative tool—namely, network administrators with Windows NT User Manager for Domains.

The basic process of assigning a user or group to a role is as follows:

1. To add a user to a Role, click the plus sign (+) to the left of the Role, in this case `HumanResources`. This displays the user's folder.

2. Click the user's folder, and then choose <u>N</u>ew, User from the Action menu. The Add User Wizard starts.

3. From the Add User and Groups dialog box, select the users or groups of users you want to add. Notice you can add from your current domain or any trusted domain listed. For this example, you should add your own name from the domain you are currently logged in to (see Figure 31.14). You can add any domain user or group, such as Everyone, Domain Users, Domain Guests, Domain Administrators, and so on. You also can add multiple users or groups.

FIGURE 31.14
Adding users and groups to a role is implemented through normal Windows NT domain security.

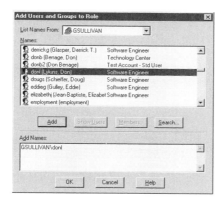

4. Click <u>O</u>K to add the users or groups to the `HumanResources` role. For this example, no users are required for the GABroker Factory package.

 TIP Each MTS package runs as a separate server process. If you configure components to run in-process, role checking is disabled.

Exporting Packages

After your application has been created, you need to export the package. A proper export will create a PAK file along with associated components such as DLLs and type libraries. It will also create an EXE file (executable application) that can be used to register the mid-tier components in this package on appropriate base client computers so that they will properly connect with the correct mid-tier server(s). In this example, ConsBill2.exe will be created.

In addition, you might want to move a package to another MTS machine for a number of reasons. Exported packages can be used to create a mid-tier utilizing multiple servers, where components are distributed across several MTS-enabled machines. Or you may simply need to move the package to a new server as part of routine maintenance or upgrading of hardware. This can be done easily using the import/export feature of the MTS Explorer. Ensure you have administrative rights on the MTS machine or the export will not create the necessary files and directories for import.

The following steps describe how to export the package ConsBill2:

1. Ensure you have the ConsBill2 package installed (see Figure 31.15).

FIGURE 31.15

Selecting the Packages Installed icon displays all components that were created using the Package Installation Wizard.

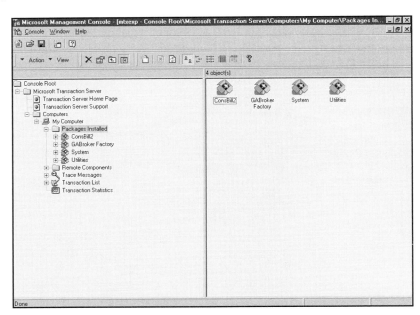

2. Click on the ConsBill2 icon in the left pane and then choose Export from the Action menu. The Export Wizard starts.

3. In the Export Package dialog box, enter the path where you would like to store the package. The MTS Explorer will create a name for you; however, you can change the name (see Figure 31.16). You have the option of saving the roles with the package, which is recommended.

FIGURE 31.16
The Export Package
dialog box.

Part
IV

Ch
31

N O T E A package file has the .pak extension. After exported, the directory containing the .pak file will also contain the DLLs and TLBs associated with the package. ▨

4. Click the Export button, and the export file will be created with the .pak extension. If you view the directory contents, you will notice it contains every DLL file along with a .pak file. You should also notice a clients subdirectory, which contains an EXE file that can be used to register the mid-tier components in this package on appropriate base client computers so that they will properly connect with the correct mid-tier server.

5. If no errors occurred during the process, this package has been successfully exported.

 T I P You can view the package file (.pak) with a text editor such as Notepad. This file lists all properties for the package and for each component.

Importing Packages into MTS

You can import packages, along with all of their associated components (DLLs, TLBs), using the MTS Explorer. The import steps, using the ConsBill2 example, follow. In order to demonstrate how to import the ConsBill2 example, you must first delete the ConsBill2 package from the machine you've been using, or use another MTS server. If you want to import the package you've just created on the same server, delete the package by right-clicking the ConsBill2 package icon in the left pane and choosing Delete from the pop-up menu (see Figure 31.17). A confirmation box will appear; click Yes. Notice that the ConsBill2 icon has been removed from the Packages Installed list. Alternatively, you can register another MTS server in your MTS Explorer and import the package on that server. Of course, you can also physically move to another MTS server and launch the MTS Explorer there.

FIGURE 31.17

Deleting packages from within the MTS Explorer will remove all components referenced to that package.

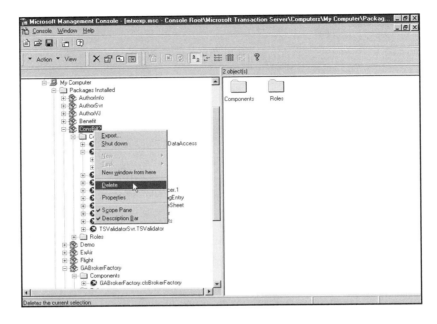

To import a package that has already been defined and exported, follow these steps:

1. Click the Packages Installed folder in the left pane and then choose New, Package from the Action menu. The Package Wizard starts.

2. Click the button labeled Install Pre-built Packages (see Figure 31.18).

FIGURE 31.18

Selecting the Install Pre-built Packages button will install a package, automatically loading and enabling all appropriate DLLs and TLBs.

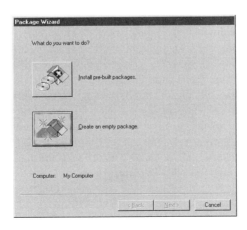

3. In the next dialog box, click the Add button and locate the package file you want to import. If the package is on a remote server, you will need to browse for it over the network or map a network drive to an appropriate share point on that computer. Remember, it will have a .pak file extension. Locate the .pak file from the ConsBill2 package export from above. Click the Next button.

4. Select the package identity by entering a username to administer this package, or you can use the default setting as the active user currently logged on. The package will run under the account specified and all database access will be through this user ID. Click the Next button.

5. An Installation Options dialog box will appear. Select the directory to install the package and its related files. You also can elect to add the Windows NT users, which are saved with Roles in the package. Click the Finish button to complete the import process.

You will notice the ConsBill2 package is now displayed in the Installed Packages list.

Setting Up MTS Clients

After mid-tier components have been created, packaged, and exported, you must still tell base clients where to find those components. It is possible to locate mid-tier components using a centrally-located service, however this has not yet been implemented as a fully-featured part of the operating system. Such a service is planned as part of the next generation of COM, currently known as COM+. For now, if you want to implement a central clearinghouse for mid-tier components, you must do most of the work yourself.

ON THE WEB

For additional information on COM+, see http://www.microsoft.com/com/.

Through its export mechanism, MTS provides an executable that makes it relatively easy to tell a base client computer where to find the mid-tier components in a package. By simply running the executable file created during the export process, appropriate entries are placed in the Registry of the base client so that it "knows" the name of the server where those components are located.

If you need to register your mid-tier components on many base client computers, you can use several different approaches to accomplish the task. Microsoft's Systems Management Server (SMS) can be used to automate the process of distributing and executing the exported package on base client machines. Alternatively, you can simply share the export directory and connect to it from the base client and manually execute the steps outlined in the next section. It is also possible to create batch files or install scripts using a variety of techniques to make the installation easier for unsophisticated users. Only the manual process is described in this chapter.

Registering Mid-Tier Components on the Base Client

Once the package has been successfully exported, a \clients directory is created (see the section "Exporting Packages" in this chapter). This directory contains an EXE file that needs to be executed on the target client machine.

Here are the steps required to setup a client application from an exported package:

1. Locate the client application, TimeEntry.exe. Copy this file to the client workstation.

2. From the exported package directory, copy the file clients\ConsBill2.exe to the client workstation.

3. Execute ConsBill2.exe, which will register certain components in the Registry.

4. Register other components such as OCXs and DLLs as required per the application. In the case of ConsBill2, see the next section, "Registering Local Components on the Base Client."

Registering Local Components on the Base Client

Application components that expose information such as properties and methods must register the information with the operating system so that it is available to other applications. This is done by executing the operating system application regsvr32.exe or an equivalent method using a Setup program or the available Registry APIs.

For the sample Time Sheet application, you must register one DLL that resides on the base client and manages interaction with mid-tier components and one OCX file containing the ActiveX grid control used to capture time sheet entries.

1. From the Start menu, select Run, and the Run dialog box will appear (see Figure 31.19).

FIGURE 31.19

The application regsvr32.exe comes with the Windows NT operating system and is used to add or delete items in the Registry.

2. Enter `regsvr32 <<path>>\GASullivan Time Sheet.ocx` in the edit box. Be sure to include the entire path.

3. Repeat step 2 for the TimeSheet.dll file.

Monitoring Transaction Statistics

Component properties can be viewed by first highlighting the component folder and then selecting View, Property View. This will display information in the right pane pertaining to component threading, associated DLL, CLSID, security, and transactions (see Figure 31.20).

You can view transactional properties by double-clicking the Transaction Statistics icon (see Figure 31.21). Current Active Components displays the number of components currently active (Active) along with the maximum number of components active during the current Microsoft (MS) Distributed Transaction Coordinator (DTC) session (Max. Active). It also displays the current number of transactions that aren't able to commit due to some sort of failure in communications or database (In Doubt).

FIGURE 31.20
Viewing component properties will display what type of threading is enabled for each installed component.

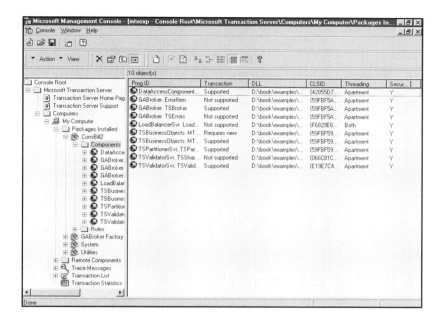

FIGURE 31.21
Total MTS transactions are displayed in the right pane. Both current and accumulative statistics are provided.

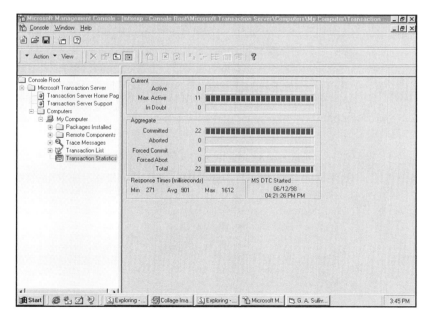

N O T E All cumulative statistics such as Aggregate Committed and Aggregate Aborted will be set to zero after the MS DTC is stopped and restarted. ▓

Aggregate Statistics displays cumulative information on commits, aborts, forced commits, forced aborts, and total number of transactions that have occurred since the MS DTC session has started. Response Times displays the time (in milliseconds) of a transaction from the point when it began to the point when it was committed. The counter named MS DTC Started depicts the time and date the current session of the MS DTC started.

From Here...

In this chapter, you learned what it takes to deploy a distributed application with Microsoft Transaction Server. You learned about using Microsoft's new management console as a common interface for all system administration work. You also explored a step-by-step procedure for creating packages, defining roles, and exporting, importing, and installing components. Finally, you learned how to monitor transactions in distributed applications using features built into the MTS Explorer.

For more information on some of the topics addressed in this chapter and the steps to take next in your exploration of Visual Studio, see the following chapters:

- ▓ See Chapter 5, "An Inside Look at Microsoft Transaction Server," for an overview of MTS and its role in enterprise applications.

- ▓ See Chapter 14, "Creating COM Components for MTS," for a general discussion of how to build mid-tier components.

- ▓ To learn more about enterprise application development and the role of Visual Studio, see Chapter 25, "Clients, Servers, and Components: Design Strategies for Distributed Applications."

- ▓ For an introduction to creating mid-tier components in Visual Basic, see Chapter 27, "Creating COM Components for MTS with Visual Basic."

- ▓ For an introduction to creating mid-tier components in Visual J++, see Chapter 28, "Creating COM Components for MTS with Visual J++."

- ▓ For an introduction to creating mid-tier components in Visual C++, see Chapter 29, "Creating COM Components for MTS with Visual C++."

CHAPTER 32

Using MSMQ with Visual Basic

by Mark A. Wolff and Patrick E. Tobey

In this chapter

Introducing MSMQ with Visual Basic

Microsoft Message Queue (MSMQ) Server release 1 is a new feature of the Windows NT operating system that makes it easy to integrate applications that would have been difficult to integrate before. MSMQ provides reliable communication of mission-critical information over unreliable networks. Today, companies are challenged with integrating a plethora of existing applications in such a way as to present management with a consolidated, near-real-time view of the customer. MSMQ provides a reliable, easy way to meet these challenges.

Most modern applications use tightly coupled, synchronous communication that makes such integration difficult because of complex design and data synchronization issues inherent with tightly coupled communication. Conversely, MSMQ is based on a message queuing model in order to offer an asynchronous, loosely coupled, reliable network communication (see Figure 32.1).

FIGURE 32.1

The MSMQ Message Queuing Model demonstrates the movement of messages through a complete MSMQ environment regardless of synchronous or asynchronous communication.

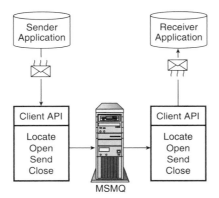

Many organizations want their applications to be aware of each other's business events by using a push model, whereby data delivery services push information and applications to users. All MSMQ features are totally protocol independent, so developers can concentrate on their applications and VB code without having to worry about communication protocol translation issues.

MSMQ supports a full set of COM components that enable it to be accessed from Visual Basic. MSMQ can also be accessed from Microsoft Internet Information Server (IIS), Microsoft Transaction Server (MTS), Visual C++, Visual J++, and Microfocus COBOL.

Using the MSMQ connector, MSMQ can work seamlessly with other products, such as IBM's MQ Series for interoperability with legacy systems. MSMQ works on clustered Windows NT servers to provide administrators with the ability to configure MSMQ services for fault-tolerant, high-availability operations.

▶ For more detailed information about IBM MQ Series and other companion products, **see** Chapter 7, "An Inside Look at the Microsoft Message Queue," **p. 167**

MSMQ can use the Crypto Application Programming Interface (API) to encrypt, protect, and sign messages to protect them from being changed during transmission, even over unsecured networks such as the Internet. MSMQ provides for centralized systems management. Its architecture is dynamic directory service based, and MSMQ is fully integrated with other Microsoft products, such as IIS and MTS. MSMQ also works with Active Server Pages (ASP), providing the capability to send and receive messages through the COM interfaces. Additionally, it is also fully integrated with the Windows NT security environment.

Finally, Visual Basic programming for MSMQ is easy because MSMQ has just five simple APIs (Open, Close, Send, Receive, and Locate).

In this chapter, we'll begin by installing the MSMQ ActiveX COM control. Then, we'll discuss MSMQ programming using Visual Basic 6. A brief presentation of MSMQ queues using the MSMQ API will follow, detailing how to Create, Locate, Open, Close, and Delete queues. Then we'll work with MSMQ messages and the MSMQMessage COM object. Finally, we'll devote some time to error handling with MSMQ. Now, let's get started.

Programming MSMQ Using Visual Basic 6

Visual Basic 6 provides a perfect medium for MSMQ Server development. The capability to implement complex messaging models is accomplished by the MSMQ ActiveX COM control. In the following sections, these important topics relating to Visual Basic 6 development are covered:

Part
IV
Ch
32

- Learn how to install the impressive ActiveX control into a Visual Basic project.
- Learn the basics of development with MSMQ queues.
- Learn the basic development issues of sending and retrieving messages.
- Discover error-handling practices useful to a successful implementation of a message queuing application.

Now that you have a brief overview, you are ready to begin your MSMQ experience.

Installing the MSMQ ActiveX Control

Installing the MSMQ ActiveX control gives you access to the ActiveX objects that provide the methods and properties to use the MSMQ features. This installation assumes that the following components are already in place:

- MSMQ Client software
- Visual Basic 5 or higher

▷ For more information about installing the client software, **see** "Client Installation," **p. 181**

To install the ActiveX control into a Visual Basic project, follow these steps:

1. Choose Project, References from the menu. The References dialog box appears.

2. Select the reference that you want to add. In this case, select Microsoft Message Queue Object Library (see Figure 32.2). Click OK or hit Enter.

FIGURE 32.2

The References dialog box allows you to use another application's objects in your code by setting a reference to that application's object library.

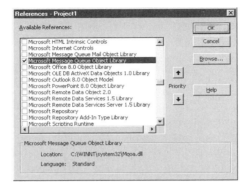

After the installation of the ActiveX control, you are ready to begin working with queues and messages. Use Visual Basic's Object Browser to look at the available MSMQ objects, methods and properties prior to jumping into programming for MSMQ.

To view the MSMQ classes in the Object Browser, follow these steps:

1. Choose View, Object Browser from the menu. The Object Browser should appear, showing all the libraries that are referenced in your project.

2. Select MSMQ from the libraries selection box. You should see the classes, methods, and properties of the MSMQ ActiveX objects. Figure 32.3 shows you the main MSMQ class objects.

FIGURE 32.3

The MSMQ class objects allow you to create and open queues and send and retrieve messages.

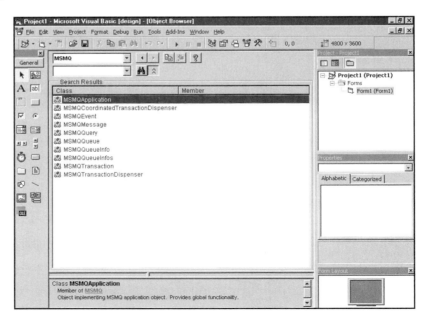

ON THE WEB

For more information on the ActiveX objects you just installed, refer to the MSMQ documentation or visit Microsoft's Web site for MSMQ at `http://www.microsoft.com/MSMQ/`.

TIP Additional documentation is supplied when the MSMQ Client Software is installed using the Windows NT 4 Option Pack. This documentation is located at C:\iishelp\msmq\htm\testtoc.htm. This HTML file allows you access to abundance of information about the MSMQ Server including COM and ActiveX support.

Now that you have the ActiveX control loaded into your Visual Basic project, you are ready to begin working with queues, the core of MSMQ.

Working with Queues

Taking advantage of MSMQ requires you to work with message queues. As stated previously, a queue is a staging area for waiting messages to be accessed by applications. When two applications communicate through MSMQ Server, one acts as a sender and the other acts as a receiver (see Figure 32.4).

FIGURE 32.4
The Message Queue Model illustrates how MSMQ uses the sender/receiver model to send messages between queues.

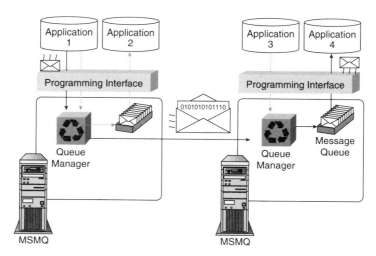

Surprisingly, implementing and manipulating queues is quite easy. The basic actions one can perform on a message queue are as follows:

- Creating a queue
- Locating an existing queue
- Opening a queue
- Closing a queue
- Deleting a queue

Creating a Queue

Prior to being able to send or retrieve messages with MSMQ, you must create a queue. Creating a queue requires an instance of the MSMQQueueInfo object, which allows access to the properties and methods of the queue. The Create method of this object allows you to create your queue, although some information needs to be supplied prior to this call. The only property that is required is the PathName property.

This queue property supplies the following three valuable attributes:

- The location where MSMQ stores the queue's eventual messages.
- Whether the queue is public or private.
- The name of the queue.

The syntax for the PathName property is machinename\queuename for public queues or, machinename\Private$\queuename for private queues.

N O T E   The PathName property is not case sensitive.

 T I P   If the desired queue is to be created on the local machine, you can use a shortcut by substituting a period (.) for the machine name. For example, .\queueForTesting generates a queue named queueForTesting located on the local machine.

Creation of private queues are only allowed on the local machine; therefore, elimination of the machine name is also permitted.

The following code illustrates setting of the PathName property:

```
Dim objTimeSheet As New MSMQQueueInfo
objTimeSheet.PathName = "KC-Wolf\TimeSheetQueue"
```

After setting the PathName property, there are many optional properties that you might want to set. These properties are outlined in Table 32.1. Remember that the PathName property is the only property that is required to be set prior to creating a queue.

Table 32.1   MSMQ Queue's Optional Creation Properties

Property	Explanation
Authenticate	Specifies whether or not the queue only accepts authenticated messages.
BasePriority	Determines the base priority for all messages that are sent to a public queue.
Journal	Specifies whether or not a retrieved message is logged in a queue journal. The valid values are MQ_JOURNAL and MQ_JOURNAL_NONE.

Property	Explanation
JournalQuota	Maximum size (in kilobytes) of the queue journal.
Label	Application-generated description of the queue. Mainly used by MSMQ administrator.
PrivLevel	Specifies the type of message that the queue will accept. Private, public, or both.
Quota	Maximum size (in kilobytes) of the queue.
ServiceTypeGuid	Type of service provided by the queue.

Now that you have specified the PathName and any other optional parameters for the queue, you are ready to actually create the queue. All that is necessary to create the queue is a call to the Create method. See Figure 32.5 for a view of the queue that you are about to create.

```
objTimeSheet.Create
```

FIGURE 32.5
The MSMQ Explorer allows you to view and administrate queues that are either created using an application or the Explorer itself.

Part

IV

Ch

32

Locating an Existing Queue

Creating a queue is one way of obtaining a reference to a queue; the other is locating an existing queue. The use of the MSMQQuery object's LookupQueue method enables querying for public queues registered in the Message Queue Server Information Store. A query can be based on one or more criteria. Table 32.2 outlines the parameters of the LookupQueue method that can be used as criteria during your search.

Table 32.2 `LookupQueue` **Method Parameters**

Property	Description
QueueGuid	Identifier of the queue
ServiceTypeGuid	Type of service provided by the queue
Label	Label of the queue
CreateTime	Time when queue was created
ModifyTime	Time queue was created and the last time `Update` was called. In other words, the last time queue properties were changed.

In Visual Basic, to locate an existing queue with a label named MSMQ_Test, you would write code similar to the following:

```
Dim objExistingQueues As MSMQQueueInfos
Dim objMSMQQuery As New MSMQQuery
Set objExistingQueues = objMSMQQuery.LookupQueue( Label:="MSMQ_Test")
```

One problem exists with this approach. As you probably have already noticed, each one of these parameters can only accept one value to query on. You can only search for one Label name. Microsoft supplies relationship parameters that, in conjunction with simple Boolean comparison operators, add extra versatility to the LookupQueue location query feature.

Table 32.3 outlines the Boolean operators that are available to developers. Also, Table 32.4 shows the relationship between the standard criteria parameters and their equivalent relationship parameter. Information from these two tables can be used together to produce an impressive array of search possibilities for existing MSMQ queues.

Table 32.3 `LookupQueue` **Boolean Operators**

Boolean Operator	Description
REL_EQ	Equal To
REL_NEQ	Not Equal To
REL_LT	Less Than
REL_GT	Greater Than
REL_LE	Less Than or Equal To
REL_GE	Greater Than or Equal To
REL_NOP	Ignore associated criteria parameter

Table 32.4 Comparison of Criteria and Relationship Parameters

Relationship Parameter	Criteria Parameter
RelServiceType	ServiceTypeGuid
RelLabel	Label
RelCreateTime	CreateTime
RelModifyTime	ModifyTime

The following code illustrates the use of criteria parameters and their corresponding relationship parameters coupled with a boolean operator. This example locates all queues located on the MSMQ server that have a label not equal to (REL_NEQ) the value of Time Sheet Queue.

```
Dim nQueueCounter As Integer
Dim objQueue As MSMQQueueInfo
Dim objMSMQQuery As New MSMQQuery
Dim obExistingQueues As MSMQQueueInfos
nQueueCounter = 0
Set objExistingQueues = objMSMQQuery.LookupQueue(Label:=
➥"Time Sheet Queue ", RelLabel:=REL_NEQ)
ObjExistingQueues.Reset
Set objQueue = objExistingQueues.Next
While Not objQueue is Nothing
    MsgBox "This queue was found "+ objQueue.Label
    nQueueCounter = nQueueCounter + 1
    Set objQueue = objExistingQueues.Next
Wend
MsgBox "Number of queues located: "+CStr( nQueueCounter )
```

N O T E   For more detailed information about the Boolean operators and the Relationship parameters, refer to the MSMQ documentation supplied by Microsoft.

Making a call to the LookupQueue method returns a collection of queues that meet the criteria specified by you. Navigating through this collection is handled with the Reset and Next methods of the MSMQQueueInfo's object. The Reset method moves you to the beginning of the collection; similarly, the Next method advances through the collection one queue at a time.

To cycle through a collection of queues returned from a previously executed query, you might write the following Visual Basic code:

```
Dim objFoundQueue As New MSMQQueueInfo
objExistingQueues.Reset   'Ensuring you are at the beginning
                          'of the collection
Set objFoundQueue = objExistingQueues.Next
While NOT objFoundQueue Is Nothing
    'Do some actions to the queue
    Set objFoundQueue = objExistingQueues.Next
Wend
```

Part IV

Ch 32

At this point, you have created or located a queue for use, but nothing can be done with a queue until it has been opened for receiving and sending of messages. Now that you have the queue, let's open it.

Opening a Queue

Working with a queue, such as sending and receiving messages, can't be performed until the queue is opened. Opening a queue is performed by a call to the Open method of the MSMQQueueInfo object, which returns a MSMQQueue object for you to work with.

The format for the open method is

```
Open (IAccess, ShareMode)
```

Prior to the opening of a queue, you must determine the values for the IAccess and the ShareMode parameters. Specifying the IAccess parameter requires you to know which of the following operations you are willing to allow applications to perform against your queue:

- Sending messages to the queue
- Retrieving messages from the queue
- Peeking at messages located in the queue

Sending or retrieving messages from the queue is relatively straightforward, but peeking at messages needs a slight explanation. Peeking at the message enables an application to view the contents of the message without removing the message from the queue. In other words, this feature enables the application to receive the message, while still allowing other applications to receive the same information.

Next, you must determine what sharing mode you are willing to give requesting applications. This parameter will be determined by the choice that is made for the access mode (IAccess) parameter. In other words, if you are opening the queue for sending or peeking, you have no other option but to give the application full access to your queue. On the other hand, if you prefer to only allow retrieving privileges, you have the opportunity to use either sharing modes. Table 32.5 outlines the possible values for the IAccess and ShareMode parameters.

Table 32.5   Possible Values for IAccess and ShareMode Parameters

Access Modes	Sharing Modes
MQ_SEND_ACCESS	MQ_DENY_NONE
MQ_RECEIVE_ACCESS	MQ_DENY_RECEIVE_SHARE
MQ_PEEK_ACCESS	

When determination of the two parameters has been accomplished, you are ready to open a queue. The following code illustrates how to open a queue for sending messages and for retrieving messages, respectively.

```
Dim objTimeSheetSendingQueue As MSMQQueue
Set objTimeSheetSendingQueue = objTimeSheet.Open(MQ_SEND_ACCESS, MQ_DENY_NONE )
```

or

```
Set objTimeSheetSendingQueue = objTimeSheet.Open(MQ_RECEIVE_ACCESS, MQ_DENY_NONE
)
```

Now that you have an object reference to a queue, you can start sending and retrieving messages. Refer to the "Working with Messages" section of this chapter for more information on how to accomplish this.

Closing a Queue

Closing a queue enables the application to close a physical connection to MSMQ. The closure of a queue doesn't destroy the queue on MSMQ, but only closes the cursor to the server. Any MSMQQueue objects that were opened using this queue will still exist after the closing occurs; therefore, you must eliminate the object through Visual Basic code.

The following Visual Basic code illustrates opening a queue and then closing the queue that was just opened:

```
Dim objQueue As MSMQQueue
Set objQueue = objTimeSheet.Open(MQ_SEND_ACCESS, MQ_DENY_ACCESS )
objQueue.Close
```

 T I P Continuous opening and closing of a queue should be avoided. If your application plans on using the same queue continuously over time, avoid frequent opening and closing of the target queue. This technique increases performance tremendously.

Deleting a Queue

Now that you have a queue that is no longer necessary to your application, you can delete the queue from MSMQ. The action deletes the queue and all messages that are not either retrieved or stored in the journal within the queue. This step isn't necessary if you plan on using the queue later in your development or even later in the future.

The following Visual Basic code illustrates deleting the queue that you created in the "Creating a Queue" section previously discussed:

```
objTimeSheet.Delete
```

Now that you have an understanding of MSMQ queues, you can move on to sending messages to the queue and retrieving messages from the queue. The following sections discuss the necessary elements of MSMQ messages.

Working with Messages

Every MSMQ Server message is an instance of the MSMQMessage COM object. The MSMQMessage object provides numerous properties that you might need to set within your Visual Basic code. MSMQ provides default values for most of them. You must provide property values only in those cases where predetermined values either are not sufficient for your needs or are not possible. Thus, MSMQ Server message programming is very simple, while at the same time, more sophisticated features are still supported.

MSMQ possesses functionality to basically handle two operations on messages:

- Sending messages to a queue
- Retrieving a sent message from a queue

Now that you have an understanding of MSMQ queues and a basic overview of MSMQ messages, you are ready to jump into creating and sending a message to your timesheet queue.

Sending a Message

Sending a message requires an instance of the MSMQ ActiveX object, MSMQMessage. Instantiating a MSMQMessage object gives you access to methods and properties that allow you to create and send messages. While sending a message, there are many properties that might be set, for example, the body of the message. Table 32.6 shows the properties of the MSMQMessage object.

Table 32.6   Properties of the MSMQMessage Object

Property	Description
Ack	When MSMQ posts acknowledgement messages to the administration queue, this property specifies the type of that message. Possible values are:
	MQMSG_ACKNOWLEDGEMENT_FULL_REACH_QUEUE
	Posts a positive acknowledgement if the message reaches the queue prior to the time-to-reach-queue timer expires; otherwise, posts a negative acknowledgement.
	MQMSG_ACKNOWLEDGEMENT_FULL_RECEIVE
	Posts a positive acknowledgement if the message is retrieved prior to the time-to-be-received timer expires; otherwise, posts a negative acknowledgement.
	MQMSG_ACKNOWLEDGEMENT_NACK_REACH_QUEUE
	Posts a negative acknowledgement if the message reaches the queue. No positive acknowledgement exists.
	MQMSG_ACKNOWLEDGEMENT_NACK_RECEIVE
	Posts a negative acknowledgement if an error occurs and the message cannot be retrieved from the queue.
	MQMSG_ACKNOWLEDGEMENT_NONE
	No acknowledgements are posted. This is the default value.

Property	Description
AdminQueueInfo	The actual queue that acknowledgements are posted to if the ACK property is other than MQMSG_ACKNOWLEDGMENT_NONE.
Body	The information that is stored in the message.
CorrelationID	An application-defined identifier that a receiving application can use to identify a message.
Delivery	The method in which MSMQ delivers the message. Possible values include:
	MQMSG_DELIVERY_RECOVERABLE
	Guaranteed method of delivery. During every node hop along the MSMQ route, the message is either forwarded on to the next node or stored locally in a backup file. This method is the slowest method, but even during a machine crash, the message is never lost.
	MQMSG_DELIVERY_EXPRESS
	Default method of delivery. The message is stored in memory until delivery is performed.
Label	An application-defined string describing the message.
MaxTimeToReachQueue	Time limit value that specifies the time, in seconds, within which a message must arrive at its destination queue. If the time expires prior to the arrival of the message, MSMQ discards the message.
MaxTimeToReceive	Time limit value that specifies the time, in seconds, within which a message must be retrieved from the target queue. If the time expires prior to any retrieval of the message, MSMQ discards the message.
Priority	Specifies the message's priority during routing and placement in the queue. The higher the value, the faster the routing occurs and the higher the message is stored in the destination queue. Messages that are sent with equivalent priorities are routed and placed in the queue in chronological order.
ResponseQueueInfo	The queue with which the receiving application might send response messages back to the sending application.

Part

IV

Ch

32

Although many properties described in Table 32.6 are important to the successful sending of messages to a destination queue, the Body property is the primary parameter for the MSMQMessage object. As stated, this property is responsible for storing the contents of the message. The Body property can contain a string value, an array of bytes, or any ActiveX object that both the sending and receiving application are able to process. Figure 32.6 demonstrates a typical message that was sent to the timesheet queue, viewed using the MSMQ Explorer.

FIGURE 32.6

Through the MSMQ Explorer, the MSMQ administrator can view the contents of a message waiting in the queue.

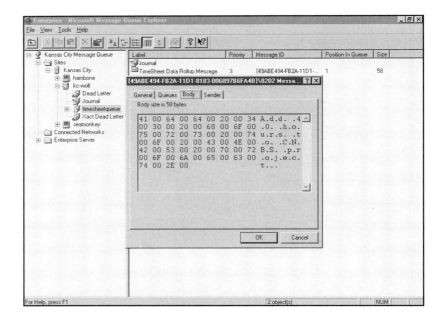

Now that you have the basis for creating a message, you can create a message and set some properties. The following coding example demonstrates a message being created for future sending:

```
Dim objTimeSheetMessage As New MSMQMessage
objTimeSheetMessage.Body = "Add 40 hours to test project"
objTimeSheetMessage.Label = "Rollup Message For Test Project"
objTimeSheetMessage.Priority = 7
objTimeSheetMessage.MaxTimeToReceive = 180
objTimeSheetMessage.Ack = MQMSG_ACKNOWLEDGEMENT_NACK_RECEIVE
Set objTimeSheetMessage.AdminQueueInfo = objAdminQueue
```

Upon further examination of the previous code, notice that a new MSMQMessage object was instantiated and the Body, Label, and Priority properties were immediately set. This message also has an added feature for the MSMQ administrator. This message sits in the destination queue waiting for 180 seconds or until retrieved by another application; otherwise, if the message is not retrieved prior to the 180 seconds, a negative acknowledgement is sent to the queue that is associated with the objAdminQueue object. The MSMQ administrator should be able to use the information supplied in the administration queue to generate a plan for more successful retrieval of messages.

Now that you have created a message and set its properties, you are ready to move on and finally send the message to a previously created and opened queue. Sending a message is quite simple, as long as the properties for the message are correctly supplied. The MSMQMessage object supplies a Send method that allows you to send a created message to a destination queue. The destination queue must be supplied (through a parameter to the method) for proper sending. For example, if you wanted to send the previously created message to the `TimeSheetQueue` that was opened in a previous section, you would write the following code:

```
objTimeSheetMessage.Send objTimeSheetSendingQueue
```

This sends off a message to the destination queue specified by the `objTimeSheetSendingQueue` object. When the message arrives, it appears similar to Figure 32.7 within the MSMQ Explorer. This message stays in the queue for the seconds supplied by the `MaxTimeToRecieve` property and deletes itself if either an application retrieves it or the time limit expires.

FIGURE 32.7
The MSMQ Explorer allows you to view your queued messages, similar to the way that Microsoft Exchange allows you to view email messages waiting in your Inbox.

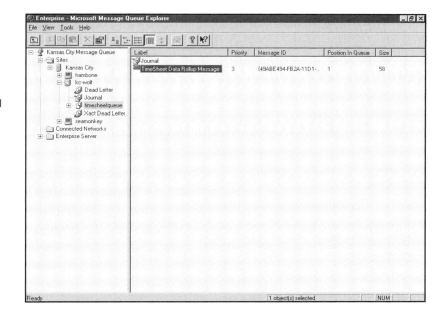

Part
IV

Ch
32

Retrieving a Message

Now that you have a message waiting for retrieval in the `TimeSheetQueue` queue, you must be able to retrieve it from an application. Prior to writing your Visual Basic code, you'll need an understanding of the retrieval process. MSMQ offers two methods of retrieval for messages from the queue:

- Reading messages synchronously
- Reading messages asynchronously

Reading messages synchronously from the queue forces execution to be blocked until either a message becomes available or the message timeout value expires. Reading messages asynchronously from the queue is handled by the queue firing events as a message arrives in the queue, and the events are handled by the application.

▶ For more information on synchronous and asynchronous concepts, **see** Chapter 7, "An Inside Look at the Microsoft Message Queue," **p. 167**

Now that you have an understanding of the methods of retrieval, you will learn how to retrieve the message that you sent in the previous section. The message was sent to the queue with the label TimeSheetQueue; therefore you must locate the queue and retrieve the message from it.

The following code shows locating the queue labeled TimeSheetQueue and opening it for retrieval:

```
Dim objExistingQueues As MSMQQueueInfos
Dim objTimeSheet, objTimeSheetQueue As New MSMQQueueInfo
Dim objMSMQQuery As New MSMQQuery
Set objExistingQueues = objMSMQQuery.LookupQueue
➡(Label:= "TimeSheetQueue")
objExistingQueues.Reset
Set objTimeSheet = objExistingQueues.Next
Set objTimeSheetQueue = objTimeSheet.Open
➡(MQ_RECEIVE_ACCESS, MQ_DENY_NONE)
Set objTimeSheetMessage = objTimeSheetQueue.Peek
➡(ReceiveTimeout:=60000)
```

TIP The Peek method of the MSMQQueueInfo object contains an optional parameter named WantBody. This parameter specifies whether the receiving application wants the body of the message retrieved. Because setting this parameter to FALSE causes the message retrieved to be considerably smaller in size, performance of your application increases tremendously.

The previous code allows you to peek at the messages that are stored in the queue. Basically, you are checking for the existence of any messages that are located in the queue that was searched on. This method peeks until either the ReceiveTimeout parameter expires or a message is located. For this example, if a message is not located after 60000 milliseconds, or one minute, the method returns. By checking the value of the objTimeSheetMessage object, you can determine if a message was located.

N O T E If the reference to the object returned from the Peek method is equal to Nothing, your method didn't locate a message in the queue.

When you have located a message in the queue, you can retrieve it. To retrieve a message in the queue, write the following Visual Basic code:

```
Set objTimeSheetMessage = objTimeSheetQueue.Receive
➡(ReceiveTimeout:=60000)
MsgBox objTimeSheetMessage.Label + "has the following body:
➡"+ objTimeSheetMessage.Body
```

TIP The ReceiveTimeout parameter for the Peek and Receive methods of the MSMQQueueInfo object is an optional parameter. Setting this parameter is recommended because the retrieving application blocks processing until a message is located, thereby ultimately locking the application indefinitely.

The message that the application retrieves is the message that has the highest priority, but if two or more messages have equivalent priorities, the message that has the longest waiting time in the queue will be retrieved.

Error Handling with MSMQ

Error handling with MSMQ is simple enough. MSMQ can report errors for either the properties that you pass in from Visual Basic or for the operation MSMQ is performing. When an error occurs, MSMQ passes back an error value to your Visual Basic application, where error handling is done just as it is in any Visual Basic program. All the MSMQ classes pass back return values, and every MSMQ object has a list of possible values to check for. The list of possible exceptions is far too long to cover here, but the concept is simple. For example, the MSMQMessage object can return values such as MQMSG_CLASS_NORMAL for a normal message, or if the sending application doesn't have access rights to the destination queue, a MSMSG_CLASS_NACK_ACCESS_DENIED is returned. In Visual Basic, this can be tested for as follows:

```
Handler:
If (Err = MSMSG_CLASS_NACK_ACCESS_DENIED) Then
    MsgBox "The sending application does not have access rights to
    ➥the destination queue. "
    Exit Sub
Else
    MsgBox "Unexpected error! "
End If
```

Part
IV

Ch
32

Again, using the same MSMQMessage object as an example, if a MQMSG_CLASS_NACK_Q_EXCEED_QUOTA value is returned, this means that the destination queue is full.

This could be tested for by using the following code:

```
If (Err = MQMSG_CLASS_NACK_Q_EXCEED_QUOTA) Then
    MsgBox "Error!  The destination queue is full! "
    Exit Sub
Else
    MsgBox "Unexpected error! "
End If
```

Error values that are generated from the properties your Visual Basic application passed to MSMQ are returned to your application in the optional status array of MOMSGPROPS, MQQUEUEPROPS, and MQQMPROPS. If your Visual Basic application specifies a NULL array in the property structure, MSMQ won't report any errors to your application. The value returned from any call is of the highest-severity error encountered. To determine which property caused the error, your application must parse the property status array.

From Here...

MSMQ Server version 1 is a state-of-the-art feature of Windows NT that provides loosely-coupled and reliable network communication services. MSMQ is an excellent solution for organizations that have multiple applications that must communicate reliably over less-than-reliable networks. Further, because MSMQ is a standard part of the Windows NT operating system, it's possible to easily integrate applications that would have been difficult to integrate before. Finally, MSMQ's simple API provides intelligent default settings to simplify application design and make it possible for developers to concentrate on coding the application instead of complex designs.

For more information on some of the topics this chapter addresses and where to go next in your exploration of the MSMQ Server, see the following chapters:

- To learn about MSMQ Server installation procedures and how MSMQ ties into an N-tier queuing model, see Chapter 7, "An Inside Look at the Microsoft Message Queue."

- For further insight into the use of ActiveX controls and COM components, see Chapter 11, "Using COM Components and ActiveX Controls."

- To explore the creation capabilities of Visual Basic, see Chapter 26, "Building Client Front Ends with Visual Basic."

- To learn how to incorporate Microsoft Transaction Server concepts into a message queuing model, see Chapter 27, "Creating COM Components for MTS with Visual Basic."

Team Development with Visual Studio

Using the Visual Component Manager and the Microsoft Repository

by Jody C. Socha

In this chapter

Using the Visual Component Manager

The ability to share information is one of the main goals of software development. As such, another goal is software systems created to support application development. Better ways of sharing software developed in one area with other areas, sharing requirements data with the design team, sharing design information with the development team, and assessing change impact across areas of a development effort need to be generated to support the growing complexity of modern software development.

Microsoft has introduced two powerful tools to aid in accomplishing these goals: the Visual Component Manager and the Microsoft Repository. The Microsoft Repository is a specially designed database coupled with a powerful engine providing for the central storage and integration of design information. The Visual Component Manager is a tool for managing and sharing components using the Microsoft Repository as its storage mechanism. This chapter provides an overview of these tools and discusses how you can begin using them in your development environment.

Modern technologies, such as Microsoft's Component Object Model (COM) architecture, have changed the face of software development. This modern technology has allowed much of new software to be configured as a series of independent components integrated together to form an application. This new component-based development has many advantages in that it allows for flexible development architectures and higher incidences of software reuse.

However, component-based development has generated several new problems; one of the biggest is a dramatic increase of the complexity of managing the software environment. Instead of one large project, software development has evolved into a large number of smaller projects. Tracking and managing these projects and the components has become a major challenge for software developers. Added to this situation is the large number of third-party components that are being used in development today.

Microsoft's Visual Component Manager, shown in Figure 33.1, provides one solution to this situation. The Visual Component Manager provides a convenient mechanism for storing component information in a centralized database. It provides capabilities to categorize components, provide descriptive information about those components, search for components that meet certain criteria, use those components in your development projects, and share components by allowing connections to other Visual Component Manager databases.

The following two sections provide an overview of how to use the Visual Component Manager. The first section describes how to set up the Visual Component Manager and how it interacts with your development environment. The second section describes how to customize the Visual Component Manager and presents strategies for sharing components developed by you and others.

FIGURE 33.1

The Visual Component Manager provides a convenient location for inventorying your software development components.

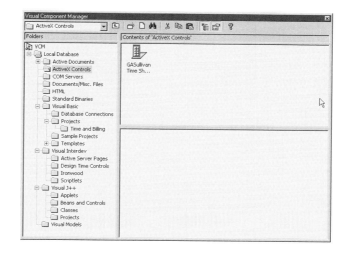

Setting Up the Visual Component Manager

The Visual Component Manager is installed for you when you install Visual Studio or any of its development tools: Visual Basic (VB), Visual J++, Visual InterDev, or Visual C++. In addition, when you use it with Visual Basic, the Visual Component Manager must be selected as an add-in in the add-in manager. At that time, the Visual Component Manager icon appears in the Visual Basic toolbar, and a Visual Component Manager menu item appears in Visual Basic's View menu.

N O T E As part of the installation process you can elect not to have the Visual Component Manager installed by using the Custom settings option. ▧

At this point, to run the Visual Component Manager, perform one of the following tasks:

▧ In Visual Basic, click the Visual Component Manager icon or select View, Visual Component Manager from the menu.

▧ In Visual J++ or Visual InterDev, select View, Other Windows, Visual Component Manager.

▧ In Visual C++, select Tools, Visual Component Manager.

The Visual Component Manager should automatically appear as a Visual Basic add-in. If it doesn't, add the following line to the VBAddIN.ini file on your system. This file should be located in your computer's Windows or WinNT directory.

```
VCMMgr.Connect=1
```

Part

V

Ch

33

N O T E The Visual Component Manager can also interact with the Visual Modeler to enable sharing of models and classes.

When selected, the Visual Component Manager activates and connects to its local database. If necessary, it configures the database as required by both the repository engine and the Visual Component Manager. Of course, if the tables are already present, this step is skipped in the installation process.

N O T E In reality, the Visual Component Manager configures the local database with its required tables and its required Tool Information Model information.

CAUTION

If you use a Visual Component Manager database that was created using an earlier version of the Visual Component Manager, it generates a `Wrong Repository Version` error. You must first convert the old database using the Microsoft Repository Migration Wizard.

For more information about the Microsoft Repository Migration Wizard, see the section "The Microsoft Repository Migration Wizard" later in this chapter.

After the database is configured, the Visual Component Manager requests whether you want to refresh its information on the various components installed on your system. If you say no, you can always refresh data from within the Visual Component Manager at any time. However, unless you have a specific reason to defer the refresh, you should say yes to begin the refresh. The refresh process can take a few minutes to perform depending on your system. When the refresh is complete, the Visual Component Manager user interface will be visible.

The Visual Component Manager will also configure several default component folders in the database. The default component folders provide a convenient location to browse for components. The following list shows the types of folders that are installed. More information on component folders and the types of components administered by the Visual Component Manager is covered in the following sections.

Active Documents	Visual Basic Templates
ActiveX Controls	Visual InterDev Active Server Pages
COM Servers	Visual InterDev Design Time Controls
Documents/Misc. Files	Visual InterDev Scriptlets
HTML	Visual J++ Applets
Standard Binaries	Visual J++ Beans and Controls
Visual Basic Database Connection	Visual J++ Classes
Visual Basic Projects	Visual J++ Projects
Visual Basic Sample Projects	Visual Models

Navigating in the Visual Component Manager

Before you begin using the Visual Component Manager, some things you should notice about the user interface are

- The Visual Component Manager is always on top of your Visual Basic project.

- The Visual Component Manager can't be minimized to an icon, nor can it be maximized to fill the window. However, it can be resized using standard windows resizing methods.

- Whenever Visual Basic is minimized to an icon, the Visual Component Manager is minimized with it.

- On the other hand, the Visual Component Manager isn't directly part of the Visual Basic Integrated Development Environment (IDE), and can be moved outside of Visual Basic's window.

- If you open a different project or create a new one, the Visual Component Manager user interface stays open and shows the new projects name in its title bar.

- Finally, if you open up multiple copies of Visual Basic, each copy can have its own Visual Component Manager open.

The Visual Component Manager has a Windows Explorer-like user interface, consisting of a toolbar and three panes: Folders, Folder Content, and Component Properties. In addition to the panes, the user interface provides a toolbar for controlling the display.

Each of the three panes provides the following capabilities:

- Folders pane—The folders pane displays the various collections of components that are available through the Visual Component Manager. The folders are displayed in a standard tree view. There are three types of items visible in the pane. The topmost icon represents the Visual Component Manager icon and provides the root item for the tree. The next level of icons represents the various databases with which the Visual Component Manager is connected. The remaining icons represent all the component folders available on that database. Each component folder consists of other component folders and/or a set of components. Selecting any folder in the tree view causes that item's contents to be displayed in the contents pane. Right-clicking on any item causes a pop-up menu to be displayed with an appropriate set of options for that item.

- Folder contents pane—The folder contents pane displays the contents of the currently selected folder item. The icons could represent a database, a component folder, or a component. Selecting an item causes that item's properties to be displayed in the property pane. Right-clicking on any item causes a pop-up menu to be displayed with an appropriate set of options for that item. Double clicking an item initiates the default action for that item.

- Component properties pane—The property pane lists all the properties and values for the currently selected item.

N O T E   To see the default action for item, right-click on it. The item displayed in bold is the default action that is performed when the item is double clicked. ▨

You might want to leave the Visual Component Manager user interface open while using Visual Basic. Because it is always open and on top of the your tool's IDE, the following tips can be used to facilitate navigation between the two interfaces:

- The Folder Contents pane is the only pane that you really need open to navigate through the interface. Close the other two panes by right-clicking in the Folder Contents pane and selecting View, Folder Outline and View, Properties Pane.
- Change the display of the Folder Contents pane to a list by right-clicking in that pane and selecting either View, List or View, Details from the pop-up menu.
- Also, hide the status bar by right-clicking in that pane and selecting View, Status Bar from the pop-up menu. The toolbar can also be turned off in a similar fashion, if desired.
- Resize the Visual Component Manager user interface to a size that you prefer and move it to an appropriate location on the desktop. Alternatively, move the user interface to a position so that it docks into the IDE.

As shown in Figure 33.2, you now have a smaller version of the user interface, but you still have access to all the Visual Component Manager options. You can access the component folders by using the drop-down list on the toolbar. The drop-down list provides a fully expanded view of all the component folders available. Alternatively, you can navigate up and down folder levels by using the up one level toolbar button or by double clicking on a folder icon, respectively. Double-clicking in an empty space in the pane also moves up one level. Right-clicking any item gives you the full range of options for that item, including the capability to change the display options (select View in the pop-up menu) and to do searches (select Find).

FIGURE 33.2

Reposition the Visual Component Manager in your IDE so that it is always available if you need it.

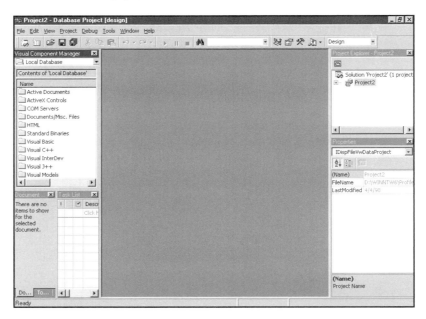

Using a Selected Item

The Visual Component Manager provides two items for storing and organizing components: Repository Database and Component Folder. By default, the Visual Component Manager connects to the local repository database and provides several predefined and automatically populated folders for you to use.

A component in the Visual Component Manager is not limited to just COM components. *Component* is a rather loose term that includes almost anything you would want to share for code development. At any time you can use any component in your Visual Basic project by either double-clicking that item or by selecting its default item in the pop-up menu. The various types of components that can be stored in the Visual Component Manager are listed in Table 33.1.

Table 33.1   The Visual Component Manager Provides Several Different Types of Objects to Interact With

Items	File Types
COM server	.dll, .exe
COM library	.dll
Standard binaries	.dll, .exe
ActiveX controls	.ocx
Active document	.vbd
VB project	.vbp
VB project group	.vbg
VB sample project	.vbp
Form templates	.frm
MDI form templates	.frm
Class templates	.cls
Code procedure template	.bas
Control set templates	.frm
Menu templates	.frm
Property page templates	.pag
User control templates	.ctl
User document templates	.dob
Database connections	.cls
Visual J++ project	.vjp
Java class	.class

Part
V

Ch
33

continues

Table 33.1   Continued

Items	File Types
Java applet	.java
Html file	.htm, .html
Visual model	.mdl
Document/misc. file	any

Another item provided by the Visual Component Manager is the component shortcut. *Component shortcuts* are special items in the Visual Component Manager that store the location of the specified component. They are similar to standard Windows shortcuts, except that they store the database and component folder where the item can be found. If you right-click on a shortcut, you actually have the same menu options that you do for the type of item to which the shortcut points.

For the various components, there are sets of actions available for use in your development environment. Not all actions apply to every component. The available actions are listed in Table 33.2.

Table 33.2   The Visual Component Manager Provides a Set of Actions for Using Components

Action	Description
Add to Project	Provides a reference to the specified server into the project, or adds the appropriate object to the currently open project.
Add to Toolbox	Causes the associated control to be loaded in the project's toolbox. Only that control is added directly to the toolbox.
Add to Project Group	Generates a Visual Basic Group, if one is not present, containing both the currently loaded project and the Visual Component Manager selected project.
Open	Closes the currently open project and opens the selected one.
Install on this computer	Moves the associated files to the local computer and performs any necessary installation steps, such as registering a COM server.
Save to Disk	Moves the associated files to the local computer.
Load the Document/File	Opens the document in the appropriate application for that type of file.

CAUTION

Not all actions apply in every development environment. Naturally, you can't add a Visual Basic project to Visual J++.

CAUTION

Although you can run the Visual Component Manager from Visual C++, the Visual Component Manager doesn't interact directly with Visual C++ at all. You need to save any desired items to disk and configure them manually.

Searching

Often you might not know what component you need or where it might be located in the database and folder structure. Therefore, a method of searching for components that meet certain criteria is provided by the Visual Component Manager. To start a search, select the Find Item(s) toolbar button.

There are three tabs available on the search screen: Description, History, and Related Files. You can enter search criteria on any or all the tabs.

On the Description tab, enter the desired search string into the Containing text box, select a type or types of components, and identify the component properties to search in (see Figure 33.3). You must select at least one Search In item. Leaving the Containing text box blank returns all components of the specified type.

Part
V
Ch
33

FIGURE 33.3
The Visual Component Manager offers several different techniques for searching for a desired component.

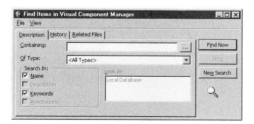

The Visual Component Manager provides a special type of search criteria called keywords. *Keywords* are text tags added to a component, placing it into a specific category. To use a keyword in a search, select the ellipsis button (…) following the Containing text box. The Item Keywords dialog box appears, as shown in Figure 33.4. Use this screen to select the keyword(s) you want to use in your search criteria.

FIGURE 33.4

Keywords provide a quick and easy search mechanism in the Visual Component Manager.

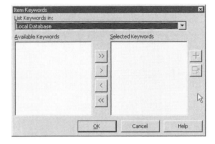

The History tab enables you to narrow your search by using historical data (see Figure 33.5). Fields are available to search by author's name, a date range, a specified period for how old the component can be, or criteria for the maximum and minimum number of times the component has been used. The last criteria might be particularly useful for an organization collecting metrics on reuse.

FIGURE 33.5

The Visual Component Manager enables searching based on the history of a component.

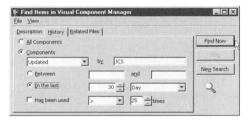

The Related Files tab is used to limit the search to files only containing certain types of supporting files or to a specified file (see Figure 33.6).

FIGURE 33.6

The Visual Component Manager enables searching based on available files.

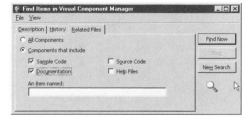

When the search criteria is specified, use Find Now to start the search, Stop to stop a search in progress, and New Search to start with a fresh search. The results are shown in the pane below. Right-click on the found item to either open the item's corresponding component folder in the Visual Component Manager user interface or to use the item directly with your project.

The Visual Component Manager and the Visual Modeler

The Visual Component Manager provides some advanced capabilities for managing models developed with the Visual Modeler. You can interact with models the same way as other components—namely, you can publish models for others to use, search for models, and get models and submodels for use in your project.

However, an exciting advanced feature is the Visual Component Manager's capability to expose the various classes that make up a model. Thus, you have the ability to import only a selected class or classes into your model, without having to import the whole model.

▶ For specific details on how the Visual Component Manager and Visual Modeler interact with each other, **see** Chapter 36, "System Modeling and the Microsoft Visual Modeler," **p. 1029**

Customizing the Visual Component Manager

You aren't locked in to the default Visual Component Manager folders and components and can easily reconfigure them. You can add new items, change the descriptive information about an item, and even connect to other repository databases to view the component information on a different computer. This section provides an overview of how to customize various aspects of the Visual Component Manager.

Adding Component Folders

You can add your own component folders anywhere in the component folder hierarchy. Navigate in either the Folders or Folder Contents pane to the level where you want to add the folder. Click the right mouse button anywhere in the pane and select New, Folder as appropriate (or select the New Folder toolbar item). After the folder is created, it shows up in the user interface with a name of New Folder, where it can easily be renamed as desired. The name you give it should indicate the type of components that can be stored in the folder. You can later view the types allowed in a folder by right-clicking that folder and selecting New in the pop-up menu.

> **N O T E** The New Folder option isn't available at the root level of the folder hierarchy. Only databases can be added at that level.

Adding Components and the Publishing Wizard

Adding items is also a straightforward process and is accomplished in one of several ways:

- Publish command—In your development environment, bring up a project's shortcut menu and select Publish. Alternatively, bring up the shortcut menu on a source code file and select Build Outputs.

- Refresh—If you have added a component to your system through an installation process, you can simply refresh the appropriate folder or category in the Visual Component Manager. The Visual Component Manager should then automatically find the new component and add it for you.

Part
V

Ch
33

■ New Item command—Right-click and select New, Component from the shortcut menu. Alternatively, select the New Item toolbar button.

■ Drag and Drop—You can add components by dragging the appropriate file from any file viewer (such as Windows Explorer) on top of the folder where you want the component stored. The Visual Component Manager automatically determines the type of component you are trying to add.

CAUTION

An item added to the Visual Component Manager might not be immediately visible to other instances of the user interface that are open. You might need to refresh the other windows if visibility of the newly added component is desired.

If any of these actions are performed, the Visual Component Manager initiates its Publish Wizard. The Publish Wizard walks you through all the information needed to add the component successfully. Figures 33.7 through 33.11 show you the various screens of the Publish Wizard.

FIGURE 33.7

Designate the folder to store the new component. Use the two command buttons to add a new folder or open a different repository database, respectively.

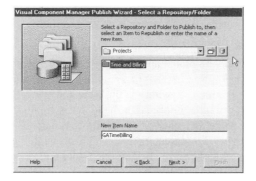

FIGURE 33.8

Provide information describing the item being added.

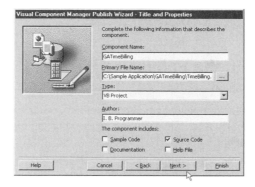

FIGURE 33.9
Provide a description and assign keywords to the item.

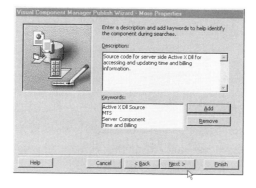

FIGURE 33.10
Confirm the files that the Visual Component Manager will associate with the component. Add or remove files as necessary.

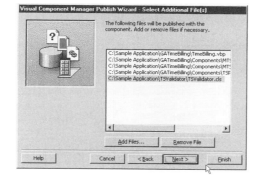

FIGURE 33.11
Identify any files that require registration if used by another developer. In the example, no files require registration.

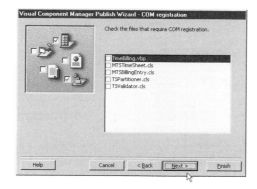

In general, the screens walk you through the following steps:

1. Designate the component folder in which to store the component.
2. Provide the component property information.

N O T E Not all screens in the Publish Wizard will be shown if the information they need is already known or not applicable. ▓

Editing Item Information

Right-clicking on any component folder provides several menu options. The menu options allow you to do the following:

▓ Change a folder's name, description, or associated keywords.

▓ Move items around from one folder to another either on the same repository database or across databases.

▓ Republish a component that starts the publishing wizard and prompts for updated information on the selected component.

▓ Check the properties of a component (see Figure 33.12).

FIGURE 33.12

Description information can be updated in the Properties window. Keywords can also be added and removed.

▓ For certain default folders, provide the capability to import local information.

▓ Refresh the user interface with the latest information in the Visual Component Manager database.

▓ Perform standard Windows tasks of cut, copy, paste, and rename.

N O T E The delete and rename options aren't available for the predefined folders provided by the Visual Component Manager. ▓

Some additional information about moving items follows:

▓ The cut, copy, paste, and paste shortcut commands only work inside the Visual Component Manager. Thus, items can't be copied and pasted between the Visual Component Manager and another application.

- Cut, copy, and paste functions can also be performed using the appropriate toolbar buttons.

- The same functionality is available using the mouse to drag items from one folder to another. Dragging an item with the left mouse button attempts a move if the destination folder is in the same database or a copy if the destination folder is in a different database. Dragging an item with the right mouse button prompts you to select either Move Here, Copy Here, Copy Shortcut Here, or Cancel.

- Pasting or moving a component folder moves or copies the folder and all its contents.

Configuring Keywords

You aren't limited to the list of keywords provided by the Visual Component Manager and can specify your own. On the keyword selection screen, select the command button with the plus sign on it (see Figure 33.13). You will then be prompted for the new keyword.

FIGURE 33.13
The Visual Component Manager allows you to assign keywords to an item from its list of all previously defined keywords.

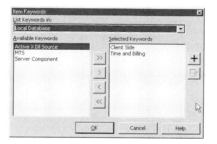

You can also edit an existing keyword by selecting the command button with the pad and pencil icon. Change the word as needed.

N O T E   Changing a keyword only makes the change for the current item. In reality, you are adding a new keyword. All other components still use the original form of the keyword.

CAUTION
After a keyword is added, it can't be deleted from the system.

Local Versus Remote Databases

The Visual Component Manager is capable of linking to other databases, including those on other computers. This capability enables the sharing of components between team members or between development teams. This section provides information on how to connect to the remote databases and how to use the components installed there.

Part
V

Ch
33

The term *local database* is slightly misleading. It is actually a default, Microsoft Access-style database that the Visual Component Manager configures on your computer. The Visual Component Manager assumes that the default database is the only one you need on your computer, hence the name local database. There is no reason, however, you can't add another database that is located on your local computer.

TIP If you installed Visual Studio in its default location, the Visual Component Manager default database is located at C:\Program Files\Microsoft Visual Studio\Common\Tools\Vcm\Vcm.mdb. If for some reason, you need to clean out the current Visual Component Manager information, simply delete or rename this database, and the Visual Component Manager will create a new one. There is no way to change the location or name of the local database.

To add another database to the Visual Component Manager, right-click in the Folders pane and select Repository Database in the resulting pop-up menu. You will be given the following three options for adding a database:

- Open a database—Use this option to open an existing database.
- Create a database—Use this option to create a new database configured for use with the Visual Component Manager.
- Most recently used list—You can reopen a previously closed database by selecting it from the list appearing in the menu.

When you select either Open or Create, you will be prompted for the type of database you want to use, either Microsoft Access (MDB) or SQL Server. The next action depends on the database type you select. If you select Access, you will be prompted for the name of the database you want to use. (Either select one from the file list or enter a name for a new one.) If you select SQL Server, you will be prompted for the ODBC data source to use.

At this point, the Visual Component Manager either creates or opens the specified database for you. If you selected open, and the database is not already configured for use with the Visual Component Manager, you will be prompted as to whether you want the database configured or not. Selecting Yes configures the database as necessary and adds an icon for the database in the user interface. Selecting No cancels the operation. If you select create, the database you specify will be configured automatically and added to the user interface.

When the Visual Component Manager configures a database, it adds the same tables to the database that it added to the local database. Also, it sets up the same predefined component folders that it added to the local database. However, it doesn't automatically load information about components on your system into these predefined folders as it did with the local database.

CAUTION

If you use the Create New Database option and you accidentally specify an existing database, the Visual Component Manager automatically configures that database with the necessary tables. This action can't be undone. It is safer in the long run to always use Open Database, even when creating a new database. Select Open Database, type in the name of the new database when appropriate, and select Yes when prompted about adding tables. If, after specifying the database, you realize you picked the wrong one, you have one more chance to abort the operation.

When you no longer need access to an added database, right-click on the database icon or a component folder under that database in the Folders Pane. Then select Repository Database, <u>C</u>lose.

N O T E   You can't close the local database in the Visual Component Manager.

Using Components on Remote Databases

When you have connected to a database, you can interact with the remote database in many of the same ways you can interact with the local database. However, there are some exceptions.

You can't add an item directly to a database on a remote computer. Rather, you must first copy the component's associated file to any desired location on the remote computer. You can then add the component to its appropriate folder on the remote computer by using several of the options presented earlier.

The default options for items on remote databases have the same behavior, with one exception. ActiveX controls and servers must first be installed on the local computer before they can be used. To do this, right-click on the desired ActiveX item and select Install on my system. The item is then installed on your computer and added to your project as appropriate. You should notice that the default action is grayed out in the pop-up menu.

Part
V

Ch
33

N O T E   When Install on my system is selected, the component is added to its appropriate folder in the local database. Unless the desired component's version is updated on the remote computer, you should use the local version from then on.

You might find it advantageous to add shortcuts on the local database to components on remote databases that you will access often. Having a shortcut still allows you to interact with a component without having to physically copy the component's file to your local computer (see previous paragraph for exception on ActiveX items). You won't have to keep the remote database connection open at all times either. Instead, if you initiate an action on a shortcut and the database pointed to by the shortcut is not open, the Visual Component Manager automatically opens the remote database and performs the appropriate action on the appropriate item.

The Visual Component Manager only automatically updates user interface data with remote database data when the remote database is opened or the Visual Component Manager is started. If an update has been made on the remote database since the last time you opened that database, you need to issue either the Refresh all items in folder or Refresh all folders command on that database.

Visual Component Manager Strategies

Now that you are familiar with all the aspects of using the Visual Component Manager, you should give consideration to how you might want to configure your development environment in order to take full advantage of its features. The configuration you want to consider depends on whether you are developing independently, as part of a small team, or as part of a large team or multiteam setting. This section provides a discussion of some of the issues you should consider when using the Visual Component Manager.

Individual Use   In the simplest environment, where you are one developer working alone, use the default Visual Component Manager settings as much as possible. In other words, you should only use the local database for storing and tracking components. Also use the predefined folders if possible. That way, you can let the Visual Component Manager do all the work of updating the latest information on components throughout your system. Of course, doing so requires storing templates and sample applications in their appropriate subdirectories of the Visual Basic installation directory.

N O T E   By using the local database as much as possible, you also simplify coordination with other repository-based tools you might use in the future. Such tools will probably also attempt to use the local database by default.

What you might want to do, however, is add component folders inside the Visual Component Manager's predefined folders to subcategorize the folders as desired. This is particularly true for the Project and Document folders, where you need to manage items manually.

Development Team Use—Segregated Team   A segregated development team is one in which the team has decided that a centralized location for sharing data isn't necessary. Such an environment is probably rare these days and probably consists of few developers that are working somewhat independently of each other.

The biggest asset of the Visual Component Manager in this environment is to simplify the sharing and reuse of components. Each developer should be encouraged to use the Visual Component Manager to manage his local components as described previously in the "Individual Use" section. In addition, he should attempt to provide quality descriptive information for his components. Effective use of the description and keyword properties on components could prove invaluable in the future.

If each developer does so, he can easily browse the component information on other computers by connecting to the appropriate Visual Component Manager database. The need to interrupt other developers for the location of certain files or to create shared directories would be greatly reduced. Instead, only the default repository database is configured for sharing between computers.

> **CAUTION**
>
> One downside to using the Visual Component Manager in a team environment is that it does not interact with all tools equally. For example, very few options are available for Visual C++.

Integrated or Multiple Team Use   An integrated development team is one in which the need for centralized sharing of components and software is required. The team is too large or too interdependent to allow developers to work on their own. In this environment, the Visual Component Manager is used for sharing and distributing components among team members through a centralized repository database. When team members have finished development on a component, they add that component to the centralized database for other team members to access.

In addition, if third-party tools are acquired for use on a project, those tools components can be located on the central database for the whole team to access. Maximum benefit is derived from adding third-party tools that use a COM-based interface in their software.

> **N O T E**   At the time this chapter was written, Microsoft was in the process of encouraging third-party vendors to develop COM interfaces for their software and to have these components automatically registered into the repository database on installation. The objective is to provide developers with a standardized interface for browsing and using components from all vendors. ▮

In this scheme, one computer should be designated as the central repository for all component information (see Figure 33.14). On that computer, a new database file should probably be created other than the local database. This prevents an instance of the Visual Component Manager running on the central component server from automatically updating information in the central database. Although the new centralized database can use the Access format, a SQL Server database is recommended for performance and security concerns.

Some organizations might expand the centralized database concept and decide to set up

Part
V

Ch
33

FIGURE 33.14
A hierarchical database structure can enable sharing and distributing components across projects and depart-ments.

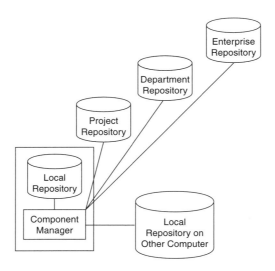

multiple databases. In one scenario, databases are set up in a hierarchical structure. Project teams or projects can share one database, related projects or a department can share another, and the organization as a whole can share an enterprisewide server. In this hierarchical struc-ture, the higher-level databases don't necessarily contain all the information in the lower data-bases they represent. Instead, only those components that need to be shared at that level are moved to that server. A designated individual could then keep each of the databases in sync with each other by dragging and dropping components from one database to another inside the Visual Component Manager.

▶ Under the hierarchical database structure, the Visual Component Manager can play a similar role as the central source for reusable components in an organization. For more information about this reuse role, **see** Chapter 10, "Creating Reusable Components," **p. 263**

N O T E   Organizations need to decide who moves components from one database to another and the procedures for making such a move. ▨

CAUTION

The Visual Component Manager doesn't provide replication capabilities for the databases it uses. Thus components can't be automatically synchronized across multiple repository levels. The repository and database engines are needed for this arrangement and require an advanced understanding of the repository architecture that is beyond the scope of this book.

The predefined folders provided by the Visual Component Manager can be used if desired, but aren't necessary. Most likely, the team should take time to configure component folders with names and attributes that most facilitate the component distribution process. The component folder names should probably be more project specific than type specific.

TIP In a large team environment, good descriptions and keywords become even more important. The project team should take the time to prepare a list of approved and recommended keywords and strongly encourage their use.

Individual developers should make full use of their local databases and the Visual Component Manager as much as possible. When developing new components or projects, they should continue to use their version control software, such as Visual SourceSafe, until the component is complete. At this point, they can add the component to the appropriate location in the centralized database and let the rest of the team know that it has been added. An alternative to using SourceSafe is to set up different the Visual Component Manager databases or component folders for managing development versus production components. However, the capabilities of SourceSafe make it the better tool for managing components in development.

▷ For a comparison of the Visual Component Manager, Visual SourceSafe, and Microsoft Transaction Server as tools for managing reusable components, **see** Chapter 10, "Creating Reusable Components," **p. 262**

Security Considerations The Visual Component Manager doesn't have native security built into it, and neither does the repository engine that the Visual Component Manager uses. Thus, security must be provided at the database level. At the present time, you can set up SQL Server databases to validate users either by requiring passwords or by using trusted connections. The appropriate Data Source driver for the database prompts the user for username and password, as necessary.

Although Access provides the capability to password protect MDB files, the Visual Component Manager doesn't offer a method for providing the password when it connects to the file. One possible workaround is to control access by setting the MDB file's sharing properties in Windows Explorer, if available.

Beyond password protection, it's not possible to control user access to specific type of components or component folders. Such an activity would involve an extremely advanced understanding of the repository's and Visual Component Manager's underlying structures.

Part
V

Ch
33

Looking at the Microsoft Repository

CAUTION

Visual Studio 6 ships with Microsoft Repository 2. Previous editions of Visual Studio included version 1 of the repository. The old repository database is incompatible with the new version. See the section "The Microsoft Repository Migration Wizard" later in this chapter for more information on conversion issues.

From a technical perspective, the repository is made up of a database with a set of interfaces that can be used to access the data in the database, which describes just about every database application in existence. Thus, with some careful planning, the repository can be used to store just about anything.

In reality, the Microsoft Repository is meant to serve a more specific purpose. Namely, that purpose is to store information describing applications and information systems. The reason for the generic structure in design is that the repository must be flexible enough to handle all the different types of information needed for designing systems. For example, suppose you have a Visual Basic application that uses ODBC to access a Microsoft SQL Server database to manage a store's inventory. The repository could be used to store the various Visual Basic forms, classes, methods, and properties that comprise the code. Another portion of the repository would describe the SQL Server database tables, columns, stored procedures, and triggers. In addition, the repository could be used to organize any requirements and design documents used in developing the system. Thus, the repository would contain a complete description of the application in one central location.

Together, these two perspectives combine to create a potentially powerful effect. The flexible architecture of a repository should allow you to store just about any information about a system that you want:

- Lifecycle phases—Store requirements documents, design documents and models, and implemented code and test structures.
- System components—Store code and test structures, database layouts, and hardware and networking configurations.
- Project management—Store project plans, task and to do lists, and possibly even cost estimates.
- Miscellaneous—Store the information on project team members and important project contacts.

However, simply storing all this information doesn't unlock the true power of using a repository. The real benefit isn't derived until the various pieces of data stored in the repository are integrated together to form a single, complete picture of the system. Now you can determine which sections of code will be impacted if you change the name of a column in the database. Alternatively, you can see which parts of the Visual Basic application use the interface to the C++ OLE server that you want to rewrite. Theoretically, you could see what happens to the accounting application used in the Atlanta office if a change is made to the inventory maintenance application in the Detroit office. It's this capability to measure the impact of a change across a system or systems that makes the repository so potentially powerful.

The remainder of this section describes how the Microsoft Repository is organized. Later sections provide information on how to use and configure the repository.

ON THE WEB

See the Microsoft Web site, `http://msdn.microsoft.com/repository/`, for the latest information on the repository.

Microsoft Repository Architecture Overview

Consider the repository as a series of layers controlling access to the shared data at the center. The repository itself is organized into three basic components. The following list describes those components, and Figure 33.15 illustrates them.

FIGURE 33.15
The Microsoft Repository is organized into several layers designed to give specific applications access to a generic interface.

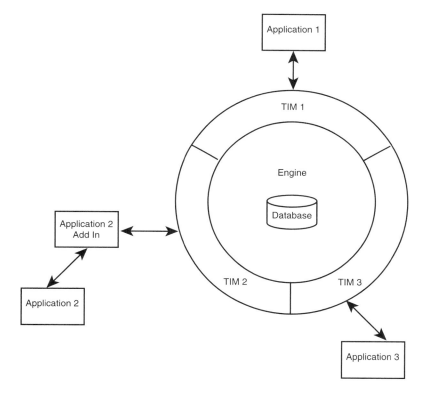

- Database—A relational database where the information about applications and projects is stored.
- Microsoft Repository Engine—A set of software that provides the basic operations for accessing repository information in the form of objects. The engine helps to ensure the enforced consistency of the database's information.
- Tool Information Model (TIM)—A set of unique interfaces designed to pass specific types of data in to and out of the repository. A different TIM is used to describe the type of information stored by development tool. One special TIM is the Type Information Model that provides the building blocks for defining other TIMs.

Around the outside of the repository are the various tools that use it. Each of these applications shares information with the repository by communicating with the appropriate TIMs. (It is possible for an application to talk to more than one TIM to store its data.) The TIM then talks to the engine through the API, which, in turn, stores and retrieves information in the database.

Each of these layers and the role of the external applications are discussed in more detail in the following sections.

Database   The heart of the repository is a standard relational database. The repository engine is restricted to interacting with only a Microsoft Access or SQL server database. However, if the repository engine isn't instructed to use a specific database, it uses a default repository database on that computer. The default database for the repository is created when the repository is installed on the computer.

N O T E   The location of the default repository database is ..\MSApps\repostry\repostry.mdb in the Windows subdirectory on the current computer. ▓

If you are curious, there are basically two sets of tables in the database. The first are the tables that the engine uses to store the repository's structural information. These tables store the information that describes the various TIMs that have been created and form a sort of repository dictionary. The second set of tables is used to store the data you are interested in. It includes a mix of initial repository tables and new tables created to store additional information required by the various TIMs. The base set of tables used by the repository engine is documented in Microsoft's *Repository Programmer's Guide*. Other tables are documented with their associated TIM, if at all.

CAUTION

Because the repository uses a relational database, you might be tempted to use a tool such as Microsoft Access to interact with the database directly. However, you are strongly encouraged not to do this because the conceptual nature of the repository makes the table relationships quite complex. In addition, the repository engine and type information models do all data integrity enforcement. Adding information directly to the database can completely undermine the rules enforced by these external layers.

The Microsoft Repository Engine   The engine manages data in the repository. Together the engine and the database form the repository itself. All the other components are a series of interfaces used to access the information in the repository.

The engine provides the main control mechanism for the repository. It controls how data is written and read to/from the database, and it controls the basic repository structure. It offers the necessary consistency checking to ensure the integrity of the data.

The engine provides a set of COM interfaces that can be called to perform various functions, such as connecting to the repository database. This set of interfaces is documented in Microsoft's *Repository Programmer's Guide*.

Tool Information Models and the Type Information Model   Tool Information Models define what information to store in the repository. The word *tool* is slightly misleading because a TIM can be used to store information from more than one tool. You have the option of creating your own TIMs or using any predefined TIMs that are available. More information on existing TIMs and tools that use them is provided in later sections of this chapter.

If you intend to write your own TIMs, you need to become familiar with the Type Information Model. The Type Information Model is a special model that is used by a TIM to describe itself to the repository. In general, the objects in a TIM derive themselves from the more generic objects described in the Type Information Model. The Type Information Model provides the following basic objects:

- `ClassDef`—Anything about which you want the repository to store information.
- `CollectionDef`—The classes that form the parent and children of a relationship or initiate the action in a relationship.
- `InterfaceDef`—The exposition of the classes, properties, collections, and behaviors to the outside world.
- `MethodDef`—A function or service that a class performs.
- `PropertyDef`—A piece of data about a class.
- `RelationshipDef`—An association between two or more classes.
- `ReposRoot`—The core object in the repository from which all navigation begins.
- `ReposTypeLib`—A group of related type information objects. Also, a TIM.
- `Workspace`—An area of the repository where tool-related data can be worked on, in isolation of other data.

Also, the Type Information Model makes it possible to extend predefined TIMs by simply adding new classes, relationships, properties, methods, and interfaces to the existing model. You can also establish relationships between two different TIMs by adding a new relationship and assigning a class in one model as the relationship's source, and a class in the other model as the relationship's destination. Be careful, however, not to change the meaning of a TIM's predefined components. Outside tools might use the TIM to store data and might not store it the way you want.

Applications   Around the outside of the repository are the various applications that use it. Some tools interact with the repository directly to store their data. The Visual Component Manager is an example of such a tool. On the other hand, some tools store data in a native format and use a separate module or program to export data to the repository. The Visual Modeler is a good example. It uses its own file structure to store model data (usually with a .mdl extension.) However, it only shares data with the repository through special export/ import commands.

These applications generally fall into three categories:

- Various tools used in the development environment. These include tools such as Visual Basic, Visual C++, the Visual Modeler, or even Microsoft Word. These tools generally don't interact with the repository directly.
- Applications that examine the development tools and extract the required information in the repository. An example of this type of tool is the repository add-in for Visual Basic, which stores Visual Basic information in the repository using Microsoft's MDO Model.

■ Applications used to browse the repository to do reporting or to perform impact analysis. An example of this type of tool is the browser tool that is provided with the repository on installation.

Versioning

Not only can information be added to the repository, but it can also be marked with versioning information to indicate changes. Basically, any object added to the repository can have its previous property information stored in an earlier version of the object, allowing users to track the evolution of that object. In addition, relationship history can be maintained using a similar version control process.

> **CAUTION**
>
> Although the underlying repository structure has been changed to support versioning, this doesn't mean that this capability is immediately available. It's up to individual tools to take advantage of this feature to provide versioning of the information that tools store in the repository. At the time of this writing, no repository-based tools support versioning.

Workspaces

Workspaces are the repositories' central structure for supporting complex team-based development environments. Workspaces enable associations between multiple objects in a related environment as part of the same project or work area. Workspaces are then coupled with a new check-in, check-out mechanism to fully support development teams.

> **CAUTION**
>
> However, as with versioning, individual tools have to be configured to support workspaces. At the present time, no known tools support this capability.

The Open Microsoft Repository Concept

In an ideal environment, the repository configuration should enable you to truly open up your development environment. Of course, the world is not ideal, and there will be limitations in Microsoft's capability to support the open concept.

The first level of openness comes at the database layer. Because the repository uses an ODBC connection to a standard relational database, any commercially available database could be used for repository data storage. However, Microsoft advertises that the repository only works with its Jet database engine or SQL server.

The second level of openness deals with sharing data between tools. For example, information about classes in a design tool could be extracted to automatically create classes in a development tool. The release of the Open Information Model (OIM) should provide a strong start to meeting this requirement.

The third level of openness deals with the capability to actually replace tools. Theoretically, the repository should be capturing your tools' data in such a way that one tool could be pulled out and replaced with another similar tool. Naturally, this level of openness is unlikely. Vendors aren't going to freely give away proprietary information just so you can switch to a competitor's tool. However, if similar tools all reference the same TIMs, transitioning to a new tool can be greatly simplified. Again, the OIM should provide a good initial step in meeting this requirement.

Understanding the Basics of the Microsoft Repository

Apparently, Microsoft's basic strategy for the repository is not to require development teams and organizations to write their own repository-aware tools. Rather, they intend to work with a series of third-party vendors to provide a suite of interoperable development tools centered on using the repository. These vendors aren't necessarily discussing techniques for having their tools work together. Rather, they have agreed to provide the capability for the tools to read and write to the repository to an agreed upon set of interfaces.

However, simply because these vendors can read and write to a common repository format doesn't mean that you will instantly gain benefits from such an environment. You need to understand what the repository is and how to structure your development environment to take full advantage of it. The remainder of this section discusses issues you should consider when moving to a repository-oriented toolset.

Reexamining the Development Process

Setting up your environment to use a repository is not much different from any other software development effort you will embark upon. You need to lay out the requirements to identify what information should be captured in the repository, and how you will use that data when captured. Then, you need to design the repository by identifying what plug-ins, TIMs, and Analysis tools need to be obtained. Finally, you will need to build and test the repository when all the components are ready.

You also need to consider who will be responsible for maintaining the repository. People will be needed for system administration, developing any additional applications, and analyzing the repository's contents.

You might need to reexamine many of your development conventions. At what points in the development process will information need to be stored in the repository? How often will it need to be updated? What role will the repository play in managing change requests? Are there any coding conventions that should be revisited to enable better information transfer?

You will need to examine your environment to understand your development needs. Figure 33.16 shows the development lifecycle according to a standard waterfall approach. The waterfall method consists of a series of steps in which one step does not begin until the first has completely ended.

FIGURE 33.16
A traditional view of the software development process is the waterfall method.

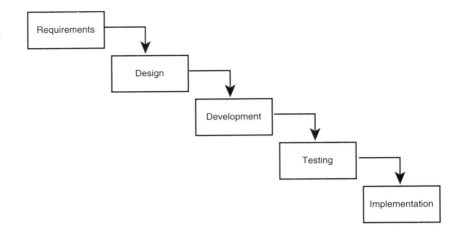

Moving to a repository-based environment means that you want to enable sharing of information between each phase of the lifecycle through centralized data storage. This new information-centered environment is shown in Figure 33.17.

FIGURE 33.17
When the repository is added to the development process, it assumes the role of a centralized, information sharing manager.

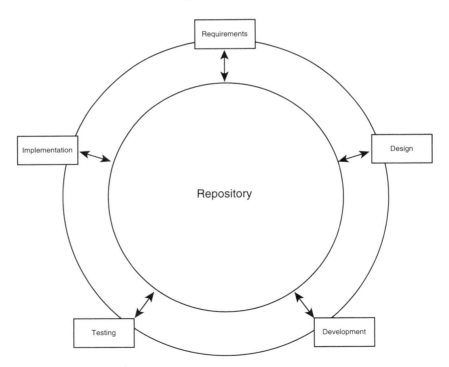

Assembling the Microsoft Repository Components

The components needed to assemble the repository are dependent on your development environment. Thus, you need to examine each phase of your development environment and determine how a repository should be used in each phase.

Consider what tools are used at each phase of your development environment. Then consider what information those tools capture. How could you benefit from sharing information between those tools, between team members and different teams, and between phases of the development lifecycle? Any location where you identify a potential benefit is a good candidate for bringing the repository into play.

Naturally, you need to consider which tools are configured to use the repository and which are not. If the tools are not configured, you will need to decide whether to switch to a repository-based tool. On the other hand, you might decide you need to build your own repository TIM or extend an existing TIM. This type of configuration information is saved for the next section.

Even if you use a repository-based tool, you need to consider the extent to which the tool interacts with the repository. Most tools store much more information in the native storage format than they export to the repository. This isn't bad, as you should aim to only store higher-level structural information in the repository and enable the tools to maintain extensive details in their local storage.

Microsoft Repository–Based Tools and Tool Information Models

So, what tools are available and how do they interact with the repository? This section provides an overview of different repository-aware tools as well as supporting Tool Information Models available from Microsoft.

Visual Basic Repository Add-in   An add-in for Visual Basic has been developed that will store information about any Visual Basic project in the repository. The add-in isn't installed automatically, however. In fact, you aren't encouraged to turn on the repository add-in just for the sake of having it. It will add processing overhead to your application with little perceived benefit.

Rather, Microsoft recommends that you defer activating the add-in to a third-party tool (or a tool of your own making) that will make use of the data in the repository. The Visual Component Manager is an example of such a tool.

If you do need to activate the add-in, simply add the following line to the VBAddin.ini file. This file is typically installed in the Windows directory on your system.

```
Repository.VBAddIn=1
```

When the add-in is activated, you can manually send information to the repository by selecting Add-Ins, Synchronize Repository. The Visual Basic add-in also comes with a set of COM interfaces that can be used to customize the behavior of the add-in.

The Microsoft Data Object Model   The Visual Basic add-In uses a special TIM known as the Microsoft Data Object (MDO) model. The MDO model enables storage of information about the current project, its components, and references.

Open Information Model   The Open Information Model (OIM) is the result of a joint venture between Microsoft and a group of third-party developers. The purpose of the OIM is to provide a single, common TIM that several different tools recognize and can use. There are several advantages to this approach.

First, the development time for new TIMs is collectively reduced. In other words, a tool with information contained in the OIM doesn't have to write its own TIM to use the repository.

Second, the TIM enables a level of information sharing between tools that wasn't previously possible. For example, the Visual Modeler stores information in an OIM subject area that is based on the Unified Modeling Language (UML) specification. As a result, model information can be shared with any tool that uses the OIM through the repository without having to use a special conversion routine. Traditionally, for four different tools to share information there would need to be six different interfaces, or conversion routines, written between each tool. Now, there only needs to be one interface, the Microsoft Repository.

There are several different subject areas covered by the OIM with several more planned for the future. At the time this chapter was written, the following subject areas are planned:

- UML—The OIM is primarily based on the UML specification and is used to specify information captured in an object model.
- Component Definition—Enables the capture of component-related information as it pertains to COM.
- Database Schema—Enables the capture of information describing the structure of a database. A variation on the schema will be implemented for each major commercial database such as SQL Server, Oracle, and DB2.
- Data Warehousing Extensions—Supports data warehousing initiatives by managing information describing the structure of the operational and data warehouse data and the mapping between them.
- Others—Additional OIM subject areas will be added in the future. Some of those additions will also aid in exposing the structure of applications to aid in reusing their components.

The Visual Modeler   The Visual Modeler uses the UML portion of the OIM to export and import information to the repository. Through this mechanism, object model information can be shared with several tools that are familiar with the OIM. Alternatively, model information can be published to the repository through the Visual Component Manager, which uses its own TIM to store information.

Data Warehousing Extensions   A potentially powerful capability of the repository lies in storing information describing the structure of an application or a database. Storing the information makes it possible to do analysis on that structure. Furthermore, it's now possible for applications to dynamically modify their behavior based on information obtained from the repository about other applications.

This concept is the heart behind the data warehousing extensions to the OIM. The repository saves the storage structure of the operational and data warehouse databases, as well as the mapping between the two structures. As a result, a set of services are enabled to automate the conversion of data from the operational environment into the data warehouse.

This concept is presented in Figure 33.18. The second layer of boxes shows the flow of data from the operational environment through a transformation process into the data warehouse where it is made available to the various Online Analysis and Processing (OLAP) tools. Below those areas lies the repository containing information describing each of those tools.

FIGURE 33.18
Data warehousing.

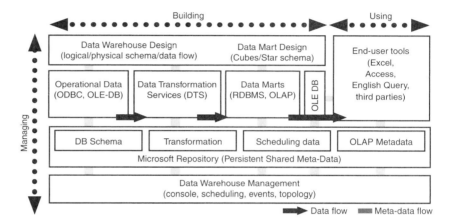

- DB Schema—Shows the layout of the operational databases.
- Transformation—Shows the relationship between the structure of the operational data and the data warehouse data.
- Scheduling Data—Used to store the timing of when the transformation process and analysis processes should occur.
- OLAP Metadata—Used to store and manage the structure of the data warehouse data.

The other two areas of the diagram show the design and management tools used to layout and control the systems involved in the data warehouse.

Each of the items shown uses the repository differently. The design tools can use the repository to store their designs and to map the design to the corresponding database implementation. Microsoft's Data Transformation Services use the repository to implement the transformation algorithms needed to move data into the warehouse. The OLAP tools can use the repository to aid in building and configuring queries needed to analyze the data warehouse data. The management tools can use the repository to schedule different events to occur and track the various databases involved in the warehouse. There isn't a section of the warehouse that the repository can't benefit in some way.

Part
V

Ch
33

The Microsoft Repository Browser   The browser is a basic analysis tool that is provided with the repository. It can usually be found within the bin directory in the repository directory in the Visual Basic installation area. Its name is Repbrows.exe and can be found in c:\Program Files\Common Files\Microsoft Shared\Repostry\ if using the standard installation.

The browser will initially connect to the default repository database, although you can connect to other databases as required (see Figure 33.19). You will either be prompted for an Access-type file or ODBC connect data if you are looking for a SQL Server database.

FIGURE 33.19

The browser can connect to other repository databases.

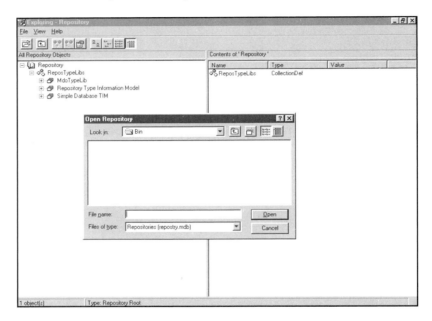

When connected, the browser uses the standard Windows tree view to show the repository structure. Figure 33.20 shows the structures of two TIMs and how they show up in the browser.

FIGURE 33.20
The browser can be used to view the MDO Model components.

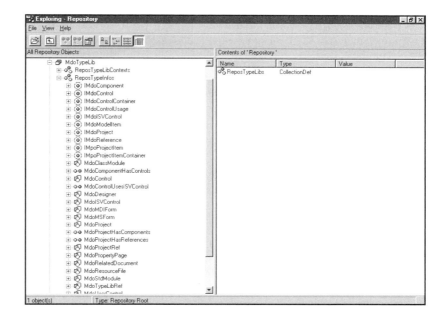

Configuring the Microsoft Repository Database

The repository is initially configured to use a default repository located on the local machine. For many situations, this local database might be adequate. However, in team-oriented environments, you might need to have everyone in the team either use (or occasionally use) a centralized database for sharing information. This centralized database should probably be a SQL server in order to handle volume and scalability issues.

Setting up this central database doesn't necessarily require understanding the underlying repository engine API structure. Whenever any repository-based tool connects to the database, the repository engine ensures that the necessary tables are installed on the database. Then, the tool itself will ensure that its TIM is configured on the system, leaving you with little work to do. So, for example, set up an Access database on the appropriate machine, connect to this database using the Visual Component Manager, and let it do all the configuration work. Any subsequent repository will also ensure that its TIM is on the repository or configure it. For a SQL server machine, connect to SQL server as the database owner and create a new database instance name. That instance name can then be connected to with the Visual Component Manager and configured appropriately.

The Microsoft Repository Migration Wizard

The database structure of the repository has changed from version 1 and needs to be upgraded for the new version. The wizard updates the core repository tables, any TIMs, and the data stored in the TIM structure. The Migration wizard wraps around the core repository OLE interfaces to perform the migration.

Part
V

Ch
33

The migration wizard doesn't change the data in the existing database, but rather moves the information to a new database. Depending on the environment, you might or might not need to run the conversion yourself. In moving the data, the Migration Wizard performs the following basic steps:

1. Enables selection of the database to convert to and from.

2. Converts the TIMs and their data while maintaining necessary internal referential integrity.

3. Provides a mechanism for having the new database assume the name of the old database. If this option is used, the old database is renamed the same except that the string _old is appended to filename. The new database is then given the same name as the old database.

4. When the tables are moved, it also moves any table owner information.

CAUTION

If you use the Migration Wizard to update the default repository database, you should rename the new database to be the same as the old database at the end of the migration. This is necessary because the name of the default repository is hard-coded to be Repostry.mdb.

However, the wizard does have limitations. It can't merge information into an already existing version 2 database, it can only move data to a new database. Also, if the repository database tables have been extended using nonstandard methods, the wizard will not be able to handle those nonstandard sections; standard extensions will be moved.

The wizard can be run in both a graphical and command line interface for initiating a conversion. The file MigRepV2.exe is the executable for the wizard. If the executable is not supplied any parameters, it will run in graphical mode. When the wizard is complete, a log file, MigRepV2.log, will have been generated containing any errors in the conversion process.

You might not need to actually run the wizard. Repository-aware tools might detect an old version of the repository and run the wizard for you. Because the tool can access the wizard using the command mode, the tool might prompt for the necessary information at startup, and isolate interaction from the wizard.

CAUTION

If you have customized the repository to add your own TIMs, you definitely want to run the wizard yourself in order to have control over the process.

The following highlights the main wizard steps:

1. Step 1 of 5—Provide the data source, username, and password of the source database, as shown in Figure 33.21. The username and password are meant only for use with SQL Server if a trusted connection is not used.

FIGURE 33.21
Providing initial information to the wizard is your first task.

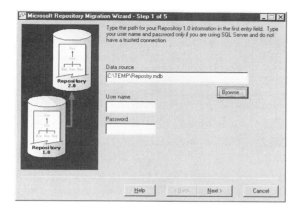

2. Step 2 of 5—A list of existing TIMs is displayed, which presents all TIMs detected in the Microsoft Repository 1. If your TIM isn't listed, you might have to use your TIM generation program to recreate the TIM and copy the table information manually. If your TIM is listed, click the Next button.

3. Step 3 of 5—Provide the data source, username, and password of the target database. Again, the username and password are meant only for use with SQL Server if a trusted connection is not used. If the target database does not exist, you will be prompted to verify that you want to create it.

4. Step 4 of 5—Information provided so far will be displayed (see Figure 33.22). Verify the information and make any corrections. Click Begin.

FIGURE 33.22
A confirmation screen shows both databases for the migration.

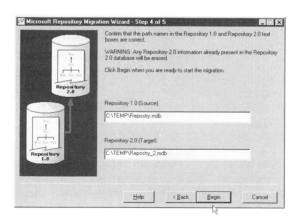

Part
V

Ch
33

5. Step 5 of 5—At this time, the migration step will begin. A progress bar keeps you informed on the progress of the migration. When complete, you will be informed of whether the conversion was successful or not. Finally, you will be prompted as to whether to name the new database the same as the old database (see Figure 33.23).

FIGURE 33.23

A prompt appears confirming the renaming of the database.

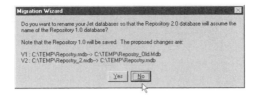

Microsoft Repository Team Members

Naturally, using a repository in your development environment requires additional human resources. Whether resource need is filled on a full-time or part-time basis depends on how extensive the repository system will be. You will have to experiment to understand how much of a strain the repository will put on development. Several roles need to be supported in a repository environment.

As with any system, someone needs to perform administration on the system. A security scheme might need to be established. The database needs to be configured and maintained. Software tools that share data with the repository need to be configured and maintained.

One or more individuals will need to provide the foundation of the repository by building and assembling the various TIMs. These individuals will need strong analytical skills, as they will determine what data needs to be stored in the repository and how that data should be obtained from the various tools. A well-designed TIM should be able to accommodate more than one tool. In addition, this team needs to analyze any commercially available TIMs, such as the MDO Model for Visual Basic, to determine if the necessary data is being captured and how that model integrates with the rest of the repository model.

You also need to consider who the users of the repository will be. Users consist of the development team as well as long term Information System (IS) planning areas. Because the repository stores information about the development environment, the repository eventually proves invaluable in analyzing your application's structure, tracking the use and reuse of software components, and analyzing the impact of change on the application or applications. Thus, everyone from the project manager, to coders, and to quality assurance can use information contained in the repository.

Regardless of how an organization wants to staff the repository team, the organization definitely wants to assign their most competent and experienced personnel. If you have a goal of a repository-based development environment, then consider that faulty data in the repository leads to faulty development decisions, leading to faulty software, leading to errors in operations. Moreover, repository data management will be more complex and abstract than any other form of development effort you are undertaking.

From Here...

In this chapter, you were presented with an overview of both the Visual Component Manager and the Microsoft Repository. The Microsoft Repository provides a central storage point for sharing information between different tools used in the development environment. The Visual Component Manager, which uses the Microsoft Repository as its storage mechanism, provides a common interface for managing and sharing components used in software development.

To get started, use and experiment with the Visual Component Manager. Start experimenting with how the Visual Component Manager interacts with your development environment and how it can play a role in component sharing.

As for the Microsoft Repository, familiarize yourself with its architecture and start researching which of your existing tools take advantage of the repository by providing some type of import/export/publishing capability. Over time, as the various TIMs and repository-based tools begin to mature, the repository will evolve into an indispensable part of your development environment.

For more information on the topics covered in this chapter, see the following chapters:

- To learn more about the data warehousing extensions to the OIM, see Chapter 4, "Creating Database-Aware Applications with Visual Studio."
- For an overview of various technologies available for developing components, see Chapter 9, "Using Microsoft's Object Technologies."
- For an overview of how the repository and the Visual Component Manager can be used to support reuse strategies, see Chapter 10, "Creating Reusable Components."
- For additional information about how COM components can be used in the development environment, see Chapter 11, "Using COM Components and ActiveX Controls."
- To learn more about how Visual SourceSafe supports sharing and managing source code, see Chapter 35, "Using Visual SourceSafe."

Part
V

Ch
33

Using the Visual Studio Analyzer

by Brad Rhodes and Larry Millett

In this chapter

Introducing the Visual Studio Analyzer

Microsoft designed Visual Studio 6 for developers of multitier applications based on COM components. Although this model provides excellent scalability, it presents some unique challenges for testing and debugging. Traditional debuggers provide detailed internal information about the execution of one or more components. In a distributed application, however, the most difficult problems arise from interactions between components. The Visual Studio Analyzer provides a detailed view of these interactions.

Developers can use the Visual Studio Analyzer alone or together with a traditional debugger. The Visual Studio Analyzer can help to isolate program defects or to identify performance bottlenecks. Quality Assurance staff can use the Visual Studio Analyzer to record a correct execution of a distributed application for comparison with new versions. New developers joining a project can use the Visual Studio Analyzer to become familiar with an application.

This chapter provides an introduction to the Visual Studio Analyzer reviewing basic concepts, installation procedures, and common operations. The chapter closes with an introduction to custom events in the Visual Studio Analyzer.

The Visual Studio Analyzer captures and logs selected events in the execution of a distributed application. Typical events might include Component Object Model (COM) function call and return, SQL query execution, Microsoft Transaction Server (MTS) component activation, NT Performance Monitor (PerfMon) counters, or any of a host of other standard events. The Visual Studio Analyzer can also capture custom events for an application. It provides a number of views for event logs so that a user can compare application events with performance or focus on a problematic interaction.

The Visual Studio Analyzer meets these goals through its event-based tracking system. Events from the event logs of Windows NT machines are merged with custom events from the distributed objects and performance data from the performance monitor. When all this data is gathered, the developer can organize, graph, or replay the events to get a feel for what the application is doing and how it is doing it.

The Visual Studio Analyzer runs within the Microsoft development environment. A Visual Studio Analyzer project includes the following components:

- A Visual Studio Analyzer project file
- One or more event logs
- One or more event filters
- One or more machines

An event log contains a detailed list of events captured during execution of an application. An event filter can be used for recording or playback: A *recording filter* determines which events are included in an event log; a *playback filter* determines which events are displayed in the selected view. Events are captured for all machines included in the project.

Visual Studio Analyzer Architecture

The Visual Studio Analyzer uses a component architecture to provide efficient and extensible event collection and distribution. The Visual Studio Analyzer Local Event Concentrator (LEC) runs on each machine included in an analysis (see Figure 34.1). LEC applies a filter to gather events on the machine and forwards them on to the Analyzer Framework. Filtering at the source will help to reduce the network traffic generated by the Visual Studio Analyzer.

FIGURE 34.1
The major components of the Visual Studio Analyzer system.

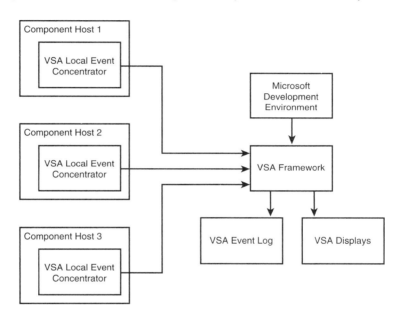

The Visual Studio Analyzer framework shown in Figure 34.1 provides the mechanism for event distribution. The framework ensures that events on a machine being analyzed are sent back to the machine requesting the analysis. This architecture enables multiple active instances of the Visual Studio Analyzer to work with the same group of machines and ensures that the selected events are routed to the right instances of the Visual Studio Analyzer.

The Visual Studio Analyzer event log records all the data selected by the recording filter. Any event forwarded to the analyzer framework is logged to the event log.

The Visual Studio Analyzer displays provide rich views of the data in the event log. Events can be viewed live, while the application runs, or later by playing back the logs.

The Developer Studio Environment coordinates the activities of the other components.

TIP

The Visual Studio Analyzer Local Event Concentrator must be installed on each machine for which you want to capture Visual Studio Analyzer events. Use the Visual Studio Analyzer Server install.

When to Use the Visual Studio Analyzer

Microsoft designed the Visual Studio Analyzer to perform three primary functions:

- Trace component interactions in a distributed application.
- Analyze application performance.
- Isolate defects in a distributed application.

The Visual Studio Analyzer differs from traditional debuggers and profilers in its focus on interactions between components. To debug an individual component of an application, use a traditional debugger. To optimize performance of an individual component, use a traditional profiler. The Visual Studio Analyzer will help you to analyze, optimize, and debug interactions among multiple components. It will also help you to isolate defective or poorly performing components, which can be debugged with traditional tools.

Analyzing Component Interactions The Visual Studio Analyzer supports analysis of component interactions, treating individual components as black boxes. Component interactions are often the most difficult aspect of an application to understand, describe, or verify. The Visual Studio Analyzer addresses these problems by

- Showing all interacting components for selected machines
- Plotting runtime relations between these components
- Showing individual events between components

The Visual Studio Analyzer can help new team members understand a distributed application. Use the Visual Studio Analyzer to trace a typical execution of the application, and then replay the event log for the new developer. When you encounter a difficult or confusing interaction, step forward and backward through the sequence until the new developer understands.

 TIP Use the Visual Studio Analyzer to familiarize a new member of a project team with an application. Record an event log for a normal execution of an application, and then review playback of that log with the new team member.

The Visual Studio Analyzer can also help to investigate the impact of changes to an application. For example, suppose a developer is working on a component of a distributed application, but is not familiar with the rest of the application. After making some business logic changes, use the Visual Studio Analyzer to compare a saved event log for a correct execution of the current system to an execution of the new version.

 TIP Record a Visual Studio Analyzer log of a correct execution of your application and save the project and log as part of the Quality Assurance documentation for the project.

Optimizing Component Interactions The Visual Studio Analyzer enables performance analysis of a distributed application by collecting timing data and performance measures for all components. The Visual Studio Analyzer provides a variety of views that allow a developer to quickly identify long-running operations. The Visual Studio Analyzer can also record selected PerfMon counters and correlate them with application events. This allows a developer to analyze not only timing but system loading as well.

The Visual Studio Analyzer differs from traditional profiling in the scope of information provided. Tools like the Microsoft Source Profiler provide information about where an individual component spends its execution time. These tools typically report time spent executing specific functions or lines of source code. By contrast, the Visual Studio Analyzer profiles execution time at the component or event level. This black-box approach reports time between events (such as COM function call and return). The Visual Studio Analyzer helps to identify the best opportunities for optimization in a distributed application. A traditional profiler helps to optimize an individual component.

Debugging Component Interactions   Sometimes it seems that all components of an application function correctly, yet the integrated application fails. The Visual Studio Analyzer helps to isolate the defect by allowing a developer to focus on important application events such as component activation and deactivation, COM method invocations, or transaction start and completion. Developers can add custom events to an application to enhance this debugging process.

Traditional debugging tools provide detailed information about execution of an individual component. The Visual Studio Analyzer, by contrast, captures high-level interactions between components to help isolate the component or set of components that is failing. When the fault is isolated, use a traditional debugger to correct the component.

Working with Events, Filters, and Views

The Visual Studio Analyzer captures detailed information about events that cross process boundaries and provides several different views of the information. Filters determine which events are collected, reducing Visual Studio Analyzer's impact on system performance and allowing an analyst to focus on specific interactions. View types include a raw Event List view, control flow diagrams, and a custom charting view.

Event Collection

In the previous section you saw several methods for analyzing distributed events. Understanding how the Visual Studio Analyzer captures events and which events can be captured will help the developer use it more efficiently.

System Events   System events are those that are coded into Microsoft delivered technologies. These include

- COM/DCOM events—Includes interface entry and departure, marshaling and unmarshaling, loading and unloading of COM/DCOM objects, and other significant COM/DCOM events.
- Database access events—Includes OLE DB, ActiveX Data Objects (ADO), and open database connectivity (ODBC).

■ MTS events—Includes the start commit and rollback of a transaction.

■ COM Transaction Integrator events.

These events are automatically available to the Visual Studio Analyzer and provide a good foundation for the analysis of the distributed application.

N O T E   The Visual Studio Analyzer doesn't capture in-process COM events except when cross-apartment marshaling takes place takes place. Use a traditional debugger or profiler to analyze in-process events. ■

Performance Monitor Events   The Visual Studio Analyzer can capture selected PerfMon counters in an application event log. This allows any performance data already available to be included with the application events.

CAUTION

Choose PerfMon counters carefully and sparingly. Each counter increases overhead for the system measured. Including too many counters might severely degrade system performance.

Custom Events   The Visual Studio Analyzer defines a set of custom interfaces that any COM/DCOM-enabled application can use to add analysis events to their application. These custom events can enhance debugging efforts or performance monitoring.

Visual Studio Analyzer Filters

The Visual Studio Analyzer can capture far more events than you want or need. Too many events can overload the network and obscure significant events for analysis. The Visual Studio Analyzer filters prevent event overload and are applied at two different points in the analysis process:

■ During event collection

■ During event viewing or playback

A Visual Studio Analyzer filter is simply a Boolean expression that selects events based on machine, process, component, event category, or other elements. The filter plays a role similar to the WHERE clause in a SQL query. The Visual Studio Analyzer includes a number of pre-defined filters; you can define and save your own filters as well.

 T I P   A new filter captures no events. In order to capture events for analysis, you must select a different recording filter or modify the blank filter to include some events.

The Visual Studio Analyzer uses filters in two different contexts: recording and viewing. A *recording filter* determines which events the Visual Studio Analyzer captures in an event log. Events excluded by the recording filter cannot be added later to the event log. A *viewing filter*

limits events retrieved from a log to generate a view. A view filter helps focus your analysis. A view filter can be more selective than the recording filter, but can never include events not selected by the recording filter.

CAUTION

Take special care in selecting Performance Monitor events for a recording filter. The Visual Studio Analyzer issues a warning if you try to select all Performance Monitor events in a filter. Performance Monitor counters fire at frequent intervals, resulting in a very large number of events, which could overload the network and severely degrade Visual Studio Analyzer's performance.

Visual Studio Analyzer Views

The real value of the Visual Studio Analyzer comes from its custom views for event analysis. These custom views include the Machine, Process, and Component diagrams. Each Visual Studio Analyzer project might contain many different event views. The events from each of the separate views might be combined in any fashion.

The Event List The Event List view is much like the Event Viewer from a Windows NT machine. See Figure 34.2 for a demonstration of the Event List view. In addition to listing events, this view is used to apply filters, sort data, and provide a mechanism for exporting event data.

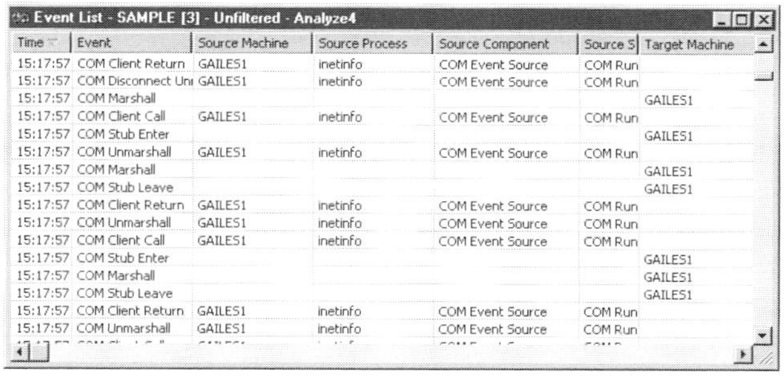

FIGURE 34.2
The Event List view is the basic view of the Visual Studio Analyzer package.

Although this view of the data isn't that flashy, the abilities of the Visual Studio Analyzer to filter, sort, and organize this data through this view provides much of its benefit.

Visual Studio Analyzer Diagrams The most impressive feature of the Visual Studio Analyzer is its capability to dynamically generate system diagrams based on event data. These custom views include the Machine, Process, and Component diagrams.

The *Machine diagram* allows the developer to track events as they travel from machine to machine. Figure 34.3 shows an example of the Machine view. As the distributed application runs, the lines between the machines in the Machine diagram will highlight and the method that is being called will be displayed.

Part
V

Ch
34

FIGURE 34.3

The Machine view allows the user to track the distributed application's interaction with machines on the network.

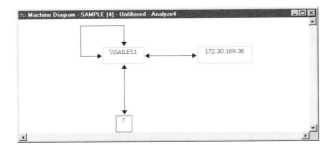

Using the animated mode of the Machine diagram allows a developer to quickly identify whether the problem is related to a specific machine or whether the distributed application is involving machines that it should not be using. After the application has finished running, the developer can use the captured events to replay the analysis session. The replay is identical to the initial capture of the data.

The Process diagram displays events at the application (process boundary) level. This diagram allows the developer to track events as they enter and exit the various processes. The processes might reside on the same machine or on a separate machine.

N O T E Almost all event views in the Visual Studio Analyzer support animated replay. When several views are open simultaneously, the animations are synchronized.

In distributed applications many processes might become involved. Some common processes in the Windows NT environment include the Microsoft Transaction Server (MTS) process and the Internet Information Server (IIS) process. If any of the distributed applications components use MTS or IIS there is a good chance the application will cross a process boundary. Any objects that are created in an Out of Process mode will also show up in a different process. Figure 34.4 shows the Process diagram.

FIGURE 34.4

The Process diagram allows the developer to see interaction between processes.

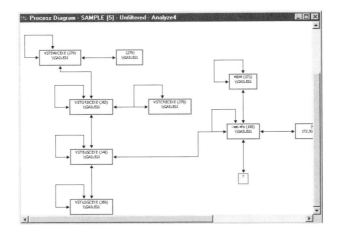

Because the same named process might reside on many different machines, the Process view includes the name of the machine where the process resides.

Because multiple instances of a process might be active on a machine, the Process view also includes the process ID, which corresponds to the PID column on the Processes tab of the Windows NT Task Manager.

Similar to the Machine diagram, the Process diagram allows the user to track the application from process to process in a dynamic mode. The COM/DCOM call that is initiating the transition shows up on the diagram and the path is highlighted.

The final rich animated diagram is the Component diagram. Similar to the Machine and Process diagrams, the Component diagram tracks the events of the application as the different components are accessed. Figure 34.5 shows the Component diagram.

FIGURE 34.5
The Component diagram allows the developer to see interaction between components.

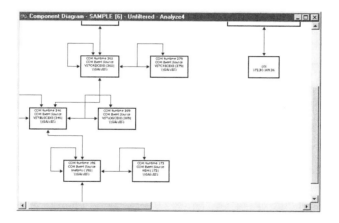

 Because the same named component might reside in several different processes on several different machines, the Component diagram includes the name of the process and the name of the machine for all the components.

The Component diagram allows the developer to identify which components come into play during execution of the application. The Component diagram should resemble the object flow diagram or state diagram often discussed in object-oriented programming concepts. Like the Machine and Process diagrams, the active link on the diagram is highlighted and the name of the method between the components is placed on the active link. The Component diagram can be replayed from the captured event data.

These three state diagrams allow the developer to analyze any distributed application from the most important levels. The developer can use the views together to analyze the applications behavior in a top-down type of approach.

Part
V

Ch
34

The Chart View The Chart view provides a Gantt chart that displays the timing of the events. This chart shows the events from the raw event list on the left and Gantt chart of the time of the call on the left. Figure 34.6 shows an example of the Gantt chart.

FIGURE 34.6
The Chart view allows the developer to see the detail timings of the distributed events.

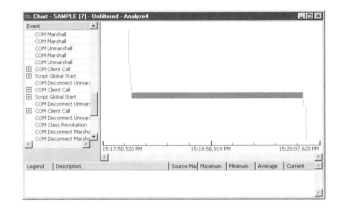

This chart provides the rich capability of being able to overlay any of the performance data from the event log on top of the chart. This allows the developer to quickly analyze possible sources for the performance of the data.

This chart understands the structure of events and allows the developer to rollup events. This allows the developer to better isolate timing down to different levels. Click the plus sign next to the rollup event to expand a level. This chart displays threaded applications as well.

Setting Up the Visual Studio Analyzer

Setting up the Visual Studio Analyzer requires two main steps. First, install it on a developer machine; second, install the Visual Studio Analyzer LEC on each machine that the Visual Studio Analyzer will analyze.

In the earlier section on Visual Studio Analyzer architecture, you saw that a machine needs the Visual Studio Analyzer LEC in order to participate in the analysis of a distributed application.

Visual Studio Analyzer Platform Requirements

The Visual Studio Analyzer runs on the following platforms:

- Windows NT 5 (Server or Workstation)
- Windows NT 4, with Service Pack 4 (Server or Workstation)
- Windows 98 with DCOM 98 or Service Pack 1
- Windows 95 with DCOM 98

N O T E The Visual Studio 6 Enterprise Edition install set includes DCOM 98. Service Pack 4 for Windows NT 4 is expected to ship shortly after Visual Studio 6. According to Bill Gates, Windows NT 5 won't ship until it is ready.

The Visual Studio Analyzer will run on Windows NT 4 with Service Pack 3, but with reduced functionality. Service Pack 4 includes libraries required to capture COM events.

On Windows 95 the operating system doesn't ship with support for services. The Visual Studio Analyzer ships an extra executable that functions as the LEC service. The application is in the Visual Studio Analyzer subdirectory and is named vales.exe. You can start this service by selecting Programs from the Start menu. Under Visual Studio 6 select Enterprise Features. Now select Visual Studio Analyzer Server and it will start. You can tell that it is running if the icon is on the Windows 95 desktop. You can start and stop event collection on the machine by right-clicking the Visual Studio Analyzer server icon.

N O T E If the Visual Studio Analyzer server program stops responding to the user interface, your server might have encountered an internal error. You can kill the server (on Windows NT only) by using the killec.exe program in the Visual Studio Analyzer subdirectory.

Using the Visual Studio Analyzer

Using the Visual Studio Analyzer on a project includes the following high-level steps:

- Create a Visual Studio Analyzer project.
- Connect to the machines that are being analyzed.
- Create event filters. Identify the Recording filter.
- Create event logs.
- Start the application.
- Open the event log.
- Refine the event collection filter.
- Analyze the data.

In the following sections, you explore the Visual Studio Analyzer project and how to set up and configure the Visual Studio Analyzer on a machine.

Create a Visual Studio Analyzer Project

The Visual Studio Analyzer uses a Visual Studio Analyzer project to store all the elements that are important to an analysis session. This allows a developer to quickly get back to the point when the project was last saved. The Visual Studio Analyzer project is a normal Visual Studio project and can be kept as a subproject to other development projects.

Part
V

Ch

34

The main elements of a Visual Studio Analyzer project include

- A list of machines the analysis involves.
- A list of event filters for this analysis. This includes one special filter known as the recording filter.
- A list of event logs that are gathered by the analysis.

There are two ways of creating a Visual Studio Analyzer project. The first and most common is to use the Visual Studio Analyzer Project Wizard. The second method for creating a project is to create a blank project and add the required elements from the project management view. For this example, you will use the Project Wizard to create a new project:

1. Select New Project from the File menu.

   This opens the Visual Studio 6 common New Project window, as shown in Figure 34.7. In the left pane of this window, under the New tab, the tree structure organizes the types of projects that can be created. The right dialog shows specific project templates for the type of project selected in the left pane.

FIGURE 34.7

The Visual Studio 6 common New Project dialog shows both the tree structure and the specific project templates.

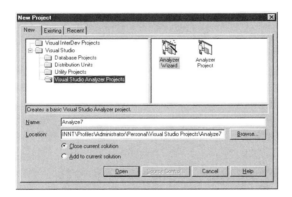

N O T E The types of projects that display in the New Project dialog depend upon the Visual Studio options that have been installed.

2. Select Visual Studio Analyzer Project in the left pane.
3. Select the Analyzer Wizard in the right pane.
4. Name the project and fill in the path where you want the project to reside.
5. Select Open to start the Project Wizard.
6. Select Yes so that the Analyzer Project Wizard will find the machines on your network that other projects in the solution are deployed to. Select Next to proceed to step 2 of the Analyzer Project Wizard.
7. Step 2 of the Analyzer Project Wizard allows you to select machines that were found to be analyzer enabled or to add machines that were not found by the Visual Studio Analyzer. Select Next to proceed to step 3.

8. Step 3 allows you to narrow down the list of components that will gather event data. You will only be looking at the COM, Web, PerfMon, and MTS event types. The others can be disabled for now.

N O T E The event categories that display in the list depend on what components have been installed on a system.

The Select Components step repeats for each machine enabled in step 2 of the Project Wizard (see Figure 34.8).

FIGURE 34.8
The Select Components step of the Project Wizard.

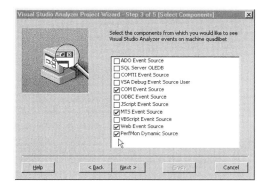

9. After going through the list of machines, the next step is to select the sample filters that you want to include in your project. Figure 34.9 shows a list of sample filters that can be included in a project. It isn't necessary to delete any of the sample filters. If you end up needing one of the sample filters, it's nice to have the template already in your project.

FIGURE 34.9
A list of sample filters that can be included in a project. Unless you are certain a sample is not needed, leave it in the project.

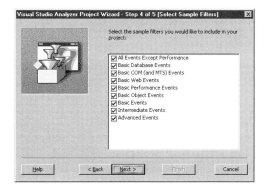

Part
V

Ch
34

10. The final step of Analyzer Project Wizard is to review your selection and click <u>F</u>inish to create the project.

You have now created a Visual Studio Analyzer project. Behind the scenes the Project Analyzer has created the recording filter and an event log. The recording filter is a filter that includes all the events selected in the Analyzer Project Wizard.

N O T E   You can create a blank project by selecting Analyzer Project as the type of Visual Studio Analyzer project to create in step 1. Make sure that you specify the recording filter and event log prior to using this new project. ▩

The Project Explorer can be used to modify all aspects of the Visual Studio Analyzer project. These modifications include

- Adding or removing machines
- Adding, removing, or editing filters
- Changing the recording filter
- Adding or removing event logs

Now that you have created the project and established the recording event filter and event logs, you can gather data by running your application. This is done by running your application the same as you always have. The events are collected by the Visual Studio Analyzer and are ready for your analysis.

To start and stop the recording of events, select the event log that is collecting the events. Choose Record events from the Analyzer menu item.

Adding Visual Studio Analyzer Events to Your Components

So far you have investigated how to use the Visual Studio Analyzer using only standard events. For a COM-based application this actually takes the developer a long way toward understanding his distributed application.

In this chapter you look at how the developer can integrate custom Visual Studio Analyzer events with applications to provide additional insight on how the applications are performing.

There are several levels of complexity to adding events to your application. The first level is to simply add an event that follows the existing Visual Studio Analyzer event model and uses one of the previously created events. The second level is to add custom parameters to your event to extend the stock events. The third is to create a new event under one of the already available categories. The fourth and most complex is to create your own event categories.

All Visual Studio Analyzer events are divided into four broad event types, as shown in Table 34.1.

Table 34.1 Visual Studio Analyzer Event Types

Type	Description
Generic	Events that describe components starting and stopping.
Inbound	Events that describe the returning of a value or result from a function or a database query.
Measured	Events that describe the measurement of an item—for example, the measurement of CPU%.
Outbound	Events that describe the calling of a function or starting of database query

Measured events are different than the other types of events. Measured events are created dynamically by the Visual Studio Analyzer going through the list of registered dynamic sources. Each dynamic source must register the categories of the events that are generated. These dynamic categories are reported to the user interface for organizing or sorting events.

Table 34.2 lists the events that are shipped with the Visual Studio Analyzer.

Table 34.2 Visual Studio Analyzer Events

Event Name	Type	Category	Description
DEBUG_EVENT_CALL	Outbound	CALLRETURN	Generated on function call.
DEBUG_EVENT_CALL_DATA	Outbound	CALLRETURN	Generated if additional data is supplied to support a function call.
DEBUG_EVENT_COMPONENT_START	Generic	STARTSTOP	Generated when a component loads an event source.
DEBUG_EVENT_COMPONENT_STOP	Generic	STARTSTOP	Generated when a component unloads an event source.
DEBUG_EVENT_ENTER	Outbound	CALLRETURN	Generated on function enter (after any time spent on the network).
DEBUG_EVENT_ENTER_DATA	Outbound	CALLRETURN	Generated if additional data is sent to support a function enter (after any time spent on the network).
DEBUG_EVENT_LEAVE_DATA	Inbound	CALLRETURN	Generated if additional data is sent to before control flow returns (before any time spent on the network).

Part

V

Ch

34

continues

Table 34.2 Continued

Event Name	Type	Category	Description
DEBUG_EVENT_LEAVE_EXCEPTION	Inbound	CALLRETURN	Generated if additional data is sent to support a function enter (after any time spent on the network).
DEBUG_EVENT_LEAVE_NORMAL	Inbound	CALLRETURN	Generated on a normal return of control (before any time on the network).
DEBUG_EVENT_QUERY_ENTER	Outbound	QUERYRESULT	Generated on the server side when a query is received from a client (after time spent on the network).
DEBUG_EVENT_QUERY_LEAVE	Inbound	QUERYRESULT	Generated on the server side when the query is returned to a client (before any time on the network).
DEBUG_EVENT_QUERY_RESULT	Inbound	QUERYRESULT	Generated on the client side when the query is returned from the server.
DEBUG_EVENT_QUERY_SEND	Outbound	QUERYRESULT	Generated on the client side when the query is sent to the server (before any time on the network).
DEBUG_EVENT_RETURN_DATA	Inbound	CALLRETURN	Generated if additional data is sent before control flow is returned.
DEBUG_EVENT_RETURN_EXCEPTION	Inbound	CALLRETURN	Generated if an exception occurs.
DEBUG_EVENT_RETURN_NORMAL	Inbound	CALLRETURN	Generated on a Normal return of control.
DEBUG_EVENT_RETURN_EXCEPTION	Inbound	CALLRETURN	Generated if an exception occurs.
DEBUG_EVENT_TRANSACTION_COMMIT	Generic	TRANSACTION	Generated when a transaction commits.
DEBUG_EVENT_TRANSACTION_ROLLBACK	Generic	TRANSACTION	Generated when a transaction rolls back.
DEBUG_EVENT_TRANSACTION_START	Generic	TRANSACTION	Generated when a transaction starts.

Adding the Firing of an Event to Your Code

In this section you'll see what code is needed to add one of the stock events to one of your components.

Given the architecture of the Event Analysis framework, it's necessary that a component register with the LEC prior to generating the event. This allows the Visual Studio Analyzer to apply filters on the event. Use the Visual Studio Analyzer COM interface `ISystemDebugEventInstall` if you are using Visual C++ and the `ISystemDEventInstallAuto` if you are using Visual Basic. This interface has the methods shown in Table 34.3.

Table 34.3 Methods of the `ISystemDebugEventInstall` COM Interface

Interface Name	Description
IsSourceRegistered	Returns `True` if this type of COM component has previously been registered for sending events to the LEC.
RegisterSource	Registers this type of COM component for sending events to the LEC. This type of COM object might begin an Event Session.
UnRegisterSource	Unregisters this type of COM component for sending events to the LEC.
RegisterEventCategory	Creates a new custom event category.
RegisterCustomEvent	Registers a user-defined event. Tells LEC that this component will generate events of this type.
RegisterStockEvent	Registers this component for sending one of the stock events from Table 34.2.
IsDynamicSourceRegistered	Reports if a component has already been registered as a dynamic event source
RegisterDynamicSource	Register this type of COM component as a source for dynamic events.
UnregisterDynamicSource	Unregisters the dynamic source.

This interface enables the component to communicate to the LEC which event capabilities the object uses. The most common use is to call `RegisterSource` when the object is registering itself as a COM object. If any custom events are needed the COM object needs to use the `RegisterEventCategory` function to create these custom events. When custom categories have been created, the COM object needs to tell the LEC which events it is capable of issuing. It does this through the `RegisterStockEvent` and `RegisterCustomEvent` interfaces.

If this object is a potential dynamic source of events, it needs to register all its events with the LEC through the `RegisterDyanmicSource` functions.

After the type of COM object has been registered, when an instance of the COM object starts on a machine it will need to create a session with the LEC. This is done through the

Part
V

Ch
34

`ISystemDebugEventFire` COM interface if you're using Visual C++ or the
`ISystemDebugEventFireAuto` if you're using Visual Basic. This interface has the methods listed
in Table 34.4.

Table 34.4 Methods of the `ISystemDebugEventFire` COM Interface

Interface Name	Description
BeginSession	Connects this instance of an object with the LEC for reporting events.
EndSession	Disconnects this instance of an object with the LEC.
FireEvent	Generates a specific event.
IsActive	Reports whether the Visual Studio Analyzer client is interested in events from the calling component

These interfaces are very straightforward to use. Prior to sending any events to the LEC you
must call the `BeginSession` interface. The programmer should also call `IsActive` on the
`ISystemDebugEventFire` interface to see if the LEC is accepting events. After verifying that it is
an active session with the LEC, you can call `FireEvent`. Of course you should only call
`FireEvent` passing events that are either stock events or already registered custom events.

 TIP IsActive returns True only if an active recording filter includes the event. If it returns False, you can short-circuit out of the code to collect information and fire the event.

Because any COM object might be instantiated an unlimited number of times on a machine, an
LEC session enables the LEC to track which realization of the COM object is sending which
events. Each object must maintain an active session the entire time that it wants to send events
to the LEC.

From Here...

This chapter shows some of the power of the new Visual Studio Analyzer tool. For those developers that are creating components for large scale applications this tool will be indispensable.
In any application that contains more than a trivial development effort, the development team
should integrate the Visual Studio Analyzer system into the project from the start. This enables
rapid fault and performance analysis when the application is being deployed. The simplicity of
the interfaces for creating internally generated events makes this task trivial.

- For more information about debugging enterprise applications, see Chapter 3, "Debugging Enterprise Applications with Visual Studio."

- For more information about COM, DCOM, and COM+, see Chapter 9, "Using Microsoft's Object Technologies."

- For more information about creating reusable COM components, see Chapter 10, "Creating Reusable Components."

Using Visual SourceSafe

by Yanni Xiao

An Introduction to Visual SourceSafe

Many large enterprisewide software development projects involve teamwork and mixed-language programming and last over an extended period of time. Developers involved might come and go through the course of a project, and the person who coded a particular section of the program might not be around later on. Additionally, many large projects are developed on a phased basis, and various versions of the software are released over time. One of the biggest challenges in managing a development project with such complexity and coordinating large teams of developers working together is keeping track of the changes made to the source code. The larger the project is, the more difficult the task. The following are some typical problems with which a development team often has to deal:

■ Team members cannot tell who worked on a module or whether certain changes have been made unless they manually keep a history log. This can be extremely time-consuming and thus impractical.

■ Files are sometimes accidentally deleted.

■ Two developers working on the same file might inadvertently overwrite each other's work, and it is difficult to negotiate turnover of control.

Microsoft Visual SourceSafe provides just the right tools for solving these problems. Its source control mechanism offers the advantages of easy and efficient team coordination and version tracking without adding a new burden to developers, and it is useful to any team development environment. This chapter describes the fundamentals of using Visual SourceSafe 6.

Visual SourceSafe is a project-oriented version control system. It provides two primary benefits to the software development process:

■ Source control

■ Version tracking

When multiple developers are working on one project, it is important to have a source control mechanism. It helps ensure that only one developer is working on a particular piece of source code at any given time so that one developer does not overwrite another developer's work. Alternatively, you can have simultaneous editing and let Visual SourceSafe automatically merge the changes made by different developers and keep the developers in sync with each other's changes.

With versioning capability, anyone can re-create an earlier version of the software, as needed. This becomes necessary when you need to re-create an old build or create a new branch of the application.

In addition to the standard benefits of using Visual SourceSafe for source control and version tracking in software development for any size team, Visual SourceSafe also offers some Web features for managing Web site development projects.

You can work with Visual SourceSafe in one of the following three ways:

■ Visual SourceSafe Explorer—The graphical user interface in Windows 95/98 or Windows NT.

■ The command-line interface in Windows 95/98 or Windows NT—You can use the Visual SourceSafe command line to run batch files and macros. In addition, you can use the command line to perform all Visual SourceSafe Explorer commands.

■ Direct integration with Microsoft Visual Test, Microsoft Access, and Microsoft Visual FoxPro, and inside the Visual Basic, Visual InterDev, Visual J++, and Visual C++ integrated development environments.

This chapter focuses only on the graphical user interface.

N O T E Various software development tools, made both by Microsoft and others, now are integrated directly with Visual SourceSafe to make it easier to use. Any tool that is part of the Integrated Development Environment (IDE) provides Tool menu selections that allow you to check files in and out of Visual SourceSafe from within the IDE. For more information, see the documentation and online Help for those products. ■

Why Use Visual SourceSafe?

Compared to older, UNIX-based version control systems, Visual SourceSafe has two unique features. First, its architecture is project-oriented rather than file-oriented. It keeps track of not only the changes made to each and every file but also the relationships among files. The key concept in understanding how to work with Visual SourceSafe is the idea of a project. A *project* is a collection of interrelated files that you store in Visual SourceSafe. You can add, delete, edit, and share files within and among projects. Second, its Windows Explorer–like interface makes it easy to use. So Visual SourceSafe actually helps the developers spend less time doing source code bookkeeping and more time programming.

Visual SourceSafe uses the reverse delta technique to keep track of project changes. That is, it stores only the latest and greatest version of each source file in the project as one complete version, plus all the changes required to go back to the previous versions. This ensures that storing old versions takes only a minimum of disk space and that you can access the current version immediately. Because the changes are not stored as files, there is no way to delete them, thus making Visual SourceSafe more reliable.

SourceSafe stores its contents like a database in its DATA directory, but only SourceSafe has access. Two files are created for each file and each project in SourceSafe, and they are stored in a subdirectory of the DATA directory. One of the two files is called the Log file. It doesn't have an extension. This is where SourceSafe information and differences between one version of the file and the next are stored. The other file is called the Data or Tip file. It has an extension of either .a or .b, and it stores the most recent version of the file or the project.

A Visual SourceSafe Network

A Visual SourceSafe network typically consists of a centralized Visual SourceSafe database on a server and several client workstations. The shared Visual SourceSafe database is where you store and track your code. To actually work on a file within Visual SourceSafe, you must obtain a copy of the file from Visual SourceSafe and place it in a working folder of your own. The Visual SourceSafe database is organized into a project tree with various projects and subprojects under a root project ($/). Visual SourceSafe associates every project with a working folder. Subprojects are created as subfolders within a project folder. You cannot choose a different working folder for each file in a project. However, each individual user can, and should, have a separate working folder for each project. This is a user-by-user setting.

Administering Visual SourceSafe

As the administrator of a Visual SourceSafe installation, you are responsible for setting up, configuring, and maintaining the installation. This section describes how to install Visual SourceSafe and use the Visual SourceSafe administration program for basic configuration and maintenance.

Setting Up and Installing Visual SourceSafe

The program SETUP.EXE is provided with the Visual Studio 6 CD-ROM to install Visual SourceSafe 6. The typical way of setting up Visual SourceSafe is to have a server installation on a network drive that is accessible to all users working on projects controlled by Visual SourceSafe and a client installation on each workstation. Although the server setup is all that is actually required, having only a server setup can generate a large volume of network traffic.

When you install Visual SourceSafe, you need two components—the Visual SourceSafe Explorer interface and the Visual SourceSafe database, which holds your project files and version information. Both are needed to use Visual SourceSafe.

The first step in creating a new Visual SourceSafe installation or upgrading an existing installation is to upgrade the server installation of Visual SourceSafe. The Visual SourceSafe administrator does this. If you are creating a new Visual SourceSafe installation, an empty Visual SourceSafe database is created for you. If an older version of Visual SourceSafe exists on the server, it will be upgraded to the new version automatically. However, be sure to back up the existing SourceSafe database before upgrading.

After an administrator has created a Visual SourceSafe installation on the server, users can run NETSETUP to copy the Visual SourceSafe executables to their hard disks to create a client installation. This setup installs, on a client computer, only the files necessary to run Visual SourceSafe. The Visual SourceSafe database or support files aren't installed. The client installation must follow a server installation and cannot be used by itself. You should perform a client installation in the following situations:

- You have heavy traffic on your network. The client option can help decrease the network volume and improve performance on the client computer compared to running SourceSafe from a server.
- You need to integrate Visual SourceSafe with one of the tools in Microsoft Visual Studio.

 During a server installation, the setup program puts a copy of the NETSETUP program in the folder in which Visual SourceSafe is installed on the server. You can double-click NETSETUP to perform a network client installation.

N O T E   To integrate SourceSafe with Visual Basic, first perform a server installation, install Visual Basic, and then either run NETSETUP to perform a network client setup or perform a client setup from disk. To integrate SourceSafe with Visual C++, perform a client setup either before or after installing Visual C++.

CAUTION

Visual SourceSafe installation places all the Visual SourceSafe files and several subdirectories (for example, WIN32, USERS, and DATA) under the main Visual SourceSafe directory, as in a database. Only the Visual SourceSafe program can create, modify, and delete files in those directories. Users should never manually change anything in those directories. All file storage is in proprietary Visual SourceSafe formats, and any change could cause unpredictable results or loss of data.

Running Visual SourceSafe Administrator

Visual SourceSafe Administrator is the administration program provided for configuring and maintaining the Visual SourceSafe installation.

To start Visual SourceSafe Administrator, complete the following steps:

1. Click the Start button.

2. Select Programs, Microsoft Visual Studio 6.0, Microsoft Visual SourceSafe from the menu.

The Visual SourceSafe Administrator main window appears, as shown in Figure 35.1.

FIGURE 35.1

The Visual SourceSafe Administrator program allows the administrator to configure and maintain the Visual SourceSafe installation.

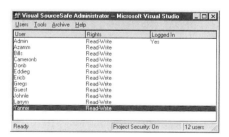

In a new installation, no password is set for the administrator. Because Visual SourceSafe security is controlled from inside Visual SourceSafe Administrator and any user who can access that program can basically do anything within Visual SourceSafe, one of the first tasks of the administrator should be to assign a password to the Admin user. You can do this by using the Change Password command on the Users menu as explained in "Maintaining the User List," the next section in this chapter.

Part

V

Ch

35

> **CAUTION**
> Write the password down in a safe place! If you forget the administrator's password, contact Microsoft Technical Support Services for help. You cannot assign a new password by running Visual SourceSafe Administrator without knowing the old one.

Maintaining the User List

As a Visual SourceSafe administrator, you are responsible for maintaining the list of Visual SourceSafe users in the database. You can use the Users menu in the Visual SourceSafe Administrator window to add, edit, or delete users and to change a user's password.

To add users, complete the following:

1. Select Users, Add User from the menu.

    Visual SourceSafe Administrator displays the Add User dialog box, as shown in Figure 35.2.

FIGURE 35.2
To add a user to the database, use the Visual SourceSafe Administrator Add User dialog box.

2. Type a name in the User Name box and a password in the Password box.

    Usernames can be up to 31 characters long, cannot begin or end with a space, and cannot include any of the special characters such as $, @, *, !, ?, ^, =.

    Passwords can be up to 15 characters long and can contain any characters. Initially set passwords to something simple, such as the username, and instruct the user to create a new password from within Visual SourceSafe.

3. To give the new user read-only rights, check the Read Only box. If this box is unchecked, the new user has read-write rights by default.

4. Click OK.

When you add a new user, Visual SourceSafe automatically creates an SS.INI file for that user based on the default SS.INI template in the \VSS\USERS\ADMIN folder. You can modify this template file to create a different default SS.INI file for each new user. For information on how to set security by user and by project, see the next section, "Setting Up Rights for Project Security."

N O T E The Visual SourceSafe database is the central database where all master copies, history, project structures, and user information are stored. A project is always contained within one database, multiple projects can be stored in one database, and multiple Visual SourceSafe databases can exist to store multiple projects. Each database is associated with a SRCSAFE.INI file. For security reasons, Visual SourceSafe's list of users and passwords is stored in a particular Visual SourceSafe database. This can be an advantage if security is the reason you want to install separate SourceSafe databases; however, to add a user to multiple Visual SourceSafe databases, you must add the user to each individual database.

To change a user's password, perform the following steps:

1. Select a user from the Visual SourceSafe Administrator user list.

2. Choose Users, Change Password from the menu.

   Visual SourceSafe Administrator displays the Change Password dialog box, as shown in Figure 35.3.

FIGURE 35.3

The Visual SourceSafe Administrator Change Password dialog box is used when a user forgets his Visual SourceSafe password.

3. In the New Password box, type a new password. (You do not need to know a user's old password to assign a new one, and Visual SourceSafe passwords are not case sensitive.)

4. In the Verify box, type the new password again to verify it.

5. Click OK.

   Visual SourceSafe Administrator changes the password.

N O T E   If a user forgets his Visual SourceSafe password, the administrator can use this dialog box to assign a new password, but cannot recover the old one. Visual SourceSafe does not prohibit you from reassigning a previously used password. Keep in mind that the Visual SourceSafe password is not meant to replace or augment your operating system or network operating system password.

As the administrator, you have a special password that is used to run Visual SourceSafe Administrator.

N O T E   As the administrator, you are responsible for controlling the location of the Visual SourceSafe database, the user list, and the access rights of each user, and for performing setup and backup duties on the database. So be careful with your password.

To change the Admin user's password, complete the following:

1. Select the Admin user from Visual SourceSafe Administrator user list.

2. Choose Users, Change Password from the menu.

   Visual SourceSafe Administrator displays the Change Admin Password dialog box, as shown in Figure 35.4. The administrator's username is always Admin.

Part

V

Ch

35

FIGURE 35.4

You can change your password in the Visual SourceSafe Administrator Change Admin Password dialog box.

3. In the Old Password box, type the old password.

You must know the old password in order to change it.

4. In the New Password box, type a new password.

5. In the Verify box, type the new password again to verify it.

6. Click OK.

Visual SourceSafe Administrator changes the Administrator password.

To delete a user, complete the following steps:

1. Select the user to be deleted from the Visual SourceSafe Administrator user list.

2. Choose Users, Delete User from the menu.

Visual SourceSafe Administrator displays the warning message Are you sure you want to delete? (see Figure 35.5).

FIGURE 35.5

The Administrator Delete User confirmation dialog box.

3. Click OK.

Visual SourceSafe deletes the selected user.

N O T E   You cannot delete the Admin user.

  If the deleted user has files checked out, a warning is not generated. To unlock and recover those files, run Visual SourceSafe as the Admin user and use the Undo Check Out command. This will leave the files in the SourceSafe database as though they were never checked out.

If the deleted user made valid changes to these files, make a backup copy of those files for emergency use. Then check the corresponding files in the SourceSafe database out to a valid user (perhaps yourself). Delete the files you just performed the Check Out on and replace them with the files containing the changes. Then check them back in.

To edit user attributes, complete the following steps:

1. Select the username to be edited from the Visual SourceSafe Administrator user list.

2. Choose <u>U</u>sers, <u>E</u>dit User from the menu.

   Visual SourceSafe Administrator displays the Edit User dialog box, as shown in Figure 35.6.

FIGURE 35.6

The Visual SourceSafe Administrator Edit User dialog box is used to change the username and access rights of the selected user.

 T I P A shortcut for displaying the Edit User dialog box is either to select the username in the Visual SourceSafe Administrator user list and then press Enter or to simply double-click the username.

3. Check/Uncheck the <u>R</u>ead Only box to give the user read-only or read-write rights. You can also change the user login name by typing a new one.

4. Click OK.

   Visual SourceSafe changes the selected user's rights and/or login name.

Setting Up Rights for Project Security

Security in Visual SourceSafe is based on user access rights. Default security in a Visual SourceSafe installation offers only two levels of access rights for the new users:

- Read-only rights—Users can see all files in all projects in the Visual SourceSafe database, but cannot change anything.

- Read-write rights—Users can see and change any file in any project in the Visual SourceSafe database.

If these two default levels of access rights are adequate for your installation, you do not need to go further. However, some Visual SourceSafe installations require more levels of security control. For these installations, you can enable project security and customize it to allow only specific users to have access to certain projects and certain commands. Four levels of access rights are available in Visual SourceSafe as described in Table 35.1.

Part

V

Ch

35

Table 35.1   User Access Rights in Visual SourceSafe

Rights	Description
Read (R)	Read-only access. Users can view files by using commands such as View and Get.
Check Out	Read-only plus Check in/out access. Users can modify files by using commands such as Check In, Check Out, and Undo Check Out.
Add (A)	Read-only plus Check in/out plus Add access. Users can add files to a project and modify the contents of a project using the Add, Delete, and Rename commands.
Destroy	Read-only plus Check in/out plus Add plus Destroy access. Users can roll back, purge, or destroy project contents.

To enable project security, perform the following:

1. Select Tools, Options from the menu in the Visual SourceSafe Administrator window.

   Visual SourceSafe Administrator displays the SourceSafe Options dialog box.

2. Click the Project Security tab.

   Visual SourceSafe Administrator displays the Project Security tab. If project security is disabled, all dialog box elements are disabled.

3. Click the Enable Project Security check box to enable project security, as shown in Figure 35.7.

FIGURE 35.7
To enable project security, use the Project Security tab in Visual SourceSafe Administrator.

4. Under Default User Rights, clear the check boxes next to the access rights you do not want to grant to the new users.

5. Click OK.

When you activate project security, you enable the security-related commands on the Tools menu: Rights by Project, Rights Assignments for User, and Copy User Rights. You can then assign rights in one of these three ways:

- Rights by Project—Shows all the users who have rights in each project and the effects of rights propagation. You can add and delete users' rights from any project and even add and delete users from the project.

- Assignments for User—Shows all the projects a user has explicit assignments in and what rights he has in each. You can add and delete assignments. However, the effect of propagation down the project list is not shown in this view.

- Copy User Rights—Acts as a template and copies one user's access rights to another user. After you copy rights, the two users have identical access rights in every project. You can, however, then individually change their access rights in specific projects.

N O T E When you add a new user and set that user's rights for a particular project, you create an assignment in the Visual SourceSafe database. Any assignment will automatically propagate down the project list until another assignment is reached. At that point in the project list, the user's rights assigned to that project would take precedence.

When you first add a user, he is given rights in the root project based on the default rights that you have established on the Project Security tab. So a user's rights in the root project ($/) form a set of default rights for that user. These default rights apply to all projects in which you do not explicitly set assignments.

To assign access rights by user, perform the following steps:

1. In the Visual SourceSafe Administrator user list, click a user.

2. Select Tools, Rights Assignments for User from the menu.

   Visual SourceSafe Administrator displays the Assignments for User dialog box, as shown in Figure 35.8. This dialog box shows all the projects the selected user has explicit assignments in and what rights he has in each. The effect of propagation down the project list is not shown in this view.

FIGURE 35.8

To assign access rights by user, use the Assignments for User dialog box in Visual SourceSafe Administrator.

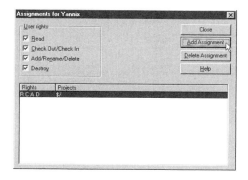

3. Under Projects, click a project.

4. Click the check boxes for the access rights you want to assign to the user.

5. Click <u>A</u>dd Assignment to display a list of projects to add the user to, or click <u>D</u>elete Assignment to delete rights for the user in the selected project.

6. Click Close.

To assign access rights by project, complete the following:

1. Select <u>T</u>ools, <u>R</u>ights by Project from the menu.

   Visual SourceSafe Administrator displays the Project Rights dialog box, as shown in Figure 35.9.

FIGURE 35.9

To assign access rights by project, use the Project Rights dialog box in Visual SourceSafe Administrator.

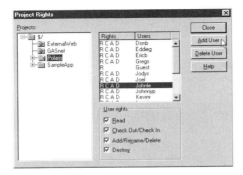

2. Under <u>P</u>rojects, click a project.

3. Under Users, click a user.

   Visual SourceSafe Administrator displays the current rights assigned to the selected users in the selected project.

4. Add or delete rights by clicking the appropriate <u>U</u>ser Rights check boxes.

5. Click <u>A</u>dd User to add a user to the currently selected project. (If the Add User button is disabled, it means that there are currently no users who do not have rights in the selected project.) Visual SourceSafe Administrator displays the Add Users for <project name> dialog box, which contains a list of users who currently do not have rights in the selected project. Click the check box next to each right you want to assign the user. Then click OK.

   Or click <u>D</u>elete User to delete a user's access to the selected project.

6. Click Close.

To copy one user's access rights to another user, complete the following:

1. In the Visual SourceSafe Administrator user list, select the user you want to copy rights assignments to.

2. Choose Tools, Copy User Rights from the menu.

   Visual SourceSafe Administrator displays the Copy Rights Assignments dialog box, shown in Figure 35.10.

FIGURE 35.10
You can use the Copy Rights Assignments dialog box in Visual SourceSafe Administrator to copy one user's access rights to another user.

3. Select the user you want to copy rights assignments from.

4. Click Copy.

After you copy rights, the two users have identical access rights in every project. If you change one user's access rights in a specific project, the changes are not duplicated for the other user, unless you use the Copy Rights Assignments command to copy user rights again.

Managing the SourceSafe Database

As the Visual SourceSafe administrator, it is your responsibility to manage the SourceSafe database. This involves database integrity check, database backup, and database cleanup.

The Visual SourceSafe DATA directory contains all your SourceSafe files and projects. Sometimes file corruption may occur due to network or operating system problems. You can use the Analyze.exe utility program from the command line to search for and fix any problems or errors in the database.

N O T E Doing a full backup of your DATA directory on a regular basis is highly recommended. ▦

Periodically, you may want to back up or archive your Visual SourceSafe database or parts of it, especially when it becomes too large. This allows you to

- Save disk space on your SourceSafe database server.
- Make the Show History command work more quickly.
- Transfer files and projects between SourceSafe databases while keeping history information intact.

In earlier versions of Visual SourceSafe, archiving and restoring were only available from the command line. Now, you can archive databases from the Visual SourceSafe Administrator program, as shown in Figure 35.11.

Part
V

Ch

35

FIGURE 35.11

Archive and Restore commands are available from the Archive menu in the Visual SourceSafe Administrator main window.

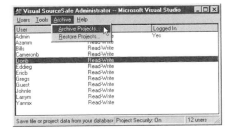

To archive a database, complete the following steps:

1. Click Archive, Archive Projects from the menu to display the Archive Wizard.

2. Select the project you want to archive.

3. Click OK.

4. In step 1 of the wizard, click Add if you would like to add additional projects to the archive. Then click Next.

5. In step 2 of the wizard, specify how you want the project to be archived and the name of the archive file. Then click Next.

6. In step 3 of the wizard, specify the version range you would like archived and add any comment you have to the comment box. Then click Finish to complete the archive.

To restore a database, perform the following:

1. Open the database into which you want to restore information.

2. Click Archive, Restore Projects from the menu to display the Restore Wizard.

3. In step 1 of the wizard, specify the archived file that contains the project you want to restore to the database. Then click Next.

N O T E   The archive file may contain projects from a different database.

4. In step 2 of the wizard, select the project(s) you want to restore to the database. Then click Next.

5. In step 3 of the wizard, specify where you want the project(s) restored to and add any comment you have to the comment box. Then click Finish to complete the restore.

Once every few weeks, you should clean the TEMP directory pointed to by the Temp_Path initialization variable in the SrcSafe.ini file. Visual SourceSafe normally puts files in its TEMP directory while running and deletes them before quitting. Some circumstances (for example, having to restart), however, can cause files to remain in the TEMP directory and thus waste disk space.

To clean the temporary directory, perform the following steps:

1. Click Tools, Clean up Temp Directory from the menu in the Visual SourceSafe Administrator main window.

The Clean Up Local Temporary Files Directory dialog box is displayed.

2. Click OK.

> **CAUTION**
>
> To keep user actions from interfering, you need to lock the database before you analyze, archive and restore databases, and clean temporary directory. To lock a Visual SourceSafe database, select Tools, Lock SourceSafe Database from the menu in the Visual SourceSafe Administrator main window. You should ask users to quit Visual SourceSafe before locking the database.

Using SourceSafe to Manage Code

Your source code is a precious resource, and you need to manage this resource properly and effectively. If you are working on a team-based project or a complex system for a customer, it is important to have a source control and version tracking mechanism to help you achieve these goals. Visual SourceSafe provides you with the right tools.

Using Visual SourceSafe Explorer

Many of the actions in Visual SourceSafe take place in the Visual SourceSafe Explorer. Its graphical user interface is modeled after Windows Explorer for ease of use and logical representation of your project files.

To start Visual SourceSafe, perform the following steps:

1. Click the Start button.

2. Select Programs, Microsoft Visual Studio 6.0, Microsoft Visual SourceSafe from the menu.

3. The Visual SourceSafe Explorer window is displayed, as shown in Figure 35.12. By default, the window is made up of three panes—the left project pane, the right file pane, and the lower results pane—as well as the toolbar, status bar, menus, and so on.

FIGURE 35.12

The Visual SourceSafe Explorer window is the main user interface of the Visual SourceSafe program.

Part

V

Ch

35

The left side of the Visual SourceSafe Explorer window shows the project tree with a root project ($/) at the top of the tree. It lists all the projects and subprojects currently under version control and gives a hierarchical display of them represented as folders. Of course, the tree list is expandable and collapsible. A plus sign (+) or a minus (-) sign next to a project indicates the existence of subprojects.

When you select a project on the list, the right side of the Visual SourceSafe Explorer window displays all the files contained in that project and the status information of those files. The Name column displays the names of all files in the project as well as a file icon next to each file, which provides a visual cue as to whether it is shared by two or more projects, whether it is checked out, and so on. The User column shows the name of the user if the file is checked out. The Date-Time column displays the date/time of the last modification if it is checked in, or the date/time when the file was checked out. For checked-out files, the Check Out Folder column gives the folder that the file was checked out to. The current project and working folder fields are shown at the top. Below the project list and file list is the results window for some operations.

Organizing Your Files into Visual SourceSafe Projects

Visual SourceSafe is not only for source code but also for any other files (for example, DLLs, graphics, documentation, and executables) you want to keep track of. To use Visual SourceSafe for source control and version tracking, you should store all your files in Visual SourceSafe and organize them into Visual SourceSafe projects.

Visual SourceSafe is project-oriented. Before you can do anything with files, you must have a project to place the files in. Therefore, when you begin working with Visual SourceSafe, the first thing to do is to create one or more projects and subprojects. For example, you are developing a system called Polaris, and various developers on your team are working on three subsystems: CrossReference, RuleEngine, and TransactionLoader, each of which has a physical server subdirectory in which to maintain all related files. Under each subdirectory, you might also have several different groups of files. Under TransactionLoader, for instance, you might have two other subdirectories: SQL and Documentation. When you are setting up your projects, it is always a good idea to mirror this directory structure in a Visual SourceSafe project tree. In Visual SourceSafe, you would create a project called $/Polaris. Under it, you would create three subprojects: CrossReference, RuleEngine, and TransactionLoader. Under $/Polaris/TransactionLoader, you would create two subprojects: SQL and Documentation.

To create a new project in Visual SourceSafe, complete the following steps:

1. Select the project under which the new project will be created.
2. Choose File, Create Project from the menu in Visual SourceSafe.

    Visual SourceSafe displays the Create Project dialog box, shown in Figure 35.13.

FIGURE 35.13

The Create Project dialog box in Visual SourceSafe enables you to define projects.

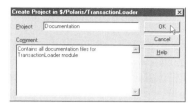

N O T E To create a project, you need read-write permissions on the root folder or the project folder in which you are creating a subproject folder. If Project Security has been enabled, you need Add/Rename/Delete rights on the folder within which you want to create a new project/subproject.

3. Type a name for the new project.

4. Type a comment and describe why you are creating this project.

5. Click OK.

Note that your new project name now appears in the Visual SourceSafe project tree. Continue to use the Create Project command to build the project tree structure that mirrors your actual file directory structure. After you create the project tree, you can add your files to the appropriate project or subproject by using the Add Files command.

To add files to a Visual SourceSafe project, perform the following steps:

1. Select the project to which the files will be added.

2. Choose File, Add Files from the menu in Visual SourceSafe Explorer.

Visual SourceSafe displays the Add Files dialog box, shown in Figure 35.14.

FIGURE 35.14

You can add files to your project in the Add Files dialog box.

3. Select the files to be added to the project. You can specify a file on any drive and folder, and that file is copied into the current Visual SourceSafe project. You must have the Add access right to use this command.

4. Click Add.

Visual SourceSafe pops up another Add Files dialog box for the comment. After you click OK, the files you added no longer appear in the File Name box because they are already part of a Visual SourceSafe project.

Part
V

Ch

35

5. Click Close.

TIP Don't keep executable files in Visual SourceSafe projects unless they take a long time to build. Do not take up space in Visual SourceSafe when you can compile and link to build an executable on demand.

Visual SourceSafe associates every project with a working folder. To actually work on a file within a Visual SourceSafe project, you must obtain a copy of the file from Visual SourceSafe and place it in a working folder of your own for that project. Your working folder can be a directory on your hard disk, or on a network drive, and it can be an existing folder or a new folder that Visual SourceSafe creates for you. When you set a working folder for a project, you make an assignment for the entire project list, including all subprojects under that project. You can, however, explicitly set a working folder for any subproject. A working folder is set per user, per project.

To set a working folder for a Visual SourceSafe project, complete the following:

1. Select the project from the project tree.

2. Choose <u>F</u>ile, Set <u>W</u>orking Folder from the menu in the Visual SourceSafe Explorer window.

    Visual SourceSafe displays the Set Working Folder dialog box, shown in Figure 35.15.

FIGURE 35.15

You must designate a working folder before you can start working on any files in a Visual SourceSafe project.

3. Click the Drives arrow and click a drive. In the Folders box, double-click an existing folder.

    If you want to create a new folder, type the new folder name in the <u>N</u>ame box and click <u>C</u>reate Folder.

4. Click OK.

Visual SourceSafe Explorer displays your working folder path above the file list.

N O T E You must specify a working folder to perform any action that takes a file out of Visual SourceSafe, including the Check Out, Get Latest Version, and Merge commands. When you attempt to use any of these commands without a working folder, Visual SourceSafe displays a message asking if you would like to set a working folder. Click OK to set a working folder. Visual SourceSafe displays the Set Working Folder dialog box. ▪

Basic Operations in Visual SourceSafe

As a developer on a project under source control, you will use the following four basic commands on a daily basis. They are available from the SourceSafe menu in the Visual SourceSafe Explorer window, as shown in Figure 35.16.

FIGURE 35.16
Four basic operations in Visual SourceSafe are Get Latest Version, Check Out, Check In, and Undo Check Out.

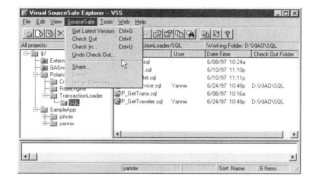

- Get Latest Version—This command enables you to copy one or more files into your working folder as read-only so you can compile or view them.

- Check Out—This command enables you to copy one or more files into your working folder as writable so you can edit them.

- Check In—This command copies one or more files you checked out back to Visual SourceSafe with all the changes you made.

- Undo Check Out—This command enables you to revert back to the state of the file before you checked it out. Use this as an alternative to using Check In.

To get the most recent version of a file, complete the following steps:

1. In Visual SourceSafe Explorer, select the file(s) in the file list.
2. Choose SourceSafe, Get Latest Version from the menu.

   Visual SourceSafe copies the file(s) from the current project into your working folder for read-only.

To check out a file, perform the following:

1. In Visual SourceSafe Explorer, select the file(s) in the file list.
2. Choose SourceSafe, Check Out from the menu.

   The Check Out command creates a writable copy of the file from the project in your working folder. The icon by the file you checked out will change to give you a visual cue: a checked out file icon will be bordered in red, and will contain a red check mark.

Part

V

Ch

35

CAUTION

Do not use the Get command to fetch files on which you plan to make changes. First of all, the files on your local computer will be read-only, so you will have to change their properties, and then you will not be able to check them back in when you are finished (because Visual SourceSafe doesn't know you were planning to change them—they are not checked out to you).

To check in one or more files to Visual SourceSafe project, perform the following:

1. In Visual SourceSafe Explorer, select the file(s) in the file list.

2. Choose <u>S</u>ourceSafe, Check <u>I</u>n from the menu.

   Visual SourceSafe displays the Check In or Check in Multiple dialog box, shown in Figure 35.17.

FIGURE 35.17

The Check In dialog box is used to copy your changes into the Visual SourceSafe database and create new versions of the file(s).

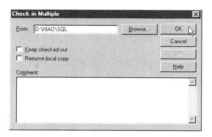

3. Type a comment in the Co<u>m</u>ment box.

4. Other options.

   If you want to continue working on the file(s) after you check in your changes, click <u>K</u>eep checked out. If you want to remove the copy of the file(s) in your working folder after the check-in is complete, click Remove <u>l</u>ocal copy. By default, Visual SourceSafe leaves a read-only copy of the file in your working folder when you check in a file. If you want to see the differences between the version of the file you are checking in and the version you checked out, click <u>D</u>iff. This option is only for checking in a single file.

5. Click OK.

The icon by the file you checked in will change again to give you a visual cue: A checked-in file icon will be appear as a simple icon, with no border or special coloring.

In any multiuser project, no file should be checked out for longer than it takes to make and test the changes to the file. If a file is kept checked out for several days by one programmer, other programmers will not receive the benefit of changes that have been made to it.

Sharing Code Between Projects

Sharing is a feature that enables the user to access the same file from multiple projects. This is useful for users who have several different projects that share common components. Changes made to the component in one project will be reflected in all other projects sharing this component. This feature saves time and resources by avoiding duplication of effort and storage.

There is only one master copy of a shared file, thus, any changes actually checked in propagate to all of the projects that share the file. *Branching* is like a shared file but without the dynamic link. Changes made to the file in one project will not be reflected in other projects. This feature is used when you must have a snapshot of all the files in a project at a particular moment for testing purposes or to create customized or parallel versions of a project. Visual SourceSafe tracks branches by making each development path a different project. Different project names keep the branches distinct.

To share the current version of a file with another project using a drag-and-drop operation, complete the following:

1. In Visual SourceSafe Explorer, click the project containing the file or files you want to share with another project.
2. Click the file or files you want to share.
3. Drag the file from its location in the file list to a different project in the project list.

Visual SourceSafe performs the share operation with no confirmation message. Visual SourceSafe does not allow you to share a file with a project that already contains that file. Alternatively, you can use the Share command:

1. In Visual SourceSafe Explorer, click the project you want to share files into.
2. Choose SourceSafe, Share from the menu.

    Visual SourceSafe displays the Share dialog box, shown in Figure 35.18.

FIGURE 35.18
The Visual SourceSafe Share dialog box has options for sharing files.

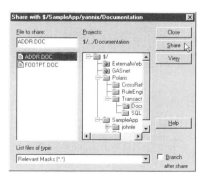

N O T E   Inside the Visual SourceSafe database, there is only one copy, the master copy, of the shared file; each project to which the file belongs simply has a pointer to it. When you change the file in any one project, Visual SourceSafe immediately updates it in all the projects that share it.

Part
V

Ch

35

3. In the Share dialog box project list, click the project containing the files you want to share.

4. Under File to Share, click the file(s) you want to share.

5. Click Share.

The file you share becomes part of the current project. All subsequent changes you make to the file are immediately part of the file in all projects that share it.

CAUTION

You cannot share files among multiple databases. For this reason, you should always organize your files into projects within a single database whenever possible.

N O T E   If a file is shared by multiple projects, destroying or purging it in one project does not delete the file from the Visual SourceSafe database, and therefore will not free any disk space. ▨

You can share any file from any project with any other project to which you have access. When a file is shared by multiple projects, the icon for that file in the file list changes from a single file to overlapping files, as shown in Figure 35.19.

FIGURE 35.19

The file icons representing unshared and shared files are different.

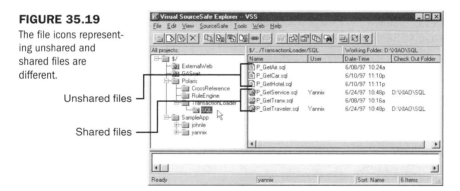

N O T E   To see which project the file is shared with, right-click the file, and select Properties. Click the Links tab of the Properties dialog to see a list of project names.

You also can use the command-line Links command to show a list of all projects that are sharing a file. ▨

To share and branch a file using the Share command, complete the following:

1. In Visual SourceSafe Explorer, click the project you want to share and branch file into.

2. Choose SourceSafe, Share from the menu to display the Share dialog box, as shown in Figure 35.20.

FIGURE 35.20

Using the Share dialog box to share and branch a file for separate use in another project.

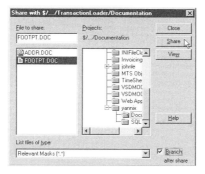

3. In the Share dialog box project list, click the project containing the file you want to share and branch.

4. Under File to Share, click the file you want to share and branch.

5. Click Branch After Share check box.

6. Click Share.

When a file is shared and branched, the icon for that file in the file list does not change to show overlapping files. This is because it is a separate copy of the file, not just a link to it.

Alternatively, you can use the file branching pop-up menu.

1. In Visual SourceSafe Explorer, right-click the file to be branched and drag it to the new project.

2. Release the mouse button and select Share and Branch from the pop-up menu.

N O T E Don't add the same file separately to multiple projects. Instead, share the file among projects.

Sometimes, a fix made to a branched file needs to be updated with the original project. The Merge Branches command allows you to combine any changes between separated files. The merge always goes in one direction, from the project in which the file was changed into the project or projects in which you want the changes to appear.

To merge branched files, perform the following steps:

1. In Visual SourceSafe Explorer, click the file into which you want to merge the changes.

2. Choose SourceSafe, Merge Branches from the menu.

   Visual SourceSafe displays the Merge dialog box, shown in Figure 35.21.

3. In the Merge dialog box, click the project containing the version of the file from which you want to merge the changes. You can then enter a comment when Visual SourceSafe prompts for one.

4. Click Merge.

Part
V

Ch

35

FIGURE 35.21
The Merge dialog box copies all the changes made in one branch of a file to another branch.

After you complete the merge operation, changes merged into a file are immediately part of any project sharing the file.

N O T E   Only ASCII and ANSI text files can be merged. You must have the Check Out access right in the project being merged into, and the Read access right in the project being merged from, to use the Merge Branches command. ▨

Version Tracking in Visual SourceSafe

In addition to various source control capabilities of Visual SourceSafe, version tracking capability is another primary benefit of using Visual SourceSafe in your software development process.

Visual SourceSafe tracks versions not only of files, but also of projects. Whenever developers check out files, make changes to them, and check them back into a Visual SourceSafe project, Visual SourceSafe tracks all the details of changes made on a file and project level. This history tracking feature enables developers to do a number of things:

- Compare two versions of a file or project and find out the differences.
- Track the history of any changes made to each file or project, when the changes were made, who did it, and what comments were made.
- Retrieve previous project versions for bug fixes or other purposes. By tracking project history, Visual SourceSafe enables you to readily retrieve previous versions of an entire application. This can help you resolve bugs reported from older versions and make sure they have been fixed in the current version.

N O T E   The number of versions of a given file that Visual SourceSafe can store is limited to 32,767. ▨

Visual SourceSafe tracks versions of files and projects by showing version numbers, labels, and date/time. You can label a specific version of a project with a descriptive string as a way to freeze a moment in the development cycle. This way, you can easily find and work with a project that has been identified as significant in the development cycle.

To label a project, complete the following:

1. In Visual SourceSafe Explorer, click a project.

2. Select File, Label from the menu.

   Visual SourceSafe displays the Label dialog box, shown in Figure 35.22.

FIGURE 35.22
The Label dialog box is used to assign a label to the specified version or current version of a file or project.

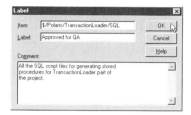

3. In the Label box, type a descriptive string of up to 31 characters.
4. Type a comment.
5. Click OK.

N O T E It is not recommended to label a file. When you label a project with a string, all the files in that project are labeled with that string. ▪

You can view the history of changes to any file or project by using the Show History command on the Tools menu. From the history dialog boxes, you can access a variety of other functions such as View, Get, and Share. You can also see details and print reports on the history of files and projects.

To show the file or project history, perform the following steps:

1. Select the file (project) of which you want to see the history from the file (project) list.
2. Choose Tools, Show History from the menu in Visual SourceSafe or click the right mouse button and select Show History from the pop-up menu.

   Visual SourceSafe displays the History dialog box, shown in Figure 35.23.

FIGURE 35.23
The History dialog box lists the versions, starting with the most recent.

Part
V

Ch
35

3. Click a command button in the History dialog box.
4. Click Close.

You can use the Show Differences command in Visual SourceSafe to compare the differences between two text files: You can compare two files on your computer; a file on your computer and a file stored in Visual SourceSafe; or versions of the same file both stored in Visual SourceSafe projects. To display differences between two versions of the same file, both stored in Visual SourceSafe projects, complete the following:

1. In Visual SourceSafe Explorer, select the file in the file list.

2. Choose Tools, Show History from the menu.

3. Select two versions in the History dialog box.

4. Click Diff.

   Figure 35.24 shows file differences in Visual format, which is the default view. You can choose three different formats to view the differences: Visual, SourceSafe, or UNIX.

FIGURE 35.24
The File Differences dialog box uses the Visual format as the default.

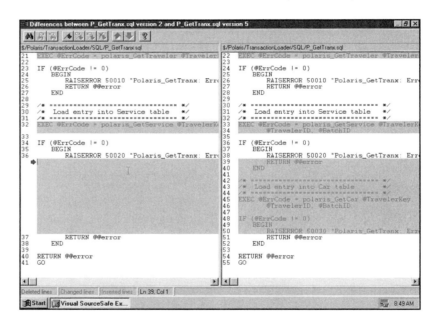

Visual SourceSafe displays the Compare file in the left pane of the display and the To file in the right pane of the display. Lines that differ between two versions are displayed in several contrasting colors. By default, for example, deleted lines are shown in blue, changed lines are shown in red, and inserted lines are displayed in green.

5. Click the Close button.

 You can set the colors in the Difference tab of the SourceSafe Options dialog box.

Using SourceSafe to Manage Web Content

Developing and managing a large-scale World Wide Web site involves a lot more than just writing HTML syntax. A large number of documents (for example, HTML files, script language files, and graphic format files), many developers, and lots of updates are normally involved in the process for submitting and updating Web page content. Typical source control and version tracking features of Visual SourceSafe can help Webmasters and Web administrators manage the task just like any other software development project. Visual SourceSafe 6 also has several Web features specifically designed to aid in managing Web sites. These Web features include

- Check Hyperlinks—Checks a collection of Web pages and reports any broken links.
- Deploy—Publishes Web content to a live Web server.
- Site Map—Generates a site map based on a collection of Web pages stored in the Visual SourceSafe project.

This section outlines these Visual SourceSafe Web features, which can be used along with the basic Visual SourceSafe features for source control and version tracking in Web site development projects.

Organizing a Web Site into a Project Tree

To use Visual SourceSafe as a Web site management tool, you need to first organize your Web site into a logical hierarchy of directories or folders, as in any other project. Then you can create the projects and subprojects in Visual SourceSafe Explorer and add your Web files to the project tree. By organizing the Web site into a Visual SourceSafe project tree, you get the standard benefits that version control has to offer to software developers. That is, it helps manage and coordinate the team by keeping track of changes and file versions and archiving your files.

For example, G. A. Sullivan has two Web site projects: $/ExternalWeb and $/GASnet. The former is for external purposes; the latter is for internal purposes, and available only to G. A. Sullivan employees. These two projects build completely different Web sites hosted on completely different servers. Some of the files between the two Web sites are different, but some are the same. When an HTML file is changed, this change might affect only one site, or it might affect both sites. It is important to copy the modified file to the right places. The sharing feature in Visual SourceSafe can help track and manage multiple webs automatically, just like any other projects. If a file is used on both sites, it can be shared between both Web projects. So whenever a change is made to this file in either project, that change is automatically reflected in both.

In addition to all the standard benefits of using Visual SourceSafe for source control and version tracking, some special benefits exist for Web projects. The next several sections describe how to designate a project as a Web project and how to use the three new Web features in Visual SourceSafe.

Part
V

Ch
35

Designating Web Projects

In order to use the Web features in Visual SourceSafe, the project first needs to be designated as a Web site project. Your Visual SourceSafe administrator can do this by using the Visual SourceSafe Administrator program.

To designate a project as a Web project, complete the following:

1. Select Tools, Options from the menu in the Visual SourceSafe Administrator main window.

   The Visual SourceSafe Administrator displays the SourceSafe Options dialog box.

2. Click the Web Projects tab on the SourceSafe Options dialog box.

   The Web Projects tab appears, as shown in Figure 35.25.

FIGURE 35.25
The Web Projects tab in the SourceSafe Options dialog box is used for designating a project as a Web project.

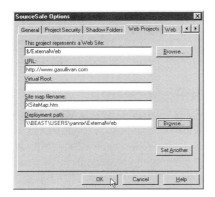

The Web Projects tab contains the following five text input fields:

- This Project Represents a Web Site—Type the name of the project into this field, or use the Browse button next to the field to select the project. All the other settings specified in the fields below apply to this project. This field must be filled in before you can designate the project as a Web project.

- URL—Type the uniform resource locator (URL) address for the Web site into this field. Either this field or the next field must be filled in.

- Virtual Root—Some Web server software supports this. If you have specified a virtual root in your server software, you should specify it here, without an initial slash.

- Site Map Filename—Type the name of the file you want Visual SourceSafe to use when it creates a site map. This field is optional. The site map file created by Visual SourceSafe will be an HTML file with links to all the HTML files in your Web project. With some minor customization, you can then add the resulting site map file to your Web site.

- Deployment Path—Specify one or more deployment locations for your Web site. A deployment location can be local or remote. You must specify a deployment path in order to deploy your project as a Web site, but you do not need to do so in order to designate the project as a Web project. You can use the Browse button next to this field to search for servers on your network. See the "Testing and Deploying Web Content" section later in the chapter for more details on deployment paths.

Once a project is designated as a Web project and you restart the Visual SourceSafe program, Visual SourceSafe Explorer displays the designated project with a special icon to indicate that it is a Web project. The Web project icon has a small global image superimposed on it. Whenever a Web project is selected, the commands on the Visual SourceSafe Web menu become enabled. Visual SourceSafe then can quickly check broken links among the project files, create a site map of the HTML files in the project and its subprojects, and automatically deploy the files to an Internet server location when they are ready. See Figure 35.26 for the Web menu in Visual SourceSafe.

FIGURE 35.26

The commands on the Visual SourceSafe Web menu are enabled whenever a Web project is selected.

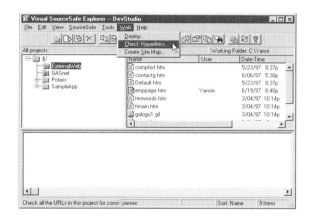

NOTE You can remove a Web project designation by using the Web Projects tab in the SourceSafe Options dialog box, from the Visual SourceSafe Administrator. Simply clear the URL and Virtual Root fields and then click OK.

Checking Hyperlink Integrity

As a Webmaster or Web administrator, you want to make sure not to publish your Web page content with broken links to a live Web server. One of the Web features available in Visual SourceSafe—Check Hyperlinks—makes it easy to test for bad links before you publish your Web page content to the server. You can choose to check the files in your working folder or those in the Visual SourceSafe project. Visual SourceSafe provides you with a report of any broken hyperlinks. You can access the Check Hyperlinks dialog box by choosing Web, Check Hyperlinks from the menu in Visual SourceSafe (see Figure 35.27). The broken links report is shown in Figure 35.28.

Part
V

Ch
35

FIGURE 35.27

In the Check Hyperlinks dialog box, you can request a report of any broken hyperlinks.

FIGURE 35.28

The Check Hyperlinks command reports broken hyperlinks.

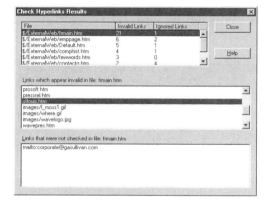

In earlier versions of Visual SourceSafe only internal hyperlinks and jumps within your Web site in the same Visual SourceSafe project tree were checked. Visual SourceSafe 6 allows you to check hyperlinks and jumps outside the project, including jumps to sites on the World Wide Web. Visual SourceSafe checks all links among your HTML files, and displays any potential problems. For example, the file frmain.htm in the project $/ExternalWeb/ refers to another file stlouis.htm, but this file does not exist in the same project. This hyperlink is, therefore, listed as invalid.

Visual SourceSafe checks only the links in HTML tags, including the <A HREF> tag. Links to other Web pages created using code, such as VBScript or Java, are not checked but only listed in the bottom list of the Check Hyperlinks result window, as shown in Figure 35.28.

Creating a Site Map

Another Web feature available in Visual SourceSafe 6 is creating site maps. Site maps are often helpful to the Web users. They provide a list of hyperlinks to the Web site's contents to help make user navigation easier. Visual SourceSafe can create a site map for your Web site easily by generating a new HTML file and writing out a list of links to all the HTML files within your Web site project. The name of this new site map HTML file was set by your Visual SourceSafe administrator, when the project was initially designated as a Web project (refer to Figure 35.25 in the section "Designating Web Projects"). The Create Site Map dialog box is displayed when you choose Web, Site Map from the menu in Visual SourceSafe (see Figure 35.29).

FIGURE 35.29

The Create Site Map dialog box enables you to create a site map.

 TIP Category names in the site map file are taken directly from your Visual SourceSafe project name, so you should use unique and descriptive strings as names for your Web site projects. Once the HTML site map file is created, you can add it into your project by using the Add Files command. If you add the file to your Web site project, be sure to check it out before running the Create Site Map command.

Testing and Deploying Web Content

Deploy is another Web feature in Visual SourceSafe 6. It can be used to send a Web project to one or more test servers or live Web servers that have been designated by the Visual SourceSafe administrator. Servers can reside on either local networks or on the Internet. If a server is outside the local network, it is reached by File Transfer Protocol (FTP). Your Visual SourceSafe administrator specified the deployment path when the project was initially designated as a Web project (refer to Figure 35.25 in the section "Designating Web Projects"). Because this command can potentially publish a Web project to the entire World Wide Web, Visual SourceSafe requires you to have Destroy-level access rights in the project in order to use it. Figure 35.30 shows the Deploy dialog box in Visual SourceSafe, which you can access by choosing Web, Deploy from the menu.

FIGURE 35.30

The Deploy dialog box enables you to send Web files to a server.

N O T E You can deploy any project that has been designated as a Web project, regardless of the types of files it contains. That is, it does not necessarily have to be an actual Web site. A single command then sends the entire project to the local or remote locations you have specified. In previous versions of Visual SourceSafe you could deploy only the entire project; Visual SourceSafe 6 now allows you to deploy individual files as well.

From Here...

Visual SourceSafe provides easy-to-use, project-oriented version control for managing software and Web site development. In addition to basic source control and versioning capabilities, Visual SourceSafe provides advanced functionality including branching and merging to support customization and parallel development and Web features for managing Web site contents. Most features in Visual SourceSafe are easily executed through its graphical interface, Visual SourceSafe Explorer. The configuration and maintenance of Visual SourceSafe installation are

Part
V

Ch

35

straightforward using its administrative program, Visual SourceSafe Administrator. Visual SourceSafe can definitely help the developers spend less time doing source code bookkeeping and more time coding. It fills a critical need in any team-based software and Web site development environment.

ON THE WEB

The very latest information on Visual SourceSafe can always be found on Microsoft's Web site at `http://www.eu.microsoft.com/ssafe/`.

The Visual Studio suite is specifically designed for team-oriented software development environment and contains many features supporting a team and its individual software developers. Refer to the following chapters for more information related to team development with Visual Studio:

- To learn about using Visual SourceSafe with Visual InterDev, see Chapter 19, "Advanced Visual InterDev Concepts.""

- To learn about the Microsoft Repository and the Visual Component Manager, products from Microsoft for organizing reusable software components, see Chapter 33, "Using the Visual Component Manager and the Microsoft Repository."

- To learn about the object-modeling tool from Microsoft, the Microsoft Visual Modeler, see Chapter 36, "System Modeling and the Microsoft Visual Modeler."

System Modeling and the Microsoft Visual Modeler

by Linda Callender Pannock

In this chapter

Understanding the Microsoft Visual Modeler

Object modeling, sometimes referred to as *visual modeling*, has existed within the software industry for many years under different names. Object modeling is one of the first steps in envisioning a system and communicating this vision through drawings or diagrams. As you model a system, you continually add design detail. Formally, object modeling is conducted as part of the system development process, and the model is delivered within a document or as part of a supporting tool. However, for every project, there may be a different modeling language or notation used to describe or draw the object model. Informally, the object model is roughly produced on a whiteboard, hand-drawn on a piece of paper (sometimes, a napkin), or created with a tool and language that only a small group of personnel understand well.

In the past, analysis and design were considered two separate activities during system development. The waterfall method and spiral method software methodologies supported the notion that first you analyze and then you design a system. As the industry has matured, the iterative process has emerged as a more practical and natural way of solving development problems when building a system.

ON THE WEB

There are many strategies for developing a project using the iterative process. The Microsoft Solutions Framework is a discipline based upon multiple processes for building a development process to be followed on a project. For more information on the Microsoft Solutions Framework, visit http://www.microsoft.com/solutionsframework/.

The Rational Objectory Process is a software methodology for developing software based on the iterative process. For more information of the Rational Objectory Process, visit http://www.rational.com/products/o_process/. It should be noted that in the near future there will be a superset of the Rational Objectory Process entitled the Rational Unified Process (RUP). The Rational Unified Process will replace the Rational Objectory Process.

Briefly stated, the iterative process breaks down a system development problem into multiple and manageable iterations. The features of the system are divided. Each iteration starts with the system from the last iteration and adds a new set of features. For an iteration, the development team revisits the design of the system and starts the analysis and design of new features to the product.

With the emergence of the iterative process, analysis and design are used throughout the development lifecycle. This analysis and design of a system are known as object modeling or visual modeling. Today, object modeling is used when an architect or developer needs either to rethink a design or to start thinking about a new problem. The Microsoft Visual Modeler is the tool within Visual Studio Integrated Development Environment (IDE) that supports this activity.

The Visual Modeler supports building models to design a system iteratively. A model is a collection of design elements that are interrelated. A model captures the relationships between design elements and the related details. Diagrams are the mechanisms that allow you to view the models from different perspectives. The diagrams support these different perspectives for the analysis of the object model. The difference between the concepts of the model and the diagrams is critical to distinguish because it affects how the Visual Modeler can be used.

The Visual Modeler was developed in conjunction with Rational Software Corporation; it is based on a subset of the Rational Rose product and integrated into Visual Studio. The Visual Modeler uses the emerging standard for notation or language, the Unified Modeling Language (UML), for all modeling activities. By utilizing the same language for analysis and design, you can use the tool naturally as you are thinking through a problem, instead of focusing on whether you are in analysis or design.

ON THE WEB

UML is a modeling language developed under the leadership of Rational Software Corporation and "The Three Amigos": Grady Booch, James Rumbaugh, and Ivar Jacobson. Together, with the contributions of many companies within the software industry, they reached a coherent level of consensus on the language that has caused UML to become a standard for building models and their associated diagrams for reusing designs or models. For more information on UML, refer to `http://www.rational.com/uml/`.

As the object-modeling tool for the Visual Studio Integrated Development Environment, the Visual Modeler is located under the Enterprise Tools program group within Visual Studio. It is an enterprise tool because the Visual Modeler is used in many different ways through the process of using Visual Studio. The Visual Modeler is integrated with multiple tools within Visual Studio: Microsoft Repository, Visual Component Manager, Visual SourceSafe, Visual Basic, and Visual C++. Today, Visual J++ is not integrated with the Visual Modeler; however, this does not preclude the fact that an object model from the Visual Modeler can be a model for something that will be written in Visual J++.

Understanding an object model for a system is important in comprehending the system's design; however, managing and maintaining all object models for the corporation is of key importance in lowering software development costs. The object models for all the corporation's systems can be kept in the Microsoft Repository. In this manner, the models or design patterns can be reused for other system designs where possible. These models may reflect effective design mechanisms or they may reflect the business domain for an organization.

The Microsoft Visual Component Manager acts as a front end to Microsoft Repository databases. It can be used to store components that may be reused in applications. The components may be accompanied by the model as documentation for the component. For someone who uses a component, it is helpful to visualize the component through a UML object model to understand the component's functionality and design details.

Throughout the modeling process, you can control your model through Visual SourceSafe. You can control your models by easily executing commands from the Visual Modeler within SourceSafe.

The Visual Modeler has the capability to generate skeleton code or forward engineer a model into Visual Basic and Visual C++. Therefore, it is integrated with Visual Basic and with Visual C++ in Visual Studio. Building on a component in an object model, you can generate the skeleton code through a code generation wizard in the Visual Modeler. You can also reverse engineer Visual Basic code into an object model. The capability of forward and reverse engineering has a powerful impact in that it allows the source code and the associated object model to be synchronized throughout the project lifecycle. In this manner, as a team develops code, the model can be periodically updated and the integrity of the system design can be checked easily.

Using the Visual Modeler in a Project

The next section will walk you through how to use the modeler effectively from the start of a project. You start with an empty model in the Visual Modeler. This will be saved as an .mdl file. You will build a skeletal base model and then learn how the Visual Modeler easily assists you in studying the model to build a system based on good design principles. Building a system for reusability implies that a system design is modeled using encapsulation and good abstraction.

Encapsulation is used so that objects (classes, modules, and controls) allow clients to see only a limited and specific interface. The implementation details are hidden from the object's clients. Developing a system with encapsulation is very important in software development. Without it, developers can innocently build components that depend on the specific internal design of another component. If the component is later modified, one seemingly simple change can result in a cascading series of additional required changes to multiple components.

A class or component should be cohesive and have low coupling to other classes or components. Obtaining the correct abstraction requires some time devoted to thinking about the abstractions for classes or components within the model. In fact, abstractions of class and components are recognized as so critical when modeling a system for reuse that some projects include a team role of `Abstractionist` on the project. The Visual Modeler supports the object modeling technique of discovering and understanding abstractions for a system. It is not the goal of this chapter to teach good design principles, but simply to show how the tool can easily assist you in focusing on areas that support good design.

TIP If you do not have an understanding of UML or any modeling language, it is best to learn the fundamentals of UML before learning the Visual Modeler. Otherwise, you may find yourself frustrated by not knowing the language rather than the tool. For example, normally a first-time programmer learns a little about a programming language (C++, for example) before learning the development tools that support the language.

You can use the Visual Modeler Help index. At the index, type in UML and then double-click UML Notation. In the Topics Found dialog box, use the UML notation to start at the beginning.

Figure 36.1 shows the tool when it is first started. The model browser is the top left window, and the documentation window is the bottom left window. The *model browser* shows the design elements in the model. Standard browsing techniques can be used to navigate the model in the browser window. There are two toolbars: Standard and Toolbox. The Standard toolbar has the Print icon, File Save icon, and other required features for working within the Visual Modeler. The Toolbox toolbar, located to the right of the Standard toolbar, is specific to UML and is used for building the model from the toolbox icons. It starts at the cursor icon in the toolbar.

FIGURE 36.1

A view of the Visual Modeler with an empty model.

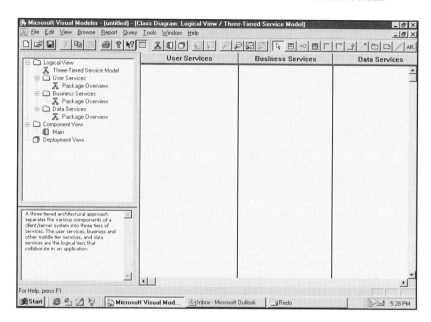

Every design element has a documentation field associated with it. The documentation field can be edited directly in the documentation window. In addition, every design element has a specification where the modeler can input the appropriate details for that design element. When you enter a description in a documentation window, it is automatically included in the design element specification. Viewing the documentation window can be turned off by using the View Documentation icon on the Standard toolbar or by toggling View, Documentation.

The Visual Modeler starts with a special class diagram known as a three-tiered service model. The three-tiered service model is a form of class diagram and is used as the highest level diagram (refer to Figure 36.1). It separates the class diagram into three tiers, assisting the user in thinking and envisioning the model in terms of a multitier architecture.

A *multitier architecture* is a paradigm used to complement other modeling techniques. A three-tier architecture is often used, although more tiers are possible. This architecture frequently has a direct correspondence to the physical location of components: desktop computers for client components, middle-tier servers with business-rule objects, and database servers.

▶ For more information about the three-tier architecture, **see** Chapter 25, "Clients, Servers, and Components: Design Strategies for Distributed Applications," **p. 727**

The three tiers can be described as follows:

- *User services* provide the visual interface for presenting information and gathering data in an application. User services connect users with the application and request the business or data services needed by users to execute business tasks.

- *Business services* respond to requests from users (or other business services) to execute a business task. They accomplish this by requesting the data services needed and applying formal procedures and business rules to the relevant data. This protocol insulates users from direct interaction with the database. Because business rules tend to change more frequently than the specific business tasks they support, they're ideal candidates for encapsulating into components that are physically separate from the application logic itself.

- *Data services* maintain, access, and update data. They also manage and satisfy requests to manipulate data initiated by business services. Separating data services allows the data structure and access mechanisms to be maintained, modified, or if necessary, even rearchitected without affecting business or user services.

Creating the Object Model

There are no exact steps to follow when creating an object model. The goal is to capture your ideas as they naturally occur in the thought process of solving a problem. Usually, the start of object modeling is experimenting with abstractions of classes and their relationships. As modeling progresses and the abstractions become better understood, experimentation may happen through thinking about the properties and methods of classes and their interactions, or it may happen with defining the details of the relationships between classes. Basically, each modeler solves design problems differently. The Visual Modeler has many easy-to-use techniques to accomplish the same task. Therefore, as the modeler thinks of ideas, they can be quickly committed to paper.

One of the goals of modeling is to create a system that has reused components from other systems and has supplied a repository with more components. Reusable components cannot be built without good encapsulation of the solution and exposing only what is necessary for clients. Normally, good abstractions for classes may take a few iterations when designing for reuse. As the team gains experience with an executing system, it may require revisiting the object model to rethink some of the abstractions for reuse. The Visual Modeler provides the flexibility and maneuverability to support this type of process for building a system.

Creating Classes

You start creating an object model by building the classes and their relationships. Given that the class is the primary design element in modeling, there are multiple ways of building the classes within your model:

- Select Tools, Class Wizard. You can build a class, complete with the details of methods and properties through the Class Wizard. Figure 36.2 shows a dialog box for completing the arguments for a class method. Notice the language option as well. You can choose Visual Basic, Visual C++, or Visual Java.

FIGURE 36.2

Building the
`GetTimeSheetForData`
method for the
`TSBroker` class
through the Visual
Modeler Class Wizard.

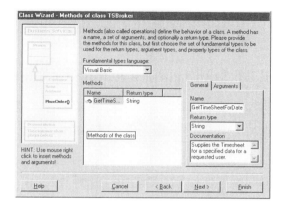

On a class diagram, right-click and select Class Wizard. Again, you can build a class, complete with methods and properties through the Class Wizard.

On the Toolbox toolbar, select the class icon and place the cursor on the diagram, left-click, click <<NewClass>> in the class element, and type the class name.

In the Browser window, select the package in which you want the class included, right-click, and select New, Class.

Select Tools, Create, Class from the menu and then click on the diagram where you want the class placed, left-click, click <<NewClass>> in the class element, and type the class name.

Import a model from a petal file. A petal file is a model represented as an ASCII file for portability among different platforms. You import a petal file by selecting File, Import from the menu. Figure 36.3 shows the dialog box for importing a petal file.

FIGURE 36.3

Importing Error.ptl,
which contains classes
for error mechanisms,
into a model.

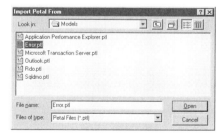

Creating an Interface Class

An *interface class* provides only the interface, and not the implementation. It is defined as an interface class through the stereotype for a class. On a class diagram, there are multiple ways of creating an interface class. Following are the ways to build an interface class:

Using the Toolbox toolbar, click the Interface icon (also known as the lollipop), click on the diagram where you want the class located, and type in the name of the interface class.

■ In the browser window, right-click the desired associated logical package, and select New, Interface. The new interface class is added at the end of the chosen package list. Figure 36.4 shows the IBroker interface class that was created in the Browser window under Business Services. The stereotype, <<Interface>>, appears within the class on the class diagram, whereas the browser window uses the interface icon.

FIGURE 36.4
The interface class, IBroker, as it was created through the browser windows.

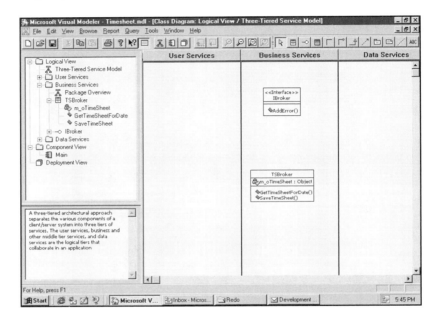

■ Select Tools, Create, Interface from the menu. Move the cursor to the location for the interface class and click on the diagram.

Creating Relationships

All relationships are created in a similar manner. To create relationships between two classes, click the appropriate relationship icon in the Toolbox toolbar. Drag the relationship between the two classes, click the first class, and drag the relationship to the second class. Figure 36.5 shows a generalization relationship between the IBroker class in the Timesheet sample and the TSBroker class.

N O T E The Visual Modeler does not support the Realizes relationship to reflect the implementation of interface classes. Therefore, to show this in the Timesheet sample, a generalization relationship was used and the viewer must understand that an interface class will require an implementation class and the relationship is always a Realizes relationship. In UML, this relationship is shown with a dashed generalization symbol. ■

FIGURE 36.5

The relationship between the `IBroker` interface class and the `TSBroker` class, shown using the generalization relationship supported within the Visual Modeler.

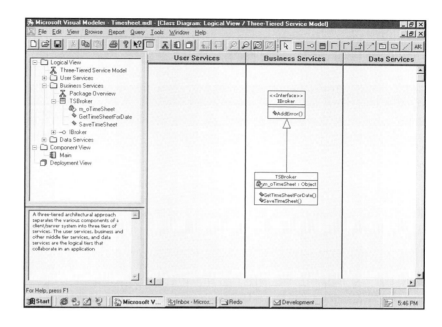

The different types of relationships are

- Association—By definition, there is no specific client or supplier.
- Aggregation—The first class is the "part-of" class relating to the second class, the whole.
- Generalization—The first class is the subclass, and the second class is the superclass.
- Dependency—The first class is the client class, and the second class is the supplier.

As shown in Figure 36.6, all relationships have a specification as well. To open a relationship specification, simply click the relationship on the diagram, right-click, and select Open Specification.

FIGURE 36.6

The specification for the relationship between the `TSBroker` and `IBroker` classes.

The type of relationship determines the details with the specification. In Figure 36.6, the relationship may be given a name, the visibility can be specified, and any documentation can be detailed in the documentation box.

> **T I P**   Browsing Tip: Within a specification, you can navigate the hierarchy of specifications through the Browse button. You can navigate via Browse Parent, Browse Selection, Select in Browser, or more importantly, Show Usage. Show Usage will deliver a list of all the class diagrams where the associated design element has been used on a class diagram. Selecting Report, Show Usage from the menu can access show usage as well.

To directly work on the class diagram instead of using the specification dialog box, click the relationship line and type the name of the relationship. An association relationship has two roles and multiplicity that can be specified. To insert the role name or multiplicity directly on the diagram, right-click the relationship line; then either select Role Name and enter the role name on the class diagram, or select Multiplicity and select the required multiplicity.

Creating Properties and Methods

The notation for a class is broken down into three areas called *compartments*. The first compartment is for the name of the class, the second is for properties, and the third is for methods.

To add methods (also known as operations) to a class, you have three choices:

- On a class diagram, place the cursor on the class, right-click, select New Method, and enter the method name. Adding the signature is optional at this time. Simply use the Enter key to enter more methods in the class.

  Once you have at least one method available, if you prefer, you can use the Insert key to include more methods. In addition, you can change the visibility type directly on the class on the diagram. Select the class, select the visibility icon, and select the new visibility type. Figure 36.7 shows the LoadBalancer class from the Timesheet sample and illustrates the methods for all the classes.

- On a class diagram, double-click the class for the class specification, select the Methods tab, right-click, select Insert, and enter the new method.

- In the model browser, select the class, right-click, and select New, Method.

To add properties (also known as attributes) to a class, you have three choices:

- On a class diagram, place the cursor on the class, right-click, select New Property, and enter the property name. Adding the initial value is optional at this time. Simply use the Enter key to enter more properties for the class.

- On a class diagram, double-click the class for the class specification, select Properties tab, right-click, select Insert, and enter the new property. Figure 36.8 illustrates the insertion of the m_oParent property for LoadBalancer class.

- In the model browser, select the class, right-click, and select New, Property.

FIGURE 36.7

The object model with the methods reflected in the three-tiered diagram.

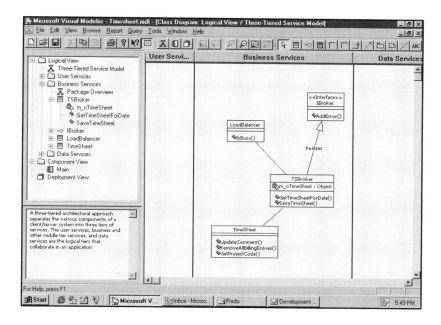

FIGURE 36.8

Within the specification for the class, a property may be added.

Creating Packages

Packages serve two purposes within UML. The logical package is for manageability purposes and for dividing the problem into smaller sets. The component package becomes a physical breakdown on a computer system. This breakdown usually comes in the form of a directory on a system.

To create a logical package, the following options are available:

- In the Model Browser, select the Logical View or the package in which you want to insert your new package. Select New, Package and then type the package name.
- Select Tools, Create, Package in the menu.

On the Toolbox toolbar, select the package icon, click and drop the icon on the diagram where you want the package placed, and type the name of the package.

T I P If you double-click a package, a new diagram will be opened, as opposed to the package specification. The specification can be viewed by selecting the package in the model browser and double-clicking it.

If it is necessary to add classes to the new package, there are different options:

- In the model browser, select the desired class and drag it to the package where you want to insert it.

- In the Toolbox toolbar, select the class icon and drop it on the class diagram for the package. There will be a list of classes in the model to select by clicking the name of the class, or you can specify a new class name.

A package has a compartment like the class icon does. The associated design elements of a package may or may not be shown on the diagram within this compartment. However, unlike the class compartment, the package compartment is not editable.

Creating Components and Component Diagrams

One of the next steps in building an object model is to think about where the software should execute and in what form. The Component View serves this purpose of modeling the physical view of the system. There are five kinds of stereotypes offered for components: ActiveX, DLL (Dynamic Link Library), EXE (executable), Applet, and an Application. Following are the multiple ways to create a component:

- In the model browser, select the Component View or package where you want to add a component. Right-click and select New, Component. The new component will be added at the bottom of the list. Type the name of your new component. Double-click the component to complete the component specification.

- In the model browser, double-click a component diagram. In the Toolbox toolbar, select the component icon and click it on the component diagram. Type the name of your new component. Double-click the component to complete the component specification.

- In the menu, select Tools, Create, Component. Click on the component diagram where you want the component placed. Type the name of your new component. Double-click the component to complete the specification.

Figure 36.9 reflects the GABroker component specification from the Timesheet sample. This component is a .dll and is designed to contain a TSBroker class, an ErrorItem class, and a TSErrors class.

FIGURE 36.9
The newly added component, GABroker.

Mapping Classes to a Component

One of the key activities of establishing components is to think about which classes belong to the component. There are multiple ways to assign classes to a component:

- In the component specification, select the Realizes tab and then select the class or classes that you want assigned to the component (see Figure 36.10). The three associated classes are identified with a check mark by the class name.

FIGURE 36.10
Assigning classes to a component can be accomplished via the Realizes tab of the Component Specification dialog box.

- In the class specification, select the Components tab, select the component you want to assign to the class, right-click, and select Assign.
- In the browser, select the class and drag it on the component where it should be assigned. You can also do this by selecting the component and dropping it on the assigned class.

Creating Deployment Diagrams

There can be only one deployment diagram within a model. The deployment diagram is used to model exactly where the software will execute on what hardware, known as a node. Building a deployment diagram, you are visualizing where the components and classes will operate as instances, and which nodes will communicate with one another. Therefore, a deployment diagram has only two design elements available: the node and the connection.

The following are different means to create a deployment diagram:

- In the browser, double-click the Deployment View. You cannot create a deployment diagram because there is only one deployment view within a model.
- Select Browse, Deployment Diagram from the menu.
- In the Standard toolbar, click the Browse Deployment Diagram icon.

As with all design elements in the Visual Modeler, nodes and connections also have specifications. For every node there can be multiple processes executing on it; these processes are listed in the node specification.

Using the Visual Modeler to Assess an Object Model

Now that you have the ability to create a model, you need to know how the tool supports your efforts in studying your model to build a better design. The goal of this section is for you to understand how the Visual Modeler can help you solve system issues or visualize your system without bogging you down in operating the tool. You will see some model browsing techniques so that you can experiment with abstractions of classes or with establishing clean encapsulations of the classes and components. You also will see techniques for experimenting with the model to determine if your components are reusable as they are, or if your components could be better if they were grouped a little differently.

Building Diagrams to Focus on a Subject Area

One way to think about a problem is through analyzing a particular mechanism of a system design. For example, in the Timesheet sample, you may want to focus on the solution for the error handling and have the need for a single diagram containing only those design elements. There are several ways to quickly build a diagram for focusing on certain design elements supporting a solution:

- You can start with a diagram that already has the classes you want on it. You can hide the classes or delete the classes that you do not want to see on the diagram. Select the classes that you want to eliminate from the diagram and Select Query, Hide Selected Classes. To further refine the selection of hiding classes, select only the supplier classes, only the client classes, or both; these can be selected in the Hide Selected Elements dialog box.

■ You can create a new diagram in the browser window by right-clicking the appropriate package and selecting New, Class Diagram. Select Query, Add Classes from the menu. A dialog box will appear as shown in Figure 36.11. It will contain a list of classes to choose from the associated package.

FIGURE 36.11

The dialog box for quickly adding class design elements to a class diagram.

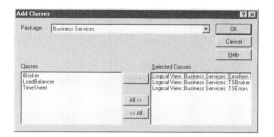

■ Start with an empty class diagram, as just discussed. Place the class critical for analyzing in the diagram. Select the class and select Query, Expand Selected Classes. In the Expand Selected Elements dialog box, select the number of levels, suppliers, or client classes you want to include on the diagram (see Figure 36.12). Choose Relations, and select the appropriate relationships you need to examine. Another use of the Relation selection is to study the generalization relationships in the object model.

FIGURE 36.12

Select the options for expanding the model in a diagram that depicts the selected classes.

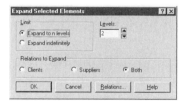

TIP Select View, Browser from the menu, if you want to eliminate the browser window and have more space for your diagram.

The Reassign command (located in Edit, Reassign) replaces one design element within a diagram with a chosen design element. This allows a user to evaluate the new design element within the context of where the replacement took place. As an example, replacing TimeSheet with MTSTimeSheet results in the design element reflecting MTSTimeSheet (from Data Services) in the diagram. This will not permanently reassign the TimeSheet to the User Services package; it will only reassign the design element for the diagram.

CAUTION

You can delete a class from a class diagram by using the Delete key or selecting Edit, Delete from the menu. This will not delete the class from the model; it will delete the class only from the diagram.

To delete a class from the model, use Edit, Delete from model. You may want to run Report, Show Usage on a class before deleting the class from the model. This command will produce a report to let you know which diagrams are using the class.

Analyzing Properties or Methods

To start examining the properties or methods within this view, you may want to have a few methods showing on each class within your diagram. To choose only certain methods or properties within the class, do the following: Click a class, right-click, and select Options. The pop-up menu allows you to Show All Properties or Methods, Suppress Properties or Methods, and Select Properties and Methods. In addition, you can show the signature for methods by using the Show Method Arguments command. Figure 36.13 shows the dialog box for selecting properties and methods on the TSBroker class from the Timesheet Sample.

FIGURE 36.13

The dialog box for selecting properties and methods to be displayed on a class within a class diagram.

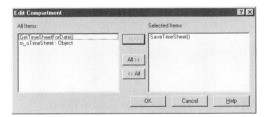

 T I P You can click a property or method shown on a class diagram, and it will expand to show the types and signature, respectively.

Another way to alter the information displayed in the diagram is to select the class or classes and use Edit, Diagram Object Properties. The look and feel of the diagram can be set for the current diagram.

Browsing the Model Diagrams

The three types of UML diagrams supported by the Visual Modeler are the class diagram, component diagram, and the deployment diagram. As a model grows and the number of diagrams grows, there are browsing capabilities to manage these diagrams within the tool. The Standard toolbar buttons for Browse Class Diagram and Browse Component Diagram invoke a mechanism for selecting from a list of the respective type of model diagram. If the Browse Deployment Diagram button is used, it immediately brings up the deployment diagram, since there is only one per model.

As you are thinking through a design problem, you can use the Browse Parent and Browse Previous Diagram from the Standard toolbar to help navigate through a hierarchy of diagrams. The Standard toolbar also includes a zoom-out and zoom-in to view an entire diagram or sections, depending on your modeling activity.

Moving Classes Within the Architecture

At this point, you may decide that there is a more logical grouping for a set of classes, or that you want a certain class to be within a business services tier instead of in a data services tier. For example, suppose that the TimeSheet class needed to move to the User Services. On the three-tiered class diagram, simply select the TimeSheet class, move it to the User Services package, right-click, and select Relocate. The class will automatically be moved to the logical package, User Services. The relocate command can also be executed by selecting Edit, Relocate from the menu.

Another mechanism for relocating classes may be found in the browser windows. Select the class you want to relocate and drag it to the new logical package. (You must be aligned with the package name for the tool to understand where the class should be newly associated.)

Controlling the Object Model with Microsoft Visual SourceSafe

Once your object model has become stable, you should start controlling the object model. Microsoft Visual SourceSafe is a tool for managing the artifacts of a project. The artifacts may be source code files, documentation files, or the object model.

▶ For details on how to use Visual SourceSafe, **see** Chapter 35, "Using Visual SourceSafe," **p. 997**

The Visual Modeler and Visual SourceSafe have been integrated so that a user can place an object model under control through the Visual Modeler. The commands that are required to control an object model are under Tools, SourceSafe.

It is important to begin controlling your object model as soon as the model is stabilized to gain the advantages of managing your project using SourceSafe. You must have a project file set up for your object model so that you can add your model to it. You can add the model file to the project through the Visual Modeler. Once the object model is open in the Visual Modeler, Select Tools, SourceSafe, Add to Source Control from the menu. The dialog box for adding the object model to SourceSafe is shown in Figure 36.14. Notice that you can choose to keep the model checked out under your current username. Figure 36.15 shows the results of executing the Add to SourceSafe command in the Visual Modeler to add the model to the Timesheet sample project.

FIGURE 36.14

The dialog box for adding an object model to Visual SourceSafe.

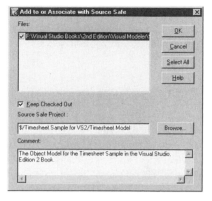

FIGURE 36.15

The Timesheet sample object model, Timesheet.mdl, has been placed under control in Visual SourceSafe and remains checked out to the user.

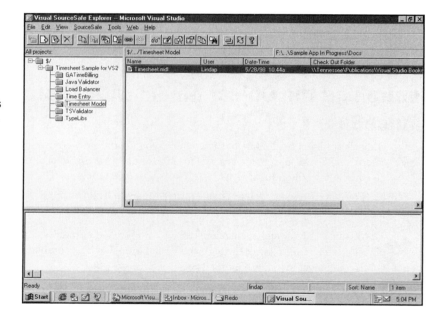

Once the model is under control, you can choose to check in or check out the model, or simply get the latest version of the object model. If you do not want to save the changes in the model, you can do an Undo Check Out, and this will restore the version in Visual SourceSafe to the version before it was checked out. In addition, you can start Visual SourceSafe by selecting Tools, SourceSafe, Start Explorer from the menu.

Generating Code from the Model

After you create a model, the Visual Modeler can automatically generate class code and function stubs, with comments, for your project. Currently, the forward engineering is supported for Visual Basic and Visual C++. You can choose to let the Visual Modeler automatically generate code for your entire model, or select specific elements of the model. You can also control what is generated and how it looks by configuring options in the Code Generation Wizard. You can configure your options by selecting Tools, Edit Model Properties; there you can specify in the Visual C++ tab or the Visual Basic tab some details on how the code generator should produce the source code.

To use the Code Generation Wizard, follow these steps:

1. In an open model, select the components that need to have code generated, select Tools, Generate Code or right-click and select Generate Code. As a Visual Basic example, select the GABroker component in the browser window. If you want to select just a class, then the class will need to be assigned to a component. If the class is not assigned to a component, the tool will lead you through the assigning.

2. The Select Classes dialog box appears (see Figure 36.16). You now can add classes beyond the selected GABroker component.

FIGURE 36.16
Use the Select Classes dialog box to determine the classes for which code will be generated.

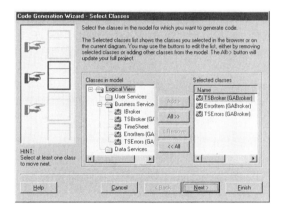

3. Click Next. The Preview Classes dialog box appears (see Figure 36.17).

4. If you choose to preview the code before it is generated (recommended), highlight a specific class and click the Preview button. You'll see a series of four dialog boxes that allow you to tune your code: Class Options, Property Options, Role Options, and Method Options. Click the Finish button to return to the Preview Classes dialog box. Repeat with another class, if desired.

FIGURE 36.17

With the Preview Classes dialog box, you can preview the code that will be generated for a specific class and change any options as required before actually generating the code.

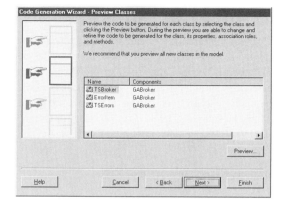

5. When you are finished previewing classes, click the <u>N</u>ext button in the Preview Classes dialog box. The General Options dialog box appears. In the General Options dialog box, you can select options that control the generation of comments, debugging code, and other additions that may make your code easier to understand and debug. Make your selections and click <u>N</u>ext.

6. Review the information in the Finish dialog box. At this point, you can go back and change any of your settings by clicking the <u>B</u>ack button; otherwise, click <u>F</u>inish.

7. A progress dialog box appears to keep you apprised of the code-generation process. The Code Generation Wizard presents a Summary dialog box when finished.

8. To review the results of the process, use the Summary and Log pages to see what occurred. Naturally, you can also review the generated code in Visual Basic (see Figure 36.18). In the object model, however, some new methods or properties will be added depending on the selections for each class from the Preview dialogs discussed earlier.

There are several items in Figure 36.18 that should be pointed out. First, in the Related Documents of the project, there is listed the Timesheet.mdl from where the code was generated. The documentation from the specification of class TSBroker is used as comments in the source file.

> **CAUTION**
>
> The ##ModelID should not be changed by the developer because this is used by the Visual Modeler for mapping the classes and their components during the round-trip engineering process.

To browse the associated source code with a component from the Visual Modeler, select the component in a diagram, and then select <u>B</u>rowse, <u>S</u>ource Code from the menu. The appropriate Visual development tool, Visual Basic or Visual C++, will start and the associated source code will be displayed in the project.

FIGURE 36.18
The Visual Basic code generated for the GABroker.dll component.

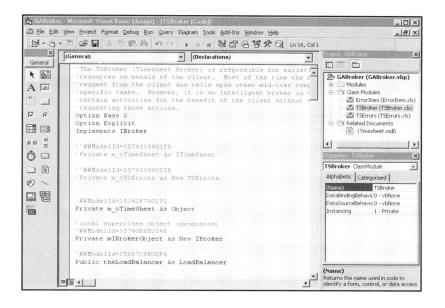

N O T E *Round-trip engineering* allows you to keep your model in sync with your code, and vice versa. Round-trip engineering is really just a combination of code generation and reverse engineering. With round-trip engineering, however, you get the advantage of having code and comments properly formatted by the Code Generation Wizard so that they, with any changes, can be properly imported back into the model and so that changes in the model can be reinserted into the code. As you can see, the Visual Modeler is a tool that truly supports the iterative development process.

To generate Visual C++ code from the Load Balancer Server component in the browser window, follow these steps:

1. In the browser window, select the component for code generation. In the Timesheet model, select LoadBalanceSvr with a right mouse click and then select Generate Code.

2. Select the project to use for the generated Visual C++ code in the dialog box (see Figure 36.19).

FIGURE 36.19
The dialog box for selecting the Visual C++ project for forward engineering a component.

3. Once the project is selected, the code is generated. There will be a summary and a log that can be reviewed for any errors in the code generation. The generated code is shown in Figure 36.20.

FIGURE 36.20
The generated code for a Visual C++ component.

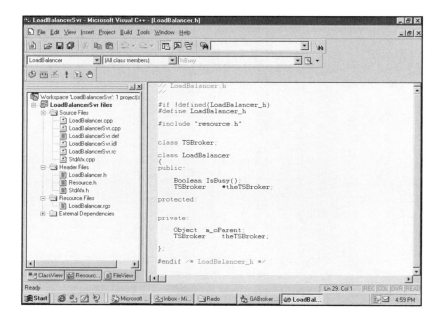

Aligning the Code and the Object Model

Even if you have never performed any design work on your application, the Visual Modeler can read through your Visual Basic code and create an object model that contains all classes, modules, controls, and relationships. This can be very useful for improving your system architecture, adding objects, doing additional design work, finding reusable code, or acquainting new people with the existing system.

Through the Reverse Engineering Wizard for Visual Basic, you can customize what types of objects and relationships are created and drawn. To bring up the Reverse Engineering Wizard and set configuration options, follow these steps:

1. Load your model, if you haven't already done so (choose File, Open from the menu), or start with an empty model.

2. Choose Tools, Visual Basic, Reverse Engineering Wizard from the menu.

3. The dialog box will ask which project should be reverse-engineered. Once the project is chosen, the Visual Modeler will start Visual Basic and bring up the chosen project.

4. The Selection of Project Items dialog box appears (see Figure 36.21). In this dialog box, you select only those components on which you want to focus. In this example, the GABroker project was chosen, so only the three modules can be selected.

FIGURE 36.21

The Selection of Project Items dialog box allows you to save your project and model before the reverse-engineering process as a precaution.

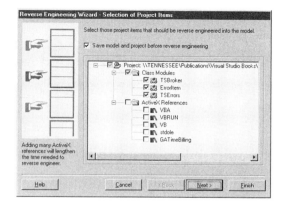

5. The Assignment of Project Items dialog box appears (see Figure 36.22). The standard Logical View includes (by default) three packages reflecting the typical three-tiered service model. Drag components from the Selected Project Items list into the desired packages in the Logical View packages list.

FIGURE 36.22

Use the Assignment of Project Items dialog box to group your components into packages.

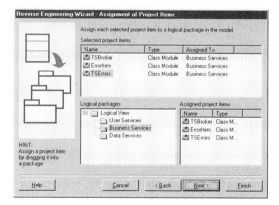

6. By highlighting a package, you can see which components have been included in that package in the Assigned Project Items list. When you are satisfied with the assignments, click the Next button.

7. The Finish dialog box appears, outlining the process that is about to occur. The Finish dialog box summarizes the impending reverse-engineering process to give you the opportunity to review the outcome before it occurs.

8. A Progress dialog box appears that provides the status of the reverse-engineering process. When it is complete, a Summary dialog box appears, allowing you to review the additions or changes made to your model.

After importing all the various elements from the project, the Visual Modeler returns the complete model (see Figure 36.23) and an initial diagram attempting to space and group the various elements in a readable format. You will find that you may need to do some reorganizing to make the diagram more readable.

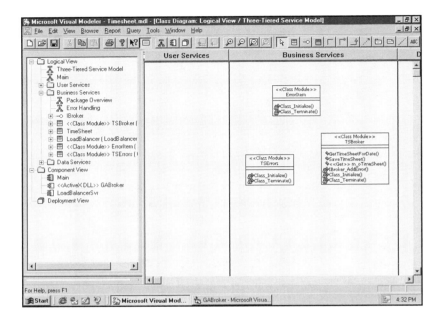

From Here...

So, where does the Visual Modeler fit into the software development lifecycle? Wherever the developer wants to use it. Normally, you would begin with the Visual Modeler from the start of a project. However, for those developers or projects that start with code first or those who need to justify object modeling as a first activity, a recommendation is to reverse engineer some of the pre-existing code. Once you can visualize the model, you will quickly see areas of improvement to the overall design for the model. The important concept to remember is to do object modeling during software development to understand how code decisions affect a system design or how design decisions affect the software. For more information on some of the topics addressed in this chapter, see the following chapters:

- For a thorough overview of the support provided for object-oriented development by Microsoft tools, see Chapter 9, "Using Microsoft's Object Technologies."

- To further understand the importance of reuse within an organization, see Chapter 10, "Creating Reusable Components."

- For in-depth information on the multitier architecture, see Chapter 25, "Client, Servers, and Components: Design Strategies for Distributed Applications."

- For information on other tools that support teams of developers who must work effectively together, see Chapter 33, "Using the Visual Component Manager and the Microsoft Repository," and Chapter 35, "Using Visual SourceSafe."

Appendix

The Sample Application Suite

by Don Benage

In this appendix

An Overview of the Sample Application Suite

This appendix describes the sample application suite. The sample is a Timesheet application used by consultants to enter information about the hours worked on various projects that will ultimately be used to drive both payroll and billing applications. The application isn't intended to be a complete, customer-ready application. Its primary purpose is to instruct and to be used as a demonstration of various technologies, so we have endeavored to write code that is clearly presented and commented. Elegant and highly optimized code that is of an obscure nature has been avoided.

Sample Company Characteristics

The name of the "fictitious" company being used is G. A. Sullivan (the name of the organization that wrote this book.) For the purposes of this sample, we have imagined that G. A. Sullivan has some different characteristics than those of the real company. The fictitious company is a U.S.-based firm that employs in excess of ten thousand people. There are thousands of consultants, hundreds of project managers, and dozens of human resources (HR) personnel. In other words, it is important that the applications scale well!

Actors/Roles

Employees for G. A. Sullivan can take on one of three roles:

- Consultant
- Project Manager
- Human Resources (HR)

All the actors in the system might be referred to collectively as employees. A Project Manager might also be a Consultant, but at any moment in time he will be acting in a single role (either Project Manager *or* Consultant, but not both). A Project Manager who is maintaining his own timesheet is acting in the Consultant role.

A basic use-case diagram for the overall system is shown in Figure A.1.

FIGURE A.1
The three different actors and the main use cases for the system at a very high level.

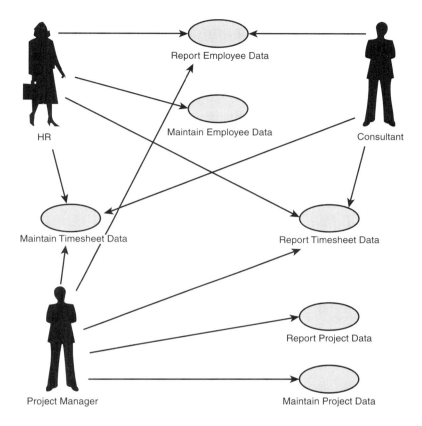

Business Rules

A few simple business rules for these various actors are outlined in the following:

- A Consultant is allowed access only to her personal timesheet. Consultants are allowed to view their own employee data, including their payroll information, but they cannot maintain this information. They must contact HR to make a change on their behalf. Consultants have primary responsibility for creating their own timesheets, however both HR and Project Managers can override information on a timesheet they are authorized to access (see the following) if necessary.

- Project Managers have access to their own data (acting in the role of Consultant) and can also access information about those Consultants who are currently assigned to a project they (the project managers) are managing. Project Managers don't have access to payroll information from the employee file. Project Managers are responsible for creating new projects, and they are the only employees able to do so.

■ Human Resources personnel have access permissions for all employee and timesheet information, but don't use the project files in any way. HR employees are the only people who can enter employee information for newly hired personnel. HR personnel can see all employee data, including payroll information, and they can override any timesheet information. All HR personnel are considered "god-like." Separate roles haven't been created for HRAdmin and HRManager, for example, which would certainly need to be created for a real system of this magnitude.

An Architectural Overview

A multitier architecture, both physical and logical, is used in this application. A simplified physical architecture is shown in Figure A.2.

FIGURE A.2

In an actual implementation, there will potentially be many clients of the various types outlined here, one or more mid-tier servers, and one or more back-end databases.

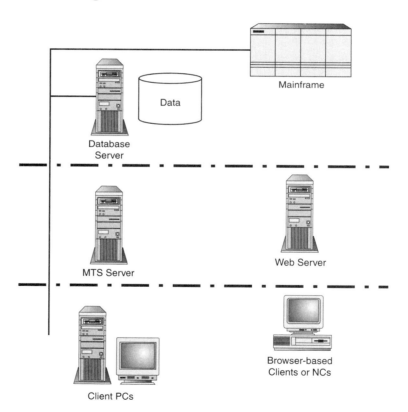

Mainframe

Data

Database Server

MTS Server

Web Server

Client PCs

Browser-based Clients or NCs

Clients

Three different front ends to the Timesheet maintenance portion of the application will be used:

- Visual Basic (VB) client—A Visual Basic front end using an ActiveX grid control
- Internet Explorer (IE) client—An Internet Explorer–based front end using the same ActiveX grid control
- Java client—A cross-platform, browser-based front end using a Java applet

The Visual Basic front end communicates directly with COM-based components running under Microsoft Transaction Server (MTS). In the case of the browser-based clients, the client communicates directly with the Web server, and Active Server Pages (ASP) scripting communicates with the MTS components on behalf of the client.

The VB client uses an ActiveX grid control to interact with the user as timesheet data is being entered (see Figure A.3). Some simple data validation and subtotaling is done directly within the grid control as it is being entered. Further validation to ensure that there are no obvious errors is performed before the information is passed (by value) to the middle tier. The validation done on the client is of the type that is unlikely to change as business conditions change (for example, a maximum of 24 hours/day or only numbers entered in numeric fields). Similar processing is done in the IE client (see Figure A.4) and Java client. The important point is to avoid network round trips for validation that is very unlikely to change and perform further validation that might change as a result of business conditions on the mid-tier.

FIGURE A.3
This Visual Basic client uses an ActiveX grid control.

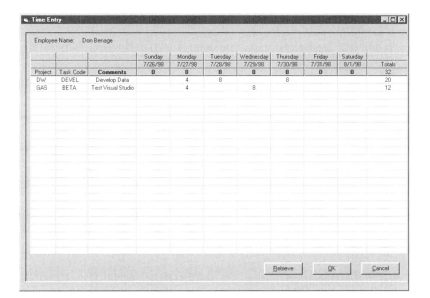

FIGURE A.4

The Internet Explorer browser-based client uses the same ActiveX grid control used in the VB client.

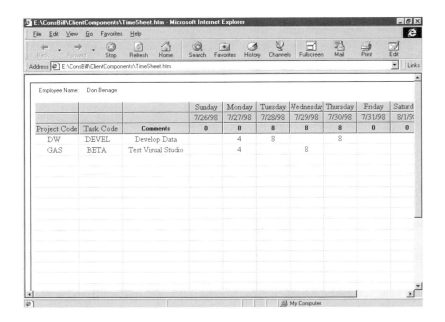

In addition to the user interface, the clients also make use of a client-resident object that holds the timesheet information as a collection of billing entries. When information is ready to be submitted to the mid-tier, all relevant state information is packaged into a variant array and passed to a mid-tier component that unpacks the array and makes the state information (temporarily) available to mid-tier components. When mid-tier processing is complete and persistent data has been stored, or an error condition has been detected and reported, the mid-tier state is destroyed.

Mid-Tier Components

In the middle tier a similar architecture is used for the various subsystems. The architecture required to support the Maintain Timesheet Data use case is used as an example for the two other systems (Employee Maintenance and Project Management). A high-level component diagram for the mid-tier is shown in Figure A.5.

Certain timesheet data and other state information will be instantiated in the mid-tier to represent various entities (for example, employee or project data). Most of the classes representing these entities are not shown in the included diagrams for simplification. The focus in the current document is on the control classes that implement the business logic and manage the flow of information among the tiers.

A Broker component will be used to enlist mid-tier resources on behalf of the client. Most of the time the broker receives a request from the client and calls upon other mid-tier components to do specific tasks. However, it is an intelligent broker in that it performs certain activities for the benefit of the client without the client requesting those actions. For example, the first thing the broker does when activated is to call a LoadBalancer component to see whether this particular MTS server is currently too busy to accept another client.

FIGURE A.5

The multitier architecture of the sample application.

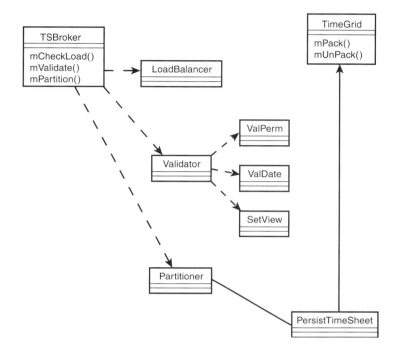

After determining that the server is available for additional client activity, the client's request is evaluated by the broker, which then employs a Validator component to apply role-based security and business logic to determine whether the request is a valid one. If the request is valid, a Partitioner is called to retrieve data from the back-end database(s). A Data Access component that implements (and encapsulates) the currently acceptable data-access technology from Microsoft (ADO for this release) is used to actually store and retrieve data under the direction of the Partitioner.

It wasn't our intention to implement a sophisticated load-balancing algorithm in this system. It's most important that our architecture supports a basic load-balancing strategy that can be performance profiled, tuned, and adjusted for better performance. The load balancer reads some Windows NT Performance Monitor counters and applies simple logic to determine whether or not the server is too busy. If so, the name of another MTS server is passed to the client, which then connects to the other server.

Some thought needs to go into this area to deal with the tougher questions:

- How do you evenly distribute clients across multiple servers even if the "first" server isn't too busy?

- How do you make sure that all the servers aren't too busy and eventually tell the client "sorry" after the client has a frustrating wait while attempting to connect to the servers?

Again, the focus is not on an elegant scheme, but a sound architecture. The sample application provided doesn't address all the issues previously listed. Some of these problems are not trivial. At any rate, many of these features will be implemented in the next release of these technologies, currently under development. They are jointly referred to under the blanket heading of COM+, the next generation of COM.

The logic for the Validator should be very straightforward to implement based upon the rules defined previously. For example, after checking to see what role the current user belongs to, the following logic applies to a user requesting a time sheet:

- If user is in the role HR, the answer is always Yes.
- If user is in the role Consultant and she wants to modify her own timesheet, Yes.
- If user is in the role Project Manager and he wants to modify a timesheet for a Consultant working on a project that the Project Manager is managing, Yes.
- Otherwise, No.

The Partitioner, like the LoadBalancer, is another area where the specific scheme we implemented is not as important as the fact that the architecture supports partitioning. The Employee table (and related tables) are partitioned based on the employee's last name. Project data won't be partitioned. All project information that is added to the system will be replicated by SQL Server so that all database servers maintain identical copies of project related data.

All mid-tier objects for a particular broker run on the same server. Although the Validator or Partitioner components could be split out on separate MTS servers, we have chosen to design this system so that they all remain on the same MTS server. Each mid-tier MTS server implements a complete collection of our mid-tier components, and is capable of using multiple SQL Server databases to store information under the direction of the Partitioner.

Database

Multiple MS SQL Server databases running SQL Server 6.5 or greater are on the back end. As previously outlined, these servers have partitioned Employee files, but all project data will be replicated to each SQL Server. Appropriate constraints and declarative referential integrity are used to help maintain the integrity of the database, although our mid-tier objects never try to do anything illegal!

Summary

This description of the sample application was accurate as the book went to press. For the final version of this document, as well as the sample application itself, check the Web site `http://www.gasullivan.com/vstudio/`.

Index

Special Edition Using Visual Basic 6

—Jeff Spotts

Special Edition Using Visual Basic 6 is designed to serve as an easy-to-use reference: The individual topics and material are organized so that they are easy to locate and read, and the authors teach Visual Basic (VB) in a straightforward manner and at a steady, consistent pace. After teaching the reader the VB programming language, the book progresses into more advanced topics, such as creating ActiveX controls, using Visual Basic with Active Server Pages, creating distributed applications, and VB database programming. *Special Edition Using Visual Basic 6* builds on the success of the bestselling previous edition of this book. This new edition incorporates changes to Visual Basic 6 and additional hands-on examples throughout the book, making it even easier to learn the topics within Visual Basic.

$39.99 USA/$57.95 CAN   *Intermediate–Advanced*

ISBN: 0-7897-1542-2   *900 pages*

Special Edition Using Visual C++ 6

—Kate Gregory

Special Edition Using Visual C++ 6 focuses on making you productive with Visual C++ as quickly as possible. It uses a straightforward approach to teaching Visual C++, and this approach enables you to move quickly to more advanced topics such as database capabilities, creating ActiveX controls and documents, and enterprise features. *Special Edition Using Visual C++ 6* builds on the success of the bestselling previous edition of this book. This new edition includes coverage of all the new features of version 6 and expands the coverage of such topics as Active Server Pages and Visual C++, memory management, and ActiveX Data Objects (ADO).

$39.99 USA/$57.95 CAN   *Intermediate–Advanced*

ISBN: 0-7897-1539-2   *900 pages*

Special Edition Using Visual InterDev 6

—Steve Banick

Special Edition Using Visual InterDev 6 provides the reader with an easy-to-use reference to the newest version of Microsoft's Visual InterDev. This book teaches Internet application development with Visual InterDev in a steady, yet concise pace. After presenting foundational information for developing with Visual InterDev, this book quickly progresses into more advanced topics such as Dynamic HTML, scriptlets, ActiveX controls, ADO, database development, security, administration, optimization, and more.

Price: $39.99 USA/$57.95 CAN   *Intermediate–Advanced*

ISBN: 0-7897-1549-X   *750 pages*

Programming Windows 98/NT Unleashed

—Viktor Toth

Programming Windows 98/NT Unleashed is the ideal reference for anyone creating applications for 32-bit Windows. This authoritative resource delivers what you need to know to design, code, and implement cutting-edge Windows applications. This book brings you up to speed on the enhancements of the Windows environment, including newer technologies, such as programming Microsoft's Distributed Internet Architecture (DNA) and Active Desktop. This book helps you learn to use common controls to quickly and easily add functionality to your applications. You learn to modify your programs to interact with the outside world using messaging (MAPI) and technology (TAPI) and to create your own Internet applications. The coverage of Microsoft Windows 98 makes the information contained in this book extremely important for all Windows programmers and developers.

$49.99 USA/$71.95 CAN

ISBN: 0-672-31353-7

Intermediate–Advanced

984 pages

Add to Your Sams Library Today with the Best Books for Programming, Operating Systems, and New Technologies

To order, visit our Web site at www.mcp.com or fax us at

1-800-835-3202

ISBN	Quantity	Description of Item	Unit Cost	Total Cost
0-7897-1542-2		Special Edition Using Visual Basic 6	$39.99	
0-7897-1539-2		Special Edition Using Visual C++ 6	$39.99	
0-7897-1549-X		Special Edition Using Visual InterDev 6	$39.99	
0-672-31353-7		Programming Windows 98/NT Unleashed	$49.99	
		Shipping and Handling: See information below.		
		TOTAL		

Shipping and Handling

Standard	$5.00
2nd Day	$10.00
Next Day	$17.50
International	$40.00

201 W. 103rd Street, Indianapolis, Indiana 46290   1-800-835-3202 — Fax

Book ISBN 0-672-31489-4